Autodesk Revit 2027 Black Book

By
Gaurav Verma
Matt Weber
(CADCAMCAE Works)

Edited by
Kristen

ISBN # 978-1-77459-220-5

DEDICATION

To teachers, who make it possible to disseminate knowledge
to enlighten the young and curious minds
of our future generations

To students, who are the future of the world

THANKS

To my friends and colleagues

To my family for their love and support

Training and Consultant Services

At CADCAMCAE WORKS, we provide effective and affordable one to one online training on various software packages in Computer Aided Design(CAD), Computer Aided Manufacturing(CAM), Computer Aided Engineering (CAE), Computer programming languages(C/C++, Java, .NET, Android, JavaScript, HTML and so on). The training is delivered through remote access to your system and voice chat via Internet at any time, any place, and at any pace to individuals, groups, students of colleges/universities, and CAD/CAM/CAE training centers. The main features of this program are:

Training as per your need

Highly experienced Engineers and Technician conduct the classes on the software applications used in the industries. The methodology adopted to teach the software is totally practical based, so that the learner can adapt to the design and development industries in almost no time. The efforts are to make the training process cost effective and time saving while you have the comfort of your time and place, thereby relieving you from the hassles of traveling to training centers or rearranging your time table.

Software Packages on which we provide basic and advanced training are:

CAD/CAM/CAE: CATIA, Creo Parametric, Creo Direct, SolidWorks, Autodesk Inventor, Solid Edge, UG NX, AutoCAD, AutoCAD LT, EdgeCAM, MasterCAM, SolidCAM, DelCAM, BOBCAM, UG NX Manufacturing, UG Mold Wizard, UG Progressive Die, UG Die Design, SolidWorks Mold, Creo Manufacturing, Creo Expert Machinist, NX Nastran, Hypermesh, SolidWorks Simulation, Autodesk Simulation Mechanical, Creo Simulate, Gambit, ANSYS and many others.

Computer Programming Languages: C++, VB.NET, HTML, Android, JavaScript, and so on.

Game Designing: Unity.

Civil Engineering: AutoCAD MEP, Revit Structure, Revit Architecture, AutoCAD Map 3D and so on.

We also provide consultant services for Design and development on the above mentioned software packages

For more information you can mail us at:
cadcamcaeworks@gmail.com
info@cadcamcaeworks.com

Table of Contents

Chapter 3 : Architectural Designing-II

Chapter 4 : Project Management

Chapter 5 : Revit Family, Conceptual Mass, and Title Block

Chapter 6 : Structural Designing

Chapter 7 : Steel Structural Designing

Chapter 8 : System Design

Chapter 9 : Performing Analysis

Chapter 10 : Inserting and Collaborating Data

Chapter 11 : Massing and Site Creation

Chapter 12 : View Management

Chapter 13 : Annotating Model

Chapter 14 : Macro Management and Visual Scripting (Introduction)

Chapter 15 : Residential Building Project

Chapter 16 : Precast

Preface

Autodesk Revit is a Building Information Modeling (BIM) software which is used to design buildings parametrically and with drafting elements. Using this software, you can create architectural, structural, and MEP designs of a building. You can generate plan views, elevations, schedules, legends, and sections of a building by using this tool. Autodesk Revit is well capable of sharing data with other users allowing them to simultaneously work on same project.

To support education, Autodesk gives free educational version of the Autodesk Revit to students with a license of 1 year. You can get your free version of software by visiting the following link:

https://www.autodesk.com/education/edu-software/overview

The **Autodesk Revit 2027 Black Book** is the 8th edition of our series on Autodesk Revit. This book is designed to help beginners in understanding the workflow in Revit and how simple BIM models are created. The book follows a step by step methodology. In this book, we have tried to give real-world examples with real challenges in designing. We have tried to reduce the gap between educational use of Autodesk Revit and industrial use of Autodesk Revit. The book covers almost all the information required by a beginner to master Autodesk Revit. The book covers Architectural Design, Structural Design, Project Management, Revit Family Components, MEP, Mass and Site Creation, Drafting, Data Management and Collaboration, Macros, Visual Scripting, and Precast. A residential building project is given in this book which revises major topics discussed throughout the book. Some of the salient features of this book are :

In-Depth explanation of concepts

Every new topic of this book starts with the explanation of the basic concepts. In this way, the user becomes capable of relating the things with real world.

Topics Covered

Every chapter starts with a list of topics being covered in that chapter. In this way, the user can easy find the topic of his/her interest easily.

Instruction through illustration

The instructions to perform any action are provided by maximum number of illustrations so that the user can perform the actions discussed in the book easily and effectively. There are about 1140 small and large illustrations that make the learning process effective.

Tutorial point of view

At the end of concept's explanation, the tutorial make the understanding of users firm and long lasting. Major topics of the book have tutorials that are real world projects. Also, most of the tools in this book are discussed in the form of tutorials.

For Faculty

If you are a faculty member, then you can ask for video tutorials on any of the topic, exercise, tutorial, or concept. As faculty, you can register on our website to get electronic desk copies of our latest books, self-assessment, and solution of practical. Faculty resources are available in the **Faculty Member** page of our website (**www.cadcamcaeworks.com**) once you login. Note that faculty registration approval is manual and it may take two days for approval before you can access the faculty website.

Formatting Conventions Used in the Text

All the key terms like name of button, tool, drop-down etc. are kept **bold**.

Free Resources

Link to the resources used in this book are provided to the users via email. To get the resources, mail us at ***cadcamcaeworks@gmail.com*** with your contact information. With your contact record with us, you will be provided latest updates and informations regarding various technologies. The format to write us mail for resources is as follows:

Subject of E-mail as ***Application for resources of ________book***.
Also, given your information like
Name:
Course pursuing/Profession:
Contact Address:
E-mail ID:

Note: We respect your privacy and value it. If you do not want to give your personal informations then you can ask for resources without giving your information.

About Authors

The author of this book, Gaurav Verma, has written and assisted in more than 18 titles in CAD/CAM/CAE which are already available in market. He has authored **AutoCAD Electrical Black Books** and **SolidWorks Electrical Black Books**. He has also authored books on various modules of Creo Parametric and SolidWorks. He has provided consultant services to many industries in US, Greece, Canada, and UK. He has assisted in preparing many Government aided skill development programs. He has been speaker for Autodesk University. He has assisted in preparing AutoCAD Electrical course for Autodesk Design Academy. He has worked on Sheetmetal, Forging, Machining, and Casting designs in Design and Development departments of various manufacturing firms.

If you have any query/doubt in any CAD/CAM/CAE package, then you can contact the authors by writing at cadcamcaeworks@gmail.com

For Any query or suggestion

If you have any query or suggestion, please let us know by mailing us on ***cadcamcaeworks@gmail.com***. Your valuable constructive suggestions will be incorporated in our books and your name will be addressed in special thanks area of our books on your confirmation.

Chapter 1

Introduction to Revit

Topics Covered

The major topics covered in this chapter are:

- ***Introduction to BIM***
- ***Role of Revit in BIM***
- ***Installing Autodesk Revit***
- ***Starting Projects and Families in Revit***
- ***File Menu Options***

INTRODUCTION TO BIM

Building Information Modeling (BIM) is a concept and process used to represent the data related to construction and maintenance of a building in organized manner. In BIM concept, a 3D model of the building is designed with all the design information embedded to related component of building. For example, if a beam/column is created using BIM concept then all the parameters like material, size, weight, shape, time taken for construction, cost, and so on are embedded to beam/column in model and can be retrieved whenever required. BIM is not a new thing as it was started in 1980s. Now a days, the software using BIM technology are becoming cheaper and hence the BIM software are finding greater uses in common building design applications too.

INTRODUCTION TO AUTODESK REVIT

You may ask why I am talking so much about BIM in a book of Revit! This is because Autodesk Revit is a BIM software. Figure-1 shows the broad spectrum of functions which Revit is capable of doing. Autodesk Revit is a parametric software which means everything you create in the software will have specific parameters so that the same object/structure can be created in real-world. One benefit of parametric software is that you can modify any object of Revit by modifying the related parameters at any time during designing.

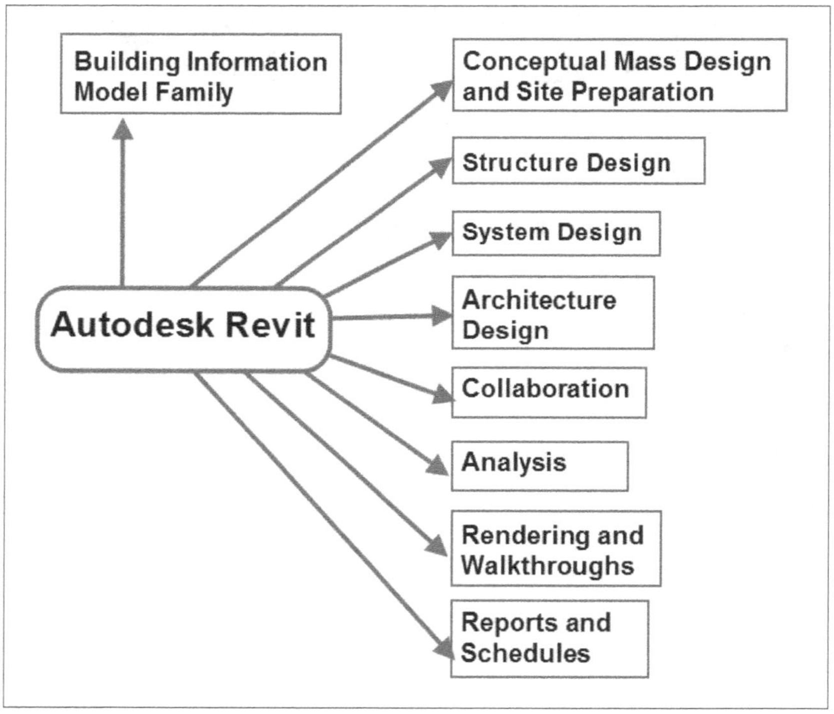

Figure-1. Basic functions of Autodesk Revit

Revit also maintains bidirectional associativity between various objects generated by 3D Building model which means if an object (door, window, etc.) is changed in one view then that change will propagate in all the connected views.

DOWNLOADING AND INSTALLING AUTODESK REVIT STUDENT VERSION

- Reach the link : **https://www.autodesk.com/education/edu-software/overview** from your web browser. The web page will be displayed as shown in Figure-2.

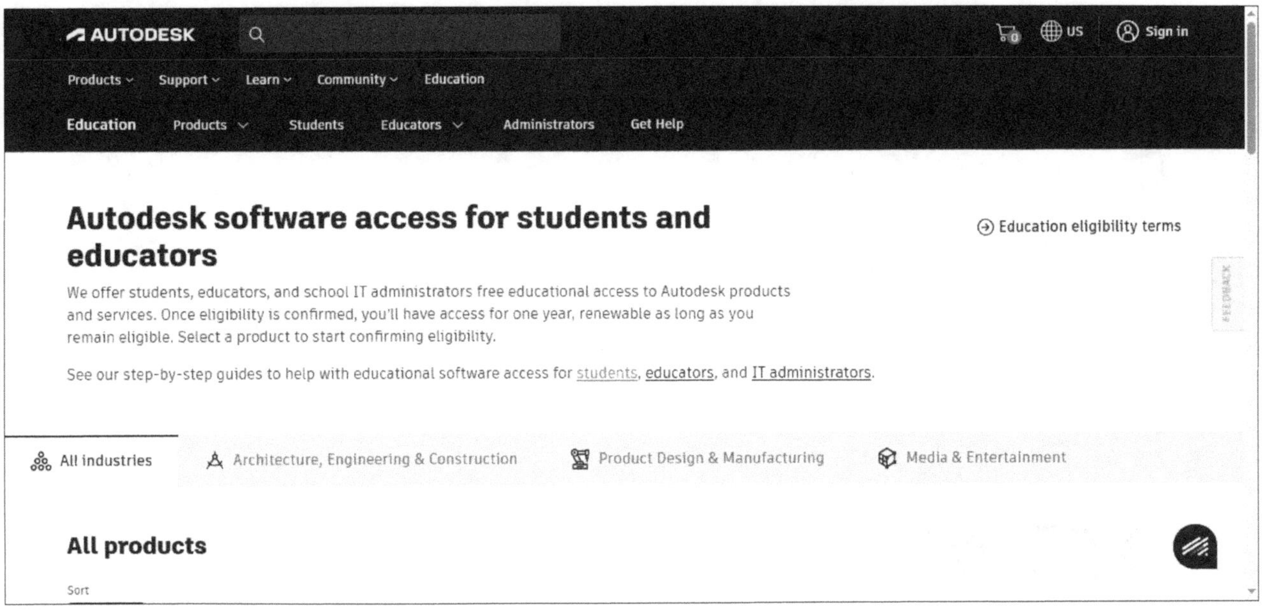

Figure-2. Educational software sign in

- Click on the **Sign in** button at top right corner. A web page to enter your Autodesk account credentials will be displayed; refer to Figure-3.

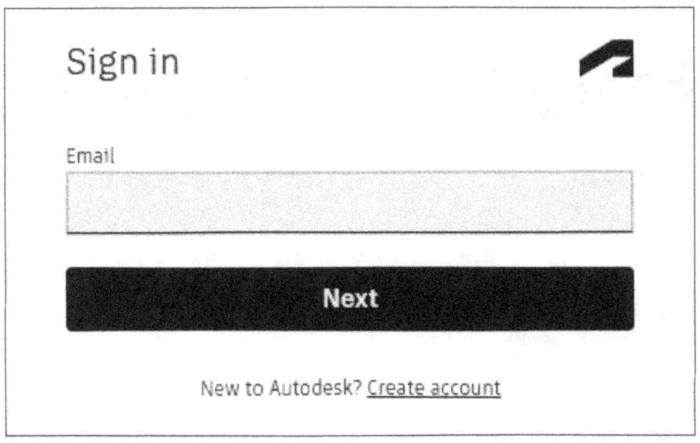

Figure-3. Sign in page

- Enter your credentials if you have an Autodesk student/educator account already created otherwise click on the **Create account** button, create an educator/student account and then sign in. A web page to access software with educational license will be displayed. Scroll down on the displayed page and click on the **Select** link button for **Revit**; refer to Figure-4. The web page to get access to the software will be displayed; refer to Figure-5.

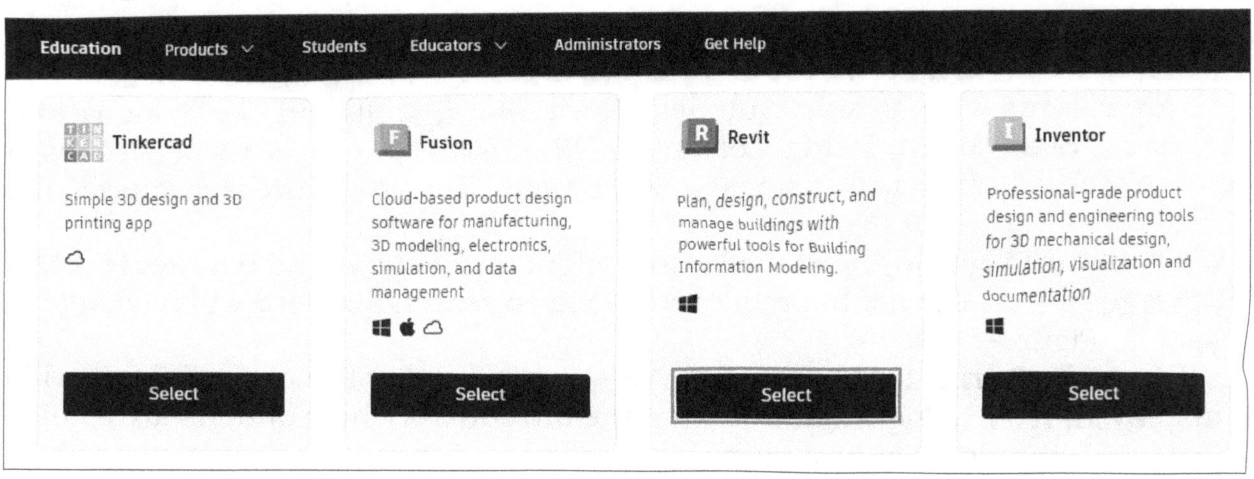

Figure-4. Select button for Revit

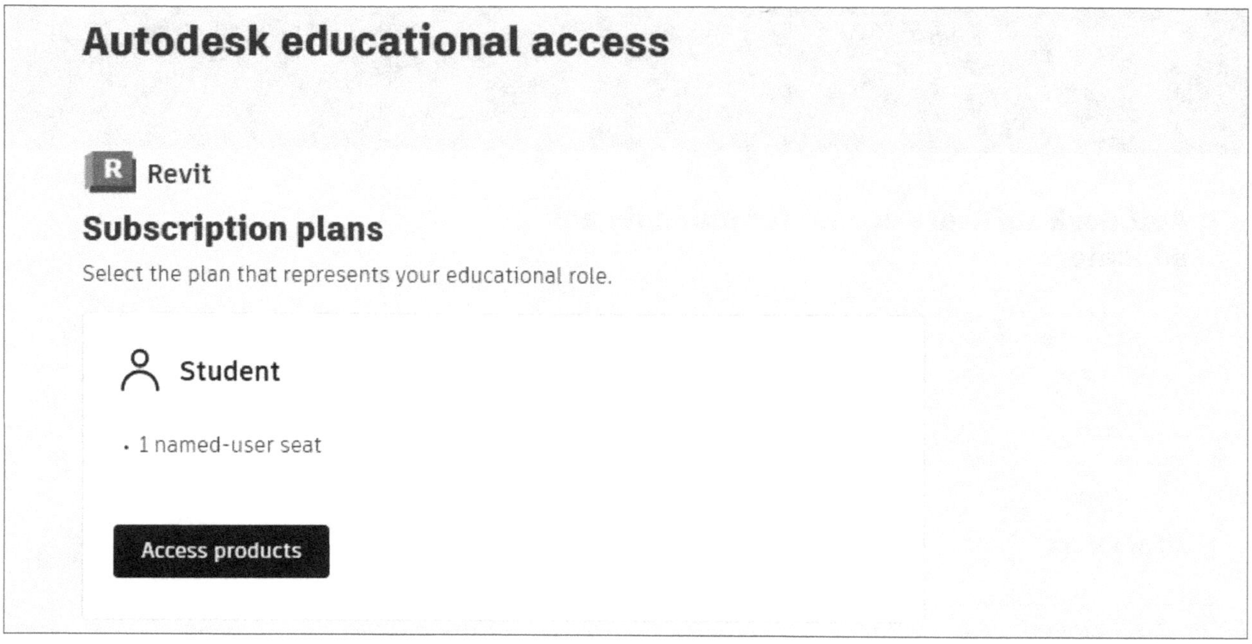

Figure-5. Webpage for accessing subscription

- Click on the **Access products** link button from the web page. The web page will be displayed as shown in Figure-6.

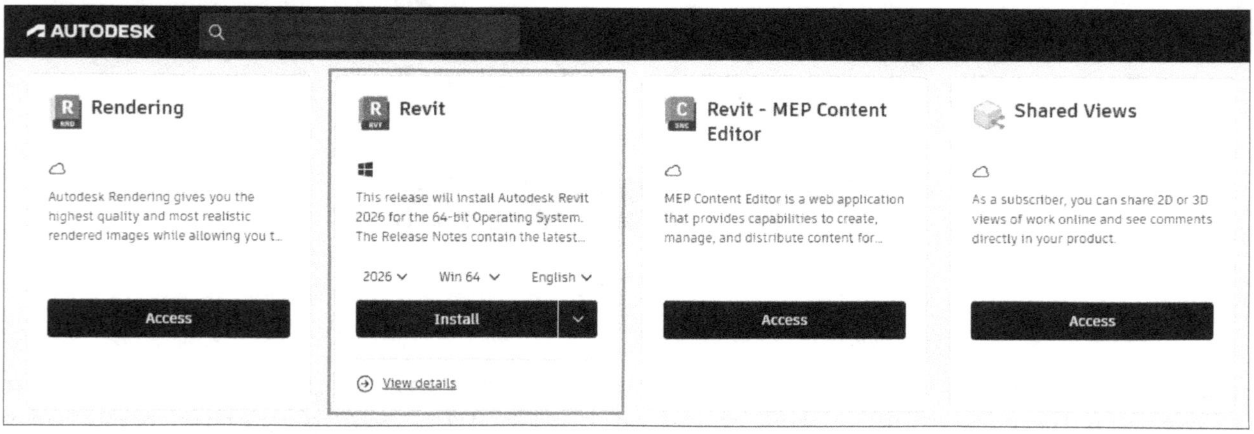

Figure-6. Webpage for downloading Revit

- Click on the **Install** button for **Revit** software and then select the **Accept** button from pop-up displayed. After downloading, installation of software will start.
- Accept the license terms of software and install the software at desired location.

STARTING AUTODESK REVIT

There are various ways to start Autodesk Revit after installation like using Desktop Icon, using Start Menu, using Cortana in Windows 10, etc. We will discuss the standard method which is by using the **Start** Menu. The procedure is discussed next.

- Click on the **Start** button at the bottom left in the Taskbar and type **Revit 2027** in the search box. The list of programs related to search keyword will be displayed; refer to Figure-7.
- Click on the **Revit 2027** option from the list. The start page of application will be displayed; refer to Figure-8. Note that the introductory help options are available in **Learn** drop-down of first page.

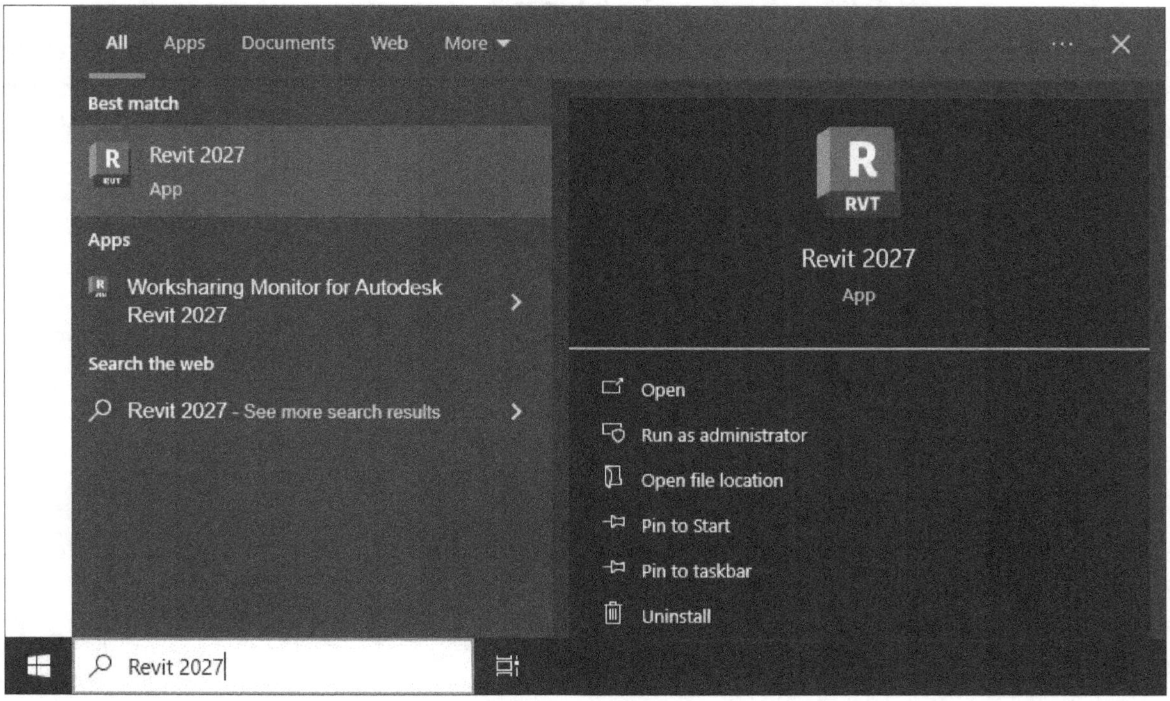

Figure-7. Revit in Start Menu

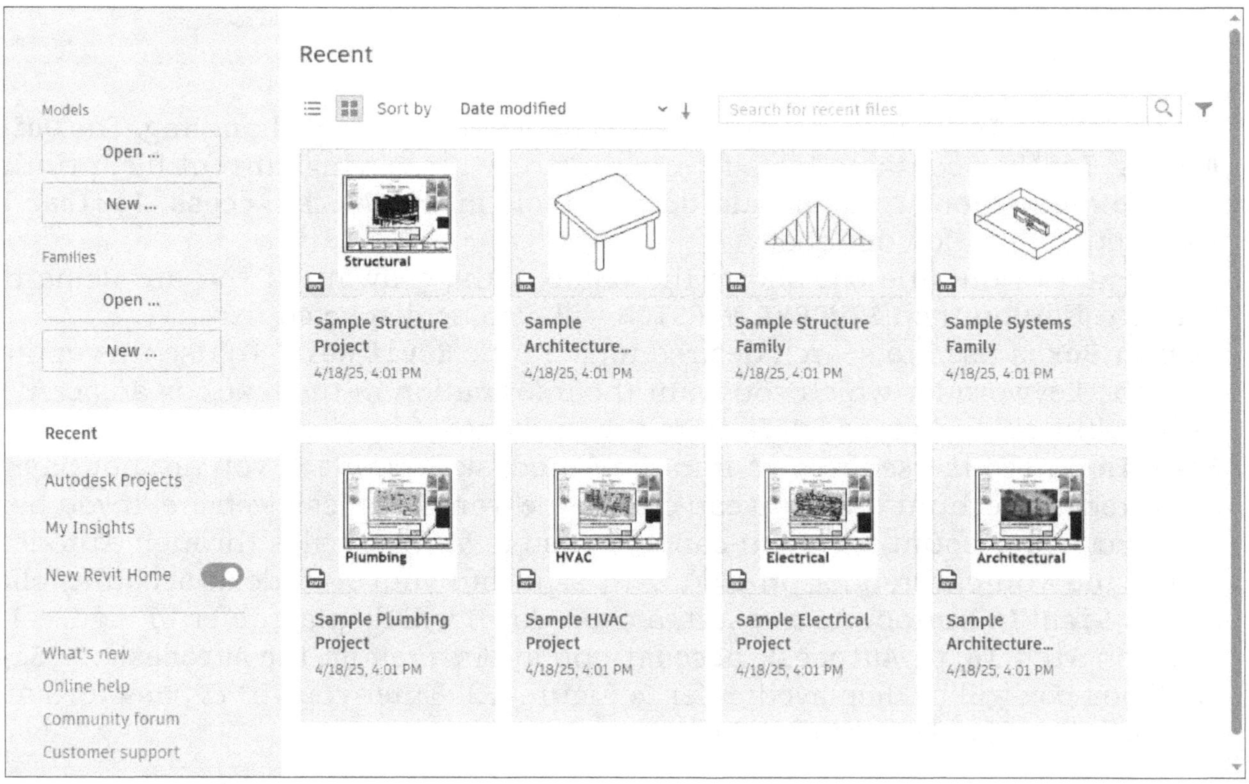

Figure-8. Revit application start page

USER INTERFACE

The first thing you need to know while learning a software is to understand various components of the user interface of the software. Various components of the Autodesk Revit User Interface after opening a sample project are annotated.

Various options of user interface after starting a project are discussed next.

Ribbon

Ribbon is a toolbox below the Title Bar in which tools are placed under different tabs; refer to Figure-9. These tabs are further divided into panels. Each panel has a number of tools which perform function of same genre shows the locations of **Ribbon**, **Tabs**, and **Panels** in the user interface.

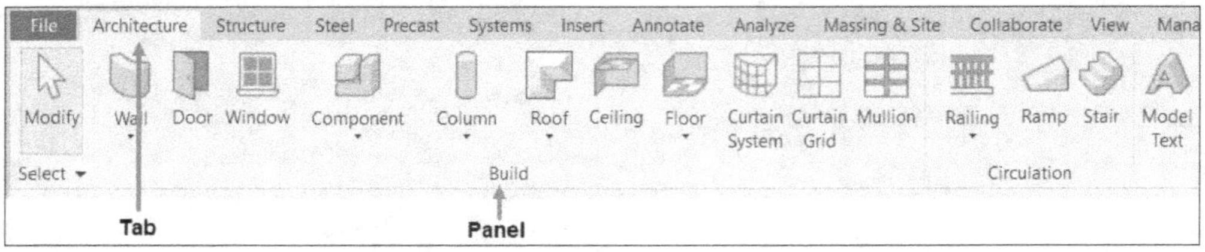

Figure-9. Ribbon

Title Bar

Title bar is the top strip containing quick access tools, name of the document, and connectivity options; refer to Figure-10.

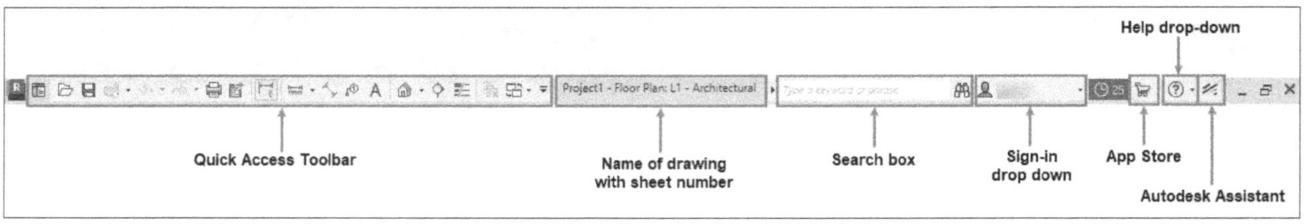

Figure-10. Title bar

- **Quick Access Toolbar** contains tools that are common for file handling. The **Quick Access Toolbar** contains tools for creating new file, saving current file, printing the file, and so on. You can add desired tools in the **Quick Access Toolbar** by using customization options.
- The center of the title bar shows the name of the drawing. If you are using the Student Edition then **STUDENT VERSION** will also be displayed here.
- **Search Box** is used to search desired topic in the **Revit Help**. To use this option, type the keyword for which you want the information in the text box adjacent to **Search** button and press **ENTER** from the keyboard.
- **Sign In** button is used to sign into the Autodesk account. If you are not having an Autodesk account then you can create one from Autodesk website. If you have an Autodesk account then you can save and share your files through Autodesk cloud and you can render on cloud. To sign into your Autodesk account, click on the **Sign In** button. As a result, a drop-down will display; refer to Figure-11. Click on **Sign In to Autodesk account** option. As a result, the **Autodesk - Sign In** dialog box will be displayed; refer to Figure-12. Enter your ID & password and click on the **Sign In** button to login.

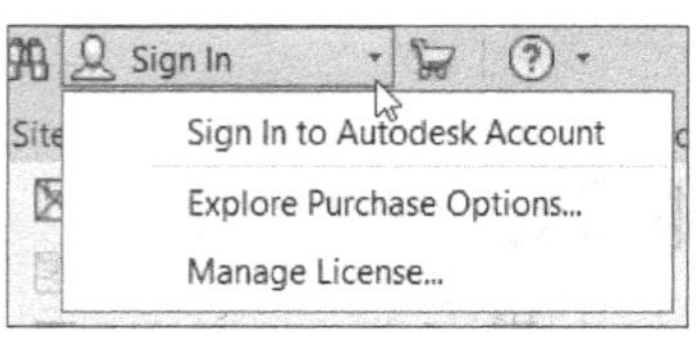

Figure-11. Sign In option

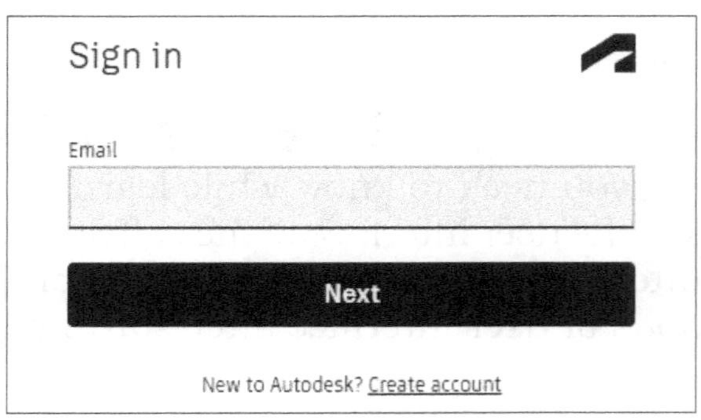

Figure-12. Autodesk Sign in dialog box

- **Autodesk App Store** button in the **Title Bar** is used to install or share apps for Autodesk products. Click on the **Autodesk App Store** button. The **Autodesk APP STORE** web page will open in the browser where you can buy or try various apps as needed; refer to Figure-13 (Apps shown in figure might be different in your case).

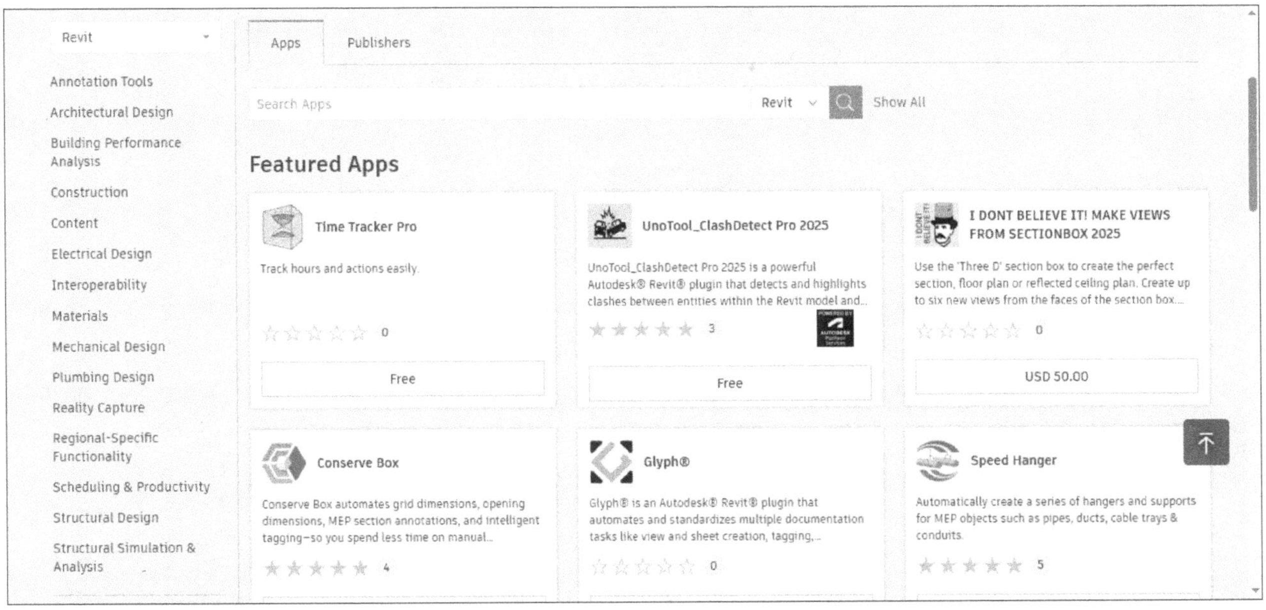

Figure-13. Autodesk App Store webpage

- The **Help** button is used to display online help of Autodesk Revit on the Autodesk server. If you click on the down arrow next to **Help** button then a list of options will be displayed; refer to Figure-14. Select desired option to check related information.

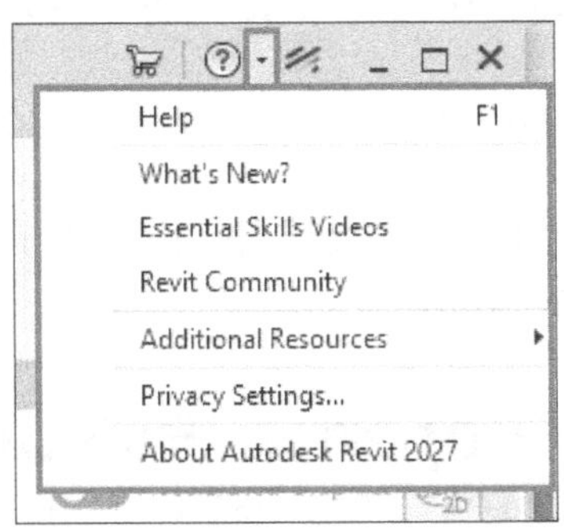

Figure-14. Help menu

Autodesk Assistant

The **Autodesk Assistant** tool is used to allow user to ask questions and receive guidance, suggestions, and step by step solutions directly within the software via AI. The procedure to use this tool is discussed next.

- Click on the **Autodesk Assistant** tool from the **Title bar**. The **Autodesk Assistant** dialog box will be displayed; refer to Figure-15.

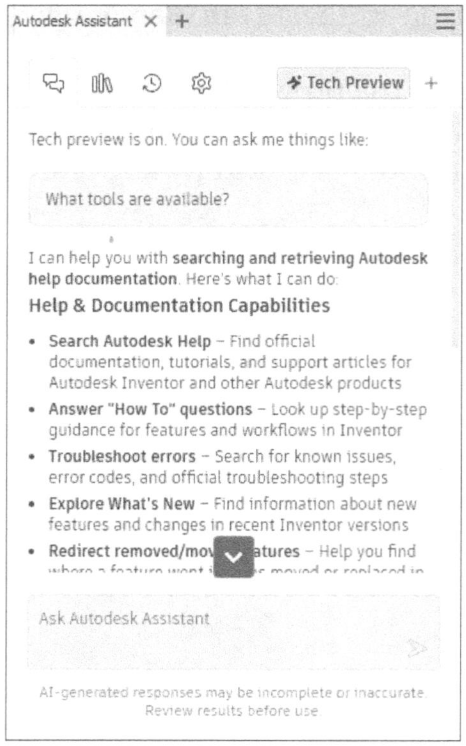

Figure-15. Autodesk Assistant dialog box

- Click on the **Prompt Library** button to provide a collection of sample prompts that user can use to interact with the assistant effectively.
- Click on the **Chat History** button to view and return to your previous conversation with the Autodesk Assistant.
- Click on the **Settings** button to manage the assistant's preferences and options within the software.
- Click on the **New chat** button to start a new conversation with the Autodesk Assistant.
- Type and enter the prompt in input field similar to ChatGPT and other AI tools to get response for your queries.

Properties Palette

The options in the **Properties Palette** are used to modify properties of the components selected from the view port. For example, Figure-16 shows the **Properties Palette** displayed on selecting a viewport.

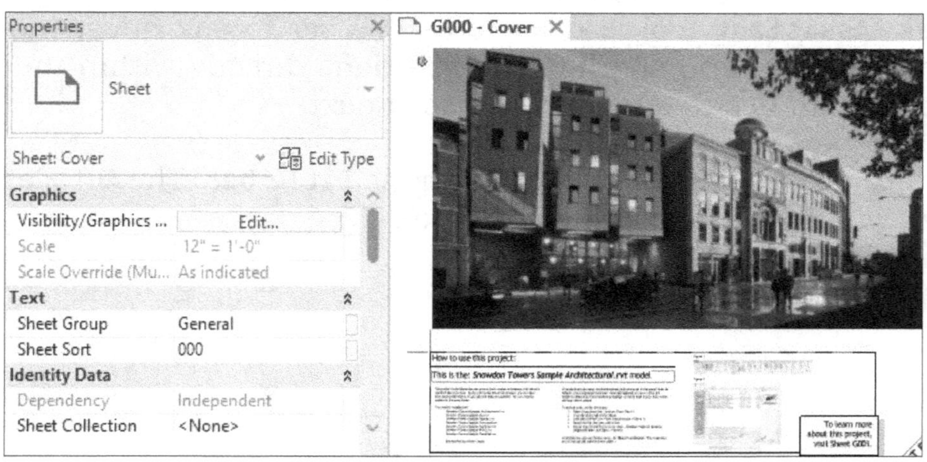

Figure-16. Properties Palette for viewport

Project Browser

Project Browser is used to switch between various views, sheets, and objects in the current Revit project. By default, the **Project Browser** is available below **Properties Palette**; refer to Figure-17. You can drag and place it at desired location in interface.

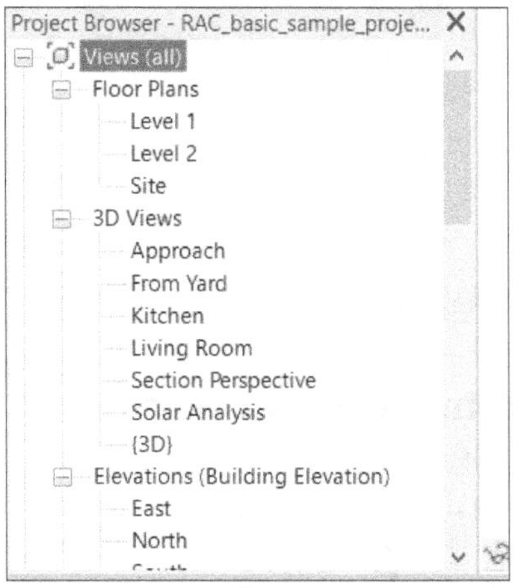

Figure-17. Project Browser

Status Bar

Various options of the **Status Bar** are annotated in Figure-18. The left area of the **Status Bar** shows tips or hints on what to do after you have selected a tool. When you highlight an element or component, the status bar displays the name of the family and family type.

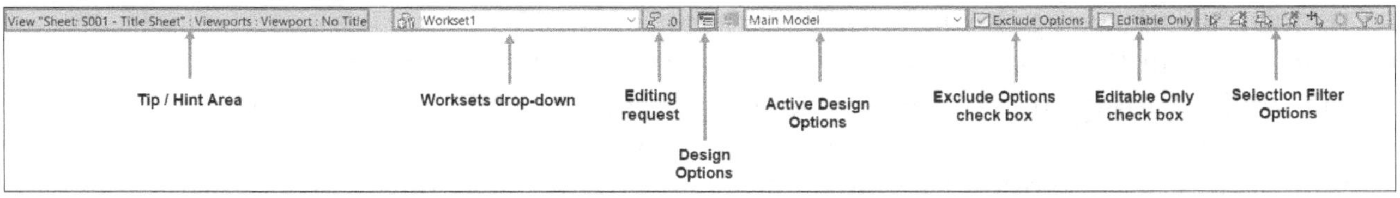

Figure-18. Status bar options

- Select desired workset from the **Worksets** drop-down that you want to share with your team member for simultaneously working. You will learn more about these options later in this book.
- Click on the **Editing request** option from the **Status Bar** to check the requests sent by your team members for editing.
- Select the **Design Options** button from the **Status Bar** to create different design sets. Design sets are used to represent different possibilities of design like one design set will have Revolving door at entrance and other design set will have double door at entrance. Select desired option from the Active Design Option to selected desired design set. You will learn more about design sets later.
- Select the **Exclude Options** check box to exclude all the components from selection which are not part of design options.
- Select the **Editable Only** check box to exclude all the components from selection which are not available for editing.
- Click on desired button from the **Selection Filter** area to toggle activation or de-activation of selection of related objects.

View Control Bar

There are various toggle and switch options to change the view of model available in the **View Control Bar** below the graphics area; refer to Figure-19.

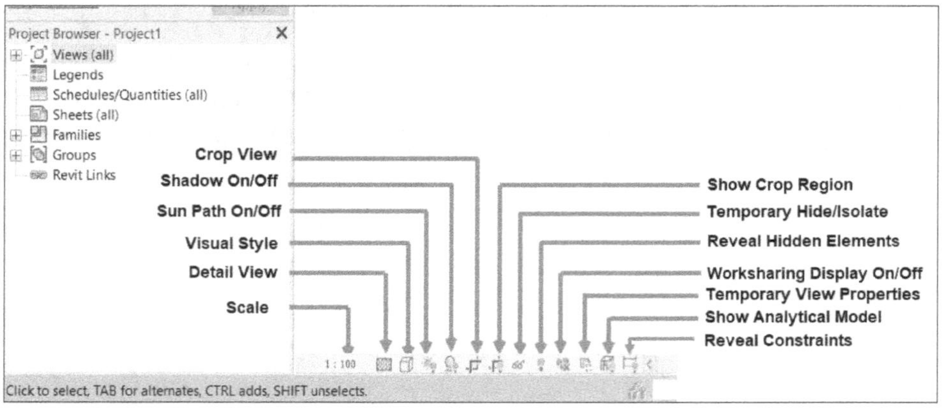

Figure-19. View Control Bar

- Click on the **Scale** option from the **View Control Bar** to change the scale of drawing unit and real size of building.
- Click on the **Detail View** option and select desired option to specify the level of details, you want to see in the graphics area. There are three options to define level of detail viz. **Coarse**, **Medium**, and **Fine**.
- Select desired option from the **Visual Style** to define the display style. You can display objects as shaded, realistic, wireframe, and so on.
- Toggle the Sun Path On or Off to include or exclude the effect on Sun on the building by using the **Sun Path On/Off** option. The Sun Path is activated to study the effect of Sun light and shadow on the building.
- Click on the **Shadows On/Off** toggle option from the **View Control Bar** to display or hide shadows of building and surrounding.
- Click on the **Crop View** button in the **View Control Bar** to crop the view using sketch boundary. If your view is not cropped yet then **Do Not Crop View** is displayed on hovering the cursor over this button. On clicking this button, the crop view will be displayed; refer to Figure-20. To edit the crop boundary, double-click on it. The modify sketch mode will be activated. Click on the lines and drag the key points to modify shape. You can also use the sketching tools to create desired crop boundary; refer to Figure-21. Click on the **OK** button from the **Modify|Edit Sketch** contextual tab to create crop.

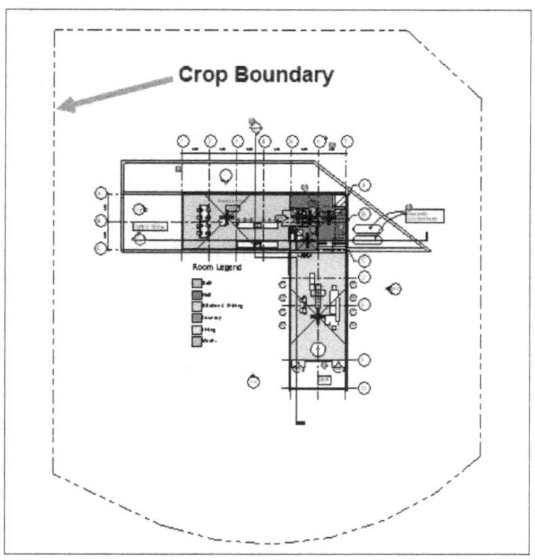

Figure-20. Crop boundary displayed

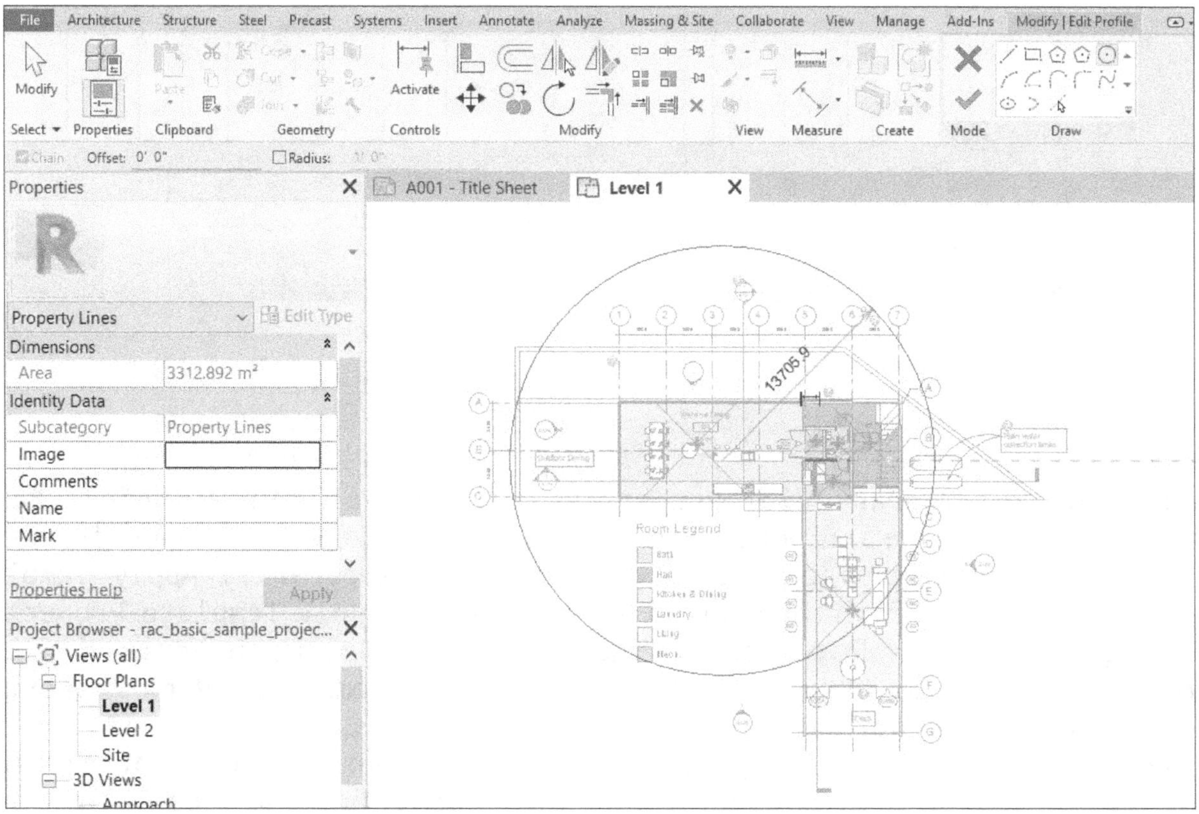

Figure-21. Modifying boundary curve

- Click on the **Show/Hide Crop Region** button from the **View Control Bar** to display or hide crop region.
- Select the objects to be isolated or hidden and then click on desired option from the **Temporary Isolate/Hide** flyout; refer to Figure-22.

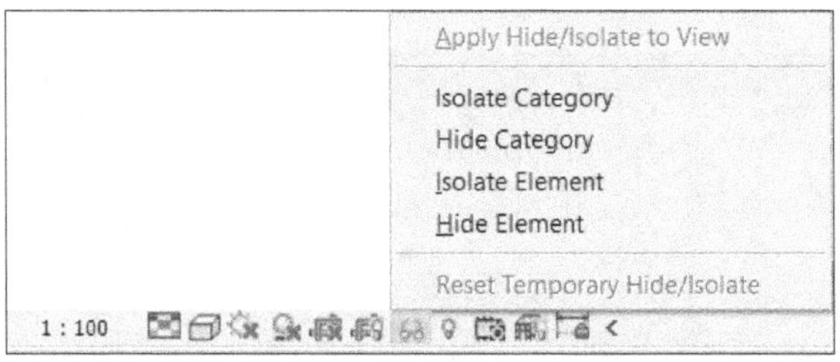

Figure-22. Temporary Hide Isolate flyout

- Click on the **Reveal Hidden Elements** option from the **View Control Bar** to display all the hidden elements.
- Select the **Worksharing Display Off** option from the **View Control Bar** to define parameters related to worksharing; refer to Figure-23. Select the **Worksharing Display Off** option from the flyout to hide highlighting shared objects. Select the **Worksets**, **Model Updates**, **Owners**, or **Checkout Status** options from the shortcut menu to use respective worksharing display modes. Click on the **Worksharing Display Settings** option from the flyout to set color codes for components based on selected display mode. On selecting this option, the **Worksharing Display Settings** dialog box will be displayed; refer to Figure-24. Set desired color codes in various tabs of dialog box to define how objects will be distinguished. Click on the **OK** button from the dialog box to apply settings.

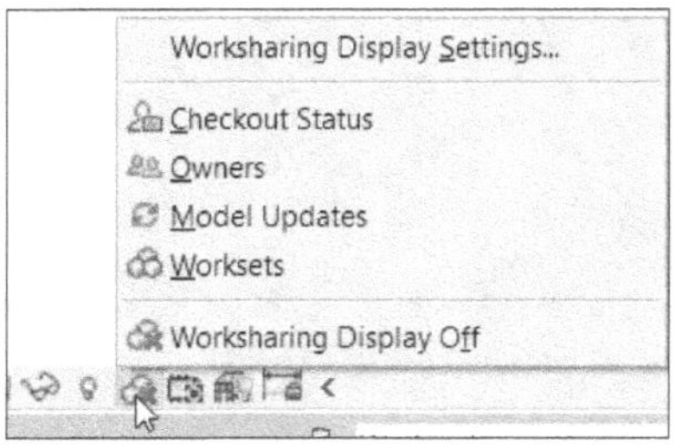

Figure-23. Worksharing flyout

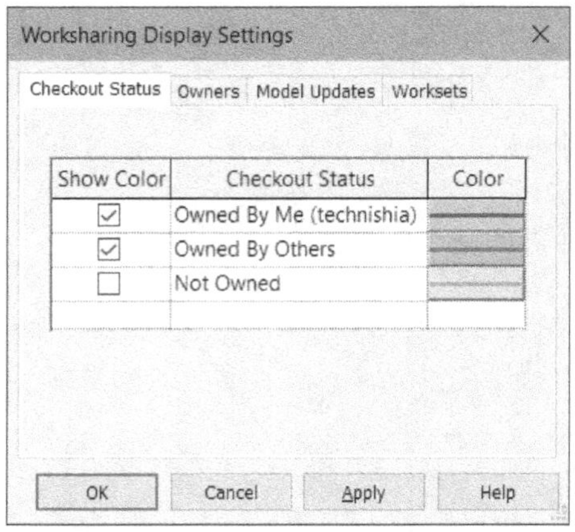

Figure-24. Worksharing Display Settings dialog box

- Click on the **Temporary View Properties** option from the **View Control Bar** to manage and enable temporary views. The **Temporary View Properties** flyout will be displayed; refer to Figure-25. Click on the **Temporarily Apply Template Properties** option from the flyout. The **Temporarily Apply Template Properties** dialog box will be displayed; refer to Figure-26. Set desired parameters in the dialog box and click on the **OK** button. Click on the **Enable Temporary View Properties** option from the flyout to enable the applied properties.
- Click on the **Show/Hide Analytical Model** option from the **View Control Bar** to display or hide analytical model created after performing analyses.

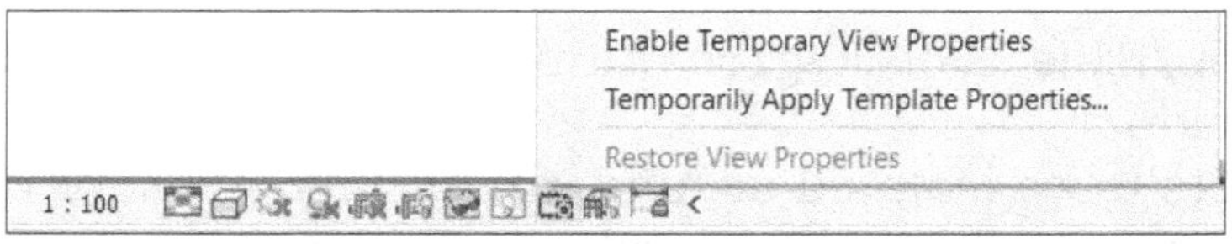

Figure-25. Temporary View Properties flyout

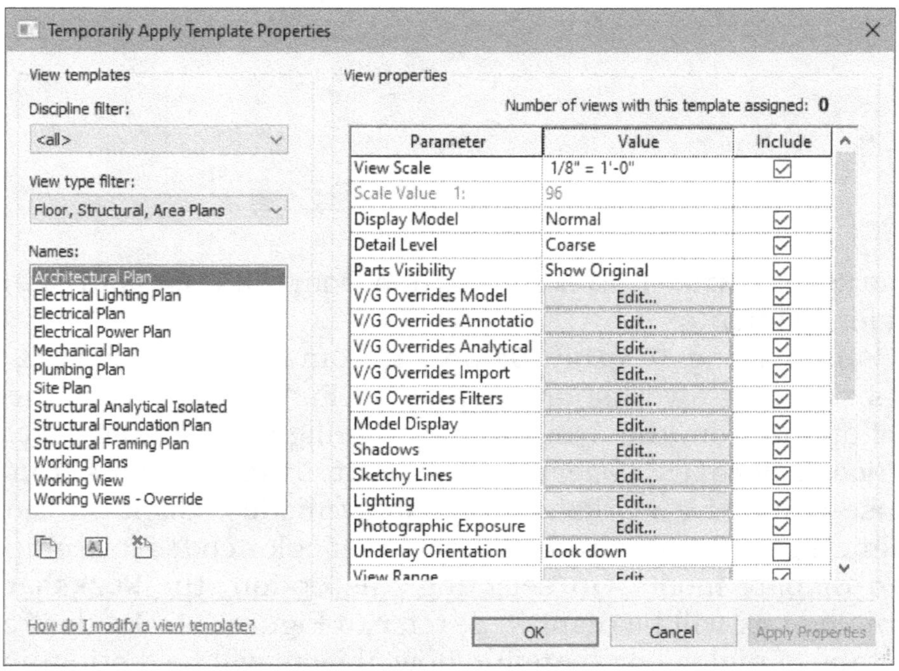

Figure-26. Temporarily Apply Template Properties dialog box

- Click on the **Reveal Constraints** option from the **View Control Bar** to display constraints applied to the model.

FILE MENU

The options in the **File** menu are used to manage functions related to files like opening a file, creating a new file, exporting a file, and so on. The **File** menu is displayed on clicking **File** button from the left in the **Ribbon**; refer to Figure-27. Various options of the **File** menu are discussed next.

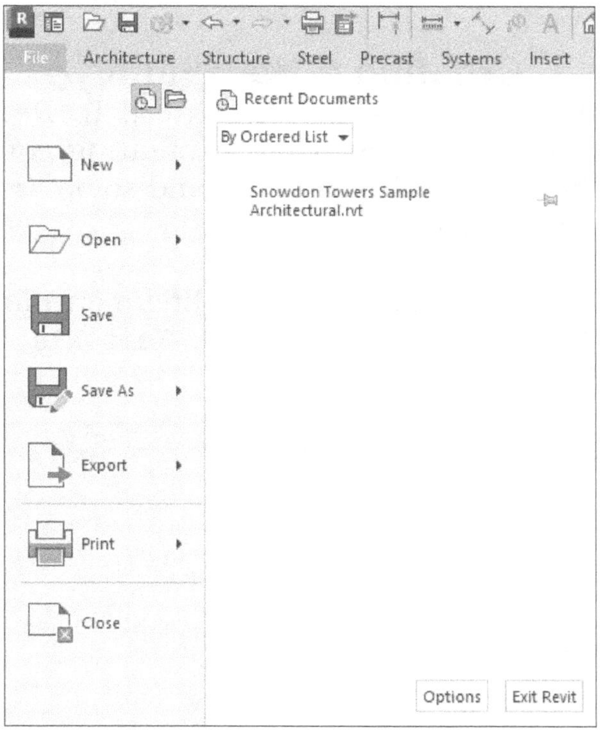

Figure-27. File menu

Creating a New Project

In Autodesk Revit, a project is a systematic collection of drawings that describes every aspect of construction project. A project may have architectural, structural, and system drawings arranged systematically. The procedure to create a new project is given next.

- Click on the **Project** tool from the **New** cascading menu in the **File** menu (**File->New->Project**). The **New Project** dialog box will be displayed; refer to Figure-28.

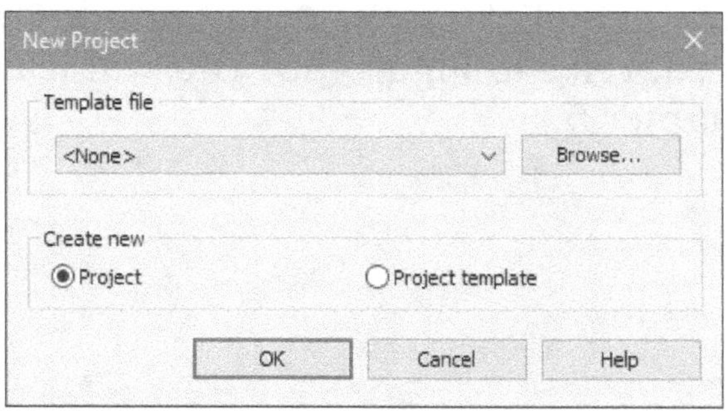

Figure-28. New Project dialog box

- Select desired template from the **Template file** drop-down. A project template provides a base for new project which includes view templates, loaded families, settings (such as units, fill patterns, line styles), and geometry, if desired.

- By default, the **Project** radio button is selected in the dialog box and hence a new project file is created. If you want to create a project template then select the **Project template** radio button. Note that the file extension for Revit project file is ***.rvt** and file extension for Revit project template is ***.rte**.
- After selecting desired parameters, click on the **OK** button from the dialog box. A new project will be created and displayed in the Application window.

Creating a New Family

Here, Family is not Mummy-Papa-Son-Daughter!! In Revit, Family means the architectural/structural/MEP blocks used in creating construction project. For example, Door, Duct, Column, TV Stand, Wire, and so on are different families. The procedure to create a new family is given next.

- Click on the **Family** tool from the **New** cascading menu in the **File** menu (**File-> New-> Family**). The **New Family - Select Template File** dialog box will be displayed; refer to Figure-29.

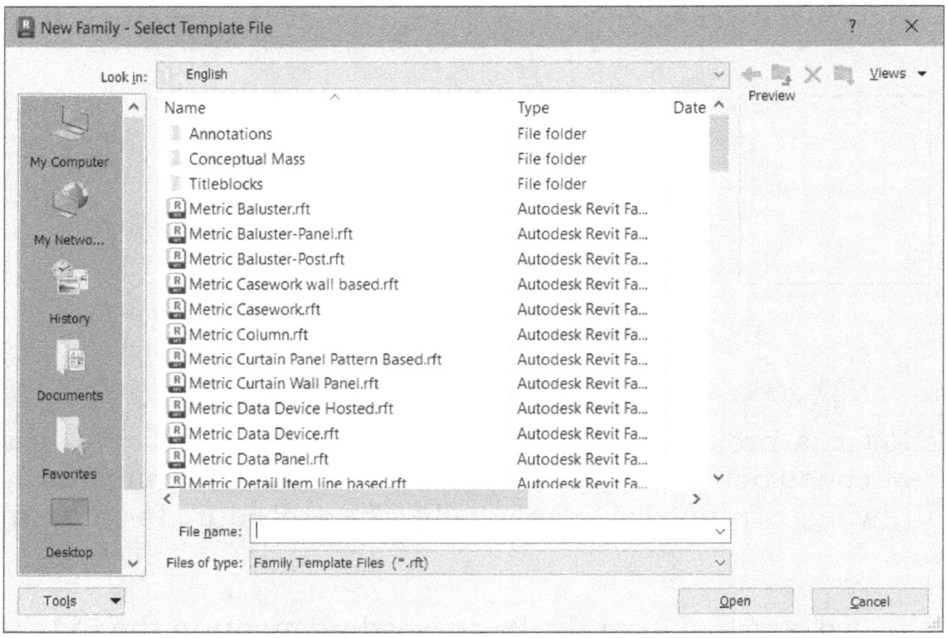

Figure-29. New Family-Select Template File dialog box

- Select desired template and click on the **Open** button. The environment to create family will be displayed; refer to Figure-30. You will learn about family creation and editing in the Chapter 5.

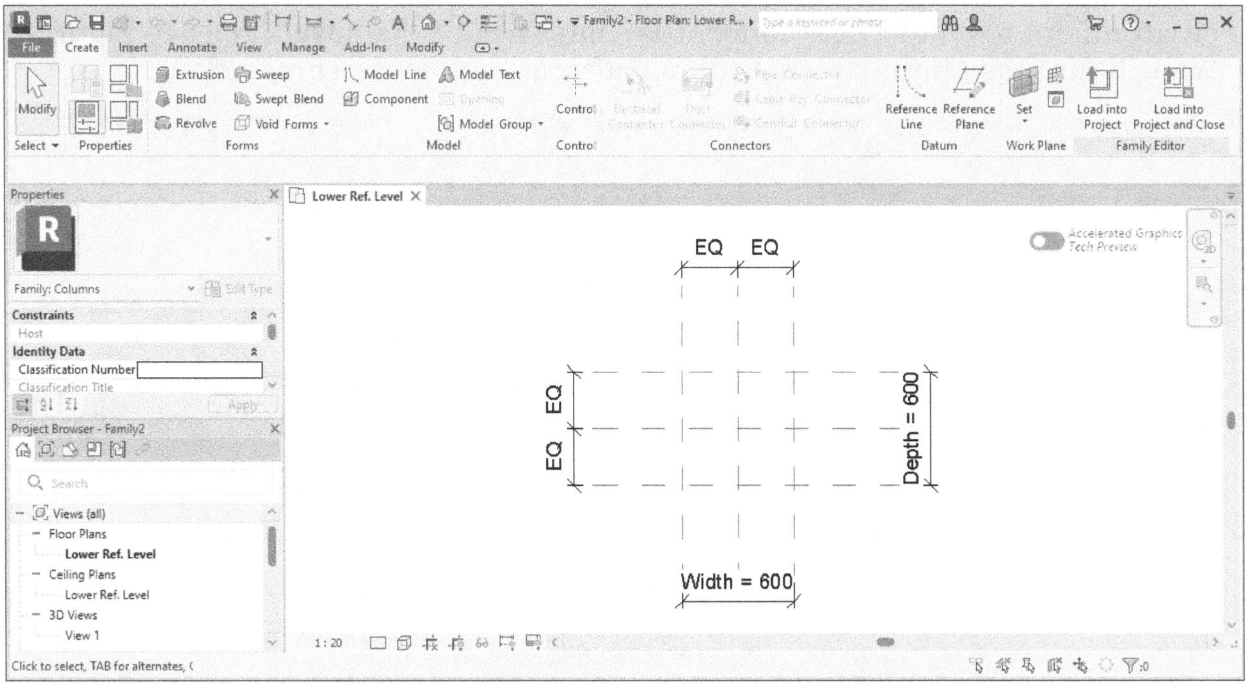

Figure-30. Family environment of Revit

Creating New Conceptual Mass

The Conceptual Mass is a conceptual representation of various elements of construction to explore earlier design ideas and perform initial analyses. The procedure to create a new conceptual mass is given next.

- Click on the **Conceptual Mass** tool from the **New** cascading menu in the **File** menu (**File->New->Conceptual Mass**). The **New Conceptual Mass-Select Template File** dialog box will be displayed; refer to Figure-31.

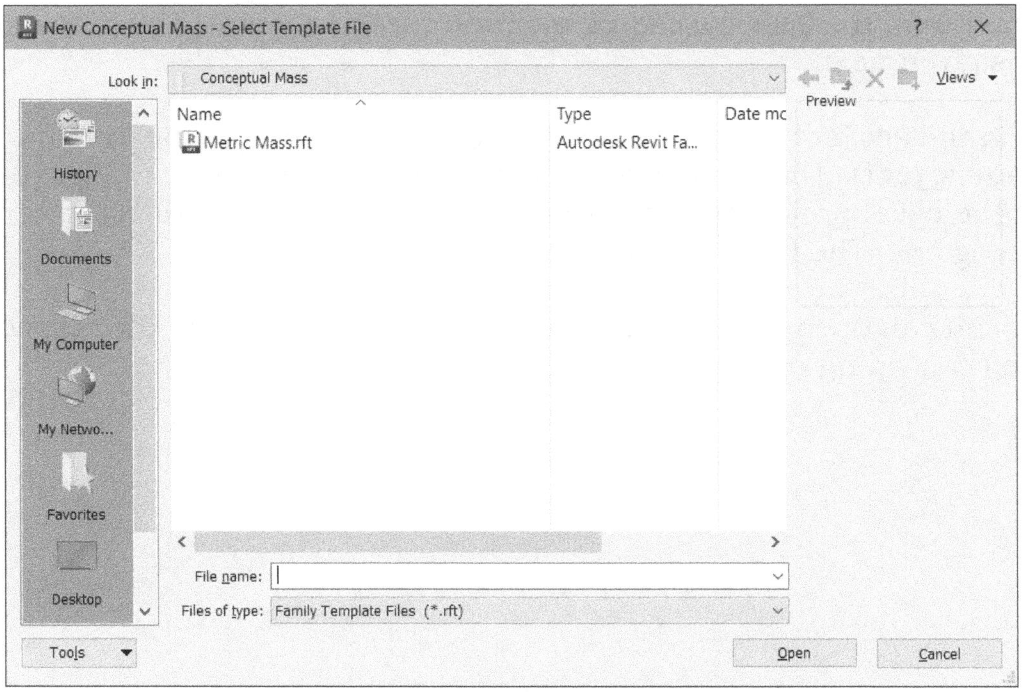

Figure-31. New Conceptual Mass-Select Template File dialog box

- Select desired template from the dialog box and click on the **Open** button. The environment to edit/create conceptual mass will be displayed; refer to Figure-32. We will discuss about conceptual mass creation later in this book.

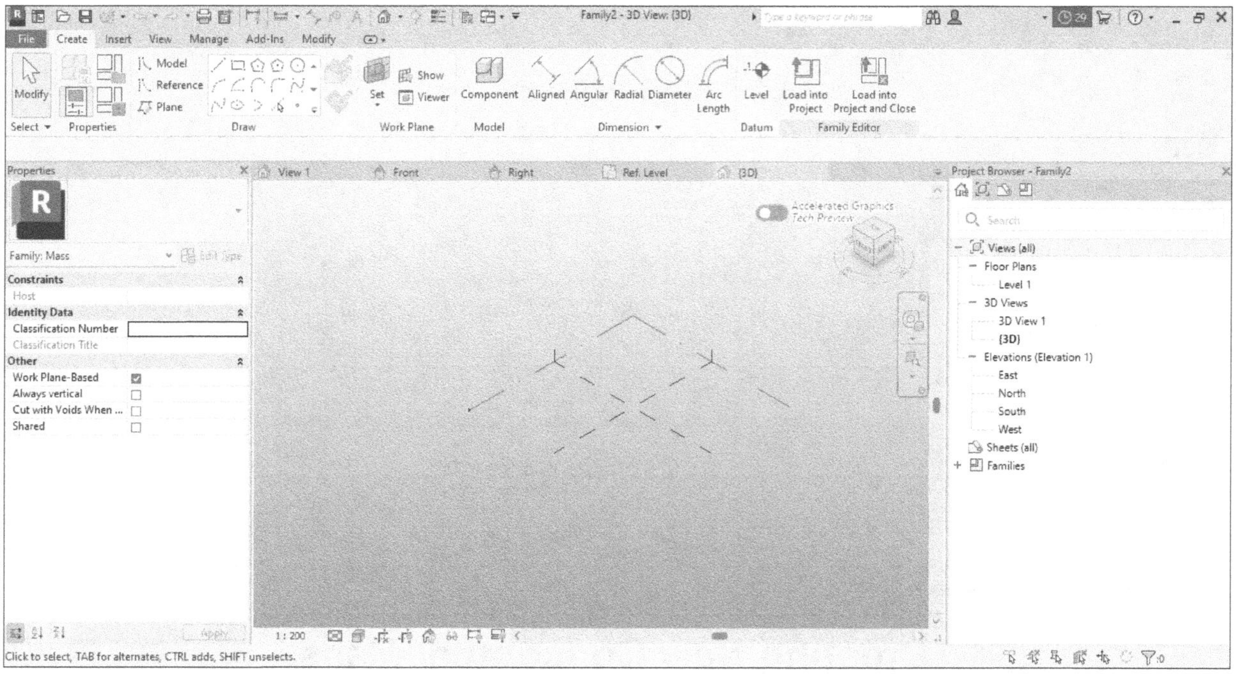

Figure-32. Environment to edit or create conceptual mass

Similarly, you can use the **Title Block** and **Annotation Symbol** tools in the **New** cascading menu of the **File** menu to create new title block template and annotation symbols, respectively.

Opening a Project File

You can open an earlier created Revit project for editing or review by using the **Project** tool from the **Open** cascading menu in the **File** menu. The procedure to use this tool is given next.

- Click on the **Project** tool from the **Open** cascading menu of the **File** menu (**File->Open->Project**). The **Open** dialog box will be displayed; refer to Figure-33.
- Select the file of project that you want to open and click on the **Open** button from the dialog box. The file will be displayed.

Note that you can open the other files in the same way by using the respective tools in the **Open** cascading menu of **File** menu.

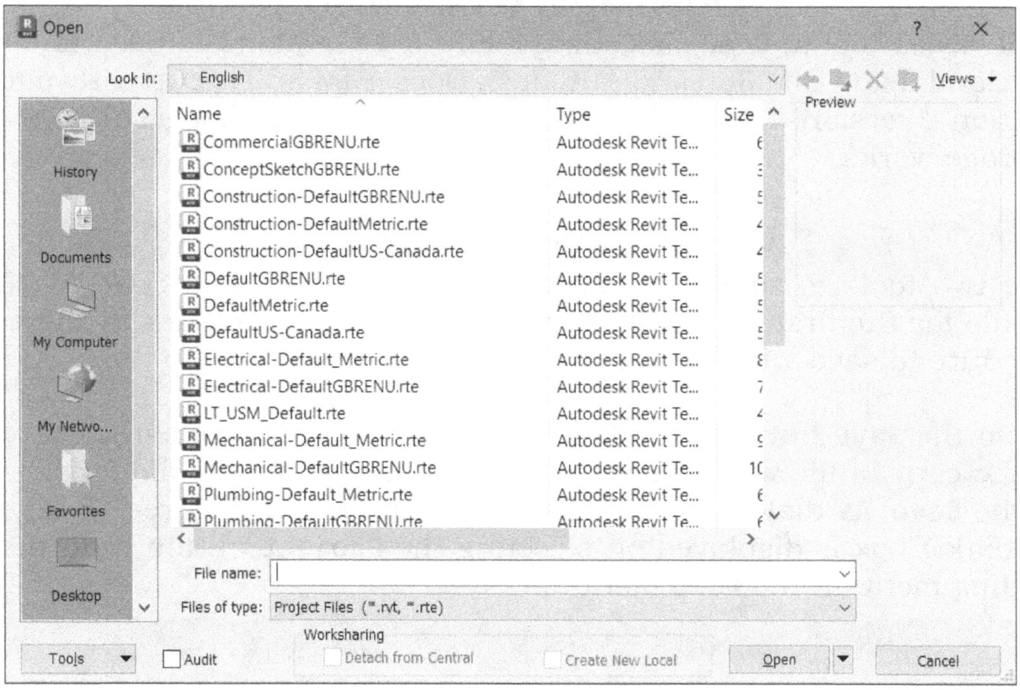

Figure-33. Open dialog box

Opening File in Revit

You can open any supported file in Revit by using a single tool named **Open**. The procedure to use this tool is given next.

- Click on the **Open** button from the **File** menu. The **Open** dialog box will be displayed; refer to Figure-34.

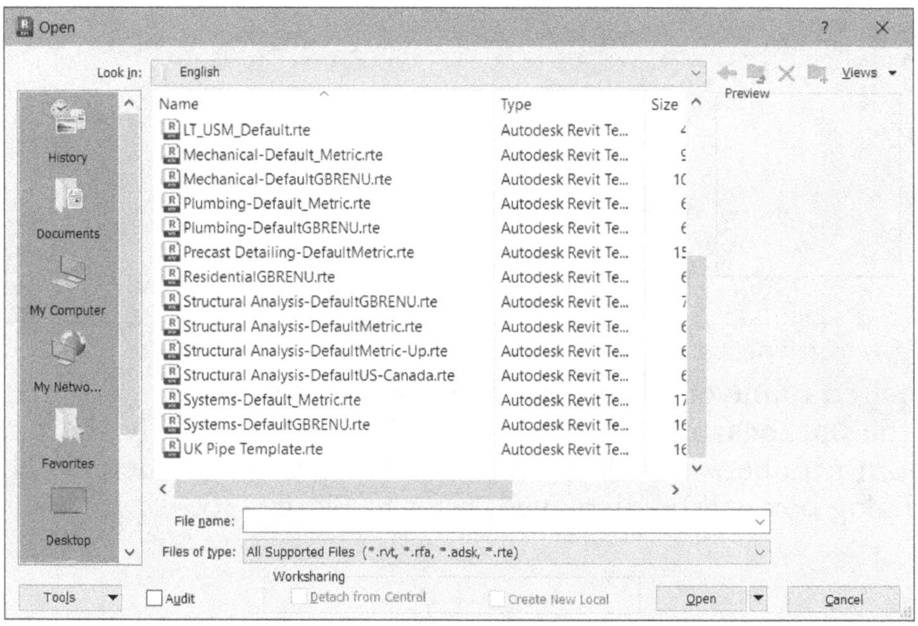

Figure-34. Open dialog box

- Select desired type of file from the **Files of type** drop-down. The files of selected type will be displayed in the dialog box.
- Double-click on the file to open it or select the file and click on the **Open** button from the dialog box. The selected file will open.

Opening a Cloud Model

The **Cloud Model** tool in **Open** cascading menu of **File** menu is used to open model saved on cloud using BIM 360 and Autodesk Docs. BIM 360 is currently not available for educational version. This tool works in the same way as Google drive or any other cloud storage works.

Saving a File

There are two tools to save a file created in Revit; Save and Save As. If you are saving a file for the first time then **Save** and **Save As** tools work in the same way. The procedure to save a file is given next.

- Click on the **Save** button from the **File** menu. If you have earlier saved the file then the copy of file will be updated. If you are saving the file for the first time then the **Save As** dialog box will be displayed; refer to Figure-35. Note that the same dialog box is displayed on selecting the **Project** button from the **Save As** cascading menu in the **File** menu.

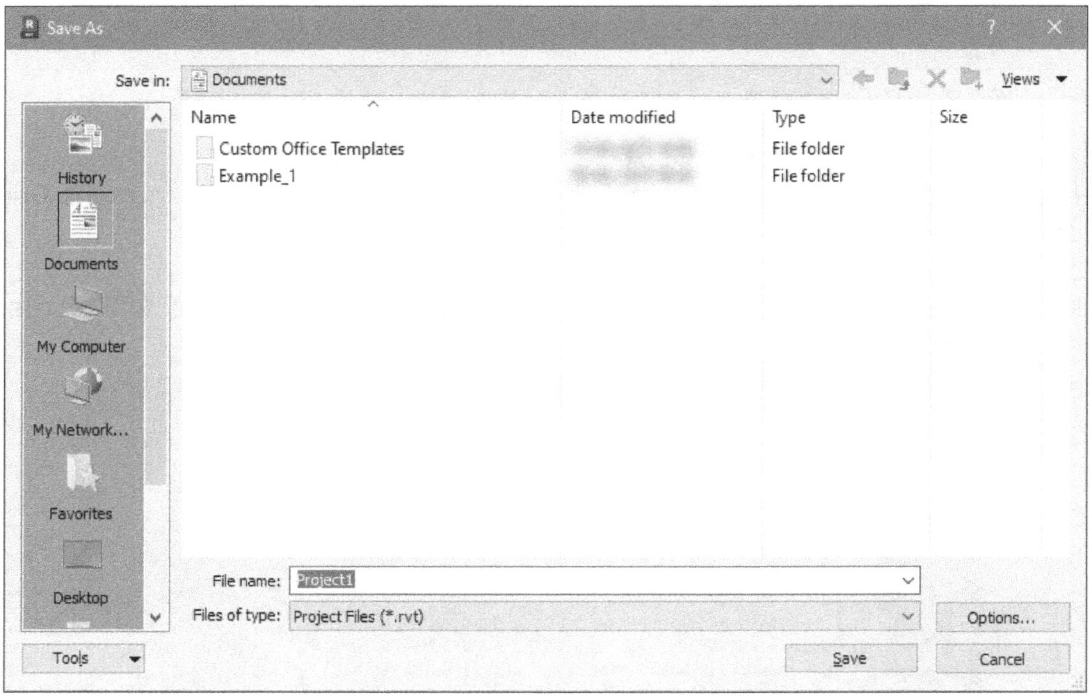

Figure-35. Save As dialog box

- Specify desired name of the file in **File name** edit box.
- Click on the **Options** button from the dialog box to modify the options related to maximum number of backups and work sharing parameters. The **File Save Options** dialog box will be displayed; refer to Figure-36.

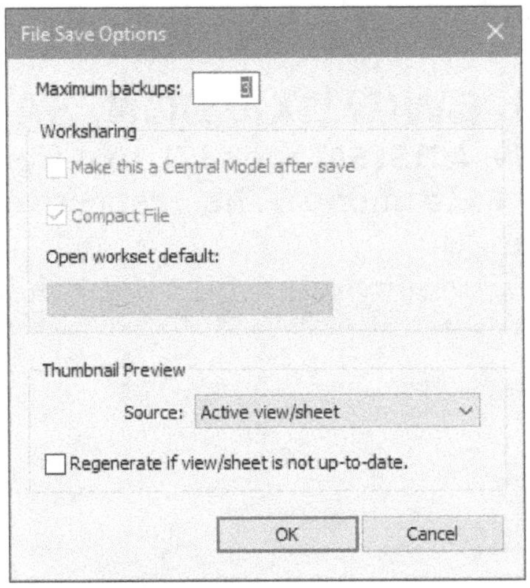

Figure-36. File Save Options dialog box

- In the **Maximum backups** edit box, specify the maximum number of backups to be created for the current file.
- In the **Worksharing** area, set desired parameters to share the saved file with other team members.
- Select desired option from the **Source** drop-down in the **Thumbnail Preview** area to select the source for preview of the project. Click on the **OK** button to apply the file save options.
- After setting all desired parameters, click on the **Save** button from the dialog box to save the file.

Note that in the same way, you can save a project, family, template, or library using respective options from the **Save As** cascading menu.

Exporting Files

The export options in Revit are used to export selected file/project/object for other software. There are various tools in the **Export** cascading menu of the **File** menu to export file in different formats; refer to Figure-37.

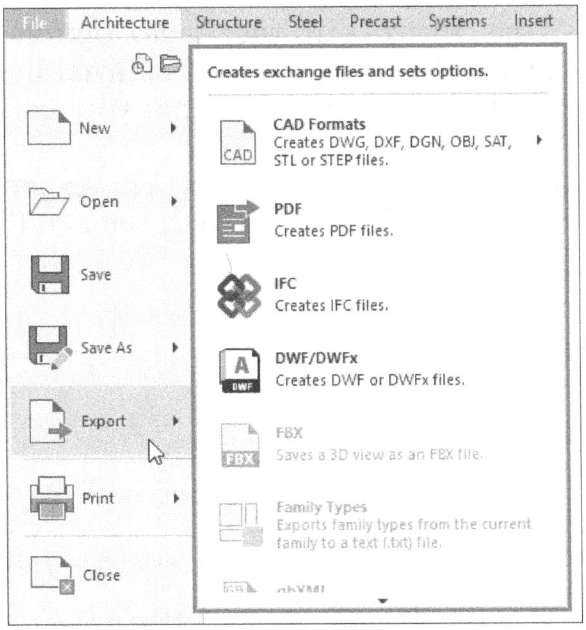

Figure-37. Export cascading menu

Various options in the **Export** cascading menu are discussed next.

Exporting File in DWG, DXF, DGN, SAT, or STL format

- Click on the **DWG**, **DXF**, **DGN**, **ACIS(SAT)**, or **STL** tool from the **Export->CAD Formats** cascading menu in the **File** menu. The respective **Export** dialog box will be displayed; refer to Figure-38.

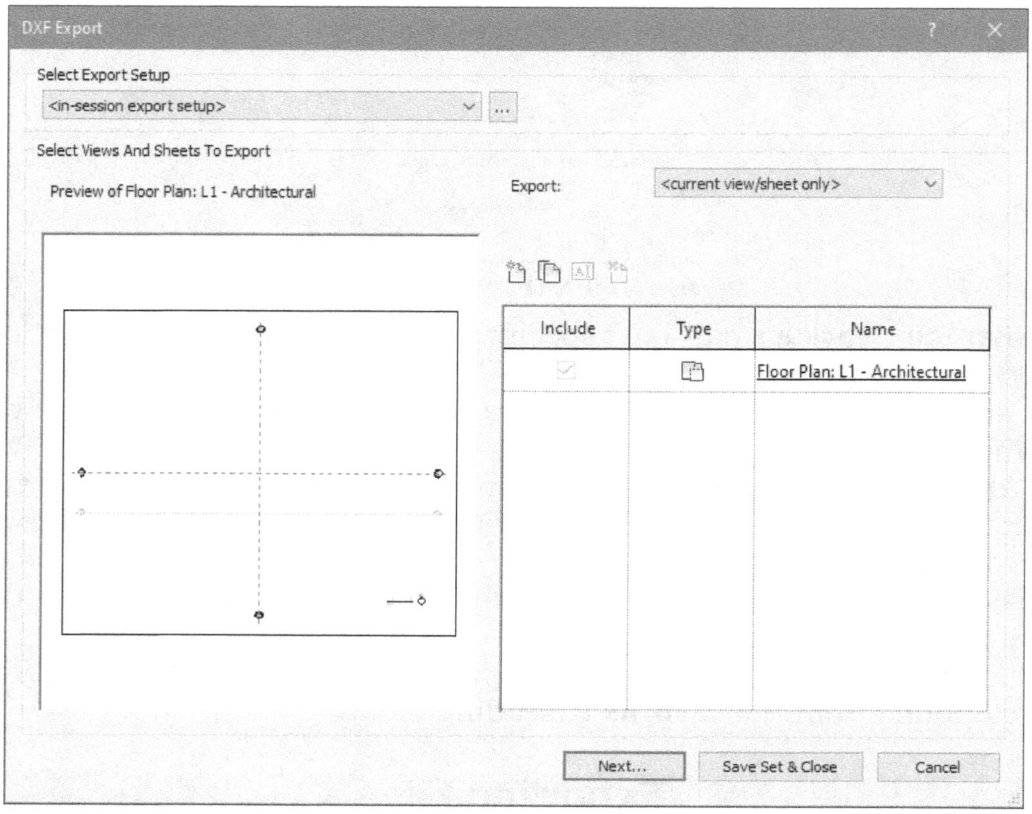

Figure-38. DXF Export dialog box

- Select the **<in-session view/sheet set>** option from the **Export** drop-down in the **Select Views And Sheets To Export** area of the dialog box. The **Show in List** drop-down will become available in the dialog box.
- Select the **All views and sheets in the Model** option from the **Show in List** drop-down. All the views and sheets will be displayed in the list box.
- Select the check boxes for views and sheets that you want to include in exported file.
- Click on the **Next** button from the dialog box. The **Export CAD Formats - Save to Target Folder** dialog box will be displayed; refer to Figure-39.

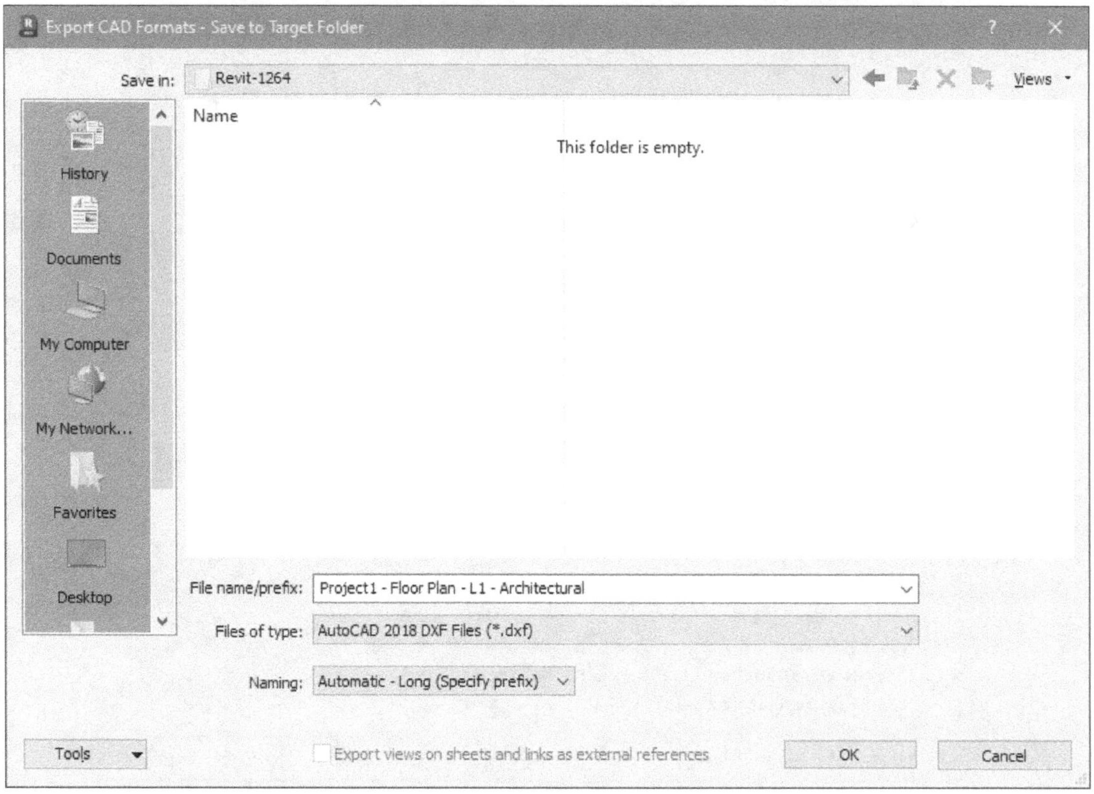

Figure-39. Export CAD Formats-Save to Target Folder dialog box

- Specify desired name for dxf and click on the **OK** button.

You can use the options in the **Export** cascading menu in the same way.

PRINTING VIEWS AND SHEETS

The tools in the **Print** cascading menu are used to prepare and print the views and sheets of model. Various tools of this cascading menu are discussed next.

Print Setup

The **Print Setup** tool is used to set the parameters for printing model. If you want to create a printout different from default settings then this is the tool to be used. The procedure to use this tool is given next.

- Click on the **Print Setup** tool from the **Print** cascading menu of the **File** menu. The **Print Setup** dialog box will be displayed; refer to Figure-40.
- Select desired profile from the **Name** drop-down. The respective options will be set in the dialog box.
- Set desired paper size in the **Size** drop-down. There are some common page sizes available in this drop-down like A3, A4, Legal, and so on. If you want to specify a custom size then select the **Custom** option from the **Size** drop-down.
- Set the orientation and other parameters as desired.
- Click on the **Save As** button from the dialog box and specify new name for the profile in **Name** edit box displayed. After specifying name, click on the **OK** button from the **New** dialog box.
- Click on **OK** button from the dialog box.

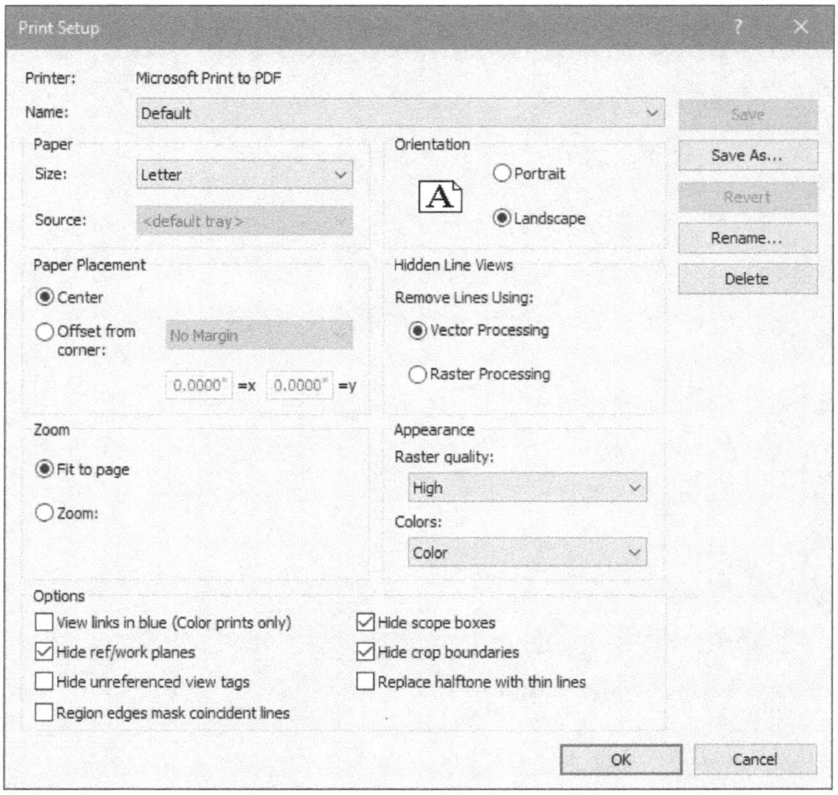

Figure-40. Print Setup dialog box

Print Preview

The **Print Preview** tool is used to check the preview of print before taking the physical printout. The procedure to use this tool is given next.

- Click on the **Print Preview** tool from the **Print** cascading menu of the **File** menu. The preview window will be displayed; refer to Figure-41.

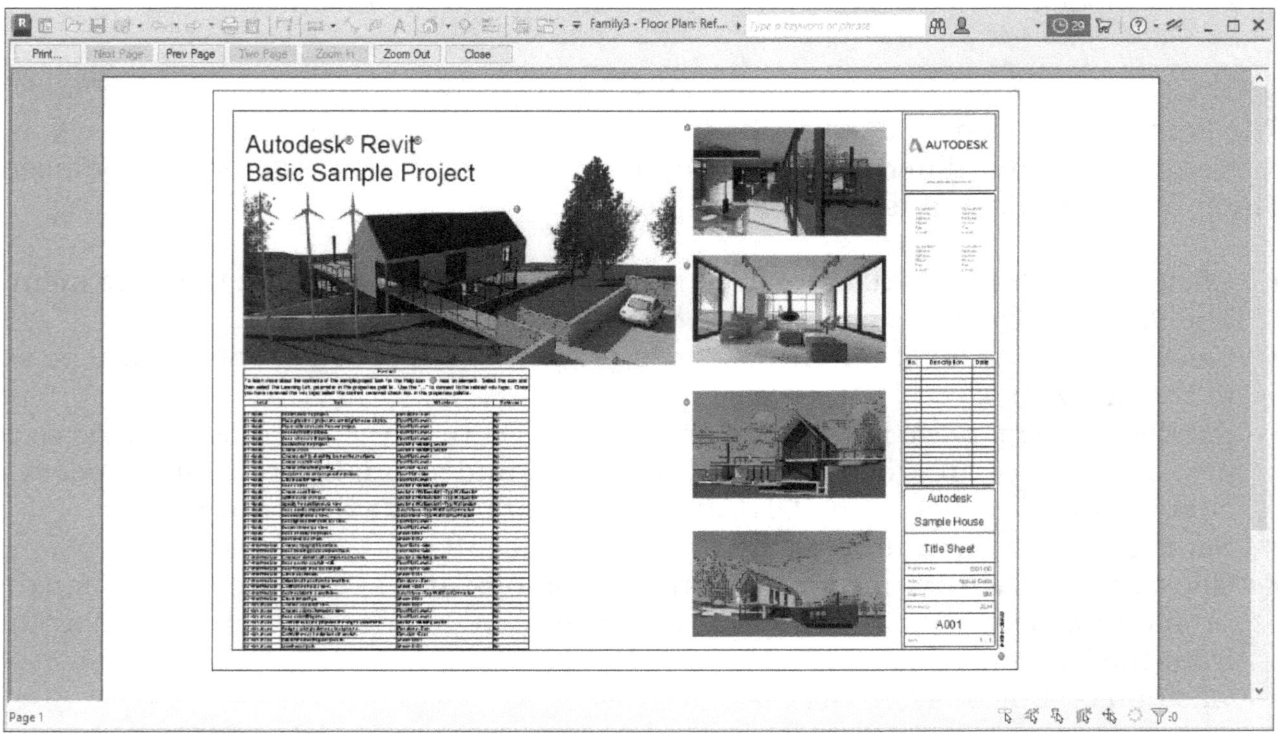

Figure-41. Print preview window

- Click on the **Next Page** and **Prev Page** buttons to check previews of different pages to be printed.
- Click on the **Zoom In** and **Zoom Out** buttons to enlarge or diminish the view.
- Click on the **Close** button to exit the window. If you want to print the documents during preview then click on the **Print** button from the preview window. The options for printing are discussed in next topic.

Printing Documents

The **Print** tool is used to take print out of drawing created in Revit. The procedure to use this tool is given next.

- Click on the **Print** tool from the **Print** cascading menu of the **File** menu. The **Print** dialog box will be displayed; refer to Figure-42.

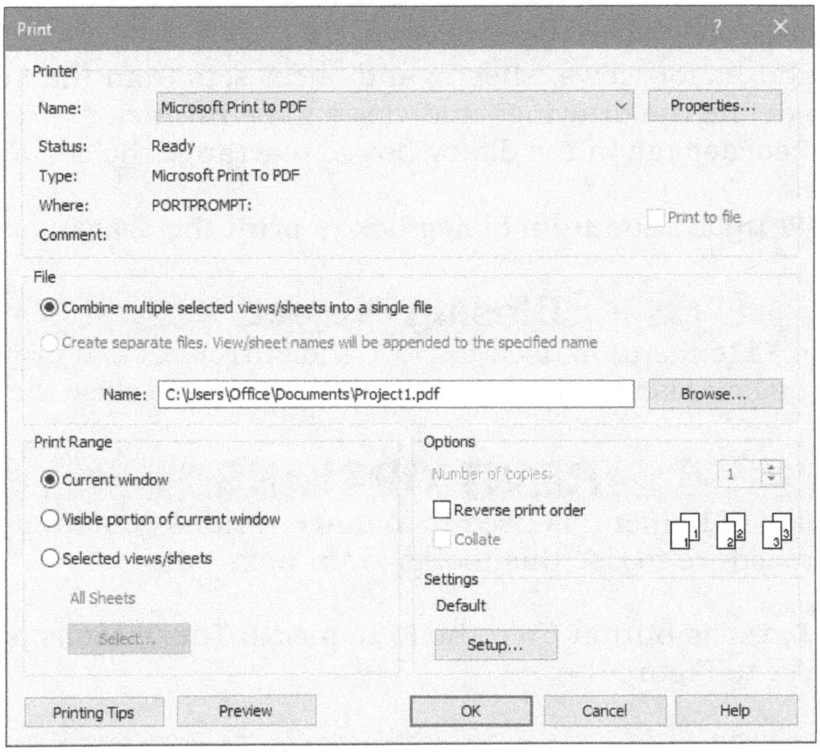

Figure-42. Print dialog box

- Select desired radio button from the **Print Range** area of the dialog box. Select the **Current window** radio button if you want to print objects displayed in current window only. Select the **Visible portion of current window** radio button to print the objects that are visible in current window. Select the **Selected views/sheets** radio button if you want to print only selected sheets and views. The **Select** button below the radio button will become active. Click on the **Select** button. The **View/Sheet Set** dialog box will be displayed. Select the sheets/views that need to be printed and click on the **OK** button.
- Set the number of copies to be printed using the **Number of copies** spinner in the **Options** area of the dialog box.
- Click on the **OK** button from the dialog box to take the printouts.

Batch Printing

The **Batch Print** tool is used to print multiple drawings of current project. The procedure to use this tool is given next.

- Open the project you want to print and make sure it is saved with latest changes. Click on the **Batch Print** tool from the **Print** cascading menu of the **File** menu. The **Batch Print** dialog box will be displayed; refer to Figure-43.

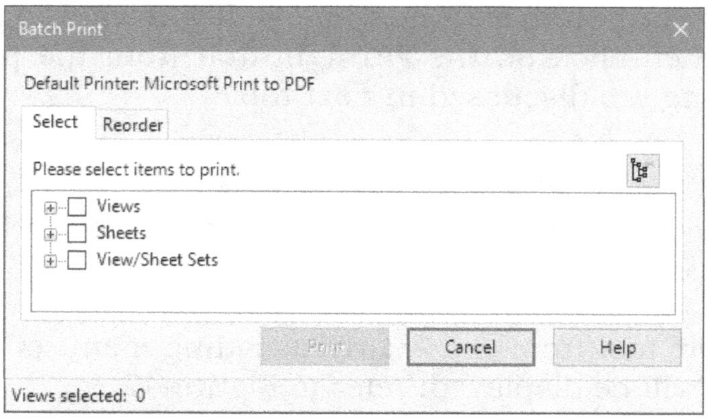

Figure-43. Batch Print dialog box

- Select check boxes for views, sheets, and sheet sets from the **Select** tab in the dialog box to define the drawings and views to be printed.
- Click on the **Reorder** tab in the dialog box to rearrange the sequence of drawings to be printed.
- Click on the **Print** button from dialog box to print the drawings.

Closing Project

The **Close** tool in **File** menu is used to close the current active project displayed in graphics area. You can also use the shortcut **CTRL+W** keys to close the current project.

REVIT OPTIONS

The **Options** tool of **File** menu is used to manage various general parameters of the software. The procedure to use this tool is given next.

- Click on the **Options** button from the **File** menu. The **Options** dialog box will be displayed; refer to Figure-44.

General Page

- By default, the **General** page of dialog box is displayed. If not displayed by default, select the **General** option from the left area in the dialog box.
- Select desired option from the **Save reminder interval** drop-down to define the time after which a save reminder will be displayed if you have not saved your current open model after modifications. Select the **No reminders** option from drop-down if you do not want to display a save reminder.
- Select desired option from the **Synchronize with Central reminder interval** drop-down to set synchronization for save reminders when worksharing.
- Set desired values in the **When number of journals exceeds** edit box to define number of journals after which cleanup will begin. Click in the **Delete journals older than (days)** edit box and specify desired value to define how much older files will be deleted.
- Using the **Worksharing update frequency** slider, you can define the time (in seconds) after which the model you are sharing with others will be updated.
- Select desired option from the **Default view discipline** drop-down to define which discipline of software will be displayed by default after starting the software.

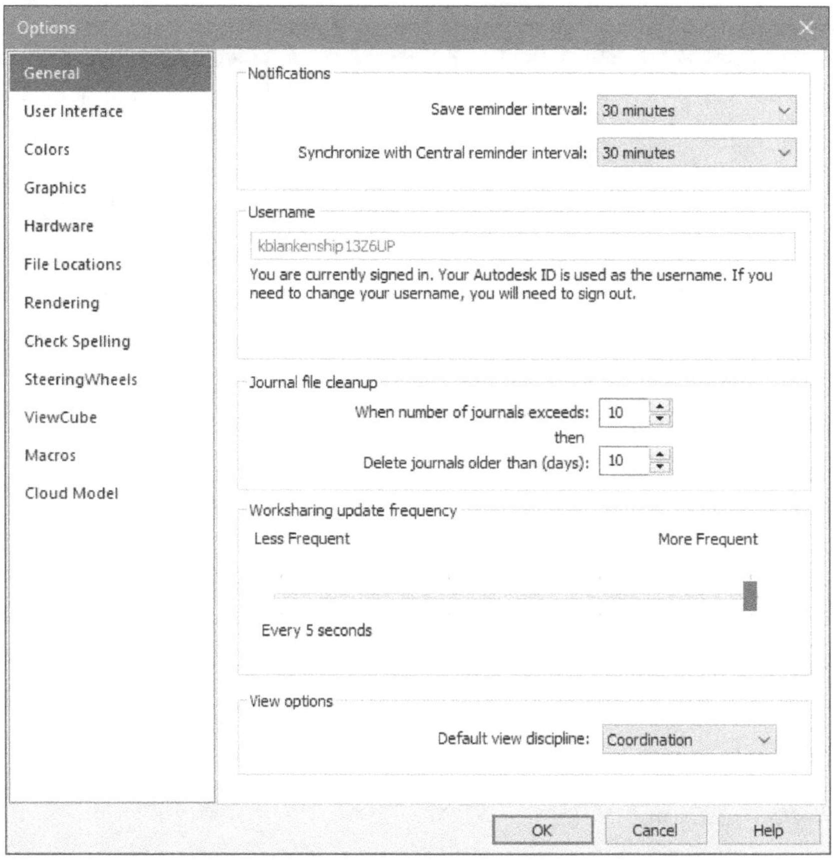

Figure-44. Options dialog box

User Interface Page

- Select desired check boxes from the **Tools and analyses** area to define which tools will be displayed in the default user interface of software.

Customizing Keyboard Shortcuts

- Click on the **Customize** button for **Keyboard shortcuts** option to customize general shortcuts. The **Keyboard Shortcuts** dialog box will be displayed; refer to Figure-45. Select desired option from the **Assignments** area of dialog box and press desired shortcut keys to be assigned to that option. After pressing keys, click on the **Assign** button. If you have pressed unique shortcut keys for the option then they will be assigned but if the shortcut keys are not unique then the **Duplicate Shortcut** dialog box will be displayed; refer to Figure-46. Click on the **OK** button if you want to allow duplicate assignment of shortcut keys. You need to press the shortcut keys and while holding the keys, press Arrow keys to cycle between options bound to shortcut keys. Press **SPACEBAR** to execute the option. You can use the **Import** and **Export** buttons in the dialog box to import and export shortcut keys data in XML format. After setting desired parameters, click on the **OK** button from the dialog box.

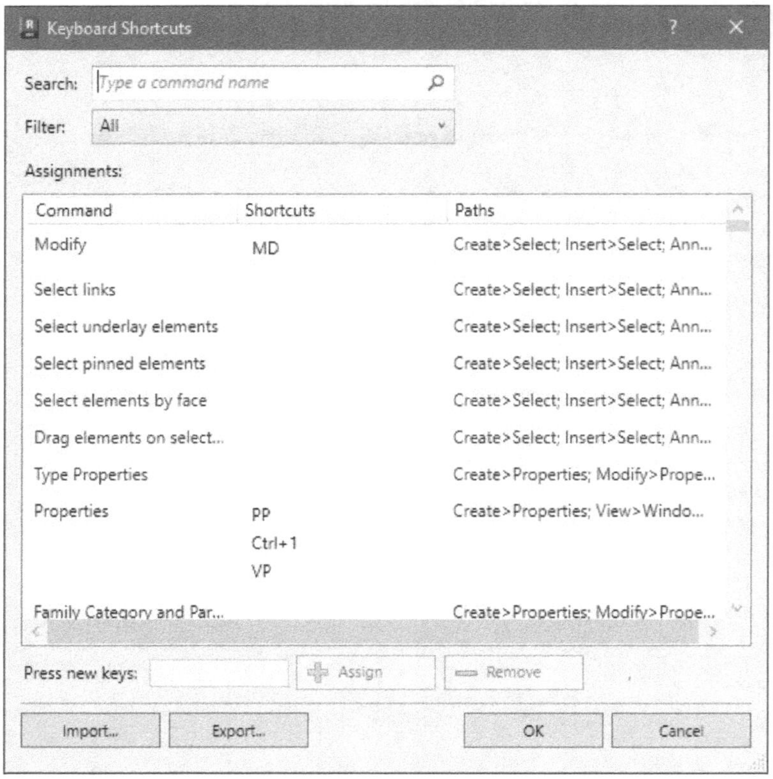

Figure-45. Keyboard Shortcuts dialog box

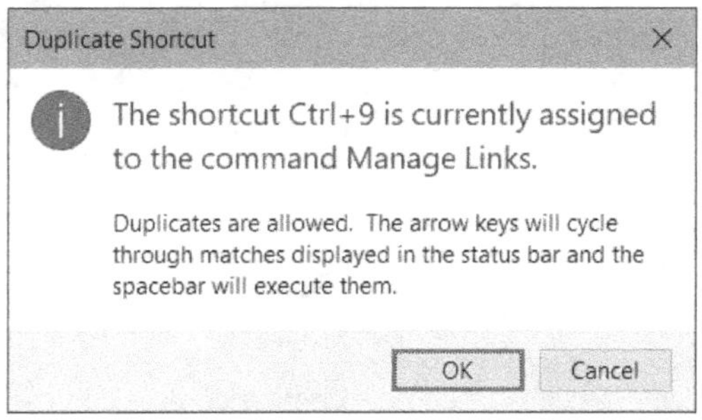

Figure-46. Duplicate Shortcut dialog box

Customizing Double-Click Actions

- Click on the **Customize** button for **Double-click actions** in the dialog box to define what functions will it do when double-clicked on a specific object. On clicking this button, the **Customize Double-click Settings** dialog box will be displayed; refer to Figure-47. Click in the **Double-click action** field for desired element from the table in the dialog box and select desired option. After setting desired parameters, click on the **OK** button from the dialog box.

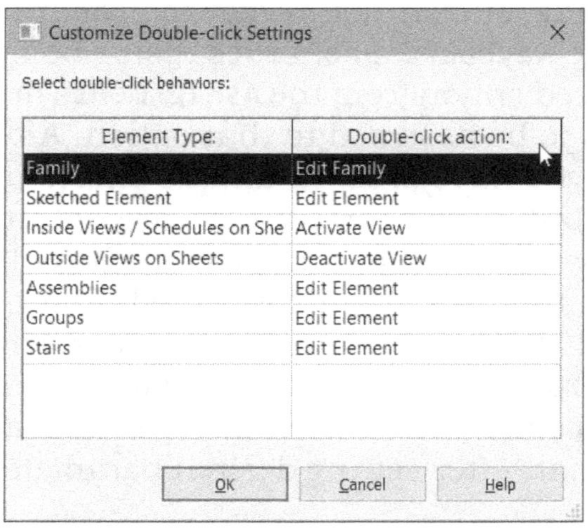

Figure-47. Customize Double-click Settings dialog box

- Select desired option from the **Tooltip assistance** drop-down to define the level up to which tooltip information will be displayed when you hover the cursor on any tool or option in the interface.
- Select the **Enable Recent Files List at Home** check box to display recently used files in the home screen after starting software.

- Select desired option from the **Project Environment** drop-down of **Ribbon tab switching** area to define whether you will return to previous tab after exiting modification mode or you will stay on the **Modify** tab.
- Similarly, select desired option from the **Family Editor** drop-down to define how you will exit the modification mode for family objects.
- Select the **Display the contextual tab on selection** check box to display related modification contextual tab when you select an object.
- Select desired option from the drop-down of **View switching** area to define how views will be switched when using shortcut keys.

Colors Page

- Select desired option from the **Active theme** drop-down to define the theme in which interface of software will be displayed. Select the **Dark** option from the drop-down to display interface elements in darker colors.
- You can also set custom colors by using drop-downs in the **Canvas colors** area of dialog box.

Graphics Page

The options in the **Graphics** page of dialog box are used to define colors and graphics mode of software interface; refer to Figure-48.

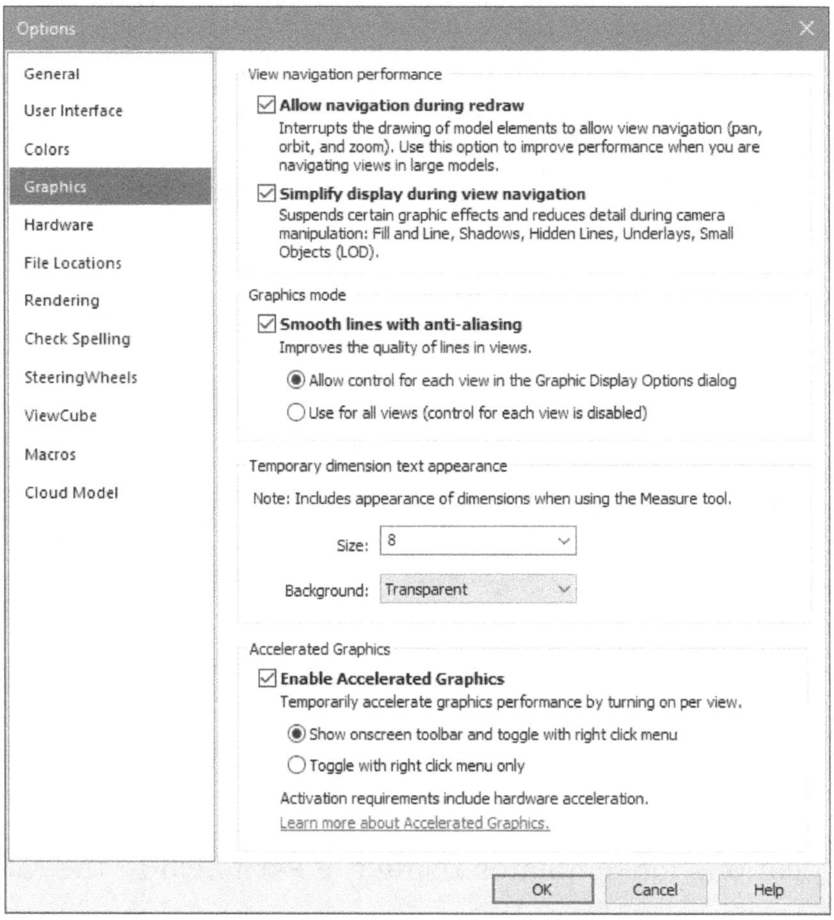

Figure-48. Graphics page

- Select the **Allow navigation during redraw** check box to allow navigation of model (using pan, orbit, and zoom tools) while drawing model elements.

- Select the **Simplify display during view navigation** check box to remove graphic effects while performing navigation maneuvers.
- Select the **Smooth lines with anti-aliasing** check box from the **Graphics mode** area to smoothen display of lines in various views. After selecting the check box, select desired radio button.
- Specify desired value in **Size** drop-down to define size of temporary text. Select desired option from the **Background** drop-down to define whether background for temporary text will be transparent or opaque.
- Select **Enable Accelerated Graphics** check box from **Accelerated Graphics** area to accelerate the graphics performance temporarily for walkthroughs and rendering.

Hardware Page

The options in **Hardware** page are used to activate hardware acceleration using graphic card installed in your system.

File Locations Page

The options in the **File Locations** page are used to define locations for various templates and files; refer to Figure-49. Various options of this page are discussed next.

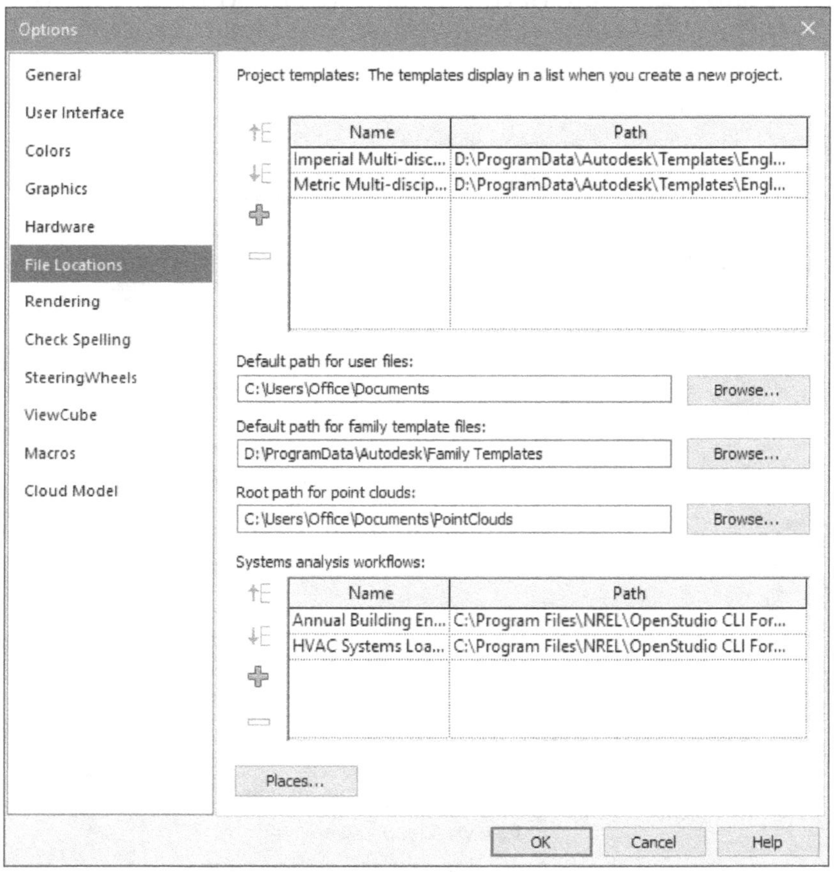

Figure-49. File Locations page

- Set desired locations for templates using the **Path** field in the table at the top of dialog box.
- Click on the **Browse** button for **Default path for user files** field and set default location for saving files created in the software.

- Similarly, set desired locations for family template files and point clouds.
- Using the options of **Systems analysis workflows** area, you can set the template file for workflow of common analyses.

Similarly, you can set parameters in other pages of **Options** dialog box. After setting desired options in the dialog box, click on the **OK** button.

Since, the Revit software is able to perform multiple tasks like structural designing, architectural designing, and system designing so we have named the chapters accordingly. We will start with Architectural Design in next chapter and then we will continue to structural and system designing.

SELF-ASSESSMENT

Q1. Describe the term BIM for Construction Industry.

Q2. In Autodesk Revit, if an object (door, window etc.) is changed in one view then that change will propagate in all the connected views. (T/F)

Q3. Which of the following options cannot be used for starting Autodesk Revit in Microsoft Windows 10?

a. Desktop Icon
b. Start menu
c. Cortana
d. Control Panel

Q4. Which of the following interface elements are used to modify properties of selected component?

a. Properties Palette
b. Project Browser
c. Ribbon
d. Status Bar

Q5. The **Sun Path On/Off** toggle button is used to check the effects of Sun heat and shadow on the building analysis. (T/F)

Q6. The **Conceptual Mass** tool is used to create conceptual representation of various objects used in Revit drawing. (T/F)

Q7. You cannot change shortcut keys applied to common functions of software by default. (T/F)

Q8. What is the primary purpose of the Ribbon in Autodesk Revit?

A. To display project details
B. To organize tools under different tabs and panels
C. To manage file settings
D. To control the user's login credentials

Q9. Which of the following is NOT a component of the Title Bar in Autodesk Revit?

A. Quick Access Toolbar
B. Project Browser
C. Sign In Button
D. Help Button

Q10. What does the Quick Access Toolbar in Revit allow you to do?

A. Customize the interface layout
B. Access common file handling tools
C. Modify component properties
D. Switch between different project views

Q11. What is the function of the Search Box in Autodesk Revit?

A. To search for design templates
B. To find topics in Revit Help
C. To search for project files on the cloud
D. To locate family components

Q12. Which option in the Title Bar is used to install or share apps for Autodesk products?

A. Help Button
B. Quick Access Toolbar
C. Autodesk App Store Button
D. Sign In Button

Q13. What is the purpose of the Properties Palette in Revit?

A. To manage project templates
B. To switch between different views
C. To modify properties of selected components
D. To control user access permissions

Q14. Where is the Project Browser typically located in the Revit interface?

A. Above the Title Bar
B. Below the Properties Palette
C. On the Ribbon
D. In the View Control Bar

Q15. What does the Status Bar display when you highlight an element or component?

A. The name of the family and family type
B. The current project settings
C. The file size and status
D. The last modified date

Q16. Which option in the Status Bar allows you to create different design sets?

A. Worksets
B. Design Options
C. Editing Requests
D. Temporary View Properties

Q17. What is the purpose of the View Control Bar in Revit?

A. To manage project settings
B. To switch between different user accounts
C. To toggle view options like scale and detail level
D. To export project files

Q18. Which of the following options in the View Control Bar is used to crop the view using a sketch boundary?

A. Crop View
B. Temporary Isolate/Hide
C. Reveal Hidden Elements
D. Worksharing Display Off

Q19. What does the File menu in Revit allow you to do?

A. Customize interface colors
B. Manage functions related to files like open, save, export
C. Create new families only
D. Adjust system performance settings

Q20. Which tool is used to create a new project in Autodesk Revit?

A. Family Tool
B. Conceptual Mass Tool
C. Project Tool
D. Annotation Symbol Tool

Q21. Which tool in Revit is used to export files in DWG, DXF, DGN, SAT, or STL formats?

A) Export to PDF
B) Export CAD Formats
C) Print Setup
D) Save As

Q22. What option should you select to export all views and sheets in the model?

A) Selected Views
B) Current Window
C) All Views and Sheets in the Model
D) Custom Views

Q23. After selecting views and sheets to export, which button should you click to proceed?

A) Cancel
B) Back
C) Next
D) Finish

Q24. What file extension is associated with a Revit project file?

A) *.rte
B) *.rvt
C) *.dwg
D) *.pdf

Q25. Which tool allows you to prepare and print views and sheets of a model?

A) Batch Print
B) Print Setup
C) Print Preview
D) Print

Q26. In the Print Setup dialog box, what option allows you to define custom paper size?

A) Page Layout
B) Custom Size
C) Print Range
D) Paper Settings

Q27. What is the purpose of the Batch Print tool?

A) To print a single view
B) To save files in batches
C) To print multiple drawings of the current project
D) To export files in bulk

Q28. What is the shortcut key to close the current active project in Revit?

A) CTRL+P
B) CTRL+S
C) CTRL+W
D) CTRL+O

Q29. Which page in the Options dialog box allows you to manage general software parameters?

A) User Interface
B) General
C) Hardware
D) Colors

Q30. How can you customize keyboard shortcuts in Revit?

A) By editing the Options file
B) Through the Customize button in the Keyboard Shortcuts dialog box
C) By changing the File menu settings
D) By modifying the Revit.ini file

Q31. What action does the Double-click action customization allow you to define?

A) Print settings
B) View switching
C) Function when double-clicking an object
D) Export format

Q32. Which theme option in the Colors page of the Options dialog box displays interface elements in darker colors?

A) Light Theme
B) Dark Theme
C) Classic Theme
D) Custom Theme

Q33. In the Graphics page of the Options dialog box, which checkbox allows navigation of the model while drawing?

A) Simplify Display During Navigation
B) Allow Navigation During Redraw
C) Smooth Lines with Anti-Aliasing
D) Enable High-Quality Graphics

Q34. In the Print Preview tool, which button allows you to check previews of different pages to be printed?

A) Zoom In
B) Next Page and Prev Page
C) Print
D) Close

Q35. What option should be selected to print only the objects visible in the current window?

A) Selected Views/Sheets
B) Current Window
C) All Views and Sheets
D) Custom View

Q36. Which dialog box is displayed when you click on the Print tool from the Print cascading menu?

A) Export CAD Formats
B) Print Setup
C) Print
D) Batch Print

Q37. What does the "Reorder" tab in the Batch Print dialog box allow you to do?

A) Change the print settings
B) Add new views for printing
C) Rearrange the sequence of drawings
D) Save the print configuration

Q38. Which option in the Options dialog box allows you to define the theme in which the interface is displayed?

A) Colors
B) General
C) User Interface
D) File Locations

Q39. In the Graphics page of the Options dialog box, which option smooths the display of lines in various views?

A) Simplify Display During Navigation
B) Allow Navigation During Redraw
C) Smooth Lines with Anti-Aliasing
D) Enable High-Quality Rendering

Q40. What is the purpose of the "Tooltip Assistance" option in the Options dialog box?

A) To display tooltips for keyboard shortcuts
B) To define the level of tooltip information displayed when hovering over a tool
C) To customize the appearance of tooltips
D) To disable all tooltips

Chapter 2

Architectural Designing

Topics Covered

The major topics covered in this chapter are:

- ***Starting A New Project***
- ***Creating Grids***
- ***Creating Walls***
- ***Creating Doors***
- ***Loading Autodesk Family***
- ***Modification Tools***
- ***Creating Windows***
- ***Placing Components***
- ***Creating Columns***

STARTING A NEW PROJECT

In the previous chapter, you have learned to start a project with standard templates. Here, we will start a project with no predefined template and then we will prepare the hierarchy of the project. The procedure to start and manage a revit project is given next.

- Click on the **Project** tool from the **New** cascading menu of the **File** menu. The **New Project** dialog box will be displayed.
- Select the **<None>** option from the **Template File** drop-down and select the **Project** radio button from the **Create new** area. Click on the **OK** button from the dialog box. The **Undefined System of Measurement** dialog box will be displayed; refer to Figure-1.

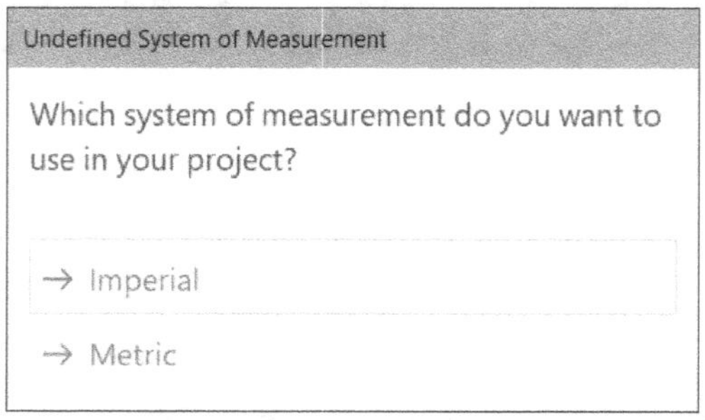

Figure-1. Undefined System of Measurement

- Select the **Imperial** or **Metric** button from the dialog box to start project in respective units. Most of the building designers use Imperial unit system. On selecting the button, the project will open in the application window. By default, the Floor plan sheet opens in the application window.

Now, we will start with Architectural Design. The tools to create architectural design are available in the **Architecture** tab of **Ribbon**; refer to Figure-2.

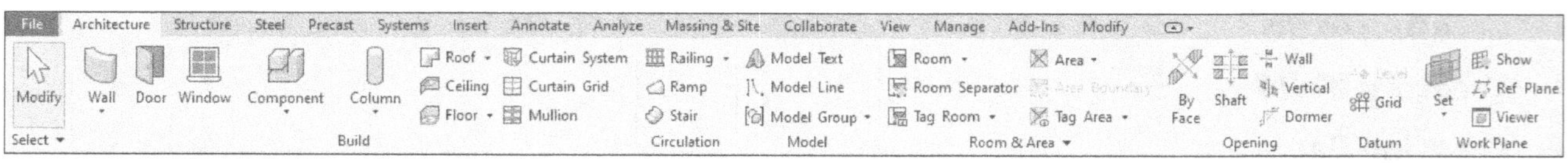

Figure-2. Architecture tab in Ribbon

Various tools of this tab are discussed next.

CREATING GRID

Grid is used as reference to create various construction objects in the model. The tool to create grid is available in the **Datum** panel of the **Architecture** and **Structure** tabs of the **Ribbon**. The procedure to create grid is given next.

- Click on the **Grid** tool from the **Datum** panel in the **Ribbon**. The **Modify|Place Grid** contextual tab will be displayed in the **Ribbon**; refer to Figure-3 and you will be asked to specify starting point of the grid.

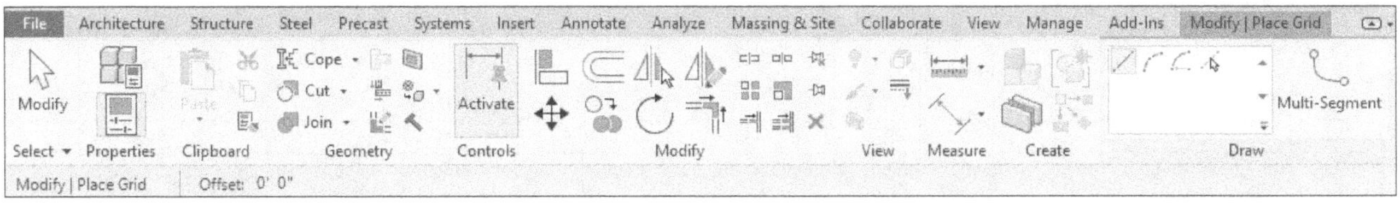

Figure-3. Modify | Place Grid contextual tab

- Click at desired location to specify starting point of grid line. You will be asked to specify end point of the line. Click to place the grid line. Note that while moving the cursor to specify end point, the angle and distance values are automatically displayed to assist you. If you want to create an arc grid then select desired **Arc** tool from the **Draw** panel in the contextual tab and create desired arc grid.
- Click on the number or alphabet in the grid balloon to change its value. The new grids will take progressive value automatically.
- Press **ESC** to exit the tool.

CREATING WALLS

The tools to create walls are available in the **Walls** drop-down of the **Build** panel in the **Ribbon**; refer to Figure-4. The procedure to create different types of walls is given next.

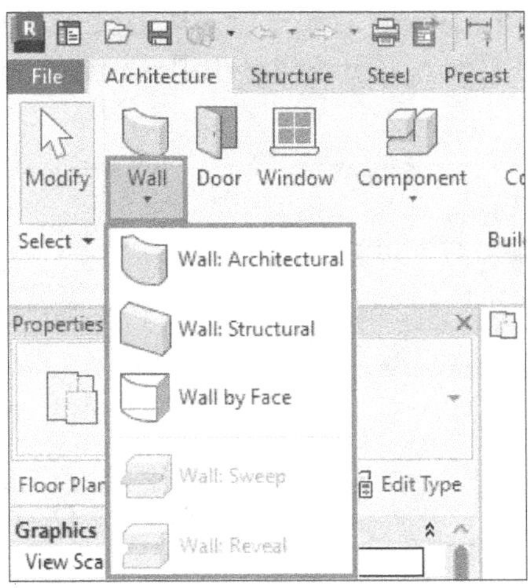

Figure-4. Wall drop-down

Creating Architectural Wall

Architectural Walls are created where load is not endured by walls. In such cases, the walls act as enclosure for a room. Note that by default, architectural walls do not appear in structural model. The procedure to create architectural wall is given next.

- Click on the **Wall: Architectural** tool from the **Wall** drop-down in the **Build** panel of **Architecture** tab in the **Ribbon**. The **Modify|Place Wall** contextual tab will be displayed in the **Ribbon** and options related to wall will be displayed in the **Property Palette**; refer to Figure-5.

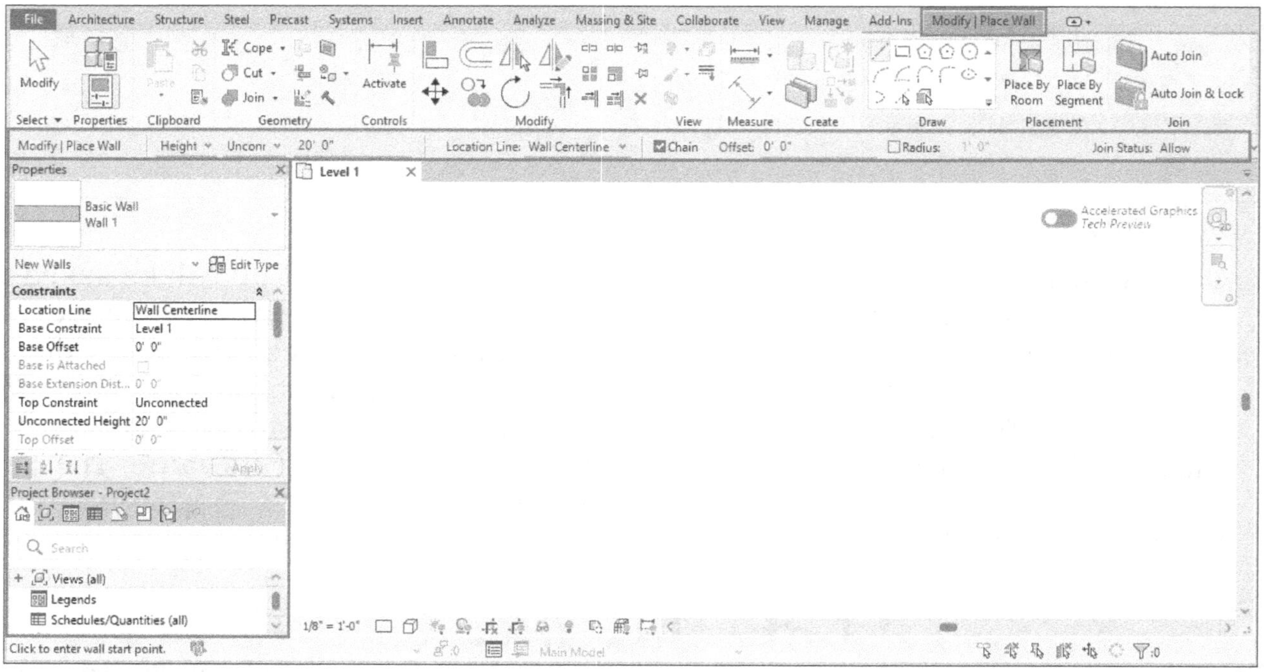

Figure-5. Options to create wall

- Click on the **Type Selector** drop-down at the top in the **Properties Palette** to change the type of wall; refer to Figure-6.
- Click on the **Location Line** option from the **Properties Palette** and select desired option from the displayed drop-down to define the reference line for placing wall; refer to Figure-7.

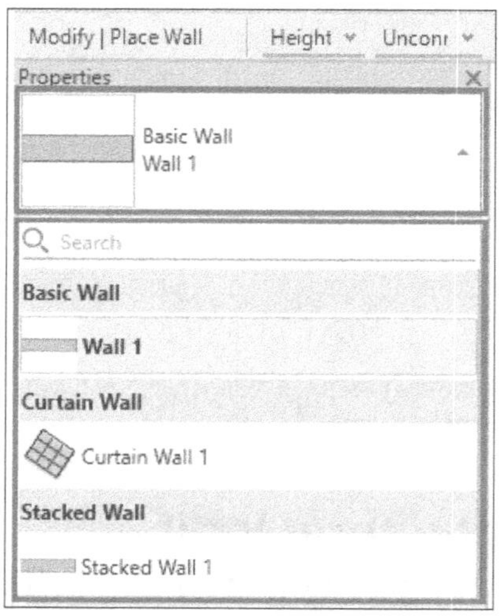

Figure-6. Wall Type Selector drop-down

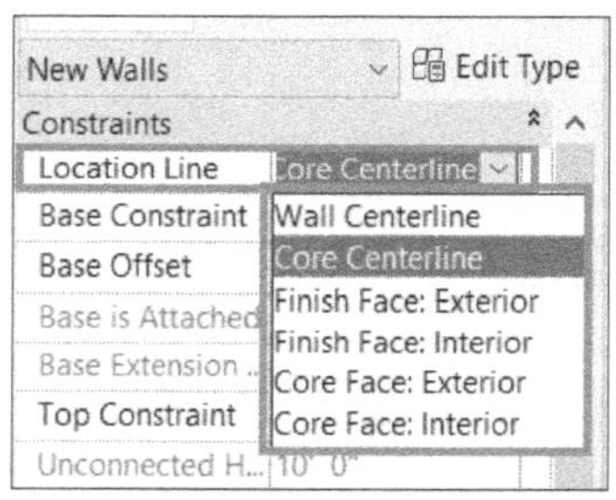

Figure-7. Location Line drop-down

- Select desired option from the **Base Constraint** drop-down to define where base of wall will be placed. You can select different levels from this drop-down.
- Specify desired value in **Base Offset** edit box to offset wall base from selected level. The wall base will be placed at a height of specified value from the base level.
- Select desired option from the **Top Constraint** drop-down to define the level up to which the wall will be created. If you want to specify the height of wall by a value then select the **Unconnected** option from the drop-down and specify desired value in **Unconnected Height** edit box below the drop-down.
- If you have selected a level option from the **Top Constraint** drop-down then you can define the offset distance for top of wall by using the **Top Offset** edit box.

- Set the **Allow** option in **Join Status** drop-down of **Options Bar** to make walls join at intersections. If you select **Disallow** option from the **Join Status** drop-down then walls will not be joined and behave as separate objects during analysis.
- If there are other construction objects above or below the walls then you can select the **Top is Attached** or **Base is Attached** check boxes from the **Properties Palette**.
- Select desired option from the **Cross-Section** drop-down to define whether wall is straight vertical, slanted (inclined from vertical axis), or tapered. Note that to create a tapered wall, you need to make structure of selected wall type as variable. To create a slanted wall, select the **Slanted** option from the **Cross-Section** drop-down and specify slant angle value in the **Angle From Vertical** field of **Properties Palette**. Preview of slanted wall will be displayed as shown in Figure-8 when drawing wall. To make structure of wall variable, click on the **Edit Type** button from **Properties Palette** after activating **Wall** tool and selecting a basic wall type; refer to Figure-9. The **Type Properties** dialog box will be displayed; refer to Figure-10. Click on the **Edit** button from the **Structure** field of dialog box. The **Edit Assembly** dialog box will be displayed; refer to Figure-11. Select the **Variable** check box for **Structure** field as shown in Figure-11. Click on the **OK** button from the **Edit Assembly** dialog box and then **Type Properties** dialog box.
- After making structure of wall as variable, select the **Tapered** option from the **Cross-section** drop-down and specify related parameters in fields below the drop-down to create a tapered wall; refer to Figure-12.

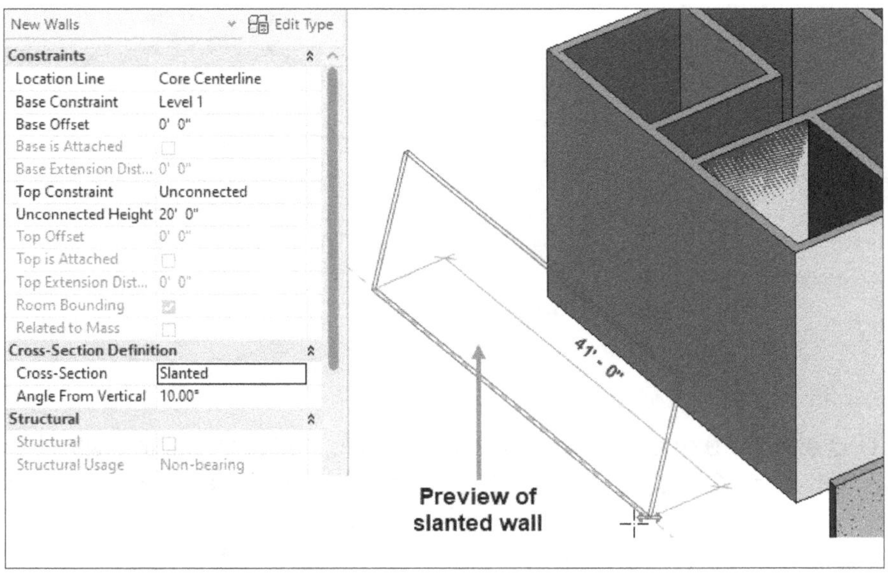

Figure-8. Preview of slanted wall

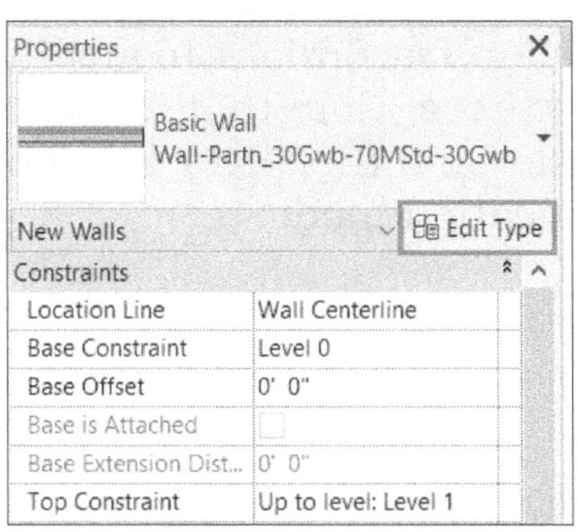

Figure-9. Edit Type button

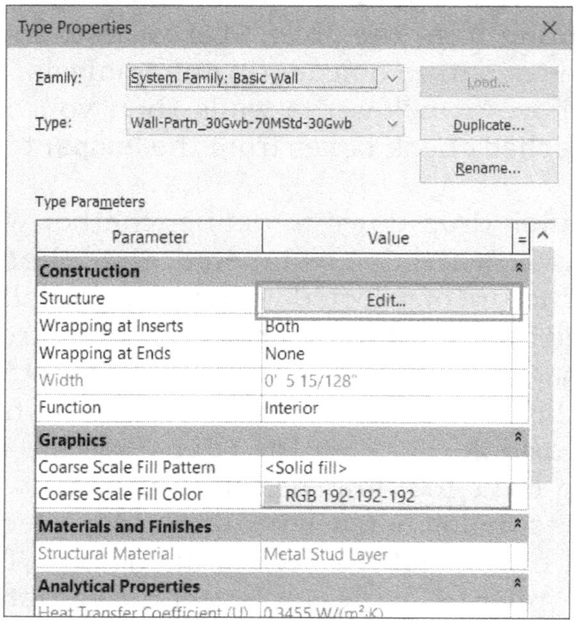

Figure-10. Type Properties dialog box

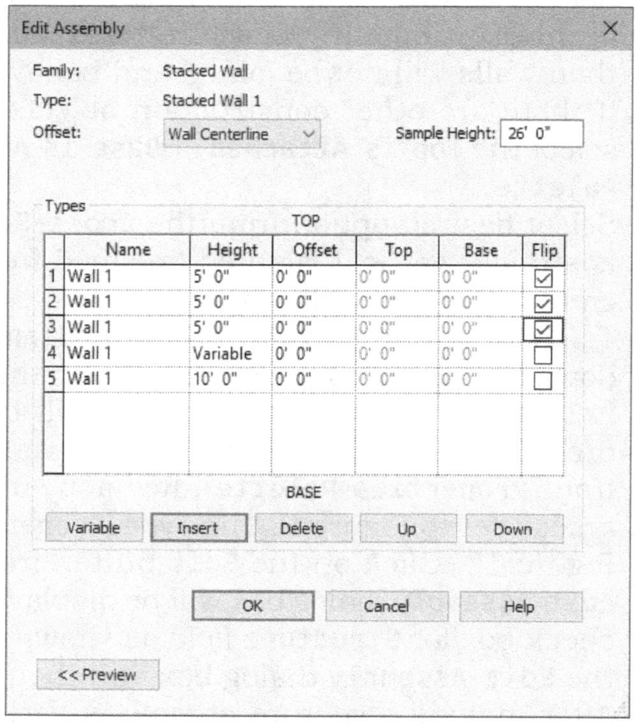

Figure-11. Edit Assembly dialog box

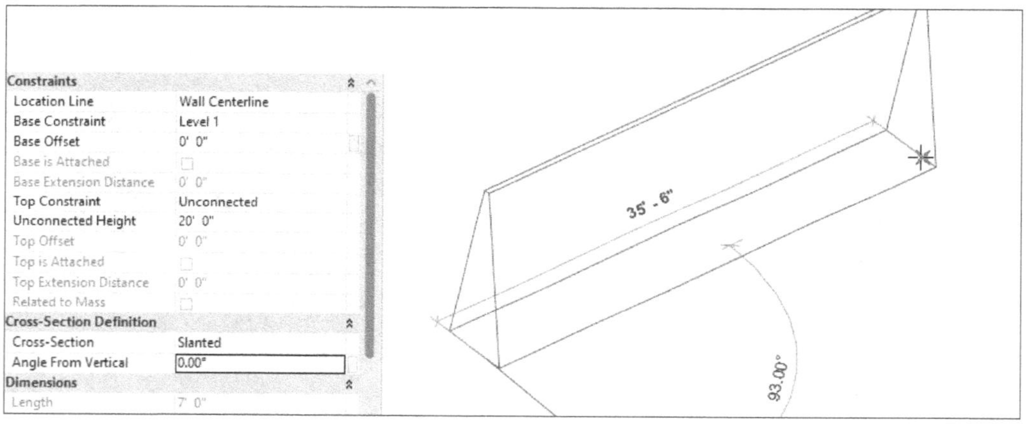

Figure-12. Preview of tapered wall

- Select desired shape from the **Draw** panel in the **Modify|Place Wall** contextual tab. You can select **Arc**, **Circle**, **Line**, **Ellipse**, and **Polygon** tools to create different shapes for wall.
- Draw the walls at desired location; refer to Figure-13. Press **ESC** twice to exit the tool.
- To modify walls, select them from the drawing area (press and hold the **CTRL** key while selecting multiple walls). The options to modify walls will be displayed in the **Ribbon** and **Properties Palette**. Note that if you want to remove any wall from the selection then press and hold the **SHIFT** key while selecting.
- Press **ESC** to exit the modification mode.

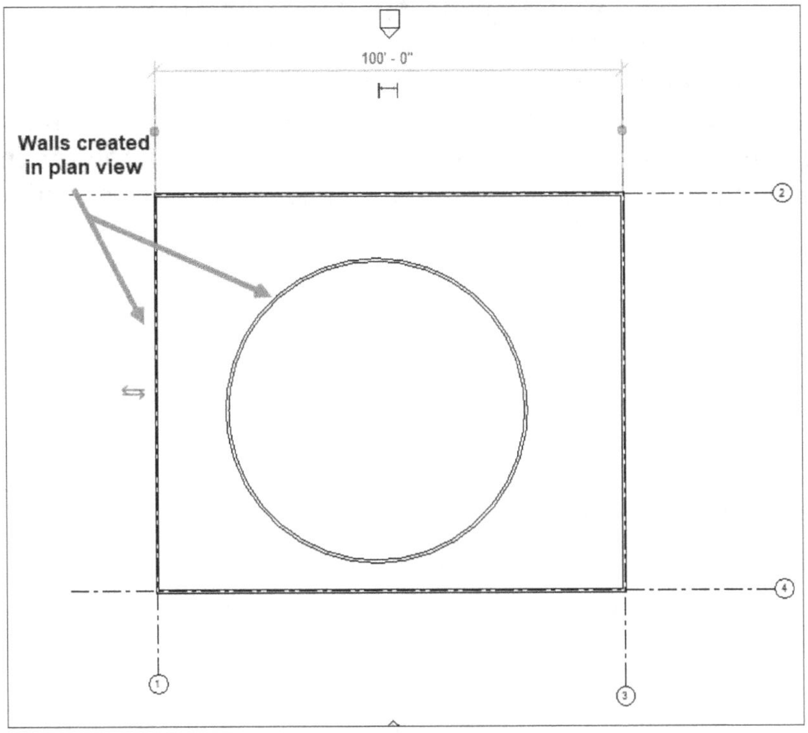

Figure-13. Walls created

Hosted walls

The **Hosted Wall** tool is used to create and host a wall on existing wall. The existing wall is a Host Wall and the newly created wall is a Hosted Wall. Hosted Wall ensures accuracy in design and construction. It also used to add dependent elements like finishes, layers, or special structures. The procedure to use this tool is discussed next.

- Create or import the architectural wall and click on the **Hosted Wall** tool from **Constraint** panel in the **Modify|Place Wall** contextual tab of the **Ribbon**. You will be asked to select the boundary of the wall.
- Select desired boundary of the wall as a host wall. The hosted wall will be created; refer to Figure-14.

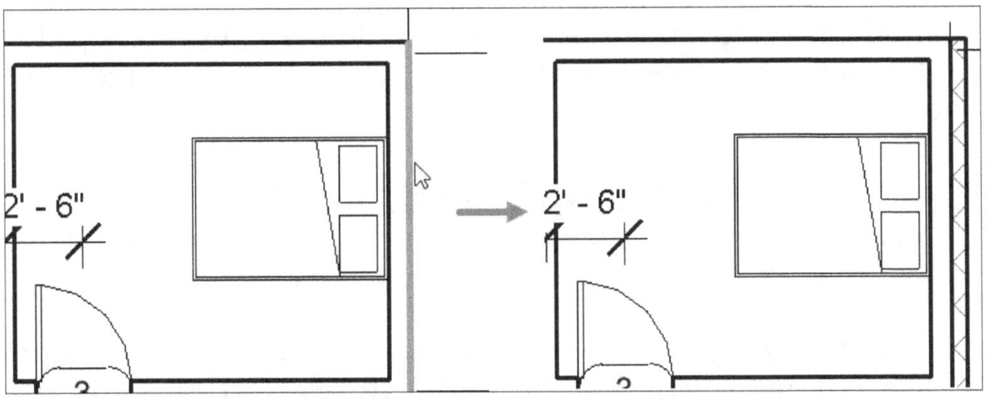

Figure-14. Hosted wall created

- You can edit the offset values of the hosted wall from **Properties Palette**.

Note that there will be some extra options active in the **Properties Palette** while modifying the wall like **Room Bounding** and **Structural** check box. Select the **Room Bounding** check box if you want to create a room boundary by using created walls. Select the **Structural** check box and apply desired parameters to convert selected architectural walls to structural walls.

Creating Structural Walls

The structural walls are load bearing walls with rebars in them. The procedure of creating structural walls is similar to architectural walls. The only difference is that options in **Structural** rollout of **Properties Palette** are active for structural walls; refer to Figure-15 (Note that some options will be active in **Properties Palette** when modifying an earlier created structural wall). These options are discussed next.

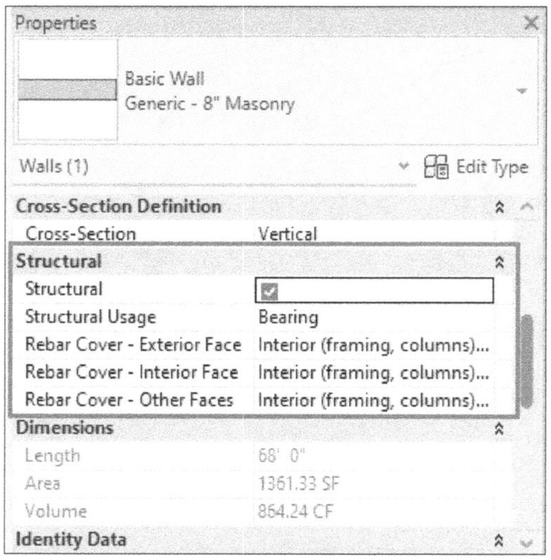

Figure-15. Structural rollout of Properties Palette for wall

- By default, the **Structural** check box is selected for a structural wall. Clear this check box if you want to create an architectural wall.
- Select desired option from the **Structural Usage** drop-down to define what is the type of structural wall. Select **Non-bearing** option if the wall does not bear vertical loads (floor, roof, walls above it etc.) and hence it will not be included in structural analysis. Select the **Bearing** option if the wall will be taking up loads applied on the building. Select the **Shear** option if the wall is specifically designed to bear shear forces (wind loads and seismic loads) in the structure. Select the **Structural Combined** option if the wall is to bear both vertical loads and shear loads. Generally, perimeter walls of building are load bearing and building core/ shafts are created using shear structural walls.
- Select desired rebar cover options from the **Rebar Cover** drop-downs in the **Structural** rollout to define how rebars of wall will be covered. You will learn more about rebar cover later in this book.

Creating Wall by Face

The **Wall by Face** tool in **Walls** drop-down is used to create wall using shape and size of selected faces. The procedure to use this tool is given next.

- Click on the **Wall by Face** tool from the **Walls** drop-down in the **Build** panel of **Architecture** tab in the **Ribbon**. The **Modify|Place Wall** contextual tab will be displayed with options to place walls and you will be asked to select faces of Mass objects (A short note about Mass objects is given in next topic).
- Click on the **Default 3D View** tool from the **Quick Access Toolbar** to change the view to 3D so that you can see the faces of mass objects.
- Select the face of mass object. The wall will be created; refer to Figure-16.

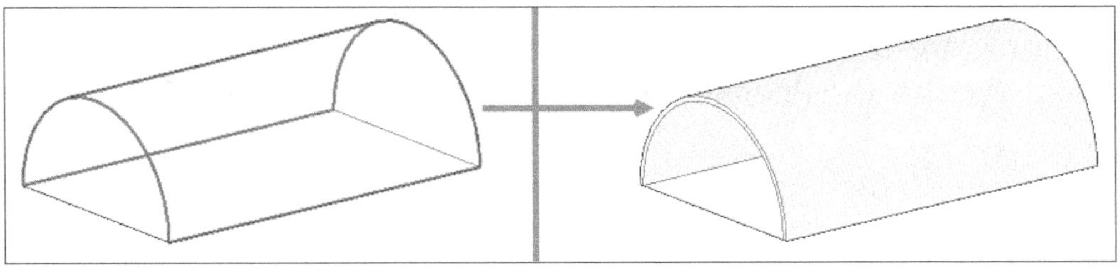

Figure-16. Creating walls by faces

- Set the other options of wall as discussed earlier.
- Press **ESC** to exit the tool.

Short Note on Mass Objects

Mass objects are 3D objects that can be used as reference to create building objects. The tools to create and insert mass objects are available in the **Massing & Site** tab of the **Ribbon**. Here, you will learn about simple procedure of inserting mass objects. You will learn more about mass objects later in this book.

- Click on the **Place Mass** tool from the **Conceptual Mass** panel of the **Massing & Site** tab of the **Ribbon**; refer to Figure-17. Since, you are activating this tool for the first time, the **Revit** information box will be displayed asking you whether to load the mass objects. Click on the **Yes** button. The **Load Family** dialog box will be displayed; refer to Figure-18.

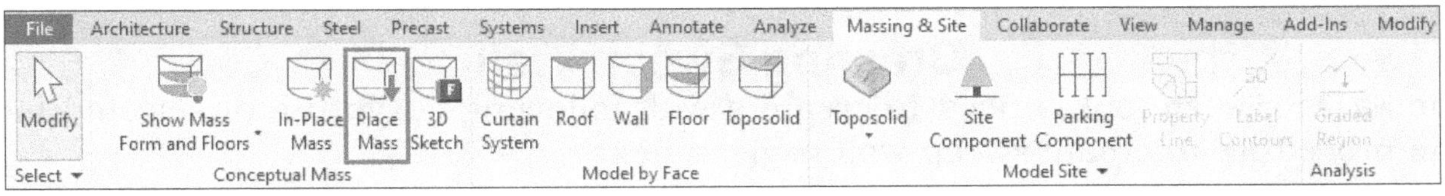

Figure-17. Place Mass tool

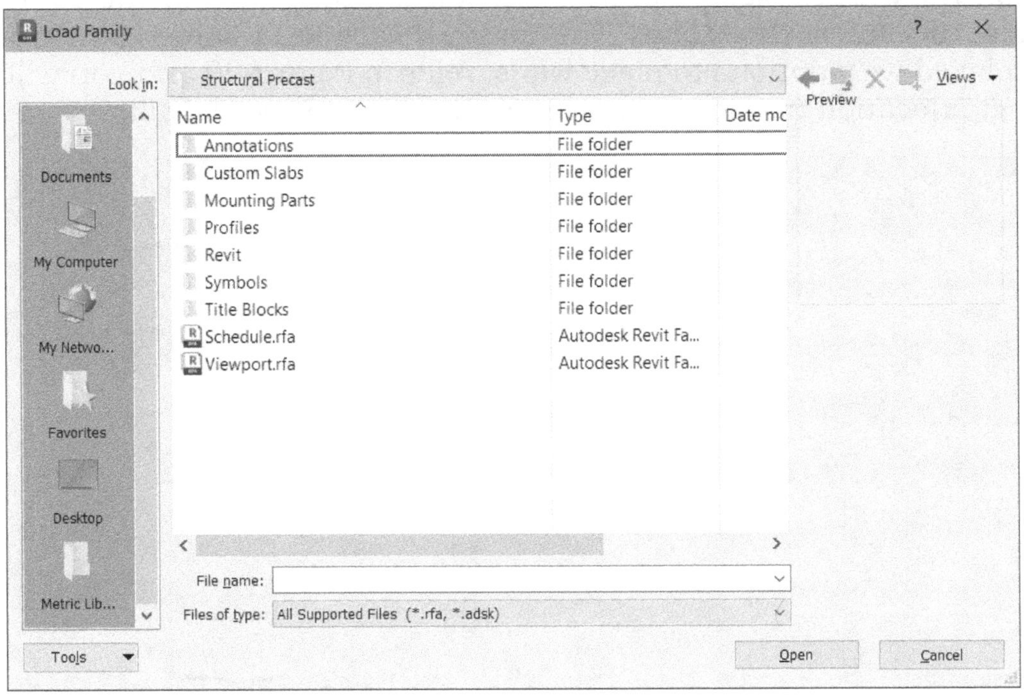

Figure-18. Load Family dialog box

- Browse to the **Mass** folder and select desired mass object to be loaded. (For information, Mass folder is available at C:\ProgramData\Autodesk\RVT 2027\Libraries\English Imperial location of the local hard drive).

- After selecting the mass object, click on the **Open** button from the dialog box. The selected mass object will get attached to the cursor and parameters for the object will be displayed in the **Properties Palette**; refer to Figure-19.

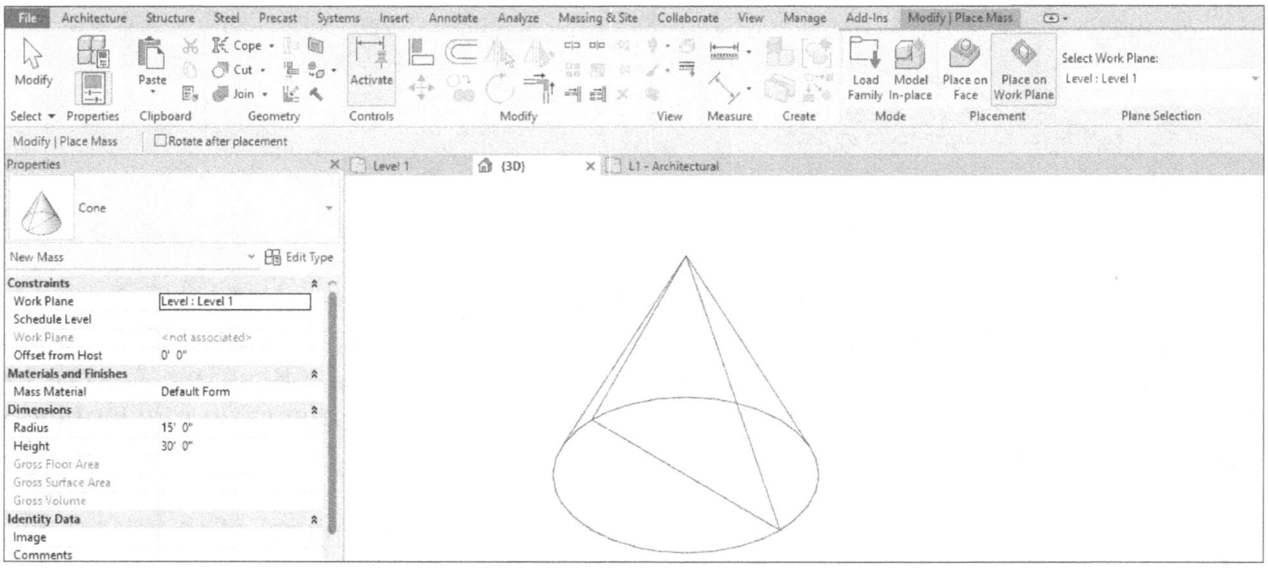

Figure-19. Options to modify and place mass objects

- Set desired parameters and click at desired location to place the mass object.
- Press **ESC** twice to exit the tool.

Creating Sweep Wall

The **Wall: Sweep** tool is used to create a wall following curvature of selected face. The procedure to create sweep wall is given next.

- Click on the **Wall: Sweep** tool from the **Walls** drop-down in the **Build** panel of **Architecture** tab in the **Ribbon**. The **Modify|Place Wall Sweep** contextual tab will be displayed with options to place walls; refer to Figure-20 and you will be asked to select a location on face of another wall to create sweep wall.

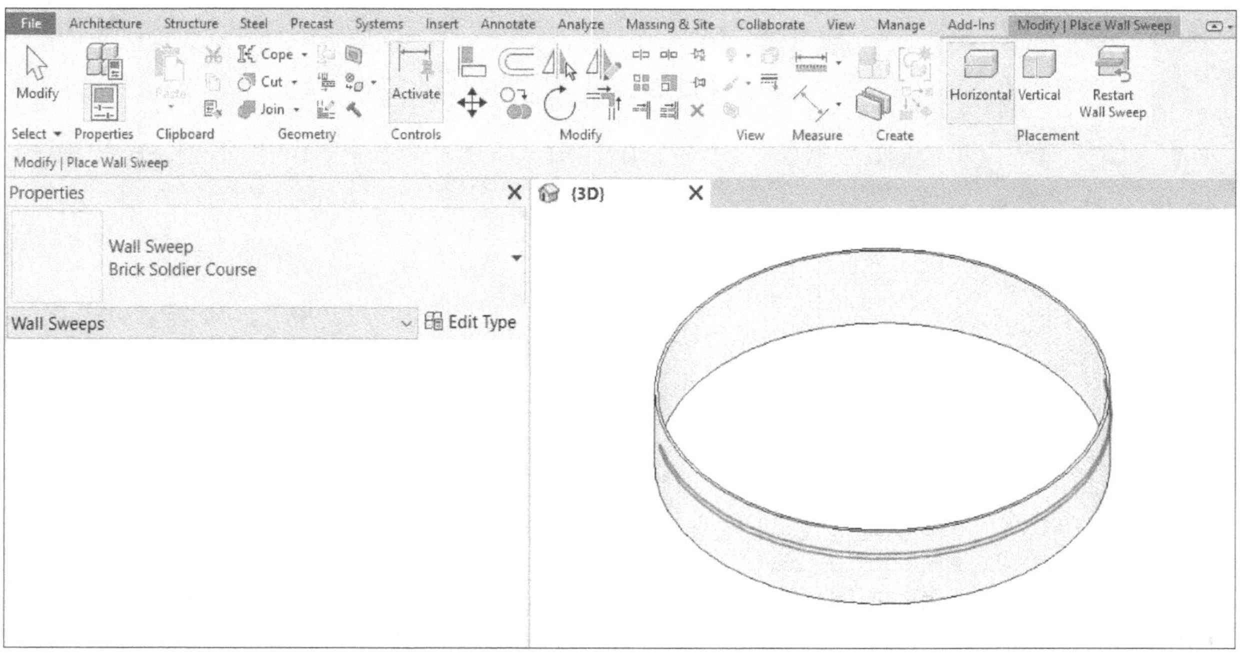

Figure-20. Options for sweep wall

- Click on the **Horizontal** or **Vertical** button from the **Placement** panel of **Modify|Place Wall Sweep** contextual tab in the **Ribbon** to create horizontal or vertical sweep wall.
- Click at desired location on the wall to create sweep wall; refer to Figure-21.

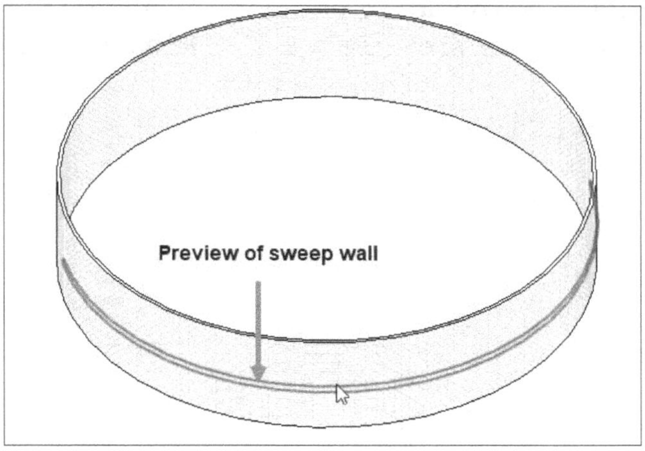

Figure-21. Creating sweep wall

- After creating sweep wall, click on the **Restart Wall Sweep** tool to create another wall or press **ESC** to exit the tool.

Creating Reveal Wall

The **Wall: Reveal** tool is used to create groove in the selected walls. The procedure to use this tool is given next.

- Click on the **Wall: Reveal** tool from the **Walls** drop-down in the **Build** panel of **Architecture** tab in the **Ribbon**. The **Modify|Place Reveal** contextual tab will be displayed with options to place walls; refer to Figure-22 and you will be asked to select a location on face of another wall to create sweep wall.

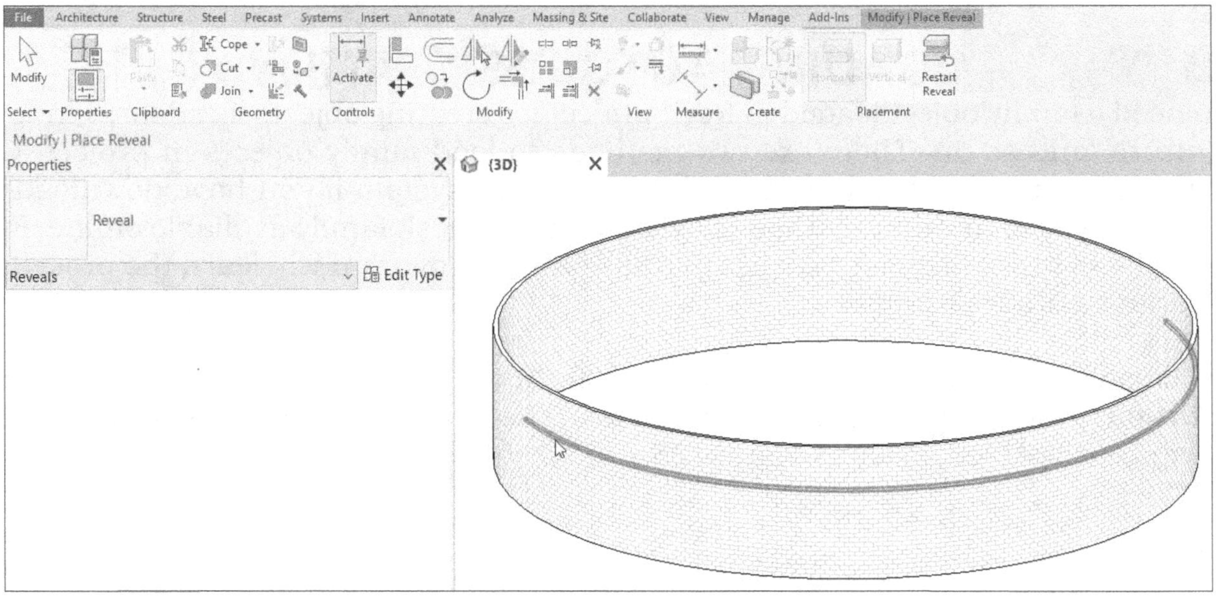

Figure-22. Options for reveal

- The options for reveal are same as discussed for wall sweep. Click at desired location on face of earlier created wall. The reveal will be created.
- After creating desired reveals, press **ESC** to exit the tool.

CREATING DOORS

Doors are created to allow entry and exit through the building. The **Door** tool is used to create doors at specified locations. The procedure to create doors is given next.

- Click on the **Door** tool from the **Build** panel in the **Architecture** tab of the **Ribbon**. The options to create doors are displayed in **Ribbon** and **Properties Palette**; refer to Figure-23.

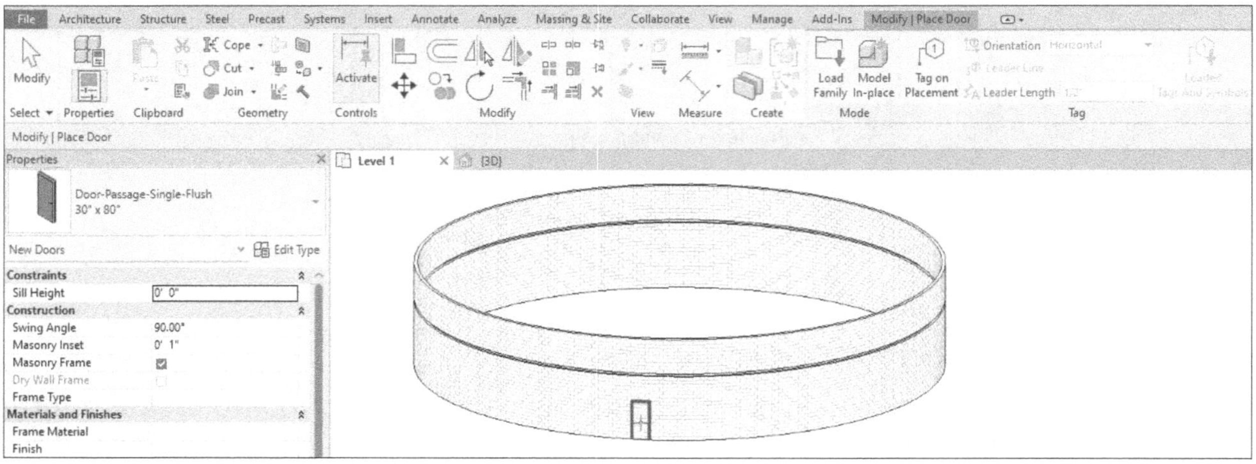

Figure-23. Options to create doors

- Select desired door type from the **Type Selector** drop-down at the top in the **Properties Palette**. If desired door type is not available in the drop-down then click on the **Load Family** tool from the **Mode** panel in the **Modify|Place Door** contextual tab. The **Load Family** dialog box will be displayed. Open the **Door** folder in the dialog box and double-click on desired family to load it. You can also load revit object families from Autodesk cloud which is discussed in next topic.
- Specify desired parameters for door in the **Properties Palette**.
- Click at desired location on a wall to place door.

LOADING AUTODESK FAMILY

You need a family object loaded in Revit project for creating objects like door, windows, furniture, and so on. There are two methods to load family objects in project. One is by using family files saved in local drive of your system if you have downloaded/ created the files. Another method is by loading Autodesk family available online. First method has been discussed earlier in this chapter. Now, you will learn the procedure of loading Autodesk families.

- Click on the **Load Autodesk Family** tool from the **Load from Library** panel in the **Insert** tab of **Ribbon**; refer to Figure-24. The **Load Autodesk Family** dialog box will be displayed; refer to Figure-25.

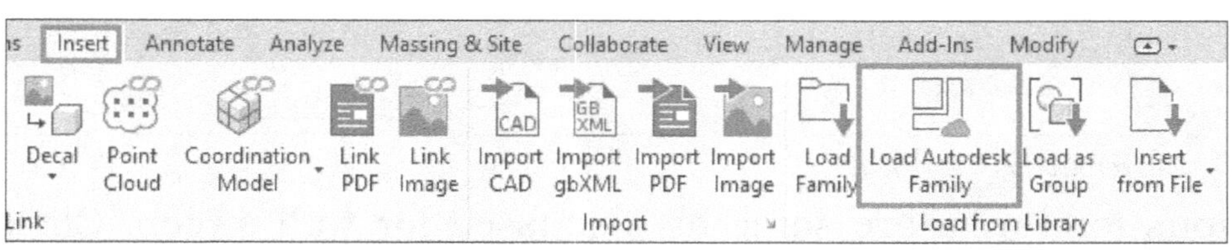

Figure-24. Load Autodesk Family tool

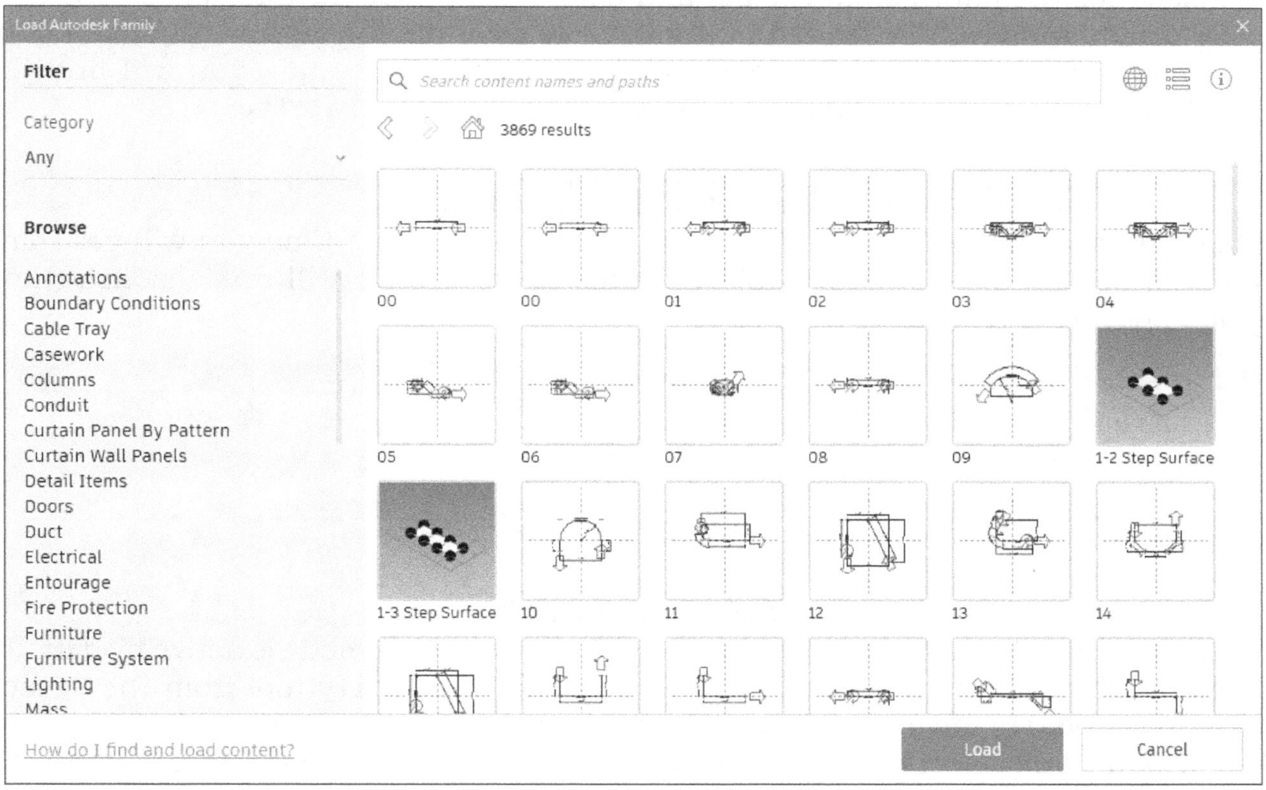

Figure-25. Load Autodesk Family dialog box

- Select desired category from the **Browse** section at the left in the dialog box. Available related families will be displayed on the right in the dialog box; refer to Figure-26.

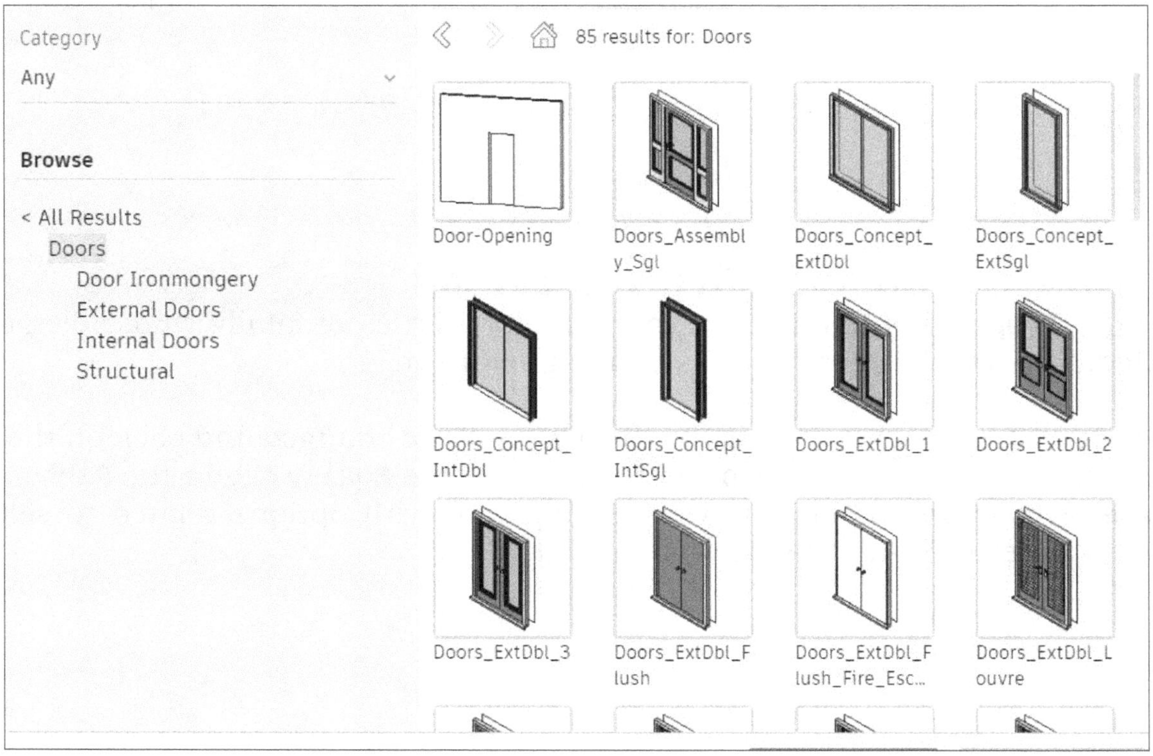

Figure-26. Families of selected category

- Select desired family from the list and click on the **Load** button from dialog box. Selected family will be loaded in library. For example, if you have loaded a door family then on clicking the **Door** tool from **Architecture** tab, you will find the selected door family in **Types** drop-down of **Properties Palette**.

MODIFY TOOLS

While inserting family parts in the Revit model, most of the time you will get some common options in the **Modify** tab; refer to Figure-27. We will now discuss these options of the **Modify** tab one by one.

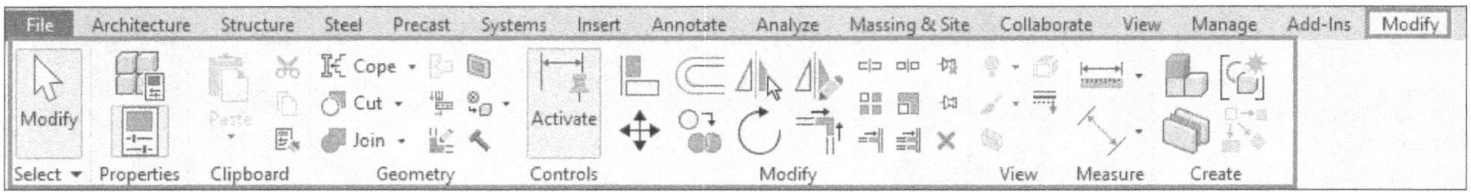

Figure-27. Modify tab in Ribbon

Selection Mode

Whenever there is no other tool active in Revit, the selection mode is active by default. To manually activate the selection mode, click on the **Modify** tool from the **Select** panel in the **Modify** tab of the **Ribbon**. The selection mode will be activated. Expand the **Select** panel and select the check boxes to apply respective filters; refer to Figure-28.

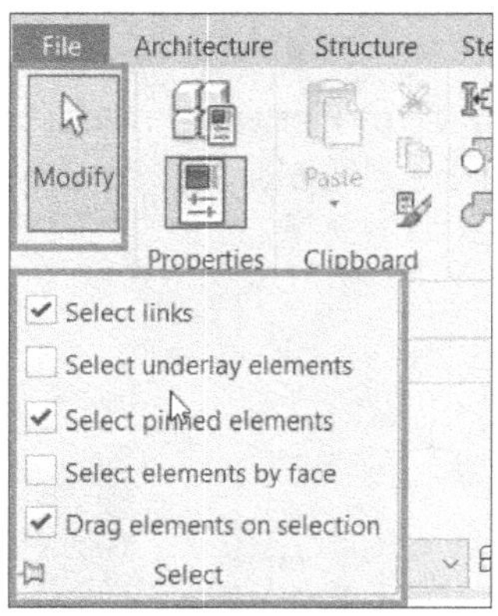

Figure-28. Expanded Select panel

Type Properties

The **Type Properties** tool is used to modify properties of family whose element is selected. The procedure to use this tool is given next.

- Select the object whose family properties are to be changed and click on the **Type Properties** tool from the **Properties** panel of the **Modify** tab in the **Ribbon**. The **Type Properties** dialog box will be displayed with options related to selected object; refer to Figure-29 (for wall family).

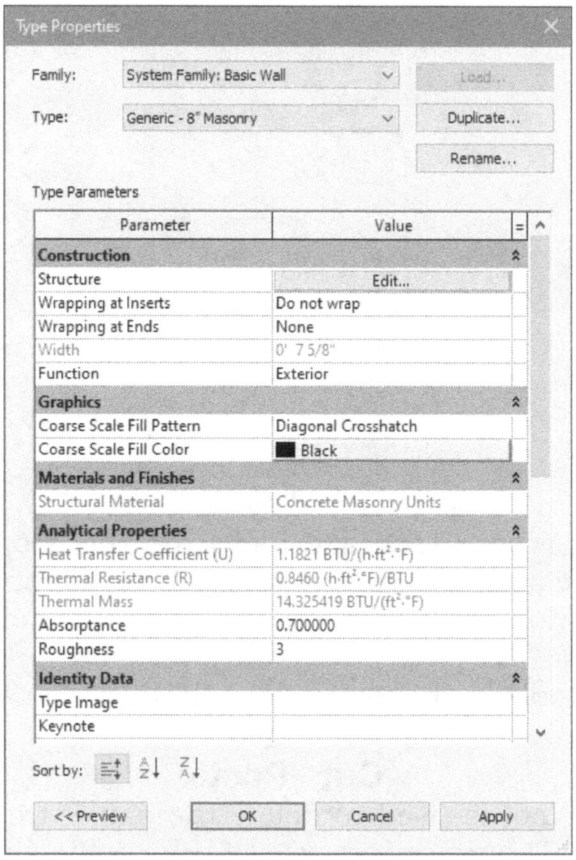

Figure-29. Type Properties dialog box

- Set desired parameters in fields of **Type Parameters** table.
- Click on the **Preview** button from the dialog box to check the preview of applied parameters.
- Click on the **OK** button from the dialog box to apply the parameters.

Modifying Properties of Elements

The **Properties** button is selected by default when you select an object in the model. When this button is selected, the **Properties Palette** is displayed.

Clipboard Operations

The operations like cut, copy, and paste are collectively called clipboard operations. These operations are discussed next.

Copying Objects

- Select the objects that you want to copy. To select multiple objects, press and hold the **CTRL** key while selecting. To remove any object from selection, press and hold the **SHIFT** key while selecting the object to be removed. The **Modify** contextual tab will be displayed in the **Ribbon**.
- Click on the **Copy to Clipboard** button. The selected objects will be copied in clipboard.

Pasting Objects

The **Paste** tools will be active only if you have used the **Copy** tool or **Cut** tool before it; refer to Figure-30.

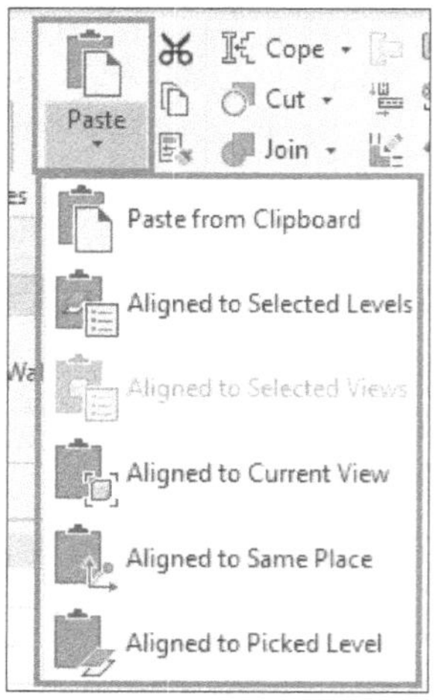

Figure-30. Paste tools

- Click on the **Paste from Clipboard** tool from the drop-down to paste copied elements. You will be asked to specify location for pasting copied elements.
- Click at desired location to place elements. The copied elements will be placed.

You can use the other tools in the **Paste** drop-down in the same way.

Cut - Paste

The **Cut to Clipboard** tool is used to delete the object from current position and save it in the clipboard. The procedure to use this tool is given next.

- Select the objects to be cut to clipboard and click on the **Cut to Clipboard** tool from the **Clipboard** panel in the **Modify** tab of the **Ribbon**. The selected objects will be removed from display and placed in the clipboard.
- Click on desired option from the **Paste** drop-down and place the cut objects.

Matching Type Properties

The **Match Type Properties** tool is used to apply the properties of first selected object on second similar selected object. The procedure to use this tool is given next.

- Click on the **Match Type Properties** tool from the **Clipboard** panel of the **Modify** tab in **Ribbon**. You will be asked to select the master object whose properties are to be copied.
- Select desired object. You will be asked to select the object whose properties are to be changed.
- Select the objects one by one whose properties are to be changed and press **ESC** to exit the tool.

Applying Coping to Steel Frame

The **Apply Coping** is used in steel frames to connect two frame members fixed in each other by removing portions from one or both the frames. (You will learn about steel frames later in this book). The procedure to use this tool is given next.

- Click on the **Apply Coping** tool from **Cope** drop-down in the **Geometry** panel of **Modify** tab in the **Ribbon**. You will be asked to select the first object to be notched.

- Select the two joining steel frame members one by one. The coping operation will be applied; refer to Figure-31. Note that while coping, the first selected frame member will be cut to accommodate.

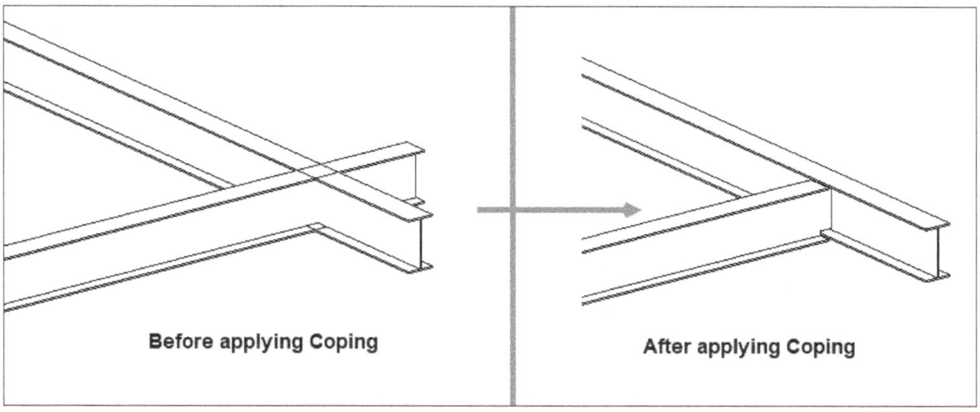

Figure-31. Applying Coping to steel frame

Removing Coping

The **Remove Coping** tool is used to remove notching earlier applied to the steel frame. The procedure to use this tool is given next.

- Click on the **Remove Coping** tool from **Cope** drop-down in the **Geometry** panel of **Modify** tab in the **Ribbon**. You will be asked to select the elements whose coping is to be removed.
- Select the element which was cut on applying coping. You will be asked to select frame member that was used for cutting element.
- Select the other member. The coping will be removed; refer to Figure-32.

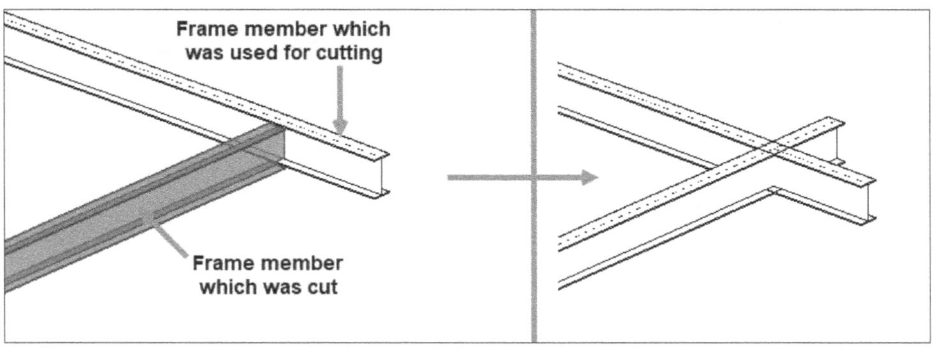

Figure-32. Removing coping

Cutting Elements using Geometry

The **Cut Geometry** tool is used to cut selected geometry based on selected object. The procedure to use this tool is given next.

- Click on the **Cut Geometry** tool from the **Cut** drop-down in the **Geometry** panel of **Modify** tab in the **Ribbon**. You will be asked to select the object to be cut.
- Select desired object from which other selected object will be cut. You will be asked to select cutting object.
- Select the object that intersects with first selected object and is parallel to earlier selected object. The cut operation will be applied; refer to Figure-33.

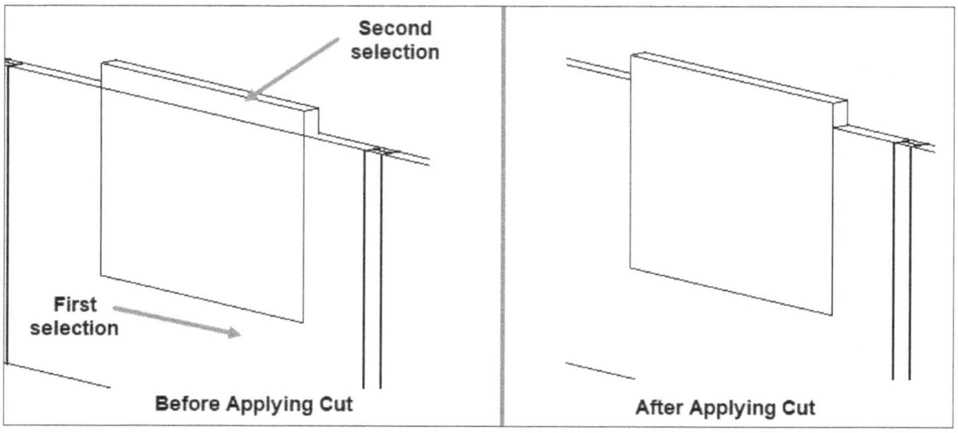

Figure-33. Applying cut

Uncut Geometry Tool

The **Uncut Geometry** tool is used to reverse the cut created by using the **Cut Geometry** tool earlier discussed. The procedure to use this tool is given next.

- Click on the **Uncut Geometry** tool from the **Cut** drop-down in the **Geometry** panel of the **Modify** tab in the **Ribbon**. You will be asked to select the object which was cut by using the **Cut Geometry** tool earlier.
- Select desired object from the drawing area. You will be asked to select the tool object which was used to cut the other object. The object will be uncut; refer to Figure-34.

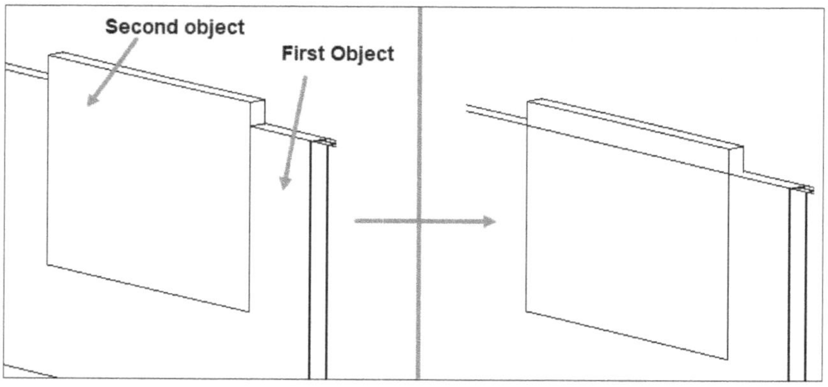

Figure-34. Applying Uncut geometry tool

Joining Geometry

The **Join Geometry** tool is used to combine two or more objects so that there is not visible parting line between them and they share the same properties of texture and hatching. The procedure to use this tool is given next.

- Click on the **Join Geometry** tool from the **Join** drop-down in the **Geometry** panel of the **Modify** tab in the **Ribbon**. You will be asked to select the first geometry to be joined.
- Click at desired object, you will be asked to select the second object.
- Select the second object. The two objects will be joined together; refer to Figure-35.

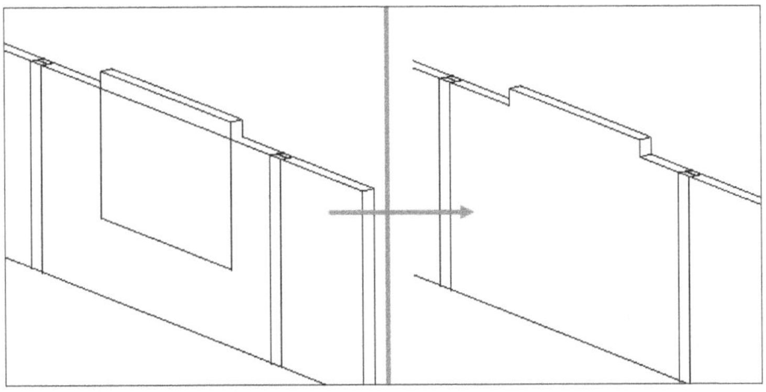

Figure-35. Joining walls

Unjoin Geometry

The **Unjoin Geometry** tool is used to unjoin the objects earlier joined by using the **Join Geometry** tool. The procedure to use this tool is given next.

- Click on the **Unjoin Geometry** tool from the **Join** drop-down in the **Geometry** panel of **Modify** tab in the **Ribbon**. You will be asked to select the body to be unjoined.
- Select earlier joined geometry. The objects will be unjoined.

Switching Join Order

The **Switch Join Order** tool is used to switch the order in which two objects were joined. If the cut was made in first object while joining then on switching, it will be made in second object. The procedure to use this tool is given next.

- Click on the **Switch Join Order** tool from the **Join** drop-down in the **Geometry** panel of **Modify** tab in the **Ribbon**. You will be asked to select the first object.
- Select the first object. You will be asked to select the other object of joined pair.
- Select the second object with which you want to switch join order. The order will be switched.

Join/Unjoin Roof

The **Join/Unjoin Roof** tool is used to connect or disconnect roof with walls. Note that there must be roofs to join before using this tool. The procedure to use this tool is given next.

- Click on the **Join/Unjoin Roof** tool from the **Geometry** panel in the **Modify** tab of the **Ribbon**. You will be asked to select at the edge of roof to join/unjoin.
- Click at desired edge of roof. You will be asked to select the face of wall/roof with which earlier selected roof will be joined/unjoined; refer to Figure-36.
- Select connected face of wall/roof. The roof will be joined. Note that if the roof is already joined then the error message dialog box will be displayed as shown in Figure-37.

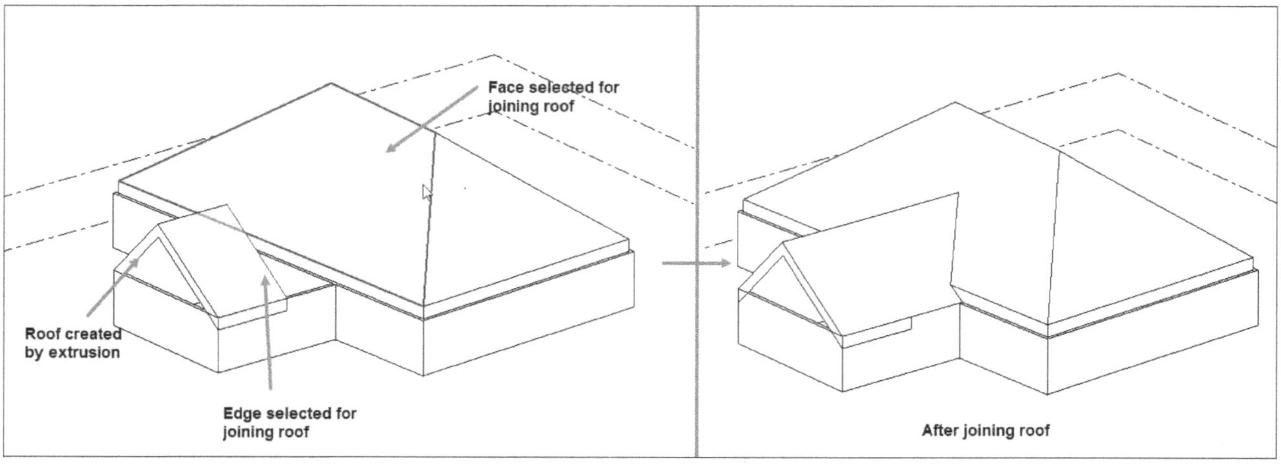

Figure-36. Joining roofs

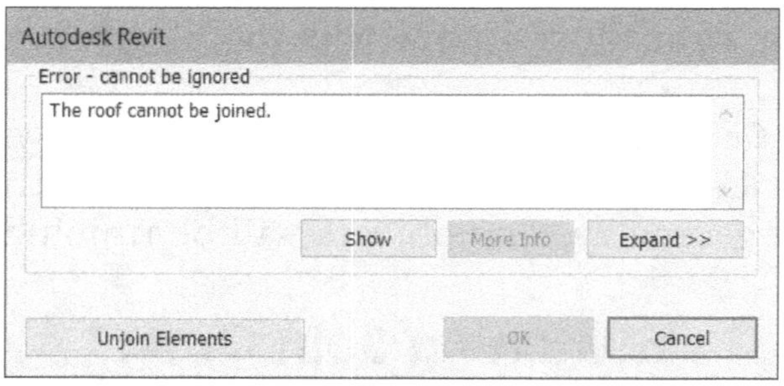

Figure-37. Autodesk Revit message box

- Click on the **Unjoin Elements** button from the dialog box if you want to unjoin the already joined elements.

Beam/Column Joins

The **Beam/Column Joins** tool is used to define how columns or beams join together. The procedure to use this tool is given next.

- Click on the **Beam/Column Joins** tool from the **Geometry** panel in the **Modify** tab of the **Ribbon**. Small arrows will be displayed on the intersecting beams/columns; refer to Figure-38.

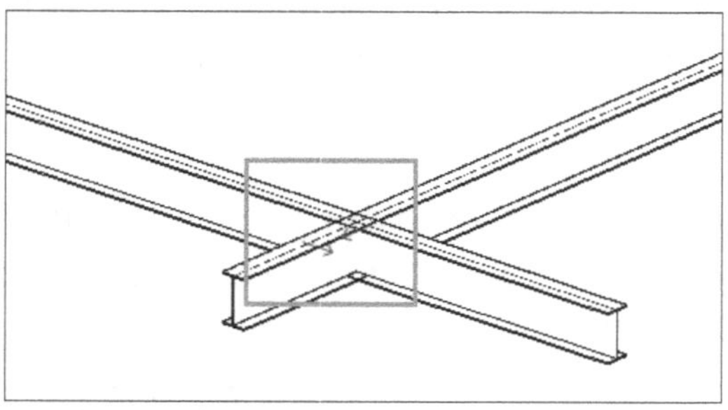

Figure-38. Intersecting beams with arrows for joint

- Select desired arrow. The section of selected beam will be trimmed. Click again on the beam/column to un-trim it. Figure-39 shows the beams joined after trimming.
- Press **ESC** to exit the tool

Wall Joins

The **Wall Joins** tool is used to modify the joints of walls. The procedure to use this tool is given next.

- Click on the **Wall Joins** tool from the **Geometry** panel in the **Modify** tab of the **Ribbon**. You will be asked to select a joint of walls; refer to Figure-39.
- Click at the bottom of wall joints when a rectangle is displayed; refer to Figure-40. The options to modify wall joint will be displayed in the **Configuration** panel of the **Ribbon**; refer to Figure-41.

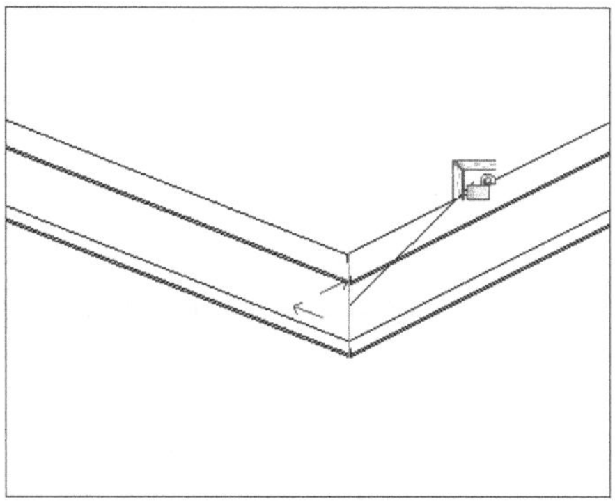

Figure-39. Beams after joining

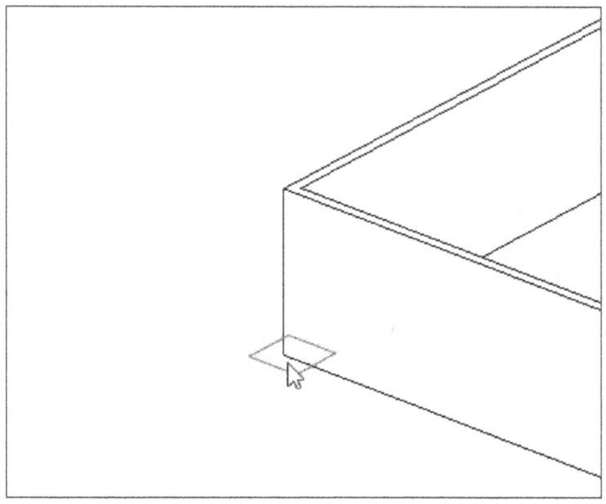

Figure-40. Selecting the wall joint

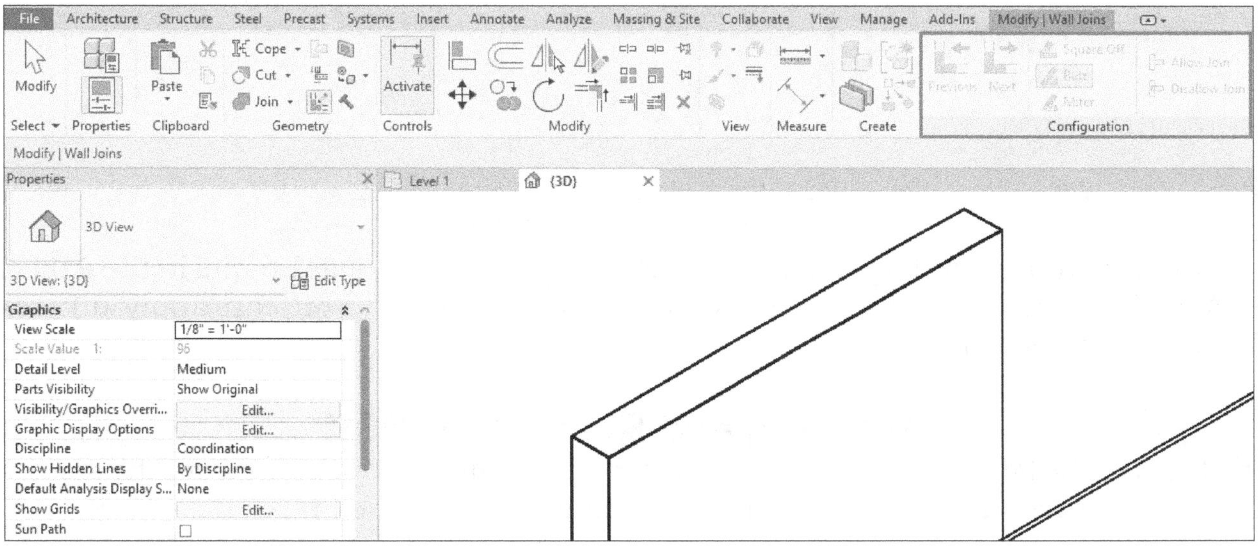

Figure-41. Options for modifying wall joint

- Select desired option from the **Ribbon** to modify wall joint.

Splitting Faces

The **Split Face** tool is used to split the face of selected walls/roofs/floors. These split faces can later be applied different material properties. The procedure to use this tool is given next.

- Click on the **Split Face** tool from the **Geometry** panel in the **Modify** tab of **Ribbon**. You will be asked to select the face which you want to split in regions.
- Select desired face. The **Modify|Split Face > Create Boundary** contextual tab will be displayed with options to create boundary for splitting; refer to Figure-42.

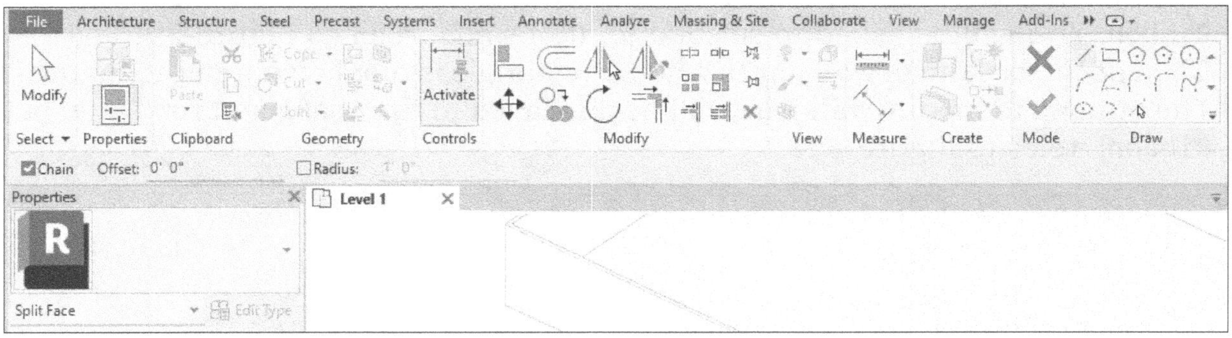

Figure-42. Options for creating split boundary

- Create a closed loop boundary on selected face using the tools in **Draw** panel of the **Ribbon**; refer to Figure-43.

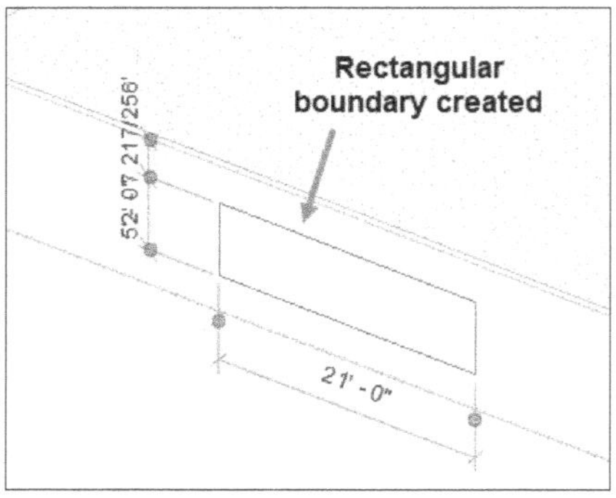

Figure-43. Boundary creation for split

- After creating boundary, click on the **OK** button from the **Model** panel in the **Ribbon**. A region will be created on the selected face to which you can apply different material properties.

Applying and Removing Paint

The tools in the **Paint** drop-down are used to apply and remove paint from the selected faces. The procedure to apply and remove paint is discussed next.

Applying Paint

- Click on the **Paint** tool from the **Paint** drop-down in the **Geometry** panel of **Modify** tab in the **Ribbon**. The **Material Browser** window will be displayed; refer to Figure-44.
- Select desired material texture from the browser and click on the faces on which you want to apply the material/paint. If the **Textures** or **Realistic** option is selected from the **Visual Style** flyout in the **Bottom Bar** then applied paint textures will be visible in graphics area; refer to Figure-45.
- Close the browser after applying material.

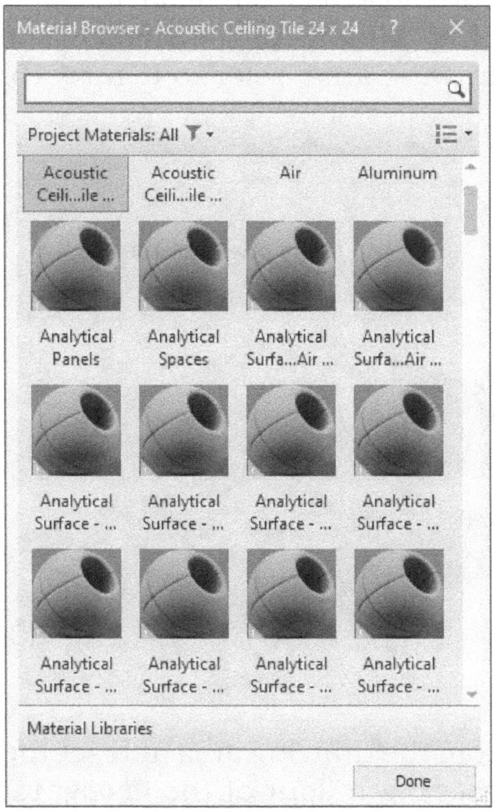

Figure-44. Material Browser

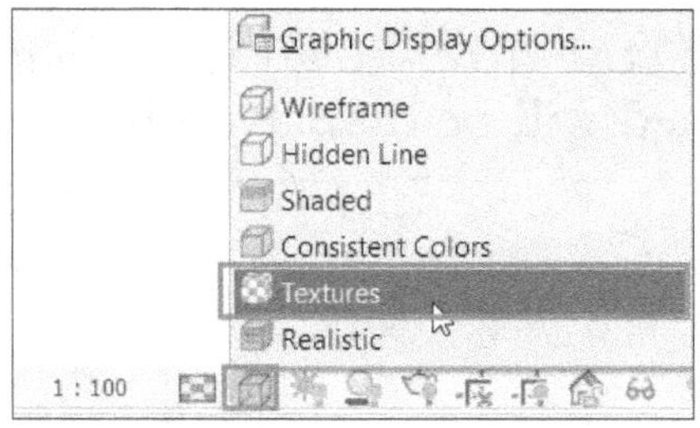

Figure-45. Textures option

Removing Material

- Click on the **Remove Paint** tool from the **Paint** drop-down in the **Geometry** panel of the **Modify** tab in the **Ribbon**. You will be asked to select the faces whose material/ paint is to be removed.
- Select desired faces. The material will be removed.
- Press **ESC** to exit the tool.

Demolish

The **Demolish** tool is used to mark selected objects as demolished. This tool is very useful when you need to demolish some parts of building before creating new construction. Using this tool, you can mark the timing of demolishing in your work plan based on phase selected. Note that the object will be displayed in phases before current phase but it will be demolished in the next phases and current phase. The procedure to use this tool is given next.

- Click on the **Demolish** tool from the **Geometry** panel in the **Modify** tab of the **Ribbon**. You will be asked to select the objects to be demolished in current phase.
- Click on desired elements to demolish them. The selected elements will be removed from the display in current phase and next phases.
- Press **ESC** to exit the tool.

Un-demolish

If you have demolished some elements by mistake then you can un-demolish them by using following procedure.

- Scroll down in the **Properties Palette** and select the **Show All** option from the **Phase Filter** drop-down in the **Phasing** rollout. All the elements including the demolished will be displayed in the drawing area; refer to Figure-46.

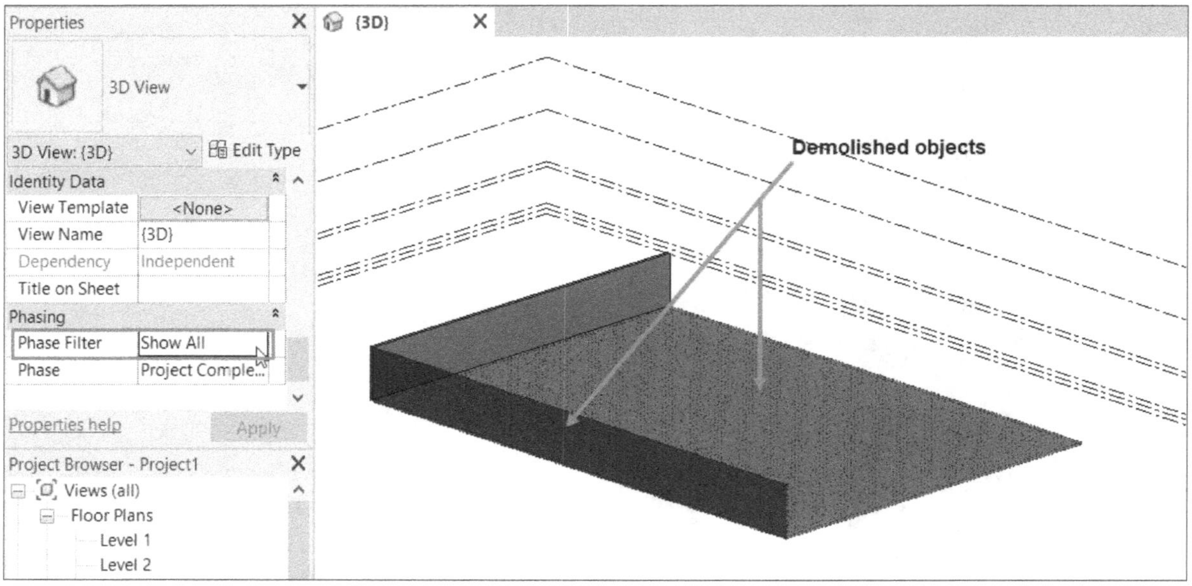

Figure-46. Displaying demolished objects

- Select the earlier demolished objects from the drawing area and set the **None** option from the **Phase Demolished** field in **Phasing** rollout of the **Properties Palette**. The selected objects will be un-demolished.
- Press **ESC** to exit the tool.

Activating Controls and Dimensions

The **Activate** tool is used to display pins, constraints, and temporary dimensions for multiple selected objects. The procedure to use this tool is given next.

- Select multiple objects from the drawing area whose temporary annotations are to be displayed and click on the **Activate** button from **Controls** panel of **Modify** tab in the **Ribbon**. The annotations will be displayed; refer to Figure-47.

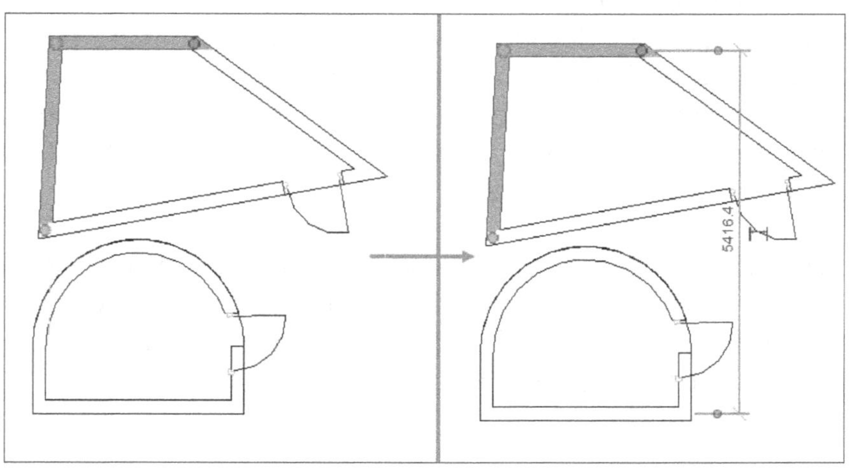

Figure-47. After selecting Activate button

Aligning Objects

The **Align** tool is used to align selected elements to point/line used as reference. The procedure to use this tool is given next.

- Click on the **Align** tool from the **Modify** panel in the **Modify** tab of the **Ribbon**. You will be asked to select a line or point to be used as reference for alignment.
- Click on desired line or point. You will be asked to select the objects to be aligned.
- Select desired objects. The objects will be aligned; refer to Figure-48.
- Press **ESC** to exit the tool.

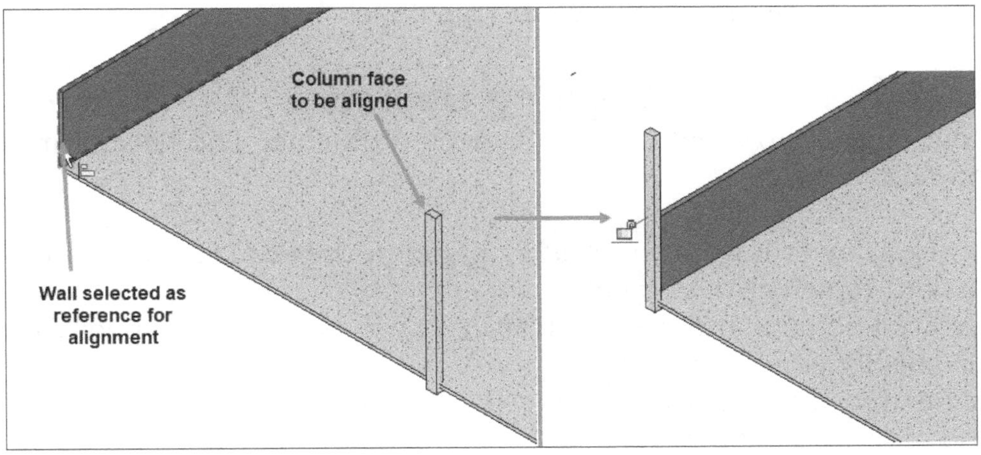

Figure-48. Aligning objects

Moving Objects

The **Move** tool is used to move selected objects at specified location. The procedure to use this tool is given next.

- Click on the **Move** tool from the **Modify** panel in the **Modify** tab of the **Ribbon**. You will be asked to select the objects to be moved.
- Select desired objects and press **ENTER**. You will be asked to specify start point for moving objects.
- Click at desired location to specify the start point. You will be asked to specify the location where you want to move the objects; refer to Figure-49.

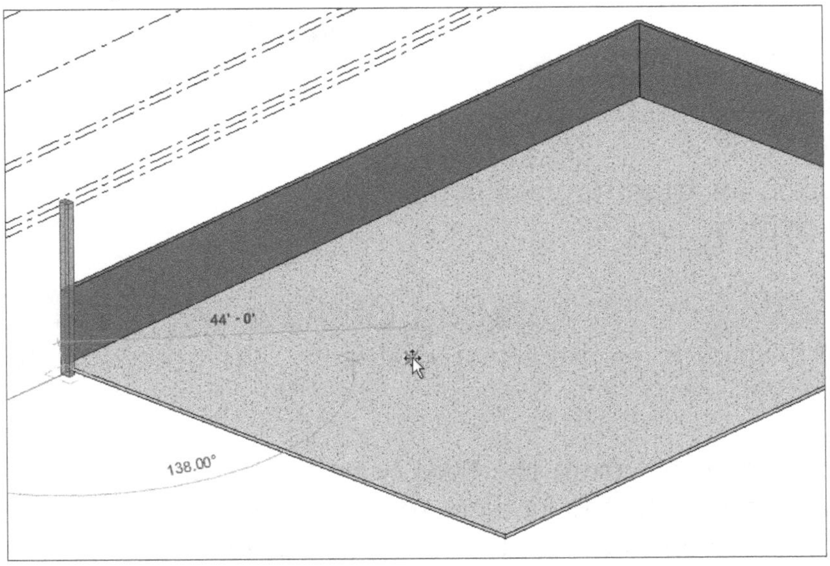

Figure-49. Moving objects

- Click at desired location to place the objects.

Applying Offset

The **Offset** tool is used to copy or move selected object at specified distance. The procedure to use this tool is given next.

- Click on the **Offset** tool from the **Modify** panel in the **Modify** tab of the **Ribbon**. You will be asked to select a wall or line to be offset.
- Specify desired offset value in the **Offset** edit box in **Options Bar**.
- Select desired wall to be offset. Offset copy of selected object will be created if the **Copy** check box is selected in the **Options Bar**. If you want to move selected object at specified offset distance then clear this check box.

Copying Objects

The **Copy** tool is used to create copy of selected objects. The procedure to use this tool is given next.

- Click on the **Copy** tool from the **Modify** panel in the **Modify** tab of the **Ribbon**. You will be asked to select the objects.
- Select desired objects and press **ENTER**. You will be asked to specify the reference point for specify copy distance.
- Click at desired location to specify reference point. You will be asked to specify target location for copying; refer to Figure-50.

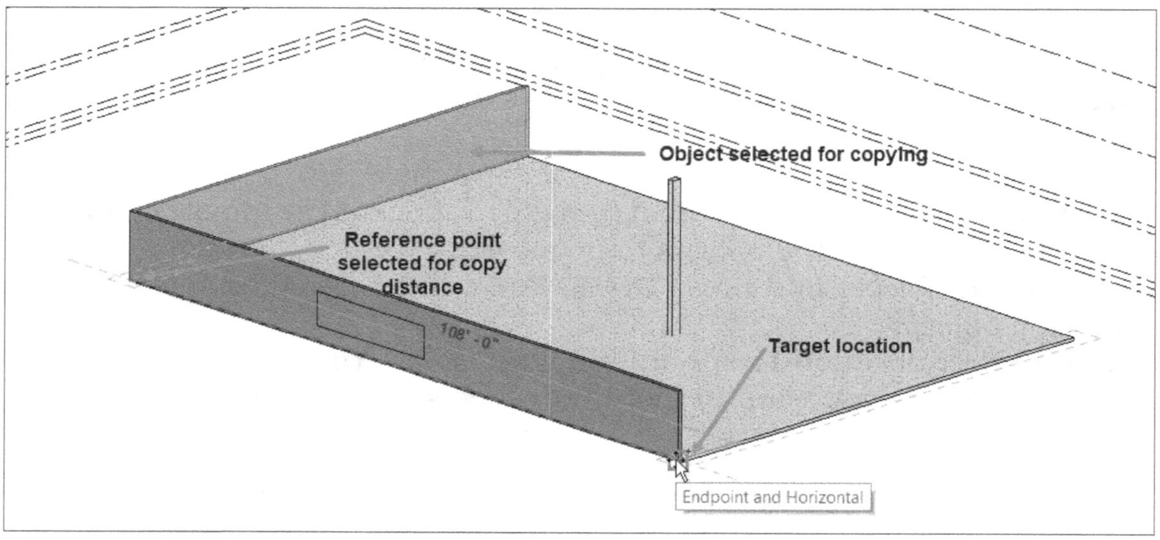

Figure-50. Copying objects

- Click on desired location to place copy.
- Press **ESC** to exit the tool.

Rotating Objects

The **Rotate** tool is used to rotate selected objects. The procedure to use this tool is given next.

- Click on the **Rotate** tool from the **Modify** panel in the **Modify** tab of the **Ribbon**. You will be asked to select the object to be rotated.
- Select desired object(s) to be rotated and press **ENTER**. You will be asked to specify starting point for rotating object.
- Click at desired location to specify the start point of rotation. You will be asked to specify end point of rotation.
- Click at desired location to rotate the object.

Creating Mirror Copy by Selecting Axis

The **Mirror - Pick Axis** tool is used to create a mirror copy of selected objects about selected axis. The procedure to use this tool is given next.

- Click on the **Mirror - Pick Axis** tool from the **Modify** panel in the **Modify** tab of the **Ribbon**. You will be asked to select the objects to be mirrored.
- Select desired object(s) to be mirrored. Note that you can press and hold the **CTRL** key for selecting multiple objects. If you want to de-select an object from selected objects then press and hold the **SHIFT** key while selecting object. After selecting objects, press **ENTER**. You will be asked to select a face to define reflection axis.
- Select desired face. The mirror copy will be created; refer to Figure-51.

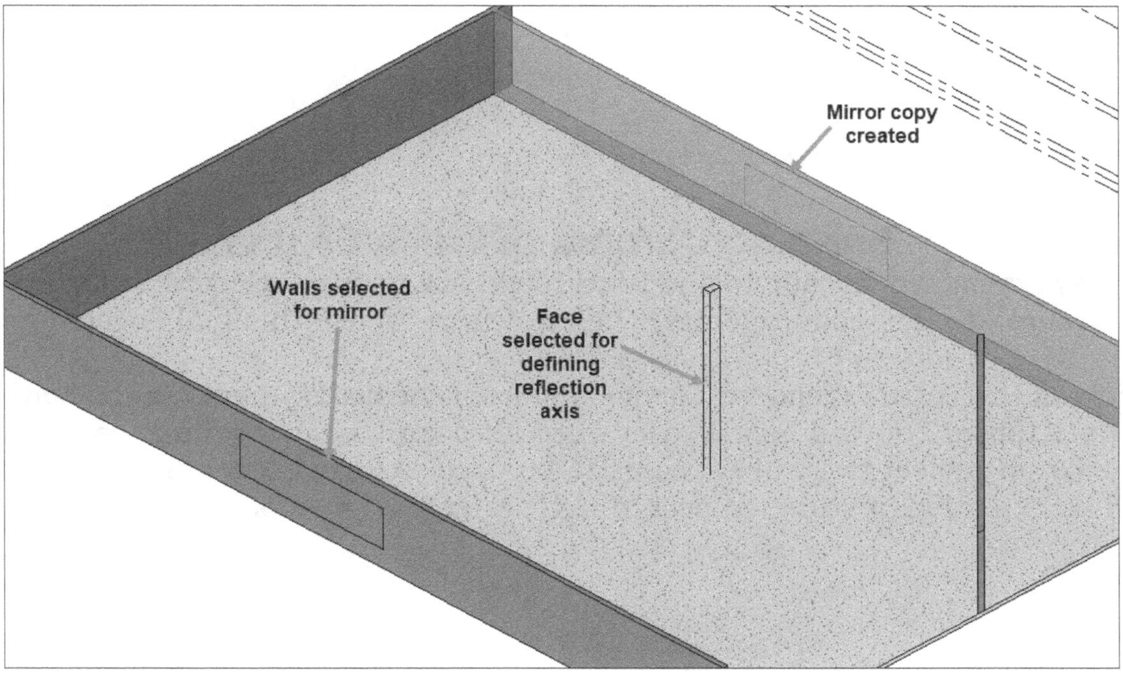

Figure-51. Creating mirror copy

Creating Mirror Copy by Drawing Axis

The **Mirror - Draw Axis** tool is used to create mirror copy of selected objects with respect to drawn reflection axis. The procedure to use this tool is given next.

- Click on the **Mirror - Draw Axis** tool from the **Modify** panel in the **Modify** tab of the **Ribbon**. You will be asked to select the objects to be mirrored.
- Select multiple objects while holding the **CTRL** key and press **ENTER**. You will be asked to specify start point of the reflection axis.
- Click at desired locations to specify start point and end point of reflection axis; refer to Figure-52. Mirror copies will be created.

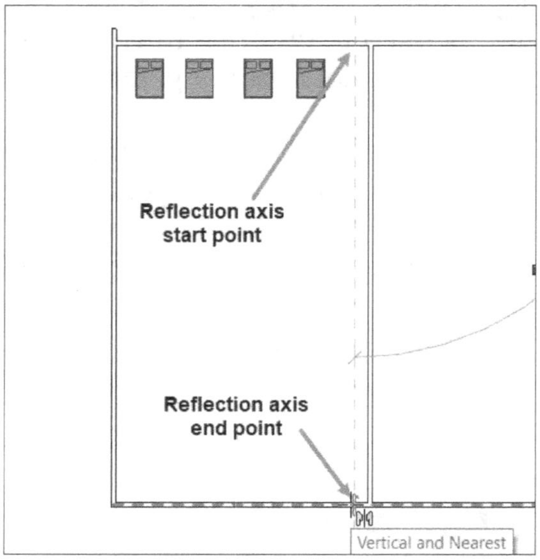

Figure-52. Drawing reflection axis

Forming Corners of Walls/Beams

The **Trim/Extend to Corner** tool is used to extend or trim selected walls/beams to form corners at intersection points. The procedure to use this tool is given next.

- Click on the **Trim/Extend to Corner** tool from the **Modify** panel in the **Modify** tab of the **Ribbon**. You will be asked to select first wall/beam to make corner.
- One by one select two walls/beams to be used to form corner. The walls/beams will be extended or trimmed accordingly; refer to Figure-53.

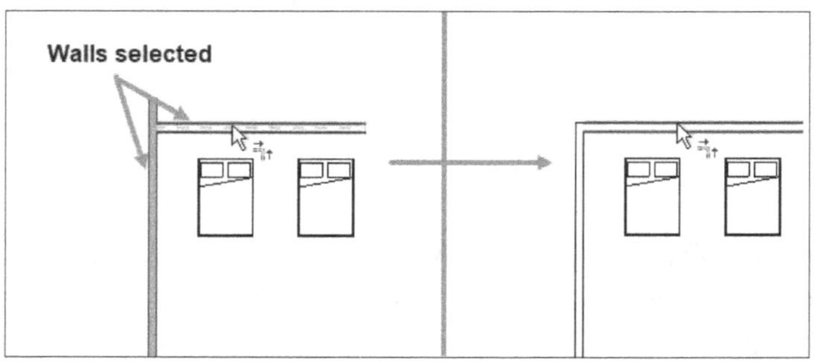

Figure-53. Trimming walls to form corner

Splitting Elements

The **Split Element** tool is used to split selected walls and other linear objects at specified points. The procedure to use this tool is given next.

- Click on the **Split Element** tool from the **Modify** panel in the **Modify** tab of the **Ribbon**. You will be asked to specify a point on the wall where you want to split it.
- Click at desired location on the wall to split it; refer to Figure-54.
- After splitting walls, press **ESC** twice to exit the tool.

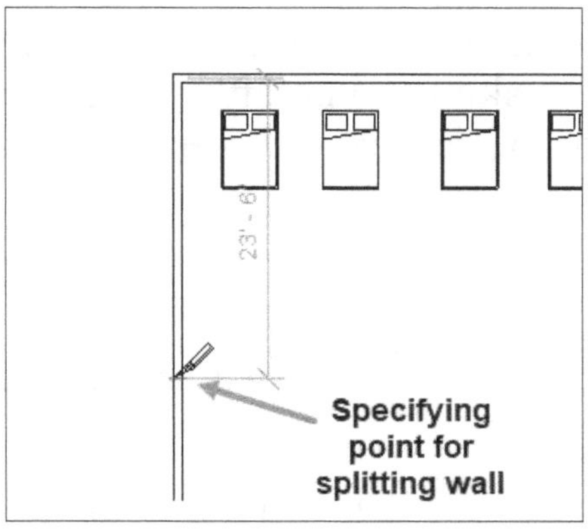

Figure-54. Splitting wall

Splitting with Gap

The **Split with Gap** tool is used to split walls and apply gap of specified value in the two wall segments. The procedure to use this tool is given next.

- Click on the **Split with Gap** tool from the **Modify** panel in the **Modify** tab of the **Ribbon**. You will be asked to specify the point where the wall should split.
- Specify desired gap value in the **Joint Gap** edit box of **Options Bar** and click at desired location. The wall will be split and specified gap will be applied.

Creating Array of Objects

The **Array** tool in **Modify** tab is used to create multiple instances of selected objects. The procedure to use this tool is given next.

- Select the objects that you want to array and click on the **Array** tool from the **Modify** panel in the **Modify** tab of the **Ribbon**. The options related to **Array** tool will be displayed in the **Array** panel of the **Ribbon** and you will be asked to specify the start point for array; refer to Figure-55.

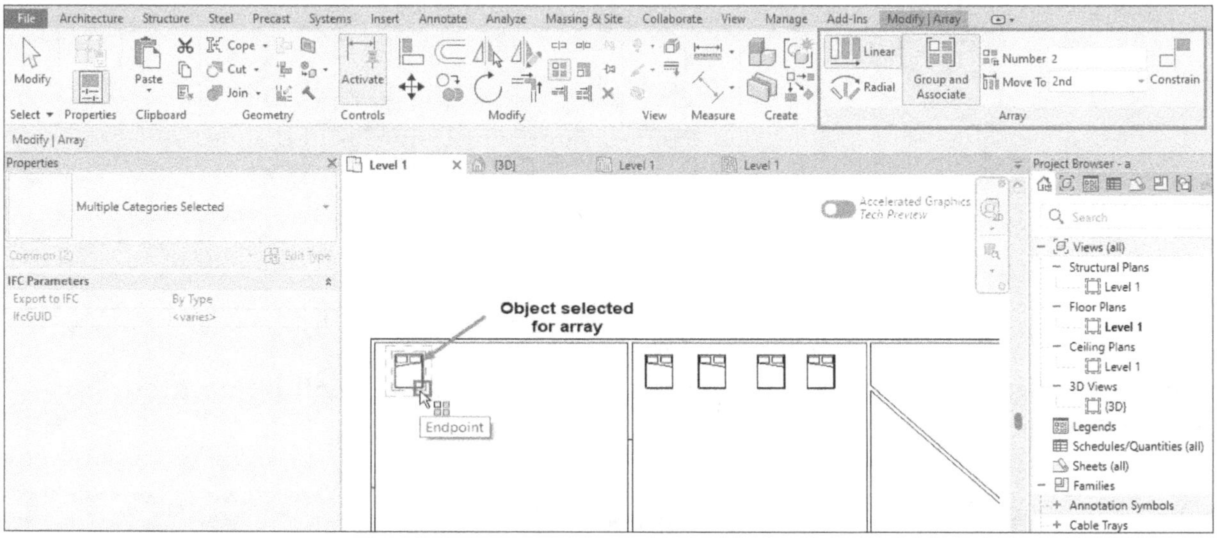

Figure-55. Options for array

- Specify the number of instances to be created in the **Number** edit box of **Options Bar** and click in the drawing area to define starting point of reference line for distance between two instances.

- Click on one of the key point of object and then click at desired distance in the direction in which you want to create the pattern. The preview pattern will be displayed and you will be asked to specify number of instances.
- Specify desired number of instances and press **ENTER**. The pattern will be created; refer to Figure-56.

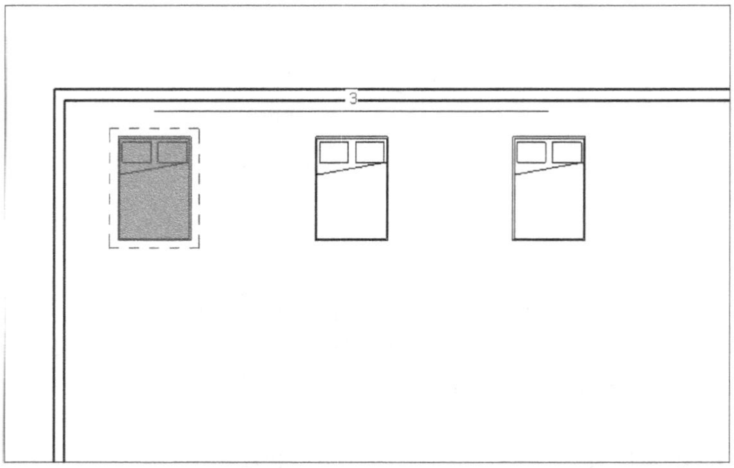

Figure-56. Pattern created

Creating Circular Pattern

- After activating the **Array** tool, click on the **Radial** button from the **Options Bar**. You will be asked to specify starting and location of second instance in radial array.
- Click on the **Place** button from the **Options Bar** and specify the location of center point for circular pattern.
- Now specify the start point and location of 2nd instance of array object; refer to Figure-57. Preview of array will be displayed and you will be asked to specify the number of instances to be created.

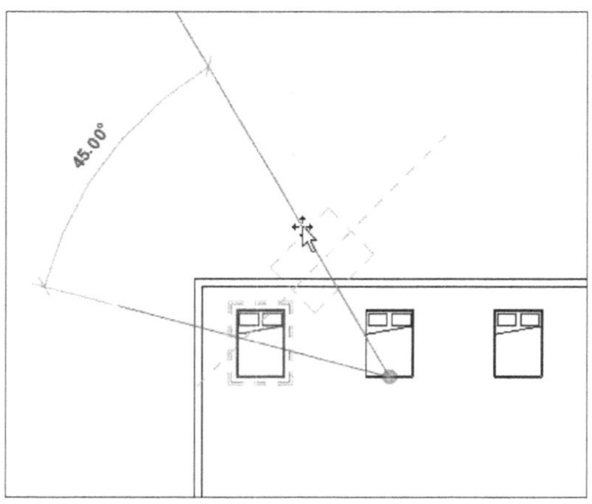

Figure-57. Creating circular array

- Enter desired number in edit box displayed. The array will be created.
- Press **ESC** to exit the tool.

Scaling

The **Scale** tool is used to scale up or scale down selected objects. You can select lines, walls, images, and other imported objects to scale. The procedure to use this tool is given next.

- Select the objects that you want to scale and click on the **Scale** tool from the **Modify** panel of **Modify** tab in the **Ribbon**. You will be asked to specify origin point for scaling model.
- Click at desired location to specify the origin point. You will be asked to specify the drag point.
- Click to specify the drag point to be used as reference for scaling. You will be asked to specify new position of drag point of scaling up/down.
- Click at desired location to scale up/down; refer to Figure-58. The selected object will be displayed.

Figure-58. Scaling the image

Trim/Extend Single Element

The **Trim/Extend Single Element** tool is used to trim or extend selected objects up to another selected object. The procedure to use this tool is given next.

- Click on the **Trim/Extend Single Element** tool from the **Modify** panel of **Modify** tab in the **Ribbon**. You will be asked to select the object to be used as reference of boundary.
- Select desired line or wall to be used as reference for trimming/extending. You will be asked to line or wall to be trimmed.
- Select the portion of wall/line you want to keep if you are trimming the walls/lines. The wall/line will be trimmed; refer to Figure-59.

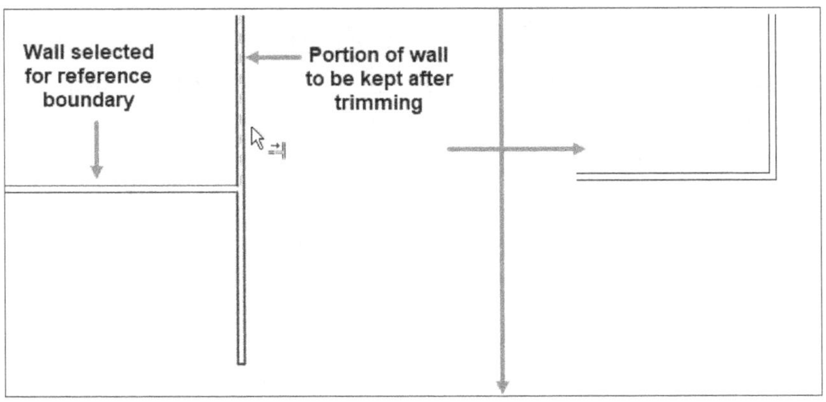

Figure-59. Trimming wall

- Press **ESC** to exit the tool.

You can use the **Trim/Extend Multiple Elements** tool in the same way.

Pin and Unpin Objects

The **Pin** tool is used to fix the model at its place so that it cannot move accidently. The procedure to pin an object is given next.

- Click on the **Pin** tool from the **Modify** panel in the **Modify** tab of the **Ribbon**. You will be asked to select the object(s) to be pinned and press **ENTER**. Options to define pin parameters will be displayed in the **Properties Palette**; refer to Figure-60.
- Select desired level from the **Level** drop-down to which you want to pin the selected objects.
- Select the **Moves With Nearby Elements** check box if you want to allow movement of pinned objects when its connected objects are moved.
- Press **ESC** to exit the tool. Now, when you try to drag the pinned objects, you will find that they are fixed.

If you want to unpin any object then click on the **Unpin** tool from the **Modify** panel in the **Modify** tab of **Ribbon** and select the pinned object(s). After selecting the objects, press **ENTER**.

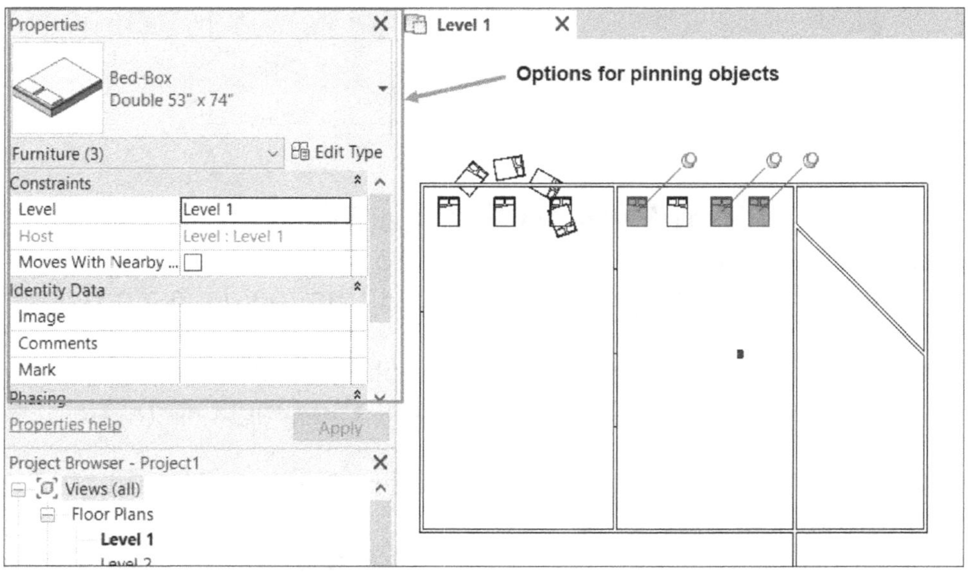

Figure-60. Options for pinning objects

Hiding Objects

The tools in the **Hide** drop-down are used to hide objects; refer to Figure-61. Note that this drop-down is active only after selecting an object. Various options in this drop-down are discussed next.

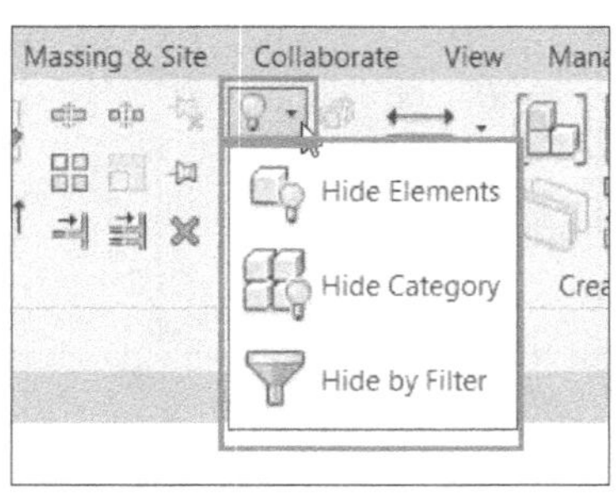

Figure-61. Hide drop-down

Hide Elements

The **Hide Elements** tool in **Hide** drop-down is used to hide selected objects. Select the options that you want to hide and click on the **Hide Elements** tool from the **Hide** drop-down in the **View** panel of **Modify** tab in the **Ribbon**. The objects will be hidden.

Hide Category

The **Hide Category** tool is used to hide all the objects that have same category as selected object has. After selecting the object, click on the **Hide Category** tool. All the objects of same category will be hidden.

Hide By Filter

The **Hide by Filter** tool is used to hide objects by specifying filters. The procedure to use this tool is given next.

- Click on the **Hide by Filter** tool from the **Hide** drop-down in the **View** panel of **Modify** tab in the **Ribbon**. The **Visibility/Graphic Overrides for Floor Plan** dialog box will be displayed; refer to Figure-62.

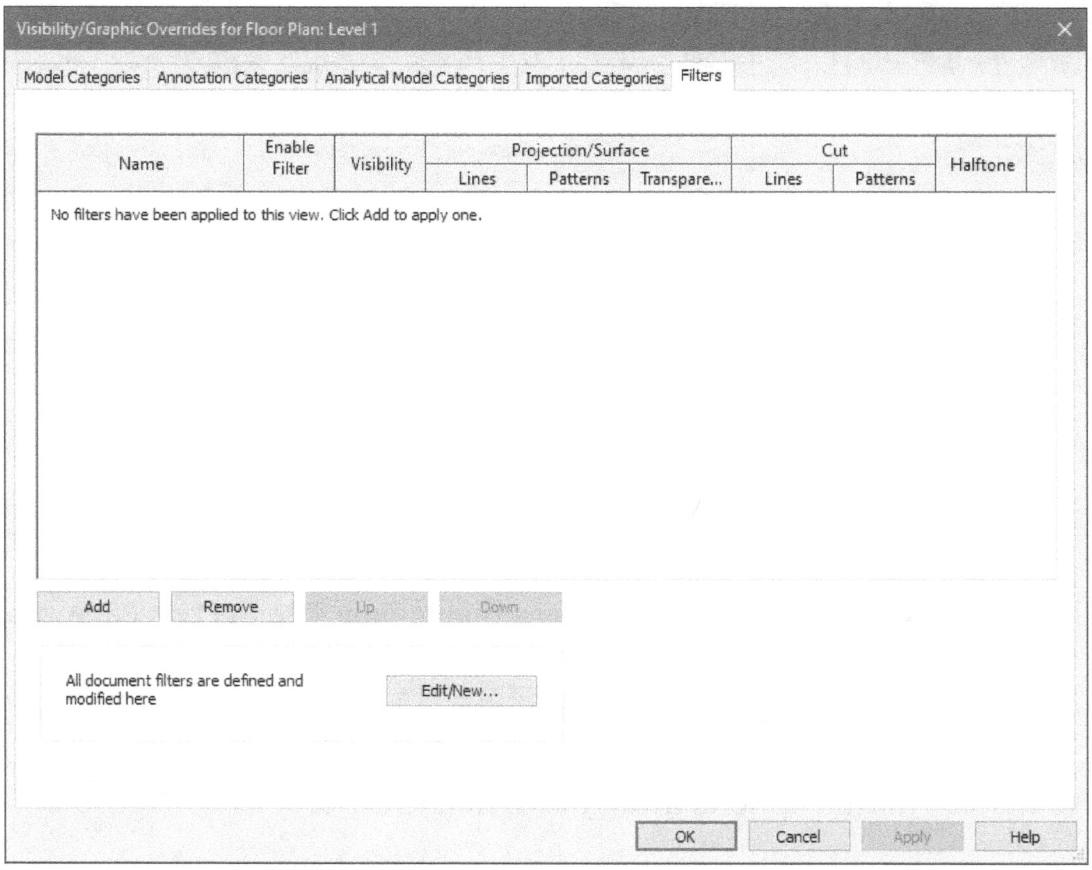

Figure-62. Visibility Graphics Overrides for Floor Plan dialog box

- Click on the **Add** button from the dialog box. The **Add Filters** dialog box will be displayed; refer to Figure-63.

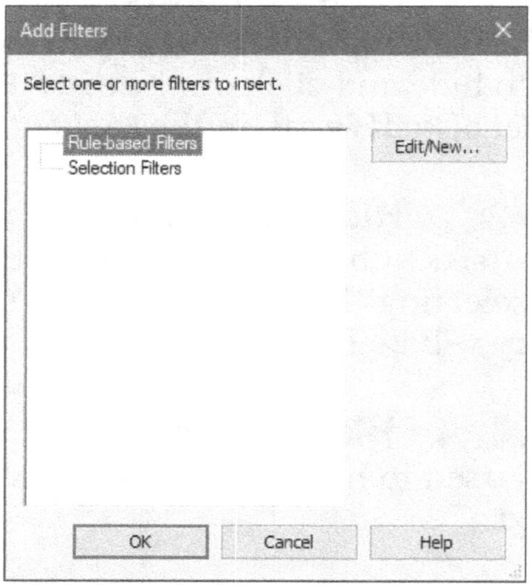

Figure-63. Add Filters dialog box

- Select desired filter from the list box. If desired filter is not available in the list then click on the **Edit/New** button from the dialog box. The **Filters** dialog box will be displayed; refer to Figure-64.

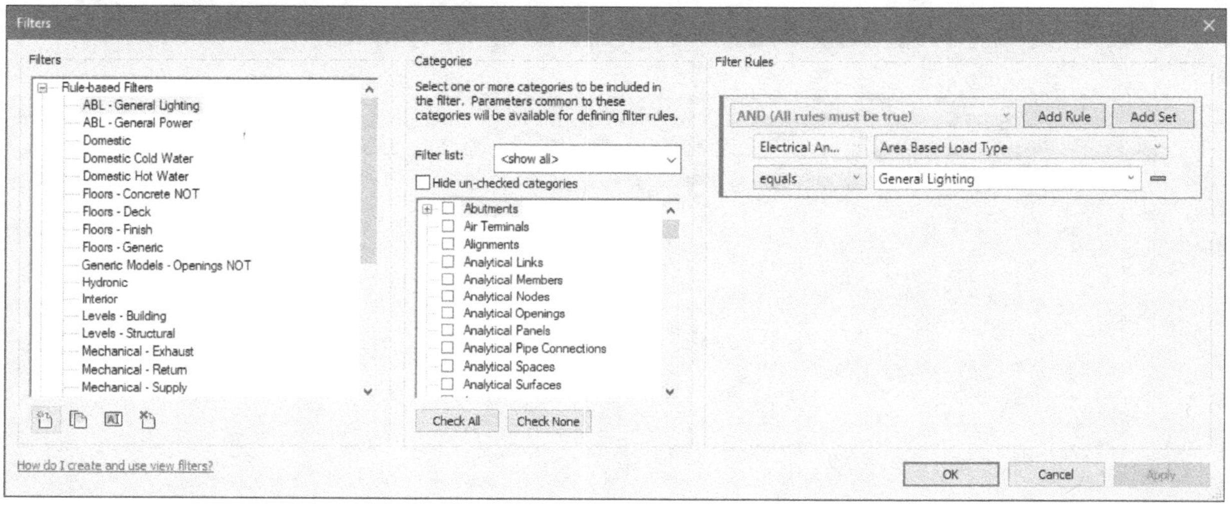

Figure-64. Filters dialog box

- Click on the **New** button from the **Filters** dialog box. The **Filter Name** dialog box will be displayed.
- Specify desired name in the dialog box and click on the **OK** button. The new filter will be added in the **Filters** area of the dialog box.
- Select the newly added filter and clear the **Hide un-checked categories** check box to display all the options available to define filter; refer to Figure-65.

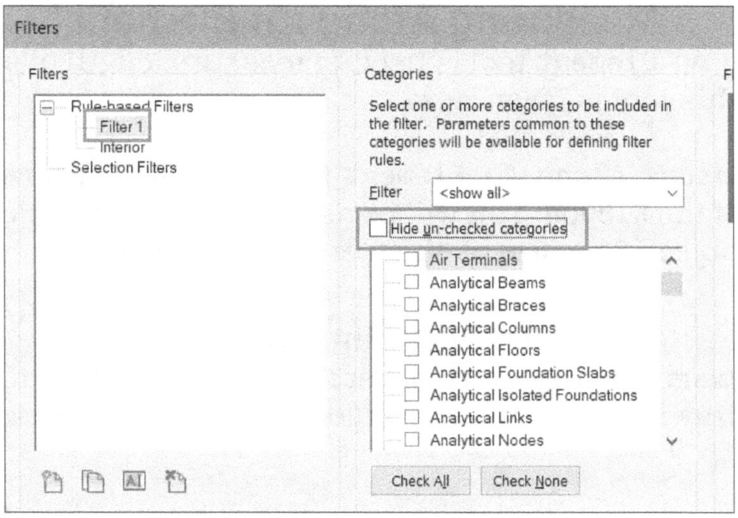

Figure-65. Options for filters

- Select check boxes for categories you want to hide from the drawing area and click on the **OK** button from the **Filters** dialog box. The **Add Filters** dialog box will be displayed again.
- Select desired filter from the dialog box and click on the **OK** button. The filter will be applied.
- Clear the **Visibility** check box for filter in the **Visibility/Graphic Overrides for Floor Plan** dialog box to hide items of selected filter.
- Click on the **OK** button from the **Visibility/Graphic Overrides for Floor Plan** dialog box to apply filter.

You can use other options in **View** panel of **Modify** tab of **Ribbon** in the same way.

Measuring Between Two References

The **Measure Between Two References** tool is used to measure distance between two objects. The procedure to use this tool is given next.

- Click on the **Measure Between Two References** tool from the **Measure** panel of the **Modify** tab in the **Ribbon**. You will be select the first reference point for measurement.
- One by one click on two points between which you want to measure distance. The distance will be displayed; refer to Figure-66.

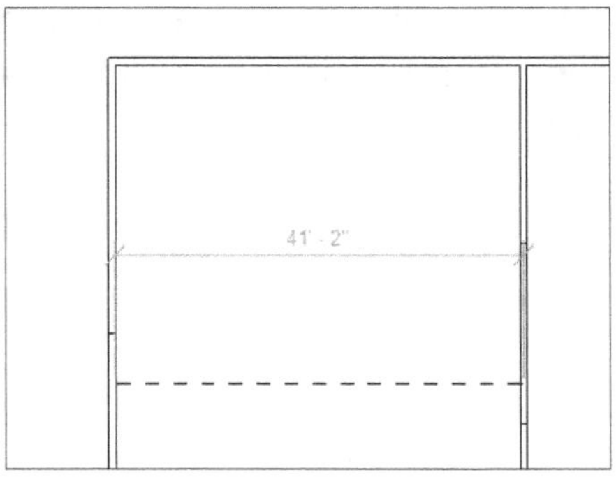

Figure-66. Measuring distance

- You can select another group of two points to measure distance between them. Press **ESC** twice to exit the tool.

Measuring Along An Element

The **Measure Along An Element** tool is used to measure length of selected object. The procedure to use this tool is given next.

- Click on the **Measure Along An Element** tool from the **Measure** drop-down in the **Measure** panel of the **Ribbon**. You will be asked to select the object to be measured.
- Select desired object. The size of object will be displayed.

Creating Dimensions

The tools in the **Dimension** drop-down of **Measure** panel are used to apply dimensions to the objects in drawing area; refer to Figure-67. Various tools in this drop-down are discussed next.

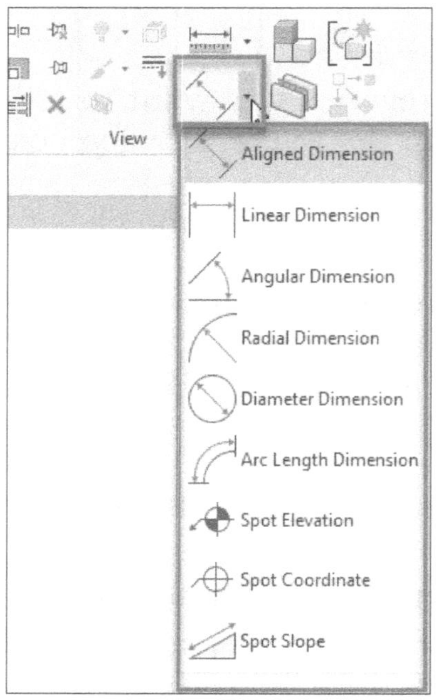

Figure-67. Dimension drop-down

Creating Aligned Dimension

The **Aligned Dimension** tool is used to create dimension aligned to selected object. The procedure to use this tool is given next.

- Click on the **Aligned Dimension** tool from the **Dimension** drop-down in the **Measure** panel of the **Ribbon**. You will be asked to select the object.
- Click on two points of object that you want dimension. The dimension will get attached to the cursor; refer to Figure-68.

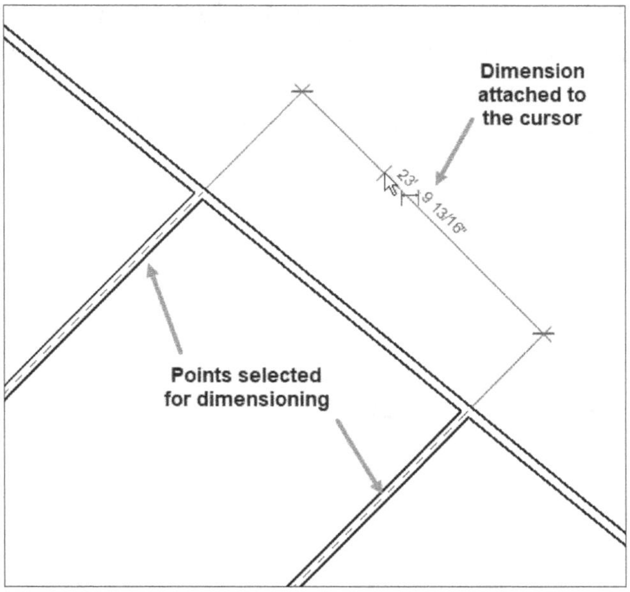

Figure-68. Creating aligned dimension

- Click at desired location to place the dimension.

You can use the **Linear Dimension** tool in the same way.

Creating Angular Dimension

The **Angular Dimension** tool is used to create angle dimension for inclined objects. The procedure to use this tool is given next.

- Click on the **Angular Dimension** tool from the **Dimension** drop-down in the **Measure** panel of the **Modify** tab in the **Ribbon**. You will be asked to select the references to be dimensioned.
- Click on two inclined lines/walls. The dimension will get attached to cursor; refer to Figure-69.

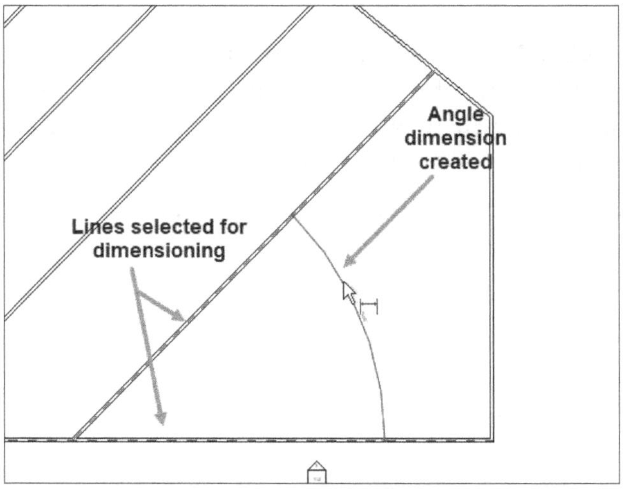

Figure-69. Creating angular dimension

- Click at desired location to place the dimension.

Creating Radial Dimension

The **Radial Dimension** tool is used to apply radius dimension to selected circular objects. The procedure to use this tool is given next.

- Click on the **Radial Dimension** tool from the **Dimension** drop-down in the **Measure** panel of **Modify** tab in the **Ribbon**. You will be asked to select arc of object to be dimensioned.
- Click on desired object. The dimension will get attached to cursor; refer to Figure-70.

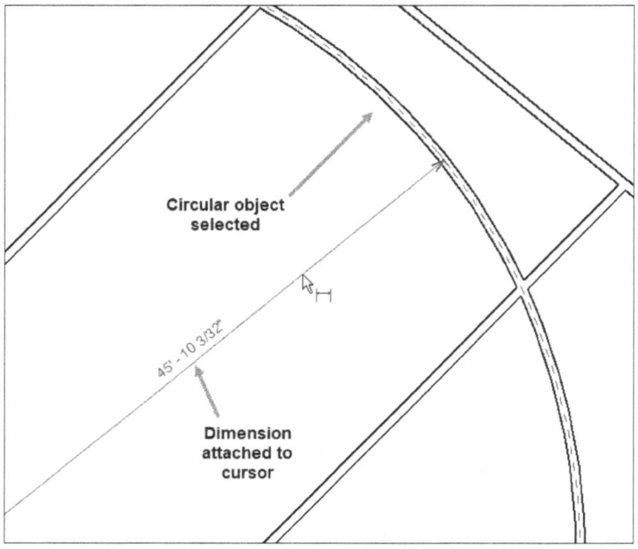

Figure-70. Creating radial dimension

- Click at desired location to place the dimension.

You can use the **Diameter Dimension** and **Arc Length Dimension** tools in the same way.

Creating Spot Elevation Mark

The **Spot Elevation** tool is used to create elevation mark at selected point. Note that the elevation of value of current selected point is displayed in the mark. The procedure to create elevation mark is given next.

- Click on the **Spot Elevation** tool from the **Dimension** drop-down of the **Measure** panel in the **Modify** tab of **Ribbon**. You will be asked to select an object.
- Click at desired object to apply elevation mark. The elevation mark with leader will get attached to cursor; refer to Figure-71.

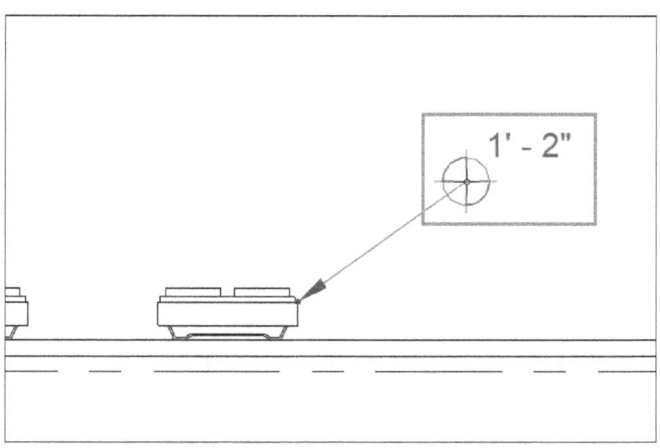

Figure-71. Elevation mark attached to cursor

- Click at desired locations to place the mark.

Spot Coordinate

The **Spot Coordinate** tool is used to display coordinate of selected point on the object. The procedure to use this tool is same as discussed for **Spot Elevation** tool.

Spot Slope

The **Spot Slope** tool is used to mark slope of selected object.

Creating Assembly

The **Create Assembly** tool is used to combine multiple objects into one element so that they are displayed as single object in schedules and other tables. The procedure to use this tool is given next.

- Click on the **Create Assembly** tool from the **Create** panel in the **Modify** tab of **Ribbon**. The **Edit Assembly** toolbox will be displayed; refer to Figure-72.

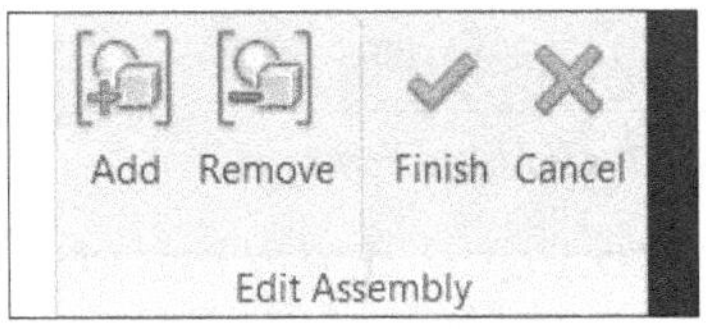

Figure-72. Edit Assembly toolbox

- Click on the **Add** button from the toolbox. You will be asked to select the objects to be added in the assembly.
- Click on the objects to add them in assembly. If you want to remove any object from the assembly then click on the **Remove** button from toolbox and select desired object.
- After selecting the objects, click on the **Finish** button. The **New Assembly** dialog box will be displayed; refer to Figure-73.

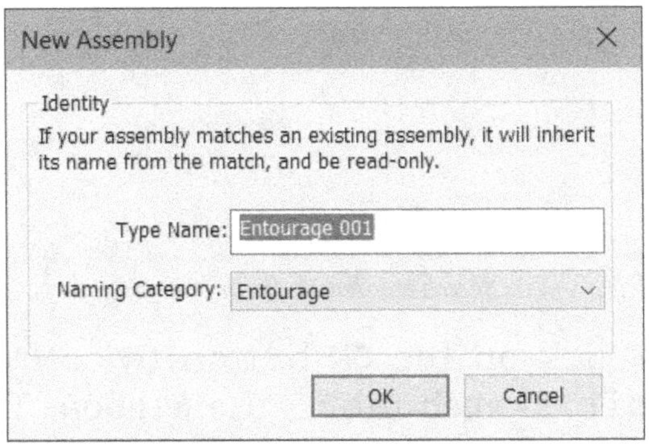

Figure-73. New Assembly dialog box

- Select desired option from the **Naming Category** drop-down in the dialog box and specify desired name in the **Type Name** edit box.
- Click on the **OK** button from the dialog box. The assembly will be created.

Creating Parts

The **Create Parts** tool is used to divide selected object into multiple parts. The procedure to use this tool is given next.

- Click on the **Create Parts** tool from the **Create** panel of **Modify** tab in the **Ribbon**. You will be asked to select the object that you want to divide.

- Select the object to be divided and press **ENTER**. The tools to divide or merge parts will be displayed in the **Modify** tab; refer to Figure-74.

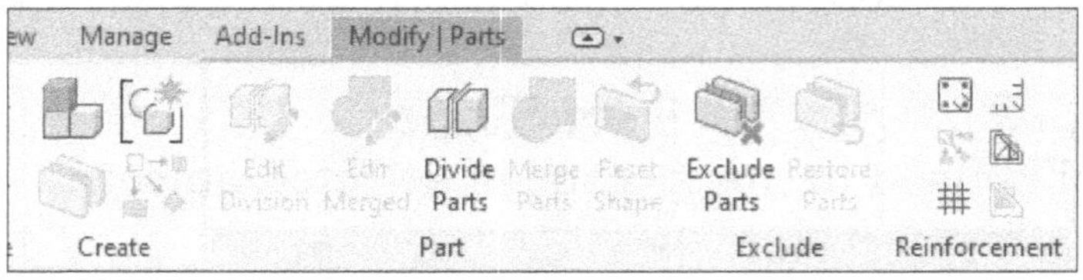

Figure-74. Tools for creating parts

- Click on the **Divide Parts** button from the **Part** panel in the **Modify** tab of **Ribbon**. The options to divide the part will be displayed in the **Ribbon**; refer to Figure-75.

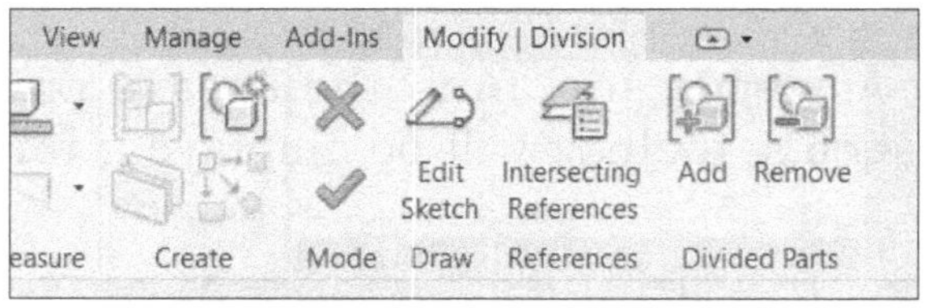

Figure-75. Modify|Division tab

- Click on the **Edit Sketch** button and draw curves that intersect with the selected elements; refer to Figure-76.

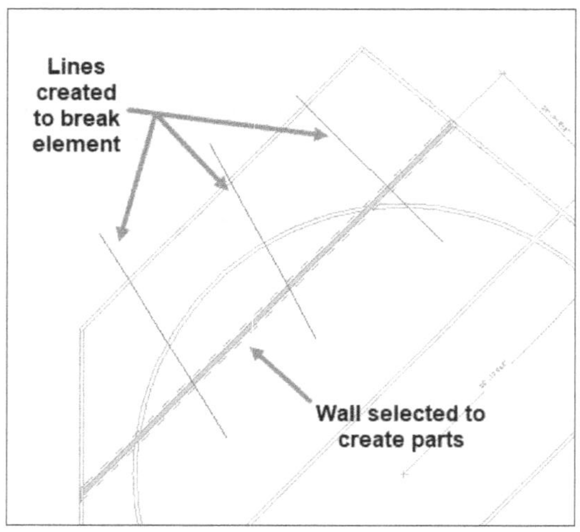

Figure-76. Sketch created to divide element

- After creating sketch, click on the **OK** button twice from the **Mode** panel of the **Modify|Division > Edit Sketch** tab in the **Ribbon**. The selected object will be divided at the intersection.

Creating Groups

Groups are used to collectively use objects. Using groups, you can copy multiple objects and reuse them in drawing. The procedure to create a group is given next.

- Click on the **Create Group** tool from the **Create** panel in the **Modify** tab of the **Ribbon**. The **Create Group** dialog box will be displayed; refer to Figure-77.

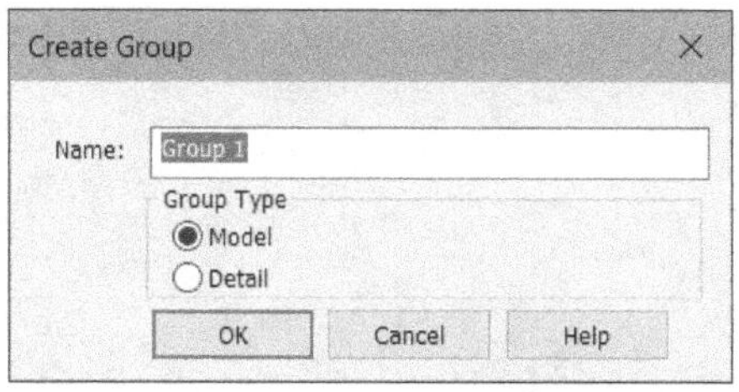

Figure-77. Create Group dialog box

- Specify desired name of group in the **Name** edit box. Select desired radio button to define type of group.
- Click on the **OK** button from the dialog box. The **Edit Group** toolbox will be displayed; refer to Figure-78.

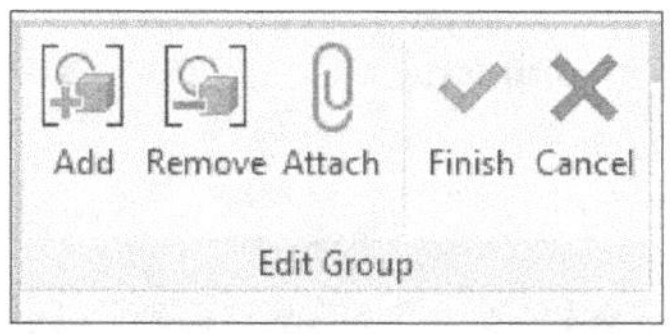

Figure-78. Edit Group toolbox

- Click on the **Add** button from the toolbox to add objects in the group. You will be asked to select objects.
- Select all the objects that you want to add to the group.
- If you want to remove any object from the group then click on the **Remove** button and select the objects.
- Click on the **Finish** button from the **Edit Group** toolbox to create the group.

After creating group, if you select any of the object of created group then whole group will get selected and the **Modify|Model Groups** or **Modify|Attached Detail Groups** contextual tab will be displayed. Use the options in the **Group** panel of contextual tab to edit or ungroup the group.

Create Similar

The **Create Similar** tool is used to active the tool for creating objects similar to selected one. The procedure to use this tool is given next.

- Click on the **Create Similar** tool from the **Create** panel of **Modify** tab in the **Ribbon** after selecting the object (like wall). The tool to create selected object will be activated.

CREATING WINDOWS

The **Window** tool is used to create windows in the walls. The procedure to use this tool is given next.

- Click on the **Window** tool from the **Build** panel in the **Architecture** tab of the **Ribbon**. You will be asked to click on the location where you want to place the window.
- Select desired type of window from the drop-down at the top in the **Properties Palette** and set desired parameters.
- Click at desired location on the wall to place the window; refer to Figure-79.

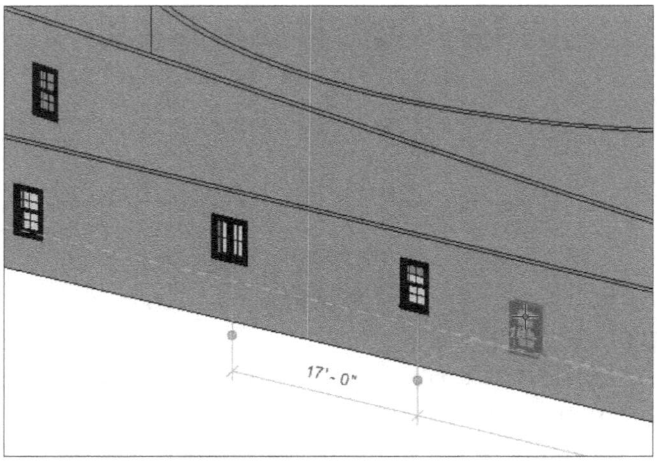

Figure-79. Placing windows

- Press **ESC** twice to exit the tool.

PLACING COMPONENTS

The **Place a Component** tool is used to place components like bed, picture frame, and other Revit family objects. The procedure to place component is given next.

- Click on the **Place a Component** tool from the **Component** drop-down in the **Build** panel of **Architecture** tab in the **Ribbon**. A component will get attached to the cursor and related properties will be displayed in the **Properties Palette**.
- Set desired parameters for the object in the **Properties Palette**. Click on the **Load Family** tool from the **Mode** panel in the **Modify** tab if you want to load a different Revit family object as discussed earlier.
- Click at desired location to place the component; refer to Figure-80.

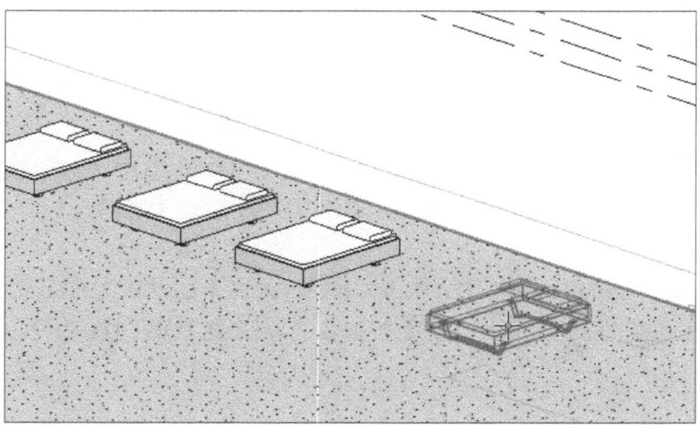

Figure-80. Placing component

- Press **ESC** twice to exit the tool.

Model In-Place

The **Model In-Place** tool is used to create user defined objects in the model. Like, you can create desired shaped table in the model. Note that unlike the Revit family objects, the objects created by using this tool are local and cannot be used in another drawing. The procedure to use this tool is given next.

- Click on the **Model In-Place** tool from the **Component** drop-down in the **Build** panel of **Architecture** tab in the **Ribbon**. The **Family Category and Parameters** dialog box will be displayed; refer to Figure-81.

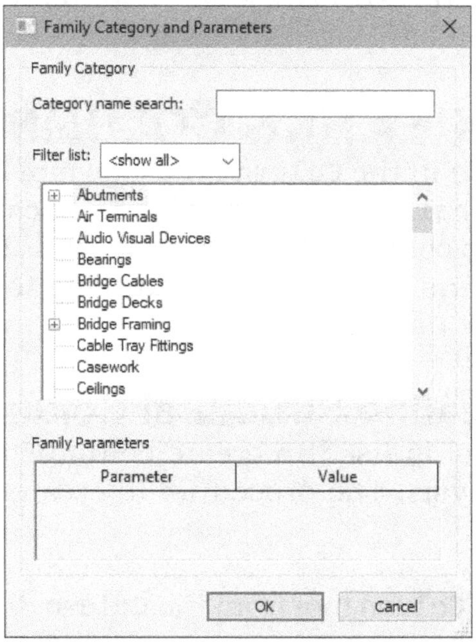

Figure-81. Family Category and Parameters dialog box

- Select desired option from the list box and click on the **OK** button. The **Name** dialog box will be displayed.
- Specify desired name for the object and click on the **OK** button from the dialog box. The **In-Place Editor** tools will be displayed in the **Ribbon**; refer to Figure-82.

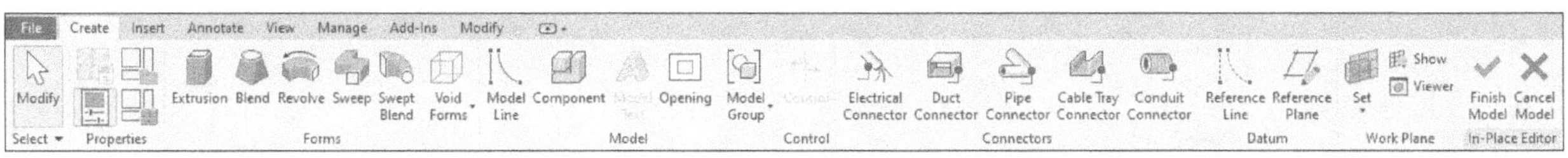

Figure-82. In-Place Editor tools

- Click on desired tool from the **Form** panel in the **Create** tab of **Ribbon**. The tools to draw sketch will be displayed.
- Create the sketch and perform desired 3D operations to create the model; refer to Figure-83.

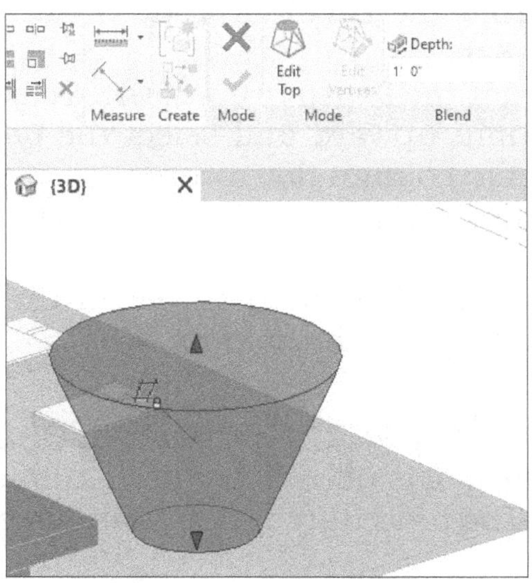

Figure-83. Creating blend object

- Click on the **Finish Model** button from the **In-Place Editor** panel of **Modify|Blend** contextual tab to exit the solid modeling environment. Note that we have selected the **Blend** tool so **Modify|Blend** contextual tab is displayed in the **Ribbon**, if you select a different tool then respective **Modify** contextual tab will be displayed.
- Press **ESC** to exit the tool.

CREATING COLUMNS

There are two tools available in the **Column** drop-down of **Architecture** tab in **Ribbon** to create columns; **Structural Column** and **Column: Architectural**. The **Structural Column** tool is used to create columns that bear the load. The **Column: Architectural** tool is used to create columns that are for beautifying the building. The procedures to create these columns are discussed next.

Creating Structural Columns

The **Structural Column** tool is used to create columns that bear the load and are included in structural analysis. The procedure to create structural column is given next.

- Click on the **Structural Column** tool from the **Column** drop-down in the **Build** panel of **Architecture** tab in the **Ribbon**. A column will get attached to the cursor and **Properties Palette** will be displayed with respective options; refer to Figure-84.

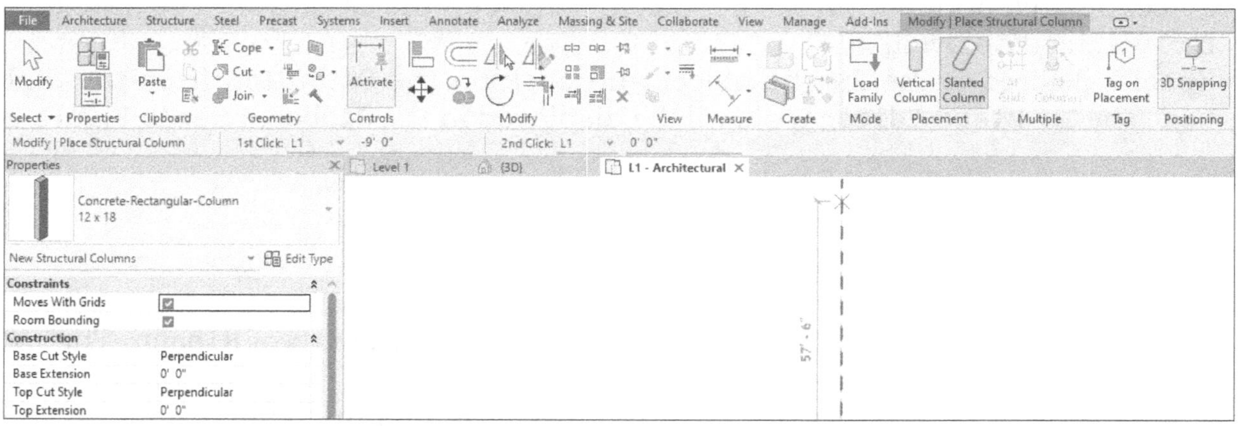

Figure-84. Options for placing structural column

- Select desired option from the **Level** drop-down to specify starting location of column in the **Options Bar**.
- Select desired option from the **Depth** drop-down. Select the **Height** drop-down if you want to create column upward and select the **Depth** option from the drop-down if you want to create column downwards.
- Select desired option from the drop-down next to **Depth** drop-down to define the location of end point of column.
- Set the other parameters as discussed earlier in the **Properties Palette** and click at desired location to place the column.

Creating Architectural Column

The **Column: Architectural** tool is used to create columns that do not have any role in bearing load of building. The procedure to create architectural column is given next.

- Click on the **Column: Architectural** tool from the **Column** drop-down of **Build** panel in the **Architecture** tab of the **Ribbon**. The column will get attached to cursor and related options will be displayed in the **Properties Palette**; refer to Figure-85.

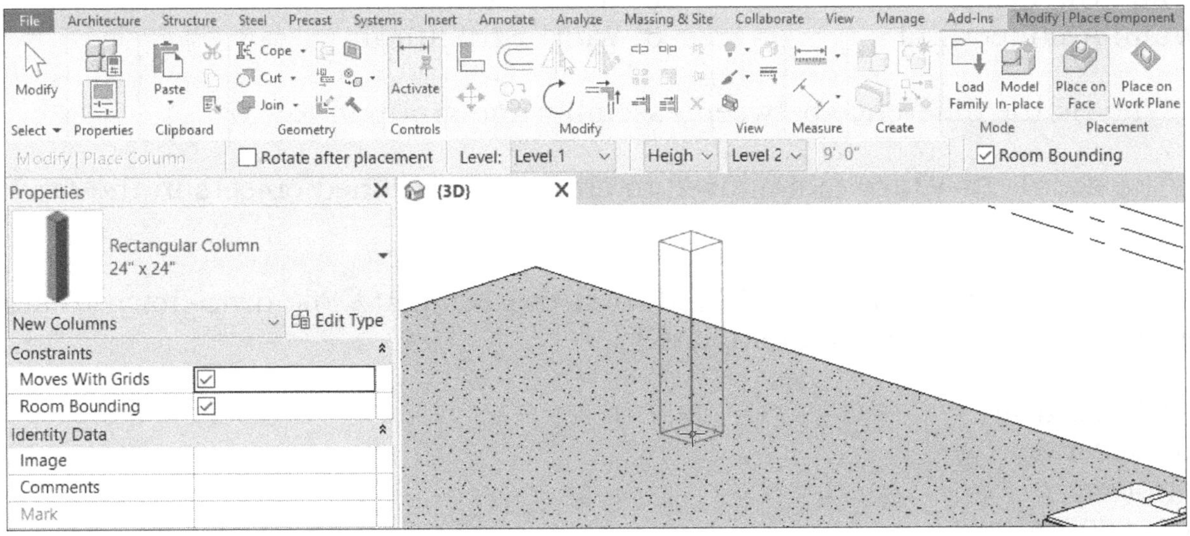

Figure-85. Options for architectural column

- Select desired shape of column from the drop-down at the top in the **Properties Palette**. If desired column is not available in the drop-down then click on the **Load Family** tool from the **Mode** panel in the **Modify** tab and load desired columns.
- Specify desired parameters in the **Properties Palette**. Select the **Moves With Grids** check box if you want the column to move when grid is moved. Note that the column should be placed on grid point if you want this check box to function. Select the **Room Bounding** check box if the columns as reference for defining room boundary.
- Click at desired locations to place the columns.
- Press **ESC** to exit the tool.

In this chapter, you have learned the basic tools of architecture design and modification tools. In the next chapter, you will work on some more architectural design tools and apply them in practical.

SELF-ASSESSMENT

Q1. Which of the following options in the **Template File** drop-down of **New Template** dialog box allows you to choose unit system for the project later?

a. None
b. Systems Template
c. Construction Template
d. Structural Template

Q2. Architectural Walls are created where load is not endured by walls. (T/F)

Q3. To create a tapered wall, you need to make structure of selected wall type as variable. (T/F)

Q4. Which of the following tools is used to create wall by using curvature of selected face of another wall?

a. Wall : Sweep
b. Wall by Face
c. Wall : Architectural
d. Wall : Structural

Q5. What is the difference between assembly and group in Revit?

Q6. The **Model In-Place** tool is used to create user defined objects in the drawing. (T/F)

Q7. Which option should be selected from the Template File drop-down to start a project without a predefined template?

A. Architectural
B. Structural
C. <None>
D. Conceptual

Q8. What is displayed after selecting the template and clicking OK when starting a new project?

A. Units Conversion dialog
B. Undefined System of Measurement dialog
C. Load Family dialog
D. Project Browser

Q9. What is typically the default unit system chosen by most building designers?

A. Metric
B. Metric-Imperial
C. Imperial
D. SI Units

Q10. Which panel contains the Grid tool in the Ribbon?

A. Structure Panel
B. Datum Panel
C. Annotation Panel
D. Drawing Panel

Q11. What happens when you click on the number or alphabet in the grid balloon?

A. It deletes the grid
B. It rotates the grid
C. It duplicates the grid
D. It allows you to change its value

Q12. What is the purpose of architectural walls in Revit?

A. Load bearing
B. Structural support
C. Enclosure for a room
D. Electrical routing

Q13. Which drop-down in the Properties Palette lets you choose where the base of a wall will be placed?

A. Top Constraint
B. Base Offset
C. Base Constraint
D. Cross-Section

Q14. What must be enabled to convert a straight wall to a tapered wall?

A. Join Status
B. Unconnected Height
C. Room Bounding
D. Variable structure in wall type

Q15. Which tool is used to create a wall based on the shape of a mass object's face?

A. Wall: Sweep
B. Wall by Face
C. Wall: Reveal
D. Place Mass

Q16. What is the primary function of Mass objects in Revit?

A. Define electrical systems
B. Create door and window frames
C. Act as references for building design
D. Provide structural analysis

Q17. What does the Wall: Sweep tool do?

A. Deletes a wall
B. Creates a groove
C. Places a wall along a curved face
D. Measures wall thickness

Q18. What is the purpose of the Wall: Reveal tool?

A. Create grooves on walls
B. Offset wall height
C. Attach top of wall
D. Modify wall base

Q19. If a desired door type is not available in the Type Selector drop-down, what should you do?

A. Create a new type manually
B. Exit and restart Revit
C. Load Family from the Mode panel
D. Choose the closest available type

Q20. What tool do you use to access and load online Autodesk family content?

A. Place Mass
B. Load Family
C. Load Autodesk Family
D. Insert Library

Q21. What does the Modify tool in the Select panel activate?

A. Wall Modification
B. Selection Mode
C. Type Properties
D. Load Library

Q22. Which tool allows editing the parameters of a selected family object?

A. Type Selector
B. Load Autodesk Family
C. Type Properties
D. Options Bar

Q23. What is the purpose of the Properties button when an object is selected in the model?

A. To align the object
B. To access clipboard tools
C. To display the Properties Palette
D. To apply paint

Q24. Which key should you hold to select multiple objects?

A. ALT
B. CTRL
C. SHIFT
D. TAB

Q25. What is the function of the Cut to Clipboard tool?

A. Paste elements from the clipboard
B. Apply paint to elements
C. Copy elements without deleting them
D. Delete and store selected elements in the clipboard

Q26. Which tool is used to apply properties of one object to another similar object?

A. Copy Tool
B. Match Type Properties Tool
C. Join Geometry Tool
D. Offset Tool

Q27. What does the Apply Notching Coping tool do in steel frames?

A. Removes paint from frames
B. Joins two steel members
C. Removes part of one or both frames for connection
D. Mirrors steel members

Q28. How is Remove Notching Coping used?

A. By trimming the intersecting frame
B. By using Rotate tool
C. By selecting the cut member and the member used for cutting
D. By selecting only one of the members

Q29. Which tool reverses the effect of the Cut Geometry tool?

A. Unjoin Geometry
B. Join Geometry
C. Uncut Geometry
D. Offset

Q30. What happens when you use the Join Geometry tool?

A. The selected objects are rotated
B. Objects are separated
C. The objects share texture and appear seamless
D. One object is demolished

Q31. What is the function of the Switch Join Order tool?

A. Changes join tool to align
B. Reverses the order of cut in joined objects
C. Switches mirror axis
D. Splits faces into two

Q32. What happens when the Join/Unjoin Roof tool is used and the roof is already joined?

A. An error is ignored
B. The wall is deleted
C. A warning dialog is displayed
D. The tool automatically unjoins the roof
Q33. Which tool helps in defining how beams and columns join?

A. Wall Joins
B. Beam/Column Joins
C. Join Geometry
D. Trim/Extend Tool

Q34. What tool is used to split the face of walls/floors/roofs to apply different materials?

A. Mirror Axis Tool
B. Split Face Tool
C. Cut Geometry
D. Rotate Tool

Q35. How can paint be removed from a face?

A. Use the Offset tool
B. Use the Remove Paint tool
C. Use the Rotate tool
D. Use the Join tool

Q36. What does the Demolish tool do?

A. Permanently deletes the object
B. Hides the object in all phases
C. Marks objects as demolished in current and future phases
D. Converts objects to temporary annotations

Q37. How can you un-demolish an object?

A. Reapply the demolish tool
B. Use Join tool
C. Set "None" in Phase Demolished in Properties Palette
D. Press ESC repeatedly

Q38. What is the function of the Activate tool?

A. Deletes objects
B. Displays annotations like pins and dimensions
C. Aligns objects
D. Rotates objects

Q39. The Align tool aligns objects to:

A. Text styles
B. Dimensions
C. Line or point references
D. Clipboard

Q40. Which tool is used to move objects from one place to another?

A. Offset
B. Move
C. Rotate
D. Mirror

FOR STUDENT NOTES

Chapter 3

Architectural Designing-II

Topics Covered

The major topics covered in this chapter are:

- ***Creating Roofs***
- ***Creating Ceilings and Floors***
- ***Creating Curtain Grid, Mullions, and Curtain System***
- ***Creating Ramps, Railings, and Stairs***
- ***Creating Model Items like model text, model line, and groups***
- ***Creating Rooms, Areas, Room tags, and Area tags***
- ***Creating Openings in Roofs, Floors, and Ceilings***

INTRODUCTION

In previous chapter, you have learned some of the tools for creating architectural components. In this chapter, we will continue these tools and later create architectural models for practice.

CREATING ROOFS

The tools to create roofs are available in the **Roof** drop-down of **Build** panel in the **Architecture** tab of **Ribbon**; refer to Figure-1. The tools in this drop-down are discussed next.

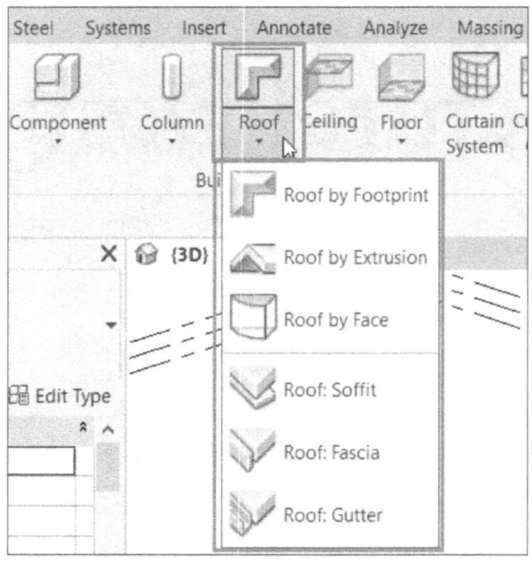

Figure-1. Roof drop-down

Creating Roof by Footprint

The **Roof by Footprint** tool is used to create roof by selecting boundary elements like walls. Note that you can also use a closed loop sketch to define boundary of roof. The procedure to use this tool is given next.

- Click on the **Roof by Footprint** tool from the **Roof** drop-down in the **Build** panel of **Architecture** tab in the **Ribbon**. The **Modify|Create Roof Footprint** contextual tab will be displayed in the **Ribbon**; refer to Figure-2.

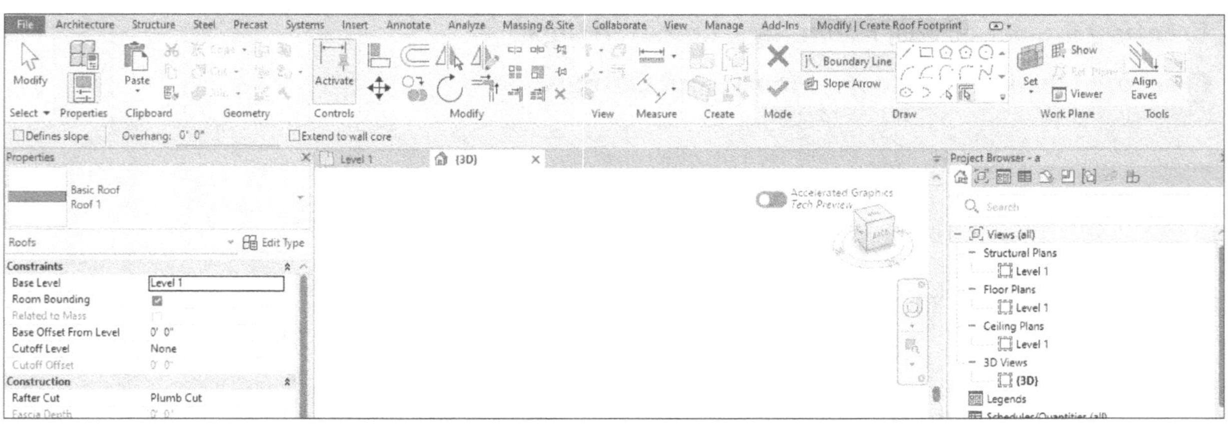

Figure-2. Create Roof Footprint contextual tab

- Select the walls that form a closed boundary and click on the **OK** button from the contextual tab. Preview of the roof will be displayed. You can also use sketching tools in the **Draw** panel of contextual tab to create boundary for roof.

- Set desired parameters in the **Properties Palette**. The roof will be modified accordingly; refer to Figure-3.

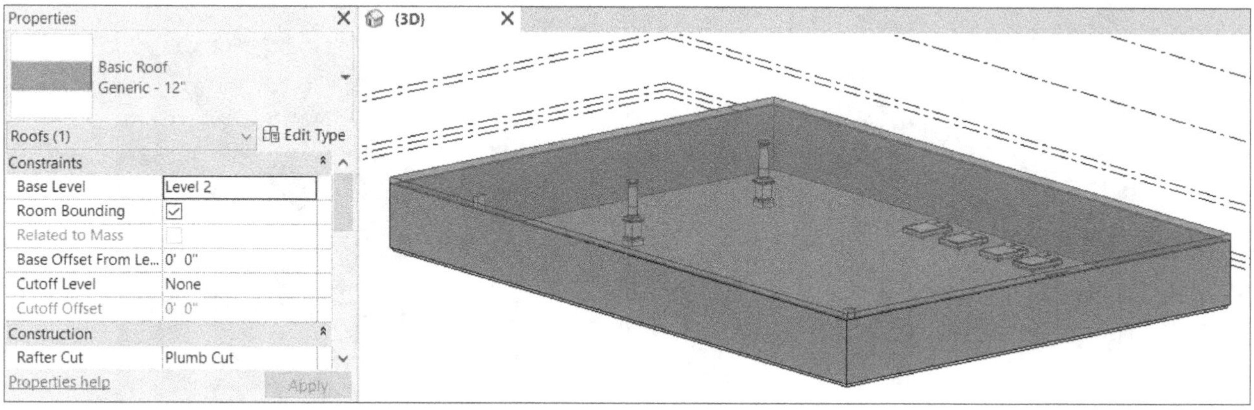

Figure-3. Preview of roof

- Note that when you are creating a roof using footprint then you can align the height and overhangs of eaves on different sides of roof by using the **Align Eaves** tool from the **Tools** panel of **Modify|Create Roof Footprint** contextual tab of **Ribbon**; refer to Figure-2. The Eaves are the overhanging portion of roof from the walls generally created to keep rain water off the walls and to prevent the ingress of water at the junction where the roof meets the wall. Figure-4 shows baselines selected with different overhangs for creating roof. To align eaves, click on the **Align Eaves** tool from the contextual tab and while holding the **CTRL** key, all the eaves to be aligned. The eaves will be aligned as per first selected eave. By default, the **Adjust Overhangs** toggle button is selected to overhangs of selected eaves are aligned. If you want to align height of eaves then select the **Adjust Height** toggle button next to **Align Eaves** tool in **Ribbon**.

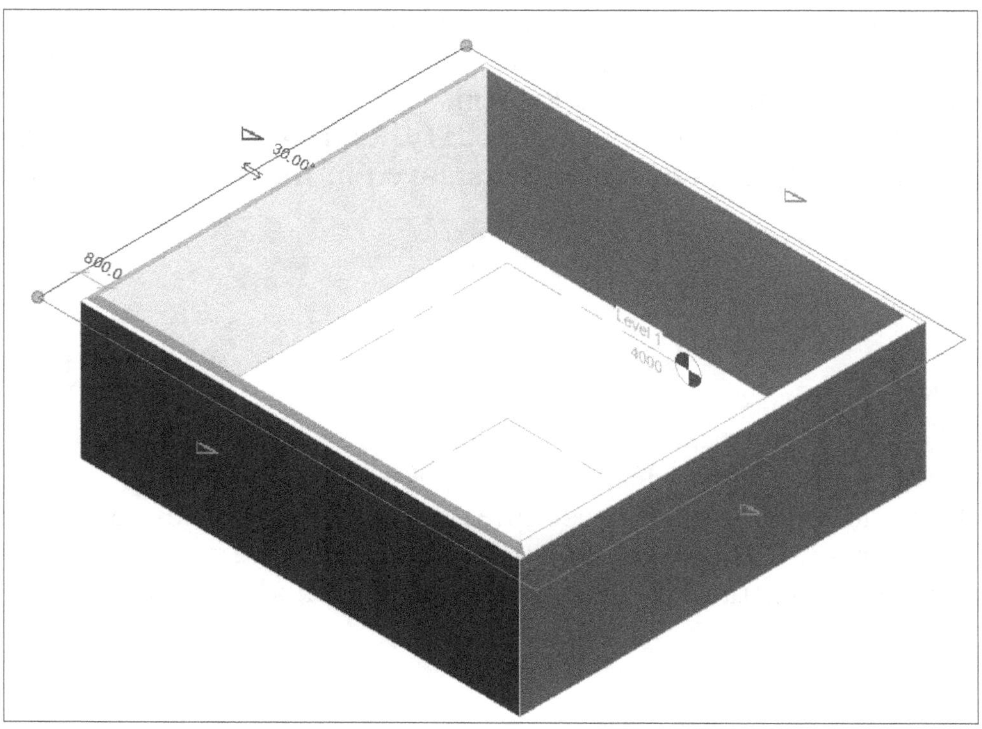

Figure-4. Roof model lines with different overhangs

- Select the **Room Bounding** check box to set extents of roof as per the boundary of room.

- Select desired option from the **Rafter Cut** drop-down of **Properties Palette** to define how eaves of roof will be created; refer to Figure-5.

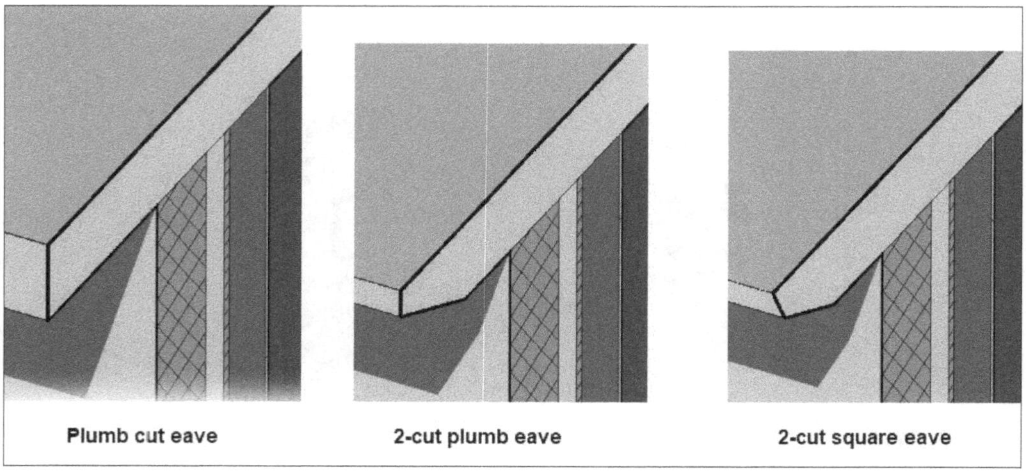

Figure-5. Rafter cut types

- Select desired option from the **Rafter or Truss** drop-down in the **Properties Palette** to define whether base of roof will be measured from inside of wall or outside of wall.
- Set desired value in the **Slope** edit box to define the slope of roof surface. After setting desired parameters, click on the **Apply** button to apply modifications in roof.
- Press **ESC** to exit the tool.

Modifying A Roof

There are various options in **Properties Palette** and contextual tab that are displayed on selecting a roof while modifying it. These options are discussed next.

Editing Footprint

After selecting the roof, click on the **Edit Footprint** tool from the **Mode** panel in the **Modify|Roofs** contextual tab of the **Ribbon**; refer to Figure-6. The options to edit footprint of roof will be displayed in the **Modify|Roof > Edit Footprint** contextual tab of **Ribbon**. The footprints of roof are displayed in the form of pink colored lines.

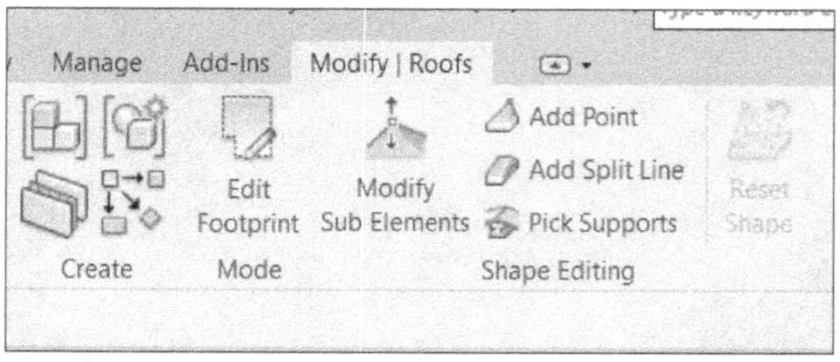

Figure-6. Modify Roof contextual tab

You can select and delete any of these lines and draw new lines to edit the shape of roof; refer to Figure-7. Click on the **OK** button from the **Mode** panel in the **Modify|Roof > Edit Footprint** contextual tab of **Ribbon**. Preview of modifying roof will be displayed.

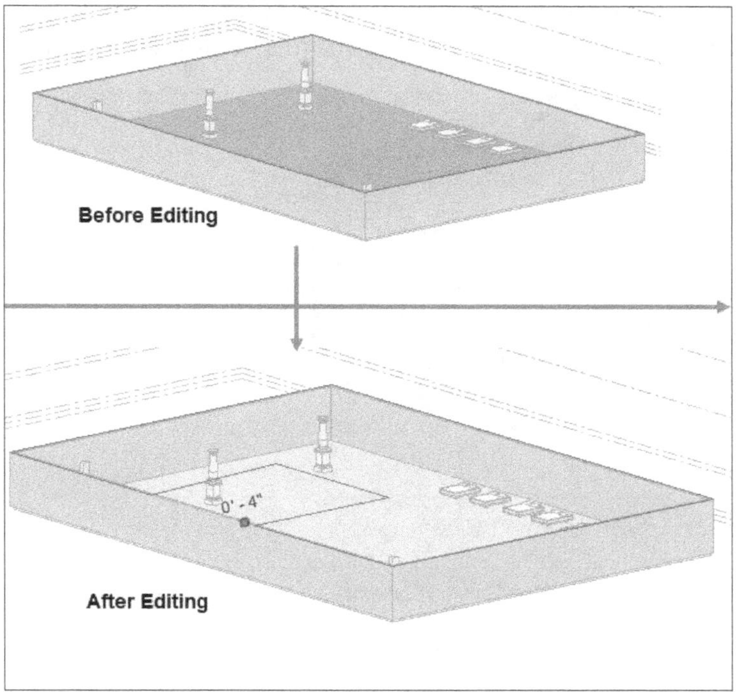

Figure-7. Editing roof footprint

Creating Roof By Extrusion

The **Roof By Extrusion** tool is used to create a roof by extruding selected section. The procedure to use this tool is given next.

- Click on the **Roof By Extrusion** tool from the **Roof** drop-down in the **Build** panel of **Architecture** tab in the **Ribbon**. The **Work Plane** dialog box will be displayed; refer to Figure-8.

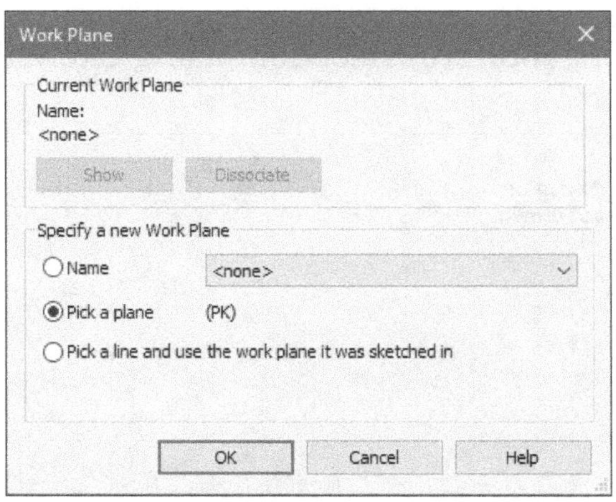

Figure-8. Work Plane dialog box

- If you want to select a work plane by name then select the **Name** radio button and select desired plane from drop-down next to it. If you want to select a face to define work plane then select the **Pick a plane** radio button. If you want to use the plane of selected line as work plane then select the **Pick a line and use the workplane it was sketched in** radio button. After selecting desired radio button, click on the **OK** button from the dialog box. We have selected the **Pick a plane** radio button in our case. So, we are asked to select a face to define plane.

- Select desired reference for sketching plane; refer to Figure-9. The **Roof Reference Level and Offset** dialog box will be displayed; refer to Figure-10.

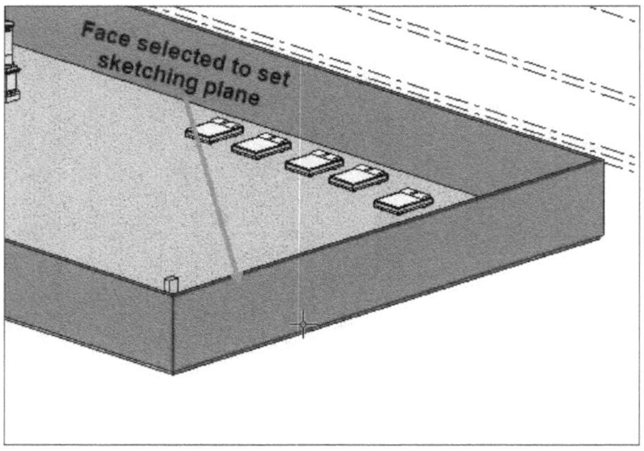

Figure-9. Selecting face

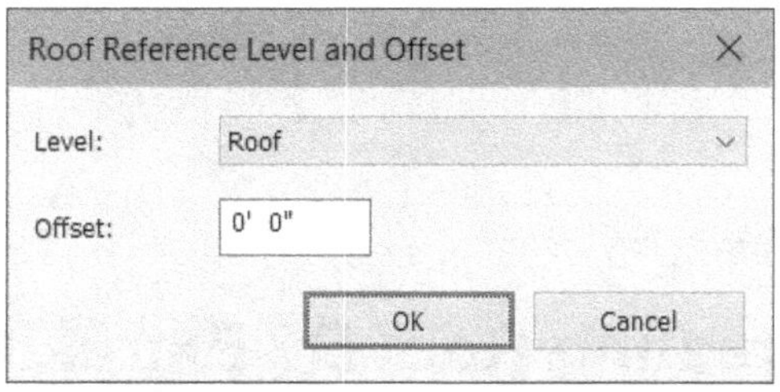

Figure-10. Roof Reference Level and Offset dialog box

- Set desired option in the **Level** drop-down and specify the offset value in the **Offset** edit box if you want to create the plane at specified offset distance from the reference. Click on the **OK** button from the dialog box. The work plane will be created and you will be asked to draw the cross-section of roof.
- Click on the **Show** button from the **Work Plane** panel in the **Ribbon** to display work plane created.
- Draw desired shape of roof cross-section using sketching tools in the **Ribbon**; refer to Figure-11.

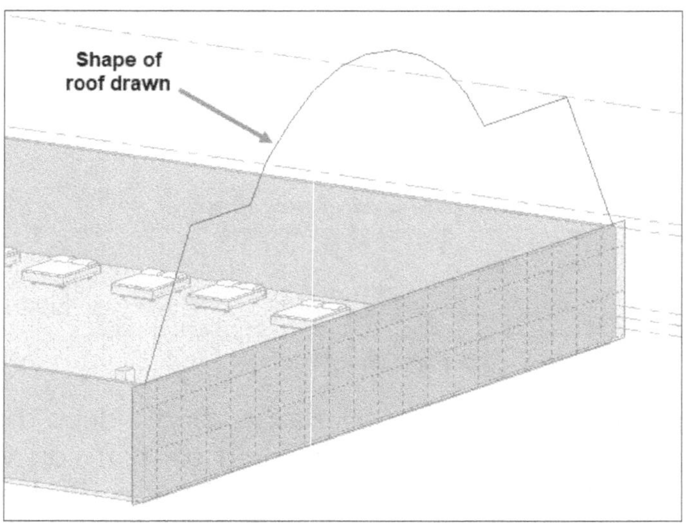

Figure-11. Drawing roof cross-section shape

- Click on the **OK** button from the **Mode** panel in the **Ribbon**. Preview of roof will be displayed; refer to Figure-12.

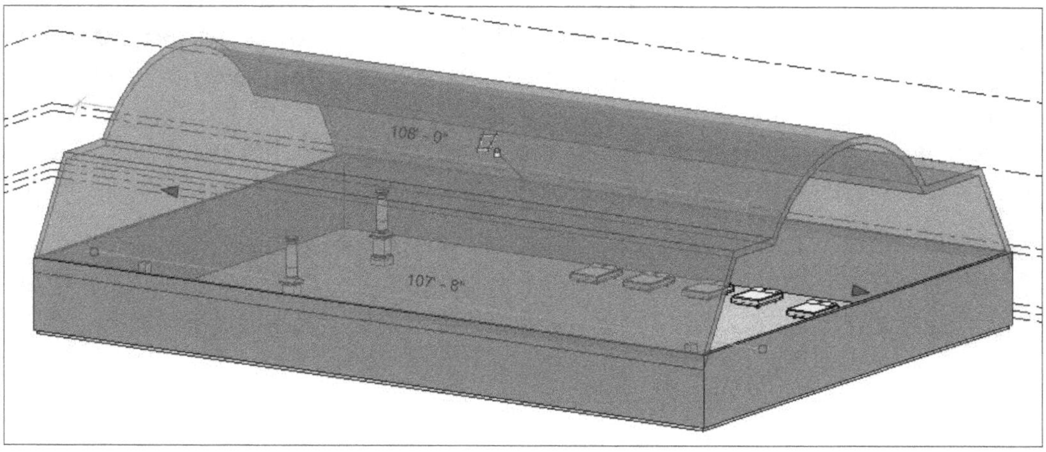

Figure-12. Preview of roof

- You can edit this roof in the same way as discussed earlier.
- Press **ESC** to exit the tool.

Creating Roof By Face

The **Roof By Face** tool is used to create a roof by using selected face as boundary reference. The procedure to use this tool is given next.

- Click on the **Roof By Face** tool from the **Roof** drop-down in the **Build** panel of **Architecture** tab in the **Ribbon**. You will be asked to select face for creating roof and options related to roof will be displayed in the **Properties Palette** & **Ribbon**.
- Select desired face to be used as boundary reference; refer to Figure-13.

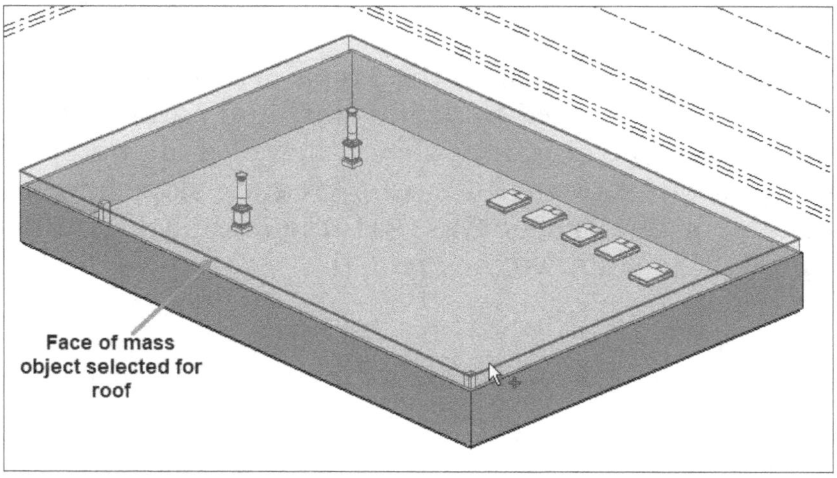

Figure-13. Selecting face for creating roof

- After selecting desired faces, click on the **Create Roof** tool from the **Multiple Selection** panel in the **Modify|Place Roof by Face** contextual tab of the **Ribbon**. The roof will be created. Press **ESC** to exit the tool.
- Select the newly created roof and modify it as required.

Creating Roof Soffit

The **Roof: Soffit** tool is used to create soffit under the roof to fill space between roof and wall. A soffit is used to decorate the roof architecturally as well as provide structural base for roof. The procedure to use this tool is given next.

- Click on the **Roof: Soffit** tool from the **Roof** drop-down in the **Build** panel of **Architecture** tab in the **Ribbon**. The **Modify|Create Roof Soffit Boundary** contextual tab will be displayed in the **Ribbon** and you will be asked to create boundary for roof soffit.
- Set desired work plane using the **Set** tool in the **Work Plane** panel of the **Ribbon** and create desired boundary; refer to Figure-14.

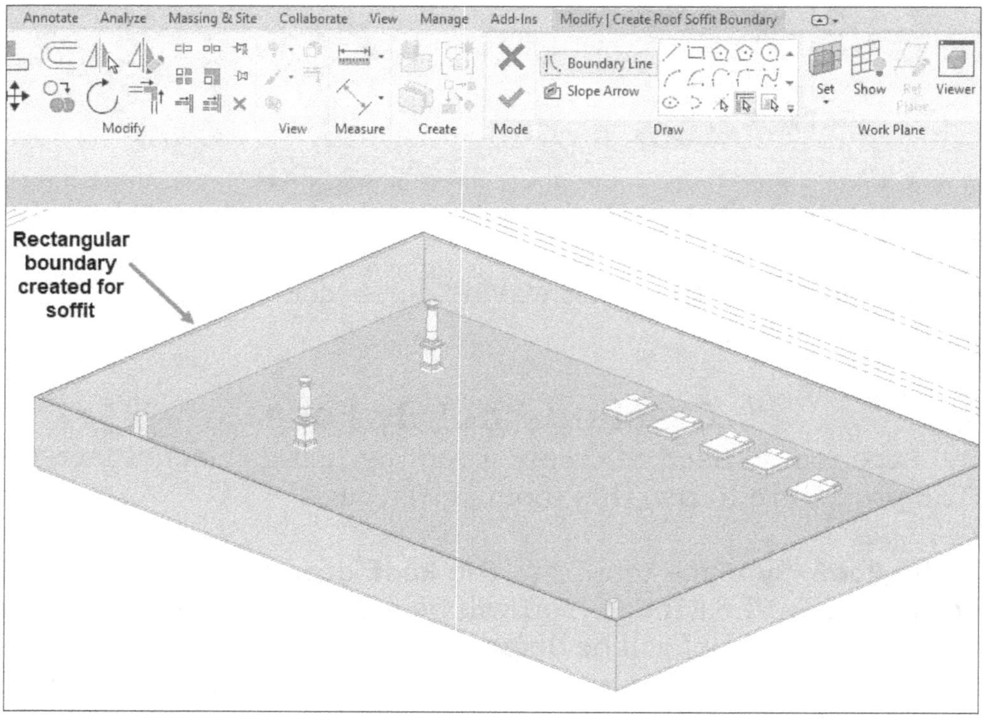

Figure-14. Creating boundary for soffit

- After creating the boundary, click on the **Slope Arrow** button if you want to apply slope to soffit. You will be asked to define start and end point for slope arrow.
- Specify the start point starting from sketch line of roof and specify at end point at desired location; refer to Figure-15. After creating slope line, specify the height offsets if applicable in the **Properties Palette** and click on the **OK** button from the contextual tab. The soffit will be created.

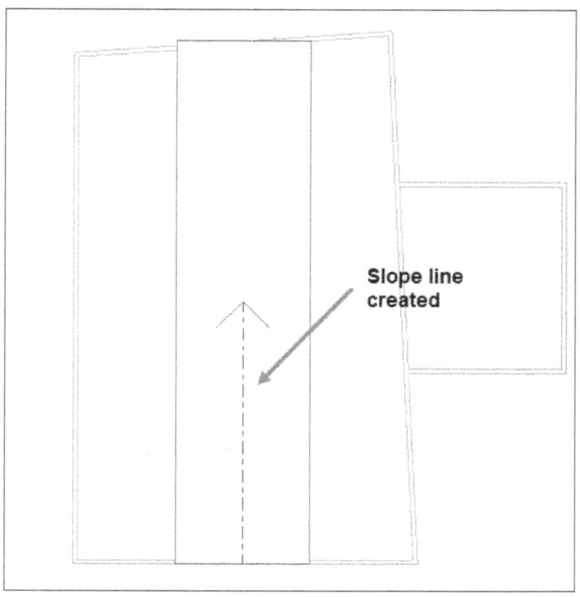

Figure-15. Slope line created

- Modify the soffit as required and press **ESC** to exit the tool.

Creating Roof Fascia

The **Roof: Fascia** tool is used to create fascia about the roof. The procedure to create fascia is given next.

- Click on the **Roof: Fascia** tool from the **Roof** drop-down in the **Build** panel of **Architecture** tab in the **Ribbon**. You will be asked to select the edges of roof, soffit, or another fascia.
- Click on desired geometry. The fascia will be created; refer to Figure-16.

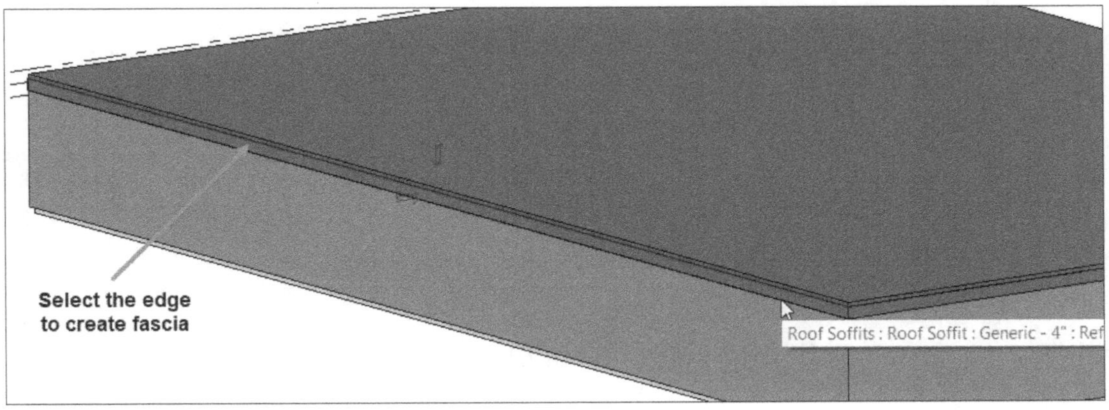

Figure-16. Selecting edge for fascia

Creating Roof Gutter

The **Roof: Gutter** tool is used to create gutter for roof so that rain water can be directed to drain pipes. The procedure to create gutter is given next.

- Click on the **Roof: Gutter** tool from the **Roof** drop-down in the **Build** panel of **Architecture** tab in the **Ribbon**. You will be asked to select the edge of roof, soffit, fascia or model line to create gutter.
- Select desired edge from model. The gutter will be created.
- Modify the gutter and press **ESC** to exit the tool.

Creating Ceiling

The **Ceiling** tool is used to create ceiling. The procedure to create ceiling is given next.

- Click on the **Ceiling** tool from the **Build** panel of **Architecture** tab in the **Ribbon**. The **Modify|Place Ceiling** contextual tab will be displayed in the **Ribbon** and you will be asked to select the area bounded by walls to create ceiling.

There are two ways to create ceiling using this tool, Automatic and sketch. Both the ways are discussed next.

Automatic Ceiling

- Make sure the **Automatic Ceiling** button is selected in the **Ceiling** panel of contextual tab. Select desired boundary; refer to Figure-17. The ceiling will be created. Note that a warning message may be displayed telling you to check the view parameters as created ceiling is not visible.

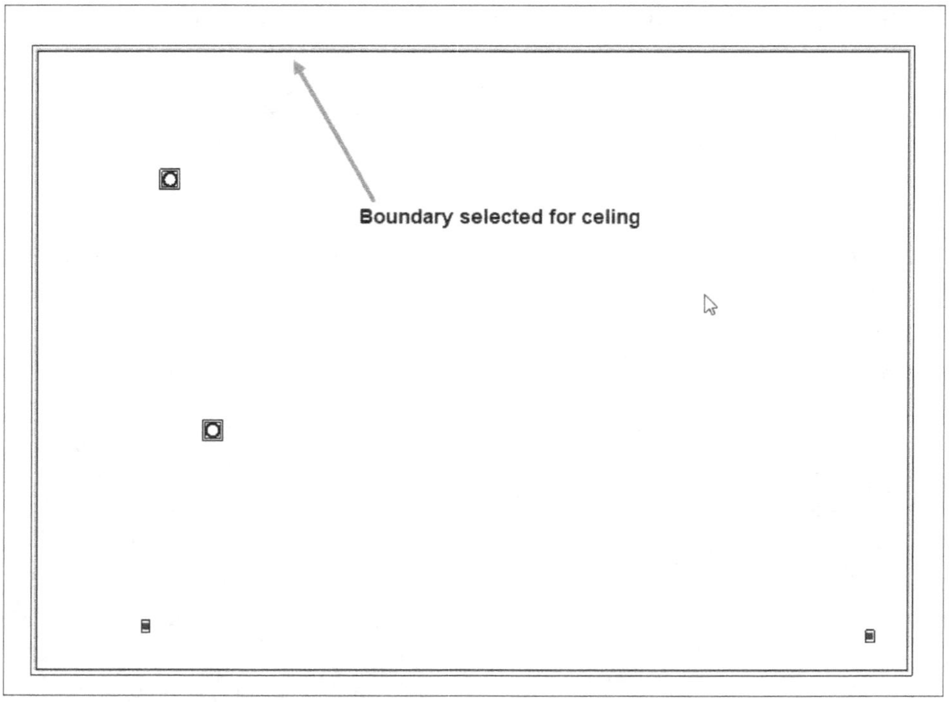

Figure-17. Selecting boundary for ceiling

You will learn about modifying visibility of objects later in this book.

Sketch Ceiling

The **Sketch Ceiling** option is used to create ceiling using sketched boundary.

- After activating the **Ceiling** tool, click on the **Sketch Ceiling** tool from the **Ceiling** panel in the **Modify|Place Ceiling** panel of the **Ribbon**. The **Modify|Create Ceiling Boundary** contextual tab will be displayed in the **Ribbon**.
- Create desired boundary and click on the **OK** button to create ceiling.
- Press **ESC** to exit the tool.

CREATING FLOOR

The tools to create different types of floors are available in the **Floor** drop-down of **Build** panel of **Ribbon**; refer to Figure-18. The procedures to use these tools are discussed next.

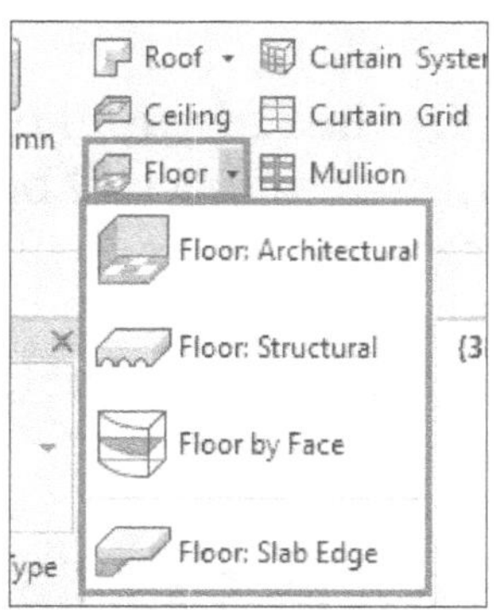

Figure-18. Floor drop-down

Creating Architectural Floor

The **Floor: Architectural** tool is used to create an architectural floor. The procedure to use this tool is given next.

- Click on the **Floor: Architectural** tool from the **Floor** drop-down in the **Build** panel of **Architecture** tab in the **Ribbon**. The **Modify|Create Floor Boundary** contextual tab will be displayed in the **Ribbon** and you will be asked to pick walls to create floor boundary.
- Select desired walls or create desired boundary by using the sketching tools in the **Draw** panel of **Ribbon**.
- Select desired floor type from the **Type** drop-down at the top in the **Properties Palette**; refer to Figure-19.

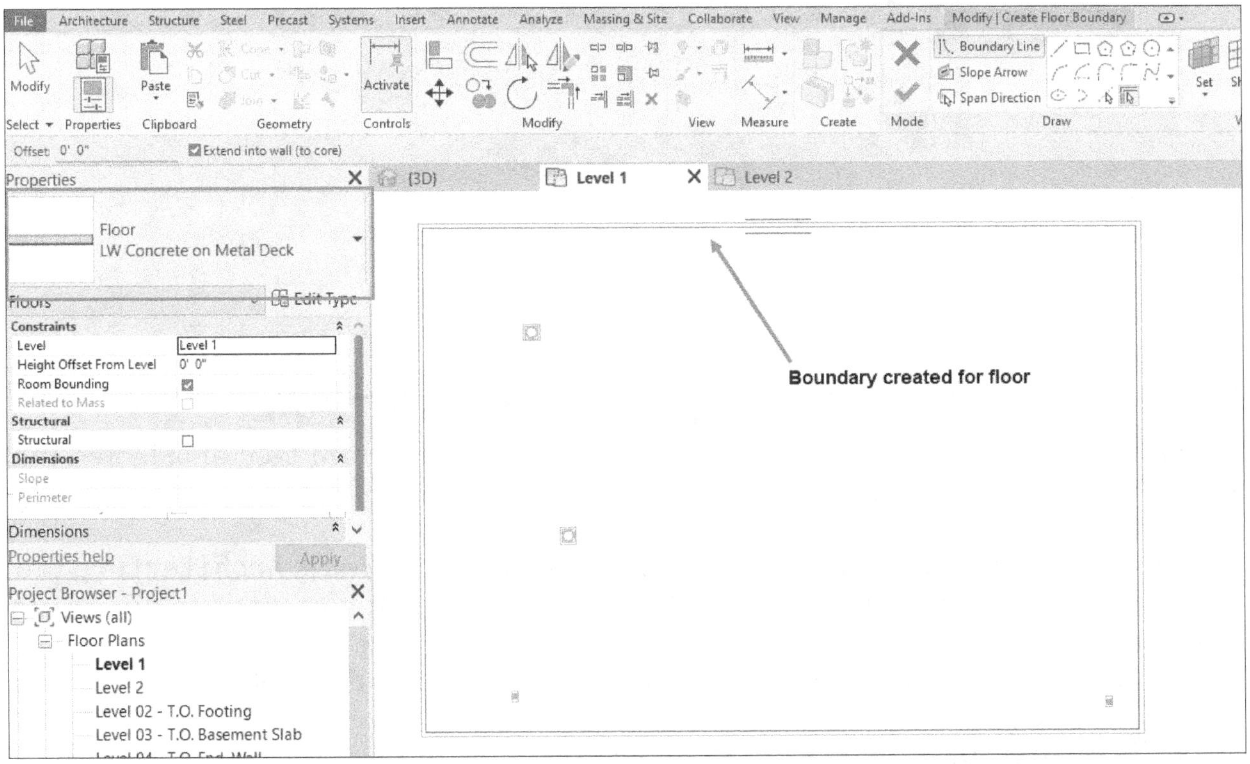

Figure-19. Creating boundary for floor

- Set the other parameters as required and click on the **OK** button from the **Mode** panel in the **Ribbon**. The floor will be created.

Creating Structural Floor

The **Floor: Structural** tool is used to create structural floor. The procedure to create structural floor is given next.

- Click on the **Floor: Structural** tool from the **Floor** drop-down in the **Build** panel of **Architecture** tab in the **Ribbon**. The **Modify|Create Floor Boundary** contextual tab will be displayed in the **Ribbon**.
- Create the boundary as discussed earlier and click on the **OK** button.

Creating Floor By Face

The **Floor by Face** tool is used to convert face of mass object into architectural floor. The procedure to use this tool is discussed in Chapter 11.

Creating Floor Slab

The **Floor: Slab Edge** tool is used to create floor slab along the selected edge. The procedure to use this tool is given next.

- Click on the **Floor: Slab Edge** tool from the **Floor** drop-down in the **Build** panel of **Ribbon**. You will be asked to select edge of floor, slab edge, or model line to create slab.
- Select desired edge. The slab will be created; refer to Figure-20.
- Modify the slab as discussed earlier and press **ESC** to exit.

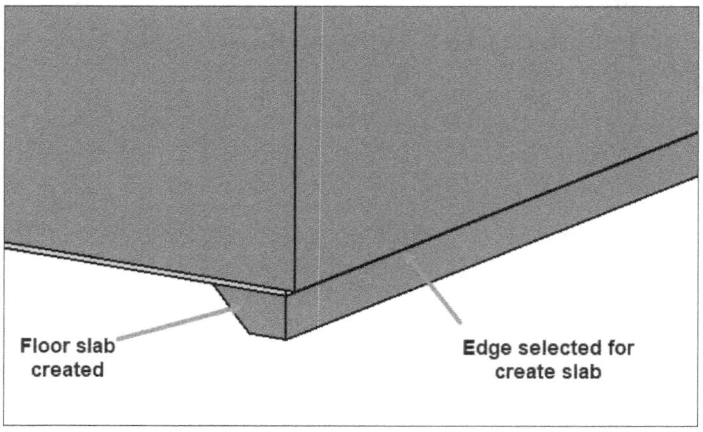

Figure-20. Creating floor slab

CREATING CURTAIN SYSTEM

The **Curtain System** tool is used to create curtain system from face of selected mass object. The procedure to use this tool is given next.

- Click on the **Curtain System** tool from the **Build** panel in the **Architecture** tab of the **Ribbon**. You will be asked to select a face on which you want to add curtain system.
- Select desired faces of a mass object. (Procedure to place mass objects is discussed in next topic.)
- Specify desired parameters in the **Properties Palette**.
- Click on the **Create System** tool from the **Multiple Selection** panel of the **Modify|Place Curtain System by Face** contextual tab of the **Ribbon**. The curtain will be created; refer to Figure-21. Press **ESC** to exit the tool.

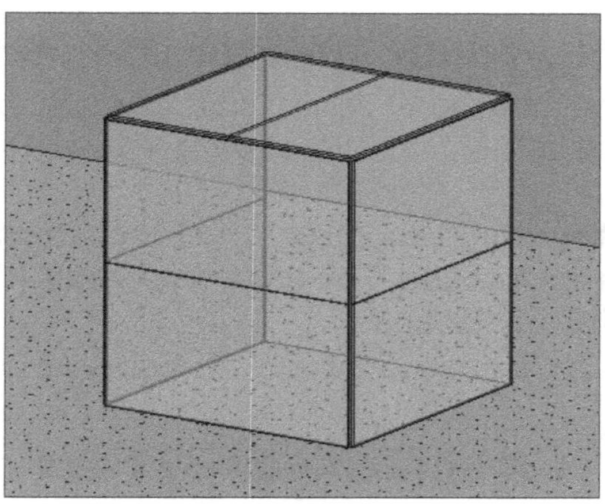

Figure-21. Curtain system created on mass object

Placing Mass Objects and Setting Visibility in Architectural Drawing

You can place the mass objects by using the **Place a Component** tool discussed in previous chapter. The procedure to place and set visibility of mass objects is given next.

- Click on the **Place a Component** tool from the **Component** drop-down in the **Build** panel of **Architecture** tab in the **Ribbon**. The **Modify|Place Component** contextual tab will be displayed in the **Ribbon**.
- Click on the **Load Family** button in the contextual tab and open the **Mass** folder; refer to Figure-22.

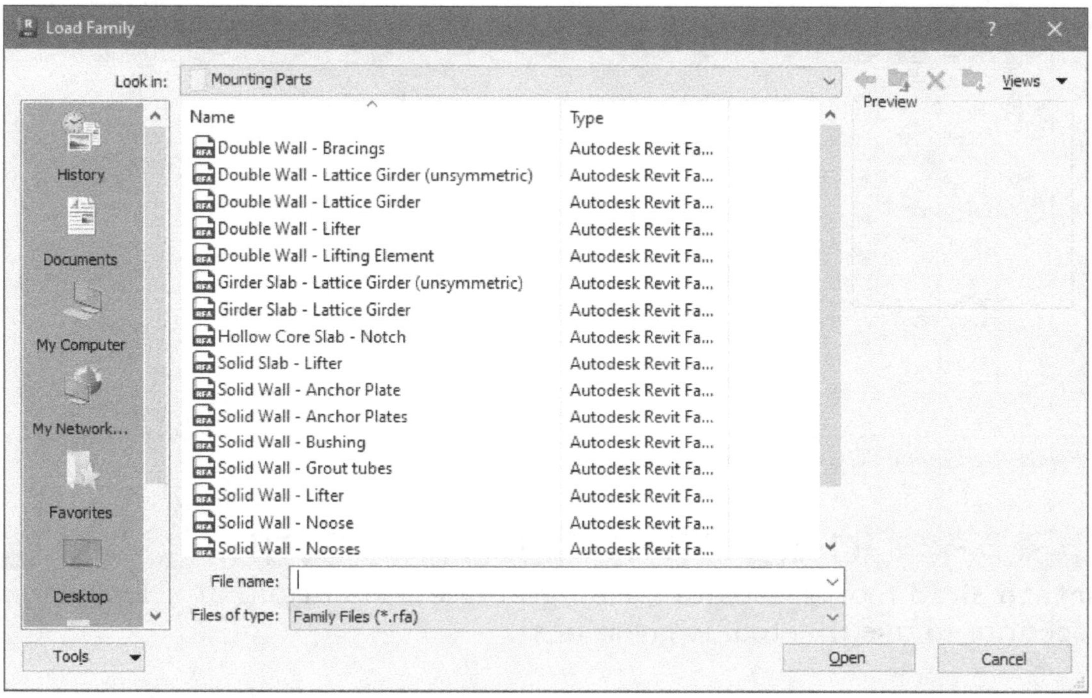

Figure-22. Mass components available by default

- Open desired mass and place it at desired location in the model. Press **ESC** twice to exit the tool. Note that the mass objects will not be displayed by default in Architectural projects.
- Type **VV** from keyboard. The **Visibility/Graphics Overrides** dialog box will be displayed; refer to Figure-23. Scroll down in the dialog box and select check box for **Mass** under **Visibility** column.
- Click on the **OK** button, the mass objects will be displayed.

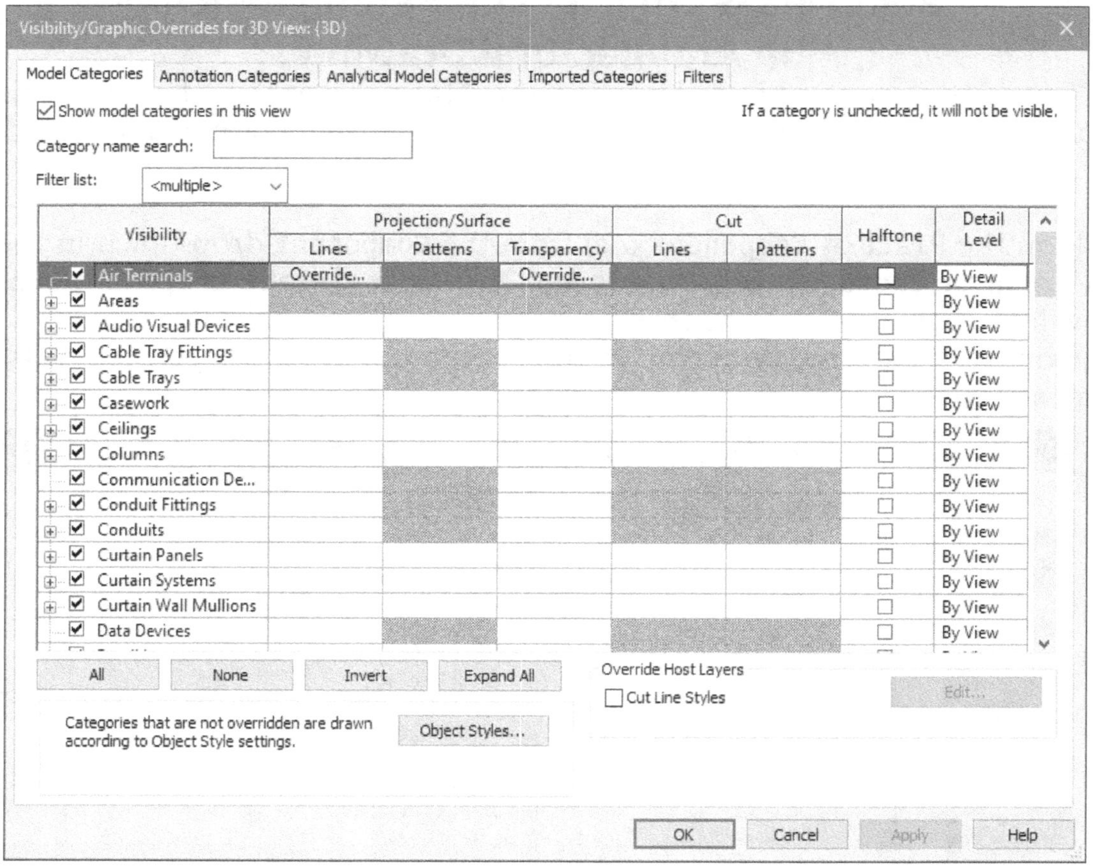

Figure-23. Visibility Graphics Overrides dialog box

CREATING CURTAIN GRID

The **Curtain Grid** tool is used to create grid lines on curtain at selected locations. The procedure to use this tool is given next.

- Click on the **Curtain Grid** tool from the **Build** panel in the **Architecture** tab of the **Ribbon**. You will be asked to specify the location of grid line.
- Click at desired locations on the curtain or curtain system to create grid lines; refer to Figure-24.

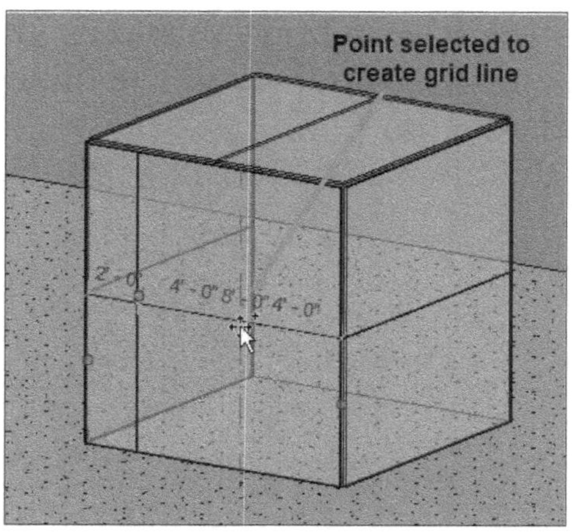

Figure-24. Creating curtain grid lines

- Press **ESC** twice to exit the tool.

CREATING CURTAIN WALL MULLION

The **Mullion** tool is used to create mullions on curtain grids. The procedure to use this tool is given next.

- Click on the **Mullion** tool from the **Build** panel of **Architecture** tab in the **Ribbon**. The **Modify|Place Mullion** contextual tab will be displayed and you will be asked to select curtain grids for creating mullions.
- Select desired type of mullion from the **Type** drop-down at the top in the **Properties Palette**.
- Click on the grid lines to create mullions; refer to Figure-25.

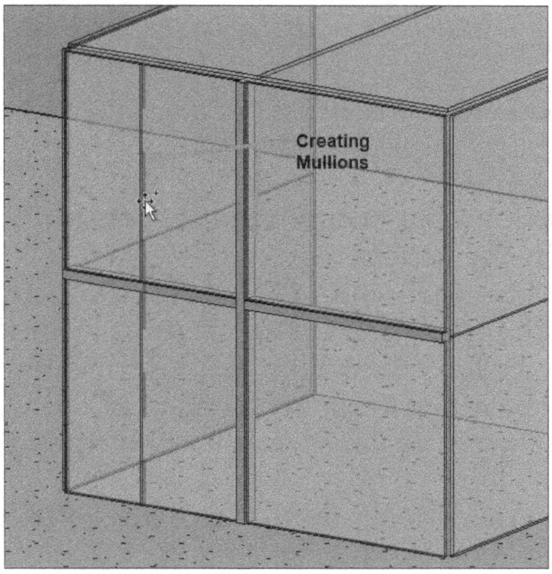

Figure-25. Creating Mullions

- Press **ESC** to exit the tool.

ADDING RAMP

The **Ramp** tool is used to create ramp between two levels in the building. The procedure to use this tool is given next.

- Click on the **Ramp** tool from the **Circulation** panel of **Architecture** tab in the **Ribbon**. You will be asked to specify the starting point of ramp.
- Click at desired location to specify starting point of ramp. You will be asked to specify end point of the ramp.
- Click at desired location to specify the length of ramp; refer to Figure-26. You can specify the ramp's run length in parts and the intermediate portion is automatically created as landing; refer to Figure-27.

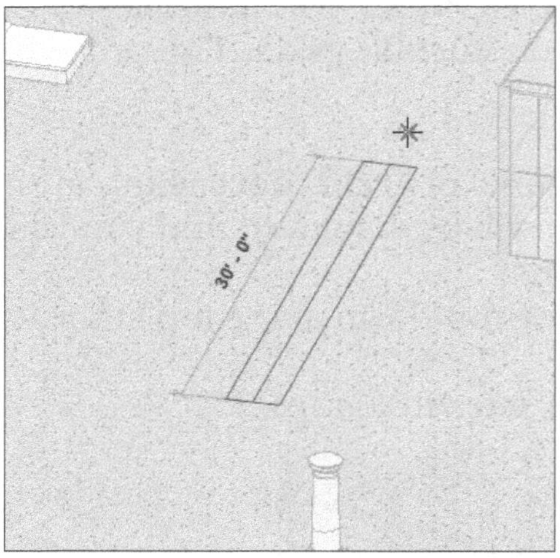

Figure-26. Specifying start point and end point of ramp

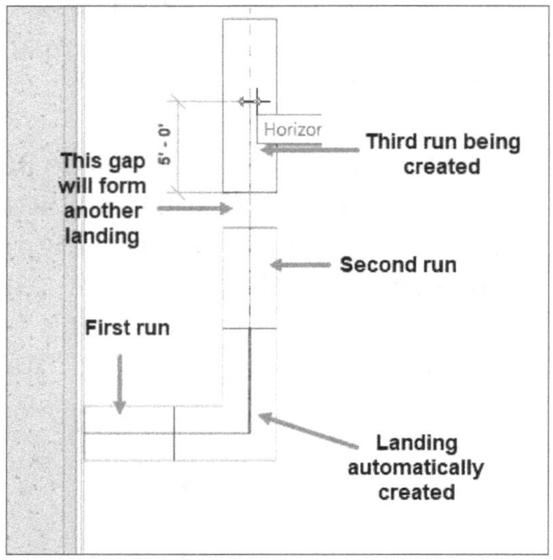

Figure-27. Creating ramp in parts

- Set desired parameters in the **Properties Palette** and click on the **OK** button from the **Mode** panel in the **Ribbon**.
- By default, the slope of ramp is set to **12:1** if you want to change the slope of ramp then select it and click on the **Edit Type** button from the **Properties Palette**. The **Type Properties** dialog box will be displayed; refer to Figure-28.
- Set desired value of slope in the **Ramp Max Slope(1/x)** edit box under the **Dimensions** rollout. Note that the lower the value specified in this edit box, the higher will be the slope.
- Set the other parameters as desired and click on the **OK** button. The ramp will be modified accordingly.

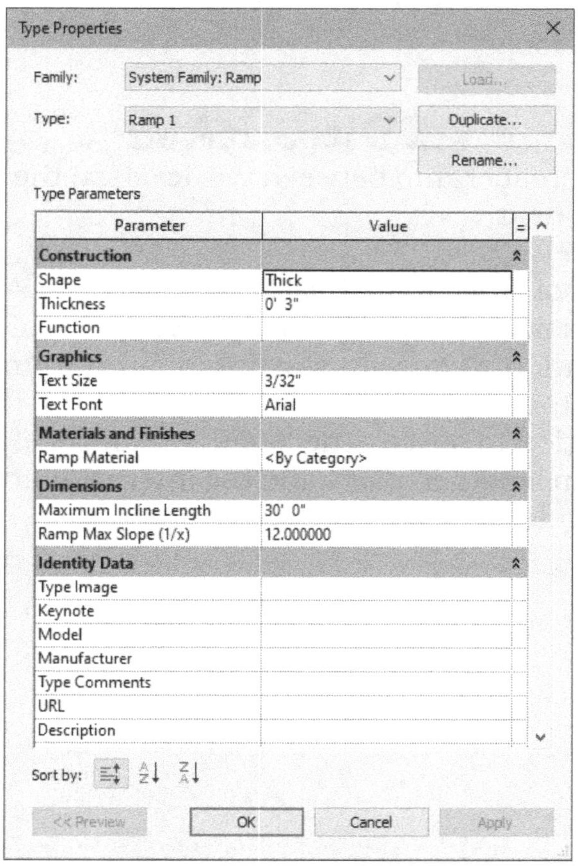

Figure-28. Type Properties dialog box

If a warning message is displayed while creating the ramp telling you to increase the slope then you need to increase it from this dialog box.

ADDING STAIR

The **Stair** tool is used to create stairs in the building. The procedure to create stair is given next.

- Click on the **Stair** tool from the **Circulation** panel of **Architecture** tab in the **Ribbon**. The **Modify|Create Stair** contextual tab will be displayed along with options in **Properties Palette**. Also, you will be asked to specify the starting point of stair.
- Select desired type of stair from the **Components** panel of the **Modify|Create Stair** contextual tab.
- Click to specify the start point of stair. You will be asked to specify the end point of stair.
- Click in between the length of stairs if you want to create stairs in parts and generate landing between two parts of stairs. Click at the end of stair length to complete stair.
- If you want to connect another run of stairs then click on desired stair type from the **Components** panel again and draw the stairs in conjunction; refer to Figure-29.

Figure-29. Stair created

CREATING RAILING

The tools in the **Railing** drop-down are used to create railings using sketch lines or stairs as reference; refer to Figure-30. The procedures to use these tools are discussed next.

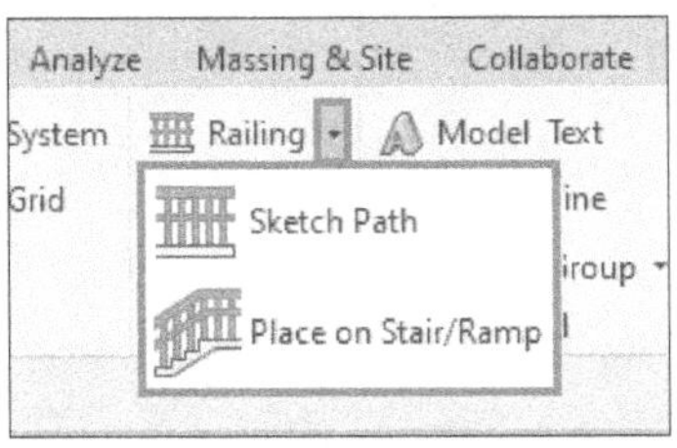

Figure-30. Railing drop-down

Sketching Railing Path

The **Sketch Path** tool is used to create railing by creating sketch lines. The procedure to create railing is given next.

- Click on the **Sketch Path** tool from the **Railing** drop-down in the **Circulation** panel of **Architecture** tab in the **Ribbon**. The **Modify|Create Railing Path** contextual tab will be displayed in the **Ribbon** and you will be asked to draw line sketch for railing.
- Draw the sketch of railing; refer to Figure-31.
- Click on the **OK** button from the **Mode** panel to create railing; refer to Figure-32.

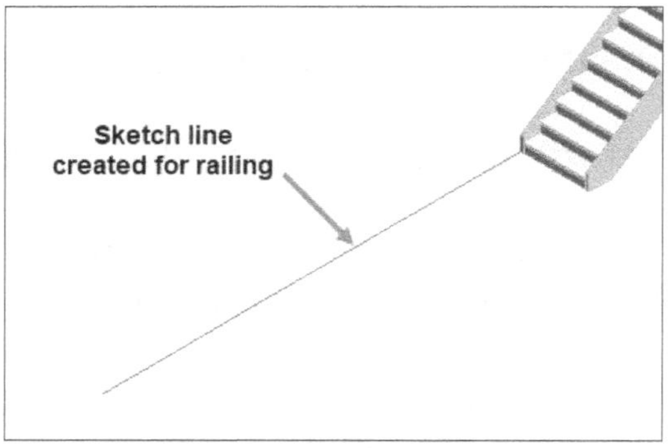

Figure-31. Sketch created for railing

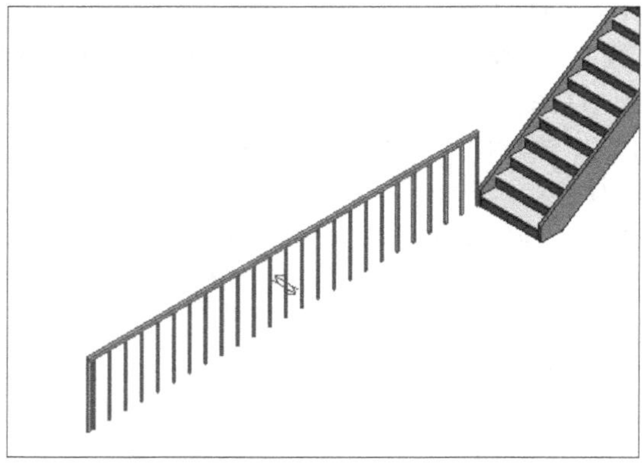

Figure-32. Railing created

Placing Railing on Stairs/Ramps

The **Place on Stair/Ramp** tool is used to create railing on stairs or ramps. The procedure to create railing on stairs or ramps is given next.

- Click on the **Place on Stair/Ramp** tool from the **Railing** drop-down in the **Circulation** panel of **Ribbon**. The options to place railing will be displayed.
- Select desired option from the **Position** panel to define the location where railings will be placed on stairs or ramps.
- Click on the stairs or ramps on which you want to create railing.
- Press **ESC** to exit the tool.

CREATING MODEL TEXT

The **Model Text** tool is used to create desired text to annotate specified areas of building. The procedure to use this tool is given next.

- Click on the **Model Text** tool from the **Model** panel in the **Architecture** tab of the **Ribbon**. The **Edit Text** dialog box will be displayed; refer to Figure-33.

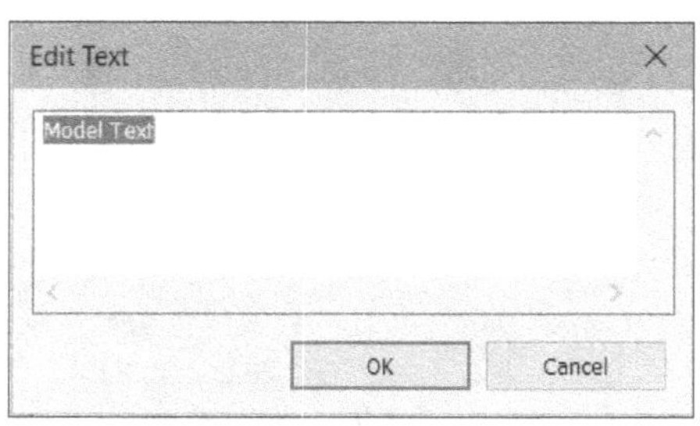

Figure-33. Edit Text dialog box

- Specify desired text in the editing space of this dialog box. Note that you can specify multiline text in this dialog box.
- After specifying the text, click on the **OK** button from the dialog box. The text will get attached to cursor.
- Click at desired location place the text; refer to Figure-34. Note that if you place text on face of a mass object then it will be automatically embossed.

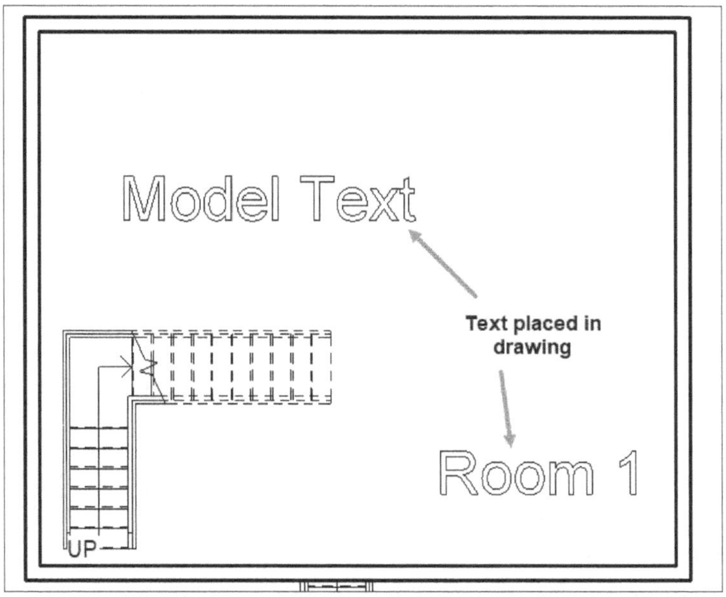

Figure-34. Placing text in drawing

- Select the text and modify the parameters in **Properties Palette** to modify text properties.

CREATING MODEL LINE

The **Model Line** tool is used to create line sketch in the drawing that can be used as reference for other features. The procedure to use this tool is given next.

- Click on the **Model Line** tool from the **Model** panel in the **Architecture** tab of **Ribbon**. You will be asked to specify start point of model line.
- Create desired sketch using tools in the **Draw** panel of **Modify|Place Lines** contextual tab of **Ribbon**.

PLACING MODEL GROUP

The **Place Model Group** tool is used to place model groups, detail groups, and associated detail groups in the drawing area like a group named kitchen will have all the kitchen elements. The procedure to use this tool is discussed next.

- Select desired model group earlier created from the **Groups** category in the **Project Browser**; refer to Figure-35 and click on the **Place Model Group** tool from the **Model Group** drop-down in the **Model** panel of **Architecture** tab in the **Ribbon**. The **Modify|Place Group** contextual tab will be displayed; refer to Figure-36. You will be asked to place the group.

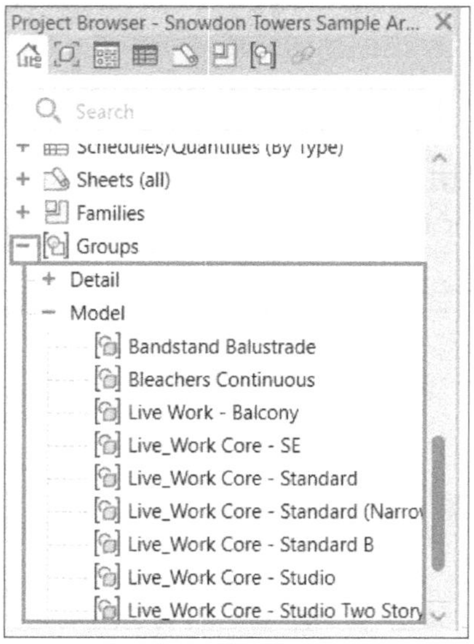

Figure-35. Groups in Project Browser

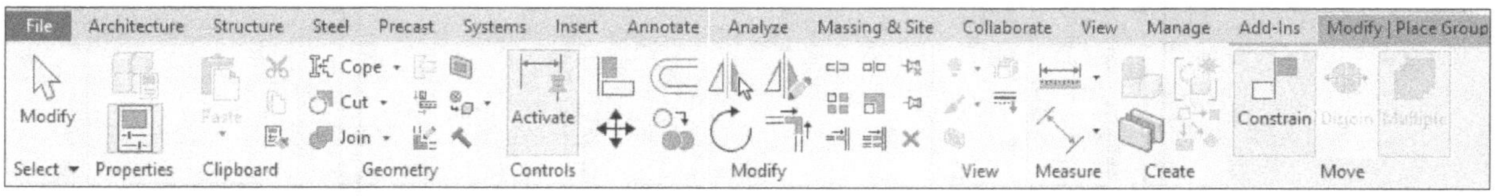

Figure-36. Options to modify model group

- Click in the drawing area at desired location(s) to place the group(s). The group(s) will be placed; refer to Figure-37.

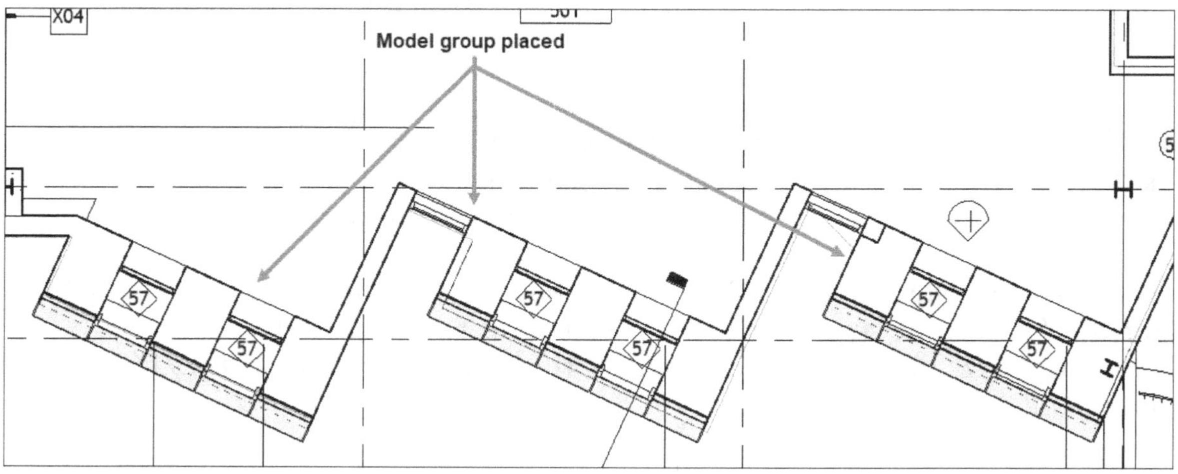

Figure-37. Model groups placed

- After placing desired number of groups, press **Enter** to exit the tool.

Create Group

Groups are used to collectively use objects. Using groups, you can copy multiple objects and reuse them in drawing. The procedure to use this tool is discussed in Chapter 2.

Load as Group into Open Projects

The **Load as Group into Open Projects** tool allows you to load the current project as a group into another open project or family. The procedure to use this tool is discussed next.

- Click on the **Load as Group into Open Projects** tool from the **Model Group** drop-down in the **Model** panel of **Architecture** tab in the **Ribbon**. The **Load into Projects** dialog box will be displayed; refer to Figure-38.

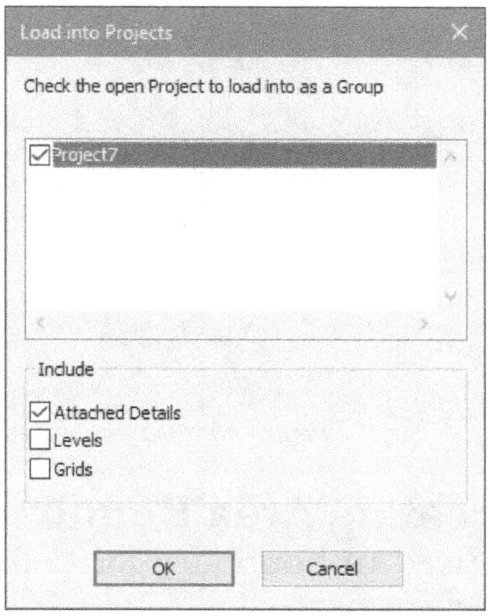

Figure-38. Load into Projects dialog box

- Select desired open project(s) from the list to be loaded in the drawing area as a group and click on the **OK** button. The project will be loaded as a group.

ROOM MARKINGS AND CALCULATIONS

The tools in the **Room & Area** panel are used to mark different sections of building for basic calculations. Before marking room in specified area of drawing, you need to create area bound by selected boundaries of the drawing. The procedure to create area is given next.

- Click on the **Area Plan** tool from the **Area** drop-down in the **Room & Area** panel of **Architecture** tab in **Ribbon**. The **New Area Plan** dialog box will be displayed; refer to Figure-39.
- Select desired option from the **Type** drop-down to define a type for area marking. For example, you can mark area as rentable, vacant, safety zone etc.
- Select desired option from the level list to define on which level the area will be created.
- After setting desired parameters, click on the **OK** button from the dialog box. A message box will be displayed telling you that Revit will automatically area boundary lines as per the external walls drawn earlier. Click on the **Yes** button to create the area feature; refer to Figure-40. Click on the **No** button if you want to manually define the boundary for area plan. If you have selected **No** button then you need to use **Area Boundary** tool to define the boundary.

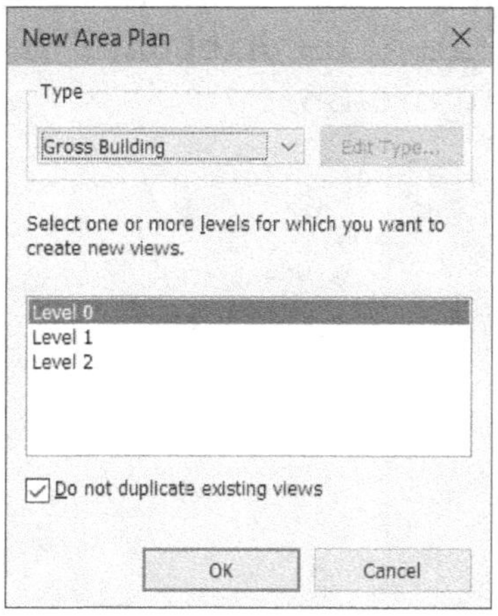

Figure-39. New Area Plan dialog box

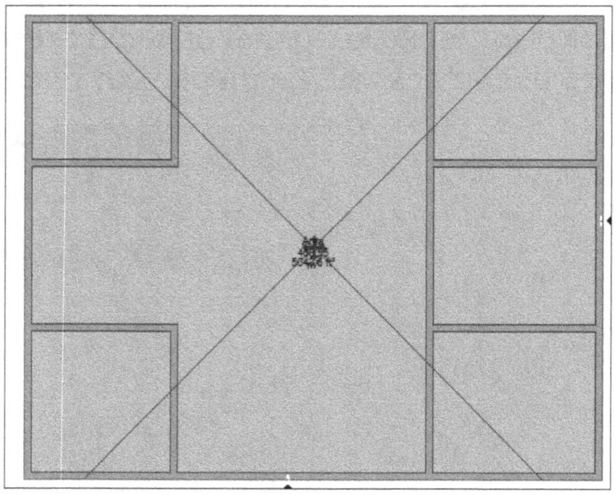
Figure-40. Area feature created

Creating Area Boundary

The **Area Boundary** tool is used to boundary for defining area in plan view. The procedure to use this tool is given next.

- Click on the **Area Boundary** tool from the **Room & Area** panel in the **Architecture** tab of the **Ribbon**. The **Modify|Place Area Boundary** contextual tab will be displayed in the **Ribbon**; refer to Figure-41.

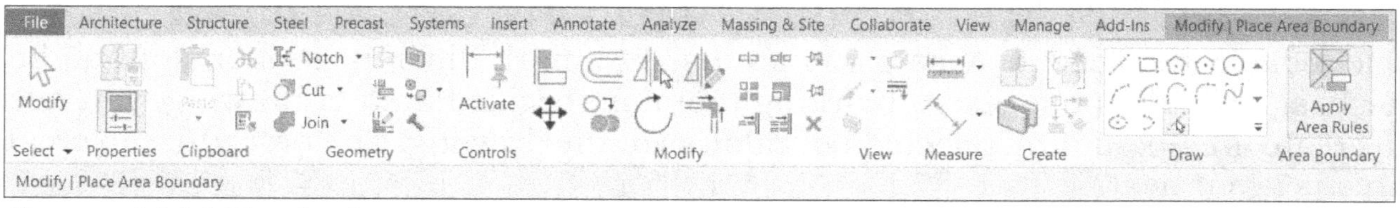

Figure-41. Modify Place Area Boundary contextual tab

- Use the tools in **Draw** panel to create the boundary as discussed earlier; refer to Figure-42.

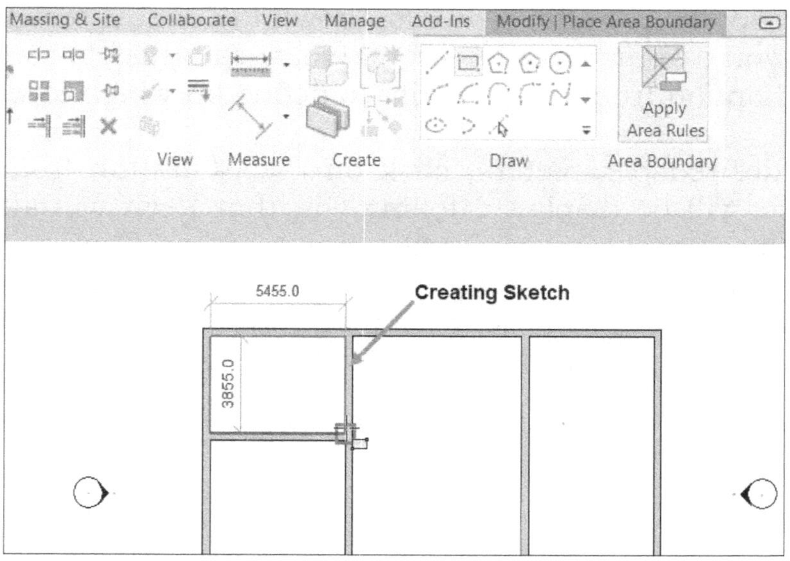

Figure-42. Creating area boundary

Area

The **Area** tool is used to create an area earlier defined by walls and boundary lines. The procedure to use this tool is discussed next.

- Click on the **Area** tool from **Room & Area** panel in the **Architecture** tab of the **Ribbon**. The area marking will get attached to cursor and you will be asked to specify the inserting point.
- Click in the drawing area at desired location bound by area boundary created using **Area Boundary** tool to define an area. The area will be created; refer to Figure-43.

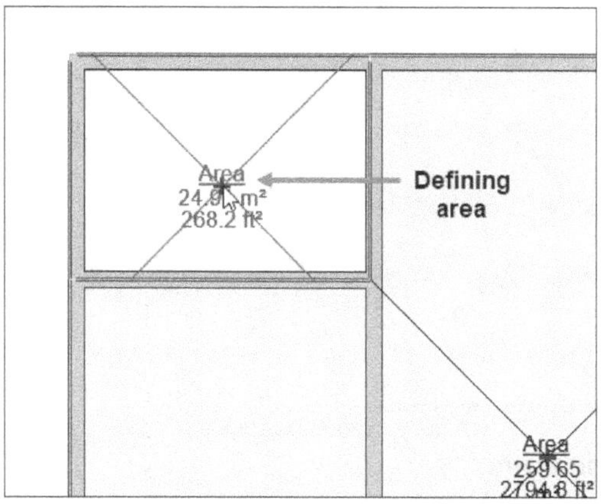

Figure-43. Creating area

- Press **ESC** to exit the tool.

Creating Room Markings

The **Room** tool is used to define a closed region bound by walls or boundary lines as room. The procedure to create room marking is given next.

- Click on the **Room** tool from the **Room & Area** panel in the **Architecture** tab of **Ribbon**. The room marking will get attached to cursor and you will be asked to specify the insertion point.
- Click in the areas bounded by walls to mark them as rooms; refer to Figure-44.

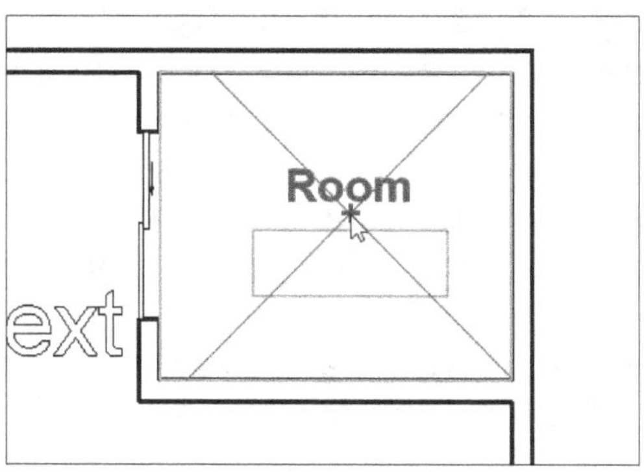

Figure-44. Creating room

- Press **ESC** to exit the tool.

Re-center Reference

The **Re-center Reference** tool is used to reposition the reference lines of all the rooms in the view back to the center of rooms. The procedure to use this tool is discussed next.

- Click on the **Re-center Reference** tool from **Room** drop-down in the **Room & Area** panel of **Architecture** tab in the **Ribbon**. You will be asked to specify the location.
- Click in the 3D view area at desired location to re-center the room. The room will be re-centered; refer to Figure-45.
- Press **ESC** to exit the tool.

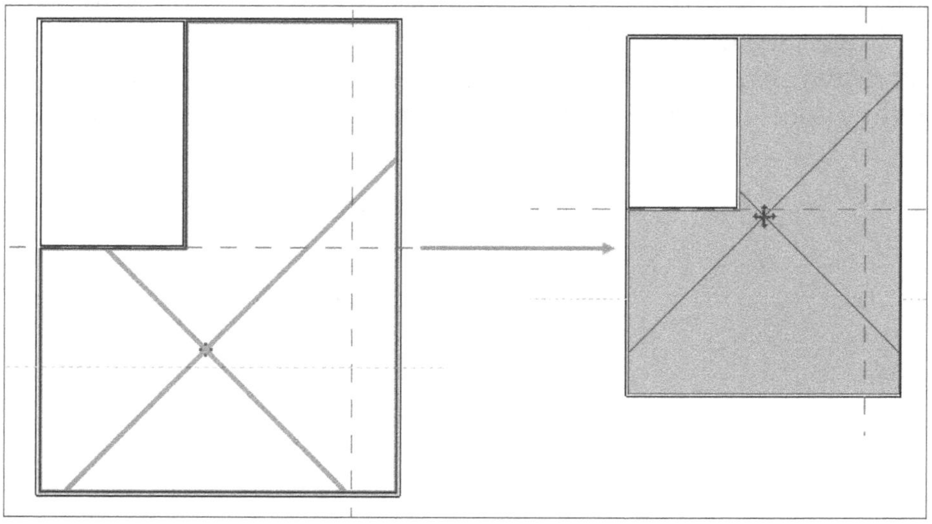

Figure-45. Performing recenter

Creating Room Separator

The **Room Separator** tool is used to create a separation line where you do not want to create walls for separation but want to make separation mark. The procedure to use this tool is given next.

- Click on the **Room Separator** tool from the **Room & Area** panel of **Architecture** tab of the **Ribbon**. You will be asked to specify the location of separator.
- Click at desired location on the wall to create separator line and click desired location to specify end point of the line.
- Press **ESC** to exit the tool.

Creating Tags for Rooms and Objects

The tools in **Tag Room** drop-down are used to apply tags to rooms and other objects like door, stairs, and so on. These tools are discussed next.

- Click on the **Tag Room** tool from the **Tag Room** drop-down in the **Room & Area** panel of **Ribbon**. You will be asked to click in the location where you have placed room mark.
- Click at desired location where you want to place the tag.
- To edit the tag of room, double-click on the tag number to modify tag.

Tagging All Not Tagged objects

- Click on the **Tag All Not Tagged** button from the **Tag Room** drop-down in the **Room & Area** panel of **Ribbon**. The **Tag All Not Tagged** dialog box will be displayed; refer to Figure-46.

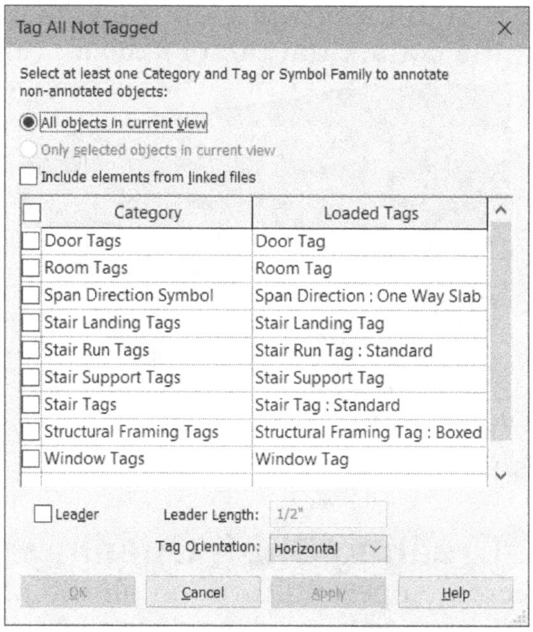

Figure-46. Tag All Not Tagged dialog box

- Select the check boxes from the dialog box and click on the **OK** button.

You can use the other tagging tools of **Room & Area** panel in the same ways.

CREATING OPENINGS

The tools in the **Opening** panel are used to create different types of openings in the model. Various tools of this panel are discussed next.

Opening By Face

- Click on the **By Face** tool from the **Opening** panel in the **Architecture** tab of the **Ribbon**. You will be asked to select a planar face on which you want to create the opening.
- Click on desired face of roof or floor. The **Modify|Create Opening Boundary** contextual tab will be displayed in the **Ribbon**; refer to Figure-47.

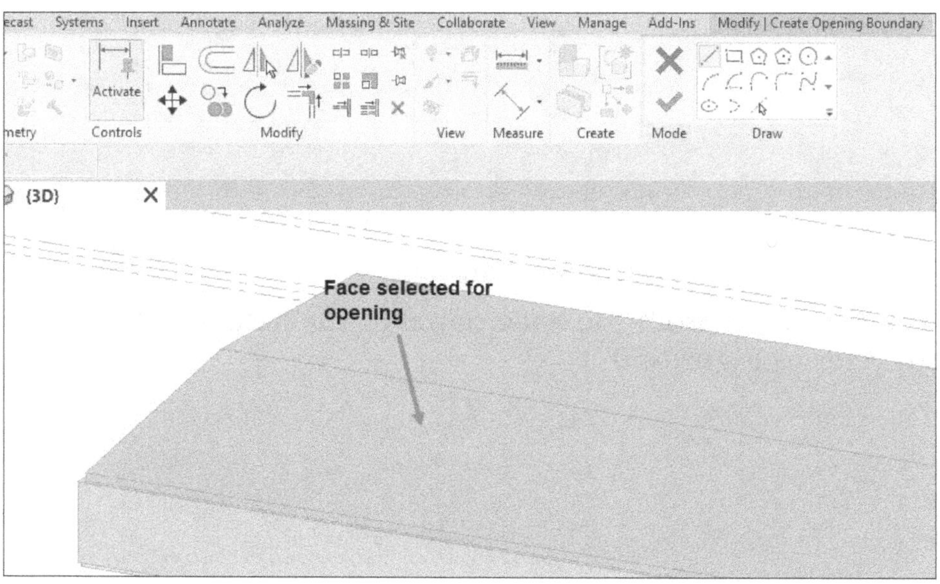

Figure-47. Face selected for opening

- Create the closed loop sketch for opening on the face and click on the **OK** button from the **Mode** panel in the contextual tab of **Ribbon**; refer to Figure-48.

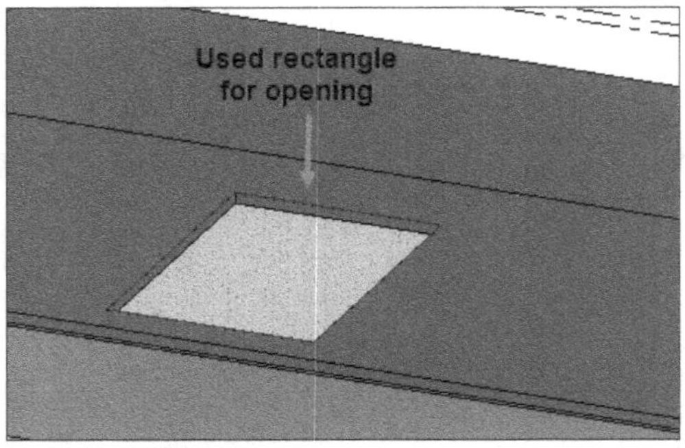

Figure-48. Opening created

- Press **ESC** to exit the tool.

Creating Shaft Opening

The **Shaft** tool is used to create opening through all the objects that are above and below the sketch drawn. The procedure to use this tool is given next.

- Click on the **Shaft** tool from the **Opening** panel in the **Architecture** tab of the **Ribbon**. The **Modify|Create Shaft Opening Sketch** contextual tab will be displayed in the **Ribbon** and related options will be displayed in the **Properties Palette**.
- Set desired base constraint and top constraint in the **Properties Palette** and draw the sketch of shaft opening; refer to Figure-49.

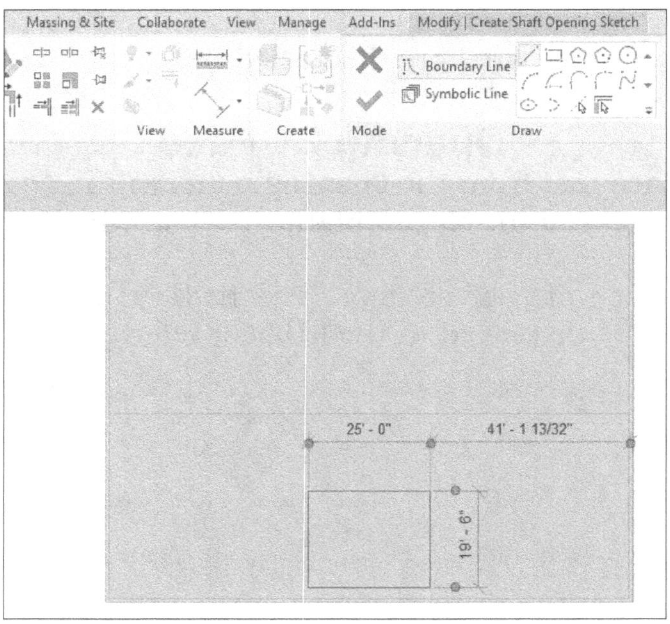

Figure-49. Creating sketch for shaft opening

- Click on the **OK** button from the **Mode** panel in the **Ribbon**. The shaft opening will be created; refer to Figure-50.

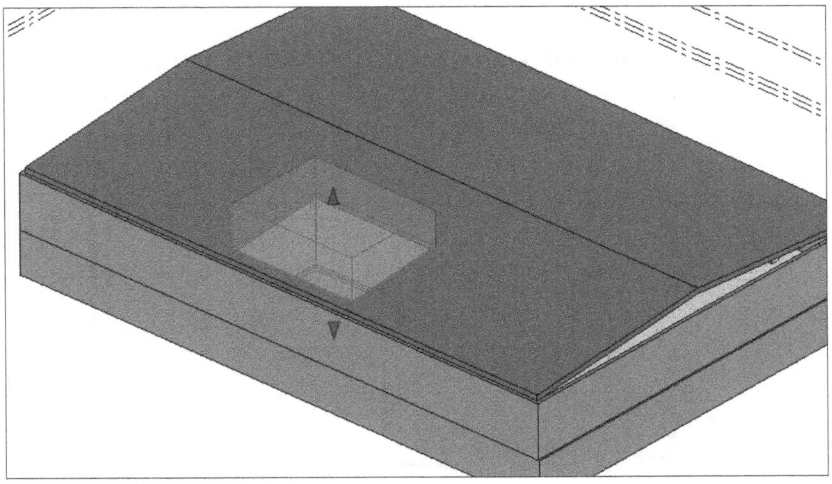

Figure-50. Shaft opening created

Creating Wall Opening

The **Wall** tool in **Opening** panel is used to create opening in the selected wall. The procedure to create wall opening is given next.

- Click on the **Wall** tool from the **Opening** panel in the **Architecture** tab of **Ribbon**. You will be asked to select the wall on which opening is to be created.
- Click on desired wall. You will be asked to specify start point of rectangle.
- Draw a rectangle of desired parameters on the wall; refer to Figure-51. Note that you can modify the parameters of wall opening by clicking on the dimensions displayed.

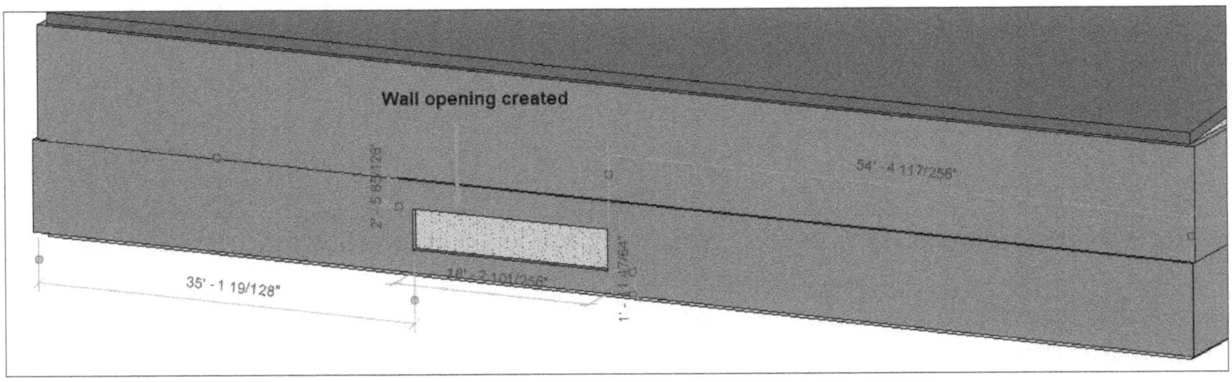

Figure-51. Wall Opening

- Press **ESC** to exit the tool.

Creating Vertical Opening

The **Vertical** tool in **Opening** panel is used to create vertical opening in floor, roof, and ceiling. This tool works in the same way as **By Face** tool in **Opening** panel. Note that **By Face** tool creates opening perpendicular to selected face while **Vertical** tool creates a vertical opening.

Creating Dormer Opening

The **Dormer** tool is used to dormer opening in the roof. First create the dormer on the roof and then select the boundaries to create dormer opening.

Practical 1

Create an architectural model for the drawing shown in Figure-52.

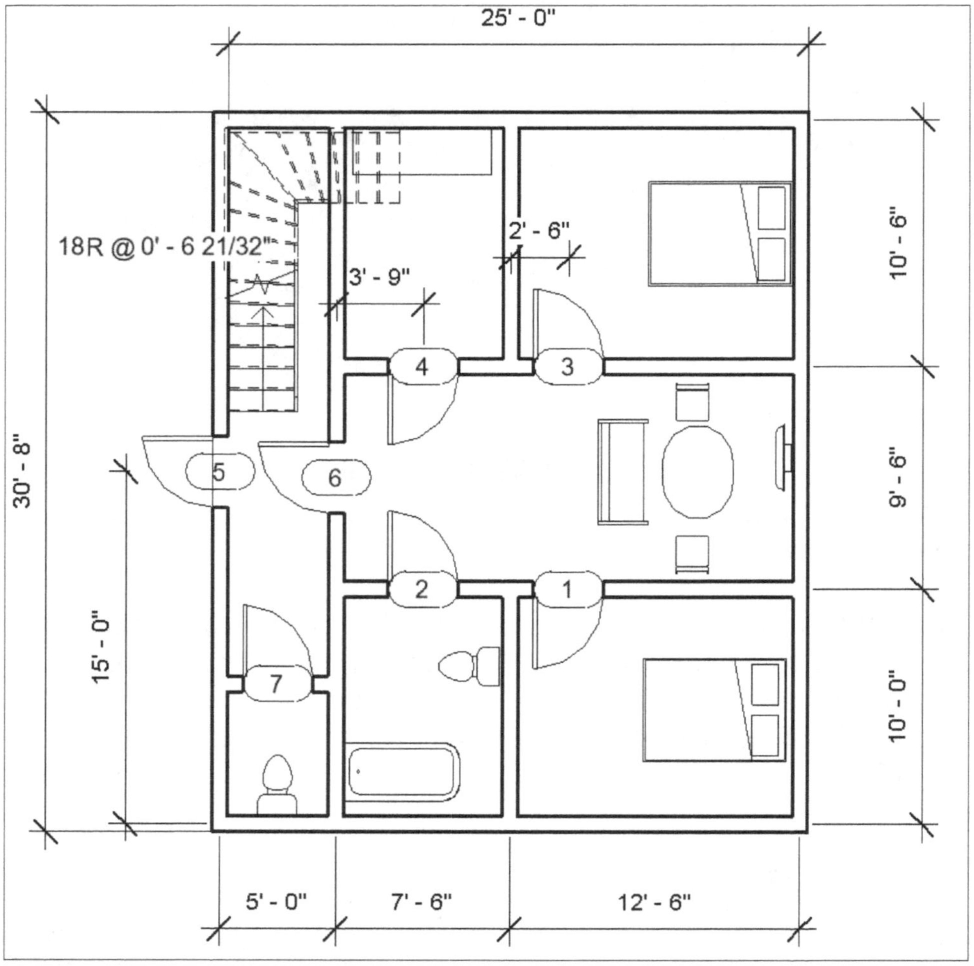

Figure-52. Drawing for practical 1

Steps

To create this architectural model, we need to perform following operations:

- Create the walls as per the plan given in Figure-52.
- Place the doors and furniture.
- Create stairs.
- Create floor and ceiling.
- Create opening for stairs on ceiling.

We will now perform each of the operations one by one.

Starting a new Project

- Start Autodesk Revit if not started yet.
- Click on the **Project** tool from the **New** cascading menu of the **File** menu. The **New Project** dialog box will be displayed.
- Select the **Construction Template** option from the drop-down in dialog box and click on the **OK** button. If the default set unit is not feet and inches then set it by using the **Project Units** tool from the **Settings** panel in the **Manage** tab of **Ribbon**.

Creating Walls

- Click on the **Wall: Architectural** tool from the **Build** panel in the **Architecture** tab of **Ribbon**. The **Modify|Place Wall** contextual tab will be displayed in **Ribbon** along with related parameters in **Properties Palette**.
- Set the **Base Constraint** as **Level 1** and **Top Constraint** as **Up to level: Level 2** in the **Properties Palette**.
- Select the **Generic - 6" Masonry** option from the **Type** drop-down at the top in the **Properties Palette**.
- Draw the line sketch for walls as shown in Figure-53.

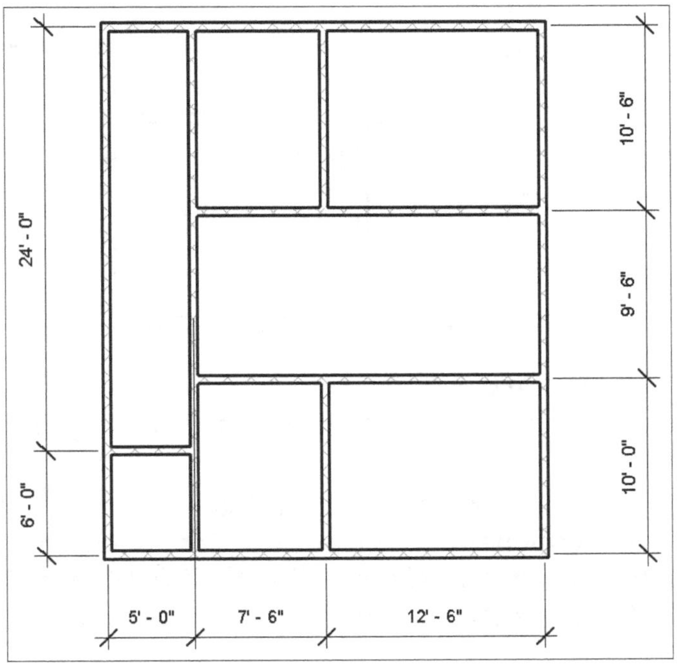

Figure-53. Walls drawn for practical 1

Creating Doors

- Click on the **Door** tool from the **Build** panel of **Architecture** tab of **Ribbon**. You will be asked to specify the location of door.
- Select the **Single-Flush 36" x 80"** option from **Type** drop-down in **Properties Palette**.
- Place the doors on the walls as per Figure-52. Note that you can change the direction of door opening by using the arrows displayed after placing the door; refer to Figure-54. After placing all the doors, the sketch will be displayed as shown in Figure-55.

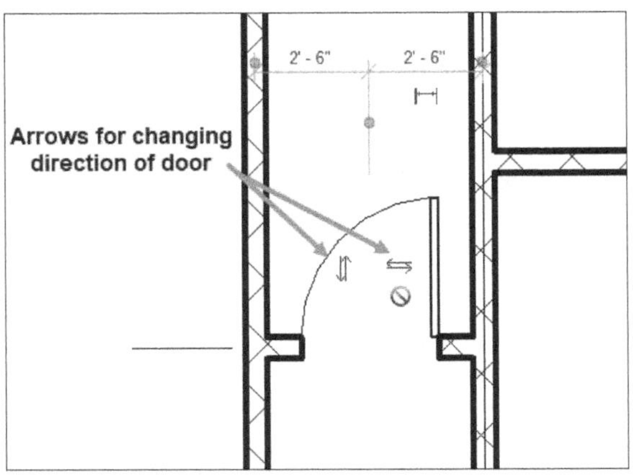

Figure-54. Changing direction of door

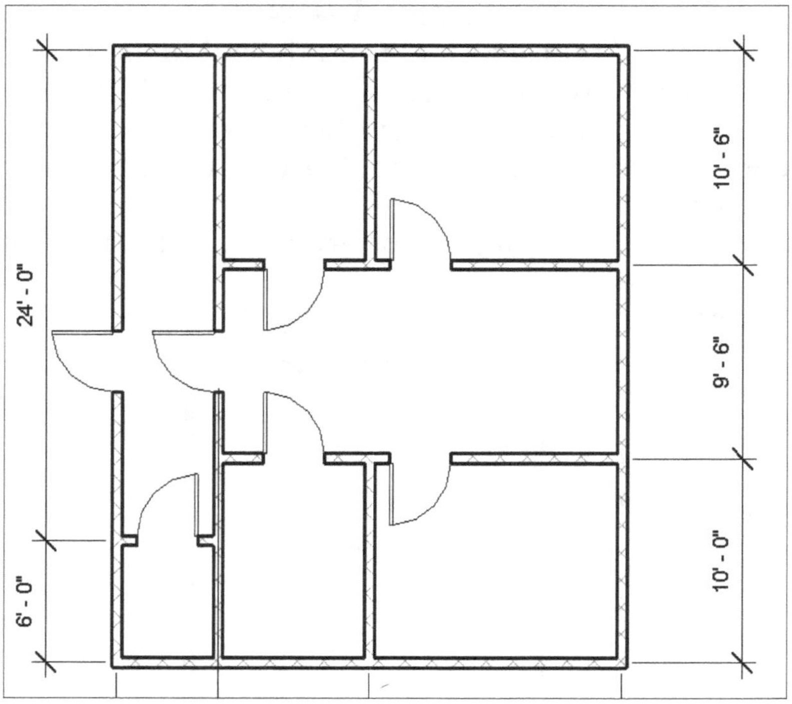

Figure-55. After placing doors

- Select the doors one by one and set the dimensions as per Figure-52.

Placing Furniture

- Click on the **Place a Component** tool from the **Component** drop-down in the **Build** panel of **Architecture** tab in the **Ribbon**. The **Modify|Place Component** contextual tab will be displayed in the **Ribbon** and you will be asked to place a component attached to cursor.
- Click on the **Type** drop-down at the top in the **Properties Palette** and select the **Bed-Box Double 53" x 74"** option from the drop-down. If the option is not available then click on the **Load Family** tool from the **Mode** panel in contextual tab and load the furniture. The bed will get attached to cursor.
- Click in the drawing to place the beds; refer to Figure-56. Press **ESC** twice to exit the tool.
- Select a bed recently placed and click on the **Rotate** tool from the **Modify** contextual tab. You will be asked to specify start point and end point for rotation.
- Rotate the bed as shown in Figure-57. Similarly, rotate the other bed and move it to desired location using arrow keys of Keyboard.

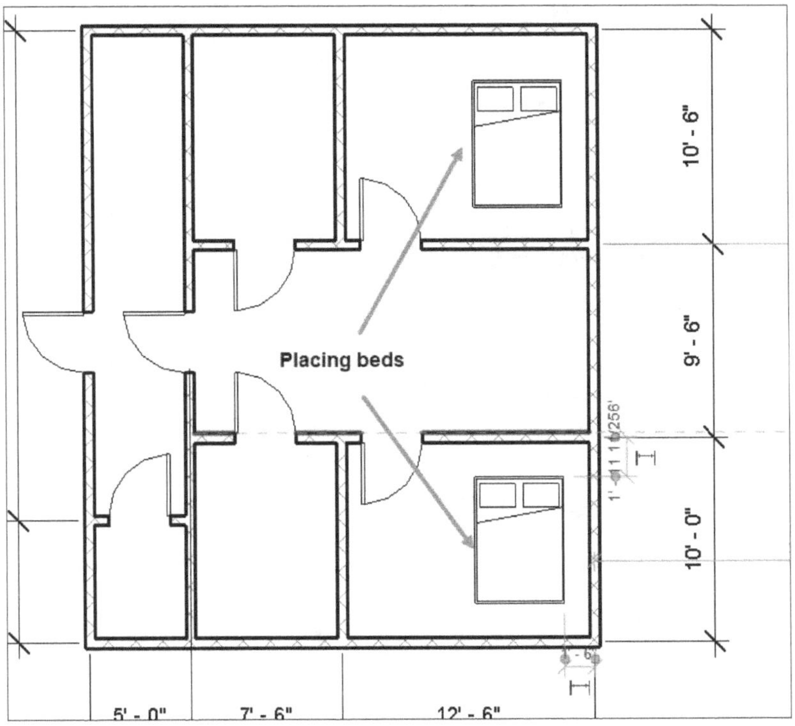

Figure-56. Placing beds

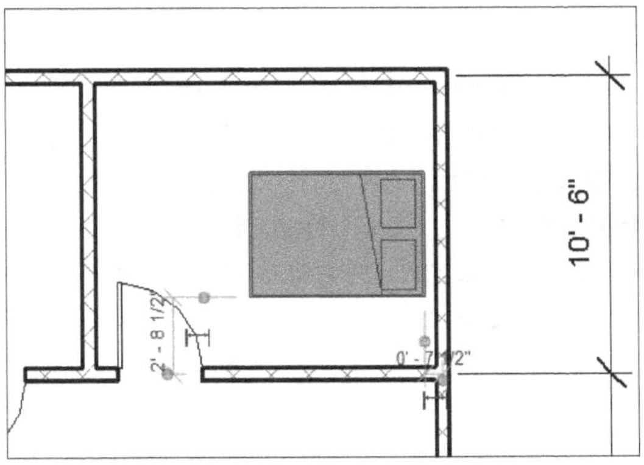

Figure-57. Bed after rotating

- Click on the **Place a Component** tool again and place the other furniture items & components.

Creating Stairs

- Click on the **Stair** tool from the **Circulation** panel in the **Architecture** tab of **Ribbon**. The **Modify|Create Stair** contextual tab will be displayed with related options in **Properties Palette**.
- Click on the **Edit Type** button from the **Properties Palette**. The **Type Properties** dialog box will be displayed.
- Click on the **Duplicate** button from the dialog box and set the parameters as shown in Figure-58.

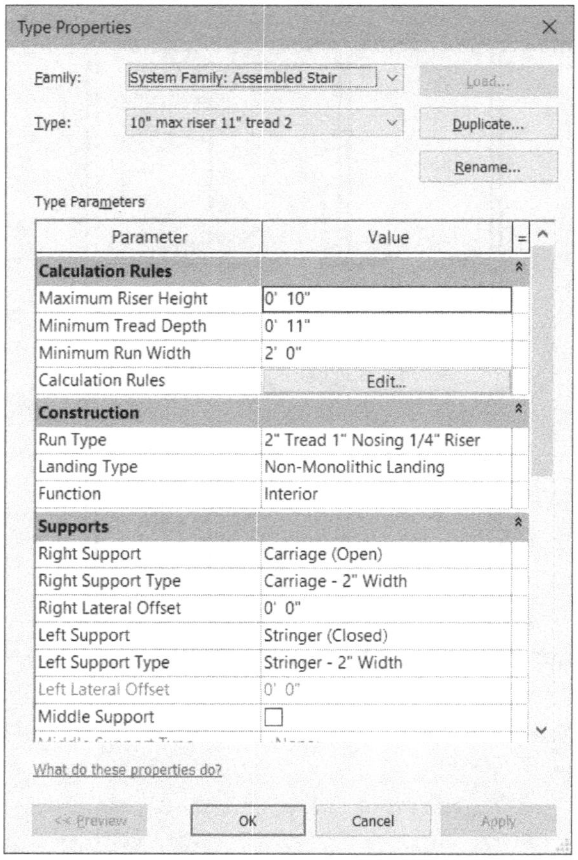

Figure-58. Parameters for new stair type

- After setting the parameters, click on the **OK** button from the dialog box. The newly created stair pattern will be selected automatically.
- Select the **Exterior Support: Left** option from the **Location Line** drop-down in the **Options Bar**. Click near the main gate to specify start point stairs and create 6 steps of stairs; refer to Figure-59.

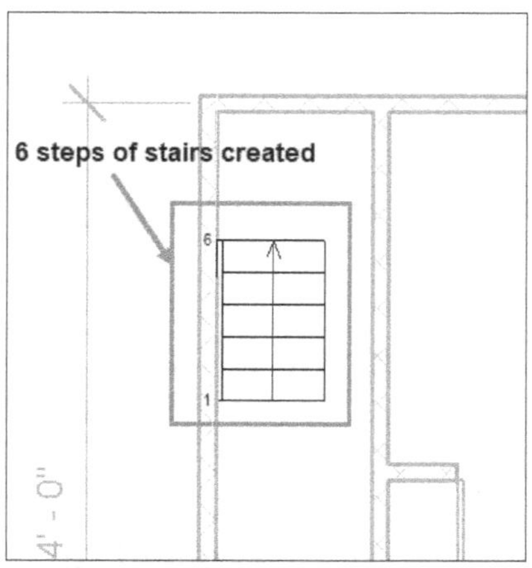

Figure-59. Placing steps of stairs

- Select the **Exterior Support: Right** option from the **Location Line** drop-down in the **Options Bar** and create rest of the stairs as shown in Figure-60.

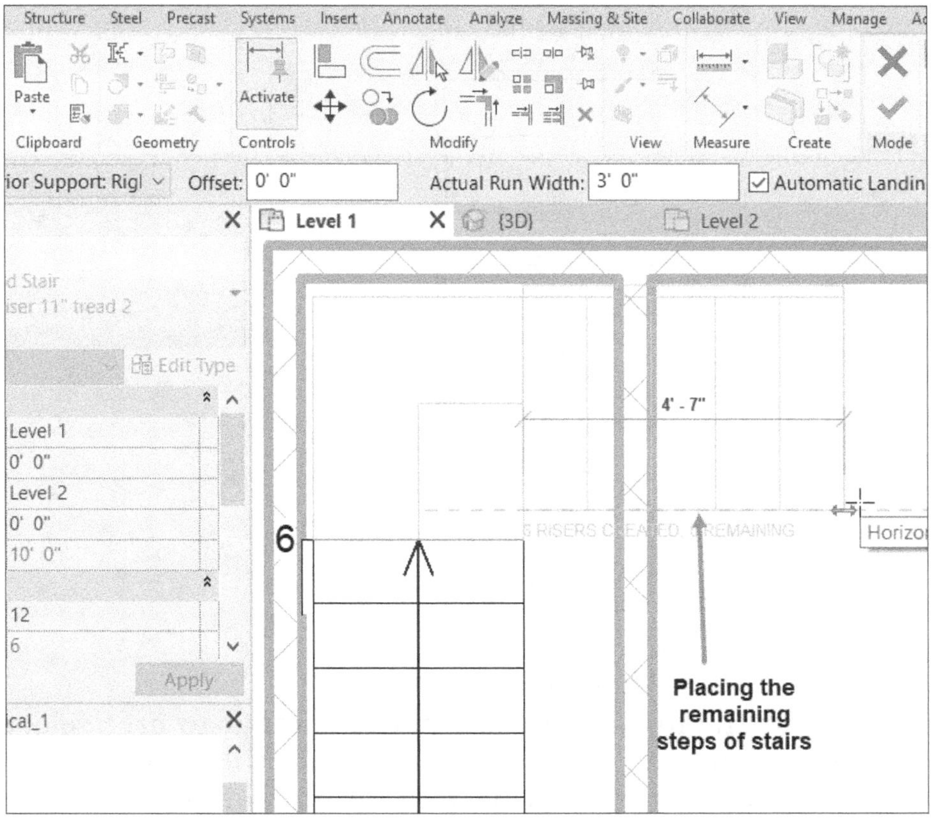

Figure-60. Creating stairs

- Click on the **OK** button from the **Mode** panel in contextual tab to create the stairs.

Annotations

You will learn about annotation tools later in this book. For completing this practical, we are using some of the annotation tools.

- Click on the **Aligned** tool from the **Dimension** panel in the **Annotate** tab of **Ribbon**. The **Modify|Place Dimensions** contextual tab will be displayed with dimensioning options in the **Options Bar** and **Properties Palette**; refer to Figure-61.

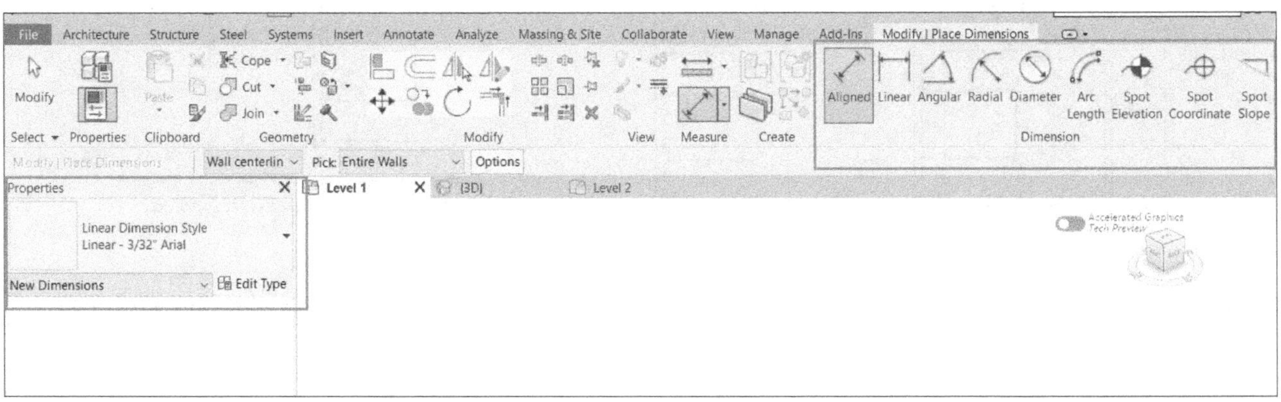

Figure-61. Options to create dimensions

- Select the **Wall centerlines** and **Entire Walls** options from the drop-downs in the **Options Bar**. Click on the **Options** button in the **Options Bar** and clear all the check boxes from the **Auto Dimension Options** dialog box displayed. Click on the **OK** button from the dialog box to apply the changes.
- Click on the wall that you want to dimension. The dimension will get attached to cursor; refer to Figure-62.

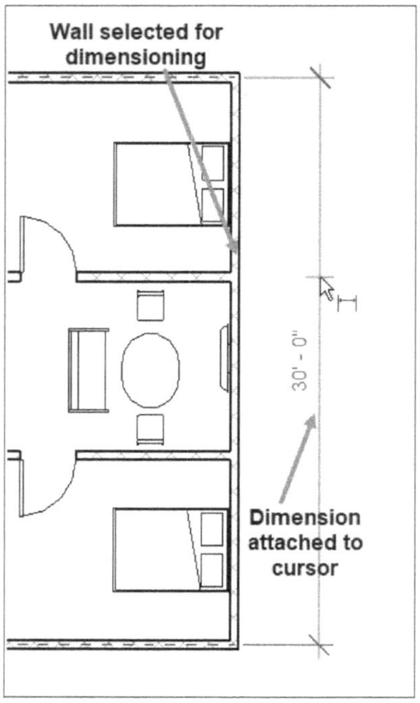

Figure-62. Creating dimension

- Click one by one at the middle of walls perpendicular to first selected wall that you want to dimension; refer to Figure-63. Select the other intermediate walls in the same way and then click at desired locations in empty area to place the dimensions; refer to Figure-64.

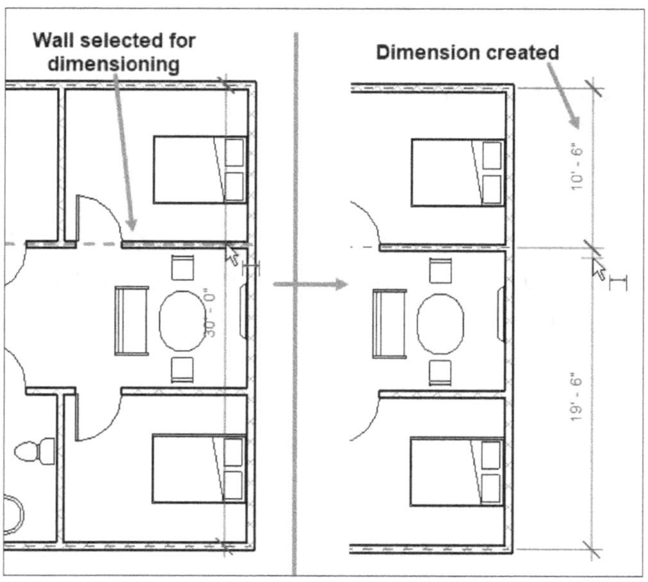

Figure-63. Dimensioning wall

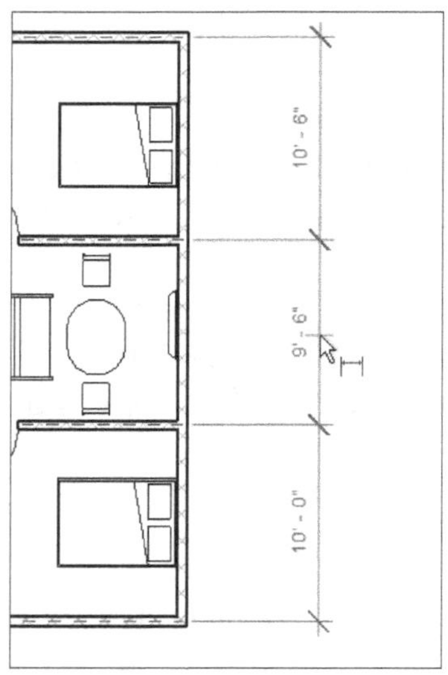

Figure-64. Dimension created

- Create the other dimensions in the same way; refer to Figure-65.

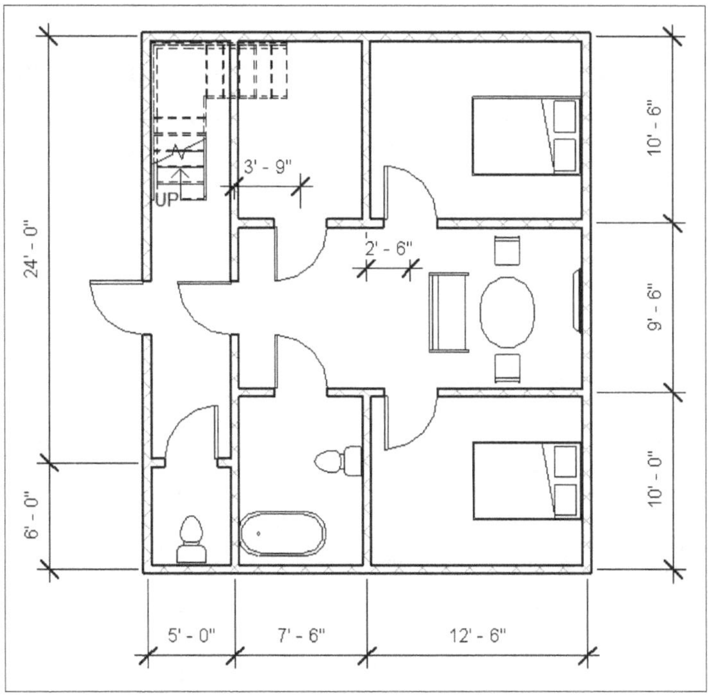

Figure-65. Practical after creating dimensions

- Press **ESC** to exit the **Dimension** tool.
- Click on the **Tag All** tool from the **Tag** panel in the **Annotate** tab of **Ribbon**. The **Tag All Not Tagged** dialog box will be displayed; refer to Figure-66.

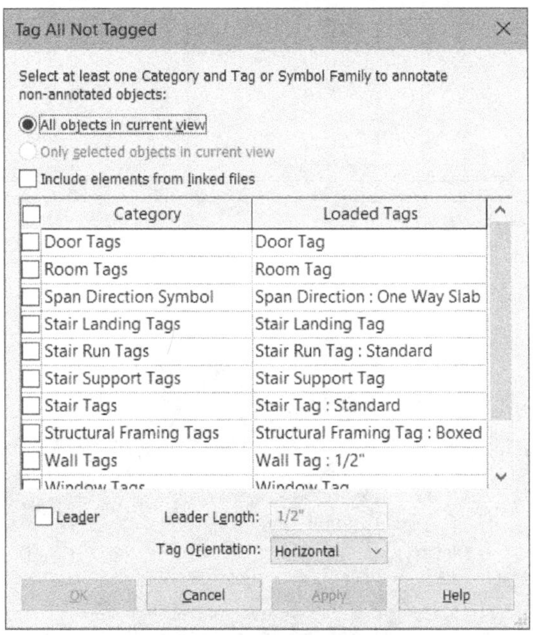

Figure-66. Tag All Not Tagged dialog box

- Select check boxes for **Door Tags** and **Stair Tags** options in this dialog box and click on the **OK** button from the dialog box. The final drawing will be displayed.

PRACTICE 1

Create the model of a hotel building as per the layout in Figure-67.

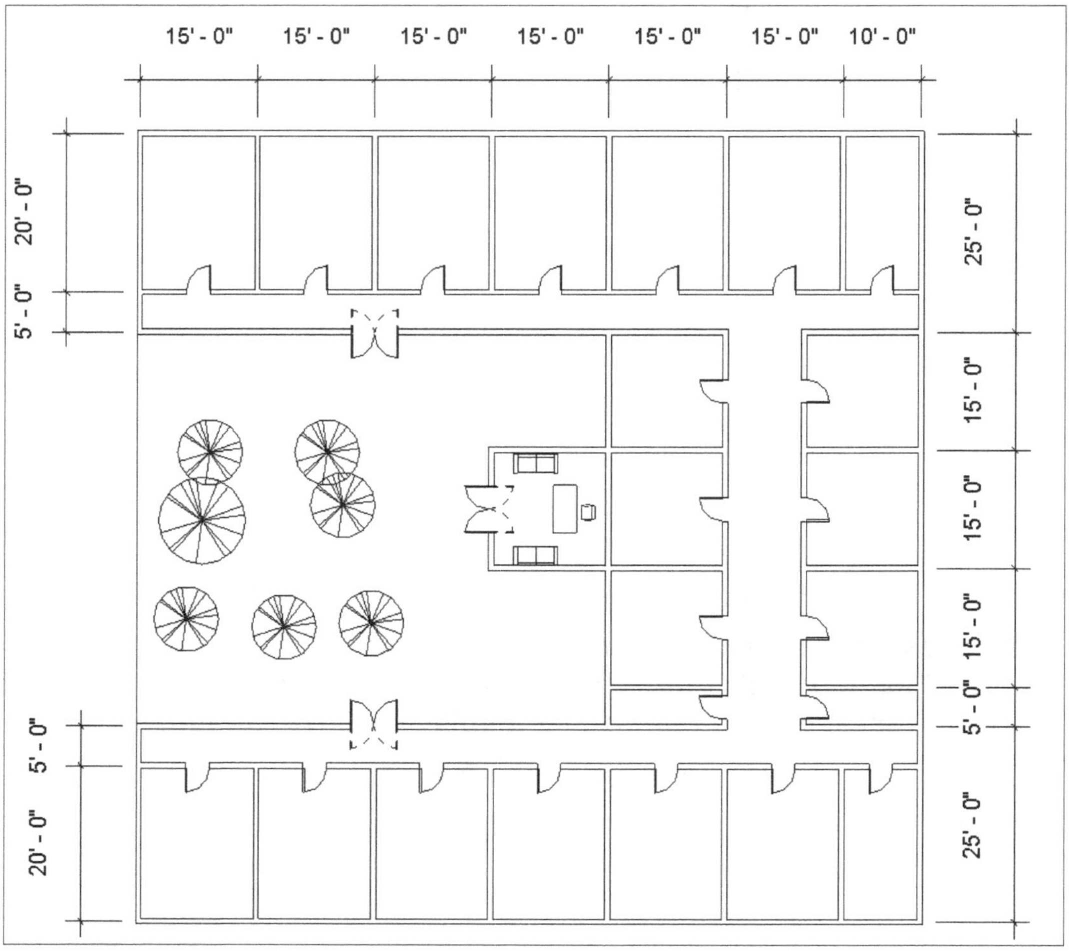

Figure-67. Level 1 layout of Practical 1

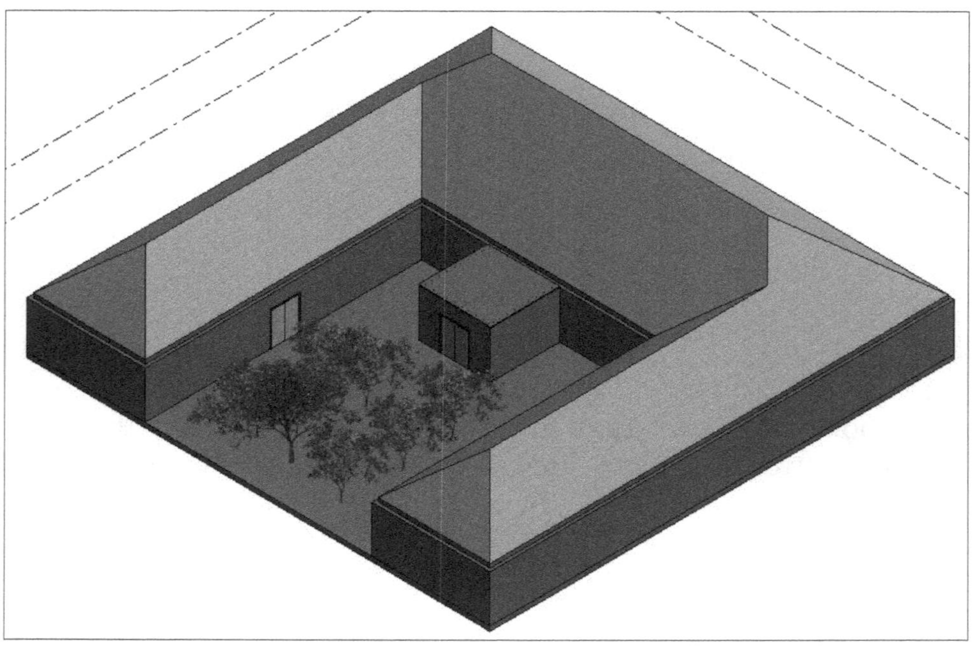

Figure-68. 3D model for Practice 1

SELF ASSESSMENT

Q1. The **Roof by Footprint** tool is used to create roof by selecting boundary elements like walls. (T/F)

Q2. The Eaves are the overhanging portion of roof from the walls generally created to keep rain water off the walls and to prevent the ingress of water at the junction where the roof meets the wall. (T/F)

Q3. Which of the following tools is used to create roof by using desired sketch section?

a. Roof by Footprint
b. Roof by Extrusion
c. Roof by Face
d. Roof: Soffit

Q4. A soffit is used to decorate the roof architecturally as well as provide structural base for roof. (T/F)

Q5. The **Roof: Gutter** tool is used to create gutter for roof so that rain water can be directed to drain pipes. (T/F)

Q6. What is the difference between ceiling and rood?

Q7. What is the difference between architectural floor and structural floor?

Q8. Which of the following tools is used to create openings through all the objects above and below the sketching plane?

a. By Face
b. Shaft
c. Wall
d. Vertical

Q9. Which tool is used to create a roof by selecting boundary elements like walls?

A. Roof by Extrusion
B. Roof by Face
C. Roof by Footprint
D. Roof Soffit

Q10. What is the function of the Align Eaves tool?

A. Align curtain grids
B. Adjust height and overhangs of roof eaves
C. Sketch ceiling boundary
D. Extrude roof sections

Q11. What does the Rafter Cut option in the Properties Palette define?

A. Slope of the wall
B. Visibility of curtain grids
C. How eaves of the roof will be created
D. Shape of the ceiling

Q12. Which tool allows you to create a roof by extruding a cross-section?

A. Roof: Soffit
B. Roof: Fascia
C. Roof by Face
D. Roof by Extrusion

Q13. In Roof by Extrusion, what must be defined before drawing the cross-section?

A. Ceiling boundary
B. Gutter type
C. Work plane
D. Curtain wall

Q14. What is the purpose of the Roof: Soffit tool?

A. Create slope for roof
B. Decorate and fill space under roof
C. Measure wall thickness
D. Set room bounding

Q15. What is the Roof: Fascia tool used for?

A. Extrude floor edges
B. Add fascia about the roof
C. Adjust ceiling visibility
D. Load mass objects

Q16. Which tool is used to add gutters to a roof?

A. Roof: Fascia
B. Curtain Grid
C. Roof: Gutter
D. Roof by Footprint

Q17. What are the two methods to create ceilings using the Ceiling tool?

A. Automatic and Boundary
B. Automatic and Sketch
C. Manual and Structural
D. Structural and Sketch

Q18. Which of the following tools is used to create an architectural floor?

A. Floor: Structural
B. Floor: Architectural
C. Curtain System
D. Roof: Soffit

Q19. The Floor: Slab Edge tool creates what?

A. Curtain system
B. Ceiling grid
C. Slab along floor edge
D. Floor boundary

Q20. Which tool is used to create curtain systems on selected mass faces?

A. Curtain Grid
B. Place Component
C. Curtain System
D. Curtain Wall

Q21. What must be enabled in Visibility/Graphics Overrides to display mass objects?

A. Ceilings
B. Floors
C. Mass
D. Roof

Q22. The Curtain Grid tool is used for what purpose?

A. Create mullions
B. Apply slope
C. Add grid lines to curtain
D. Place ceilings

Q23. Which tool is used to create mullions on curtain grids?

A. Roof: Fascia
B. Curtain System
C. Mullion
D. Grid Tool

Q24. Which tool is used to create a ramp between two levels in a building in Revit?

A. Stair tool
B. Ramp tool
C. Sketch Path tool
D. Model Line tool

Q25. What is the default slope of the ramp in Revit?

A. 10:1
B. 14:1
C. 12:1
D. 8:1

Q26. How do you change the slope of a ramp?

A. Using the Edit Text dialog box
B. In the Draw panel
C. By clicking Edit Type in the Properties Palette
D. By changing floor level

Q27. Which tool is used to draw stairs in Revit?

A. Ramp tool
B. Railing tool
C. Stair tool
D. Room tool

Q28. What happens when you click between the length of a stair while drawing it?

A. The stair is deleted
B. A landing is created
C. The stair is turned into a ramp
D. Nothing happens

Q29. What does the Sketch Path tool in the Railing drop-down do?

A. Places railing on walls
B. Adds railing using predefined paths
C. Sketches railing path manually
D. Draws staircases

Q30. Which tool is used to place railing directly on stairs or ramps?

A. Model Text tool
B. Place on Stair/Ramp tool
C. Tag Room tool
D. Shaft tool

Q31. What does the Model Text tool allow you to do?

A. Create a model line
B. Annotate building areas with 3D text
C. Create a ramp
D. Place railing

Q32. Which of the following is used to mark room boundaries without walls?

A. Room tool
B. Tag All Not Tagged
C. Room Separator tool
D. Shaft tool

Q33. Which panel contains tools for marking and calculating areas in a building?

A. Circulation panel
B. Model panel
C. Opening panel
D. Room & Area panel

Q34. How can you tag all untagged rooms or objects in Revit?

A. Click on Model Line tool
B. Use Tag Room tool
C. Use Tag All Not Tagged option
D. Click on Stair tool

Q35. What is the function of the Shaft tool in the Opening panel?

A. Creates an opening in walls only
B. Creates an opening perpendicular to a surface
C. Creates vertical opening through multiple levels
D. Tags rooms automatically

Q36. What tool would you use to create an opening on the face of a roof or floor?

A. Shaft tool
B. By Face tool
C. Vertical Opening tool
D. Dormer Opening tool

Q37. Which opening tool is specifically used for roofs where dormers are present?

A. By Face tool
B. Wall Opening tool
C. Dormer Opening tool
D. Vertical Opening tool

Q38. What is true about the Vertical Opening tool?

A. Creates horizontal openings
B. Works like the Room tool
C. Creates vertical openings in floors, roofs, or ceilings
D. Only works on walls

Q39. What tool is used to create a separation line without building walls in Revit?

A. Room tool
B. Room Separator tool
C. Shaft tool
D. Wall Opening tool

Q40. Which option in the Room & Area panel is used to apply tags to rooms and objects like doors and stairs?

A. Tag Room
B. Room Separator
C. Room tool
D. Area Plan

FOR STUDENT NOTES

Chapter 4

Project Management

Topics Covered

The major topics covered in this chapter are:

- ***Creating and Managing Material***
- ***Defining Object Styles for Project***
- ***Snap Setting***
- ***Defining Project Information***
- ***Defining Project Parameters***
- ***Creating and Editing Shared Parameters***
- ***Creating Global Parameters***
- ***Transferring Project Standards***
- ***Defining Project Units***
- ***Settings***
- ***Managing Panel Schedule Templates***
- ***Analysis Display Style***
- ***Creating Design Options***
- ***Inquiry Tools***

INTRODUCTION

The tools in **Manage** tab of Autodesk Revit are used to manage various parameters related to project and elements used in the project; refer to Figure-1. You can define snap parameters, units for project, link management, phase definition, and so on using options in this tab. Various tools in this tab are discussed next.

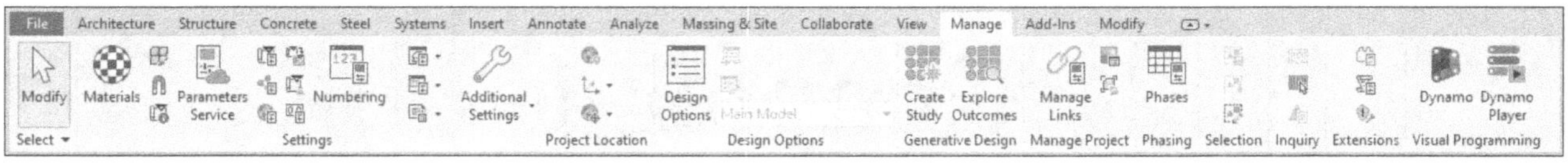

Figure-1. Manage tab

CREATING AND MANAGING MATERIALS

Autodesk Revit has a large library of different types of materials used in building design. There are hundreds of material types available for applying to different elements in the building project but still there is always a need of customizing the materials. The **Materials** tool in **Settings** panel of **Manage** tab in **Ribbon** is used to create, customize, and manage materials. The procedure to use this tool is given next.

- Click on the **Materials** tool from the **Settings** panel in the **Manage** tab of the **Ribbon**. The **Material Browser** dialog box will be displayed; refer to Figure-2.

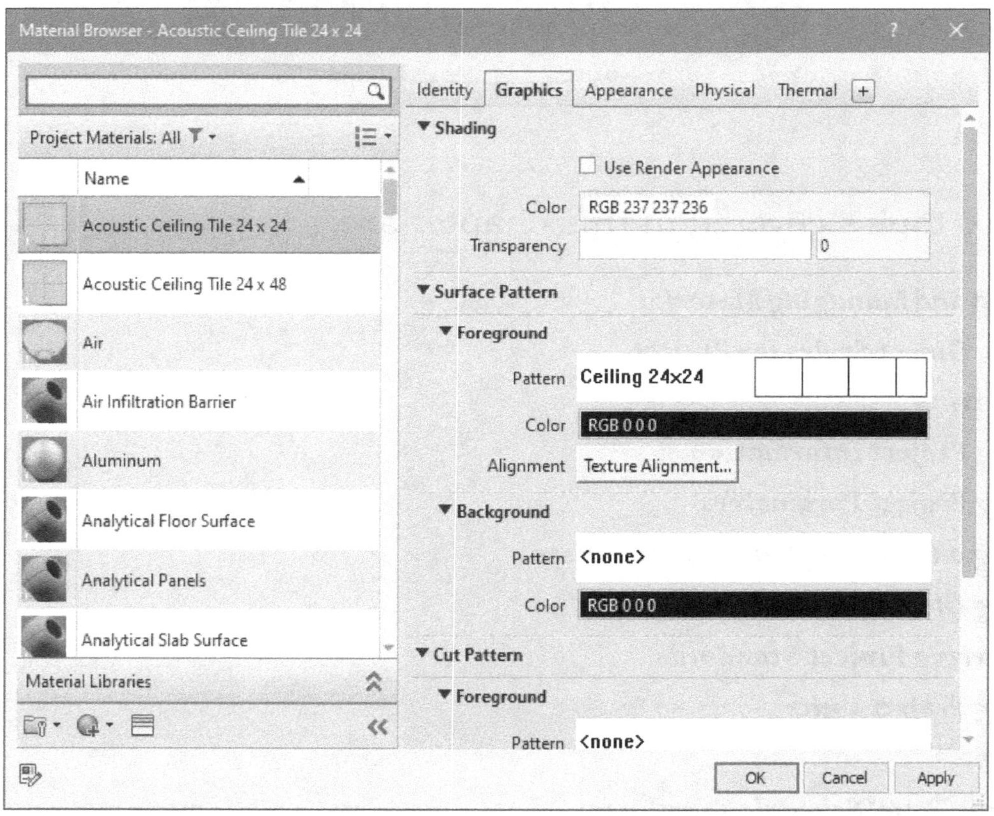

Figure-2. Material Browser

- Select desired material which you want to modify. The related parameters will be displayed on the right in the dialog box.

Graphic Parameters

- Select the **Graphics** tab in this dialog box to specify graphic parameters for the material like color, transparency, foreground color, background color, patterns, and so on. Set desired parameters to change the appearance of material.

Identity Parameters

- Click on the **Identity** tab in the dialog box to modify parameters like manufacturer, cost, class, description, Revit key note, and so on. The dialog box will be displayed as shown in Figure-3.

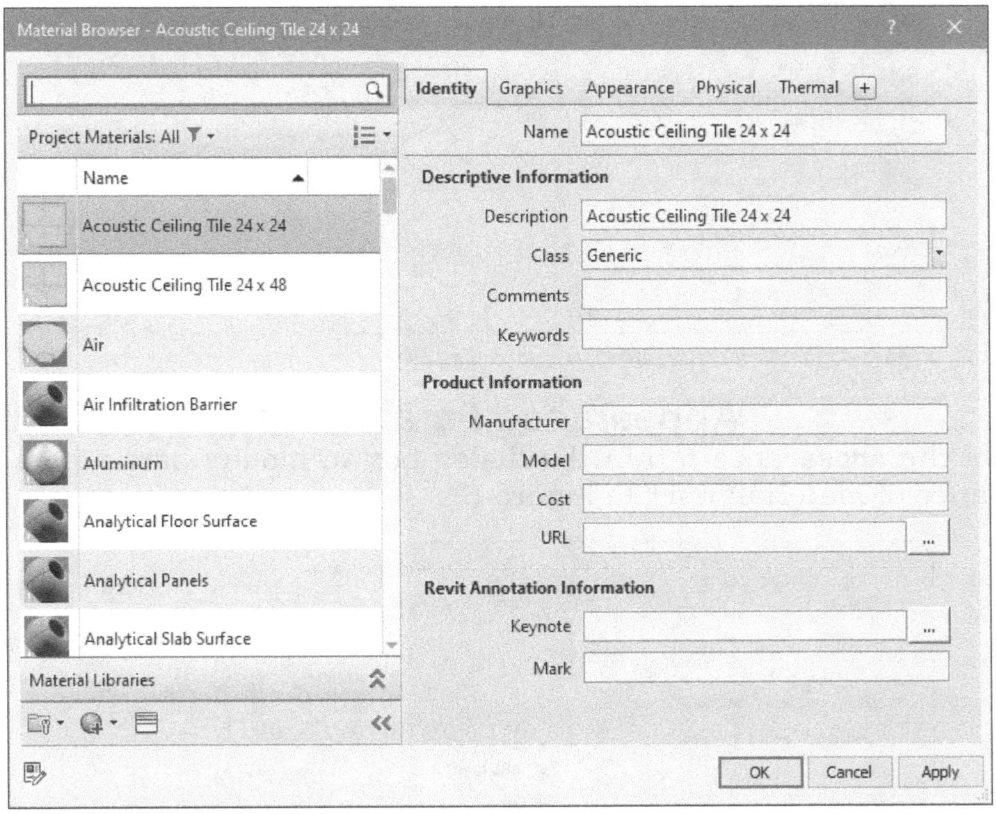

Figure-3. Identity tab in Material Browser

- The options in **Descriptive Information** area of the dialog box are used to define general description of material, their class in Revit library, user comments/notes, and keywords for searching this material in library.
- The options in **Product Information** area are of greater importance to management of building construction. This information defines from where to purchase the material, what is the model of material, what is per unit cost of material, and shopping website for material. Note that information provided here is reflected in various schedules and cost estimation chart.
- The options in **Revit Annotation Information** area are used to define keynote and marks displayed in annotated Revit drawings of project. Set the parameters as desired. Figure-4 shows a sample information for parameters.
- After setting desired parameters, click on the **Apply** button to modify material.

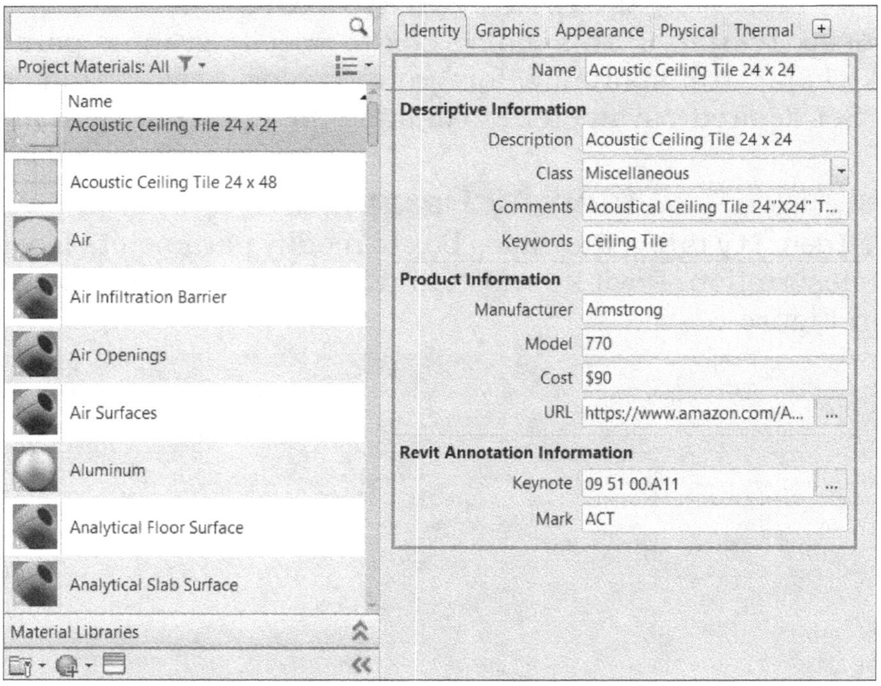

Figure-4. Sample identity information for ceiling tile

Appearance Parameters

- Click on the **Appearance** tab in the dialog box to modify parameters related to appearance of material; refer to Figure-5.

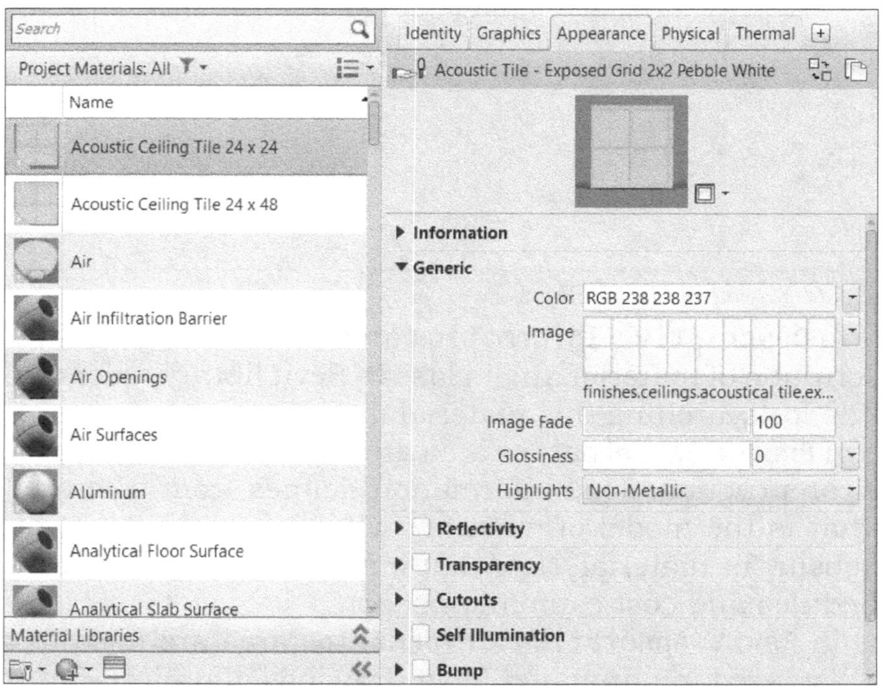

Figure-5. Appearance tab

- Set desired appearance parameters, sample image, glossiness, highlight, reflectivity, transparency, self illumination, bumps, tints, and so on in respective rollouts of this tab. Note that these parameters, directly affect the appearance of material in rendering and high quality model display. The parameters specified in **Appearance** tab do not affect the physical and thermal properties of material.

Physical Parameters

- Click on the **Physical** tab in the dialog box to modify parameters related to physical properties of material; refer to Figure-6. These properties directly affect the results of structural analyses.

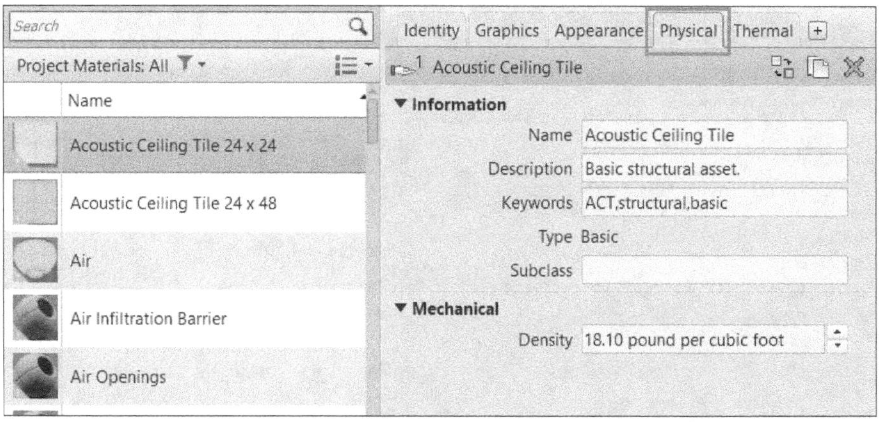

Figure-6. Physical tab

- Expand the **Information** and **Mechanical** rollouts of the dialog box and set desired parameters in respective edit boxes.

Thermal Parameters

- Click on the **Thermal** tab in the dialog box to modify thermal parameters of selected element; refer to Figure-7. These parameters affect both structural and heating/cooling analysis of the building when materials are applied.

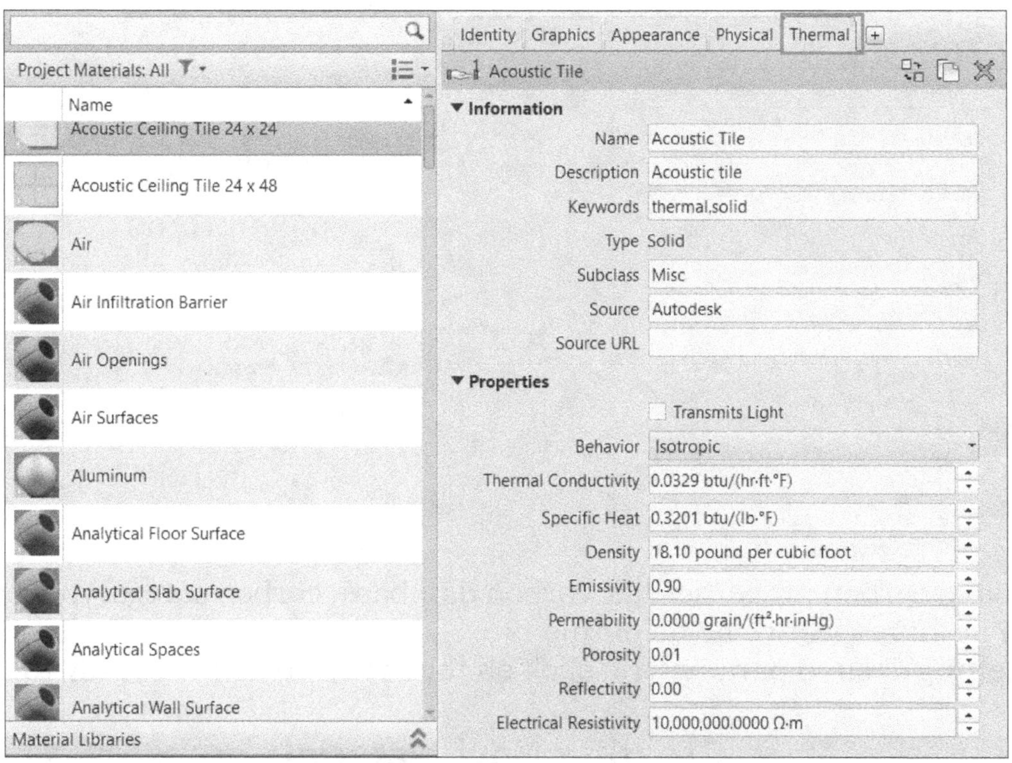

Figure-7. Thermal tab

- Set desired thermal properties like conductivity, emissivity, electrical resistance, porosity and so on in respective fields of this tab.
- After setting desired parameters, click on the **Apply** button to modify material.

Carbon Parameters

- Click on the [+] button and click on the **Carbon** option from drop-down displayed to define material properties related to carbon emission for making environment friendly buildings. The **Asset Browser** dialog box will be displayed; refer to Figure-8.

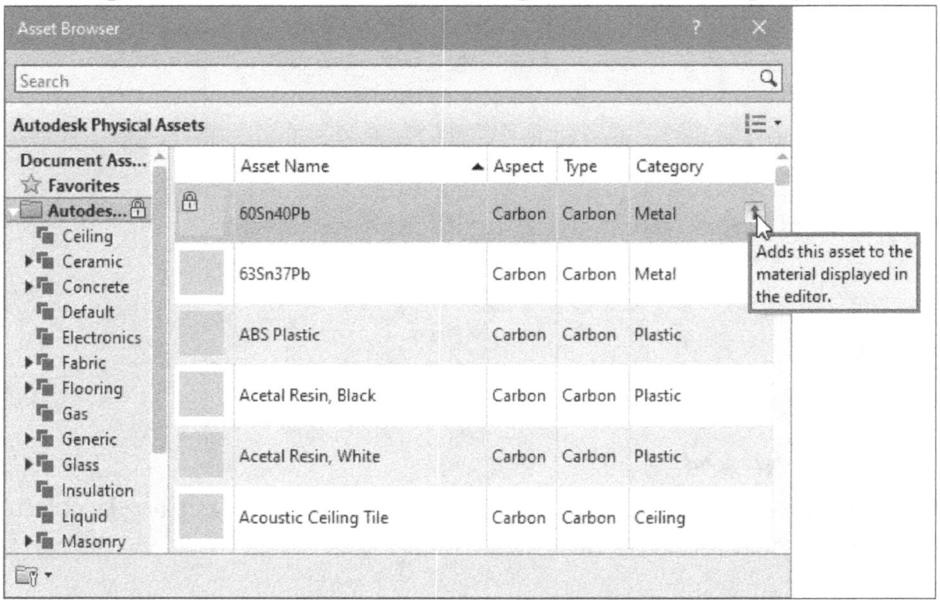

Figure-8. Asset Browser dialog box

- Click on the **Adds this asset to the material displayed in the editor** button. The carbon parameters will be displayed in the **Carbon** tab; refer to Figure-9.

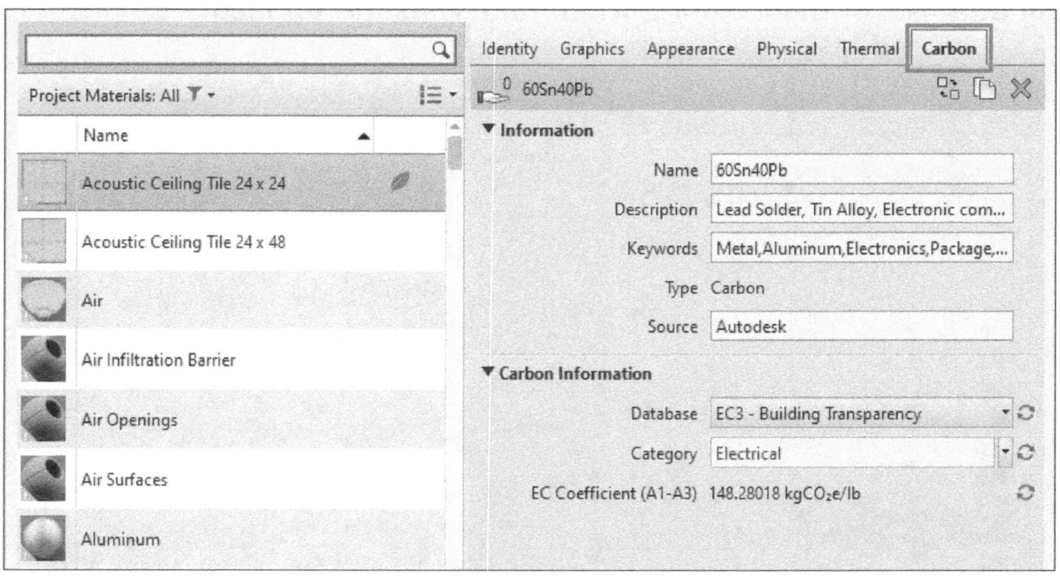

Figure-9. Carbon tab

- Set desired carbon properties like carbon database, carbon category, ec coefficient, and so on in respective fields of this tab.
- After setting desired parameters, click on the **Apply** button to modify the material.

Creating New Material

You can create a new material by using the **Create New Material** tool in the bottom toolbar of the dialog box. The procedure to create material is given next.

- Click on the **Create New Material** tool from the **Creates and duplicates materials** drop-down at the bottom in the dialog box; refer to Figure-10. The new material will be added in the material list and related parameters will be displayed in the dialog box; refer to Figure-11.

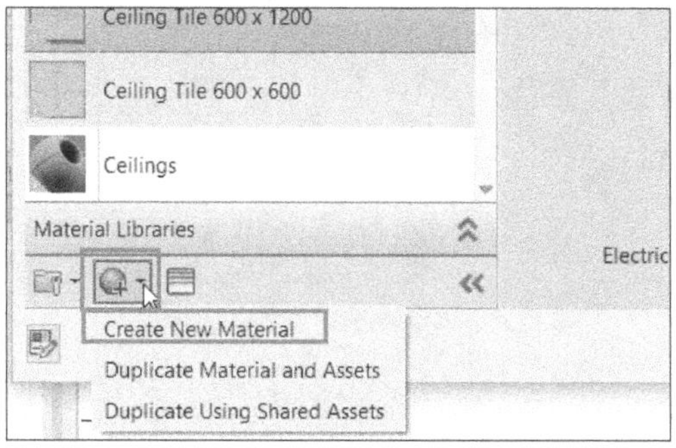

Figure-10. Create New Material tool

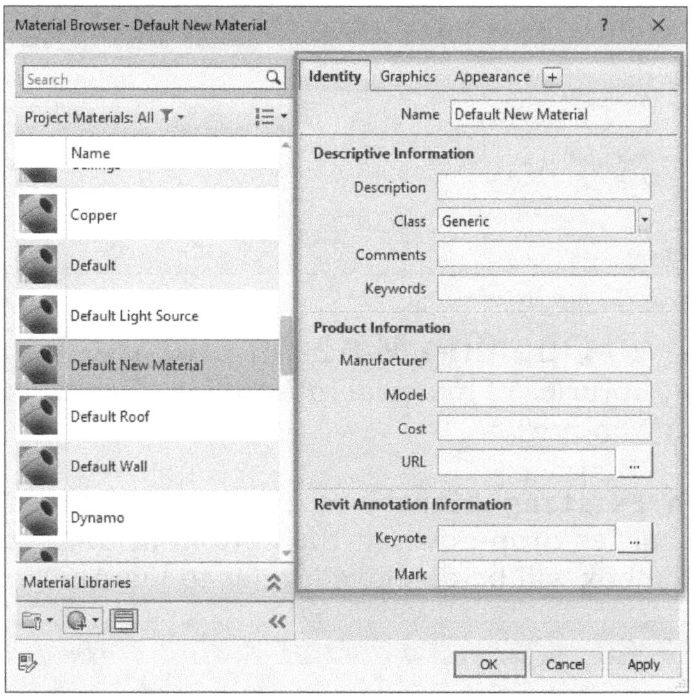

Figure-11. New material added

- Click on the [+] button to specify advanced properties like physical property and thermal property. Note that these advanced properties are to be extracted from existing properties. For example, click on the [+] button and click on the **Physical** option from drop-down displayed. The **Asset Browser** dialog box will be displayed; refer to Figure-12.
- Expand desired category from the left and double-click on the asset property you want to use for defining property of new material. The parameters will be copied.
- Close the **Asset Browser** dialog box and modify the properties of new material as desired. Similarly, you can apply thermal properties to the new material.
- Set desired parameters for new material as discussed earlier and click on the **OK** button.

Similarly, you can use the **Duplicate Selected Material** tool from the **Creates and duplicates materials** drop-down to create duplicate copy of selected material. Use the **Duplicate Using Shared Assets** tool from the drop-down to create duplicate copy of material while keeping the properties linked to original material.

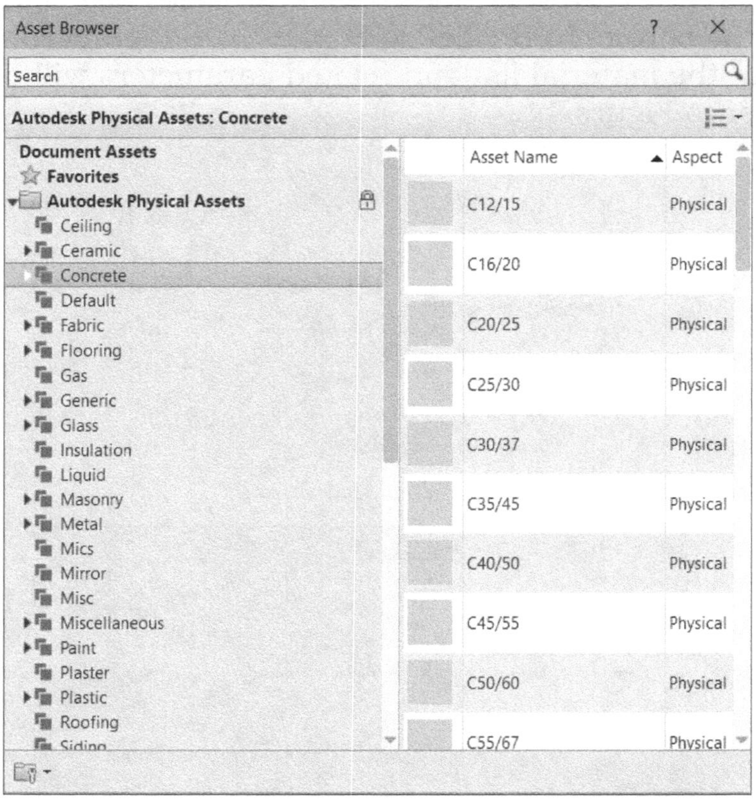

Figure-12. Asset Browser

Opening Material Library

You can use different libraries of material in Autodesk Revit. The procedure to open a material library is given next.

- Click on the **Open Existing Library** tool from the **Creates, opens and edits user-defined libraries** drop-down at the bottom in the **Material Browser**. The **Select File** dialog box will be displayed; refer to Figure-13.

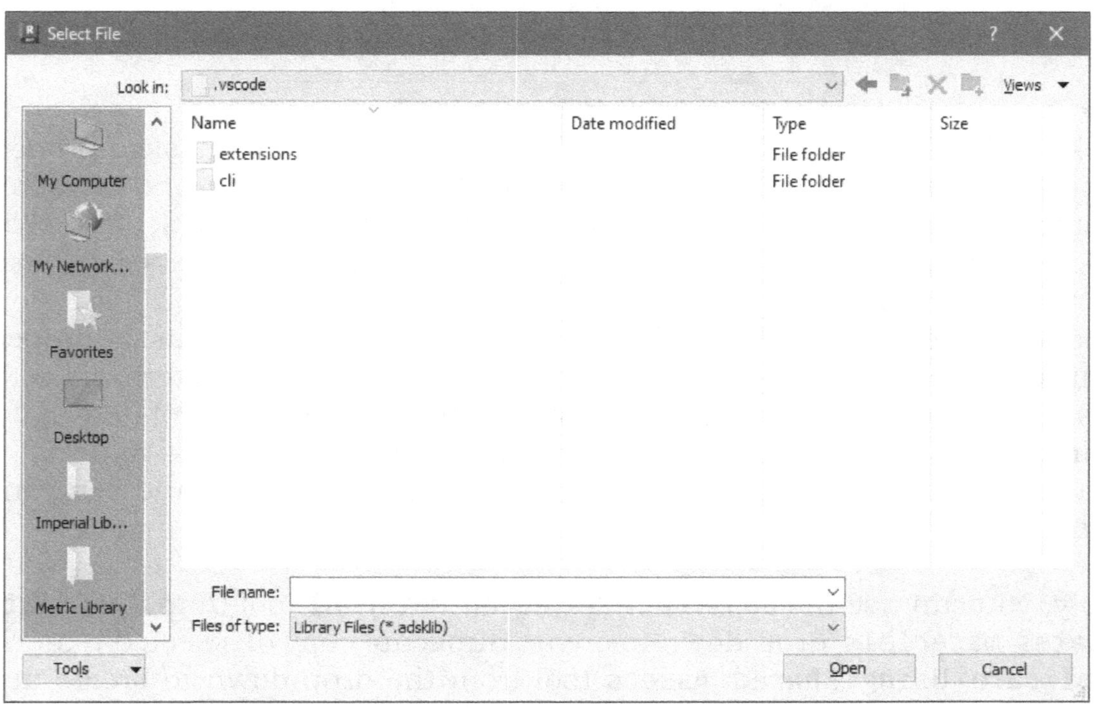

Figure-13. Select File dialog box

- Select desired material library and click on the **Open** button from the dialog box. The materials from selected library will be added in the list.

Similarly, you can perform other material related operations in the **Material Browser**. After setting desired parameters, click on the **OK** button from the **Material Browser** to exit.

DEFINING OBJECT STYLES FOR PROJECT

The **Object Styles** tool in **Settings** panel is used to define color, line weight, line type, material, and other style parameters for different elements. The procedure to use this tool is given next.

- Click on the **Object Styles** tool from the **Settings** panel in the **Manage** tab of **Ribbon**. The **Object Styles** dialog box will be displayed as shown in Figure-14.

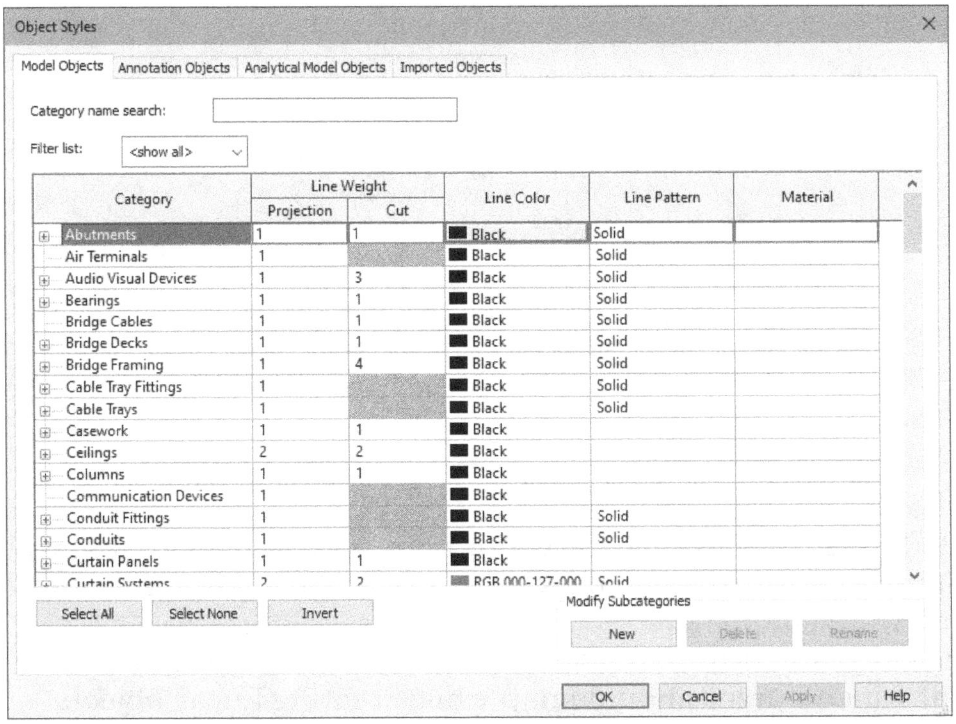

Figure-14. Object Styles dialog box

- You can change the color, pattern, material, and line weight for different objects using their respective fields in the dialog box. By default, the **Model Objects** tab is selected and hence, options to modify model objects are displayed.
- Click on the **Annotation Objects**, **Analytical Model Objects**, and **Imported Objects** tabs to modify their display styles.
- After setting desired parameters, click on the **OK** button from the dialog box.

SNAP SETTING

In Autodesk Revit, snaps are used to guide cursor at some specific points during selection like end points of object, center points for circular objects, and so on. The procedure to use this tool is given next.

- Click on the **Snaps** tool from the **Settings** panel in the **Manage** tab of **Ribbon**. The **Snaps** dialog box will be displayed; refer to Figure-15.

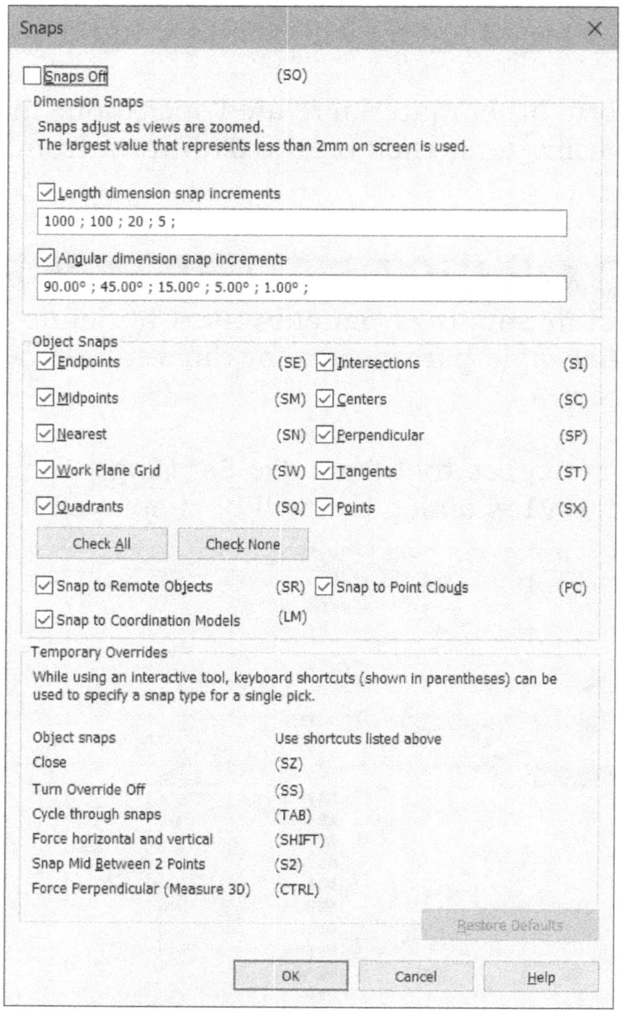

Figure-15. Snaps dialog box

- Select the **Snaps off** check box if you do not want to use snaps while selection. All the options in this dialog box will be deactivated. Clear this check box if you want to activate snapping.
- Select the **Length dimension snap increments** check box and define the distance interval at which cursor should snap while creating linear objects.
- Select the **Angular dimension snap increments** check box and define the angles at which cursor should snap while creating arc, circle, elliptical, or other round objects.
- Select check boxes for key points to be used for snapping from the **Object Snaps** area of the dialog box. You can click on the **Check All** button to select all the key points or you can click on the **Check None** button to de-select all the key points from snapping.
- You can use the shortcuts displayed at the bottom in the dialog box to temporarily override the snap type for single point selection.
- After setting desired parameters, click on the **OK** button from the dialog box.

DEFINING PROJECT INFORMATION

The **Project Information** tool is used to define description and other general details of project. The procedure to use this tool is given next.

- Click on the **Project Information** tool from the **Settings** panel in the **Manage** tab of **Ribbon**. The **Project Information** dialog box will be displayed; refer to Figure-16.
- Set desired values in the fields of **Identity Data** and other rollouts.

Route Analysis Settings

The route analysis settings are used to define the objects that are not counted as obstacle while creating automatic route for hvac, piping, or electrical system.

- Click on the **Edit** button for **Route Analysis Settings** field in the **Project Information** dialog box. The **Route Analysis Settings** dialog box will be displayed; refer to Figure-17.

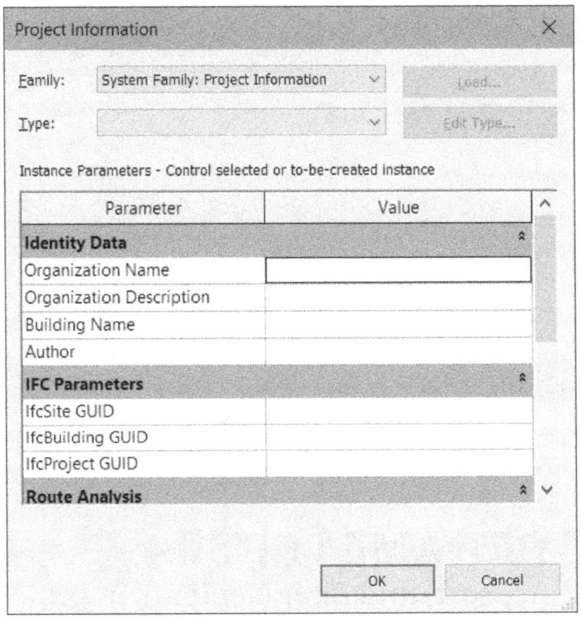

Figure-16. Project Information dialog box

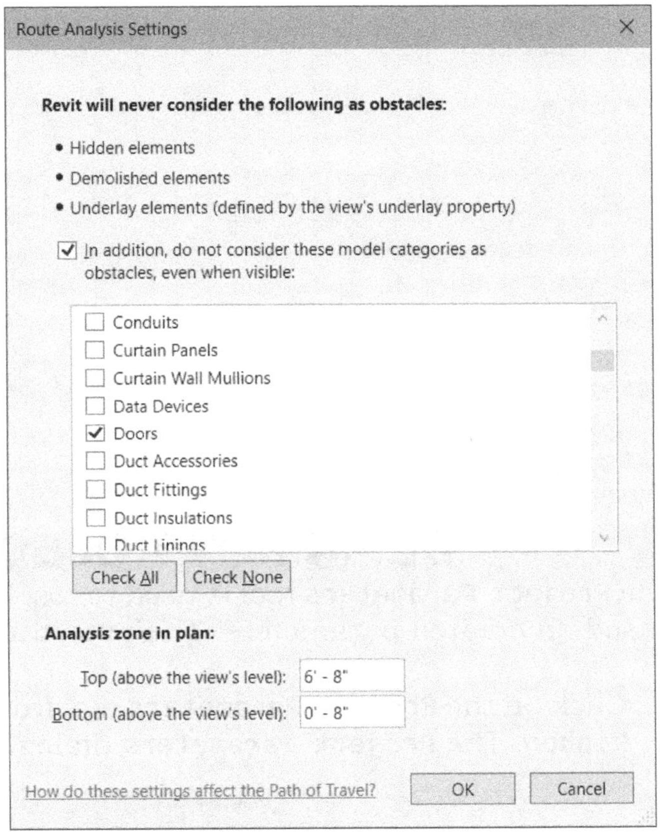

Figure-17. Route Analysis Settings dialog box

- Select desired check boxes for the elements which are not to be considered as obstacles for routing from the list box in the dialog box. If you want to select all the check boxes then click on the **Check All** button and if you do not want to select any check box then click on the **Check None** button.
- Specify desired upper and lower limit of analysis zone in respective edit boxes of **Analysis zone in plan** area of the dialog box.
- Click on the **OK** button from the dialog box to apply the route settings.
- Click on the **OK** button from the **Project Information** dialog box to apply project information.

PARAMETERS SERVICE

The **Parameters Service** tool is used to manage shared parameter and import them into an active Revit session. Note that you must be connected to internet for using this tool. On clicking this tool, the **Parameters Service** dialog box will be displayed with list of parameters available online; refer to Figure-18. You must have Administrator rights to modify the shared parameters on cloud.

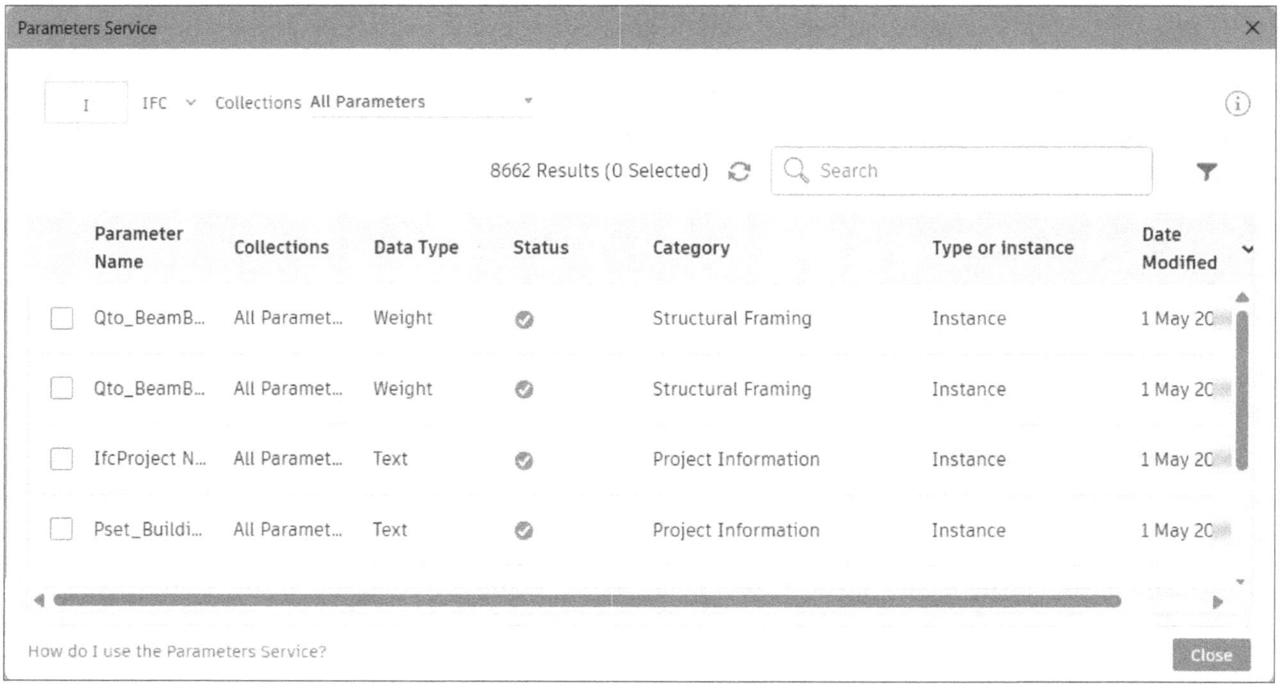

Figure-18. Parameters Service dialog box

DEFINING PROJECT PARAMETERS

The **Project Parameters** tool is used to reschedule, sort, and filter elements in project based on created parameters. The procedure to use this tool is given next.

- Click on the **Project Parameters** tool from the **Settings** panel in the **Manage** tab of **Ribbon**. The **Project Parameters** dialog box will be displayed; refer to Figure-19.

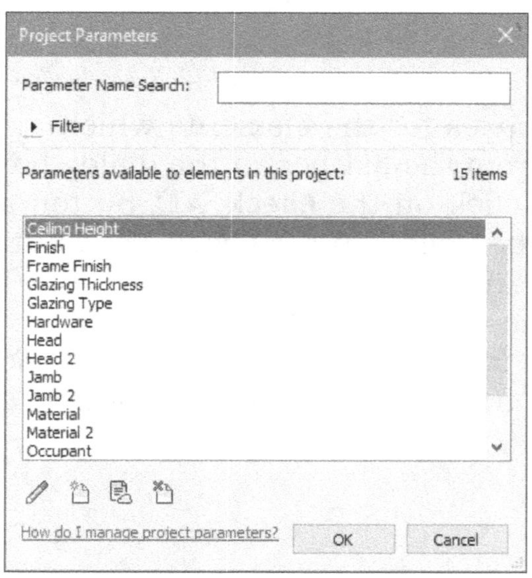

Figure-19. Project Parameters dialog box

- Select desired parameter from the dialog box. You can specify keywords for searching desired parameter in the **Parameter Name Search** edit box. If you want to create a new project parameter, then click on the **New Parameter** button from the dialog box. The **Parameter Properties** dialog box will be displayed; refer to Figure-20.

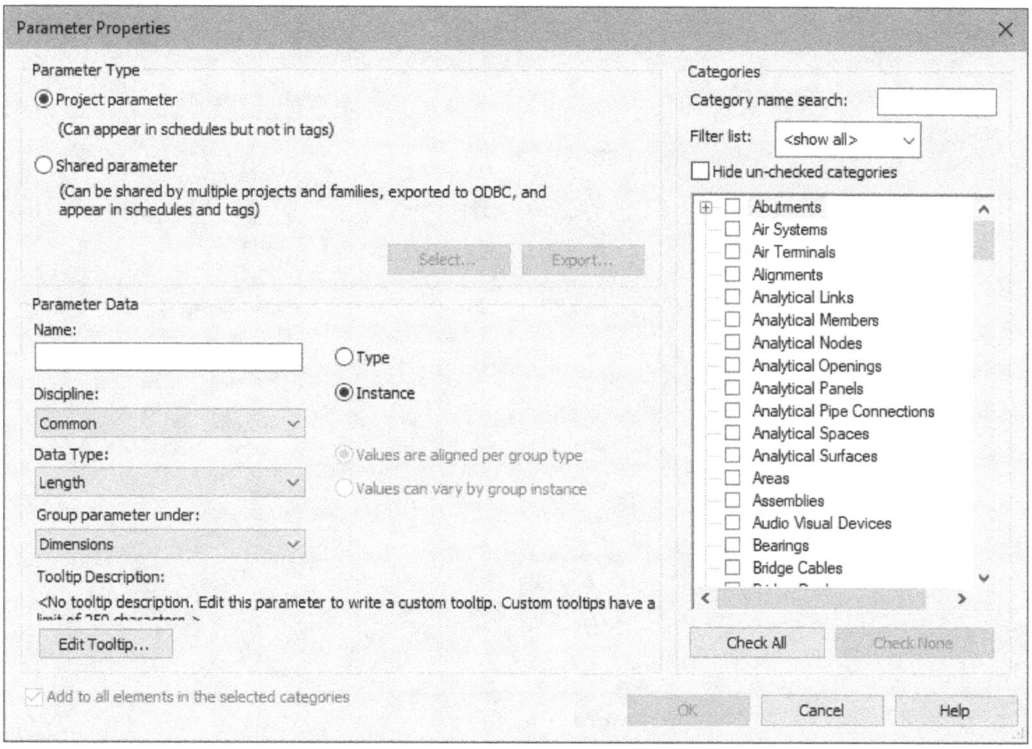

Figure-20. Parameter Properties dialog box

Creating Project Parameter

- By default, the **Project parameter** radio button is selected in the dialog box and hence parameters specified in this dialog box will only appear in schedules. The parameters are specific to current project and cannot be shared with other projects. For example, if you want to create a parameter called duct length for ducts in current project then you should create it after selecting the **Project parameter** radio button.
- Specify desired name for parameter in the **Name** edit box like Duct length.
- Select desired options from the **Discipline**, **Type of Parameter**, and **Group parameter under** drop-downs to define what type of parameter you want to create.
- If you want to specify a tool tip for new parameter then click on the **Edit Tooltip** button at the bottom in the dialog box. The **Edit Tooltip** dialog box will be displayed; refer to Figure-21.

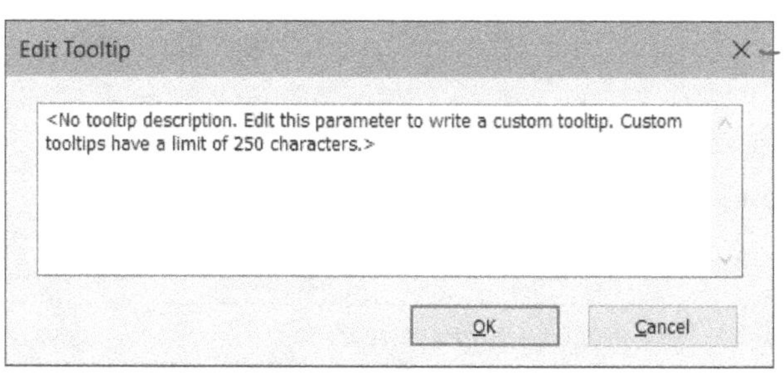

Figure-21. Edit Tooltip dialog box

- Clear the text in the box and type desired tooltip. Click on the **OK** button to create the tooltip.
- Select the check box(es) for category(s) to which you want to apply the newly created parameter; refer to Figure-22.

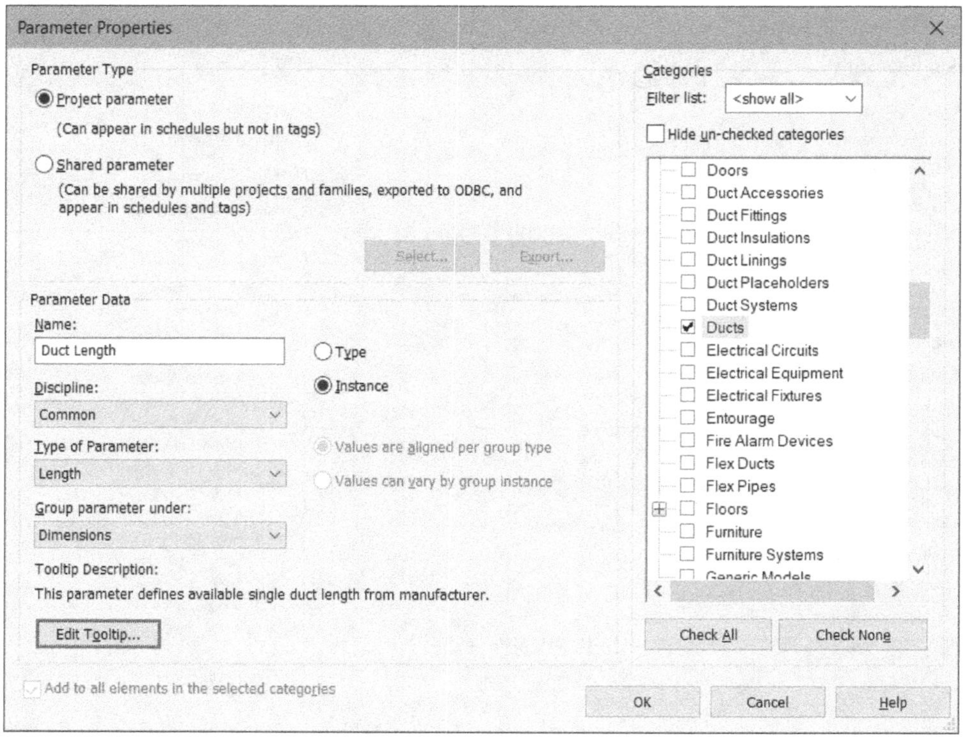

Figure-22. Duct length parameter created

- Click on the **OK** button from the dialog box to create the parameter. The **Project Parameters** dialog box will be displayed again. Click on the **OK** button to exit the dialog box. Now, if you create a new schedule for ducts then you will find newly created parameter in the **Schedule Properties** dialog box; refer to Figure-23.

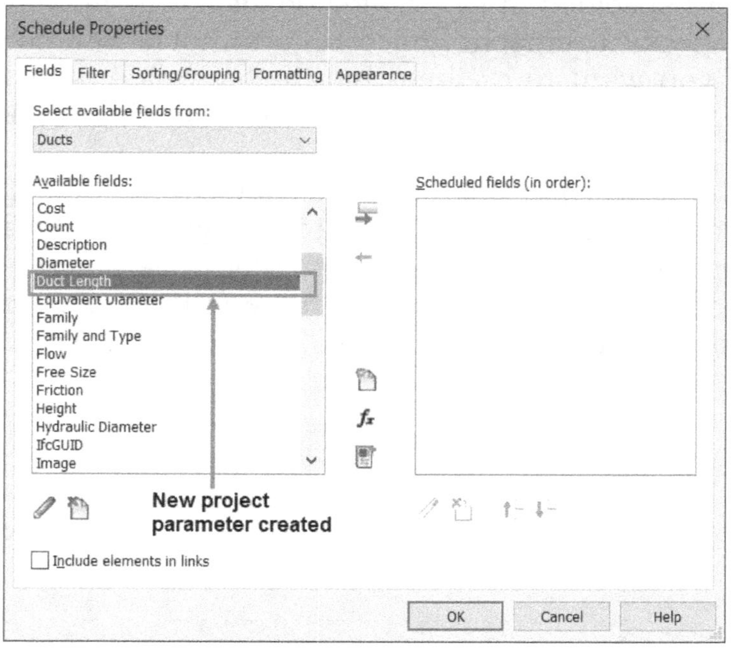

Figure-23. New project parameter created

Adding Shared Parameter

- Select the **Shared Parameter** radio button from the **Parameter Properties** dialog box if you want to create a parameter that can be shared within multiple projects and can also be used in tags, schedules etc. On selecting this radio button, the **Discipline** and **Type of Parameter** drop-downs will become inactive.
- Click on the **Select** button from the dialog box to select the shared parameters group in which new parameter will be added. If no shared parameters file is selected by default then a message box will be displayed asking you whether to select a parameter file or not. Select the **Yes** button from message box. The **Edit Shared Parameters** dialog box will be displayed; refer to Figure-24. Using **Browse** button, select pre-existing library or create a new parameters library and then click on the **OK** button from the **Edit Shared Parameters** dialog box. The **Shared Parameters** dialog box will be displayed; refer to Figure-25.

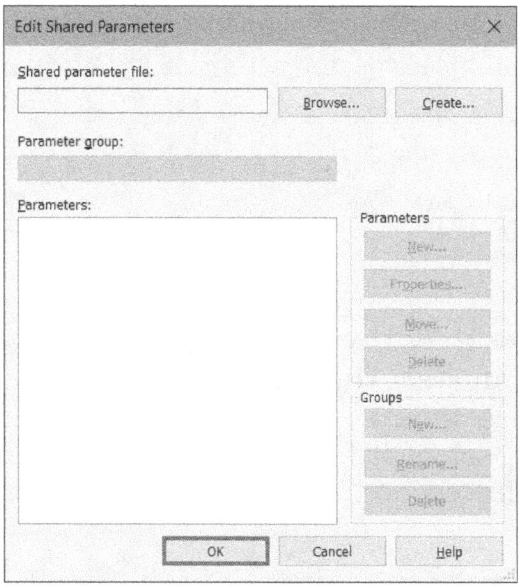

Figure-24. Edit Shared Parameters dialog box

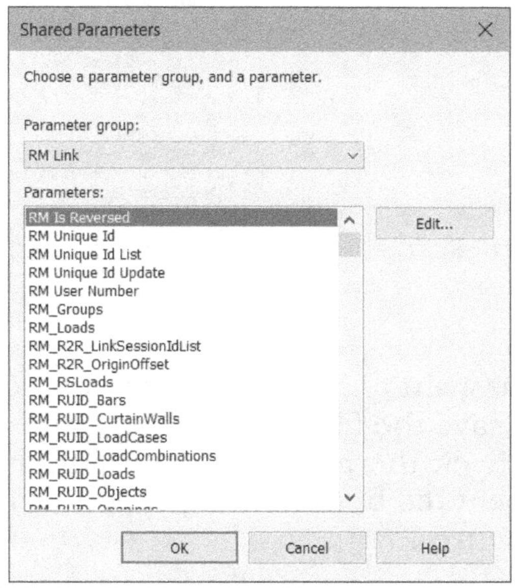

Figure-25. Shared Parameters dialog box

- Select desired group from the **Parameter group** drop-down and then select desired parameter from the **Parameters** area. The selected parameter will be added in current project. Click on the **OK** button from the dialog box. The **Parameter Properties** dialog box will be displayed again and the selected parameter will be displayed automatically in the **Name** field of dialog box.
- Select desired option from the **Group parameter under** drop-down to define the group in which the selected parameter will be placed in the current project.
- Select the check box(es) for category(s) in which you want to add the selected parameter from the **Categories** area of the dialog box.
- Click on the **OK** button from the dialog box to add parameter. The **Parameter Value** dialog box will be displayed asking you to specify the value for current elements.
- Specify desired values and click on the **OK** button. The parameter will be included in the respective categories of the project. Click on the **OK** button from the **Project Parameters** dialog box to exit the tool.

CREATING AND EDITING SHARED PARAMETERS

The **Shared Parameters** tool is used to create and edit shared parameters used in multiple projects. The procedure to sue this tool is given next.

- Click on the **Shared Parameters** tool from the **Settings** panel in the **Manage** tab of **Ribbon**. The **Edit Shared Parameters** dialog box will be displayed; refer to Figure-26.
- Click on the **Browse** button to load the shared parameter file and open desired parameter file.

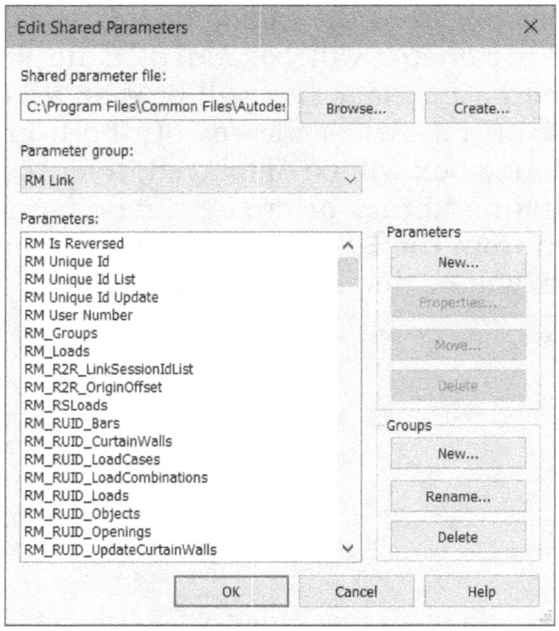

Figure-26. Edit Shared Parameters dialog box

- If you want to create a file for shared parameters then click on the **Create** button and save the file with desired name and location.
- To check the properties of a parameter, select it from the list and click on the **Properties** button. The properties of selected parameter will be displayed; refer to Figure-27.

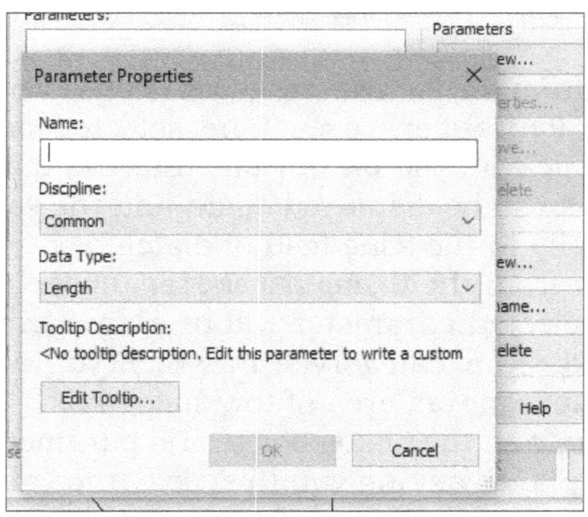

Figure-27. Parameter Properties dialog box

- To move selected parameter in different group, click on the **Move** button. The **Move To Group** dialog box will be displayed; refer to Figure-28.

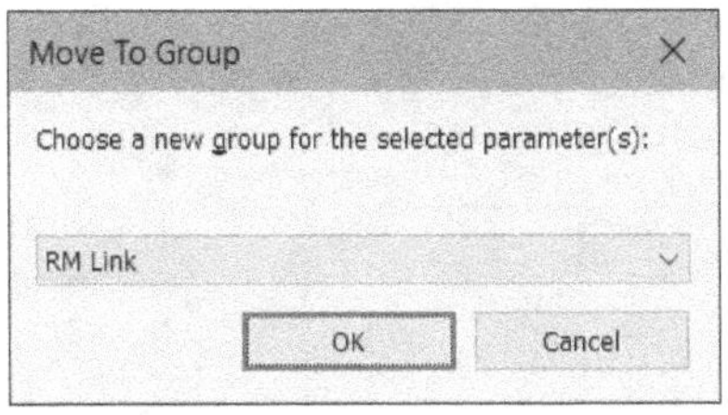

Figure-28. Move To Group dialog box

- Select desired group from the drop-down and click on the **OK** button.

Creating New Shared Parameter

- Click on the **New** button from the **Parameters** area of the dialog box. The **Parameter Properties** dialog box will be displayed as shown in Figure-29.

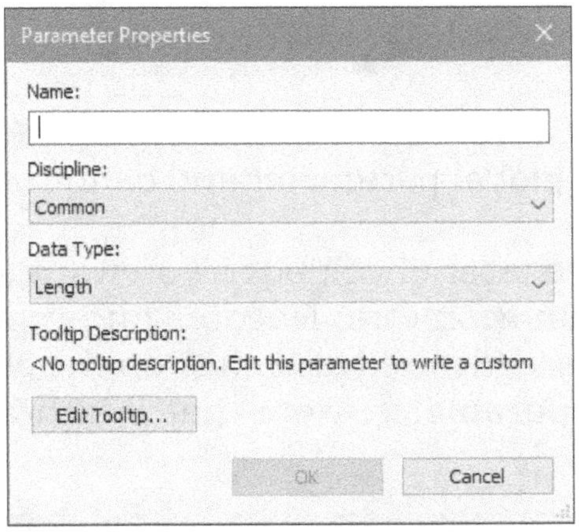

Figure-29. Parameter Properties dialog box

- Specify the name of new parameter in **Name** edit box.
- Select desired discipline and type of parameter from respective drop-downs in the dialog box.
- Click on the **Edit Tooltip** button and create desired tool tip.
- Click on the **OK** button from the dialog box. The new parameter will be created.

Similarly, you can create, rename, and delete parameter group by using the respective tools in the **Groups** area of the dialog box.

After setting desired parameters, click on the **OK** button from the **Edit Shared Parameters** dialog box.

CREATING GLOBAL PARAMETERS

The global parameters are used to define values of other parameters either by reporting or by modifying the values based on formulae. The procedure to create and manage global parameters is given next.

- Click on the **Global Parameters** tool from the **Settings** panel in the **Manage** tab of **Ribbon**. The **Global Parameters** dialog box will be displayed; refer to Figure-30.
- Click on the **New Global Parameter** button from the bottom in the dialog box. The **Global Parameter Properties** dialog box will be displayed as shown in Figure-31.

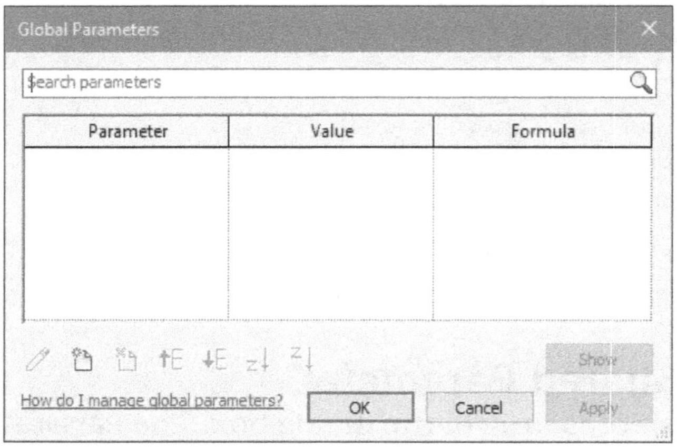

Figure-30. Global Parameters dialog box

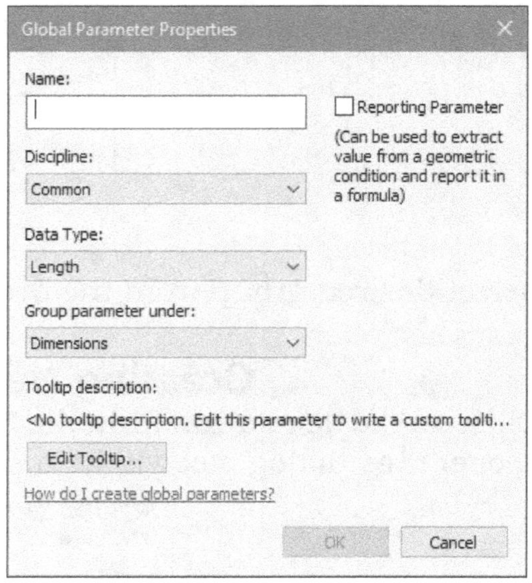

Figure-31. Global Parameter Properties dialog box

- Specify desired name for global parameter and define other properties as discussed earlier.
- Select the **Reporting Parameter** check box if you want to use this global parameter for extracting values from geometric features and report them in formulae.
- Set the other parameters as desired and click on the **OK** button. Refer to Figure-32 for example of a global parameter. Note that Width and Room width are report parameters.

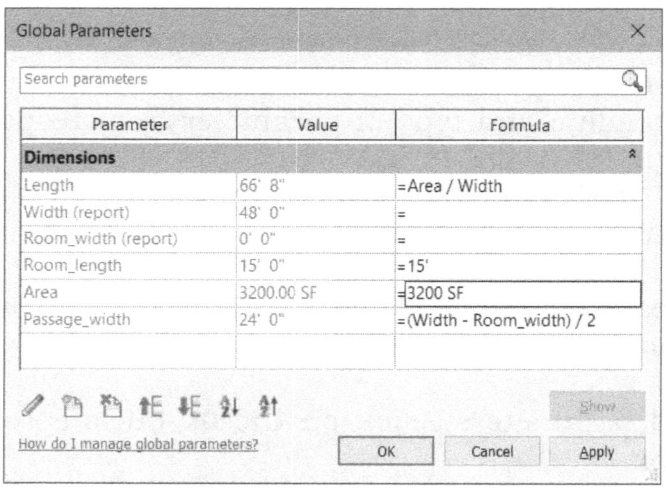

Figure-32. Global Parameters defined

- Click on the **OK** button from the dialog box to create the parameters.

Assigning Parameters

After creating global parameters, the next thing is to assign them to dimensions. Assume that we want to assign parameters to dimensions as shown in Figure-33.

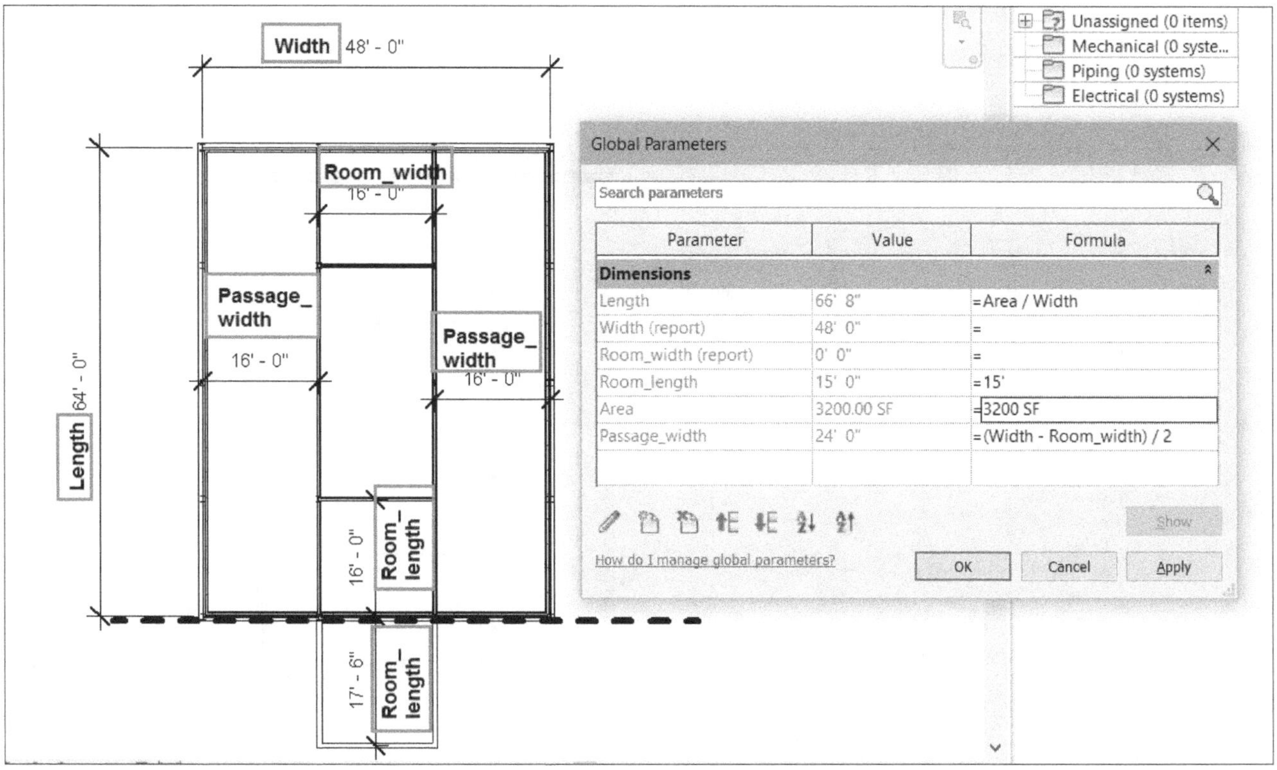

Figure-33. Assigning parameters

- To assign a global parameter, select desired dimension from the view. The **Modify|Dimensions** contextual tab will be displayed in the **Ribbon**.
- Select desired parameter for dimension from the **Label** drop-down; refer to Figure-34. The selected parameter will be assigned and all other global parameters that are using this parameter will be modified automatically.

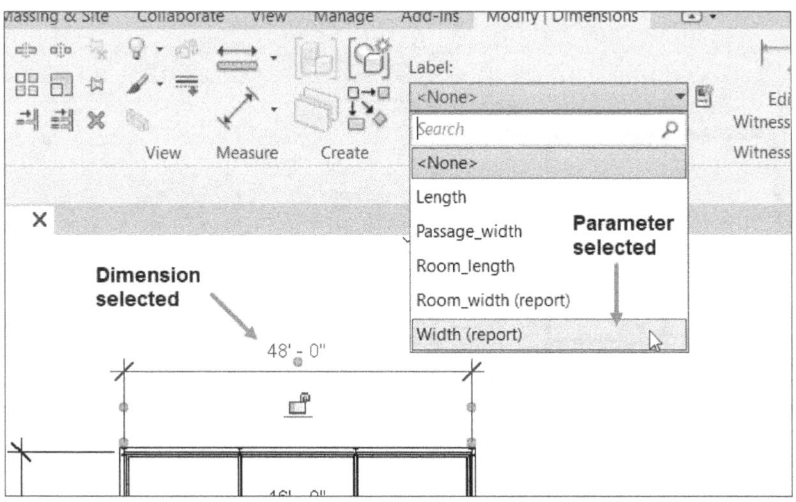

Figure-34. Assigning label

- You can assign the other parameters in the same way.
- To display label of dimension(s), select the dimension(s) and select the **Show Label in View** check box from the **Other** rollout of **Properties Palette**; refer to Figure-35.

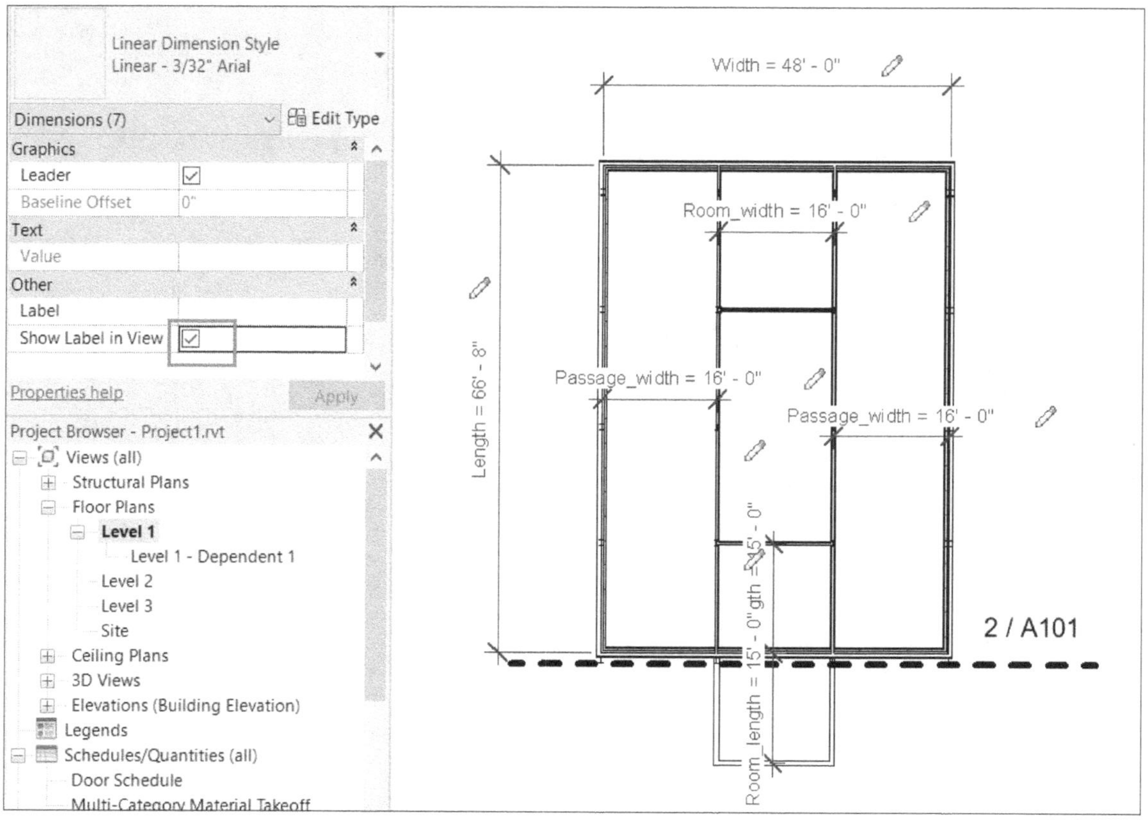

Figure-35. Displaying labels in views

After assigning labels, now you use the **Global Parameters** dialog box to modify the building. For example if you change the area to 3600 then Length parameter will automatically change to 75' in dialog box and if you click **Apply** button then the model will also change.

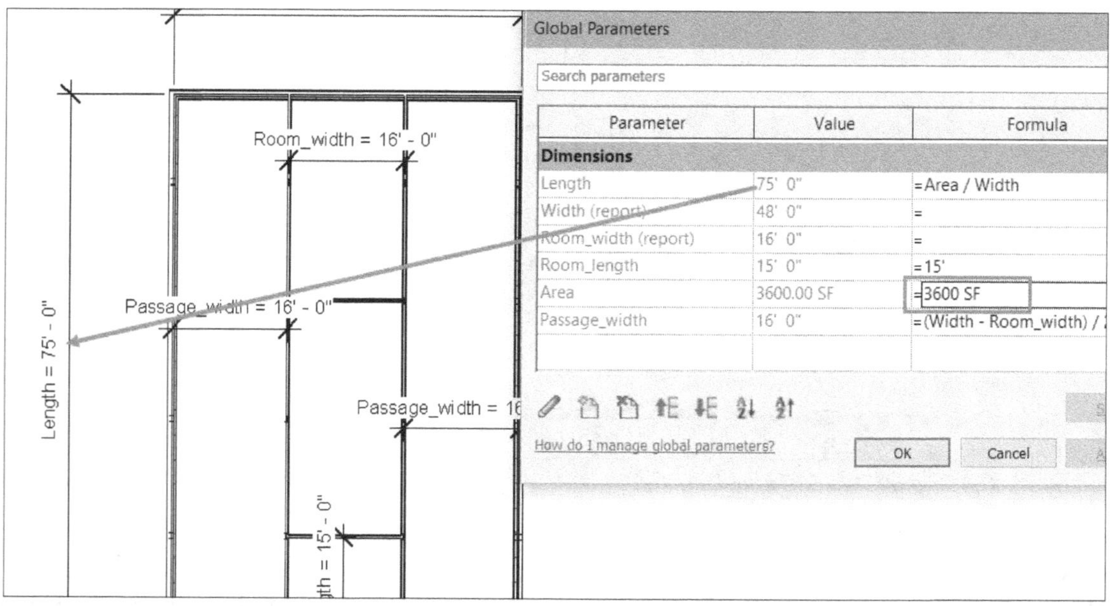

Figure-36. Changing global parameters

TRANSFERRING PROJECT STANDARDS

The **Transfer Project Standards** tool is used to transfer different styles, settings, and element types from one project to another. The procedure to use this tool is given next.

- Open the first project file from which you want to transfer the standards in Revit.
- Open the second project file in which you want to transfer the project standards.
- Click on the **Transfer Project Standards** tool from the **Settings** panel in the **Manage** tab of **Ribbon**. The **Select Items to Copy** dialog box will be displayed; refer to Figure-37.

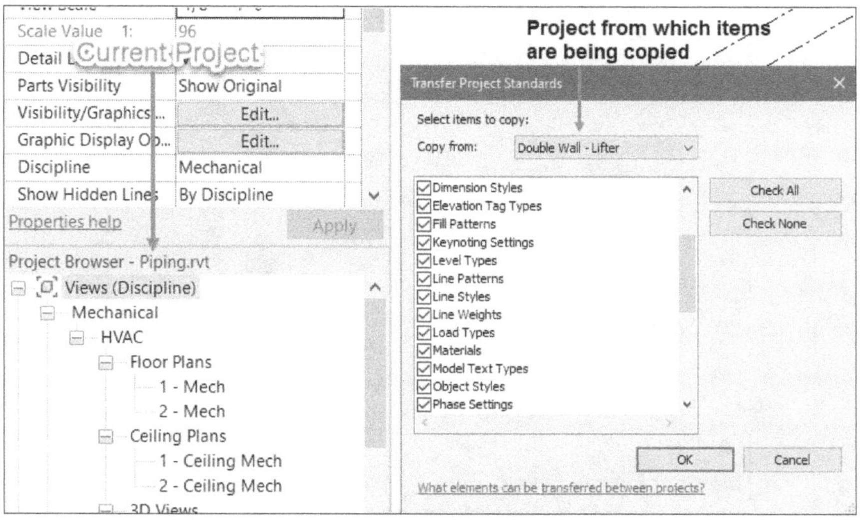

Figure-37. Transferring Project Standards

- Select check boxes for items to be copied in current project and then click on the **OK** button. If there are duplicates in the projects then the **Duplicate Types** dialog box will be displayed; refer to Figure-38.

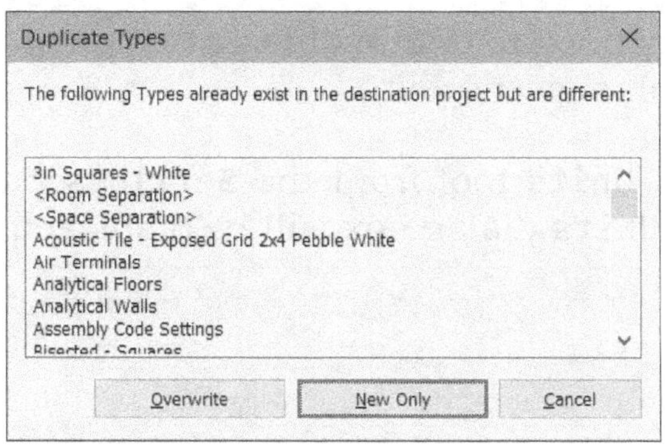

Figure-38. Duplicate Types dialog box

- Click on desired button. The software will transfer items accordingly.

PURGING UNUSED ITEMS

The **Purge Unused** tool is used to delete all the unused families and item types from the project. Using this tool helps reduce the size of project file. The procedure to use this tool is given next.

- Click on the **Purge Unused** tool from the **Settings** panel in the **Manage** tab of **Ribbon**. The **Purge Unused** dialog box will be displayed with list of all the elements that are not used in the project and not other element depend on them; refer to Figure-39.

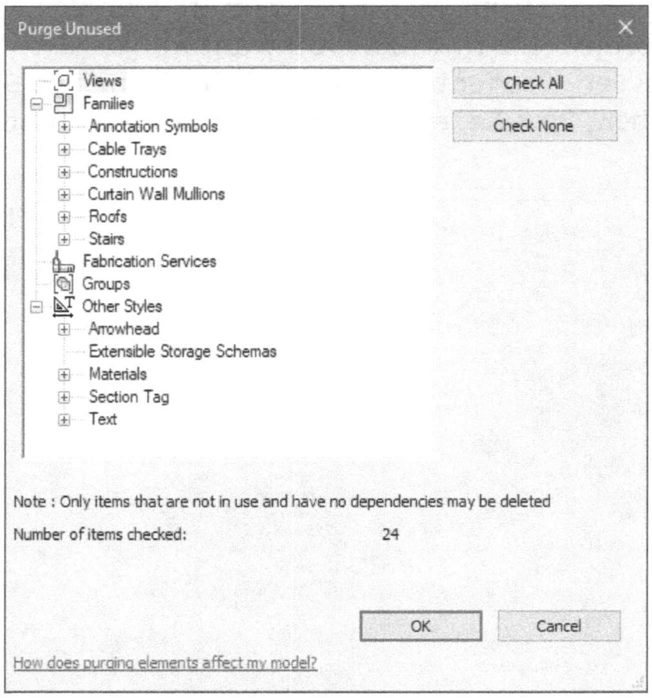

Figure-39. Purge Unused dialog box

- Click on the **OK** button from the dialog box to perform purging.

DEFINING PROJECT UNITS

The **Project Units** tool is used to define different types of units for the project. The procedure to use this tool is given next.

- Click on the **Project Units** tool from the **Settings** panel in the **Manage** tab of **Ribbon**. The **Project Units** dialog box will be displayed; refer to Figure-40.

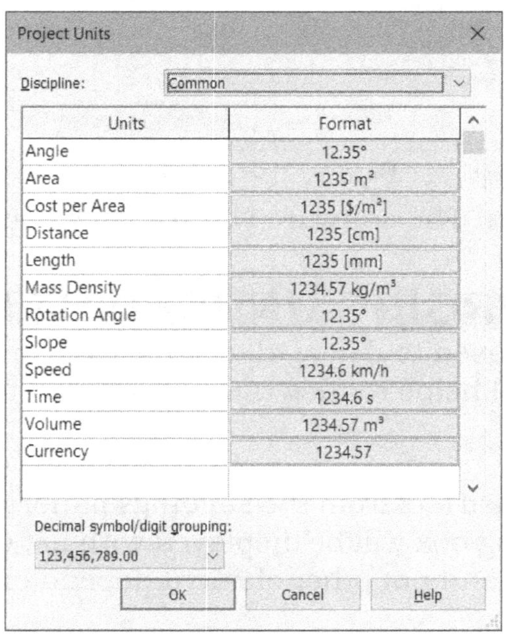

Figure-40. Project Units dialog box

- Click on the button next to the unit to be modified. The **Format** dialog box will be displayed with respective options; refer to Figure-41.

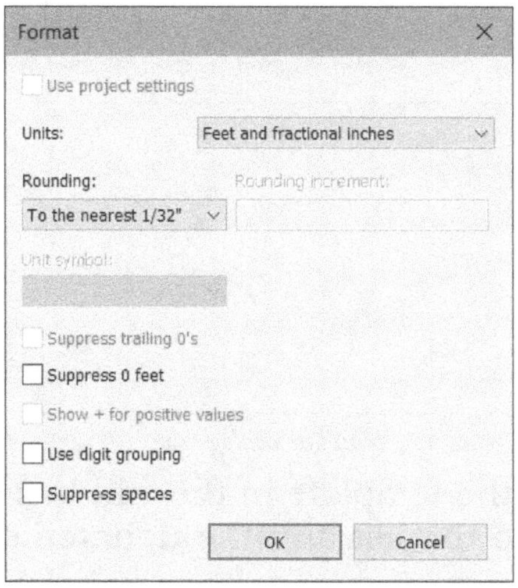

Figure-41. Format dialog box

- Select desired unit from the **Units** drop-down and set the other parameters as desired.
- Click on the **OK** button from the dialog box to define formatting for unit. The **Project Units** dialog box will be displayed again.
- Select desired option from the **Decimal symbol/digit grouping** drop-down to define how decimal and digit grouping will be used in units.
- Click on the **OK** button from the **Project Units** dialog box.

NUMBERING

The **Numbering** tool is used to create, edit, or apply a numbering template to the project. The procedure to use this tool is discussed next.

- Click on the **Numbering** tool from the **Settings** panel in the **Manage** tab of **Ribbon**. The **Numbering Options** dialog box will be displayed; refer to Figure-42.

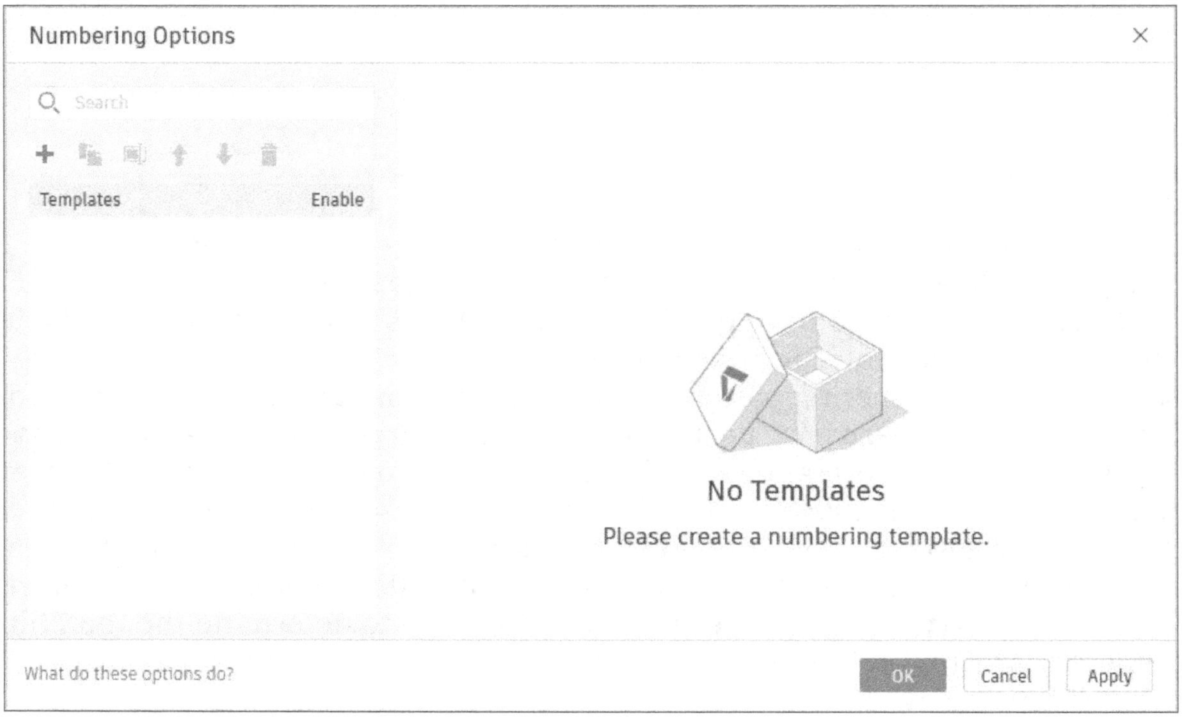

Figure-42. Numbering Options dialog box

- Click on the **Add** button, the **Create new template** dialog box will be displayed; refer to Figure-43.

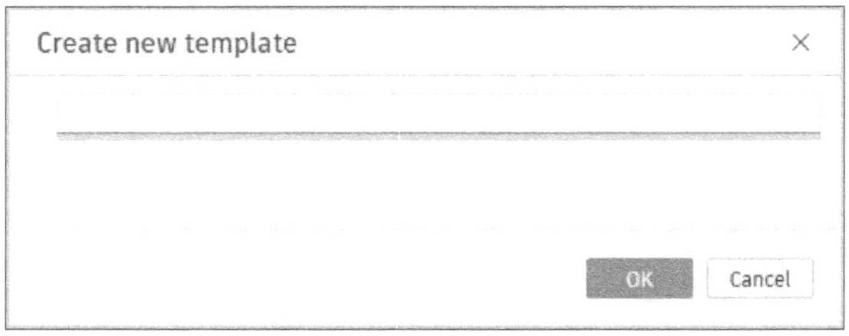

Figure-43. Create new template dialog box

- Specify desired name of the template in the edit box and click on **OK** button. The template will be added to the list and the updated dialog box will be displayed; refer to Figure-44.

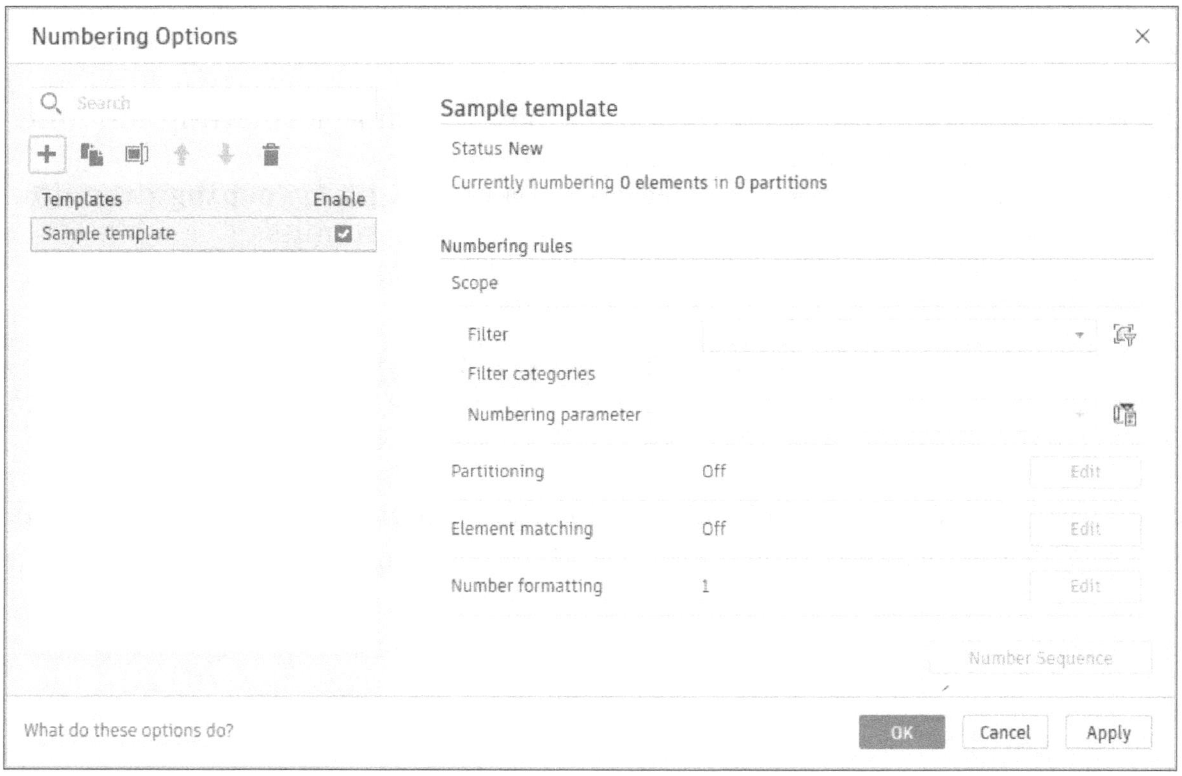

Figure-44. Updated dialog box

- Select desired filter for the project from **Filter** drop-down of **Scope** area, the filter categories will be displayed in the **Filter categories** area. Alternatively, click on the **Filters** button to apply filters, the **Filters** dialog box will be displayed which is discussed later in this chapter.
- Select desired numbering parameter to be used from **Numbering parameter** drop-down. Click on the **Project parameters** button from the **Numbering parameter** area to reschedule, sort, and filter elements in the project, the **Project Parameters** dialog box will be displayed which has been discussed earlier in this chapter.
- Click on the **Edit** button of **Partitioning** area to separate elements into the assigned numbering partitions, the **Partitioning** dialog box will be displayed.
- Click on the **Edit** button of **Element matching** area to determine the matching of elements for numbering based on their geometry, the **Element matching** dialog box will be displayed.

- Click on the **Edit** button of **Number formatting** area to specify how numbering values are formatted for elements assigned by the numbering template, the **Number formatting** dialog box will be displayed.
- After specifying desired parameters of template, click on **Apply** button to create the template.
- Click on the **Duplicate** button, the **Rename duplicated template** dialog box will be displayed to specify the name of duplicated template.
- Click on the **Rename** button, the **Rename** dialog box will be displayed to rename the original created template.
- Click on the **Move up** or **Move down** button to adjust the priority of template for numbering.
- Click on the **Delete** button to delete the selected template.
- After specifying desired parameters, click on **OK** button to close the dialog box. The numbering template will be applied to the project; refer to Figure-45.

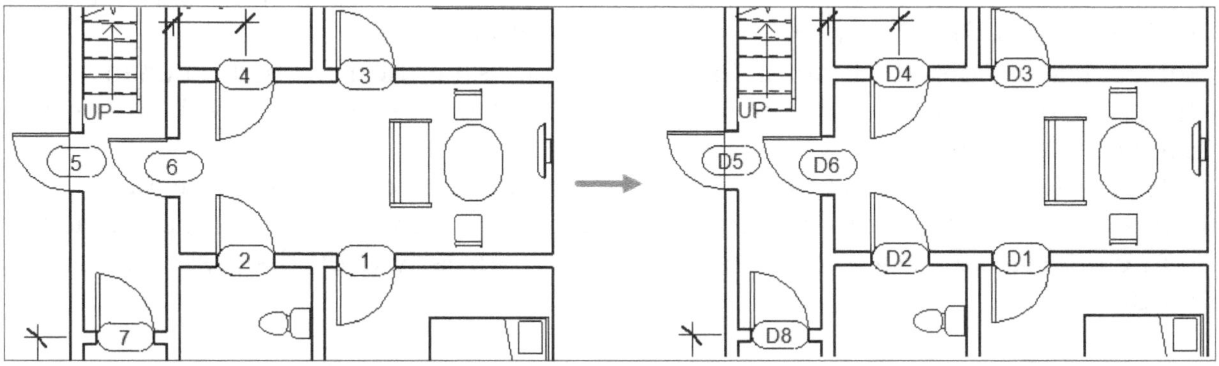

Figure-45. Numbering template applied

SETTINGS

The tools for defining settings of different systems of project are available at the right in **Settings** panel; refer to Figure-46. Some of the setting tools like **Structural Settings**, **Connection Settings**, **Mechanical Settings**, **Electrical Settings**, **Fabrication Settings**, and so on have been discussed later in their respective chapters. The rest of the tools in this panel are discussed next.

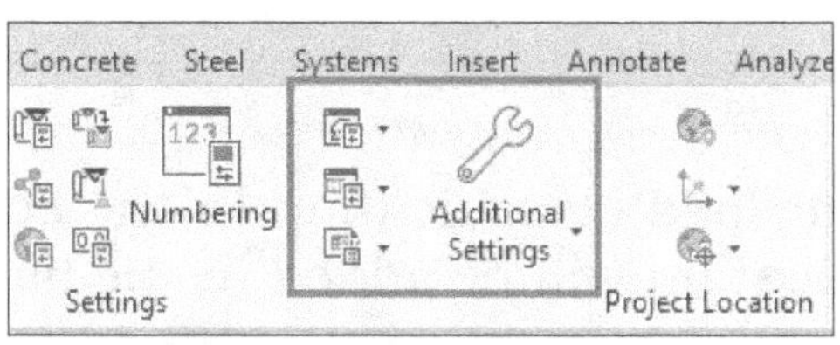

Figure-46. Tools for defining settings

LOAD CLASSIFICATION SETTINGS

The **Load Classifications** tool is used to define classifications for different types of loads. The classifications also reflect in schedules and help identify the sources for different types of electrical loads in the Project. The procedure to define load classification settings is given next.

- Click on the **Load Classifications** tool from the **MEP Settings** drop-down in the **Settings** panel of the **Manage** tab in the **Ribbon**. The **Load Classifications** dialog box will be displayed; refer to Figure-47.

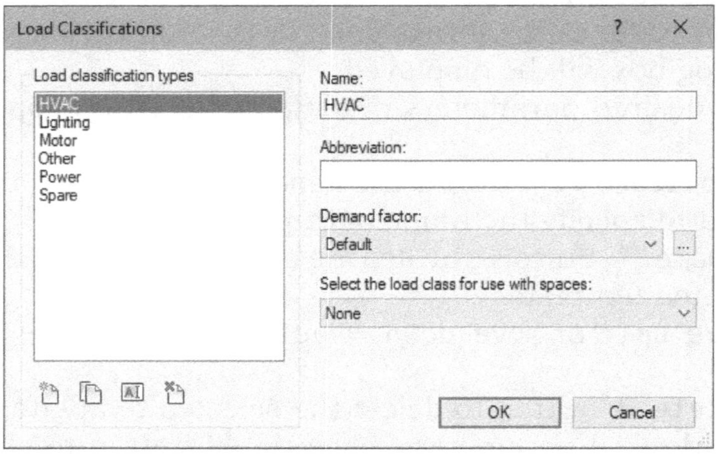

Figure-47. Load Classifications dialog box

- Select desired option from the **Load classification types** list box. The related options will be displayed in the right of the dialog box.
- Select desired demand factor for selected classification from the **Demand factor** drop-down. The procedure to create and edit demand factor will be discussed later in this chapter.
- Select desired load class from the **Select the load class for use with spaces** drop-down at the bottom in the dialog box. There are mainly two types of electrical load classes; Lighting and Power which have already been discussed in previous chapters.

Creating New Load Classification

- Click on the **New** button from the bottom in the **Load Classifications** dialog box. The **Name** dialog box will be displayed as shown in Figure-48.

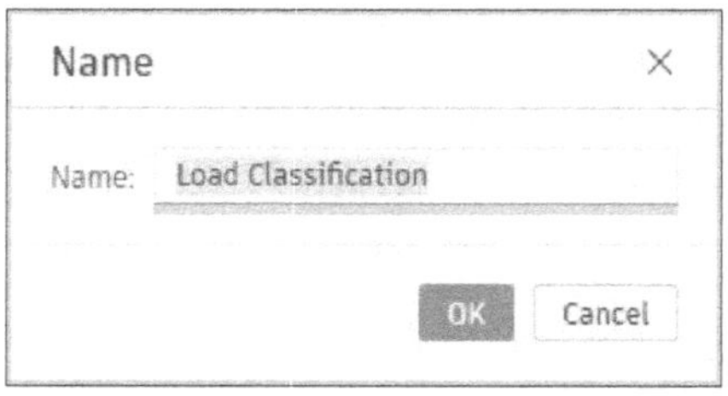

Figure-48. Name dialog box

- Specify desired name for load classification in the edit box and click on the **OK** button. The new classification will be added in the list box; refer to Figure-49.

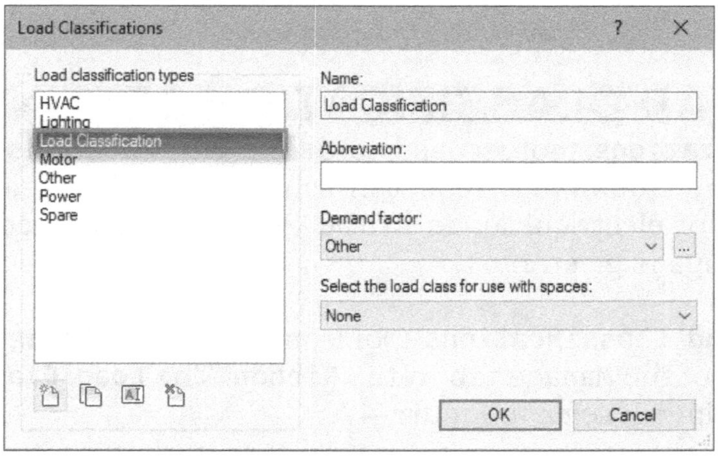

Figure-49. New classification type added

- Set desired parameters in drop-downs on the right in the dialog box and click on the **OK** button to define classification settings.

Similarly, you can duplicate, rename, or delete the classification by using the respective tool at the bottom in the **Load Classifications** dialog box.

Demand Factors Settings

The demand factor is used to define actual load consumption by objects based on their total load capacity. For example, there are 10 bulbs of 100W connected to a circuit and the load factor is 75% then net load of ten bulbs will be 750W (75% of 10x100W). The procedure to define load factor for different objects is discussed next.

- Click on the **Demand Factors** tool from the **MEP Settings** drop-down in the **Settings** panel of **Manage** tab in the **Ribbon**. The **Demand Factors** dialog box will be displayed as shown in Figure-50.
- Select desired factor type from the **Demand factor types** list box on the left in the dialog box. The related parameters will be displayed on the right.

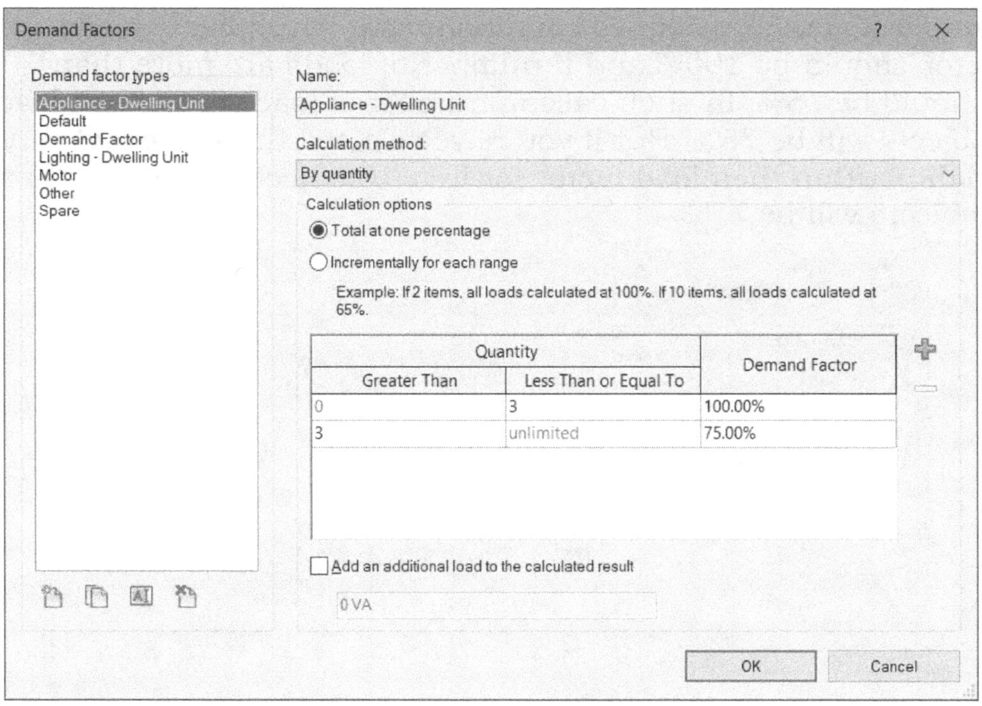

Figure-50. Demand Factors dialog box

Constant Demand Factor

- Select desired calculation method for demand factor from the **Calculation method** drop-down. Select the **Constant** option if you want to define a fixed value of demand factor. The options in dialog box will be displayed as shown in Figure-51. Specify desired value of demand factor in respective edit box.

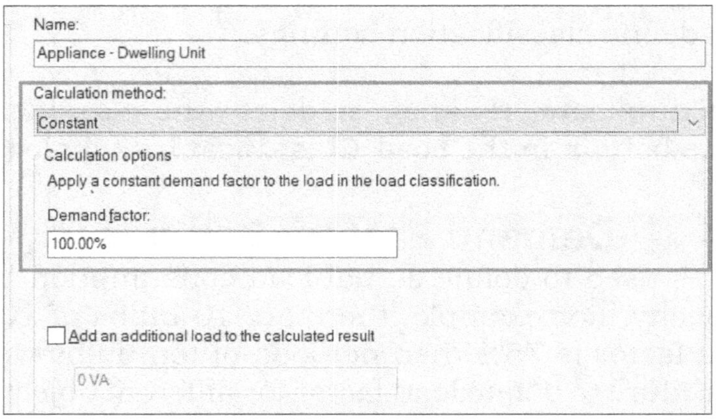

Figure-51. Constant calculation method

Demand Factor By Quantity

- Select the **By quantity** option if you want to vary the value of demand factor based on number of loads connected to circuit. The options in the dialog box will be displayed as shown in Figure-52. Select the **Total at one percentage** radio button if you want to define a fixed value for all the objects based on their quantity. For example, if you have defined conditions that if number of loads are 0-10 then load factor should be 100% and if number of loads are more than 10 then load factor should be 75%. In such case, if number of loads is 11 then load factor for all 11 objects will be 75%. But if you have selected the **Incrementally for each range** radio button then load factor for first 10 objects will be 100% and for the rest of objects will be 75%.

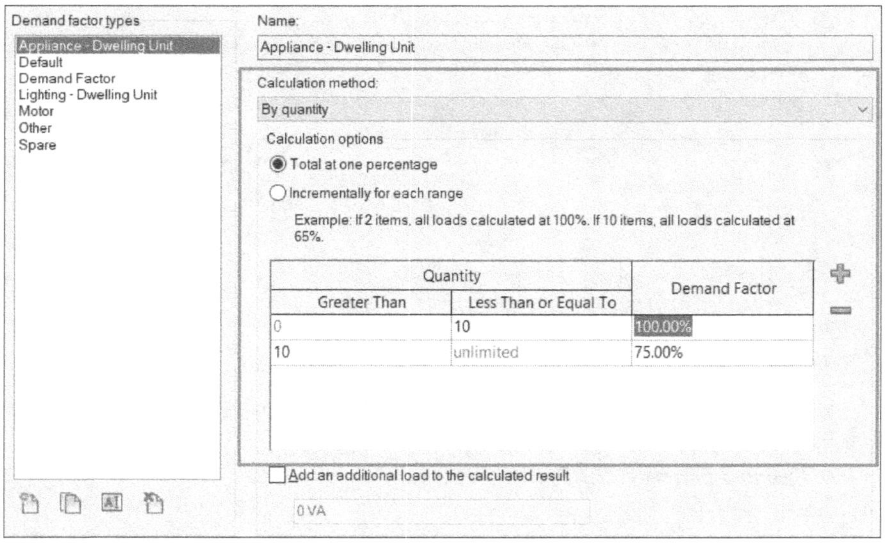

Figure-52. By quantity calculation method

- Click on the **+** button next to the table to create a new range and specify desired quantity & demand factor.
- To delete a load range, select the related field and then click on the **-** button.

Demand Factor By Load

- Select the **By load** option from the **Calculation method** drop-down if you want to define demand factor for objects based on their load value. The options in the dialog box will be displayed as shown in Figure-53.

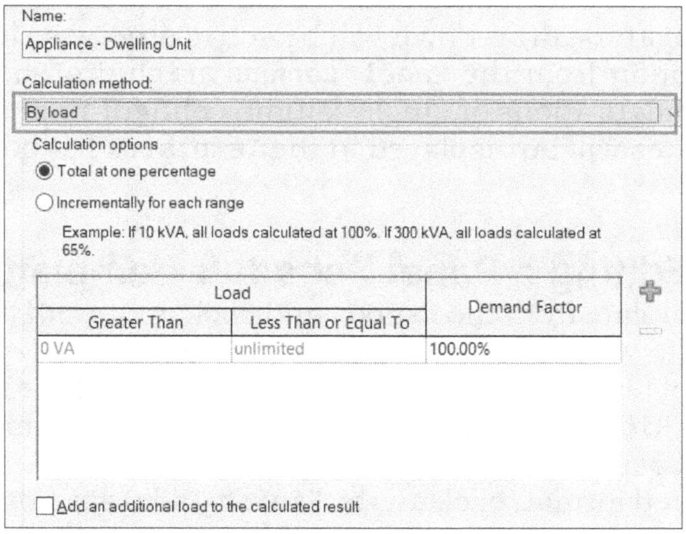

Figure-53. By load calculation method

- Set desired parameters as discussed for **By quantity** option.
- Select the **Add an additional load to the calculated result** check box if you want to add additional load of specified value to the calculated load result.
- Set the other parameters as discussed earlier and click on the **OK** button. Click on the **Load Classifications** dialog box to exit.

MANAGING PANEL SCHEDULE TEMPLATES

The **Manage Templates** tool is used to manage different types of panel schedule templates. The procedure to use this tool is given next.

- Click on the **Manage Templates** tool from the **Panel Schedule Templates** drop-down in the **Settings** panel of **Manage** tab in the **Ribbon**. The **Manage Panel Schedule Templates** dialog box will be displayed; refer to Figure-54.

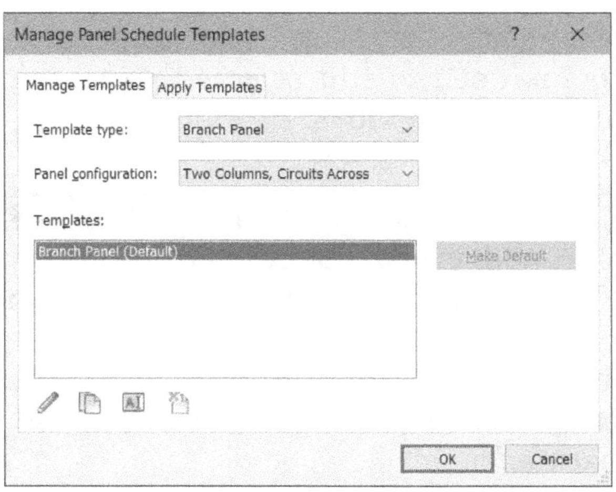

Figure-54. Manage Panel Schedule Templates dialog box

- Select desired option from the **Template type** drop-down to define what type of template you want to manage.

- If you have selected **Branch Panel** option from the **Template type** drop-down then the **Panel configuration** drop-down will be active otherwise it will be deactivated. Select desired option from the **Panel configuration** drop-down. You can select Two Columns configurations or single column configuration from the drop-down. The list of templates will be displayed in the **Templates** list box based on specified parameters.

Editing a Panel Schedule Template

- Select desired template from the list box and click on the **Edit** button. The options to modify template will be displayed; refer to Figure-55.
- Modify the table of template by using the tools in **Modify Panel Schedule Template** contextual tab of **Ribbon**. Tools in the contextual tab are same as generally found in common database management software.
- After setting desired format, click on the **Finish Template** button from the **Ribbon**. The template will be updated automatically.

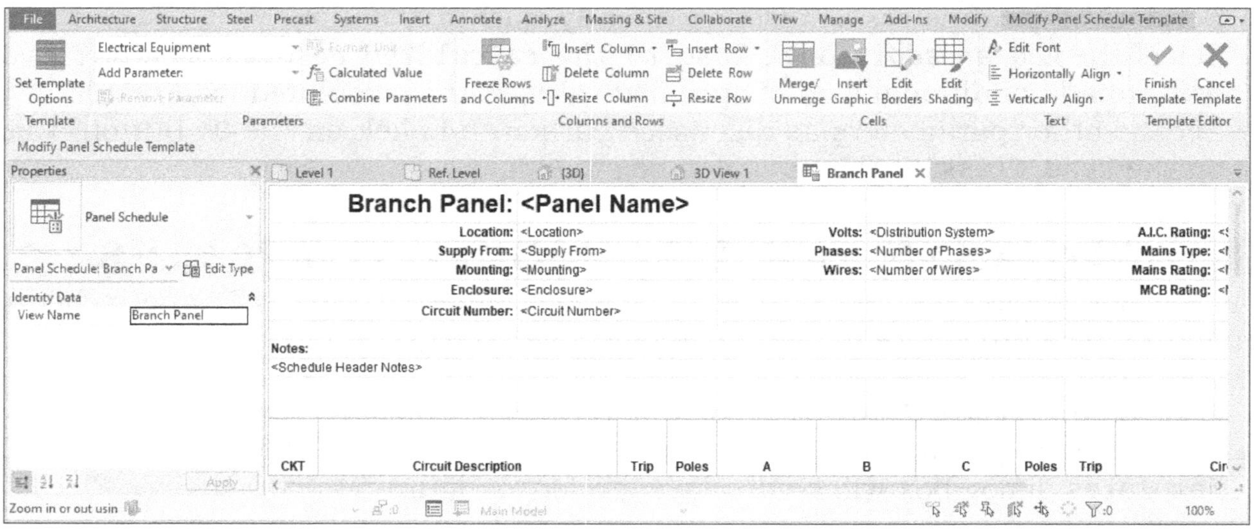

Figure-55. Modify Panel Schedule Template contextual tab

The **Edit a Template** tool is used to edit selected panel template and works in the same way as editing panel schedule does.

EDITING FILL PATTERN

The **Fill Patterns** tool in **Additional Settings** drop-down is used to modify and create fill patterns. The procedure to use this tool is given next.

- Click on the **Fill Patterns** tool from the **Additional Settings** drop-down in the **Settings** panel of **Manage** tab in the **Ribbon**. The **Fill Patterns** dialog box will be displayed; refer to Figure-56.
- Select desired radio button from the **Pattern Type** area of the dialog box to display the relative types of patterns.
- Select desired pattern from the list which you want to edit and click on the **Edit fill pattern** button at the bottom in the dialog box. The **Edit Pattern Properties** dialog box will be displayed; refer to Figure-57.

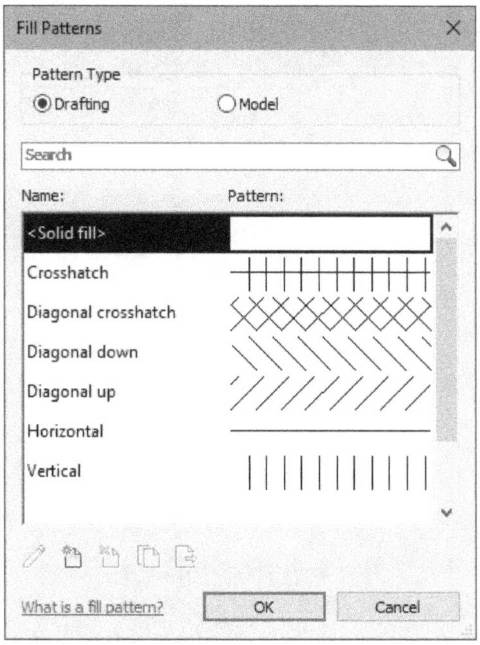

Figure-56. Fill Patterns dialog box

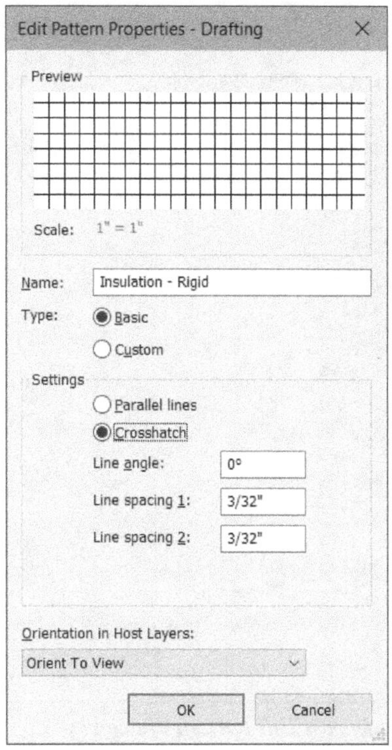

Figure-57. Edit Pattern Properties dialog box

- Specify desired name of pattern in the **Name** edit box.
- Select the **Basic** radio button from the **Type** section if you want to create fill pattern using lines only. On selecting this radio button, the options to define orientation, angle, and spacing between two lines will be displayed. Set desired parameters and check the preview in **Preview** area at the top in the dialog box.
- Select the **Custom** radio button to define custom settings for fill pattern. The dialog box will be displayed as shown in Figure-58.

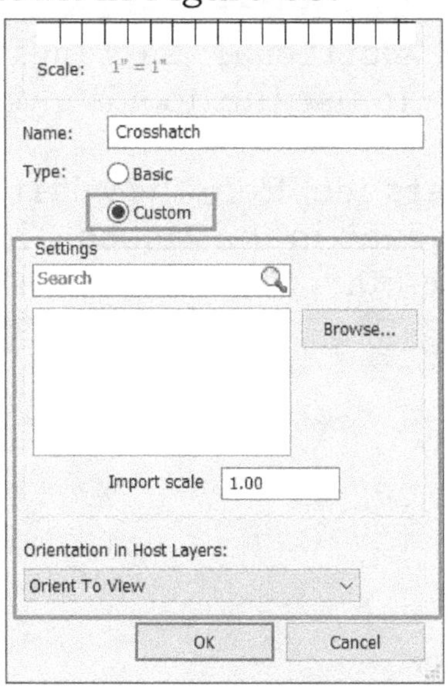

Figure-58. Options for custom type fill patterns

- Click on the **Browse** button from the dialog box to load custom pattern. The **Import Fill Pattern** dialog box will be displayed; refer to Figure-59.

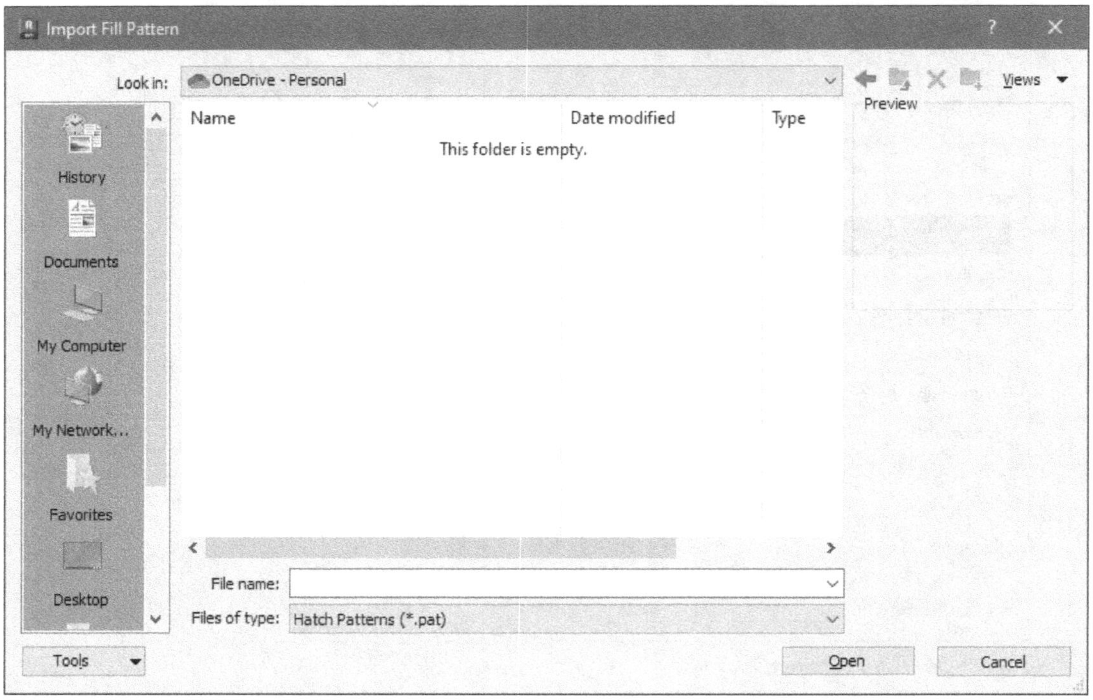

Figure-59. Import Fill Pattern dialog box

- Select desired pattern file in the dialog box and click on the **Open** button. The list of patterns will be displayed in the **Settings** area of the dialog box.
- Set the other parameters as desired and click on the **OK** button to modify pattern.

Similarly, you can use the **New fill pattern**, **Delete fill pattern**, and **Duplicate fill pattern** tools of this dialog box.

MODIFYING MATERIAL ASSETS

The **Material Assets** tool in **Additional Settings** drop-down is used to define material assets. The procedure to use this tool is given next.

- Click on the **Material Assets** tool from the **Additional Settings** drop-down in the **Settings** panel of **Manage** tab in the **Ribbon**. The **Asset Editor** dialog box will be displayed; refer to Figure-60.

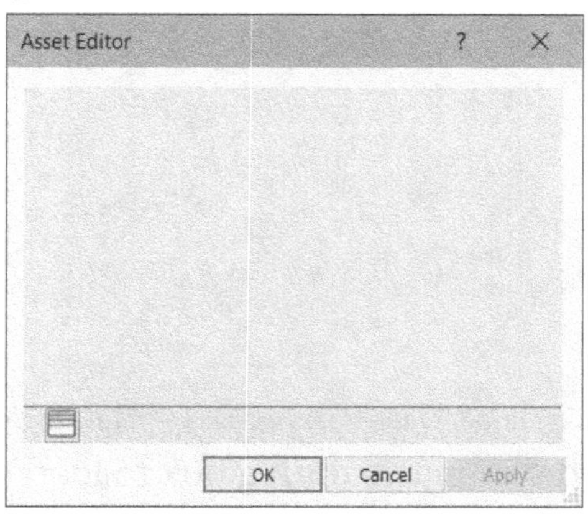

Figure-60. Asset Editor dialog box

- Click on the **Asset Browser** button at the bottom in the dialog box. The **Asset Browser** will be displayed as shown in Figure-61.

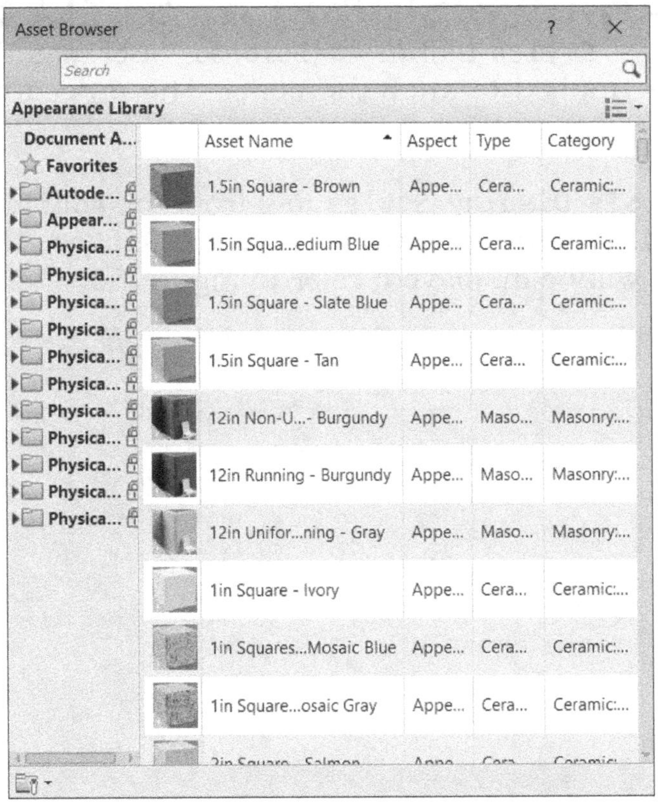

Figure-61. Asset Browser

- Double-click on desired material. The related options will be displayed in the **Asset Editor**; refer to Figure-62.

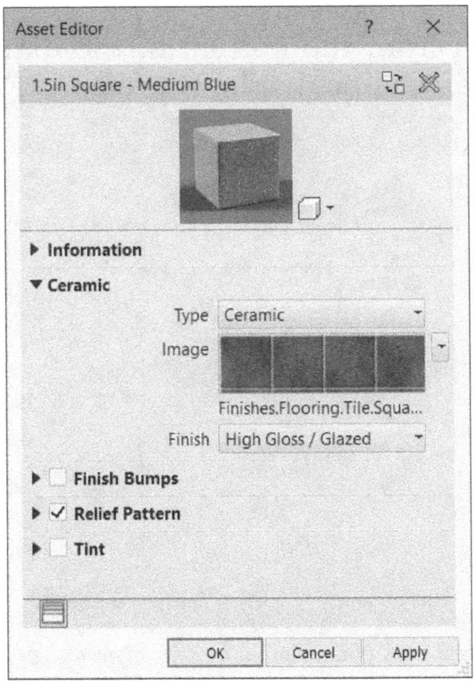

Figure-62. Asset Editor dialog box

- Modify the parameters in various rollouts as desired and click on the **OK** button. The selected material will be modified accordingly.

ANALYSIS DISPLAY STYLES

The **Analysis Display Styles** tool in **Additional Settings** drop-down is used to modify display styles applied to analysis model. The procedure to use this tool is given next.

- Click on the **Analysis Display Styles** tool from the **Additional Settings** drop-down in the **Settings** panel of **Manage** tab in the **Ribbon**. The **Analysis Display Styles** dialog box will be displayed; refer to Figure-63.

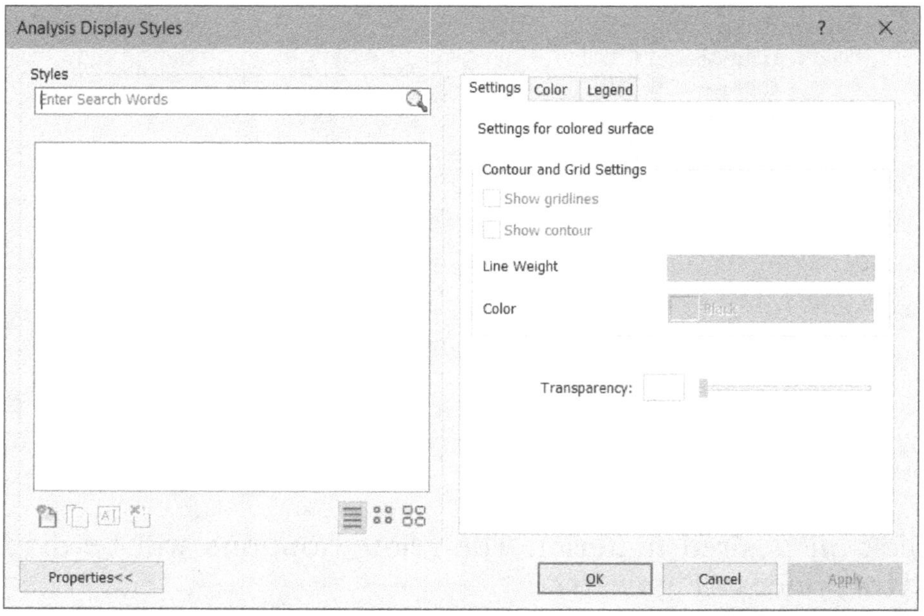

Figure-63. Analysis Display Styles dialog box

- Click on the **New** button from the bottom of the dialog box. The **New Analysis Display Style** dialog box will be displayed; refer to Figure-64.

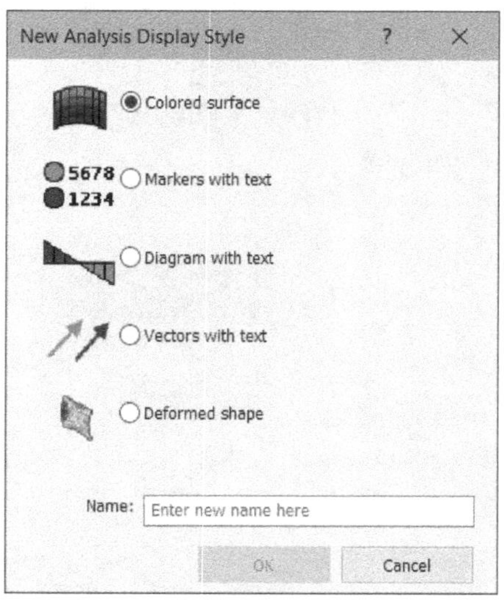

Figure-64. New Analysis Display Style dialog box

- Select desired radio button and specify name for style in the edit box.
- Click on the **OK** button from the dialog box. The new style will be added in the left area of the dialog box and related options will be displayed; refer to Figure-65 (for Surface display style).

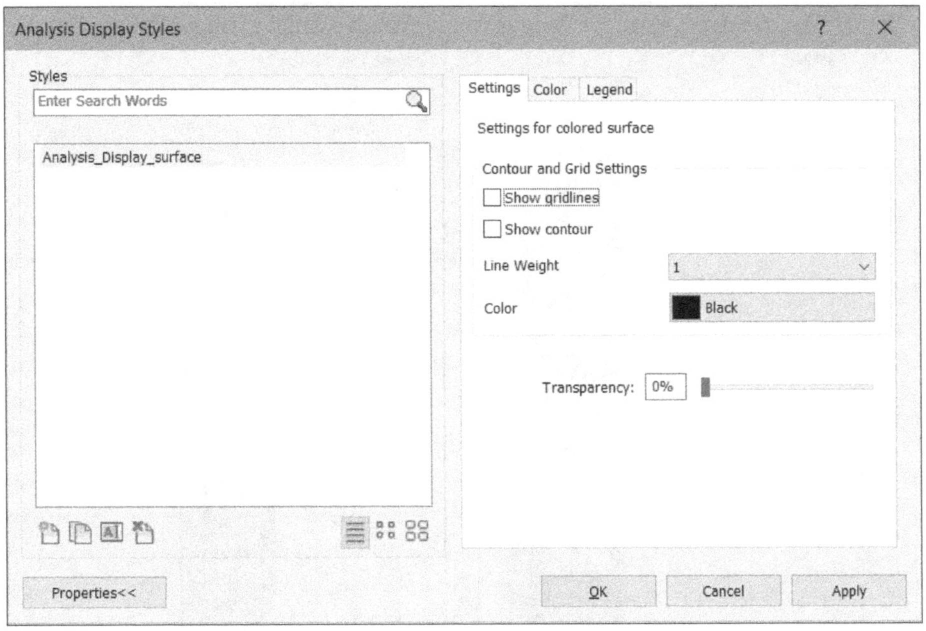

Figure-65. Display style added in the list

- Set desired contour and grid parameters in the **Settings** tab. If you have created a marker with text style, diagram with text style, or vector with text style then options in **Settings** tab will be displayed as shown in Figure-66.

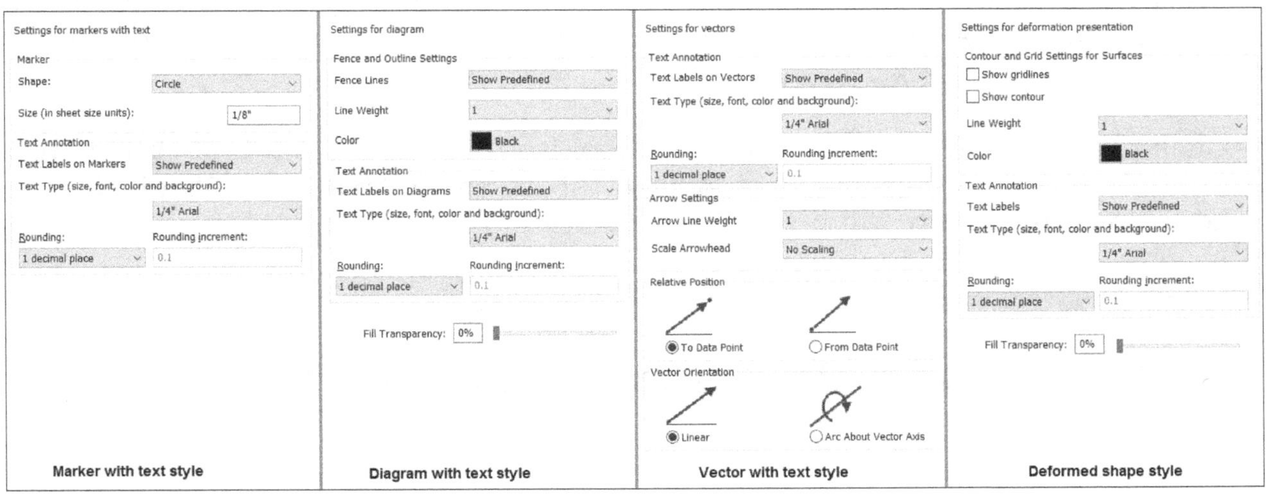

Figure-66. Settings tab for different styles

- Click on the **Color** tab to modify color of analysis display graphics; refer to Figure-67. Set desired color method by using **Gradient** or **Ranges** radio button.
- Click on the **Legend** tab to modify the legend displayed in analysis model. The options will be displayed as shown in Figure-68.
- Set desired parameters in this tab and click on the **Apply** button to apply modifications.
- You can duplicate, rename, or delete selected style by using respective button from the bottom in the dialog box.
- Click on the **OK** button from the dialog box to apply the settings.

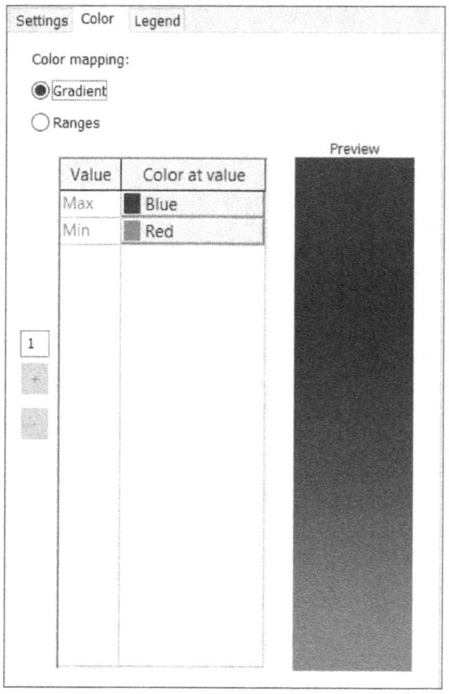

Figure-67. Color tab

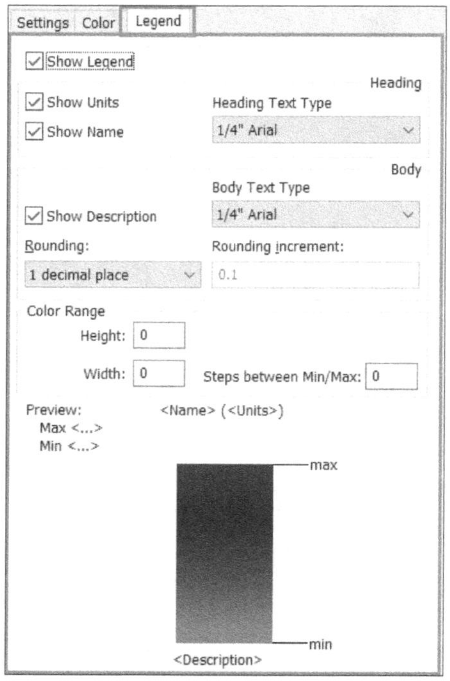

Figure-68. Legend tab

MANAGING SHEET ISSUES/REVISIONS

The **Sheet Issues/Revisions** tool is used to manage sheet issue numbers and revision numbers. You can also use this tool to control visibility of tags. The procedure to use this tool is given next.

- Click on the **Sheet Issues/Revisions** tool from the **Additional Settings** drop-down in the **Settings** panel of **Manage** tab in the **Ribbon**. The **Sheet Issues/Revisions** dialog box will be displayed; refer to Figure-69.

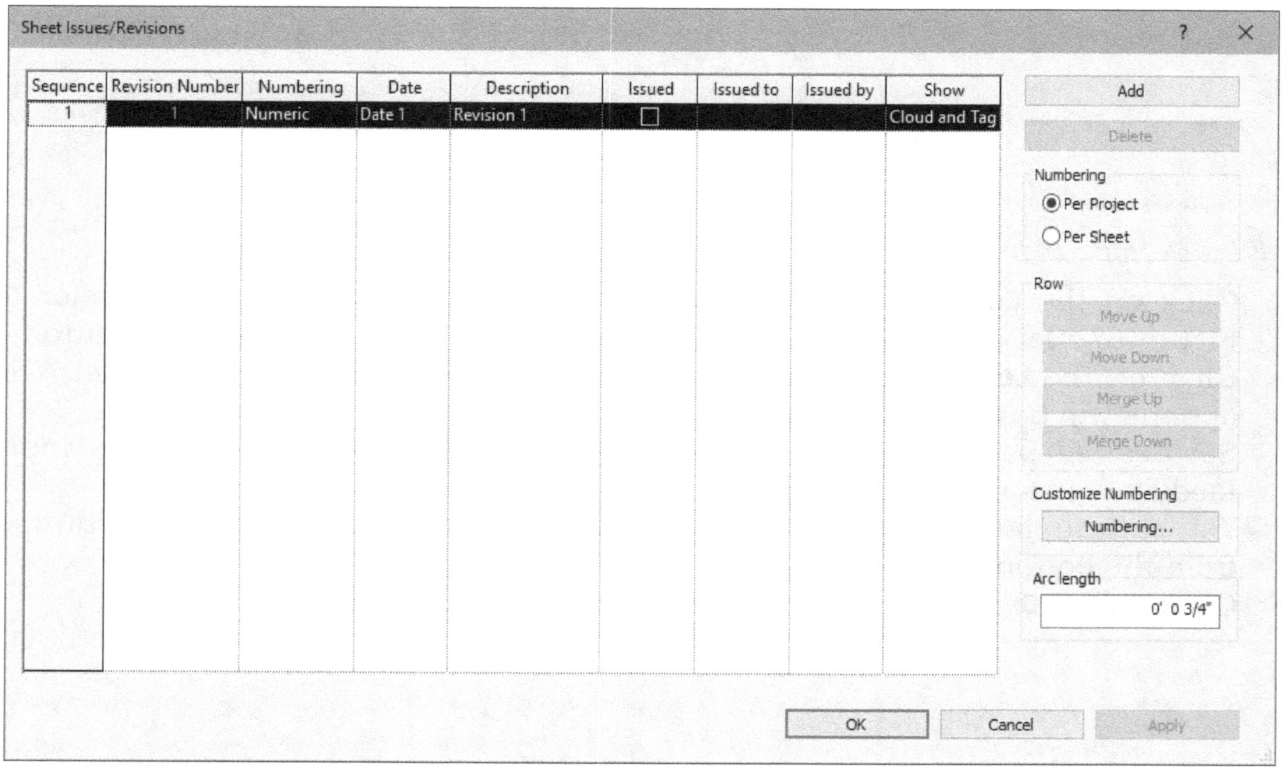

Figure-69. Sheet Issues Revisions dialog box

- Click in different fields of the table to modify the values.
- If you want to add a new revision then click on the **Add** button from the dialog box.
- You can set the revision numbering based on per sheet or per project by selecting respective radio button from **Numbering** area of the dialog box.
- Set the other parameters like numbering options, row position & merging by using respective button from the dialog box.
- Specify desired size of minimum arc length used for creating revision cloud in the **Arc length** edit box.
- Click on the **OK** button from the dialog box to apply settings.

MODIFYING LINE STYLES

The **Line Styles** tool in **Advanced Settings** drop-down is used to modify the properties of various line styles used in project. The procedure to use this tool is given next.

- Click on the **Line Styles** tool from the **Additional Settings** drop-down in the **Settings** panel of the **Manage** tab in the **Ribbon**. The **Line Styles** dialog box will be displayed; refer to Figure-70.

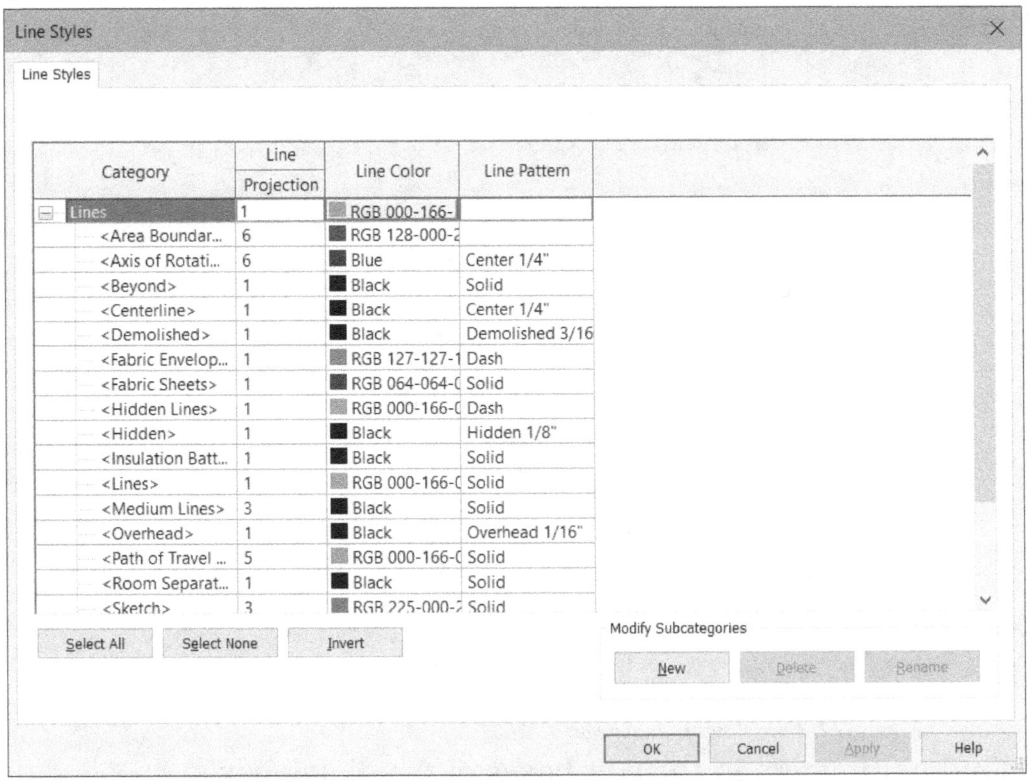

Figure-70. Line Styles dialog box

- Set desired color and other parameters for various lines in the line category.
- If you want to add a new sub-category of line then click on the **New** button from the **Modify Subcategories** area of the dialog box. The **New Subcategory** dialog box will be displayed; refer to Figure-71.

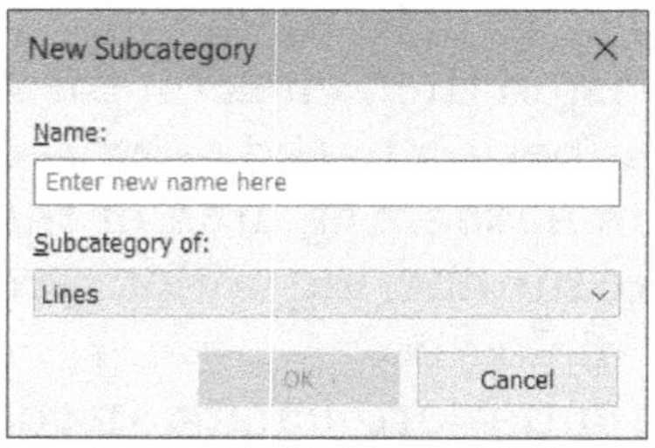

Figure-71. New Subcategory dialog box

- Set desired name of line subcategory in the **Name** edit box and click on the **OK** button.
- After setting desired parameters, click on the **OK** button.

SETTING LINE WEIGHT

The **Line Weights** tool in the **Additional Settings** drop-down is used to set thickness of lines for different annotation scales. The procedure to use this tool is given next.

- Click on the **Line Weights** tool from the **Additional Settings** drop-down in the **Manage** tab of **Ribbon**. The **Line Weights** dialog box will be displayed; refer to Figure-72.

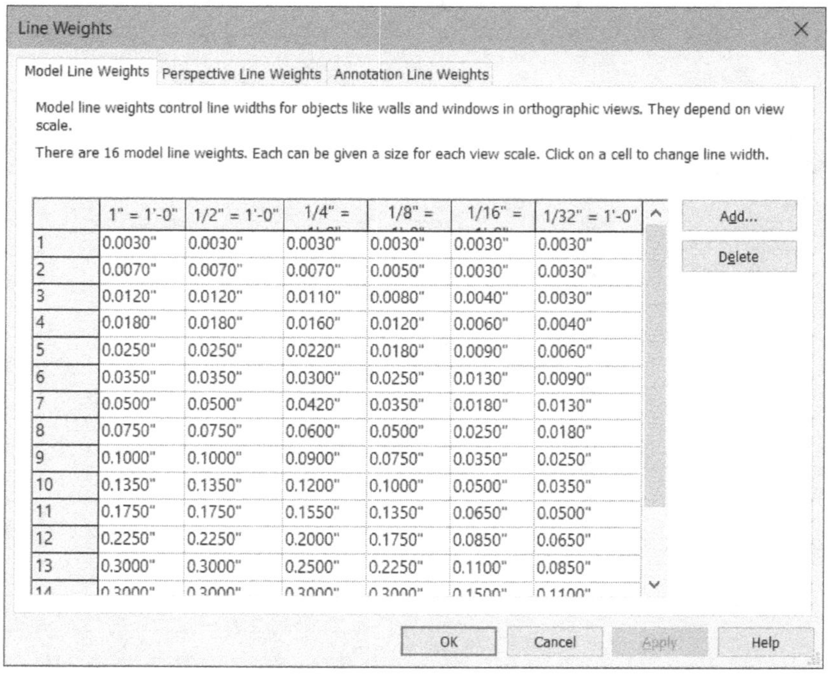

Figure-72. Line Weights dialog box

- Set desired parameters in the edit boxes of the dialog box.
- If you want to add a new scale then click on the **Add** button. The **Add Scale** dialog box will be displayed; refer to Figure-73.

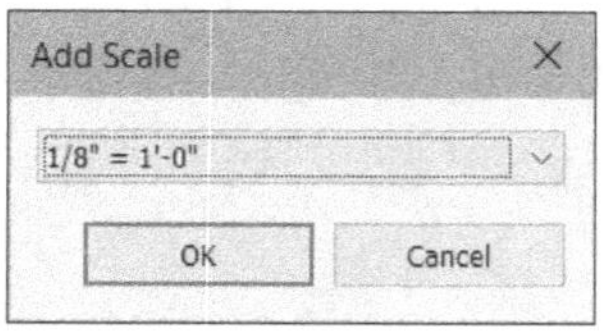

Figure-73. Add Scale dialog box

- Set desired parameters in the dialog box and click on the **OK** button.
- Similarly, you can set parameters for the **Perspective Line Weights** and **Annotation Line Weights** in their respective tabs of the dialog box.

- After setting desired parameters, click on the **OK** button from the **Line Weights** dialog box.

SETTING LINE PATTERNS

The **Line Patterns** tool is used to set line patterns for different line styles. The procedure to use this tool is given next.

- Click on the **Line Patterns** tool from the **Additional Settings** drop-down of the **Manage** tab in the **Ribbon**. The **Line Patterns** dialog box will be displayed; refer to Figure-74.

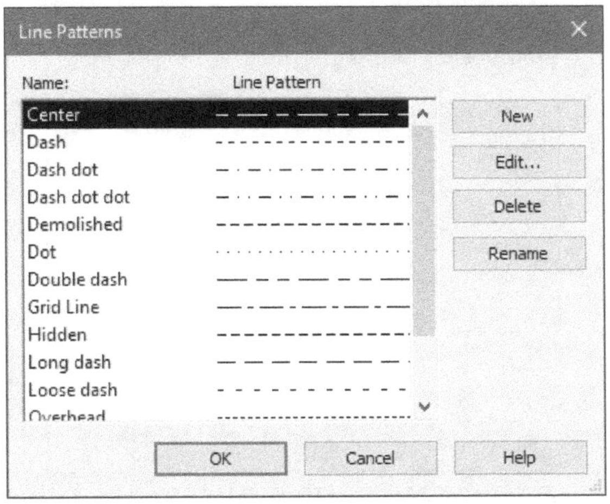

Figure-74. Line Patterns dialog box

- Double-click to change the line pattern. The **Line Pattern Properties** dialog box will be displayed; refer to Figure-75.

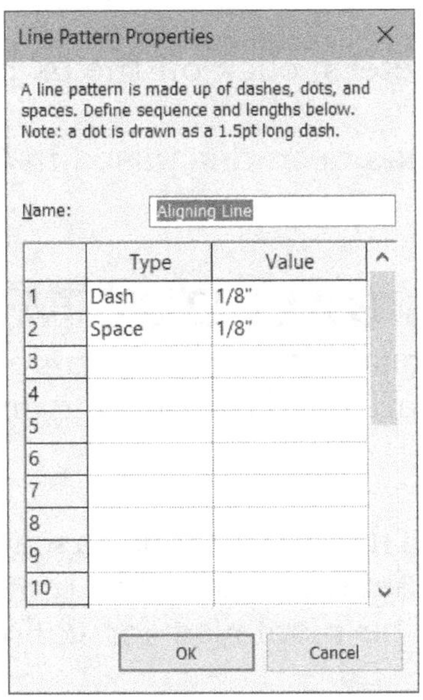

Figure-75. Line Pattern Properties dialog box

- Click in the field of **Type** column and select desired option. Click in the fields of **Value** column and set desired values.
- Click on the **OK** button from the **Line Pattern Properties** dialog box to apply parameters.
- You can use the other options in the dialog box as discussed earlier. Click on the **OK** button from the **Line Patterns** dialog box.

SETTING PARAMETERS FOR HALFTONE AND UNDERLAY

The **Halftone / Underlay** tool in **Additional Settings** drop-down is used to display style of halftone and underlay objects imported in the model. The procedure to use this tool is given next.

- Click on the **Halftone / Underlay** tool from the **Additional Settings** drop-down of the **Settings** panel in the **Manage** tab of the **Ribbon**. The **Halftone/Underlay** dialog box will be displayed; refer to Figure-76.

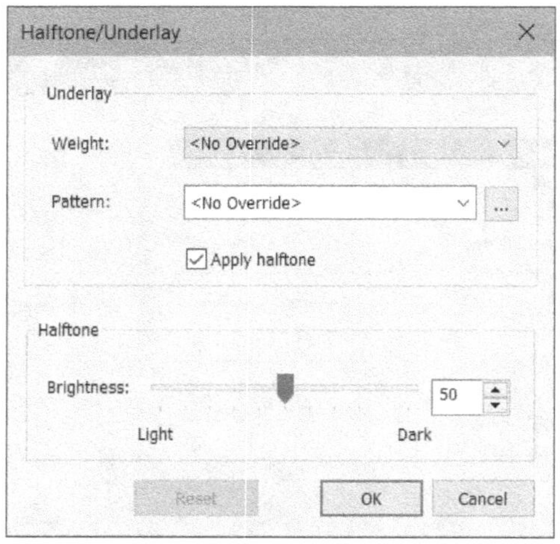

Figure-76. Halftone/Underlay dialog box

- Select desired options from the **Weight** and **Pattern** drop-downs to define boundary line thickness and pattern for underlays.
- Using the **Brightness** slider, you can set brightness of halftone elements inserted in the model.
- After setting desired parameters, click on the **OK** button.

The procedure of sun setting has been discussed in Chapter 12 so we will skip this tool here.

SETTING CALLOUT TAG STYLE

The **Callout Tag** tool in **Additional Settings** drop-down is used to specify properties of callout tags. The callout tags are used to annotate different elements. The procedure to use this tool is given next.

- Click on the **Callout Tag** tool in **Annotations** cascading menu from the **Additional Settings** drop-down of the **Settings** panel in the **Manage** tab of **Ribbon**. The **Type Properties** dialog box will be displayed for callout tag system family; refer to Figure-77.

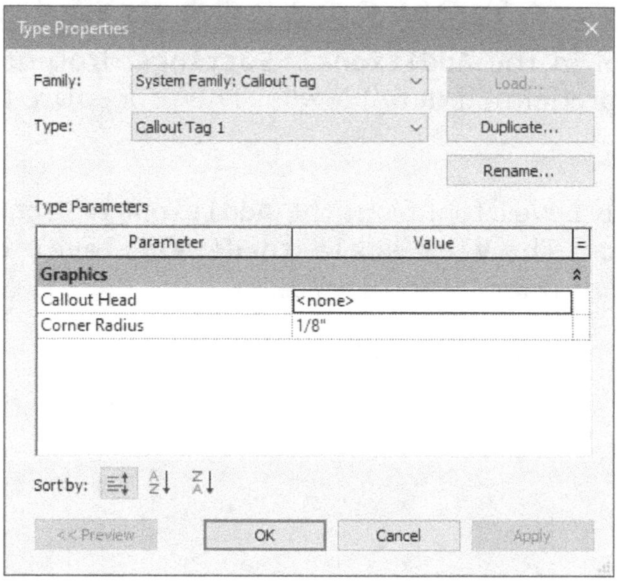

Figure-77. Type Properties dialog box for Callout tag

- Set desired parameters for callout tag in the **Type Parameters** area of dialog box.
- Click on the **OK** button from the dialog box to apply changes.

Similarly, you can set style for elevation tag, section tag, and arrow heads by using respective tools from the drop-down.

SETTING TEMPORARY DIMENSION PROPERTIES

The **Temporary Dimensions** tool in **Additional Settings** drop-down is used to set properties of temporary dimensions. The procedure to use this tool is given next.

- Click on the **Temporary Dimensions** tool in **Annotations** cascading menu from the **Additional Settings** drop-down of the **Manage** tab in **Ribbon**. The **Temporary Dimension Properties** dialog box will be displayed; refer to Figure-78.

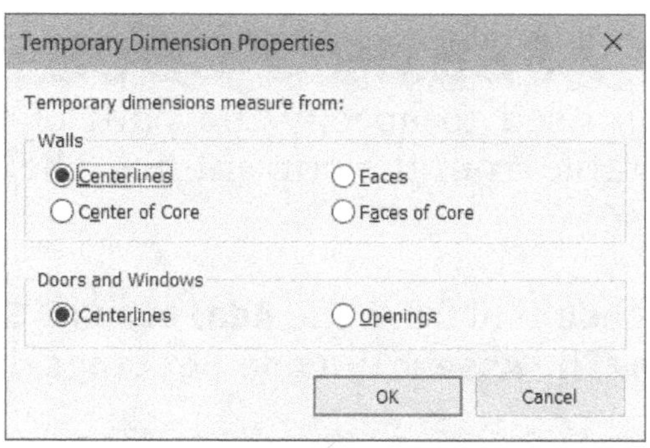

Figure-78. Temporary Dimension Properties dialog box

- Select desired radio button from the **Walls** area to define the object to be used as reference for measuring temporary dimensions of walls.
- Similarly, you can select reference for doors and windows from the **Doors and Windows** area of the dialog box.
- After setting desired parameters, click on the **OK** button.

SETTING ANNOTATION SCALES FOR DETAIL LEVELS

The **Detail Level** tool in the **Additional Settings** drop-down is used to specify annotation scales for predefined detail levels. The procedure to use this tool is given next.

- Click on the **Detail Level** tool from the **Additional Settings** drop-down in the **Manage** tab of **Ribbon**. The **View scale-to-detail level correspondence** dialog box will be displayed; refer to Figure-79.

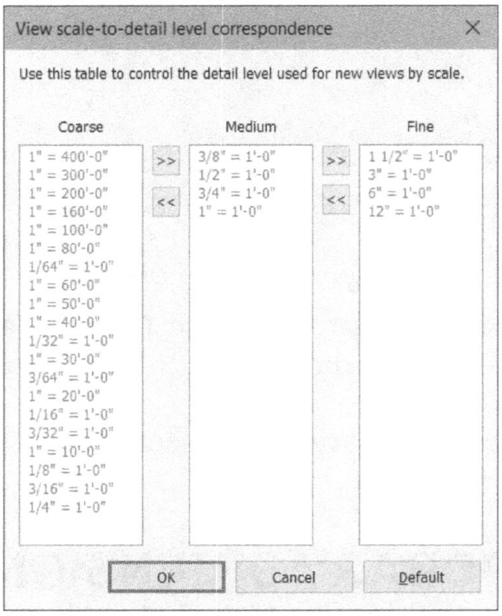

Figure-79. View scale-to-detail level correspondence dialog box

- Use the **>>** or **<<** buttons in the dialog box to shift last scale value of one detail level into another.
- After setting desired parameters, click on the **OK** button from the dialog box to apply.

ASSEMBLY CODE

The **Assembly Code** tool is used to specify the path of the assembly code file or reload the assembly code table from the current file. The procedure to use this tool is discussed next.

- Click on the **Assembly Code** tool from the **Additional Settings** drop-down in the **Manage** tab of the **Ribbon**. The **Assembly Code Settings** dialog box will be displayed; refer to Figure-80.

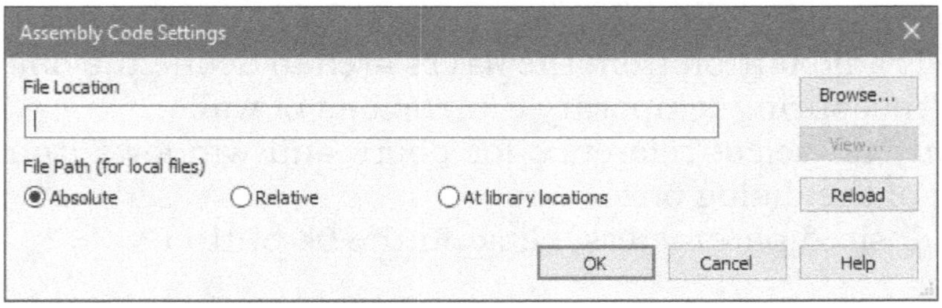

Figure-80. Assembly Code Settings dialog box

- Select desired radio button from **File Path** area to specify the path for local files. Select the **Absolute** radio button to specify a particular folder located on the local PC or a network server. Select the **Relative** radio button to locate the assembly code file in the same directory as the project file or central model. Select the **At library locations** radio button to find the assembly code file where the stand-alone installation or network deployment specified.
- Click on the **Browse** button, the **Browse for Assembly Code File** dialog box will be displayed; refer to Figure-81.

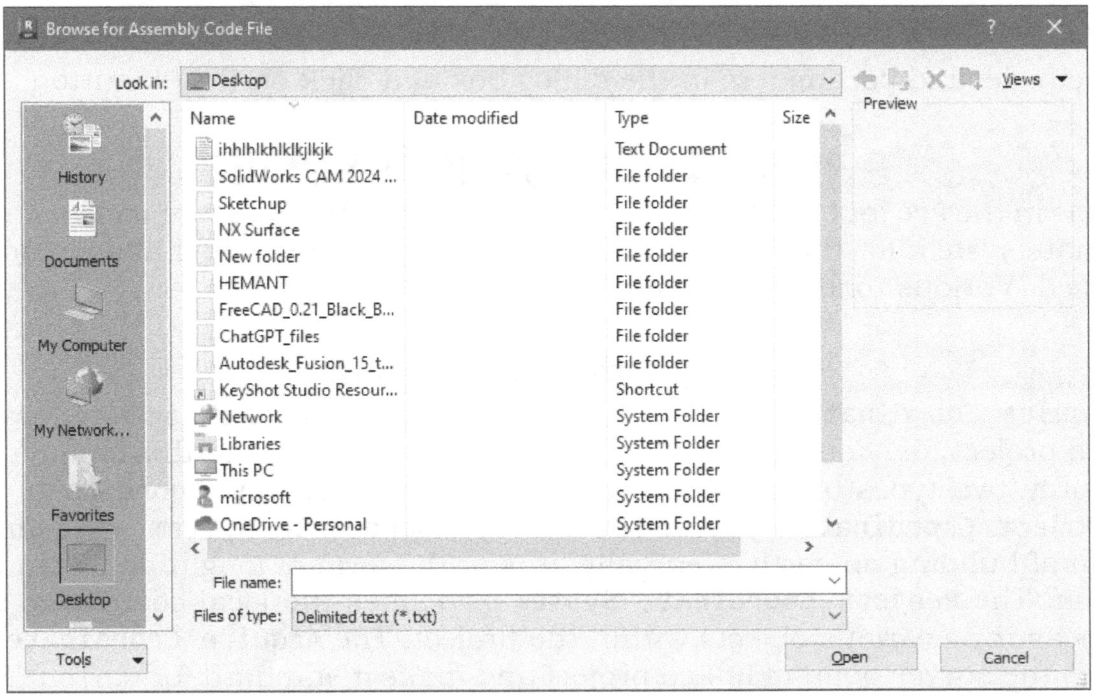

Figure-81. Browse for Assembly code file dialog box

- Select desired code file from the dialog box and click on the **Open** button. The path of the file will be displayed in the **File Location** area of the dialog box.
- Click on the **View** button from the dialog box, the **Assembly Code** dialog box will be displayed showing the assembly code.
- Click on the **Reload** button from the dialog box to refresh the assembly code file from the current project file.
- After specifying desired parameters, click on **OK** button from the dialog box.

MULTIPLE VALUES INDICATION

The **Multiple Values Indication** tool is used to define how a parameter's value is displayed when multiple elements with different values for that parameter are selected. The procedure to use this tool is discussed next.

- Click on the **Multiple Values Indication** tool from the **Additional Settings** drop-down in the **Manage** tab of **Ribbon**. The **Multiple Values Indication** dialog box will be displayed; refer to Figure-82.

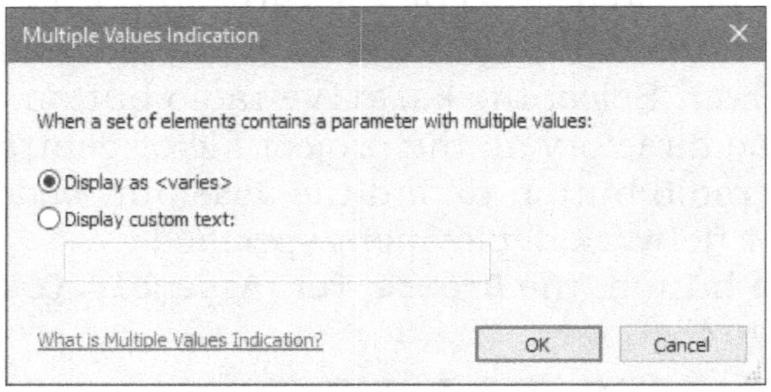

Figure-82. Multiple values indication dialog box

- Specify desired parameters in the dialog box and click on the **OK** button.

PROJECT LOCATION TOOLS

The tools in the **Project Location** panel are used to define geographical location and coordinate system for the project. The **Location** tool in this panel has already been discussed. Various tools of this panel are discussed next.

Acquiring Coordinate

The **Acquire Coordinates** tool is used to acquire the coordinate system location of a linked project file. You will learn about linked projects later in this chapter. There are mainly two types of coordinate systems in Revit; **Survey Coordinate System** and **Project Coordinate System**. The **Survey Coordinate System** defines the location of building on earth. Generally, it is in the form of longitude, latitude, and elevation. The **Project Coordinate System** defines the local coordinate system from measuring various objects within the project. The **Acquire Coordinates tool** acquires the survey point of linked project and make it standard for current project. The procedure to use this tool is given next

- Click on the **Acquire Coordinates** tool from the **Coordinates** drop-down in the **Project Location** panel of **Manage** tab in the **Ribbon**. You will be asked to select the linked project whose coordinate systems are to be used.
- Select desired linked project. The coordinate system will change accordingly.

Note that by default these points are not displayed in the model. To display them, open the **Visibility/Graphics Overrides** dialog box by clicking on **Visibility/Graphics** tool in **Graphics** panel of **View** tab in **Ribbon** and select the check boxes for **Project Base Point & Survey Point** options in the **Site** category; refer to Figure-83.

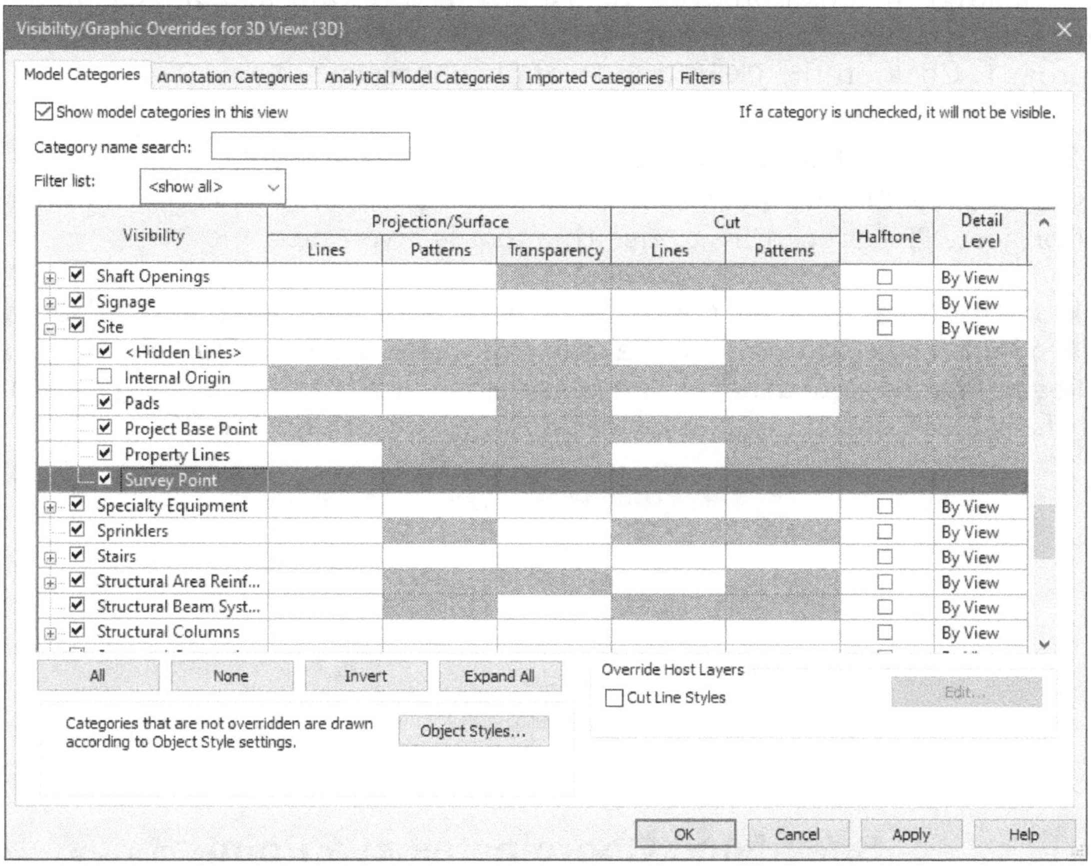

Figure-83. Displaying coordinate points

Publishing Coordinate System

The **Publish Coordinates** tool is used to check the project coordinate system of current model and apply it to linked model. The procedure to use this tool is given next.

- Click on the **Publish Coordinates** tool from the **Coordinates** drop-down in the **Manage** tab of **Ribbon**. You will be asked to select linked project.
- Select desired linked project. The **Location and Site** dialog box will be displayed; refer to Figure-84.

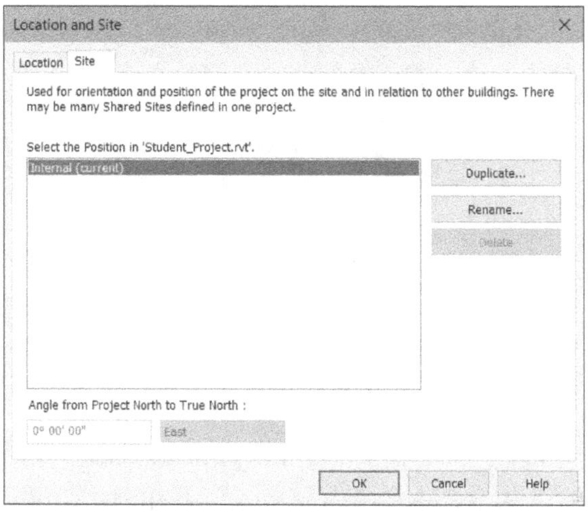

Figure-84. Location and Site dialog box

- Select desired site position from the list box. If you want to change global location of project then click on the **Location** tab in the dialog box and set desired location for project. Click on the **OK** button to apply changes.

Resetting Shared Coordinates

The **Reset Shared Coordinates** tool is used to remove shared coordinates from the current project. The procedure to use this tool is given next.

- Click on the **Reset Shared Coordinates** tool from the **Coordinates** drop-down in the **Project Location** panel of **Manage** tab in the **Ribbon**. On selecting this tool, the **Reset Shared Coordinates Success** message box will be displayed confirming that the shared coordinates have been reset; refer to Figure-85.

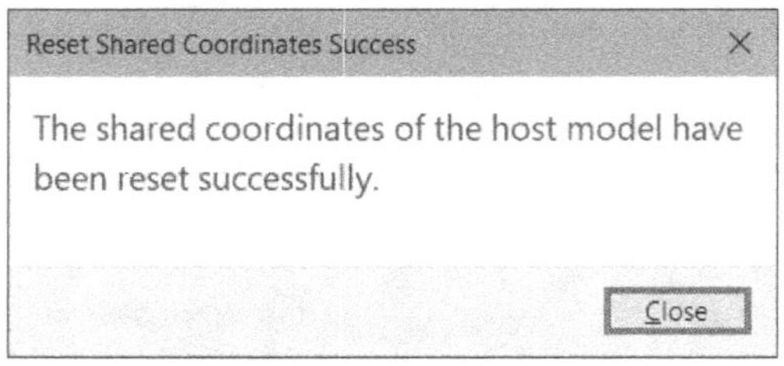

Figure-85. Reset Shared Coordinates Success message box

- Click on the **Close** button to exit the message box.

Specifying Coordinates at a Point

The **Specify Coordinates at Point** tool is used to define desired location as shared coordinate point for linked model. The shared model will be repositioned according to specified point. The procedure to use this tool is given next.

- Click on the **Specify Coordinates at Point** tool from the **Coordinates** drop-down in the **Project Location** panel of **Manage** tab in the **Ribbon**. You will be asked to select reference point for shared coordinate.
- Click at desired location on base model. The **Specify Shared Coordinates** dialog box will be displayed; refer to Figure-86.

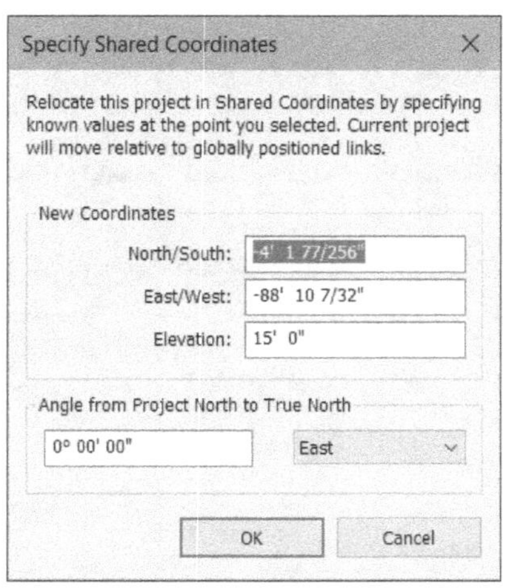

Figure-86. Specify Shared Coordinates dialog box

- Set desired values of different coordinates and click on the **OK** button. The position of linked model will change accordingly.

Reporting Coordinate System

The **Report Shared Coordinates** tool is used to display shared coordinates of linked model. The procedure to use this tool is given next.

- Click on the **Report Shared Coordinates** tool from the **Coordinates** drop-down in the **Project Location** panel of **Manage** tab in the **Ribbon**. You will be asked to select the location of object in project whose coordinates are to be checked.
- Click at desired entity in the model. The coordinates will be displayed in **Options Bar**; refer to Figure-87.

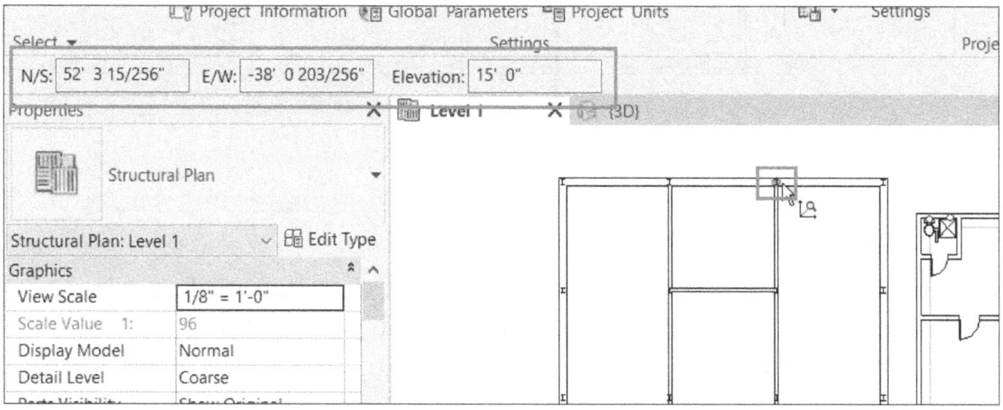

Figure-87. Coordinates displayed in Options Bar

PROJECT POSITIONING

The tools in the **Position** drop-down of **Project Location** panel are used to define the position of project model with respect to shared coordinate system; refer to Figure-88. The tools in this drop-down are discussed next.

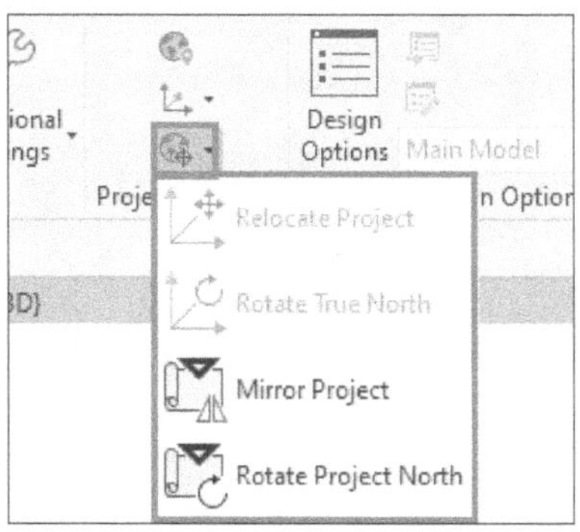

Figure-88. Position drop-down

Relocating Project

The **Relocate Project** tool is used to change the position of model with respect to shared coordinate system in Plan view. The procedure to use this tool is given next.

- Click on the **Relocate Project** tool from the **Position** drop-down in the **Project Location** panel of **Manage** tab in the **Ribbon**. You will be asked to specify start point for moving the project.
- Click at desired location on project model. You will be asked to specify end point for movement; refer to Figure-89.

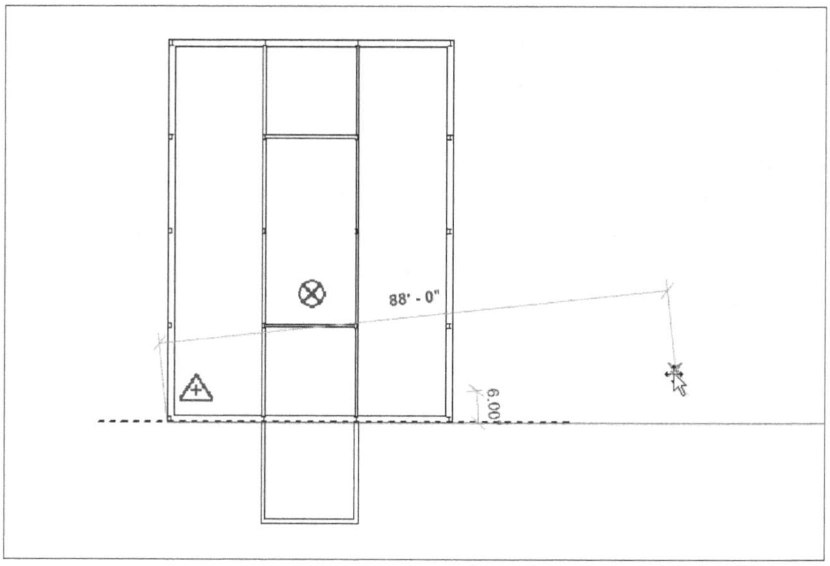

Figure-89. Relocating project

- Move the cursor at desired angle and type the distance value where you want to relocate the project. Press **ENTER** to relocate or you can click at desired position to relocate the project.

Rotating True North

The **Rotate True North** tool is used to rotate the true north of model to change orientation of model on Earth. Make sure you have selected **True North** option in **Orientation** field for current plan in **Properties Palette**; refer to Figure-90. The procedure to use this tool is given next.

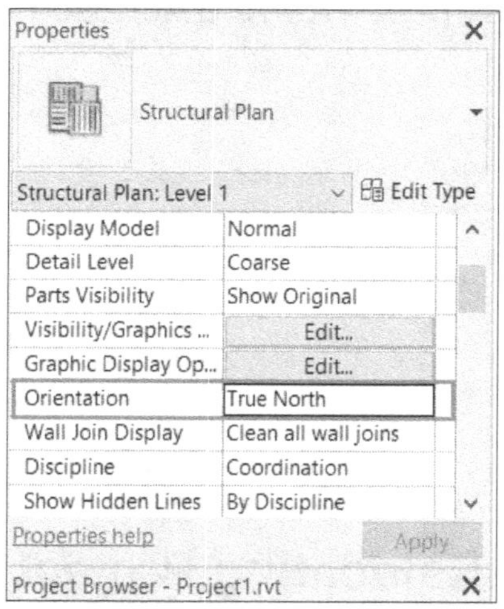

Figure-90. True North option selected

- Click on the **Rotate True North** tool from the **Position** drop-down in the **Project Location** panel of **Manage** tab in the **Ribbon**. You will be asked to specify start point for rotation and related options will be displayed in the **Ribbon**; refer to Figure-91.

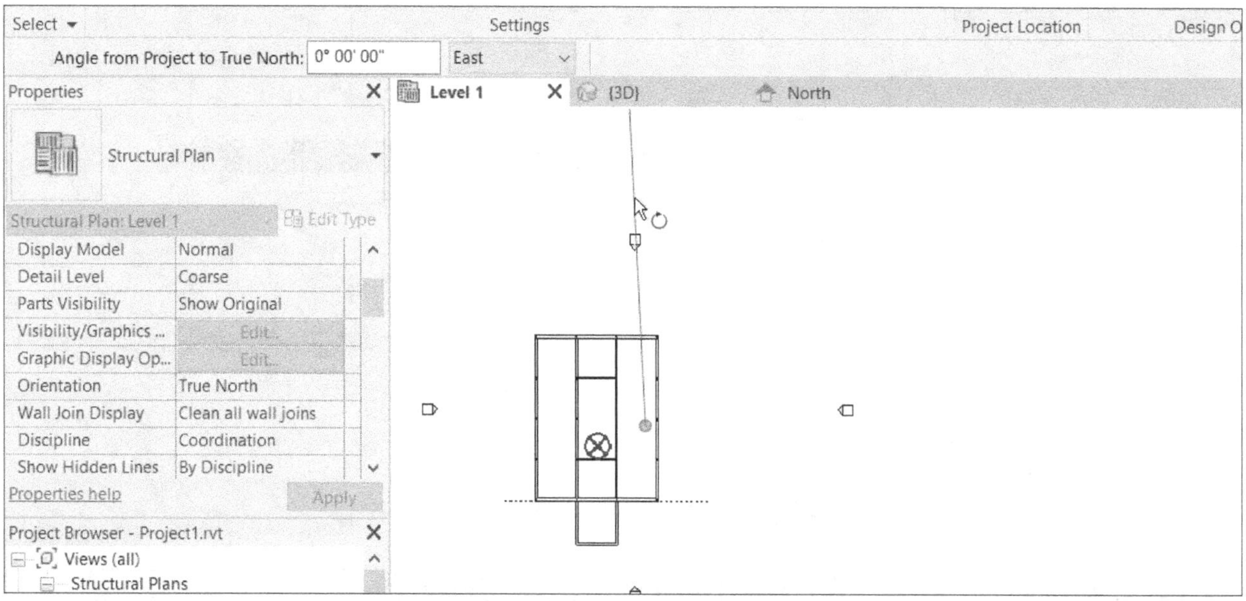

Figure-91. Options for rotation of true north

- Click at desired location to specify start point. You will be asked to specify end point of rotation ray.
- Click at desired angle or you can specify desired values in the **Ribbon** and press **ENTER** to apply rotation. The model will rotate accordingly.

Mirroring Project

The **Mirror Project** tool is used to flip the project with respect to selected reference axis. The procedure to use this tool is given next.

- Click on the **Mirror Project** tool from the **Position** drop-down in the **Project Location** panel of **Manage** tab in the **Ribbon**. The **Mirror Project** dialog box will be displayed; refer to Figure-92.

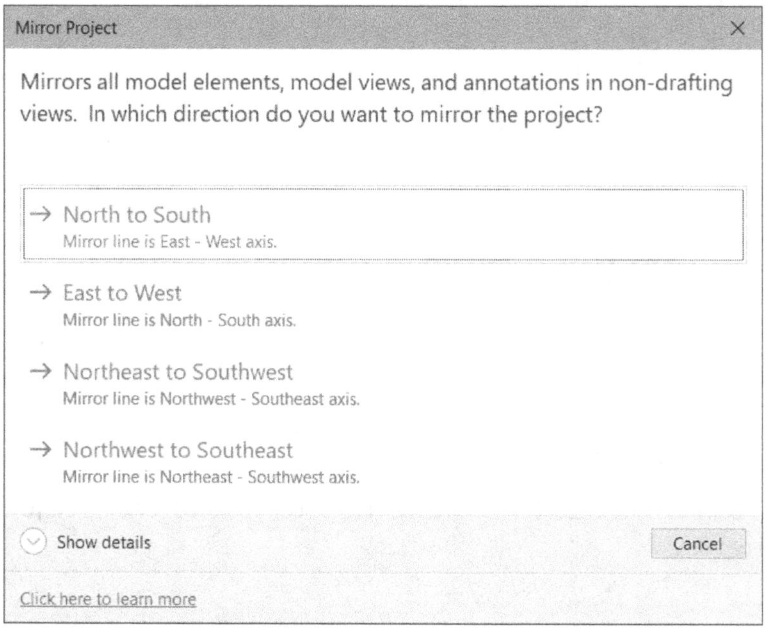

Figure-92. Mirror Project dialog box

- Select desired option to use respective mirror line. The model will get mirrored and a warning box will be displayed tell you that all elements have been mirrored; refer to Figure-93.

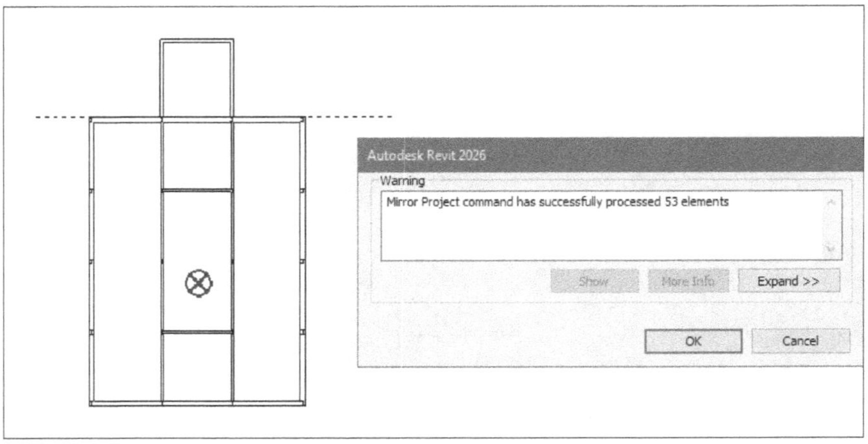

Figure-93. Project after mirroring

- Click on the **OK** button from the warning box.

Rotating Project North

The **Rotate Project North** tool is active only when **Project North** option is selected in the **Orientation** field of **Properties Palette** for structural plan. This tool is used to rotate the project north by specified angle value. The procedure to use this tool is given next.

- Click on the **Rotate Project North** tool from the **Position** drop-down in the **Project Location** panel of **Manage** tab in the **Ribbon**. The **Rotate Project** dialog box will be displayed; refer to Figure-94.

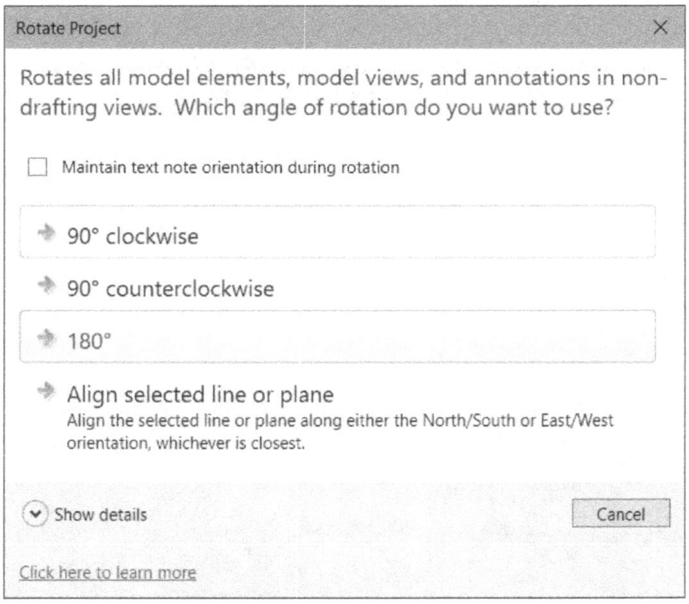

Figure-94. Rotate Project dialog box

- Select desired button from the dialog box to rotate the project. The model will rotate accordingly.

CREATING DESIGN OPTIONS

There is a time during designing when you need to check two different design options after making base model. For example, in Figure-95 you want to check the position of a room on the both sides of an already created room and based on the feedback from your client, you will keep the final design. In such cases, rather than keeping two different project files, you can use the **Design Options** tool to create two design options. The procedure to use **Design Options** tool is given next.

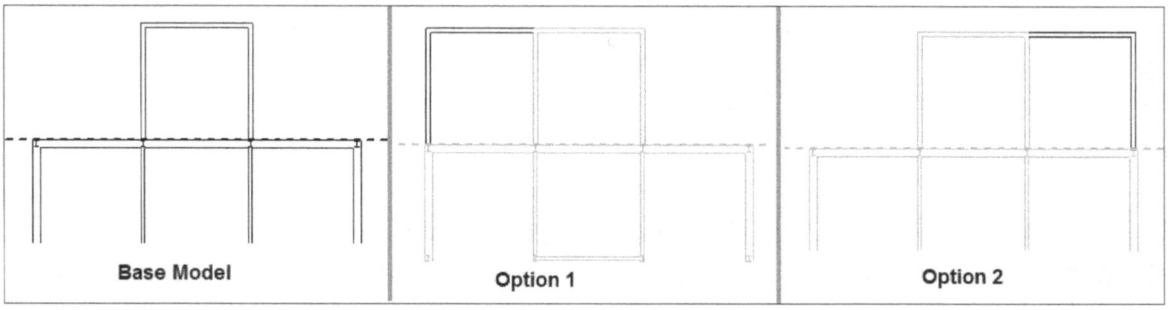

Figure-95. Design options

- Click on the **Design Options** tool from the **Design Options** panel in the **Manage** tab of **Ribbon**. The **Design Options** dialog box will be displayed; refer to Figure-96.

Figure-96. Design Options dialog box

- Click on the **New** button from the **Option Set** area of the dialog box. An option set will be added with default Option 1 (primary).
- Click on the **New** button from the **Option** area of the dialog box. The Option 2 will be added in the design options list.
- Click on the **Close** button from the dialog box to exit.
- Now, click on the drop-down in **Design Options** panel of **Manage** tab in **Ribbon**. The list of created options will be displayed; refer to Figure-97.

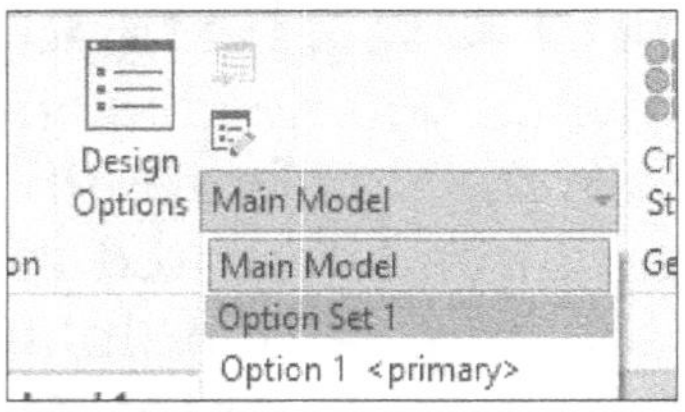

Figure-97. List of design options

- Select the Option 1 and modify the model.
- Now, select the Option 2 from the drop-down. You will see that changes made in Option 1 are not reflected in Option 2. Modify the model as you want for option 2.
- Save the file by pressing **CTRL+S**. You can create as many options as you want by using this tool.

CREATE STUDY

The **Create Study** tool is used to produce alternative design options based on specified criteria. The procedure to use this tool is discussed in chapter 14.

MANAGING LINKS

The **Manage Links** tool is used to modify parameters for linked projects/objects. The procedure to use this tool is given next.

- Click on the **Manage Links** tool from the **Manage Project** panel in the **Manage** tab of the **Ribbon**. The **Manage Links** dialog box will be displayed; refer to Figure-98.

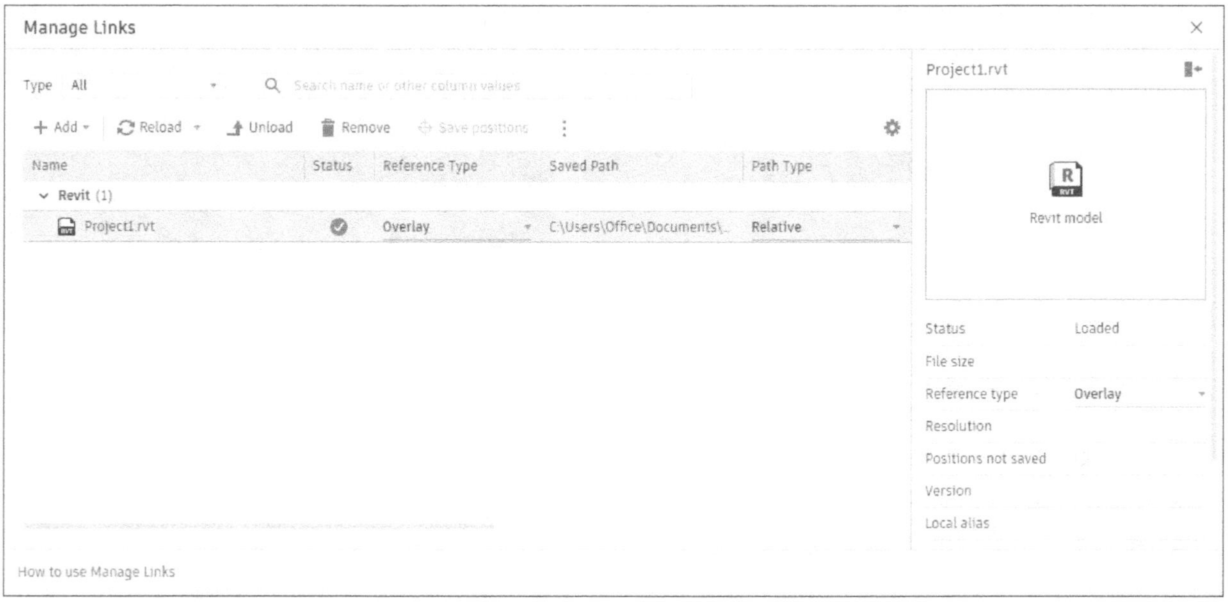

Figure-98. Manage Links dialog box

- Set desired path type from the **Path Type** column. If you have selected the **Relative** option then system will search for linked files in relative folders. For example, you have saved all the link files and current project files in same folder then system will search this folder for links even if you transfer the files in another system. If you have selected the **Absolute** option then system will search the files in exact location where they were save`d in original.

- Select the **Overlay** option from **Reference Type** field for linked object if you want create a link to the original model. This option saves memory of current project but you will need to copy the linked objects as well if you are moving project data to different computer. Select the **Attachment** option from the **Reference Type** field if you want to save a copy of linked model in current project drawing. Using this option will break the link to original model and also increase the size of current project file but now, you will not need to carry the original model file (of linked object) with the project.
- Specify other parameters as desired and click on the **OK** button.

Managing Images

The options available on selecting the **Images** option from **Type** drop-down in the **Manage Links** dialog box are used to manage raster images used in the project. The procedure to use this tool is given next.

- Select the **Images** option from **Type** drop-down in the **Manage Links** dialog box. The options to manage images will be displayed; refer to Figure-99.

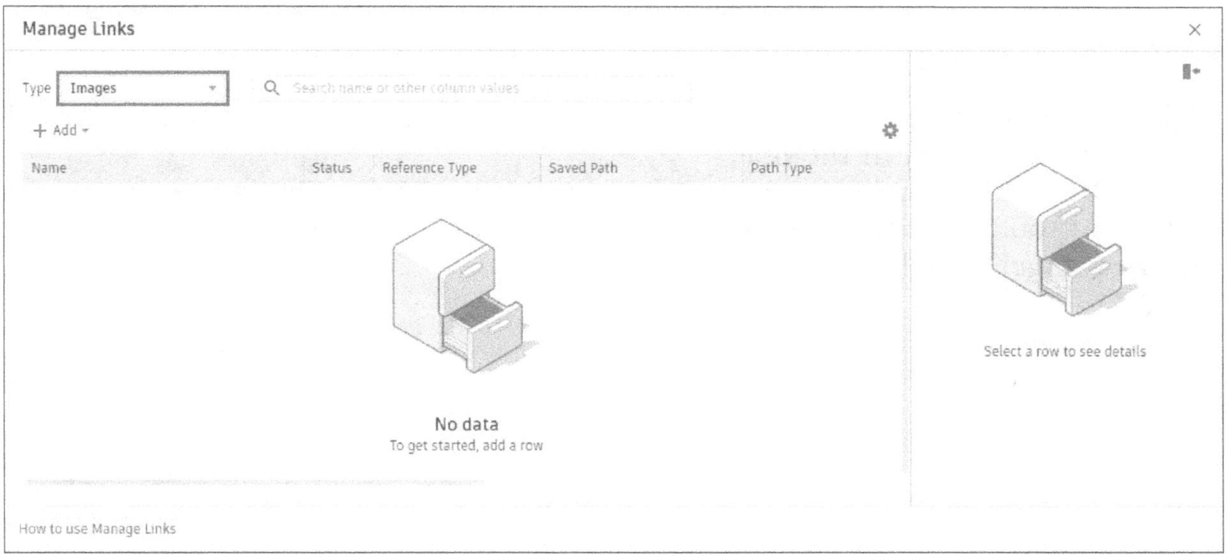

Figure-99. Images option in the Manage Links dialog box

- Select the **Images** option from **+Add** drop-down in the dialog box to add an image. The **Import Image** dialog box will be displayed; refer to Figure-100.

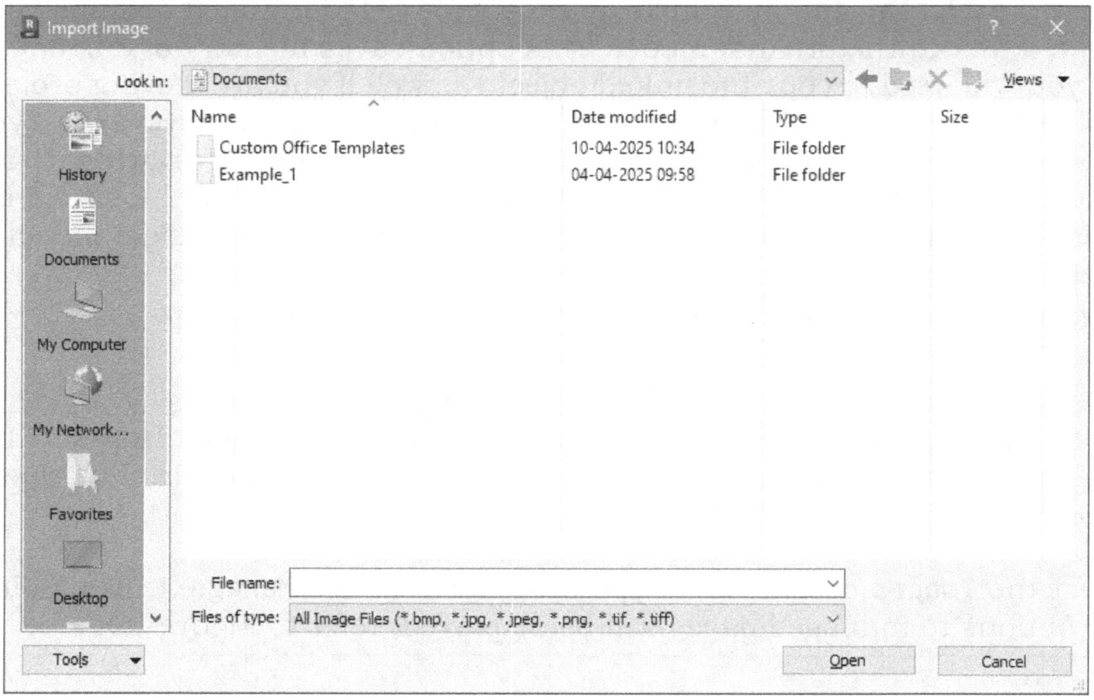

Figure-100. Import Image dialog box

- Select desired image file from the dialog box and click on the **Open** button. The image will be added in the list.
- Select the newly added image and click on the **Place Instance** button from extended toolbar in the dialog box; refer to Figure-101. The instance of selected image will get attached to the cursor.

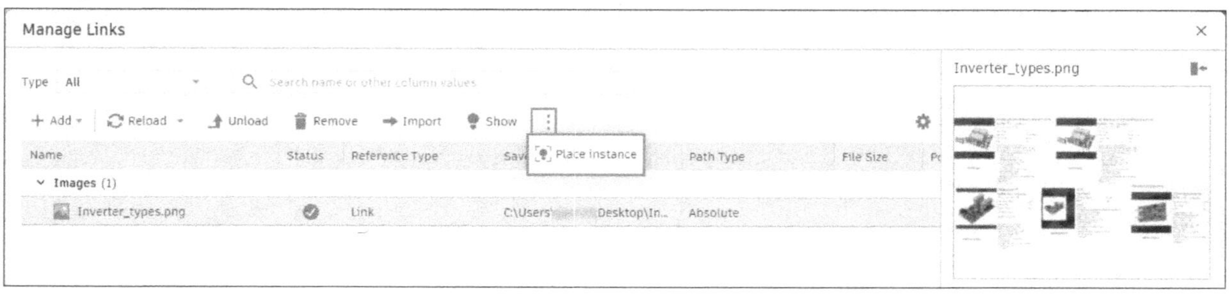

Figure-101. Place instance tool

- Click at desired location in the model to place the image.
- Similarly, you can use the other options in the **Manage Images** dialog box to delete, replace, and reload the images.
- Click on the **OK** button from the dialog box to exit.

You can use the **Decal Types** tool of **Manage Project** panel in **Manage** tab of **Ribbon** in the same way to create and manage decals.

Creating Starting View

The **Starting View** tool is used specify the view which will be displayed when you next time open the model. The procedure to use this tool is given next.

- Click on the **Starting View** tool from the **Manage Project** panel in the **Manage** tab of **Ribbon**. The **Starting View** dialog box will be displayed; refer to Figure-102.

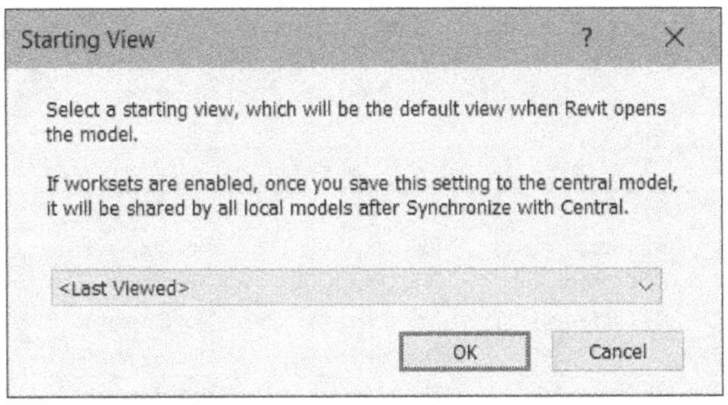

Figure-102. Starting View dialog box

- Select desired view from the drop-down in the dialog box and click on the **OK** button. The settings will be applied.

MANAGING PHASES

Phases are used to mark the status of construction. Phases can also be used to define the time point after which a specific construction can be performed. For example, if new construction is to be performed after demolition then you can create demolition as a phase and new construction as another phase. The procedure to create and manage phases is given next.

- Click on the **Phases** tool from the **Phasing** drop-down in the **Manage** tab of **Ribbon**. The **Phasing** dialog box will be displayed; refer to Figure-103.

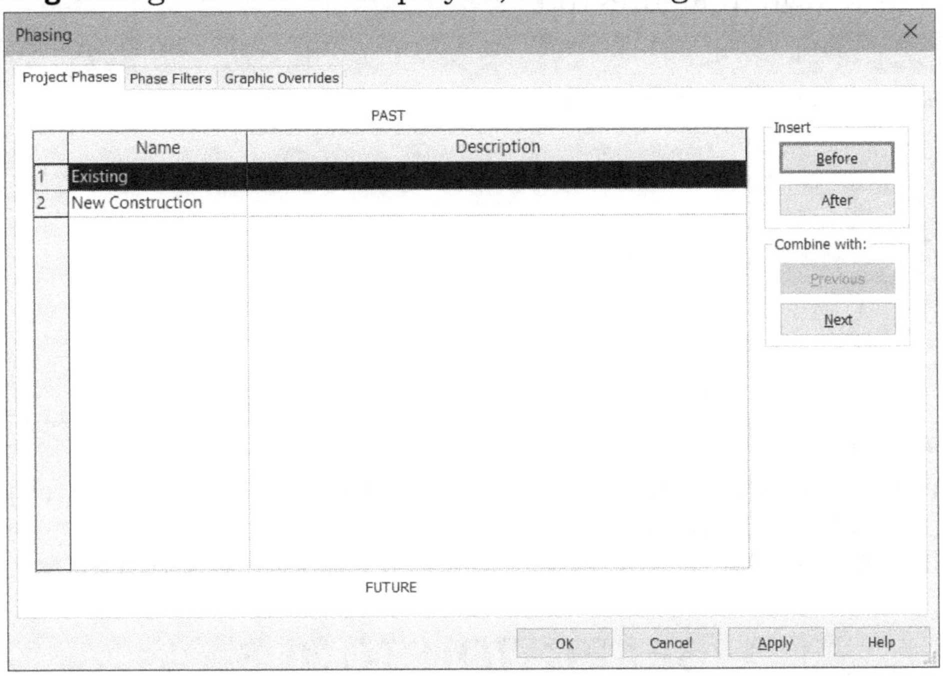

Figure-103. Phasing dialog box

- Specify desired descriptions for phases in the **Description** column.
- Click on the **Before** button to create a new phase before selected phase. Click on the **After** button to create a new phase after selected phase.
- You cannot delete a phase in Revit but you can combine selected phase with previous or next phase. To do so, click on the **Previous** or **Next** button from **Combine with** area of the dialog box.
- Click on the **Phase Filters** tab to modify parameters related to default phase filters. The options will be displayed as shown in Figure-104.

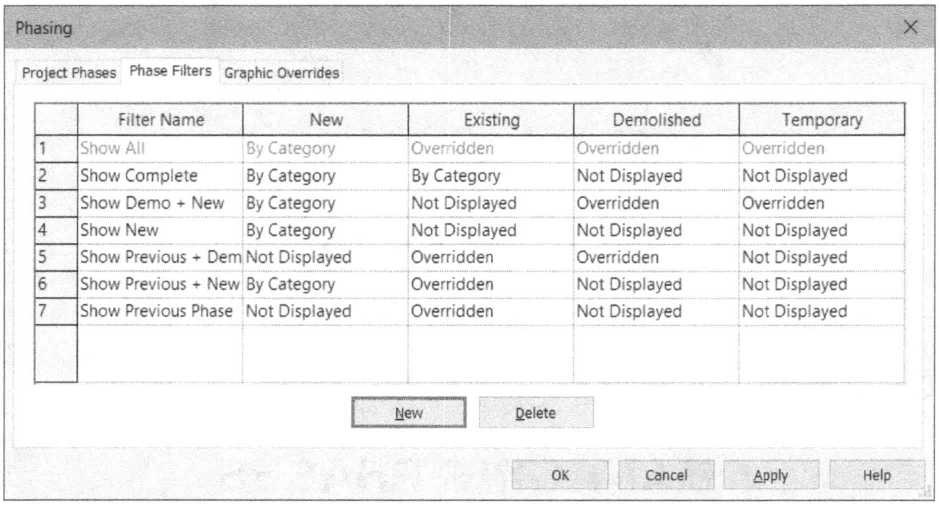

Figure-104. Phase Filters tab

- Modify the filters as desired by using options under **New**, **Existing**, **Demolished**, and **Temporary** columns.
- Click on the **New** button to create a new phase filter.
- Click on the **Delete** button to delete selected phase filter.
- Click on the **Graphic Overrides** tab to modify graphical change settings applied after selecting phase filters and phases. The options in the dialog box will be displayed as shown in Figure-105.

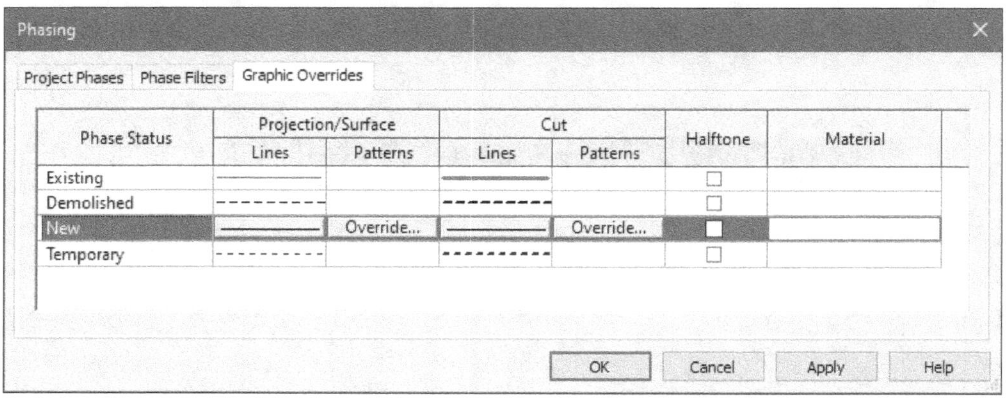

Figure-105. Graphic Overrides tab

- Set desired parameters under various columns to define how objects will be displayed in different phases.
- Click on the **OK** button from the dialog box to apply the settings.

SELECTION TOOLS

The tools in **Selection** panel are used to create and manage selections. There are three tools available in this panel; Save Selection, Edit Selection, and Load Selection. These tools are discussed next.

- Select the objects which you are going to select many times during creation of drawing. The related contextual tab will be displayed in the **Ribbon** with **Selection** panel; refer to Figure-106. Note that these tools will also be available in the **Manage** tab of **Ribbon**.

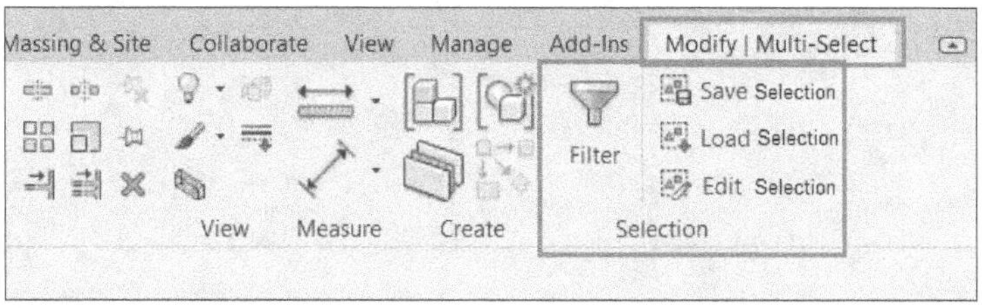

Figure-106. Selection panel

- Click on the **Save** button from the **Selection** panel. The **Save Selection** dialog box will be displayed; refer to Figure-107.

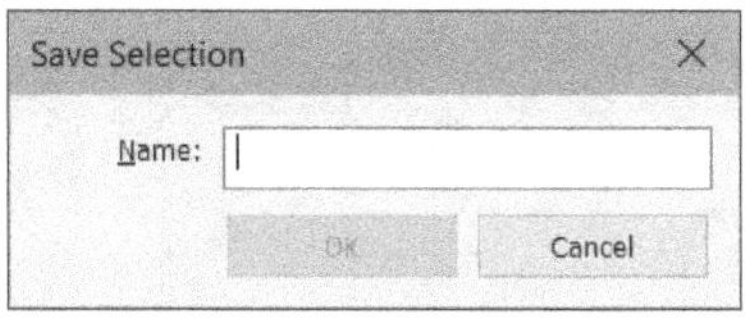

Figure-107. Save Selection dialog box

- Specify desired name for selection in the **Name** edit box and click on the **OK** button. The selection will be saved and rest of the tools in **Selection** panel will become active. Press **ESC** to exit the selection.
- Now, click on the **Load Selection** button from the **Selection** panel to select earlier saved selections. The **Retrieve Filters** dialog box will be displayed; refer to Figure-108.
- Select desired saved selection and click on the **OK** button. The objects will be selected accordingly.
- If you want to edit the earlier saved selection, then click on the **Edit Selection** button from the **Selection** panel in the **Manage** tab of **Ribbon**. The **Edit Filters** dialog box will be displayed; refer to Figure-109.

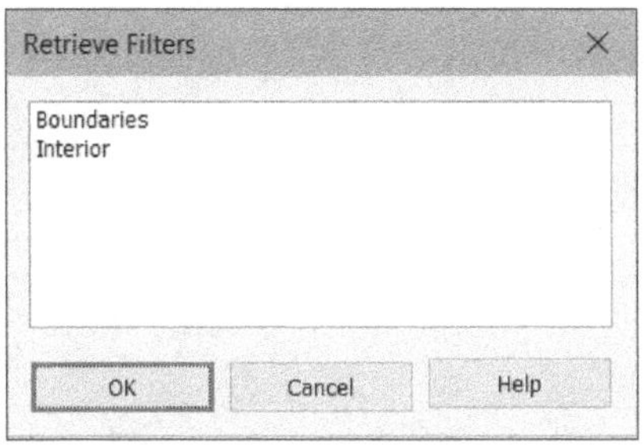

Figure-108. Retrieve Filters dialog box

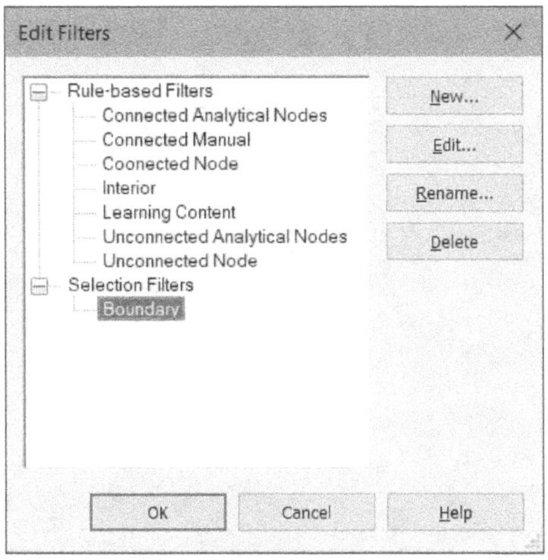

Figure-109. Edit Filters dialog box

Editing Selection Filter

- Select desired selection filter to be modified and click on the **Edit** button. The **Edit Selection Set** contextual tab will be displayed in the **Ribbon** with options to edit selection; refer to Figure-110. Note that all the elements which are not part of selection will be highlighted dark and selected objects will be in halftone.

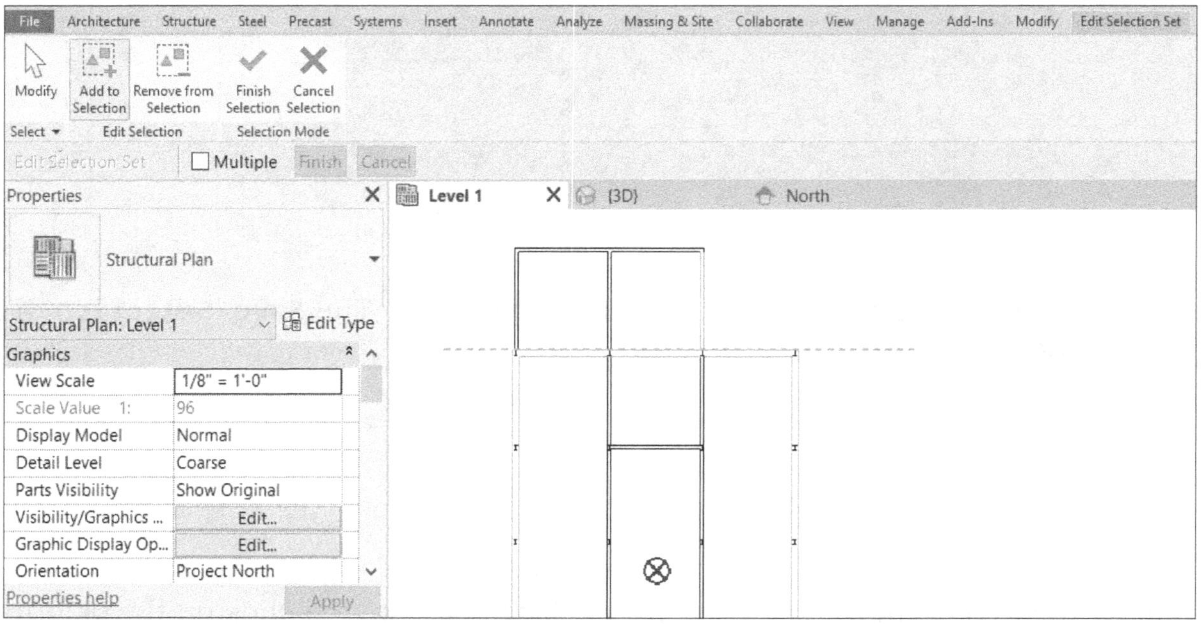

Figure-110. Edit Selection Set contextual tab

- Click on the **Add to Selection** button and select the objects to be added in current selection. Click on the **Remove from Selection** button and select the objects to be removed from selection.
- Click on the **Finish Selection** button to apply changes. The **Edit Filters** dialog box will be displayed again.

Editing Rule-based Filters

- Select desired selection filter from the **Rule-based Filters** section and click on the **Edit** button. The **Filters** dialog box will be displayed as shown in Figure-111.

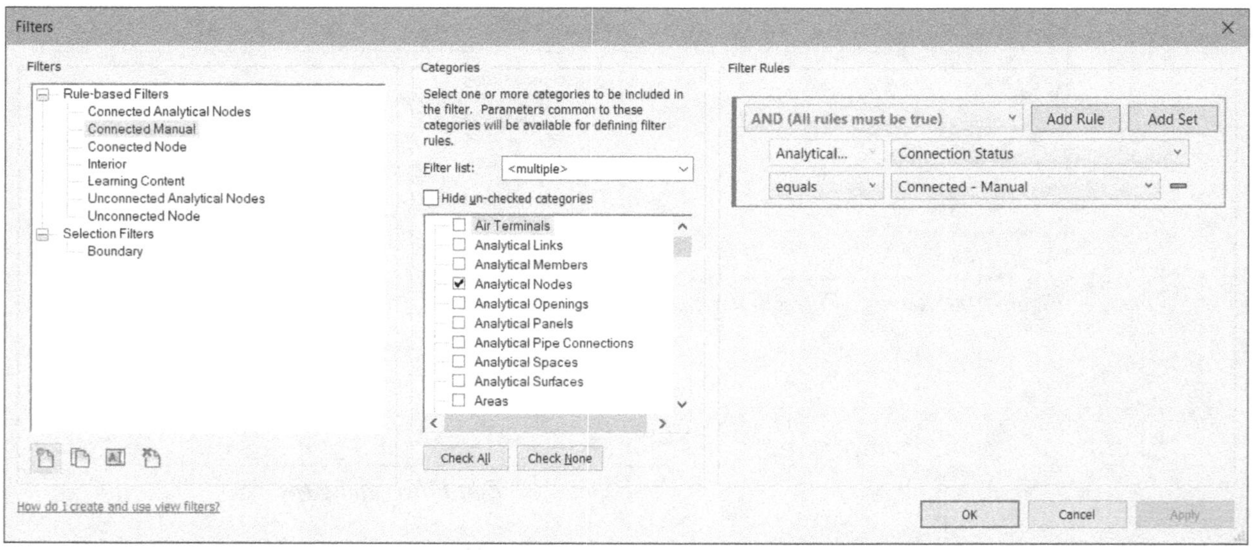

Figure-111. Filters dialog box

- Select the objects to be included in selection from the **Categories** area of dialog box.
- Select desired option from the **Condition** drop-down in **Filter Rules** section of the dialog box to define whether you want to use **AND** condition or **OR** condition. After selecting a condition, set the related parameters for conditions. For example, set analytical node objects for selection which are connected; refer to Figure-112.

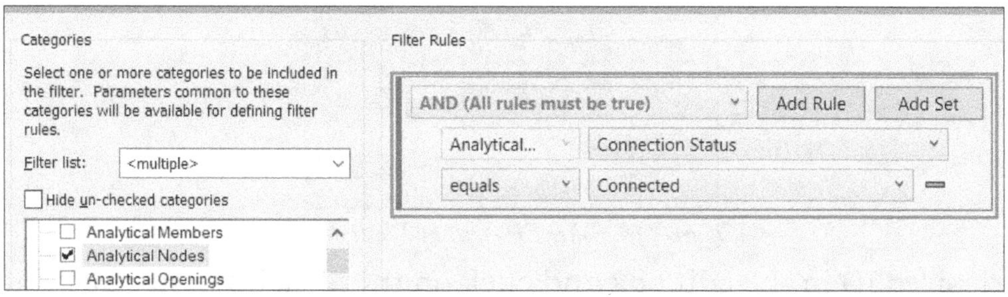

Figure-112. Rules for analytical nodes

- Click on the **Add Rule** button from the dialog box to add a new condition for selection. Click on the **Add Set** button to add a new set of filter rules. Click on the **OK** button from the dialog box to create filters.
- You can use the **New**, **Rename**, and **Delete** buttons from the **Edit Filters** dialog box as discussed earlier. Click on the **OK** button from the dialog box to apply changes.

INQUIRY TOOLS

The tools in **Inquiry** panel are used to check and report errors by using IDs of objects. Note that since ID of each object is different so, you do not need to say left 3rd wall or 4th bottom floor to guide your collaborators for editing. You can tell the ID of object to your collaborator and he/she will find the object easily. Various tools in this panel are discussed next.

IDs of Selection

The **IDs of Selection** tool is used to display diagnostic IDs of selected objects. When contacting the tech support for help of some error, the technician can identify problem causing elements easily by this ID.

- Select the object(s) whose IDs are to be checked and click on the **IDs of Selection** tool from the **Inquiry** panel of **Manage** tab in the **Ribbon**. The **Element IDs of Selection** dialog box will be displayed; refer to Figure-113.

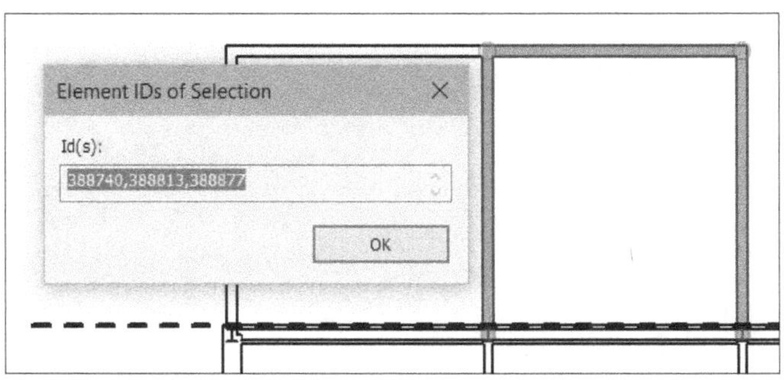

Figure-113. IDs of selection

- Click on the **OK** button from the dialog box to exit the tool.

Selection by ID

The **Select by ID** tool is used to select objects by their IDs. The procedure to use this tool is given next.

- Click on the **Select by ID** tool from the **Inquiry** panel in the **Manage** tab of **Ribbon**. The **Select Elements by ID** dialog box will be displayed; refer to Figure-114.

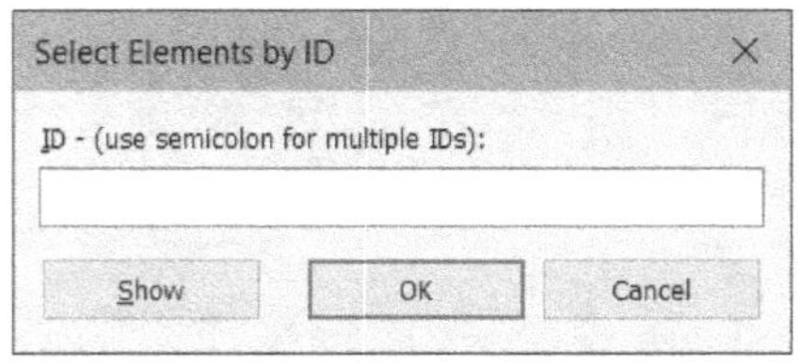

Figure-114. Select Elements by ID dialog box

- Specify desired ID in the edit box and click on the **Show** button. The related element will be highlighted; refer to Figure-115.

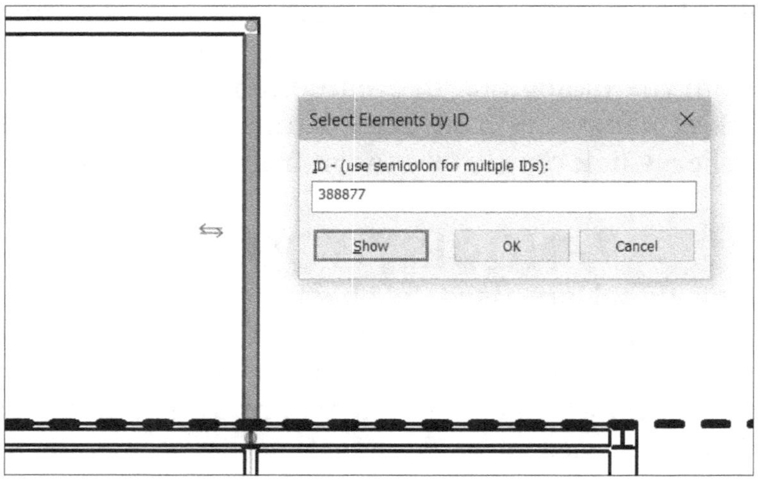

Figure-115. Showing element by ID

- Click on the **OK** button from the dialog box to select element.

Review Warnings

The **Review Warnings** tool is used to check warnings generated while creating model. The procedure to use this tool is given next.

- Click on the **Review Warnings** tool from the **Inquiry** panel in the **Manage** tab of **Ribbon**. The warning box will be displayed; refer to Figure-116.

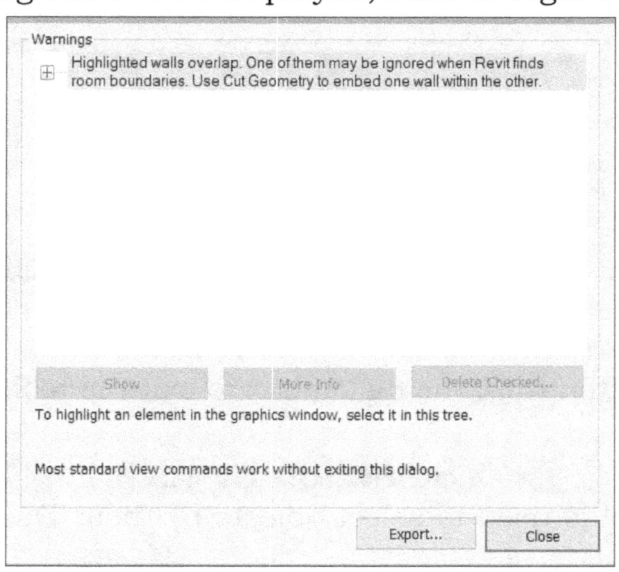

Figure-116. Warning box

- Expand the categories of warnings and select the elements in question to find them in model. You can modify the model to resolve warning.

The tools to create and manage macros and visual scripts will be discussed later in this book.

SELF-ASSESSMENT

Q1. Which of the following properties of materials affect heating/cooling analysis of the project?

a. Identity
b. Appearance
c. Physical
d. Thermal

Q2. The route analysis settings are used to define the objects that are not counted as obstacle while creating automatic route for hvac, piping, or electrical system. (T/F)

Q3. The **Transfer Project Standards** tool is used to copy all the data of one project to another. (T/F)

Q4. The **Project Units** tool is used to set precision of units for the project. (T/F)

Q5. The demand factor is used to define actual load consumption by objects based on their total load capacity. (T/F)

Q6. The **Material Assets** tool in the **Additional Settings** drop-down is used to create and manage material properties. (T/F)

Q7. The **Acquire Coordinates** tool is used to acquire the coordinate system location of current project file. (T/F)

Q8. The **Report Shared Coordinates** tool is used to display shared coordinates of linked model. (T/F)

Q9. The **Rotate True North** tool is used to rotate the true north of model to change orientation of model on Earth for various analyses. (T/F)

Q10. The **Mirror Project** tool is used to flip the project with respect to selected reference axis. (T/F)

Q11. Which tab contains the Materials tool in Autodesk Revit?

A. Annotate tab
B. View tab
C. Manage tab
D. Modify tab

Q12. What is the function of the Graphics tab in the Material Browser dialog box?

A. To edit physical properties
B. To change graphic appearance settings
C. To input manufacturer information
D. To define keynote values

Q13. Which type of information is found under the Product Information area in the Identity tab?

A. Model and cost details
B. Color and pattern settings
C. Structural loads
D. Snap types

Q14. What does the Appearance tab NOT affect in a material?

A. Rendering quality
B. Glossiness
C. Physical properties
D. Reflectivity

Q15. Which tab is used to modify thermal properties of a material?

A. Identity
B. Appearance
C. Thermal
D. Graphics

Q16. What is the purpose of the Create New Material tool?

A. To delete existing materials
B. To import object styles
C. To create a brand-new material
D. To edit graphic parameters

Q17. What happens when you use the Duplicate Using Shared Assets tool?

A. Only color is duplicated
B. Materials are copied without parameters
C. Properties remain linked to the original material
D. The material becomes non-editable

Q18. How do you open a user-defined material library in Revit?

A. Click the Materials tool
B. Click Open Existing Library in Material Browser
C. Use the Appearance tab
D. Select Duplicate Material

Q19. What is the primary function of the Object Styles tool?

A. To create new materials
B. To define object visibility
C. To manage shared parameters
D. To set styles for project elements

Q20. Which tool is used to define snap behavior in Revit?

A. Object Styles
B. Project Parameters
C. Snaps
D. Project Info

Q21. What is defined using the Project Information tool?

A. Family categories
B. View templates
C. General project description and identity data
D. Schedule templates

Q22. What does the Route Analysis Settings dialog allow you to do?

A. Create duct routes manually
B. Analyze wall thickness
C. Define elements that are not counted as obstacles
D. Link multiple files

Q23. What is the Parameters Service tool used for?

A. Creating new families
B. Editing snaps
C. Importing shared parameters into a session
D. Rendering materials

Q24. What is the main purpose of Project Parameters?

A. To change color schemes
B. To sort, filter, and reschedule elements
C. To snap to angles
D. To adjust line weights

Q25. Which option should be selected to create parameters that appear only in schedules and cannot be shared?

A. Shared Parameter
B. Appearance Property
C. Identity Property
D. Project Parameter

Q26. What must you do before adding a shared parameter to a project?

A. Save the project
B. Select or create a shared parameters file
C. Enable route analysis
D. Edit object styles

Q27. What does the Group parameter under drop-down define for a parameter?

A. The unit of measurement
B. The snap increment
C. The category grouping within the project
D. The type of physical property

Q28. Which tool is used to create and edit shared parameters in multiple projects?

A. Project Units
B. Global Parameters
C. Shared Parameters
D. Load Classifications

Q29. What should you click to load an existing shared parameter file?

A. New
B. Create
C. Browse
D. Move

Q30. Which dialog box is displayed when you move a shared parameter to a different group?

A. Edit Shared Parameters
B. Properties
C. Move To Group
D. Parameter Properties

Q31. What must be done to define the name and type of a new shared parameter?

A. Edit Tooltip
B. Select group
C. Click Move
D. Use Parameter Properties dialog box

Q32. What type of parameter can extract values from geometric features?

A. Custom
B. Reporting
C. Global
D. Shared

Q33. What should be selected from the Label drop-down to assign a global parameter to a dimension?

A. Global dimension
B. Label selector
C. Desired parameter
D. Modify tab

Q34. What happens when you change a global parameter value like area in the Global Parameters dialog box?

A. Only geometry updates
B. Dimensions remain static
C. Model updates automatically
D. Labels are removed

Q35. What tool is used to transfer styles and settings from one project to another?

A. Manage Templates
B. Transfer Project Standards
C. Load Classifications
D. Edit Shared Parameters

Q36. What is the purpose of the Purge Unused tool?

A. Import new families
B. Optimize load classification
C. Reduce file size
D. Duplicate project elements

Q37. Which dialog box lets you define how decimal and digit grouping will be used in units?

A. Format
B. Decimal
C. Units Grouping
D. Project Units

Q38. Which setting defines classifications for different electrical loads?

A. Global Parameters
B. Project Units
C. Load Classifications
D. Structural Settings

Q39. Which classification types are mainly used in electrical load classes?

A. Circuits and Fixtures
B. Lighting and Power
C. Basic and Advanced
D. Custom and Default

Q40. What is the purpose of the Demand Factor tool?

A. Increase model speed
B. Define actual load consumption
C. Create parameter files
D. Report values to labels

Q41. What happens when the "By quantity" method is selected in Demand Factor settings?

A. Load is distributed by area
B. Demand factor varies with object count
C. Fixed value is always applied
D. Objects are grouped by type

Q42. What does selecting "Incrementally for each range" do?

A. Uses same demand factor for all objects
B. Adds load to each object
C. Uses different demand factors for ranges
D. Sets one demand factor

Q43. Which option lets you define demand factor based on object's load value?

A. By quantity
B. Constant
C. Reporting
D. By load

Q44. What is the first step to manage panel schedule templates?

A. Select Load Class
B. Edit Shared Parameter
C. Click Manage Templates
D. Apply Demand Factor

Q45. Which panel configuration types can be selected for branch panels?

A. Single or multiple tabs
B. Lighting or Power
C. Two Columns or Single Column
D. Basic or Custom

Q46. What tool is used to modify fill patterns?

A. Edit Tooltip
B. Modify Panel Schedule
C. Fill Patterns
D. Pattern Loader

Q47. What does selecting the "Basic" radio button in Fill Patterns dialog allow you to do?

A. Use custom files
B. Create fill with lines only
C. Add labels
D. Edit global parameters

Q48. What should you do to import a custom fill pattern?

A. Use Edit Pattern Properties
B. Select the Basic option
C. Click Browse and load file
D. Click on Duplicate

Q49. What is the first step to access the Material Assets tool?

A. Click on the Asset Browser in the Ribbon
B. Open the Asset Editor from the Settings tab
C. Click on Material Assets from Additional Settings in the Manage tab
D. Select the desired material from the Project Browser

Q50. Which tab is used to set the color for analysis display graphics?

A. Legend
B. Gradient
C. Settings
D. Color

Q51. What action allows adding a new revision in the Sheet Issues/Revisions dialog box?

A. Clicking on the Apply button
B. Double-clicking the revision row
C. Clicking on the Add button
D. Editing the Arc length box

Q52. Which tool is used to define thickness of lines for annotation scales?

A. Line Patterns
B. Line Weights
C. Line Styles
D. Callout Tag

Q53. What does the Halftone / Underlay tool allow you to adjust?

A. Revision cloud arc length
B. Annotation scale
C. Brightness of halftone elements
D. Temporary dimension units

Q54. What dialog box is displayed when changing line patterns?

A. Line Pattern Properties
B. New Line Style
C. Line Style Editor
D. Pattern Definition Box

Q55. What is the function of the Callout Tag tool?

A. Define coordinate systems
B. Set properties of callout tags
C. Adjust brightness
D. Create sun studies

Q56. Which tool sets annotation scales for detail levels?

A. Temporary Dimensions
B. Callout Tag
C. Detail Level
D. View Override
57. What can be selected in the Assembly Code dialog box?

A. Linked project
B. Custom material
C. Absolute, Relative, or Library location
D. Callout parameters

Q58. What does the Multiple Values Indication tool do?

A. Duplicates annotation values
B. Hides tags from sheet
C. Displays custom text for differing parameter values
D. Sets dimension styles

Q59. Which coordinate system defines the location of a building on Earth?

A. Assembly Coordinate System
B. Temporary Coordinate System
C. Project Coordinate System
D. Survey Coordinate System

Chapter 5

Revit Family, Conceptual Mass, and Title Block

Topics Covered

The major topics covered in this chapter are:

- ***Creating a Revit Family Component***
- ***Creating Extrude, Revolve, Blend, and Swept Blend features***
- ***Creating Void Forms***
- ***Creating Conceptual Mass***
- ***Creating Title Blocks and Annotation Symbols***

INTRODUCTION

In the previous chapters, you have learned to create architectural drawings. You have placed various components like table, chair, and other furniture items in these drawings. These components are called Revit family objects. In this chapter, we will discuss the procedure to create different types of Revit family objects.

CREATING NEW REVIT FAMILY COMPONENT

The Revit Family components are the objects inserted in Revit drawings to represent real objects in buildings. The procedure to create Revit Family component is given next.

- Press **CTRL+D** if home screen is displaying in the application. Click on the **Family** tool from the **New** cascading menu of **File** menu. The **New Family - Select Template File** dialog box will be displayed; refer to Figure-1.

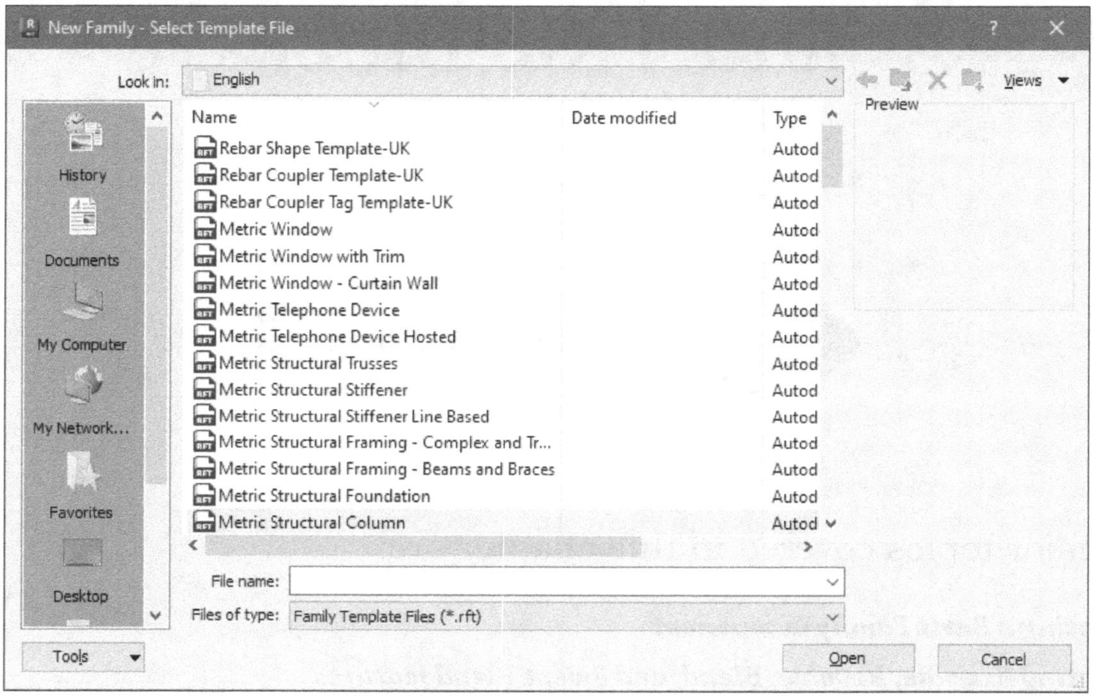

Figure-1. New Family-Select Template File dialog box

- Select desired template from the dialog box. For example, we have selected **Furniture** template in our case. After selecting the template, click on the **Open** button. The interface to create the Revit family component will be displayed; refer to Figure-2.
- Create the model of object using the tools in **Ribbon**. (You will learn about creation tools later in this chapter.)
- After creating the model, click on the **Save** button from **Quick Access Toolbar**. The **Save As** dialog box will be displayed; refer to Figure-3.

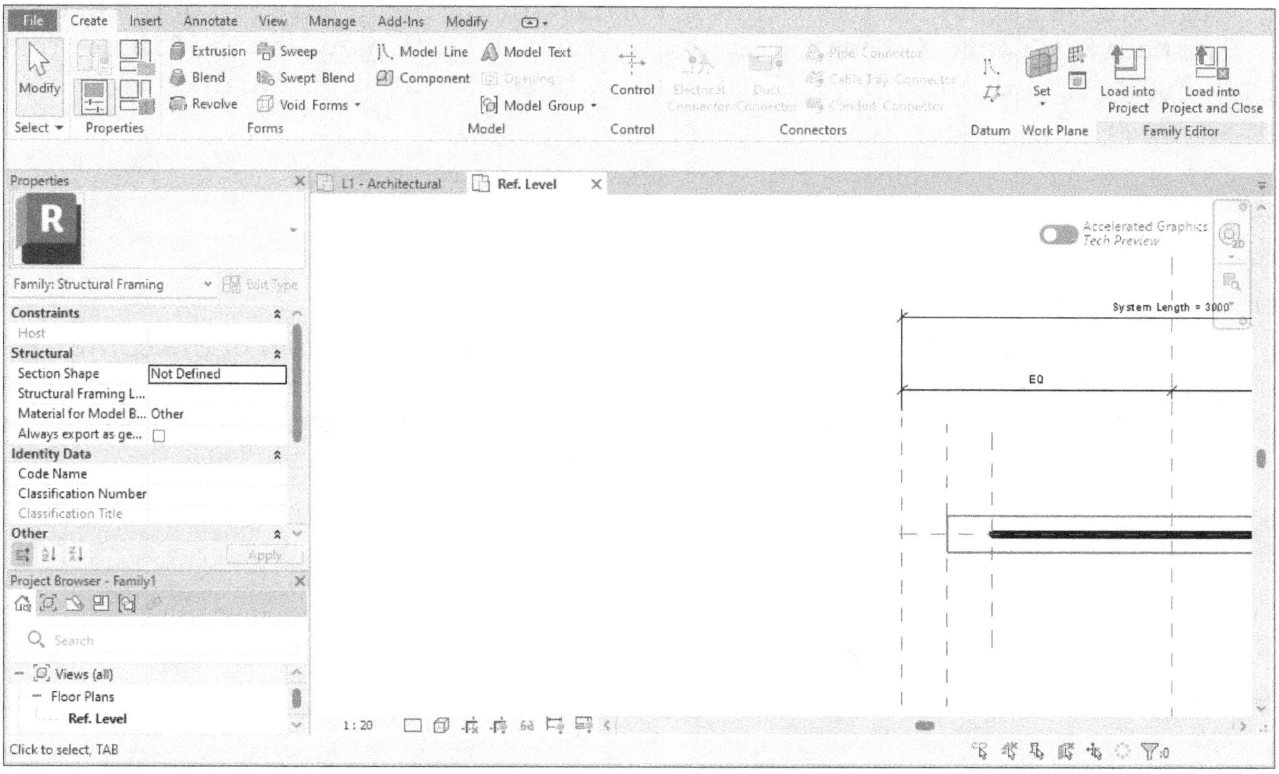

Figure-2. Interface for creating Revit Family objects

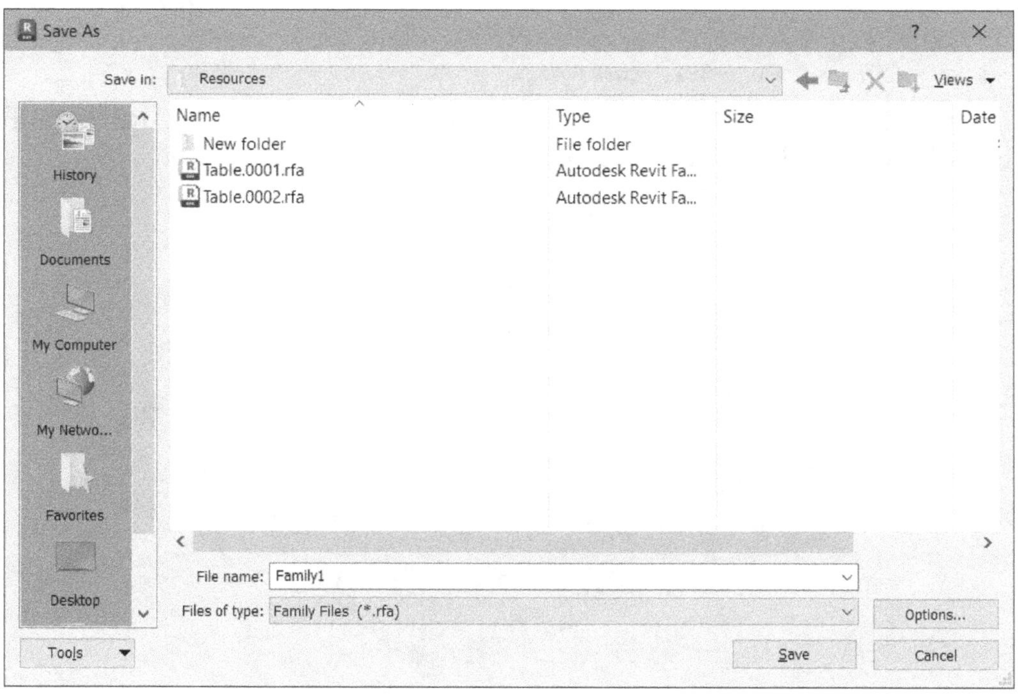

Figure-3. Save As dialog box

- Specify desired name of part and click on the **Save** button to save the file.

Various tools available in **Ribbon** to create model are discussed next.

Creating Extrusion

The **Extrusion** tool is used to create a 3D shape by adding material within the sketch boundaries up to specified height or depth. The procedure to create objects by extrusion is discussed next.

- Click on the **Extrusion** tool from the **Forms** panel in the **Create** tab of the **Ribbon**. The **Modify|Create Extrusion** contextual tab will be displayed in the **Ribbon**; refer to Figure-4 and you will be asked to draw base sketch to be extruded.

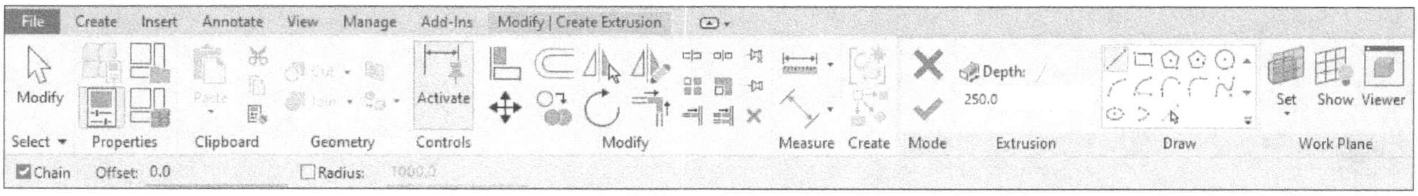

Figure-4. Modify Create Extrusion contextual tab

- Set the work plane by using **Set** tool from the **Work Plane** panel of the contextual tab as discussed earlier.
- Using the tools in the **Draw** panel, create a closed loop sketch; refer to Figure-5.

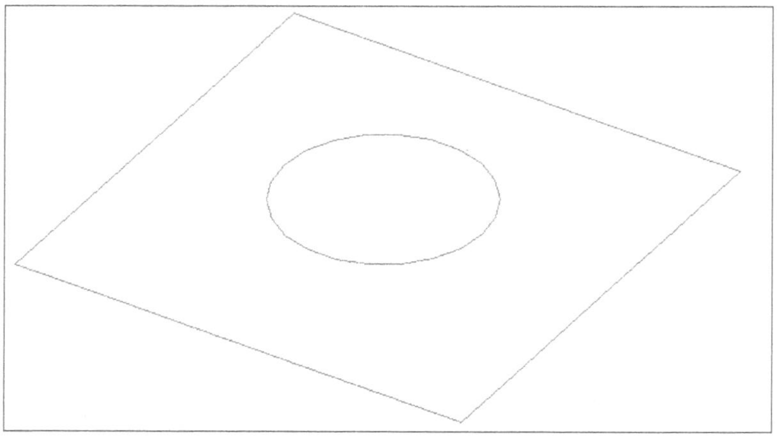

Figure-5. Sketch for extrusion

- Click on the **OK** button from the **Mode** panel in the contextual tab. Preview of extruded object will be displayed; refer to Figure-6.

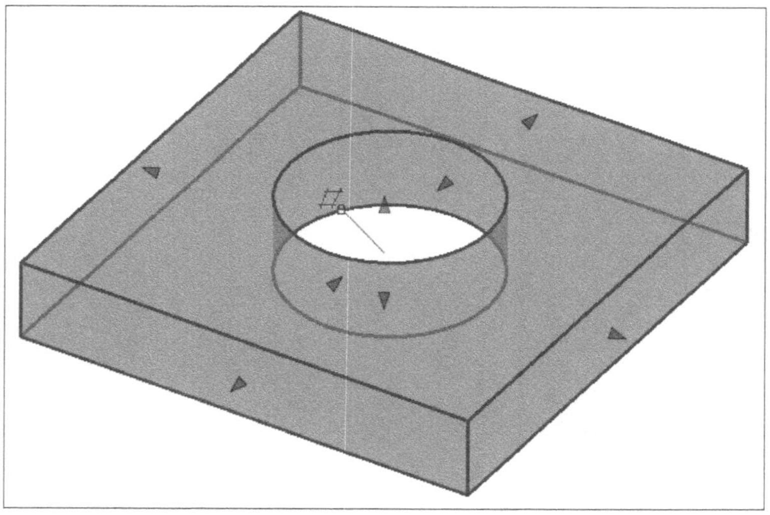

Figure-6. Preview of extrusion

- Note that you can use the arrows displayed in the preview to modify shape of extrusion. Press **ESC** to exit the tool.

Creating Blend Object

The **Blend** tool is used to create solid feature by joining two sketches. The procedure to create blend feature is given next.

- Click on the **Blend** tool from the **Forms** panel in the **Create** tab of **Ribbon**. The **Modify|Create Blend Base Boundary** contextual tab will be displayed in the **Ribbon** and you will be asked to draw closed loop sketch for base of blend feature.
- Create desired sketch using the tools in **Draw** panel of contextual tab; refer to Figure-7.

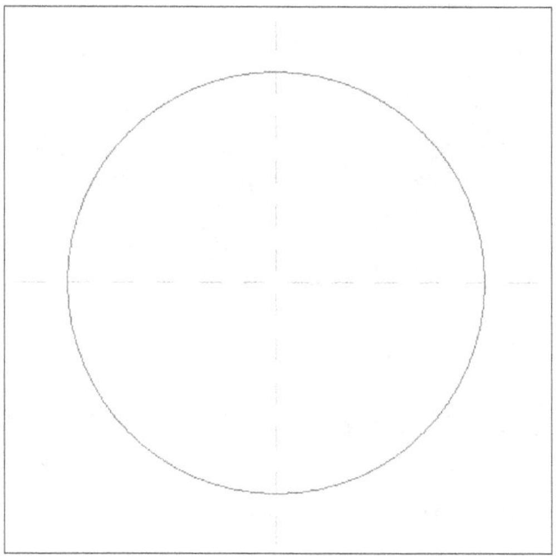

Figure-7. Base sketch

- Click on the **Edit Top** button from the **Mode** panel in the contextual tab. The options to define depth of top sketch are displayed in the **Options Bar**.
- Specify desired value of depth in the **Depth** edit box and create the top sketch; refer to Figure-8.

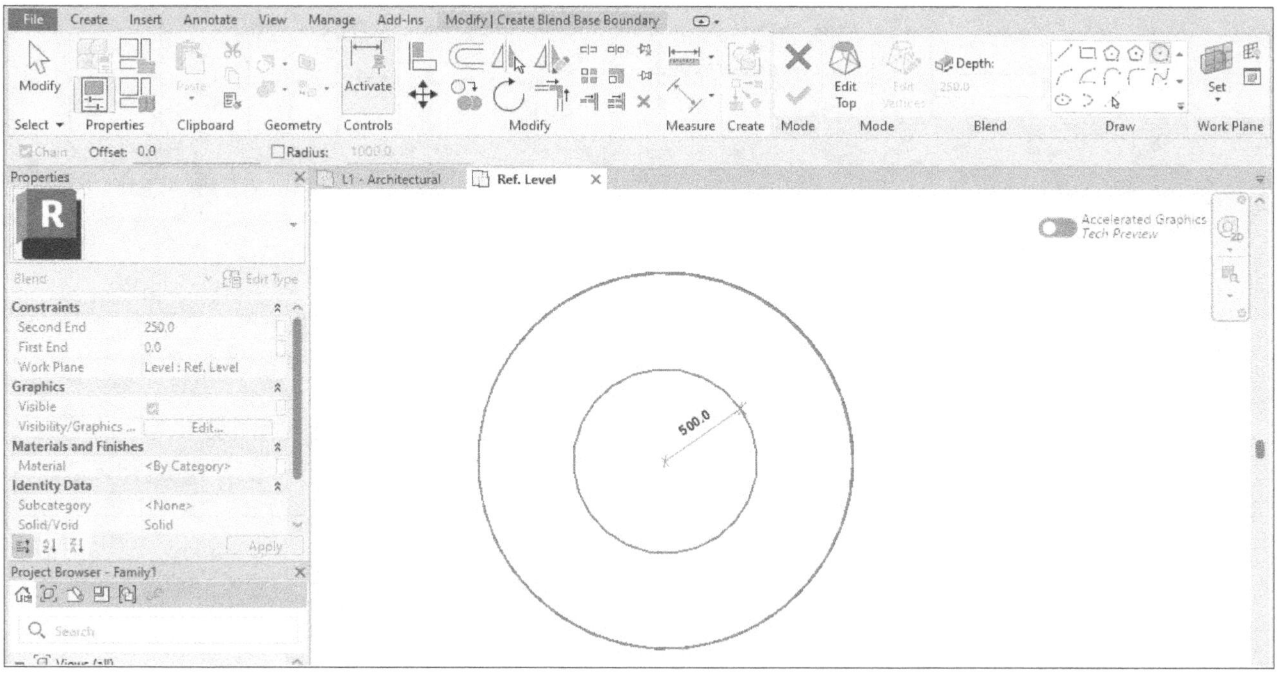

Figure-8. Creating top sketch for blend

- Click on the **OK** button from the **Mode** panel in the **Ribbon** to create the blend feature.
- Click on the **Default 3D View** tool from the **Quick Access Toolbar** to check the blend feature; refer to Figure-9.

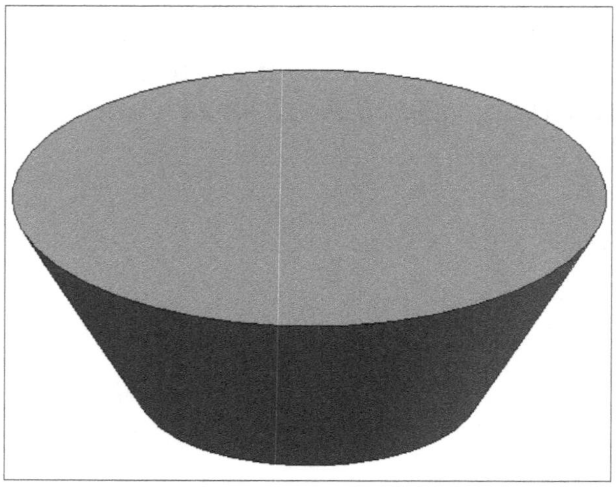

Figure-9. Blend feature created

Creating Revolve Feature

The **Revolve** tool is used to create solid feature by revolving closed loop sketch about an axis. The procedure to use this tool is given next.

- Click on the **Revolve** tool from the **Forms** panel in the **Create** tab of **Ribbon**. The **Modify|Create Revolve** contextual tab will be displayed in the **Ribbon**.
- Create desired closed loop sketch using the tools in **Draw** panel.
- Click on the **Axis Line** button from the **Mode** panel in the contextual tab and create the axis about which the sketch will be revolved; refer to Figure-10.

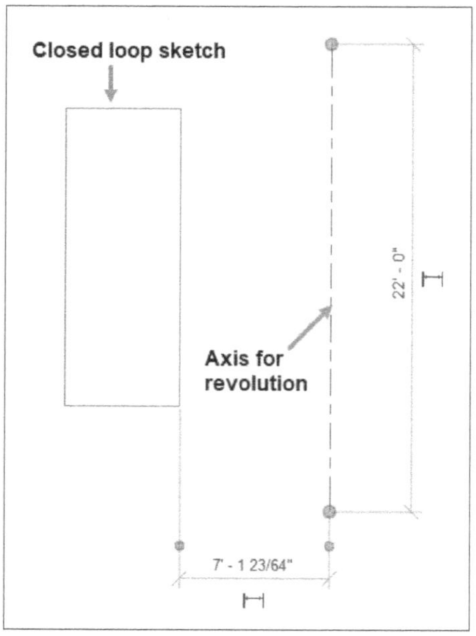

Figure-10. Sketch for revolve feature

- Set the start and end angle for revolve feature in respective edit boxes in **Properties Palette** and click on the **OK** button from the **Mode** panel in the **Ribbon**. The revolve feature will be created.
- Rotate the model in 3D view to check the feature.

Creating Sweep Feature

The **Sweep** tool is used to create solid feature by sweeping a closed loop sketch along selected path sketch. The procedure to create sweep feature is given next.

- Click on the **Sweep** tool from the **Forms** panel in the **Create** tab of **Ribbon**. The **Modify|Sweep** contextual tab will be displayed in the **Ribbon**.
- Click on **Pick Path** button from the **Work Plane** panel if you want to select edges to define path sketch. Click on the **Sketch Path** tool from the **Work Plane** panel if you want to create sketch for path. We will use the later option here.
- On clicking the **Sketch Path** tool, the **Modify|Sweep>Sketch Path** contextual tab will be displayed. Create the sketch of desired shape and size; refer to Figure-11. Note that the sketch can be open or can have one closed loop.

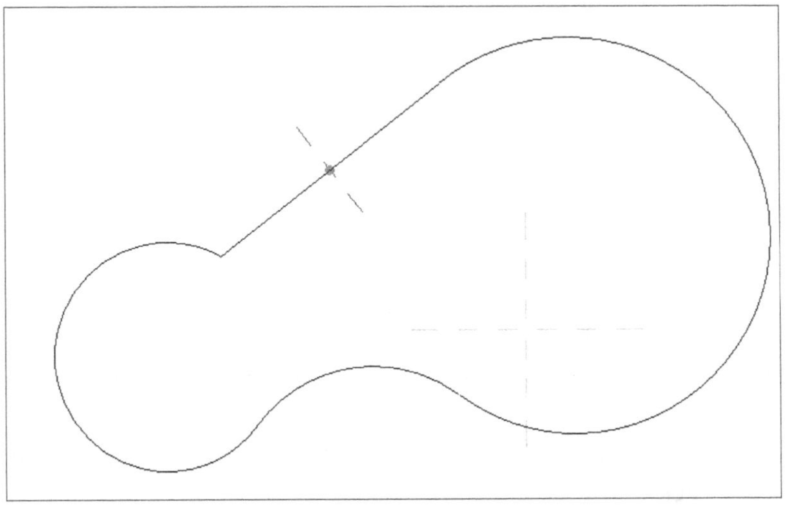

Figure-11. Sketch for sweep path

Note that the location where a red dot appears with dashed lines on the path sketch will be used as reference for creating profile of sweep section.

- After creating path sketch, click on the **OK** button from the **Mode** panel.
- Click on the **Select Profile** button from the **Sweep** panel of **Modify|Sweep** tab in the **Ribbon**. The tools in **Sweep** panel will become active.
- Click on the **Edit Profile** tool from the **Sweep** panel in the **Ribbon**. The **Go To View** dialog box will be displayed if you are not in 3D view; refer to Figure-12.

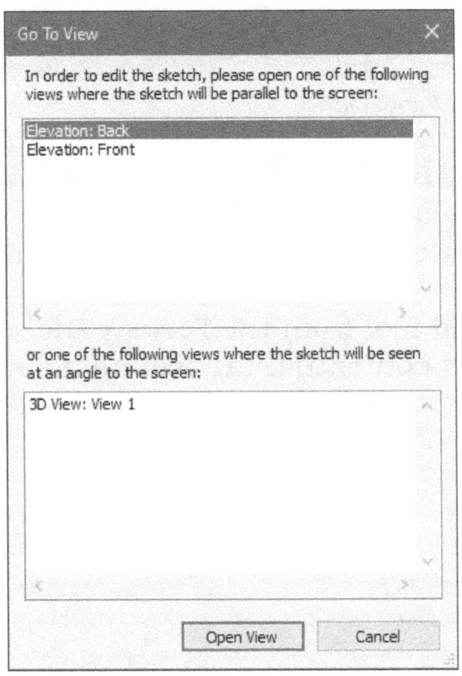

Figure-12. Go To View dialog box

- Select the **3D View: View 1** option from the dialog box and click on the **Open View** button from the dialog box. The view will be activated.
- Create desired sketch while keeping red dot as center; refer to Figure-13.

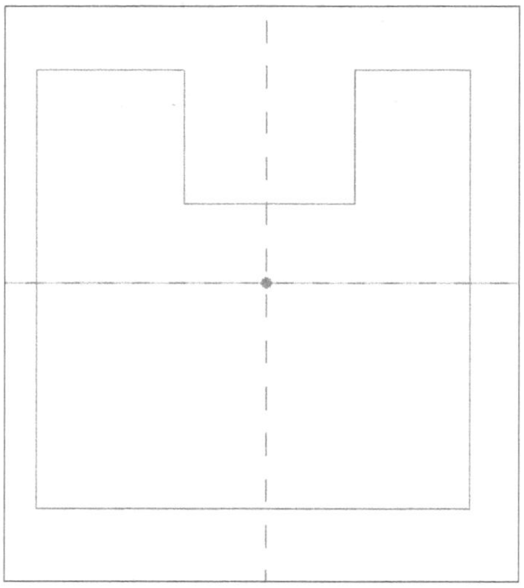

Figure-13. Sketch for sweep profile

- Click on the **OK** button from the **Mode** panel after creating the sketch. The profile will be created.
- Click on the **OK** button from the **Mode** panel again. The sweep feature will be created; refer to Figure-14.

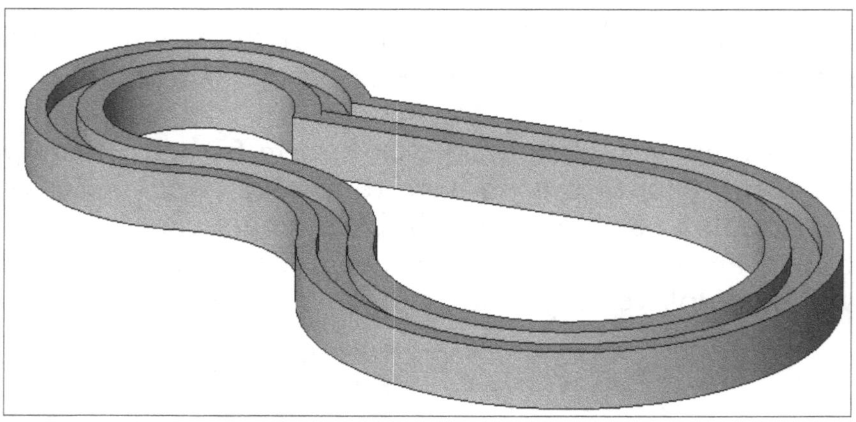

Figure-14. Sweep feature created

Creating Swept Blend Feature

The swept blend feature is a solid feature created by joining two sketches along specified path. The procedure to create swept blend feature is given next.

- Click on the **Swept Blend** tool from the **Forms** panel in the **Create** tab of **Ribbon**. The **Modify|Swept Blend** contextual tab will be displayed in the **Ribbon**; refer to Figure-15.

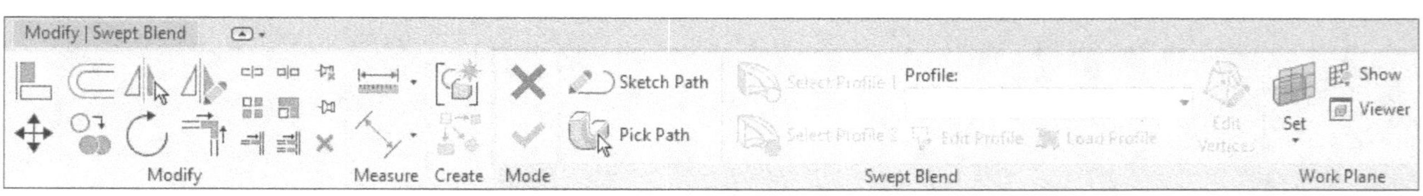

Figure-15. Modify Swept Blend contextual tab

- Click on the **Sketch Path** tool from the **Mode** panel in the contextual tab of **Ribbon**. The tools to draw path will be displayed in the **Ribbon**.
- Create desired sketch of path and click on the **OK** button from the **Mode** panel. Note that there should be only one sketch curve in path; refer to Figure-16.

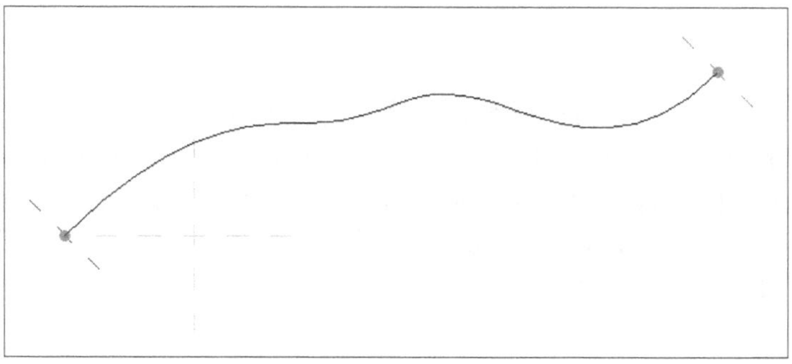

Figure-16. Sketch for swept blend path

- Click on the **Select Profile 1** button from the **Swept Blend** panel in the **Ribbon** and click on the **Edit Profile** button from the **Swept Blend** panel. The **Go To View** dialog box will be displayed.
- Select the **3D View: View 1** option from the dialog box and click on the **Open View** button. The view will be activated.
- Create the sketch of first profile; refer to Figure-17.

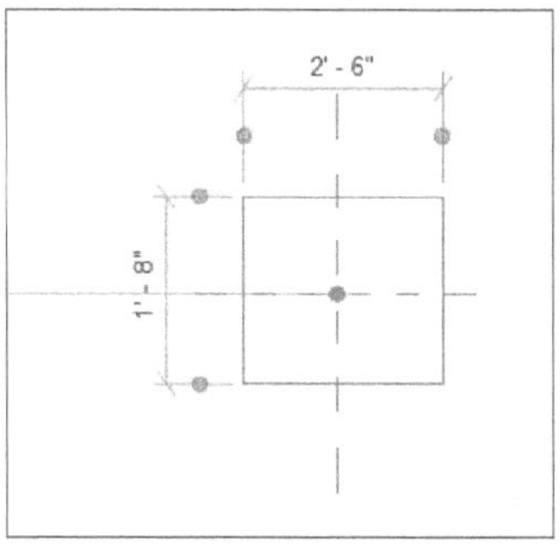

Figure-17. Sketch of first profile

- Click on the **OK** button from the **Mode** panel.
- Click on the **Select Profile 2** button from the **Swept Blend** contextual tab in the **Ribbon** and then click on the **Edit Profile** again. You will be asked to draw second profile sketch.
- Create the second profile sketch and click on the **OK** button from the **Mode** panel.
- Click again on the **OK** button from the **Mode** panel to create the feature. The swept blend feature will be created; refer to Figure-18.

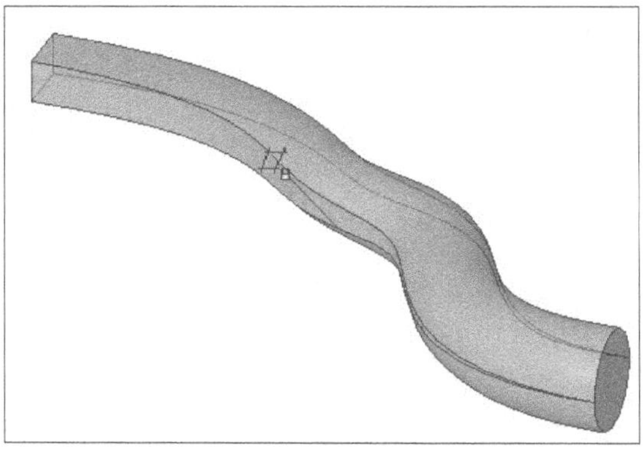

Figure-18. Swept Blend feature created

Creating Void Forms

The tools in **Void Forms** drop-down are used to remove material from the 3D object. The tools in this drop-down work in the same way as discussed earlier for creation tools. We will discuss the **Void Extrusion** tool here, you can apply the same concept to other tools.

Creating Void Extrusion

- Click on the **Void Extrusion** tool from the **Void Forms** drop-down in the **Forms** panel of **Create** tab in **Ribbon**. The **Modify|Create Void Extrusion** contextual tab will be displayed in the **Ribbon** and you will be asked to draw sketch for extrusion.
- Create a closed loop sketch on the face of 3D object earlier created; refer to Figure-19.

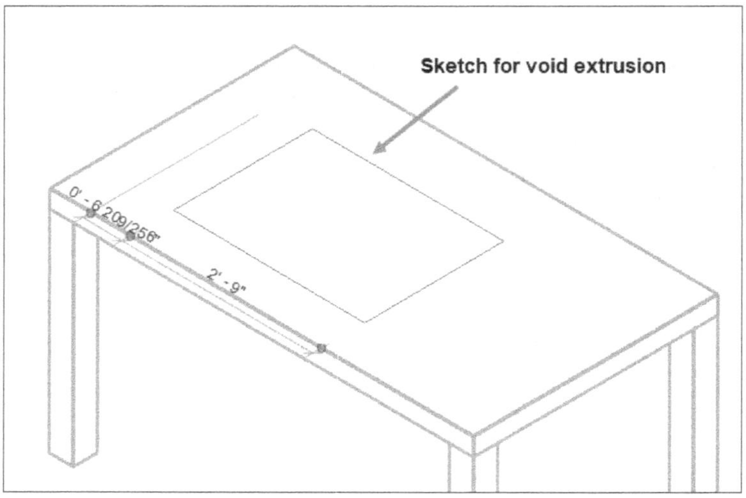

Figure-19. Sketch for void extrusion

- Specify the depth up to which you want to remove material by extruding sketch.
- Click on the **OK** button from the **Mode** panel in the **Ribbon** and click in the empty area of screen. The cut will be created; refer to Figure-20.

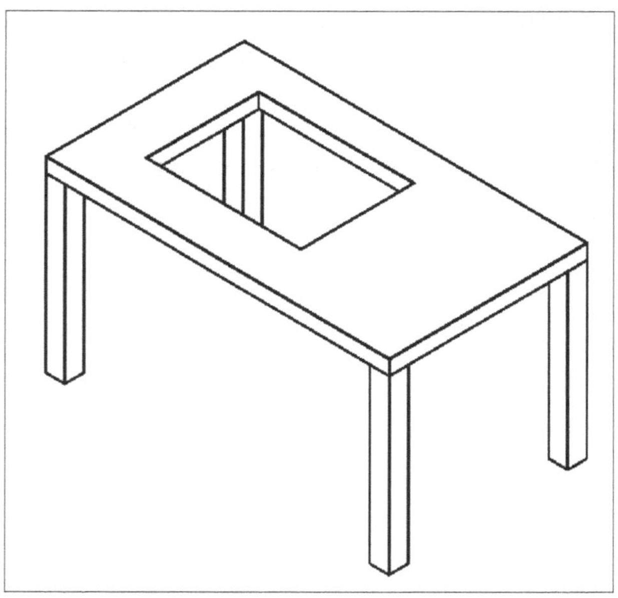

Figure-20. Extrusion cut created

You can use the other tools of **Void Forms** drop-down in the same way.

PRACTICAL 1

Till this point, you have learned about various tools used to create Revit family parts. Now, we will discuss the basic procedure of creating Revit family parts. We will create an electric motor family with different horsepower ratings like 0.75 KW, 1KW, 2KW, and 5 KW.

Starting a New Part

- Click on the **Family** tool from the **New** cascading menu of the **File** menu. The **New Family - Select Template File** dialog box will be displayed.
- Select the **Electrical Equipment** template from the dialog box and click on the **Open** button. The **Reference Level** tile will be displayed active in the viewport.

Creating Model

- Create the model of motor using the tools (**Revolve** tool) in **Forms** panel of **Create** tab in the **Ribbon**; refer to Figure-21.
- While making the sketch for revolve feature, dimension the radius of motor and shaft; refer to Figure-22. Press **ESC** twice to exit the dimension tools.

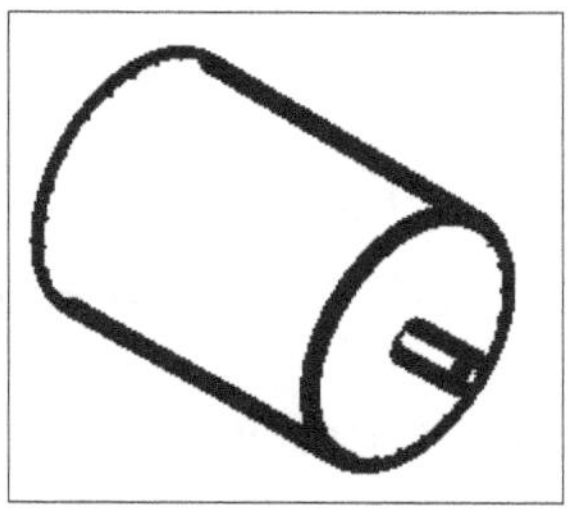

Figure-21. Model of motor created

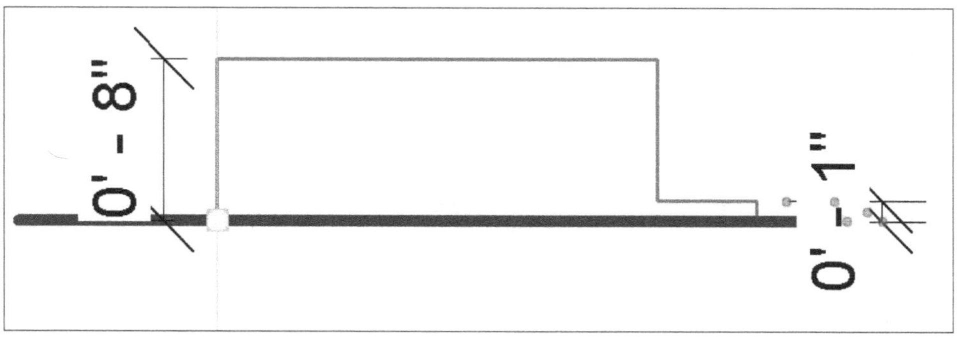

Figure-22. Sketch for motor

- Select the dimension of motor radius (8" dimension) and click on the **Create Parameter** button from the **Dimension** contextual tab in the **Ribbon**; refer to Figure-23. The **Parameter Properties** dialog box will be displayed; refer to Figure-24.

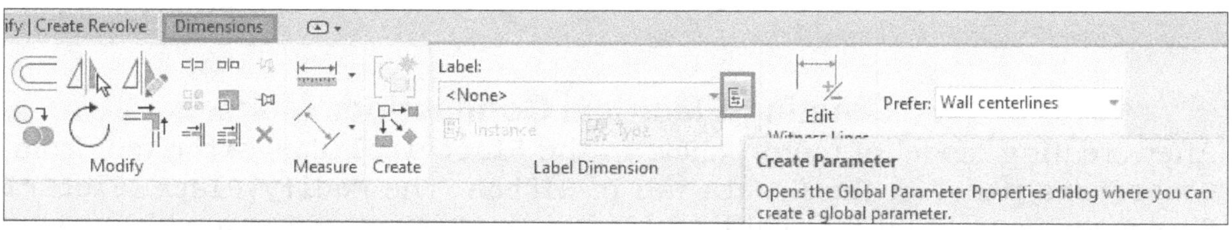

Figure-23. Create Parameter button

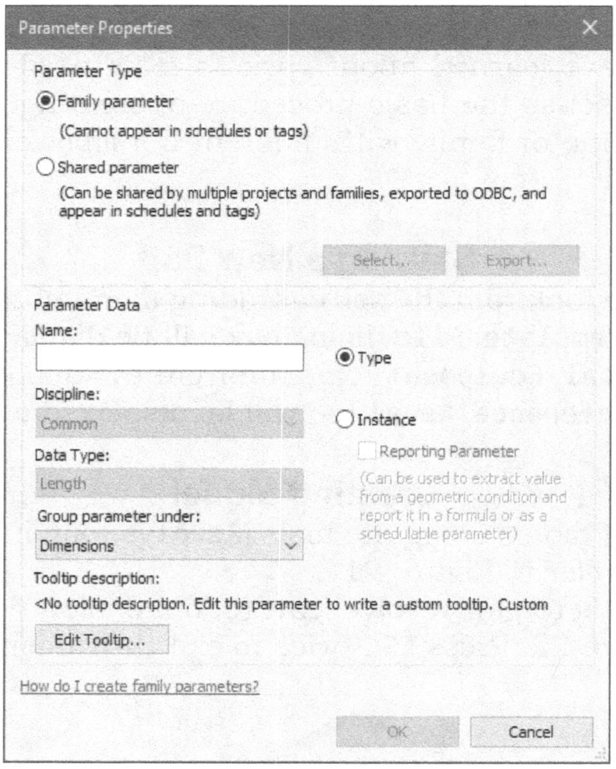

Figure-24. Parameter Properties dialog box

- Specify the name of parameter as **Motor dia** and click on the **OK** button from the dialog box.
- Similarly, create dimension parameter for other dimension (1" dimension) as **Shaft dia**; refer to Figure-25.

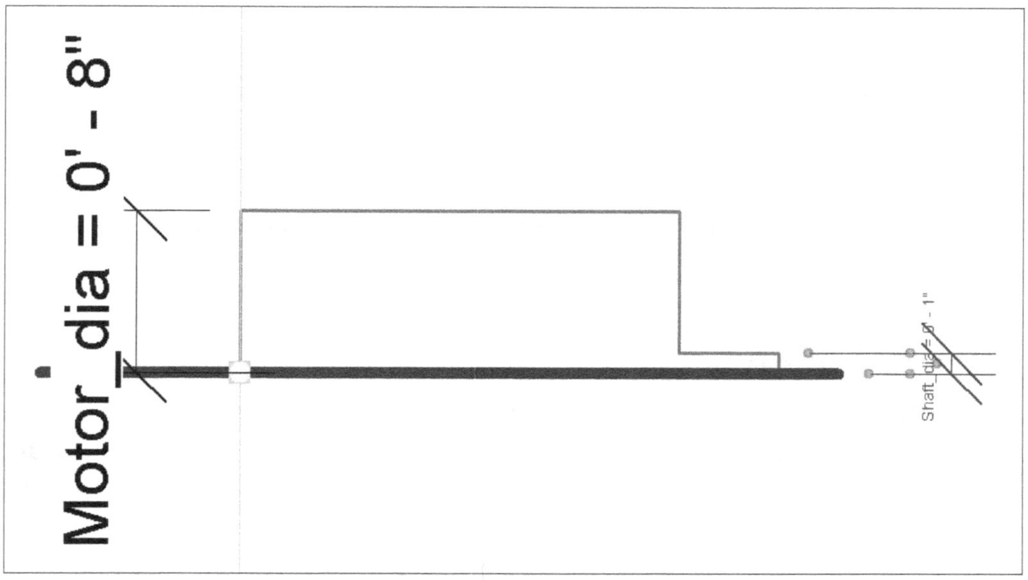

Figure-25. Parameters created for motor sketch

Creating Electrical Connections

- After creating model of motor, click on the **Electrical Connector** tool from the **Connectors** panel in the **Create** tab of **Ribbon**. The **Modify|Place Electrical Connector** contextual tab will be added in the **Ribbon** and you will be asked to specify the location of connection point.

- Click on the edge of back face of motor; refer to Figure-26. The connection will be created; refer to Figure-27.

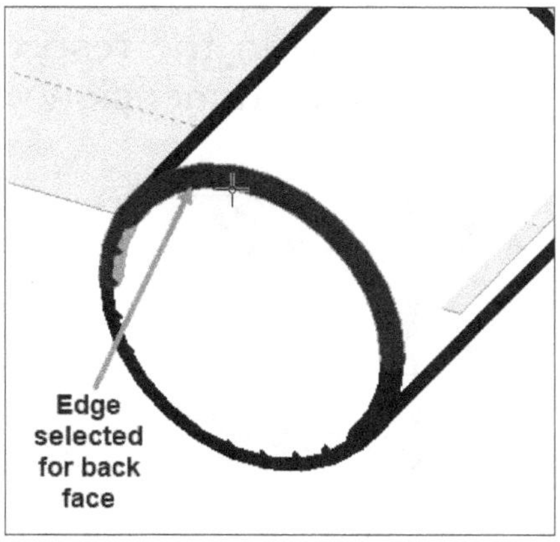

Figure-26. Selecting edge for back face of motor

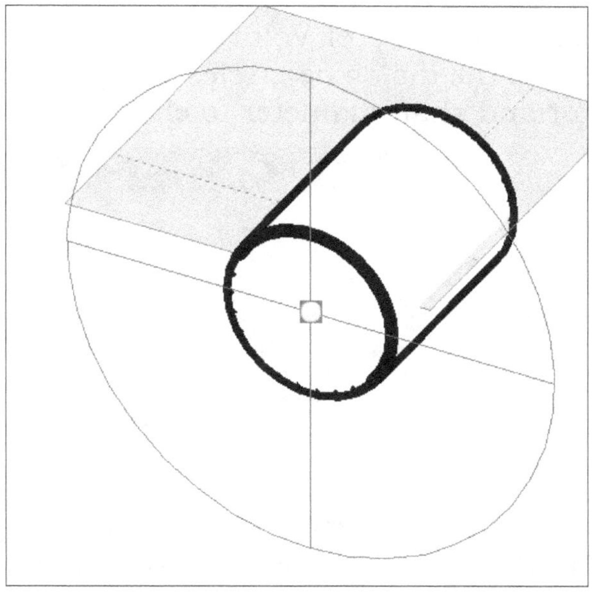

Figure-27. Connection created on motor

Defining Types of Motor

- Click on the **Family Types** tool from the **Properties** panel in the **Create** tab of **Ribbon**. The **Family Types** dialog box will be displayed; refer to Figure-28.

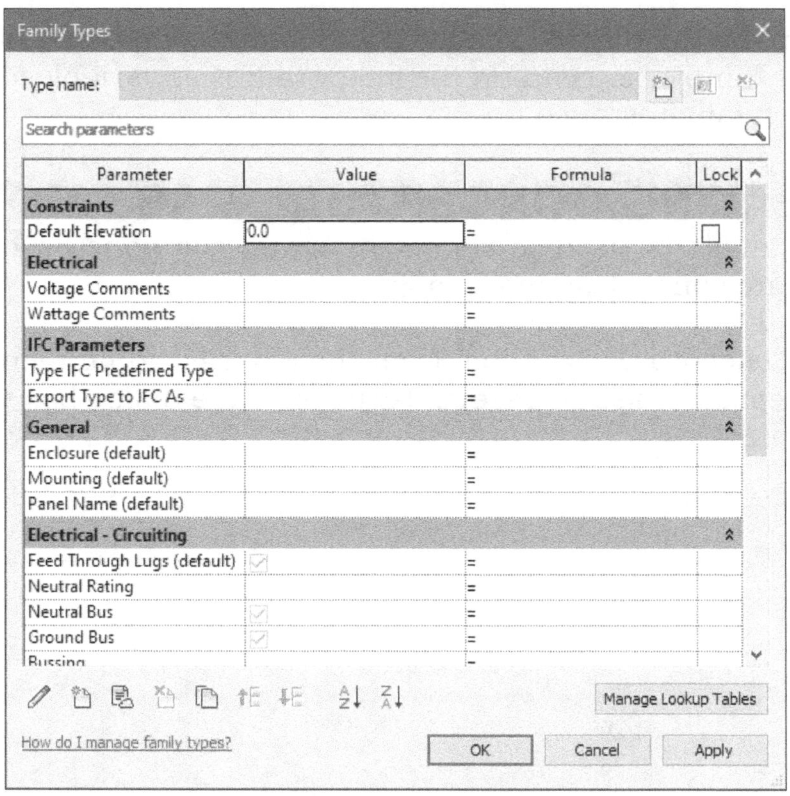

Figure-28. Family Types dialog box

- Click on the **New Type** button at the right of **Type name** edit box at the top in the dialog box. The **Name** dialog box will be displayed asking you to specify the name for new type of family component.

- Specify the name as **Motor 0.75 KW** in **Name** edit box and click on the **OK** button. The newly create name will be added in the **Type name** drop-down at the top in the **Family Types** dialog box.
- Specify the value of Voltage as 220 and Wattage as 750 in the respective edit boxes in the dialog box; refer to Figure-29. Specify desired dimension values for motor and shaft diameter to change the shape of motor.

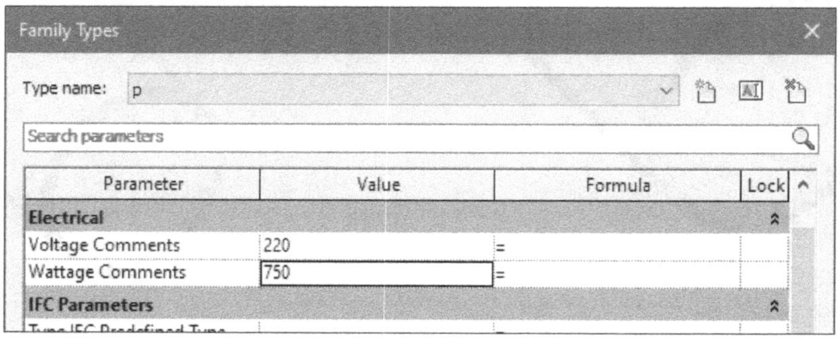

Figure-29. Creating motor types

- Click on the **New Type** button again and specify the name of family type as **Motor 1 KW**. Click on the **OK** button from the **Name** dialog box.
- Change the **Wattage** value as **1000** in the edit box.
- Click on the **New Type** button again and create the motor of 2KW and 5KW as discussed earlier.
- Click on the **OK** button from the **Family Type** dialog box.
- Save the file at desired location.

Note that you can also modify the shape/size of family component based on specified parameters. For example, you can set the motor radius as variable to modify diameter of motor in each family instance.

CREATING CONCEPTUAL MASS MODEL

The Conceptual mass is used to represent static components of buildings. The procedure to create conceptual mass is given next.

- Click on the **Conceptual Mass** tool from the **New** cascading menu of **File** menu. The **New Conceptual Mass - Select Template File** dialog box will be displayed; refer to Figure-30.

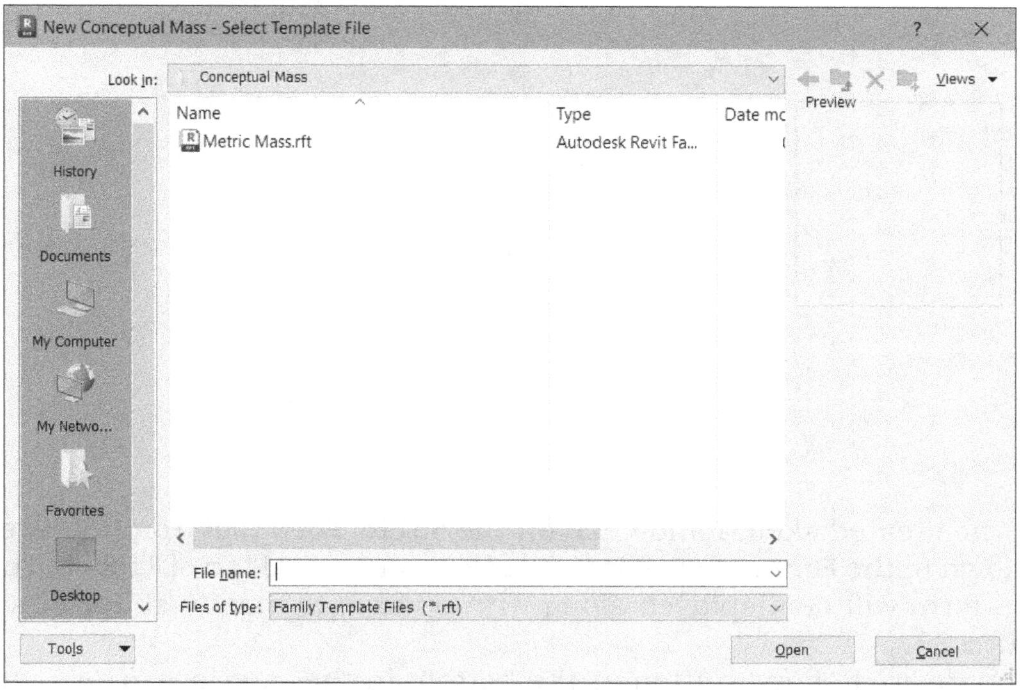

Figure-30. New Conceptual Mass-Select Template File dialog box

- Select desired template and click on the **Open** button from the dialog box. The environment to create conceptual mass will be displayed; refer to Figure-31.
- Create the base sketch for model; refer to Figure-32.

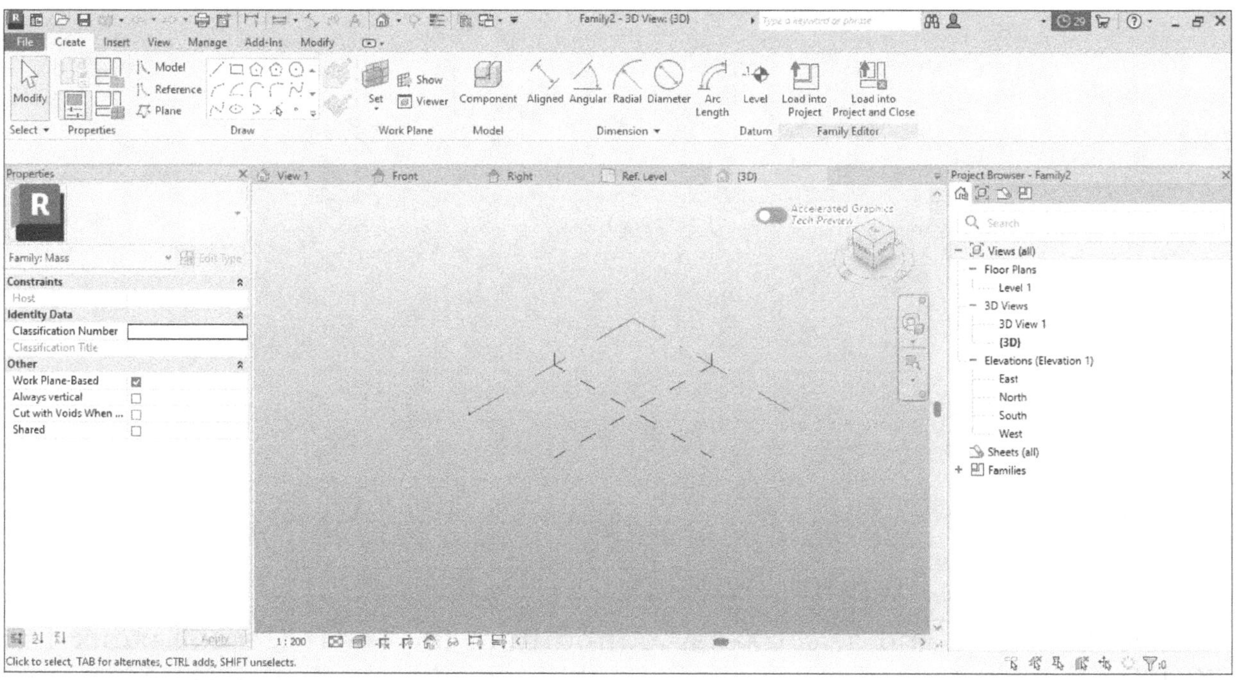

Figure-31. Environment to edit or create conceptual mass

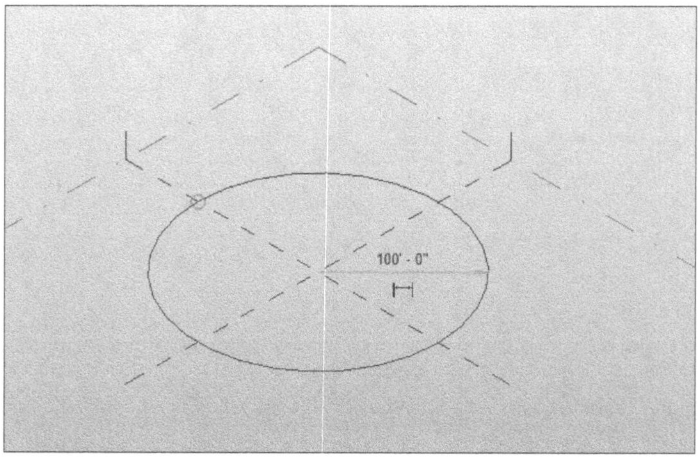

Figure-32. Base sketch created

- Select the created sketch and click on the **Solid Form** tool from the **Create Form** drop-down in the **Form** panel of **Modify|Lines** contextual tab of **Ribbon**. The preview of solid form will be displayed along with options to modify shape of solid; refer to Figure-33.
- Click on desired shape button at the bottom in the interface. The shape will be created.
- Set desired height of the shape using the dimension displayed on the form.
- You can add edges and profiles to modify the shape of conceptual mass by using **Add Edge** and **Add Profile** tools.

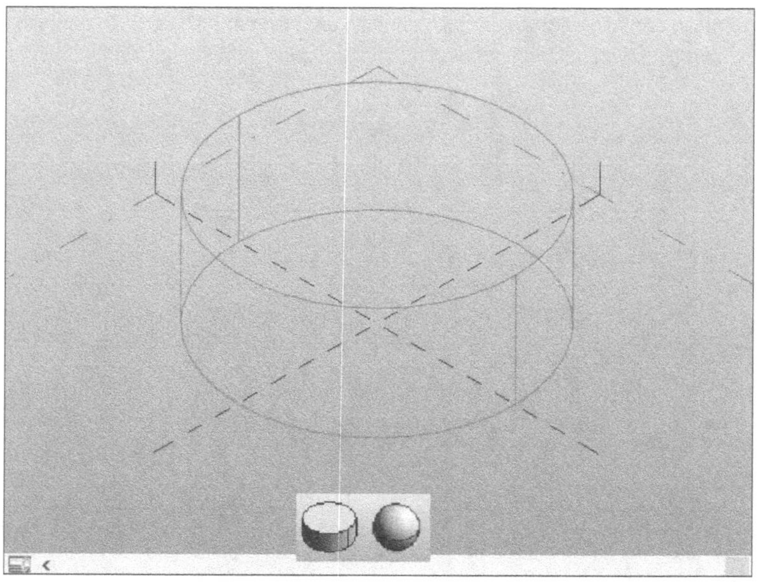

Figure-33. Preview of solid form

- Select the model and select **X-Ray** button from the **Form Element** panel of the **Modify|Form** contextual tab. You will be able to modify the model using key points; refer to Figure-34. Select desired key point and move it using arrows.

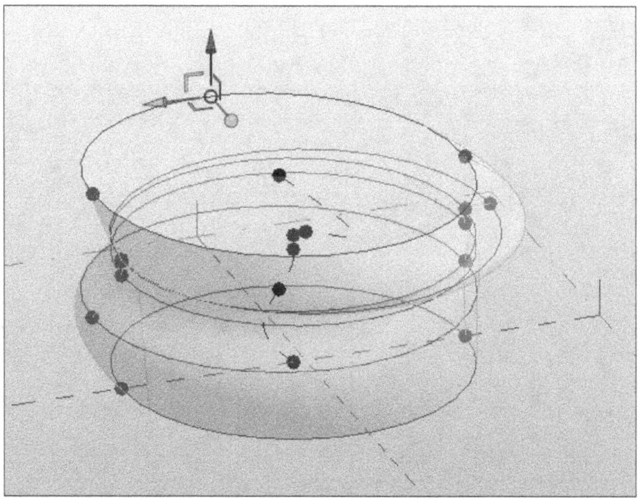

Figure-34. Conceptual model in X Ray visual style

- Click on the **Save** button from the **Quick Access Toolbar** to save the file. Click on the **Load into Project** button if a project is open in Revit and you want to load the current conceptual mass in the project.

CREATING TITLE BLOCK TEMPLATE

The title block template is used to create drawings based on specified settings. The procedure to create title block template is given next.

- Click on the **Title Block** tool from the **New** cascading menu of the **File** menu. The **New Title Block - Select Template File** dialog box will be displayed; refer to Figure-35.

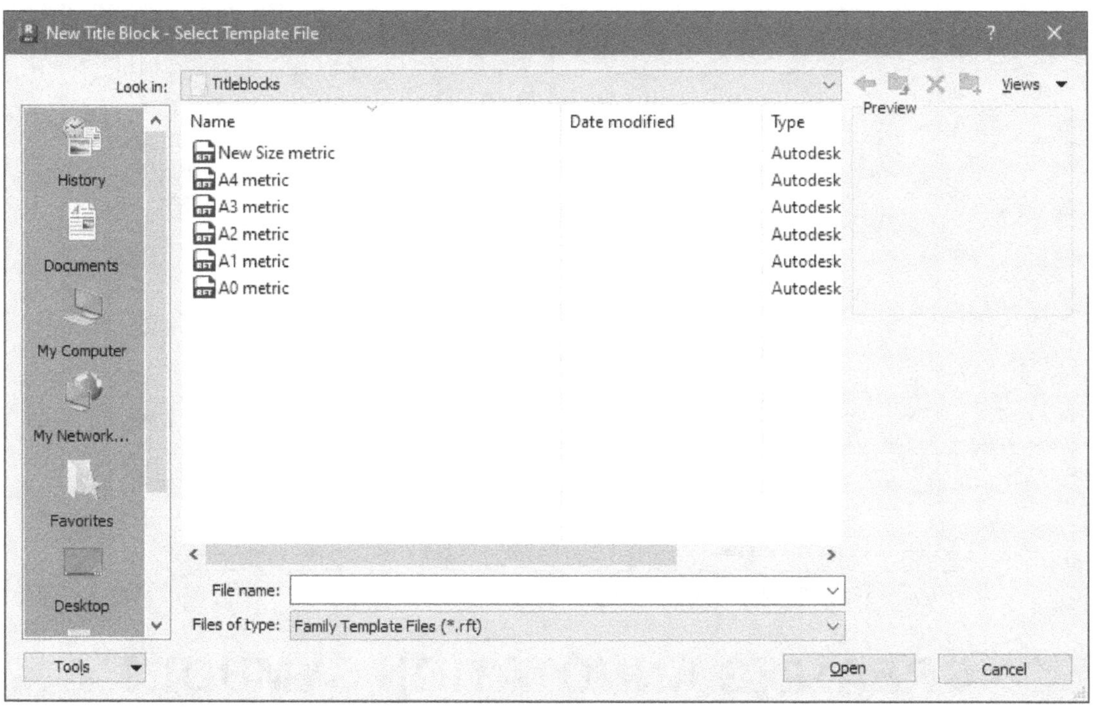

Figure-35. New Title Block-Select Template File dialog box

- Select desired template from the dialog box and click on the **Open** button. The tools to create template will be displayed; refer to Figure-36.

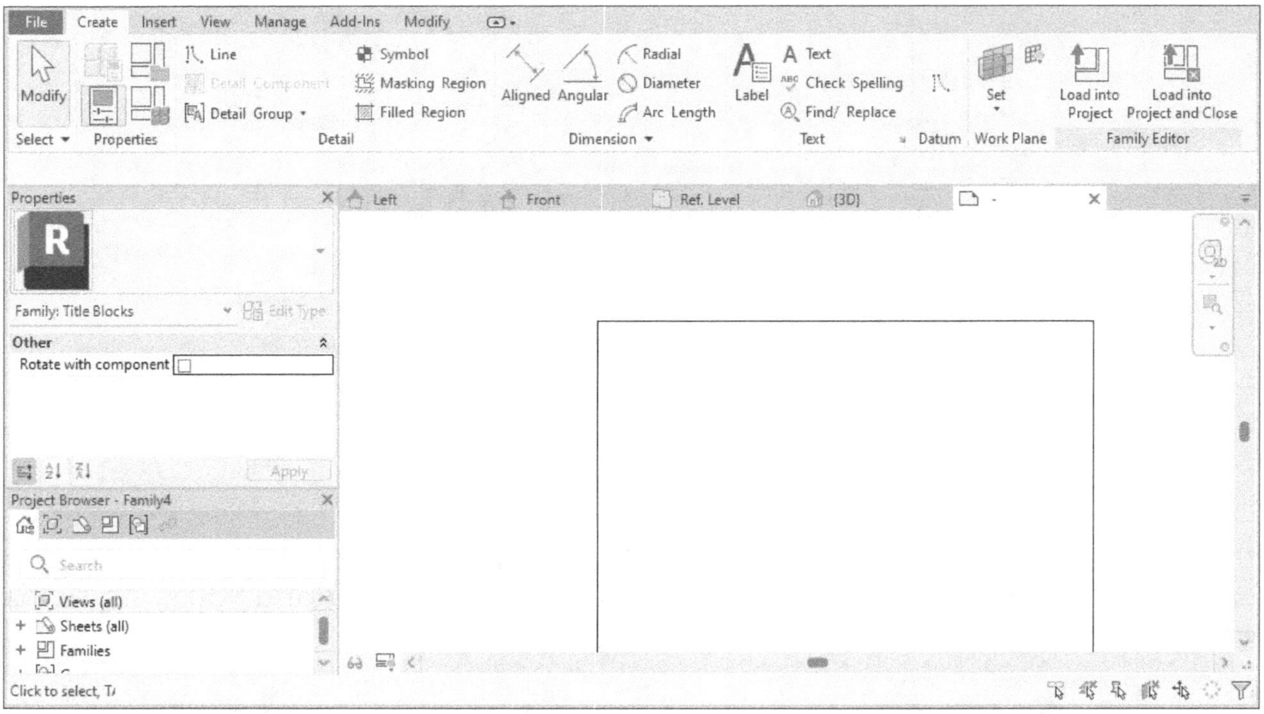

Figure-36. Tools to create template

- Click on the **Line** tool from the **Detail** panel in the **Create** tab of **Ribbon**. The **Modify|Place Lines** contextual tab will be displayed in the **Ribbon**.
- Create the template shape as desired; refer to Figure-37.

Figure-37. Title block template created

CREATING ANNOTATION SYMBOLS

The annotation symbols are used in drawing to represent objects in symbols and tags. The procedure to create annotation symbol is given next.

- Click on the **Annotation Symbol** tool from the **New** cascading menu of the **File** menu. The **New Annotation Symbol - Select Template File** dialog box will be displayed; refer to Figure-38.

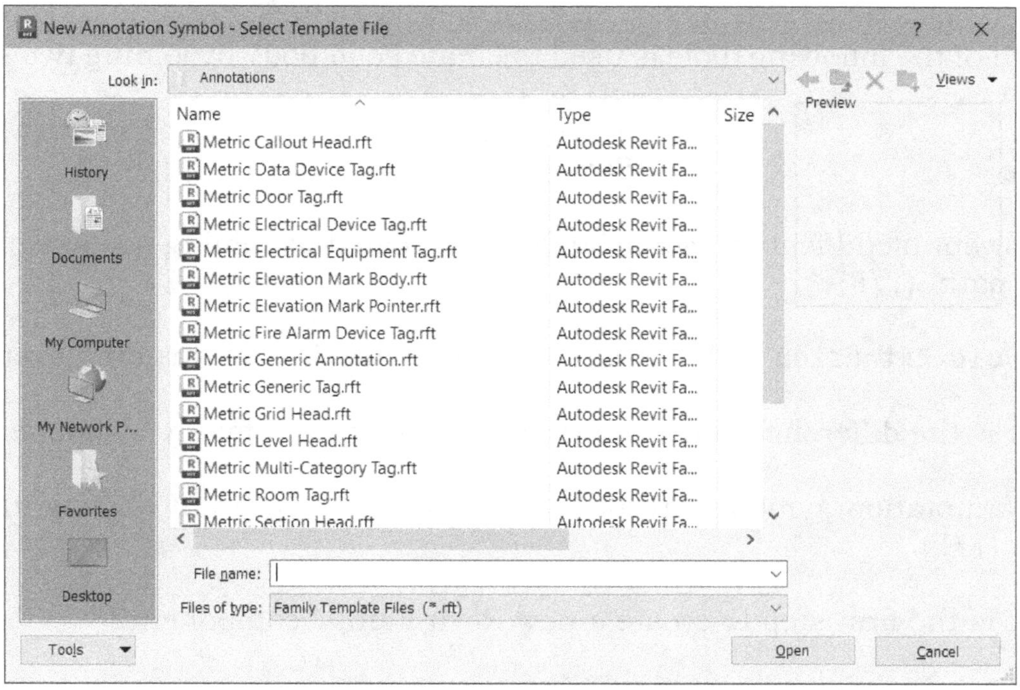

Figure-38. New Annotation Symbol-Select Template File dialog box

- Select desired template from the dialog box and click on the **Open** button. The environment to create annotative symbol will be displayed.
- Create the symbol as desired and save it for later use. The procedure to create symbol is similar to creating conceptual mass or Revit family component.

PRACTICE 1

Create the model of a standard car to be used as revit family in the Revit building model. The general dimensions of a car are given in Figure-39. Width of car is 5 feet.

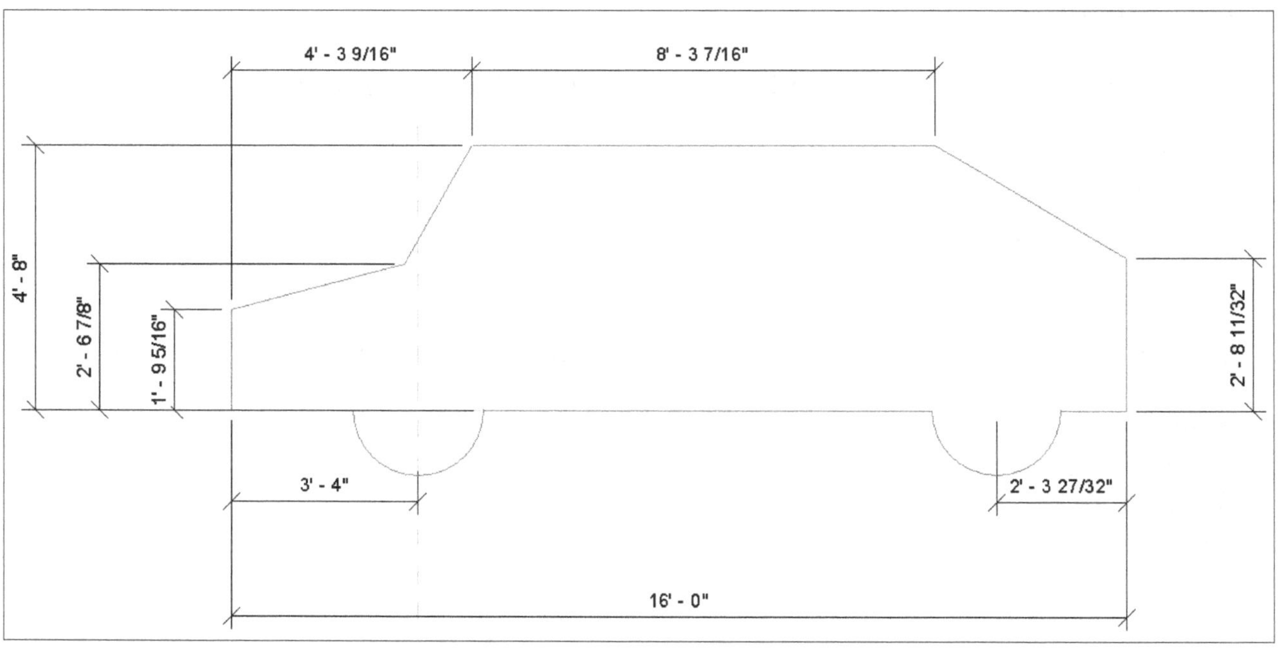

Figure-39. Car sketch

Self Assessment

Q1. The Revit Family components are objects that represent real world objects like table, chair in the project with specified properties. (T/F)

Q2. Which of the following tools is used to create solid body by joining two sketches?

a. Blend
b. Extrusion
c. Revolve
d. Sweep

Q3. The swept blend feature is a solid feature created by joining two sketches along specified path. (T/F)

Q4. The **Void Extrusion** tool is used to remove material by extruding sketch. (T/F)

Q5. What is the difference between Conceptual Mass and family component forms?

Q6. The annotation symbols are used in drawing to represent objects in symbols and tags. (T/F)

Q7. What is the first step to create a new Revit Family component?

A. Select the Extrusion tool
B. Open the Project Browser
C. Click on the Family tool from the New menu
D. Select the View tab

Q8. Which panel contains the Extrusion tool?

A. Work Plane panel
B. Draw panel
C. Mode panel
D. Forms panel

Q9. What do you need to create before using the Extrusion tool?

A. Profile view
B. A solid revolve
C. A closed loop sketch
D. A 3D path

Q10. What tool allows you to create a 3D object by joining two sketches vertically?

A. Blend tool
B. Revolve tool
C. Sweep tool
D. Extrusion tool

Q11. In the Revolve tool, what is used to define the axis of rotation?

A. Sweep path
B. Profile center
C. Axis Line
D. Sketch center

Q12. Which tool is used to create a solid by sweeping a closed loop sketch along a path?

A. Blend
B. Extrusion
C. Revolve
D. Sweep

Q13. When using the Sweep tool, what indicates the reference for creating the profile?

A. Blue arrow
B. Red dot with dashed lines
C. Axis Line
D. Green circle

Q14. What is a Swept Blend feature?

A. A feature using a single sketch
B. A feature created by revolving a sketch
C. A feature joining two profiles along a path
D. A 2D drafting tool

Q15. What is required for the path sketch in the Swept Blend tool?

A. Two intersecting curves
B. A single sketch curve
C. A closed loop sketch
D. Multiple profile intersections

Q16. Which tool removes material from a 3D object using a sketch?

A. Void Extrusion
B. Sweep
C. Blend
D. Revolve

Q17. In the Void Extrusion tool, what must the sketch be?

A. A set of open lines
B. A closed loop
C. A point reference
D. A 3D model

Q18. What must you do after setting sketch depth in Void Extrusion?

A. Close the project
B. Click on the Axis tool
C. Click OK from the Mode panel
D. Redraw the profile

Q19. Which template is selected in the example given for creating a Revit family component?

A. Wall
B. Door
C. Furniture
D. Window

Q20. What happens after you click the Open button in the New Family dialog box?

A. The Properties Palette opens
B. The interface to create the Revit family component is displayed
C. The application exits
D. A void form is created

Q21. Which toolbar is used to save a newly created family component?

A. Ribbon
B. Properties Palette
C. Project Browser
D. Quick Access Toolbar

Q22. What is the purpose of the Set tool in the Work Plane panel?

A. To adjust zoom level
B. To rotate the view
C. To define the working plane for sketching
D. To lock dimensions

Q23. What tab appears when you start an extrusion?

A. Modify|Create Void
B. Modify|Create Extrusion
C. Modify|Create Path
D. Create|Draw

Q24. Which panel contains the Edit Top button while creating a blend?

A. Draw
B. Forms
C. Mode
D. Work Plane

Q25. What must you do before creating a revolve feature?

A. Create blend profiles
B. Create an axis line
C. Activate extrusion preview
D. Set top depth

Q26. What do you click to switch to 3D view while creating a blend or sweep?

A. View Browser
B. ViewCube
C. Default 3D View tool
D. Properties Palette

Q27. What does the Sketch Path tool do when creating a sweep or swept blend?

A. Locks the path for voids
B. Edits the profile loop
C. Allows creation of a path sketch
D. Cuts the object

Q28. When using Sweep, what appears if you're not in 3D view while editing profile?

A. An error message
B. A default 2D editor
C. The Go To View dialog box
D. The Path Constraint dialog box

Q29. In Swept Blend, what follows after drawing the path sketch?

A. Editing the extrusion depth
B. Selecting ViewCube
C. Defining Profile 1 and Profile 2
D. Creating axis of revolution

Q30. Which option must be selected to sketch Profile 1 in Swept Blend?

A. Pick Axis
B. Sketch Path
C. Edit Top
D. Edit Profile

Q31. What is the visual indicator for reference while drawing a Sweep profile?

A. Green tick
B. Red dot with dashed lines
C. Blue axis
D. Orange square

Q32. What does a Void Form do in Revit?

A. Adds annotation
B. Creates a floor plan
C. Removes material
D. Locks work plane

Q33. What must be created in Void Extrusion for it to work?

A. Open path sketch
B. 2D axis
C. Closed loop sketch
D. Edge blend

Q34. Where is the Void Extrusion tool located?

A. Work Plane panel
B. Forms panel → Void Forms drop-down
C. Draw panel
D. Mode panel

Chapter 6

Structural Designing

Topics Covered

The major topics covered in this chapter are:

- ***Introduction to Structural Designing***
- ***Creating Beams and Columns***
- ***Creating Structural Trusses***
- ***Creating Braces***
- ***Creating Beam System***
- ***Defining Structural Settings***
- ***Creating Connections***
- ***Creating Foundations***
- ***Creating Structural Rebars and Area Reinforcements***
- ***Creating Fabric Area and Fabric Sheets***
- ***Creating Rebar Couplers***
- ***Modifying Rebar Covers***

INTRODUCTION

In previous chapters, you learned about architectural designing and creating family objects. In this chapter, you will learn about the structural designing of a building. The main element involved in structural designing of a building is load. Various loads involved in structural designing are given next.

Static Load

Static load is a fixed load applied slowly on the structure. Once the load reaches its final value, it remains constant. Some of the static load examples are load of floor or roof, load of heavy machinery permanently placed on structure. The loads that do not vary and remain fixed are also called dead load.

Dynamic Load

The dynamic loads are not fixed and vary with time. This includes loads due to water tanks and people. Dynamic loads are also called live loads.

Impact Load

The impact loads are those sudden impacts that should be absorbed by the structure while keeping the building safe. These impacts may be due to falling objects on the floor, mechanical machines like sheet metal press, and so on.

All these forces can be pointed load, uniformly distributed load, axial load or eccentric load. There are some environmental loads on building which are given next.

Seismic Load

Seismic load is the effect of an earthquake. An earthquake causes vibration, with compression and twisting in the structure.

Wind Load

Wind loads are caused due to high pressure of fast running wind. Wind load has more effect on high rise buildings. Wind loads are generally recurring type.

Snow Load

The snow loads are caused due to snow accumulation on the roofs and slabs of buildings. This type of load is generally considered in areas where heavy snow fall occurs.

Service Load

You need to consider state building codes and area codes for calculation of total loads. You should also consider mean recurrence interval of load. You need to decide whether you are considering building construction for 25 years, 50 years, or 100 years. Based on that you need to multiply load factor to get final load value.

Various components involved in structural designing are beams, structural walls, columns, structural slabs, trusses, braces, and so on.

The tools to create these components are discussed next.

CREATING BEAMS

The **Beam** tool in **Structure** panel of the **Ribbon** is used to create beams of different shapes and sizes. The procedure to create beams is given next.

- Click on the **Beam** tool from the **Structure** panel of **Structure** tab in the **Ribbon**. The options for beams are displayed in the **Properties Palette**; refer to Figure-1.

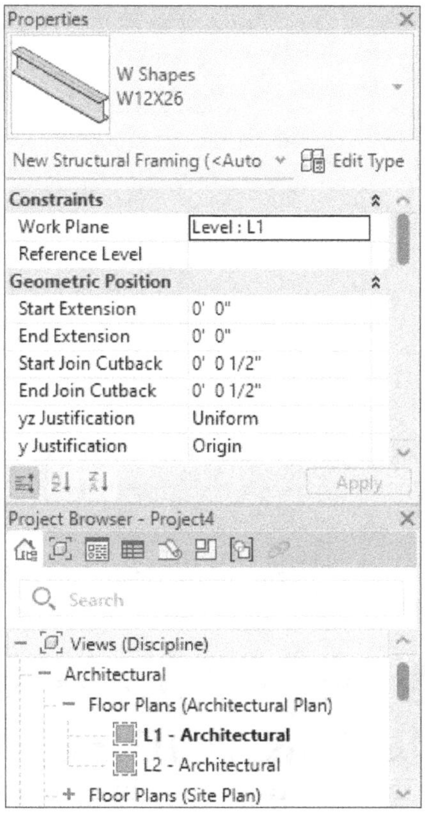

Figure-1. Beam options in Properties panel

- Select desired beam type from the drop-down at the top in **Properties Palette**. If desired beam type is not available then you can load family by using the **Load Family** tool in the **Modify|Place Beam** contextual tab of the **Ribbon** as discussed earlier.
- Select desired option from the **Placement Plane** drop-down in the **Options bar** to define the plane where beam will be created.
- Select desired option from the **Structural Usage** drop-down to define the category of beam. You can select **Girder**, **Joist**, **Purlin**, **Horizontal Bracing**, **Other** from the drop-down; refer to Figure-2.

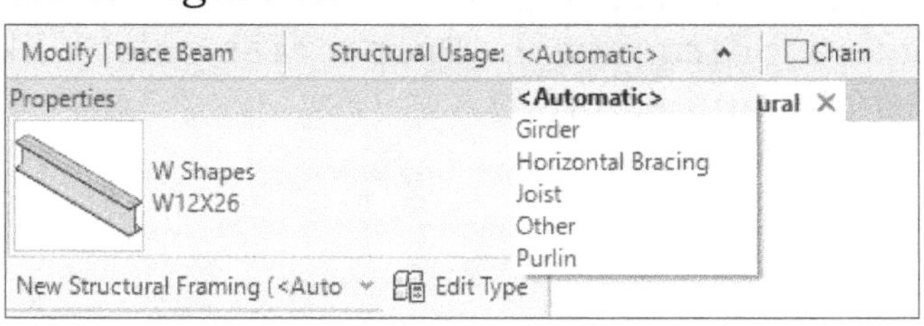

Figure-2. Structural usage drop-down

- Select desired sketching tool for beam from the **Draw** panel in the **Modify|Place Beam** contextual tab of the **Ribbon** and draw the shape of beam; refer to Figure-3.

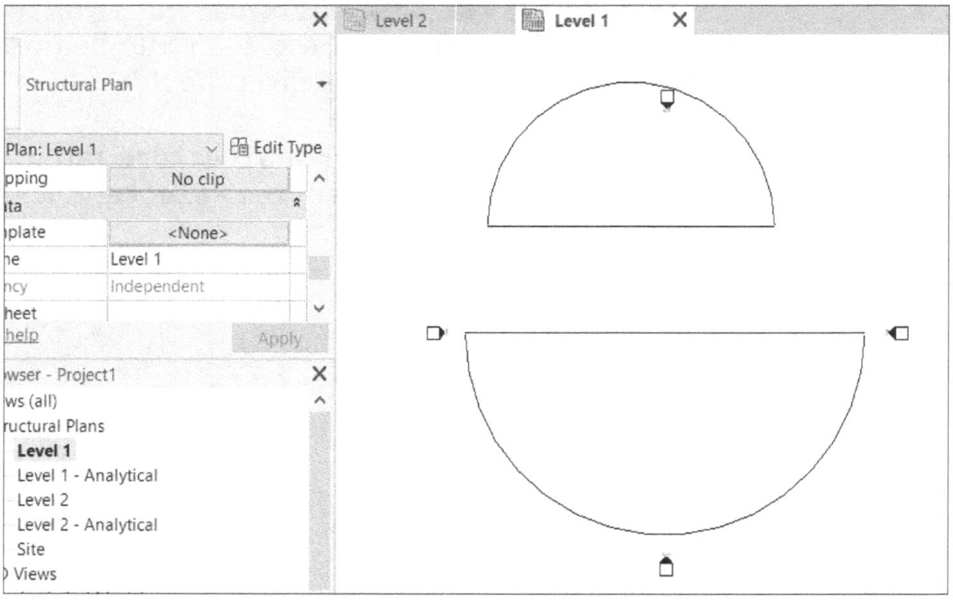

Figure-3. Beams drawn

- Select the **Chain** check box if you want to create a chain of beams.
- Press **ESC** to exit the tool.

If the beams or other structural elements are not displayed after creation then you can check whether its enabled in **Visibility/Graphic Overrides** dialog box.

CREATING THE STRUCTURAL WALL, COLUMN, AND FLOOR

The **Wall: Structural** tool is used to create load bearing walls. The procedure to create structural wall is same as architectural wall created earlier. You can create column and floor as discussed in previous chapters.

CREATING STRUCTURAL TRUSS

Structural truss is used to carry and transfer loads. The procedure to create structural truss is given next.

- Click on the **Truss** tool from the **Structure** panel in the **Structure** tab of the **Ribbon**. The **Modify|Place Truss** contextual tab will be displayed with related options in **Properties Palette**; refer to Figure-4.
- Set desired parameters for truss in the **Properties** palette like truss height, chord location, rotation angle, and so on.

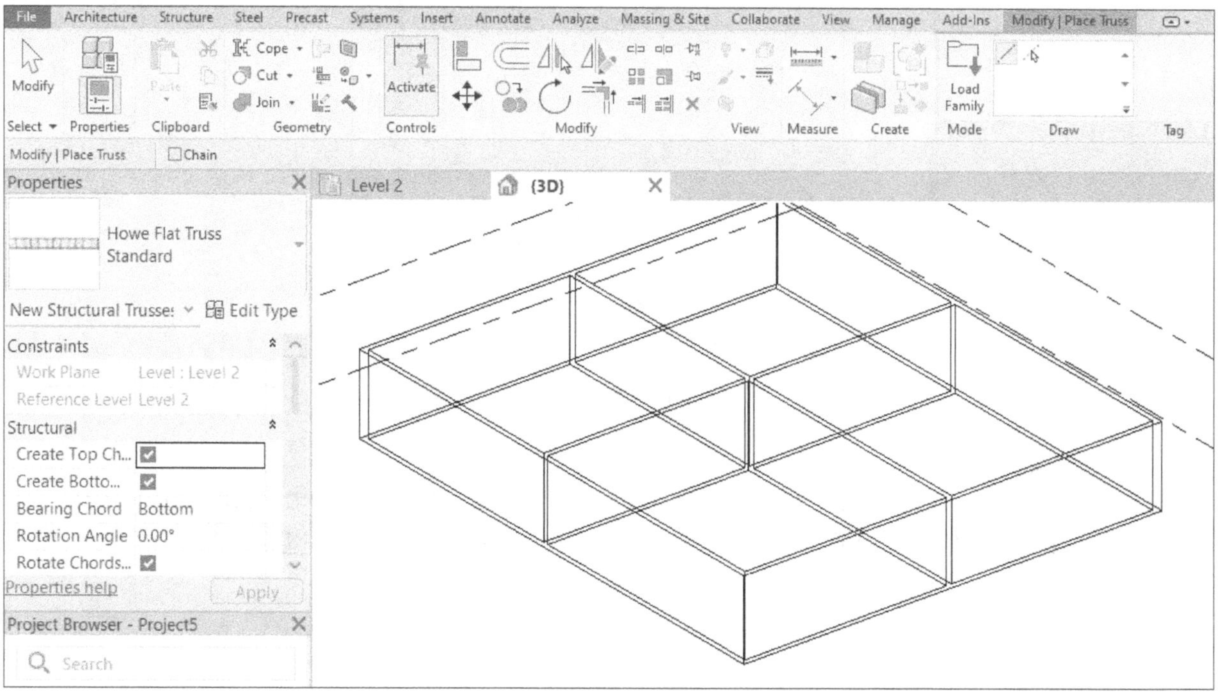

Figure-4. Options for creating truss

- Select desired placement plane from the **Placement Plane** drop-down. Select the **Chain** check box if you want to create a chain of trusses.
- Create a line sketch where you want to create trusses; refer to Figure-5. The trusses will be created.

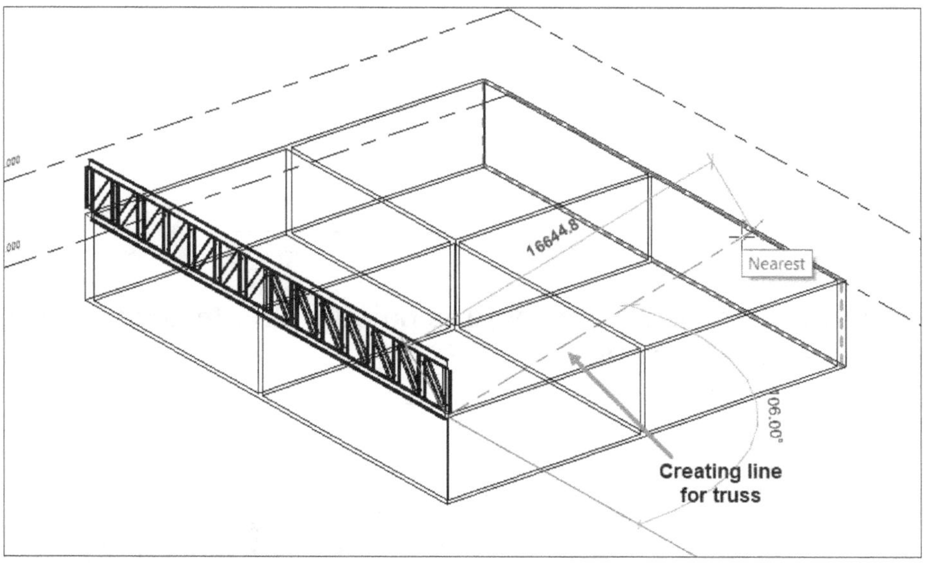

Figure-5. Creating sketch lines for trusses

CREATING BRACE

The braces are used to diagonally connect beams and columns. Braces are changed automatically based on building design. The procedure to create brace is given next.

- Select desired elevation from the Project Browser.
- Click on the **Brace** tool from the **Structure** panel in the **Structure** tab of the **Ribbon**. The **Work Plane** dialog box will be displayed; refer to Figure-6.

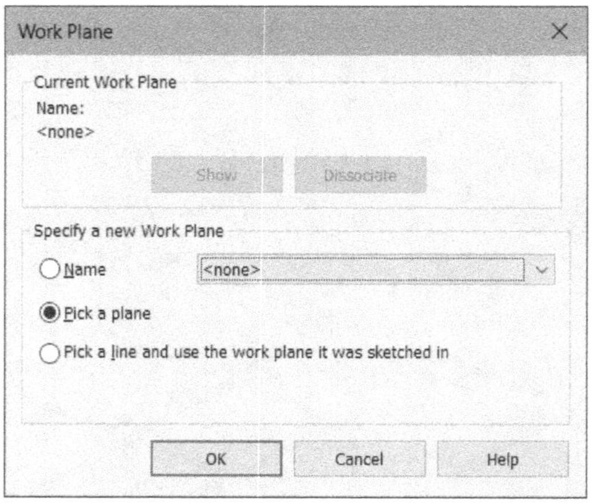

Figure-6. Work Plane dialog box

- Select desired plane where you want to create the braces and click on the **OK** button. The options to create braces will be displayed; refer to Figure-7.

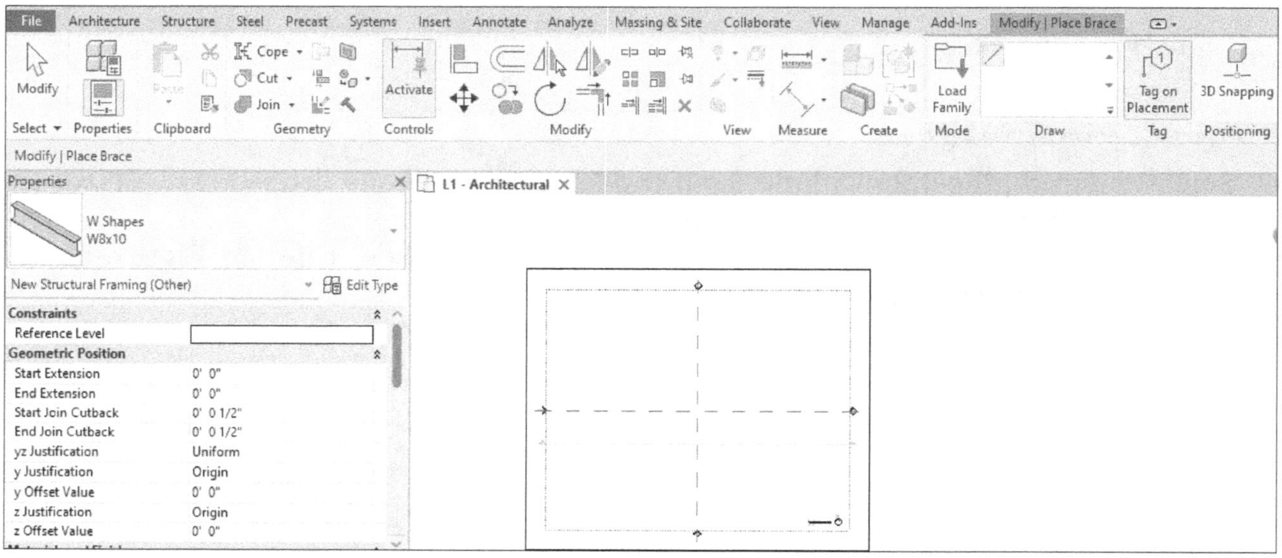

Figure-7. Options for creating braces

- Set desired parameters in the **Properties** palette. Create desired bracing by using sketch lines; refer to Figure-8.

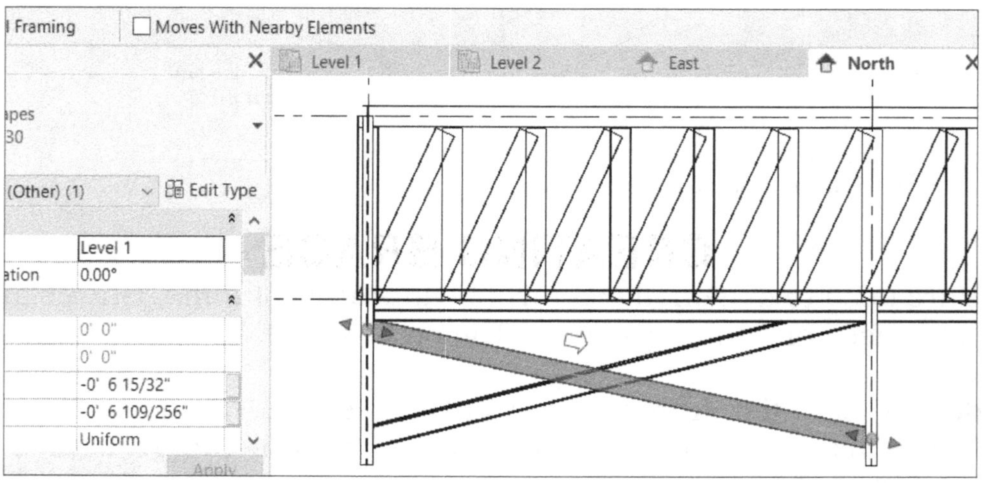

Figure-8. Bracing created

CREATING BEAM SYSTEM

The **Beam System** tool is used to create system of parallel beams. The procedure to create beam system is given next.

- Click on the **Beam System** tool from the **Structure** panel in the **Structure** tab of **Ribbon**. The options to create beam system will be displayed; refer to Figure-9. Note that the displayed contextual tab is available when automatic beam system cannot be created due to gap or multiple loops in the structure.

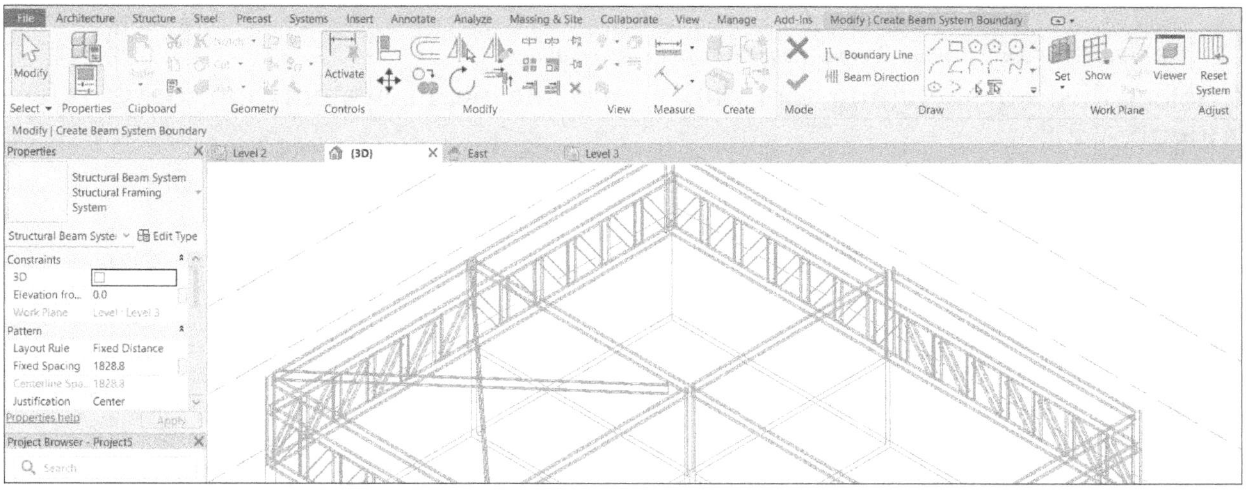

Figure-9. Options for beam structure

- Select desired beam type from the **Beam Type** drop-down in the **Pattern** rollout of **Properties Palette**. Set the other parameters like layout rule and number of lines in the **Pattern** rollout.
- Create closed boundary sketch using drawing tools. If the structure is a closed boundary where beam can be created automatically, then hover the cursor on the wall or beam to be used as direction reference for beam system. Preview of beam system will be displayed; refer to Figure-10.

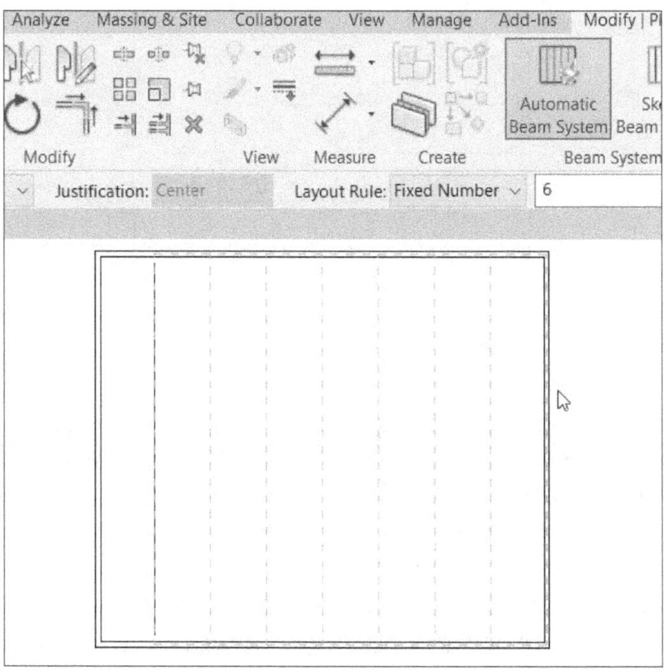

Figure-10. Preview of beam system

- Click at desired location to place the beam system. Note that by default, **Automatic Beam System** is selected in the contextual tab hence beams are automatically spaced. If you want to create the beam system manually then click on the **Sketch Beam System** button from the contextual tab. The **Modify|Create Beam System Boundary** contextual tab will be displayed; refer to Figure-11.

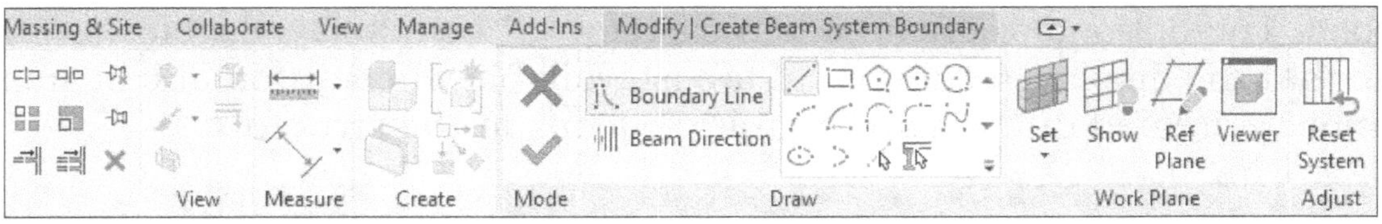

Figure-11. Modify Create Beam System Boundary contextual tab

- Select desired sketching tool and create the beam system boundary; refer to Figure-12.

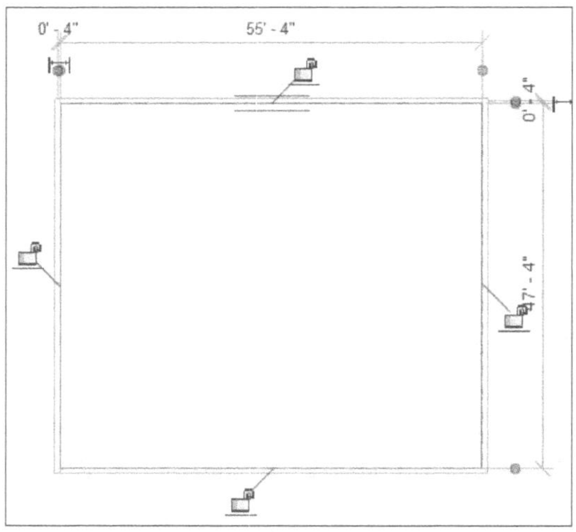

Figure-12. Boundary created for beam system

- Click on the **OK** button from the contextual tab. The beam system will be created; refer to Figure-13.

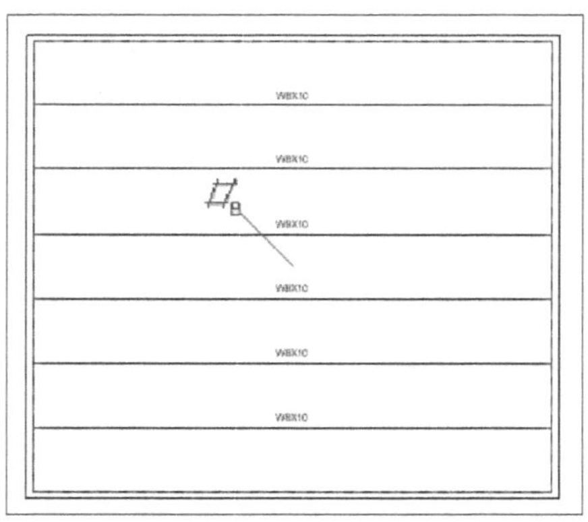

Figure-13. Beam system created

DEFINING STRUCTURAL SETTINGS

The **Structural Settings** tool is used to define parameters for structural frame. The procedure to define these settings is given next.

- Click on the inclined arrow button in the **Structure** panel of **Structure** tab in the **Ribbon**. The **Structural Settings** dialog box will be displayed; refer to Figure-14.

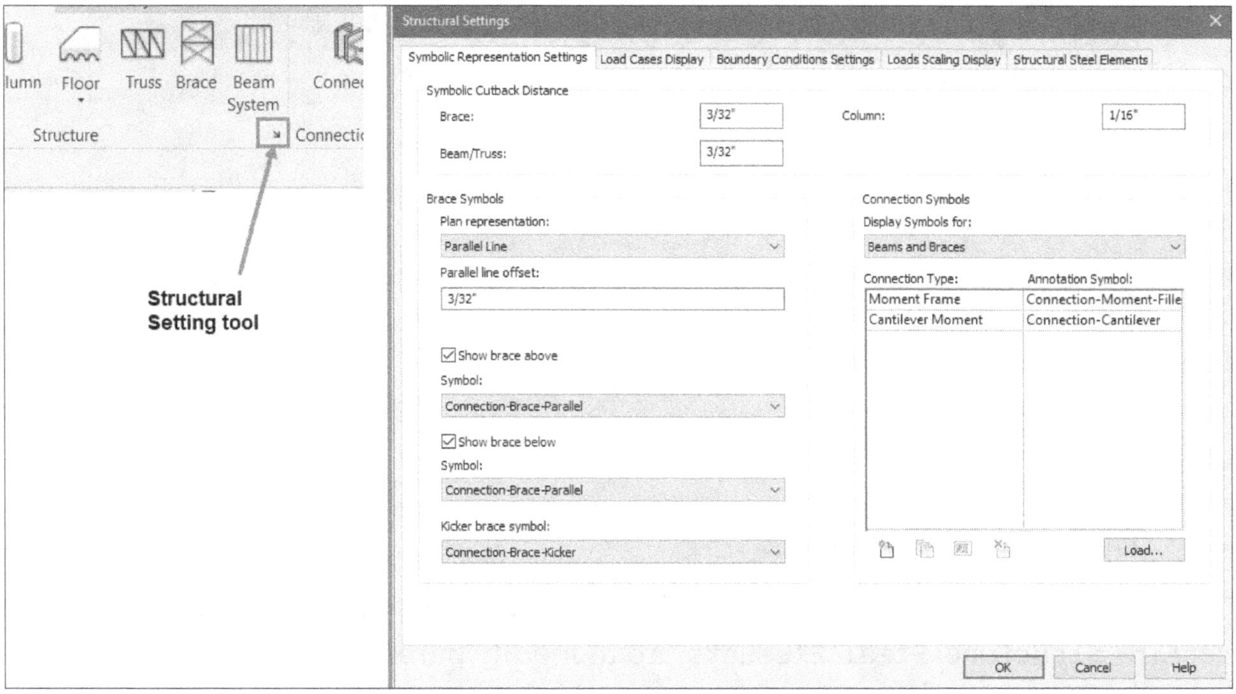

Figure-14. Structural Settings dialog box

Symbolic Representation Settings

- The options in **Symbolic Representation Settings** tab are used to define how symbols are displayed in drawing. You can set desired size of symbols in the **Symbolic Cutback Distance** area of the dialog box.
- Select **Parallel Line** option from the **Plan representation** drop-down if you want to display only parallel lines to represent braces. Select the **Line with Angle** option from the drop-down if you want to display braces as lines at angle.

Load Cases Display

The options in **Load Cases Display** tab are used to define load cases. Click in desired field to modify its value. There are mainly 8 categories of loads which are defined in the **Load Cases Display** tab. You will learn more about load cases later in Chapter 9 of the book.

Boundary Conditions Settings

The options in **Boundary Conditions Settings** tab of **Structural Settings** dialog box are used to set symbols for different boundary conditions. Select desired symbol for a boundary condition from respective drop-down. Click on the **OK** button from the dialog box to apply the changes.

Loads Scaling Display

The options in **Loads Scaling Display** tab are used define scale of display of loads in analytical model; refer to Figure-15. Select the **Use Project Settings** check box to use specified scale values for whole project. After setting desired parameters, click on the **OK** button from the dialog box to apply changes and exit.

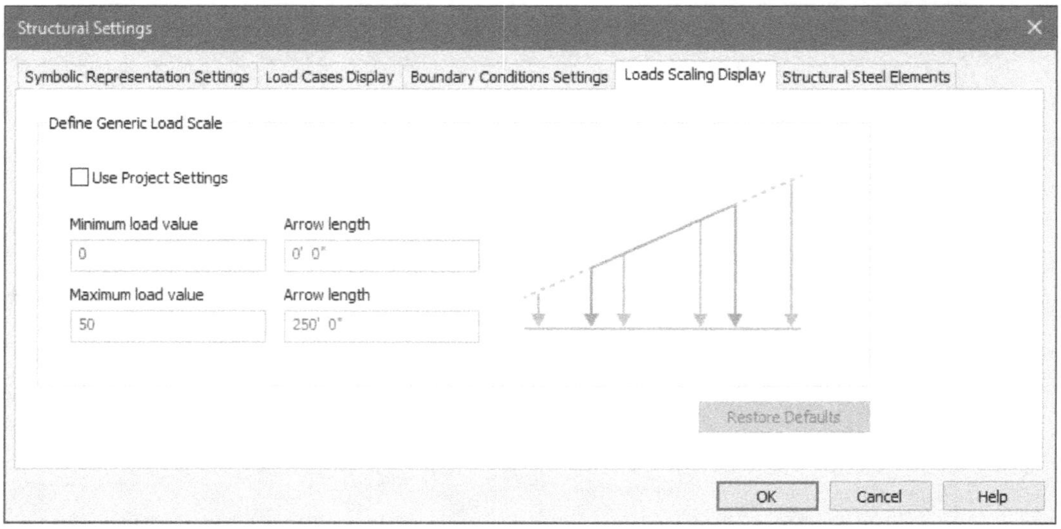

Figure-15. Loads Scaling Display tab

Structural Steel Elements

Select the **Structure Steel Elements** tab to modify parameters related to structural steel; refer to Figure-16.

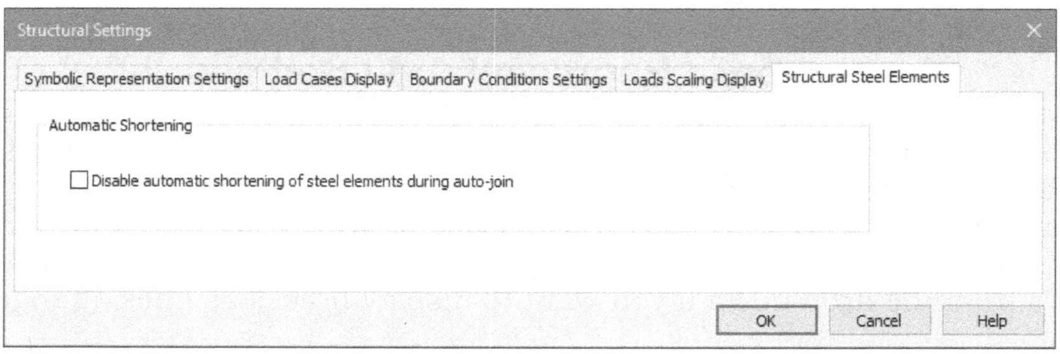

Figure-16. Structural Steel Elements tab

Select the **Disable automatic shortening of steel elements during auto-join** check box from **Automatic Shortening** area to disable the automatic shortening of steel elements during auto-join. In such case, the section where steel elements join will be added to the total length of steel elements accordingly. On selecting the check box, the **Structural Steel Elements Auto-shortening Warning** information box will be displayed telling you that additional processing time will be required for performing the operations; refer to Figure-17. Click on **OK** button from the box.

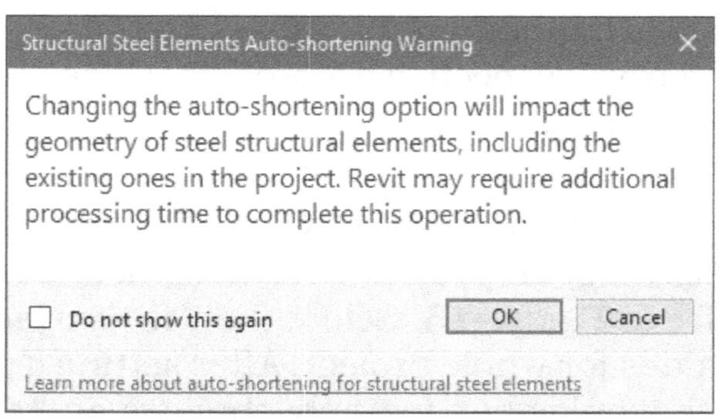

Figure-17. Structural steel elements warning dialog box

CONNECTIONS

The tools in **Connection** panel of **Structure** tab are used to define how structural frame members connect with each other. The procedure to define connection setting is given next.

Connection Settings

- Click on the inclined arrow of **Connection** panel. The **Structural Connection Settings** dialog box will be displayed; refer to Figure-18.

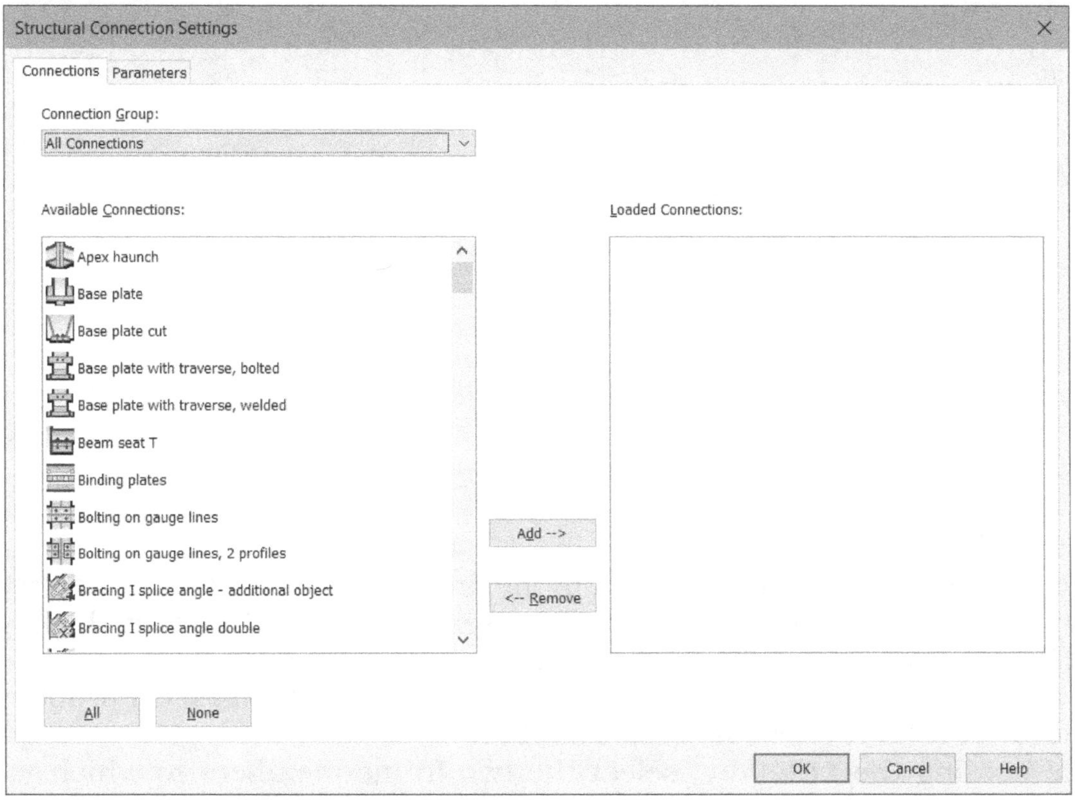

Figure-18. Structural Connection Settings dialog box

- Select desired connections types from the **Available Connections** area of the dialog box and click on the **Add-->** button. The selected connections will be loaded in the project.
- Click on the **Parameters** tab to create status parameters; refer to Figure-19. Click on the **Add** button and create desired approval status parameter.
- Click on the **OK** button from the dialog box to apply changes.

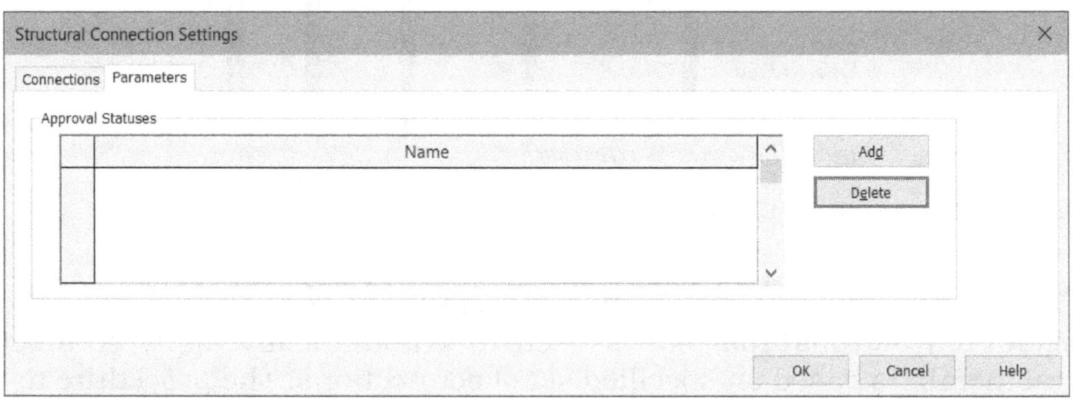

Figure-19. Parameters tab

Applying Connection

The **Connection** tool in **Connection** panel is used to define type of connection at selected intersection point of frame members. The procedure to apply connection is given next.

- Click on the **Connection** tool from the **Connection** panel of **Structure** tab of the **Ribbon**. The options to create connection will be displayed in **Properties Palette** and **Ribbon**; refer to Figure-20.

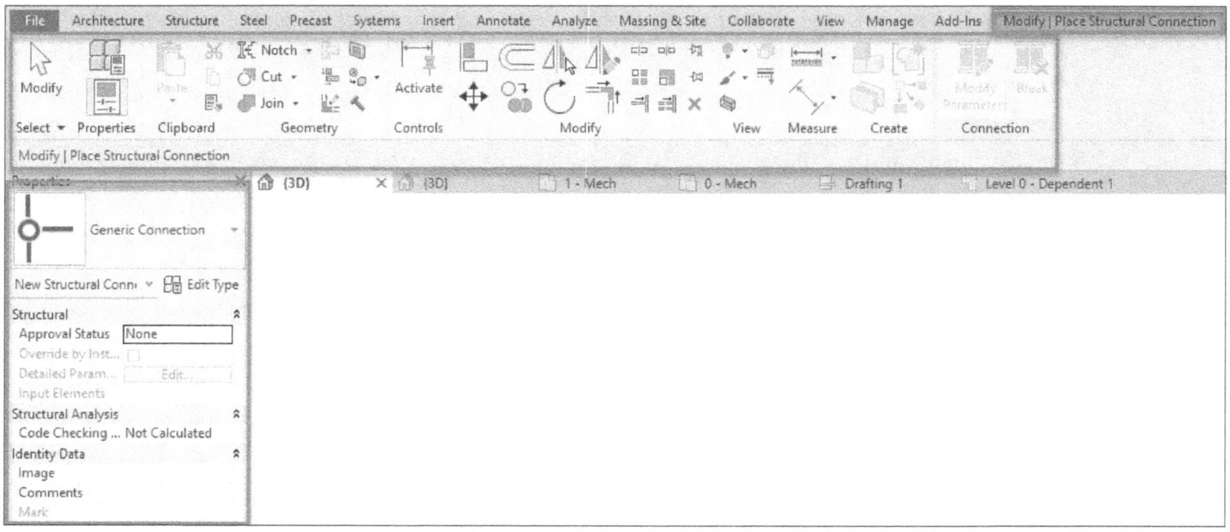

Figure-20. Options for structural connection

- Select desired type of connection from the drop-down at the top in the **Properties Palette**. Note that the connection types selected in the **Structural Connection Settings** dialog box will be displayed in the drop-down.
- Select desired approval status from the **Approval Status** drop-down in the **Structural** rollout of **Properties Palette**.
- While holding the **CTRL** key, select the two frame members to which you want to apply connection and press **ENTER**. The connection will be created; refer to Figure-21.

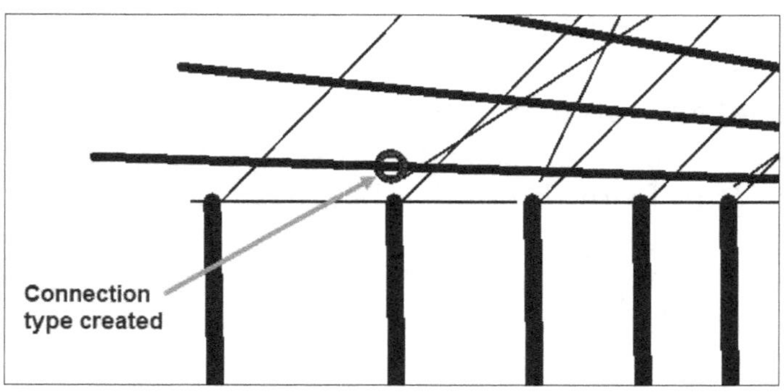

Figure-21. Connection type created

- Press **ESC** twice to exit the tool.

AUTOMATING CONNECTIONS

The **Connection Automation** tool is used to automatically apply connections to structural members based on specified set of connections. The procedure to use this tool is given next.

- Click on the **Connection Automation** tool from the **Connection** panel in the **Structure** tab of the **Ribbon**. The **Steel Connection Automation** window will be displayed; refer to Figure-22.
- Select desired connection setup to be automated from the list and click on the **Play** button. The options related to selected connection setup will be displayed; refer to Figure-23.

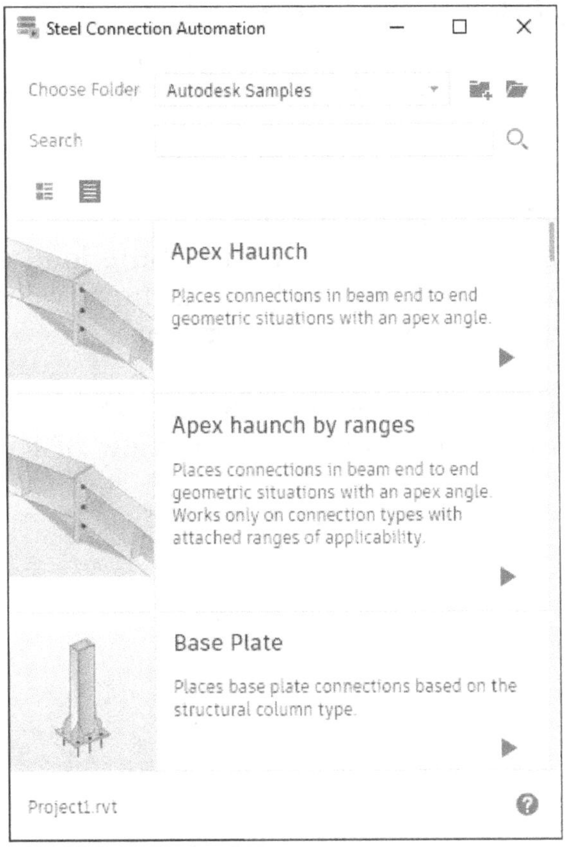

Figure-22. Steel Connection Automation window

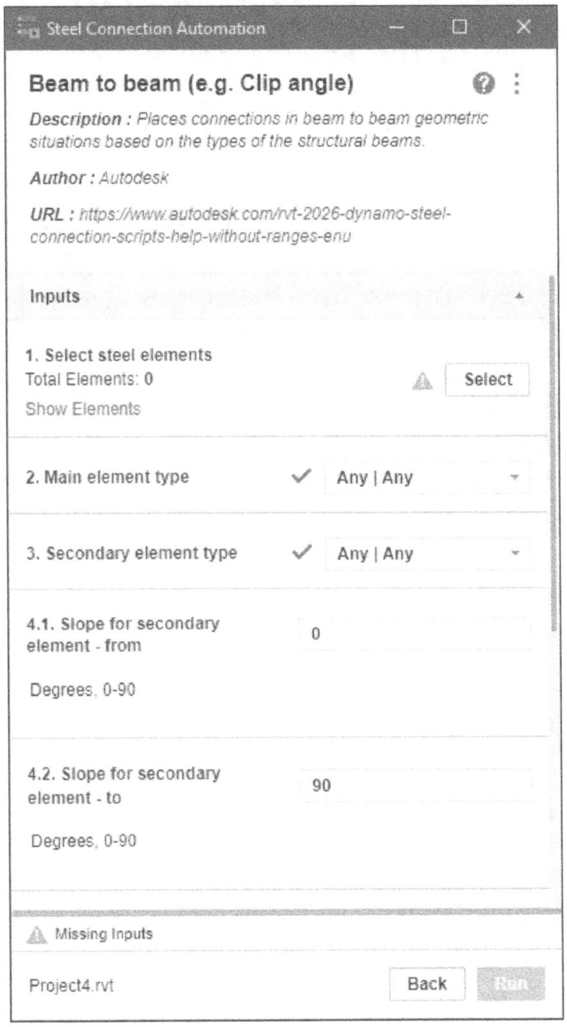

Figure-23. Connection setup parameters

- Click on the **Select** button from **Inputs** section and select all the beams/columns to be joined by selected connection type, using window selection; refer to Figure-24.

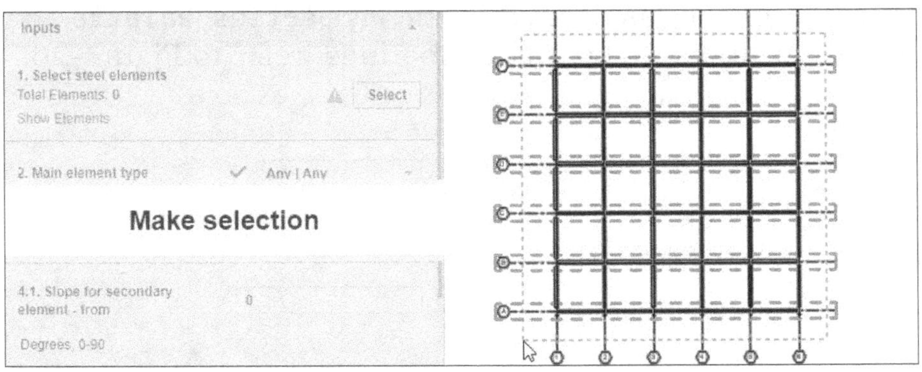

Figure-24. Selecting elements for connection

- Select desired options from the **Main element type** and **Secondary element type** drop-downs to define the type of elements to be included for creating connections.

- Similarly, you can set slopes for main and secondary elements in respective fields.
- Select desired option from the **Connection type to add in model** drop-down to define the type of connection to be created.
- After setting desired parameters, click on the **Run** button. The connections will be applied automatically.

CREATING FOUNDATIONS

The tools in the **Foundation** panel are used to create base foundation of frame members. There are three tools in Foundation panel Isolated, Wall, and Slab. The procedures to create these foundations are discussed next.

Creating Isolated Foundation

The Isolated footings are applied at the bottom of columns to distribute load safely to the bed soil. Isolate footing is applied when there are single columns at relatively long distances. The procedure to apply isolate foundation is given next.

- Click on the **Isolated** tool from the **Foundation** panel in the **Structure** tab of the **Ribbon**. The options to create footing will be displayed with preview of footing; refer to Figure-25.

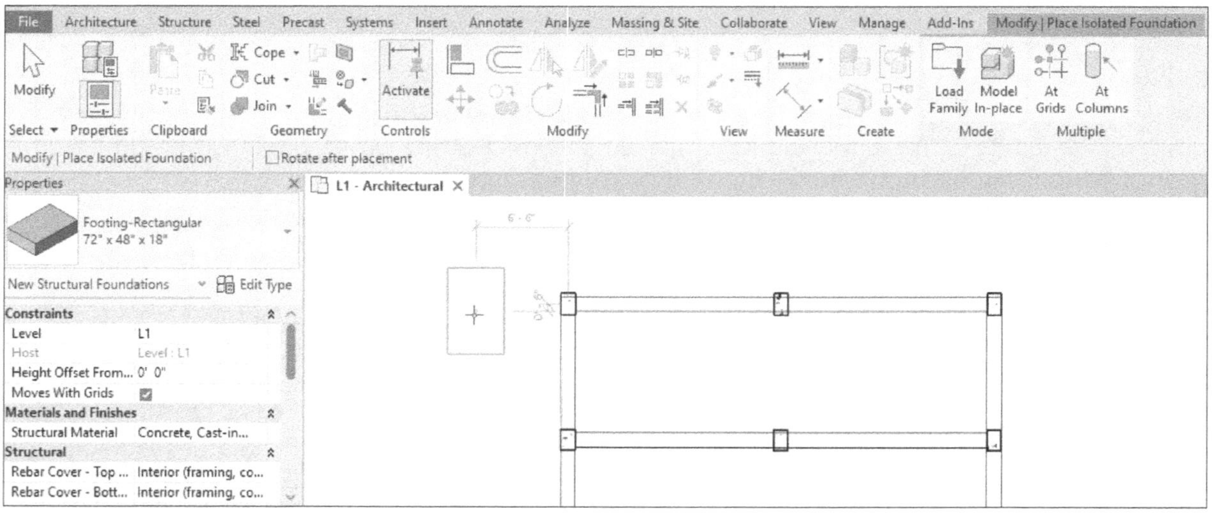

Figure-25. Options to create isolated foundation

- Select desired shape and size of footing from the drop-down at the top in the **Properties Palette**.
- Set the other parameters as desired in the **Properties Palette**.
- Click at desired locations to create the footings; refer to Figure-26.

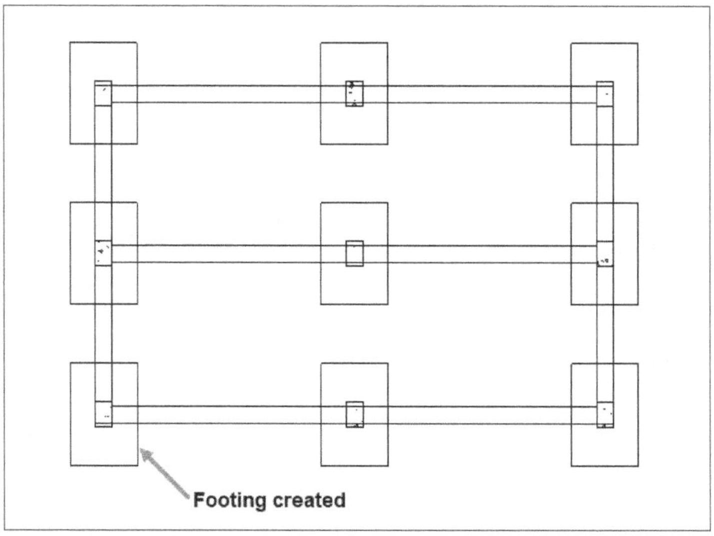

Figure-26. Creating footing for column

Creating Wall Footing

The **Wall** tool in the **Foundation** panel is used to create foundation for structural walls. The procedure to use this tool is given next.

- Click on the **Wall** tool from the **Foundation** panel in the **Structure** tab of the **Ribbon**. The options to create wall foundation will be displayed; refer to Figure-27.

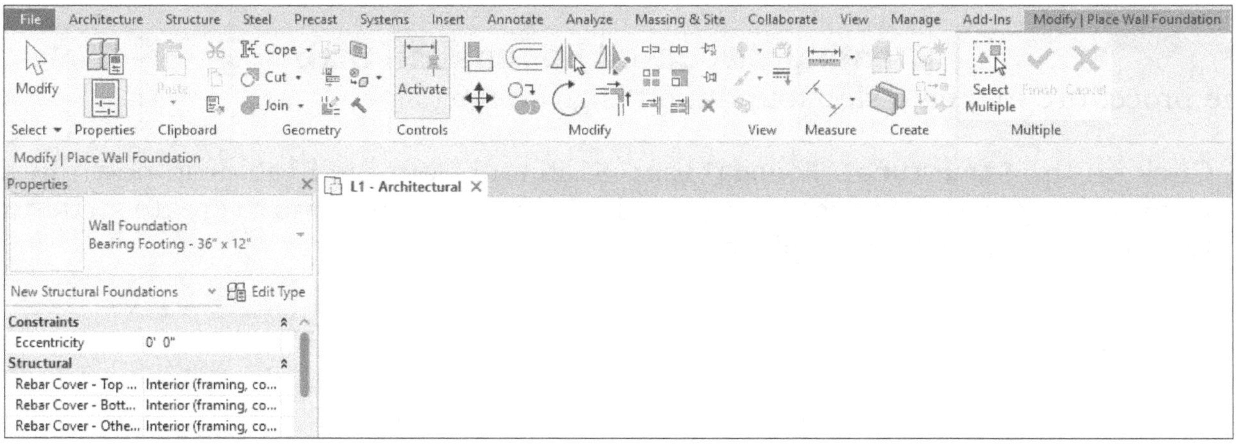

Figure-27. Wall foundation options

- Set desired shape and size of wall footing in the drop-down at the top in the **Properties Palette**.
- Set desired offset value for wall in the **Eccentricity** edit box of the **Constraints** rollout. Note that this option is available only for bearing footings.
- Set the other parameters as desired in the **Properties Palette**.
- Click at desired walls to create footings for them; refer to Figure-28.

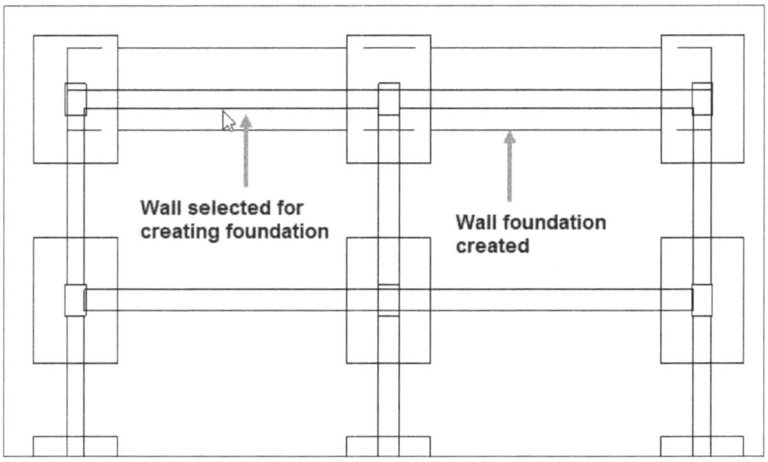

Figure-28. Wall foundation created

Creating Slab Foundation

The Slab foundation is used where other type of foundations are not required/ appropriate like directly below the floor. You can also use slab foundations to create complex foundations. There are two tools to create slab foundation; **Structural Foundation: Slab** and **Floor: Slab Edge**. The **Structural Foundation: Slab** tool is used to create independent slab at desired level. You can create complex shaped slabs by using this tool. Select the **Floor: Slab Edge** tool to create slab by using the horizontal edge of a floor.

Creating Structural Foundation Slab

The procedure to create slab foundation is given next.

- Click on the **Structural Foundation: Slab** tool from the **Slab** drop-down in the **Foundation** panel of **Structure** tab in the **Ribbon**. The options to create structural foundation slab will be displayed; refer to Figure-29.

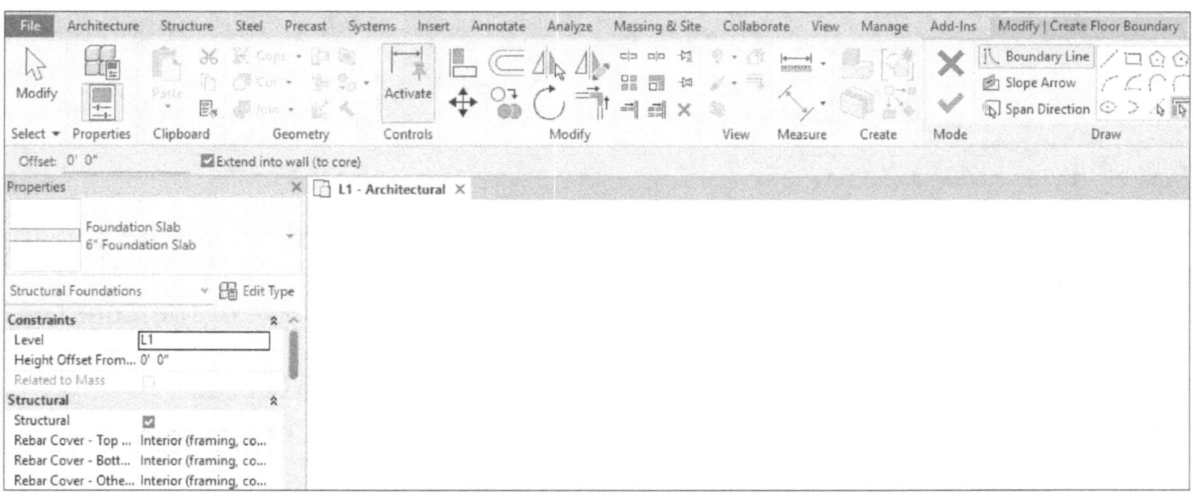

Figure-29. Options for structural foundation slab

- Select desired thickness of slab from the drop-down at the top in the **Properties Palette**.
- Set the other parameters as desired in the **Properties Palette** and create desired shape of foundation slab.

- Click on the **OK** button from the **Mode** panel in the **Modify|Create Floor Boundary** contextual tab of **Ribbon**.

Creating Floor: Slab Edge

The **Floor: Slab Edge** tool is used to create foundation slab on selected edge. The procedure to use this slab is given next.

- Click on the **Floor: Slab Edge** tool from the **Slab** drop-down in the **Foundation** panel of **Structure** tab in the **Ribbon**. The options to create slab edge will be displayed; refer to Figure-30.

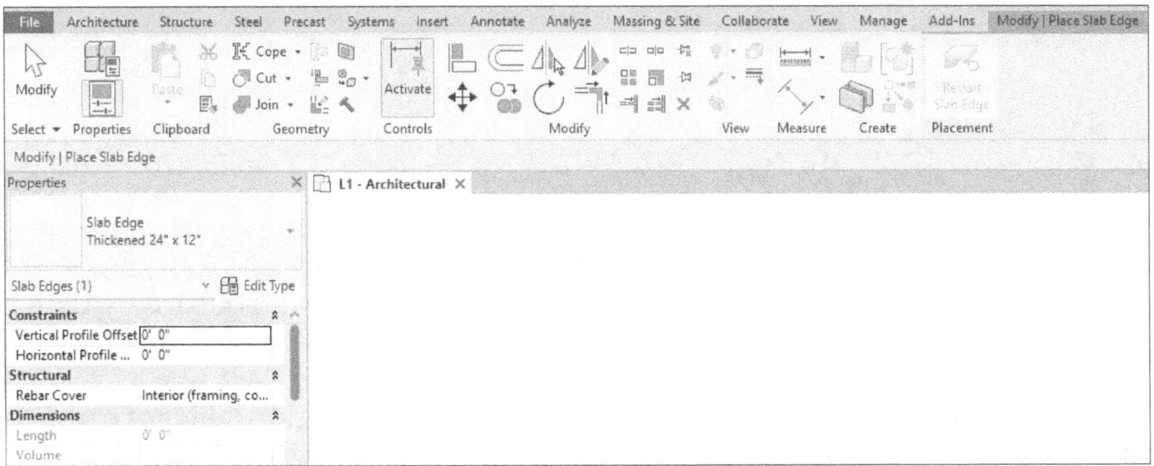

Figure-30. Options to create slab edge

- Set desired parameters in the **Properties Palette** to define shape, size, and offset for slab.
- Select the edge on which you want to create slab. The slab will be displayed; refer to Figure-31.

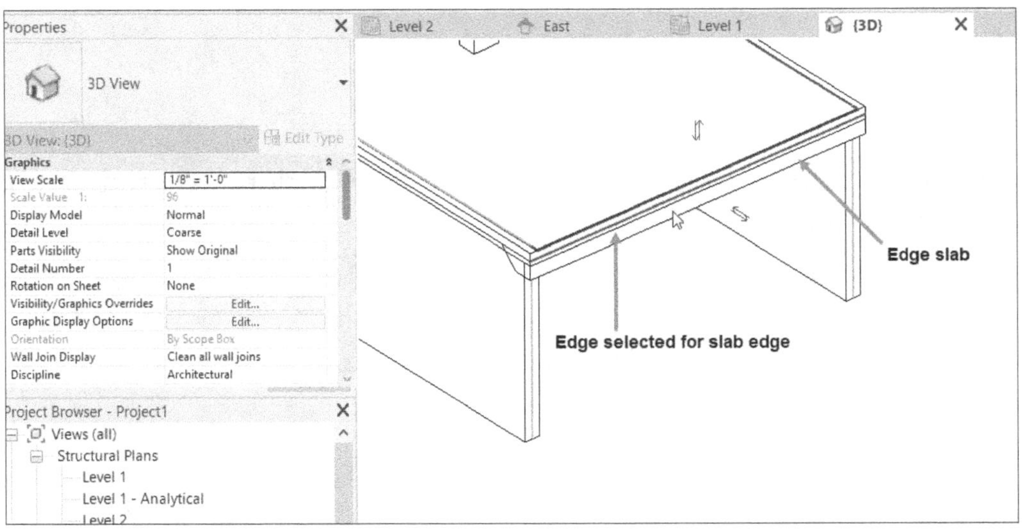

Figure-31. Edge slab created

- Click on the double arrows displayed on the slab edge to flip the slab direction.
- Press **ESC** to exit the tool. If you want to change length of slab then select it and drag the end points to modify it; refer to Figure-32.

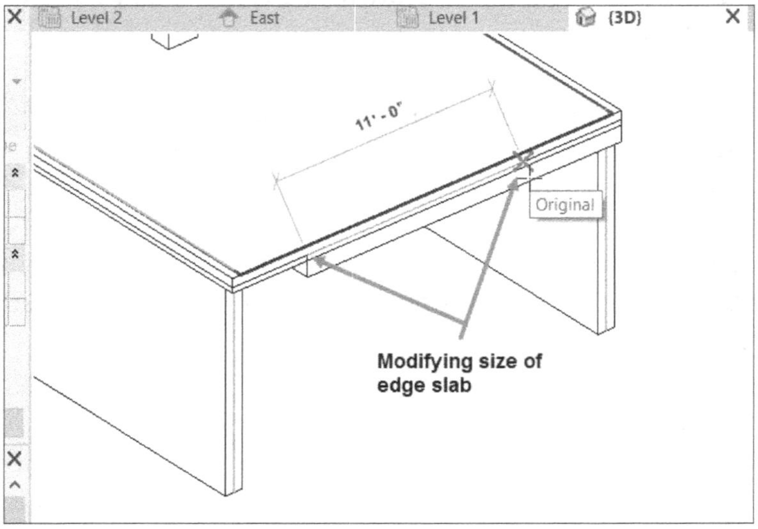

Figure-32. Modifying size of slab

STRUCTURAL REBAR

Structural rebar is used to strengthen concrete and masonry structure by using steel bar and mesh of steel wires. The procedure to create structural rebar is given next.

- Click on the **Rebar** tool from **Reinforcement** panel in the **Concrete** tab of the **Ribbon**. An information box will be displayed; refer to Figure-33.

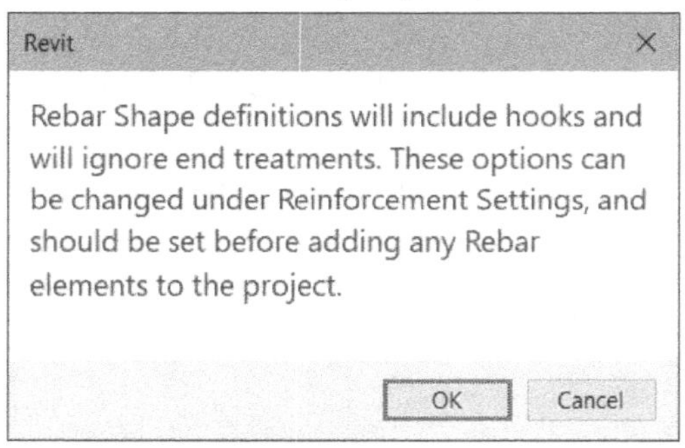

Figure-33. Revit information box

- Click on the **OK** button from the dialog box. The options to create rebar will be displayed; refer to Figure-34.

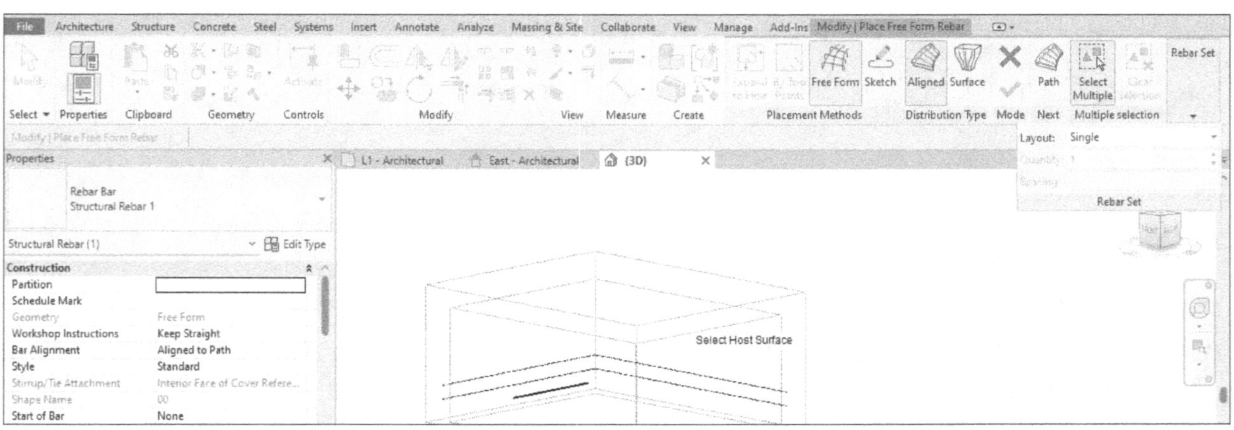

Figure-34. Options to create rebar

- Select desired masonry or concrete structure to which you want to apply rebar. (To download the shapes and family of rebar, refer to the procedure discussed in Chapter 8 of this book. To select the rebar shape, open desired 2D plan from the **Project Browser** or from the local directory. The **Rebar Shape Browser** dialog box will be displayed; refer to Figure-35. Select desired shape from the dialog box and place it in the graphics window at desired location.)

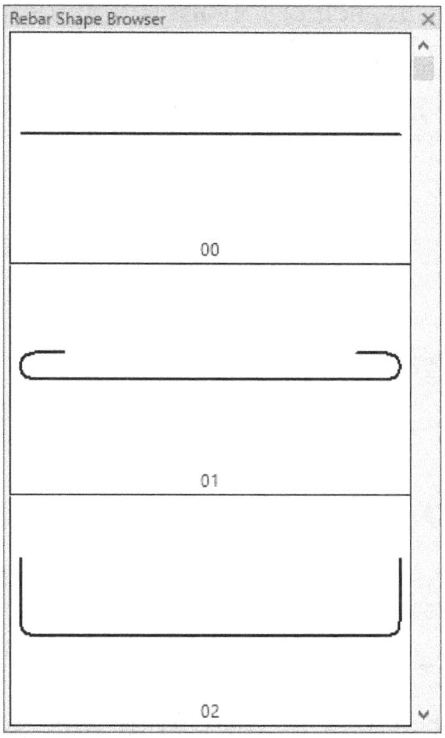

Figure-35. Rebar Shape Browser dialog box

- Set desired parameters in the **Properties Palette** and click on the **Surface** tool to define the starting face for rebar. Select desired surface to define starting face; refer to Figure-36.

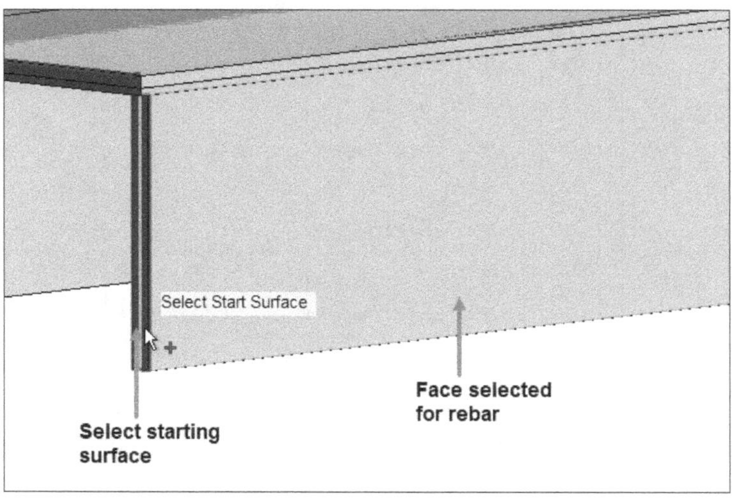

Figure-36. Face selected for rebar

- Click on the **End Surface** button from the **Next** panel in the **Modify| Place Free Form Rebar** contextual tab of **Ribbon**. You will be asked to select the surface upto which rebar will be created.
- Select desired face to be used as reference.

- Select desired option from the **Layout** drop-down in the **Rebar Set** panel of contextual tab. Select **Fixed Number** option if you want to create fixed number of rebars in the selected structure and specify number of rebars in the **Quantity** edit box. Select the **Maximum Spacing** option if you want to define space between two consecutive rebars. Similarly, you can use other options.
- Press **ENTER** to create the rebars. Press **ESC** to exit the tool.
- If you want to modify a rebar, select it from the model. The options to modify rebar will be displayed; refer to Figure-37.

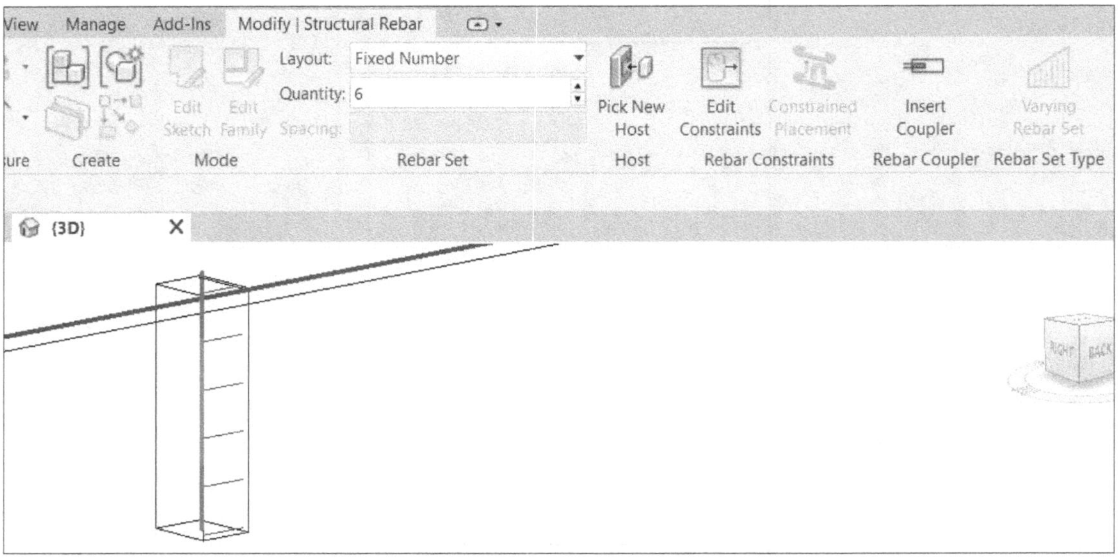

Figure-37. Options to modify rebar

- Click on the **Edit Constraints** button from the contextual tab if you want to change the start point, mid point, and end point of rebar. The bar handles will be displayed; refer to Figure-38.
- Select desired bar handle. The offset value for it will be displayed.
- Click on the value and modify it as desired.

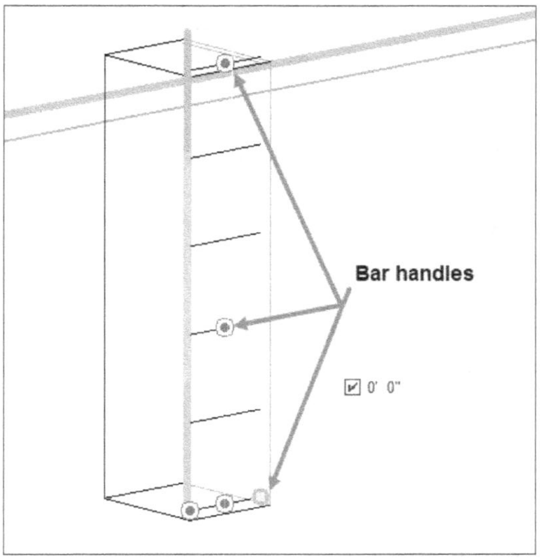

Figure-38. Bar handles on rebar

Rebar Properties

Various properties of significance are shown in **Properties Palette** on selecting a rebar; refer to Figure-39. These properties are discussed next.

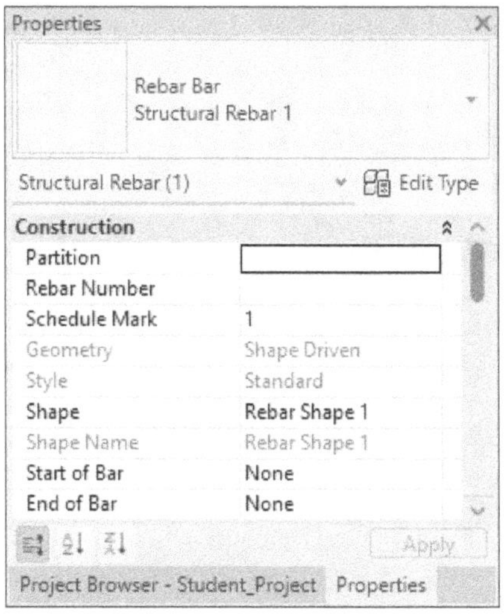

Figure-39. Rebar Properties

- The **Rebar Number** area defines the number assigned to the selected rebar and the rebar element of same type, shape, size, and partition.
- The **Schedule Mark** area defines the number that associate rebar element with a schedule mark to improve scheduling and organization.
- **Geometry** area defines the geometry of the rebar, i.e., either Shape Driven or Free Form.
- Select desired option from **Style** drop-down to specify the bend radii control of the rebar shape.
- Select desired identification number of the rebar shape from **Shape** drop-down.
- Specify desired custom identification number for the rebar shape in the **Shape Name** edit box.
- The **Start of Bar** and the **End of Bar** area define whether the start and end of the rebar has a hook, end treatment, or crank.

STRUCTURAL AREA REINFORCEMENT

The **Area** tool is used to create reinforcement for floors, walls, and foundation slabs. The procedure to use this tool is given next.

- Click on the **Area** tool from the **Reinforcement** panel of **Concrete** tab in **Ribbon**. You will be asked to select a floor or wall.
- Select desired floor, wall, or slab. A warning message will be displayed; refer to Figure-40.

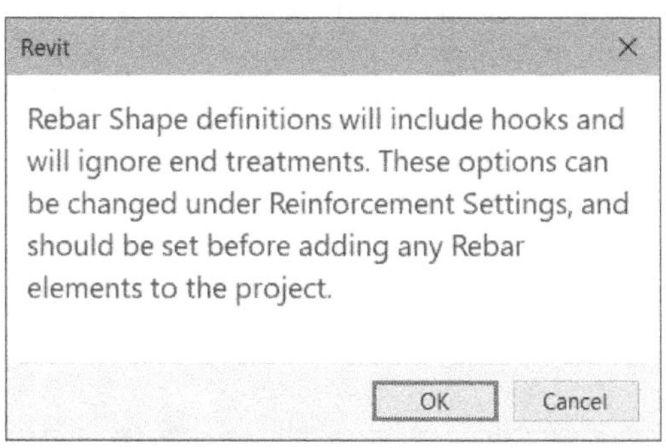

Figure-40. Warning message

- Click on the **OK** button from the dialog box. The options to create area reinforcement will be displayed; refer to Figure-41.

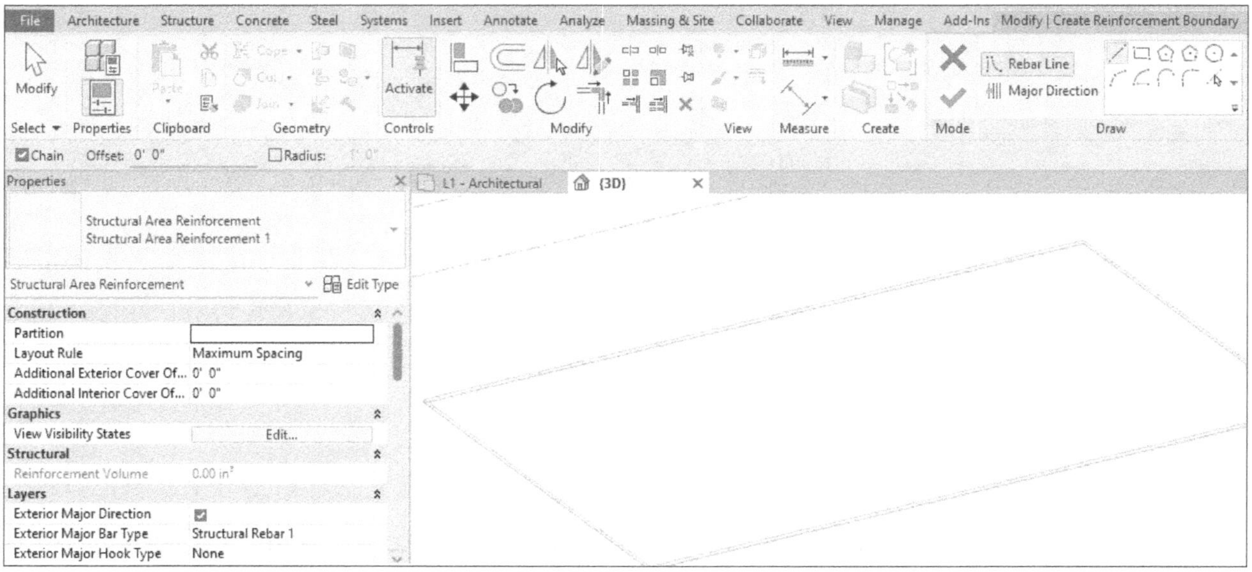

Figure-41. Options to create area reinforcement

- Set desired parameters in the **Properties Palette**. By default, **Maximum Spacing** option is selected in the **Layout Rule** drop-down of **Construction** rollout in the **Properties Palette** so you are asked to specify the distance between two rebars. Set desired values of distances in **Top Major Spacing**, **Top Minor Spacing**, **Bottom Major Spacing**, and **Bottom Minor Spacing** edit boxes of the **Layers** rollout in the **Properties Palette**.
- Select the **Fixed Number** option from the **Layout Rule** drop-down if you want to specify number of rebars in specified region. Specify desired number of rebars in **Top Major Number of Lines**, **Top Minor Number of Lines**, **Bottom Major Number of Lines**, and **Bottom Minor Number of Lines** edit boxes.
- Select desired sketching tool from the **Draw** panel and create the single loop closed sketch; refer to Figure-42.

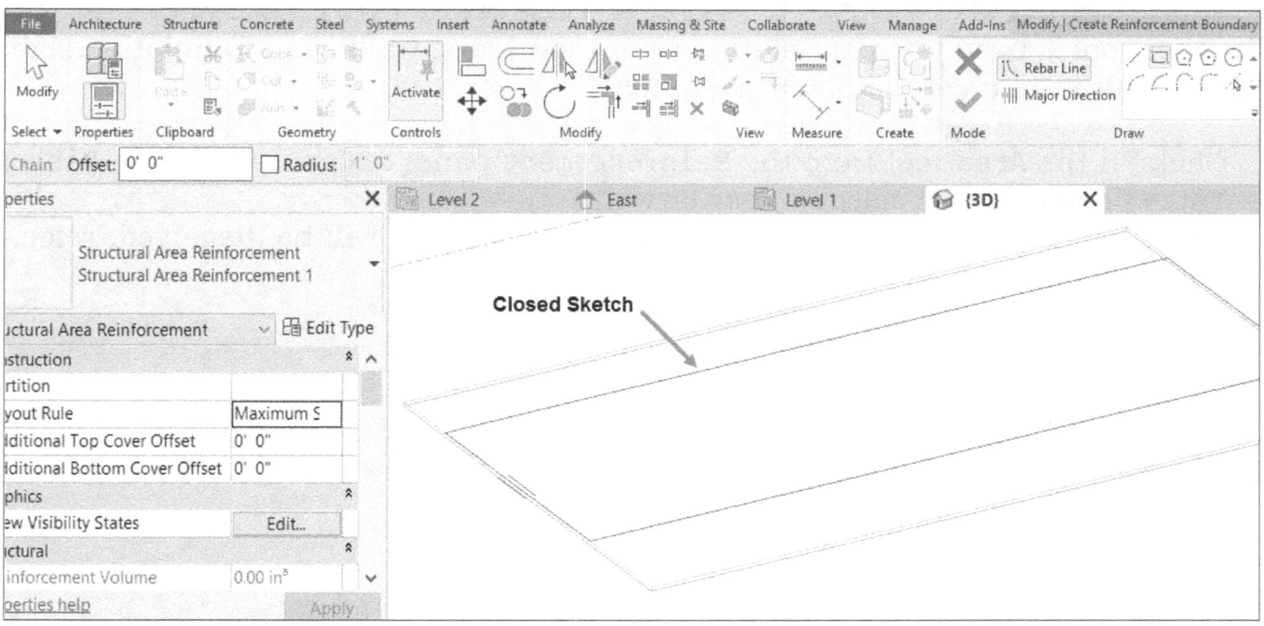

Figure-42. Sketch created for area rebar

- Click on the **OK** button from the **Mode** panel in the contextual tab. The structural area reinforcement will be created; refer to Figure-43.

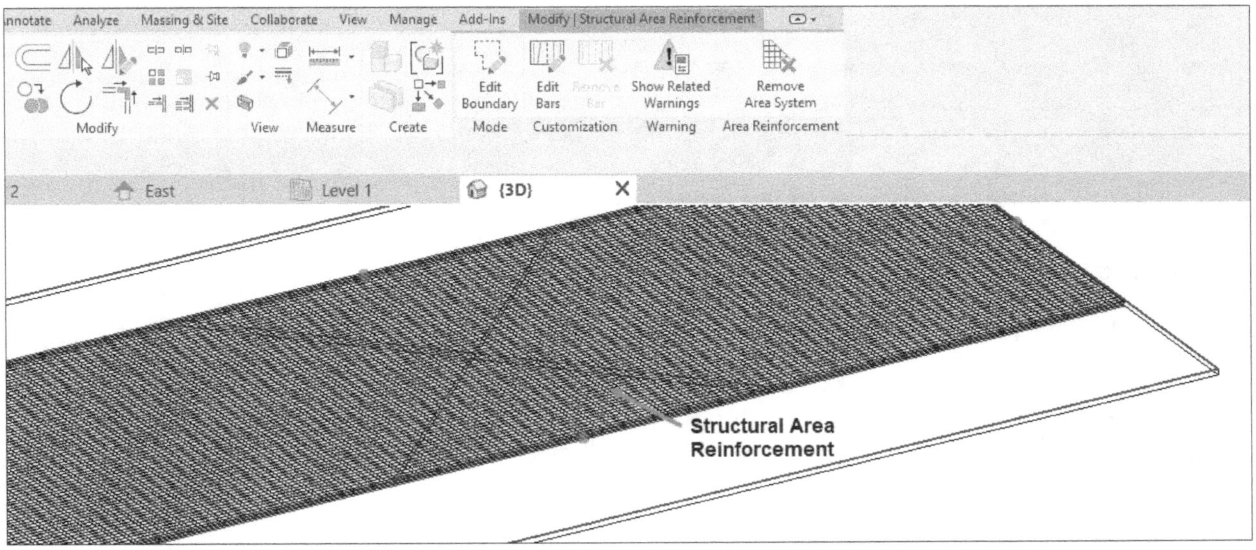

Figure-43. Structural area reinforcement created

STRUCTURAL PATH REINFORCEMENT

The structural path reinforcement is used to create reinforcement along specified direction. The procedure to create structural path reinforcement is given next.

- Click on the **Path** tool from the **Reinforcement** panel in the **Concrete** tab in the **Ribbon**. You will be asked to select a floor or wall on which you want to create rebar.
- Select desired object. A warning message will be displayed; refer to Figure-44.

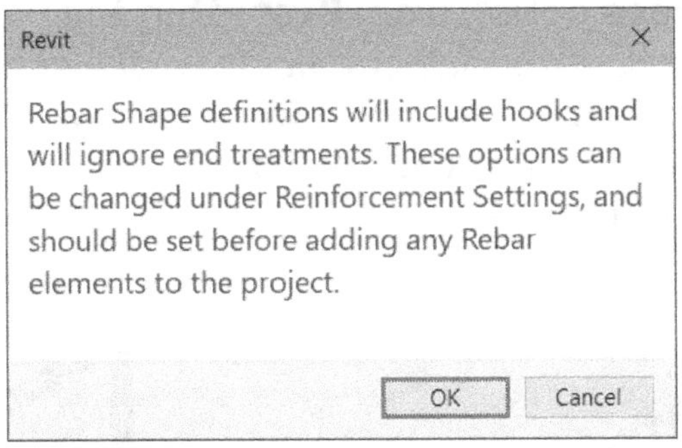

Figure-44. Warning box

- Click on the **OK** button from the dialog box. You will be asked to create direction line for rebars.
- Set desired parameters in the **Properties Palette** like define the length of rebar, spacing between two instances of rebar, and other related parameters.
- Select the **Alternating Bars** check box if you want to create alternate sequence of bars with different properties.
- Create a line or open curve at desired location; refer to Figure-45.
- Click on the **OK** button from the contextual tab. The reinforcement will be created.
- Press **ESC** to exit the tool.

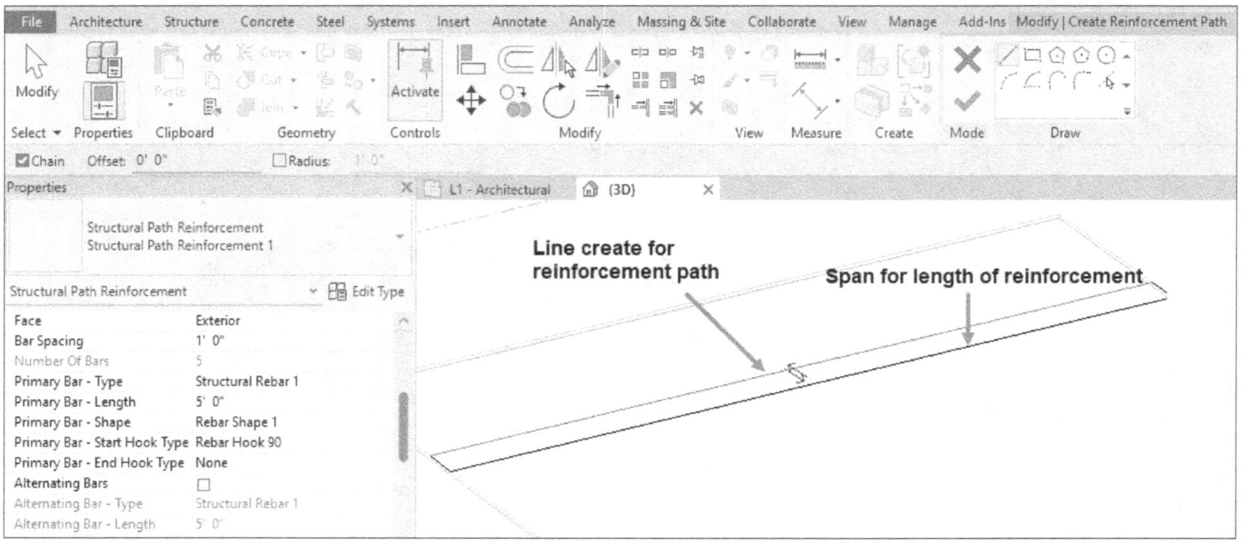

Figure-45. Creating path reinforcement

STRUCTURAL MORPHED REINFORCEMENT

The structural morphed reinforcement is used to create reinforcement along transverse bar segments or between the selected faces. The procedure to create structural morphed reinforcement is discussed next.

- Click on the **Morphed** tool from **Reinforcement** panel in the **Concrete** tab of the **Ribbon**. You will be asked to select a rebar segment or the direction for rebar.
- Set desired parameters in the **Properties Palette** as discussed earlier.
- Select **By Rebar** or **Surface** option from **Distribution** panel to create a rebar set by selecting a rebar segments or along the surface of a rebar segments, respectively.
- Select desired rebar segment. The preview of reinforcement will be displayed.
- Click on the **Finish** button from the contextual tab. The morphed reinforcement will be created; refer to Figure-46.

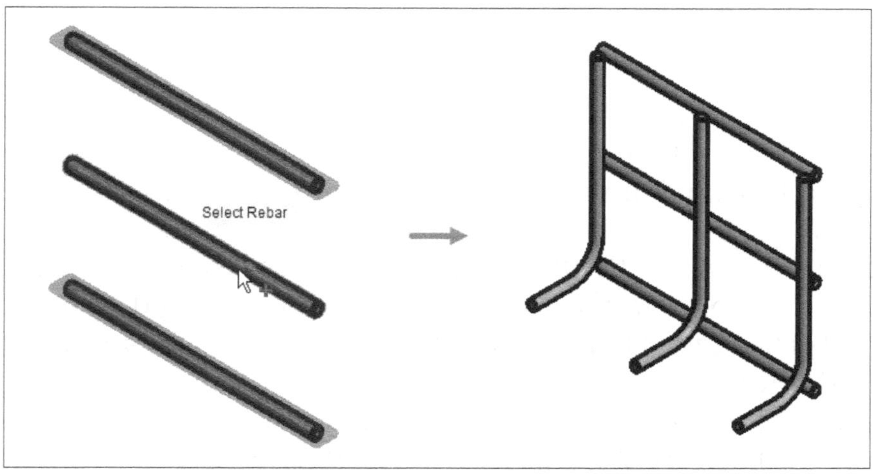

Figure-46. Morphed reinforcement created

CREATING FABRIC AREA

The **Fabric Area** tool is used to create a fabric sheet in sketched boundary. The procedure to create fabric area is given next.

- Click on the **Fabric Area** tool from the **Reinforcement** panel in the **Concrete** tab of **Ribbon**. You will be asked to select a wall or floor for creating fabric area.

- Select the floor or wall to which you want to apply fabric area. You will be asked to create boundary of fabric area and the related options will be displayed; refer to Figure-47.

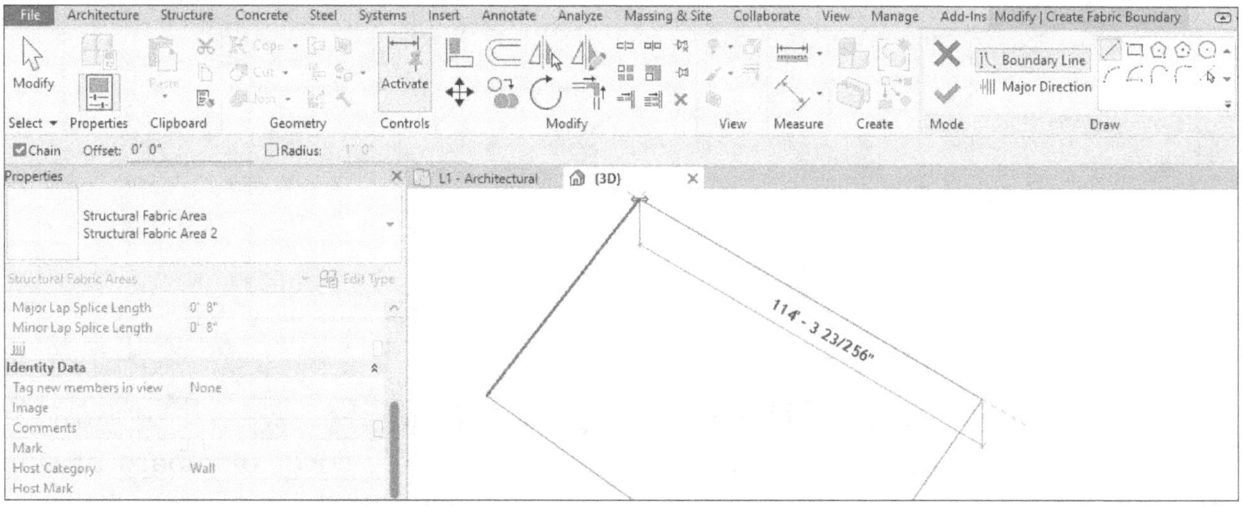

Figure-47. Options for fabric area boundary

- Set desired parameters in the **Properties Palette** like fabric sheet size, location, and so on.
- Create a closed loop sketch for fabric sheet; refer to Figure-48.

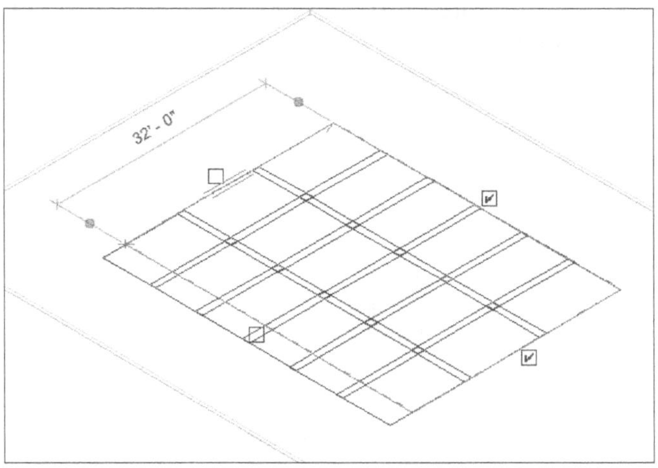

Figure-48. Preview of fabric area

- Click on the **OK** button from the **Mode** panel in the contextual tab to create the structural fabric.

CREATING FABRIC SHEET

The **Fabric Sheet** tool is used to create a block of fabric sheet. This tool is available when a Plan view is active. The procedure to use this tool is given next.

- Click on the **Fabric Sheet** tool from the **Reinforcement** panel in the **Concrete** tab of the **Ribbon**. The options to create fabric sheet will be displayed with preview of fabric sheet; refer to Figure-49.
- Set desired parameters in the **Properties Palette** and click to place the fabric sheet.
- Press **ESC** to exit the tool.

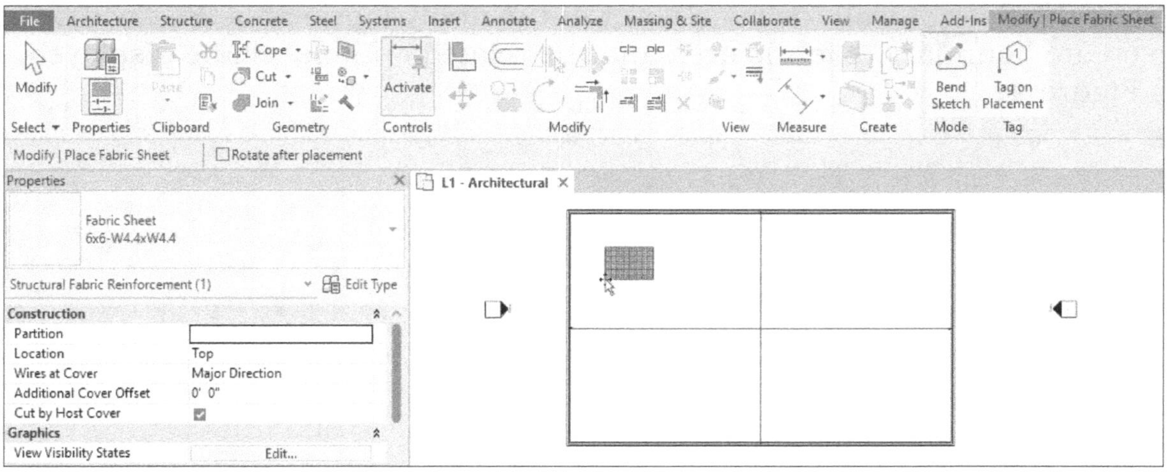

Figure-49. Options to create fabric sheet

EDITING REBAR COVER

The **Cover** tool in **Reinforcement** panel is used to modify cover of rebars in walls, slabs, and floors. The procedure to use this tool is given next.

- Click on the **Cover** tool from the **Reinforcement** panel of **Concrete** tab in the **Ribbon**. The options to modify cover will be displayed in the **Options Bar** and you will be asked to select the rebar structure.
- Select the face of wall/floor/slab with rebar or cover of rebar. The related options will be activated in the **Options Bar**; refer to Figure-50.

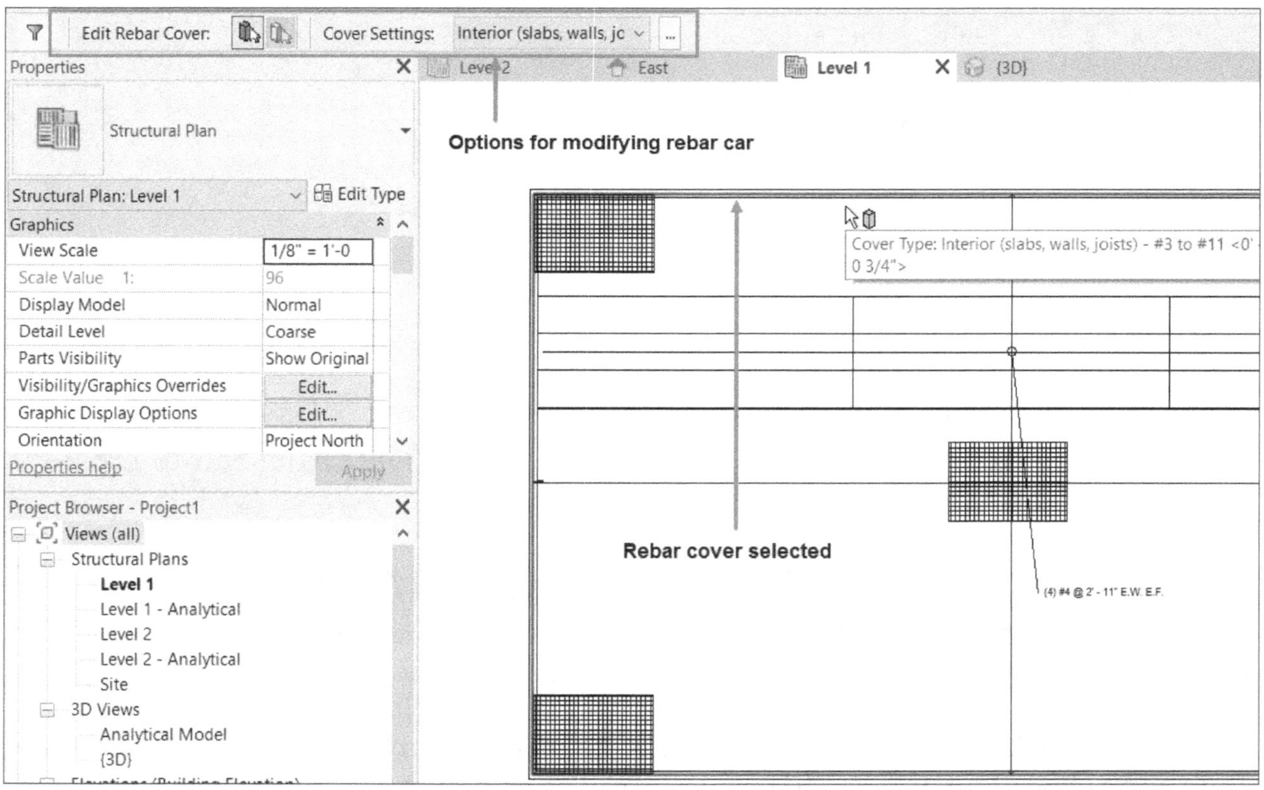

Figure-50. Modifying rebar cover

- Select desired option from the **Cover Settings** drop-down in the **Options Bar** to change the cover.
- If you want to change standard cover settings, click on the **Edit Cover Settings** button from the **Options Bar**. The **Rebar Cover Settings** dialog box will be displayed; refer to Figure-51.

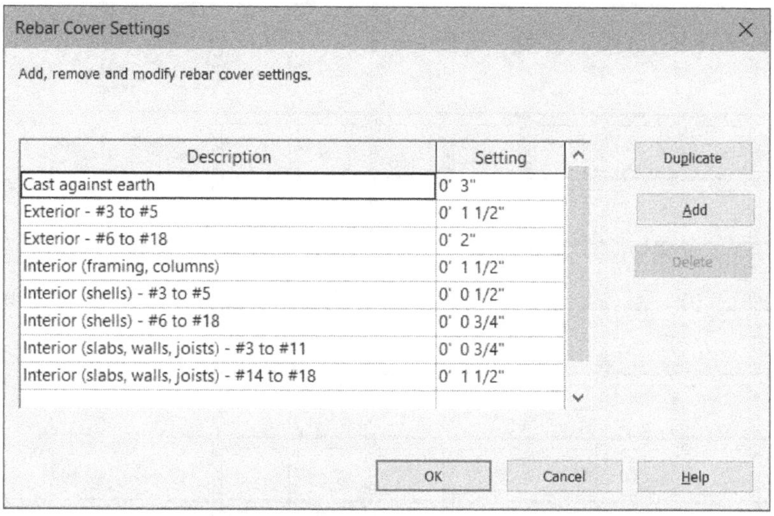

Figure-51. Rebar Cover Settings dialog box

- Set desired values in the table to modify cover parameters. Click on the **Add** button to add a new rebar cover and modify the values as desired.
- Click on the **OK** button from the dialog box to apply the changes.

The other tools in the **Structure** tab have already been discussed previous chapters.

Practical 1

Create a structure of 8 floor building of size 100'x100'. Each floor has same area of 100,000 sqft. Size of each rectangular concrete column is 12x18 sq. inch. Size of each rectangular concrete beam is 12x24 sq. inch. Footing is needed at 9 feet below ground level. The height of each level is 10 feet. The floors are created by 3" concrete on 2" metal deck. The foundation slab has a thickness of 6". Various views of structural model are given in Figure-52, Figure-53, and Figure-54.

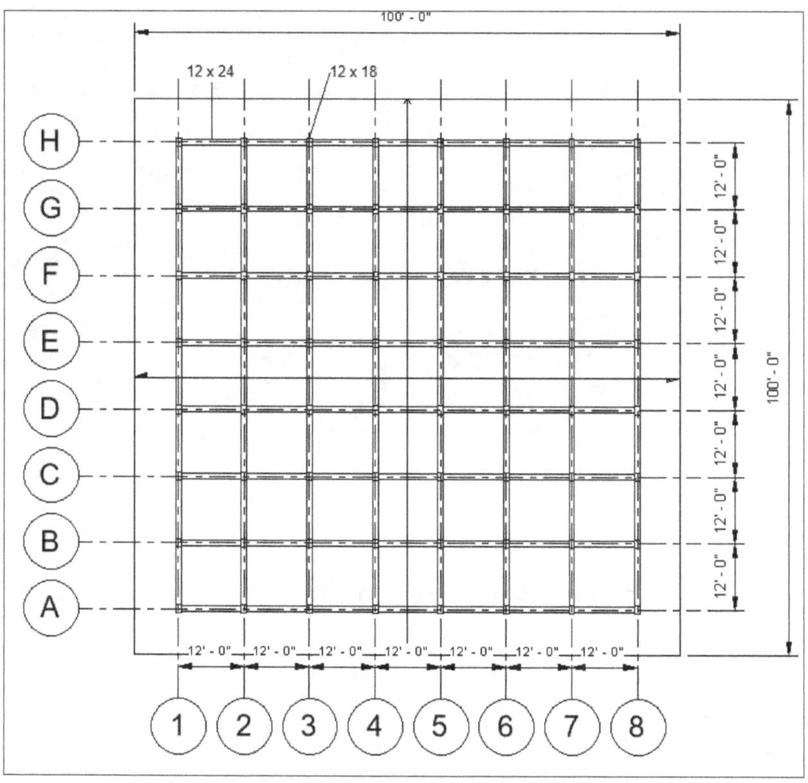

Figure-52. Plan for Practical 1

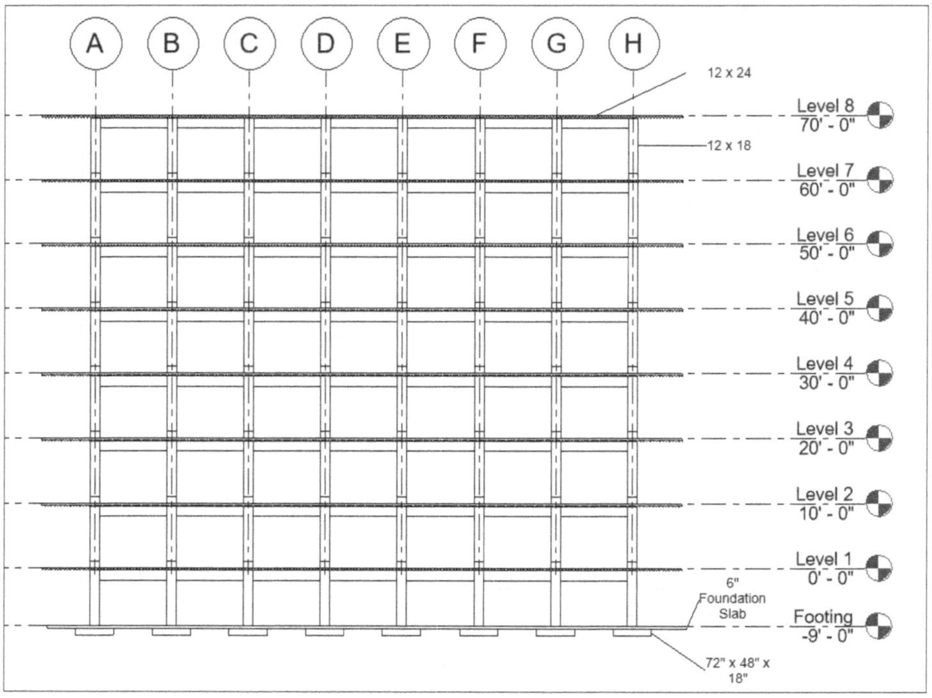

Figure-53. East elevation for Practical 1

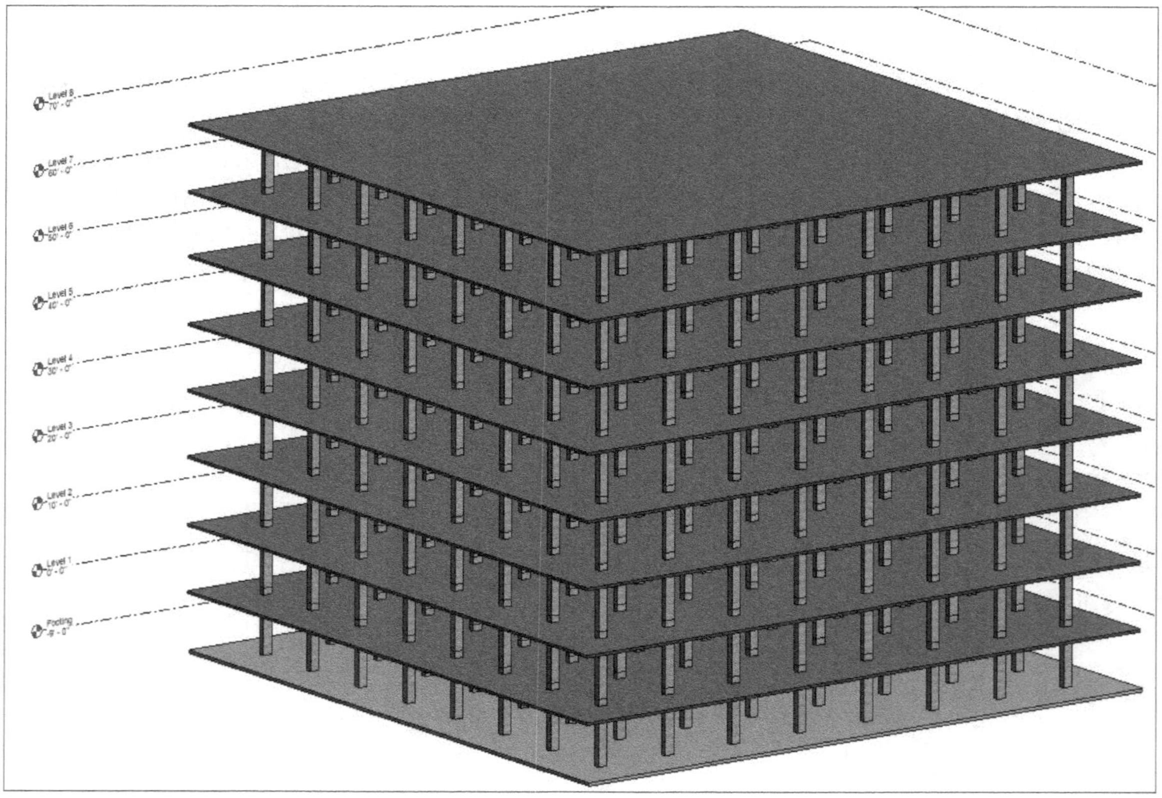

Figure-54. 3D model for Practical 1

Steps to perform:

1. Start a new project with Structural template. Create 6 levels above Level 2 and one level below Level 1.
2. Rename and dimension levels as required.
3. Create the grids for columns and beams in Level 1 plan view.
4. Create the columns below Level 1 upto Footing level.
5. Create the footings and foundation slab.

6. Create the columns between Level 1 and Level 2 at grid intersection points.
7. Create beams at the intersections of grids in Level 1 plan view.
8. Create structural floor on Level 1.
9. Copy the beams, columns, and floor to all the levels as per the model.

Procedure:

Starting A Structural Project

- Click on the **Project** tool from **New** cascading menu of the **File** menu. The **New Project** dialog box will be displayed.
- Select the **Imperial Multi-discipline** option (any other imperial structural template, if this is not available) from the **Template file** drop-down. Make sure **Project** radio button is selected in the **Create new** area of the dialog box and then click on the **OK** button. The new project file will open in Revit.

Creating Levels

- Click on the **East-Architectural** view from the **Elevations (Building Elevation)** category in the **Project Browser**. The east elevation view will be displayed; refer to Figure-55.

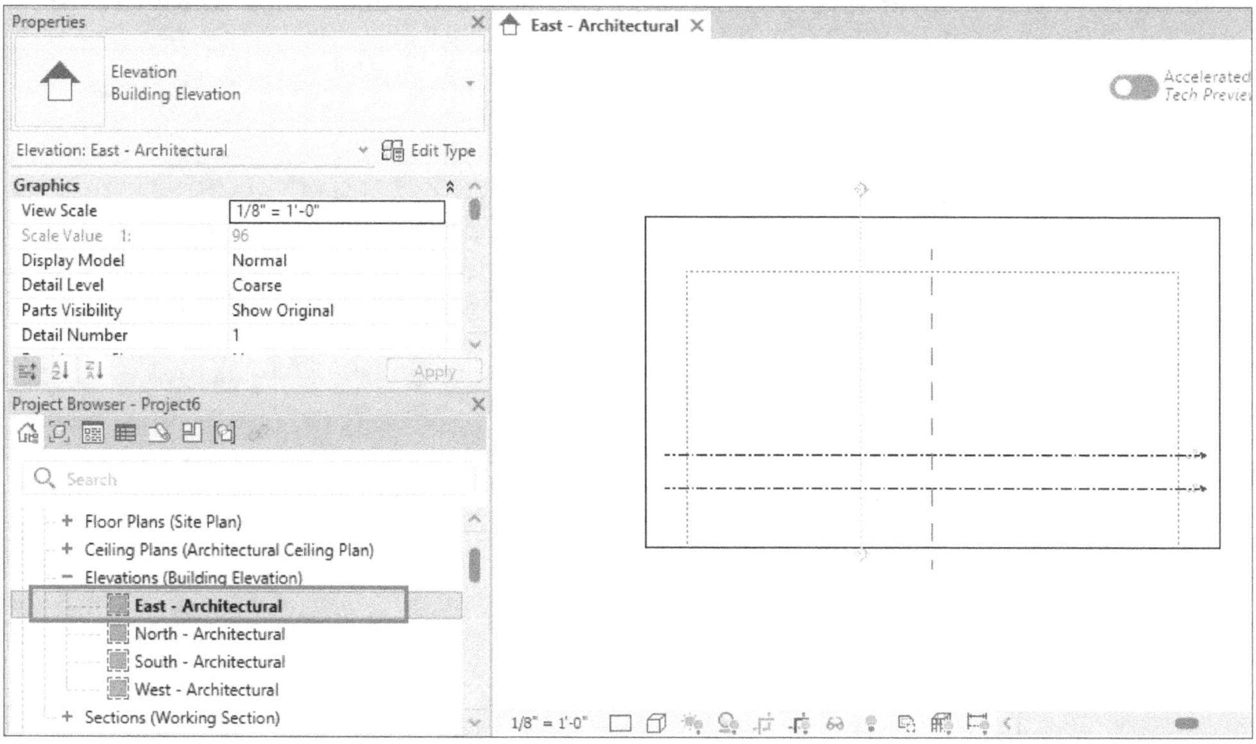

Figure-55. East elevation view

- Click on the **Level** tool from the **Datum** panel in the **Structure** tab of **Ribbon** or type **LL** from keyboard. The **Level** tool will be activated and you will be asked to specify start point for level line.
- Move the cursor at 10 feet above the Level 2 line near its end point and click to specify start point for level line; refer to Figure-56. You will be asked to specify location of level number tag.

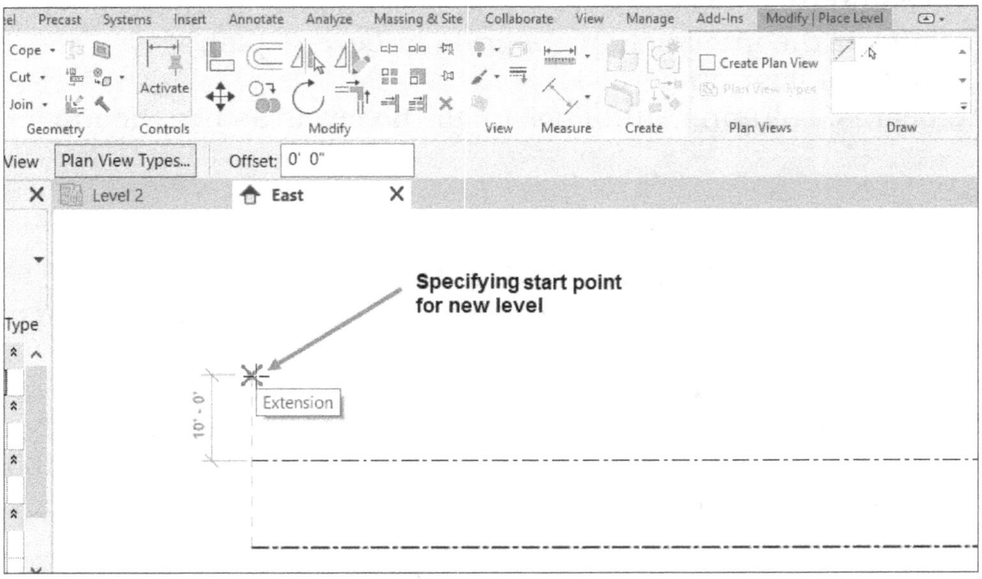

Figure-56. Specifying start point for level line

- Click at the location above Level 2 tag where cursor snaps automatically; refer to Figure-57.
- Similarly, create other levels above and below the Level 1; refer to Figure-58.

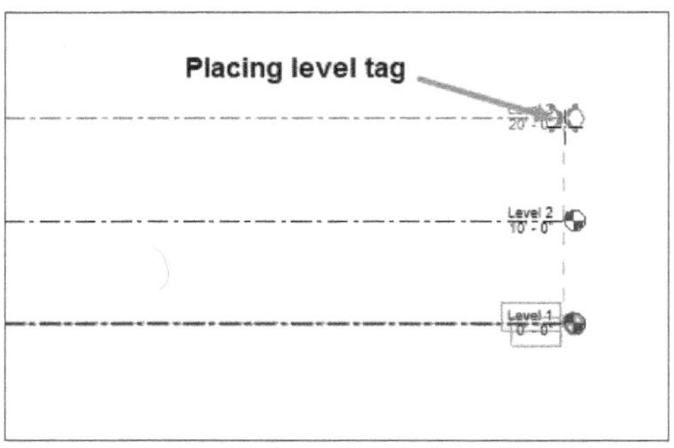

Figure-57. Placing Level tag

Figure-58. Levels created

- Double-click on the name tab of level below **Level 1** and change the name as **Footing**; refer to Figure-59. Click in the blank area of viewport. The **Confirm Level Rename** dialog box will be displayed; refer to Figure-60.

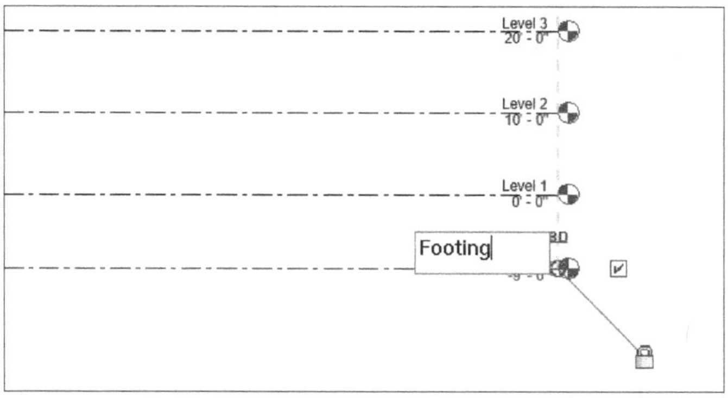

Figure-59. Specifying name of level

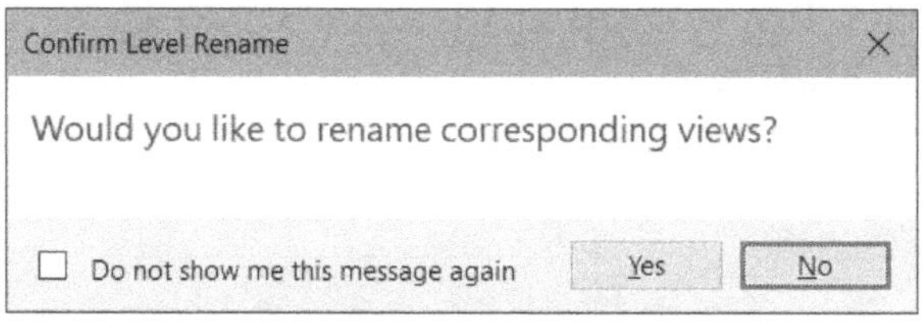

Figure-60. Confirm Level Rename dialog box

- Click on the **Yes** button to confirm change of name.

Creating Grids

- Double-click on **Level 1 Structural** from **Structural Plans** category in the **Project Browser**. The Level 1 plan view will be displayed.
- Click on the **Grid** tool from the **Datum** panel in the **Structure** tab of **Ribbon**. You will be asked to specify start point for grid line.
- Create 8 vertical grid lines as shown in Figure-61.

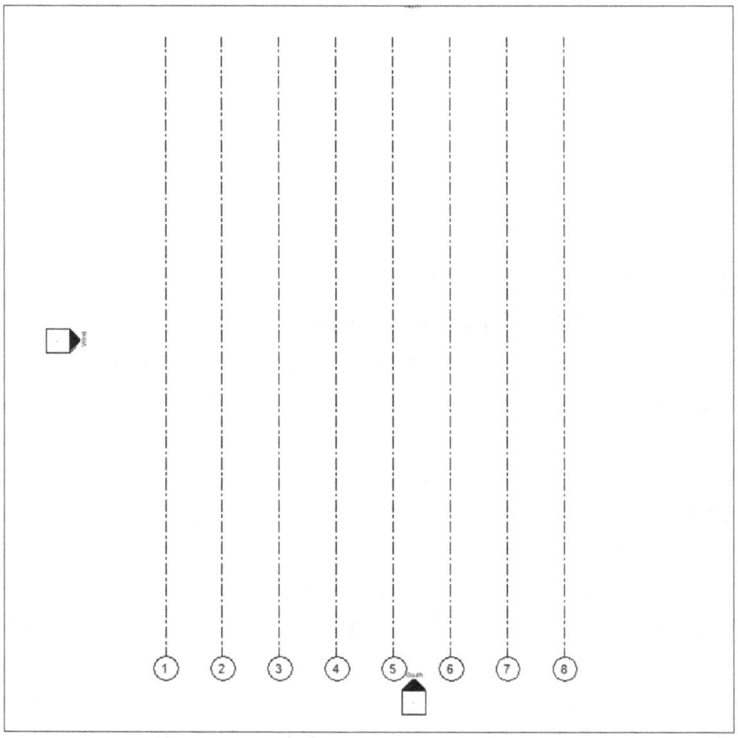

Figure-61. Vertical grid lines created

- Now, create the first horizontal grid line and rename it **A**; refer to Figure-62.

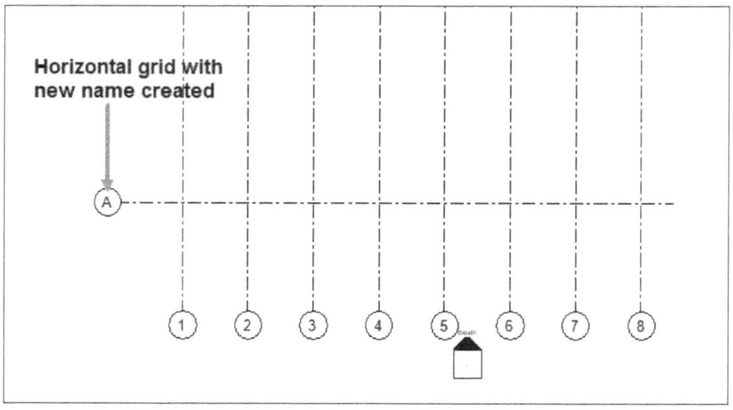

Figure-62. Horizontal grid created

- Now, create rest of the horizontal grid lines upto H with distance between two instances 12; refer to Figure-63.

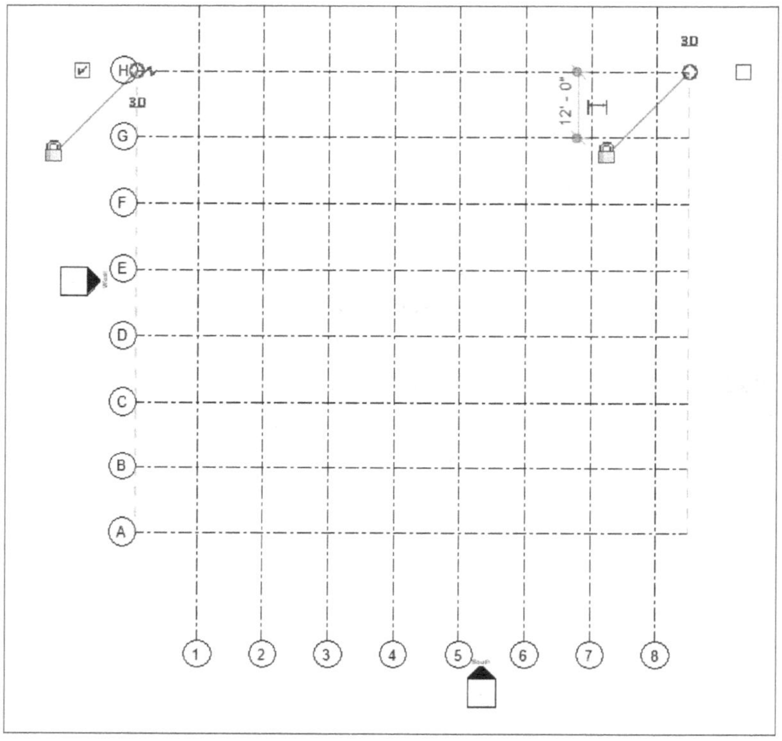

Figure-63. Horizontal grids created

Creating Columns and Beams

- Make sure the Level 1 plan is active and then click on the **Column** tool from the **Structure** tab in the **Ribbon**. The options to place columns will be displayed in the contextual tab.
- Select the **Concrete-Rectangular-Column 12x18** type from the drop-down at the top in the **Properties Palette**. Make sure the **Depth** options with **9'** value is set in the **Options Bar**; refer to Figure-64.
- Click on the **At Grids** tool from the **Multiple** panel in the **Modify|Place Structural Column** contextual tab of **Ribbon**. You will be asked to select the intersecting grid lines.
- Select all the grid lines using cross-window selection; refer to Figure-65. The preview of columns will be displayed; refer to Figure-66.

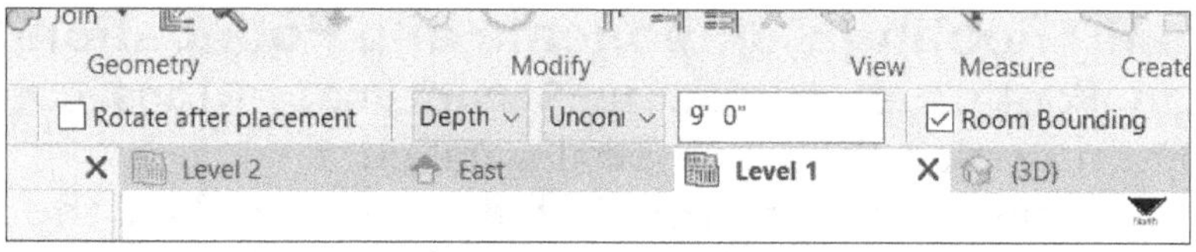

Figure-64. Options set in Options Bar

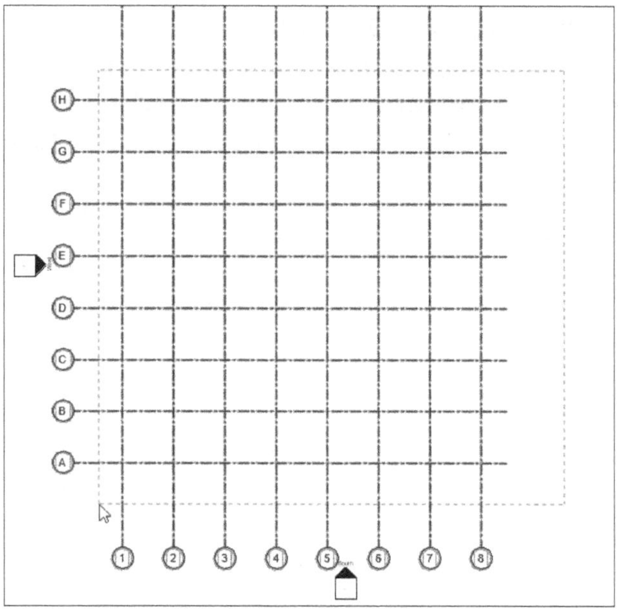

Figure-65. Selecting grid lines

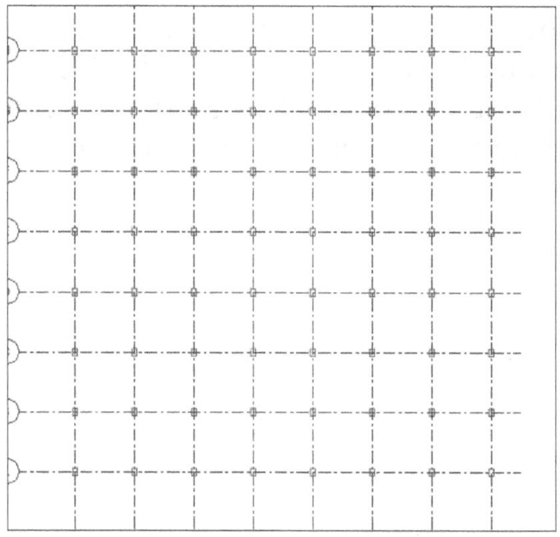

Figure-66. Columns created on grid lines

- Click on the **Finish** button from the contextual tab. The columns will be created.
- Now, set the **Height** option for column upto **Level 2** in the **Options Bar** as shown in Figure-67 and create the columns at grid intersections. Press **ESC** to exit the tool.

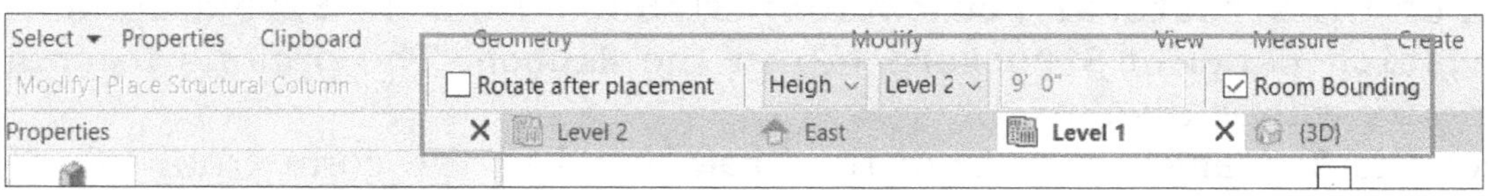

Figure-67. Options set for columns

- Create beams connecting the intersection points of grids in the same way using the **Beam** tool from the **Structure** panel in the **Structure** tab of **Ribbon**; refer to Figure-68. Make sure **Level 1** is selected in the **Placement Plane** drop-down.
- Press **ESC** to exit the tool.

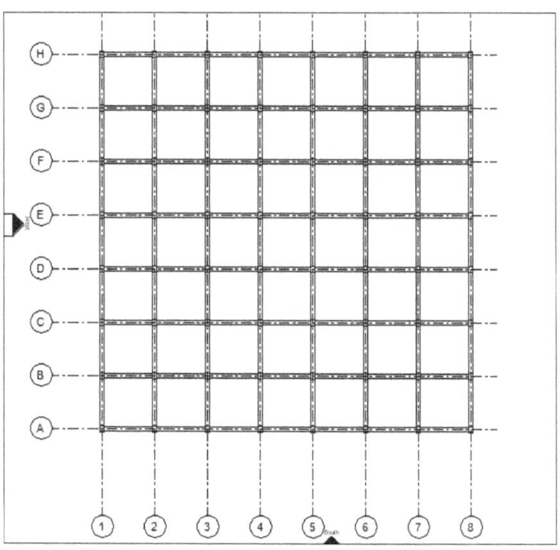

Figure-68. Placing beams on grid points

Creating Footing Components and Foundation Slab

- Double-click on Footing plan view in **Structural Plans** category of **Project Browser**. The Footing plan view will be displayed.
- Click on the **Isolated** tool from the **Foundation** panel in the **Structure** tab of **Ribbon**. The options to place footing will be displayed.
- Select the **Footing-Rectangular 72"x48"x18"** option from the drop-down at the top in the **Properties Palette** and click on the **At Grids** tool from the **Multiple** panel in the contextual tab of **Ribbon**. You will be asked to select grid lines.
- Select all the grid lines using cross-window selection as discussed for creating columns on Level 1. The preview of footings will be displayed; refer to Figure-69.

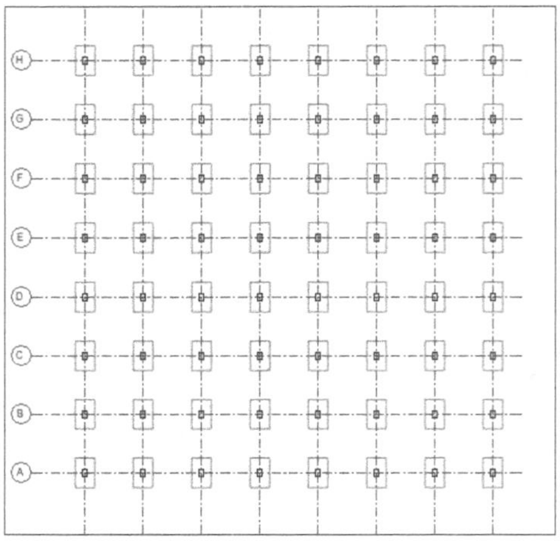

Figure-69. Footing created

- Click on the **Finish** tool from the **Multiple** panel in contextual tab to create footings. Press **ESC** to exit the tools.
- Click on the **Structural Foundation: Slab** tool from the **Slab** drop-down in the **Foundation** panel of **Structure** tab in the **Ribbon**. The options to create floor boundary will be displayed.
- Select the **Rectangle** tool from the **Draw** panel in the contextual tab of **Ribbon** and select the **6" Foundation Slab** option from the drop-down at the top in the **Properties Palette**.
- Create the rectangular boundary for slab; refer to Figure-70.

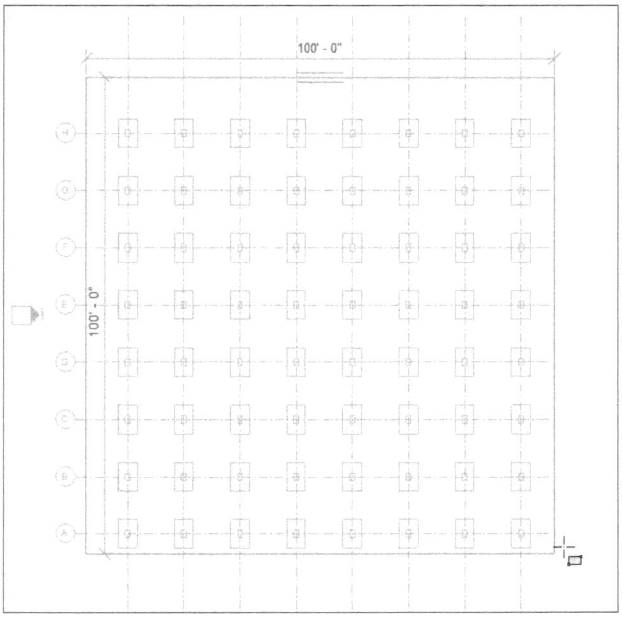

Figure-70. Creating foundation slab

- Click on the **Finish** button to create the slab. The **Modify|Structural Foundation** contextual tab will be displayed in the **Ribbon**.
- Click on the **Move** tool from the **Modify|Structural Foundation** contextual tab in the **Ribbon** and then move the foundation at desired location.

Creating Structural Floor

- Double-click on the **Level 1** in **Structural Plans** category in the **Project Browser**. The plan view will open.
- Click on the **Floor: Structural** tool from the **Floor** drop-down in the **Structure** panel of **Structure** tab in the **Ribbon**. The options to create structural floor will be displayed; refer in the **Ribbon** and **Properties Palette**.
- Select the **Floor 3" LW Concrete on 2" Metal Deck** option from the drop-down at the top in the **Properties Palette** and create the floor boundary as shown in Figure-71.

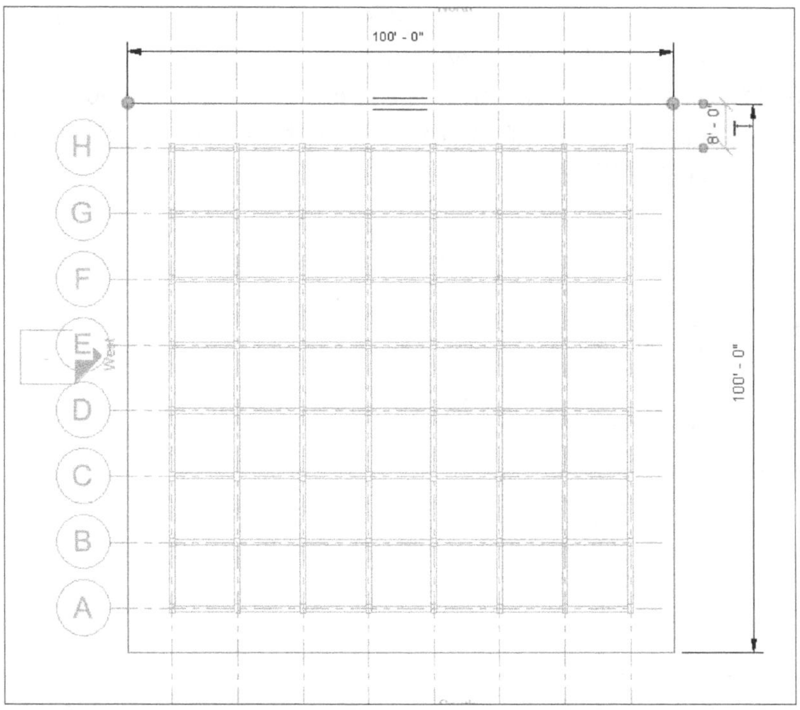

Figure-71. Structural floor boundary created

- Click on the **OK** button from the **Mode** panel in the **Modify|Create Floor Boundary** contextual tab of **Ribbon**.

Copying Elements on Different Levels

- Select the elements on **Level 1** plan view using windows selection; refer to Figure-72. The **Modify|Multi-Select** contextual tab will be displayed.

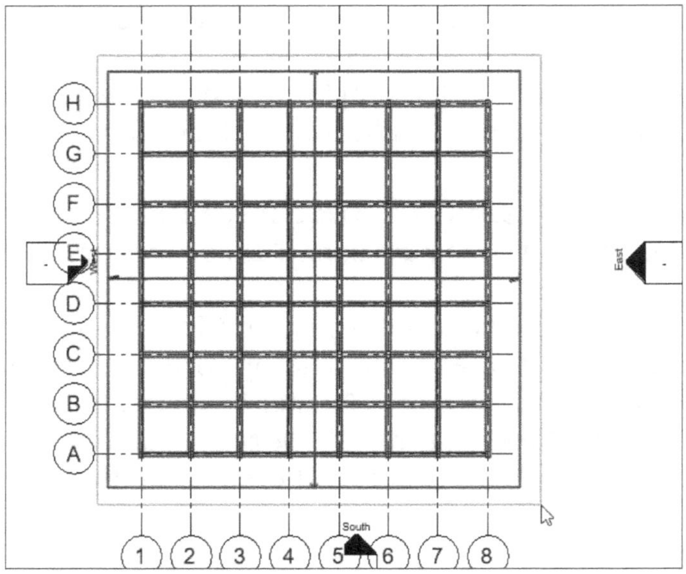

Figure-72. Selecting elements on Level 1

- Click on the **Filter** tool from the **Selection** panel in the **Modify|Multi-Selection** contextual tab of **Ribbon**. The **Filter** dialog box will be displayed with selected objects; refer to Figure-73.

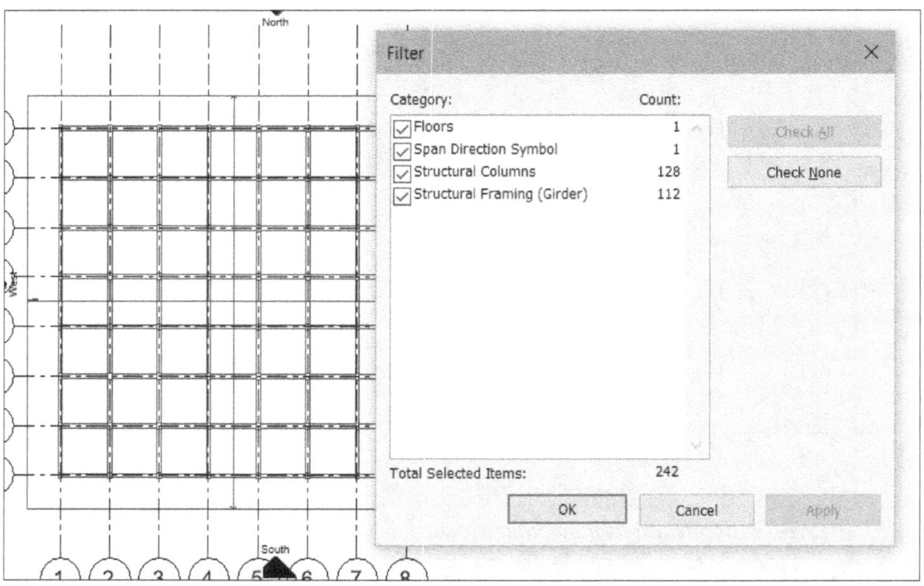

Figure-73. Filter dialog box with selected elements

- Clear the **Structural Columns** check box and click on the **OK** button. Now, the floor, beams, and direction symbol will be selected but columns will be cleared.
- Click on the **Copy to Clipboard** tool from the **Clipboard** panel in the contextual tab. The elements will be copied in clipboard.
- Click on the **Aligned to Selected Views** option from the **Paste** drop-down in the **Clipboard** panel of **Modify** tab in the **Ribbon**. The **Select Views** dialog box will be displayed.
- Select the Structural Plan Level 2, Structural Plan Level 3, Structural Plan Level 4, Structural Plan Level 5, Structural Plan Level 6, Structural Plan Level 7, and Structural Plan Level 8 from the dialog box while holding the **CTRL** key; refer to Figure-74 and click on the **OK** button. The elements will be copied.

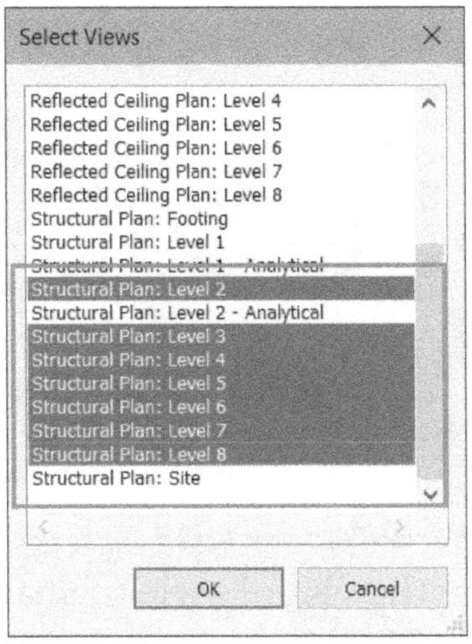

Figure-74. Structural plans selected

- If you open the 3D View then you will notice that columns are not copied to selected levels.
- Open the **Level 2** plan view and select the elements as shown in Figure-75.

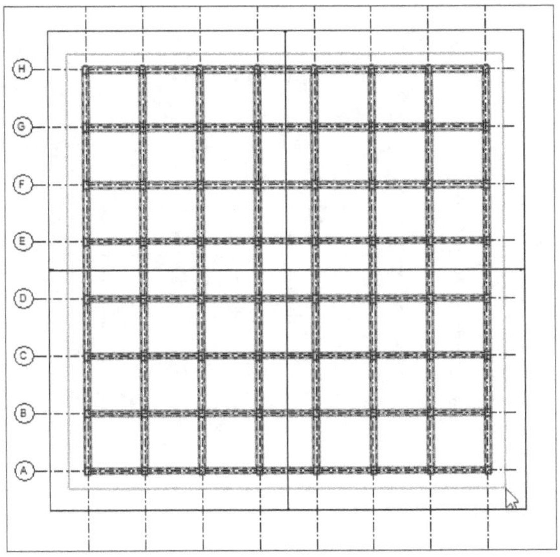

Figure-75. Elements selected for copying

- Click on the **Filter** tool from the **Modify|Multi-Select** contextual tab in the **Ribbon** and clear the **Structural Framing (Girder)** check box from the **Filter** dialog box. Click on the **OK** button from the dialog box. The columns of level 2 will be selected.
- Click on the **Copy to Clipboard** button from the **Modify|Structural Columns** contextual tab in the **Ribbon**. The columns will be selected.
- Click on the **Aligned to Selected Levels** tool from the **Paste** drop-down in the **Clipboard** panel of **Ribbon**. The **Select Levels** dialog box will be displayed.
- Select **Level 3**, **Level 4**, **Level 5**, **Level 6**, **Level 7**, and **Level 8** options from the **Select Levels** dialog box; refer to Figure-76 and click on the **OK** button. The columns will be created on all the selected levels.

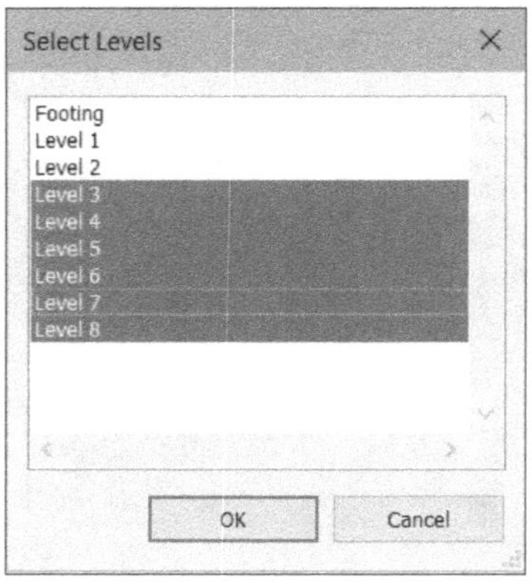

Figure-76. Select Levels dialog box

- Open the 3D view and change the visual style to **Shaded**. The model will be displayed as shown in Figure-77.

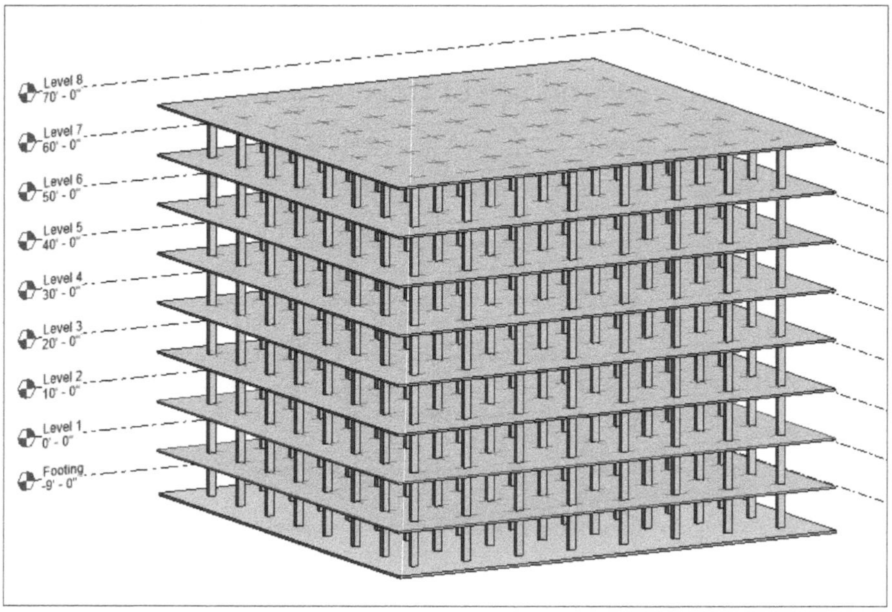

Figure-77. Model for practical 1

PRACTICE 1

Create the structural model of building as shown in Figure-78. The plan view of structure is given in Figure-79.

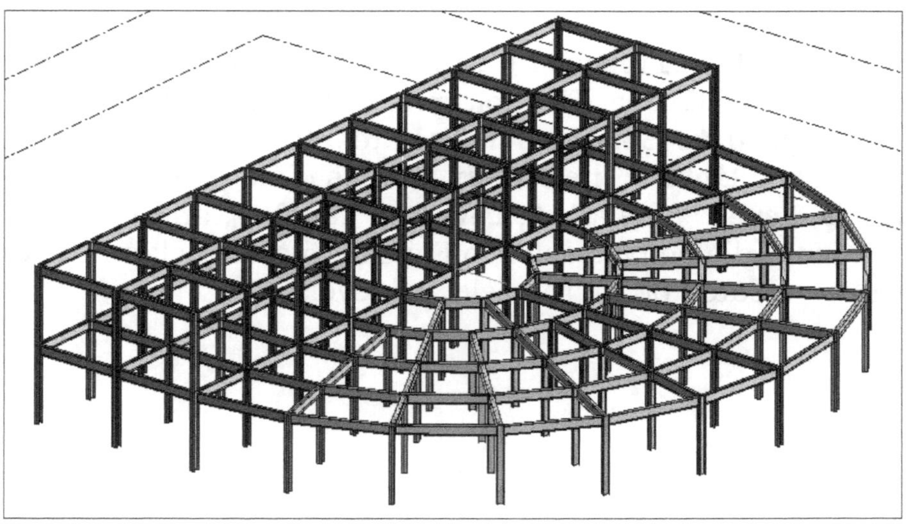

Figure-78. Structural model for Practice 1

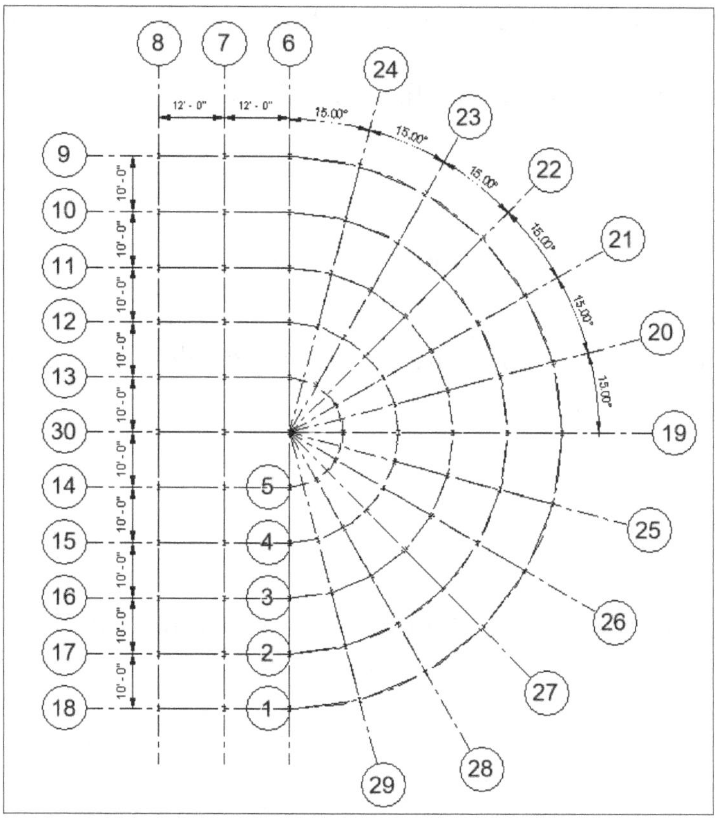

Figure-79. Plan View for Level 2

SELF ASSESSMENT

Q1. Write a short note on different type of loads applied in structural drawing.

Q2. Structural truss is used to carry and transfer loads. (T/F)

Q3. The braces are used to diagonally connect beams and columns. (T/F)

Q4. Which of the following tools is used to create a series of parallel beams?

a. Beam b. Beam System
c. Truss d. Brace

Q5. In **Load Cases** tab of **Structural Settings** dialog box, you can create 8 different types of load cases. (T/F)

Q6. Discuss the difference between analytical and physical model of structure.

Q7. Discuss the difference between connections and braces.

Q8. Isolate footing is applied to columns when there are single columns at relatively long distances. (T/F)

Q9. Structural rebar is used to strengthen concrete as well as masonry structure by using steel bar and mesh of steel wires. (T/F)

Q10. The **Fabric Area** tool is used to create a fabric sheet in sketched boundary. (T/F)

Q11. What type of load is defined as a fixed load that remains constant once applied?

A. Dynamic Load
B. Impact Load
C. Static Load
D. Seismic Load

Q12. Which load varies with time and includes people and water tanks?

A. Dead Load
B. Static Load
C. Dynamic Load
D. Snow Load

Q13. What is the effect of an earthquake on a building called?

A. Impact Load
B. Seismic Load
C. Wind Load
D. Snow Load

Q14. Which type of load is most relevant for high-rise buildings?

A. Service Load
B. Wind Load
C. Snow Load
D. Static Load

Q15. What tool is used to create beams in Revit?

A. Column Tool
B. Wall: Structural Tool
C. Beam Tool
D. Brace Tool

Q16. What option must be selected to create a series of connected beams or trusses?

A. Structural Usage
B. Chain
C. Placement Plane
D. Beam Type

Q17. What element is used to diagonally connect beams and columns?

A. Beam
B. Truss
C. Brace
D. Slab

Q18. What tool allows automatic placement of parallel beams within a boundary?

A. Beam Tool
B. Truss Tool
C. Beam System Tool
D. Connection Tool

Q19. In Structural Settings, what is used to represent how braces appear in plan view?

A. Load Combinations
B. Symbolic Representation Settings
C. Boundary Conditions
D. Load Scaling

Q20. What is the purpose of the Load Combinations tab?

A. To define structural symbols
B. To apply combined load factors for analysis
C. To draw beam boundaries
D. To create beam types

Q21. What setting controls symbol representation for different boundary conditions?

A. Structural Usage
B. Structural Settings
C. Boundary Conditions Settings
D. Placement Plane

Q22. Which tab defines how the scale of loads is displayed in the analytical model?

A. Load Cases Display
B. Symbolic Representation Settings
C. Load Combinations
D. Loads Scaling Display

Q23. What checkbox must be selected to stop automatic shortening of steel elements during auto-join?

A. Chain
B. Placement Plane
C. Disable automatic shortening
D. Structural Usage

Q24. What tool is used to define how frame members connect to each other?

A. Beam System Tool
B. Structural Usage
C. Connection Tool
D. Boundary Conditions Settings

Q25. What tool is used to automatically apply connections to selected structural members?

A. Structural Settings
B. Load Combinations
C. Connection Automation
D. Placement Plane

Q26. What is the purpose of an Isolated footing?

A. To provide support to structural walls
B. To distribute load safely to the bed soil below single columns
C. To support beams in a continuous slab
D. To reinforce the structural floor

Q27. Which tool is used to create foundation for structural walls?

A. Slab
B. Isolated
C. Wall
D. Footing

Q28. In the Wall footing creation, the "Eccentricity" option is available for which type of footing?

A. Slab footing
B. Reinforced footing
C. Bearing footing
D. Isolated footing

Q29. What is the primary use of the Structural Foundation: Slab tool?

A. To draw wall foundations
B. To create edge slabs only
C. To create independent slab at desired levels
D. To reinforce steel columns

Q30. What action flips the slab direction when using the Floor: Slab Edge tool?

A. Clicking ESC
B. Dragging the slab
C. Clicking the double arrows on the slab edge
D. Using the Offset parameter

Q31. What does the Rebar tool primarily reinforce?

A. Steel structures
B. Concrete and masonry structures
C. Timber floors
D. Fabric sheets

Q32. What option should be selected to define the space between two rebars in a set?

A. Maximum Spacing
B. Fixed Number
C. Top Major Number
D. Quantity Rule

Q33. Which layout rule is selected by default in the Area Reinforcement tool?

A. Fixed Number
B. Minimum Length
C. Equal Distribution
D. Maximum Spacing

Q34. What is used to define the path of reinforcement in Structural Path Reinforcement?

A. Rectangle loop
B. Open curve or line
C. Polygon sketch
D. Floor edge

Q35. Which view must be active to use the Fabric Sheet tool?

A. Elevation View
B. 3D View
C. Plan View
D. Section View

Q36. What does the Cover tool modify?

A. Size of rebar
B. Shape of the wall
C. Cover distance for rebars
D. Reinforcement type

Q37. Which condition is required for placing a rebar coupler between two bars?

A. Bars should be at least 10 feet apart
B. Bars should be parallel
C. Bars should be near each other at the ends
D. Bars should be perpendicular

Q38. What is the first step when starting a structural project in Revit?

A. Open Project Browser
B. Choose Plan View
C. Click on Project tool and select template
D. Define column grids

For Student Notes

Chapter 7

Steel Structural Designing

Topics Covered

The major topics covered in this chapter are:

- ***Creating Fabrication Plate***
- ***Creating Bolts***
- ***Creating Anchor Bolts***
- ***Creating Holes***
- ***Creating Shear Studs***
- ***Creating Weld Joints***
- ***Creating Corner Cuts***
- ***Creating Notch Skewed***
- ***Shortening Beams and Columns***
- ***Creating Contour Cuts***
- ***Creating Notches***
- ***Creating Miter Cuts***
- ***Creating Saw Cuts***
- ***Creating Cut Through***

INTRODUCTION

In previous chapter, you have learned about creating structural objects. You have learned to create beams, columns, foundations, rebars, and so on. In this chapter, you will learn about steel structure design. The tools to do so are available in the **Steel** tab of **Ribbon**; refer to Figure-1.

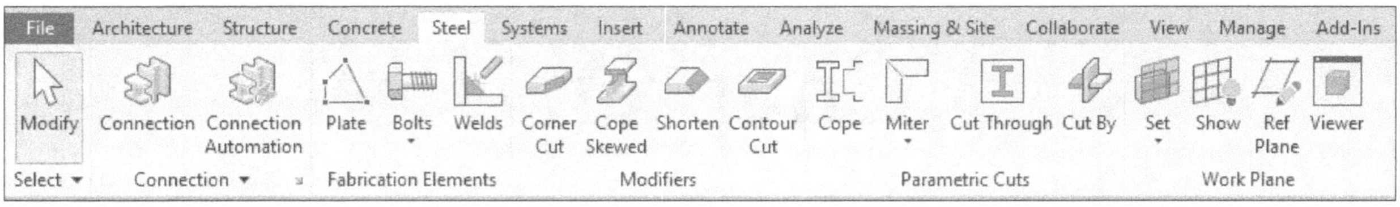

Figure-1. Steel tab

Various tools in this tab are discussed next.

CONNECTION

The **Connection** tool is used to define type of connection at selected intersection point of frame members. The procedure to use this tool is discussed in Chapter 6.

CONNECTION AUTOMATION

The **Connection Automation** tool is used to automatically apply connections to structural members based on specified set of connections. The procedure to use this tool has been discussed in Chapter 6.

CREATING FABRICATION PLATE

The **Plate** tool is used to create fabrication plate to which other structural members can be bolted or welded. The procedure to create fabrication plate is given next.

- Click on the **Plate** tool from the **Fabrication Elements** panel in the **Steel** tab of **Ribbon**. The options to create fabrication plate will be displayed; refer to Figure-2.

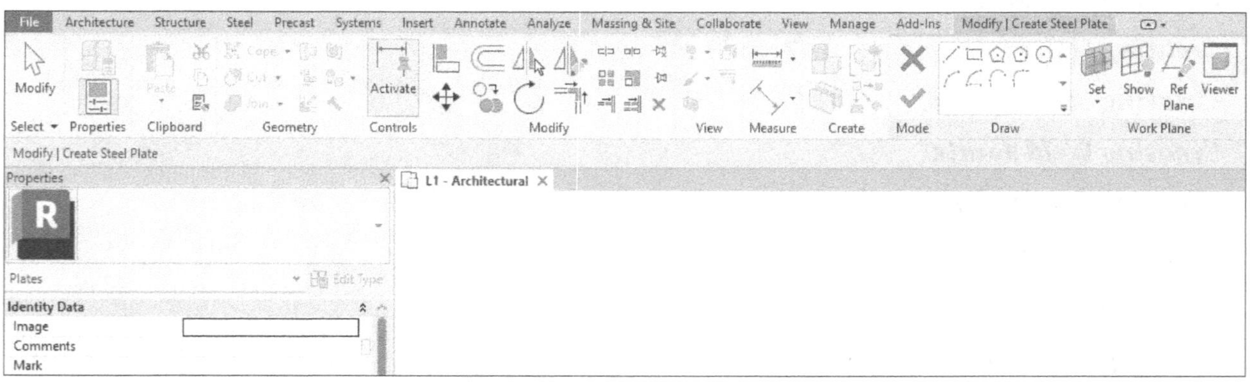

Figure-2. Options to create steel plate

- Click on the **Set** tool from the **Work Plane** panel in the **Modify|Create Steel Plate** contextual tab of the **Ribbon**. The **Work Plane** dialog box will be displayed.
- Select the **Pick a plane** radio button from the dialog box and click on the **OK** button. You will be asked to select a face/plane to be used as work plane.
- Select desired face/plane and click on the **Show** button to make sure you have selected correct plane.

- Click on desired tool from the **Draw** panel in the contextual tab and create the sketch of plate; refer to Figure-3.
- Click on the **OK** button from the contextual tab. The plate will be created; refer to Figure-4.

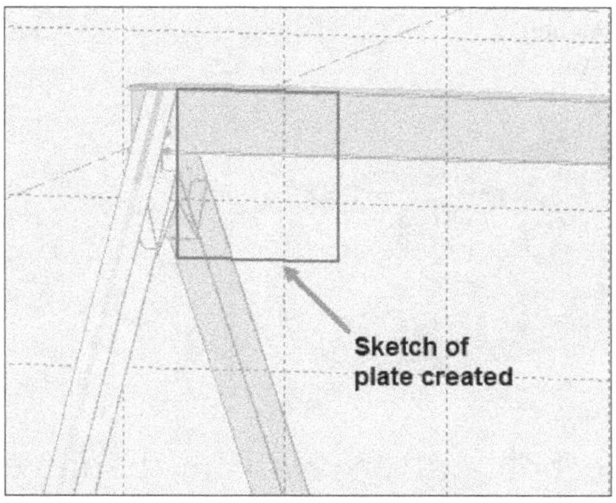

Figure-3. Sketch created for plate

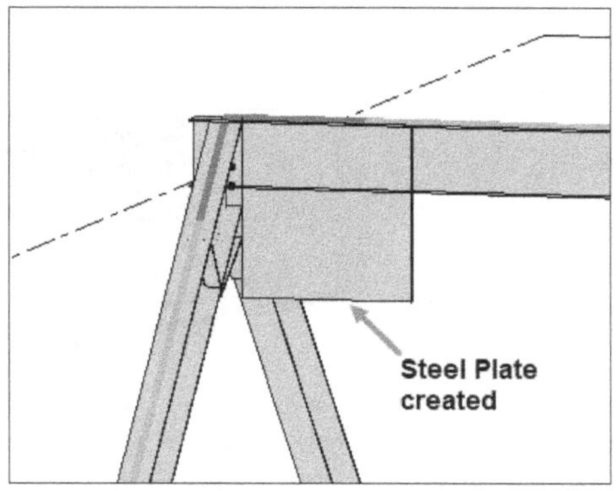

Figure-4. Steel plate created

Note that you need to make plates and other structural connections visible in the **Visibility/Graphic Overrides** dialog box; refer to Figure-5 to display the plates and other steel objects. Also, make sure **Detail Level** is set to **Fine** in the **View Control Bar**.

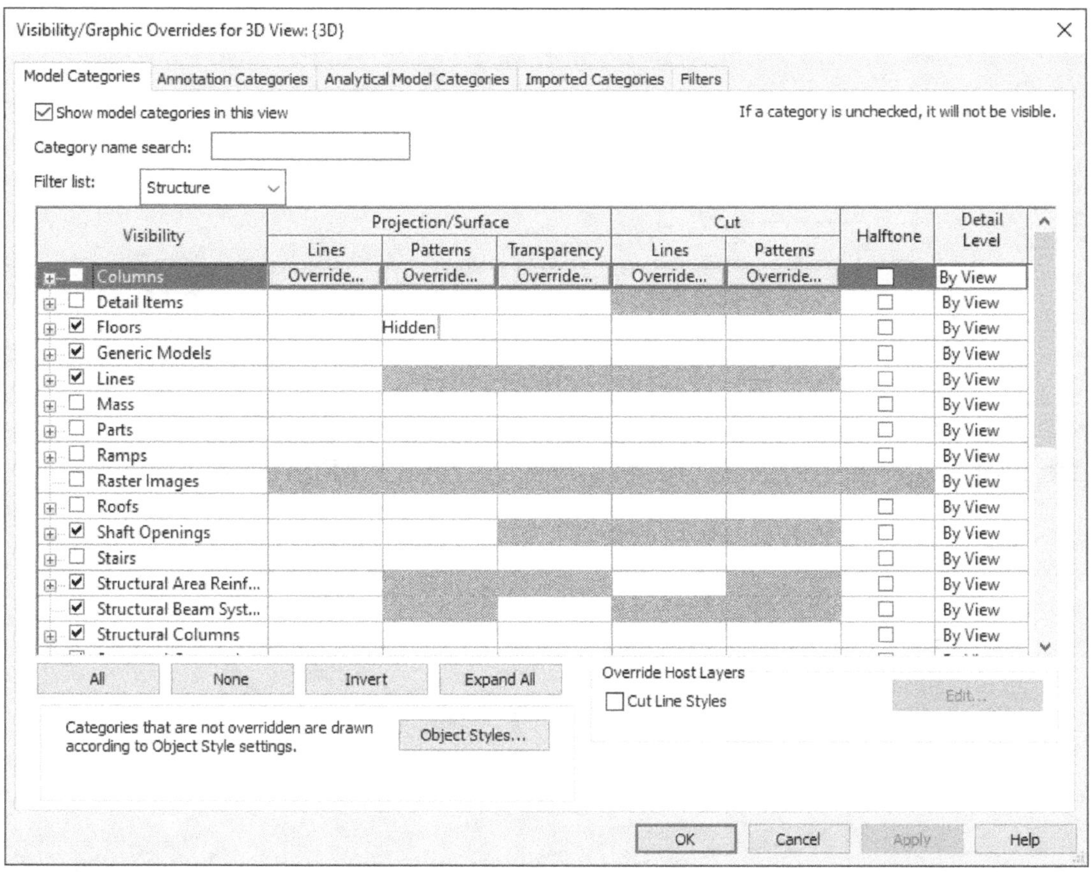

Figure-5. Visibility Graphics Overrides dialog box for steel connections

CREATING BOLTS

The **Bolts** tool is used to create bolted connection between two selected steel members. The procedure to use this tool is given next.

- Click on the **Bolts** tool from the **Fabrication Elements** panel in the **Steel** tab of **Ribbon**. You will be asked to select the frame members to be connected.
- Select the two frame members to be connected; refer to Figure-6. Press **ENTER**. You will be asked to select a plate/beam/column to define direction of bolt connection.

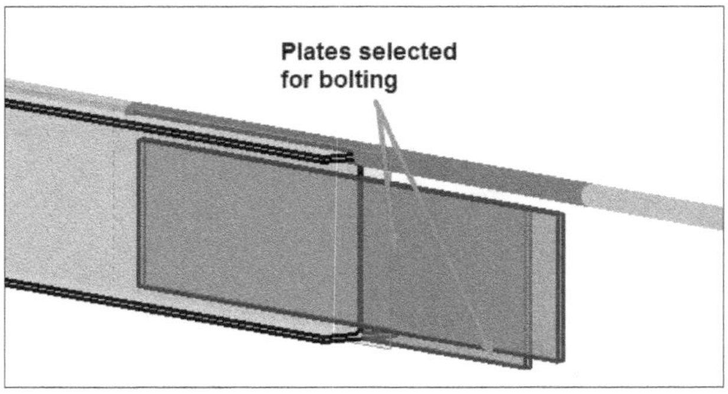

Figure-6. Plates selected for bolting

- Select desired face. The tools to create bolt pattern will be displayed; refer to Figure-7.

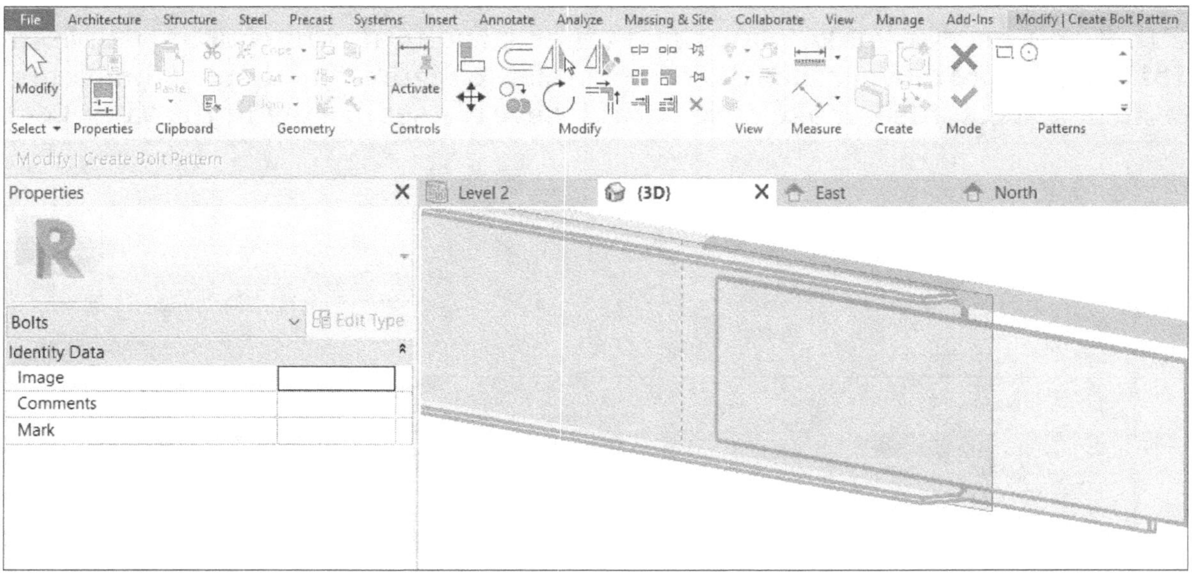

Figure-7. Tools to create bolt pattern

- Create rectangle or circle to create pattern; refer to Figure-8.

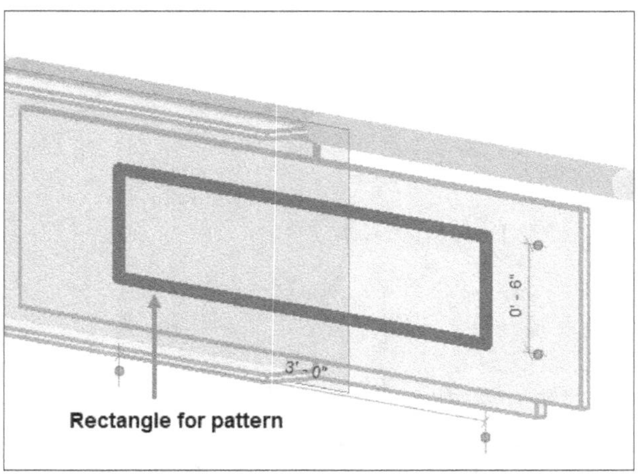

Figure-8. Pattern for bolts

- Click on the **OK** button from the contextual tab.

CREATING ANCHOR BOLTS

The **Anchors** tool is used to create anchor bolts in steel plate. The procedure to create anchor bolts is given next.

- Click on the **Anchors** tool from the **Bolts** drop-down in the **Fabrication Elements** panel of **Steel** tab in the **Ribbon**. You will be asked to select elements to be fastened by anchor bolts.
- Select desired steel plate(s) and press **ENTER**. You will be asked to select plate/ beam/column to define the direction of anchor bolt.
- Select the face of plate/beam/column. The options to create bolt pattern sketch will be displayed; refer to Figure-9.

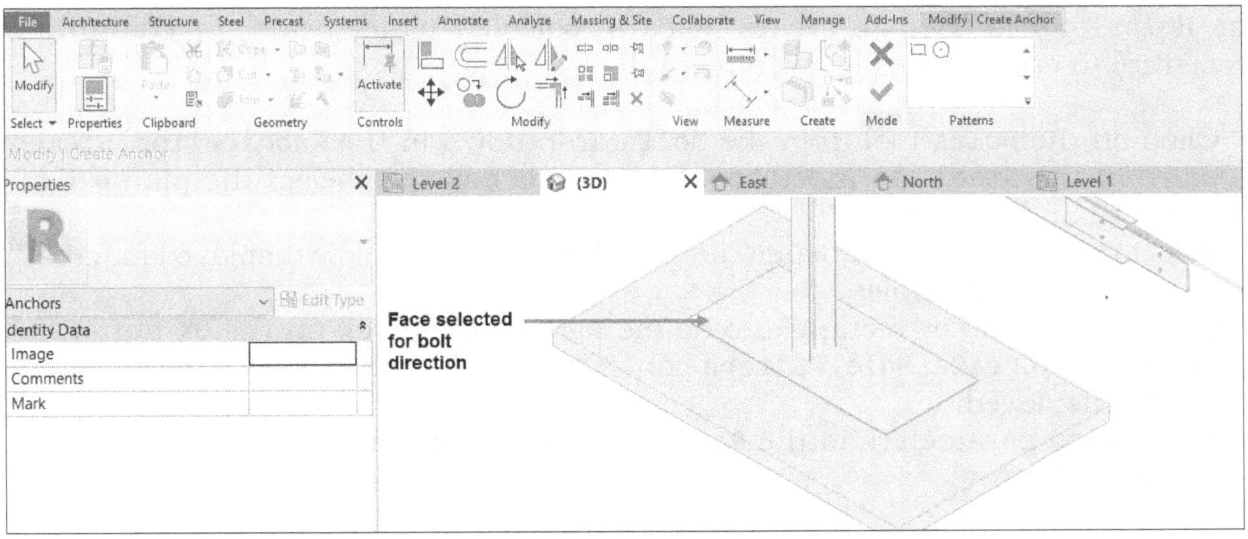

Figure-9. Options to create anchor bolt pattern

- Create desired sketch (circle or rectangle) for bolt pattern; refer to Figure-10.

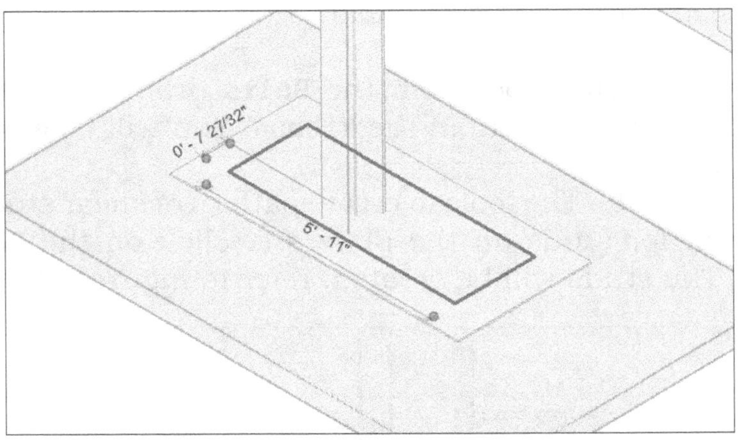

Figure-10. Sketch created for bolt pattern

- Click on the **OK** button from the contextual tab. The anchor bolt pattern will be displayed; refer to Figure-11.

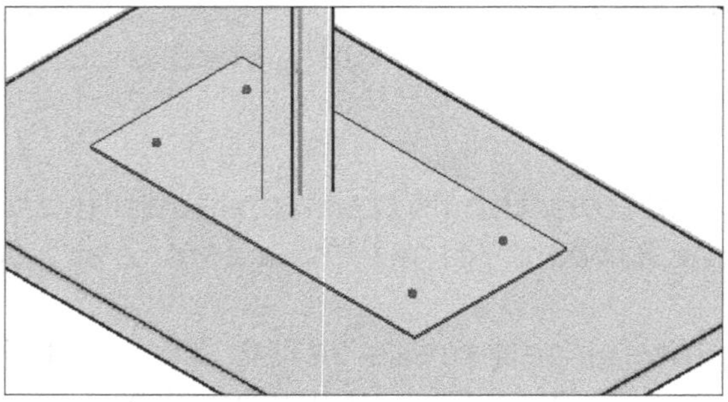

Figure-11. Anchor bolt pattern

CREATING HOLES

The **Holes** tool is used to create holes in selected plate, beam, or column. The procedure to create holes is given next.

- Click on the **Holes** tool from the **Bolts** drop-down in the **Fabrication Elements** panel of the **Steel** tab in **Ribbon**. You will be asked to select the planar face of plate/beam/column.
- Select the face of desired plate. The sketching options will be displayed for creating pattern sketch for holes.
- Create the circle or rectangle to define pattern and click on the **OK** button from the **Modify|Create Hole Pattern** contextual tab in the **Ribbon**. Preview of holes will be displayed.
- Set desired parameters in the **Properties Palette** to modify holes and click on the **Apply** button.

CREATING SHEAR STUDS

The shear studs are used to fasten sheet metal plates with concrete blocks. The procedure to create shear stud is given next.

- Click on the **Shear Studs** tool from the **Bolts** drop-down in the **Fabrication Elements** panel of the **Steel** tab in the **Ribbon**. You will be asked to select plate, beam, or column.
- Select desired steel plate. The tools to create pattern of shear stud will be displayed.
- Create the sketch for studs on the plate and click on the **OK** button from the contextual tab. The studs will be created; refer to Figure-12.

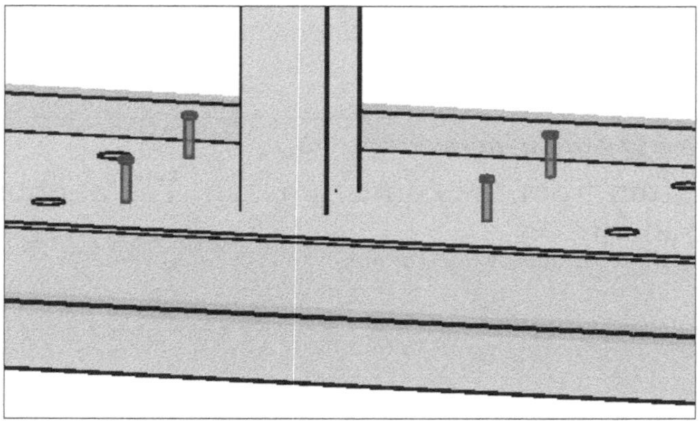

Figure-12. Studs created

CREATING WELD JOINTS

The **Welds** tool is used to create welding joints on selected plates. The procedure to create weld joints is given next.

- Click on the **Welds** tool from the **Fabrication Elements** panel in the **Steel** tab of **Ribbon**. You will be asked to select elements for welding.
- Select desired steel frame members and press **ENTER**. You will be asked to an edge for weldment.
- Select desired edge. The weldment will be created; refer to Figure-13.

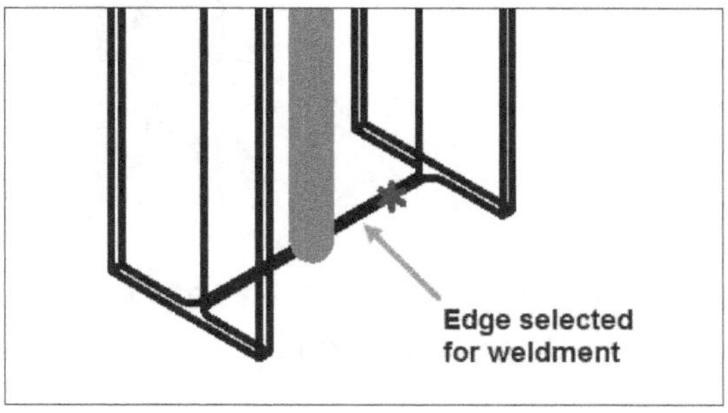

Figure-13. Weldment created

CREATING CORNER CUTS

The **Corner Cut** tool is used to create cut at the corner of a steel plate. The procedure to create corner cut is given next.

- Click on the **Corner Cut** tool from the **Modifiers** panel in the **Steel** tab of **Ribbon**. You will be asked to select the steel plate near the location where you want to create cut.
- Click at desired location. The cut will be created; refer to Figure-14.
- Set desired parameters in the **Properties Palette** to modify corner cut and click on the **Apply** button.

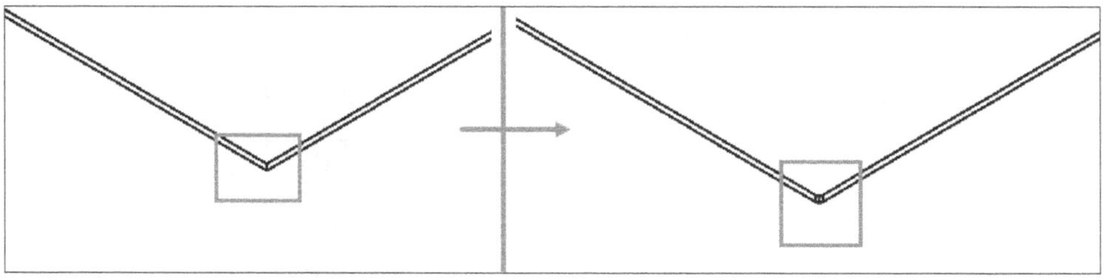

Figure-14. Corner cut created

CREATING COPE SKEWED

The **Cope Skewed** tool is used to create skewed cut on the beam or column for their inter-connections. The procedure to create skewed cut is given next.

- Click on the **Cope Skewed** tool from the **Modifiers** panel in the **Steel** tab of the **Ribbon**. You will be asked to select a beam or column.
- Select desired beam/column. The skewed cut will be displayed; refer to Figure-15.

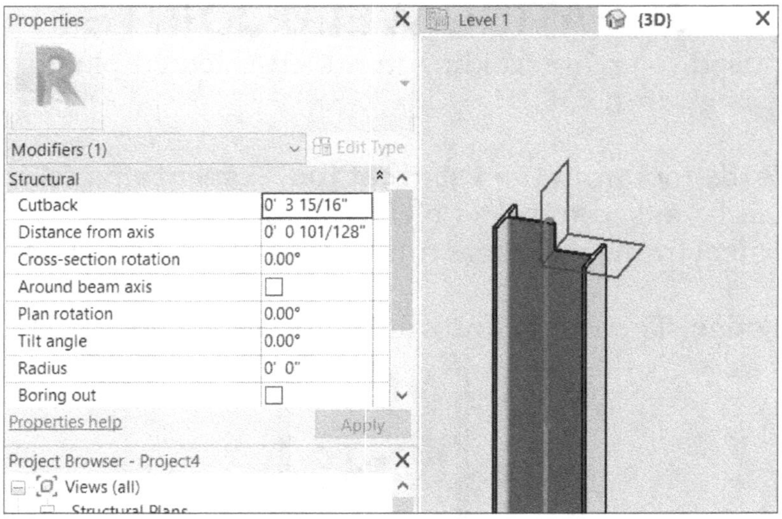

Figure-15. Notch skew cut created

- Set desired parameters in the **Properties Palette** like cutback depth, tilt angle, plan rotation, and so on. Click on the **Apply** button to set parameters.

SHORTENING BEAMS/COLUMNS

The **Shorten** tool is used to reduce the size of selected steel beam or column. The procedure to use this tool is given next.

- Click on the **Shorten** tool from the **Modifiers** panel in the **Steel** tab of **Ribbon**. You will be asked to select the beam/column to be shortened.
- Select desired beam/column. The shortened beam/column will be created; refer to Figure-16.

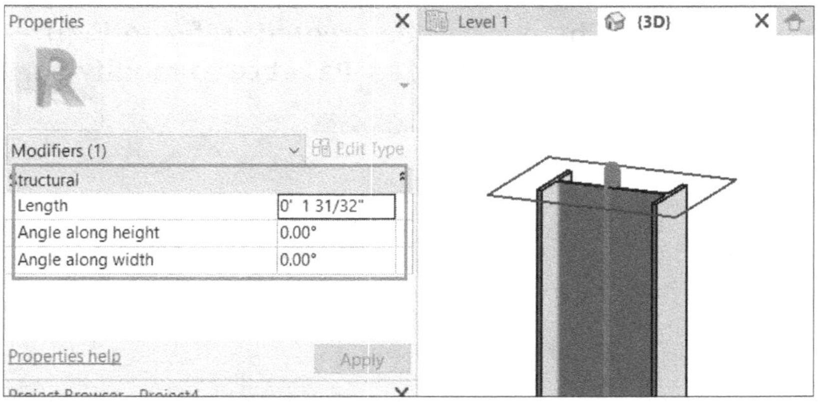

Figure-16. Shortened column

- Set desired depth value in the **Length** edit box of **Properties Palette**. Similarly, set the other parameters and click on the **Apply** button from the **Properties Palette**.

CREATING CONTOUR CUT

The **Contour Cut** tool is used to create cut based on the sketch. The procedure to create contour cut is given next.

- Click on the **Contour Cut** tool from the **Modifiers** panel in the **Steel** tab of **Ribbon**. You will be asked to select a plate, beam, or column.
- Select the planar face of desired plate, beam, or column. The tools to create contour cut sketch will be displayed.

- Create desired sketch for cut; refer to Figure-17.

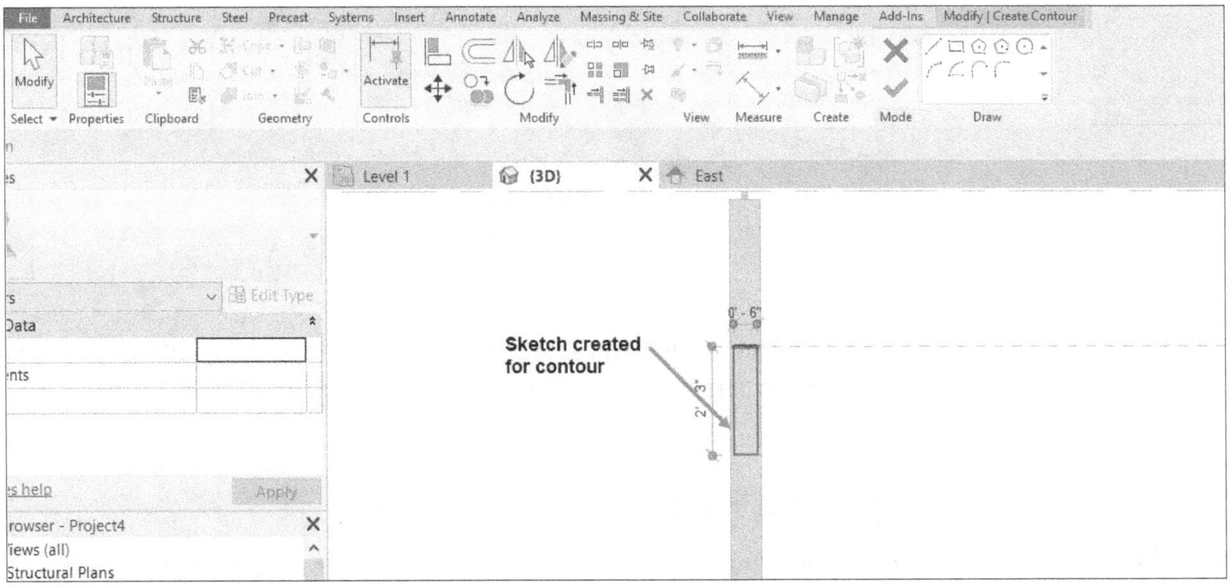

Figure-17. Sketch for contour cut

- Click on the **OK** button from the **Modify|Create Contour** contextual tab in the **Ribbon**. The cut will be created; refer to Figure-18.

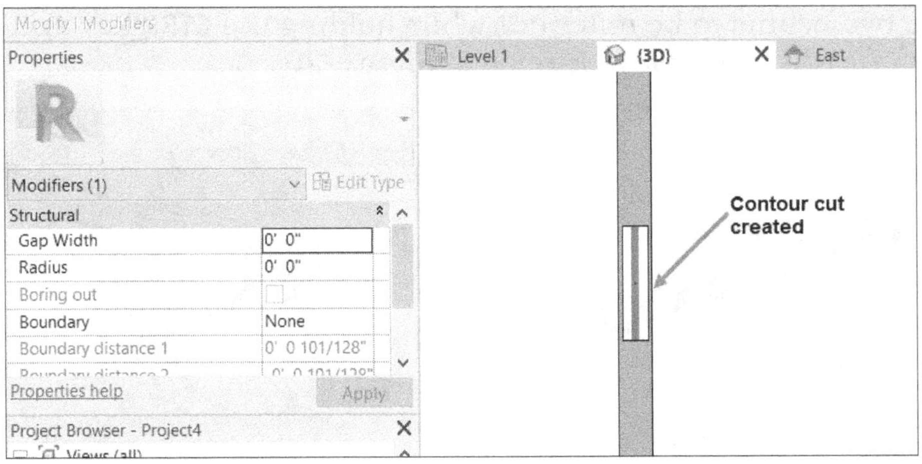

Figure-18. Contour cut created

- Set desired value of offset gap in the **Gap Width** edit box. The cut will expand by specified offset value.
- Set desired value of radius in the **Radius** edit box. Fillets will be created around the corners of cut.
- Set the other parameters as desired in the **Properties Palette** and click on the **Apply** button.

CREATING COPE

The **Cope** tool is used to create fitting cuts in the intersecting beams. The procedure to create notch cut is given next.

- Click on the **Cope** tool from the **Parametric Cuts** panel in the **Steel** tab of **Ribbon**. You will be asked to select intersecting beams.
- Select the two intersecting beams and press **ENTER**. The notch cut will be created on beams; refer to Figure-19.

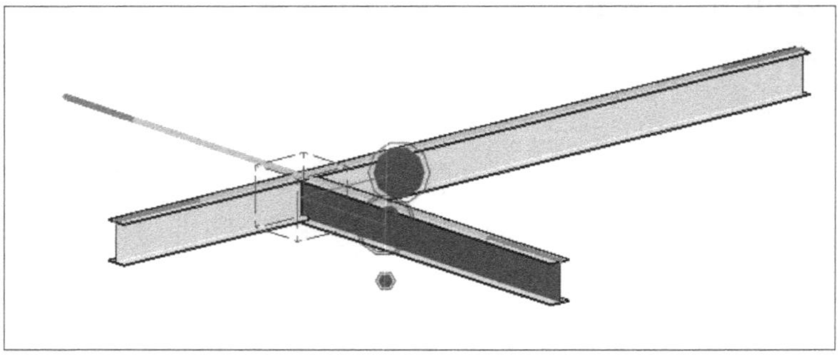

Figure-19. Notch cut

- Note that the beam with bigger blue dot is cutting tool and other beam is cut by it. Click on the smaller dot to make it cutting tool.
- Press **ESC** to exit the tool.

CREATING MITER CUT

The **Miter** tool is used to cut beams vertically at bisector line. The procedure to create miter cut is given next.

- Click on the **Miter** tool from the **Miter** drop-down in the **Parametric Cuts** panel of **Steel** tab in the **Ribbon**. You will be asked to select beams for miter cut.
- Select the two beams to be miter cut while holding the **CTRL** key and press **ENTER**. The miter cut will be displayed; refer to Figure-20.

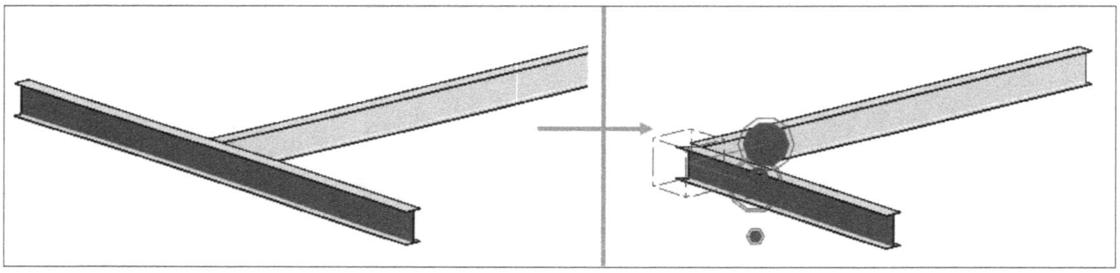

Figure-20. Miter cut created

- Press **ESC** to exit the tool.

CREATING SAW CUT-FLANGE

The **Saw cut - Flange** tool is used to cut beams to form flange cut. The procedure to perform saw cut is given next.

- Click on the **Saw cut - Flange** tool from the **Miter** drop-down in the **Parametric Cuts** panel in the **Steel** tab of **Ribbon**. You will be asked to select beams to cut in flange.
- Select the beams while holding the **CTRL** key and press **ENTER**. The saw cut will be created; refer to Figure-21.

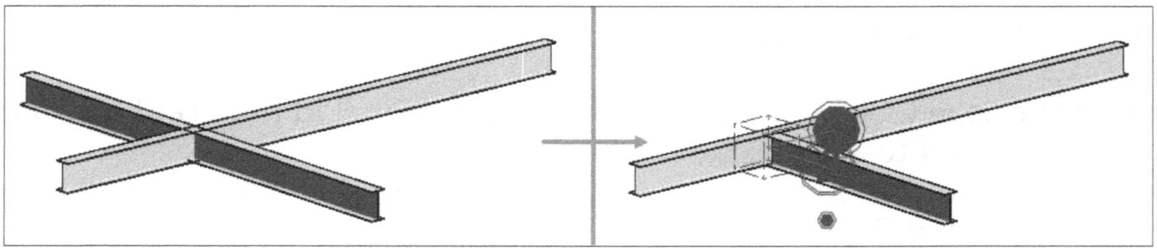

Figure-21. Saw cut created

- You can use the smaller dot to change side of cut.
- Set the other parameters as desired in the **Properties Palette** and click on the **Apply** button.

CREATING SAW CUT - WEB

The **Saw cut - Web** tool is used to cut the beam as per the intersecting web of beam. The procedure to use this tool is given next.

- Click on the **Saw cut - Web** tool from the **Miter** drop-down in the **Parametric Cuts** panel of **Steel** tab in the **Ribbon**. You will be asked to select the intersecting beams.
- Select the two intersecting beams and press **ENTER**. The saw cut will be created; refer to Figure-22.

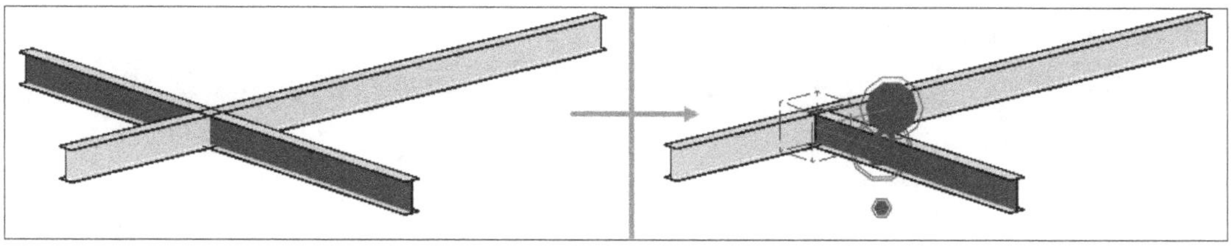

Figure-22. Web saw cut created on beams

- Click on the **Edit** button in **Modify Parameters/Detailed Parameters** field of **Properties Palette** or **Modify Parameters** tool from the **Connection** panel in **Modify|Sub-Connections** contextual tab to change properties of connection. The **Saw cut - Web** dialog box will be displayed; refer to Figure-23.

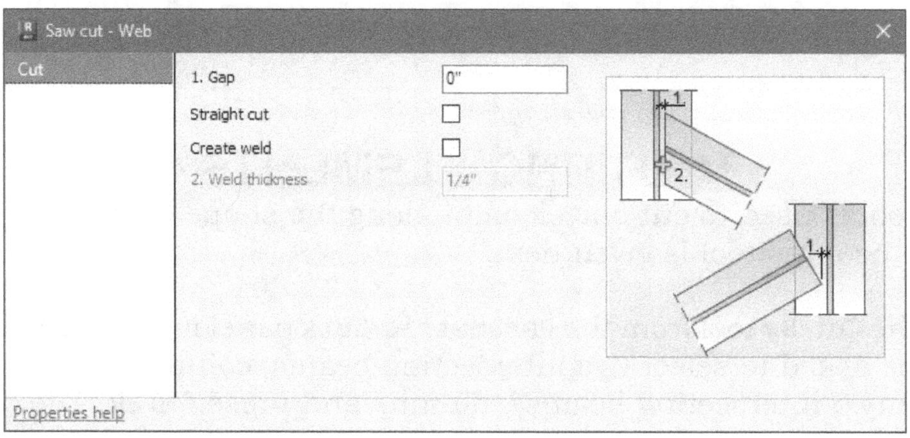

Figure-23. Saw cut-Web dialog box

- Set desired parameters in the dialog box. Specify desired value of gap at connection in the **Gap** edit box. Select the **Straight cut** check box if you want to make straight cut at the connection even if two beams are inclined. Select the **Create weld** check box if you want to make welding at the connection. On selecting the **Create weld** check box, the **Weld thickness** edit box will be active. Set desired value of thickness in the edit box. After setting desired parameters, close the dialog box.

CREATING CUT THROUGH

As the name suggests, the **Cut Through** tool is used to cut one element allowing other intersecting element passing through it. The procedure to use this tool is given next.

- Click on the **Cut Through** tool from the **Parametric Cuts** panel in the **Steel** tab of **Ribbon**. You will be asked to select the two elements for intersection cut.

- Select the two intersecting beams or columns while holding the **CTRL** key and press **ENTER**. The cut through will be created; refer to Figure-24.

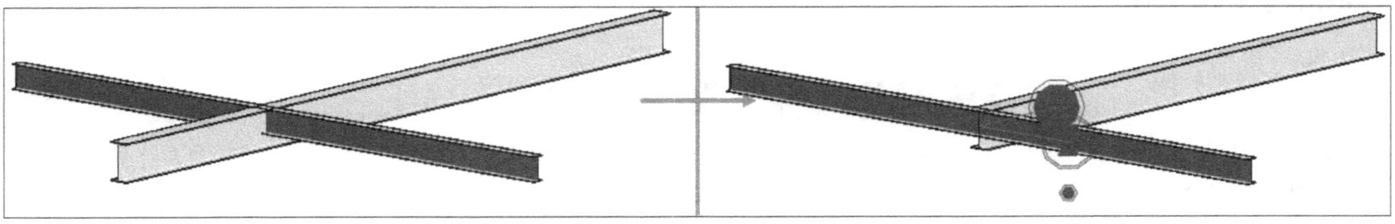

Figure-24. Cut through created

- Click on the **Edit** button from the **Modify Parameters / Detailed Parameters** field in the **Properties Palette**. The **Element contour, rule** dialog box will be displayed; refer to Figure-25.
- Set desired parameters in the dialog box and close it.
- Press **ESC** to exit the tool.

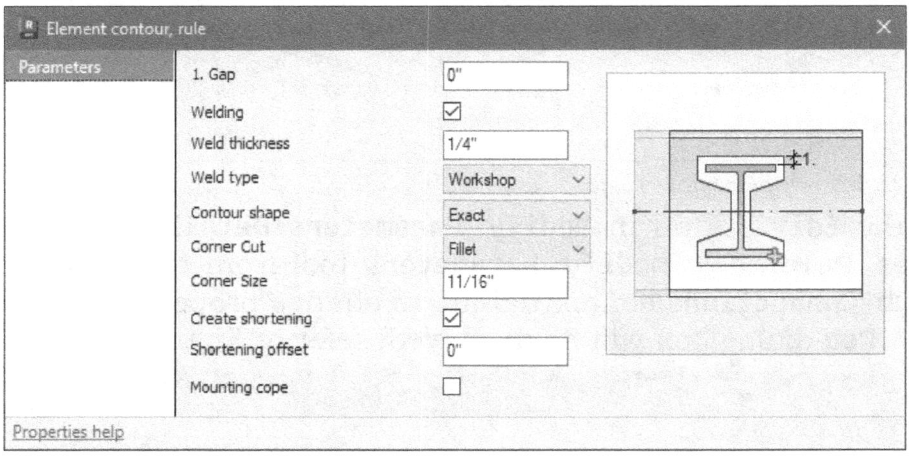

Figure-25. Element contour rule dialog box

CUTTING ELEMENTS

The **Cut By** tool is used to cut one element along the shape of another element. The procedure to use this tool is given next.

- Click on the **Cut By** tool from the **Parametric Cuts** panel in the **Steel** tab of **Ribbon**. You will be asked to select two intersecting beams/columns.
- Select the two intersecting beams/columns and press **ENTER**. The cut by will be created; refer to Figure-26.

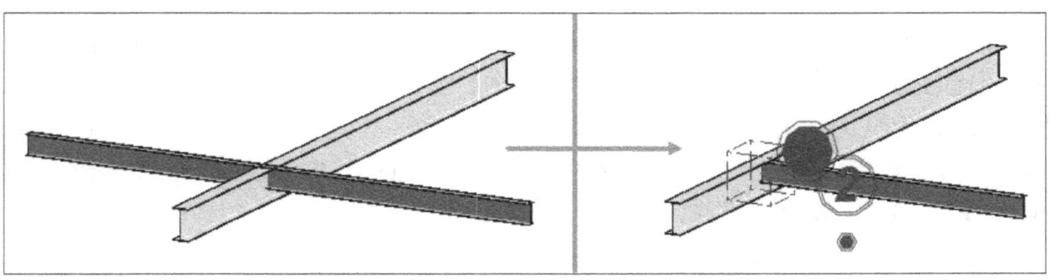

Figure-26. Cut by created

- Click on the **Edit** button from the **Modify Parameters / Detailed Parameters** field in the **Properties Palette**. The **Fitting at floor beam, free parameter** dialog box will be displayed; refer to Figure-27.

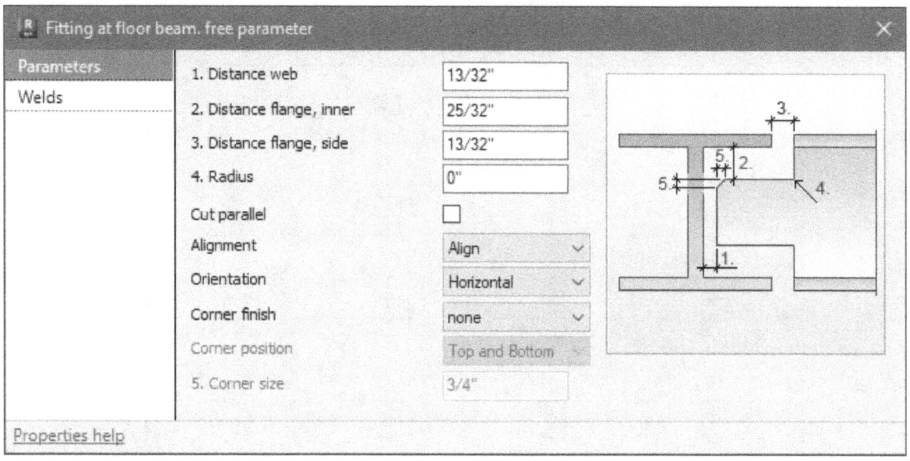

Figure-27. Fitting at floor beam free parameter dialog box

- Set desired parameters in the dialog box to modify cut and then close the dialog box.

PRACTICAL 1

Create the steel structure for an open warehouse as shown in Figure-28, Figure-29, and Figure-30 and perform various steel connections as required.

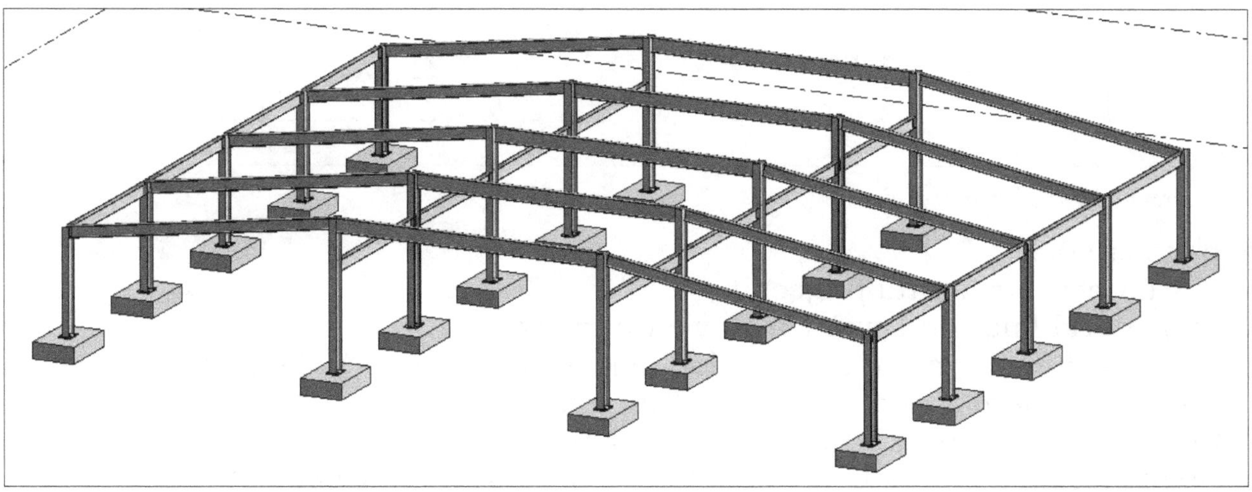

Figure-28. 3D view of steel structure

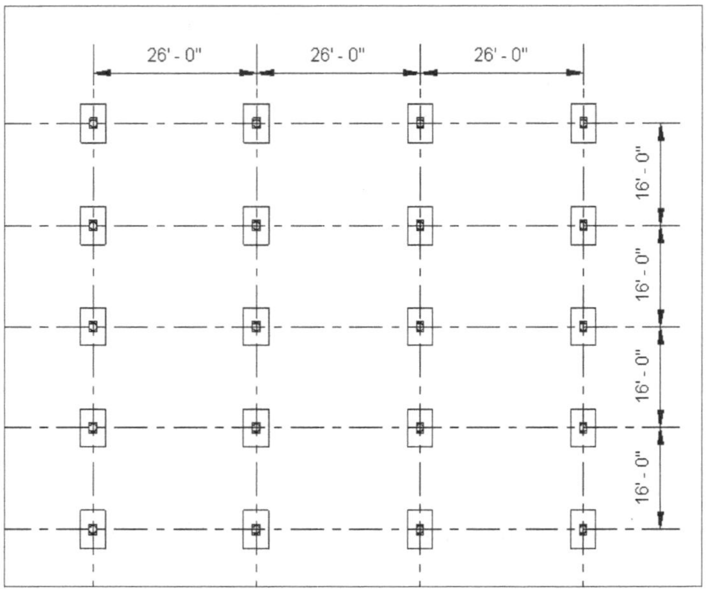

Figure-29. Plan View for Level 1

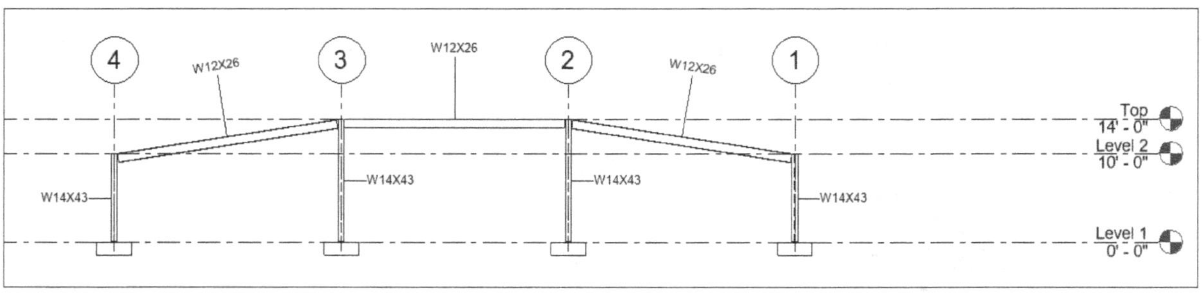

Figure-30. North plan view of model

Steps to create:

1. Start a new structural project.
2. Create grid lines on Level 1 plan view and levels.
3. Create columns on the intersection points of columns. Make sure the height of columns on grid 2 and 3 are up to Top level.
4. Create the structural beams connecting the columns.
5. Create isolated foundations for columns as shown in model.
6. Create the connection as required between various beams and columns.

Procedure:

Starting A New Structural Project

- Click on the **Project** tool from the **New** cascading menu of the **File** menu. The **New Project** dialog box will be displayed.
- Select the **Structural Template** option from the **Template file** drop-down, select the **Project** radio button from the **Create new** area of the dialog box, and click on the **OK** button. The new project will be created.

Creating Grid Lines and Levels

- Click on the **Grid** tool from the **Datum** panel in the **Structure** tab of **Ribbon**. You will be asked to specify start point of grid line.
- Create the vertical and horizontal grid lines; refer to Figure-31.

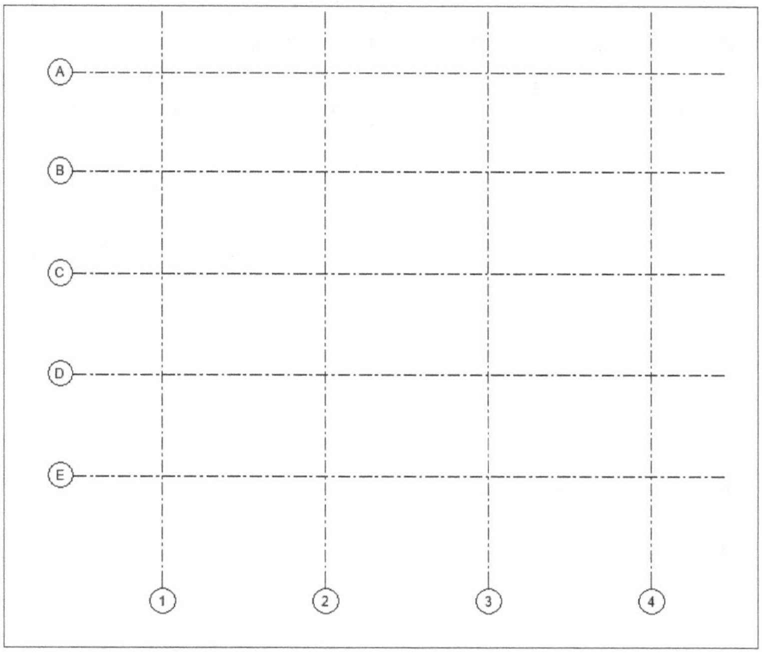

Figure-31. Grid lines for warehouse

- Open the **East** elevation view from the **Elevations** category in **Project Browser**. The view will open.
- Click on the **Level** tool from the **Datum** panel in the **Structure** tab of **Ribbon**. The options to create level will be displayed.
- Create a new level at 4 feet from the **Level 2** grid line; refer to Figure-32.

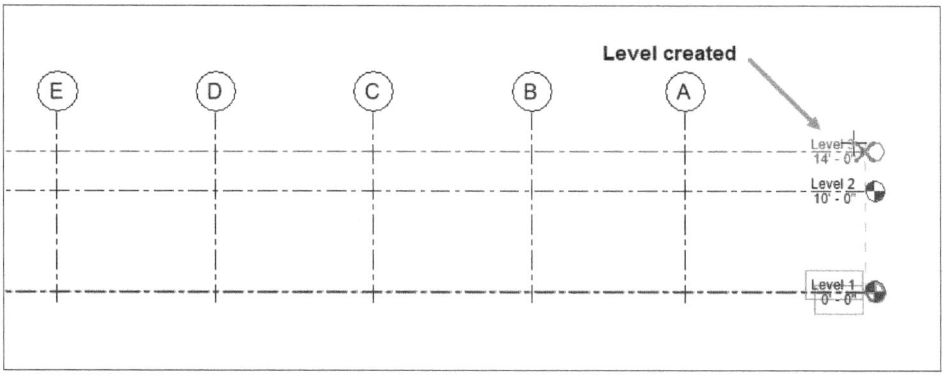

Figure-32. Level created

- Click on the **Level 3** name tag, change the name to **Top** and press **ENTER**. The **Confirm Level Rename** dialog box will be displayed; refer to Figure-33.

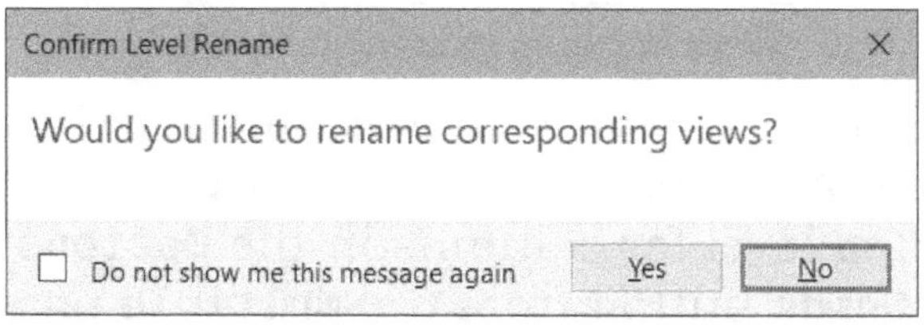

Figure-33. Confirm Level Rename dialog box

- Click on the **Yes** button from the dialog box. The level will be renamed. Press **ESC** twice to exit the tool.

Creating Columns

- Open the **Level 1** plan view from the **Project Browser**.

- Click on the **Column** tool from the **Structure** panel in the **Structure** tab of **Ribbon**. The options to create columns will be displayed.
- Select the **W14X43** option from the drop-down at the top in the **Properties Palette** and set the height of column upto **Level 2** in the **Options Bar**; refer to Figure-34.

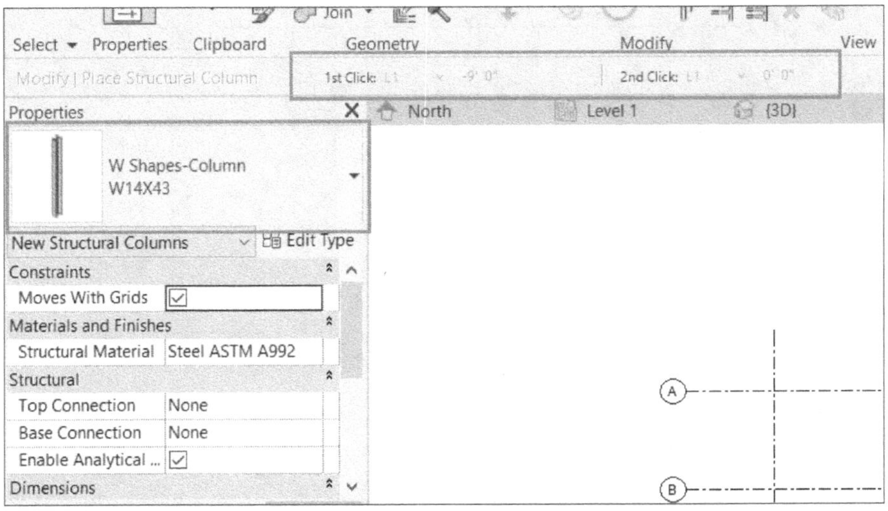

Figure-34. Options set for columns in Properties Palette and Options Bar

- Select the **At Grids** button from the contextual tab in the **Ribbon** and select the **A**, **B**, **C**, **D**, **E**, **1**, and **4** grid lines. The preview of columns will be displayed; refer to Figure-35.

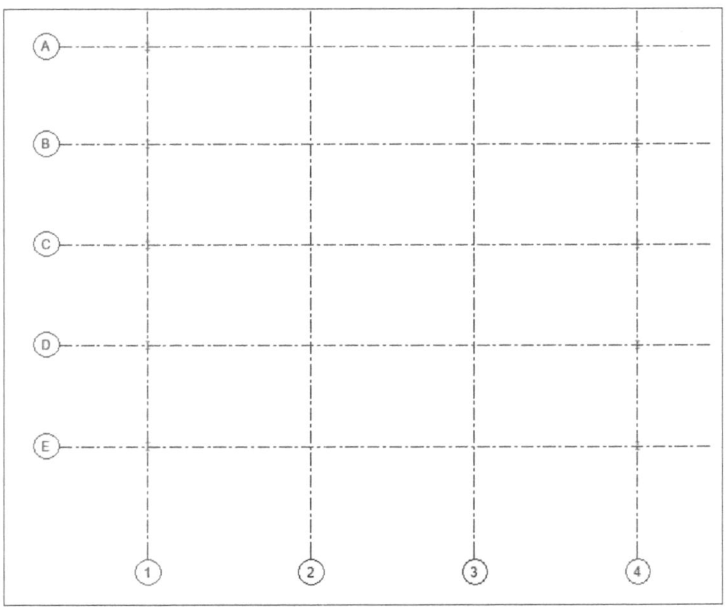

Figure-35. Grid lines selected and preview of columns

- Click on the **Finish** button from the contextual tab. The columns will be created and the **Modify|Place Structural Column** contextual tab will be displayed again.
- Set the height upto **Top** level for columns in the **Options Bar**; refer to Figure-36 and click on the **At Grids** button from the **Multiple** panel in the contextual tab of **Ribbon**. You will be asked to select the grid lines.

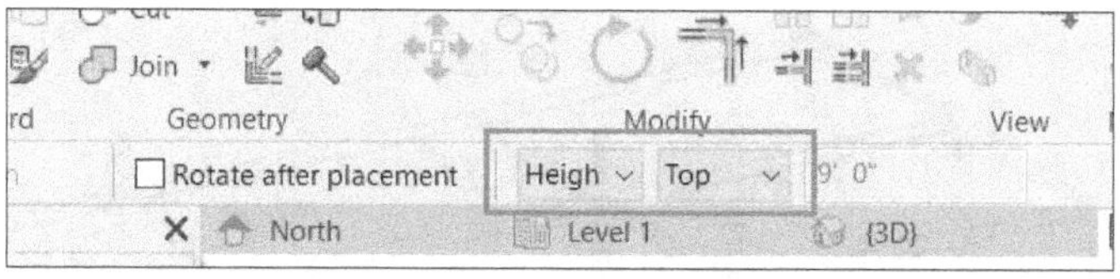

Figure-36. Height set to Top in Options Bar

- Select the **A**, **B**, **C**, **D**, **E**, **2**, and **4** grid lines from the **Level 1** plan view. The new columns will be created.
- Click on the **Finish** button from the contextual tab. The columns will be created. Press **ESC** twice to exit the tool.

Creating Connecting Beams

- Open **Level 2** plan view from the **Project Browser**.
- Click on the **Beam** tool from the **Structure** panel in the **Structure** tab of **Ribbon**. The options to create beams will be displayed.
- Select the **W12X26** option from the drop-down at the top in the **Properties Palette** and create the beams at all grid intersection points; refer to Figure-37.

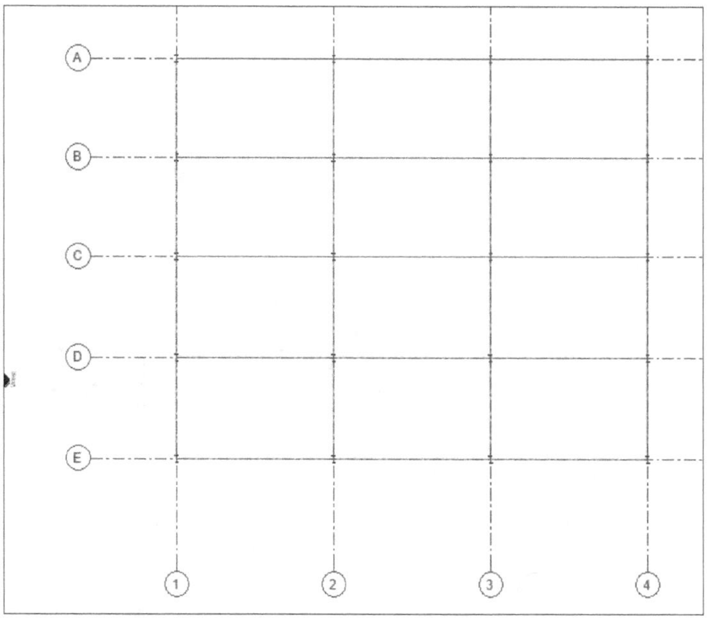

Figure-37. Beams created on grid points

- Click on the **Finish** button from the contextual tab and press **ESC** twice to exit the tool.
- Open the 3D view by clicking on the **Default 3D View** button from the **Quick Access Toolbar**. The 3D view will be displayed and you will notice that all the beams are at same level; refer to Figure-38.

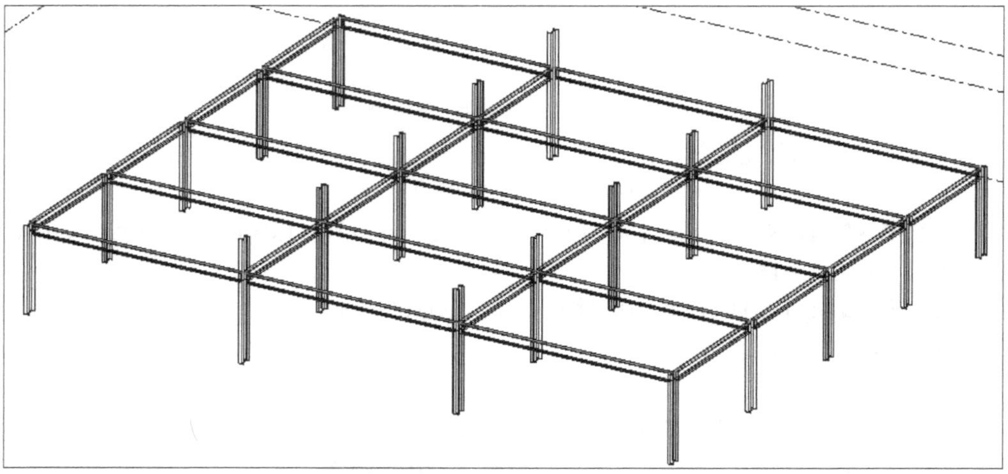

Figure-38. Beams displayed in 3D view

- Select the beams on the left side in model and set the start level offset as **4'** in the **Properties Palette**; refer to Figure-39.

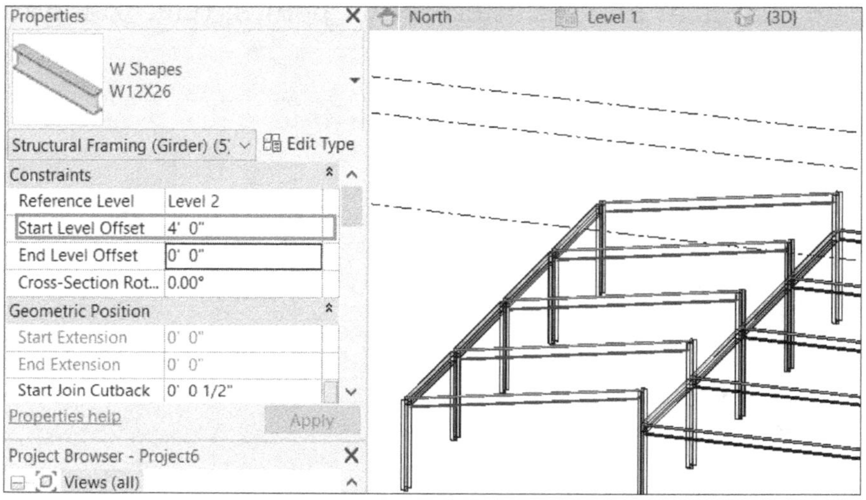

Figure-39. Setting start level offset to 4

- Similarly, set the other beams to connect with end points of columns; refer to Figure-40.

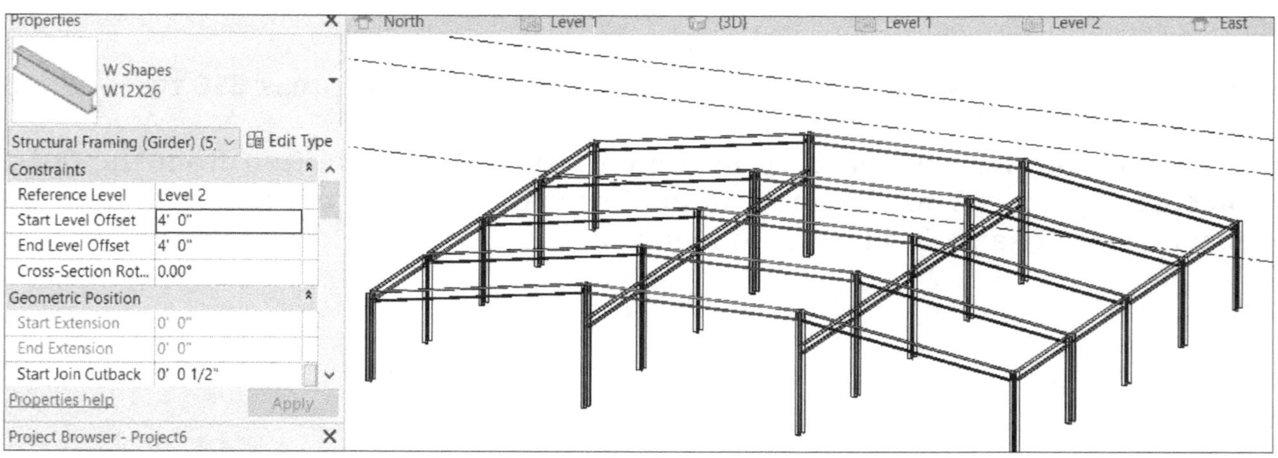

Figure-40. After setting beams

Creating Isolated Foundations

- Open the Level 1 plan view by double-clicking on the **Level 1** option from **Structural Plans** category in **Project Browser**.

- Click on the **Isolated** tool from the **Foundation** panel in the **Structure** tab of **Ribbon**. The options to create isolated foundations will be displayed in the **Ribbon** and **Properties Palette**.
- Click on the **At Grids** button from the **Modify|Place Isolated Foundation** contextual tab in the **Ribbon** and select all the grid lines. The preview of foundations will be displayed at intersection points of grid lines.
- Click on the **Finish** button from the contextual tab in the **Ribbon** and press **ESC** to exit the tool.

Creating Connections

- Open the 3D view by clicking on the **Default 3D View** tool from the **Quick Access Toolbar**.
- Click on the **Connection Settings** button (inclined arrow) from the **Connection** panel in the **Steel** tab of **Ribbon**. The **Structural Connection Settings** dialog box will be displayed.
- Select the **Base plate**, **Clip angle**, and **Seated beam connection** options from the **Available Connections** list box and click on the **Add-->** button from the dialog box. The connections will be added in the **Loaded Connections** list box; refer to Figure-41.

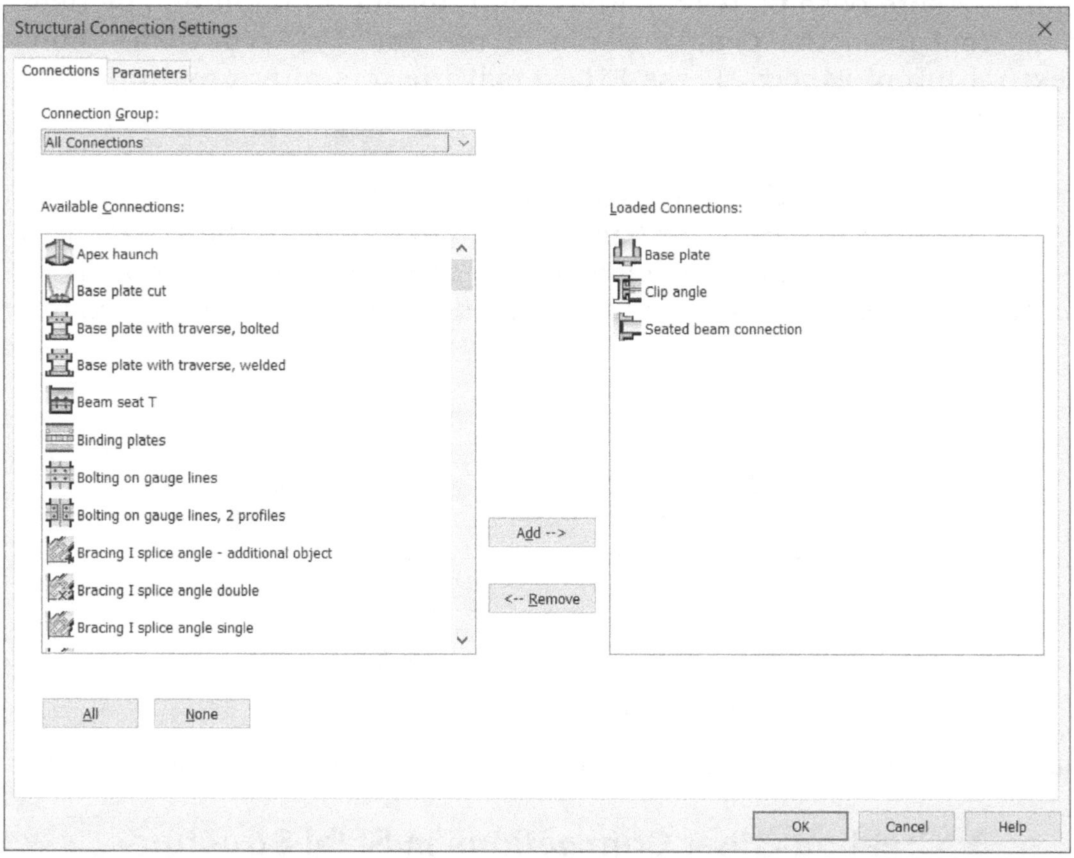

Figure-41. Structural Connection Settings dialog box with connections loaded

- Click on the **OK** button from the dialog box.
- Click on the **Connection** tool from the **Connection** panel in the **Steel** tab of **Ribbon**. The options to place connection will be displayed in the **Ribbon** and **Properties Palette**.
- Select the **Base plate** option from the drop-down at the top in the **Properties Palette**.

- Select a vertical column and select respective isolated foundation while holding the **CTRL** key. Press **ENTER** to create connection; refer to Figure-42.

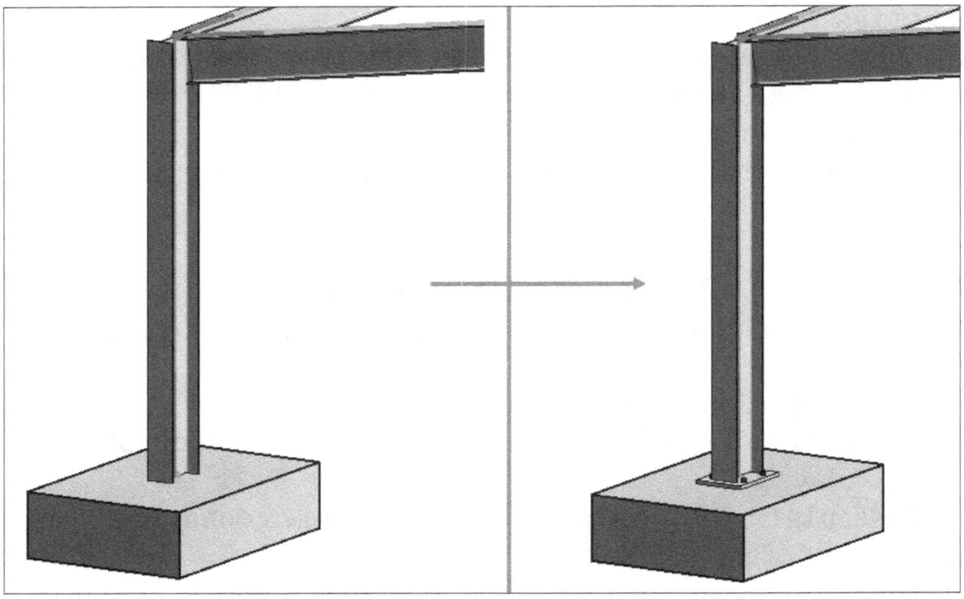

Figure-42. Base plate connection created

- Similarly, create base plates on other columns and foundations by using **Create Similar** tool from the **Create** panel in the **Modify|Structural Connections** contextual tab of **Ribbon**. Press **ESC** to exit the tool after creating all base plate connections.

Creating Notch Intersections

- Click on the **Notch** tool from the **Parametric Cuts** panel in the **Steel** tab of **Ribbon**. You will be asked to select the elements to create intersecting notch.
- Select two intersecting column and beam; and press **ENTER**. The notch intersection will be created; refer to Figure-43.

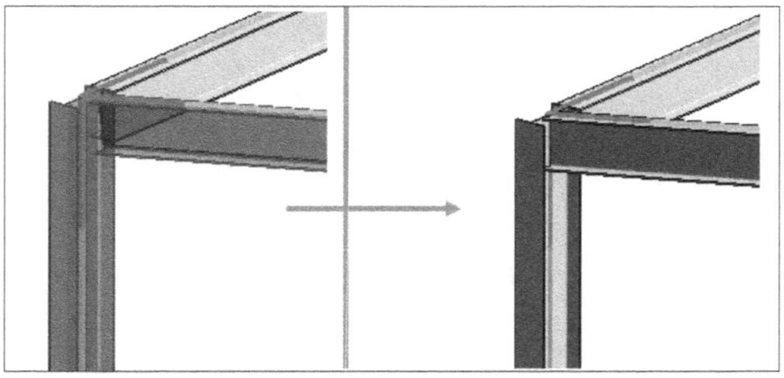

Figure-43. Creating notch intersections

- Similarly, create the notch intersections at other connection locations.

Creating Other Connections in Steel Structure

- Click on the **Connection** tool from the **Connection** panel in the **Steel** tab of **Ribbon**. The options to create connections will be displayed as discussed earlier.
- Select the **Clip angle** option from the drop-down at the top in the **Properties Palette**.
- Select an inclined beam and select the connecting column. Press **ENTER** to create the connection; refer to Figure-44.

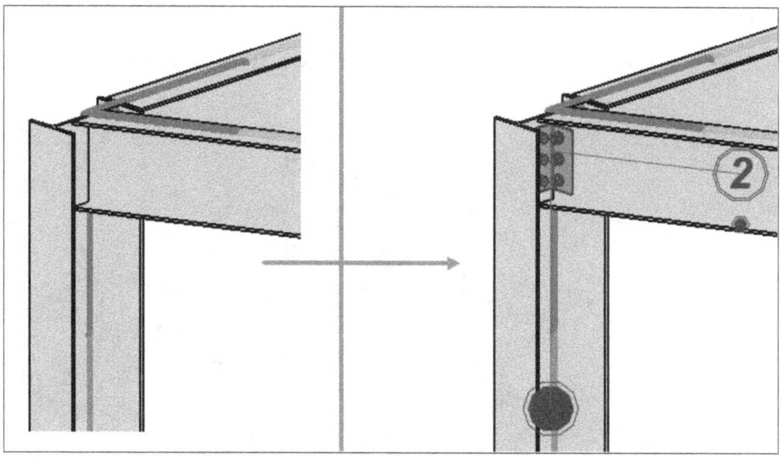

Figure-44. Clip angle connection created

- Similarly, create the clip angle connections at other inclined beam connections.
- Now, select the **Seated beam connection** option from the top drop-down in the **Properties Palette** while the **Connection** tool is active.
- Now, select the column of height upto top level and connecting beam; and press **ENTER**. The seated beam connections will be created; refer to Figure-45.

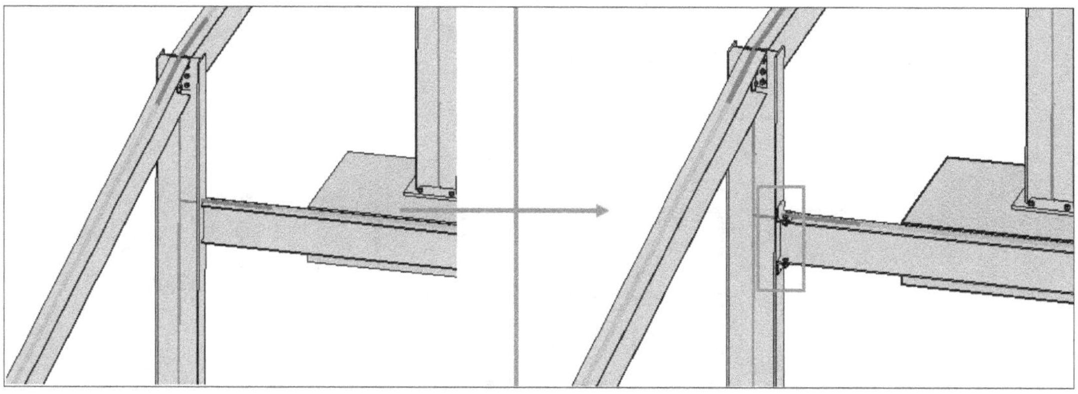

Figure-45. Creating seated beam connection

- Similarly, create the other seated beam connections. The model will be displayed as shown in Figure-46.

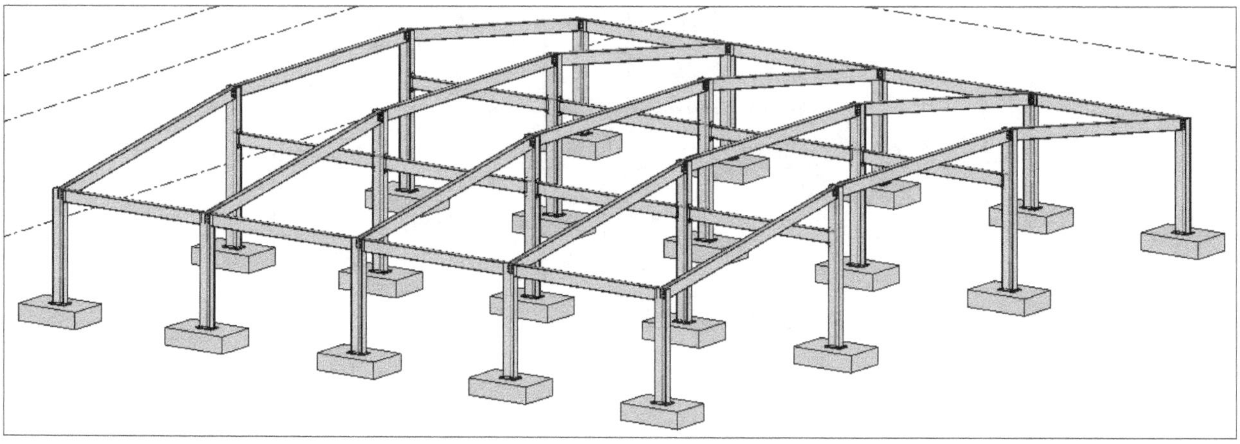

Figure-46. Model created

PRACTICE 1

Create steel structure of a hotel building as shown in Figure-47, Figure-48, and Figure-49.

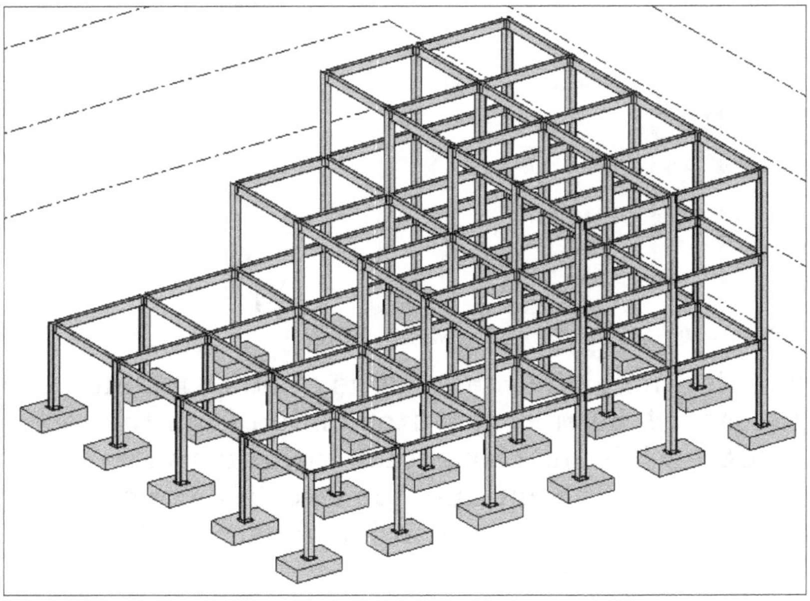

Figure-47. 3D view of Practice 1 model

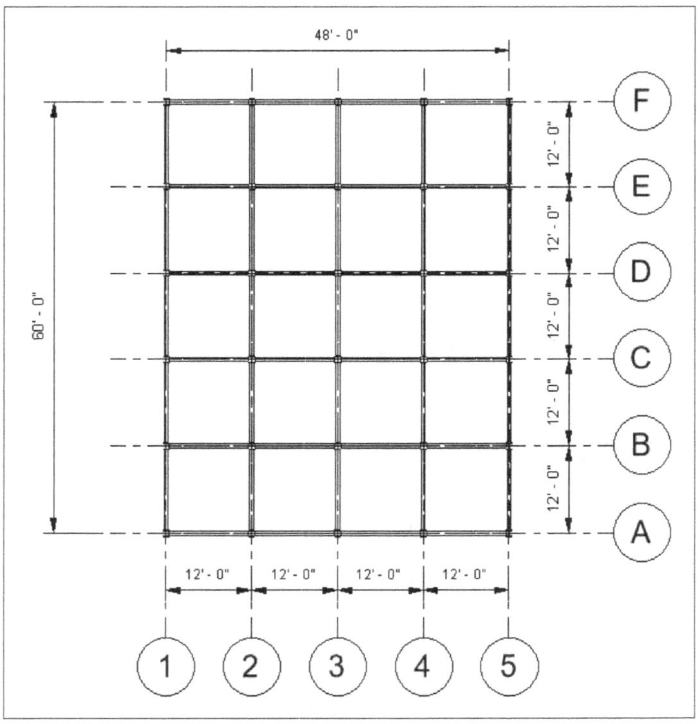

Figure-48. Practice 1 Plan View

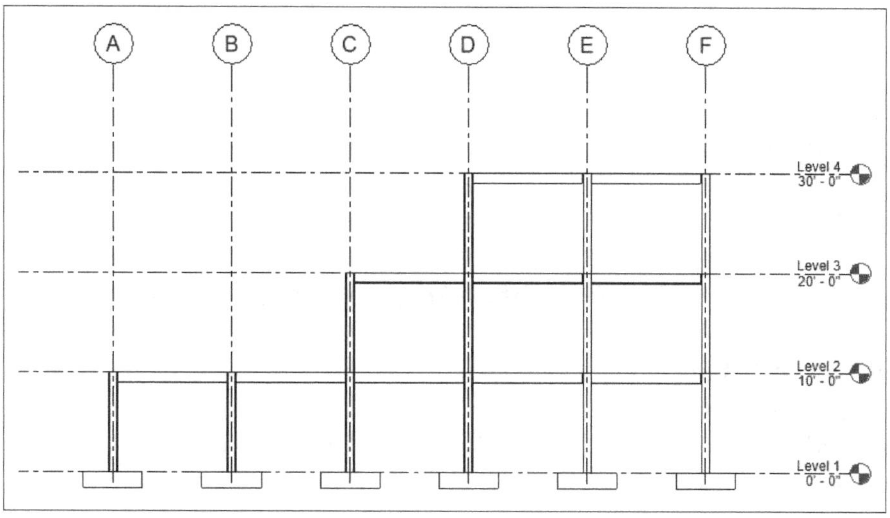

Figure-49. Practice 1 Elevation View

SELF ASSESSMENT

Q1. Discuss the importance of fabrication plate in structural design of building.

Q2. Bolt connections can be applied to two steel plates only. (T/F)

Q3. Discuss the difference between bolts and anchor bolts.

Q4. The **Holes** tool in **Steel** tab can not be used to create hole in beams and columns. (T/F)

Q5. Which of the following fasteners/fastening method is used to fasten steel plates to concrete blocks?

a. Shear Studs
b. Anchor Bolt
c. Bolt
d. Weld

Q6. Discuss the difference between Notch and Notch skewed cuts.

Q7. Discuss the use of Miter cut.

Q8. What is the purpose of the Connection tool in steel design?

A. To create shear studs between steel and concrete
B. To define connection types at intersection points of frame members
C. To generate holes in plates
D. To weld steel beams together

Q9. Which tool automatically applies structural connections based on a predefined set?

A. Connection
B. Connection Automation
C. Modifiers
D. Fabrication Plate

Q10. What must be set in the Visibility/Graphic Overrides to view steel plates?

A. Detail Level to Medium
B. Show Hidden Elements
C. Steel plates visibility ON and Detail Level to Fine
D. Wireframe display mode

Q11. What is the first step when creating a fabrication plate?

A. Select the steel plate
B. Choose the anchor bolts
C. Click the Plate tool from the Fabrication Elements panel
D. Activate the Detail Level

Q12. The Bolts tool requires selection of how many frame members?

A. One
B. Two
C. Three
D. Four

Q13. Which tool is accessed via the Bolts drop-down to create anchor bolts?

A. Holes
B. Shear Studs
C. Anchors
D. Notch Cope

Q14. What type of pattern can be used to sketch holes?

A. Ellipse
B. Rectangle or circle
C. Polygon
D. Line

Q15. What element are shear studs typically fastened to?

A. Concrete blocks
B. Wood planks
C. Beams
D. Columns

Q16. Which parameter can be set when creating a Contour Cut?

A. Welding direction
B. Radius and offset gap
C. Sketch type only
D. Detail Level

Q17. In the Notch Cope tool, what indicates which beam is used as the cutting tool?

A. Highlighted beam name
B. Red outline
C. Larger blue dot
D. Arrow icon

Q18. The Miter tool cuts beams along what?

A. Corner edge
B. Random line
C. Bisector line
D. Center axis

Q19. What tool is used to make flange cuts on beams?

A. Notch Cope
B. Contour Cut
C. Saw cut – Flange
D. Shear Studs

Q20. What setting allows a straight cut in Saw Cut - Web tool?

A. Create fillet
B. Apply angle
C. Select Straight cut checkbox
D. Use circular sketch

Q21. What is the function of the Cut Through tool?

A. Remove a beam
B. Create a fillet
C. Allow one element to pass through another
D. Extend a column

Q22. What does the Cut By tool do?

A. Weld two plates together
B. Create bolt patterns
C. Cut one element using the shape of another
D. Sketch notch pattern

Q23. What is the purpose of the Anchors tool?

A. To weld steel beams
B. To connect concrete and steel with shear studs
C. To fasten elements to steel plates using anchor bolts
D. To sketch holes in columns

Q24. After selecting a steel plate for anchors, what must be selected next?

A. The edge to cut
B. The bolt type
C. The face of plate/beam/column
D. The color of the plate

Q25. Which tool is specifically used to create welding joints?

A. Notch Cope
B. Holes
C. Welds
D. Cut Through

Q26. When using the Corner Cut tool, what must you do after selecting the plate?

A. Click on Show button
B. Sketch a bolt pattern
C. Click at the desired location to create cut
D. Select a weld edge

Q27. What does the Notch Cope Skewed tool create?

A. Hole pattern
B. Skewed cut for inter-connections
C. Contour shape
D. Anchor weld

Q28. What kind of adjustments can be made in Notch Cope Skewed tool?

A. Visibility override
B. Work plane selection
C. Cutback depth and tilt angle
D. Thread type of bolts

Q29. What action follows selecting a beam/column using the Shorten tool?

A. Create miter cut
B. Draw a rectangle
C. Enter depth value in Properties Palette
D. Activate anchor pattern

Q30. What must be created before applying a Contour Cut?

A. A bolt group
B. A connection rule
C. A contour sketch
D. A weld joint

Q31. In the Contour Cut tool, what does setting the Gap Width do?

A. Reduces the radius
B. Sets spacing between holes
C. Expands cut by specified value
D. Connects beams with anchor bolts

Q32. The Notch Cope tool is primarily used for which purpose?

A. To make vertical cuts at bisectors
B. To create fitting cuts at beam intersections
C. To create flange grooves
D. To place anchor bolts

Q33. What does the user need to press after selecting intersecting beams in Notch Cope tool?

A. ESC
B. TAB
C. ENTER
D. ALT

Q34. What does the smaller blue dot in Notch Cope indicate?

A. Hidden cut location
B. Selection for steel type
C. Tool to reverse cut
D. The current cutting tool

Q35. Which panel contains the Saw Cut – Flange tool?

A. Fabrication Elements
B. Parametric Cuts
C. Miter drop-down
D. Welds Panel

Q36. What additional feature can be activated in Saw Cut – Web?

A. Create weld with specified thickness
B. Automatic anchor bolt placement
C. Template-based plate design
D. Radius smoothening

Q37. What is the key difference between Cut Through and Cut By?

A. Cut Through uses sketch, Cut By uses edge
B. Cut Through cuts one element to allow another through, Cut By uses shape of second element
C. Cut Through is for bolts, Cut By for plates
D. Cut Through applies only to columns

Q38. Which dialog box is associated with Cut By tool?

A. Work Plane
B. Hole Parameters
C. Fitting at floor beam, free parameter
D. Notch Cut Pattern

FOR STUDENT NOTES

Chapter 8

System Design

Topics Covered

The major topics covered in this chapter are:

- ***Introduction***
- ***Creating HVAC System***
- ***Defining HVAC Settings***
- ***Creating and Modifying HVAC Ducts***
- ***Placing Duct Placeholders, Duct Fittings, Duct Accessories, and Mechanical Equipment***
- ***Converting and Creating Flexible Ducts***
- ***Creating Air Terminal, Fabrication Parts, and Multi-Point Routing***
- ***Creating Piping and Plumbing System***
- ***Creating Electrical Layout***

INTRODUCTION

In previous chapter, you have learned about architectural and structural designing. In this chapter, you will learn about creating various building systems like HVAC, Mechanical, Electrical, Plumbing, and Piping. These tools are available in the **Systems** panel of the **Ribbon**; refer to Figure-1.

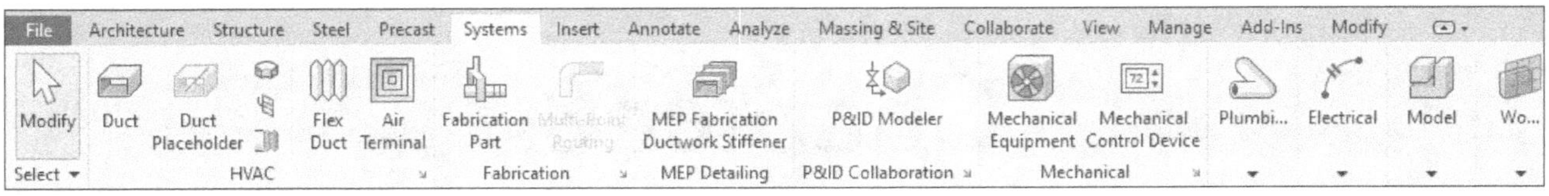

Figure-1. Systems contextual tab

HVAC SYSTEM

The tools in the **HVAC** panel of **Systems** tab are used to create Heating, Ventilation, and Air Conditioning (HVAC) systems. The HVAC system is used to thermally control a confined region and create comfort level. Various tools used to create HVAC system are given next.

Defining HVAC Settings

The **Mechanical Settings** tool is used to set parameters for HVAC. The procedure is given next.

- Click on the inclined arrow of **HVAC** panel in the **Systems** tab of **Ribbon**. The **Mechanical Settings** dialog box will be displayed; refer to Figure-2.

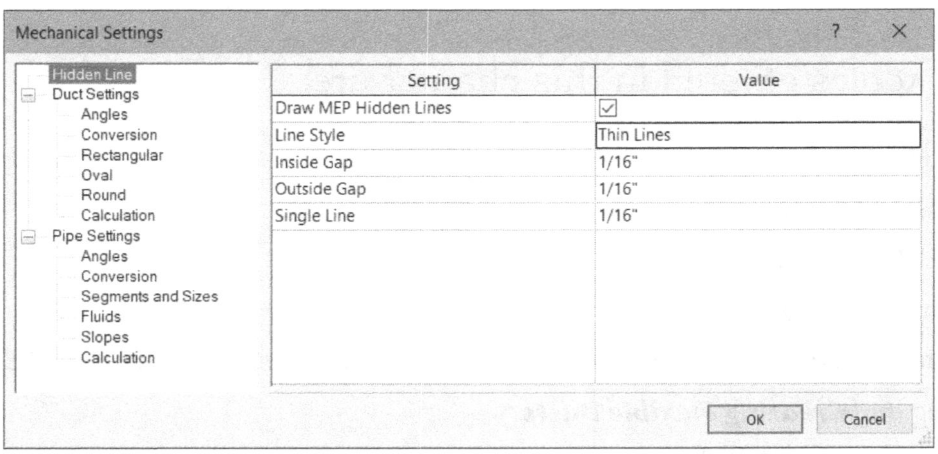

Figure-2. Mechanical Settings dialog box

- By default, the **Hidden Line** option is selected in the left area of the dialog box. Select the **Draw MEP Hidden Lines** check box to display hidden MEP lines. Select desired option from the **Line Style** field for hidden MEP lines. Select the thickness of different lines in respective fields of the dialog box.

Duct Settings

- Select the **Duct Settings** option from the left area of the dialog box. The related options will be displayed; refer to Figure-3.
- Select the **Use Annot. Scale for Single Line Fittings** check box to use size specified in the **Duct Fitting Annotation Size** edit box of the dialog box.
- Specify desired density and viscosity of air in the **Air Density** and **Air Dynamic Viscosity** fields of the dialog box.

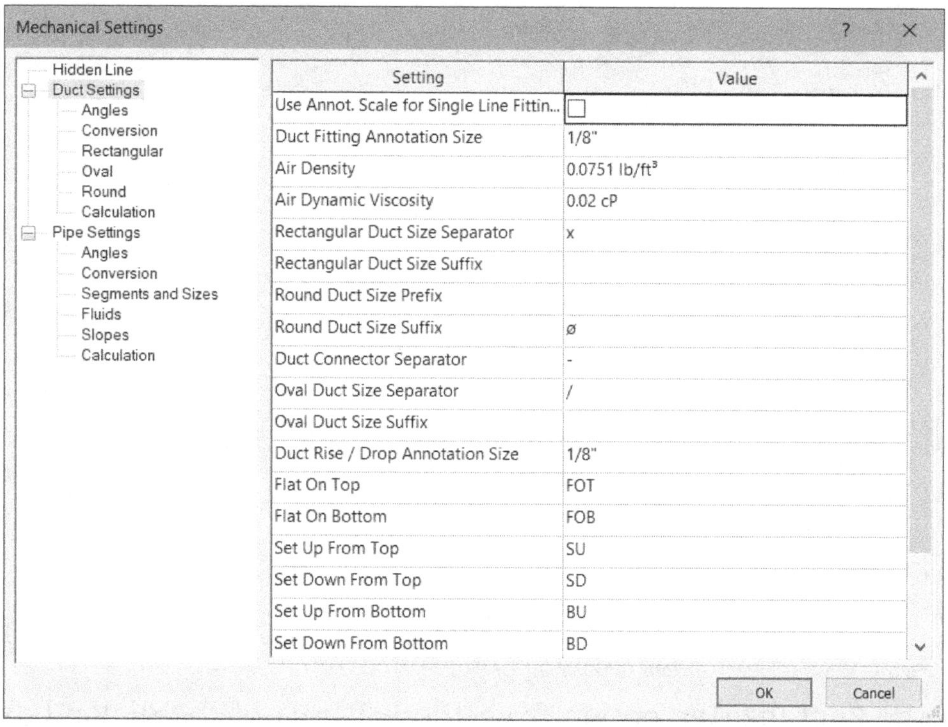

Figure-3. Duct Setting options

- Set desired parameter in the **Rectangular Duct Size Separator** field to define symbol to be used as separator in dimension of rectangular duct. For example, 'x' in 12" x 12" rectangular duct.
- Set desired parameter in the **Rectangular Duct Size Suffix** field to define symbol to be added after size of rectangular duct.
- Similarly, you can set prefix, suffix, separator and other parameters for round and oval ducts.
- Select the **Angles** option from the left area of the dialog box if you want to define how duct components will be aligned for connections. If you select the **Use any angle** radio button then duct fittings will use all the available supported angles for connection. If you select the **Set an angle increment** radio button then duct fittings can rotate by specified angle increment. If you select the **Use specific angles** radio button then the fittings will snap to angle values selected in the table. Generally, the **Use specific angles** radio button is selected in industry work because all the fittings are available at some predefined angle values in market.
- Select the **Conversion** option from the left area of the dialog box to define how duct route lines will be converted to ducts. The options will be displayed as shown in Figure-4. Select desired option from the **System** drop-down to define for which system of HVAC, you want to define conversion parameters. After selecting the system, click in the value field of **Duct Type** setting from the table and select desired option from the drop-down displayed. Using this drop-down, you can define the shape of duct and type of fittings that can be automatically applied during route conversion. Using value field of **Middle Elevation** setting, you can define the height of duct from the base level. You can set the duct type and height for both main and branch ducts by using options of respective tables in the dialog box. If you want to add flexible duct for branch connections then select the **Flex Duct Round : Flex - Round** option from the **Flex Duct Type** field in **Branch** table of dialog box.

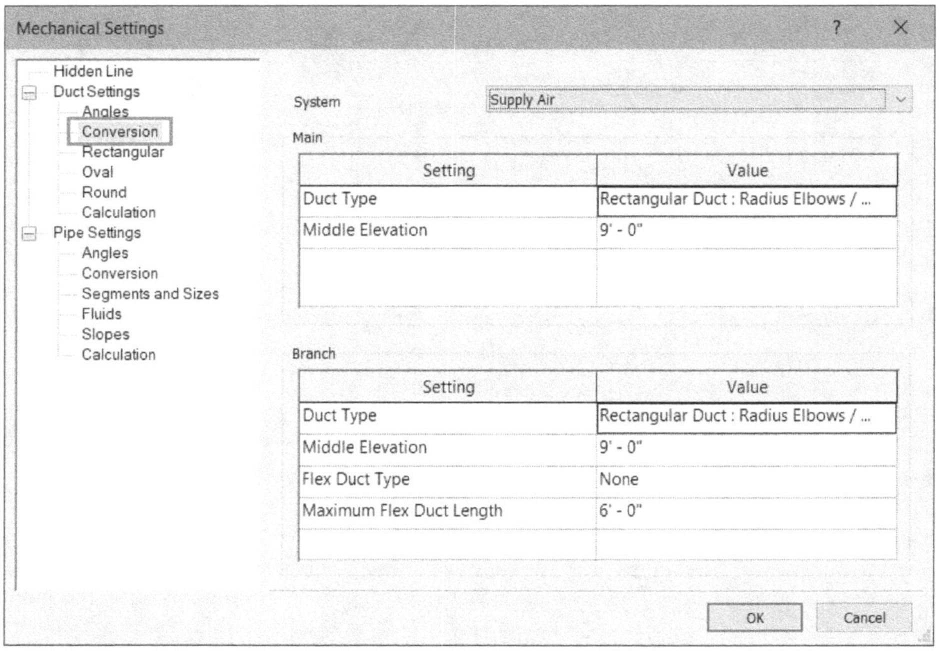

Figure-4. Conversion options for ducting

- Click on the **Rectangular** option from the left area of the dialog box and select the sizes of rectangular duct sections that can be used in creating HVAC system.
- Similarly, using the **Oval** and **Round** options at the left in the dialog box, you can select respective shaped section sizes for ducting.
- Click on the **Calculation** option from the left in the dialog box to define how pressure drop will be calculated along the duct segments during analysis. After selecting this option, select desired method from the **Calculation Method** drop-down.
- Similarly, you can set parameters for piping in this dialog box. These options will be discussed later in this chapter. Click on the **OK** button from the dialog box to apply settings.

Creating Duct

The **Duct** tool is used to create duct passage for HVAC. The flow of air occurs through these ducts in the building. The procedure to create duct is given next.

- Click on the **Duct** tool from the **HVAC** panel in the **Systems** tab of **Ribbon**. The options to create duct will be displayed; refer to Figure-5.
- Select desired type of duct from the drop-down at the top in the **Properties Palette**. Note that the drop-down is divided into three sections; **Oval Duct**, **Rectangular Duct**, and **Round Duct**. Select desired fitting option from the section to use it for creating HVAC duct. For example, if you have selected **Radius Elbows/ Tees** option from the **Rectangular** section then a rectangular duct will be created. If there is a need of rotation in the duct path then elbow will be created and if there is an intersection of duct lines then a tee will be created at the intersections. Make sure to load desired duct type families in project as discussed earlier.
- Select desired option from the **Reference Level** drop-down in the **Properties Palette** to define at what level the duct will be created. Similarly, set the justification of duct in respective fields of **Properties Palette**.
- Specify the width and height of duct in the **Width** and **Height** edit boxes of **Options Bar**.

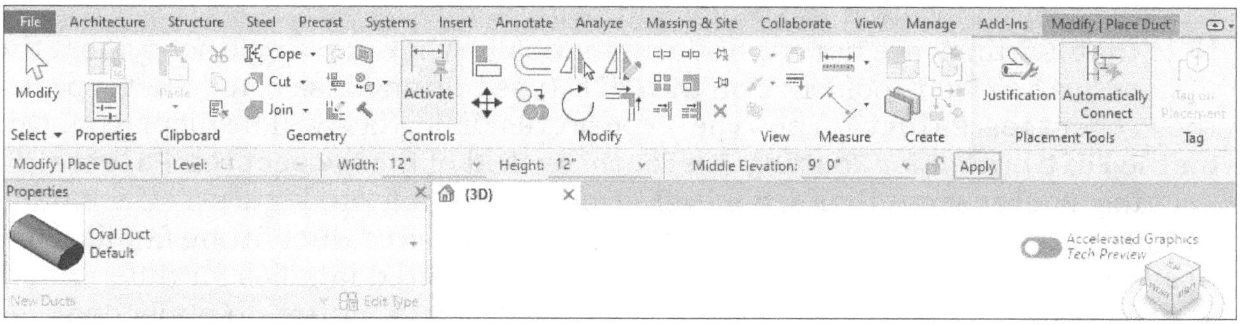

Figure-5. Options for creating duct

- Set desired value in **Middle Elevation** edit box of **Options Bar** to define height or depth of duct from selected reference level. A negative value will move the duct downward and positive value will move the duct upward with specified value.
- Click on the **Lock** button in **Options Bar** to lock the elevation of duct.
- Select the **Automatically Connect** button from the **Placement Tools** panel in the **Modify|Place Duct** tab of **Ribbon** so that ducts automatically get connected while creating them.
- Select the **Inherit Elevation** toggle button from the **Placement Tools** panel if you want the new duct to inherit elevation level from connecting duct. Select the **Inherit Size** toggle button if you want the new duct to inherit size of connected duct.
- Select the **Tag on Placement** button from the contextual tab if you want to place tag while creating duct. Note that this button will be active when you are working on elevation or plan view.
- Select desired air type for duct in the **System Type** drop-down in the **Properties Palette** like select **Supply Air** option if you are using it for supplying fresh air. Select the **Exhaust Air** option if you want the duct for exhaustion. Select the **Return Air** option if you want the duct to be used as return duct for HVAC machine.
- If you want extra air to flow through duct apart from standard flow value based on calculations by air terminals then specify desired value in **Additional Flow** edit box of **Properties Palette**.
- After setting desired parameters, click to specify the start point of duct. You will be asked to specify end point of duct; refer to Figure-6.

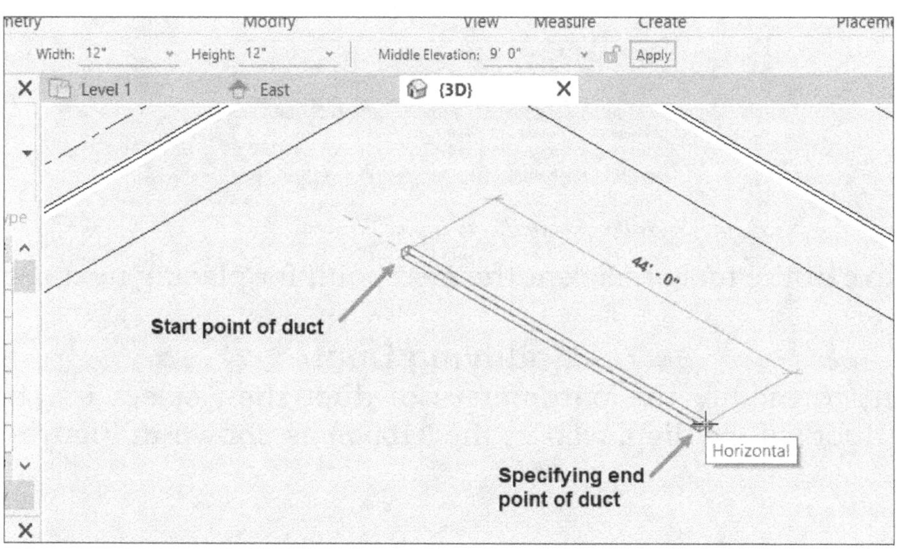

Figure-6. Creating duct

- Click at desired location to specify end point of duct.
- Note that if fittings are not applied automatically while creating duct system then after activating **Duct** tool, click on the **Edit Type** button for selected duct type from the **Properties Palette**. The **Type Properties** dialog box will be displayed. Click on the **Edit** button for **Routing Preferences** field of the **Properties Palette**. The **Routing Preferences** dialog box will be displayed; refer to Figure-7. Click on the **Load Family** button from the dialog box and load desired duct fitting families to be used in duct routing. After loading families, set desired families for different type of fittings in the dialog box; refer to Figure-8. Click **OK** button to apply changes.

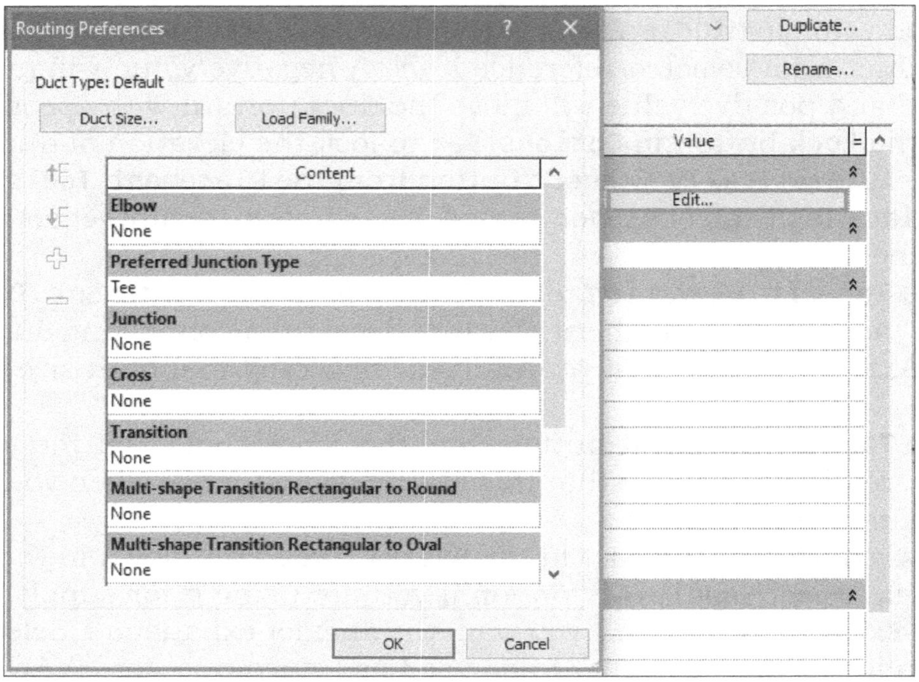

Figure-7. Routing Preferences dialog box

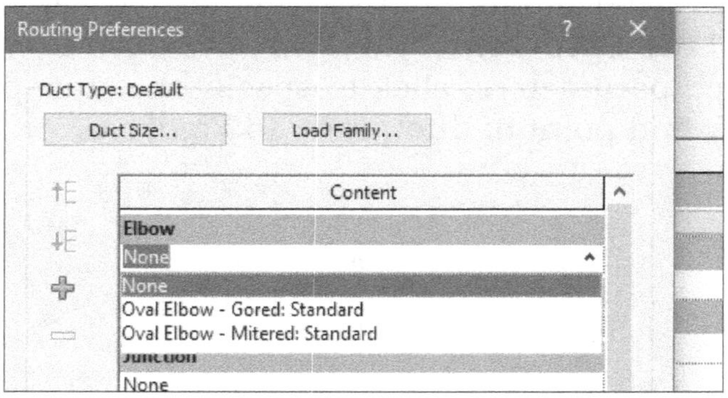

Figure-8. Assigning families to Elbow fittings

- Press **ESC** to exit the tool or click at the next point for placing next segment of duct.

Modifying Duct

- If you want to modify the parameters of duct then select it. The options for modifying duct will be displayed in the **Ribbon** as shown in Figure-9.

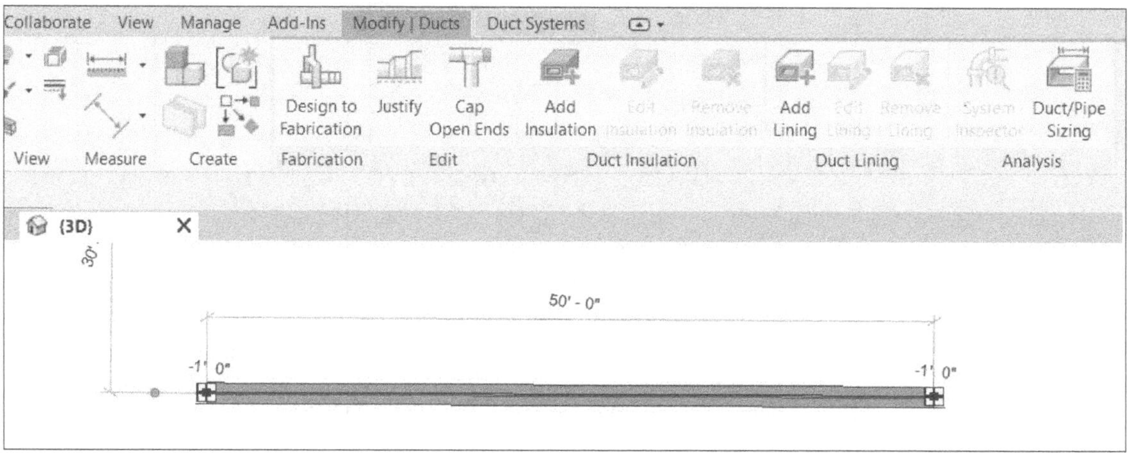

Figure-9. Options to modify duct

- Click on the **Add Insulation** button from the **Duct Insulation** panel of the **Modify|Ducts** contextual tab in the **Ribbon** to add insulating material around duct for reducing heat loss. The **Add Duct Insulation** dialog box will be displayed; refer to Figure-10.

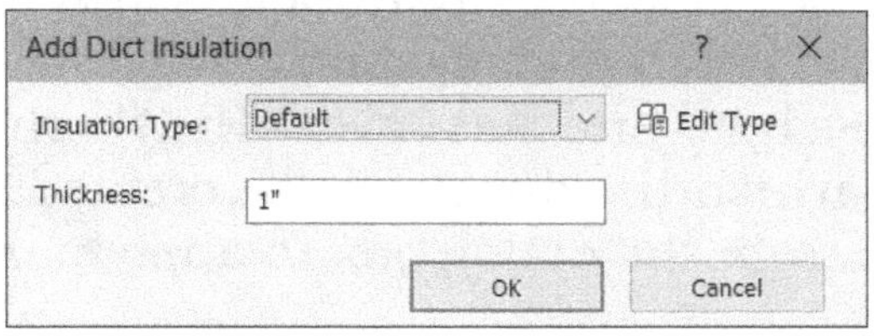

Figure-10. Add Duct Insulation dialog box

- Set desired value of insulation thickness in the **Thickness** edit box and click on the **OK** button.
- If there is already insulation on the duct then click on the **Edit Insulation** button from the **Duct Insulation** panel of contextual tab to modify it. If you want to remove the insulation then click on the **Remove Insulation** button from the contextual tab.
- Click on the **Add Lining** button from the **Duct Lining** panel of **Modify|Ducts** contextual tab in the **Ribbon** if you want to add lining inside the duct for heat insulation. The **Add Duct Lining** dialog box will be displayed; refer to Figure-11. Specify desired value of duct lining thickness and click on the **OK** button.

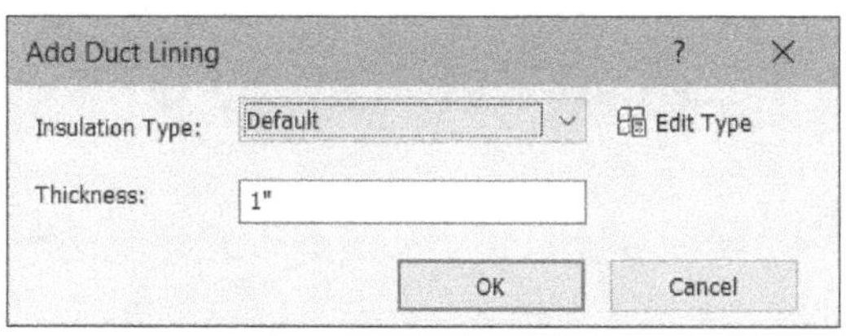

Figure-11. Add Duct Lining dialog box

- Click on the **Duct/Pipe Sizing** button from the **Analysis** panel in the **Modify|Ducts** contextual tab of **Ribbon** to change calculation parameters for duct/pipe sizing. The **Duct Sizing** dialog box will be displayed; refer to Figure-12.

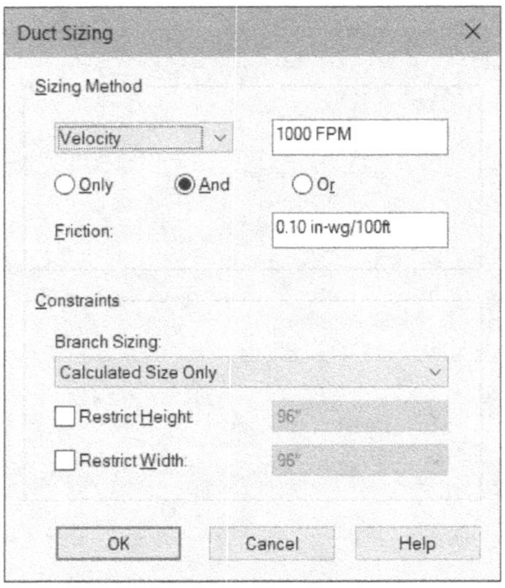

Figure-12. Duct Sizing dialog box

- Set desired parameters in the dialog box for sizing method like parameter used for sizing and its standard value. Similarly, select desired option from the **Branch Sizing** drop-down and set desired restrictions for duct sizing. Note that width and height of duct will be decided by parameters specified in this dialog box and number of branches created in duct system.
- Select the **Restrict Height** and **Restrict Width** check boxes to specify the maximum value up to which the ducts can be created for branches.
- Click on the **OK** button from the dialog box to apply parameters.

Creating Duct Placeholder

The **Duct Placeholder** tool is used to create line diagram of duct without elbows or tee fittings. This line diagram can later be converted to duct system. The procedure to use this tool is given next.

- Click on the **Duct Placeholder** tool from the **HVAC** panel in the **Systems** tab of **Ribbon**. The options to create duct placeholder will be displayed; refer to Figure-13.

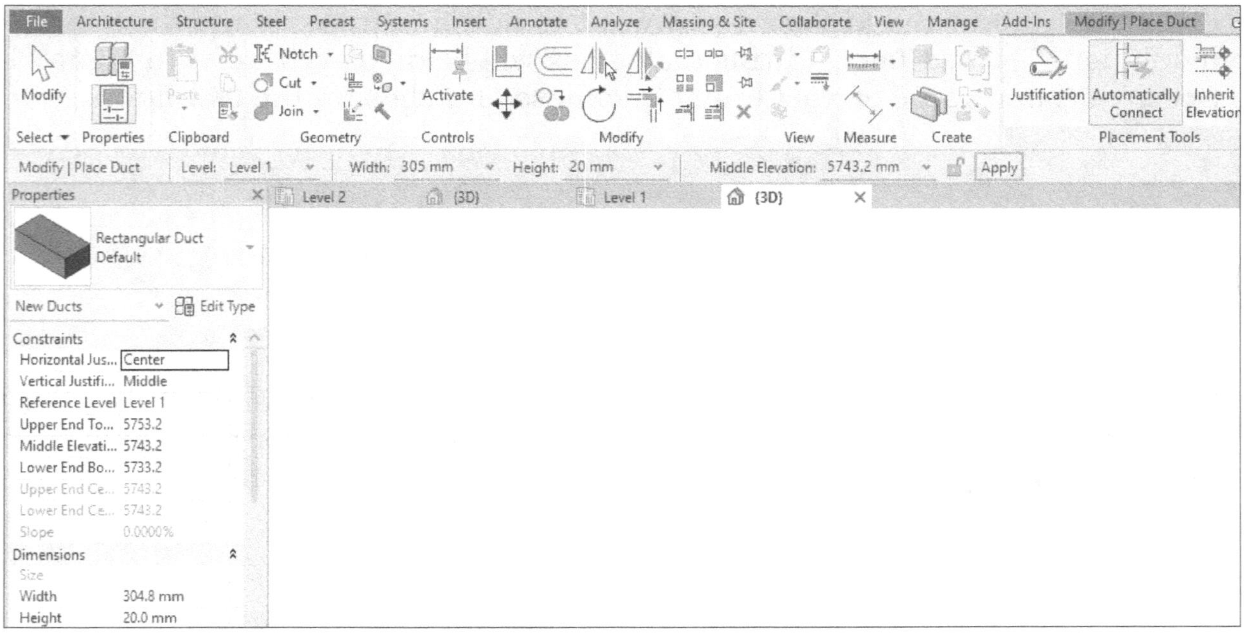

Figure-13. Options to create duct placeholder

- Click at desired location specify start point of duct placeholder. You will be asked to specify end point of the duct placeholder.
- Click to specify the end point. A line of duct placeholder will be created.
- Create the other parts of duct placeholder as desired. Once you have created desired circuit of duct placeholders, select one of the placeholder. The options to modify it will be displayed; refer to Figure-14.

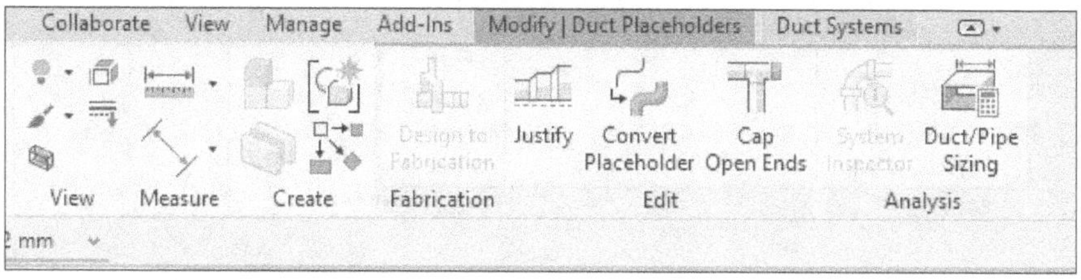

Figure-14. Options to modify duct placeholder

- Click on the **Convert Placeholder** tool from the **Edit** panel in the **Modify|Duct Placeholders** contextual tab of **Ribbon** to convert placeholder into duct; refer to Figure-15. The conversion will occur based on settings specified in the **Mechanical Settings** dialog box and **Duct Sizing** dialog box.

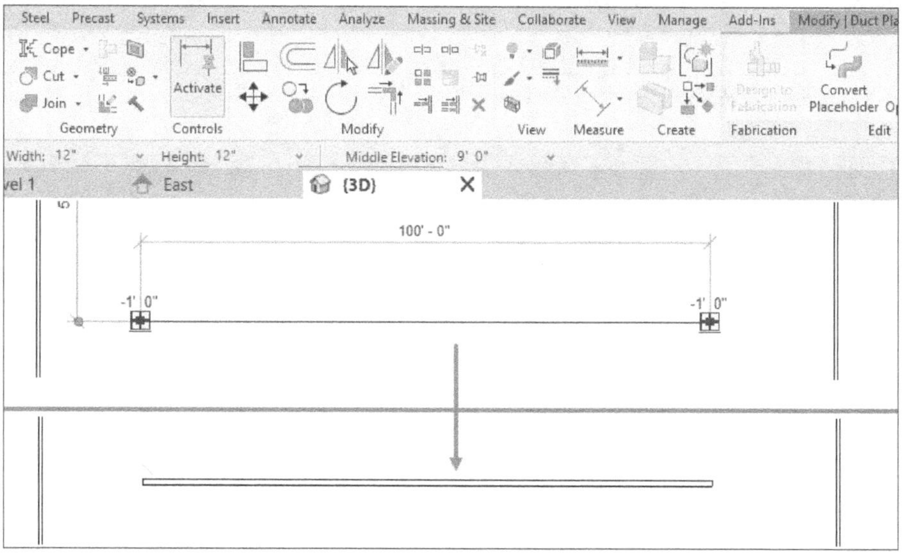

Figure-15. Converting placeholder to duct

- Set the other parameters as discussed earlier.

Applying Duct Fittings

The **Duct Fitting** tool is used to apply duct fitting to the ducts. The procedure to apply duct fitting is given next.

- Click on the **Duct Fitting** tool from the **HVAC** panel in the **Systems** tab of **Ribbon**. A message box will be displayed asking you to load duct fittings if there are no fittings loaded by default.
- Click **Yes** button to load duct fittings. The **Load Family** dialog box will be displayed; refer to Figure-16.
- Select desired fittings from the **Duct/Fittings** folder of library in the dialog box. You can select multiple objects while holding the **CTRL** key. Click on the **Open** button from the dialog box. The options to place duct fitting will be displayed; refer to Figure-17.

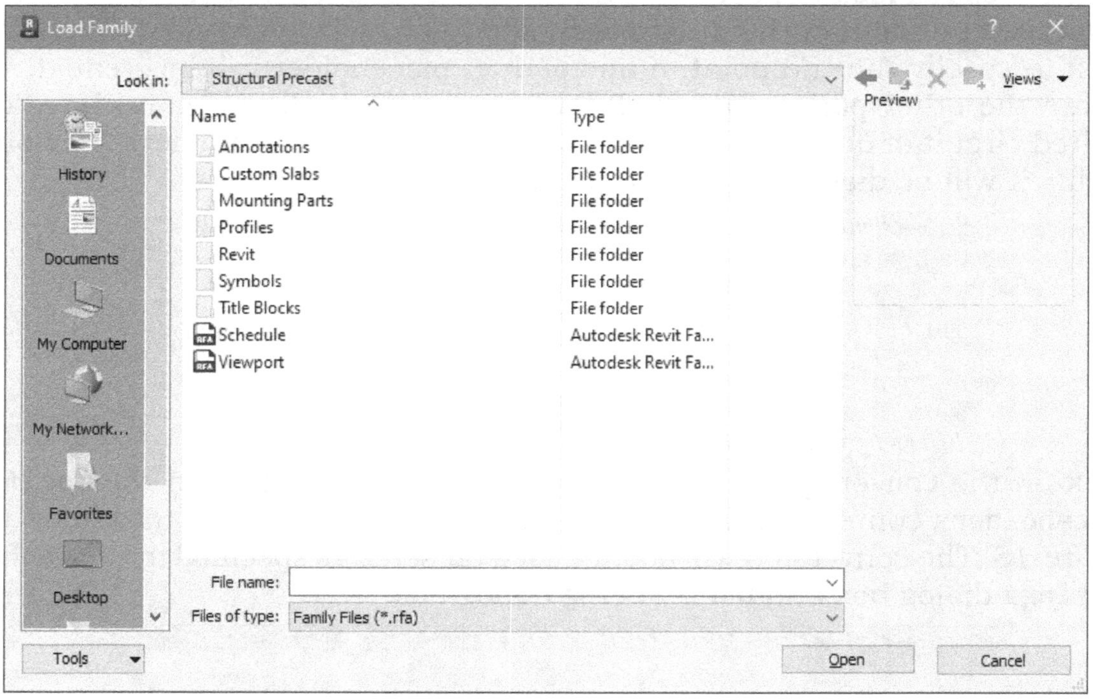

Figure-16. Load Family dialog box

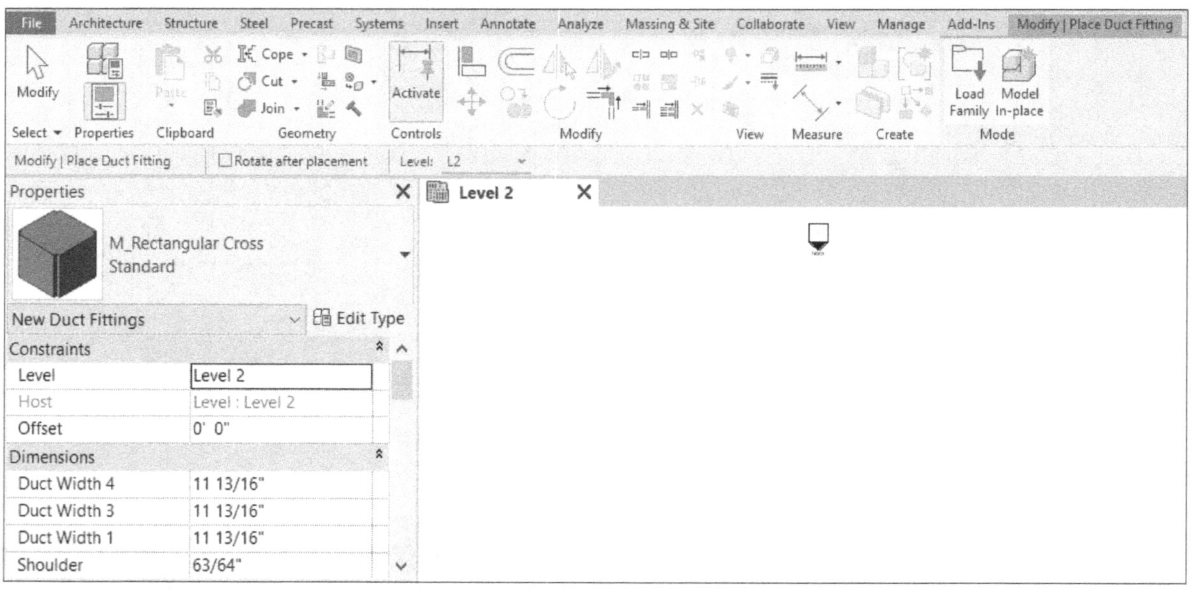

Figure-17. Options to place duct fitting

- If you have loaded multiple duct fittings then select desired fitting from the top drop-down in the **Properties Palette**. Set desired parameters in the **Properties Palette** like size of fitting, offset, level of duct, and so on.
- Click at desired location to place the fitting, like we are placing cross duct fitting at intersection of duct placeholders; refer to Figure-18.

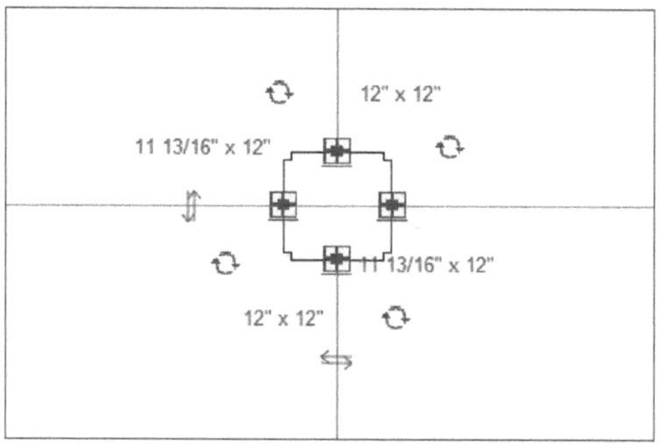

Figure-18. Duct fitting placed on intersection

- Set the other parameters as discussed earlier and press **ESC** to exit the tool.

Placing Duct Accessories

The **Duct Accessory** tool is used to place different types of accessories like dampers and filters in the duct line. The procedure to use this tool is given next.

- Click on the **Duct Accessory** tool from the **HVAC** panel in the **Systems** tab of the **Ribbon**. An information box will be displayed asking you whether to load accessories if there are no duct accessory families loaded by default.
- Click on the **Yes** button from the dialog box. The **Load Family** dialog box will be displayed.
- Select desired accessories to be loaded from the dialog box; refer to Figure-19 and click on the **Open** button. The options to place duct accessory will be displayed with duct accessory attached to cursor; refer to Figure-20.

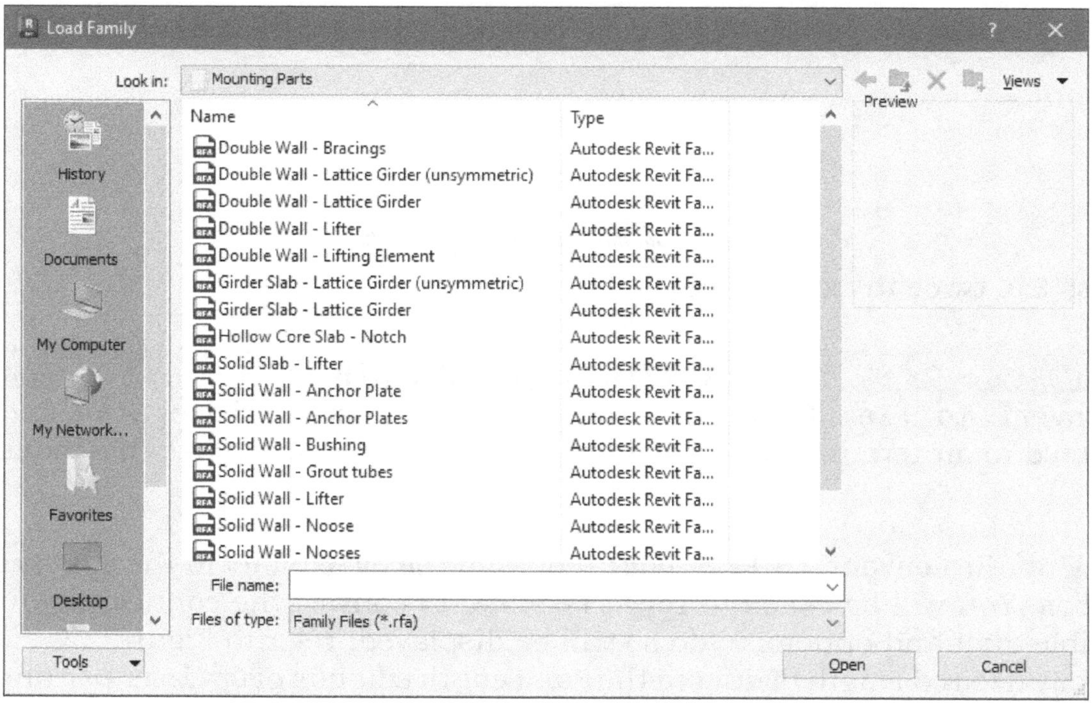

Figure-19. Loading accessories

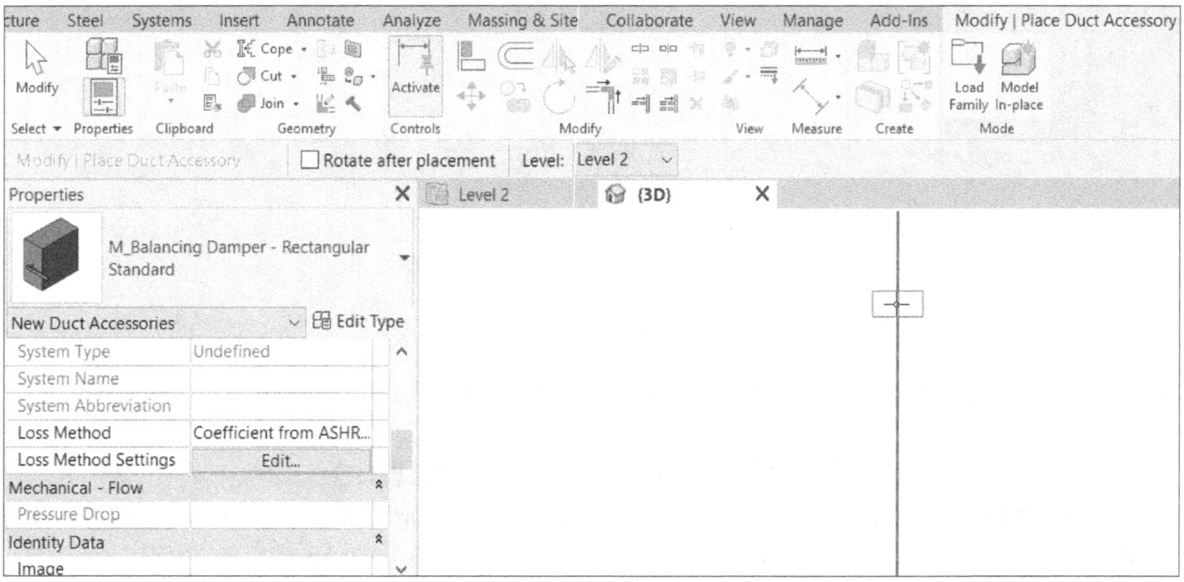

Figure-20. Options to place duct accessory

- Set desired parameters in the **Properties Palette** and click on the duct to place the accessory; refer to Figure-21.

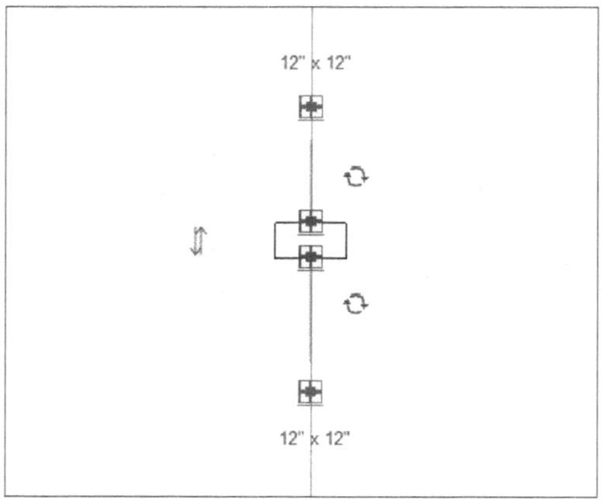

Figure-21. Balancing damper placed on duct

- Press **ESC** twice to exit the tool.

Converting to Flex Duct

The **Convert to Flex Duct** tool is used to convert selected length of duct work (connected to air terminal) into flexible duct. The procedure to use this tool is given next.

- Click on the **Convert to Flex Duct** tool from the **HVAC** panel in the **Systems** tab of **Ribbon**. You will be asked to select terminal to convert the connecting duct into flexible duct and options to do so will be displayed; refer to Figure-22.
- Specify desired length of duct in the **Max Length** edit box of **Options Bar** and select the air terminal connected to duct. The connected duct will be convert to flexible duct; refer to Figure-23. (You will learn about air terminals later in this chapter).

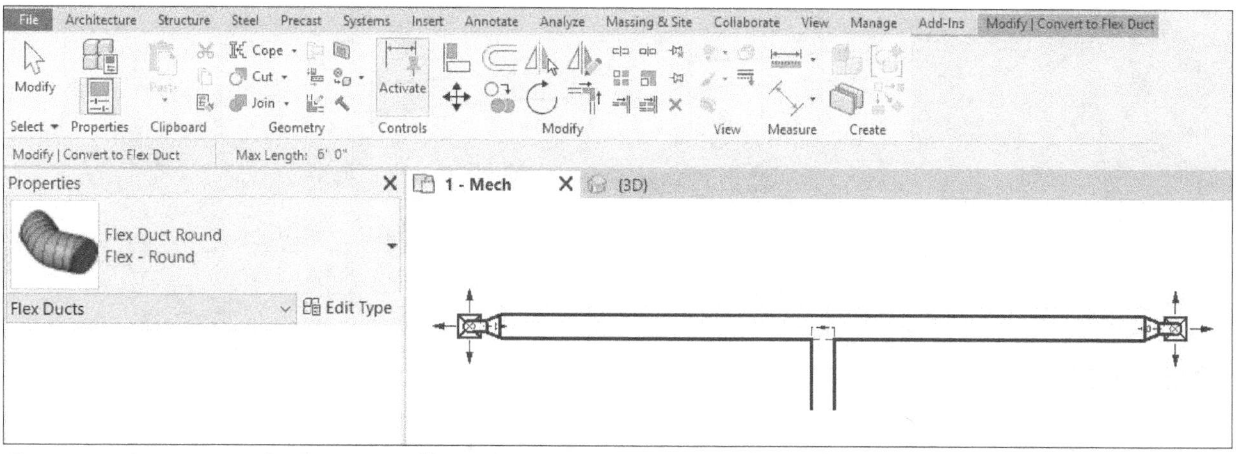

Figure-22. Options to convert duct into flex duct

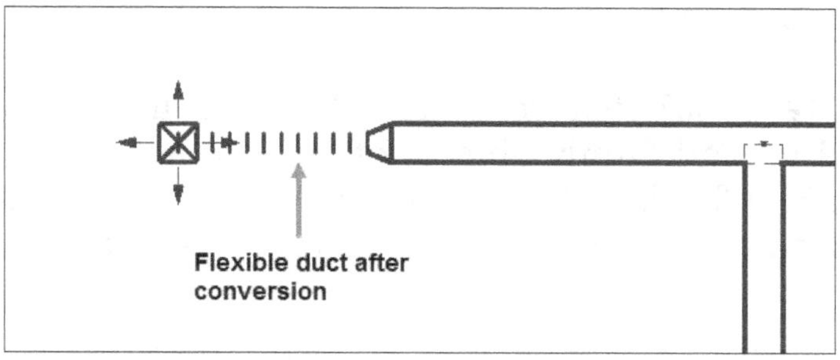

Figure-23. Flexible duct after conversion

Creating Flexible Duct

The **Flex Duct** tool is used to create flexible duct. The procedure is given next.

- Click on the **Flex Duct** tool from the **HVAC** panel in the **Systems** tab of **Ribbon**. The options to create flexible duct will be displayed; refer to Figure-24.

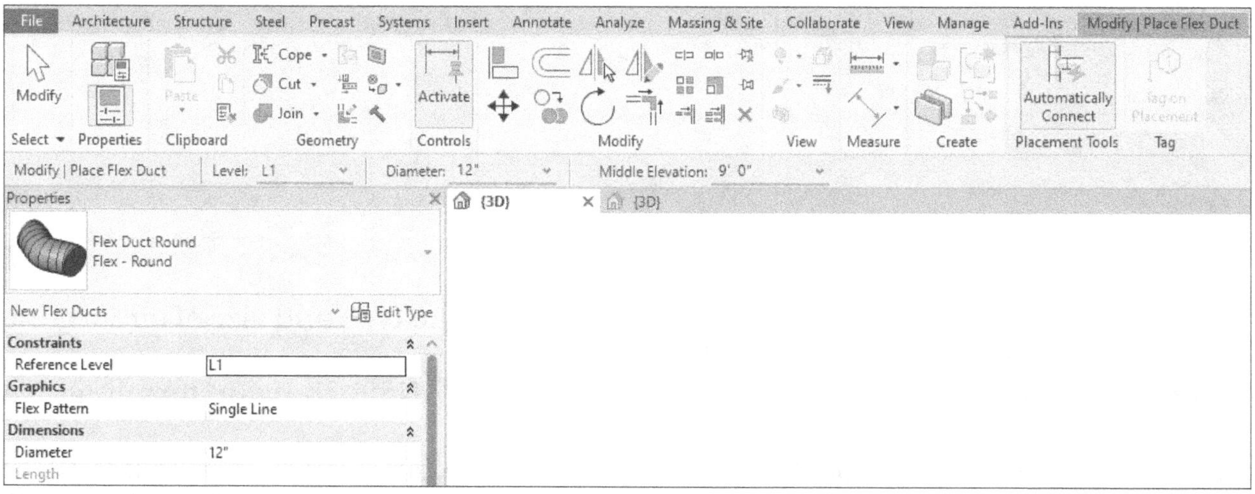

Figure-24. Options for creating flexible duct

- Set desired parameters in **Options Bar** and **Properties Palette**.
- Click at desired location to specify start point of flexible duct. You will be asked to specify next point.
- Click to specify the next point. You will be asked to specify end point/next point; refer to Figure-25. Specify desired point and press **ESC** to create the duct.

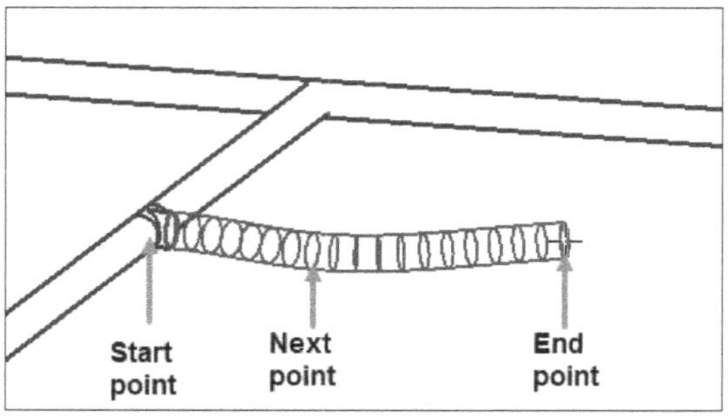

Figure-25. Creating flex duct

- Press **ESC** to exit the tool.

Creating Air Terminal

The **Air Terminal** tool is used to create diffusers and grilles. The procedure to create air terminal is discussed next.

- Click on the **Air Terminal** tool from the **HVAC** panel in the **Systems** tab of **Ribbon**. You will be asked to load family objects of air terminal.
- Load the air terminal families from Mechanical folder in Autodesk Revit content library as discussed earlier. The options to create air terminal will be displayed; refer to Figure-26.

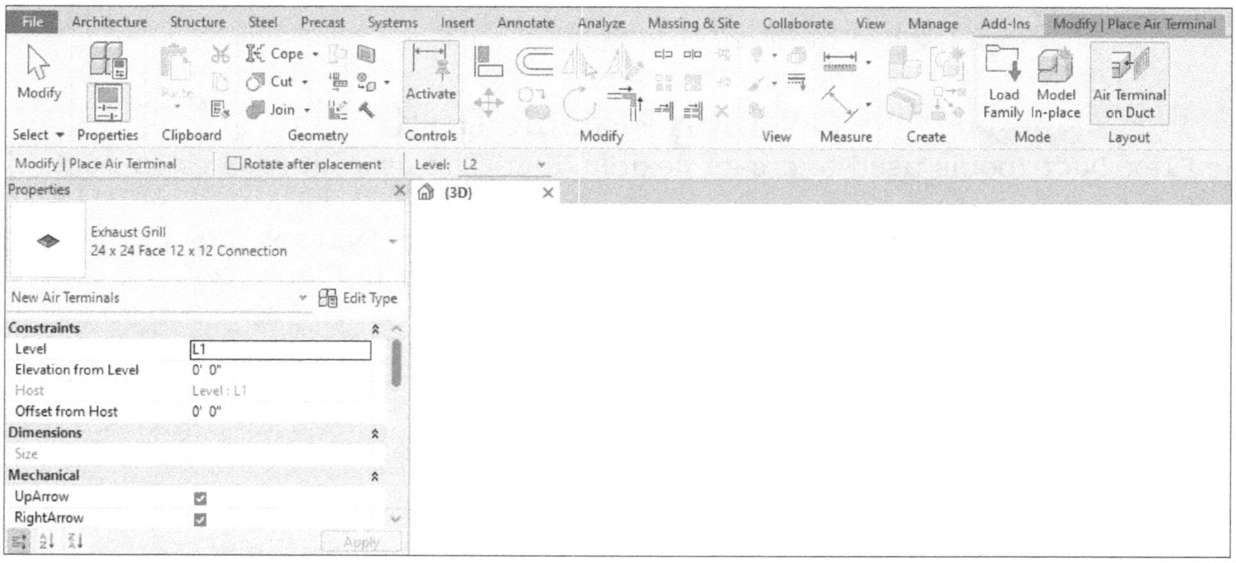

Figure-26. Options to place air terminal

- Set desired parameters in the **Properties Palette** like type and size of air terminal, level of terminal, CFM of terminal, and so on.
- Click at desired locations to place the terminals. Note that air terminals can automatically snap to duct line end points.
- Select the **Air Terminal on Duct** button from the **Layout** panel in the **Modify|Place Air Terminal** contextual tab of **Ribbon** while placing air terminals to automatically place air terminals connected to duct line.
- Press **ESC** twice to exit the tool.

Placing Fabrication Parts

The **Fabrication Part** tool is used to insert parts for ducting like elbows, reducers, and so on. Note that you need to install Fabrication CAMduct software as well from Autodesk to setup fabrication configuration if they are not displayed by default. The procedure to use this tool is given next.

- Click on the **Fabrication Part** tool from the **Fabrication** panel in the **Systems** tab of **Ribbon**. The **MEP Fabrication Parts** panel will be displayed at right in the application window.
- Click on the **Settings** button from the **MEP Fabrication Parts** panel. The **Fabrication Settings** dialog box will be displayed; refer to Figure-27.

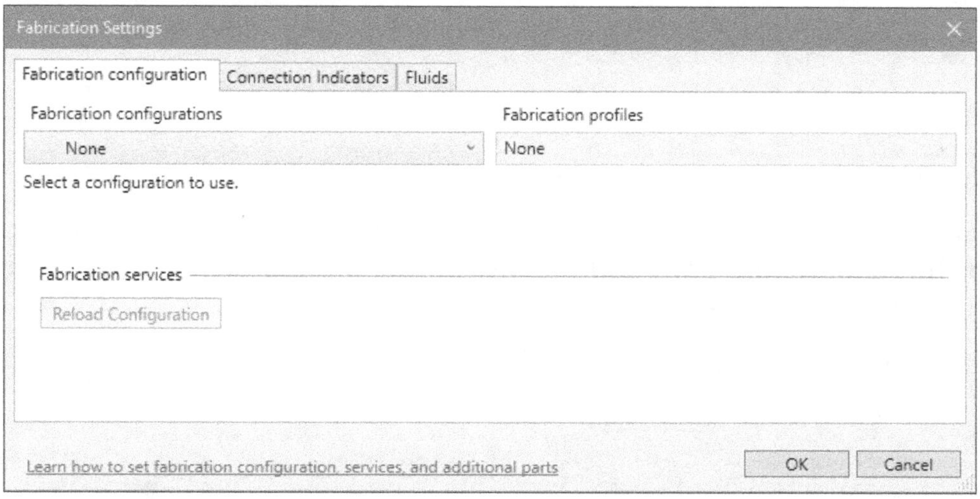

Figure-27. Fabrication Settings dialog box

- Select desired option from the **Fabrication configurations** drop-down. Select **Revit MEP Metric Content V2.41** option from the drop-down if you want to use components of metric unit system. Select the **Revit MEP Imperial Content V2.51** option if you want to use components of imperial unit system. (If the sample content is not installed by default then login in to your Autodesk account using link https://manage.autodesk.com/products/updates and select check boxes for desired content for downloading from the **Libraries** tab of the web page; refer to Figure-28. After downloading the file(s), install them in your system. Note that files are installed in C:/Users/Public/Documents/Autodesk/Fabrication <release>/ Revit MEP Imperial Content/Vx.xx and C:/Users/Public/Documents/Autodesk/ Fabrication <release>/Revit MEP Metric Content/Vx.xx directories).

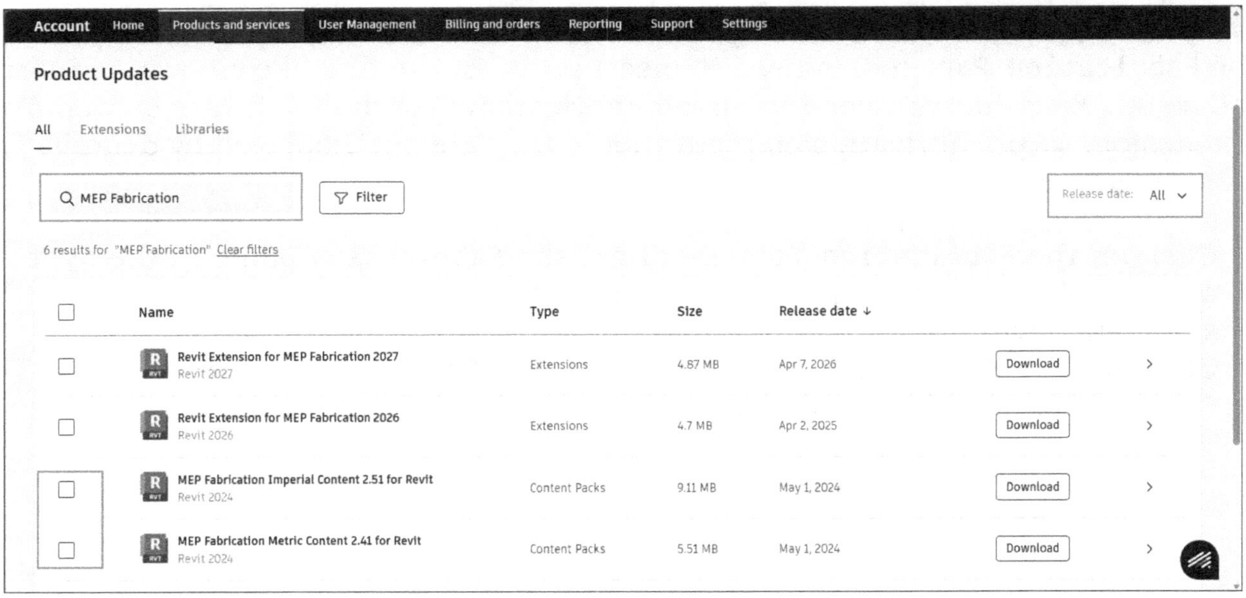

Figure-28. Autodesk account page for content

- Select all the services whose components are to be included in the project and click on the **Add** button; refer to Figure-29. The components of respective services will be loaded in the project.

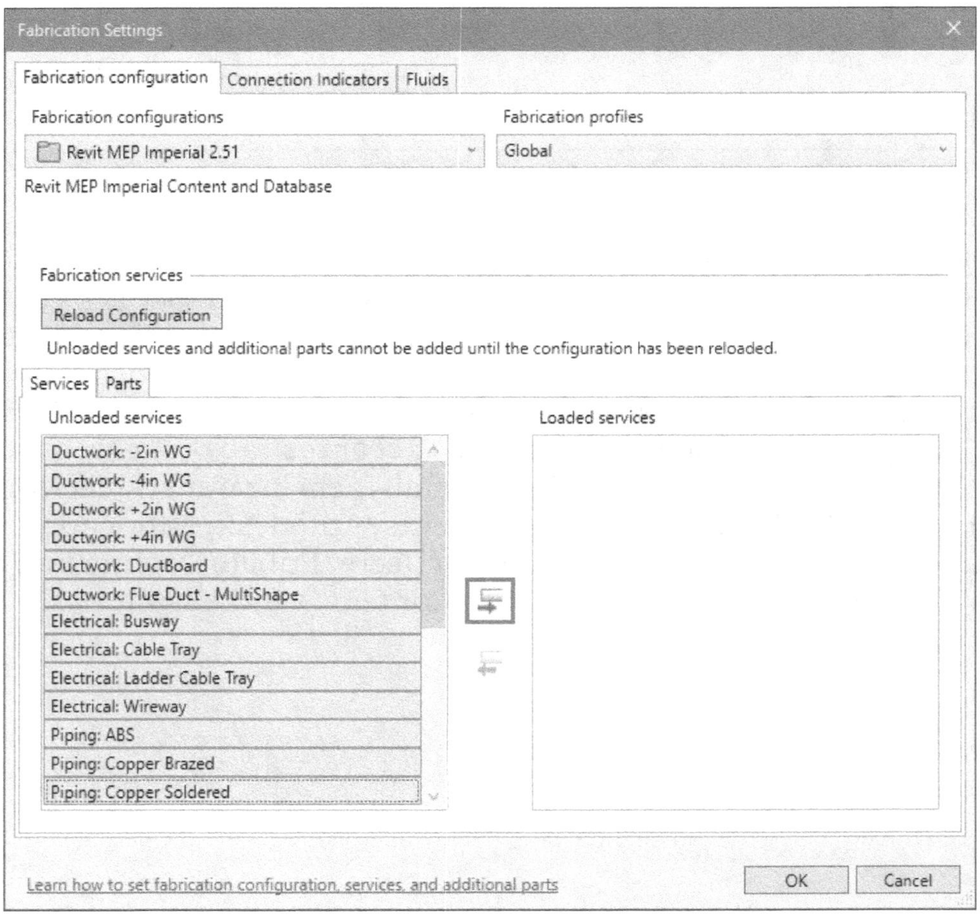

Figure-29. Loading services in project

- Click on the **OK** button from the dialog box. The components will be displayed in the **MEP Fabrication Parts** panel.

- Select desired fabrication part from the list. The options to modify and place part will be displayed in the **Modify|Place Fabrication Part** contextual tab; refer to Figure-30.

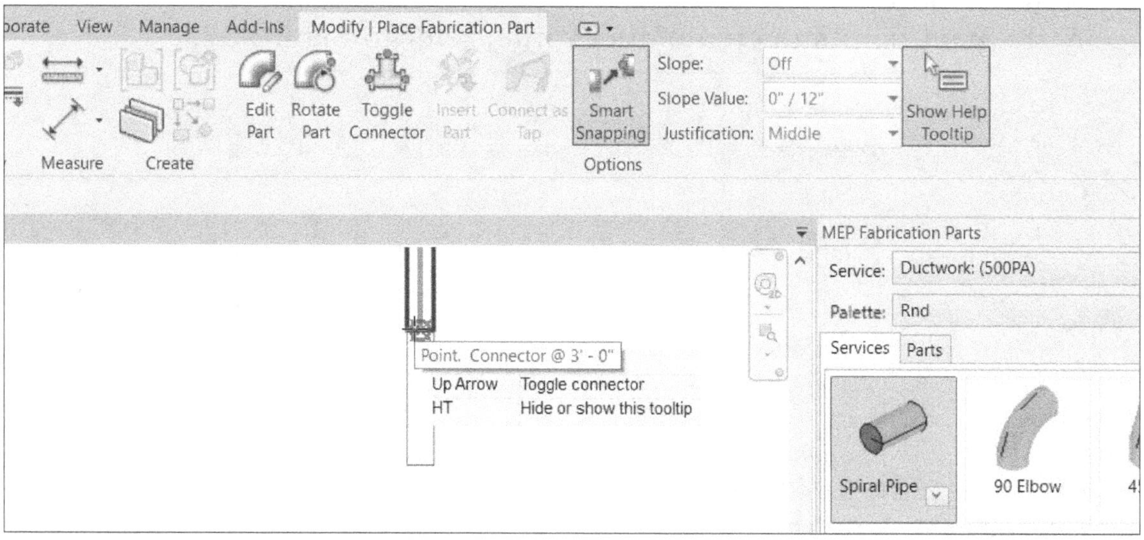

Figure-30. Options to place fabrication part

- Move the component near connection point. The component will snap automatically.
- Click on the **Toggle Connector** button to change the connection point of component if there are more than one connection points.
- Select desired material from the **Part Material** field in the **Properties Palette** and set the other parameters as desired.
- Click at desired location to place the component.
- Press **ESC** to exit the tool.

Creating Multi-Point Routing

The **Multi-Point Routing** tool is used to create a multi-point route of ducting. This tool is available only when **Fabrication Part** tool is selected in the **Ribbon**. The procedure to create multi-point route is given next.

- Click on the **Multi-Point Routing** tool from the **Fabrication** panel in the **Systems** tab of **Ribbon**. The options to create route will be displayed; refer to Figure-31.

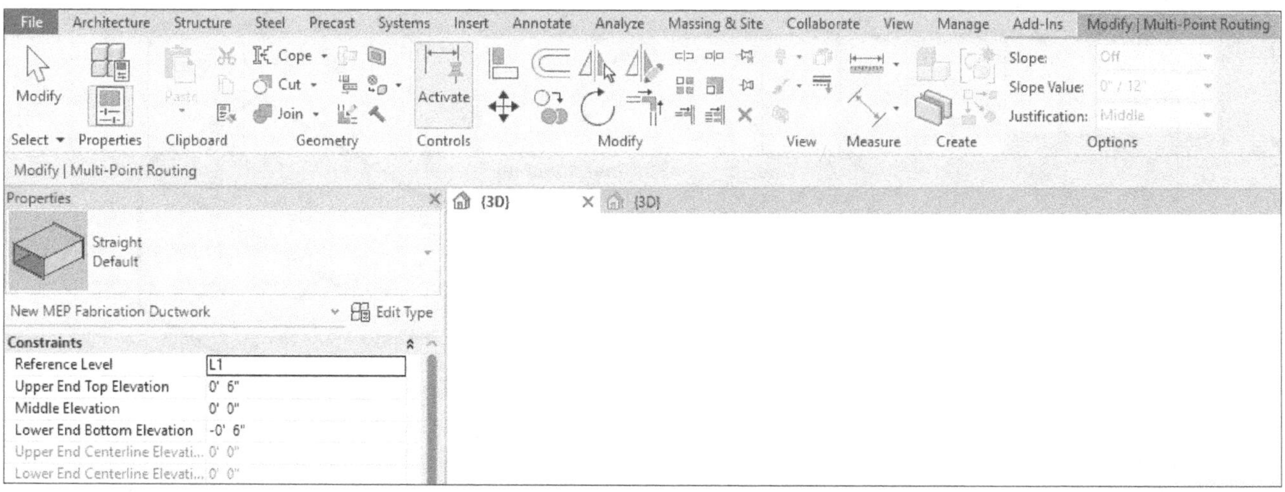

Figure-31. Options to create multipoint route

- Select desired type of duct from the drop-down at the top in the **Properties Palette** and set the other parameters like material, offset, insulation, and so on.
- Click at desired location to specify start point of route. You will be asked to specify next point of route.
- Specify the next points to create duct route; refer to Figure-32.

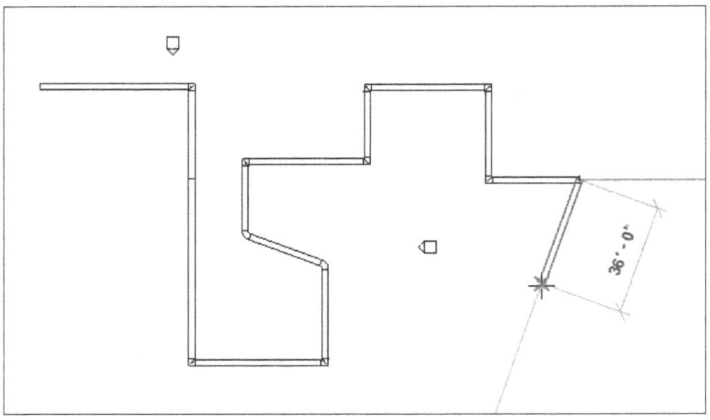

Figure-32. Creating duct route

- Press **ESC** twice to exit the tool.

Placing MEP Fabrication Ductwork Stiffener

The **MEP Fabrication Ductwork Stiffener** tool is used to place duct stiffener in MEP fabrication ducts placed by using Fabrication Part tool. The procedure to use this tool is given next.

- Click on the **MEP Fabrication Ductwork Stiffener** tool from the **MEP Detailing** panel of **Systems** tab in the **Ribbon**. If there is no part family loaded then load the duct stiffener parts as discussed earlier. The stiffener will be attached to cursor and you will be asked to specify placement location on the MEP duct; refer to Figure-33.

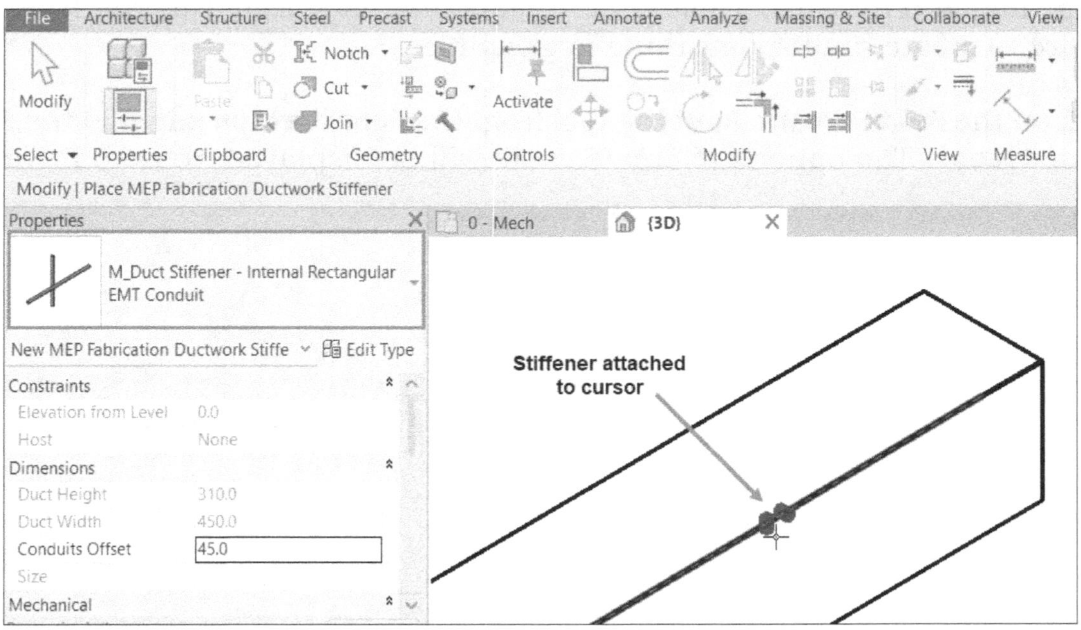

Figure-33. Stiffener attached to cursor

- Set the parameters in the **Properties Palette** as discussed earlier and click on the duct at desired location to place the stiffener.
- Press **ESC** to exit the tool.

P&ID Modeler

The **P&ID Modeler** tool in the **P&ID Collaboration** panel is used to generate a 3D piping model directly from P&ID 2D drawing stored in the cloud. Note that you will need access to Autodesk Construction Cloud to use this tool. This tool is not available for student version of the software. Visit the link https://www.youtube.com/watch?v=pLKOTo6S1BA to learn more.

Placing Mechanical Equipment

The **Mechanical Equipment** tool in the **Mechanical** panel is used to place different types of mechanical equipment in the layout. The procedure to place the equipment is given next.

- Click on the **Mechanical Equipment** tool from the **Mechanical** panel of **Systems** tab in **Ribbon**. The tools to place equipment will be displayed; refer to Figure-34.
- Select desired component from the top drop-down in the **Properties Palette**. If desired component is not available in current project then click on the **Load Family** tool from the **Mode** panel in the contextual tab and select desired component.
- Set the properties as required in the **Properties Palette** and click at desired location to place the component.

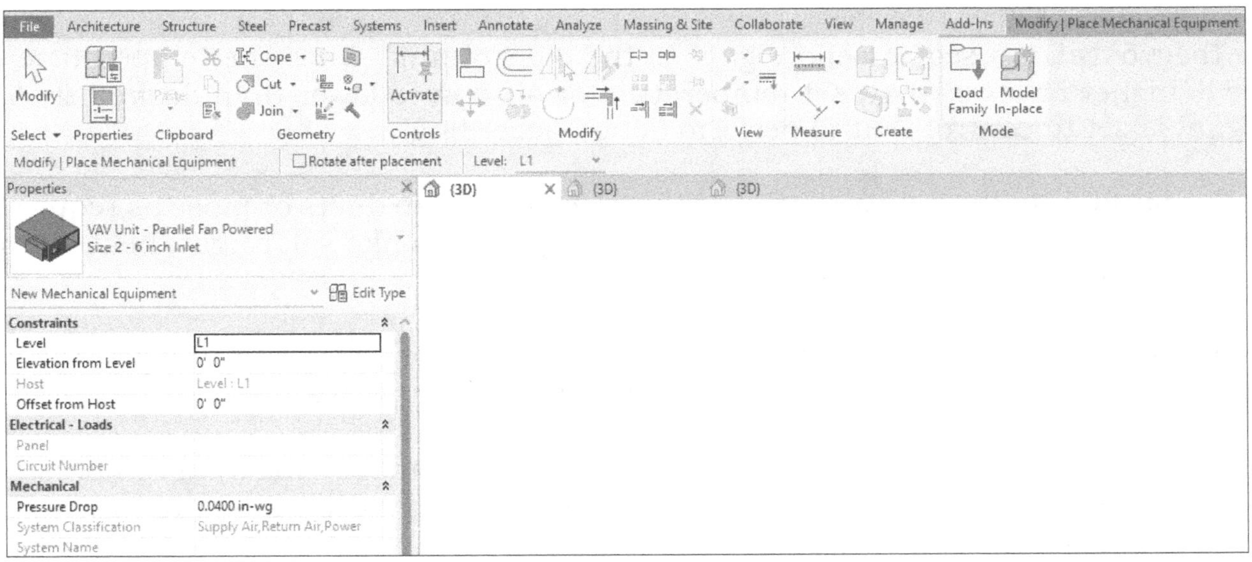

Figure-34. Options to place mechanical equipment

Placing Mechanical Control Devices

The **Mechanical Control Device** tool is used to place mechanical devices like thermostats, CO2 sensors, and so on. The procedure to use this tool is similar to using the **Mechanical Equipment** tool.

BASICS OF HVAC

The HVAC system is a combination of mechanical and electrical components used to control air flow and temperature in a specified zone. There are mainly six components of HVAC system; refer to Figure-35:

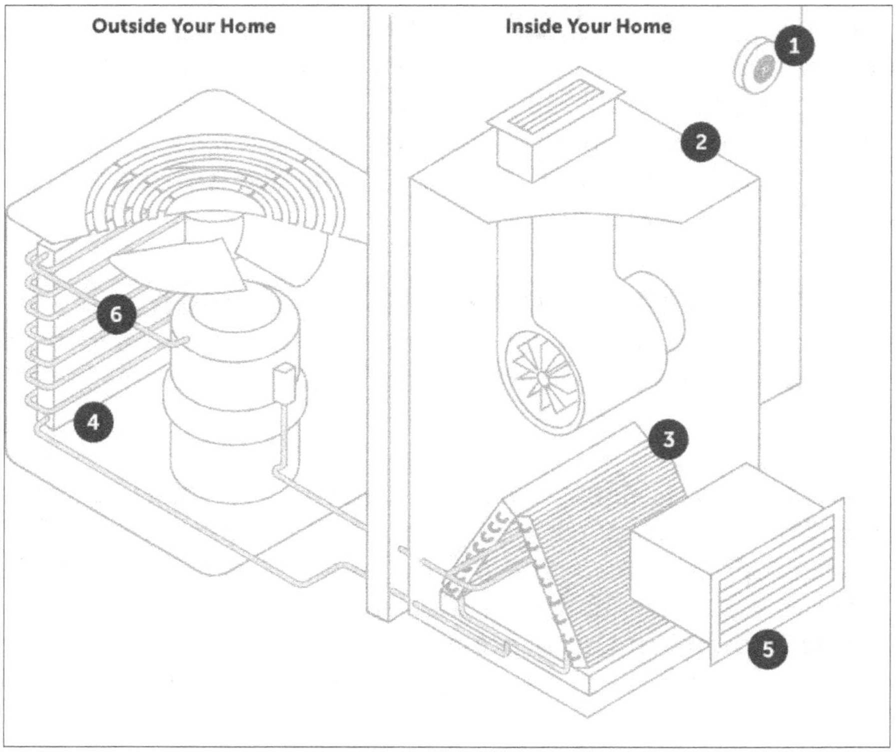

Figure-35. HVAC unit

1. **Thermostat** is used to send signal to the control unit. Once the temperature of air is higher or lower than set temperature or air flow is lower than desired then a signal is set to control unit to perform action accordingly.

2. **Furnace** is used to heat air which is then transferred to ducts or pipes as required. The Furnace can use different types of heating sources like solar light, heat pump, electrical resistance, and so on.

3. **Evaporator Coil** is used to lower the temperature of air when thermostat is set to lower temperature. This cold air is then passed through duct.

4. **Condensing unit** is used to remove heat from refrigerant coming from compressor. Due to heat, the refrigerant transforms into gas but when it cools down in condensing unit; it transforms back to liquid.

5. **Vents** are used to distribute heated or cooled air from duct system into different rooms.

6. **Refrigerant Lines** are used to distribute refrigerant through pipe lines from condenser to evaporation coil.

Calculating CFM and Planning Duct System

The air flow in HVAC is calculated in CFM (Cubic Feet per Minute). The procedure to calculate CFM requirement for given space is discussed next.

1. Calculate volume of specified region (LxWxH). For example, if there is a room of 10 feet x 10 feet x 10 feet then the volume of room is 1000 cubic feet.

2. Decide how much air change is required in the region. The minimum air change for a bed room is 5-6 times and for a smoking room it goes to 15-20 times. The table in Figure-36 defines the number of changes for different types of area.

Typical Air Changes Per Hour Table	
Residential	
Basements	3-4
Bedrooms	5-6
Bathrooms	6-7
Family Living Rooms	6-8
Kitchens	7-8
Laundry	8-9
Light Commercial	
Offices	
Business Offices	6-8
Lunch Break Rooms	7-8
Conference Rooms	8-12
Medical Procedure Offices	9-10
Copy Rooms	10-12
Main Computer Rooms	10-14
Smoking Area	13-15
Restaurants	
Dining Area	8-10
Food Staging	10-12
Kitchens	14-18
Bars	15-20
Public Buildings	
Hallways	6-8
Retail Stores	6-10
Foyers	8-10
Churches	8-12
Restrooms	10-12
Auditoriums	12-14
Smoking Rooms	15-20

Figure-36. Air changes table

3. Multiply the required air change to volume.
4. Divide the outcome value with 60 minutes to find CFM.

Based on the final CFM value, we decide the number of air terminals, the output level of HVAC machine, and so on. As per the thumb rule of conversion, 400 CFM output is produced by 1 ton air handling unit. So, if there is requirement of 700 CFM then you will need 2 ton AHU.

Now, based on your requirement and flow ratings of air vents, find out the number of vents required in the room to distribute air properly. Like if the total CFM requirement of a room is 100 CFM and flow rate of vent is 30 CFM then you will need (100/30=3.33) approximately 4 vents.

CREATING HVAC SYSTEM

There are two ways to create HVAC system; manually and automatically. You have learned about creating duct layout manually earlier in this chapter. Now, we will discuss how we can create automatic duct layout. The procedure is given next.

- Place the supply and return air vents at desired locations; refer to Figure-37.

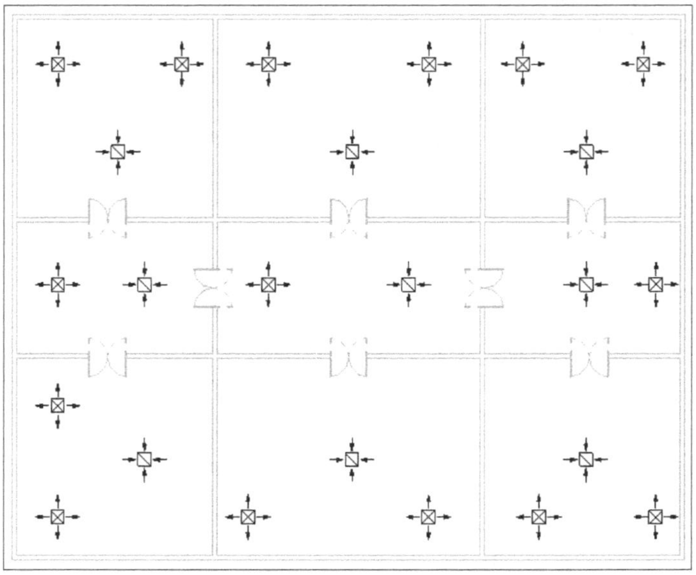

Figure-37. Air vents created

- Click on the **Mechanical Equipment** tool from the **Mechanical** panel in the **Systems** tab of **Ribbon** and place Air Handling Unit at desired location.
- Select all the supply air terminals and then select the air handling unit. The **Duct** option will be displayed in the **Create Systems** panel of **Modify|Multi-Select** contextual tab in **Ribbon**; refer to Figure-38.

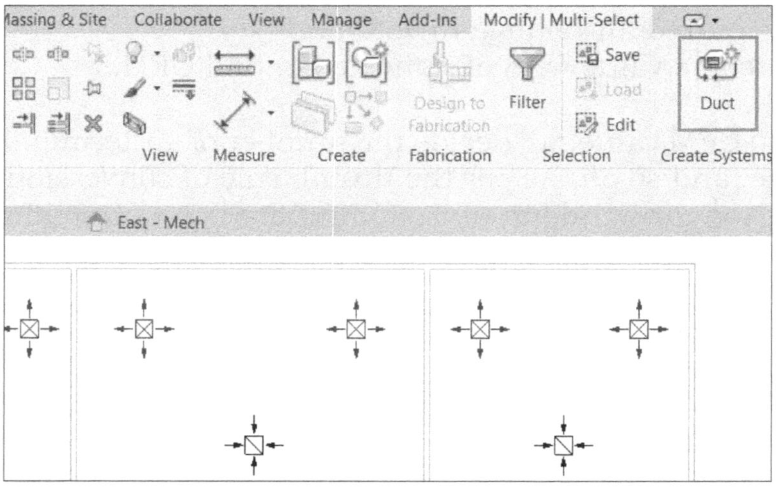

Figure-38. Duct option

- Click on the **Duct** tool. The **Create Duct System** dialog box will be displayed; refer to Figure-39. Set desired name of duct system and select desired type. Click on the **OK** button from the dialog box. The duct system will be created with respective options for editing; refer to Figure-40.

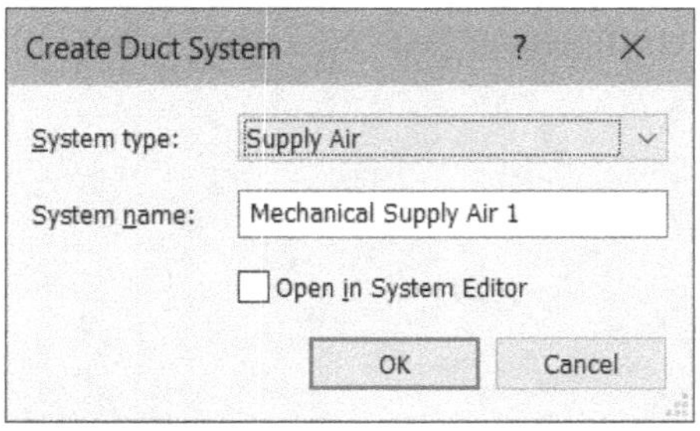

Figure-39. Create Duct System dialog box

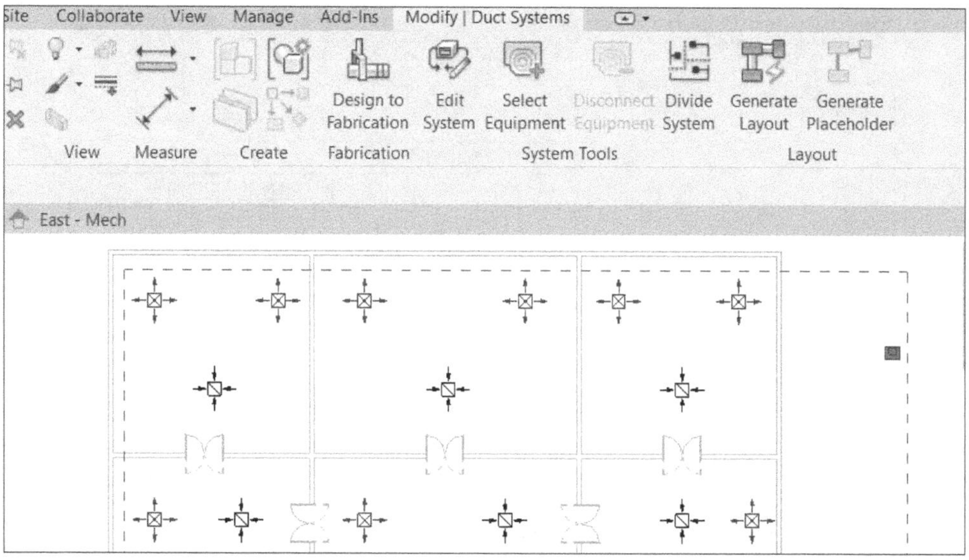

Figure-40. Duct system created

- Click on the **Generate Layout** tool from the **Layout** panel in the **Modify|Duct Systems** contextual tab of **Ribbon**. The preview of layout will be displayed; refer to Figure-41.

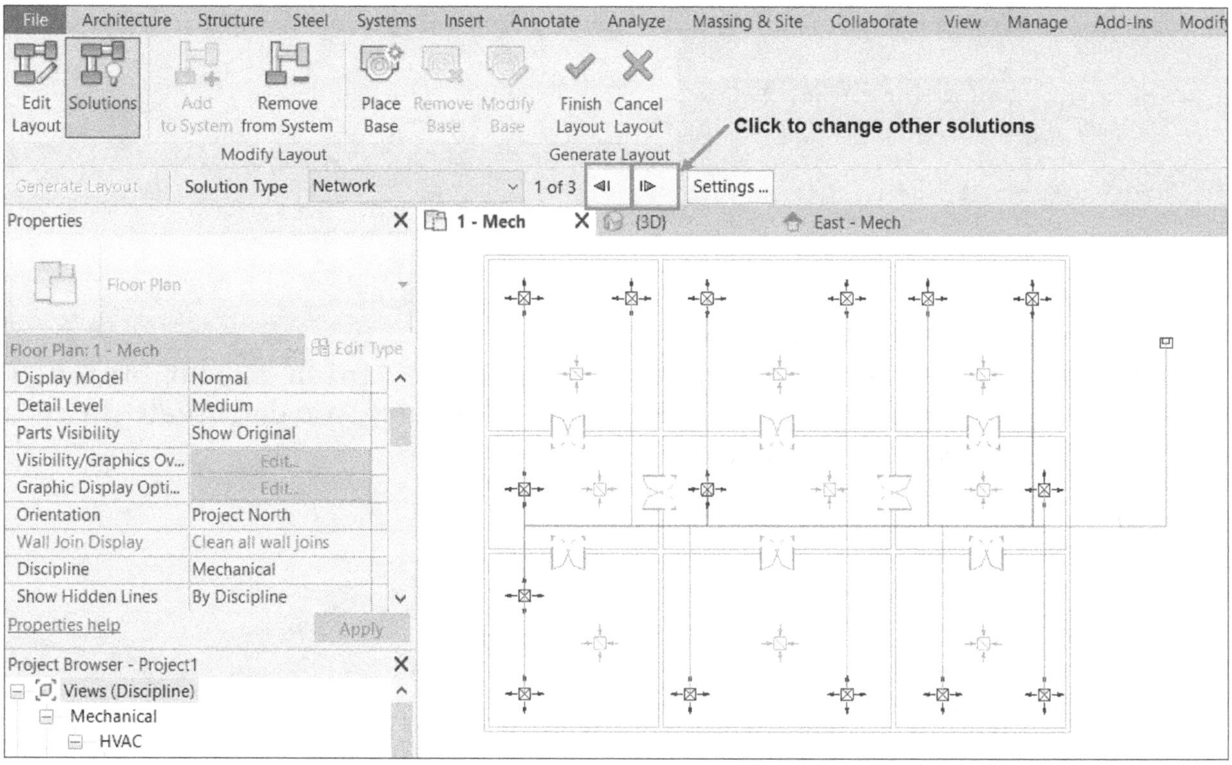

Figure-41. Options to check solutions for duct layout

- Click on the next or previous button in **Options Bar** to change layout.
- Click on the **Settings** button to modify duct setting and shape. The **Duct Conversion Settings** dialog box will be displayed; refer to Figure-42.

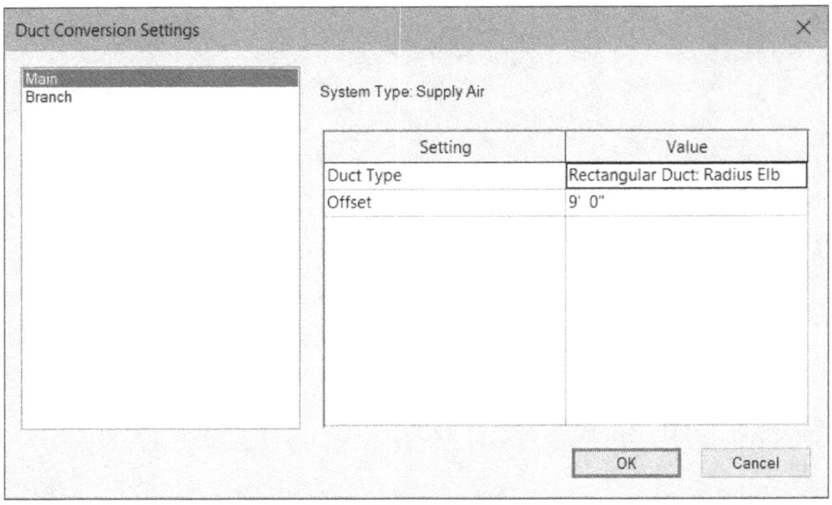

Figure-42. Duct Conversion Settings dialog box

- Click in the **Value** fields of the table to modify parameters like type of duct and offset value (height from current plane). You can convert the branch ducts into flexible ducts by using the **Flex Duct Type** field in the **Branch** page of this dialog box; refer to Figure-43. Click on the **OK** button from the dialog box to apply settings.

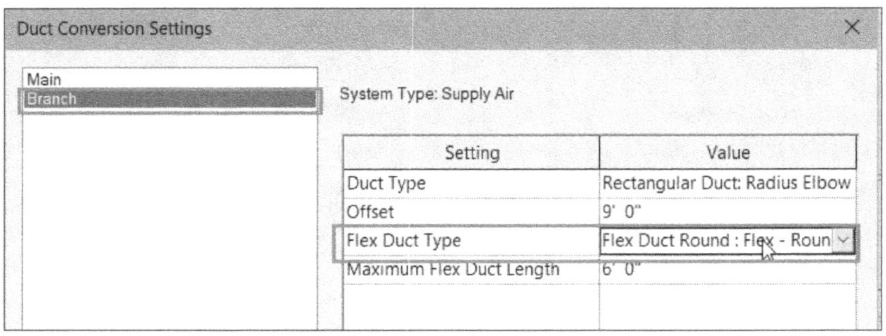

Figure-43. Converting branch ducts to flexible ducts

- Once you have set desired parameters, click on the **Finish Layout** button. The duct system will be created; refer to Figure-44. Similarly, you can create the return air system and exhaust system.

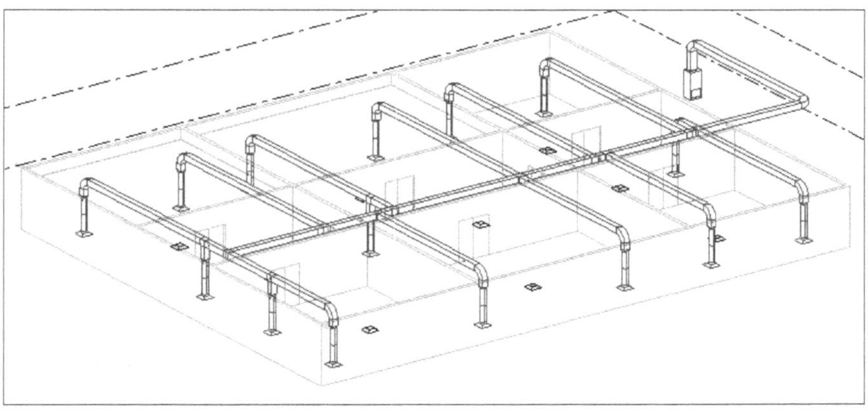

Figure-44. Duct system created

- If you find a warning in duct connections then move the air vents at appropriate locations where duct fittings can be created.

PRACTICAL (HVAC)

Create the HVAC system for the building shown in Figure-45.

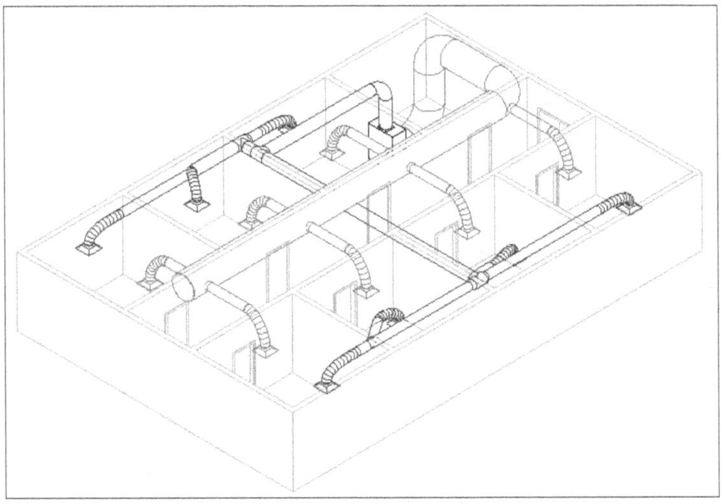

Figure-45. HVAC System for Building

Steps:

Starting a Mechanical Project and Creating Architectural Drawing

- Start Revit from the desktop or Start menu if not started yet.
- Start a new project using Mechanical Template. The environment to create mechanical system will be displayed.
- Now, we need to create architectural floor plan views for level 1 and level 2. Click on the **Floor Plan** tool from the **Plan Views** drop-down in the **Create** panel of **View** tab in the **Ribbon**. The **New Floor Plan** dialog box will be displayed; refer to Figure-46.

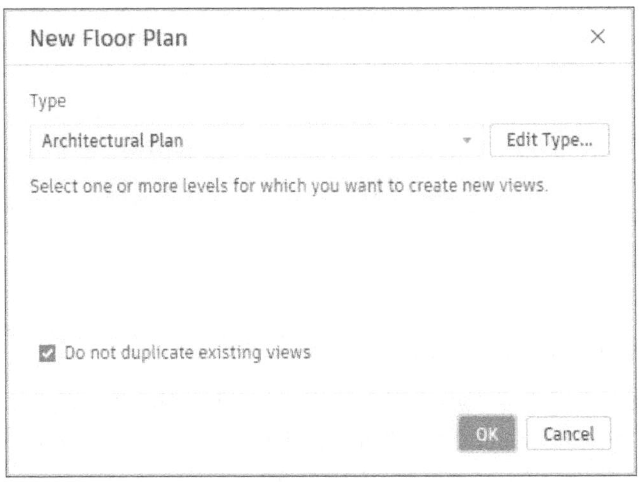

Figure-46. New Floor Plan dialog box

- Click on the **Edit Type** button from the dialog box. The **Type Properties** dialog box will be displayed; refer to Figure-47.

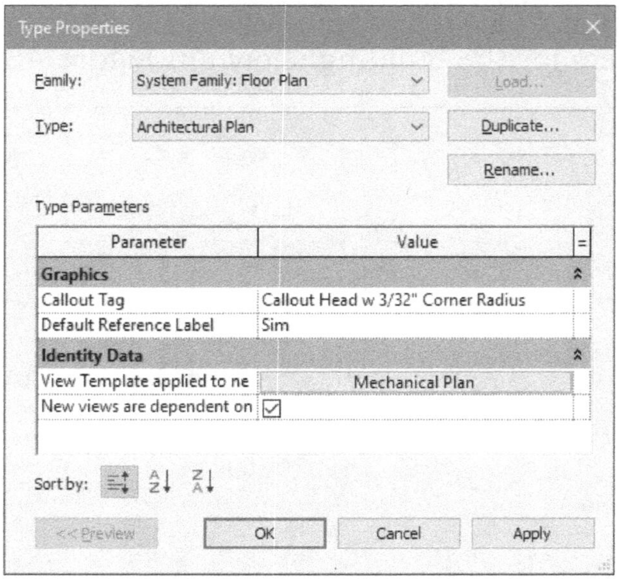

Figure-47. Type Properties dialog box

- Click on the **Mechanical Plan** button from the **Identity Date** rollout in the dialog box. The **Assign View Template** dialog box will be displayed; refer to Figure-48.

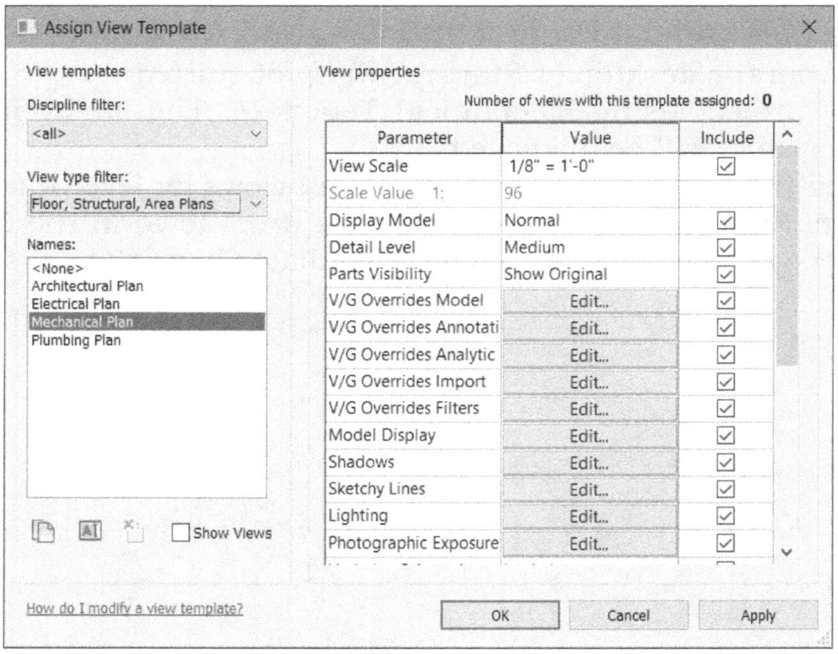

Figure-48. Assign View Template dialog box

- Select the **Architectural Plan** option from the **Names** area of the dialog box and click on the **OK** button. The **Type Properties** dialog box will be displayed again.
- Click on the **OK** button from the dialog box.
- Clear the **Do not duplicate existing views** check box and select both the levels from the dialog box. Click on the **OK** button from the dialog box. The architectural plan will be added in the **Project Browser**; refer to Figure-49.
- Double-click on the **Level 1** plan from **Floor Plans** node in **Architectural** category. The plan will be activated in drawing area.
- Create the drawing as desired; refer to Figure-50.

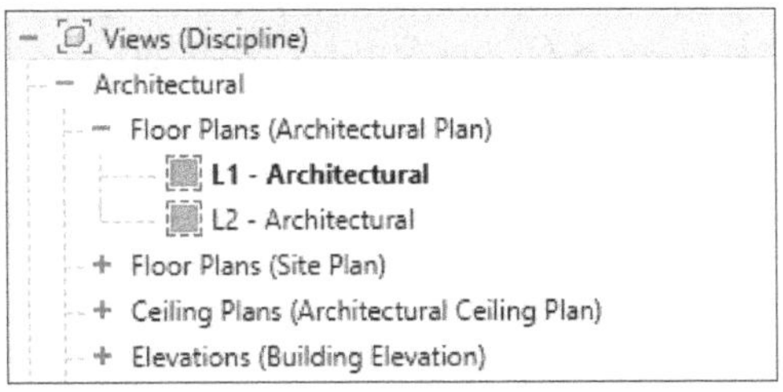

Figure-49. Architectural plan created

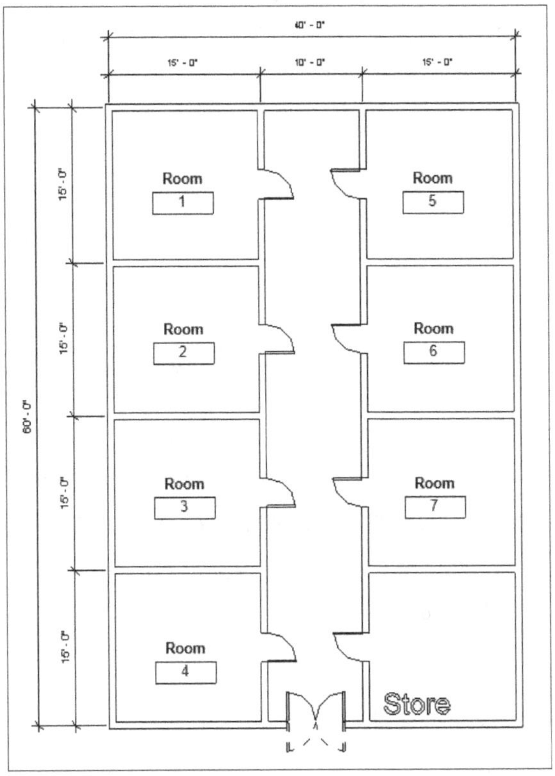

Figure-50. Room created for practical

Placing Air Handling Unit and Air Vents

- Calculate the total area for which you want to place the air handling unit. Here we have 7 rooms with 15x15 feet size. The area of each room is 225 sq feet. So the total area of all rooms to be ventilated is 1575 sq feet. We will need an AHU with minimum 1575 CFM capacity.
- Click on the **Mechanical Equipment** tool from the **Mechanical** panel in the **Systems** tab of **Ribbon**. The options to place mechanical equipment will be displayed. Load the Air Handling Units if not loaded yet in the project.
- Select the Air Handling Unit - Split System - Vertical 07 in the **Properties Palette**; refer to Figure-51.

Figure-51. Air handling unit selected

- Place the AHU in the store and press **ESC** to exit the tool.
- Click on the **Air Terminal** tool from the **HVAC** panel in the **Systems** tab of **Ribbon**. The options to place air terminal will be displayed.

- Select the **Supply Diffuser** option from the drop-down at the top in the **Properties Palette** and specify offset value from Level 1 as 8'0"; refer to Figure-52.

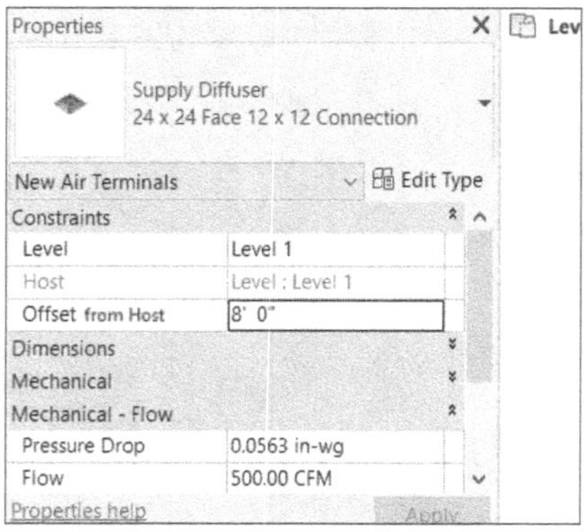

Figure-52. Parameters for supply diffuser

- Click at desired locations to place the vents; refer to Figure-53.

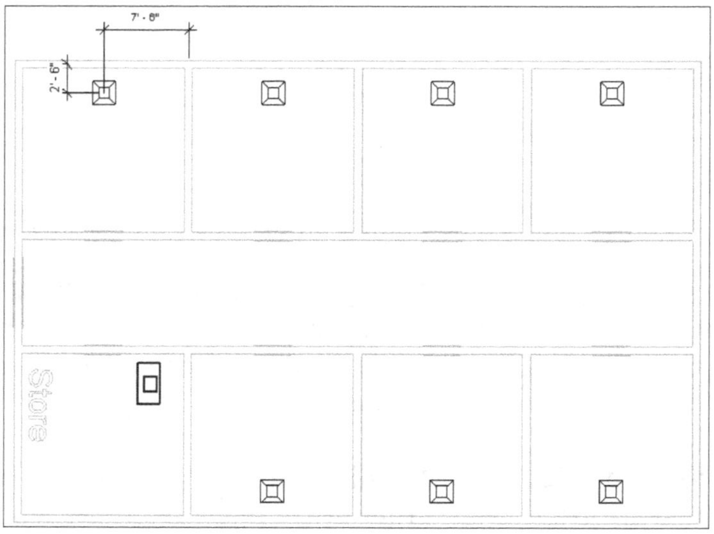

Figure-53. Diffuser vents and AHU placed

- Similarly, place the return diffusers at desired locations. Note that the CFM of return diffusers should be a little lesser than the supply diffusers; refer to Figure-54.

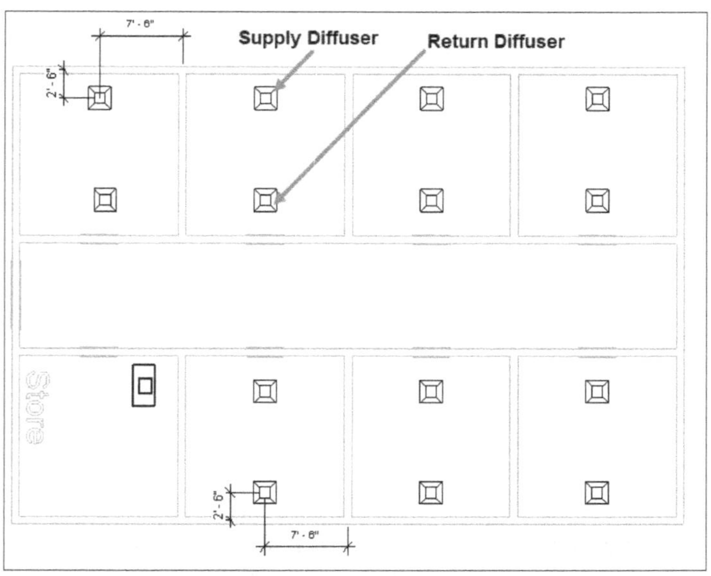

Figure-54. Return diffusers placed

Creating HVAC System

- Select all the diffuser air vents and then select the AHU. The options to create system will be displayed.
- Click on the **Duct** tool from the **Create Systems** panel of **Modify|Multi-Select** contextual tab in the **Ribbon**. The **Create Duct System** dialog box will be displayed.
- Set desired parameters and click on the **OK** button. The options to create duct layout will be displayed.
- Click on the **Generate Layout** tool from the **Layout** panel in the **Modify|Duct Systems** contextual tab of **Ribbon**. The layout will be displayed; refer to Figure-55.

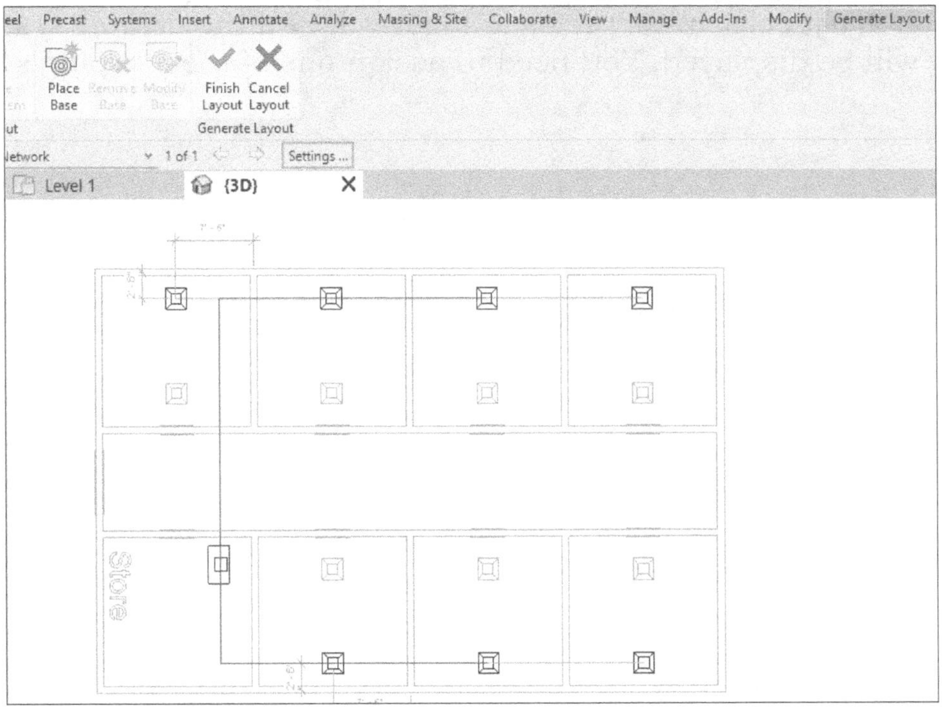

Figure-55. Options to generate layout

- Click on the **Settings** button from the **Options Bar**. The options to modify duct system will be displayed. Set the offset value as 10 feet for both main and branch ducts. Click on the **OK** button from the dialog box.
- Click on the **Finish Layout** button from the **Generate Layout** contextual tab.
- If there are warnings and errors then modify the vent locations and duct fittings as desired.
- Create the return air duct system in the same way; refer to Figure-56.

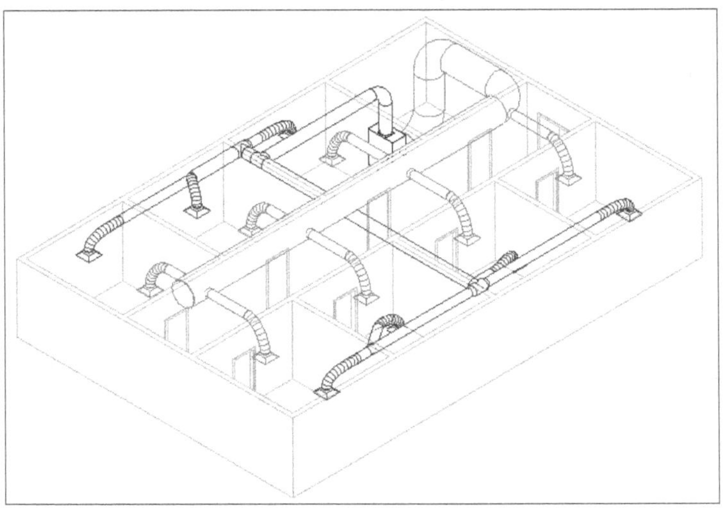

Figure-56. Return duct created

CREATING PIPING AND PLUMBING SYSTEM

The tools to create piping and plumbing system are available in the Mechanical template of Revit. The Piping system is used to create fresh water pipe lines which can be hot as well as cold. The Plumbing system is used to carry away waste water for treatment or dumping. Both the systems are created in Mechanical template of Revit. The procedure to activate plumbing floor plan and define plumbing system settings is given next.

- Expand the **Piping System** sub-node in **Piping Systems** node of the **Families** category in **Project Browser**; refer to Figure-57. All the default systems related to piping will be displayed. You need to assign one of these piping system to the pipes.

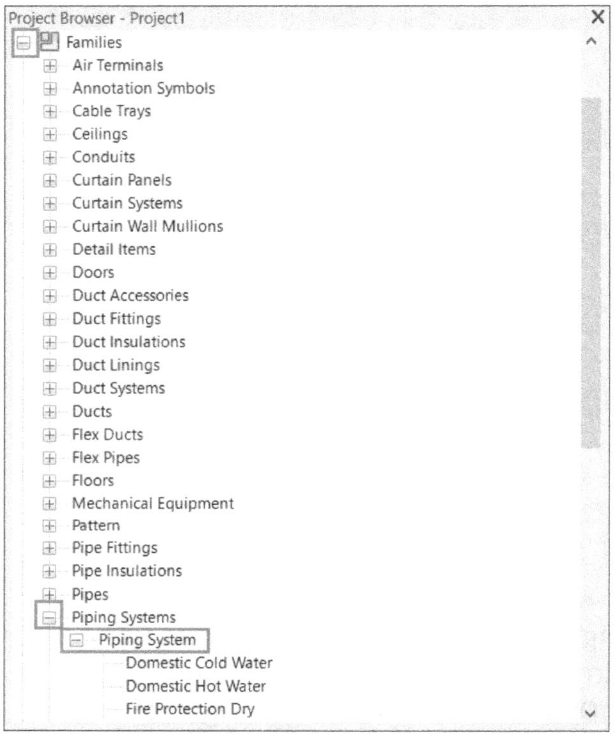

Figure-57. Default piping systems

- To modify property of any of the piping system, right-click on it. A shortcut menu will be displayed; refer to Figure-58.

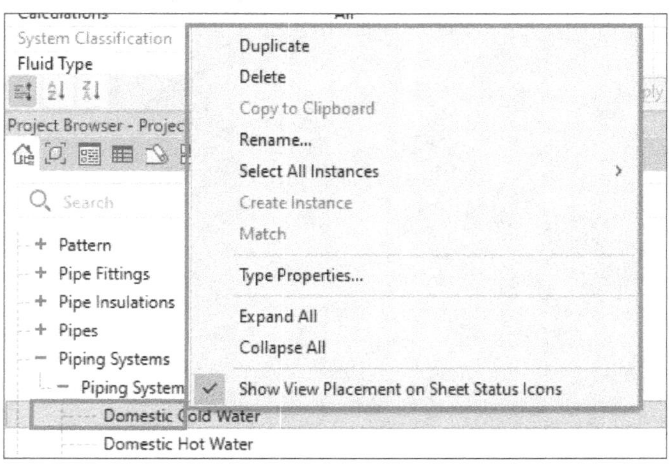

Figure-58. Shortcut menu for changing system properties

- Select the **Type Properties** option from the shortcut menu. The **Type Properties** dialog box will be displayed; refer to Figure-59.

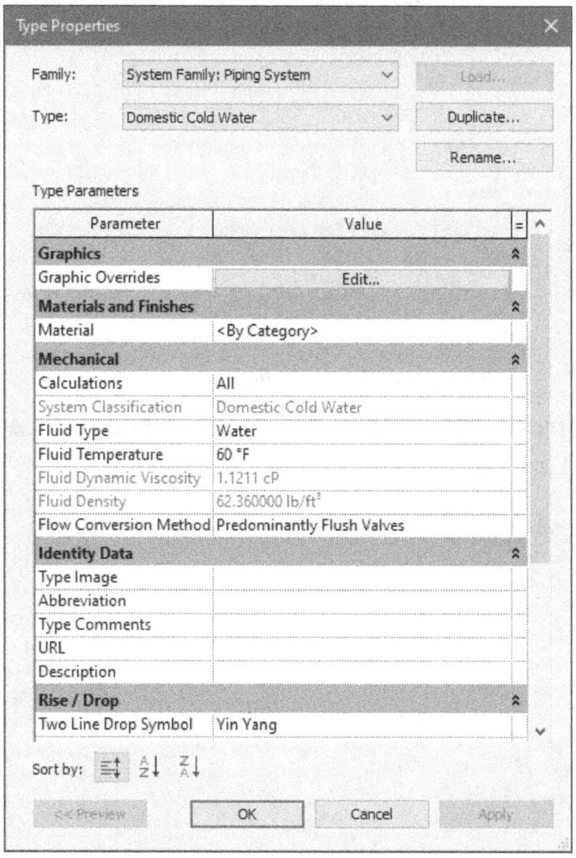

Figure-59. Type Properties dialog box

- Set desired parameters like fluid temperature, fluid type, material, and so on. If you want to change the colors of pipe lines then click on the **Edit** button for **Graphic Overrides** field of the table. The **Line Graphics** dialog box will be displayed; refer to Figure-60.

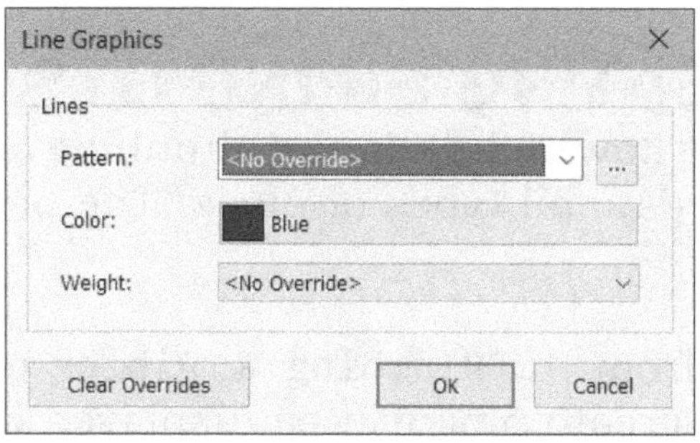

Figure-60. Line Graphics dialog box

- Set desired color, pattern, and line weight in the dialog box and click on the **OK** button. Click on the **OK** button from the **Type Properties** dialog box to apply the properties.

Activating plumbing floor plan

- Expand the nodes in **Plumbing** category of the **Views** node in **Project Browser**. The plumbing floor plans will be displayed; refer to Figure-61.

Figure-61. Plumbing floor plan

- Double-click on desired floor plan from the **Floor Plans** node to activate the drawing; refer to Figure-62.

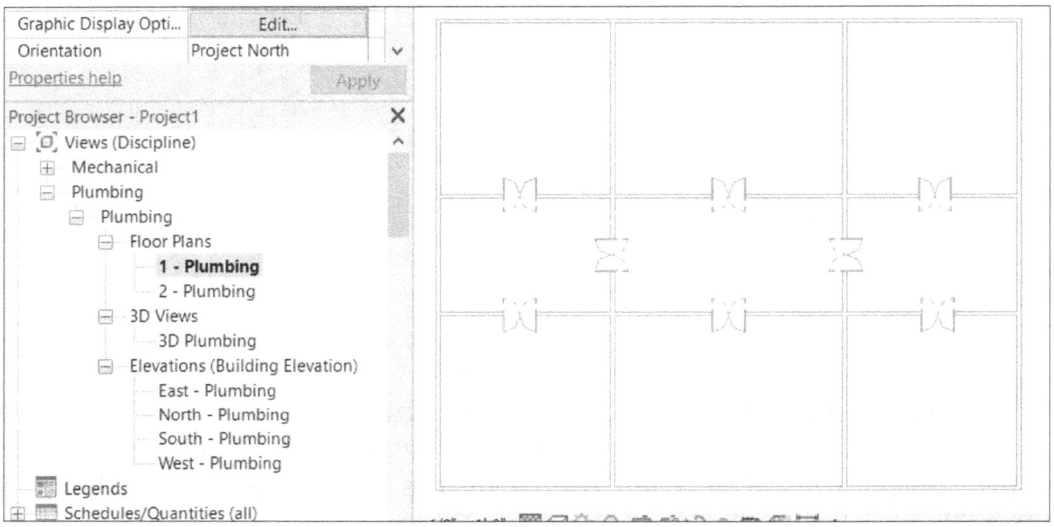

Figure-62. Plumbing floor plan activated

CREATING PIPING SYSTEM

The pipes are used to allow flow of fluid in the plumbing and piping system. In Revit, the **Pipe** tool is used to create all types of pipes. The procedure to use this tool is given next.

- Click on the **Pipe** tool from the **Plumbing & Piping** panel in the **Systems** tab of **Ribbon**. The options to create pipe will be displayed in the **Properties Palette** and **Ribbon**; refer to Figure-63.
- Set desired parameters in the **Properties Palette** like horizontal and vertical justification, offset height of pipe from selected level, system type, diameter of pipe, and so on.
- Select the **Inherit Elevation** button from the **Placement Tools** panel in the **Modify|Place Pipe** contextual tab of the **Ribbon** to make the newly created pipe have same elevation level as connecting pipe.
- Select the **Inherit Size** button from the **Placement Tools** panel in the contextual tab to make the newly created pipe have same diameter as connecting pipe.
- Select the **Add Vertical** button from the **Offset Connections** panel in the contextual tab of **Ribbon** to make vertical connection between two pipes at different elevations.

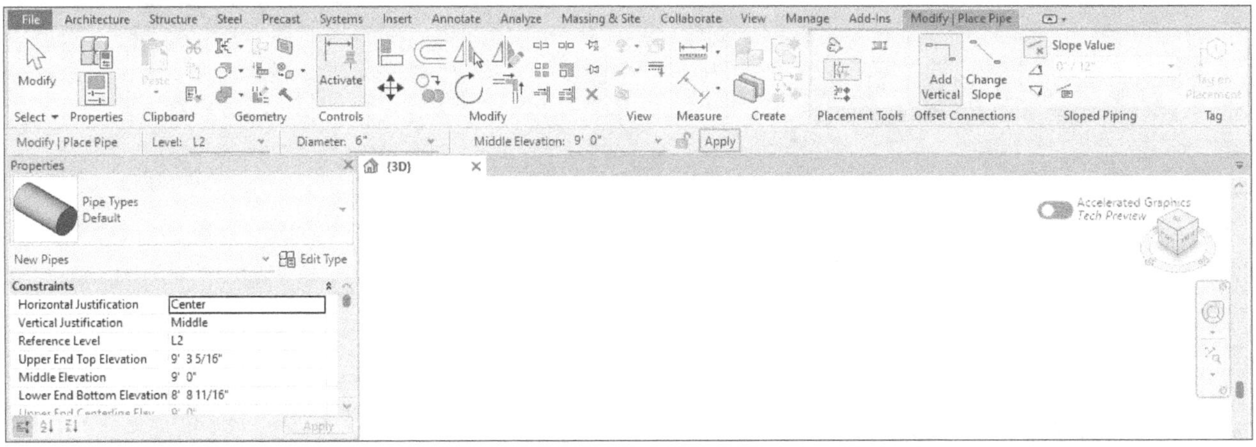

Figure-63. Options to place pipes

- Select the **Change Slope** button from the **Offset Connections** panel in the contextual tab to connect two pipes at different elevation by sloped pipe.
- Select the **Slope:Off** button from the **Sloped Piping** panel in the contextual tab to draw the pipe without slope. If you want to create inclined pipes for natural gravitational flow then select the **Slope Up** or **Slope Down** button as desired from the **Sloped Piping** panel in the contextual tab. The **Slope Value** edit box will be activated. Specify desired slope value in the edit box.
- Select the **Tag on Placement** button from the contextual tab to attach tag on pipes while creating them.
- Click at desired location to specify start point of pipe. You will be asked to specify the end point or next point of pipe.
- Click at desired location to specify next point of pipe. Once you have created the pipes, press **ESC** to exit the tool; refer to Figure-64.

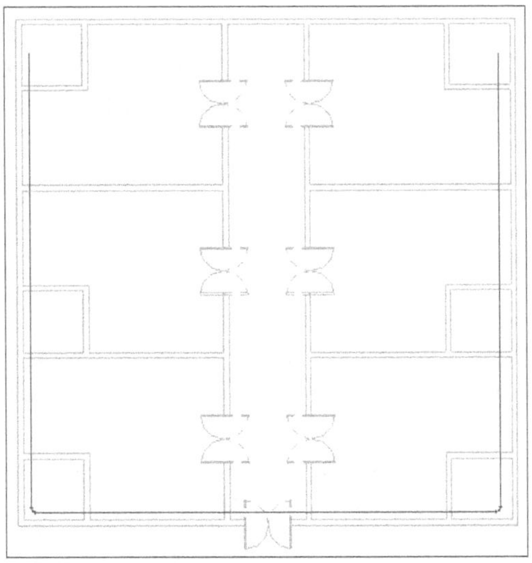

Figure-64. Pipes created

Creating Pipe Placeholder

The **Pipe Placeholder** tool is used to create schematic lines of pipe without elbow or tee. The procedure to do so is given next.

- Click on the **Pipe Placeholder** tool from the **Plumbing & Piping** panel in the **Systems** tab of **Ribbon**. The options to create pipe placeholder will be displayed; refer to Figure-65.

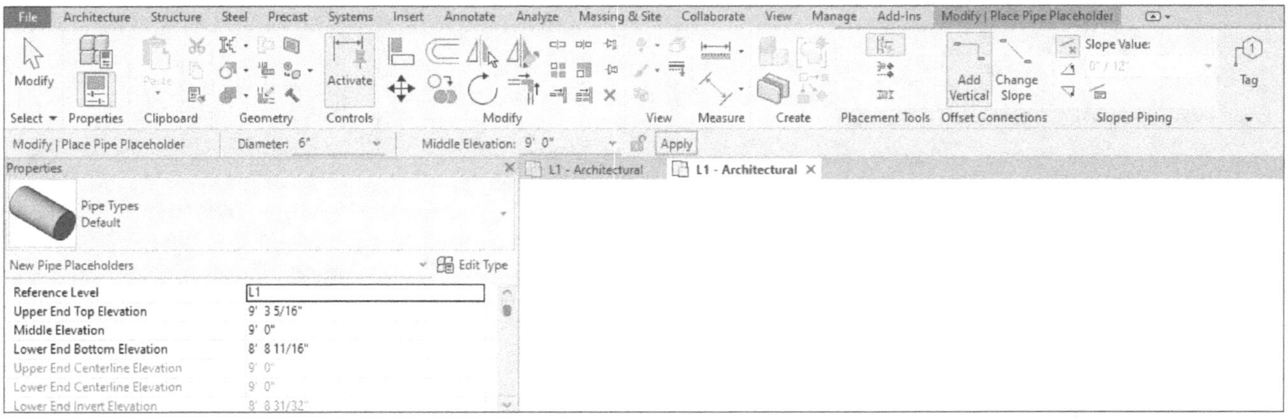

Figure-65. Options for creating pipe placeholder

- Set desired parameters in the **Properties Palette** and **Modify|Place Pipe Placeholder** contextual tab.
- Click at desired location to specify the start point. You will be asked to specify the next point.
- Click at desired locations to specify next points of placeholders. Press **ESC** to exit the tool.

Once you have created placeholders, select them, and click on the **Convert Placeholder** tool from the **Edit** panel in the **Modify|Pipe Placeholders** contextual tab of **Ribbon** to convert them into pipes.

Creating Parallel Pipes

The **Parallel Pipes** tool is used to create parallel pipes for selected pipe. The procedure to use this tool is given next.

- Click on the **Parallel Pipes** tool from the **Plumbing & Piping** panel of **Systems** tab in the **Ribbon**. The options to create parallel pipes will be displayed; refer to Figure-66.

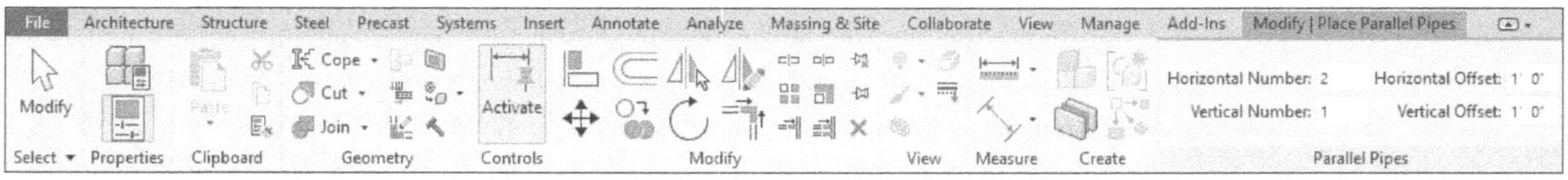

Figure-66. Modify Place Parallel Pipes contextual tab

- Specify desired value in **Horizontal Number** edit box to define number instances in horizontal direction.
- Specify the distance between two instances of parallel pipes in the **Horizontal Offset** edit box. Similarly, you can specify parameters in **Vertical Number** and **Vertical Offset** edit boxes.
- Click on desired pipe to create its multiple instances. The parallel pipes will be created; refer to Figure-67.

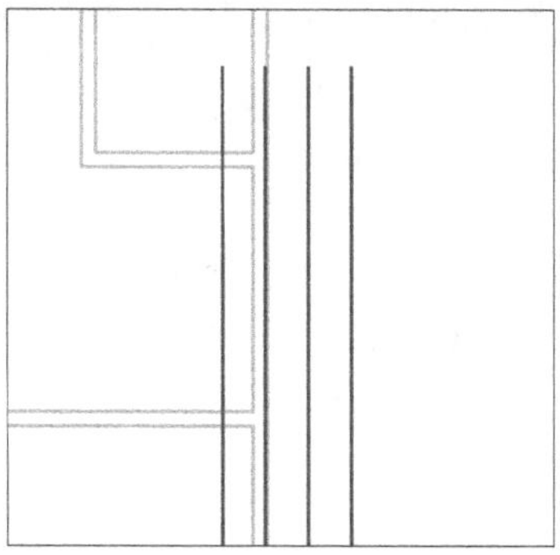

Figure-67. Parallel pipes created

Placing Pipe Fittings

The **Pipe Fitting** tool is used to place fittings like tee, elbow, cross, and union in the pipe line. The procedure to use this tool is given next.

- Click on the **Pipe Fitting** tool from the **Plumbing & Piping** panel in the **Systems** tab of **Ribbon**. The options to place pipe fitting will be displayed; refer to Figure-68.

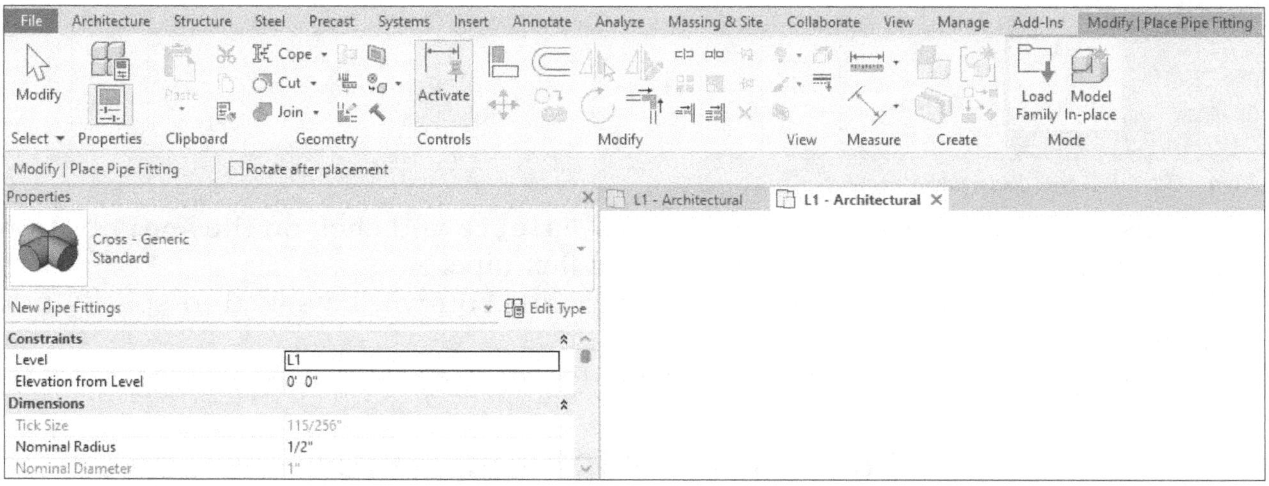

Figure-68. Options to place pipe fitting

- If there is no fitting loaded in project then a warning message will be displayed asking you to load fittings. Load desired fitting as discussed earlier.
- Select desired fitting from the drop-down at the top in the **Properties Palette**. Set desired parameters in the **Properties Palette** and **Ribbon**.
- Click at desired location to place the fitting.

Placing Pipe Accessories

The **Pipe Accessory** tool is used to place piping accessory like valve, in-line heater, and so on. The procedure to place pipe accessory is given next.

- Click on the **Pipe Accessory** tool from the **Plumbing & Piping** panel in the **Systems** tab of **Ribbon**. If there is no accessory loaded in the project then load desired accessory as discussed earlier.
- Select desired accessory from the drop-down at the top in **Properties Palette** and set desired parameters.
- Click at desired location to place pipe accessory. You can connect the piping later to this accessory.

Creating Flex Pipe

The **Flex Pipe** tool is used create flexible pipe in plumbing and piping system. The procedure to create flex pipe is given next.

- Click on the **Flex Pipe** tool from the **Plumbing & Piping** panel of **Systems** tab in **Ribbon**. The options to create flexible pipe will be displayed; refer to Figure-69.

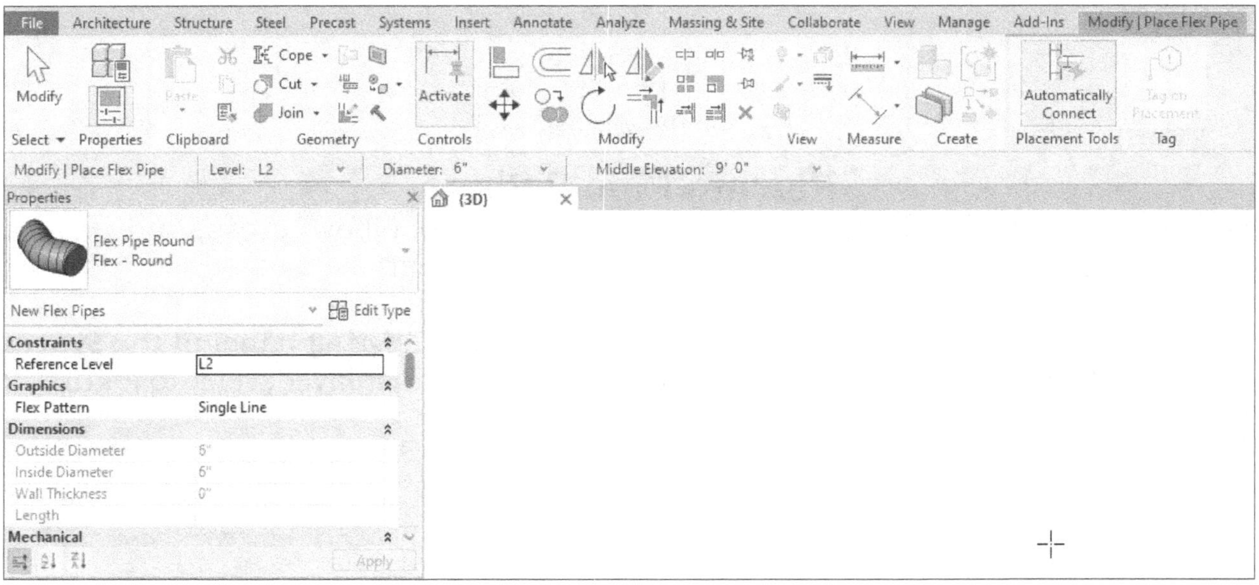

Figure-69. Options to create flexible pipe

- Set desired parameters in the **Properties Palette** and click on the **Apply** button. You will be asked to specify start point of flex pipe.
- Click at desired location to specify start point. You will be asked to specify next point.
- Click to specify the points and press **ESC** to exit the tool.

Placing Plumbing Equipment

The **Plumbing Equipment** tool is used to place plumbing equipment such as hot water heater, domestic water pump, and so on. The procedure is similar to placing mechanical equipment as discussed earlier.

Placing Plumbing Fixture

The **Plumbing Fixture** tool is used to place fixtures like water closet, sinks, tubs, and so on. The procedure to place plumbing fixture is given next.

- Click on the **Plumbing Fixture** tool from the **Plumbing & Piping** panel in the **Systems** tab of **Ribbon**. Load the fixtures if they are not loaded already. The options to place plumbing fixture will be displayed; refer to Figure-70.

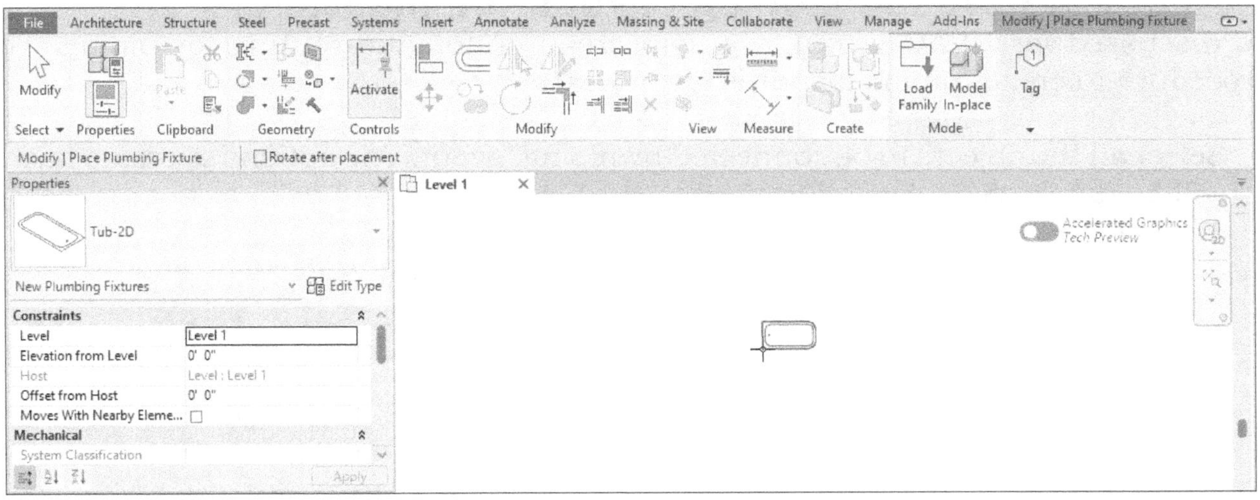

Figure-70. Options to place plumbing fixture

- Select desired fixture from the drop-down at the top in the **Properties Palette** and set desired parameter.
- Select the **Rotate after placement** check box from the **Options Bar** if you want to rotate the fixture after placing it.
- Click at desired location to place the fixture.
- Press **ESC** to exit the tool.

Placing Sprinklers

The **Sprinkler** tool is used to place sprinklers at desired location. The procedure to do so is given next.

- Click on the **Sprinkler** tool from the **Plumbing & Piping** panel in the **Systems** tab of **Ribbon**. The options to place sprinklers will be displayed; refer to Figure-71.
- Select desired sprinkler from the drop-down at the top in the **Properties Palette** and set desired parameters.
- Click on the face of wall where you want to place the sprinkler.
- Press **ESC** to exit the tool.

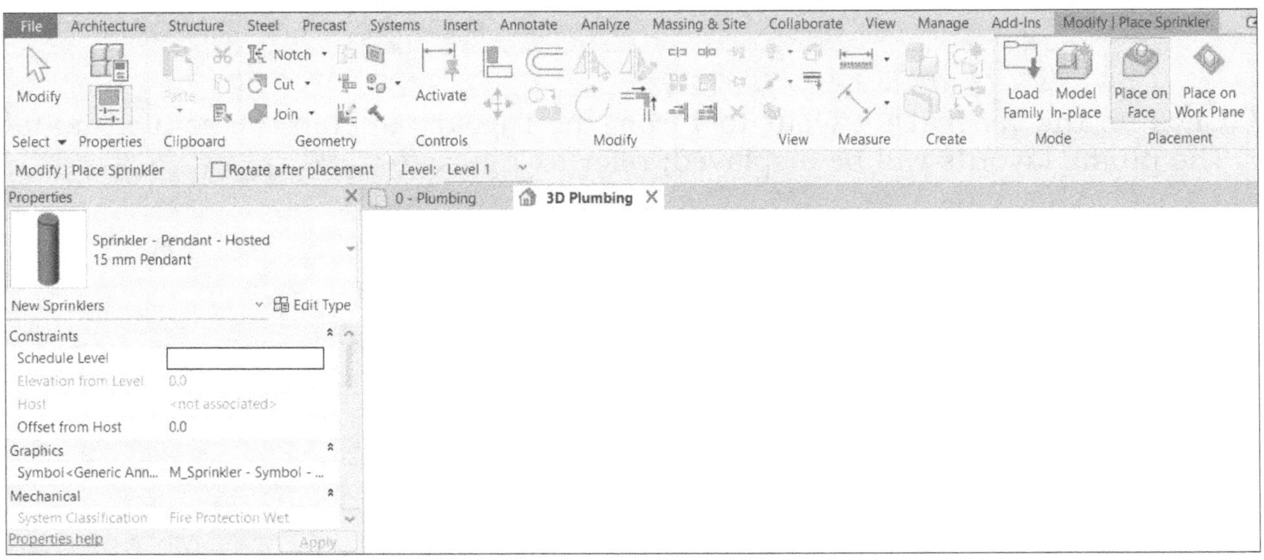

Figure-71. Options to place sprinklers

Creating Piping Layout Automatically

As discussed for HVAC layout, you can create automatic routing for piping. The procedure to create piping layout is given next.

- Select all the objects to be connected by piping layout. The options to create layout will be displayed; refer to Figure-72.

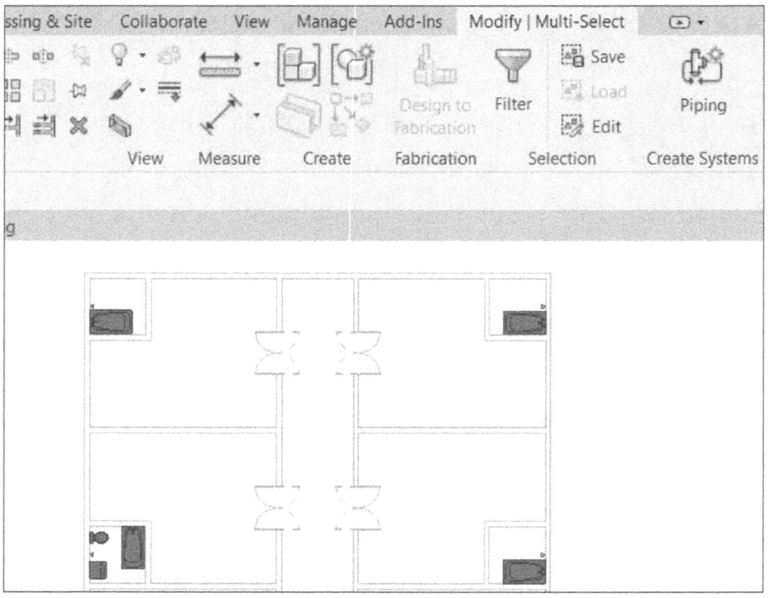

Figure-72. Option to create piping system

- Click on the **Piping** tool from the **Create Systems** panel in the **Modify|Multi-Select** contextual tab of **Ribbon**. The **Create Piping System** dialog box will be displayed.
- Select desired system type from the **System type** drop-down in the dialog box and click on the **OK** button. The options to generate layout will be displayed in the **Ribbon**; refer to Figure-73.

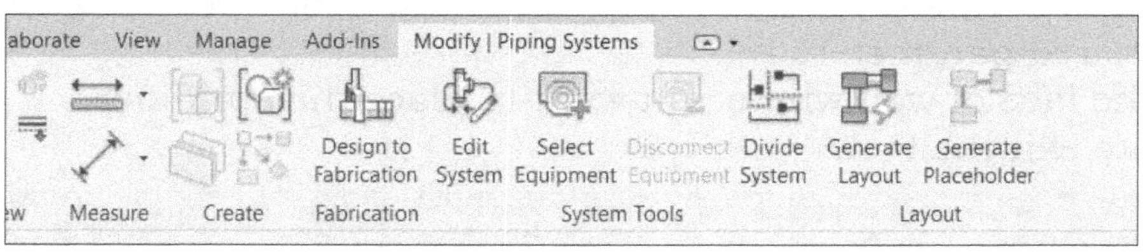

Figure-73. Options to generate piping layout

- Click on the **Generate Layout** tool from the **Layout** panel in the contextual tab. The piping layouts will be displayed; refer to Figure-74.

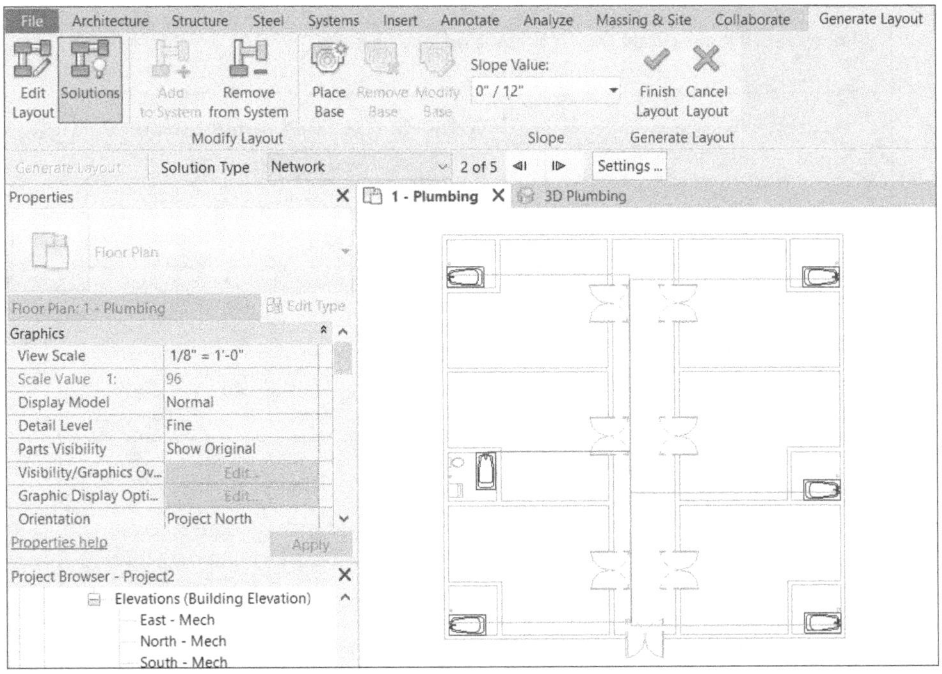

Figure-74. Preview of layouts

- Click on the **Finish Layout** button from the contextual tab to create the piping layout.

To modify settings related to piping system, click on the inclined arrow button in **Plumbing & Piping** panel of the **Systems** tab in **Ribbon**. The **Mechanical Settings** dialog box will be displayed. The options of this dialog box have been discussed earlier.

BASICS OF PIPING/PLUMBING SYSTEM

Plumbing system is used in buildings to supply water through various outlets. This water need to be drained out after use. A drainage system is used to drain out the water from the building. Drainage system is also used to drain out human wastes from the building. For plumbing system designer, plumbing and drainage systems are two sides of a coin. Piping systems are used in residential as well as commercial sites to supply and drain various fluids and gases like methane, oxygen, sulfuric acid, and so on. In Revit software, these two terms are quite mixed when using tools of **Ribbon** so knowingly we had to write Piping system in place of plumbing and drainage system in this chapter.

In any plumbing or piping system, a fixture unit value is assigned to all the fixtures based on their rate of fluid consumption during total usage hours. This value determines the size of pipe connected to them. If you want to consider simultaneous use of various fixtures connected to a single pipe in your design, then you need to increase the size of pipe accordingly. Generally, a total flow rate of all the units connected to a pipe is multiplied by factor 0.6 to 0.7 for designing cost efficient system. After determining the fixtures to be installed and pipe sizes to be selected, the next thing to consider for designing is maintaining water pressure in the system. Generally, gravity storage tank is used to supply water in piping system. The gravity method is adequate if number of users are low but if there are a lot of fixtures for water outlet then you can consider booster pump sets in your design. Figure-75 shows acceptable flow rates (per second) for some common fixtures.

Acceptable flow rates for fixtures and appliances

Fixture	Flow rate (l/s) and temperature °C
Basin	0.1 at 45 °C
Bath	0.3 at 45°C
Sink	0.2 at 60°C (hot) and 0.2 (cold)
Shower	0.1 at 42°C
Laundry tub	0.2 at 60°C (hot) and 0.2 (cold)
Dishwasher and washing machine	0.20

Figure-75. Common flow rates

When planning a water supply layout, the following must be considered:

- Pipe runs and lengths – Keep pipe runs as short as possible. Pass pipes close to fixtures to minimise the number of branches and unnecessary elbows, tees and joints. Having longer pipe runs and more fixtures will reduce flow rate, increase heat losses, and increase use of materials.
- Point of entry into the building – This should be into a utility space such as garage/ laundry and include an accessible isolating valve, line strainer, and pressure limiting valve (if required).
- Water heating system – Locate centrally to reduce the length of pipe runs to fixtures because longer pipe runs require more water to be drawn off before hot water is discharged. Install a separate point-of-use water heater for fixtures that are more than 10 m from the main water heater.
- Noise prevention – Avoid running pipes over or near bedrooms and living areas.

Note that material of pipe should not contaminate potable water supply. Some of the common materials used for domestic supply are CPVC, copper, polybutylene (PB), polyethylene (PE), polypropylene (PP-3 or PP Type 3), and cross-linked polyethylene (PEX).

The information provided here for designing a plumbing/piping system is just a drop of ocean. You must always check the local construction codes when designing a system in building.

Practical (Piping)

The base file for this practical is shown in Figure-76. Download the file from resource kit. Create the piping and plumbing system with related equipment like bath tub, bidet, sink, kitchen equipment, and so on.

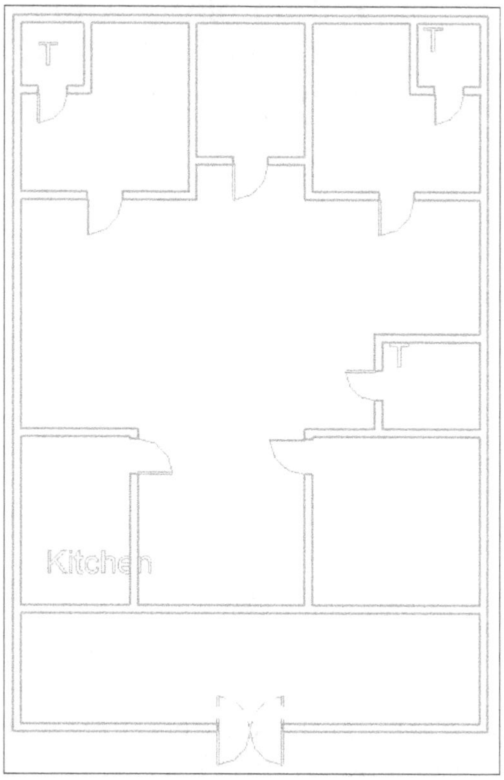

Figure-76. Architectural layout

Starting Mechanical Project with Architectural Layout

- Open the file with architectural layout of this practical and copy all the elements of architectural plan at level 1.
- Start a new file with Mechanical template.
- Paste the copied architectural plan at level 1 of mechanical project; refer to Figure-77.

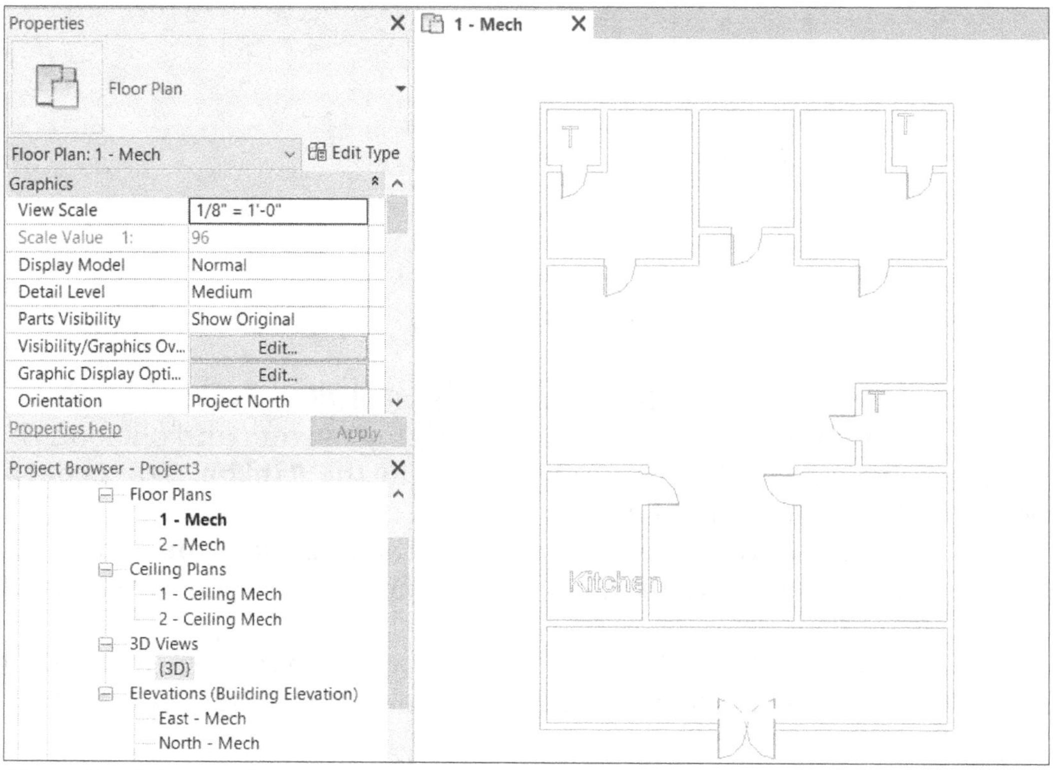

Figure-77. Architectural plan pasted on Mech level

Placing Plumbing Fixture

- Click on the **Plumbing Fixture** tool from the **Plumbing & Piping** panel of **Systems** tab in the **Ribbon**. The options to place plumbing fixtures will be displayed; refer to Figure-78.

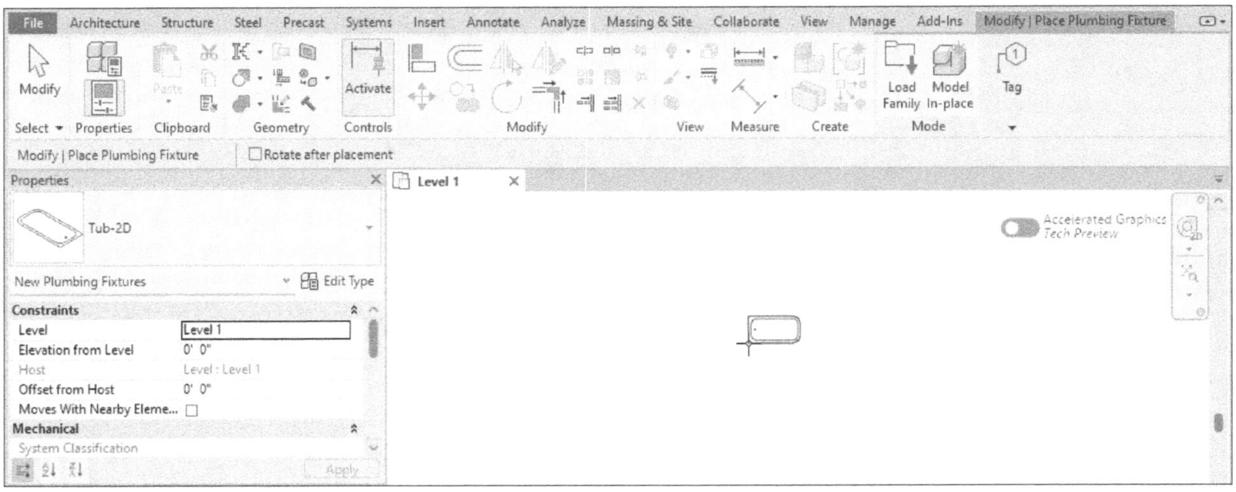

Figure-78. Options to place plumbing equipment

- Load the fixtures like bath tub, sink, kitchen unit, water closet, and so on in the Project. Place the fixtures as shown in Figure-79.

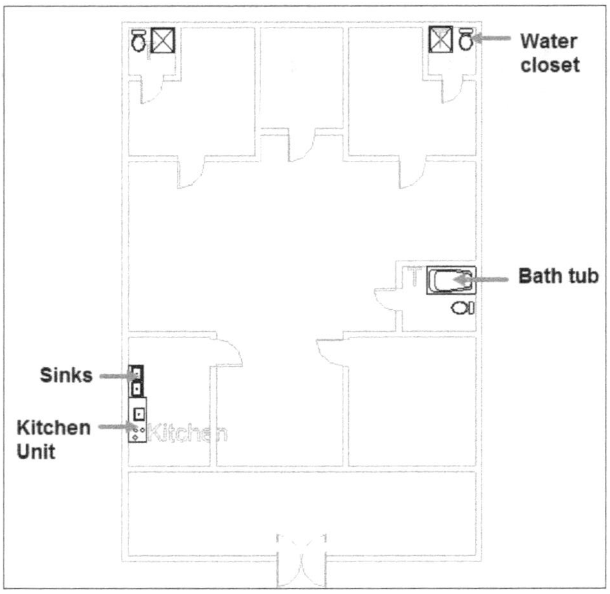

Figure-79. After placing plumbing fixture

Creating Piping Systems

- Select all the equipment to be connected by piping system and click on the **Piping** tool from the **Create Systems** contextual tab in the **Ribbon**. The **Create Piping System** dialog box will be displayed.
- Select the **Domestic Cold Water** option from the **System type** drop-down in the dialog box and click on the **OK** button. The options to generate layout will be displayed.
- Click on the **Generate Layout** tool from the **Layout** panel in the **Modify|Piping System** contextual tab of **Ribbon**. The options to generate layout will be displayed; refer to Figure-80.

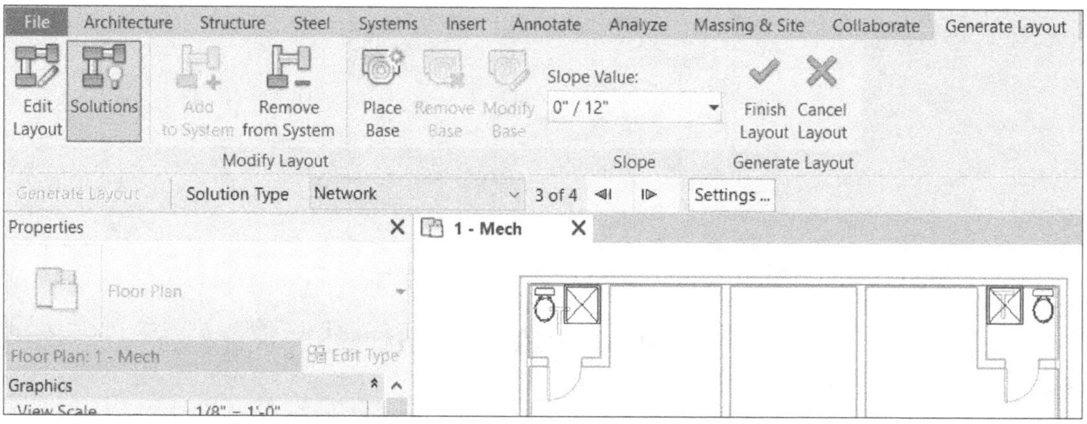

Figure-80. Generate Layout contextual tab

- Switch between the solutions till you find the suitable one. Set desired value of slope in **Slope Value** drop-down. The specified slope will allow natural flow of fluid through pipe. After setting desired parameters, click on the **Finish Layout** tool from the **Generate Layout** contextual tab in the **Ribbon**. The piping layout will be created; refer to Figure-81.

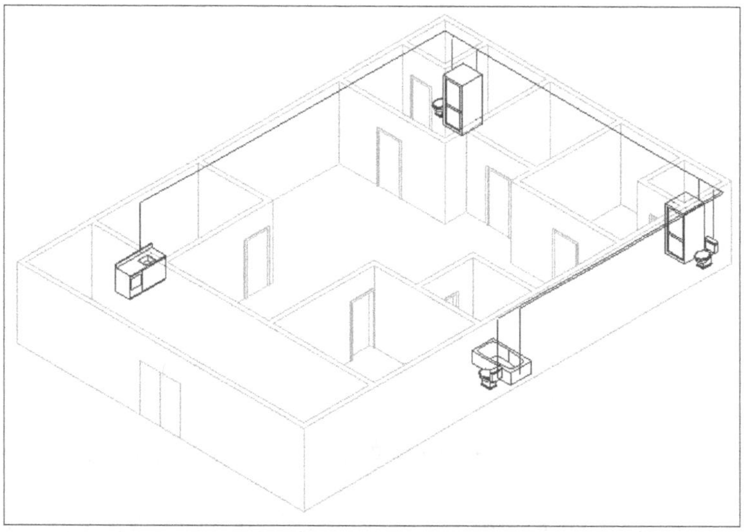

Figure-81. Piping layout created

- Create the sanitary system piping layout in the same way as discussed earlier. Make sure to set the level for piping at 0 or below the level of fixtures.
- If errors are displayed then change the locations of fixtures or modify the fittings.
- Save the project file at desired location

CREATING ELECTRICAL LAYOUT

The tools to create electrical layout of a building are available in the **Electrical** panel of **Systems** tab in the **Ribbon**. The electrical wiring is created in architectural template. You can also use Systems template to create layout. Various tools in this panel are discussed next.

Creating Wires

There are three types of wires in the **Wire** drop-down of **Electrical** panel: **Arc Wire**, **Spline Wire**, and **Chamfered Wire**; refer to Figure-82. These tools are discussed next.

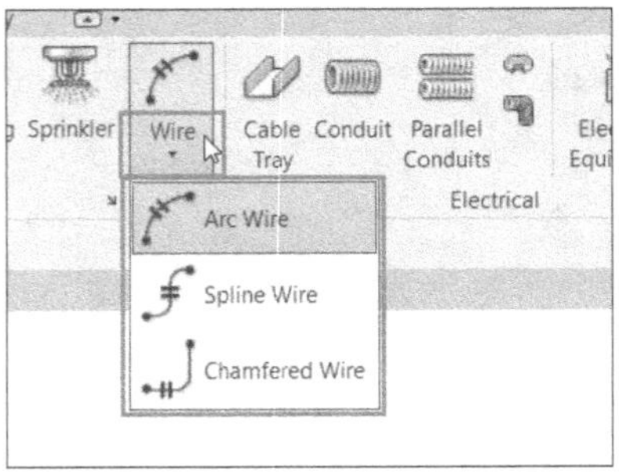

Figure-82. Wire drop-down

Creating Arc Wire

The procedure to create an arc wire is given next.

- Click on the **Arc Wire** tool from the **Wire** drop-down in the **Electrical** panel of **Systems** tab in the **Ribbon**. You will be asked to specify start point of arc wire and options to place wire will be displayed in the **Ribbon**; refer to Figure-83.

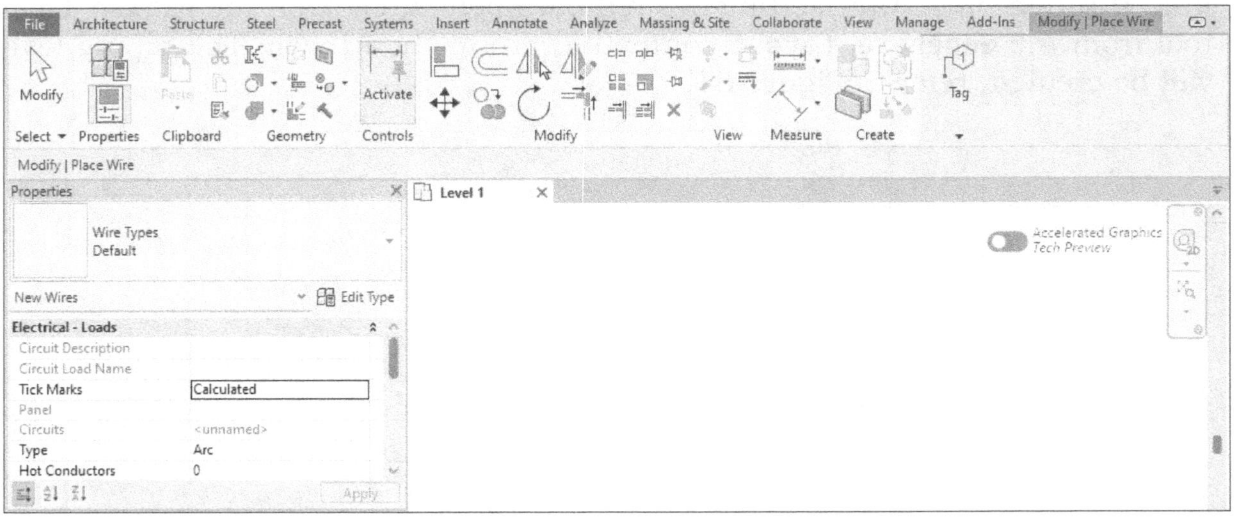

Figure-83. Options to place wire

- Set desired parameters in the **Properties Palette** like number of hot, neutral, and ground conductors, type of wire, and so on.
- Click at desired location to specify start point of wire. You will be asked to specify mid point of the wire.
- Click to specify the mid point. You will be asked to specify end point of the wire.
- Click to specify end point. The wire will be created; refer to Figure-84.

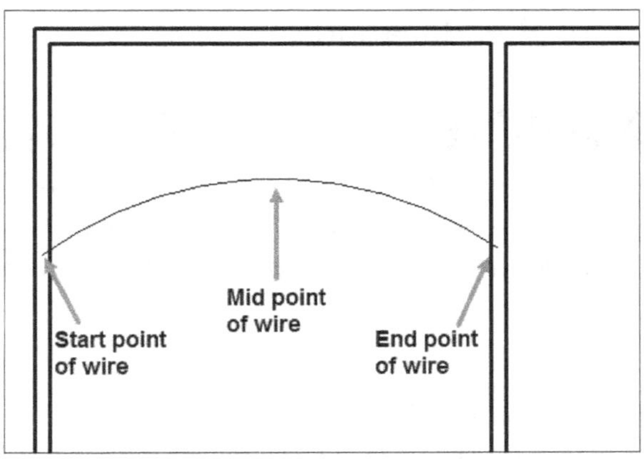

Figure-84. Arc wire created

- Press **ESC** to exit the tool.

Creating Spline Wire

The **Spline Wire** tool is used to create wire in the form of spline. The procedure to use this tool is given next.

- Click on the **Spline Wire** tool from the **Wire** drop-down in the **Electrical** panel of **Systems** tab in **Ribbon**. You will be asked to specify start point of spline wire.
- Click at desired location to specify start point of spline wire. You will be asked to specify next point of spline.
- Create the wire by specifying desired points; refer to Figure-85 and press **ESC** to exit the tool.

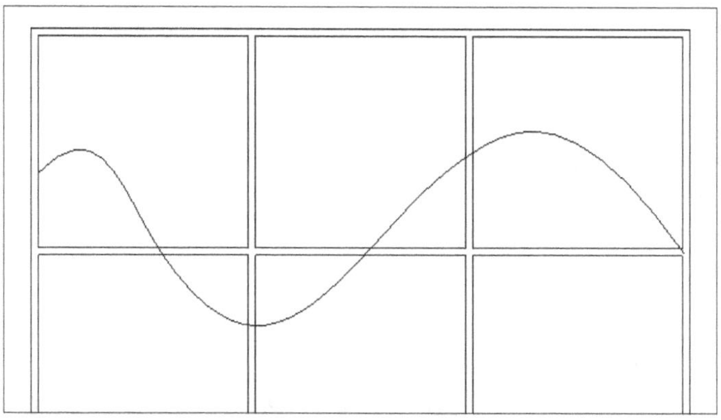

Figure-85. Spline wire created

Creating Chamfered Wire

The **Chamfered Wire** tool is used to create chamfered wires. The procedure to use this tool is given next.

- Click on the **Chamfered Wire** tool from the **Wire** drop-down in the **Electrical** panel of **Systems** tab in the **Ribbon**. You will be asked to specify start point of wire.
- Set desired options for wire as discussed earlier.
- Click to specify start point of wire. You will be asked to specify next point.
- Create the chamfered wire as per your requirement; refer to Figure-86.

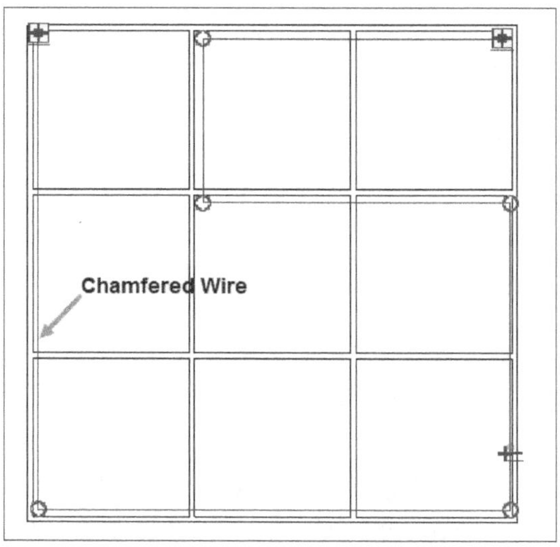

Figure-86. Chamfered wire created

Creating Cable Tray

The **Cable Tray** tool is used to create cable tray with and without fittings. The procedure to create cable tray is given next.

- Click on the **Cable Tray** tool from the **Electrical** panel in the **Systems** tab of **Ribbon**. The options to create cable tray will be displayed; refer to Figure-87.

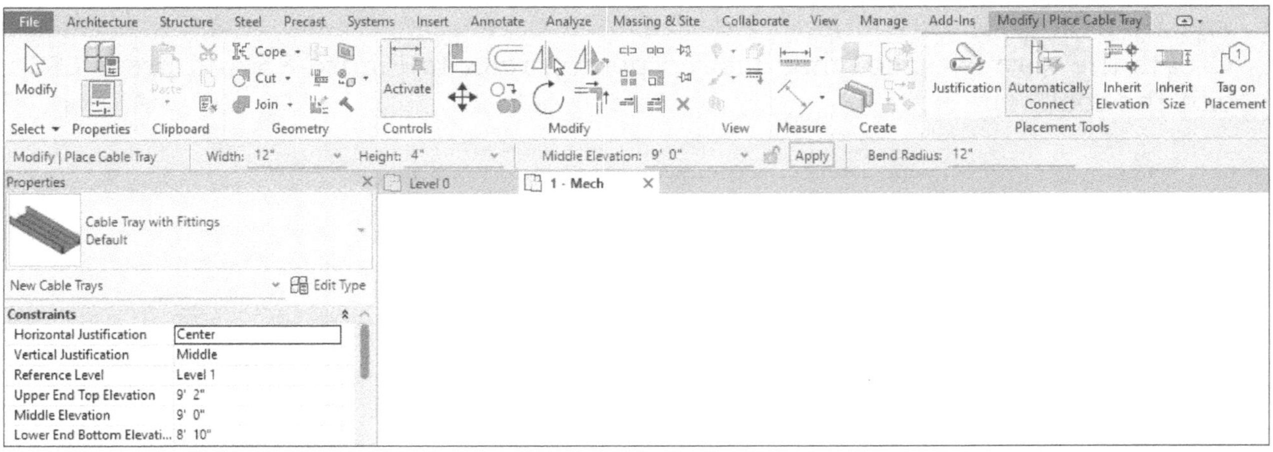

Figure-87. Options to create cable tray

- Set desired parameters in the **Properties Palette** and **Options Bar** like width & height of cable tray, height of cable tray from selected reference level, rung space, and so on.
- Click to specify the start point of cable tray. You will be asked to specify end point of cable tray.
- Click at desired location to specify end point. The cable tray will be created; refer to Figure-88.

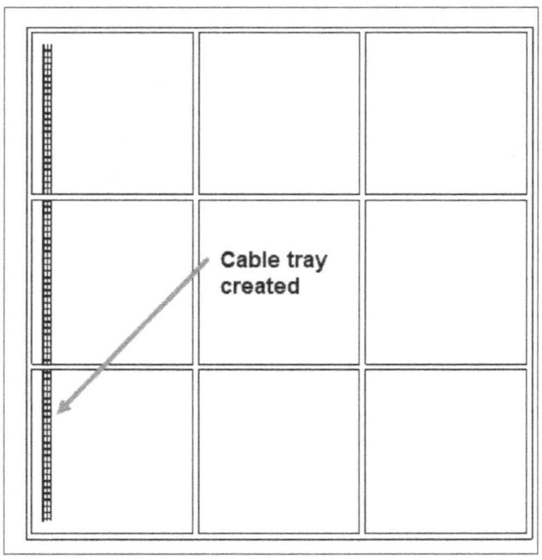

Figure-88. Cable tray created

- Press **ESC** to exit the cable tray creation mode.

Creating Conduits

The **Conduit** tool is used to create rigid conduits for wirings. The procedure to use this tool is given next.

- Click on the **Conduit** tool from the **Electrical** panel in the **Systems** tab of **Ribbon**. The options to create conduit will be displayed; refer to Figure-89.

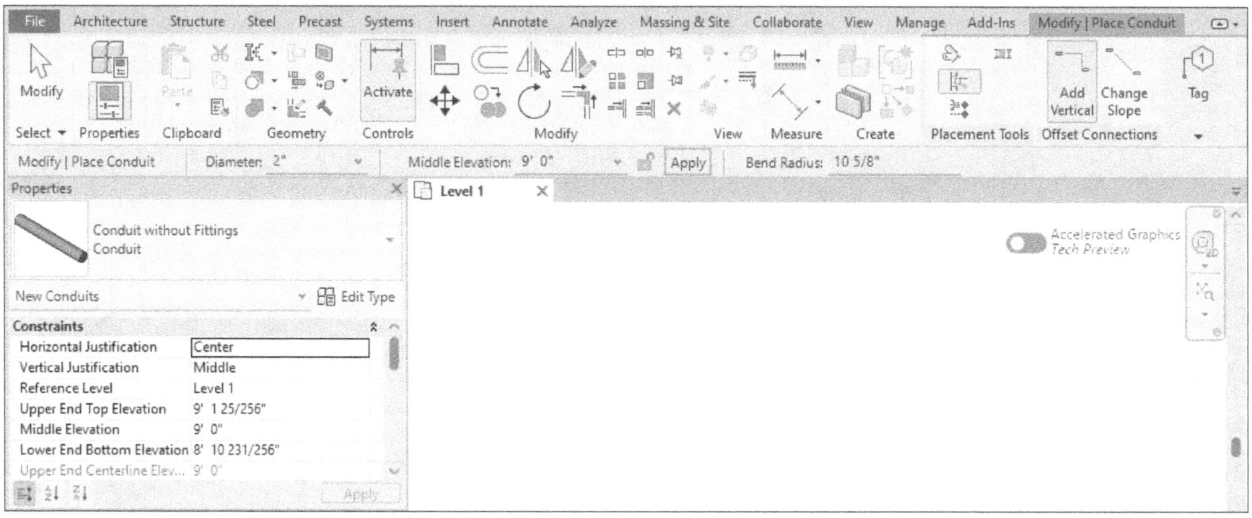

Figure-89. Options to place conduits

- Set desired parameters in the **Properties Palette** and create the conduit as discussed for cable tray.
- Press **ESC** to exit the tool. Note that conduits are by default available in the Power Floor Plans but you can make them visible in any view by using the **Visibility/ Graphics** tool.

Creating Parallel Conduits

The **Parallel Conduits** tool is used to create multiple parallel conduits based on selected conduit. The procedure to create parallel conduit is discussed next.

- Click on the **Parallel Conduits** tool from the **Electrical** panel in the **Systems** tab of **Ribbon**. The options to create parallel conduit will be displayed; refer to Figure-90.

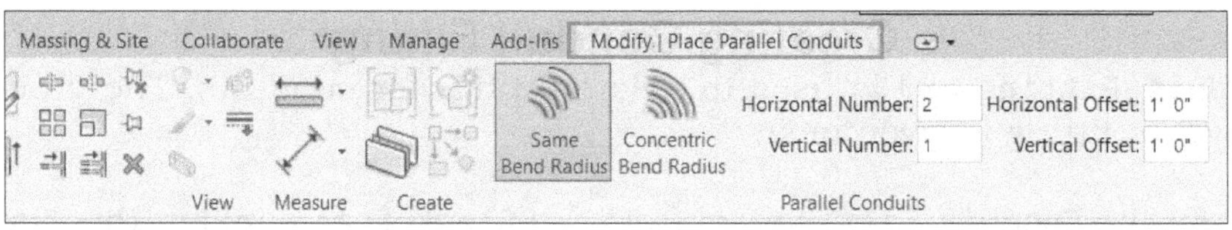

Figure-90. Options to place parallel conduit

- Set desired parameters in the contextual tab like number of conduits parallel in horizontal direction, distance between two instances, and so on.
- Click on the conduit from graphics area for which you want to create parallel conduits.
- Press **ESC** to exit the tool.

Creating Cable Tray Fitting

The **Cable Tray Fitting** tool is used to create different type of fittings like bends, crosses, tees, and so on. The procedure to create cable tray fitting is given next.

- Click on the **Cable Tray Fitting** tool from the **Electrical** panel in the **Systems** tab of **Ribbon**. The options to create cable tray fitting will be displayed; refer to Figure-91.

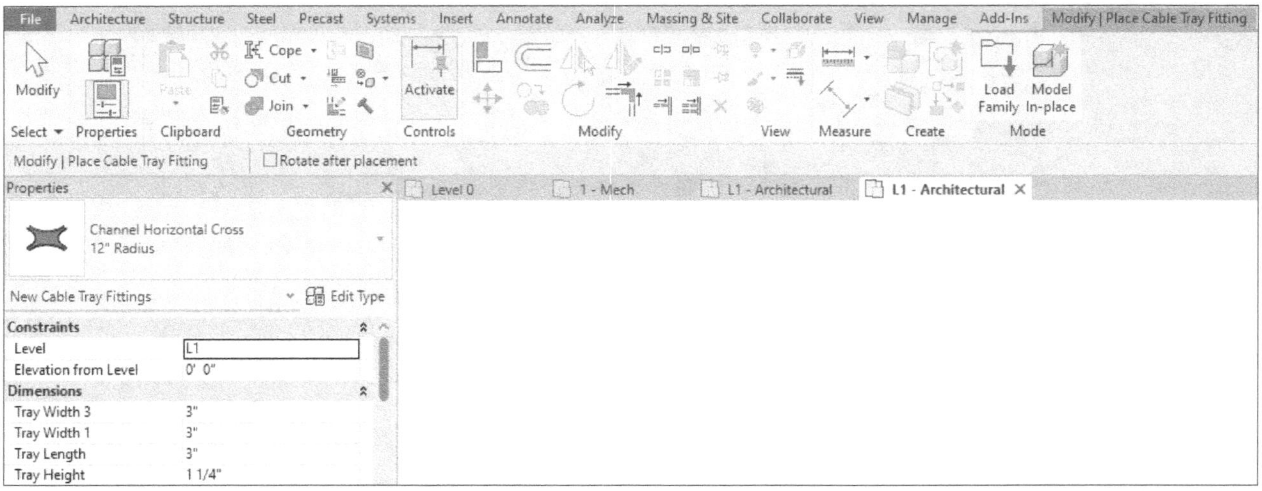

Figure-91. Options to place cable tray fittings

- Load desired types of cable tray fittings as discussed earlier.
- Set desired parameters in the **Properties Palette** and click on the cable tray to which you want to attach the fitting; refer to Figure-92.

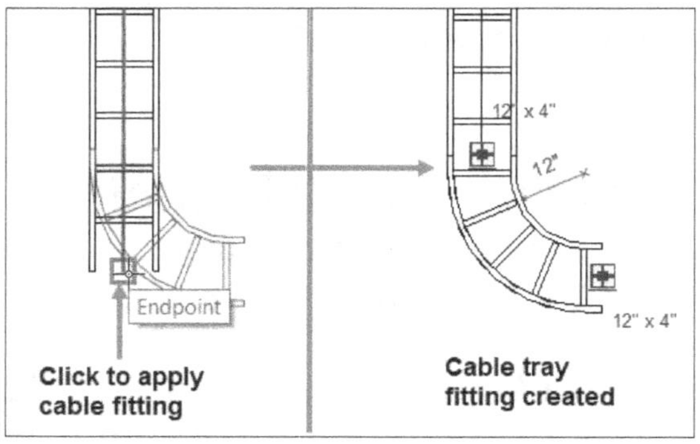

Figure-92. Cable tray fitting created

Creating Conduit Fitting

The **Conduit Fitting** tool is used to create fittings for conduits. The procedure to place conduit fitting is given next.

- Click on the **Conduit Fitting** tool from the **Electrical** panel in the **Systems** tab of **Ribbon**. You will be asked to load fittings.
- Load desired fittings. The options to place conduit fitting will be displayed; refer to Figure-93.

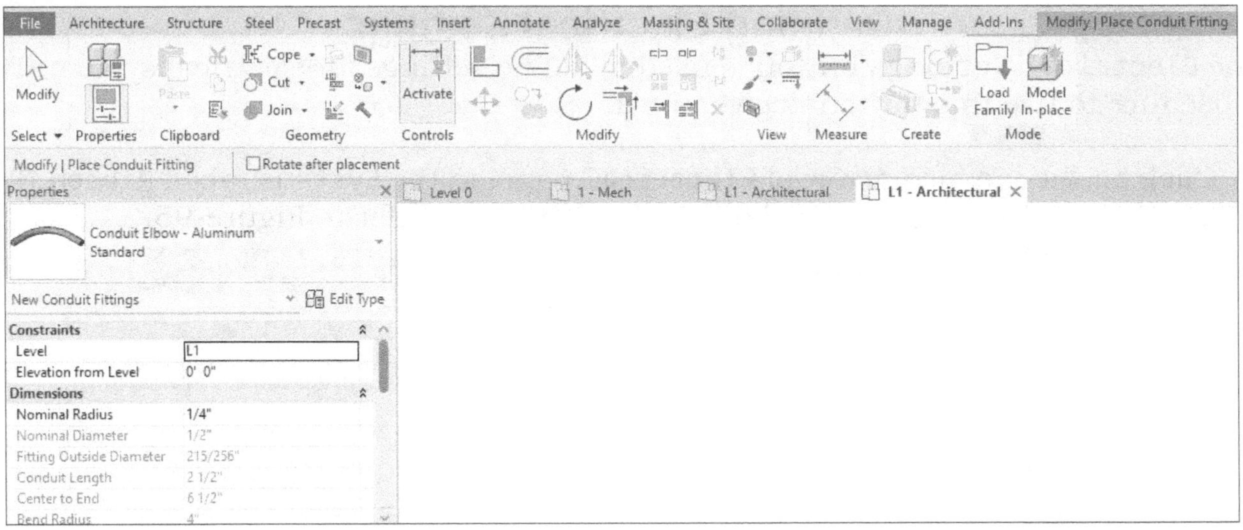

Figure-93. Options to place conduit fitting

- Click at desired location to place the fitting.

Placing Electrical Equipment

The **Electrical Equipment** tool is used to place different types of electrical equipment like panels, switch gear, push buttons, and so on. The procedure to place electrical equipment is given next.

- Click on the **Electrical Equipment** tool from the **Electrical** panel of **Systems** tab in the **Ribbon**. You will be asked to load electrical equipment.
- Load desired electrical equipment as discussed earlier. The options to place electrical equipment will be displayed; refer to Figure-94.

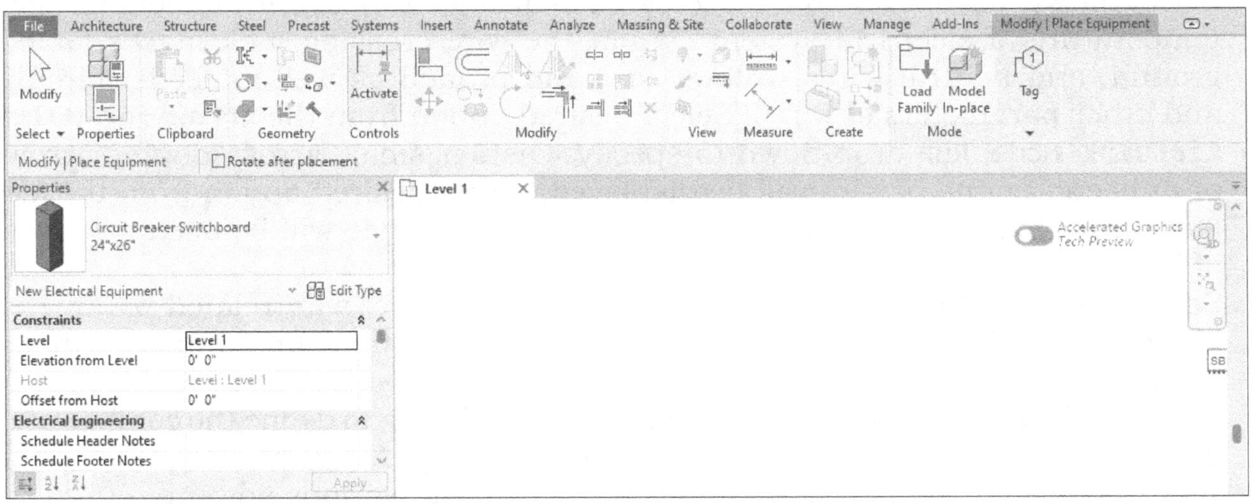

Figure-94. Options to place electrical equipment

- Select desired equipment from the **Properties Palette** and set desired parameters. You will be asked to specify location to place the equipment.
- Click at desired location to place equipment.
- Press **ESC** twice to exit the tool. You can place the devices and fixtures in the same way.

Defining Electrical Settings

The **Electrical Settings** button is used to define settings for electrical system. The procedure to use this button is given next.

- Click on the inclined arrow of **Electrical** panel in the **Systems** tab of **Ribbon**. The **Electrical Settings** dialog box will be displayed; refer to Figure-95.

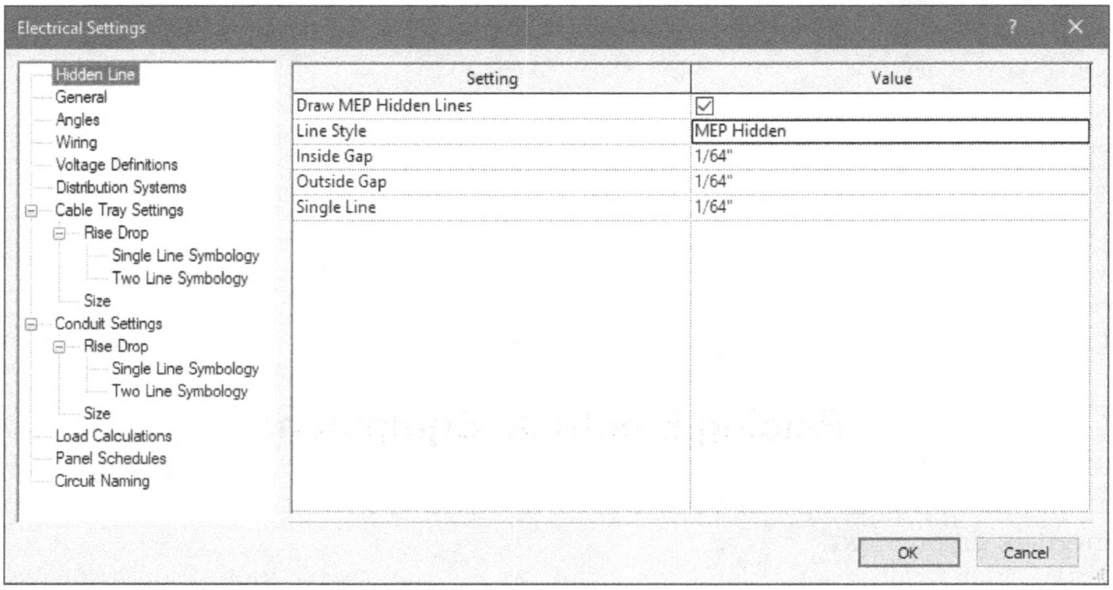

Figure-95. Electrical Settings dialog box

- Select the **General** option from the left area in the dialog box to define general parameters for electrical systems like connector separator, circuit description, and so on.
- Select the **Wiring** option from the left area in dialog box to define ambient (general) temperature of electrical system, gap at the wire crossing, tick marks for hot, ground, and neutral wires, voltage drops in branch as well as feeder circuits, and other parameters of wires. Select desired option from the **Arrow for Multi-Circuits Home Run** drop-down to specify whether single arrow, double arrows, or only end points of wire will be displayed. Select desired option from the **Home Run Arrow Style** drop-down to define which arrow style will be used for arrows of home run of wires.
- Select the **Wire Sizes** option from the left area and set wire related parameters like material of wire, temperature of wire, insulation type, and ampere capacity of wire. Similarly, set the other parameters for wiring.
- Select the **Distribution Systems** option from the left area to define the configuration to be used for distribution from three phase supply. After selecting this option, set desired value in the **Configuration** drop-downs for various power circuits. You can define the configuration as star type or delta type. Similarly, set the other parameters in this page. If you want to add more power circuits then click on the **Add** button from the bottom in the dialog box and specify desired parameters.

- Click on the **Load Calculations** option from the left area in the dialog box to define how loads will be calculated from electrical fittings installed in the building; refer to Figure-96. Select the **Sum true load and reactive load** radio button to add all the true loads and reactive loads for finding total load of building. The reactive load is a load carried by alternating current generating station in which current and voltage are out of phase. Select the **Sum apparent load** radio button to add all the apparent loads for finding total load of building. Select the **Run calculations for loads in spaces** check box to perform live load calculations while creating the model. Click on the **Load Classifications** button to define categories in which load can be specified while placing them in the drawing. On selecting this button, the **Load Classifications** dialog box will be displayed; refer to Figure-97. The options of this dialog box have been discussed earlier. Similarly, you can use **Demand Factors** button to define demand factors for various appliances.

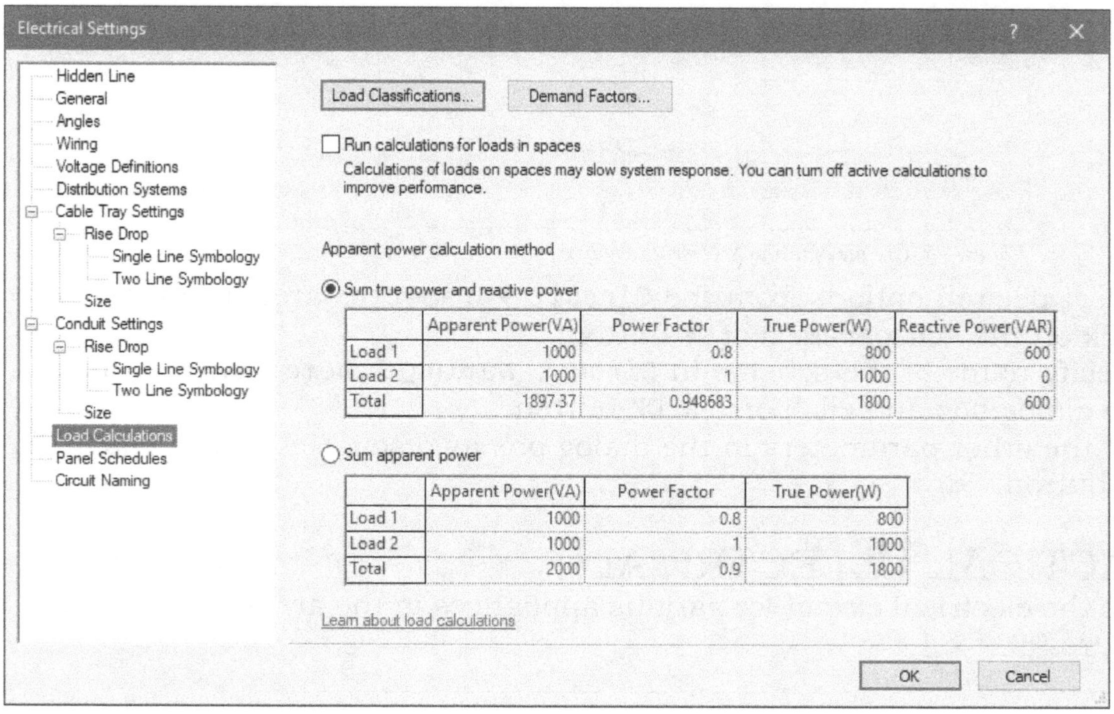

Figure-96. Load Calculations page

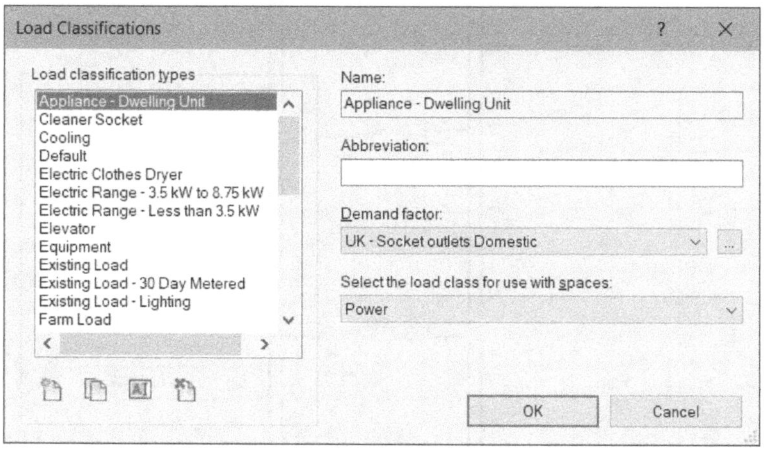

Figure-97. Load Classifications dialog box

- Select the **Panel Schedules** option from the left area in the dialog box and specify parameters to manage panel schedules.

- Select the **Circuit Naming** option from the left area to create circuit naming schemes. The options will be displayed for creating and managing new schemes. Click on the **New scheme** button from the bottom in the page. The **Circuit Naming Scheme** dialog box will be displayed; refer to Figure-98.

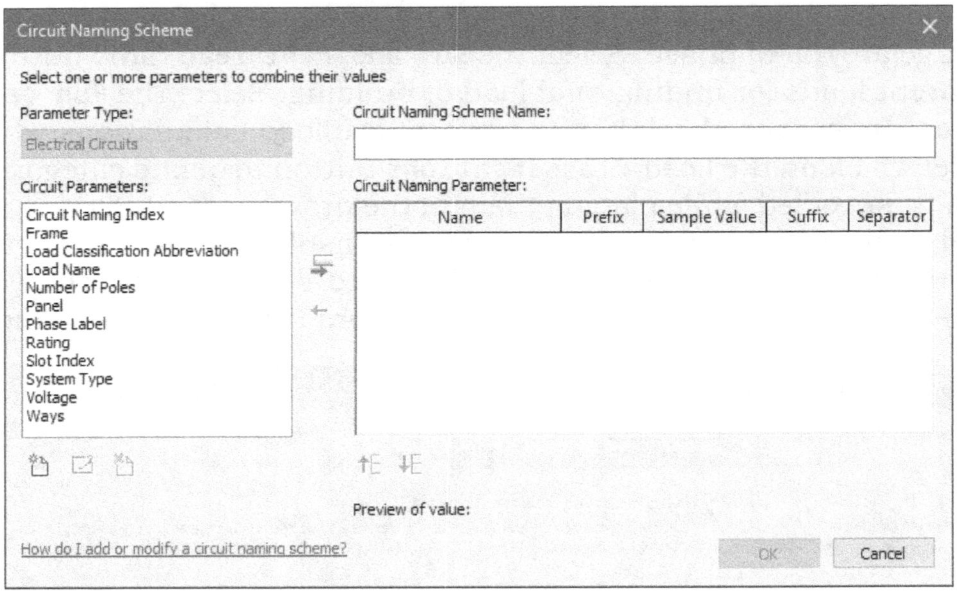

Figure-98. Circuit Naming Scheme dialog box

- Select desired options from the **Circuit Parameters** area in the dialog box and click on the **Add parameter(s)** button.
- Specify name of the scheme in **Circuit Naming Scheme Name** edit box at top in the dialog box and click on the **OK** button.
- Set the other parameters in the dialog box as discussed earlier and click on the **OK** button.

Practical (Electrical)

Create the electrical circuit for various appliances in the architectural layout shown in Figure-99.

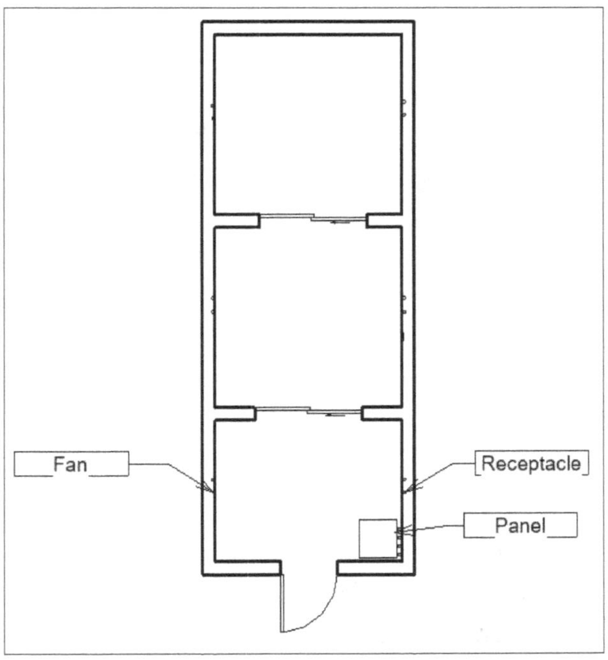

Figure-99. Layout for electrical circuit

Starting Project and Placing Electrical Equipment

- Open the file available for this practical from the resource kit of the book.
- Click on the **Electrical Equipment** tool from the **Electrical** panel in the **Systems** tab of **Ribbon**. The options to place electrical equipment will be displayed.
- Place the circuit breaker and other equipment.
- Similarly, place the receptacles, fan, light fixture, and so on; refer to Figure-100.

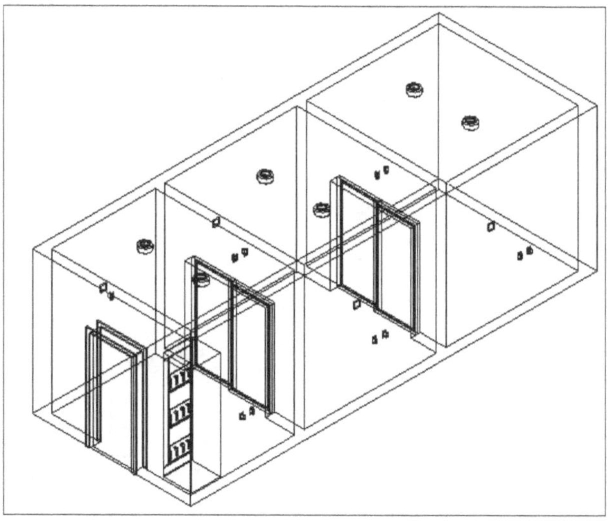

Figure-100. Placing fixtures

Creating Electrical Wiring System

- Select all the receptacles to be wired in same circuit and click on the **Power** tool from the **Create Systems** panel in the **Modify|Electrical Fixtures** contextual tab of **Ribbon**; refer to Figure-101. The circuit will be created and the related options will be displayed in the **Properties Palette**; refer to Figure-102.

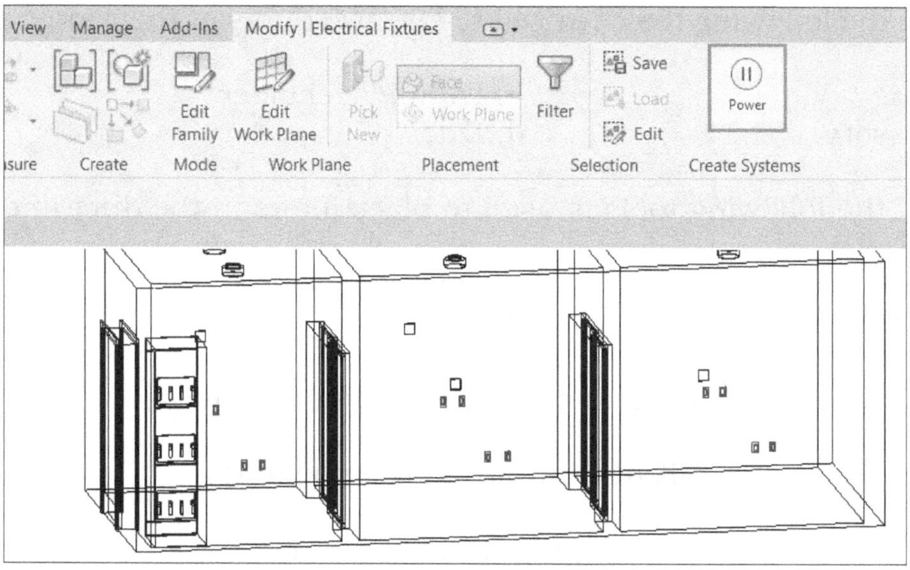

Figure-101. Options for creating power circuit

- Click on the **Select Panel** tool from the **System Tools** panel of the **Modify|Electrical Circuits** contextual tab in the **Ribbon**. You will be asked to select the panel to which you want to connect the wires.
- Click on the **Arc Wire** or **Chamfered Wire** tool from the **Convert to Wire** panel in the **Modify|Electrical Circuits** contextual tab to create related type of wiring.
- Similarly, you can create wirings for other equipment.

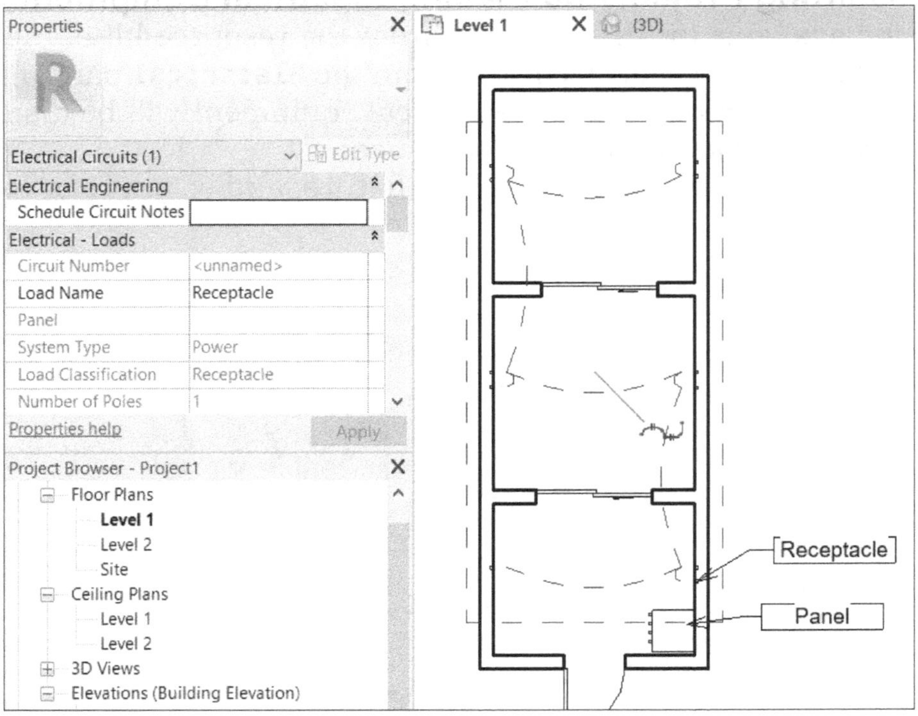

Figure-102. Options to create circuit

SELF ASSESSMENT

Q1. What is full form of HVAC in construction industry?

Q2. What is the difference between duct fittings and duct accessories?

Q3. Which of the following tools is used to join two ducts at their intersection point?

a. Duct Fitting
b. Duct Placeholder
c. Duct Accessory
d. Duct

Q4. Which of the following tools is used to place filters in the duct line?

a. Duct Fitting
b. Duct Placeholder
c. Duct Accessory
d. Duct

Q5. The .... tool is used to create diffusers and grilles.

Q6. Write a short note on HVAC unit and its components.

Q7. Discuss the method of calculating CFM of building.

Q8. Discuss the difference between piping system and plumbing system in broad scope of construction industry.

Q9. What is the purpose of the HVAC panel in the Systems tab?

A. To create electrical circuits
B. To manage piping systems
C. To create HVAC systems for thermal control
D. To draw structural elements

Q10. Which tool is used to define parameters for HVAC in Revit?

A. Duct Sizing
B. Mechanical Settings
C. Load Family
D. Duct Accessory

Q11. What does the "Draw MEP Hidden Lines" checkbox in Mechanical Settings do?

A. Displays wall thickness
B. Shows hidden MEP lines
C. Aligns duct fittings
D. Hides unused ducts

Q12. What is the function of the "Use Annot. Scale for Single Line Fittings" checkbox?

A. Shows insulation
B. Automatically places tags
C. Uses specified annotation size
D. Converts ducts to flex

Q13. In industry practice, which angle setting is commonly selected for duct fittings?

A. Use any angle
B. Set an angle increment
C. Use specific angles
D. Random angles

Q14. Which option is used to define how duct route lines are converted into ducts?

A. Calculation
B. Conversion
C. Duct Settings
D. Routing Preferences

Q15. What is the purpose of the Duct tool?

A. Draw piping networks
B. Place light fixtures
C. Create air passages
D. Tag electrical components

Q16. What does the "Inherit Size" toggle button do while placing a duct?

A. Applies lining
B. Converts to flexible duct
C. Inherits size of connecting duct
D. Adds accessories

Q17. Which drop-down allows you to define the use of duct like supply, exhaust or return?

A. Reference Level
B. Duct Type
C. System Type
D. Flex Duct Type

Q18. What is the function of the Duct Sizing dialog box?

A. Load fittings
B. Define air flow
C. Set parameters for duct sizing
D. Add accessories

Q19. What does the Duct Placeholder tool create?

A. Final duct system
B. Flexible duct
C. Line diagram of duct
D. Round duct

Q20. Which tool converts duct placeholders into actual ducts?

A. Duct Accessory
B. Routing Preferences
C. Convert Placeholder
D. Duct Fitting

Q21. What does the Duct Fitting tool allow you to do?

A. Apply fitting at intersections
B. Design HVAC schedules
C. Place ducts in ceiling
D. Add annotations

Q22. What is placed using the Duct Accessory tool?

A. Filters and dampers
B. Insulation
C. Light fixtures
D. Flex ducts

Q23. What does the Convert to Flex Duct tool do?

A. Adds air terminals
B. Converts duct placeholder
C. Converts rigid duct to flexible duct
D. Creates new fittings

Q24. Which tool is used to draw a flexible duct directly?

A. Duct Fitting
B. Duct Placeholder
C. Flex Duct
D. Duct Sizing

Q25. What is the function of the Air Terminal tool in Autodesk Revit?

A. To insert mechanical equipment
B. To create diffusers and grilles
C. To design architectural floor plans
D. To calculate CFM requirements

Q26. Which palette is used to set parameters like CFM, type, and size while placing air terminals?

A. Options Bar
B. Settings Palette
C. Properties Palette
D. System Browser

Q27. What must be installed to access fabrication configurations in Revit?

A. AutoCAD
B. Fabrication CAMduct
C. Revit Viewer
D. HVAC Plugin

Q28. Which content should be selected to use metric fabrication components?

A. Revit MEP Imperial Content V2.51
B. Revit Metric MEP Classic
C. Revit MEP Metric Content V2.41
D. Revit Fabrication Metric Pack

Q29. What is the purpose of the Multi-Point Routing tool?

A. To place control devices
B. To generate 3D piping from 2D drawings
C. To create multi-point duct routes
D. To load architectural templates

Q30. What tool is used to place duct stiffeners in Revit?

A. HVAC Reinforcement Tool
B. Mechanical Equipment Tool
C. MEP Fabrication Ductwork Stiffener
D. Fabrication Routing Connector

Q31. What is the unit for measuring airflow in HVAC systems?

A. Cubic meters
B. Liters per second
C. Cubic feet per minute
D. PSI

Q32. If a room needs 700 CFM, how much AHU tonnage is required approximately?

A. 1 ton
B. 1.5 tons
C. 2 tons
D. 3 tons

Q33. How many vents are required if room needs 100 CFM and each vent has 30 CFM capacity?

A. 2
B. 3
C. 4
D. 5

Q34. Which tool helps to create duct system automatically after selecting air terminals and AHU?

A. Air Terminal Tool
B. Mechanical Equipment Tool
C. Duct Tool
D. Create Duct System Tool

Q35. What does the Flex Duct Type field allow you to modify in Duct Conversion Settings?

A. Material of ducts
B. Length of ducts
C. Convert branch ducts into flexible ducts
D. Insulation type

Q36. What happens if there is a warning in duct connections during layout?

A. Reinstall software
B. Change duct type
C. Move vents to appropriate locations
D. Ignore the warning

Q37. What is the first step in starting a mechanical project in Revit?

A. Load air terminals
B. Place mechanical equipment
C. Start new project using Mechanical Template
D. Calculate duct size

Q38. What view template must be selected when assigning architectural plans?

A. HVAC Plan
B. Electrical Plan
C. Mechanical Plan
D. Architectural Plan

For Student Notes

Chapter 9

Performing Analysis

Topics Covered

The major topics covered in this chapter are:

- ***Introduction to Structural Analysis***
- ***Creating Boundary Conditions***
- ***Applying Loads and Load Combinations***
- ***Automating Analytical Model Creation***
- ***Performing Consistency Checks***
- ***Running Analysis on Robot Structural***
- ***Checking Systems***
- ***Creating Spaces and Apply Space Tags***
- ***Generating Reports***

INTRODUCTION

In previous chapter, you have learned to create different types of systems in architectural and structural plans of buildings. In this chapter, you will learn to perform different types of analyses like structural analysis, leakage checks for ducts and pipes, and so on.

STRUCTURAL ANALYSIS

The options to perform different type of analyses are available in the **Analyze** tab of **Ribbon**; refer to Figure-1.

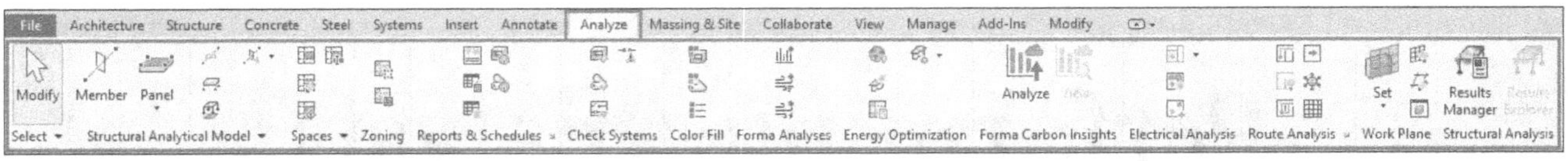

Figure-1. Analyze tab

The steps to perform a structural analysis are given next.

- Specify the boundary conditions for analysis like applying fix constraint, pin constraint, roller constraint, and so on.
- Create the loads and load cases.
- Perform adjustment in analytical model.
- Run the analysis on model.

Placing Line Analytical Member

The **Member** tool (Analytical Member) is used to place analytical line element in the project for analysis. The procedure to use this tool is given next.

- Click on the **Member** tool from the **Structural Analytical Model** panel in the **Analyze** tab of the **Ribbon**. You will be asked to specify start point of analytical member and options in **Ribbon** will be displayed as shown in Figure-2.

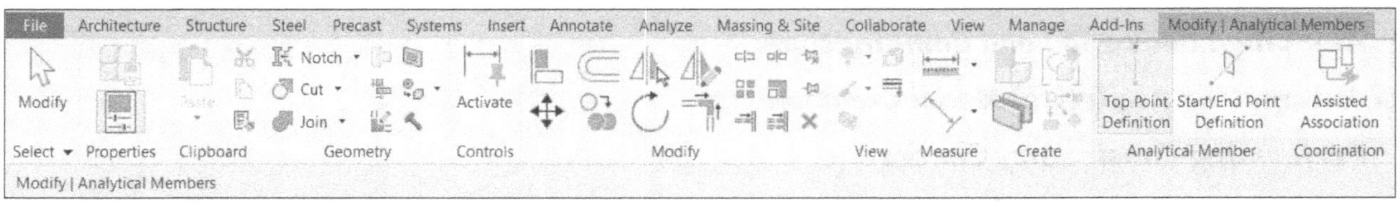

Figure-2. Modify Analytical Members tab

- Select the **Top Point Definition** button from **Analytical Member** panel in the **Modify | Analytical Members** tab of **Ribbon** to create a vertical analytical member between current level and the lower level. Select the **Start/End Point Definition** button from the **Modify | Analytical Members** tab of **Ribbon** to create a line analytical member between two points.
- Select desired options from the **Highest Associated Level** and **Lowest Associated Level** fields in the **Properties Palette** to define the range of vertical analytical member; refer to Figure-3.

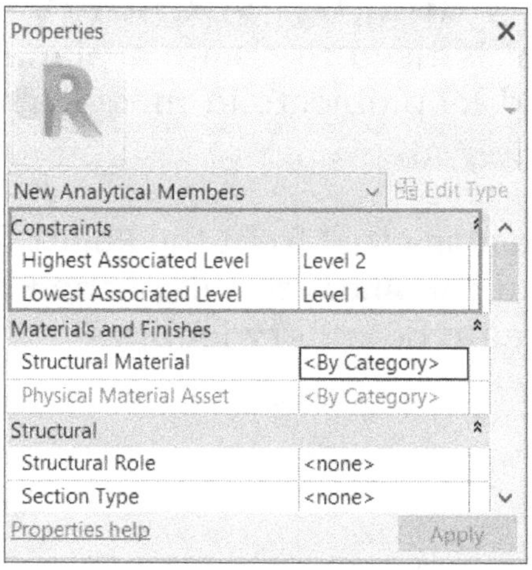

Figure-3. Constraints for analytical member

- Click in the **Structural Role** field and select the type of analytical member. For example, select the **Column** option from the field to represent column structural member of building.
- Click in the **Section Type** field and select the size of structure member; refer to Figure-4.

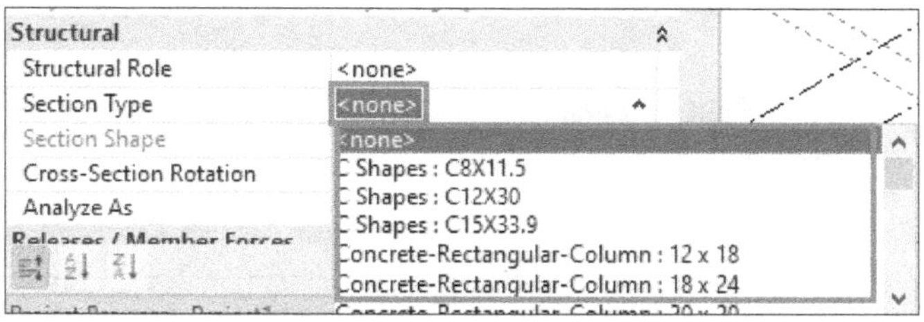

Figure-4. Section Type field

- Set desired value in **Cross-Section Rotation** field to rotate the cross-section analytical member.
- Select desired option from the **Analyze As** field to define how external applications will consider the analytical member.
- Set desired options in **Releases/Member Forces** section of **Properties Palette** to define how forces and connections will be applied to the analytical members.
- After selecting desired button, click in the Analytical Model 3D view or Analytical structure plans to place the members; refer to Figure-5.
- Press **ESC** to exit the tool.

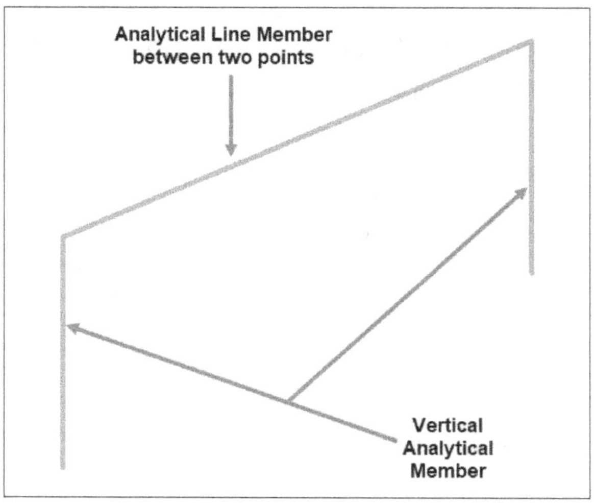

Figure-5. Line analytical members

Panel by Boundary

The **Panel by Boundary** tool is used to create a planar analytical panel using the boundaries of selected closed loop objects in model. The procedure to use this tool is discussed next.

- Click on the **Panel by Boundary** tool from the **Panel** drop-down of the **Structural Analytical Model** panel in the **Analyze** tab of the **Ribbon**; refer to Figure-6. You will be asked to select/create boundary loop.

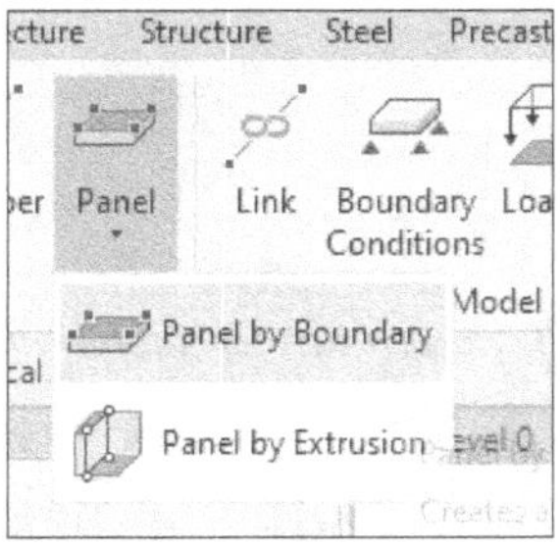

Figure-6. Panel by boundary tool

- Select desired objects or draw the closed loop sketch; refer to Figure-7.

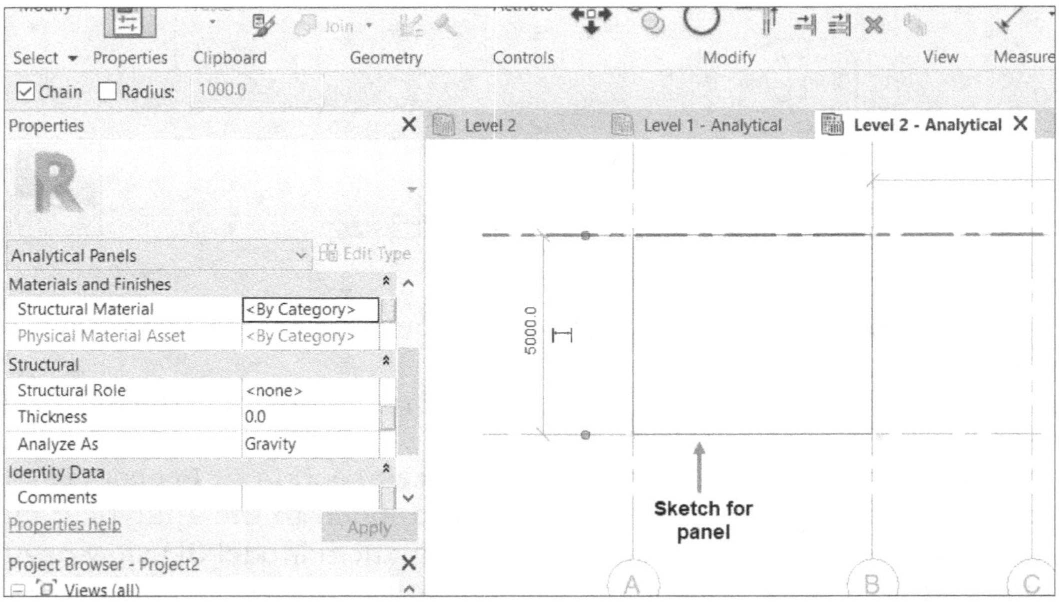

Figure-7. Sketch created for analytical panel

- Specify desired parameters in the **Properties Palette** as discussed earlier and click on the **OK** button from the **Mode** panel in **Modify|Create Analytical Panels** contextual tab of **Ribbon**. The analytical panel will be created; refer to Figure-8.

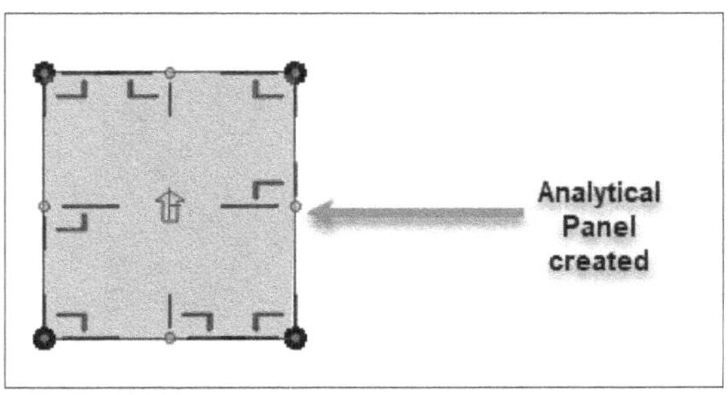

Figure-8. Analytical panel created

Panel by Extrusion

The **Panel by Extrusion** tool is used to create a analytical panel perpendicular to the current work plane using sketch curves as path. The procedure to use this tool is discussed next.

- Click on the **Panel by Extrusion** tool of the **Panel** drop-down from the **Structural Analytical Model** panel in the **Analyze** tab of the **Ribbon**; refer to Figure-9. You will be asked to select/draw path for analytical panel. The path can be straight line, an arc, or an ellipse.

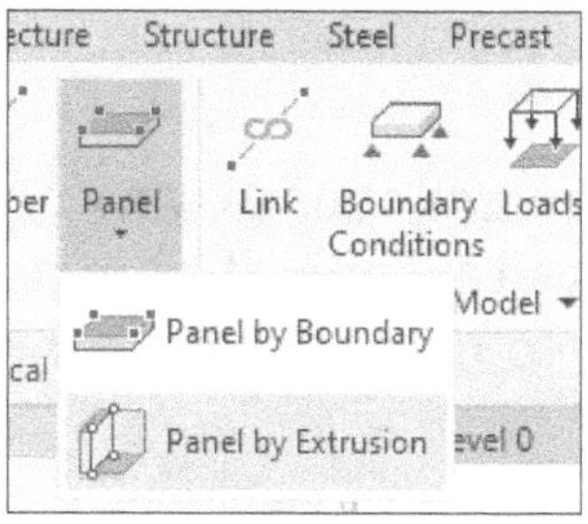

Figure-9. Panel by extrusion tool

- Draw the curves as discussed earlier. The analytical panel is extruded and its height equals 10 feet/3 meters; refer to Figure-10.

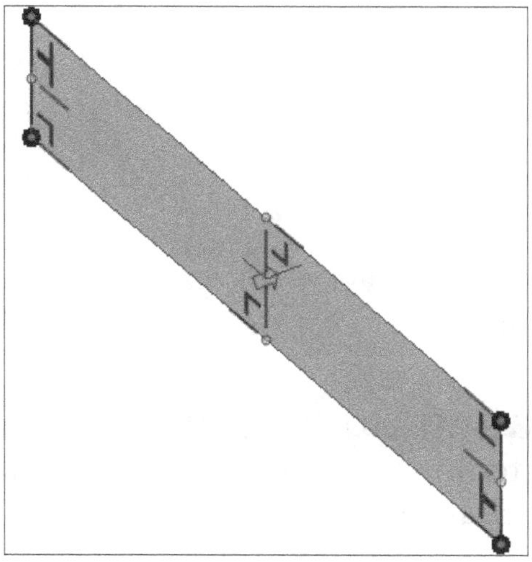

Figure-10. Panel by extrusion sketch

Creating Link Between Analytical Nodes

The **Link** tool is used to create a link between two analytical nodes for load transfer. To use this tool, the analytical nodes should be visible in graphics area by using the **Visibility/Graphic Overrides** dialog box discussed earlier; refer to Figure-11. The procedure to use this tool is given next.

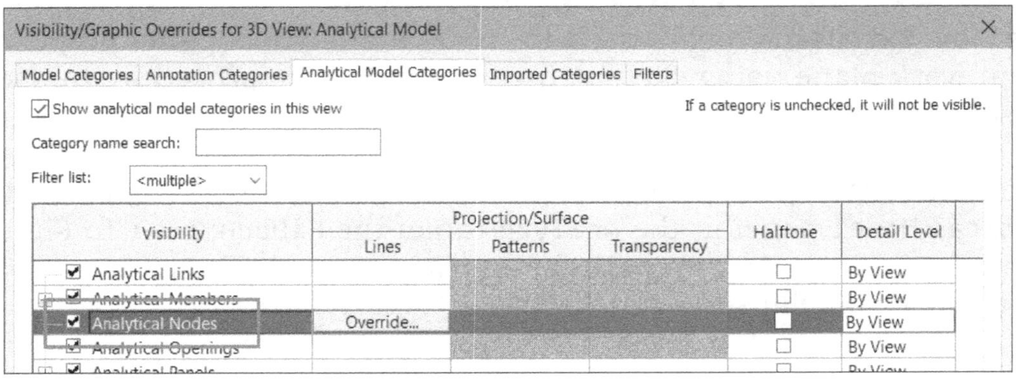

Figure-11. Displaying analytical nodes

- Click on the **Link** tool from the **Structural Analytical Model** panel in the **Analyze** tab of **Ribbon**. You will be asked to specify start point and end point of link.
- Specify the location of points to create link; refer to Figure-12.

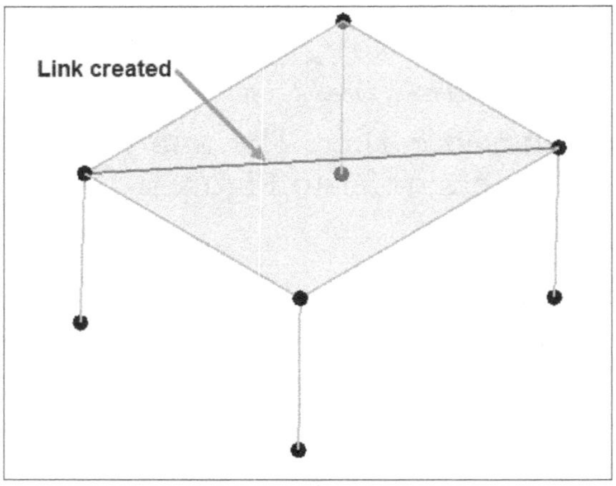

Figure-12. Link created between points

- Press **ESC** to exit the tool.

Creating Boundary Conditions

The **Boundary Conditions** tool is used to specify boundary conditions like fixing a point, line, or face. The procedure to create boundary condition is given next.

- Click on the **Boundary Conditions** tool from the **Structural Analytical Model** panel of **Analyze** tab in the **Ribbon**. The options to place boundary conditions will be displayed; refer to Figure-13. Note that if boundary condition families are not loaded by default then load the boundary condition families from the **Boundary Conditions** folder of Revit Content library; refer to Figure-14 as discussed earlier using **Load Family** tool in the **Insert** tab of **Ribbon**.

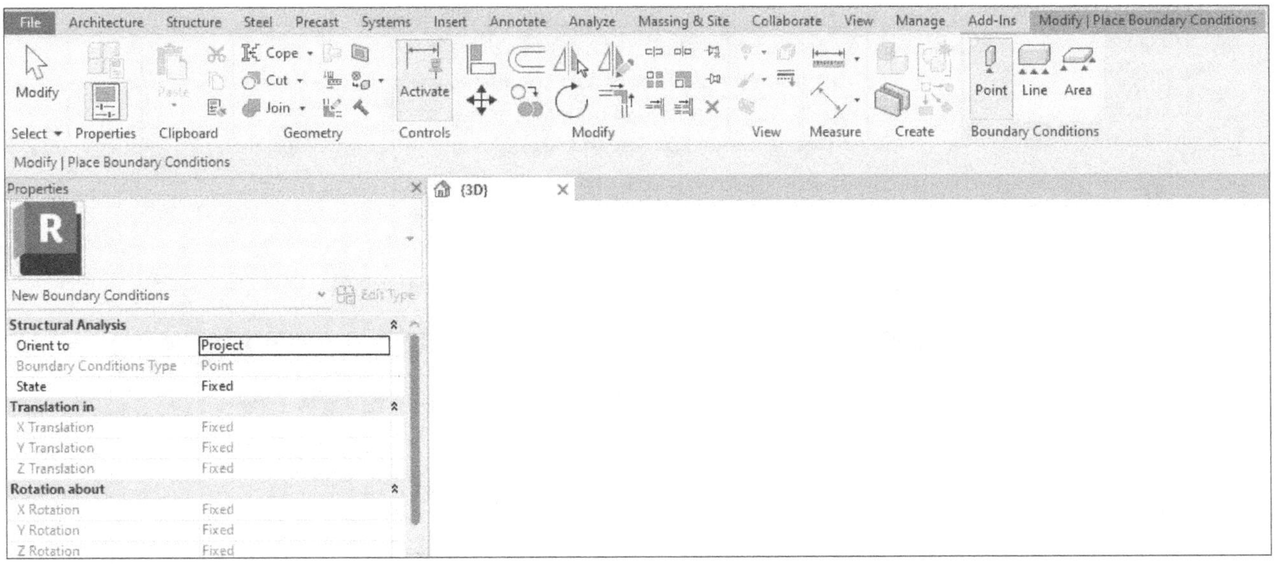

Figure-13. Placing boundary conditions

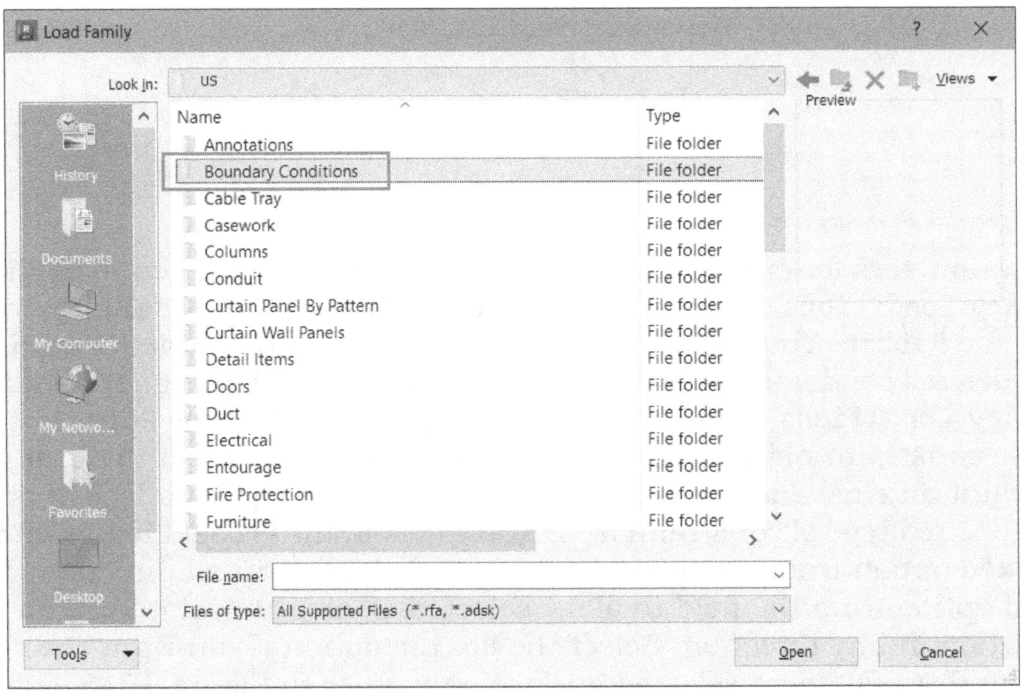

Figure-14. Boundary Conditions folder

- Note that after loading the boundary condition families, if Boundary Condition Settings are not specified earlier then the **Boundary Conditions Settings Incomplete** dialog box will be displayed; refer to Figure-15. Click on the **Close** button to exit the dialog box and then click on the **Boundary Condition Settings** tool from the expanded **Structural Analytical Model** panel of **Analyze** tab in the **Ribbon**. The **Boundary Conditions Settings** tab will be displayed in the **Structural Settings** dialog box; refer to Figure-16. Set desired family symbols in various drop-downs of the dialog box and click on the **OK** button.

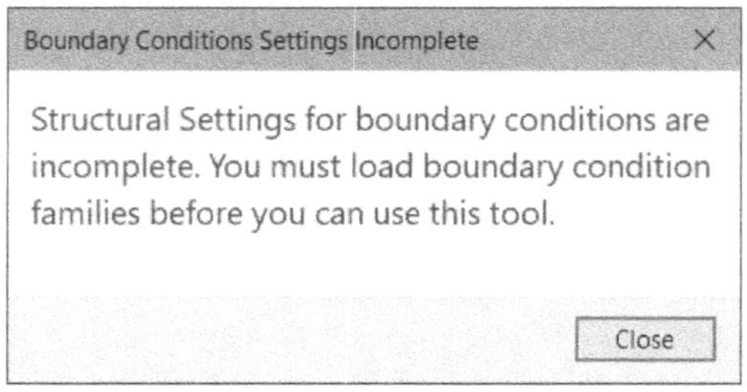

Figure-15. Boundary Conditions Settings Incomplete dialog box

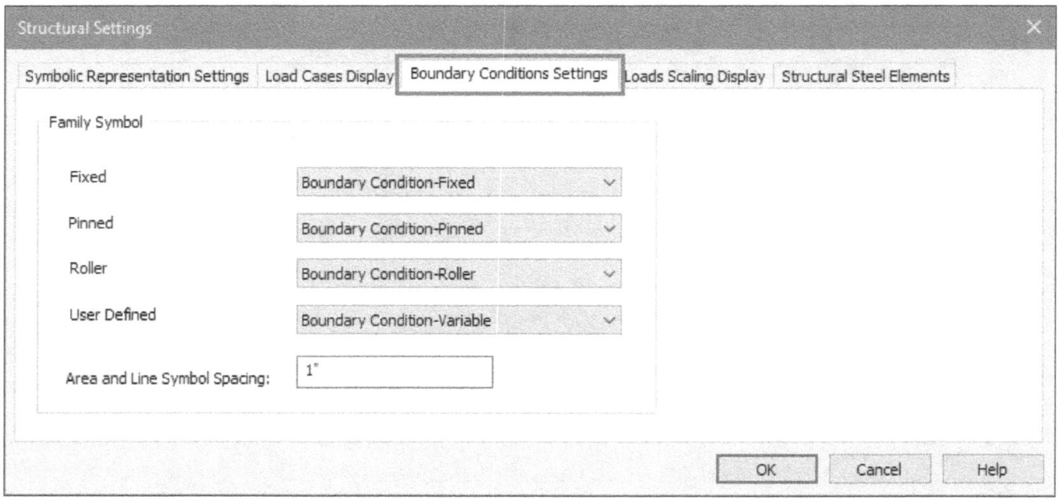

Figure-16. Boundary Conditions Settings tab

- If all parameters for creating boundary conditions are specified then click on the **Boundary Conditions** tool from the **Structural Analytical Model** panel of **Analyze** tab in the **Ribbon**. You will be asked to select desired boundary condition.
- Select desired condition option from the **Boundary Conditions** panel of **Modify|Place Boundary Conditions** contextual tab in the **Ribbon**. Select the **Point** button if you want to constraint objects at selected points. Similarly, select the **Line** button to constraint an edge and select the **Area** button to constraint a face of object.
- Select desired type of constraint from **State** field in the **Properties Palette**. Select the **Fixed** option from the field to fix selected element in all direction. Select the **Pinned** option from the field to allow selected element to rotate but do not allow translation in any direction. Select the **Roller** option if you want the element to rotate and translate on selected surface only; refer to Figure-17. Select the **User** option if you want to manually set the allowed translation and rotation directions. On selecting **User** option, the options in **Translation in** and **Rotation about** rollouts of **Properties Palette** will become active. There are three options available for each field in these rollouts; **Release**, **Fixed**, and **Spring**. Select the **Release** option to free selected direction. Select the **Fixed** option to restrict movement or rotation in selected direction. Select the **Spring** option if you want to apply spring support in selected direction. The **Spring Modulus** edit box will be displayed for respective direction. Specify desired value in the edit box.

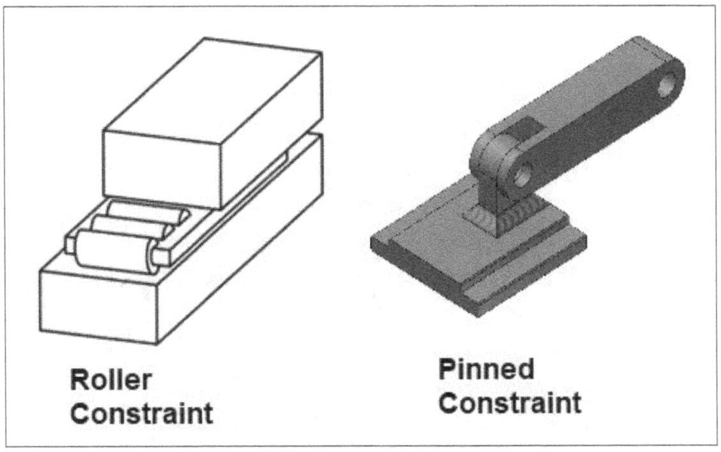

Figure-17. Roller and pinned constraints

- After setting desired parameters, click on desired objects (points, edges, or faces) to apply constraint.
- Press **ESC** to exit the tool.

Applying Loads

The **Loads** tool is used to represent various practical loads applied on a building. Using this tool, you can apply force as well as moment load. The procedure to use this tool is given next.

- Click on the **Loads** tool from the **Analytical Model** panel in the **Analyze** tab of **Ribbon**. The options to apply loads will be displayed; refer to Figure-18.

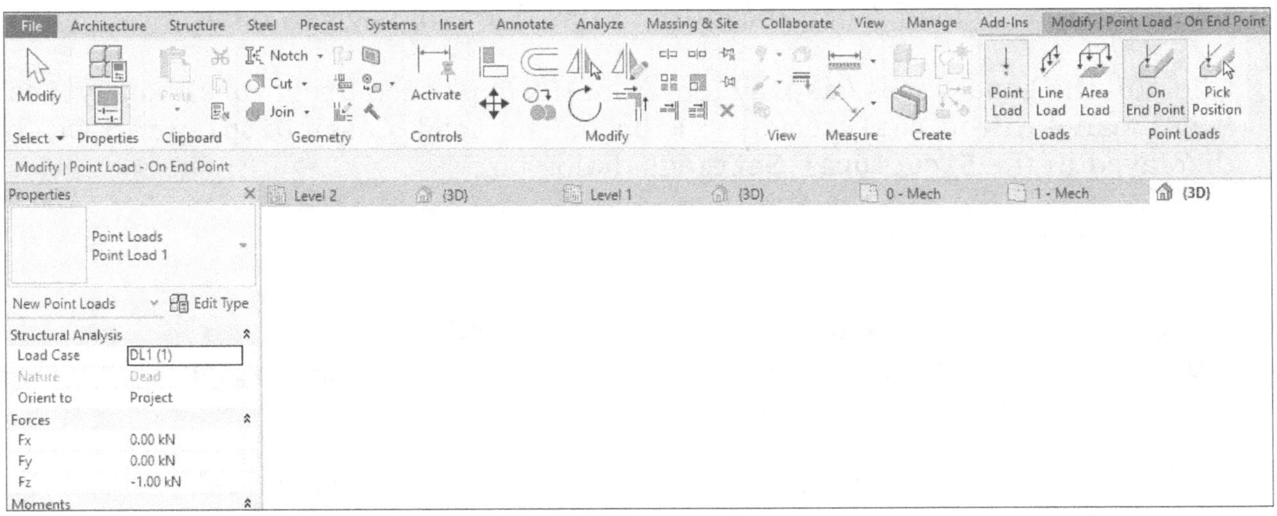

Figure-18. Options to apply loads

- Select desired option from the **Loads** panel in the **Modify|Point Load** contextual tab of the **Ribbon**. The respective options will be displayed in the **Ribbon**. Select the **Point Load**, **Line Load**, and **Area Load** options to apply loads on selected frame members likes beams, braces, columns, walls, floors etc. For other three options, you will need sketched point, line, or area.
- Set desired force values in the **Force** edit boxes of **Forces** rollout in the **Properties Palette**.
- Select the load case in which you want to create this load from the **Load Case** field in the **Properties Palette**. By default, DL (Dead Load) is selected in this field.

- Select desired entities on which you want to apply the load (floors selected in this case); refer to Figure-19.

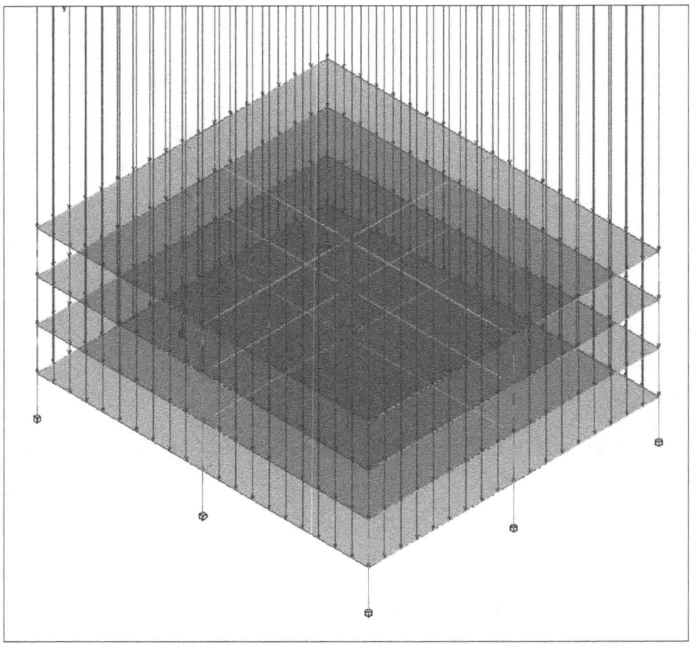

Figure-19. Preview of loads applied

- After applying load, press **ESC** to exit the tool.

Creating Load Cases

The **Load Cases Display** tool is used to create or edit load cases. A load case is used to define the type of load. The procedure to use this tool is given next.

- Click on the **Load Cases Display** tool from the expanded **Structural Analytical Model** panel in the **Analyze** tab of **Ribbon**. The **Load Cases Display** tab will be displayed in the **Structural Settings** dialog box.

The options to create load cases have been discussed earlier.

Automation Customization

The **Automation Customization** tool is used to create analytical model from physical structure model. The procedure to use this tool is given next.

- Click on the **Automation Customization** tool from the **Analytical Automation** drop-down in the **Structural Analytical Model** panel of **Analyze** tab in the **Ribbon**. The **Analytical Automation** window will be displayed; refer to Figure-20.
- Click on the **Play** button from the window to start process of creating analytical model from physical model. The options to define parameters for creation of analytical model will be displayed in the **Analytical Automation** window; refer to Figure-21.

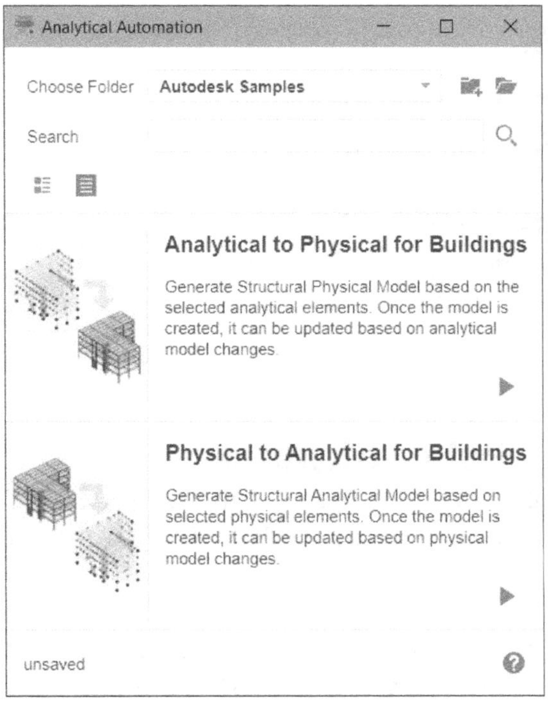

Figure-20. Analytical Automation window

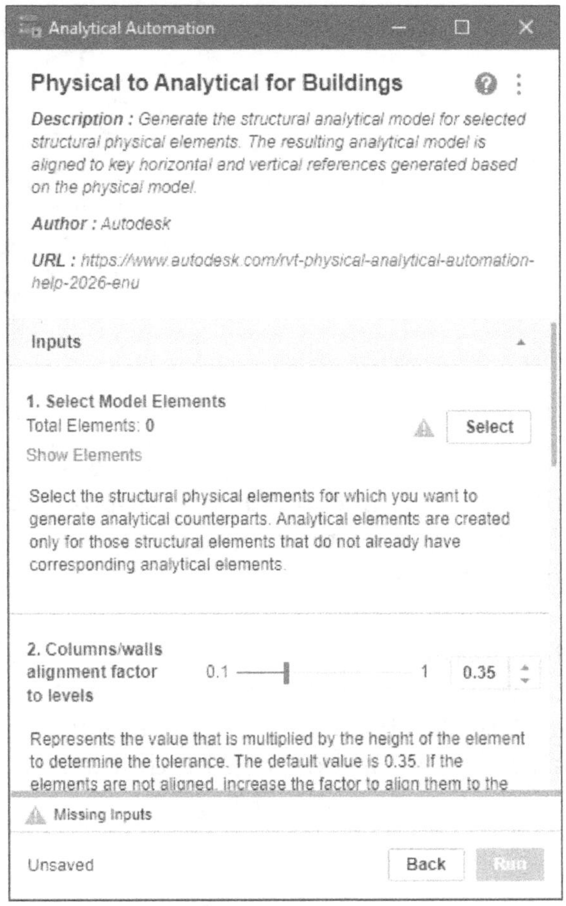

Figure-21. Parameters for Analytical Automation

- Click on the **Select** button from the **Inputs** section and select all the structural elements using window selection; refer to Figure-22.

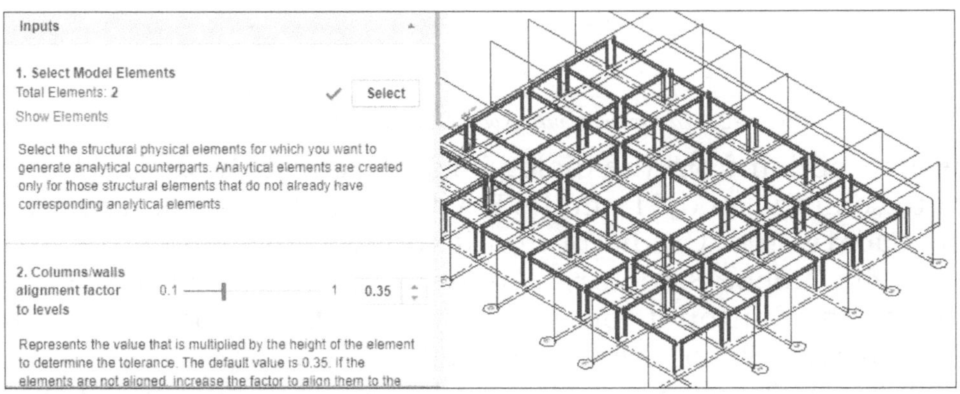

Figure-22. Physical elements selected

- Set the other parameters as discussed earlier and click on the **Run** button. The analytical model will be created; refer to Figure-23. Click on the **Close** button to exit the window.

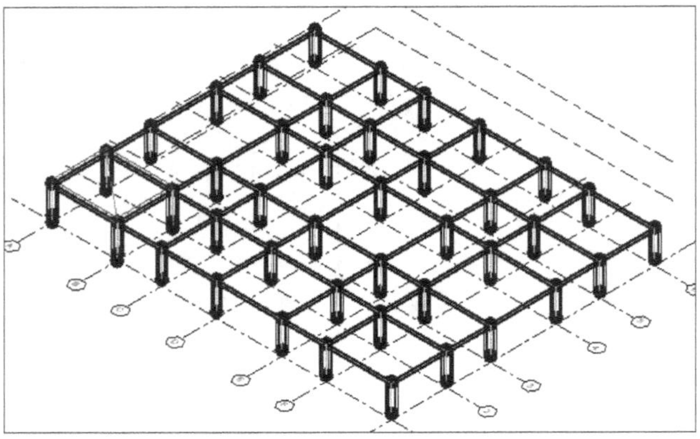

Figure-23. Analytical model generated

Running Analysis on Robot Structural

If you have installed **Autodesk Robot Structural Analysis** software then you will be able to perform structural analysis on a model. The procedure to run an analysis is discussed next.

- After preparing model for analysis, click on the **Robot Structural Analysis Link** tool from the **Robot Structural Analysis** drop-down in the **Structural Analysis** panel of **Analyze** tab in the **Ribbon**. The **Integration with Robot Structural Analysis** dialog box will be displayed; refer to Figure-24.

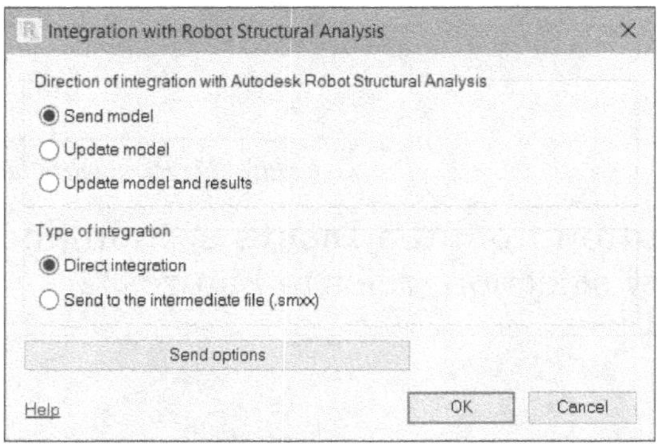

Figure-24. Integration with Robot Structural Analysis dialog box

- Select desired option from the dialog box. Select the **Send model** radio button if you want to send the model from the Revit to Robot Structural Analysis software. Select the **Update model** radio button if you want to update the model in Revit also along with Robot Structural Analysis software. Select the **Update model and results** radio button if you want to update both model and results in Revit software along with Robot Structural Analysis software.
- Set the other parameters as desired and click on the **OK** button. If you have selected the **Send** radio button then a message box will be displayed; refer to Figure-25.

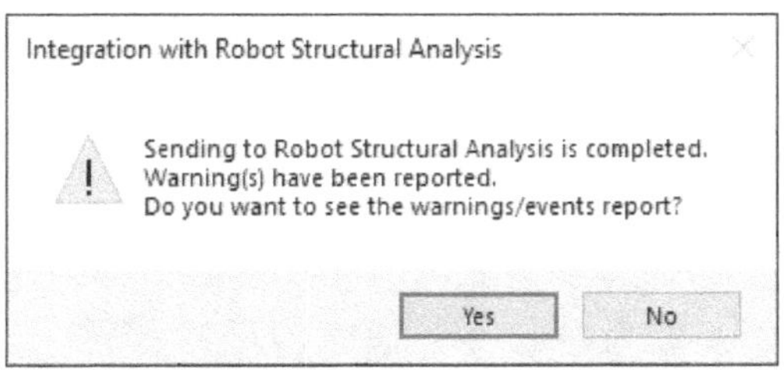

Figure-25. Message box

- Click on desired button from the dialog box. The model will be displayed in Robot Structural Analysis software; refer to Figure-26. Make sure a new structural analysis project is open in Robot Structural Analysis software. Perform the analysis as desired. (Discussion of Robot Structural Analysis software is not in scope of this book.)

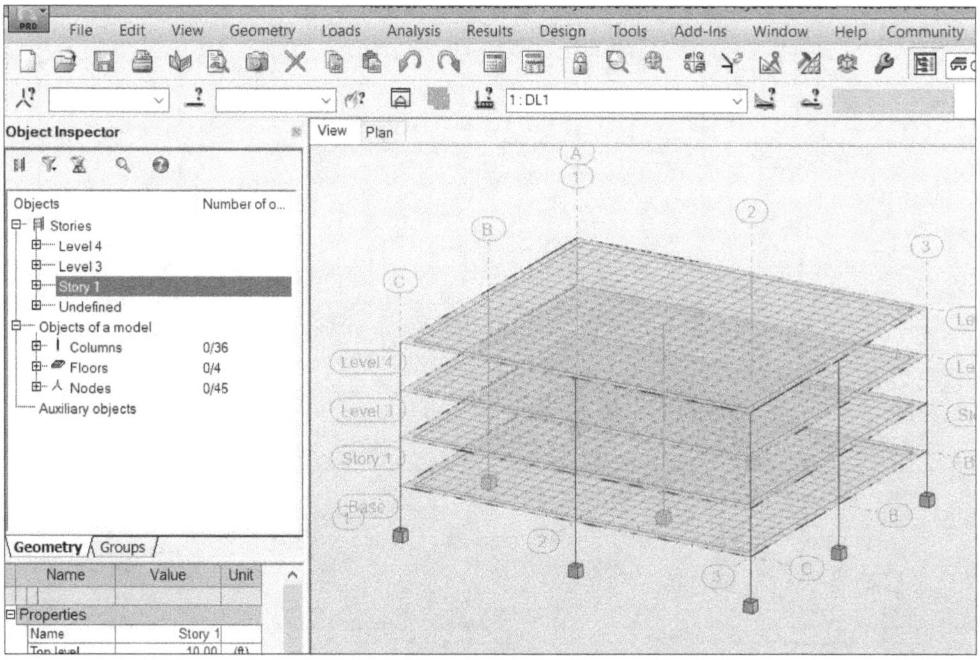

Figure-26. Model sent to Robot Structural Analysis software

Checking Systems

The tools in the **Check Systems** panel are used to check consistency of different systems like duct system, pipe system, electrical circuits, and so on. The procedures to perform various checks is given next.

Checking Duct Systems

- Click on the **Check Duct Systems** tool from the **Check Systems** panel of **Analyze** tab in the **Ribbon**. The warning signs will be displayed for different duct systems; refer to Figure-27.

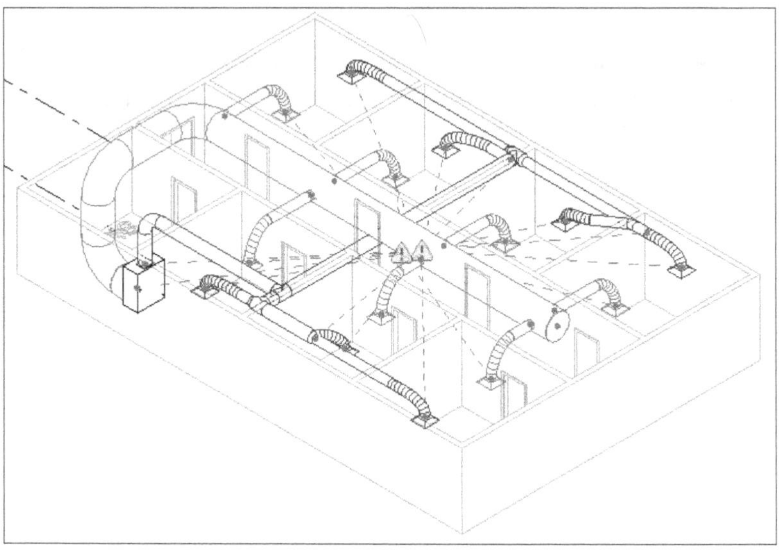

Figure-27. Duct warning systems

- Click on the warning sign to check the inconsistency in duct system; refer to Figure-28. Click on the **Expand warning dialog** button. The expanded warning box will be displayed with elements that are disconnected or connected to many elements; refer to Figure-29.

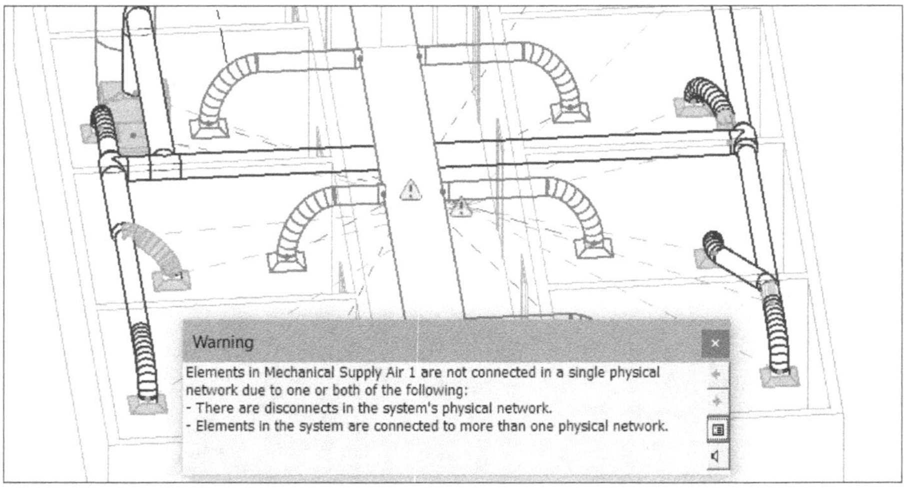

Figure-28. Warning elements for duct system

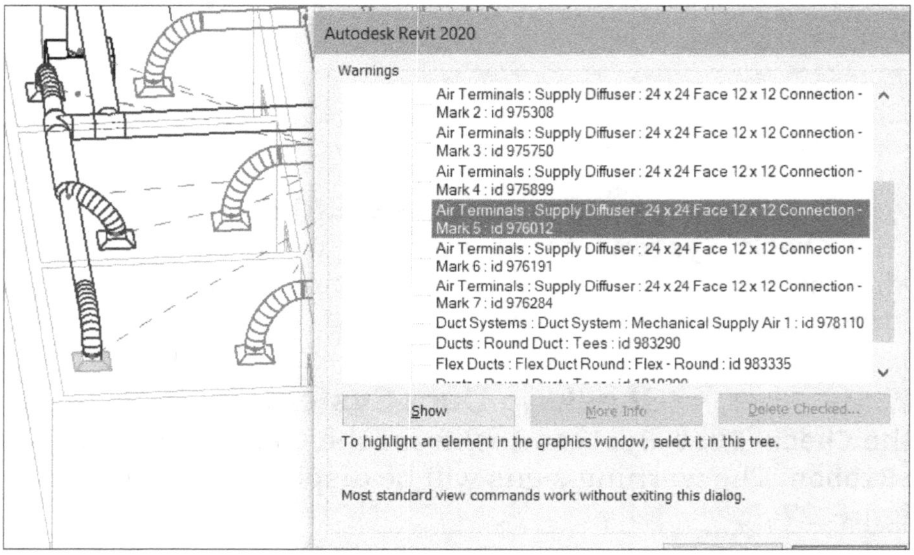

Figure-29. Elements with disconnections

- Click on the **Close** button in the dialog box to exit and modify the duct system accordingly till no warning message is displayed; refer to Figure-30.

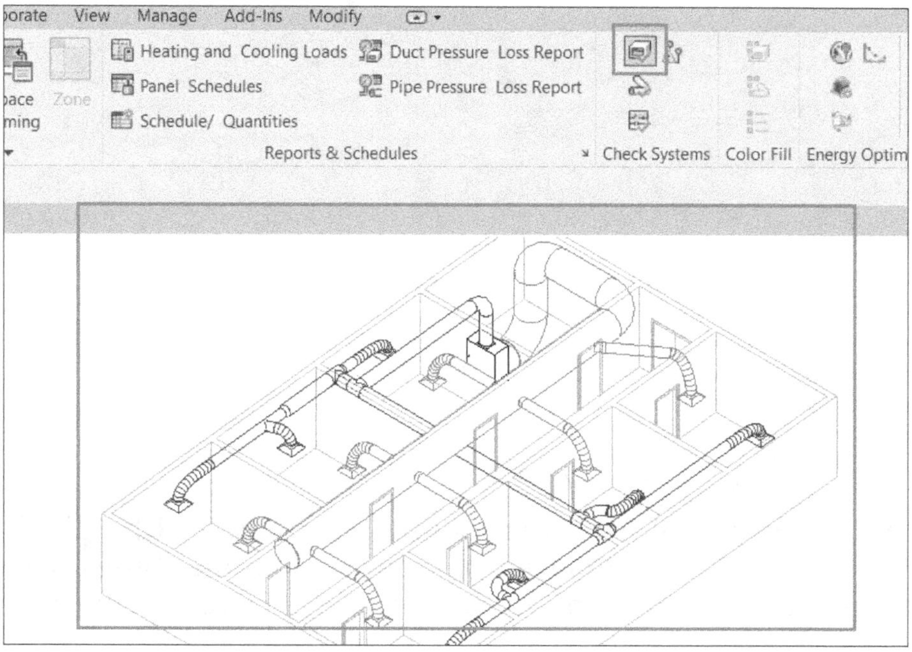

Figure-30. After modifying duct system

- You can use the other tools of **Check Systems** panel of **Analyze** tab in the **Ribbon** to perform checks in the same way.

Checking Disconnections in Route

- Click on the **Show Disconnects** tool from the **Check Systems** panel of **Analyze** tab in the **Ribbon**. The **Show Disconnects Options** dialog box will be displayed; refer to Figure-31.

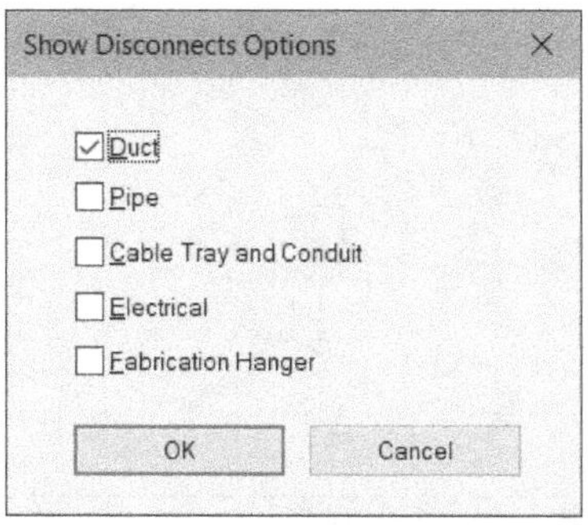

Figure-31. Show Disconnects Options dialog box

- Select the check boxes for system elements to be checked for disconnections and click on the **OK** button.
- Modify the elements and connect the disconnected elements. Once you get a completed duct system then select any of the duct in the system. The **System Inspector** tool will be displayed in the contextual tab. Click on the **System Inspector** tool to show the flow in duct system. The **System Inspector** toolbar will be displayed; refer to Figure-32.

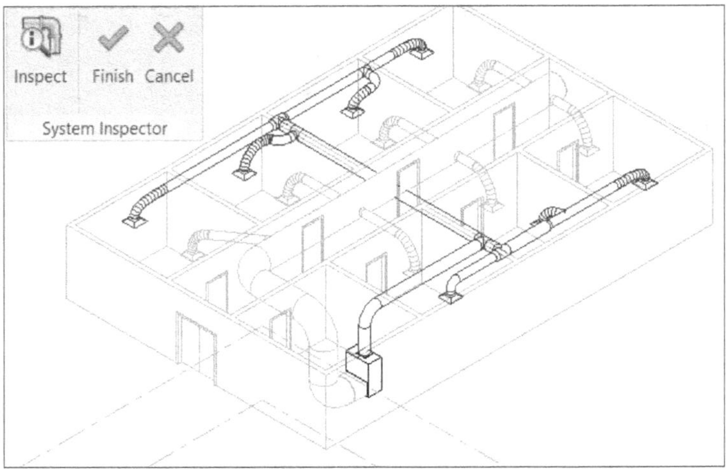

Figure-32. System Inspector toolbar

- Click on the **Inspect** tool from the toolbar. The flow will be displayed; refer to Figure-33. Note that the red lines show pressure loss and blue lines show normal flow in system. Hover the cursor on the red line to check the pressure loss in the duct system.

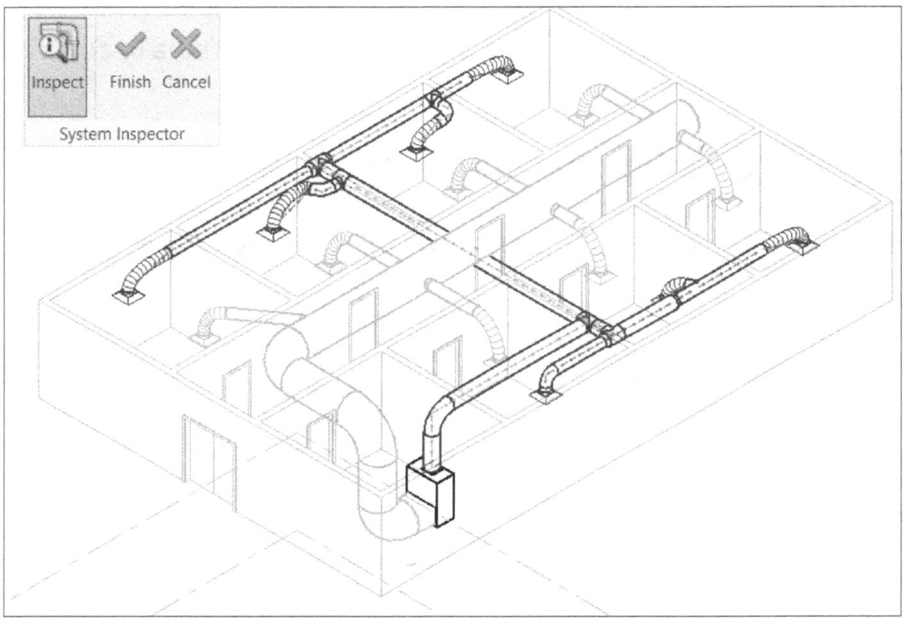

Figure-33. Checking flow in system

- Click on the **Finish** button after checking and modifying the system.

Creating Spaces

The **Space** tool is used to create analytical space for different analysis calculations. The procedure to use this tool is given next.

- Click on the **Space** tool from the **Spaces** panel in the **Analyze** tab of **Ribbon**. The options to place spaces will be displayed; refer to Figure-34. Note that if space tag is not loaded by default then an error message will be displayed. Load the **Space tag** family from **Annotations** > **Mechanical** folder of Revit content library by using **Load Family** tool as discussed earlier.

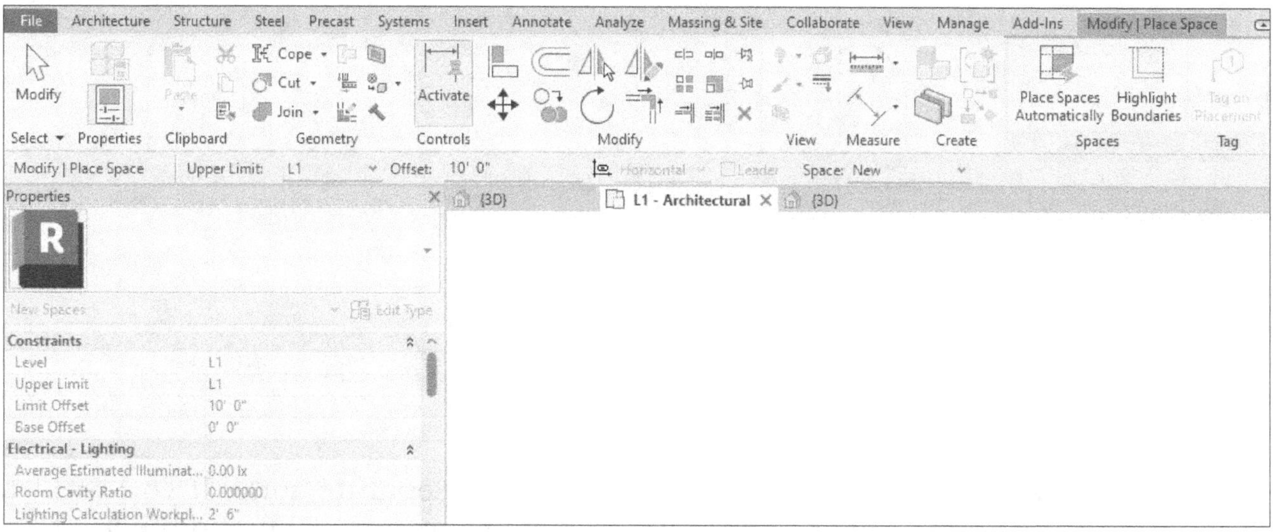

Figure-34. Options to place spaces

- Select desired option from the drop-down at the top in the **Properties Palette**. Select the **Space Tag** option if you want to create space with sequence number tag only. Select the **Space Tag With Area** option if you want to create space tag with area value displayed. Select the **Space Tag With Volume** option if you want to create space tag with volume value displayed.
- Set desired parameters in the **Properties Palette** like electrical load parameters, lighting parameters, mechanical parameters, energy analysis parameter, and so on.
- Click on the **Apply** button in the **Properties Palette** to apply parameters.
- Click in the enclosed region to which you want to assign space; refer to Figure-35.

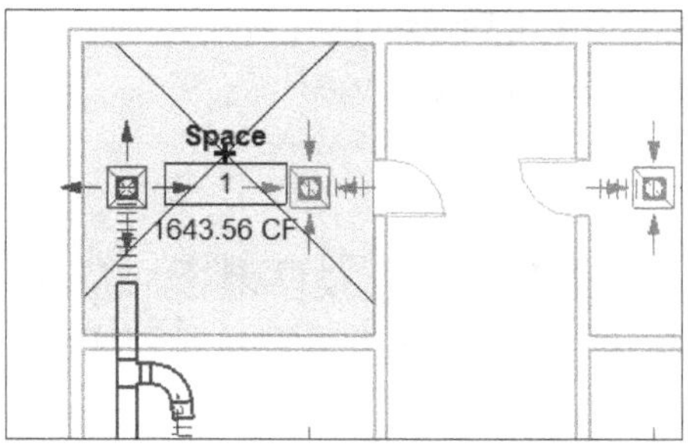

Figure-35. Space assigned with volume value

Creating Space Separator

The **Space Separator** tool is used to create separator line to divide selected space. The procedure to use this tool is given next.

- Click on the **Space Separator** tool from the **Spaces** panel of **Analyze** tab in the **Ribbon**. The options to place space separator will be displayed; refer to Figure-36.

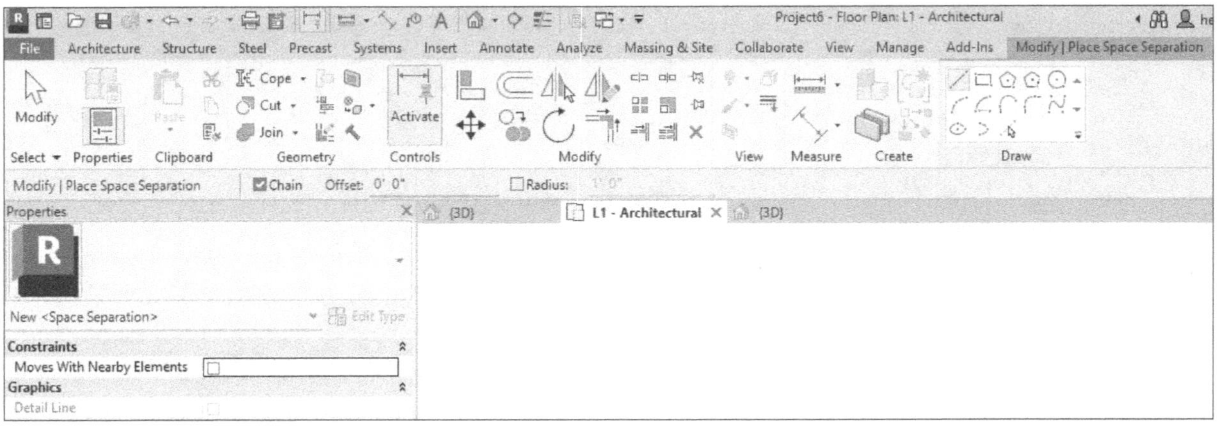

Figure-36. Space separation options

- Create a closed loop inside the space to create a separate zone. If you want to separate a portion of space then create a line, arc, or spline connecting the boundary lines; refer to Figure-37.

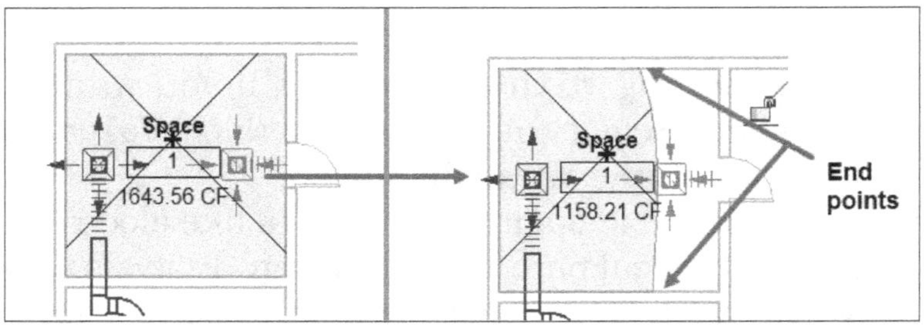

Figure-37. Separator created

- Select the **Moves With Nearby Elements** check box to allow changes of separator curve when you move the connected walls.
- Press **ESC** to exit the tool.

Applying Space Tag

The **Space Tag** tool is used to apply space tag at desired space. The procedure to use this tool is given next.

- Click on the **Space Tag** tool from the **Spaces** panel in the **Analyze** tab of **Ribbon** and hover the cursor inside a space. The tag will be displayed; refer to Figure-38.

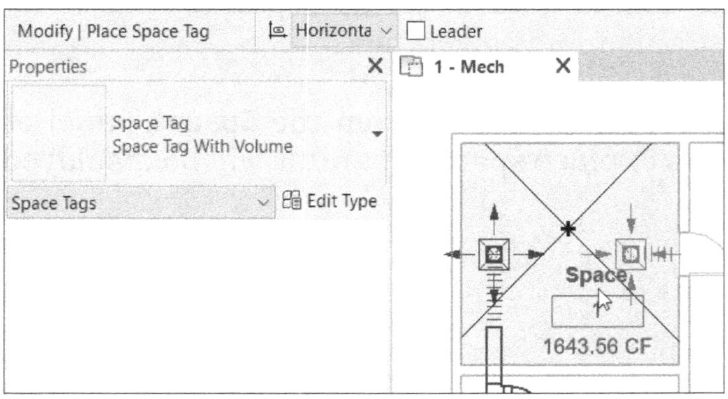

Figure-38. Preview of space tag

- Select desired space tag from the drop-down at the top in the **Properties Palette** and click inside the space to create tag.
- Press **ESC** to exit the tool.

Applying Space Naming

The **Space Naming** tool is used to assign names to various spaces in the drawing. The procedure to use this tool is given next.

- Click on the **Space Naming** tool from the **Spaces** panel of **Analyze** tab in the **Ribbon**. The **Space Naming** dialog box will be displayed; refer to Figure-39.

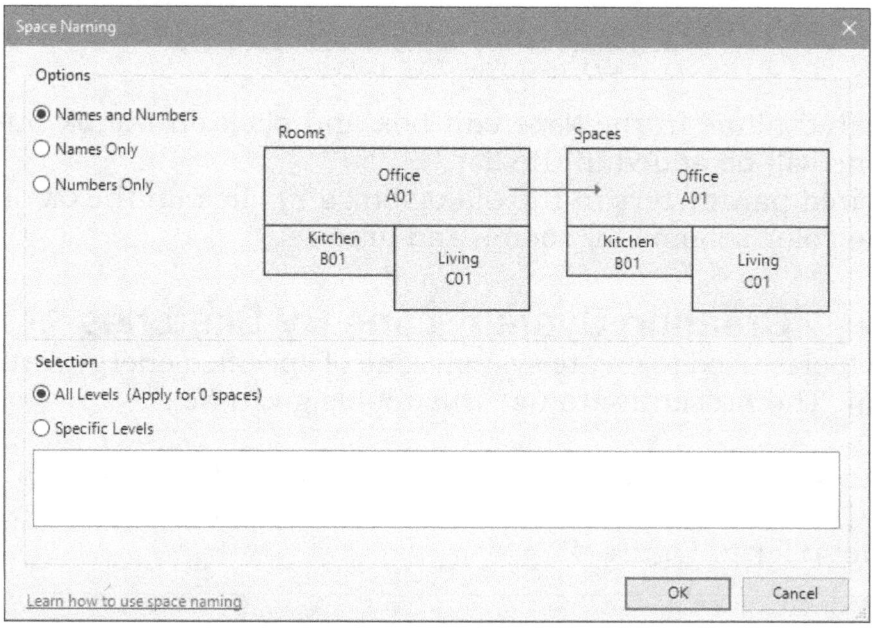

Figure-39. Space Naming dialog box

- Select desired radio buttons from the dialog box and click on the **OK** button. The tag will be modified accordingly.

Color Schemes

The **Color Schemes** tool is used to create or modify color scheme for filling of rooms and areas. The procedure to use this tool is discussed next.

- Click on the **Color Schemes** tool from the expanded **Spaces** panel of **Analyze** tab in the **Ribbon**. The **Edit Color Scheme** dialog box will be displayed; refer to Figure-40.

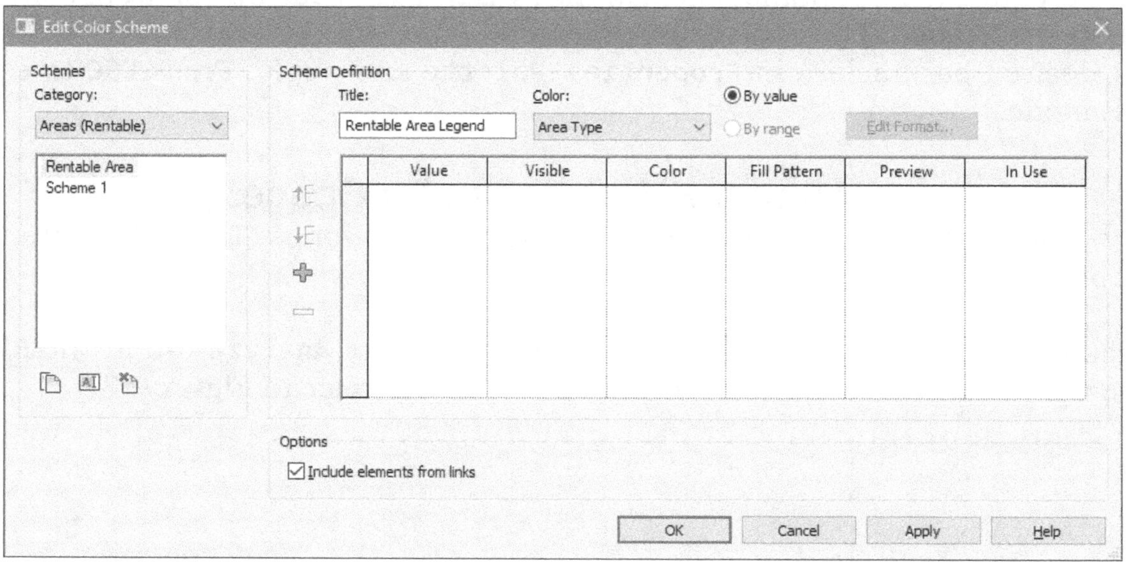

Figure-40. Edit Color Scheme dialog box

- Click on the **Add Value** button from the dialog box. The **New Color Scheme Entry** dialog box will be displayed; refer to Figure-41.

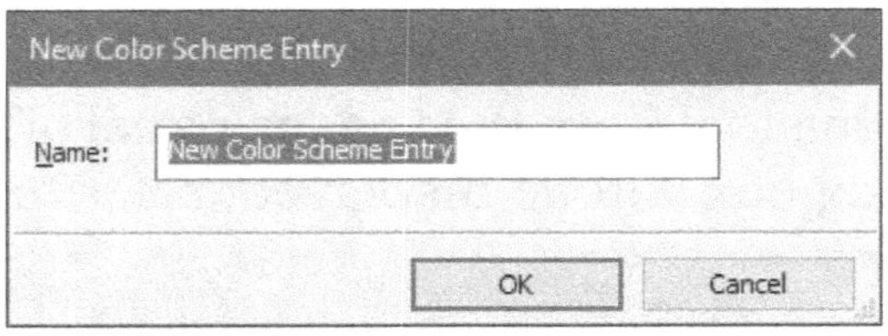

Figure-41. New color scheme dialog box

- Specify desired name in the **Name** edit box and click on the **OK** button. The new color scheme will be added in the list.
- Specify desired parameters in the dialog box and click on the **OK** or **Apply** button to apply the color scheme for rooms and areas.

Creating System Zone By Sketches

The **By Sketch** tool is used to create system zone of specified energy settings at desired sketch location. The procedure to use this tool is given next.

- Click on the **By Sketch** tool from the **Zoning** panel of **Analyze** tab in the **Ribbon**. The **Modify|Create Zone** contextual tab will be displayed with options to create system zone; refer to Figure-42.

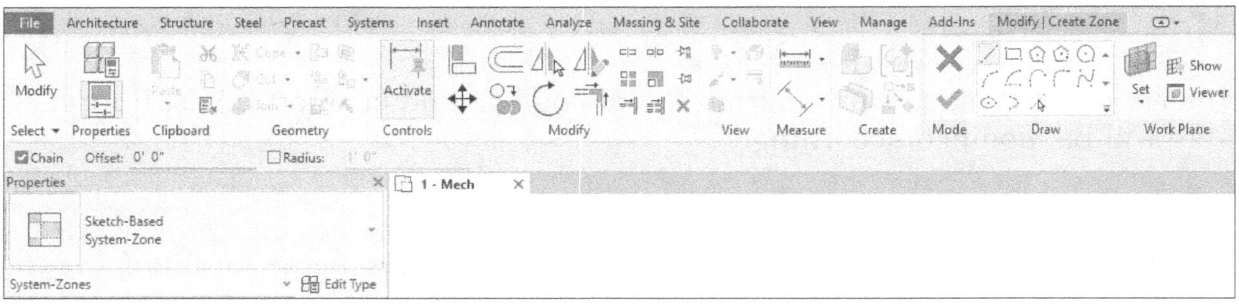

Figure-42. Modify Create Zone contextual tab

- Select desired sketch creation tool from the **Draw** panel in the contextual tab and create the closed loop boundary of system zone.
- After creating the boundary, click on the **Finish Edit Mode** button from contextual tab in the **Ribbon**. The zone will be created.
- Set desired parameters in **Properties Palette** and apply. Press **ESC** to exit the edit mode.

Defining HVAC Zones By Space

The **By Space** tool is used to define and modify HVAC zones. The procedure to use this tool is given next.

- Click on the **By Space** tool from the **Zoning** panel of **Analyze** tab in the **Ribbon**. The **Create Zone** contextual tab will be displayed; refer to Figure-43.

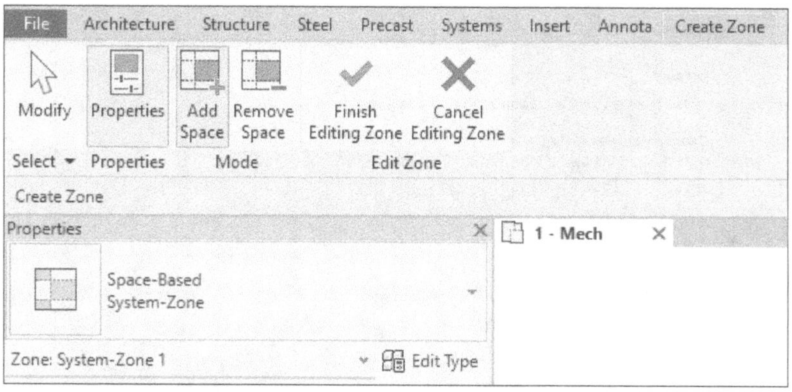

Figure-43. Create Zone contextual tab

- Select all the spaces that you want to add/remove from HVAC zone; refer to Figure-44, select the **Add Space** or **Remove Space** toggle button from **Ribbon** as needed, and click on the **Finish Editing Zone** tool from the contextual tab in the **Ribbon**.

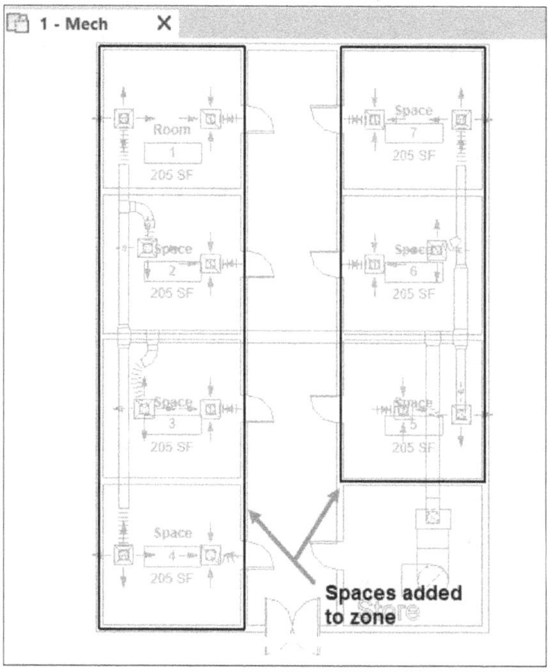

Figure-44. Spaces added to zones

- Press **ESC** to exit the tool.

Generating Duct Pressure Loss Report

The **Duct Pressure Loss Report** tool is used to generate report on how much pressure is lost in the duct system. The procedure to use this tool is given next.

- Click on the **Duct Pressure Loss Report** tool from the **Reports & Schedules** panel in the **Analyze** tab of **Ribbon**. The **Duct Pressure Loss Report - System Selector** dialog box will be displayed; refer to Figure-45.

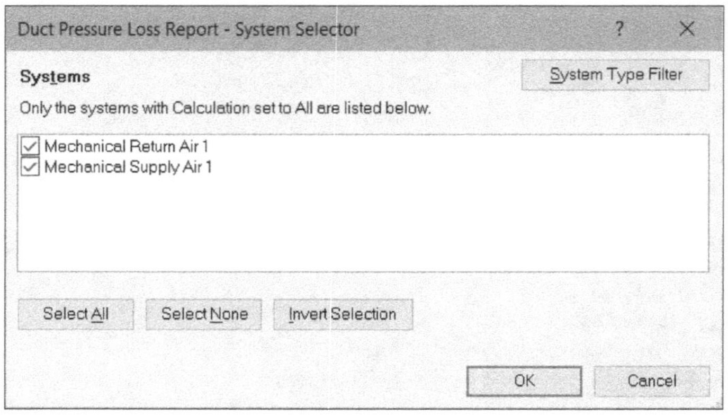

Figure-45. Duct Pressure Loss Report-System Selector dialog box

- Select the check boxes of systems for which you want to generate the loss report and click on the **OK** button from the dialog box. The **Duct Pressure Loss Report Settings** dialog box will be displayed; refer to Figure-46.

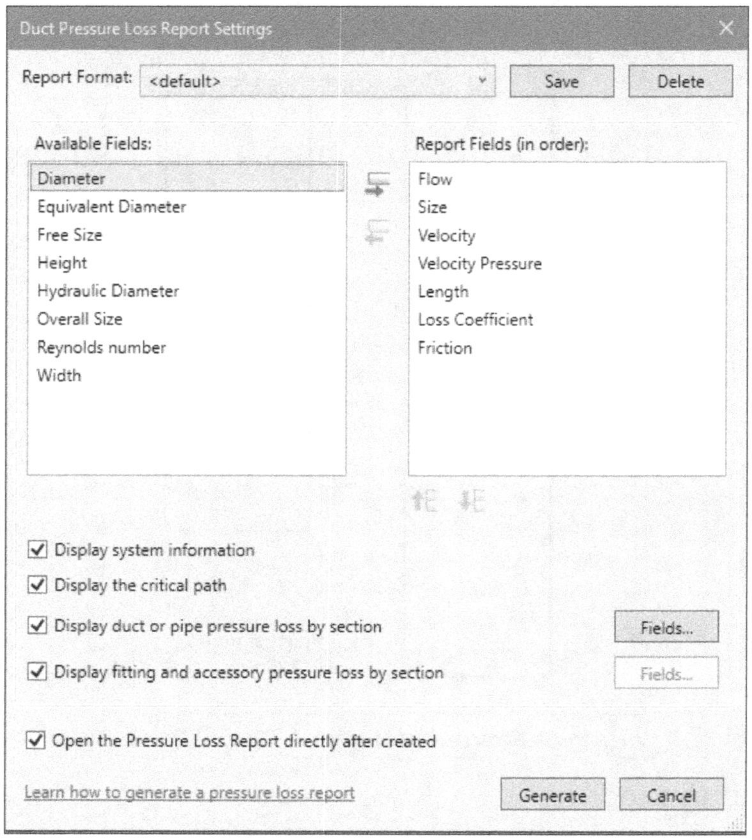

Figure-46. Duct Pressure Loss Report Settings dialog box

- Set desired fields to be included in the report and specify other parameters.
- Click on the **Generate** button from the dialog box. The **Save As** dialog box will be displayed; refer to Figure-47.

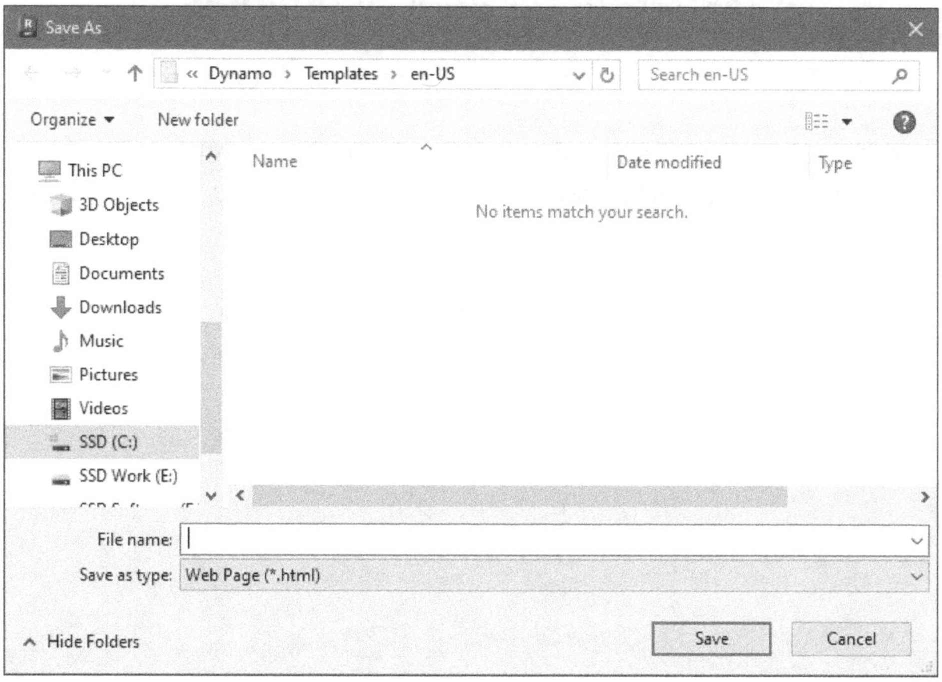

Figure-47. Save As dialog box

- Specify desired name of program in the **File name** edit box and click on the **Save** button. The file will be saved and displayed in the default web browser; refer to Figure-48.

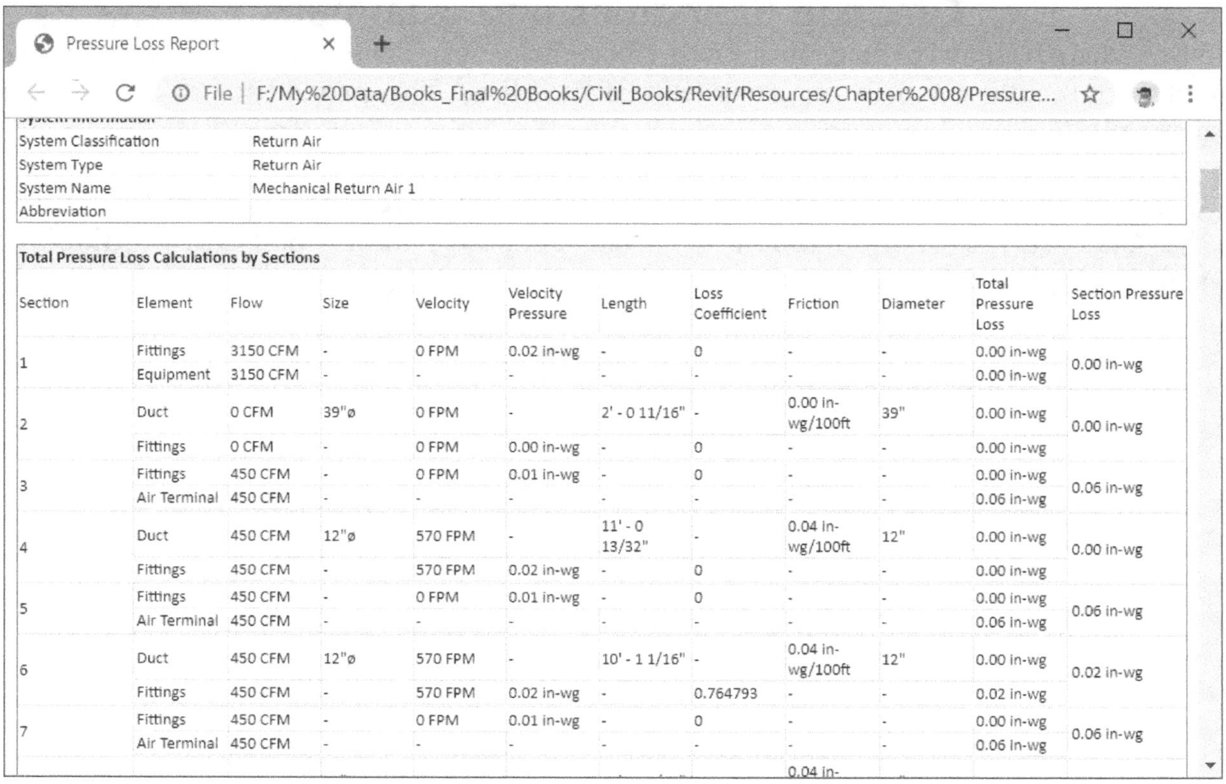

System Classification	Return Air
System Type	Return Air
System Name	Mechanical Return Air 1
Abbreviation	

Total Pressure Loss Calculations by Sections

Section	Element	Flow	Size	Velocity	Velocity Pressure	Length	Loss Coefficient	Friction	Diameter	Total Pressure Loss	Section Pressure Loss
1	Fittings	3150 CFM	-	0 FPM	0.02 in-wg	-	0	-	-	0.00 in-wg	0.00 in-wg
	Equipment	3150 CFM	-	-	-	-	-	-	-	0.00 in-wg	
2	Duct	0 CFM	39"ø	0 FPM	-	2' - 0 11/16"	-	0.00 in-wg/100ft	39"	0.00 in-wg	0.00 in-wg
	Fittings	0 CFM	-	0 FPM	0.00 in-wg	-	0	-	-	0.00 in-wg	
3	Fittings	450 CFM	-	0 FPM	0.01 in-wg	-	0	-	-	0.00 in-wg	0.06 in-wg
	Air Terminal	450 CFM	-	-	-	-	-	-	-	0.06 in-wg	
4	Duct	450 CFM	12"ø	570 FPM	-	11' - 0 13/32"	-	0.04 in-wg/100ft	12"	0.00 in-wg	0.00 in-wg
	Fittings	450 CFM	-	570 FPM	0.02 in-wg	-	0	-	-	0.00 in-wg	
5	Fittings	450 CFM	-	0 FPM	0.01 in-wg	-	0	-	-	0.00 in-wg	0.06 in-wg
	Air Terminal	450 CFM	-	-	-	-	-	-	-	0.06 in-wg	
6	Duct	450 CFM	12"ø	570 FPM	-	10' - 1 1/16"	-	0.04 in-wg/100ft	12"	0.00 in-wg	0.02 in-wg
	Fittings	450 CFM	-	570 FPM	0.02 in-wg	-	0.764793	-	-	0.02 in-wg	
7	Fittings	450 CFM	-	0 FPM	0.01 in-wg	-	0	-	-	0.00 in-wg	0.06 in-wg
	Air Terminal	450 CFM	-	-	-	-	-	-	-	0.06 in-wg	

Figure-48. Pressure loss report displayed in web browser

Similarly, you can create pipe pressure loss report by using the **Pipe Pressure Loss Report** tool in the **Reports & Schedules** panel of **Analyze** tab in the **Ribbon**.

Generating Panel Schedules

The **Panel Schedules** tool is used to generate schedules of panels used in electrical circuit of building. The procedure to use this tool is given next.

- Click on the **Panel Schedules** tool from the **Reports & Schedules** panel of **Analyze** tab in the **Ribbon**. The **Create Panel Schedules** dialog box will be displayed; refer to Figure-49.

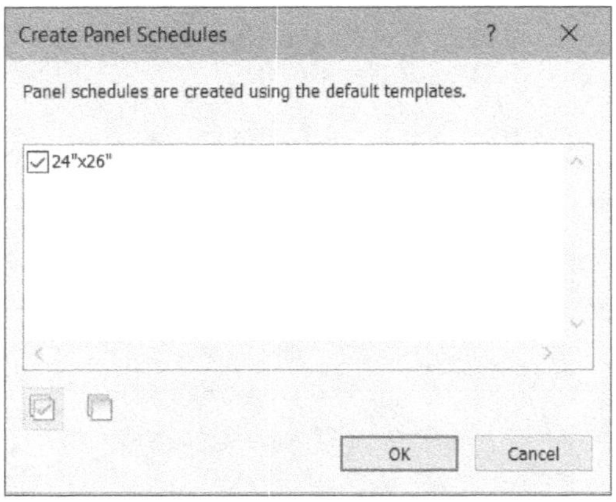

Figure-49. Create Panel Schedules dialog box

- Select check boxes for panels to be included in the report and click on the **OK** button. The panel schedule will be created.

Creating Schedules and Quantities

The **Schedule/Quantities** tool is used to create a schedule of quantities of different objects/materials used in construction of building. The procedure to use this tool is given next.

- Click on the **Schedule/Quantities** tool from the **Reports & Schedules** panel in the **Analyze** tab of the **Ribbon**. The **New Schedule** dialog box will be displayed; refer to Figure-50.

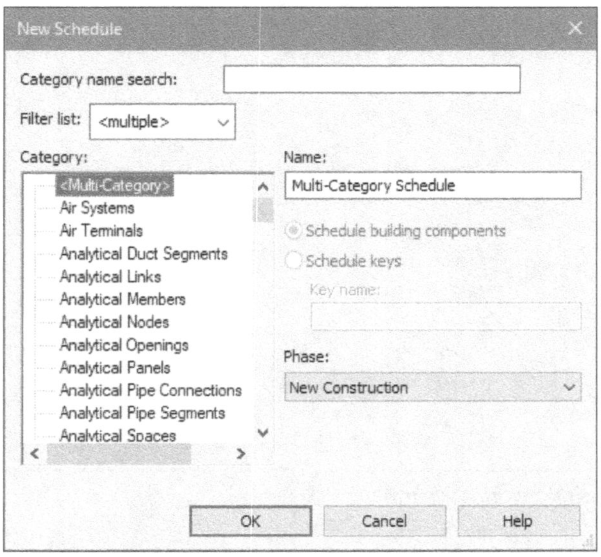

Figure-50. New Schedule dialog box

- Select desired category or search the category by its name using **Category name search** box for which you want to create schedule and click on the **OK** button from the dialog box. The **Schedule Properties** dialog box will be displayed; refer to Figure-51.

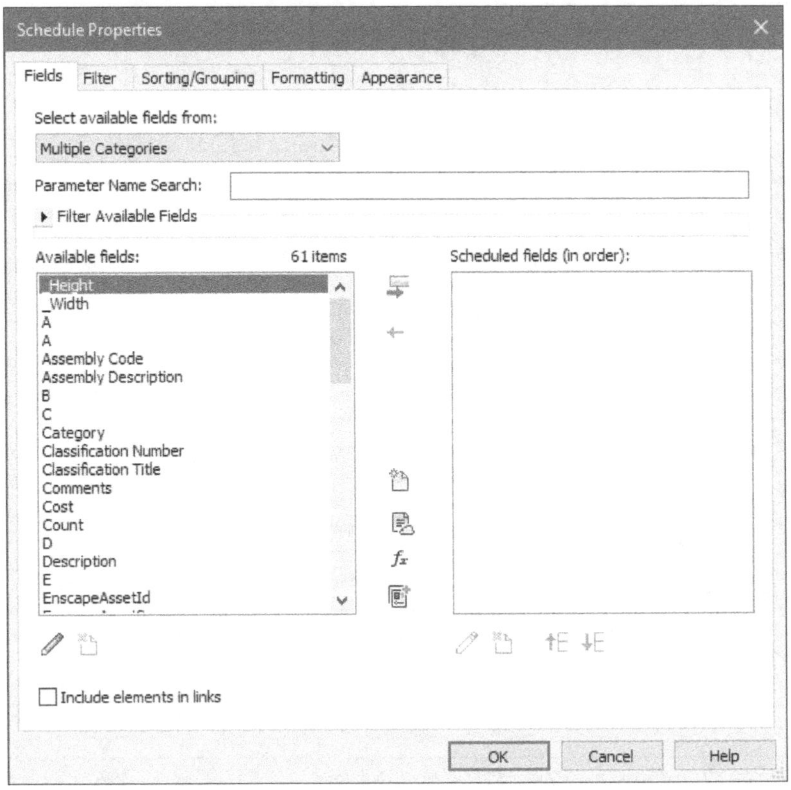

Figure-51. Schedule Properties dialog box

- Select desired option from the drop-down and add desired fields in the schedule.
- Set the parameters in other tabs of dialog box as desired and click on the **OK** button. The schedule will be created; refer to Figure-52.

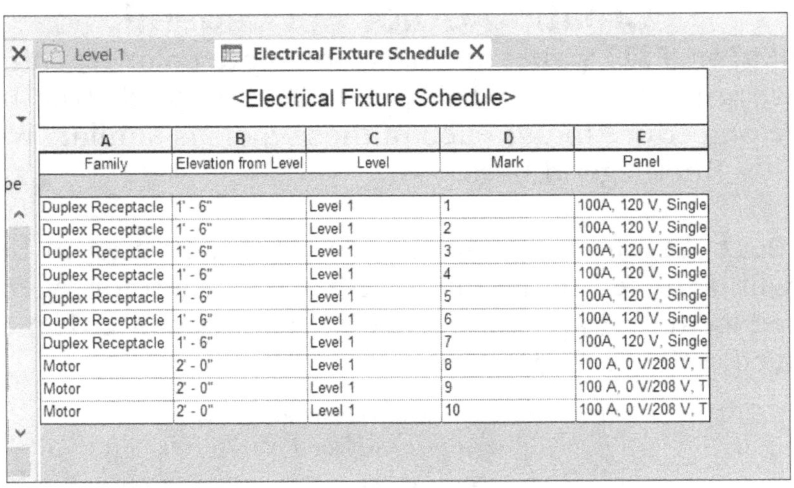

<Electrical Fixture Schedule>

A	B	C	D	E
Family	Elevation from Level	Level	Mark	Panel
Duplex Receptacle	1' - 6"	Level 1	1	100A, 120 V, Single
Duplex Receptacle	1' - 6"	Level 1	2	100A, 120 V, Single
Duplex Receptacle	1' - 6"	Level 1	3	100A, 120 V, Single
Duplex Receptacle	1' - 6"	Level 1	4	100A, 120 V, Single
Duplex Receptacle	1' - 6"	Level 1	5	100A, 120 V, Single
Duplex Receptacle	1' - 6"	Level 1	6	100A, 120 V, Single
Duplex Receptacle	1' - 6"	Level 1	7	100A, 120 V, Single
Motor	2' - 0"	Level 1	8	100 A, 0 V/208 V, T
Motor	2' - 0"	Level 1	9	100 A, 0 V/208 V, T
Motor	2' - 0"	Level 1	10	100 A, 0 V/208 V, T

Figure-52. Schedule created

Defining Building/Space Type Settings

The **Building/Space Type Settings** tool (inclined arrow) of **Reports & Schedules** panel is used to define parameters for different types of buildings and spaces. The procedure to use this tool is given next.

- Click on the inclined arrow **(Building/Space Type Settings)** button from the **Reports & Schedules** panel in the **Analyze** tab of the **Ribbon**. The **Building/Space Type Settings** dialog box will be displayed; refer to Figure-53.

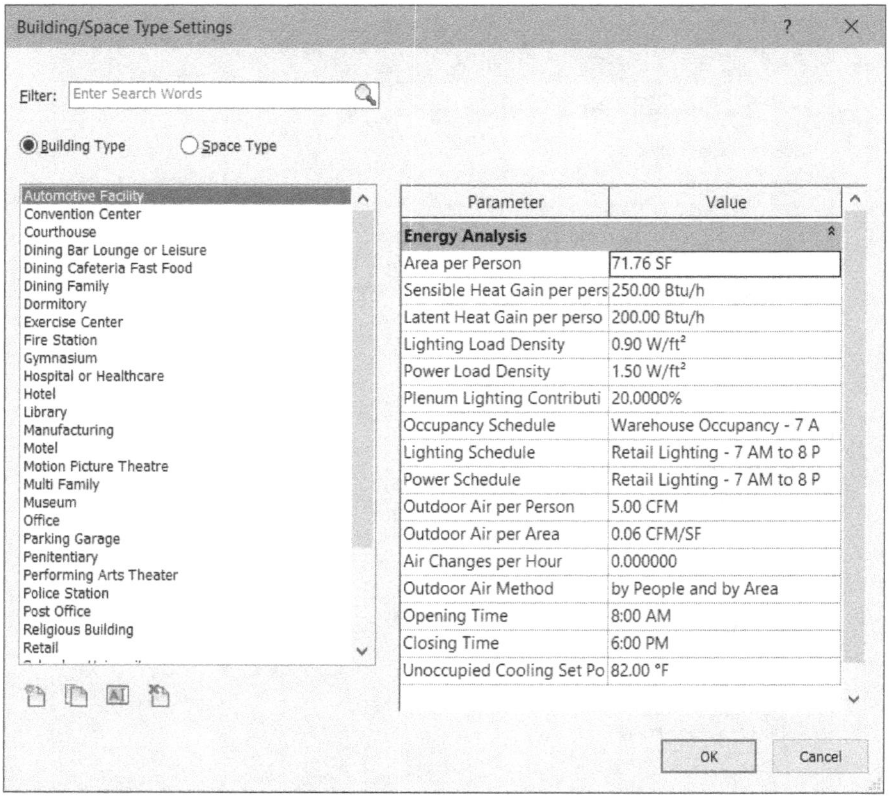

Figure-53. Building/Space Type Settings dialog box

- Select desired building type from the left list box and define various parameters in the right area of dialog box.
- Click on the **OK** button from the dialog box.

Creating Color Fill Legend

The tools in the **Color Fill** panel are used to create color legend for different flow parameters. There are three tools in this panel; **Duct Legend**, **Pipe Legend**, and **Color Fill Legend**. The procedure to use each of these tools is similar. We will discuss the procedure to create duct legend here.

- Click on the **Duct Legend** tool from the **Color Fill** panel in the **Analyze** tab of **Ribbon**. You will be asked to define placement location for legend.
- Click at desired location to place the legend. The **Choose Color Scheme** dialog box will be displayed; refer to Figure-54.

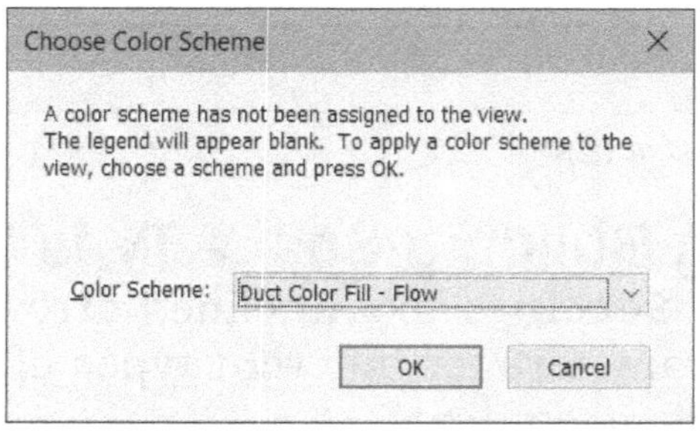

Figure-54. Choose Color Scheme dialog box

- Select desired option from the **Color Scheme** drop-down and click on the **OK** button from the dialog box. The legend will be created with color code; refer to Figure-55.

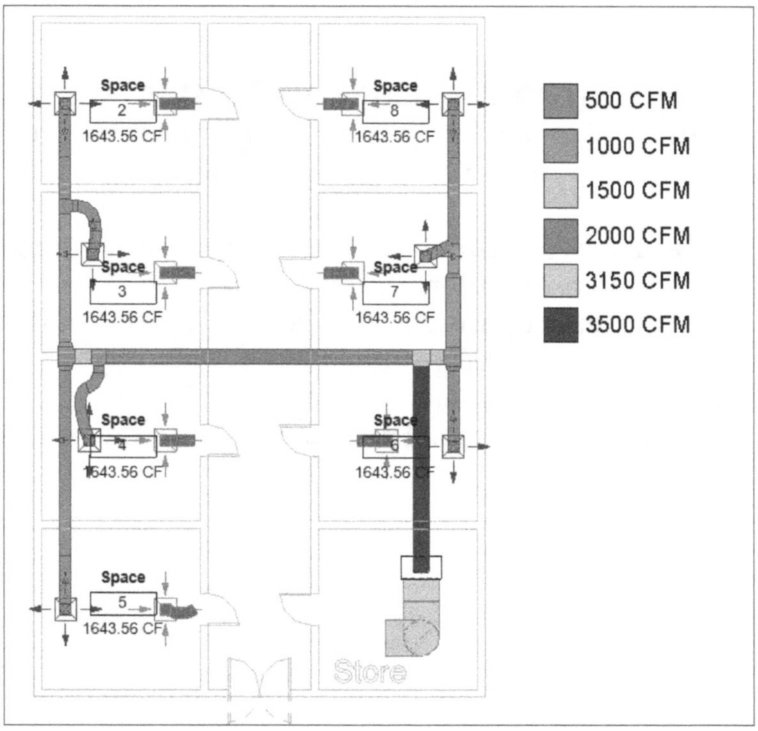

Figure-55. Duct color legend created

Forma Analysis

When the model connects to a scenario and uses contextual data and other models, Forma Analysis provides insights to help in making informed decisions related to wind analysis. This tool is specially useful for high-rise building design. The tools in this panel are activate in commercial version of this software.

Specifying Geographic Location for Project

The **Location** tool is used to specify location for current project. The procedure to use this tool is given next.

- Click on the **Location** tool from the **Energy Optimization** panel of **Analyze** tab in the **Ribbon**. The **Location and Site** dialog box will be displayed; refer to Figure-56.

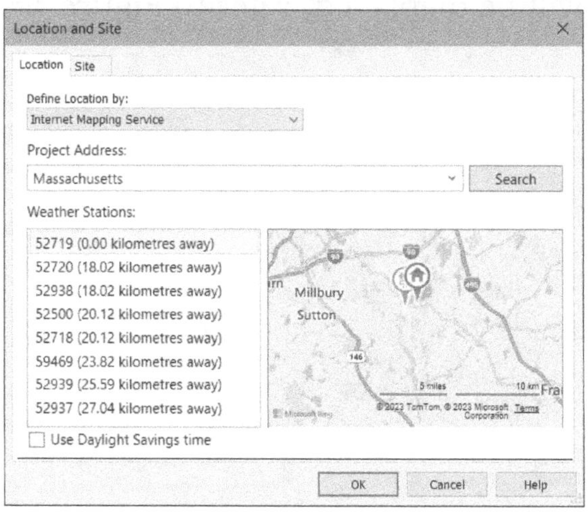

Figure-56. Location and Site dialog box

- Search desired location and set desired parameters in the dialog box like distance from the selected address, weather, and so on.
- Click on the **OK** button to apply the location.

Creating Energy Model

The **Create Energy Model** tool is used to prepare analytical model for energy simulation of building. The procedure to use this tool is given next.

- Click on the **Create Energy Model** tool from the **Energy Optimization** panel in the **Analyze** tab of **Ribbon**. An information box will be displayed telling you that the process of creating energy model will take time and you will not be able to use the Revit software in the mean time.
- Click on the **Create the Energy Analytical Model** button from the information box. Once the process is complete. The analytical model will be displayed; refer to Figure-57.

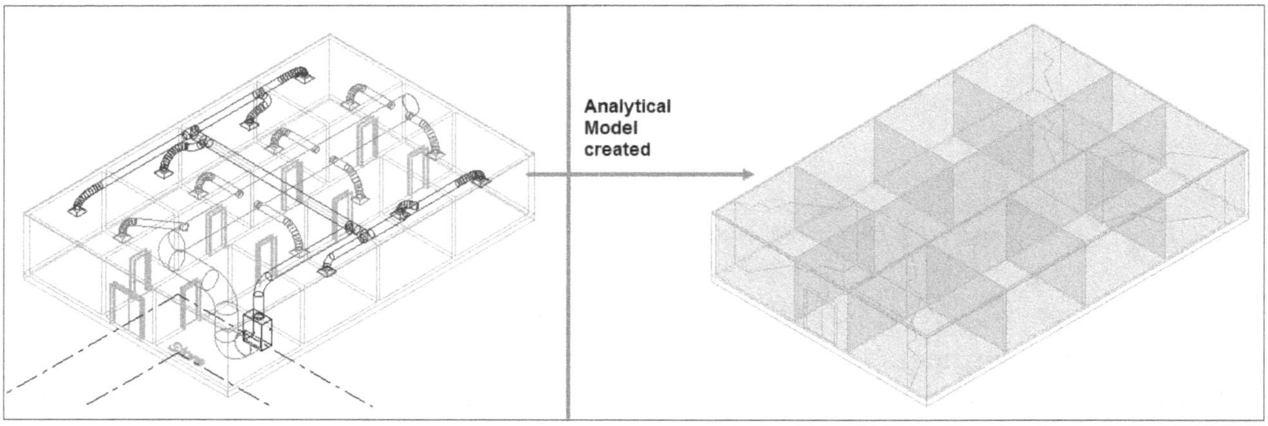

Figure-57. Analytical model

Defining Energy Model Settings

The **Energy Model Settings** tool in **Energy Optimization** panel is used to define parameters for generating analytical energy model. The procedure to use this tool is given next.

- Click on the **Energy Model Settings** tool from **Energy Model Settings** drop-down in the **Energy Optimization** panel of **Analyze** tab in the **Ribbon**. The **Energy Model Settings** dialog box will be displayed; refer to Figure-58.

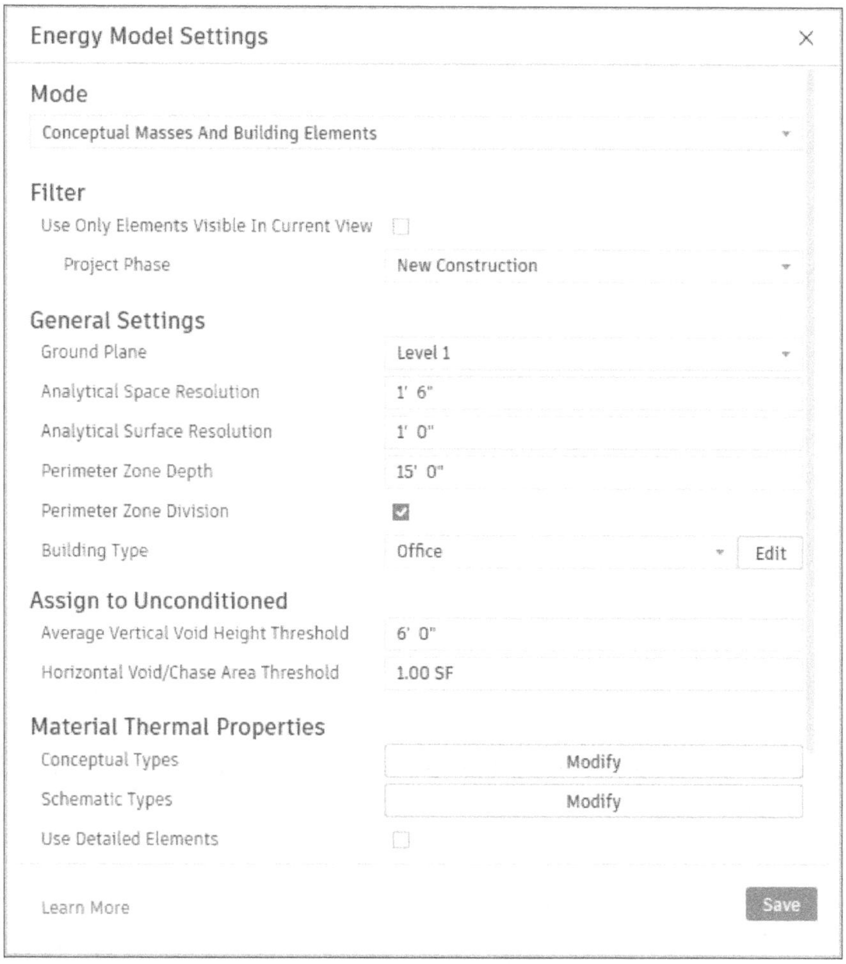

Figure-58. Energy Model Settings dialog box

- Set desired parameters for creating energy model. In **Mode** field, we define whether the building has conceptual masses or it is a building only or it is a combination of both. Selecting correct option saves processing time.
- In **Ground Plane** field, we define at what level system will assume the earth ground and stop analyzing further.
- In **Analytical Space Resolution** and **Analytical Surface Resolution** fields, we define the minimum size of analytical model elements. The lower you define element size, the more accurate you will get analysis result but at the cost of higher processing time.
- In **Perimeter Zone Depth** field, we define the depth upto which you want to check energy analysis from main entrance.
- Set desired parameters in the dialog box and click on **Save** button to apply the settings.

Energy Model Guide

The **Energy Model Guide** tool provides step by step guidance to set up and configure the energy analytical model. The procedure to use this tool is discussed next.

- Click on the **Energy Model Guide** tool from **Energy Model Settings** drop-down in the **Energy Optimization** panel of **Analyze** tab in the **Ribbon**. The **Energy Model Guide** dialog box will be displayed; refer to Figure-59.

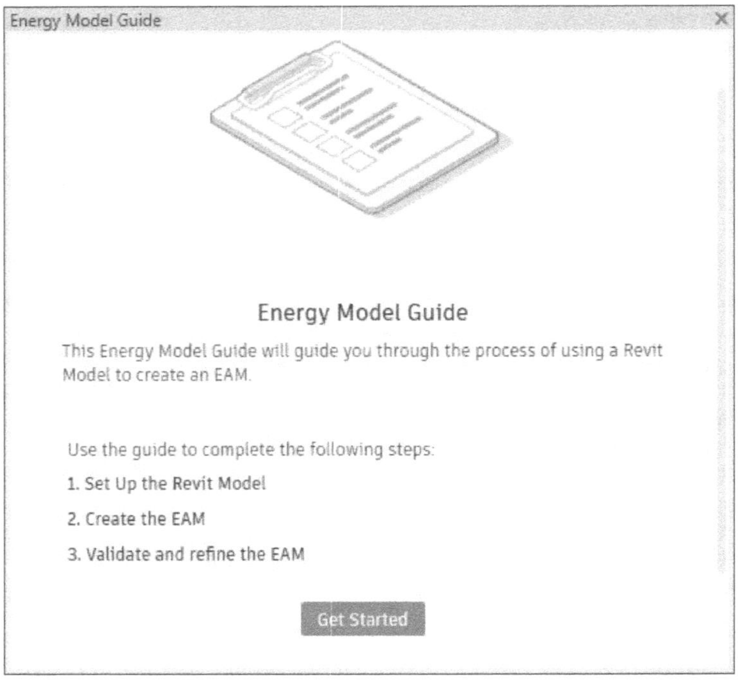

Figure-59. Energy Model Guide dialog box

- Click on the **Get Started** button, the **Set-up** page of dialog box will be displayed; refer to Figure-60.

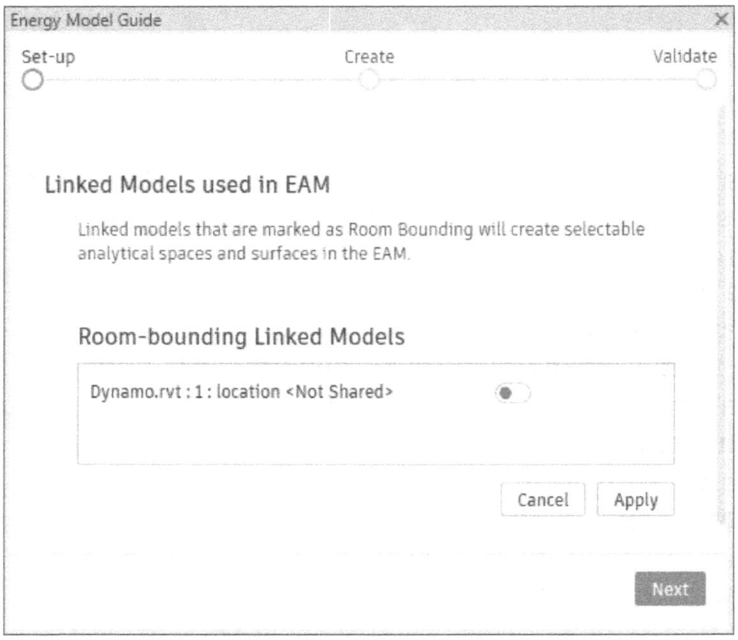

Figure-60. Set up page will be displayed with room bounding linked model

- Turn the linked model toggle button **ON** displayed in the **Room-bounding Linked Models** box if you already have analytical spaces created in some sections of the building and want to add them in current analytical model.
- Now, click on the **Apply** then **Next** button from the page. The configuration page of model will be displayed; refer to Figure-61.

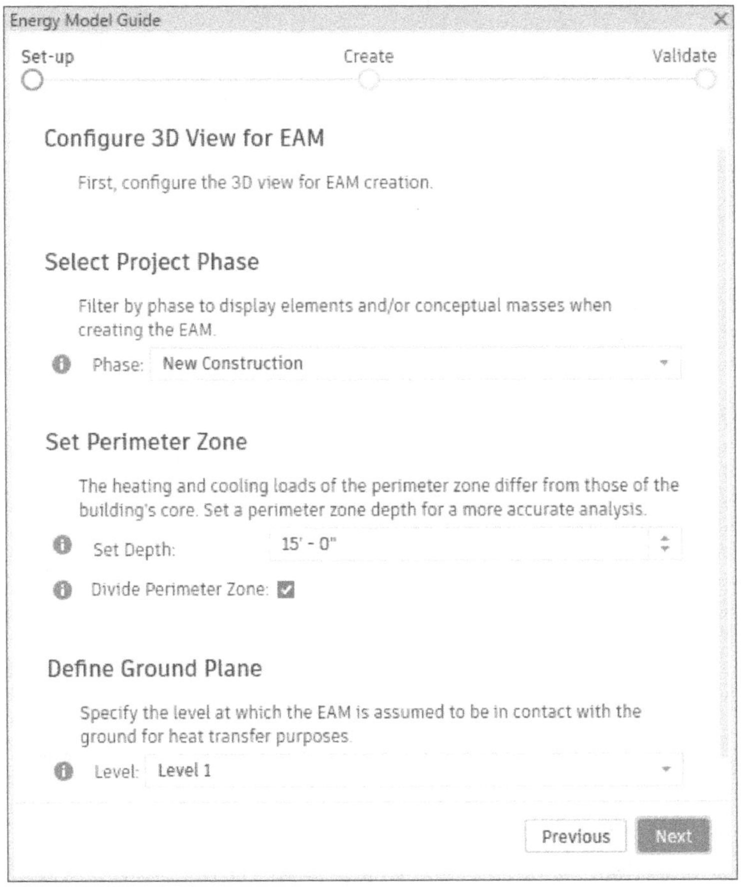

Figure-61. Configuration page of model

- Select desired phase to be used for analytical model from **Phase** drop-down of **Select Project Phase** area. The analytical model for that phase of model will be created.
- Specify desired distance to be measured inward from the exterior walls in the **Set Depth** edit box of **Set Perimeter Zone** area to define energy calculation zone. Select **Divide Perimeter Zone** check box to divide the perimeter zone at the outer corner faces.
- Select desired level at which the model is to be in contact with the ground from **Level** drop-down of **Define Ground Plane** area.
- After specifying desired parameters, click on **Next** button. The **Create** page of dialog box will be displayed; refer to Figure-62.

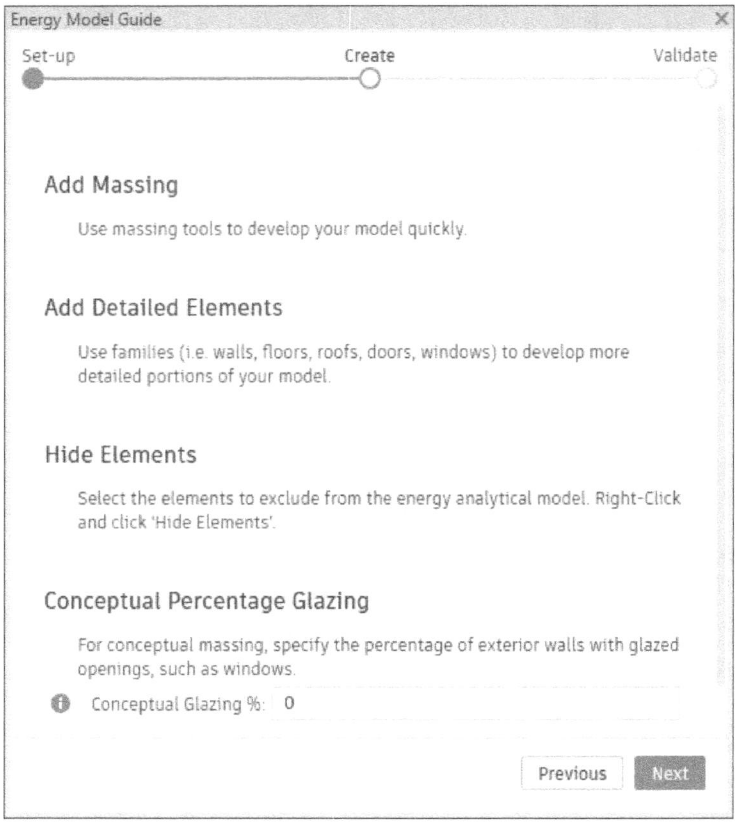

Figure-62. Create page

- Specify desired percentage of each exterior wall that has a glazed opening (windows, glasses, openings, etc.) in the **Conceptual Glazing %** edit box and click on the **Next** button. The **Schematic Types** section of **Create** page will be displayed; refer to Figure-63.

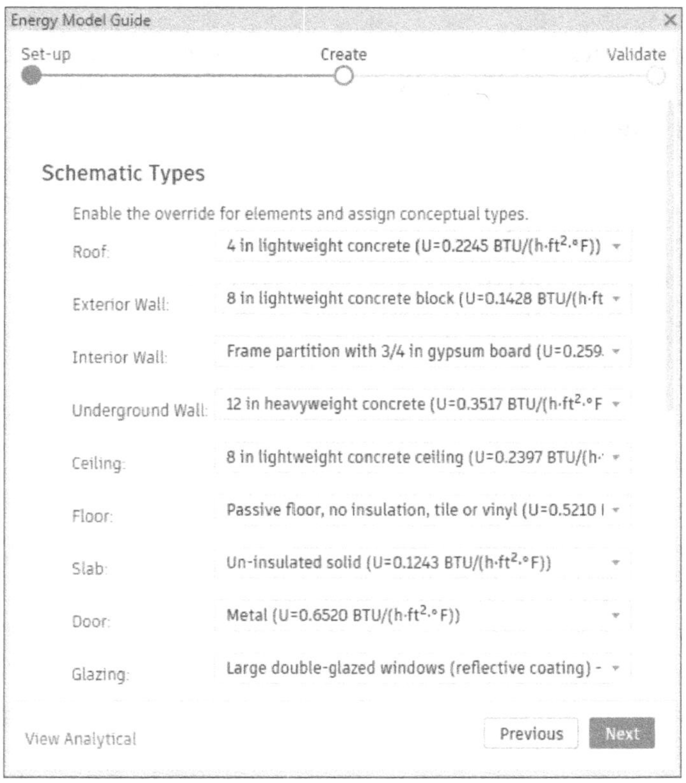

Figure-63. Schematic Types section of Create page

- Specify desired thermal properties for building elements during schematic design in the **Schematic Types** area.
- Select **Use Detailed Elements** check box from **Use Detailed Elements** area to use detailed elements in the model to create the EAM.
- Adjust the analytical resolution to optimize the performance using slider in the **Adjust Analytical Resolution** area.
- After specifying desired parameters, click on the **Next** button. A page will be displayed to set building type and add spaces; refer to Figure-64.

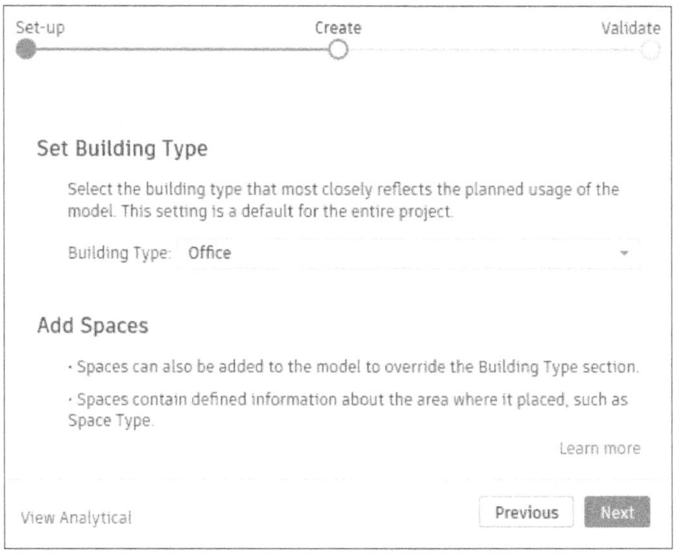

Figure-64. Page displayed to set building type and add spaces

- Select desired building type or geographic location for projects from **Building Type** drop-down in the **Set Building Type** area.
- You can also add spaces in the areas of building model for performing system analysis on the building model in the **Add Spaces** area.
- After specifying desired parameters, click on **Next** button. The **Validate** page of the dialog box will be displayed; refer to Figure-65.

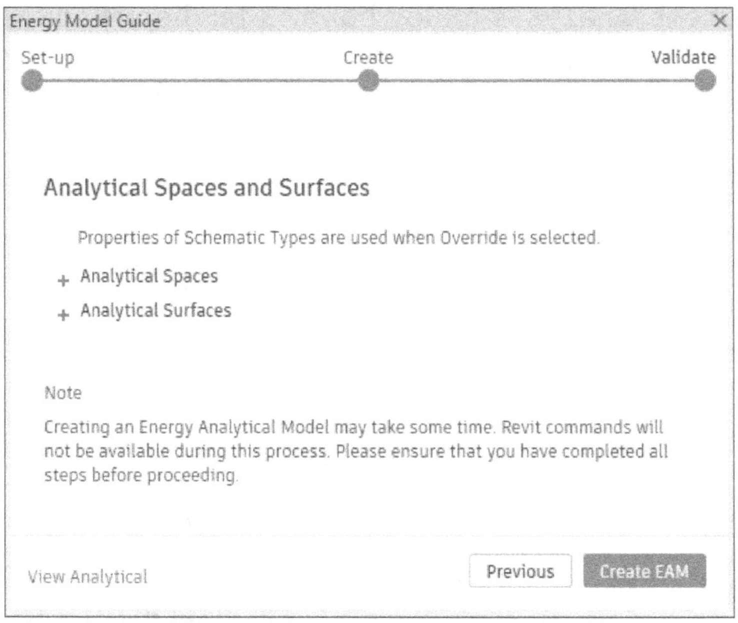

Figure-65. Validate page

- Click on the **Create EAM** button, the **Energy Analytical Model** will be displayed with the **Analytical Surfaces** and **Analytical Spaces** files opened in the graphics window; refer to Figure-66. Click on **Close** button to close the **Energy Model Guide** dialog box.

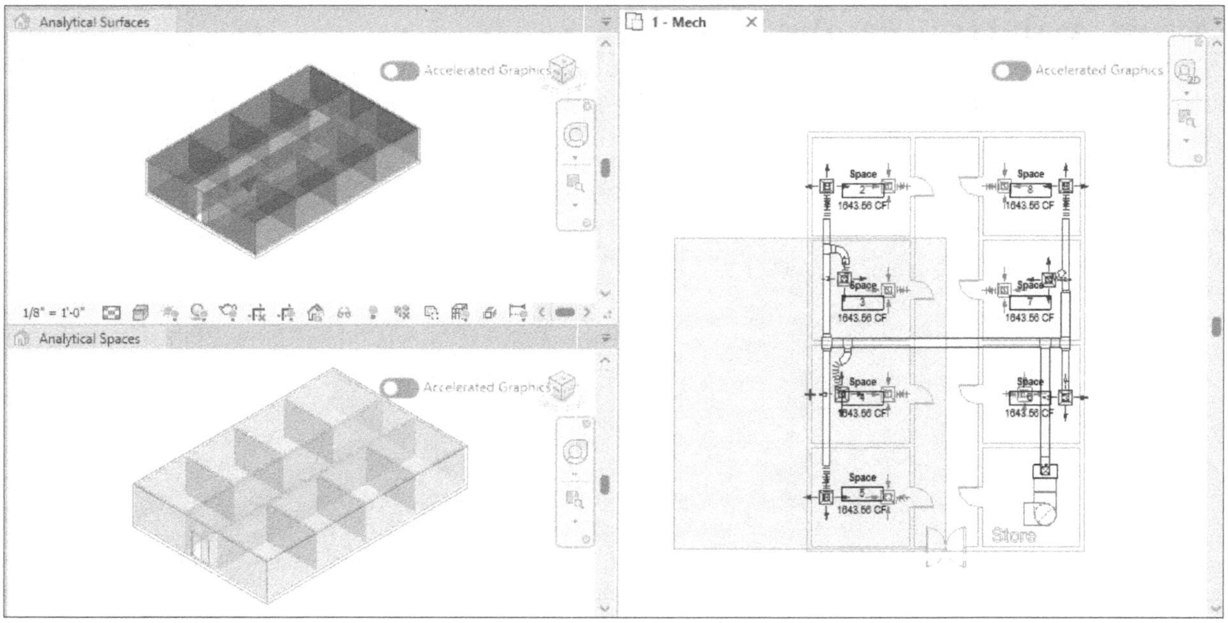

Figure-66. Energy Analytical Model created

Performing System Analysis

The **Systems Analysis** tool is used to perform analysis for various systems desired in building like HVAC system and Building energy simulation. The procedure to use this tool is given next.

- After creating HVAC system or building energy model, click on the **Systems Analysis** tool from the **Energy Optimization** panel in the **Analyze** tab of the **Ribbon**. The **Systems Analysis** dialog box will be displayed; refer to Figure-67.

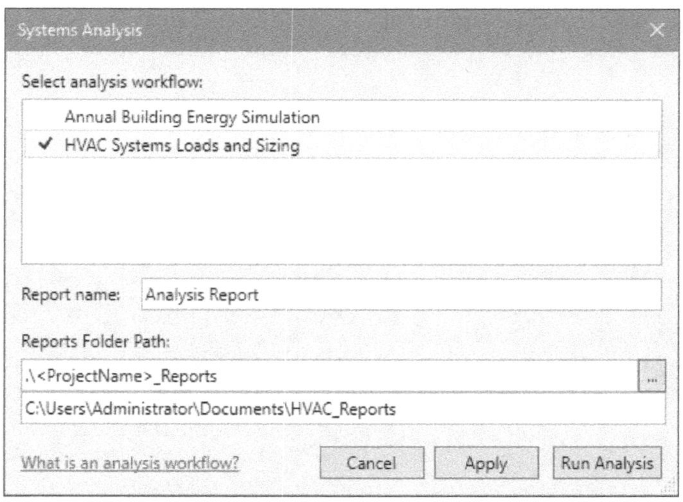

Figure-67. Systems Analysis dialog box

- Select desired option from the **Select analysis workflow** list box in the dialog box.

- Make sure to specify desired folder location in the **Reports Folder Path** field as this is where report file will be saved. After specifying parameters, click on the **Apply** then **Run Analysis** button from the **Systems Analysis** dialog box. The report calculations will run in background and once calculations are finished, the report will be generated.

Analyzing Forma Carbon Insights

The **Analyze** tool is used to generate an analytical model from the architectural and structural model of building, and upload it to the cloud. The model is then analyzed in the cloud for key sustainability and performance aspects of the building. The procedure to use this tool is discussed next.

- Click on the **Analyze** tool from **Forma Carbon Insights** panel of **Analyze** tab in the **Ribbon**. The **Energy Analytical Model Required** window will be displayed asking to create the Energy Analytical Model; refer to Figure-68.

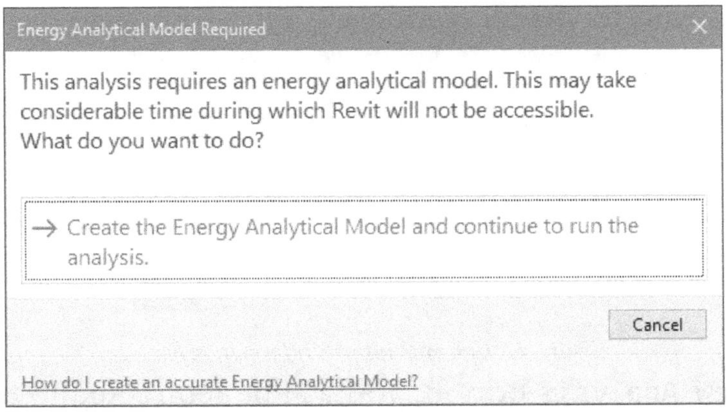

Figure-68. Energy Analytical Model Required box

- Click on the **Create the Energy Analytical Model and continue to run the analysis** button. The **Energy Analytical Model Complete** message box will be displayed; refer to Figure-69.

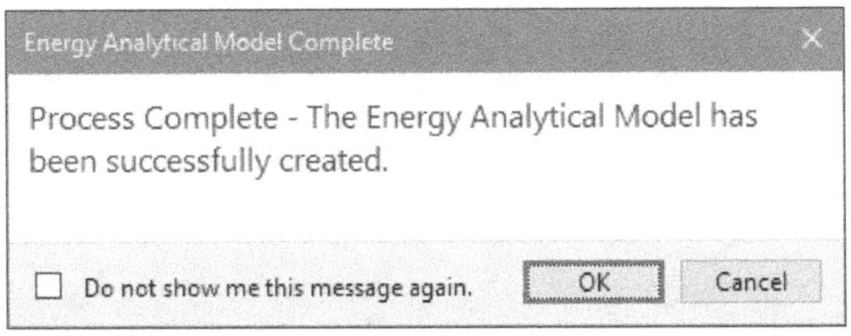

Figure-69. Energy Analytical Model Complete message box

- Click on the **OK** button from the box, the **Forma Carbon Insights** information box will be displayed; refer to Figure-70.

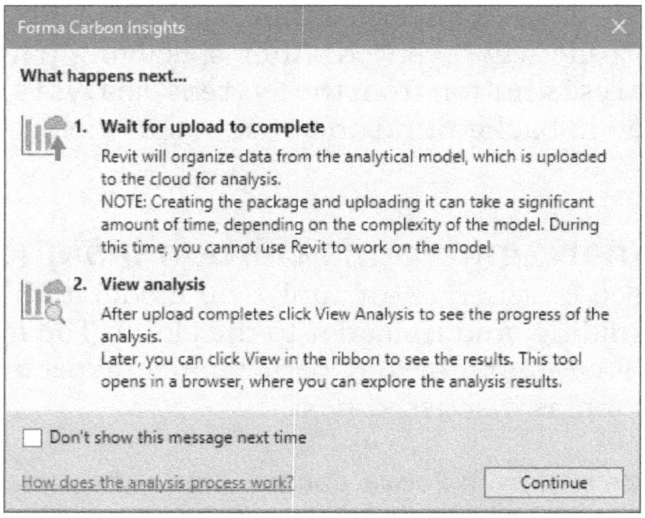

Figure-70. Forma Carbon Insights information box

- Click on the **Continue** button, the **Generate insights** information box will be displayed asking you to view the analysis; refer to Figure-71.

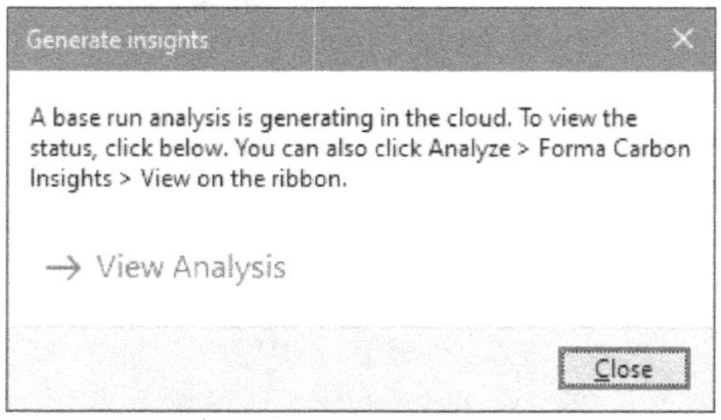

Figure-71. Generate insights information box

- Click on the **View Analysis** button, you will be redirected to the **https://forma-carbon-insights.autodesk.com** website page in your default web browser. Login using the same initials as used in **Revit Autodesk** account. You will find the model recently uploaded on Insight; refer to Figure-72. Once the analysis of model is complete, you will get the detailed insight of energy consumed by your building.

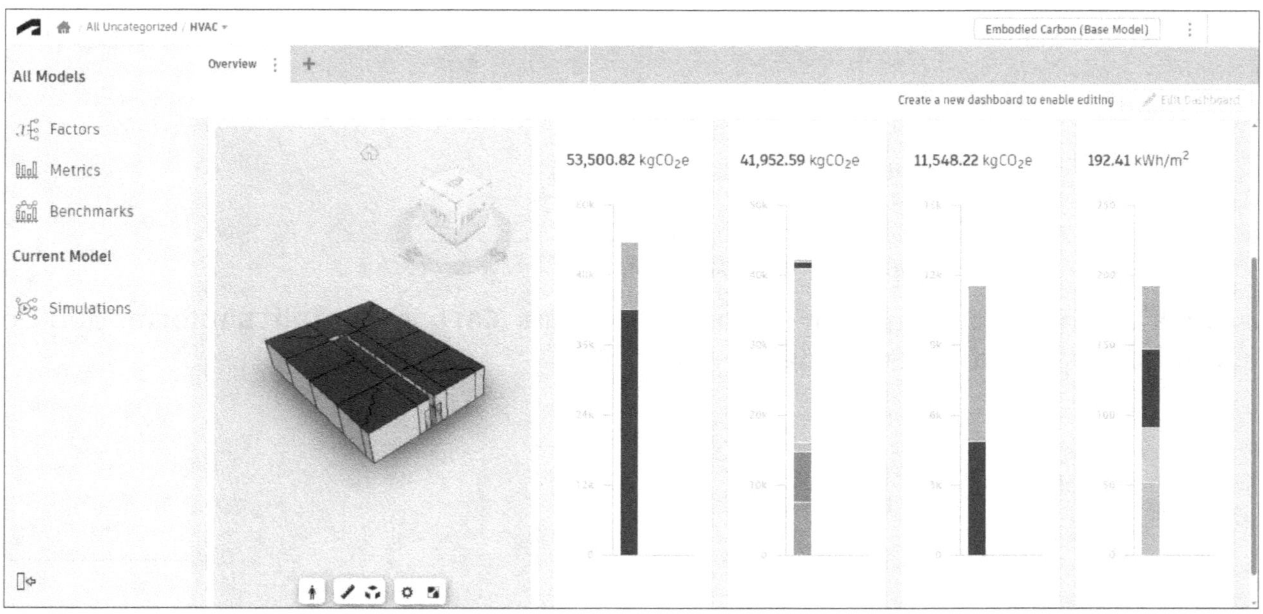

Figure-72. Energy analytical model uploaded to Insight

View

The **View** tool in **Forma Carbon Insights** panel is used to open the latest analysis results previously submitted for the active building model.

Creating Boundaries for Area Based Load

The **Area Based Load Boundary** tool is used to create boundaries for area based electrical load. The procedure to use this tool is discussed next.

- Click on the **Area Based Load Boundary** tool from the **Electrical Analysis** panel of **Analyze** tab in the **Ribbon**. The **Modify|Place Area Based Load Boundary** contextual tab will be displayed; refer to Figure-73.

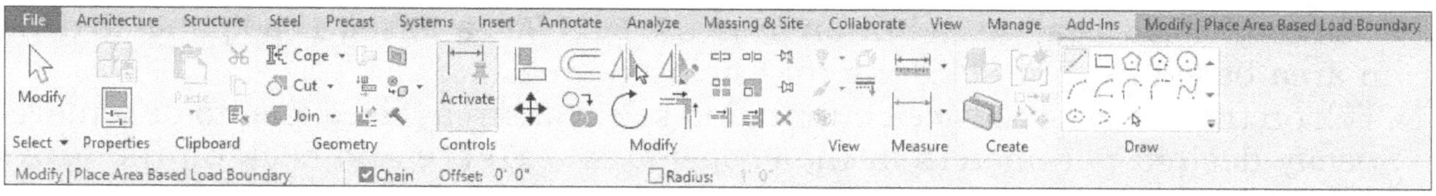

Figure-73. Options to place Area load boundary

- Creating desired boundary using tools in **Draw** panel of contextual tab in the **Ribbon** and click on the **OK** button to create the boundary.
- Press **ESC** to exit the tool.

Show/Hide Boundary Open-Ends

The **Show/Hide Boundary Open Ends** tool is used to display or hide the open ends of area based load boundary lines. The procedure to use this tool is discussed next.

- Click on the **Show/Hide Boundary Open Ends** tool from the **Area Based Load Boundary** drop-down in the **Electrical Analysis** panel of **Analyze** tab in the **Ribbon**.
- Select desired ends that you want to show or hide; refer to Figure-74.

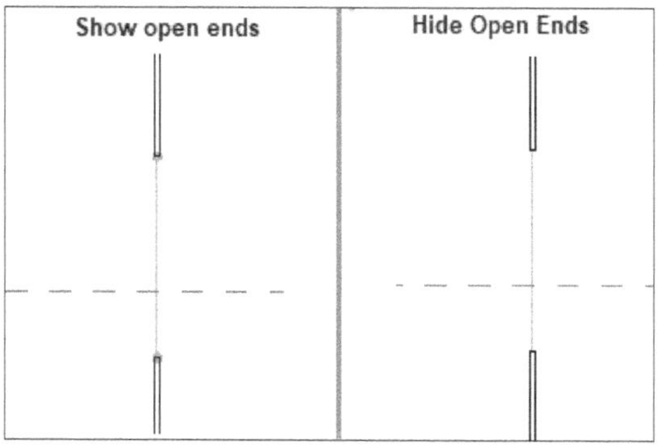

Figure-74. Showing/hiding open ends

Area Based Load

The **Area Based Load** tool is used to generate a load based on the area enclosed by the defined area load boundaries. The procedure to use this tool is discussed next.

- Click on the **Area Based Load** tool from the **Electrical Analysis** panel of **Analyze** tab in the **Ribbon**. The **Edit Area Based Load** contextual tab will be displayed; refer to Figure-75.

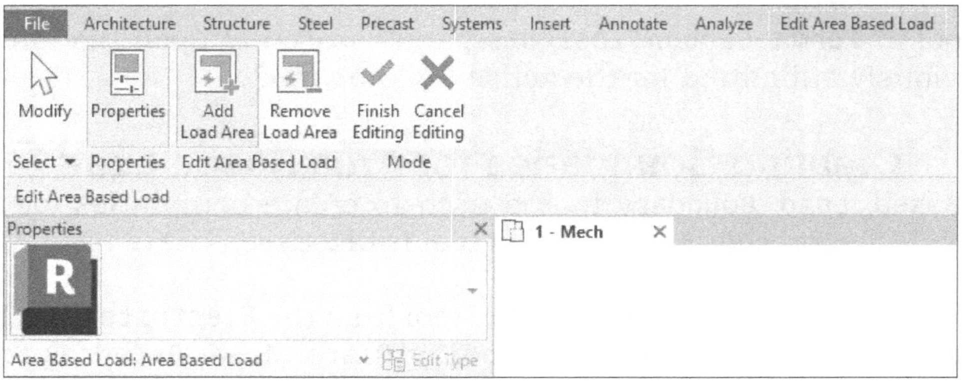

Figure-75. Options to modify place area load boundary

- Click on the **Add Load Area** button from the **Edit Area Based Load** panel to define an area based load by selecting the enclosed area.
- Click on the **Remove Load Area** button and select an area based load to be removed.
- Specify desired parameters in the **Properties Palette** and click on the **Finish Editing** button.

Equipment Load

The **Equipment Load** tool is used to define total load of equipment using the System Browser. The procedure to use this tool is discussed next.

- Click on the **Equipment Load** tool from the **Electrical Analysis** panel of **Analyze** tab in the **Ribbon**. The **Modify|Electrical Analytical Loads** contextual tab will be displayed; refer to Figure-76.

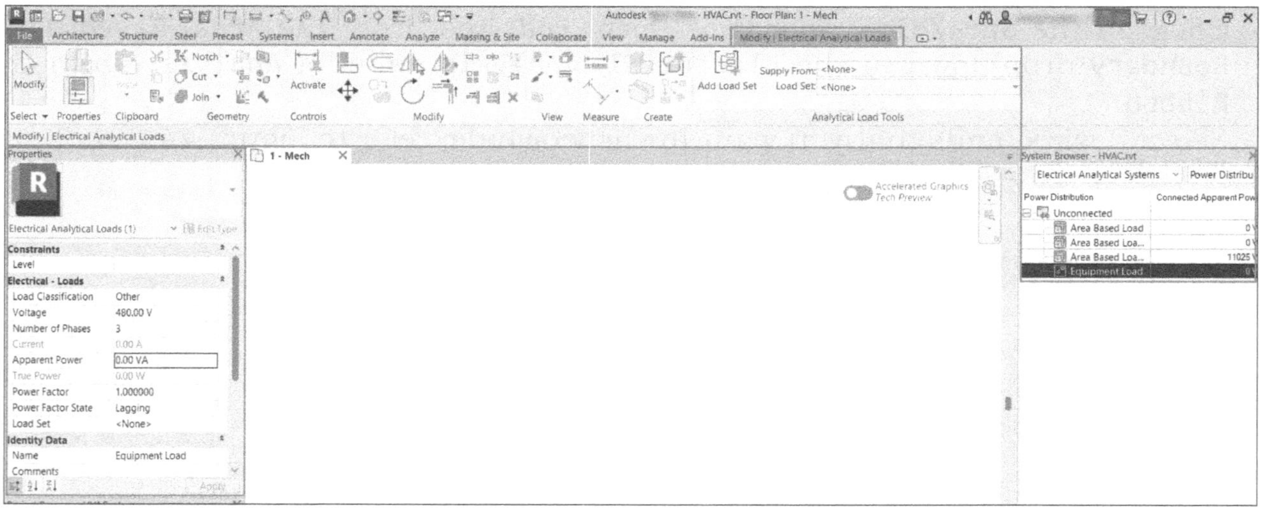

Figure-76. Modify Electrical Analytical Loads contextual tab

- Set desired load value in the **Properties Palette** as discussed earlier for equipment loads.
- Press **ESC** to exit the tool.

Path of Travel Analysis

The **Path of Travel** tool is used to display shortest path between two selected points while considering specified obstacles. This tool is active when plan view is open. The procedure to use this tool is given next.

- Click on the inclined arrow (**Route Analysis Settings**) button from the **Route Analysis** panel of **Analyze** tab in the **Ribbon**. The **Route Analysis Settings** dialog box will be displayed; refer to Figure-77.
- Select all the check boxes from the dialog box that you do not want to consider obstacles while generating the route path.
- Set desired values for bottom and top level of analysis zone in respective edit boxes, and click on the **OK** button.
- Click on the **Path of Travel** tool from the **Route Analysis** panel of **Analyze** tab in the **Ribbon**. You will be asked to specify start point and end point of the route path.

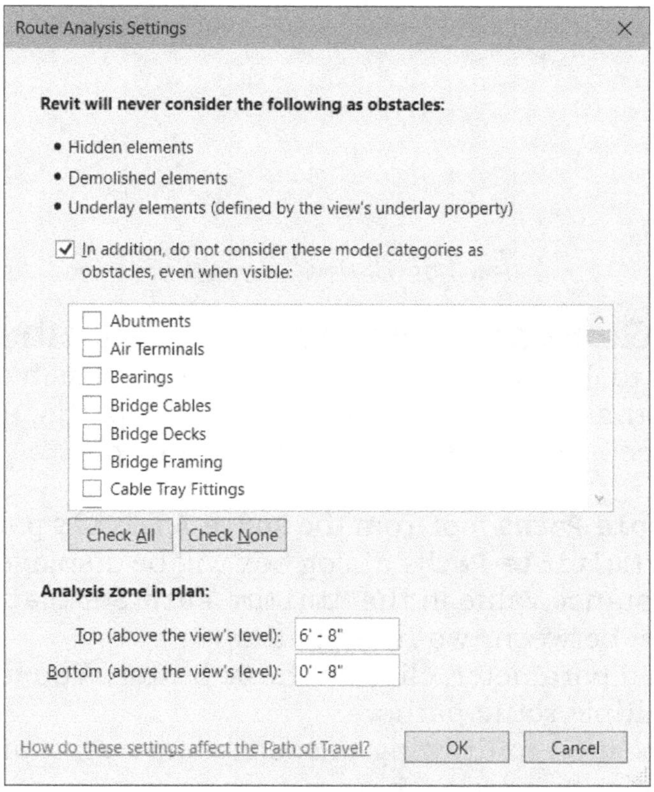

Figure-77. Route Analysis Settings dialog box

- Click at desired locations to specify start and end point of route. The route path will be displayed; refer to Figure-78.

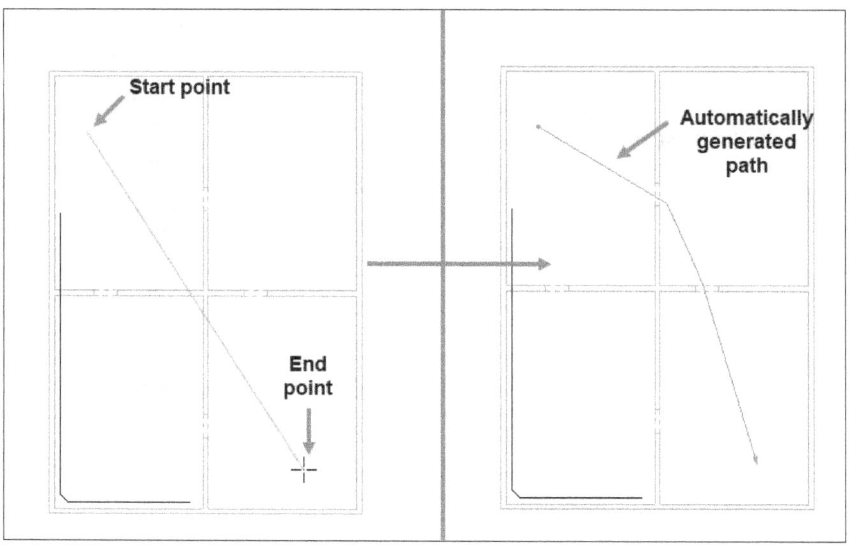

Figure-78. Route path generated automatically

- Press **ESC** to exit the tool.
- If you want to check which objects of model are being considered as obstacle then click on the **Reveal Obstacles** tool from the **Route Analysis** panel of the **Ribbon**. All the obstacles will be displayed in orange color; refer to Figure-79.

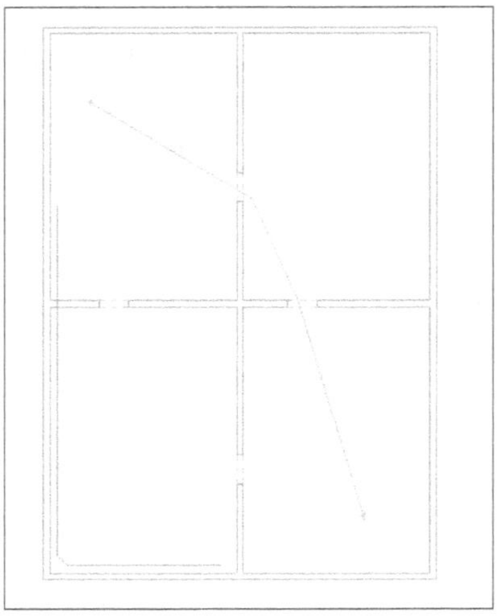

Figure-79. Displaying obstacles

Generating Multiple Route Paths

The **Multiple Paths** tool is used to generate multiple possible routes between two selected points. Note that while creating multiple route paths, the specified obstacles are avoided. The procedure to use this tool is given next.

- Click on the **Multiple Paths** tool from the **Route Analysis** panel in the **Analyze** tab of the **Ribbon**. The **Multiple Paths** dialog box will be displayed; refer to Figure-80.
- Specify desired distance value in the **Minimum Path Separation** edit box to define minimum distance between two route paths.
- After setting desired parameter, click on the **OK** button. You will be asked to specify start point for multiple route paths.
- Click at desired location in drawing to specify start point and then end point for multiple routes; refer to Figure-81.

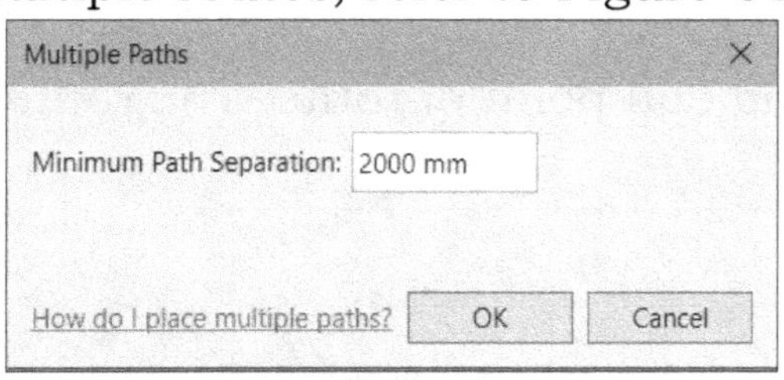

Figure-80. Multiple Paths dialog box

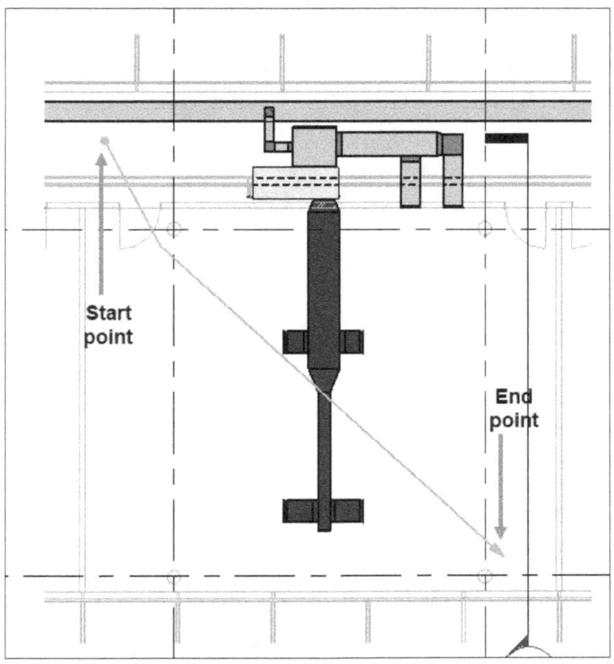

Figure-81. Start point and end point of route paths specified

- Click on the **OK** buttons from warning dialog boxes if displayed. Similarly, rectify the errors if displayed. If there are no warnings or errors then **Multiple Paths** dialog box will be displayed with preview of multiple paths; refer to Figure-82.

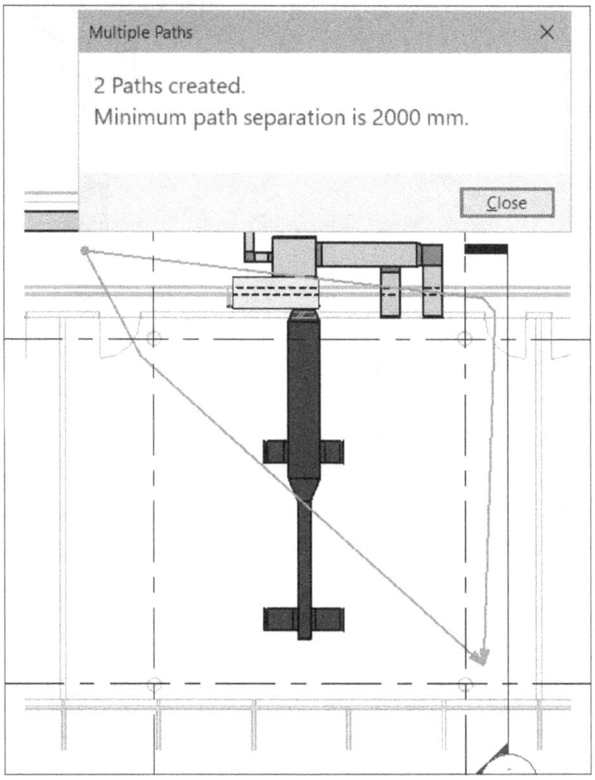

Figure-82. Multiple Paths dialog box with preview

- Click on the **Close** button from the dialog box. The paths will be generated.

Placing One Way Indicator

The **One Way Indicator** tool is used to place flow indicator symbol in the drawing. The procedure to use this tool is given next.

- Click on the **One Way Indicator** tool from the **Route Analysis** panel in the **Analyze** tab of **Ribbon**. The symbol will get attached to cursor and you will be asked to specify location for placing symbol.
- Press **SPACEBAR** from keyboard to rotate the symbol. If you want to rotate the symbol after placing then select the **Rotate after placement** check box.
- Set the other parameters as desired in the **Properties Palette** and click in the drawing area. The symbol will be placed.

Placing People Content

The **People Content** tool is used to show a person and its physical distance radius. By placing people content symbol, we make sure that route paths do not interfere with people content. The procedure to use this tool is given next.

- Click on the **People Content** tool from the **Route Analysis** panel in the **Analyze** tab of the **Ribbon**. The symbol will get attached to cursor and you will be asked to specify placement location for symbol.
- Specify desired parameters in the **Properties Palette** and click at desired location to place the symbol; refer to Figure-83. Press **ESC** twice to exit the tool.

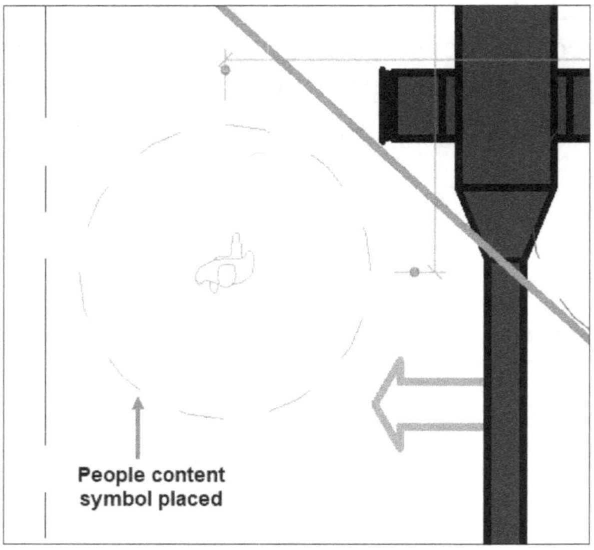

Figure-83. People content placed

Similarly, you can use the **Spatial Grid** tool to generate square or hexagonal grid in the selected room boundary.

SELF-ASSESSMENT

Q1. Which of the following entities of the analytical model can be fixed by using the **Boundary Conditions** tool?

a. Point b. Line
c. Face d. All of the options

Q2. Using the **Loads** tool, you can apply force as well as moment load on the structure of building. (T/F)

Q3. Discuss the difference between load cases and load combinations.

Q4. The **Location** tool in the **Energy Optimization** panel is used to set site for the project. (T/F)

Q5. The **Path of Travel** tool is used to display shortest path between two selected points while considering specified obstacles. (T/F)

Q6. The **People Content** tool is used to show a person and its physical distance radius in building analysis. (T/F)

Q7. Where can you find the options to perform different types of analyses in Revit?
A. Modify tab
B. Analyze tab
C. View tab
D. Insert tab

Q8. What is the first step in performing a structural analysis?
A. Creating load cases
B. Placing analytical members
C. Specifying boundary conditions
D. Running the analysis

Q9. Which tool is used to place an analytical line element in a Revit model?
A. Load tool
B. Panel by Boundary tool
C. Member tool
D. Link tool

Q10. What does the "Top Point Definition" button do?
A. Creates horizontal member
B. Defines highest load point
C. Creates vertical analytical member
D. Rotates analytical member

Q11. Which field in the Properties Palette defines how external applications consider the analytical member?
A. Section Type
B. Cross-Section Rotation
C. Structural Role
D. Analyze As

Q12. What does the Panel by Boundary tool require to create an analytical panel?
A. Load case
B. Closed loop boundary
C. Section type
D. Link

Q13. The Panel by Extrusion tool creates a panel in which orientation relative to the current work plane?
A. Parallel
B. Perpendicular
C. Diagonal
D. Horizontal

Q14. Which tool creates a link between two analytical nodes for load transfer?
A. Member tool
B. Link tool
C. Panel by Boundary
D. Boundary Conditions tool

Q15. What happens if boundary condition families are not loaded?
A. The tool crashes
B. A warning message appears
C. The Boundary Conditions Settings Incomplete dialog appears
D. The boundary conditions are auto-loaded

Q16. What does the "Pinned" option in the State field allow?
A. No movement at all
B. Free rotation and translation
C. Rotation allowed, translation restricted
D. Only translation allowed

Q17. Which load option applies load over surface areas?
A. Point Load
B. Line Load
C. Area Load
D. Moment Load

Q18. What is the default load case in the Load Case field?
A. LL (Live Load)
B. DL (Dead Load)
C. WL (Wind Load)
D. EL (Earthquake Load)

Q19. What does the Automation Customization tool do?
A. Loads load cases
B. Applies boundary conditions
C. Creates analytical model from physical model
D. Fixes system disconnections

Q20. What tool is used to send model to Robot Structural Analysis software?
A. Loads tool
B. Check Systems tool
C. Robot Structural Analysis Link tool
D. Automation Customization tool

Q21. What does the Check Duct Systems tool help identify?
A. Unsupported loads
B. Unassigned boundary conditions
C. Disconnected or overconnected duct elements
D. Missing load cases

Q22. In the Show Disconnects tool, what do red lines represent?
A. High flow
B. No flow
C. Pressure loss
D. Normal flow

Q23. Which tool is used to create analytical space for various analysis calculations in Revit?
A. Room tool
B. Space Separator tool
C. Space tool
D. HVAC tool

Q24. What should you do if the Space Tag is not loaded by default?
A. Restart Revit
B. Ignore the message
C. Load it from Annotations > Mechanical folder using Load Family
D. Reinstall the software

Q25. Which option would you select to create a space tag with area displayed?
A. Space Tag
B. Space Tag With Volume
C. Space Tag Only
D. Space Tag With Area

Q26. What does the Space Separator tool help you achieve?
A. Merge multiple spaces
B. Separate a space using lines
C. Apply color scheme
D. Connect ducts

Q27. What does the 'Moves With Nearby Elements' checkbox control in Space Separator tool?
A. Prevents moving the separator
B. Deletes space
C. Updates separator when walls move
D. Rotates the separator

Q28. What is the purpose of the Space Naming tool?
A. Define space size
B. Tag the space
C. Assign names to spaces
D. Export space data

Q29. Where do you find the Color Schemes tool in Revit?
A. View tab
B. Architecture tab
C. Analyze tab
D. Manage tab

Q30. What is the purpose of the 'By Sketch' tool under Zoning?
A. Create closed boundaries for ducts
B. Define HVAC systems
C. Create system zones using sketches
D. Create space separators

Q31. Which tool helps define or modify HVAC zones?
A. Duct tool
B. Room tool
C. By Space tool
D. Equipment Load

Q32. What report is generated using the Duct Pressure Loss Report tool?
A. Electrical report
B. Heat loss report
C. Pressure drop in duct system
D. Load summary

Q33. What is the use of the Panel Schedules tool?
A. Create HVAC diagrams
B. Schedule project deadlines
C. Generate electrical circuit panel reports
D. Generate plumbing schedule

Q34. What does the Schedule/Quantities tool generate?
A. Equipment list
B. Quantity takeoffs
C. Cost estimates
D. HVAC layout

Q35. What does the Building/Space Type Settings tool help define?
A. Electrical layout
B. Building material
C. Parameters for different building types
D. HVAC zones

Q36. What is the main purpose of the Duct Legend tool?
A. Show duct load
B. Create a color-coded duct legend
C. Display airflow direction
D. Insert duct size

Q37. Which tool is used to specify the project's real-world location?
A. Energy Settings
B. Location tool
C. Path of Travel
D. Carbon Insights

Q38. What is the purpose of the Create Energy Model tool?
A. Add lighting
B. Estimate HVAC cost
C. Create an analytical energy model
D. Add space tags

Q39. What does the Energy Settings tool allow you to configure?
A. Electrical circuit
B. HVAC layout
C. Parameters for energy simulation
D. Material strength

Q40. What is the final step in the Systems Analysis tool process?
A. Exporting to Excel
B. Creating duct network
C. Running the analysis
D. Tagging the model

Q41. What does the Analyze tool in Carbon Insights panel do?
A. Adds material
B. Creates HVAC zones
C. Uploads model to cloud for sustainability analysis
D. Paints walls

Q42. What does the Area Based Load Boundary tool define?
A. Electrical circuit
B. Wall thickness
C. Area boundaries for electrical loads
D. Pipe layout

Q43. What is the purpose of the Area Based Load tool?
A. Display heat map
B. Assign load to enclosed area
C. Tag HVAC
D. Create lighting plan

Q44. What is the Equipment Load tool used for?
A. Analyze structure
B. Define total equipment load
C. Estimate lighting
D. Size ducts

Q45. Which tool helps you calculate the shortest distance between two points?
A. Location tool
B. Duct Legend
C. Path of Travel
D. HVAC tool

Q46. What is the function of the Reveal Obstacles tool?
A. Hide ducts
B. Display objects considered as obstacles
C. Rename obstacles
D. Lock model view

Q47. What does the Multiple Paths tool generate?
A. Pressure maps
B. Multiple shortest routes
C. Material lists
D. Energy loads

Q48. What does the One Way Indicator tool do?
A. Show water direction
B. Display wind speed
C. Show direction of flow
D. Indicate panel load

Q49. What is the function of the People Content tool?
A. Place furniture
B. Show human distance radius
C. Count workers
D. Tag population zones

FOR STUDENT NOTES

Chapter 10

Inserting and Collaborating Data

Topics Covered

The major topics covered in this chapter are:

- ***Creating and Managing Links***
- ***Importing Files***
- ***Collaborating with Team***
- ***Copying and Monitoring Linked Objects***
- ***Sharing Views***

INTRODUCTION

The building projects created in Revit contain information from different sources like architectural design team, structural design team, mechanical system design team, and so on. These teams work together on same model to achieve a common goal. In this chapter, you will learn to share work with other teams and simultaneously work the model in Revit. You will also learn to insert non-native files and create links in the Revit project.

CREATING AND MANAGING LINKS

The links are used to collectively display various buildings of larger project in one file. For example, you are working on a township project in which there are 15 different types of buildings. For these 15 buildings, you have created 15 different project files and now you want to display the complete township project to your client. In such case, you will link all the building project files to a single project file where you will place the buildings and create desired renders. The tools to create and manage links of Revit are available in **Link** panel of **Insert** tab in the **Ribbon**; refer to Figure-1. The tools in this panel are discussed next.

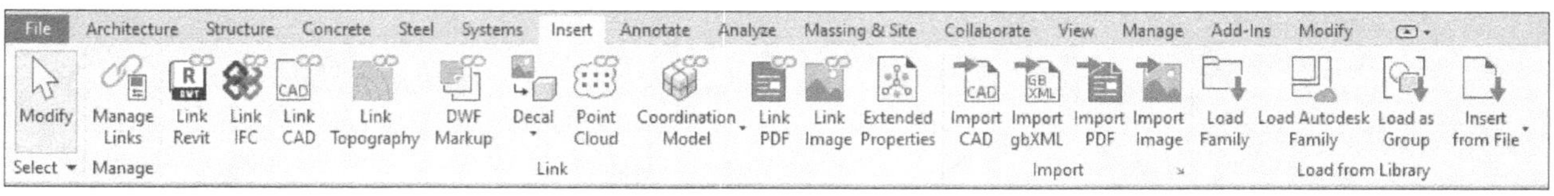

Figure-1. Link panel

Linking Revit Model

The **Link Revit** tool is used to place external Revit models in current project. The procedure to use this tool is given next.

- Click on the **Link Revit** tool from the **Link** panel in the **Insert** tab of **Ribbon**. The **Import/Link RVT** dialog box will be displayed; refer to Figure-2.

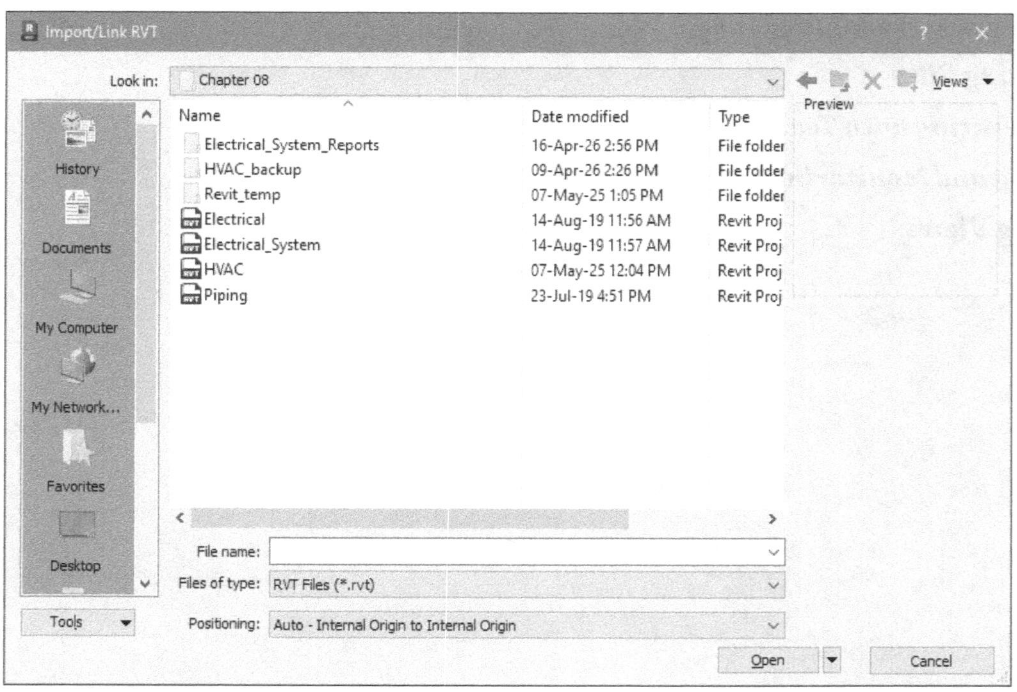

Figure-2. Import Link RVT dialog box

- Select desired file from the dialog box. Select desired option from the **Positioning** drop-down to define where the linked model will be placed in project; refer to Figure-3. By default, **Auto - Internal Origin to Internal Origin** option is selected in this drop-down and hence Revit model is automatically placed at the origin of project file. Select the **Manual - Internal Origin** option from the drop-down if you want to manually place the linked model at desired location in project while using the origin as key point.

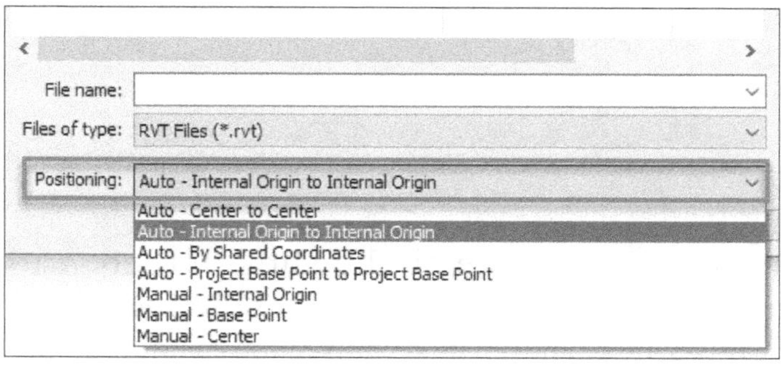

Figure-3. Positioning drop-down

- Click on the **Open** button from the dialog box. The model will get attached to the cursor; refer to Figure-4.

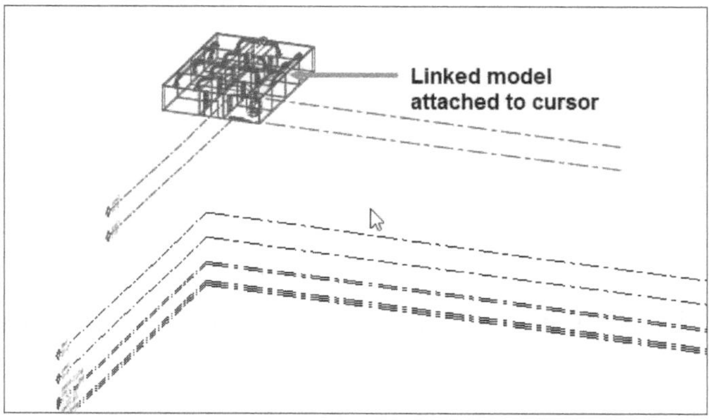

Figure-4. Revit model attached to cursor

- Click at desired location to place the linked model.

Binding Linked Model to Current Project

Once you have linked a Revit model to project, you can convert it to Revit model group. These groups are saved locally in the project file. The procedure is given next.

- Select the linked model and click on the **Bind Link** button from the **Link** panel in the **Modify|RVT Links** contextual tab of **Ribbon**. The **Bind Link Options** dialog box will be displayed; refer to Figure-5.

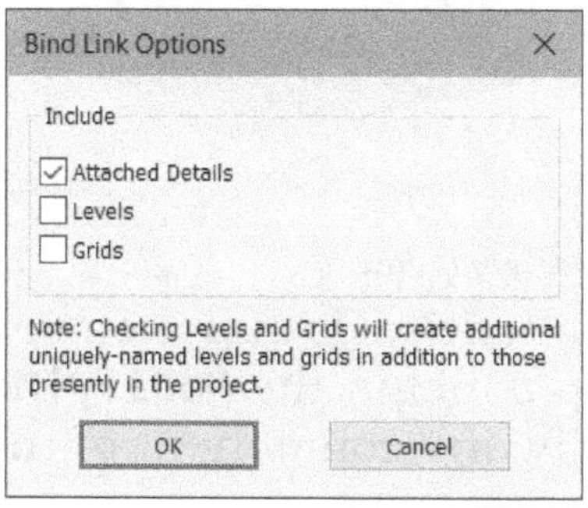

Figure-5. Bind Link Options dialog box

- Select desired check boxes from the dialog box that you want to bind with current project and click on the **OK** button. The message box will be displayed as shown in Figure-6.

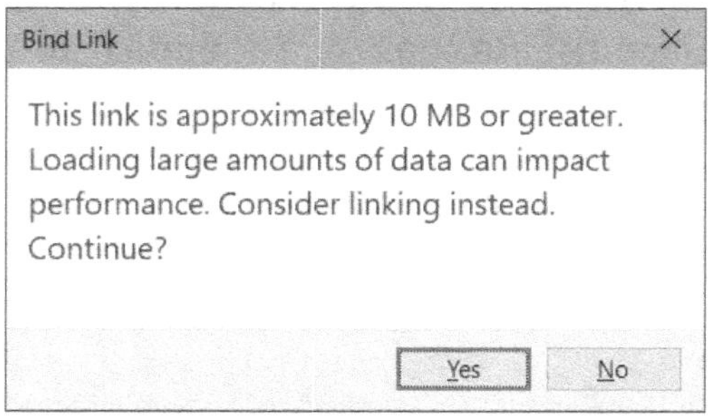

Figure-6. Bind Link dialog box

- Click on the **Yes** button to continue binding link. If there are duplicates in linking model and base model then **Duplicate Types** message box will be displayed; refer to Figure-7.

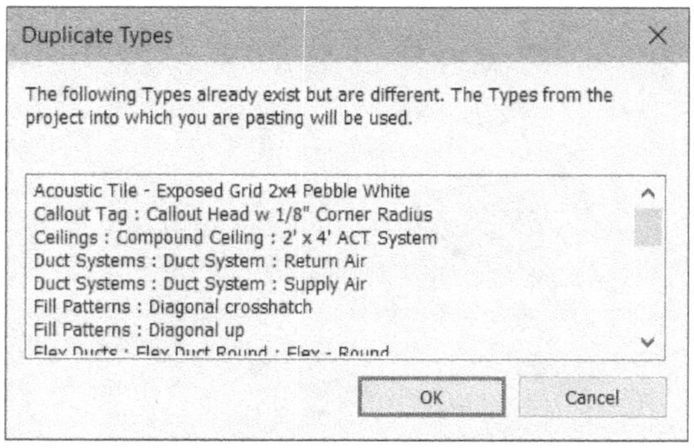

Figure-7. Duplicate Types dialog box

- Click on the **OK** button from the dialog box. The group will be created; refer to Figure-8.

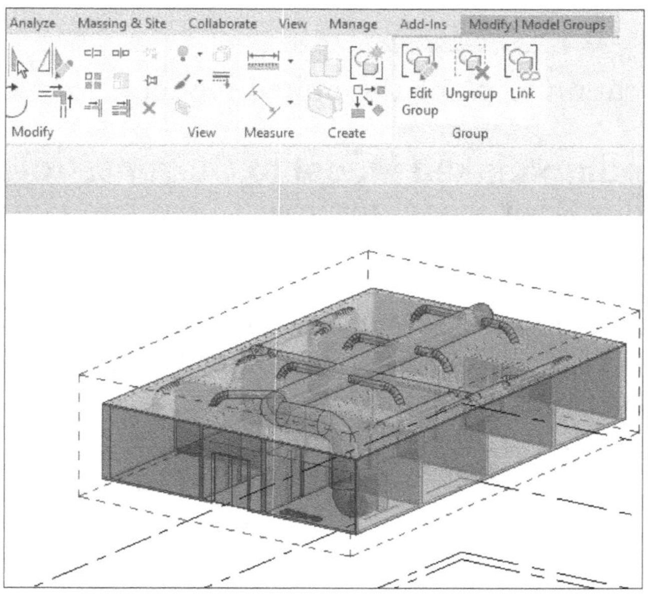

Figure-8. Model group created

- If you want to modify components of group then select the group and click on the **Ungroup** tool from the **Group** panel in the **Modify|Model Groups** contextual tab of **Ribbon**. Now, you can modify any component of the bounded model.

Note that once you have converted the link model to group, the parent model will not update automatically after changing group elements.

Linking IFC Model

The **IFCs** (Industry Foundation Classes) are used to describe architectural, building, and construction data. The procedure to link IFC model is given next.

- Click on the **Link IFC** tool from the **Link** panel in the **Insert** tab of **Ribbon**. The **Link IFC** dialog box will be created; refer to Figure-9.

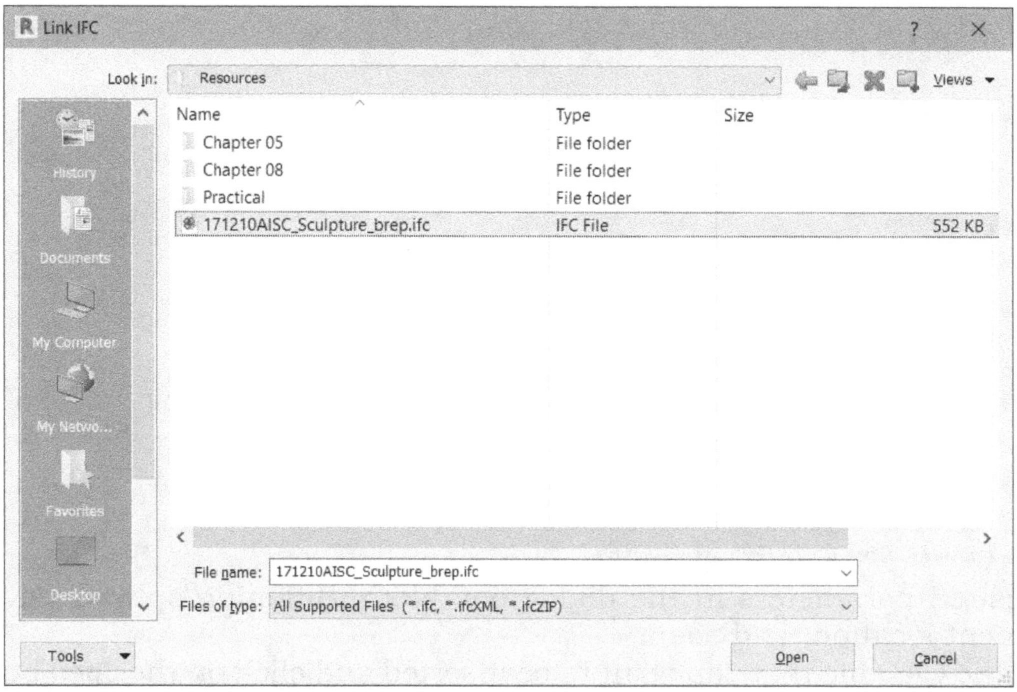

Figure-9. Link IFC dialog box

- Select desired IFC file and click on the **Open** button. The model will be placed in the project; refer to Figure-10.

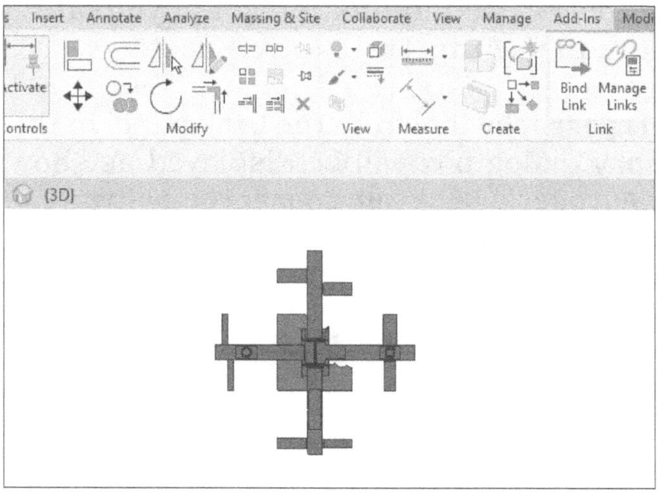

Figure-10. IFC model placed in project

Linking CAD Model

The **Link CAD** tool is used to link CAD models in current project. The procedure to use this tool is given next.

- Click on the **Link CAD** tool from the **Link** panel in the **Insert** tab of **Ribbon**. The **Link CAD Formats** dialog box will be displayed; refer to Figure-11.

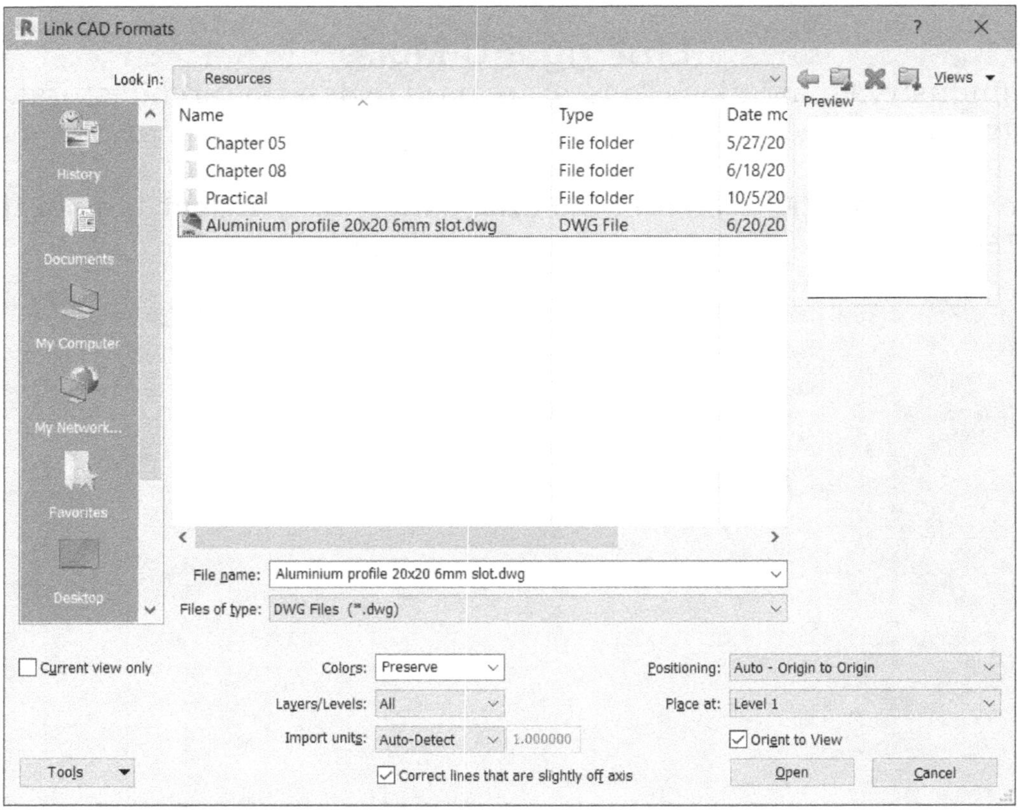

Figure-11. Link CAD Formats dialog box

- Set desired parameters in the dialog box like positioning options, level, units, placement location, and so on.
- Select the CAD file that you want to be inserted and click on the **Open** button. The model file will be placed.

Linking Topography

The **Link Topography** tool is used to link topography created in Revit or any other software. The procedure to use this tool is given next.

- Click on the **Link Topography** tool from the **Link** panel in the **Insert** tab of **Ribbon**. The **Link Topography** dialog box will be displayed as shown in Figure-12 if you have not installed **Autodesk Desktop Connector** software.

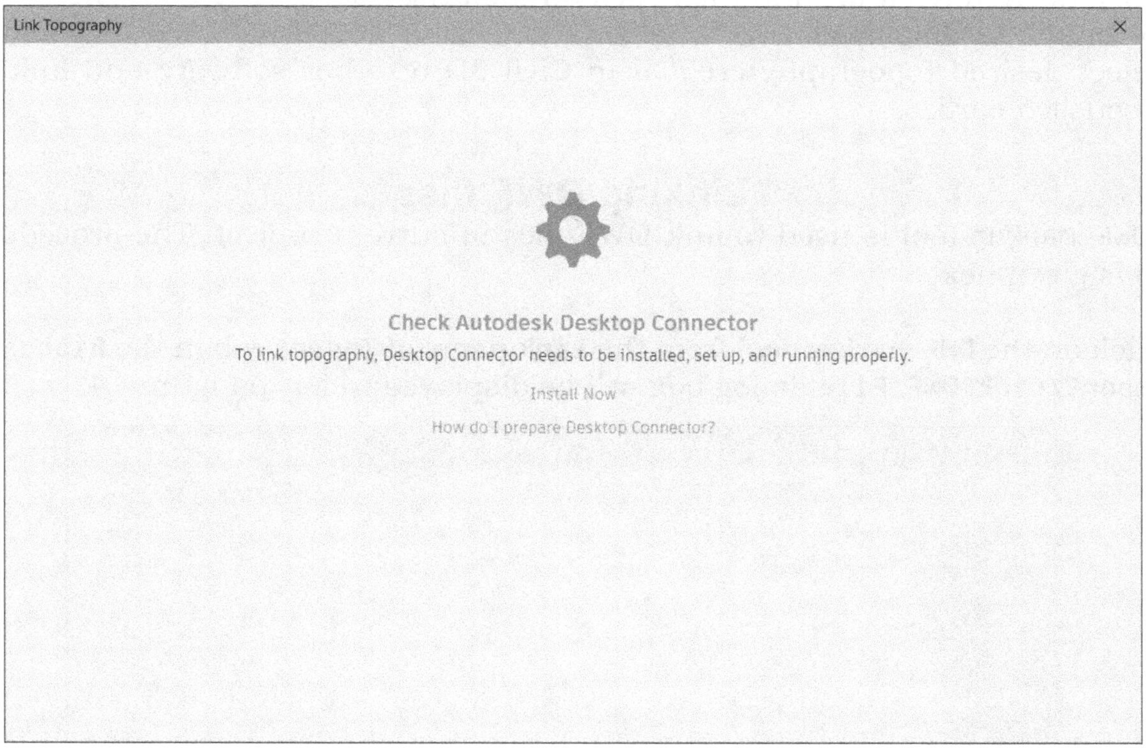

Figure-12. Link Topography dialog box

- Click on the **Install Now** button from the dialog box. The web page will be displayed as shown in Figure-13. Click on the **Desktop Connector for Windows 64-Bit** button and save at desired location. Install the software if not done yet. Save your files and restart the system even if you are not prompted after installing the software.

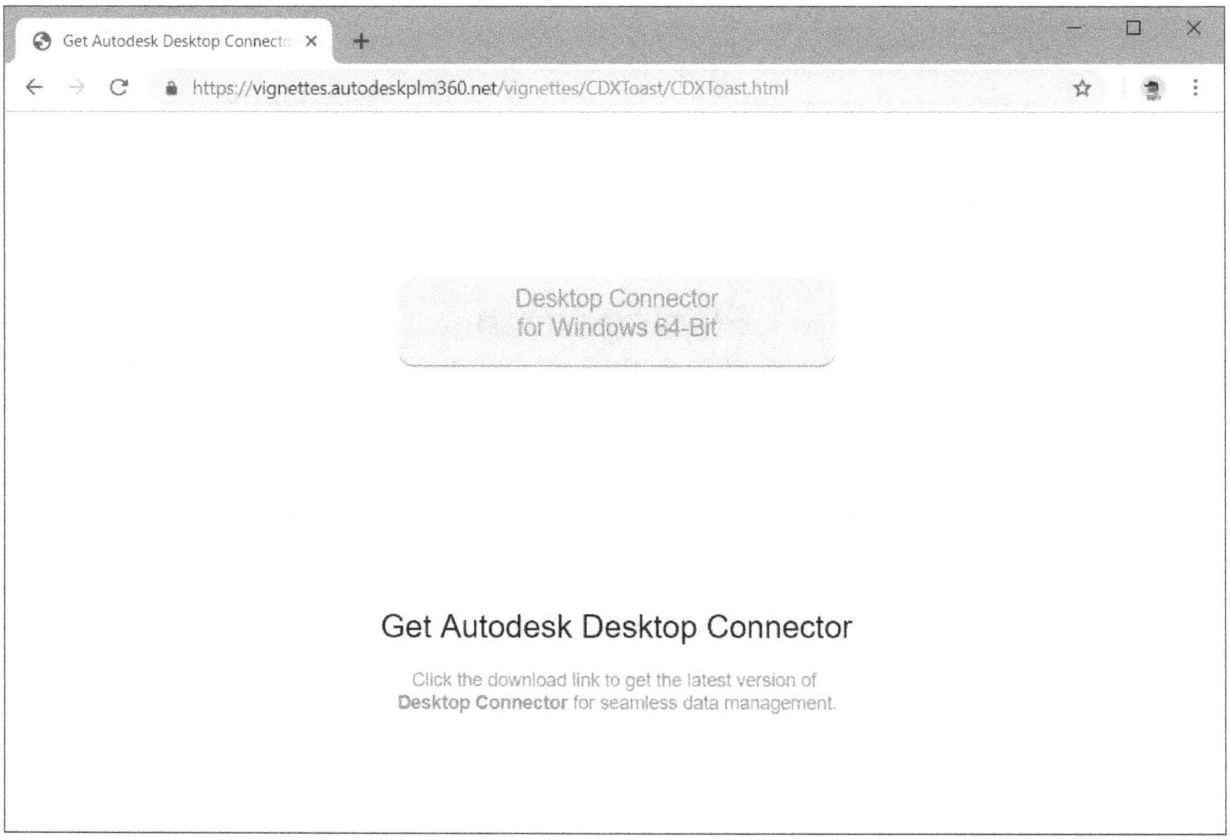

Figure-13. Option to download Desktop Connector

- Open desired Revit file and then click on the **Link Topography** tool. The BIM 360 folder will be displayed.
- Select desired topography created in Civil 3D or other software and link it as discussed earlier.

Linking DWF files

The **DWF Markup** tool is used to link DWF files in current project. The procedure to do so is given next.

- Click on the **DWF Markup** tool from the **Link** panel of **Insert** tab in the **Ribbon**. The **Import/Link DWF File** dialog box will be displayed; refer to Figure-14.

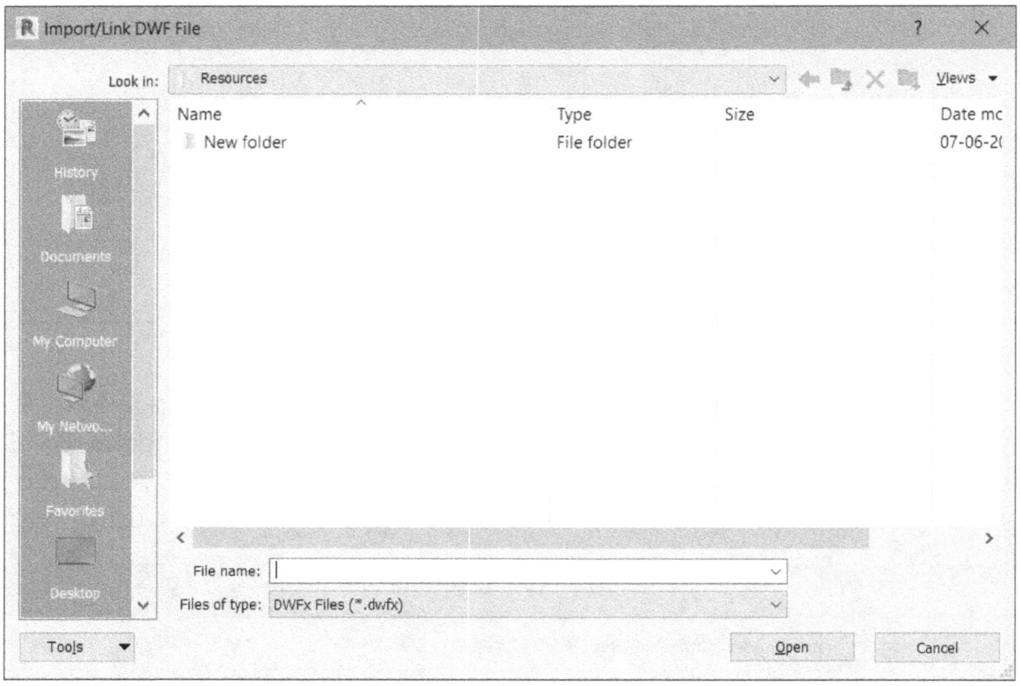

Figure-14. Import Link DWF File dialog box

- Select desired DWFx or DWF file of model and click on the **Open** button. The model will be placed.

Placing Decal

The tools in the **Decal** drop-down are used to link images in the model. The procedure to place decal is given next.

- Click on the **Place Decal** tool from the **Decal** drop-down in the **Link** panel of **Insert** tab in **Ribbon**. The **Decal Types** dialog box will be displayed; refer to Figure-15.

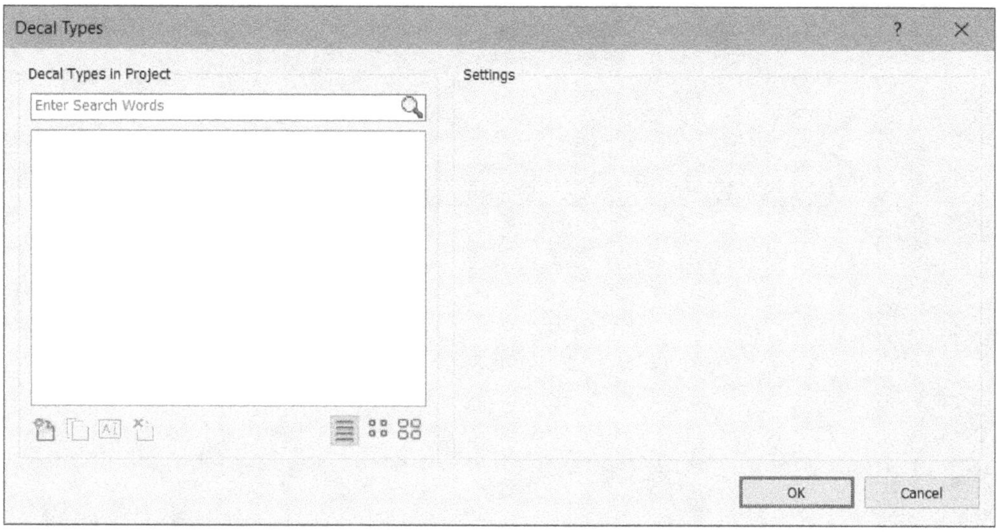

Figure-15. Decal Types dialog box

- Click on the **Create new decal** tool from the dialog box. The **New Decal** dialog box will be displayed.
- Specify desired name of decal and click on the **OK** button. The options to create decal type will be displayed; refer to Figure-16.

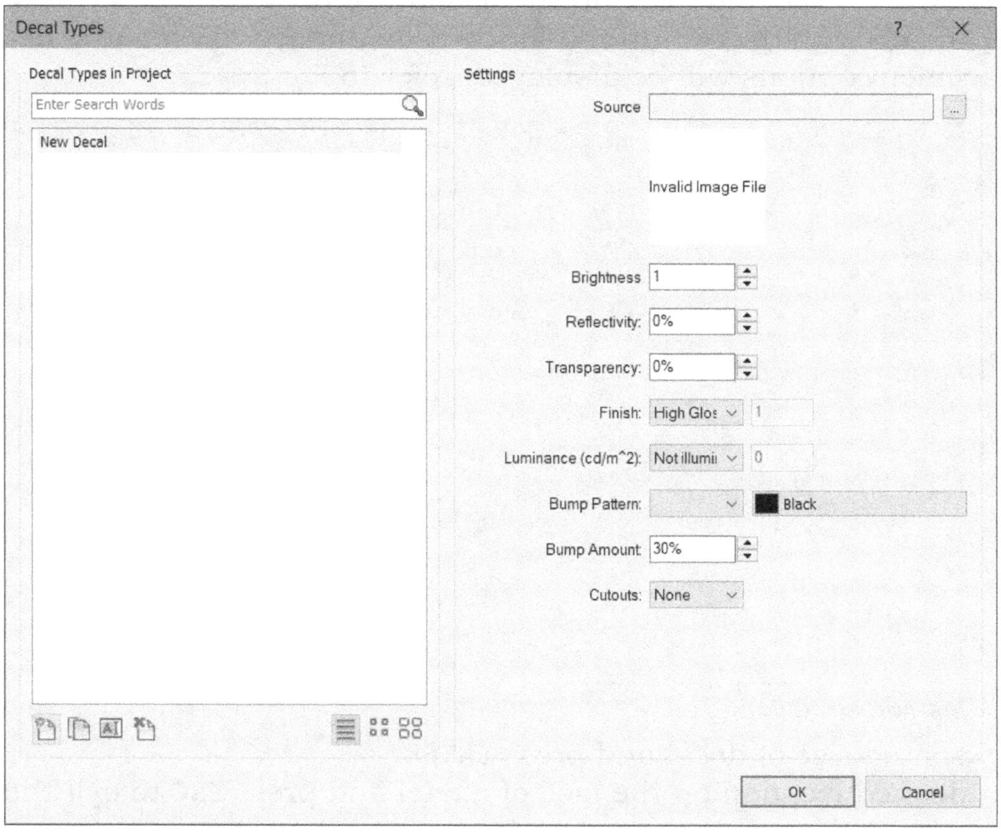

Figure-16. Options to create decal type

- Click on the **Browse** button for source in the dialog box. The **Select File** dialog box will be displayed; refer to Figure-17.

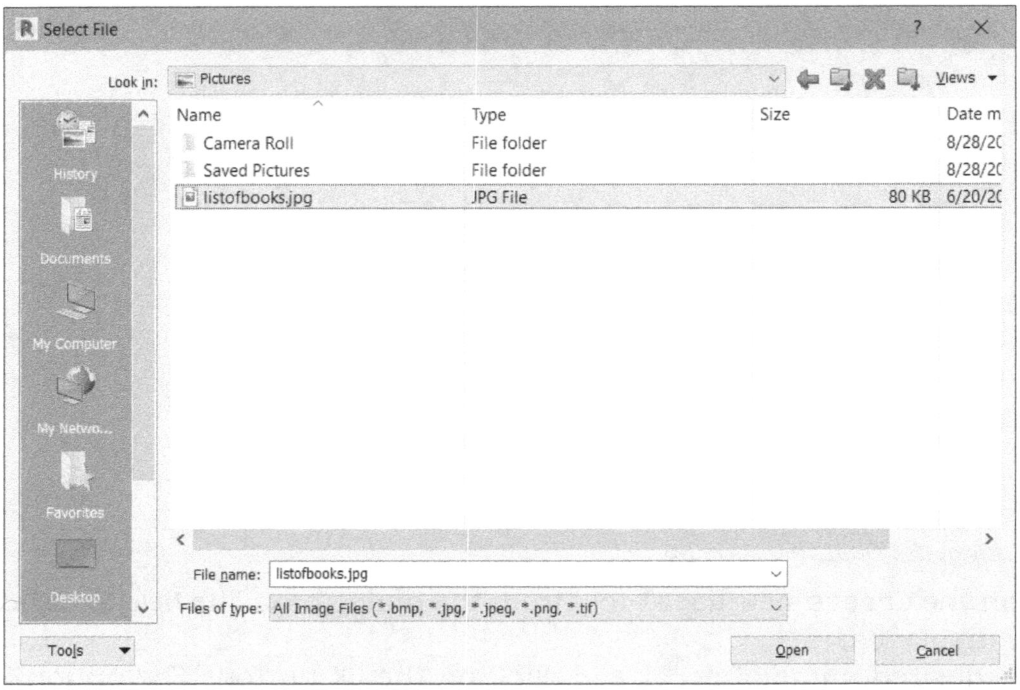

Figure-17. Select File dialog box

- Select desired image and click on the **Open** button. Set the other parameters as desired and click on the **OK** button. The decal boundary will get attached to cursor and placement options will be displayed; refer to Figure-18.

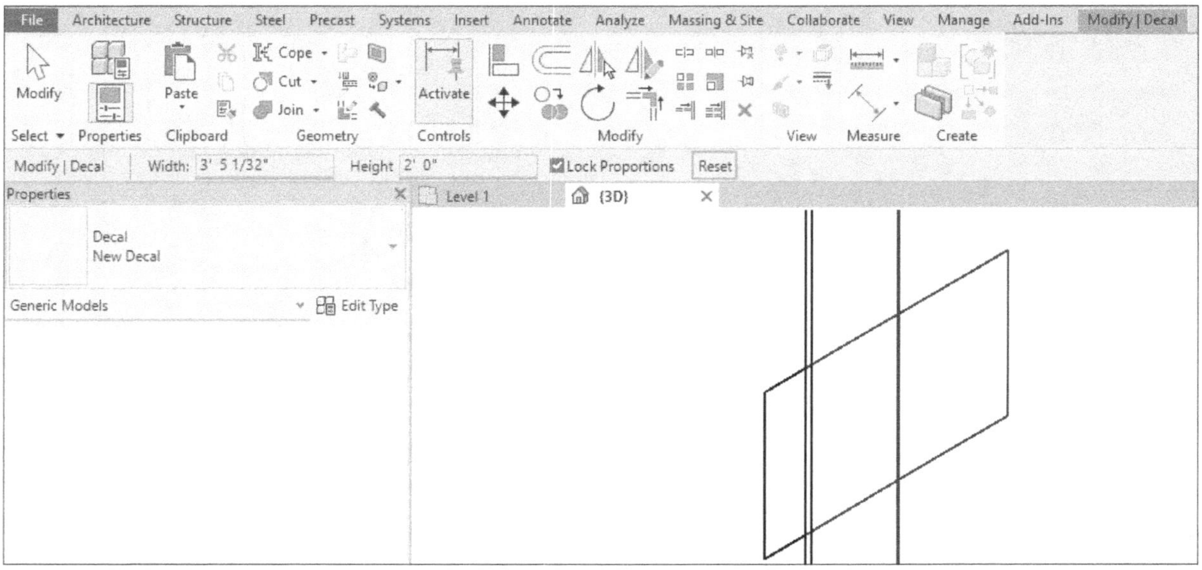

Figure-18. Decal placement options

- Specify desired size of decal and press **ENTER**.
- Click at desired location on the face of model and press **ESC** to exit the tool.

To create more types of decals, click on the **Decal Types** tool from the **Decal** drop-down of **Link** panel in the **Insert** tab of **Ribbon**.

Linking Point Cloud Data

The **Point Cloud** tool is used to link point cloud model into current project. The procedure to use this tool is given next.

- Click on the **Point Cloud** tool from the **Link** panel in the **Insert** tab of **Ribbon**. The **Link Point Cloud** dialog box will be displayed; refer to Figure-19.

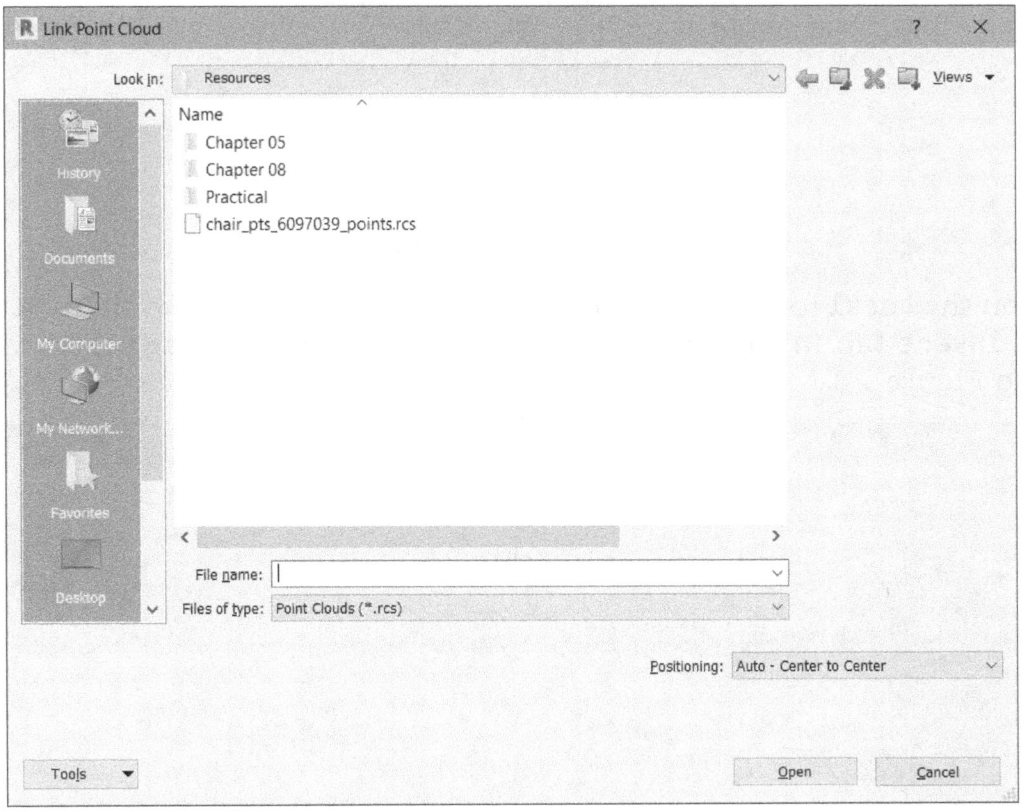

Figure-19. Link Point Cloud dialog box

- Select desired point cloud file and click on the **Open** button. The linked model will be displayed; refer to Figure-20.

Figure-20. Point cloud file placed

Linking Coordination Model

There are two tools for linking coordination model in the project which are available in the **Coordination Model** drop-down of the **Insert** tab in **Ribbon** - **Local** and **Autodesk Docs**; refer to Figure-21. Use the **Local** tool to link NavisWorks file available in your local drive. Use the **Autodesk Docs** tool if the file to be linked is stored on Autodesk Docs. Here, we will discuss the procedure to use **Local** tool for linking Coordination model. You can apply the **Autodesk Docs** tool in the same way. The procedure to use this tool is given next.

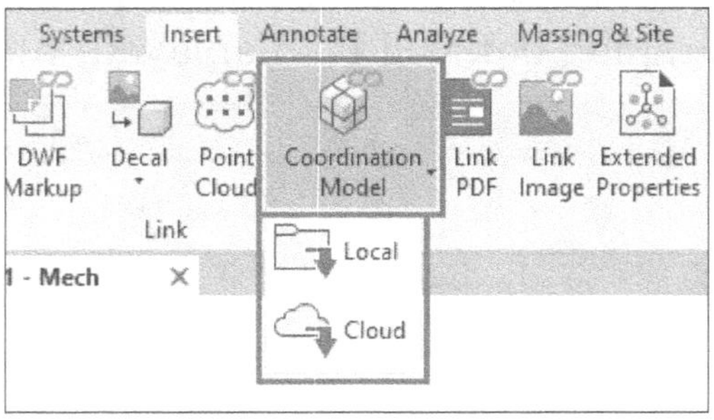

Figure-21. Coordination Model drop-down

- Click on the **Local** tool from the **Coordination Model** drop-down in the **Link** panel of the **Insert** tab in the **Ribbon**. The **Select File** dialog box will be displayed; refer to Figure-22.

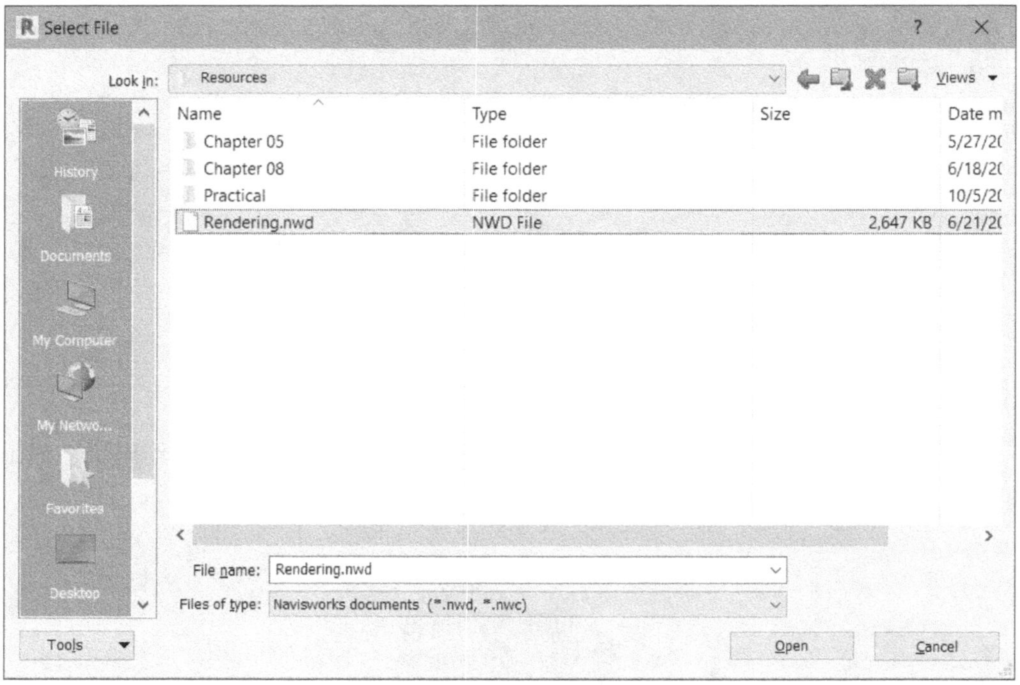

Figure-22. Select File dialog box

- Select desired Navisworks file and click on the **Open** button. The model will be linked in the current project.
- Click on the **OK** button from the dialog box.

Linking PDFs

The **Link PDF** tool is used to link selected PDF file in the project. Note that this tool is not available for 3D views. The procedure to use this tool is given next.

- Click on the **Link PDF** tool from the **Link** panel in the **Insert** tab of **Ribbon**. The **Link PDF** dialog box will be displayed; refer to Figure-23.

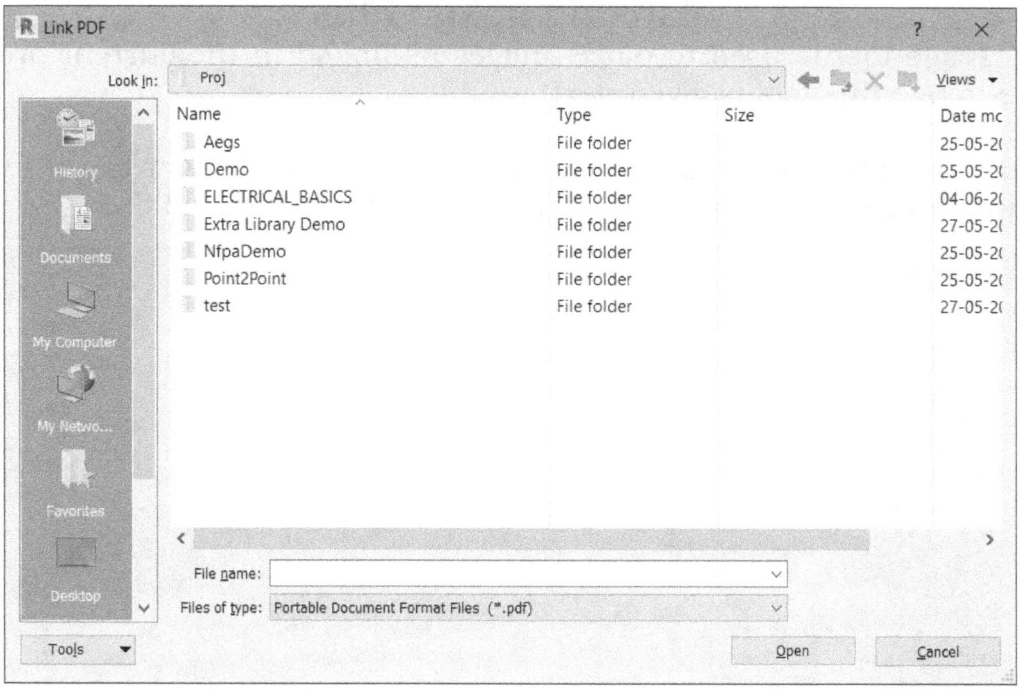

Figure-23. Link PDF dialog box

- Select desired PDF file from the dialog box and click on the **Open** button. The **Import PDF** dialog box will be displayed; refer to Figure-24.

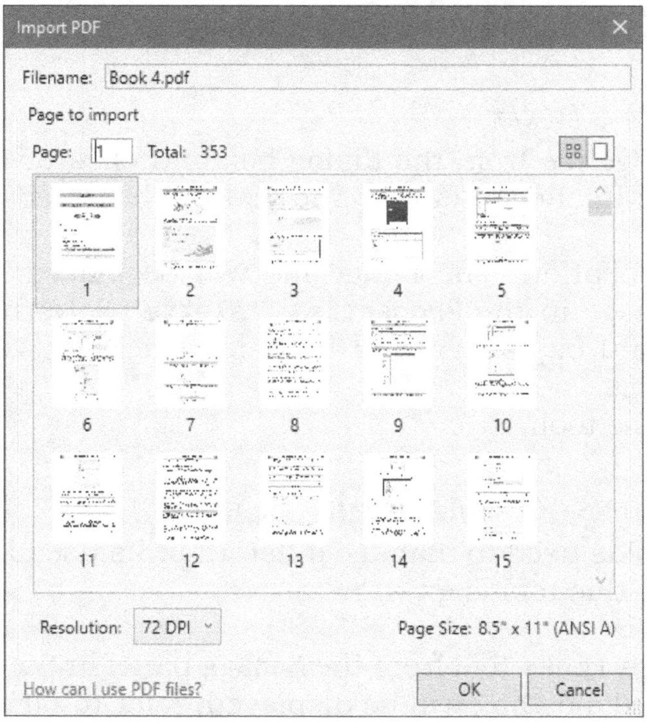

Figure-24. Import PDF dialog box

- Set desired resolution in the **Resolution** drop-down and select the page that you want to import from the **Page to import** area of the dialog box.
- Click on the **OK** button from the dialog box. You will be asked to specify location for placing raster image of linked PDF.
- Click at desired location to place the raster image. Note that you may need to make the raster image visible in the view by using the **Visibility/Graphics** tool.
- Press **ESC** to exit the tool.

Linking Image File

The **Link Image** tool is used to place images as linked in the current project. The procedure to use this tool is given next.

- Click on the **Link Image** tool from the **Link** panel in the **Insert** tab of the **Ribbon**. The **Link Image** dialog box will be displayed; refer to Figure-25.

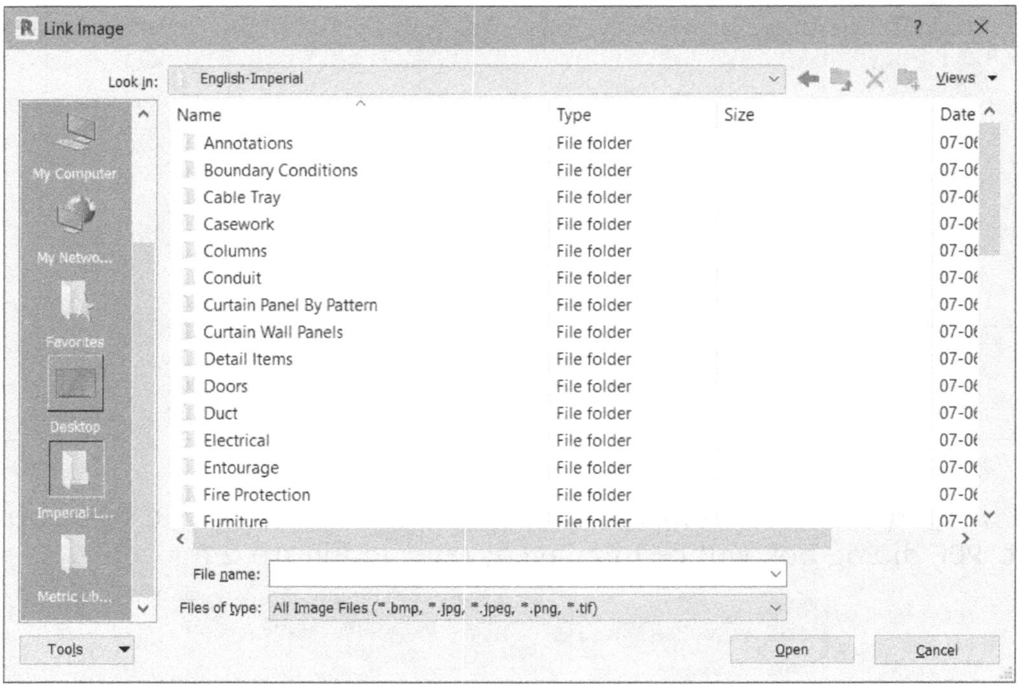

Figure-25. Link Image dialog box

- Select desired image file from the dialog box and click on the **Open** button. The image file will get attached to cursor and you will be asked to specify location for placing image.
- Click at desired location. The image file will be placed. You can specify the parameters for image in the **Properties Palette**. Note that you can place the image in foreground or background by using the **Draw Layer** option from the **Properties Palette**.
- Press **ESC** to exit the tool.

Managing Links

The **Manage Links** tool is used to manage different links used in the current project. The procedure to use this tool is given next.

- Click on the **Manage Links** tool from the **Manage** panel in the **Insert** tab of **Ribbon**. The **Manage Links** dialog box will be displayed; refer to Figure-26.
- Set desired parameters for different links using the options in different tabs of the dialog box.
- Click on the **OK** button from the dialog box.

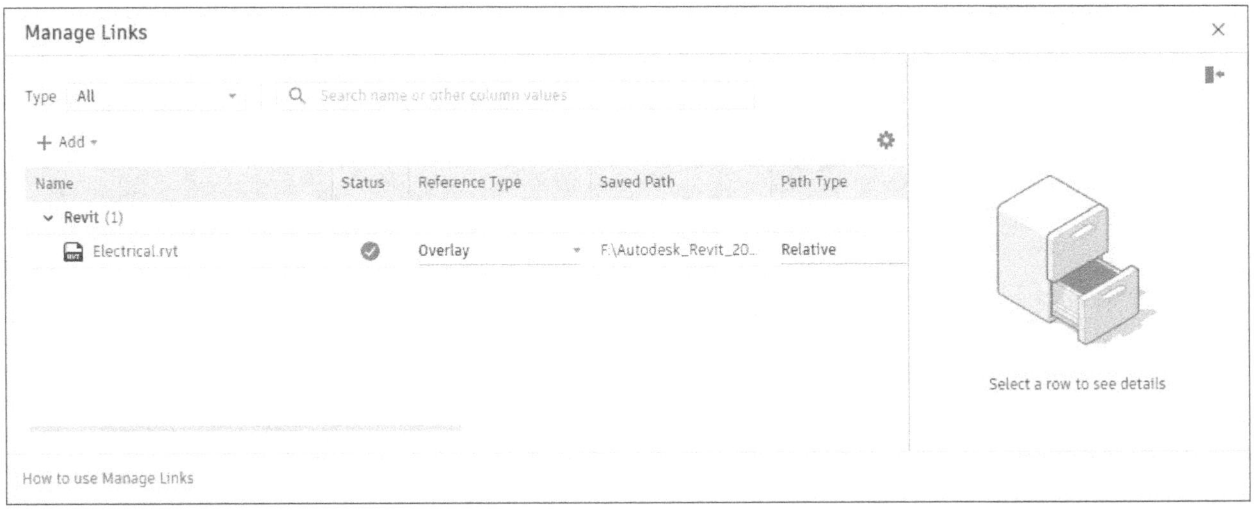

Figure-26. Manage Links dialog box

Extended Properties

Extended properties are sets of element property data stored in the cloud and linked to your models. This tool is not functional in the educational version of this software.

IMPORTING FILES

The tools in the **Import** panel of **Insert** tab in **Ribbon** are used to place local copy of data and model from other files. Various tools in this panel are discussed next.

Importing CAD Files

The **Import CAD** tool is used to import different 3D geometries and data from other CAD software. The procedure to use this tool is given next.

- Click on the **Import CAD** tool from the **Import** panel in the **Insert** tab of **Ribbon**. The **Import CAD Formats** dialog box will be displayed; refer to Figure-27.

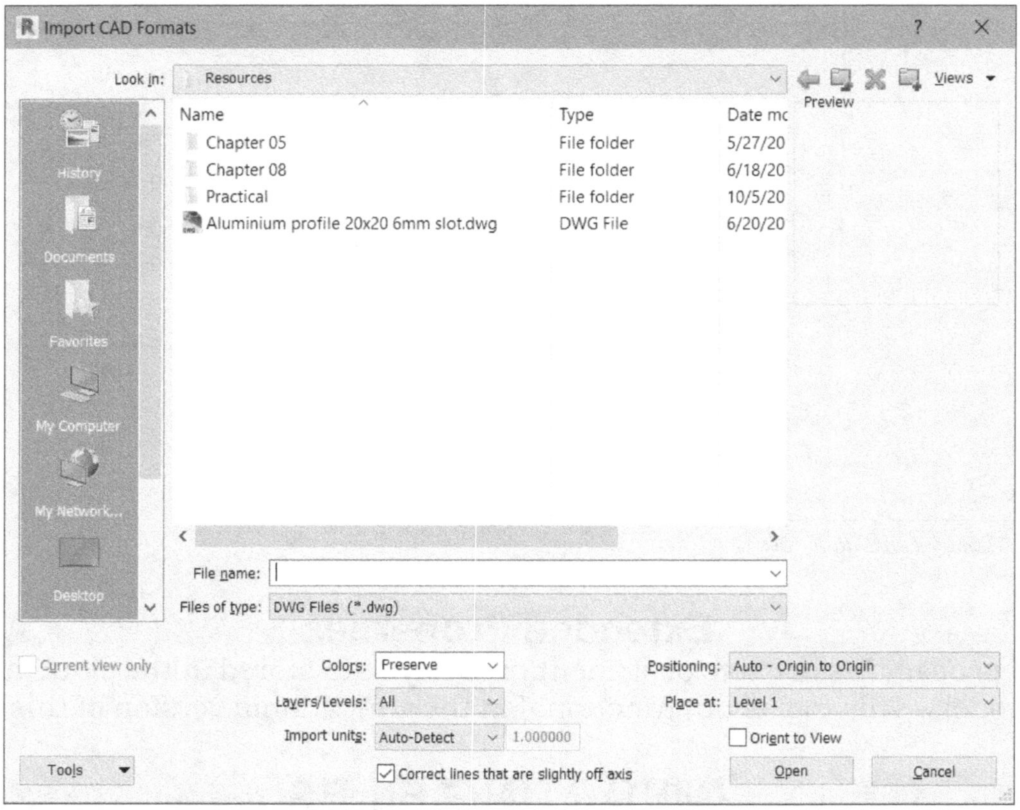

Figure-27. Import CAD Formats dialog box

- Select desired format for CAD file from **Files of type** drop-down and select desired CAD file.
- Set other parameters like color, layer, unit, and so on as desired and click on the **Open** button. By default, the **Auto - Origin to Internal Origin** option is selected in the **Positioning** drop-down of **Import CAD Formats** dialog box hence, the model file will be placed at origin. You can other options to define placement of imported CAD objects in current project.

Importing gbXML File

The **Import gbXML** tool is used to import analysis data in the form of xml report. You can create gbXML files of Revit projects by using Autodesk Green Building Studio software. The procedure to use this tool is given next.

- Click on the **Import gbXML** tool from the **Import** panel in the **Insert** tab of **Ribbon**. The **Import gbXML** dialog box will be displayed; refer to Figure-28.

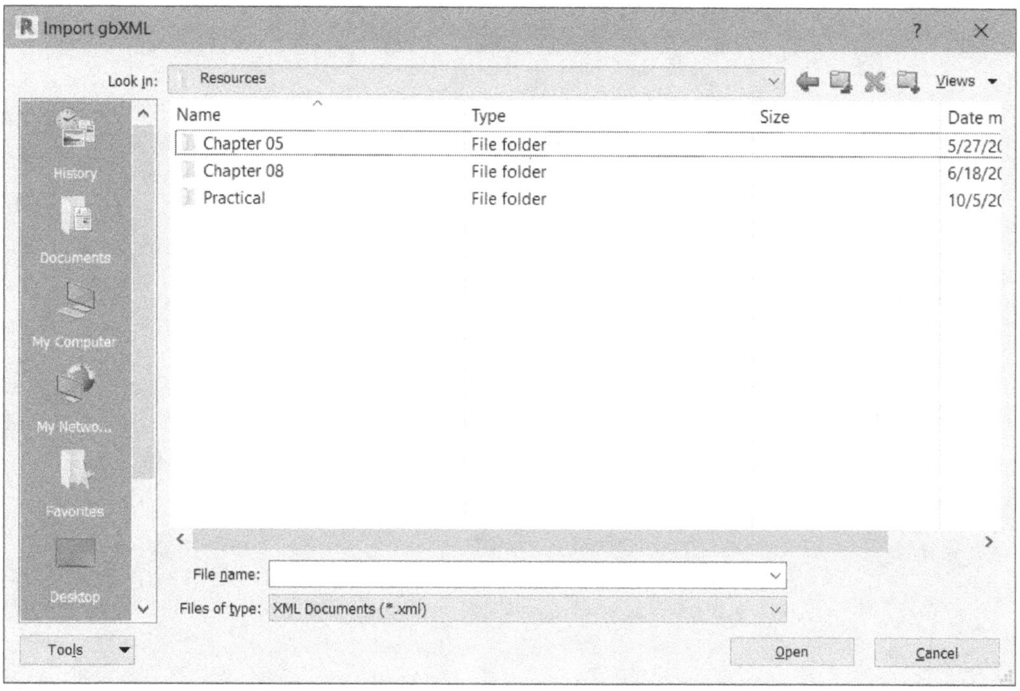

Figure-28. Import gbXML dialog box

- Select desired file and click on the **Open** button from the dialog box. The **Select data to import from the gbXML file** dialog box will be displayed; refer to Figure-29.

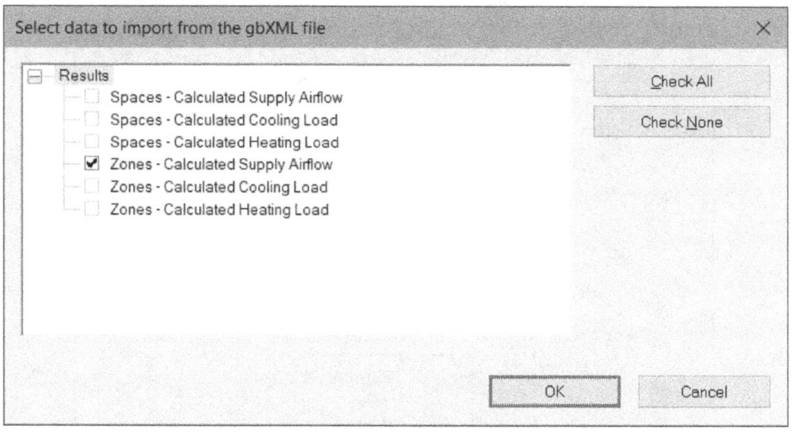

Figure-29. Select data to import from the gbXML file dialog box

- Select the check boxes for data to be loaded in the project and click on the **OK** button. The results of analysis will be loaded.

Importing PDF

The **Import PDF** tool in **Import** panel is used to place pdf file at the background of model view as image. The procedure to use this tool is given next.

- Click on the **Import PDF** tool from the **Import** panel in the **Insert** tab of **Ribbon**. The **Import Image** dialog box will be displayed; refer to Figure-30.

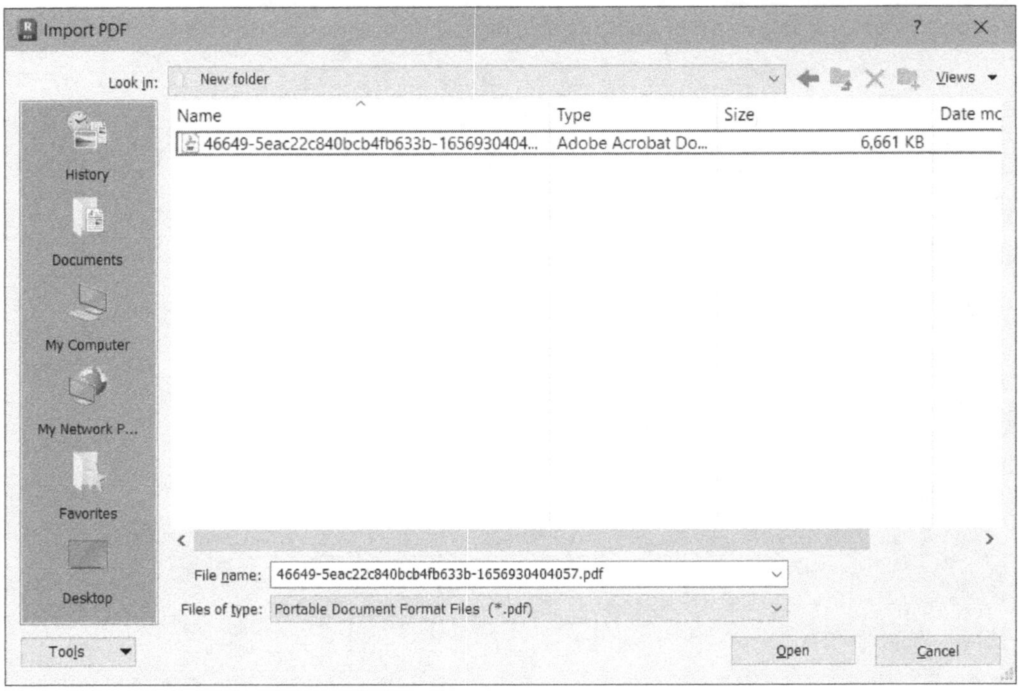

Figure-30. Import Image dialog box

- Select desired file from the dialog box and click on the **Open** button. The **Import PDF** dialog box will be displayed; refer to Figure-31.

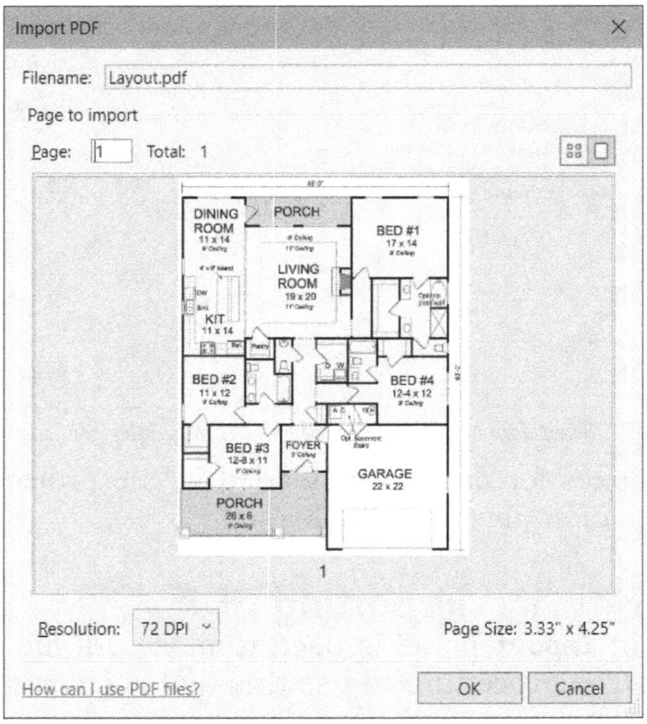

Figure-31. Import PDF dialog box

- Select desired page of PDF and resolution in the dialog box. Click on the **OK** button from the dialog box. You will be asked to specify location of PDF.
- Click at desired location to place the image. The raster image of PDF will be placed; refer to Figure-32.

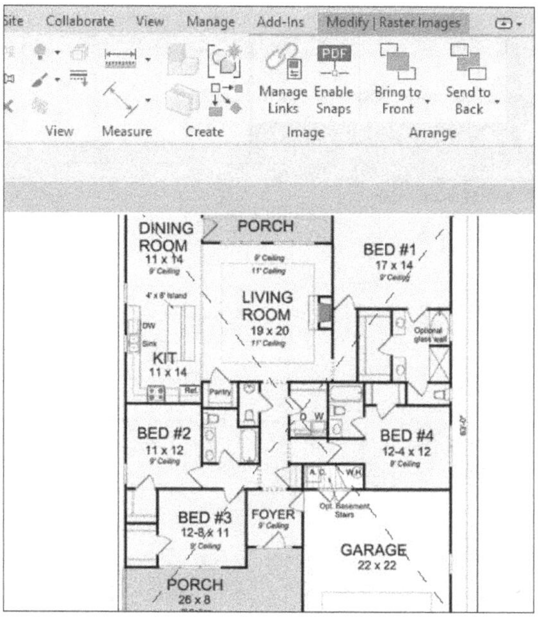

Figure-32. Raster image of pdf placed

- Press **ESC** to exit the tool. Similarly, you can use **Import Image** tool to import image file.

Inserting Views from Other Files

The **Insert Views from File** tool is used to import views and schedules from other Revit and Autodesk files. The procedure to use this tool is given next.

- Click on the **Insert Views from File** tool in **Insert from File** drop-down from the **Load from Library** panel in the **Insert** tab of **Ribbon**. The **Open** dialog box will be displayed; refer to Figure-33.

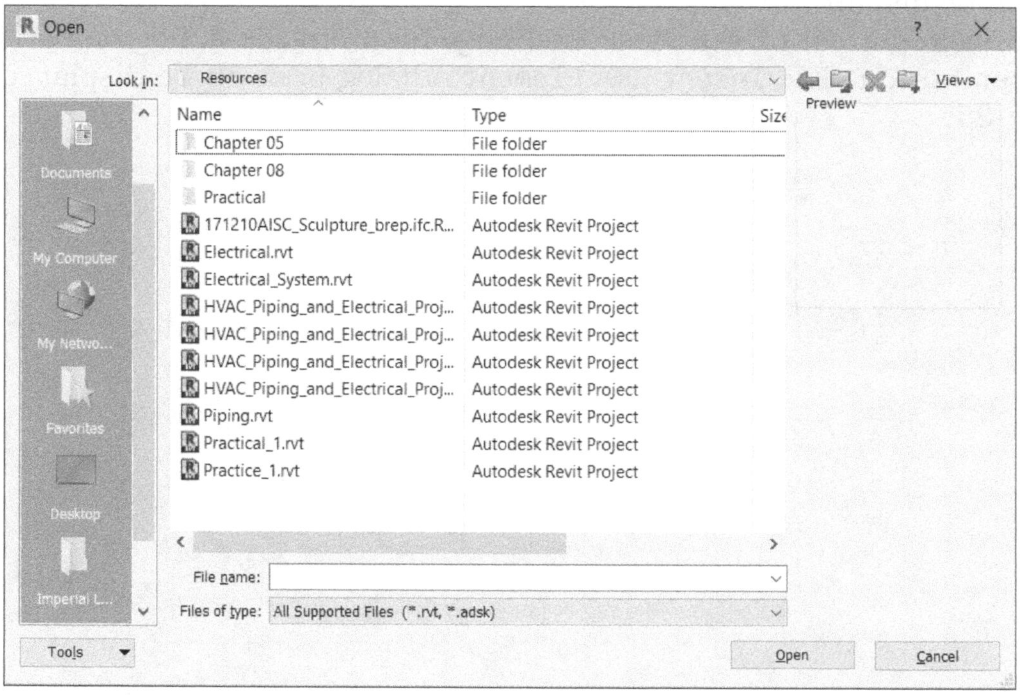

Figure-33. Open dialog box

- Select desired file from the dialog box and click on the **Open** button. The **Insert Views** dialog box will be displayed; refer to Figure-34.

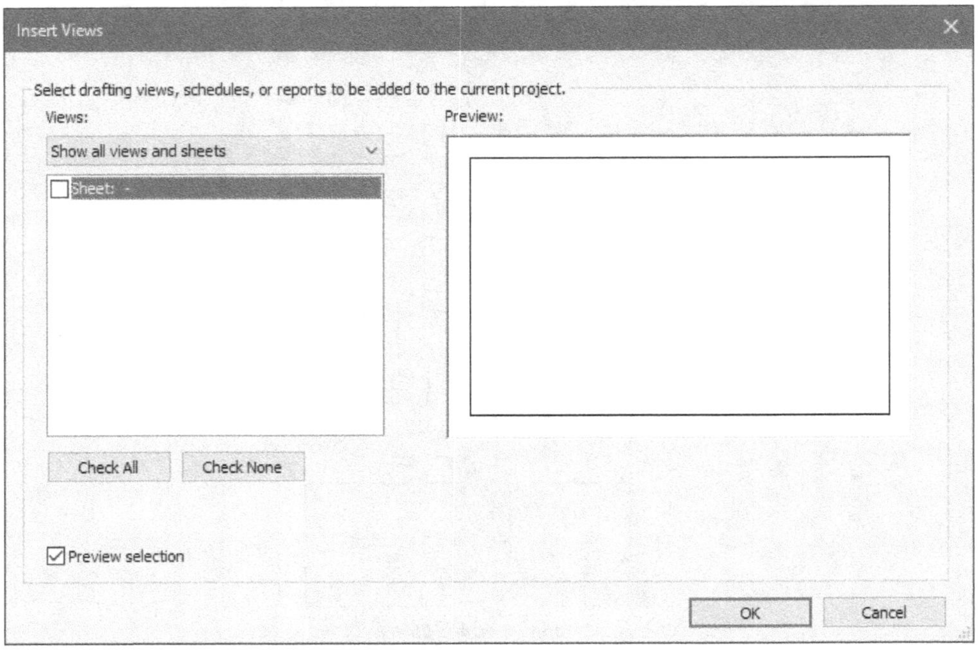

Figure-34. Insert Views dialog box

- Select desired check boxes and click on the **OK** button. The selected views and schedules will be added in the project.

Inserting 2D Elements from File

The **Insert 2D Elements from File** tool is used to insert 2D elements from selected Revit or Autodesk file in project. The procedure to use this tool is given next.

- Click on the **Insert 2D Elements from File** tool from the **Insert from File** drop-down in the **Load from File** panel of **Insert** tab in the **Ribbon**. The **Open** dialog box will be displayed.
- Select desired Revit or Autodesk exchange file from the dialog box and click on the **Open** button. The **Insert 2D Elements** dialog box will be displayed; refer to Figure-35.

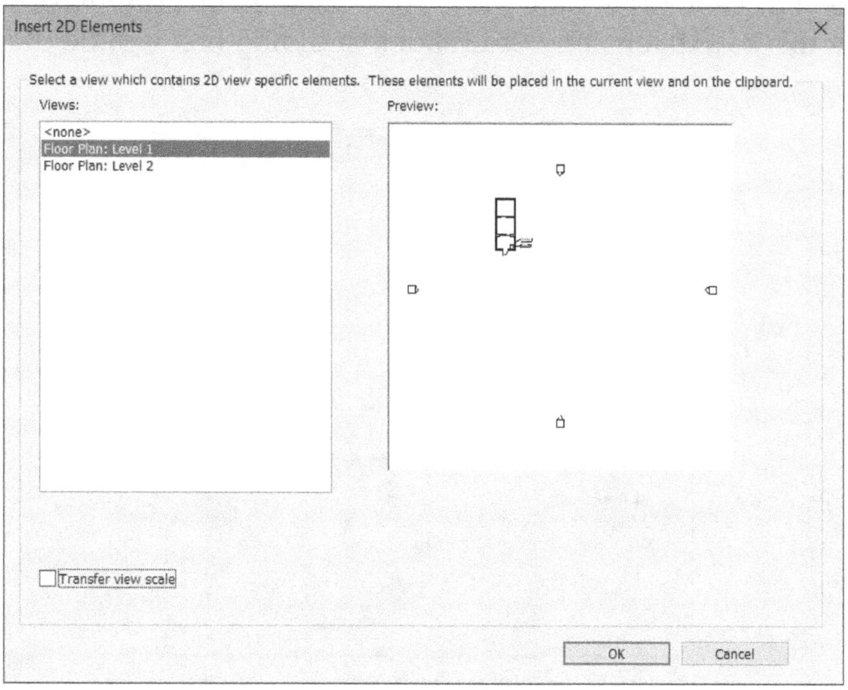

Figure-35. Insert 2D Elements dialog box

- Select desired view from which you want to copy elements and place in current view. Select the **Transfer view scale** check box to use the same scale of elements.
- Click on the **OK** button from the dialog box. You will be asked to specify location of elements.
- Click at desired location to place the elements. The elements will be placed as group.
- Click on the **Finish** button from the **Modify|Groups** contextual tab in the **Ribbon** to place elements.

The procedure to load family parts and group has been discussed earlier.

Till this point, you learned to link and import objects in a Revit project. Now, you will learn to collaborate the project file with other team members.

COLLABORATING WITH TEAM

The tools in the **Collaborate** tab of **Ribbon** are used to collaborate on current project with your team members; refer to Figure-36. Various tools in this tab are discussed next.

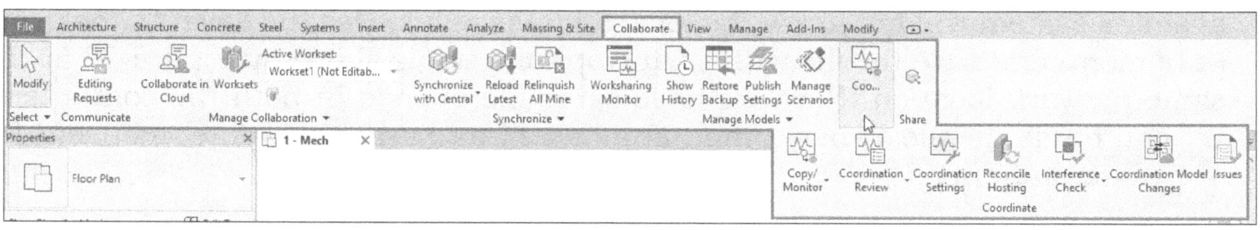

Figure-36. Collaborate tab

Collaboration of Project

The **Collaborate** tool is used to activate sharing of the current project with your team members. The procedure to use this tool is given next.

- Click on the **Collaborate** tool from the **Manage Collaboration** panel in the **Collaborate** tab of **Ribbon**. The **Collaborate** dialog box will be displayed; refer to Figure-37.

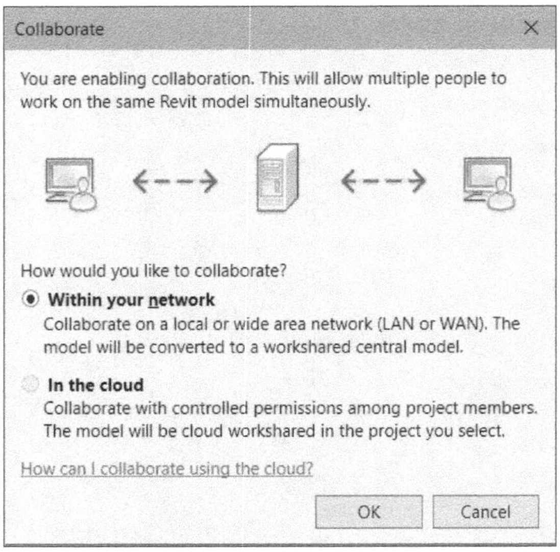

Figure-37. Collaborate dialog box

- Select the **Within your network** radio button if you want share the file in LAN or WAN. Select the **In the cloud** radio button if you want to share the project using BIM cloud.
- Click on the **OK** button from the dialog box. The file will be available for collaboration.
- Save the file at a location accessible by all your team members on a network drive. As in our case, we have saved the file on shared folder named Revit Project; refer to Figure-38.

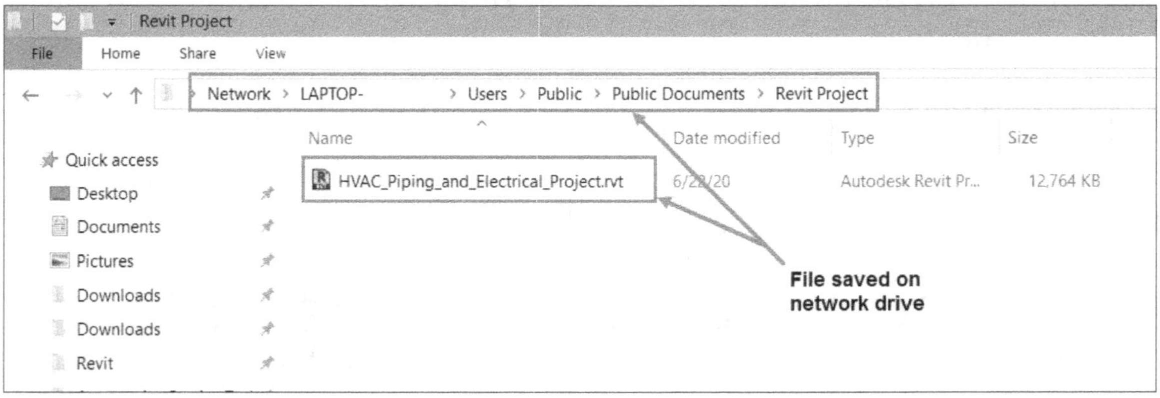

Figure-38. File saved on network

- Now, open the file in other PC on network. You might be asked to save the file again as system will not know the local address of file. Use the **Save As** tool from **File** menu and save the file with saving options set as shown in Figure-39 at the same network location. Now, we have same file opened in both the computers. We can name the file owner computer as user1 and other computer as user2 for our understanding.

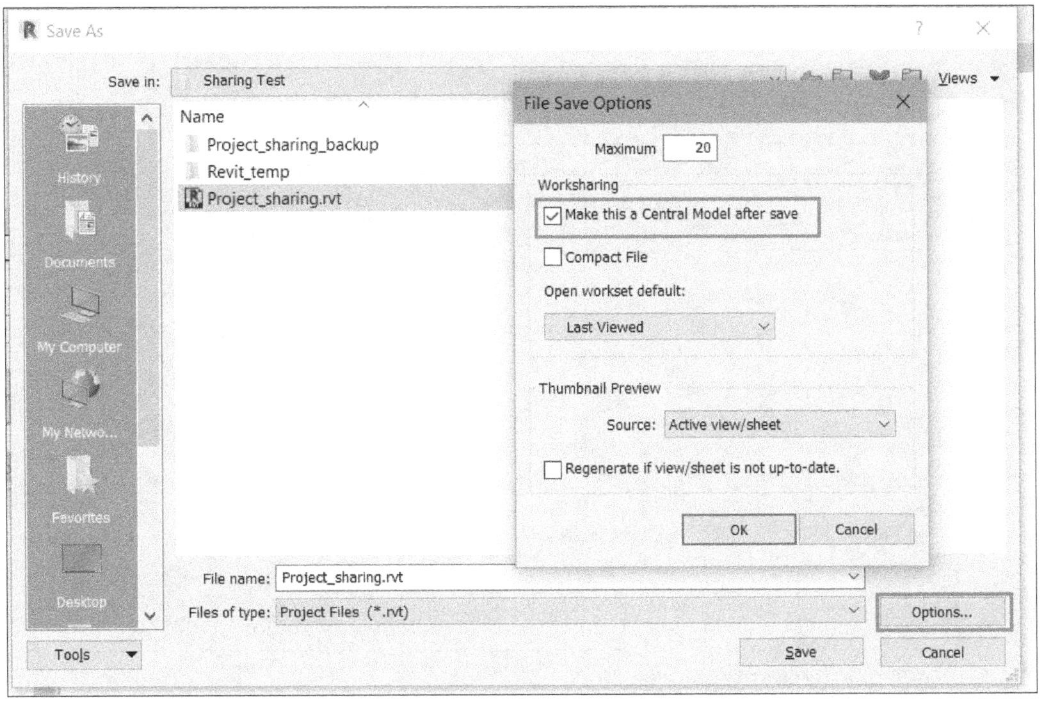

Figure-39. Save option for central file

- Click on the **Worksets** tool in user1 computer and make any of the workset as editable for you; refer to Figure-40. Click on the **OK** button and save the file using **CTRL+S**.

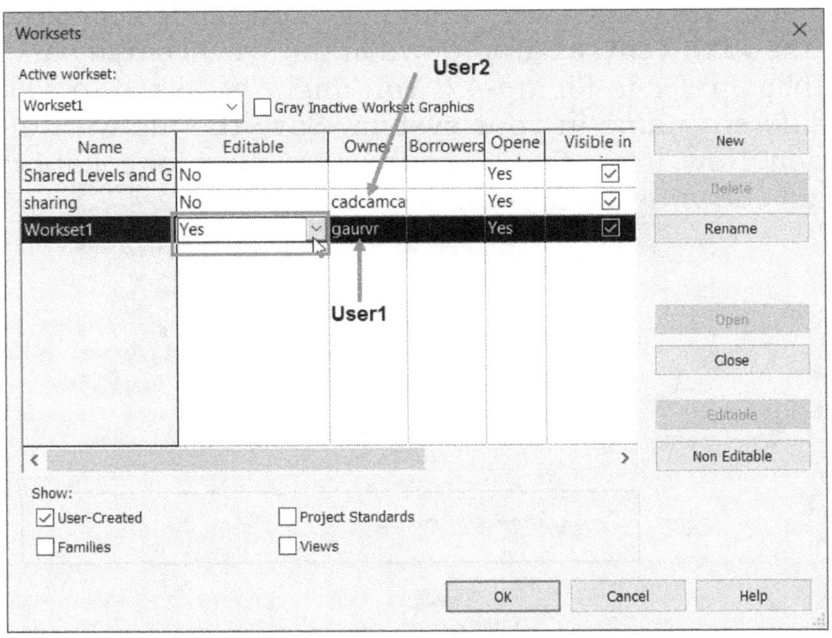

Figure-40. Making workset editable

- Similarly, make another workset editable for user2 on another PC; refer to Figure-41. Click on the **OK** button and save the file using **CTRL+S**.

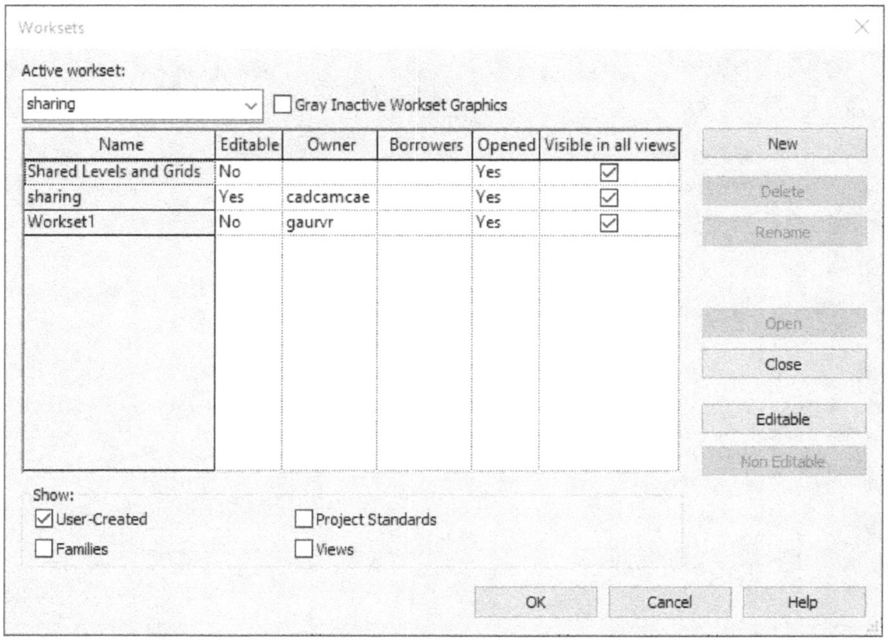

Figure-41. Workset editable on other pc

- Now, user1 (gaurvr) can work on **Workset1** workset and edit it while user2 (cadcamcae) can work on **sharing** workset. Assume user1 is making architectural model then he/she should create architectural model on Workset1. If user2 is creating structural model then he/she should create the model on sharing workset.
- After making changes, each user should click on the **Synchronize Now** tool from the **Synchronize with Central** drop-down in the **Synchronize** panel of **Collaborate** tab in the **Ribbon**; refer to Figure-42. You might be asked to save the local copy of file with different name in your system. Save the file with different name at desired location. Now, if you make a connection chart for collaboration of file then it should be as shown in Figure-43.

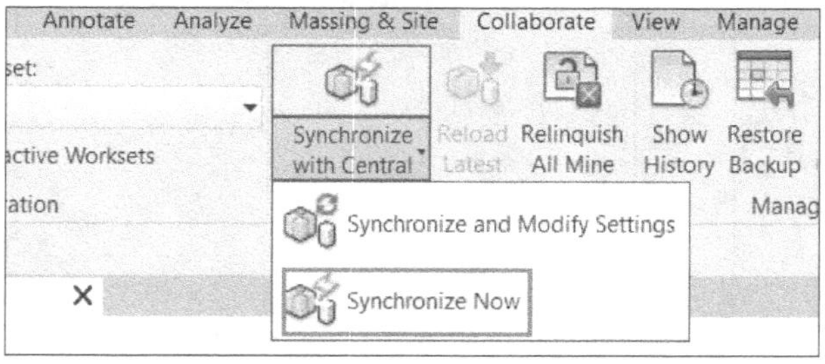

Figure-42. Synchronize Now tool

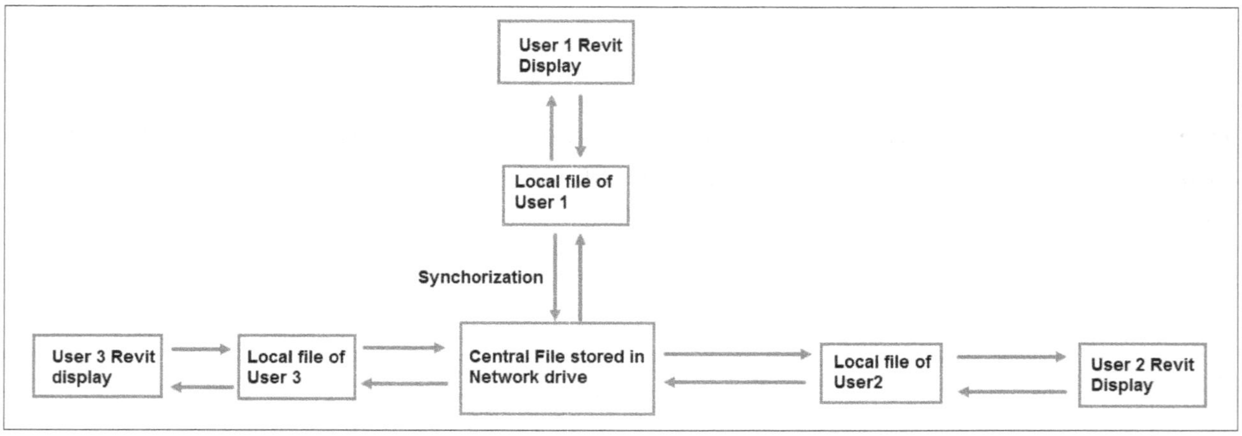

Figure-43. Collaboration synchronization chart

As shown in Figure-43, once you have created a central file at network location then each user will be asked to save local copy of the project file at local locations. Now, each user can perform desired operations on their local copies and once they click on the **Synchronize Now** tool, their model gets updated automatically.

- After making desired changes, click on the **Relinquish All Mine** tool from the **Synchronize** panel of **Collaborate** tab in the **Ribbon** to free the workset for others.
- If you are starting the software again after some time then click on the **Reload Latest** tool from the **Synchronize** panel of **Collaborate** tab in the **Ribbon** to load latest version of file from central model.

Worksharing Monitor

The **Worksharing Monitor** tool is used to check current status of shared model and various requests of editing by your team members. The procedure to use this tool is given next.

- Click on the **Worksharing Monitor** tool from the **Synchronize** panel of **Collaborate** tab in the **Ribbon**. The **Worksharing Monitor for Autodesk Revit** window will be displayed; refer to Figure-44.

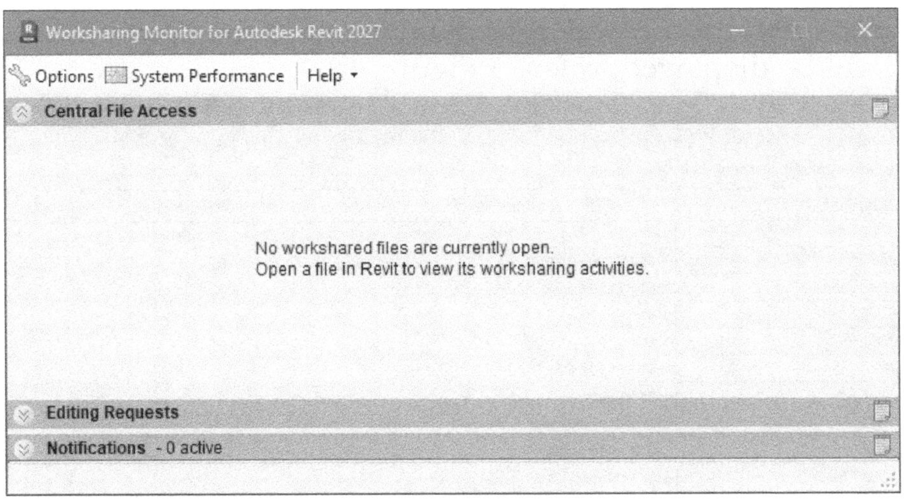

Figure-44. Worksharing Monitor for Autodesk Revit window

There are three panes in this window. The **Central File Access** pane shows information about the current project your are working with and the team members which are collaborating with you on that project. The **Editing Requests** pane shows the permissions issues on current shared project and pending requests. The **Notifications** pane shows warnings and messages related to shared project by your collaborators.

Checking History of Model Collaboration

The **Show History** tool is used to check history of changes made in the model by different users. The procedure to use this tool is given next.

- Click on the **Show History** tool from the **Manage Models** panel in the **Collaborate** tab in the **Ribbon**. The **Show History** dialog box will be displayed; refer to Figure-45.

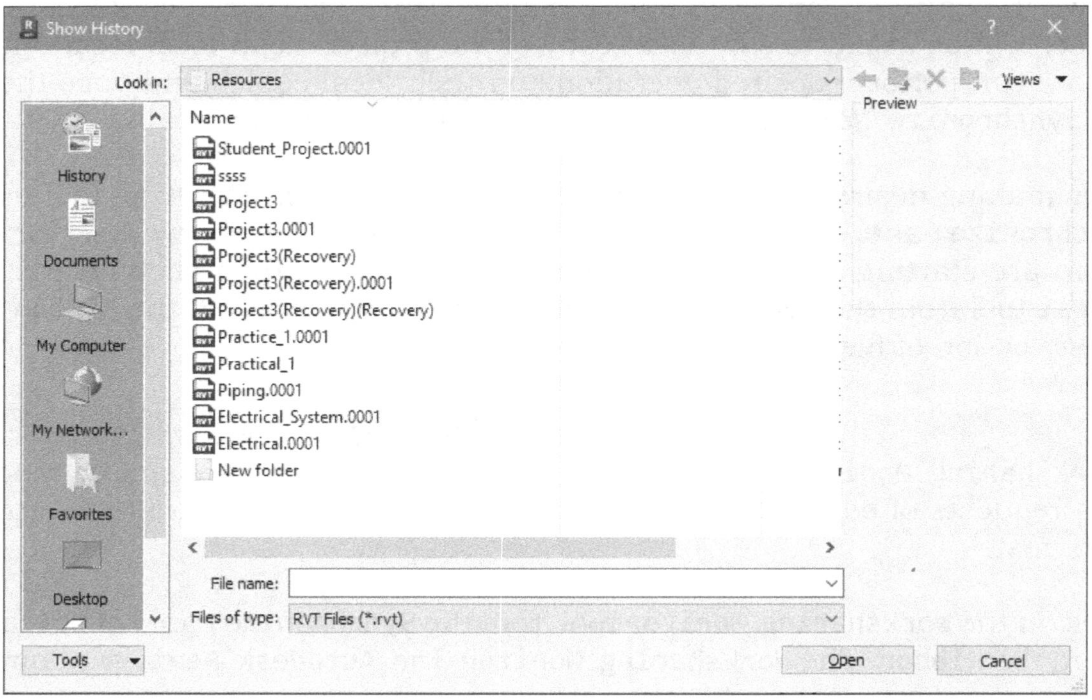

Figure-45. Show history dialog box

- Select desired file from the dialog box and click on the **Open** button. The **History** dialog box will be displayed; refer to Figure-46.

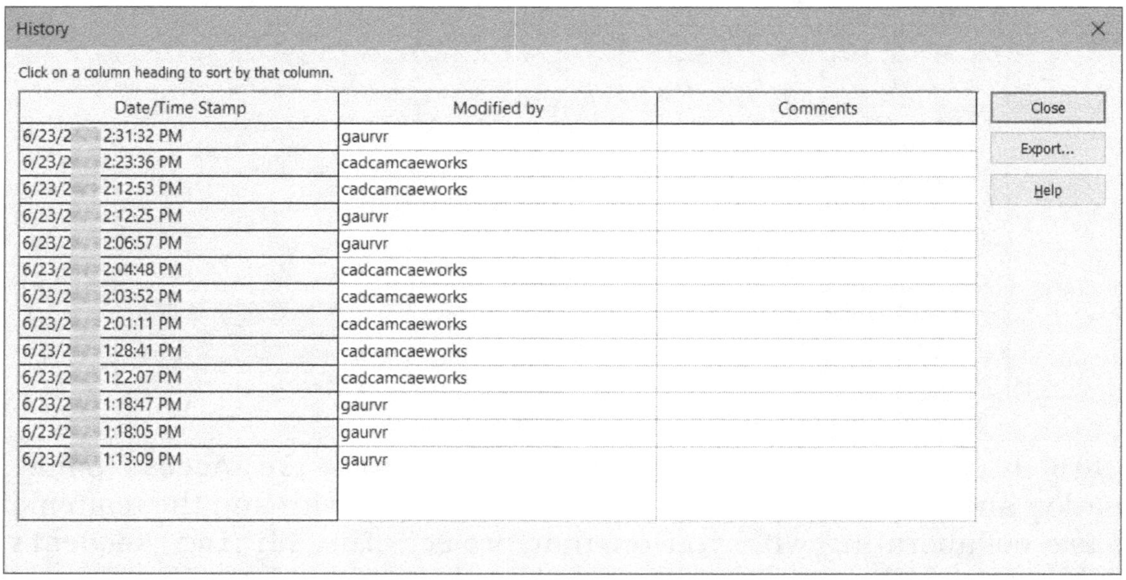

Figure-46. History dialog box

- Check the time and user who made the changes.
- Click on the **Close** button.

Restoring Backup

The **Restore Backup** tool is used to restore the backup file created automatically while different users are working the model. The procedure to use this tool is given next.

- Click on the **Restore Backup** tool from the **Manage Models** panel in the **Collaborate** tab of **Ribbon**. The **Browse For Folder** dialog box will be displayed; refer to Figure-47.

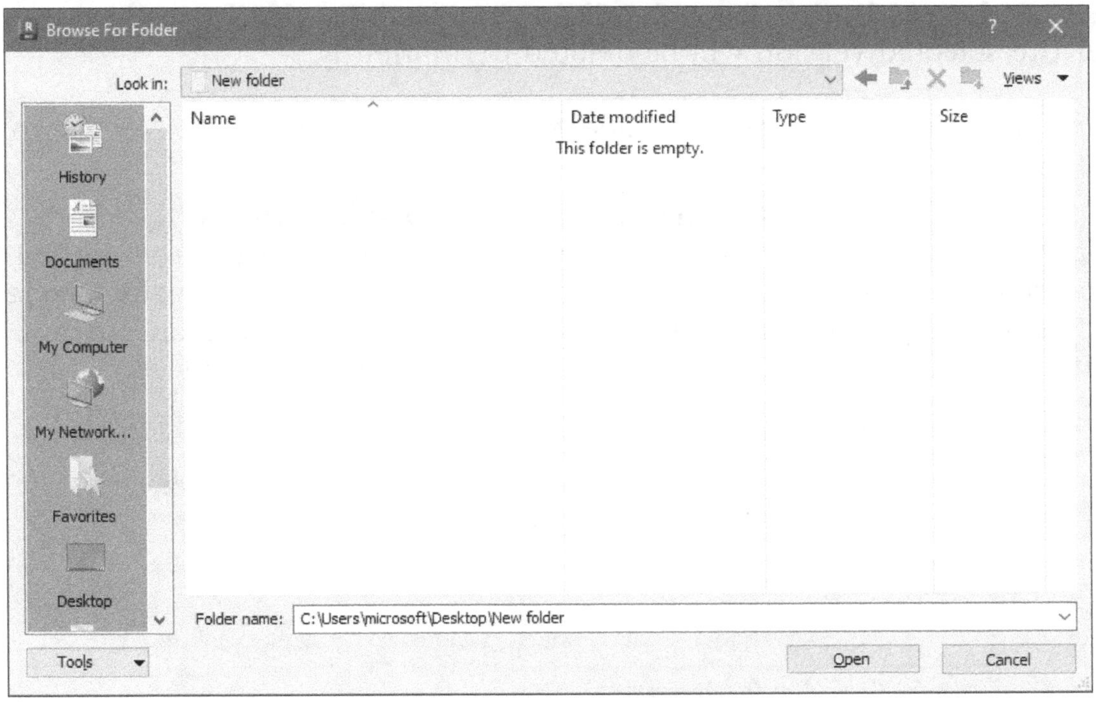

Figure-47. Browse For Folder dialog box

- Select desired folder in the dialog box where the backup files are saved automatically and click on the **Open** button. The **Project Backup Versions** dialog box will be displayed; refer to Figure-48.

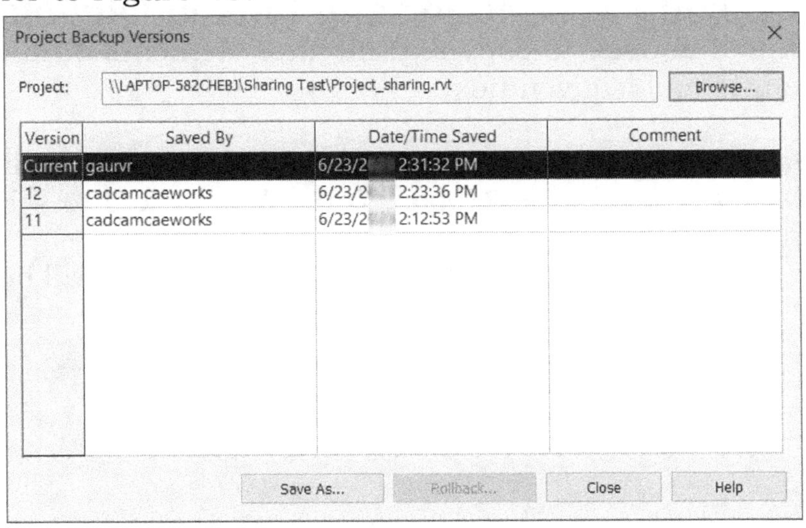

Figure-48. Project Backup Versions dialog box

- Select desired version of file and click on the **Rollback** button from the dialog box. The **Rollback Backup File** dialog box will be displayed; refer to Figure-49.

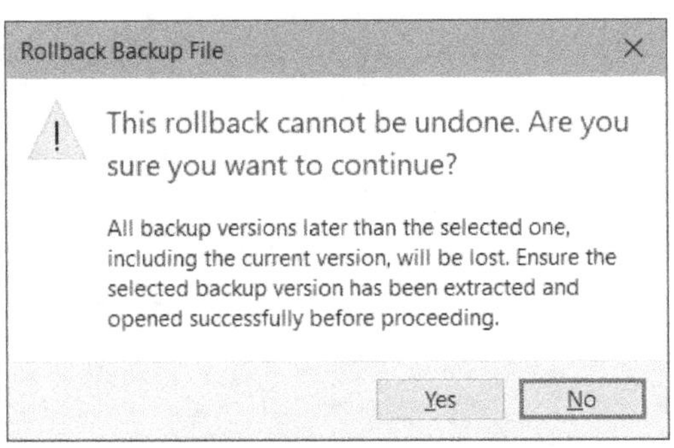

Figure-49. Rollback Backup File dialog box

- Click on the **Yes** button from the dialog box to rollback. Note that data created after the selected version will be deleted permanently.

You can use other tools of **Manage Models** panel in the same way.

Copying and Monitoring Elements

The **Copy/Monitor** tools are used to copy and monitor elements from linked files or projects; refer to Figure-50. The function of both tools, **Use Current Project** and **Select Link** is same but the **Use Current Project** tool works on current project elements and **Select Link** tool works on elements from linked files.

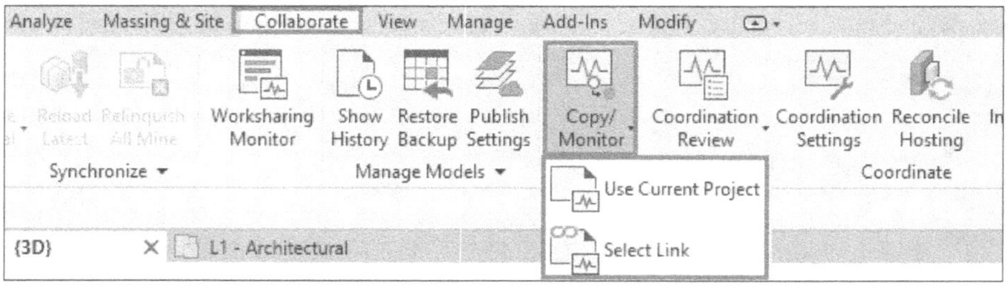

Figure-50. Copy Monitor drop-down

We will discuss the **Select Link** tool here, you can apply the same procedure for **Use Current Project** tool.

Copying and Monitoring Linked Objects

The **Select Link** tool is used to copy and monitor elements of linked models. The procedure to use this tool is given next.

- Click on the **Select Link** tool from the **Copy/Monitor** drop-down in the **Coordinate** panel of **Collaborate** tab in the **Ribbon**. You will be asked to select the revit link to be monitored.
- Select desired linked file. The **Copy/Monitor** contextual tab will be displayed; refer to Figure-51.

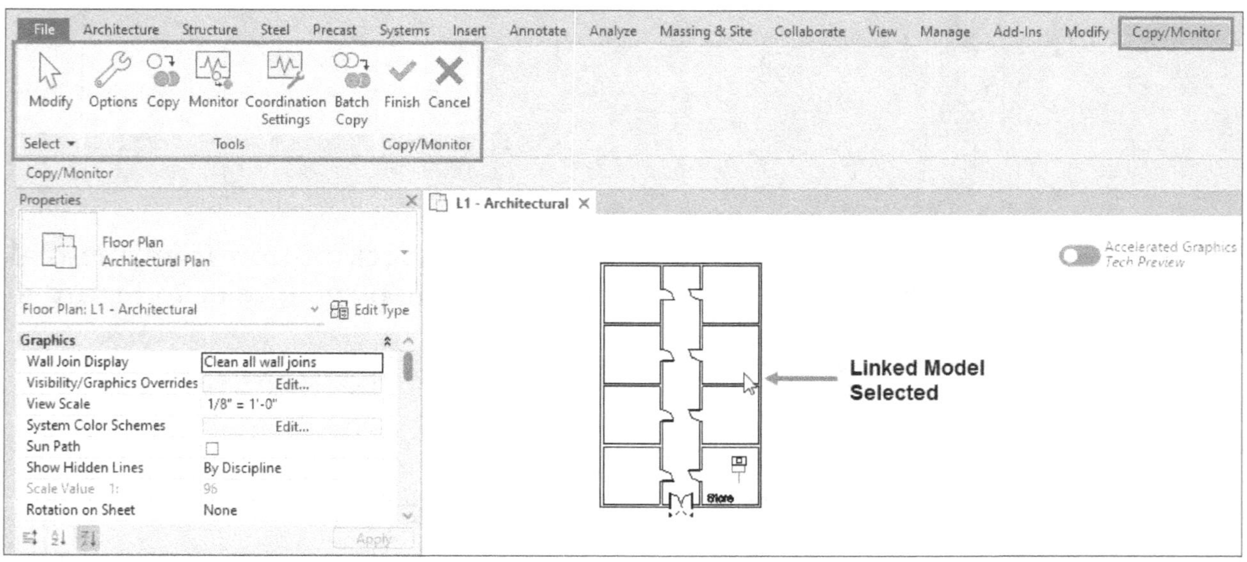

Figure-51. Copy Monitor contextual tab

- Click on the **Options** tool from the **Tools** panel in the **Copy/Monitor** contextual tab of **Ribbon** to define options related to copying and monitoring of link model. The **Copy/Monitor Options** dialog box will be displayed; refer to Figure-52.

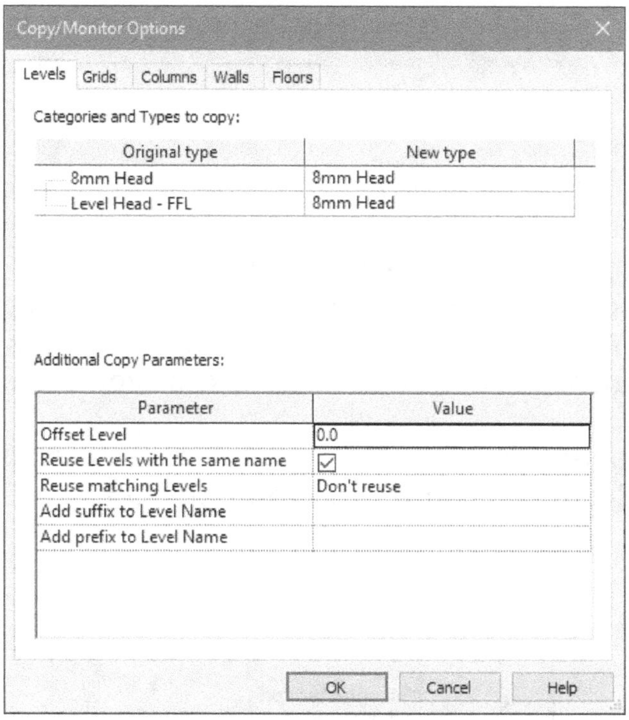

Figure-52. Copy Monitor Options dialog box

- Set desired parameters in the dialog box and click on the **OK** button to apply settings.

Copying Objects

- Click on the **Copy** tool from the **Tools** panel in the contextual tab of **Ribbon**. You will be asked to select the element to be copied.
- Select the **Multiple** check box if you want to copy multiple elements and then select multiple elements while holding the **CTRL** key.
- Click on the **Finish** button from the **Options Bar**. The copies will be created and monitoring of copied objects will be activated automatically; refer to Figure-53.

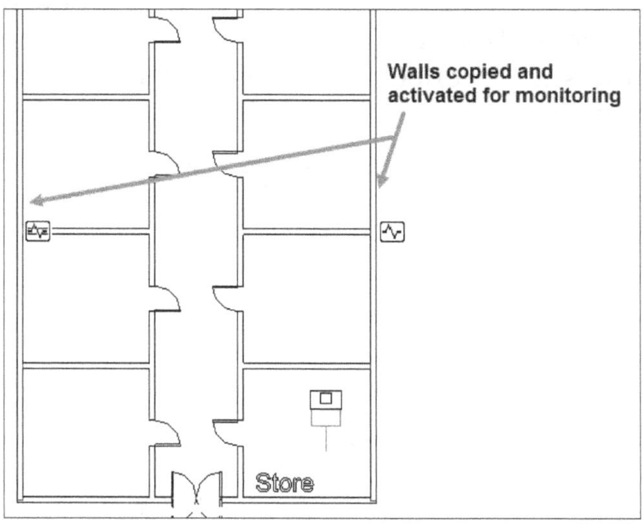

Figure-53. Copied elements

- Drag the copied elements to desired locations or change the size of elements. The warning will be displayed telling you that the element size or shape has changed; refer to Figure-54.

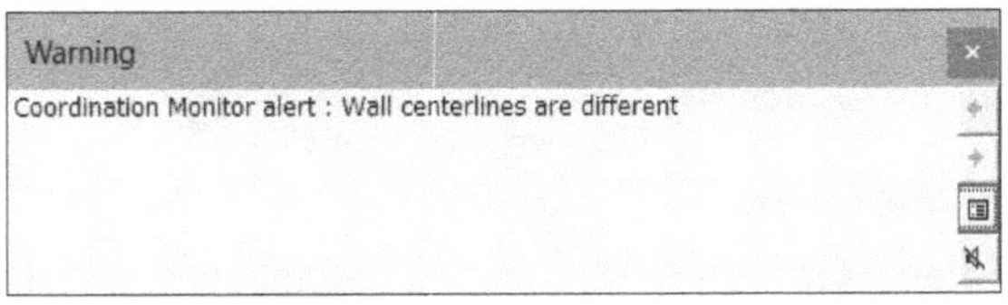

Figure-54. Warning box

Monitoring Objects

- Click on the **Monitor** tool from the **Tools** panel in the **Copy/Monitor** contextual tab of the **Ribbon**. You will be asked to select the elements to be monitored.
- Select desired element. You will be asked to select corresponding element for comparison.
- Select desired element. The monitoring will start and symbol of monitoring will be displayed on selected element; refer to Figure-55.

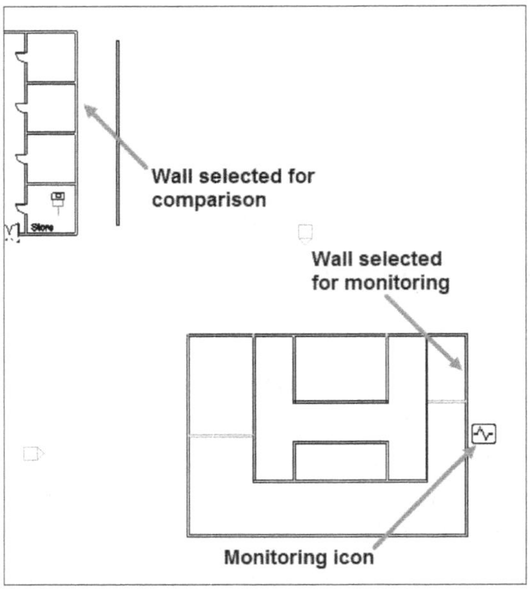

Figure-55. Element selected for monitoring

- Press **ESC** twice to exit the editing mode. Now, if you change the size of element then warning message will be displayed. Note that if you are not able to select an element then you should check the selection filters in the expanded **Select** panel; refer to Figure-56.

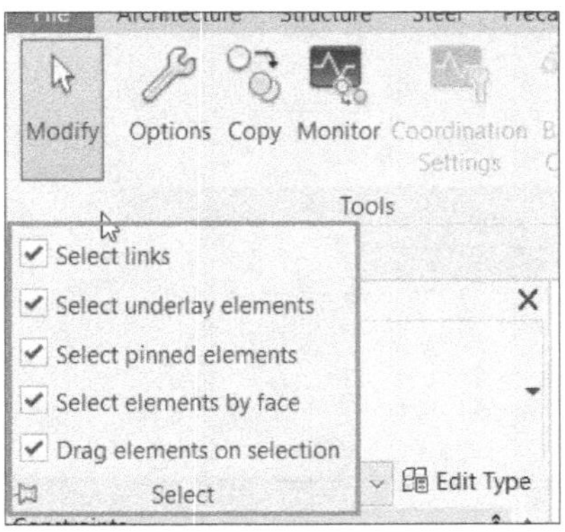

Figure-56. Expanded Select panel

- If you want to stop monitoring an element then select the element being monitored and click on the **Stop Monitoring** tool from the **Monitor** panel of the contextual tab in the **Ribbon**; refer to Figure-57.

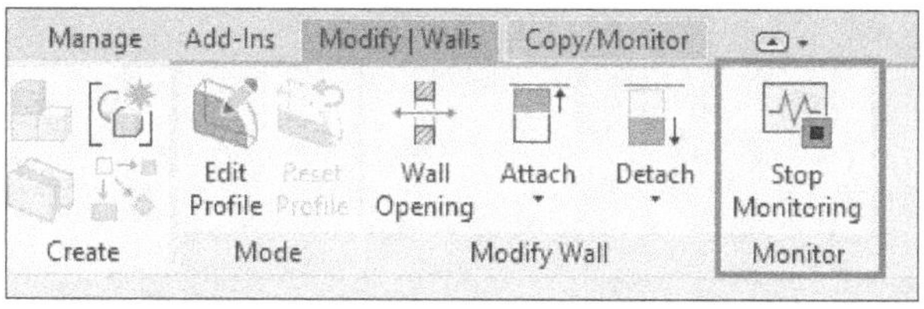

Figure-57. Stop Monitoring tool

Coordination Settings

The **Coordination Settings** tool is used to define settings related to copying and mapping of objects. The procedure to define settings is given next.

- Click on the **Coordination Settings** tool from the **Tools** panel in the **Copy/Monitor** contextual tab of **Ribbon**. The **Coordination Settings** dialog box will be displayed; refer to Figure-58.

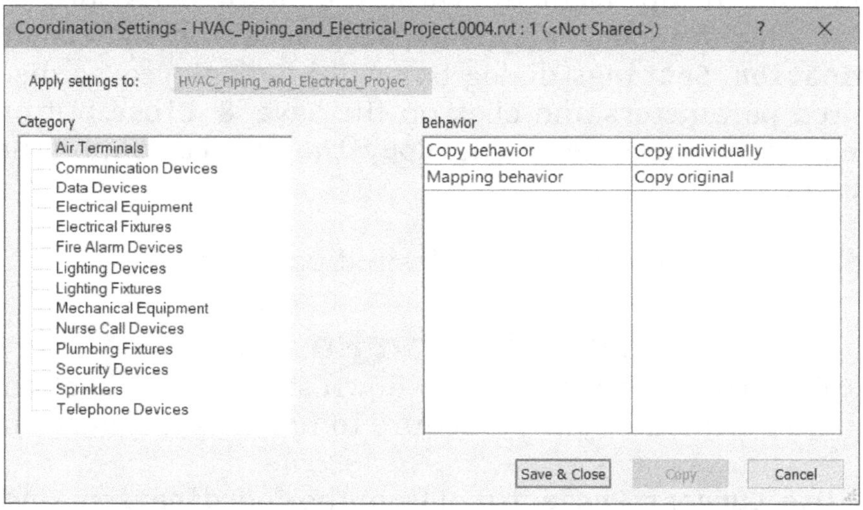

Figure-58. Coordination Settings dialog box

- Select desired category from the left area of the dialog box and define behavior like copying behavior & mapping behavior.
- Click on the **Save & Close** button from the dialog box.

Batch Copying

The **Batch Copy** tool is used to copy elements that have not yet been copied from the linked model. The procedure to use this tool is given next.

- Click on the **Batch Copy** tool from the **Tools** panel in the **Copy/Monitor** contextual tab of **Ribbon**. The **Fixtures Found** dialog box will be displayed; refer to Figure-59.

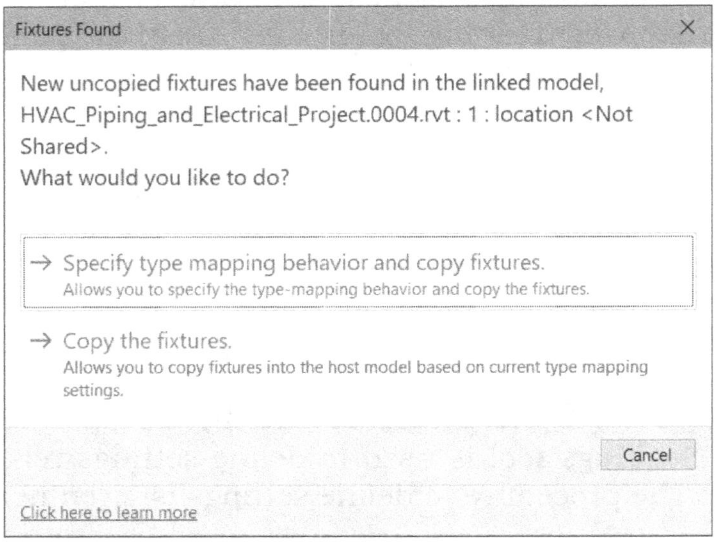

Figure-59. Fixtures Found dialog box

- Select the **Specify type mapping behavior and copy fixtures** option if you want to define mapping behavior before copying fixtures. Select the **Copy the fixtures** option if you want to copy elements without defining behavior.
- If you have selected the **Specify type mapping behavior and copy fixtures** option then **Coordination Settings** dialog box will be displayed as discussed earlier. Specify desired parameters and click on the **Save & Close** button. The fixtures will be copied. If you have selected the **Copy the fixtures** option then fixtures will be copied directly.

Click on the **Finish** button after setting desired parameters.

Coordination Review

The tools in the **Coordination Review** drop-down are used to check the modification details of monitored elements. The procedure to use this tool is given next.

- Click on the **Use Current Project** tool from the **Coordination Review** drop-down of **Coordinate** panel in the **Collaborate** tab of **Ribbon**. The **Coordination Review** dialog box will be displayed; refer to Figure-60.

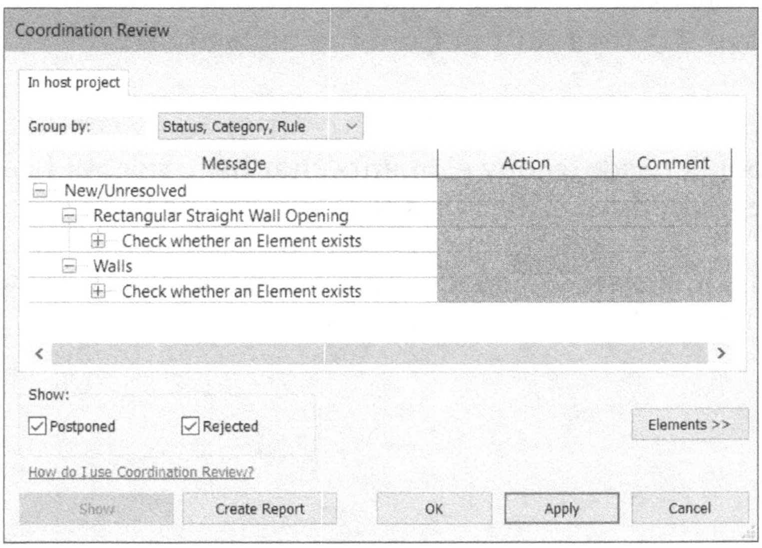

Figure-60. Coordination Review dialog box

- Select the element to be checked and click on the **Show** button. The selected element will be highlighted in the drawing area.
- Click on the **Create Report** button from the dialog box. The **Export Revit Coordination Report** dialog box will be displayed; refer to Figure-61.
- Specify desired name of file in the dialog box and click on the **Save** button. The report will be created.

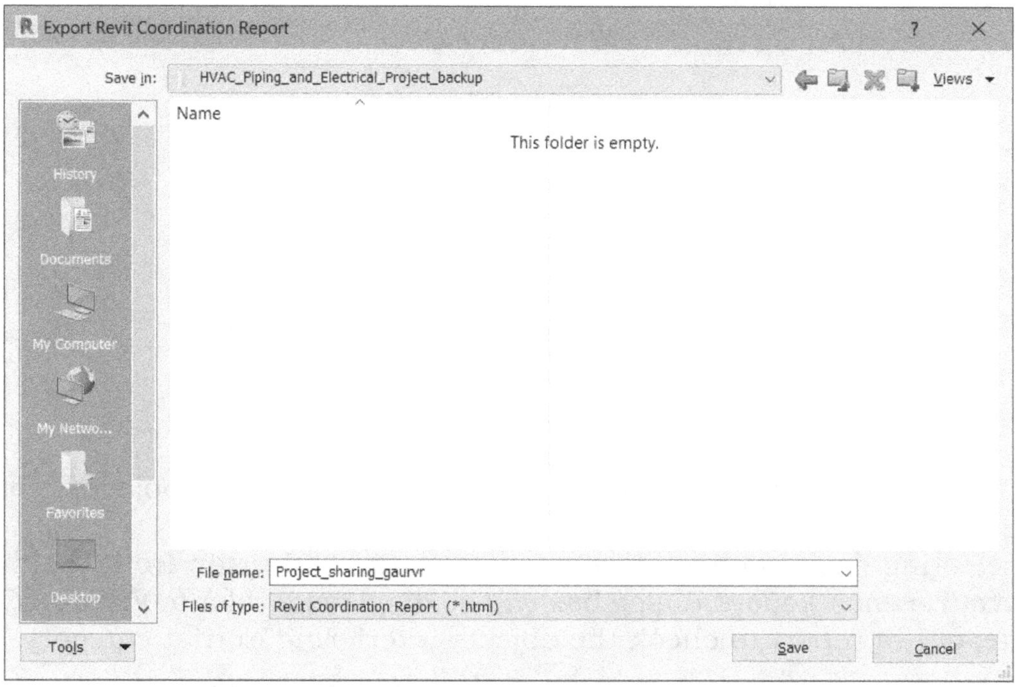

Figure-61. Export Revit Coordination Report dialog box

- Click on the **OK** button from the dialog box once review is complete.

You can use the **Select Link** tool of **Coordination Review** drop-down in the same way.

Interference Check

The tools in the **Interference Check** drop-down are used to check if there are objects in the project that are interfering with each other like, a duct line interfering with water pipe in the project. The tools in this drop-down are discussed next.

- Click on the **Run Interference Check** tool from the **Interference Check** drop-down in the **Coordinate** panel of **Collaborate** tab in the **Ribbon**. The **Interference Check** dialog box will be displayed; refer to Figure-62.

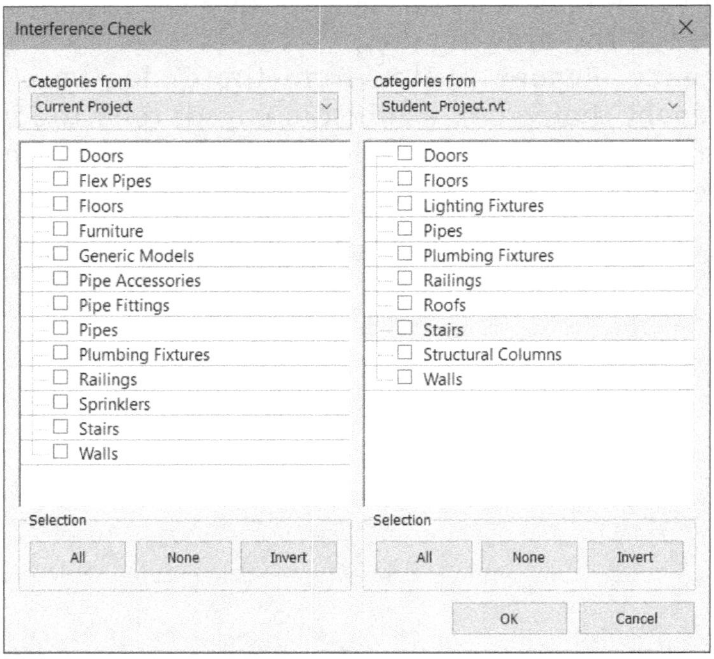

Figure-62. Interference Check dialog box

- Select the check boxes from both sides in dialog box to define objects to be checked for interference.
- After selecting desired check boxes, click on the **OK** button from the dialog box. The **Interference Report** dialog box will be displayed; refer to Figure-63. Expand the category in report to check the objects interfering in that category.

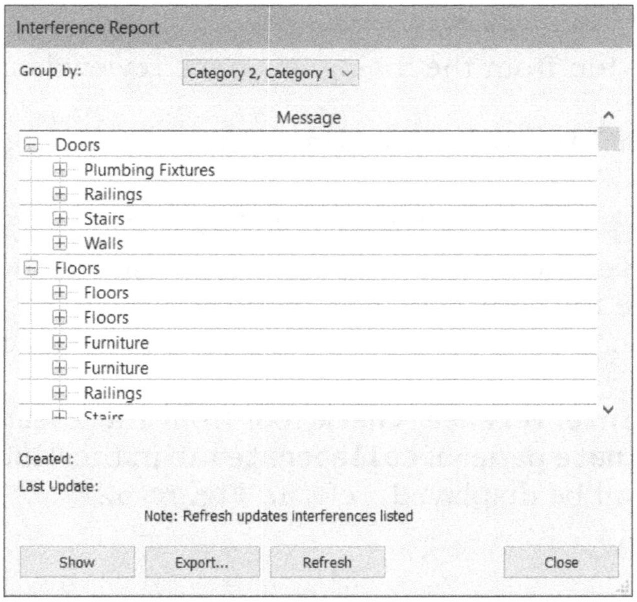

Figure-63. Interference Report dialog box

- Select desired object from the list in dialog box and click on the **Show** button to check how objects are interfering; refer to Figure-64.

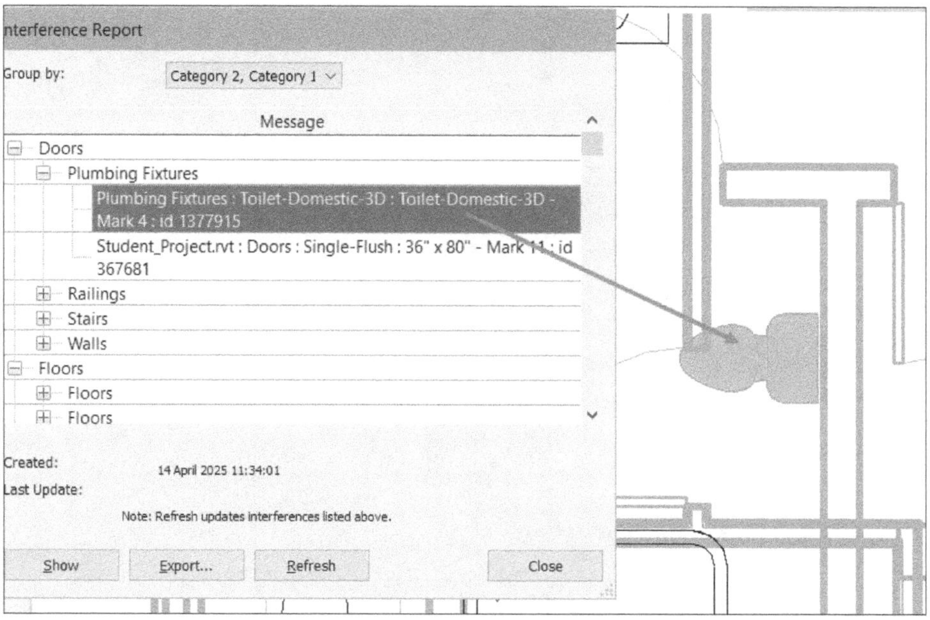

Figure-64. Interfering objects

- Click on the **Close** button from the dialog box to exit tool.

If you want to check the last report of interference again then click on the **Show Last Report** tool from the **Interference Check** drop-down.

Coordination Model Changes

The **Coordination Model Changes** tool shows a summary of changes between the current cloud-linked coordination model and its previous versions. This tool is currently not functional for educational version.

Issues

The **Issues** tool is used to show or hide the Issues panel and toggle the visibility of issue push pins. This tool is currently not functional for educational version.

The **Coordination Settings** tool has been discussed earlier and the other tools in **Coordinate** panel work in the same way.

Sharing Views of Model

The **Shared Views** tool is used to share current view of the model. The procedure to use this tool is given next.

- Click on the **Shared Views** tool from the **Share** panel in the **Collaborate** tab of **Ribbon**. The **Shared Views** task pane will be displayed at the right in the application window; refer to Figure-65.

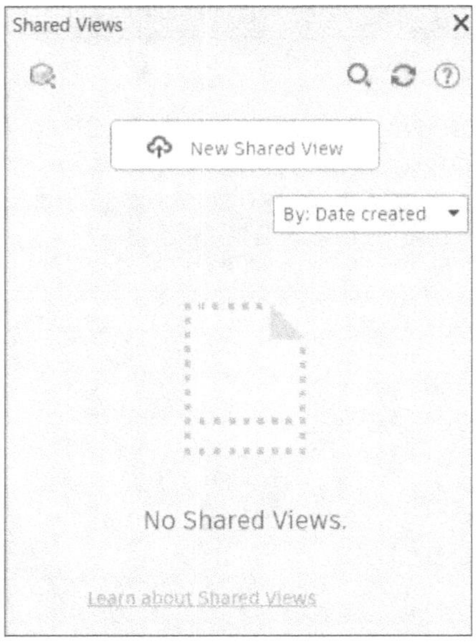

Figure-65. Shared Views task pane

- Make sure the model is saved already and then click on the **New Shared View** button from the task pane. The **Create Shared Views** dialog box will be displayed; refer to Figure-66.

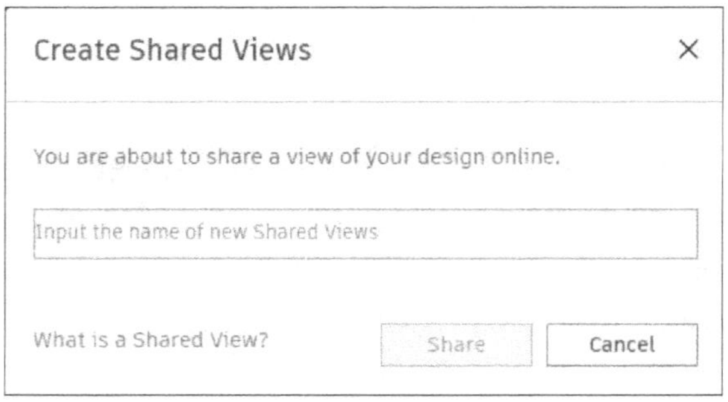

Figure-66. Create Shared Views dialog box

- Specify desired name of shared view in the edit box and click on the **Share** button. Once the process of extracting view is complete, a message box will be displayed; refer to Figure-67.

Figure-67. Message box

- Click on the **View in the Browser** link button from message box to check the view on your Autodesk Cloud account. Click on the **Copy the link** button from message box to copy link in clipboard and share it with other. Close the message box and **Shared Views** task pane, once you have shared the views.

TRANSMITTING REVIT PROJECT

The **Transmit model(s)** tool is used to copy a Revit model with all its dependent files into a folder for sharing with other. The procedure to use this tool is given next.

- Close all the models currently open in Revit, press **CTRL+D** if start page is being displayed instead of **Ribbon**, and then click on the **Transmit model(s)** tool from the **eTransmit** panel of **Add-ins** tab of **Ribbon**. The **eTransmit** dialog box will be displayed; refer to Figure-68.

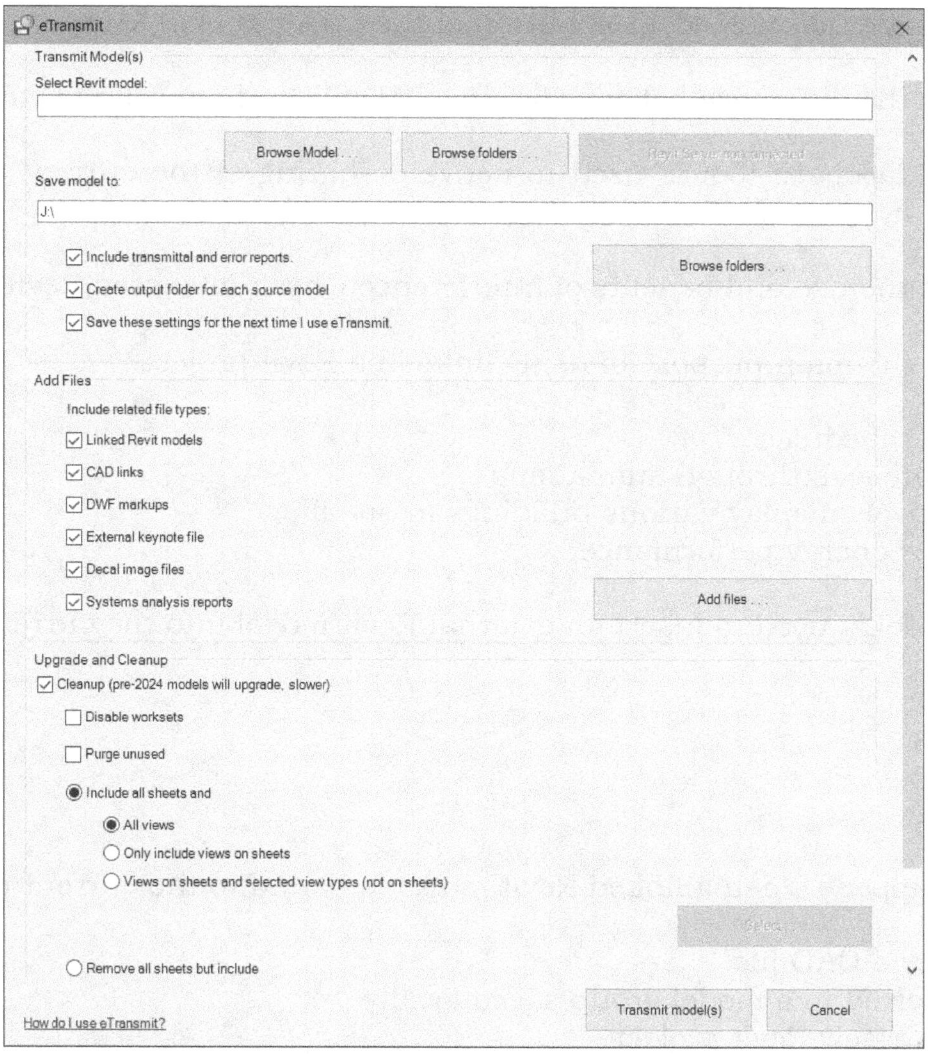

Figure-68. eTransmit dialog box

- Click on the **Browse Model** button from the **Transmit Model(s)** area of dialog box to select the model. The **Open** dialog box will be displayed.
- Select desired Revit model file from the dialog box and click on the **Open** button. The path of selected file will be displayed in the **Select Revit model** field.
- Click on the **Browse folders** button from the **Transmit Model(s)** area and specify location of folder where all the related files will be saved.
- Select check boxes for files and objects to be included when sharing project.
- If you want to add any additional file then use the **Add files** button from the **Add Files** area of dialog box.
- After setting desired parameters, click on the **Transmit model(s)** button. The location of folder will be displayed in an information box.

SELF-ASSESSMENT

Q1. Discuss the importance of using links in a Revit project.

Q2. Discuss the use of **Bind Link** button of the **Link** panel in **Ribbon**.

Q3. Discuss the difference between linking CAD file and importing CAD file.

Q4. The **Collaborate** tool is used to activate sharing of the current project with everyone on internet. (T/F)

Q5. Discuss the use and benefits of Interference Check in shared Revit project.

Q6. What is the main purpose of using links in a Revit project?

A. To create schedules
B. To generate walkthrough animations
C. To collectively display various buildings in one file
D. To analyze energy performance

Q7. Which tool is used to insert an external Revit model into the current project?

A. Link CAD
B. Bind Link
C. Link IFC
D. Link Revit

Q8. What happens when a linked Revit model is bound to the current project?

A. It becomes a CAD file
B. It is converted to a model group saved locally
C. It creates a new Revit project
D. It updates automatically with changes in the linked model

Q9. Which file format is associated with Industry Foundation Classes in Revit?

A. .dwg
B. .rvt
C. .ifc
D. .pdf

Q10. What tool is used to insert a CAD model into the current Revit project?

A. Link IFC
B. Link Topography
C. Link CAD
D. Link Image

Q11. Before using the Link Topography tool, what must be installed on the system?

A. Revit Extensions
B. Autodesk Desktop Connector
C. Navisworks Manage
D. Adobe Reader

Q12. Which tool allows you to import markup data from a DWF file?

A. Link DWF
B. Manage Links
C. DWF Markup
D. PDF Import

Q13. What must be done to place an image as a decal in a Revit model?

A. Use the Link Image tool
B. Set the image as a topography
C. Use the Place Decal tool and create a decal type
D. Link the image as a PDF

Q14. What is the purpose of the Point Cloud tool in Revit?

A. To render the model in 3D
B. To display energy simulations
C. To link point cloud data for reference
D. To manage all model groups

Q15. Which tool should be used to link a Navisworks file stored on your local drive?

A. Link Revit
B. Local under Coordination Model
C. Bind Link
D. Link Topography

Q16. What is a limitation of the Link PDF tool in Revit?

A. It only supports 3D PDFs
B. It is only available in 3D views
C. It is not available in 3D views
D. It supports only JPEG files

Q17. How can you change an image's position between the foreground and background in Revit?

A. Using the Draw Layer option in the Properties Palette
B. By selecting the Visibility/Graphics tool
C. By renaming the image
D. Through the Manage Links tool

Q18. Which tool is used to manage all the links inserted into a Revit project?

A. Link CAD
B. Manage Links
C. Insert View
D. Bind Link

Q19. What is the purpose of the Import CAD tool in Revit?

A. To export CAD models to other software
B. To modify CAD models inside Revit
C. To import 3D geometries and data from other CAD software
D. To link CAD files without importing

Q20. Which of the following options is selected by default in the Positioning drop-down of the Import CAD Formats dialog box?

A. Center to Center
B. Auto - Origin to Internal Origin
C. Auto - Center to Internal Origin
D. Manual Placement

Q21. What is the function of the Import gbXML tool?

A. To convert PDF to model
B. To import PDF as background image
C. To import analysis data in XML format
D. To export model for analysis

Q22. When importing a PDF file, which action is required to place the image?

A. Press Enter
B. Right-click to place
C. Click at the desired location
D. Drag and drop the image

Q23. What does the Insert Views from File tool allow you to do?

A. Import 3D geometry from CAD
B. Insert views and schedules from other Revit files
C. Link Excel data
D. Convert 2D elements to 3D

Q24. Which tool allows the insertion of 2D elements from another file?

A. Import PDF
B. Insert Views from File
C. Insert 2D Elements from File
D. Import CAD

Q25. What does the Collaborate tool enable in Revit?

A. Object rendering
B. File compression
C. Project sharing with team members
D. Linking CAD files

Q26. What must users do after modifying a shared project in collaboration mode?

A. Export the project
B. Save as PDF
C. Synchronize Now
D. Print the project

Q27. What is the purpose of the Worksharing Monitor tool?

A. To generate backup
B. To print collaboration report
C. To check status and editing requests
D. To export project history

Q28. Which pane in Worksharing Monitor displays permissions issues and pending requests?

A. Notifications
B. Central File Access
C. File Transfer
D. Editing Requests

Q29. What does the Show History tool allow users to do?

A. View file size changes
B. View change history with time and user details
C. Compare file versions side-by-side
D. Track file export logs

Q30. What is the primary function of the Restore Backup tool?

A. Back up your local project copy
B. Delete old files
C. Restore a previous version of the model
D. Update linked files

FOR STUDENT NOTES

Chapter 11

Massing and Site Creation

Topics Covered

The major topics covered in this chapter are:

- ***Creating and Managing Masses***
- ***Creating and Managing Site***
- ***Creating and Modifying Toposolid***

INTRODUCTION

The massing refers to creating structure in 3D form. In Revit, you can create 3D objects and represent them as architectural elements like high-rise building, vehicles, and so on. The Site tools are used to prepare site for building like preparing toposurface, parking components, and so on. These tools are available in the **Massing & Site** tab of **Ribbon**; refer to Figure-1. These tools are discussed next.

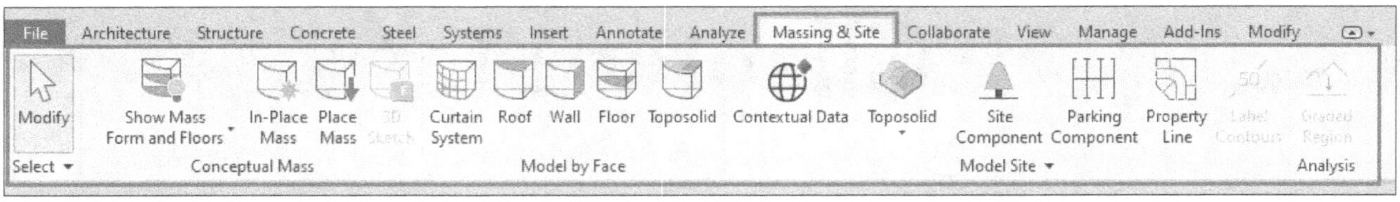

Figure-1. Massing & Site tab

CREATING AND MANAGING MASS

The tools in the **Conceptual Mass** panel are used to display, place, and create masses. These tools are discussed next.

Show Mass Settings

The tools in the **Show Mass** drop-down are used to show different types of mass elements; refer to Figure-2.

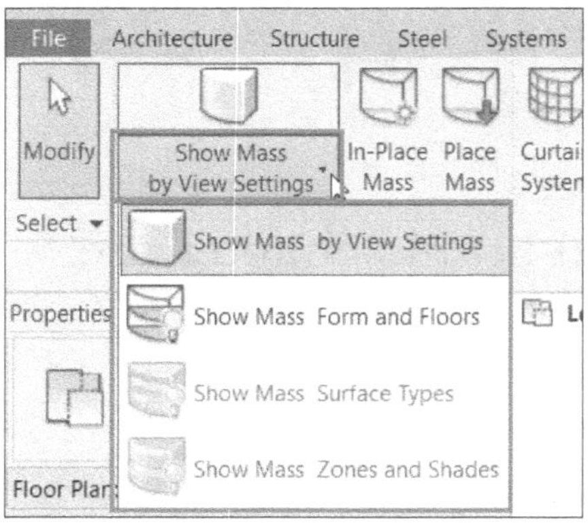

Figure-2. Show Mass drop-down

- Select the **Show Mass by View Settings** tool from the **Show Mass** drop-down if you want to display mass element based on view settings set for different views.
- Select the **Show Mass Form and Floors** tool from the **Show Mass** drop-down if you want to override view settings for masses and display them.
- Select the **Show Mass Surface Types** tool from the **Show Mass** drop-down to display shades and glazing specified for mass.
- Select the **Show Mass Zones and Shades** tool from the **Show Mass** drop-down to display mass zones and shades.

Placing Masses

The **Place Mass** tool in the **Conceptual Mass** panel is used to place conceptual masses in the model. The procedure to use this tool is given next.

- Click on the **Place Mass** tool from the **Conceptual Mass** panel of **Massing & Site** tab of **Ribbon**. The options to place mass will be displayed; refer to Figure-3.

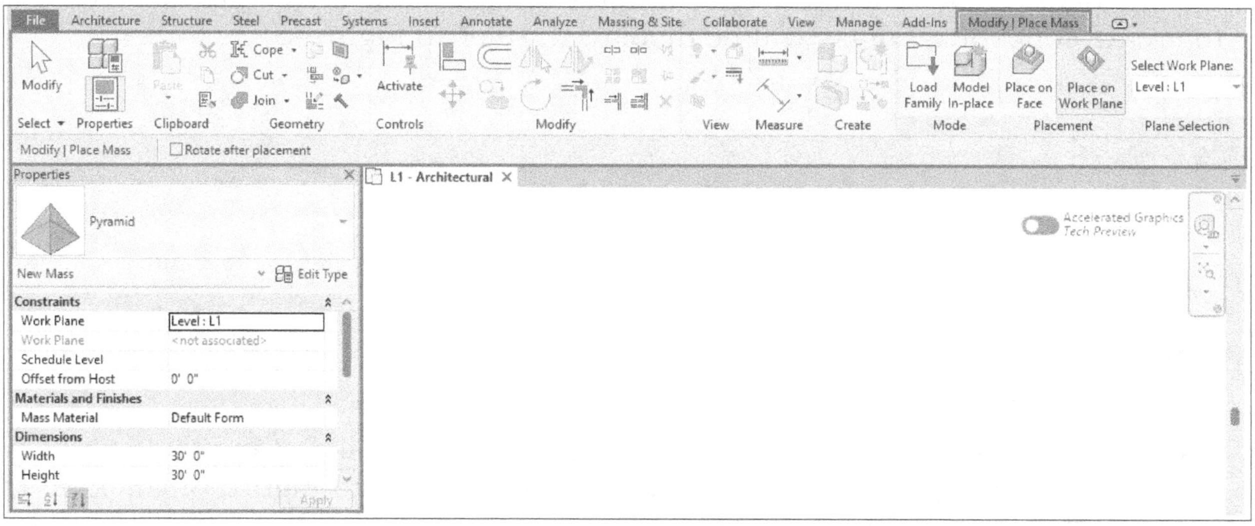

Figure-3. Options to place mass

- If no mass is loaded then click on the **Load Family** tool from the **Mode** panel in **Modify|Place Mass** contextual tab of **Ribbon**. The **Load Family** dialog box will be displayed; refer to Figure-4.

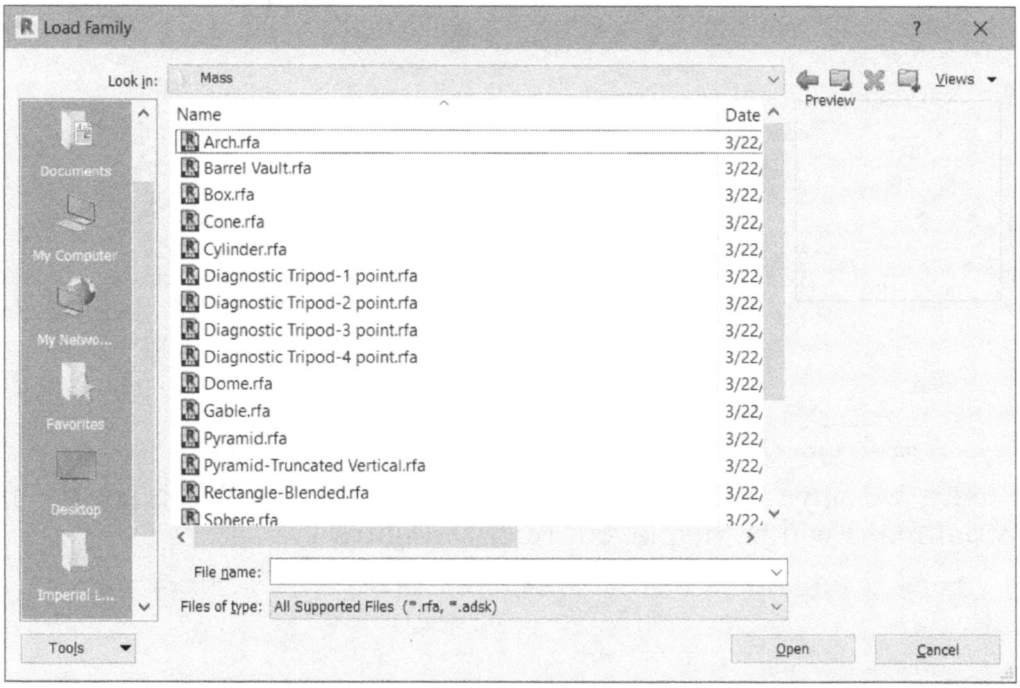

Figure-4. Load Family dialog box

- Select desired mass from the dialog box (you can select multiple mass types while holding the **CTRL** key) and click on the **Open** button. You will be asked to place selected mass.
- Click at desired location to place the model. Press **ESC** twice to exit the tool.

Creating In-Place Mass

The **In-Place Mass** tool is used to create conceptual mass at current work plane. The procedure to use this tool is given next.

- Click on the **In-Place Mass** tool from the **Conceptual Mass** panel in the **Massing & Site** tab of **Ribbon**. The **Name** dialog box will be displayed.

- Specify desired name for conceptual mass and click on the **OK** button. The tools to create conceptual mass will be displayed; refer to Figure-5.

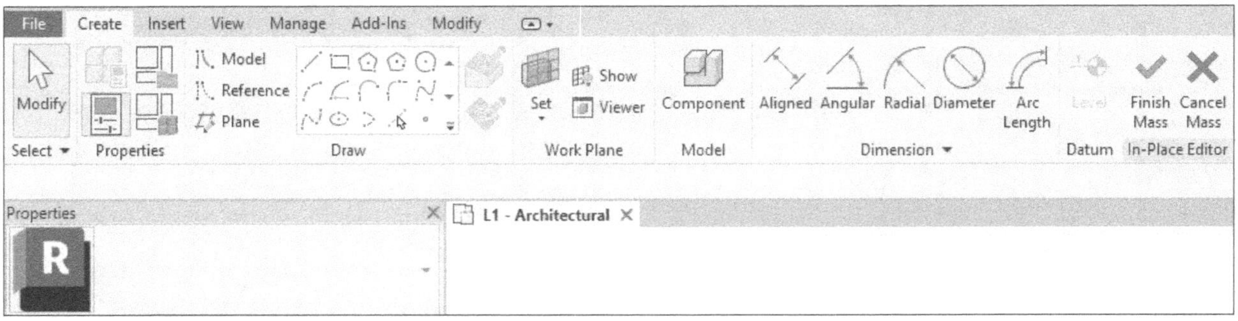

Figure-5. Options to create conceptual mass

- Create desired shape of base of conceptual mass using sketching tools and click on desired tool from the **Create Form** drop-down; refer to Figure-6. Click on the **Solid Form** tool from the drop-down if you want to create a solid conceptual mass. Click on the **Void Form** tool from the drop-down if you want to remove material from a solid body.

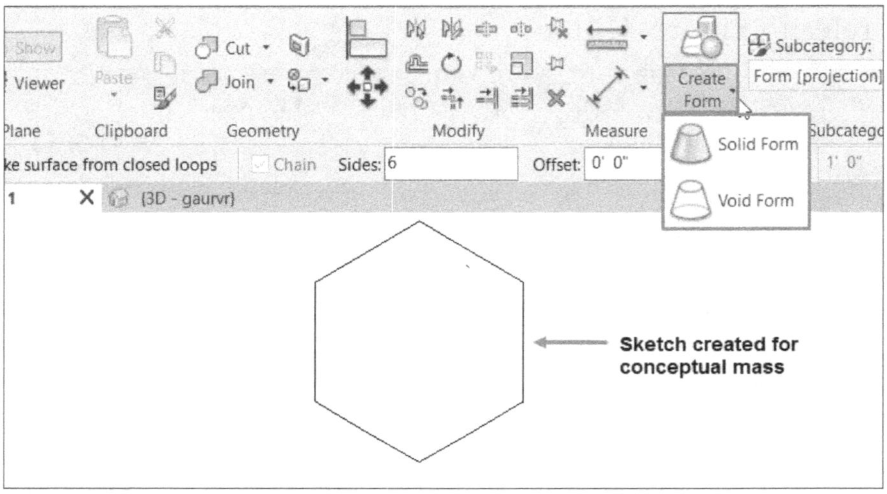

Figure-6. Create Form drop-down

- In our case, we have selected the **Solid Form** tool. On doing so, the preview of conceptual mass will be displayed; refer to Figure-7.

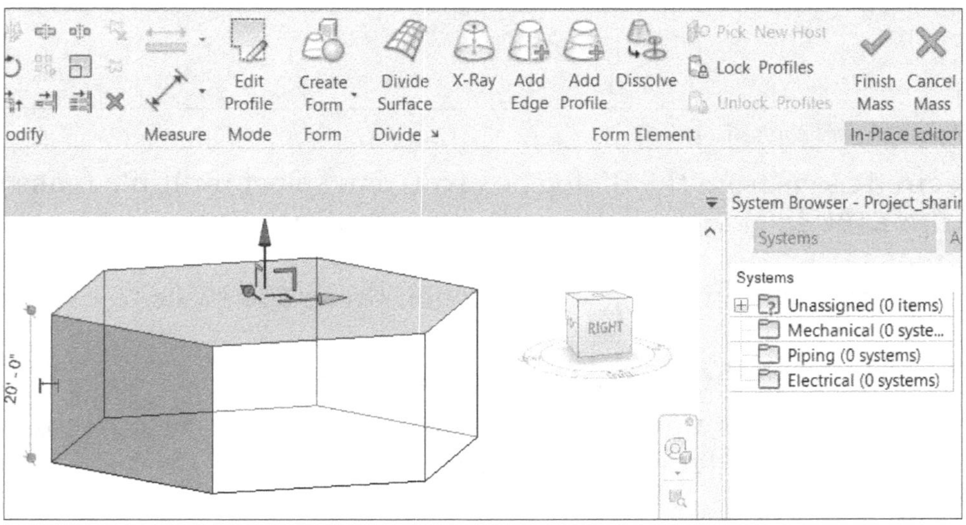

Figure-7. Preview of conceptual mass

Rest of the procedure to create conceptual mass has already been discussed in Chapter 4.

Creating 3D Sketch

The **3D Sketch** tool is used to create conceptual 3D designs in Autodesk FormIt Pro software and then import them back in current project. To use this tool, you must have installed FormIt Pro first. The procedure to use this tool is given next.

- Click on the **3D Sketch** tool from the **Conceptual Mass** panel in the **Massing & Site** tab of the **Ribbon**. The **Open FormIt** dialog box will be displayed; refer to Figure-8.

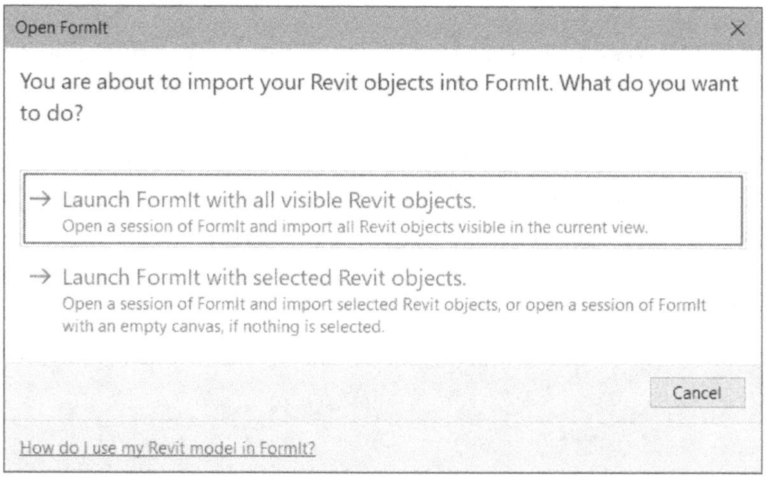

Figure-8. Open FormIt dialog box

- Select the **Launch FormIt with visible Revit objects** button to import all the visible Revit objects into FormIt for modifications. Select the **Launch FormIt with selected Revit objects** button to import only selected Revit objects into FormIt for modifications.
- We have selected the **Launch FormIt with visible Revit objects** button in our case. The current model will all visible objects will be displayed in FormIt; refer to Figure-9.

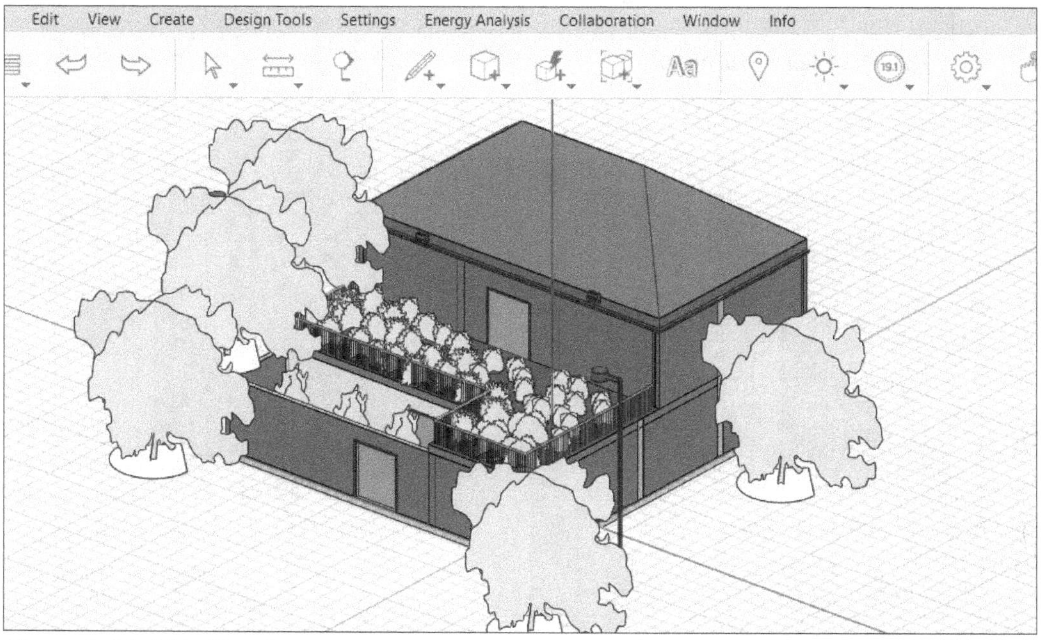

Figure-9. Model in FormIt

- The tools of FormIt are beyond the scope of this book. After modifying the model, click on the **Return to Revit** button in the **Toolbar**. You will be asked to save the FormIt file.
- Save the file in directory of your project for easy file handling. The model will be updated in the Revit application. You can close the FormIt application after changes have been updated in Revit.

Changing Face of Conceptual Model to Curtain

The **Curtain System** tool is used to change the face of conceptual mass to curtain system. The procedure to use this tool is given next.

- Click on the **Curtain System** tool from the **Model by Face** panel in the **Massing & Site** tab of **Ribbon**. You will be asked to select the faces of model to be converted to curtain.
- Select desired faces from the model and click on the **Create System** tool from the **Modify|Place Curtain System by Face** contextual tab of **Ribbon**; refer to Figure-10. The curtain system will be created; refer to Figure-11.

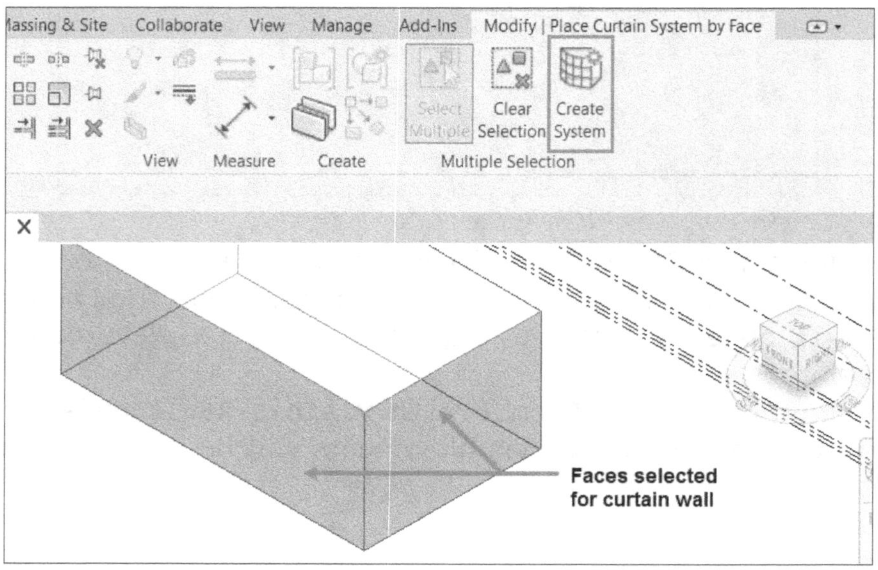

Figure-10. Create System tool

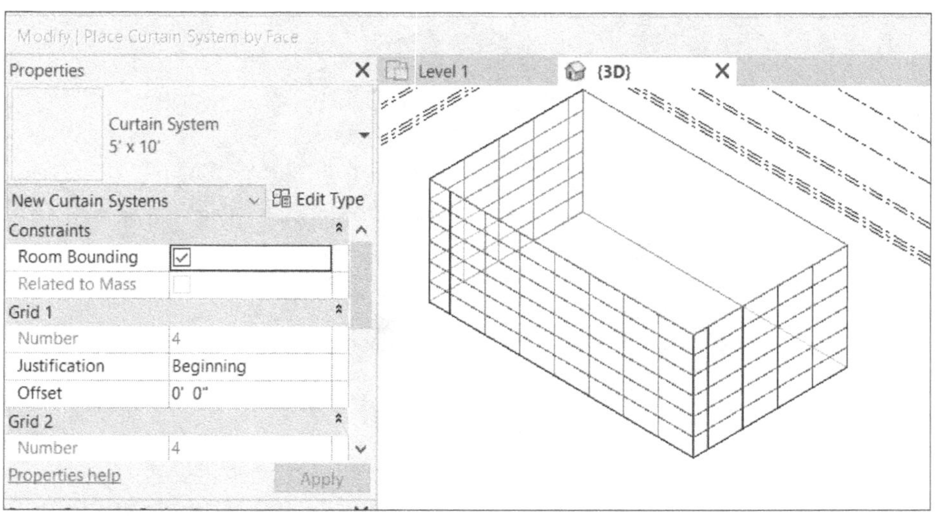

Figure-11. Curtain system created

- Set desired parameters for curtain in the **Properties Palette** and click on the **Apply** button.
- Press **ESC** to exit the tool.
- If you want to add or remove segment from the curtain system then select a grid line and click on the **Add/Remove Segments** tool from the **Curtain Grid** panel of **Modify|Curtain System Grids** contextual tab in the **Ribbon**. Now, select the grid line whose status is to be changed.

Creating Roof on Conceptual Mass

The **Roof** tool in **Model by Face** panel is used to create roof on selected face. The procedure to use this tool is given next.

- Click on the **Roof** tool from the **Model by Face** panel in the **Massing & Site** tab of **Ribbon**. The options to place roof will be displayed; refer to Figure-12.

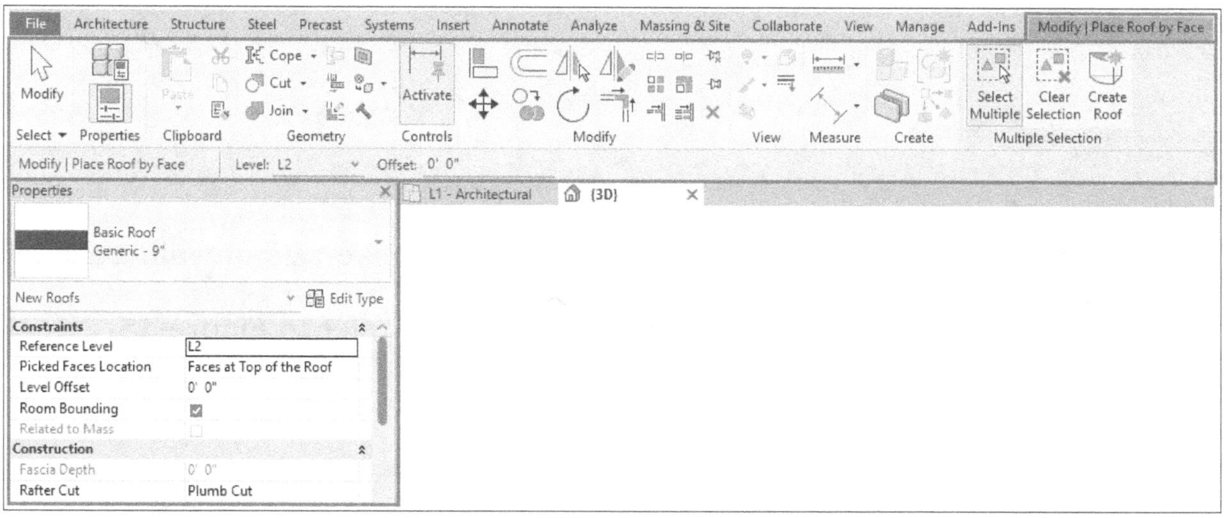

Figure-12. Options to place roof

- Select the faces on which you want to place the roof and click on the **Create Roof** tool from the **Multiple Selection** panel in the **Modify|Place Roof by Face** contextual tab of **Ribbon**. The roof will be created; refer to Figure-13.

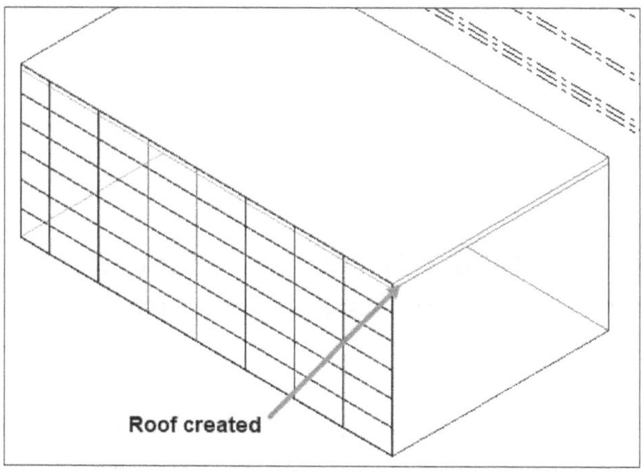

Figure-13. Roof created

- Press **ESC** to exit the tool.

Creating Wall by Face

The **Wall** tool in the **Model by Face** panel is used to create wall using selected face of mass. The procedure to use this tool is given next.

- Click on the **Wall** tool from the **Model by Face** panel of **Massing & Site** tab in **Ribbon**. The options to select face for wall will be displayed; refer to Figure-14.

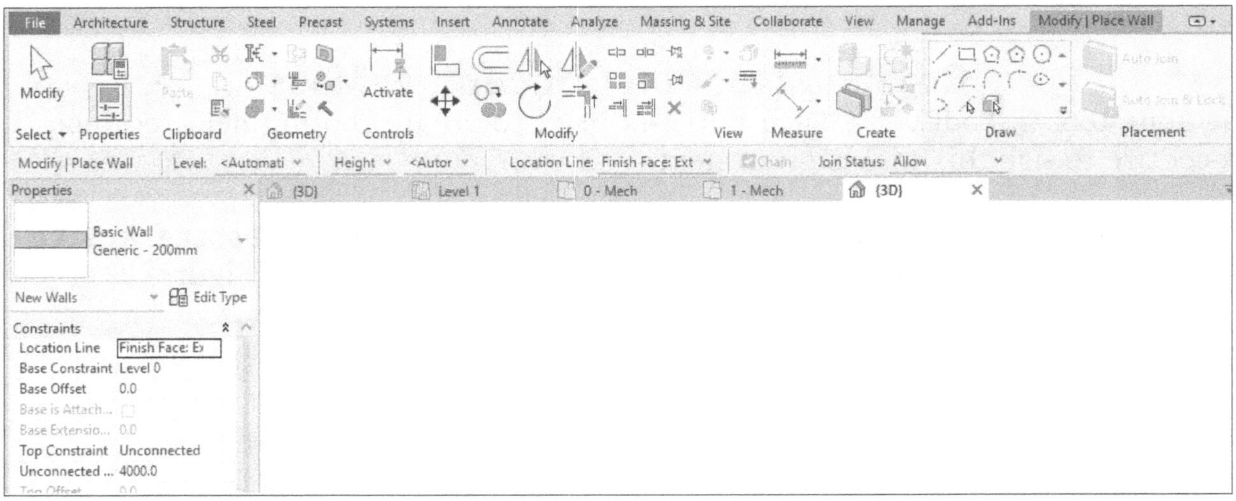

Figure-14. Options to place wall

- Set desired parameters in the **Properties Palette** like size of wall, base level, height of wall, and so on.
- Select desired vertical face. The wall will be created; refer to Figure-15.

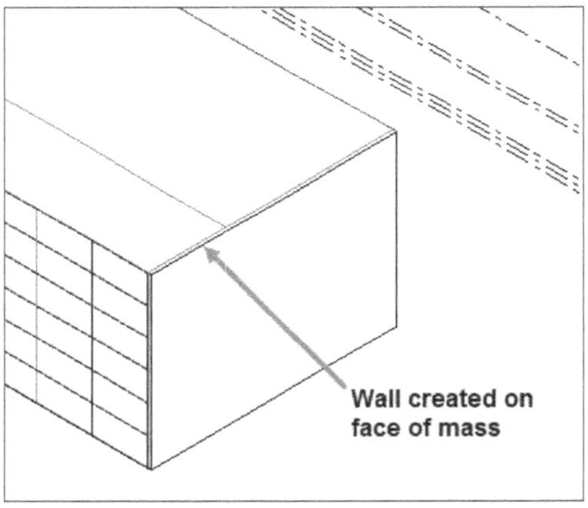

Figure-15. Wall created

- Press **ESC** to exit the tool.

Creating Floor by Face

The **Floor** tool is used to convert mass floor into building floor. The procedure to use this tool is given next.

- Click on the **Floor** tool from the **Model by Face** panel in the **Massing & Site** contextual tab of **Ribbon**. The options to create floors will be displayed; refer to Figure-16.
- Select desired mass floors while holding the **CTRL** key; refer to Figure-17 and click on the **Create Floor** tool from the contextual tab. The building floor will be created.

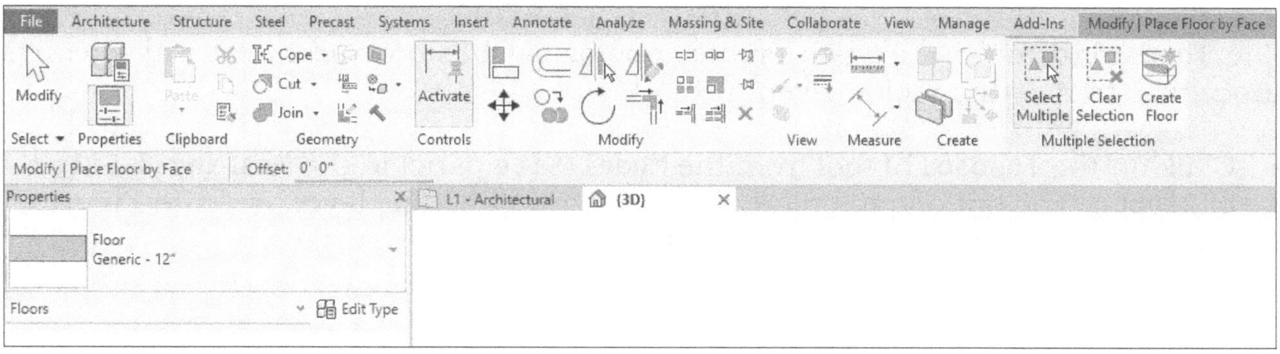

Figure-16. Modify Place Floor by Face contextual tab

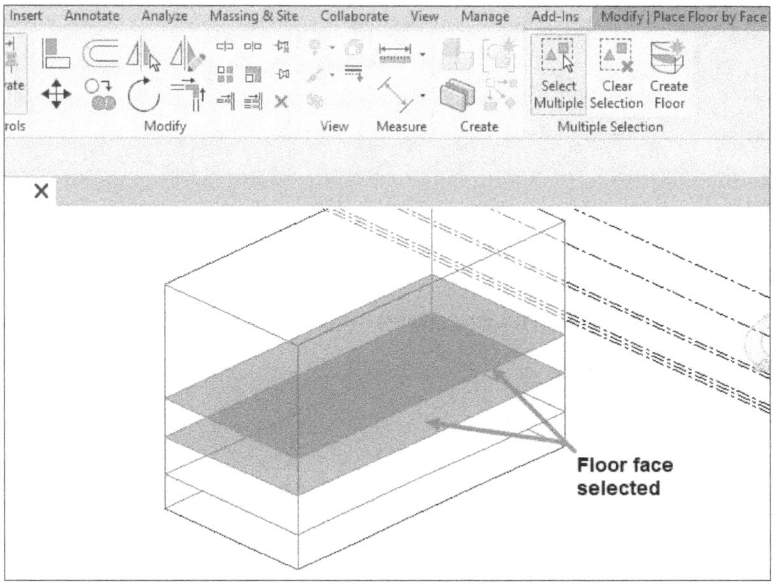

Figure-17. Floor face selected

- Press **ESC** to exit the tool. You can now edit the properties of floor by selecting it and defining parameters in the **Properties Palette**.

CREATING AND MANAGING SITE

The tools to prepare and manage site are available in the **Model Site** panel of **Massing & Site** tab in **Ribbon**; refer to Figure-18.

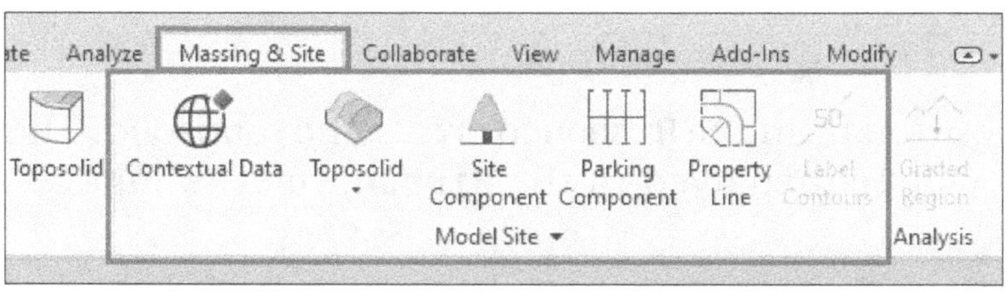

Figure-18. Model Site panel

These tools are discussed next.

Contextual Data

The **Contextual Data** is third party, location-based information used to understand real-world conditions for a forma project. This tool is active for commercial version of this software.

Creating Toposolid

The **Toposolid** tool is used to create topological base for architectural site. The procedure to use this tool is given next.

- Click on the **Toposolid** tool from the **Model Site** panel in the **Massing & Site** tab of **Ribbon**. The options to create toposurface will be displayed; refer to Figure-19 and you will be asked to specify control points for toposurface.

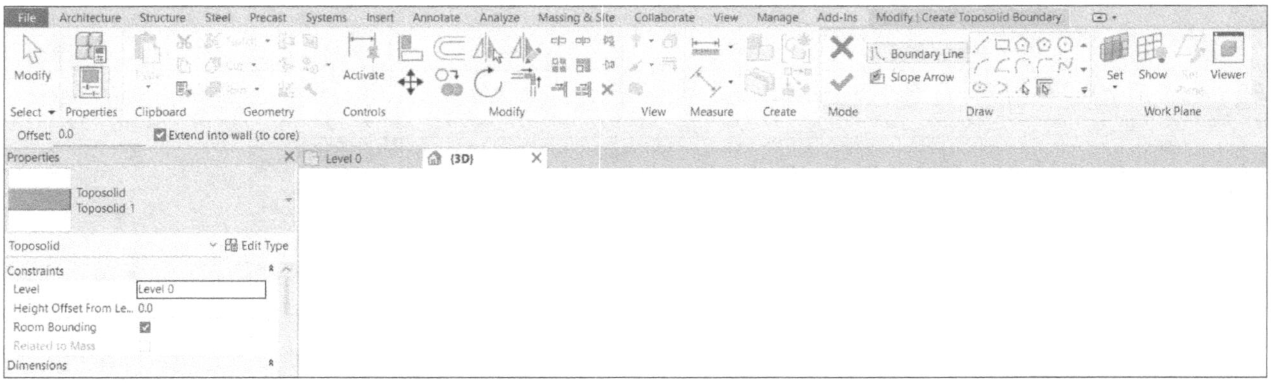

Figure-19. Options to create toposurface

- Select desired drawing tools and create boundary of toposurface; refer to Figure-20.

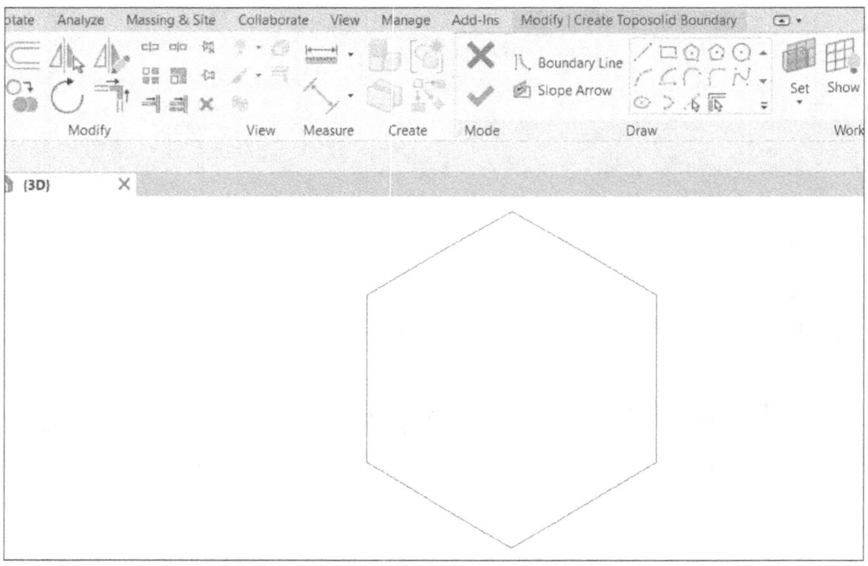

Figure-20. Creating toposolid boundary

- Click on the **OK** button from the **Ribbon** to create the toposolid. The **Modify|Toposolid** contextual tab will be displayed in the **Ribbon**; refer to Figure-21.

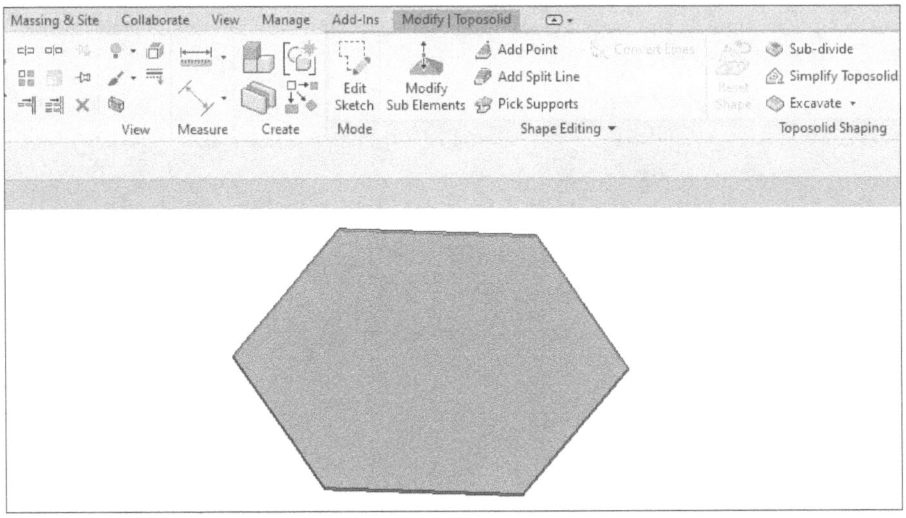

Figure-21. Modify Toposolid contextual tab

- Click on the **Modify Sub Elements** tool from the **Shape Editing** panel of contextual tab in the **Ribbon**. The points and edges of toposolid will be active for modification.
- Select desired point or edge of the toposolid and use the handles to modify shape of toposolid; refer to Figure-22.

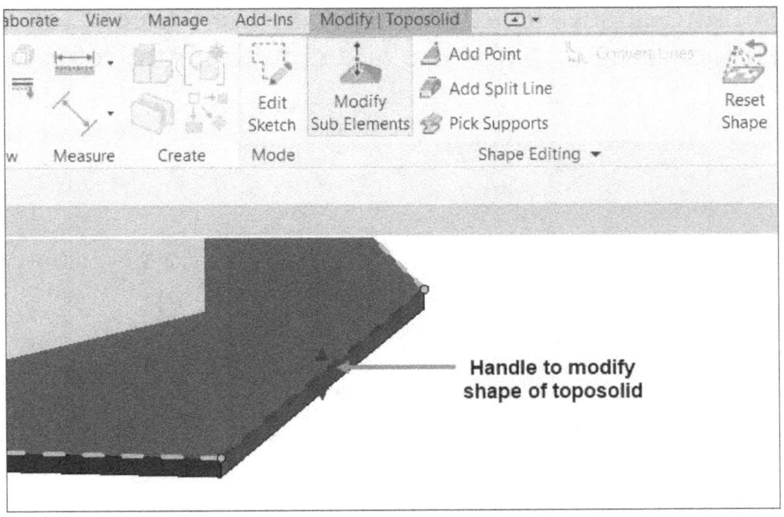

Figure-22. Handle to modify shape of toposolid

- Use the **Add Point** tool from the **Shape Editing** panel of contextual tab to add more points for modifying shape of toposolid. Similarly, you can use the other tools like **Add Split Line** and **Pick Supports**.
- Press **ESC** to exit the tool.

If you want to import the toposolid then select the **Create from Import** tool from the **Model Site** panel of **Massing & Site** tab in the **Ribbon** and select desired model file to be used for toposolid.

Placing Site Components

The **Site Component** tool is used to place different type of site components like tree, bike stand, park bench, and so on. The procedure to use this tool is given next.

- Click on the **Site Component** tool from the **Model Site** panel of **Massing & Site** tab in **Ribbon**. The options to place site component will be displayed; refer to Figure-23 and you will be asked to specify placement location of site component.

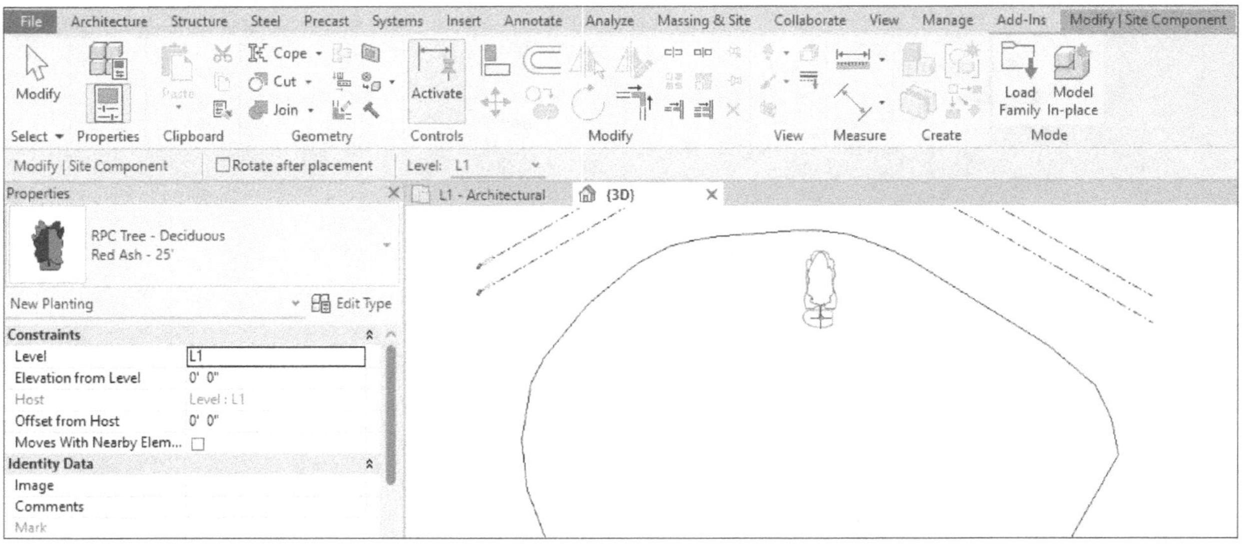

Figure-23. Options to place site component

- Select desired type of site component from the drop-down at the top in the **Properties Palette**. If you do not find desired component then click on the **Load Family** tool and load desired site component.
- Set desired level and offset elevation values in the **Properties Palette**.
- Click at desired locations to place the site components; refer to Figure-24.

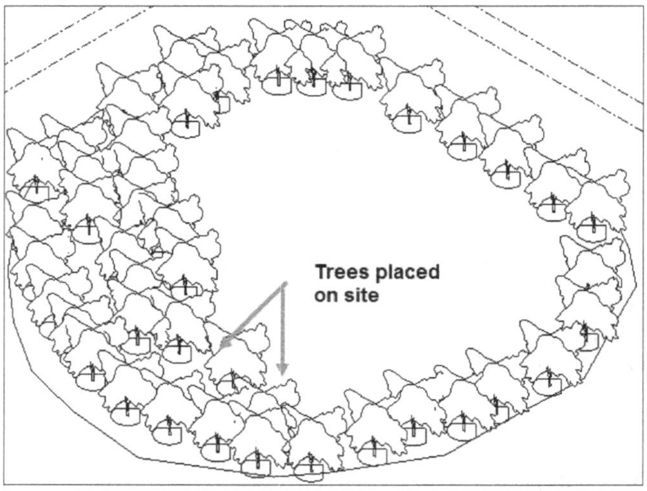

Figure-24. Placing site component

- Press **ESC** to exit the tool.

Placing Parking Component

The **Parking Component** tool is used to place different type of parking components like parking space, signs, parking island, and so on. The procedure to use this tool is given next.

- Click on the **Parking Component** tool from the **Model Site** panel in the **Massing & Site** tab of **Ribbon**. The options to place parking components will be displayed; refer to Figure-25.

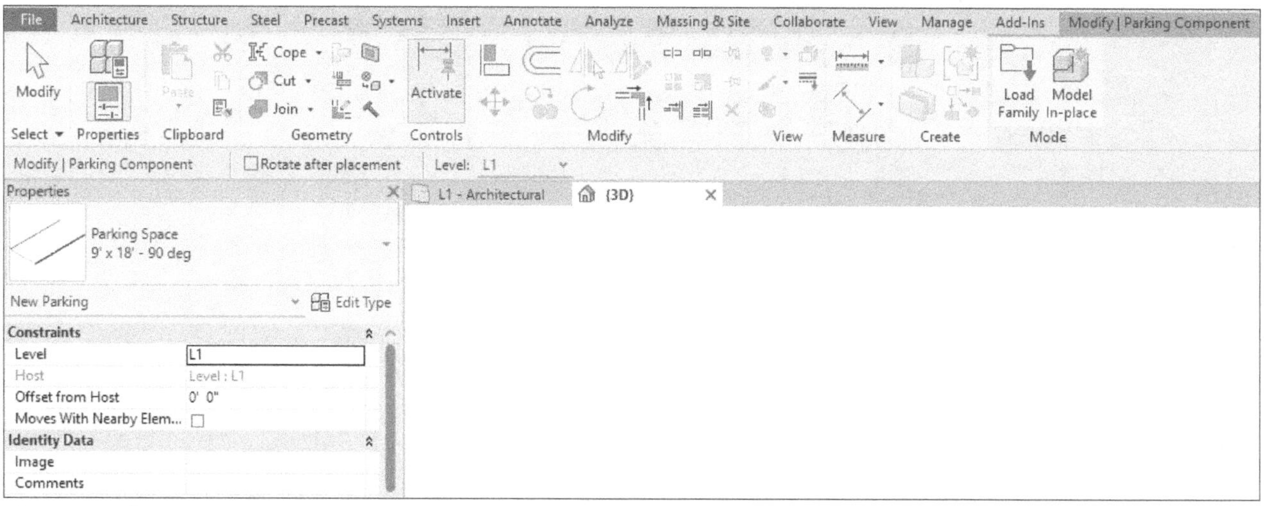

Figure-25. Options to place parking component

- Select desired component from the drop-down at the top in the **Properties Palette**. Set desired parameters and click at desired location to place the parking component.
- Press **ESC** to exit the tool.

Creating Property Line

The **Property Line** tool is available when a plan view is open. The property line is used to indicate the purpose of area bounded by them. The procedure to use this tool is given next.

- Click on the **Property Line** tool from the **Modify Site** panel of **Massing & Site** tab in the **Ribbon**. The **Create Property Line** dialog box will be displayed; refer to Figure-26.

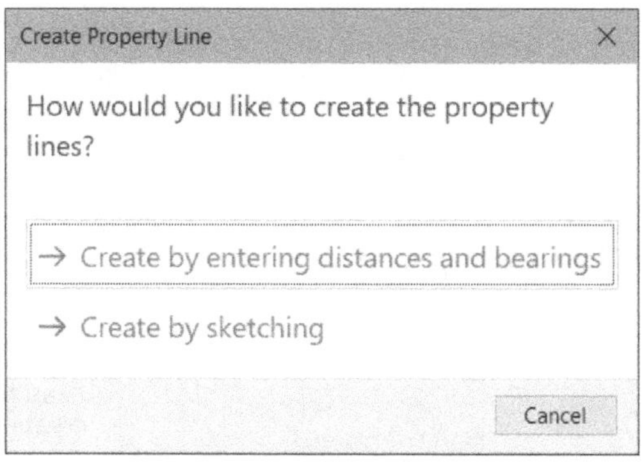

Figure-26. Create Property Line dialog box

By Specifying Distances and Bearings

- Click on the **Create by entering distances and bearings** option. The **Property Lines** dialog box will be displayed as shown in Figure-27.

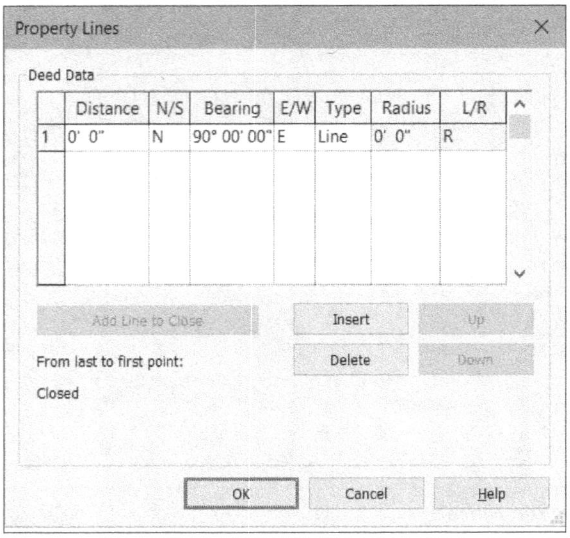

Figure-27. Property Lines dialog box

- Specify desired values of coordinates in the dialog box. To add a new point, click on the **Insert** button.
- After specifying desired coordinates, you can use the **Add Line to Close** button to connect last point with first point via a line.
- Click on the **OK** button from the dialog box to create the property line.

By Sketch

- Click on the **Create by sketching** tool from the dialog box to draw the boundaries of property line. The options to create sketch will be displayed; refer to Figure-28.
- Create the boundary for property line and set desired offset value; refer to Figure-29.

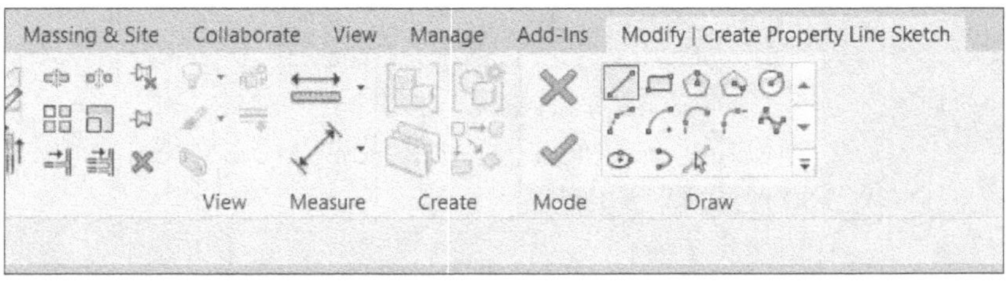

Figure-28. Modify|Create Property Line Sketch

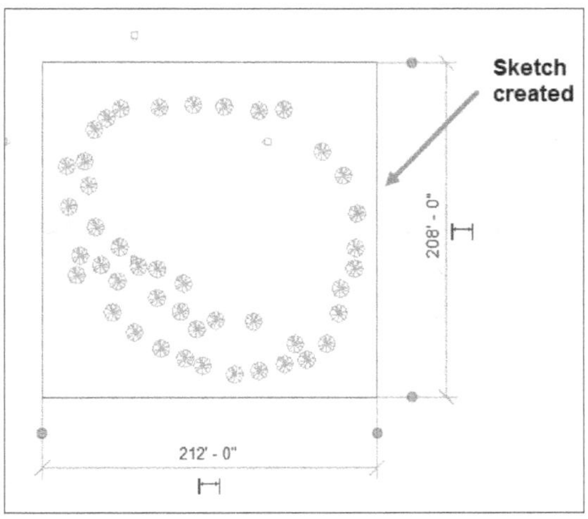

Figure-29. Sketch for property line

- Click on the **Finish Edit Mode** button from the contextual tab.

Graded Region

The **Graded Region** tool is used create regions on the toposurface with modified elevation levels. The procedure to use this tool is given next.

- Click on the **Graded Region** tool from the **Modify Site** panel in the **Massing & Site** tab of the **Ribbon**. The **Edit Graded Region** dialog box will be displayed; refer to Figure-30. Note that creating the graded region will demolish earlier created toposurface and generate a new copy of toposurface for editing.

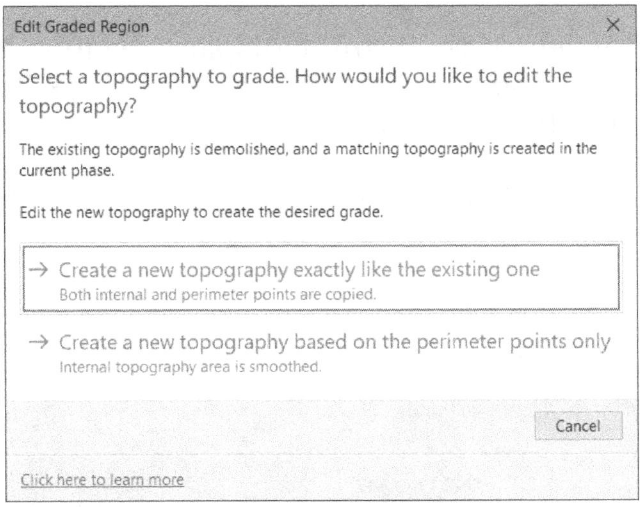

Figure-30. Edit Graded Region dialog box

- Select the **Create a new topography exactly like the existing one** option from the dialog box to create topography with both internal and perimeter points. It generates exactly same toposolid for editing as was available earlier.
- Select the **Create a new topography based on the perimeter points only** option if you want to create topography with perimeter points only. Note that the elevation values specified in toposurface due to internal points will also be lost in the process.
- After selecting desired option, click on the toposolid to be graded. The solid will be displayed with control points based on selected option; refer to Figure-31.

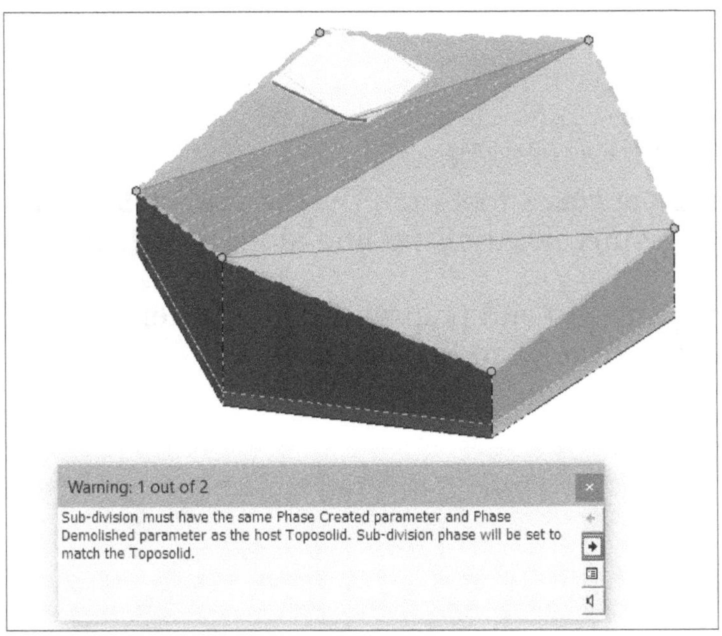

Figure-31. Points displayed after selecting toposolid

- Select desired point from the toposolid and specify desired parameters like elevation level, location, and so on. You can also drag the points to modify their location. Use the tools in **Modify|Toposolid** contextual tab to modify topography.
- Press **ESC** to exit the current modification option.

Displaying Label Contours

The **Label Contours** tool is used to display elevation level of contour lines in topography. The procedure to use this tool is given next.

- Open the plan view in which you want to display elevation levels of contour lines.
- Type **VV** from keyboard and select the **Topography** check box; refer to Figure-32. Click on the **OK** button from the dialog box.

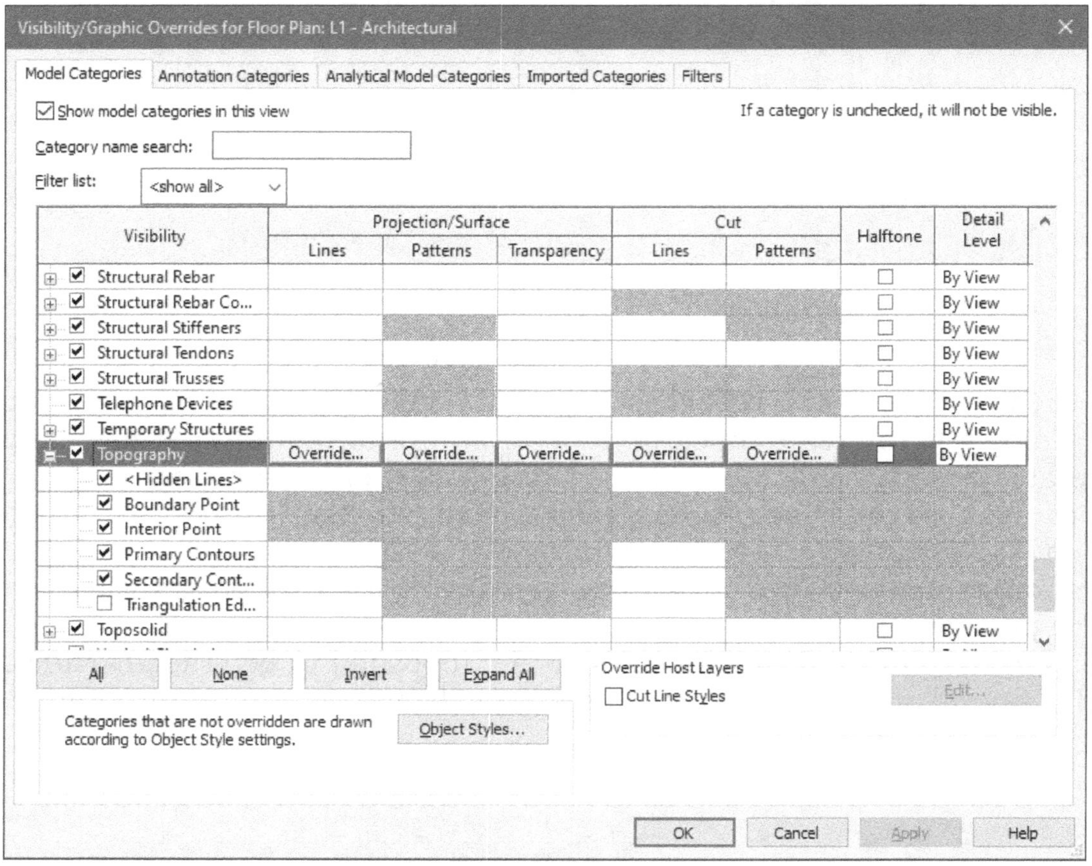

Figure-32. Visibility override for topography

- Click on the **Label Contours** tool from the **Massing & Site** tab of **Ribbon**. You will be asked to specify start point of the line along which the contour labels will be displayed.
- Specify the start point and end point of the line; refer to Figure-33. The elevation levels will be displayed; refer to Figure-34.

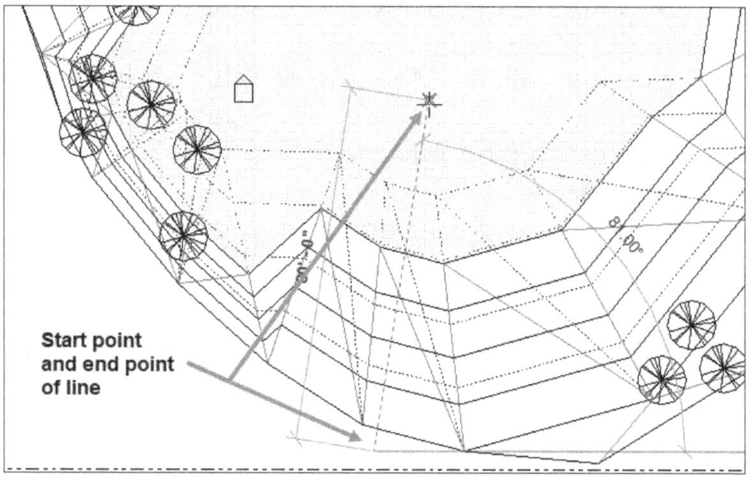

Figure-33. Creating line for contour labels

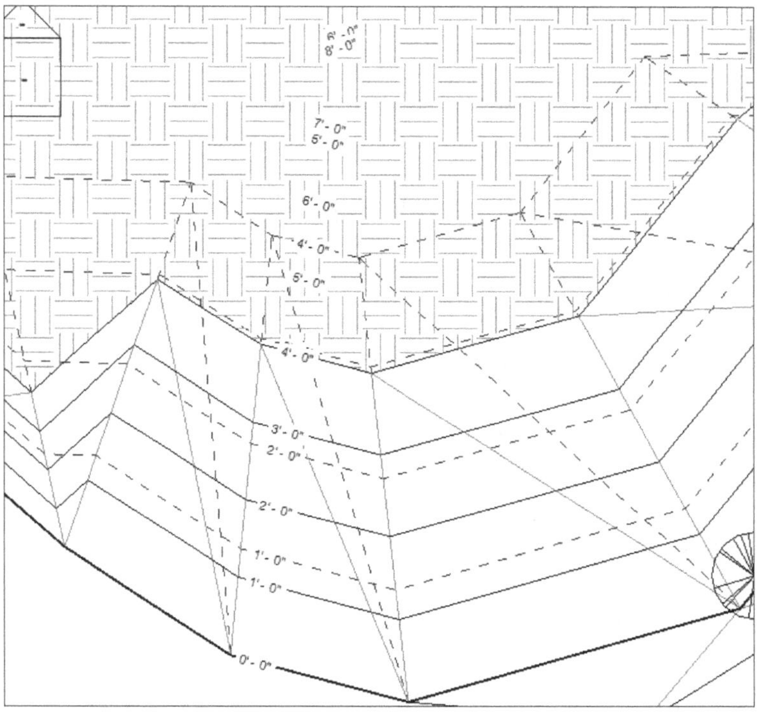

Figure-34. Elevation levels displayed

- Note that if the annotation is displayed very small or big then you need to set proper annotation scale in the **View Control Bar** at the bottom in the **Application** window.

SELF ASSESSMENT

Q1. Discuss the benefits of using Conceptual Mass in architectural design.

Q2. Discuss the use of Place Mass and In-Place Mass tools.

Q3. Which of the following objects do not fall in the category of site components?

a. Tree b. Park bench

c. Toposolid d. Swimming Pool

Q4. Using sub divide, you can modify properties of different sections of toposolid. (T/F)

Q5. What is the main purpose of the Massing & Site tab in Revit?

A. To apply materials and rendering effects
B. To manage building phases
C. To create and place masses and manage site elements
D. To analyze building performance

Q6. Which tool should be used to override view settings and display mass elements directly?

A. Show Mass Zones and Shades
B. Show Mass by View Settings
C. Show Mass Surface Types
D. Show Mass Form and Floors

Q7. What should you do if no mass is loaded while using the Place Mass tool?

A. Restart the software
B. Load the family using the Load Family tool
C. Select the Modify tool
D. Save the project first

Q8. When creating an In-Place Mass, what is the function of the Solid Form tool?

A. It removes material from a solid body
B. It allows annotation of mass
C. It creates a solid conceptual mass
D. It converts sketches to toposurfaces

Q9. What is required before using the 3D Sketch tool in Revit?

A. Autodesk Navisworks must be installed
B. The FormIt Pro software must be installed
C. The project must be rendered first
D. The model must be saved as a family

Q10. Which tool is used to convert faces of conceptual mass into curtain systems?

A. Wall
B. Curtain System
C. Roof
D. In-Place Mass

Q11. How can a user add or remove segments from a curtain system?

A. By editing wall properties
B. By selecting the Add Point tool
C. By selecting a grid line and using Add/Remove Segments
D. By creating a new mass

Q12. Which tool is used to convert selected mass floor into a building floor?

A. Floor
B. Curtain
C. Roof
D. Toposolid

Q13. What is the function of the Toposolid tool?

A. To create conceptual mass
B. To place site components
C. To create topological base for architectural site
D. To display annotation labels

Q14. How can you modify the shape of a toposolid?

A. Using the Create Roof tool
B. Using the Add Point tool in the Shape Editing panel
C. Using the Wall by Face tool
D. By exporting the model

Q15. Which tool allows placing components like trees and benches on site?

A. Property Line
B. Parking Component
C. Site Component
D. Graded Region

Q16. What is a use of the Graded Region tool?

A. To mark property boundaries
B. To create walls from faces
C. To modify elevation levels of a toposurface
D. To convert masses into roofs

Q17. What is the purpose of the Label Contours tool?

A. To define walls using faces
B. To change annotation size
C. To display elevation levels of contour lines
D. To export 3D models to FormIt

Q18. What should be done after placing a mass using the Place Mass tool?

A. Apply a floor by face immediately
B. Exit the tool by pressing ESC twice
C. Add a curtain wall automatically
D. Switch to site plan view

Q19. What does the Void Form tool do when creating an In-Place Mass?

A. Creates an annotation
B. Adds a solid volume to the model
C. Removes material from a solid body
D. Applies texture to surfaces

Q20. Which button in the 3D Sketch process imports only selected Revit objects into FormIt?

A. Launch FormIt with visible Revit objects
B. Return to Revit
C. Launch FormIt with selected Revit objects
D. Modify Selection

Q21. What step is required after selecting faces for the Curtain System?

A. Click Create System
B. Define levels
C. Sketch boundaries
D. Change visibility settings

Q22. How can a wall be created using a conceptual mass?

A. Use the Place Mass tool
B. Click on the Wall tool from Model by Face panel and select a vertical face
C. Sketch it manually on top view
D. Import from CAD

Q23. What should be done before clicking "Finish Edit Mode" in the Property Line tool when sketching?

A. Load topography
B. Change visibility graphics
C. Create the boundary sketch
D. Add a 3D sketch

Q24. What option connects the last point to the first in the Property Line dialog box?

A. Insert
B. Add Line to Close
C. Create Sketch
D. Join Ends

Q25. Which tool allows selecting only perimeter points of an existing toposolid when grading?

A. Add Split Line
B. Create a new topography with perimeter points only
C. Modify Sub Elements
D. Label Contours

Q26. What is the correct tool to place signs or parking islands in a site plan?

A. Property Line
B. Graded Region
C. Parking Component
D. Curtain System

Q27. What is displayed when you use the Label Contours tool and define a start and end point?

A. Grid lines
B. Toposolid volume
C. Elevation levels of contour lines
D. Property boundary

Q28. What is the purpose of the Modify Sub Elements tool when editing a Toposolid?

A. Add new site components
B. Change material of site surface
C. Modify points and edges of the toposolid
D. Convert it to a building floor

Q29. Which tool is used to convert a mass floor into a building floor?

A. Wall by Face
B. Floor
C. Property Line
D. Roof by Face

Q30. What should be done if a desired site component is not available in the list during placement?

A. Restart Revit
B. Use Toposolid tool instead
C. Click on Load Family to load the component
D. Use the Curtain System tool

For Student Notes

Chapter 12

View Management

Topics Covered

The major topics covered in this chapter are:

- ***Creating and Managing View Templates***
- ***Visibility and Graphics Settings***
- ***Creating Cut Profiles***
- ***Rendering***
- ***Rendering on Cloud***
- ***Creating Camera Views***
- ***Creating Walkthrough***
- ***Creating Section View***
- ***Creating Callouts***
- ***Creating Plan View, Elevation View, Drafting View, Duplicate View, and Legend View***
- ***Creating Schedules and Legends***
- ***Creating and Managing Sheets***
- ***Managing User Interface***

INTRODUCTION

Till this point, you have learned to create structural, architectural, and system designs. If you have tried to manage structural elements in architectural plans then you might have noticed that you cannot select or modify these elements. For such cases, you need to create structural views in the project. Various tools to create and manage views are available in the **View** tab; refer to Figure-1.

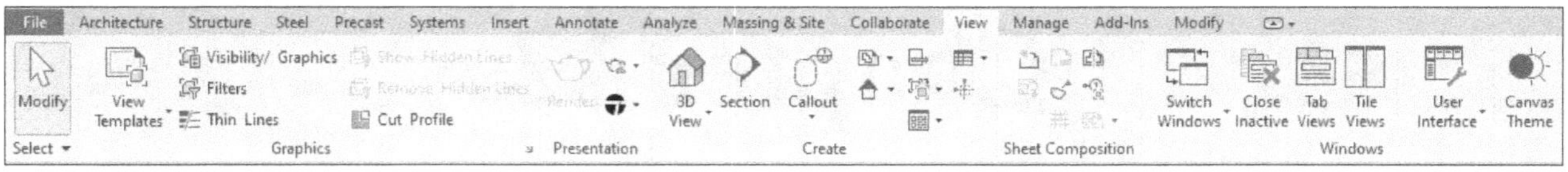

Figure-1. View tab

Creating and Managing View Templates

The tools to create and manage view templates are available in the **View Templates** drop-down; refer to Figure-2. These tools are discussed next.

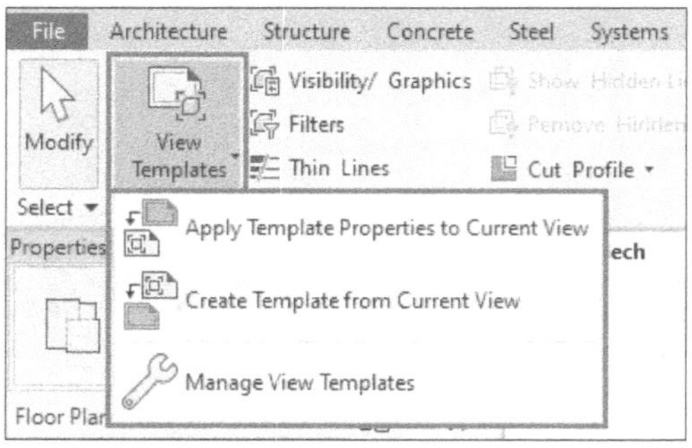

Figure-2. View Templates drop-down

Applying Template Properties to Current View

The **Apply Template Properties to Current View** tool is used to apply predefined view properties to current view. The procedure to use this tool is given next.

- Click on the **Apply Template Properties to Current View** tool from the **View Templates** drop-down in **Graphics** panel of **View** tab in the **Ribbon**. The **Apply View Template** dialog box will be displayed; refer to Figure-3.

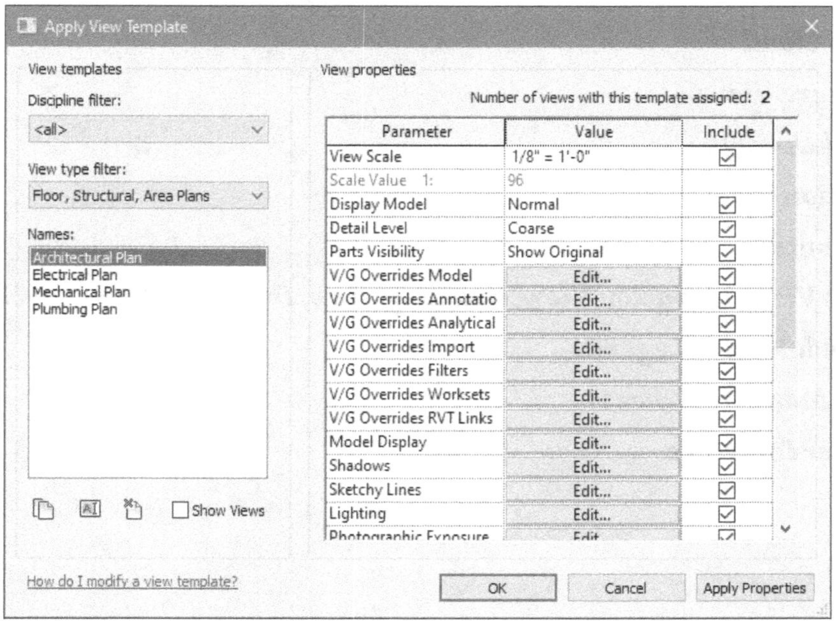

Figure-3. Apply View Template dialog box

- Select desired template from the **Names** area which you want to apply to current view.
- Set desired parameters in the **View properties** area if you want to apply custom parameters and click on the **OK** button from the dialog box. The template properties will be applied to current view.

Creating Template from Current View

The **Create Template from Current View** tool is used to create a view template using properties of current view. The procedure to use this tool is given next.

- Click on the **Create Template from Current View** tool from the **View Templates** drop-down in the **Graphics** panel of the **View** tab in **Ribbon**. The **New View Template** dialog box will be displayed; refer to Figure-4.

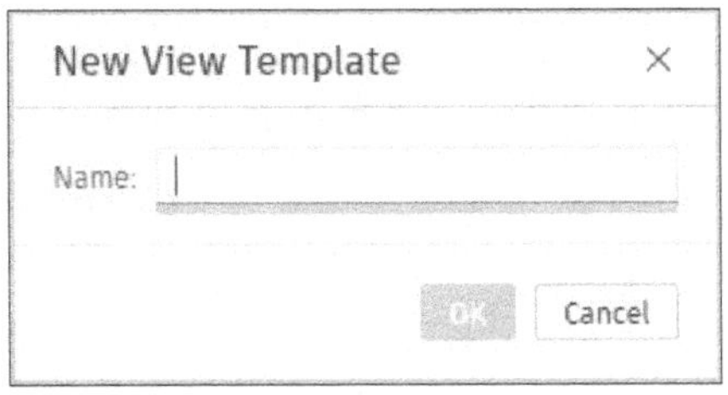

Figure-4. New View Template dialog box

- Specify desired name for the template and click on the **OK** button. The new template will be created and added in the **Names** list of **View Templates** dialog box; refer to Figure-5.

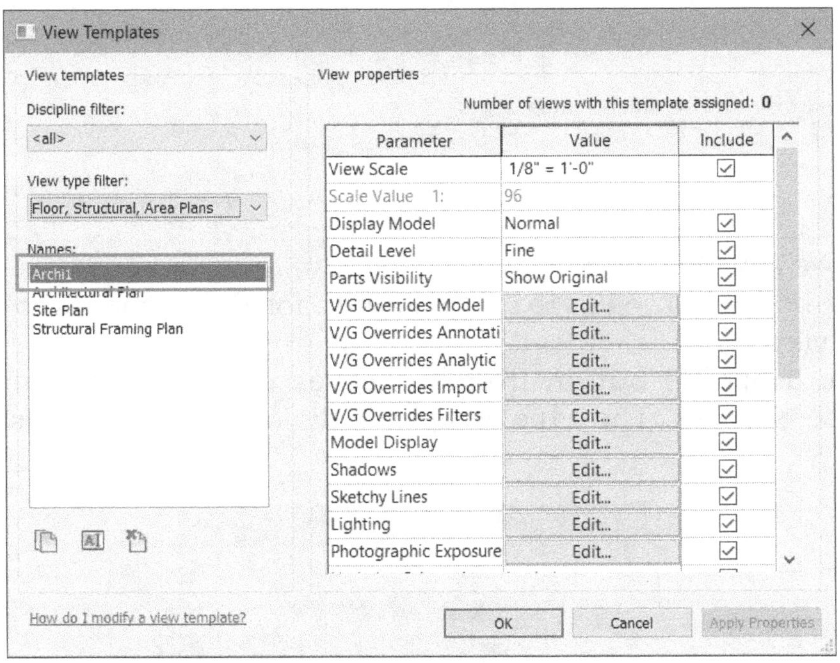

Figure-5. New template added in the list

- If you want to modify any parameter then set it in the **View properties** area of the dialog box. Click on the **OK** button from the dialog box to exit the dialog box and apply the changes.

The **Manage View Template** tool is used to modify parameters of view templates already created. On clicking this tool, the **View Templates** dialog box will be displayed as discussed earlier.

Visibility and Graphics Settings

The **Visibility/Graphics** tool in **Graphics** panel is used to modify the display settings for views. Using this tool, you can define which elements to be displayed in the view and which are to be hidden. The procedure to use this tool is given next.

- Click on the **Visibility/Graphics** tool from the **Graphics** panel in the **View** tab of **Ribbon** or type **VV** when no tool is active. The **Visibility/Graphic Overrides** dialog box will be displayed; refer to Figure-6.

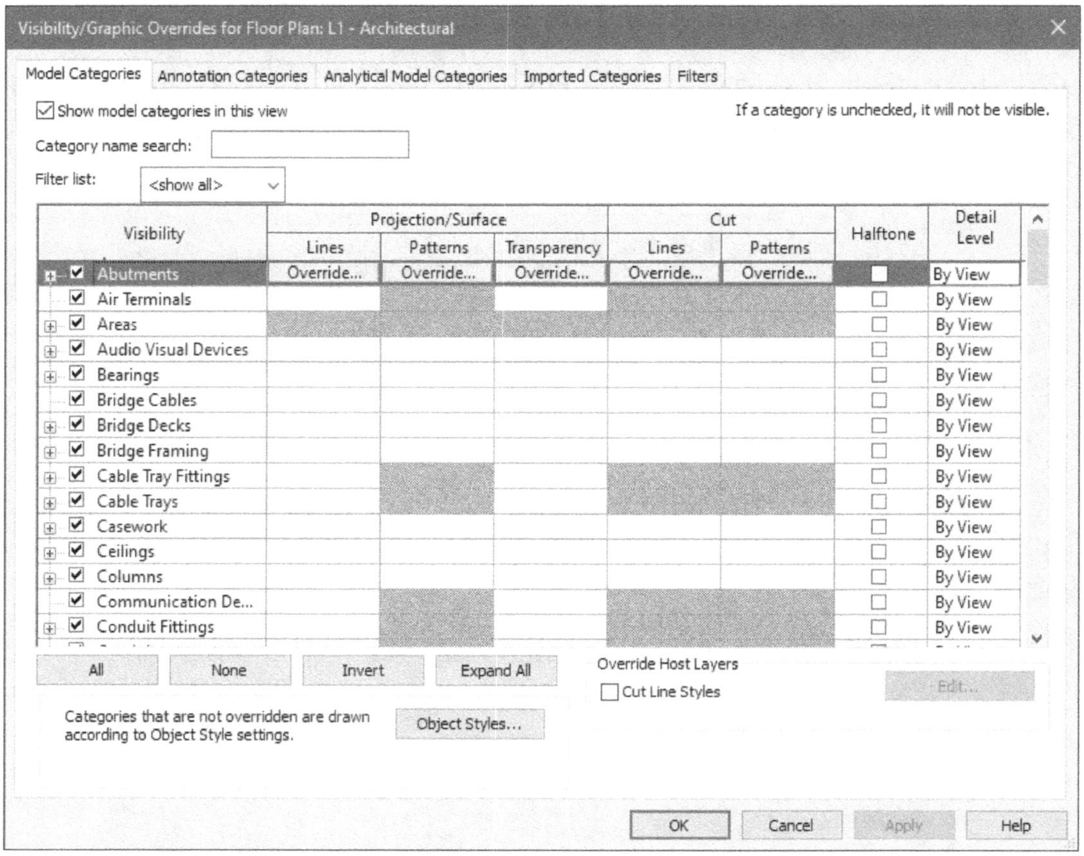

Figure-6. Visibility Graphics Overrides dialog box

- Select check boxes in the **Visibility** column for the elements to be displayed in the current view.
- Click on the **Override** button from the **Lines** column to modify the line style for respective element. The **Line Graphics** dialog box will be displayed; refer to Figure-7.

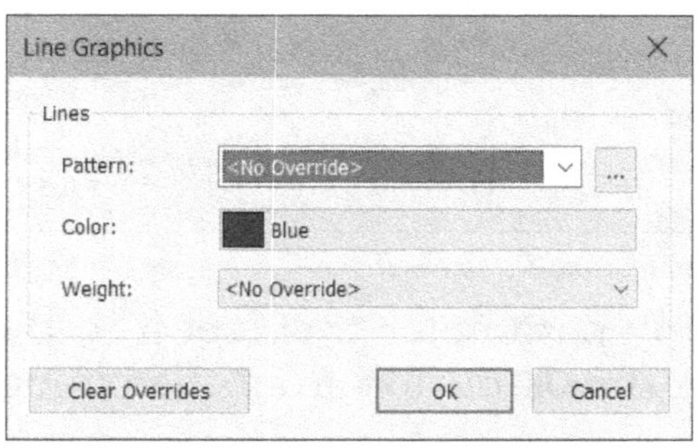

Figure-7. Line Graphics dialog box

- Select desired pattern, color, and weight for selected line. Click on the **OK** button from the dialog box to apply the changes.

- Similarly, you can specify overrides for patterns and transparency for projection/surface and cut features.
- Select the **Halftone** check box for the element to be sent in background. The selected element will be displayed in halftone (light gray colored by default).
- Select desired option from the drop-down in the **Detail View** column for desired element whose representation detail level is to be changed. There are four options available to define detail view level; refer to Figure-8. Select the **Coarse** option to display only major details of elements. Select the **Fine** option to display even minor details of elements. Select the **By View** option to display details based on view template settings. Select the **Medium** option to display medium level of details. Note that fine details consume more processing power of system.

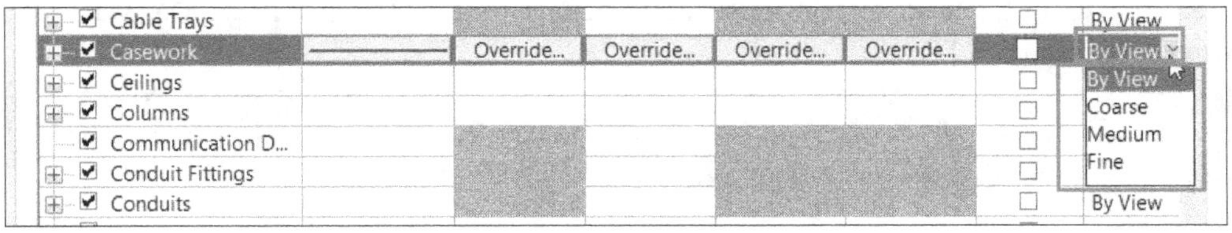

Figure-8. Detail view drop-down

- You can expand the category of elements by clicking on the **+** sign for elements in the table.
- You can set the visibility and override parameters for elements at object level by using the **Object Styles** button in the dialog box. On clicking this button, the **Object Styles** dialog box will be displayed; refer to Figure-9.

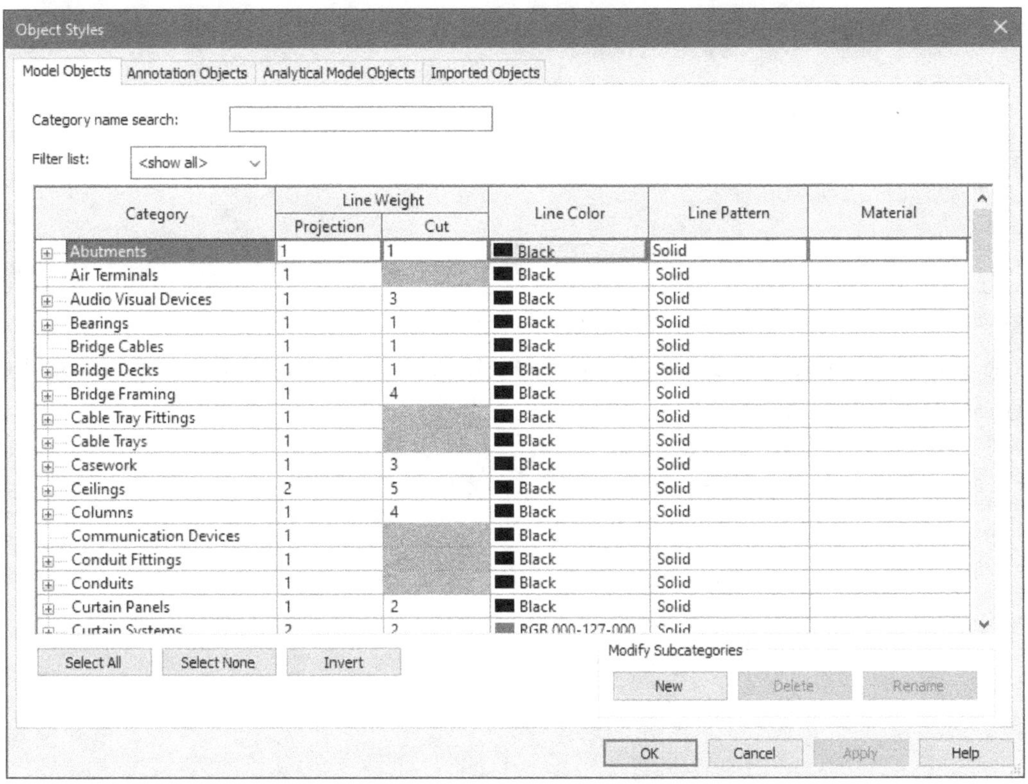

Figure-9. Object Styles dialog box

- Set desired line weight, line color, line pattern, and material for desired object in the same way as discussed earlier.

- By default, the **Model Objects** tab is selected in the dialog box and only model elements are displayed for modification. Select the **Annotation Objects**, **Analytical Model Objects**, or **Imported Objects** tab to modify view properties for respective elements.
- Click on the **OK** button from the dialog box. The **Visibility/Graphic Overrides** dialog box will be displayed again. You can modify visibility parameter for annotation objects, analytical model objects, and imported objects by using the respective tabs from the dialog box.

Setting Visibility/Overrides for Filtered Objects

- Click on the **Filters** tab from the dialog box to modify visibility of elements that qualify specified filter conditions. The options in the dialog box will be displayed as shown in Figure-10.

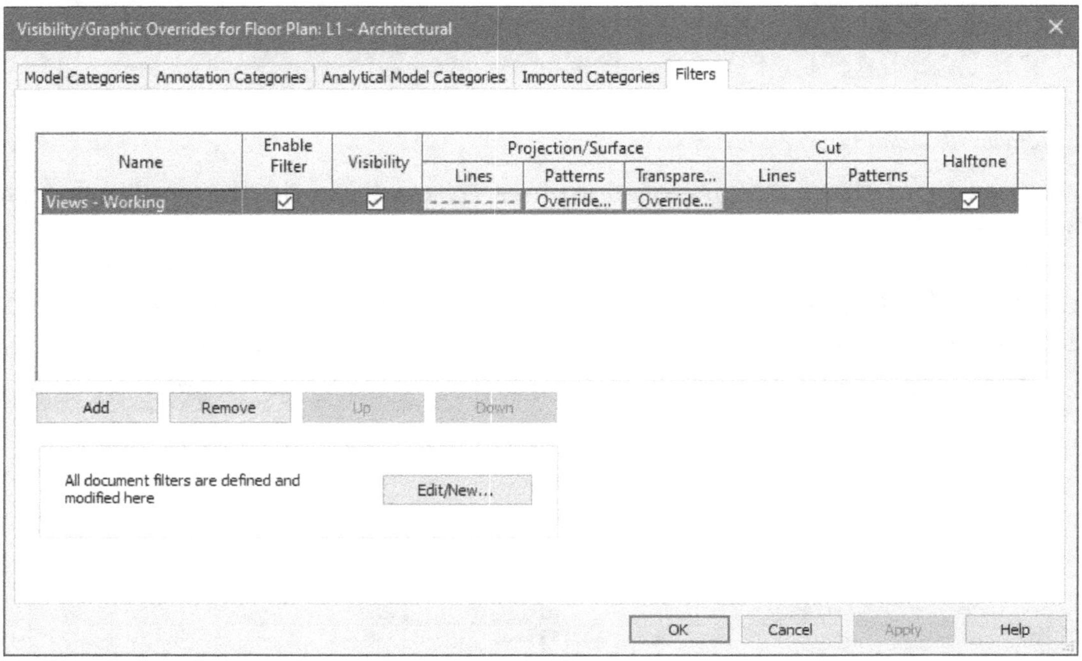

Figure-10. Filters tab in Visibility Graphic Overrides dialog box

- Click on the **Add** button from the dialog box. The **Add Filters** dialog box will be displayed; refer to Figure-11.

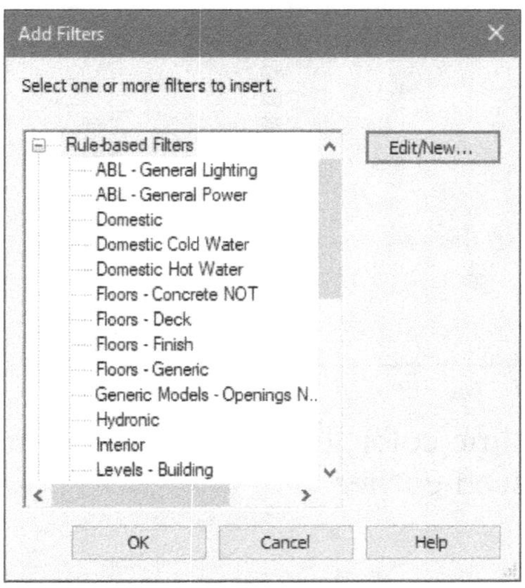

Figure-11. Add Filters dialog box

- Select desired filter from the dialog box.
- If you want create/edit a filter then click on the **Edit/New** button. The **Filters** dialog box will be displayed; refer to Figure-12. The options in this dialog box have already been discussed in Chapter 2 of this book.

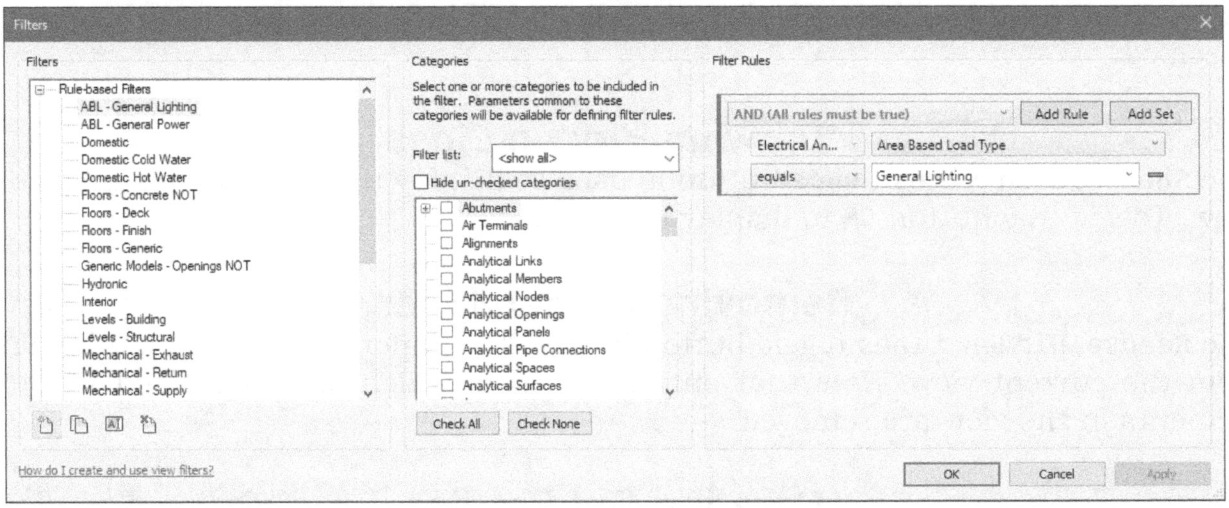

Figure-12. Filters dialog box

- Set desired parameters and click on the **OK** button from the dialog box to create the filters.
- Now, select desired filter from the **Add Filters** dialog box. The selected filter will be added in the table of **Visibility/Graphic Overrides** dialog box; refer to Figure-13.

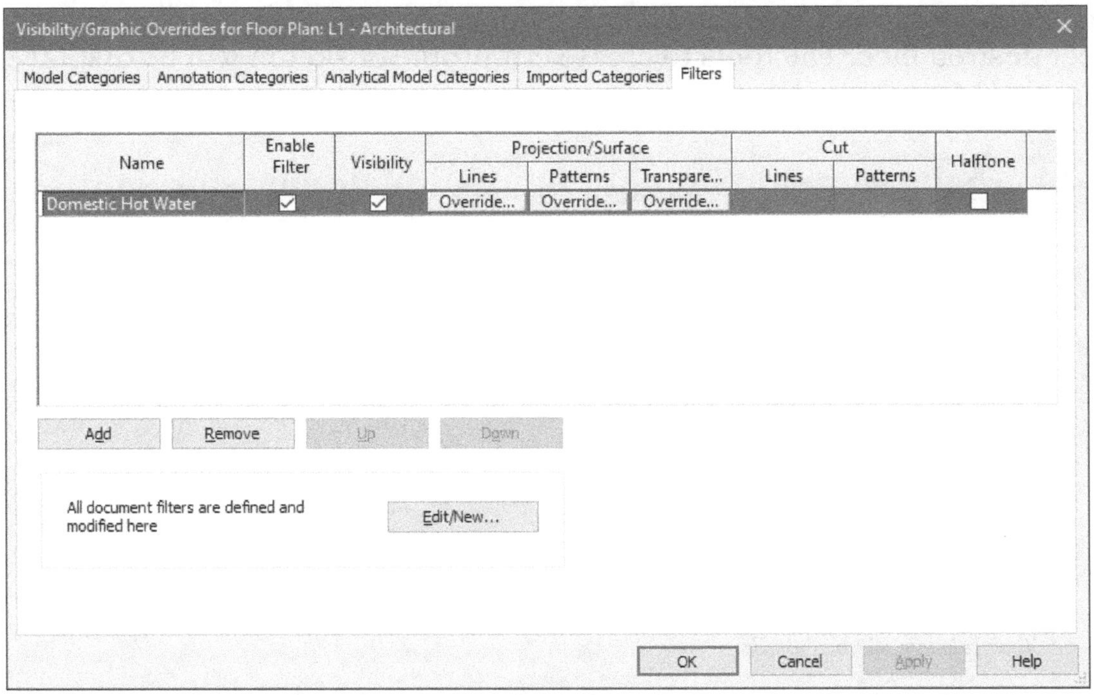

Figure-13. Filter added for overrides

- Set desired overrides and click on the **OK** button from the dialog box to apply modifications for the element visibility.

The **Filters** tool in the **Graphics** panel is used to set filters for different graphic operations. On selecting this tool, the **Filters** dialog box will be displayed. The options of this dialog box have already been discussed.

Activating Thin Lines

The **Thin Lines** toggle button in **Graphics** panel is used to activate/deactivate thin lines mode in the view. Toggle this button **ON** to display all lines in the view as thin lines. Note that although all the lines will be displayed as thin line on activating this button but if you print the view then lines will be printed as per the properties specified.

Showing Hidden Lines

The **Show Hidden Lines** toggle button is used to display the hidden lines in current view. Toggle this button **ON** to display hidden lines.

Removing Hidden Lines

The **Remove Hidden Lines** toggle button is used to temporarily remove hidden lines from the current view. Note that only those lines which are obstructed by other elements in the view are removed.

Creating Cut Profiles

The **Cut Profile** tool in **Graphics** panel is used to modify the cut profile of elements in plan view or section view. The procedure to use this tool is given next.

- Click on the **Cut Profile** tool from the **Graphics** panel in the **View** tab of the **Ribbon** when plan view or section view is open. You will be asked to select face of element whose cut profile is to be changed.
- Select desired face. The tools to create cut profile of sketch will be displayed; refer to Figure-14.

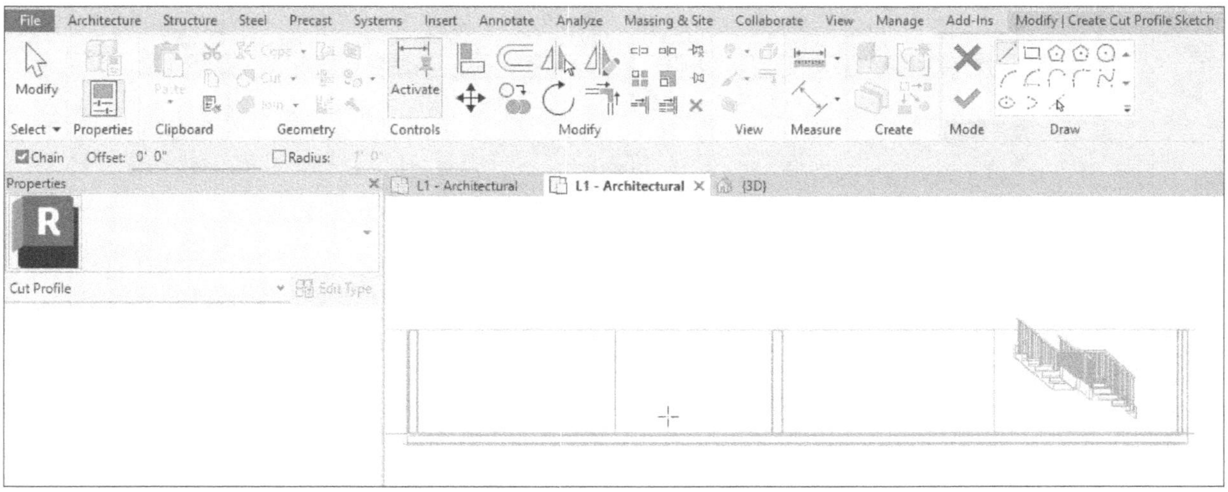

Figure-14. Tools to create sketch of profile

- Create the sketch for cut profile as desired connected to the boundary of face. Note that the profile should be open loop sketch connected to boundary; refer to Figure-15.

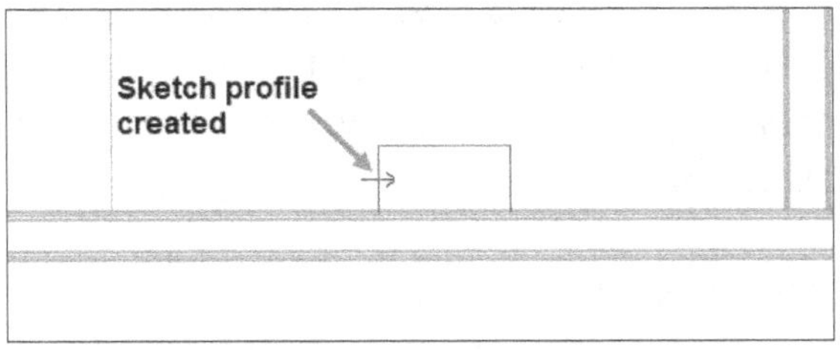

Figure-15. Sketch profile for cut

- Click on the **OK** button from the contextual tab. The cut profile will be modified; refer to Figure-16.

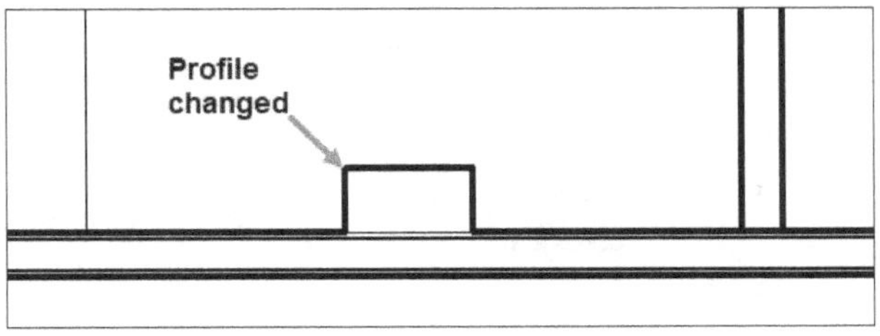

Figure-16. Changed profile of cut

Graphic Display Settings

The **Graphic Display Options** tool is used to define various parameters related to graphic display. The procedure to use this tool is given next.

- Click on the **Graphic Display Options** tool (inclined arrow) from the **Graphics** panel in the **View** tab of **Ribbon**. The **Graphic Display Options** dialog box will be displayed; refer to Figure-17.

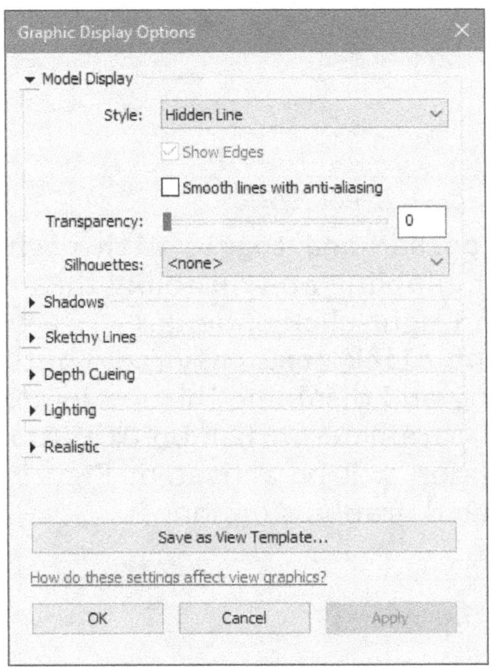

Figure-17. Graphic Display Options dialog box

- Set desired parameters for model display, shadows, sketch lines, background, lighting, and so on.
- After setting desired parameters, click on the **Apply** button to apply changes. Click on the **OK** button from the dialog box if you want to apply the changes and exit the dialog box.

Accelerated Graphics

The **Accelerated Graphics** option uses GPU (graphics card) instead of relying mainly on the CPU to increase performance while working in views of the model. The procedure to use this option is discussed next.

- Select **Enable Accelerated Graphics** check box from **Accelerated Graphics** area in the **Graphics** tab of **Options** dialog box; refer to Figure-18. The options in the **Accelerated Graphics** area will be activated.

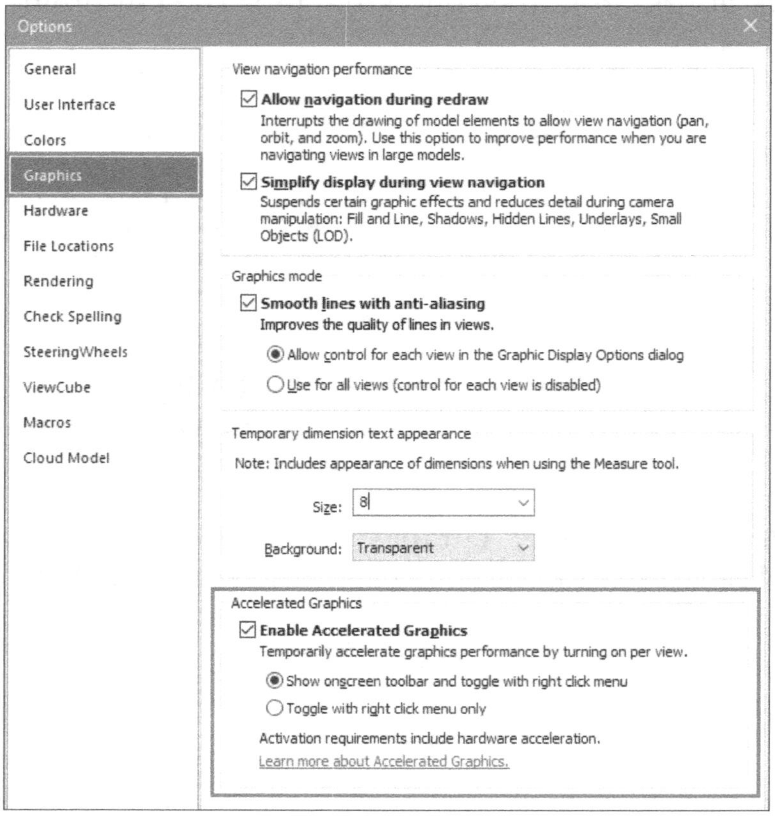

Figure-18. Accelerated Graphics option

- Select **Show onscreen toolbar and toggle with right click menu** radio button to display the option for enabling and disabling the accelerated graphics in both the onscreen toolbar and right-click options.
- Select **Toggle with right click menu only** radio button to display only the right click options for enabling and disabling the accelerated graphics.
- After specifying desired parameters, click on **OK** button from the dialog box. The accelerated graphics option will be activated. Figure-19 shows the enable and disable state of accelerated graphics option.

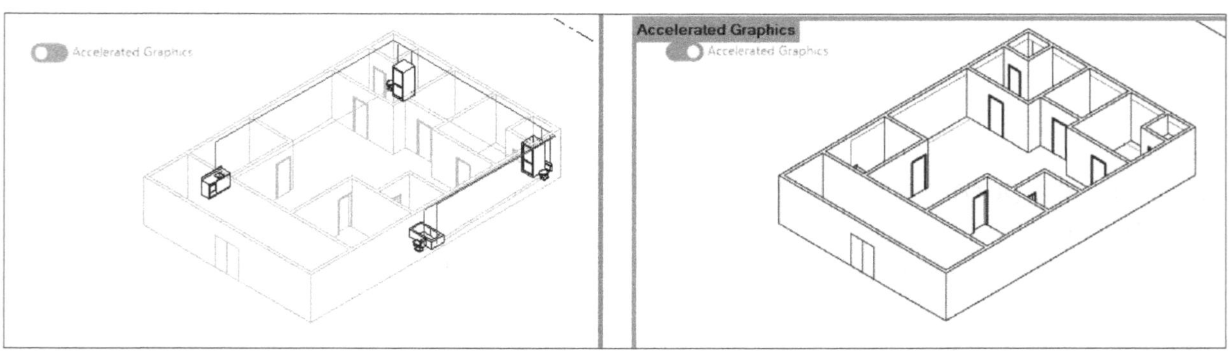

Figure-19. Enable and disable state of accelerated graphics

RENDERING

The renderings of model are used to represent the building in real material and texture in the form of an image. So, before creating a rendering image, we need to apply material and textures to the elements of building. The procedure to apply material is given next.

Applying Material

The **Materials** tool is used to apply and manage materials. The procedure to use this tool is given next.

- Click on the **Materials** tool from the **Settings** panel in the **Manage** tab of **Ribbon**. The **Material Browser** dialog box will be displayed; refer to Figure-20.

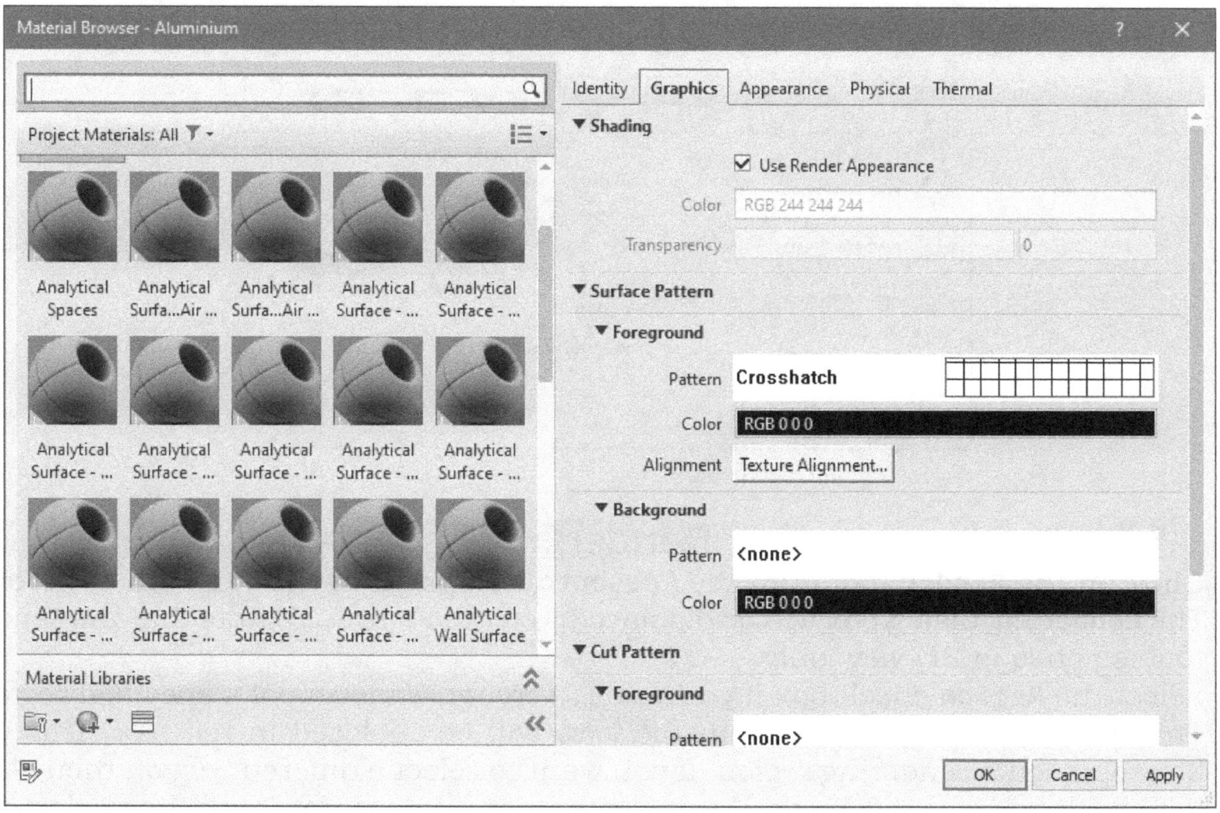

Figure-20. Material Browser dialog box

- Set desired parameters for material and click on the **Apply** button to modify them.
- If you want to create a new material then click on the **Create New Material** tool from the drop-down at the bottom in the dialog box; refer to Figure-21. The new material will be added in the library.

Figure-21. Create New Material tool

- You can modify the properties of material as discussed earlier.
- Click on the **OK** button from the dialog box.

- Click on the **Paint** tool from the **Paint** drop-down in the **Geometry** panel of **Modify** tab in the **Ribbon**. The **Material Browser** will be displayed; refer to Figure-22.
- Select desired material from the **Browser**. The cursor will change to paint icon.
- Select the faces of elements to which you want to apply material/texture.
- After applying material, click on the **Done** button from the **Browser**.

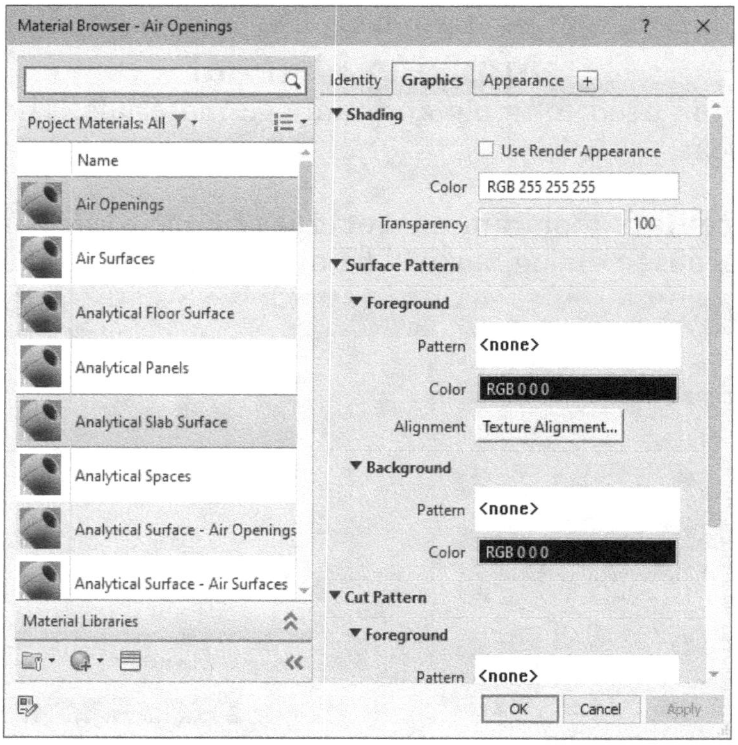

Figure-22. Material Browser

Rendering

- Click on the **Render** tool from the **Presentation** panel in the **View** tab of **Ribbon**. The **Rendering** dialog box will be displayed; refer to Figure-23. Note that the **Render** tool is active in 3D view only.
- Select the **Region** check box if you want to create rendering of a specified region. The current displaying model in the view will be enclosed in red box. This red box represents rendering region. If you want to select a different region then clear the check box, zoom & pan to keep elements in current view, and then select the **Region** check box.
- Select desired option from the **Setting** drop-down in **Quality** area of the dialog box.
- In **Output Settings** area of the dialog box, the **Screen** radio button is selected by default for resolution of render image and hence current view resolution is used for rendering. Select the **Printer** radio button to create rendering image of desired resolution and then select desired resolution from the adjacent drop-down. You can select **75 DPI**, **150 DPI**, **300 DPI**, or **600 DPI** option as resolution from the drop-down.
- Select desired option from the **Scheme** drop-down in the **Lighting** area of the dialog box to define how Sun light and artificial lights will affect in the rendering. For example, select the **Exterior: Sun and Artificial** option if you want to show lighting effect of Sun on exterior walls/elements and also want to take artificial lights into account.

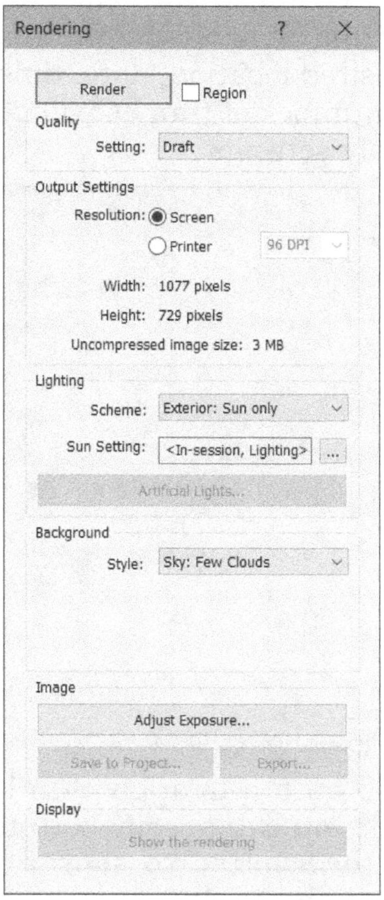

Figure-23. Rendering dialog box

Sun Settings

- Click on the **Choose a sun location** button next to **Sun Setting** field in the **Lighting** area of the dialog box. The **Sun Settings** dialog box will be displayed; refer to Figure-24. By default, **Lighting** radio button is selected in this dialog box and hence, you are asked to specify the location of Sun in azimuth & altitude coordinates. Select the **Relative to View** check box if you want to use current view as reference for positioning Sun. Click on the **Apply** button to apply settings.

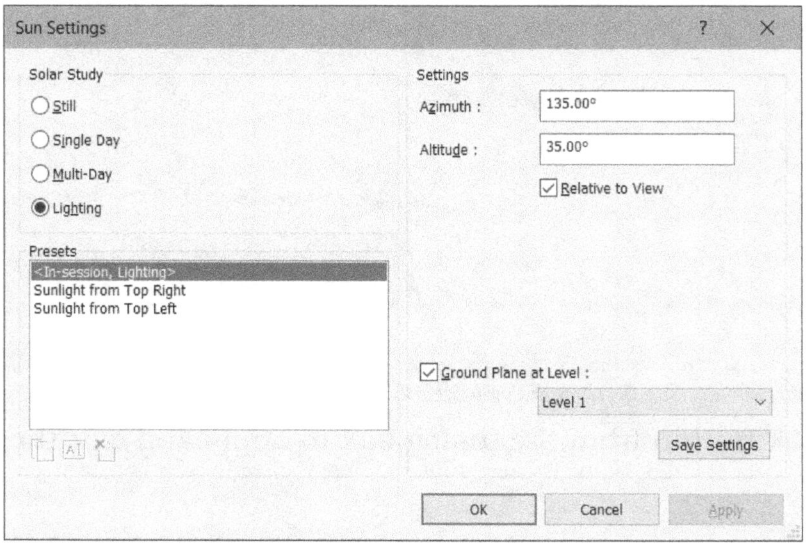

Figure-24. Sun Settings dialog box

- Select the **Multi-Day** radio button if you want to apply Sun light for specified interval of days. On selecting this option the dialog box will be displayed as shown in Figure-25. Set desired location, date, time, interval and so on. Based on specified parameters, the number of frames will be decided automatically. Click on the **Apply** button to apply settings.

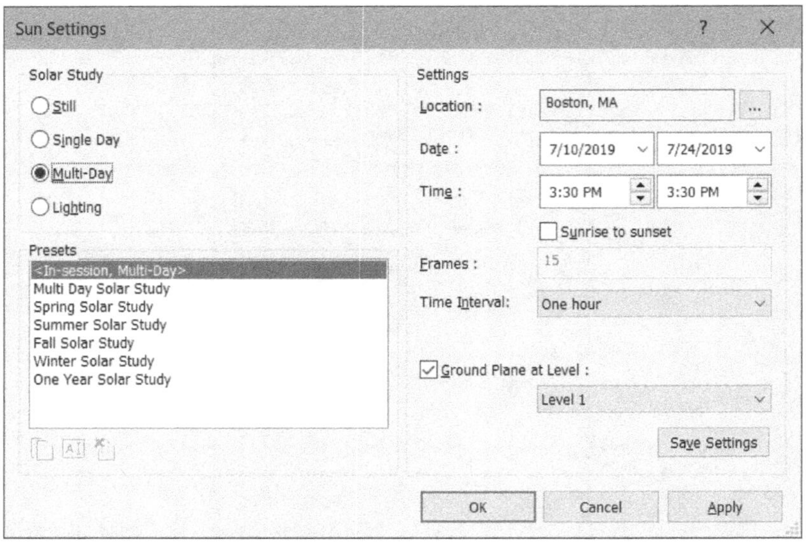

Figure-25. Sun Settings dialog box with Multi-Day radio button selected

- Select the **Single Day** radio button to apply Sun light based on time, place and location specified. Note that you can specify both the start time and end time for sun light or you can select the **Sunrise to sunset** check box to use time between sunrise and sunset. Click on the **Apply** button to apply settings.
- Select the **Still** radio button to capture light of Sun at specified location, time instant, and day. The options will be displayed as shown in Figure-26. Select the **Use shared settings** check box if you want to use settings applied in Project Settings. Click on the **Apply** button to apply settings.

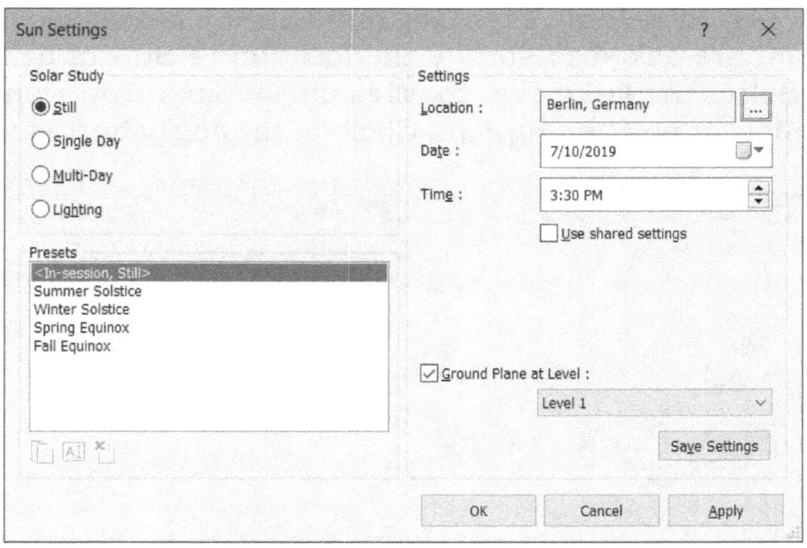

Figure-26. Sun Settings dialog box with Still radio button selected

- Click on the **OK** button from the dialog box to apply and exit the dialog box.

Artificial Light Groups

- Click on the **Artificial Lights** button from the **Lighting** area of the dialog box when artificial light option is selected in the **Scheme** drop-down of **Lighting** area in the dialog box. The **Artificial Lights** dialog box will be displayed; refer to Figure-27.

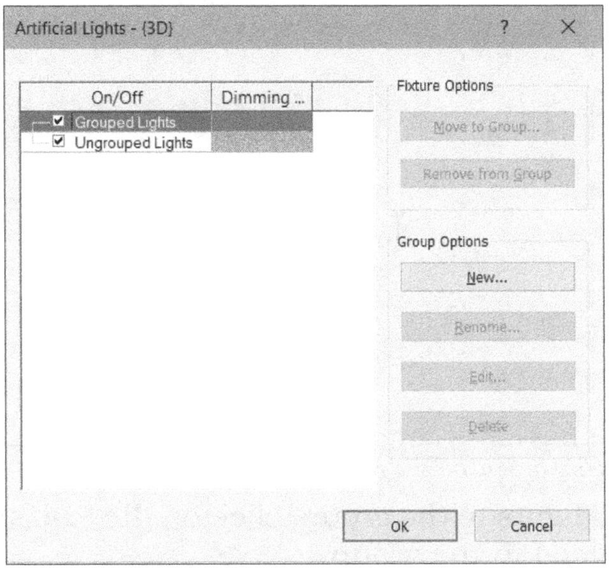

Figure-27. Artificial Lights dialog box

- Select desired group combination of lights in which you want to add a new light group and then click on the **New** button. The **New Light Group** dialog box will be displayed; refer to Figure-28.

Figure-28. New Light Group dialog box

- Specify desired name of light group and click on the **OK** button. The new light group will be added. Note that there is no light fixture added in this group. To add a light in the group, select the newly created light group and click on the **Edit** button. The **Light Group** toolbar will be displayed; refer to Figure-29.

Figure-29. Light Group toolbar

- Click on the **Add** button and select the light fixtures already placed in the model; refer to Figure-30. (Note that you need to place light fixtures by using the **Lighting Fixture** tool in the **Electrical** panel of **Systems** tab in the **Ribbon** before creating artificial light groups.)

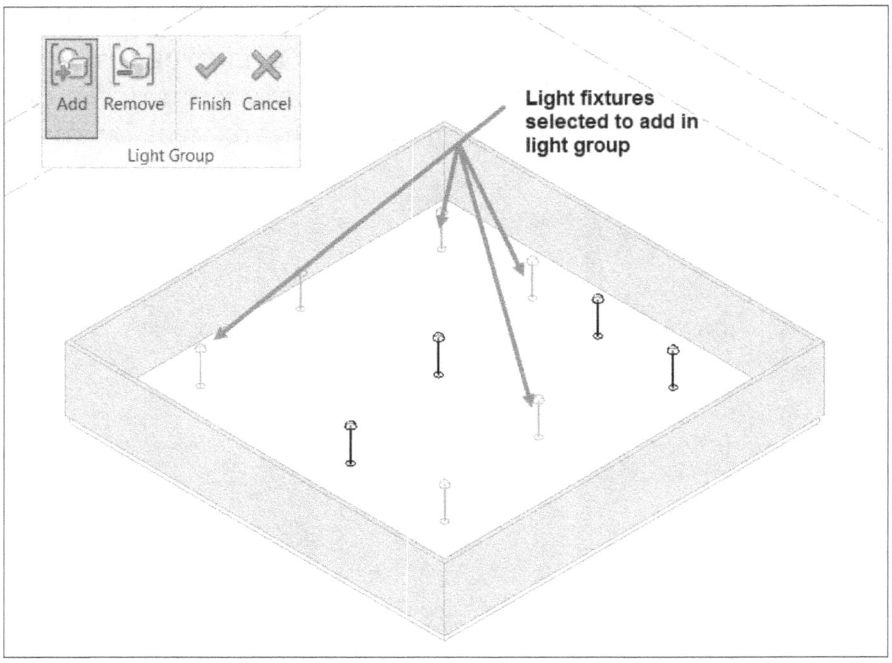

Figure-30. Adding light fixtures to group

- After adding desired lights to the group, click on the **Finish** tool from the toolbar. The lights will be added in the group.
- Click on the **Render** tool from the **Presentation** panel in the **View** tab of **Ribbon** if the tool gets deactivated.
- Select desired style of background from the **Style** drop-down in the **Background** area of the **Rendering** dialog box.

Adjusting Image Exposure

- Click on the **Adjust Exposure** tool from the **Image** area of the dialog box. The **Exposure Control** dialog box will be displayed; refer to Figure-31.

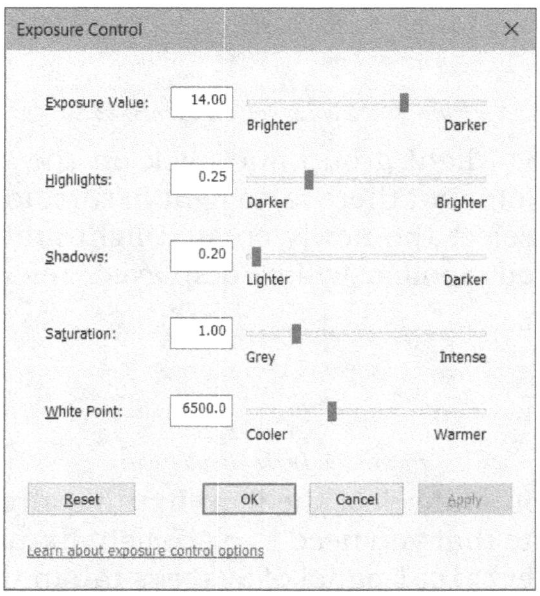

Figure-31. Exposure Control dialog box

- Set desired value of various parameters for image in different fields of dialog box and click on the **OK** button.

- After setting desired parameters, click on the **Render** button from the dialog box. The **Rendering Progress** information box will be displayed informing you about the progress of rendering. Once the process is complete, the rendering image will be displayed; refer to Figure-32.

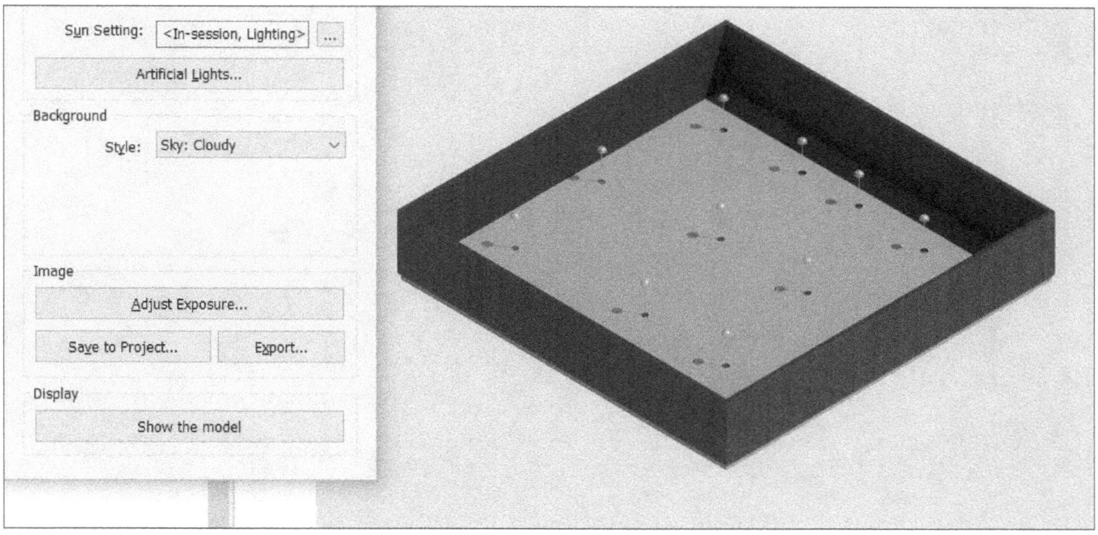

Figure-32. Rendering created

- Click on the **Save to Project** button to save the rendering image into current project. The **Save To Project** dialog box will be displayed; refer to Figure-33.

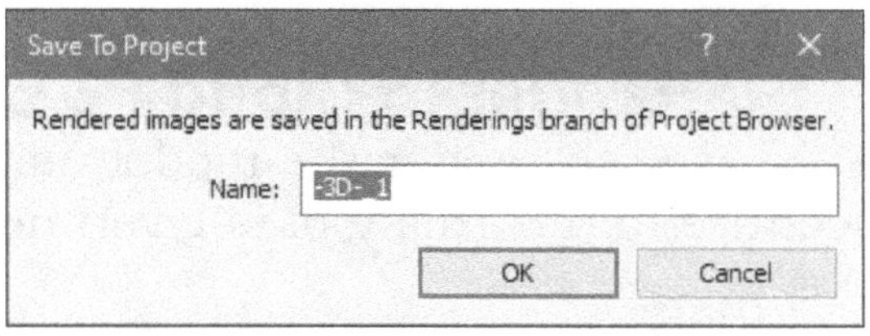

Figure-33. Save To Project dialog box

- Set desired name of image in the **Name** field of dialog box and click on the **OK** button. The rendering will be added in the **Project Browser**; refer to Figure-34.

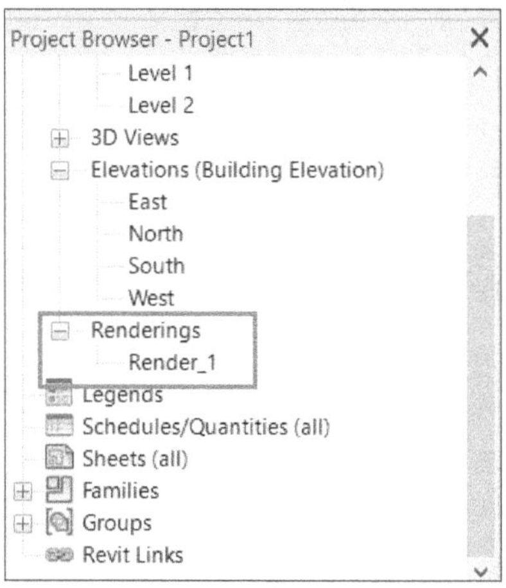

Figure-34. Rendering added in Project Browser

- Click on the **Export** button from the dialog box to save the image in local drive in desired format. The **Save Image** dialog box will be displayed; refer to Figure-35.
- Specify desired name and format for image file and then click on the **Save** button to save the file.

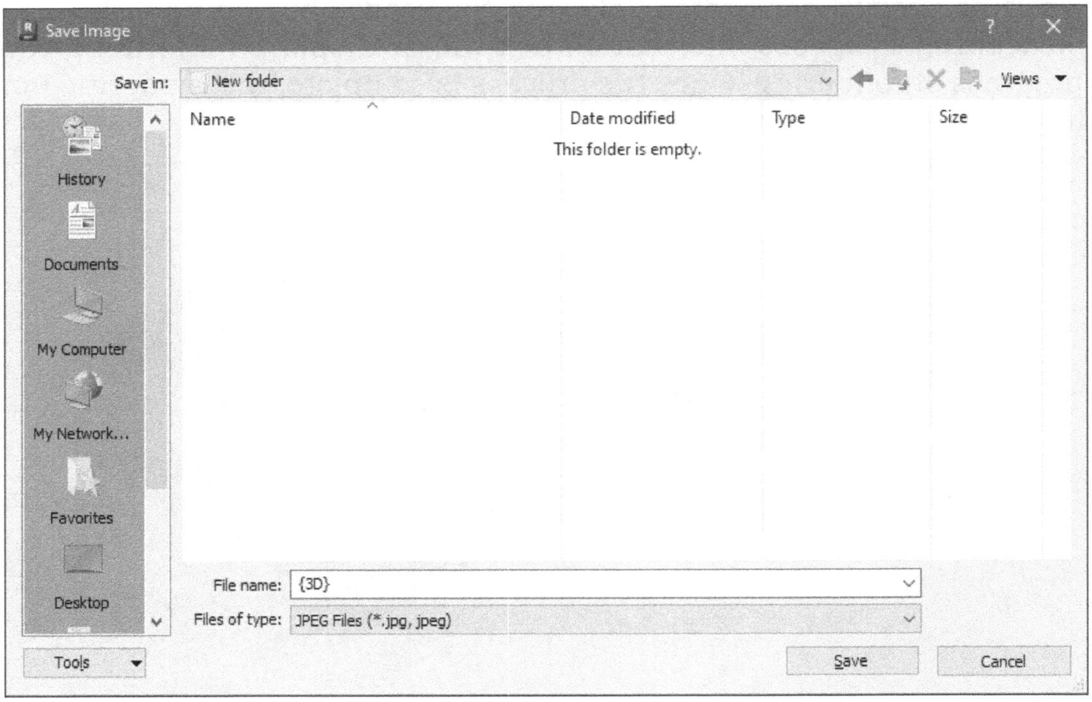

Figure-35. Save Image dialog box

Click on the **Show Model** button from the **Rendering** dialog box to display the model again. Click on the **Close** button at top right corner of dialog box to exit the tool.

Render in Cloud

The **Render in Cloud** tool is used to render the model using computation power of Autodesk Cloud. The procedure to use this tool is given next.

- Click on the **Render in Cloud** tool from the **Cloud Rendering** drop-dowm in the **Presentation** panel of **View** tab in the **Ribbon**. The **Render in Cloud** dialog box will be displayed; refer to Figure-36.

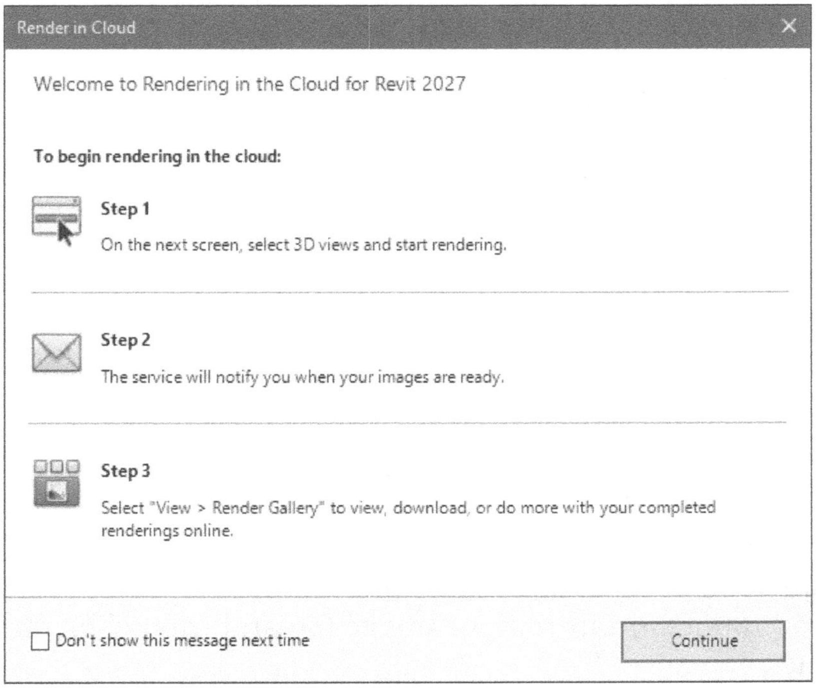

Figure-36. Render in Cloud dialog box

- Click on the **Continue** button from the dialog box. The **Render in Cloud** dialog box will be displayed as shown in Figure-37.

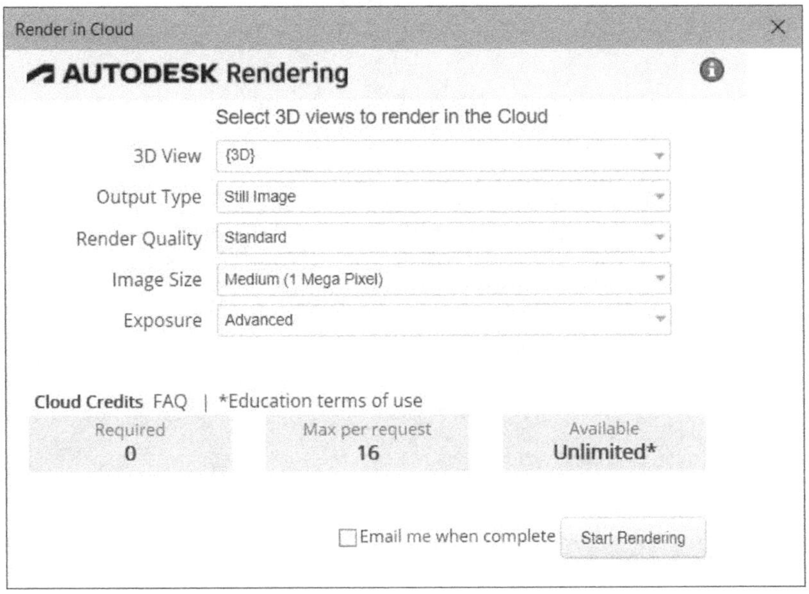

Figure-37. Render in Cloud dialog box

- Set desired parameters in various drop-downs of the dialog box.
- Select the **Email me when complete** check box so that system notifies you when rendering process is complete.
- After setting desired parameters, click on the **Start Rendering** button. The notification of rendering process will be displayed; refer to Figure-38.

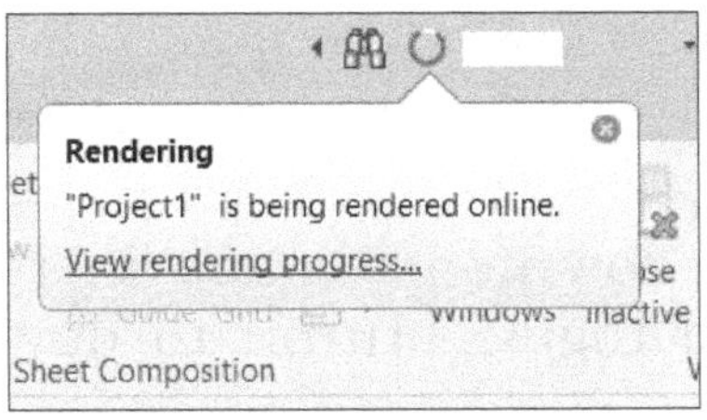

Figure-38. Notification of rendering

- Once the rendering process is complete, expand drop-down of your Autodesk account and click on the **View Completed Renderings** option; refer Figure-39. All of your cloud renderings will be displayed in the web browser.

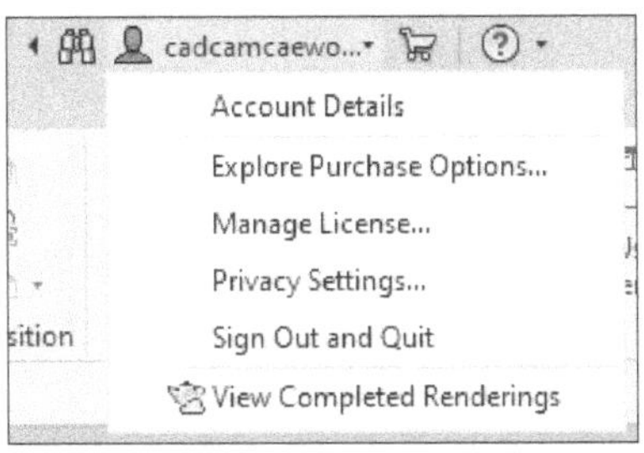

Figure-39. View Completed Renderings option

- Click on desired rendering to check and further edit it. The rendering will be displayed with related tools; refer to Figure-40.
- Click on the **Download** button from the toolbar in web page to download the rendering in local drive. The options to download as image will be displayed; refer to Figure-41.

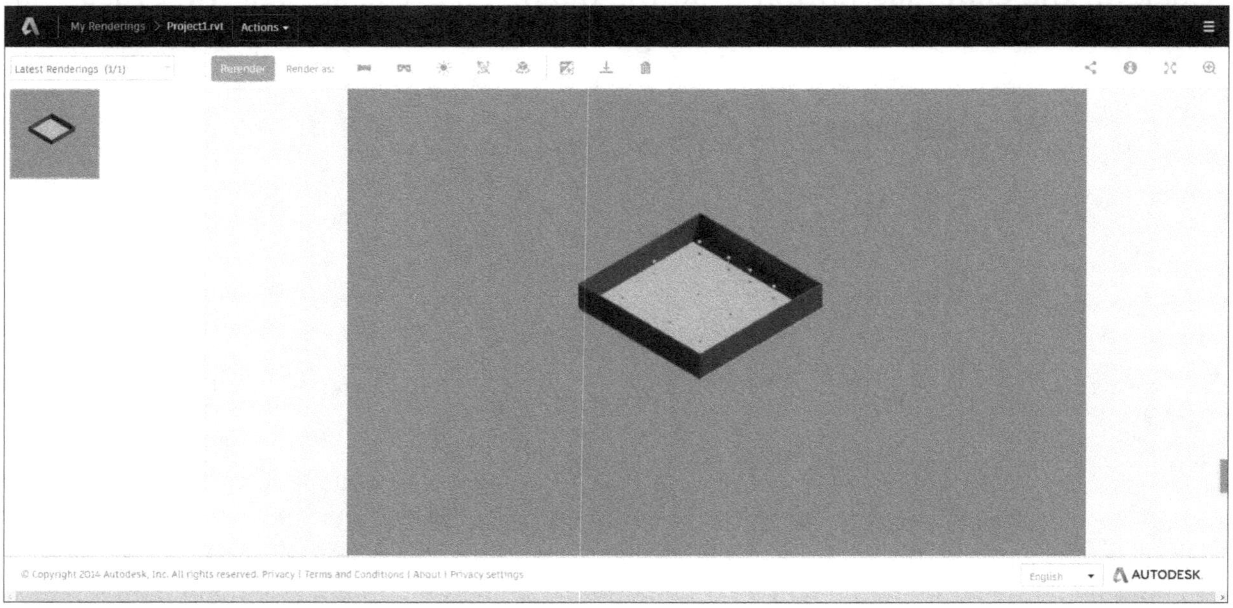

Figure-40. Rendering on cloud

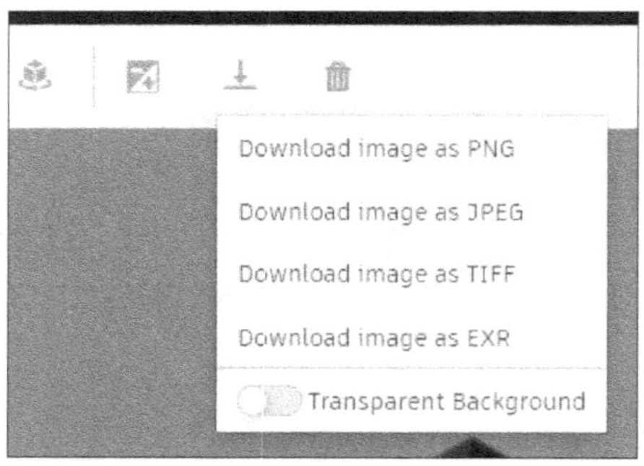

Figure-41. Download options

- Select desired option to download image in respective format. Select the **Transparent Background** toggle button to download rendering image with transparent background.
- Click on **Panorama** button to render current model as panorama image. The option for defining panorama image settings will be displayed; refer to Figure-42.

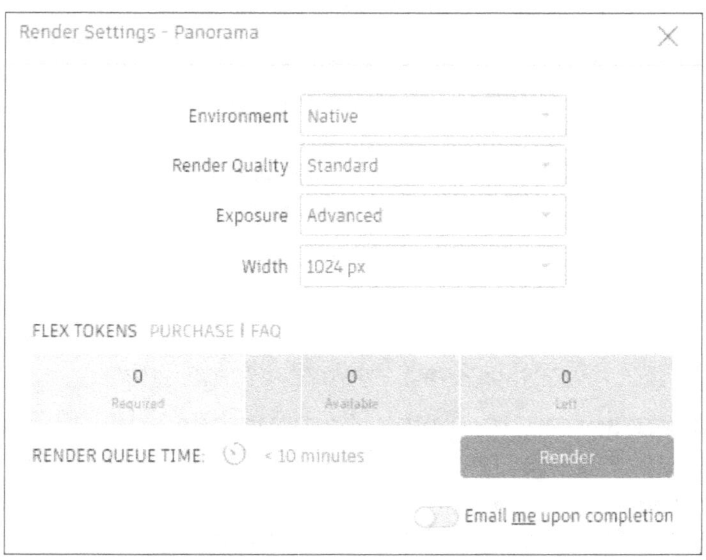

Figure-42. Render Settings-Panorama

- Set desired parameters in the dialog box and click on the **Render** button. In a few minutes, the panorama image will be displayed.
- Similarly, you can use the Stereo Panorama, Solar Study, Illuminance, and Turntable renderings.
- Click on the **Post-processing** button to define exposure and image adjustment parameters; refer to Figure-43. Set desired parameters and click on the **Apply** button.

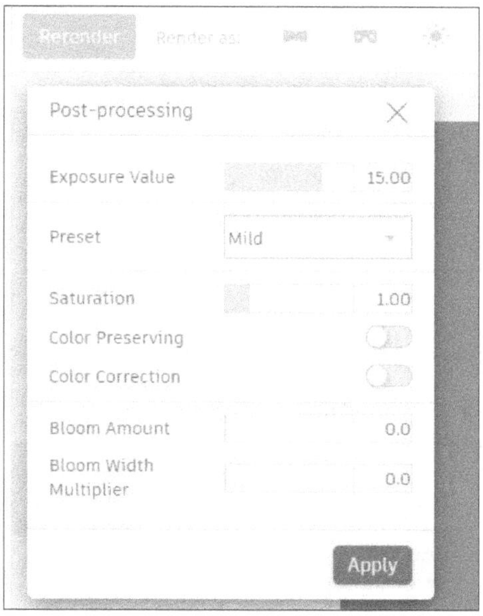

Figure-43. Post-processing options

Render Gallery

The **Render Gallery** tool in **Presentation** panel is used to display gallery of renderings on Autodesk cloud; refer to Figure-44. The other tools of render gallery have already been discussed.

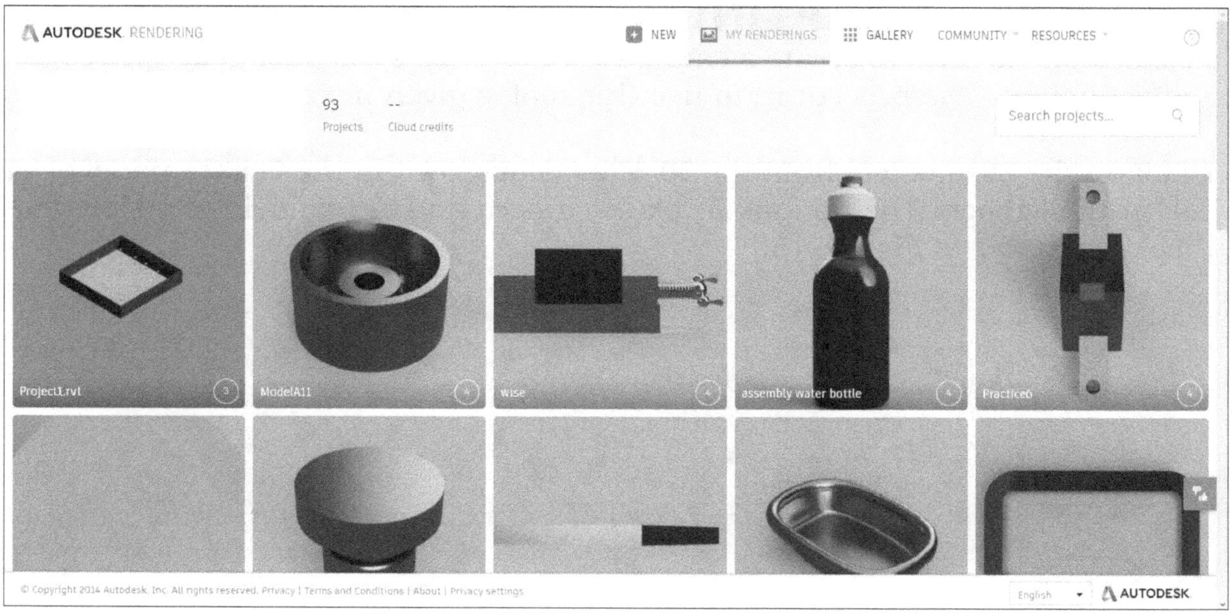

Figure-44. Render gallery

Creating Default 3D View

The **Default 3D View** tool is used to create a 3D view of model and add it in **Project Browser**. The procedure to use this tool is given next.

- Click on the **Default 3D View** tool from the **3D View** drop-down in the **Create** panel of **View** tab in the **Ribbon**. The 3D view will be created; refer to Figure-45.

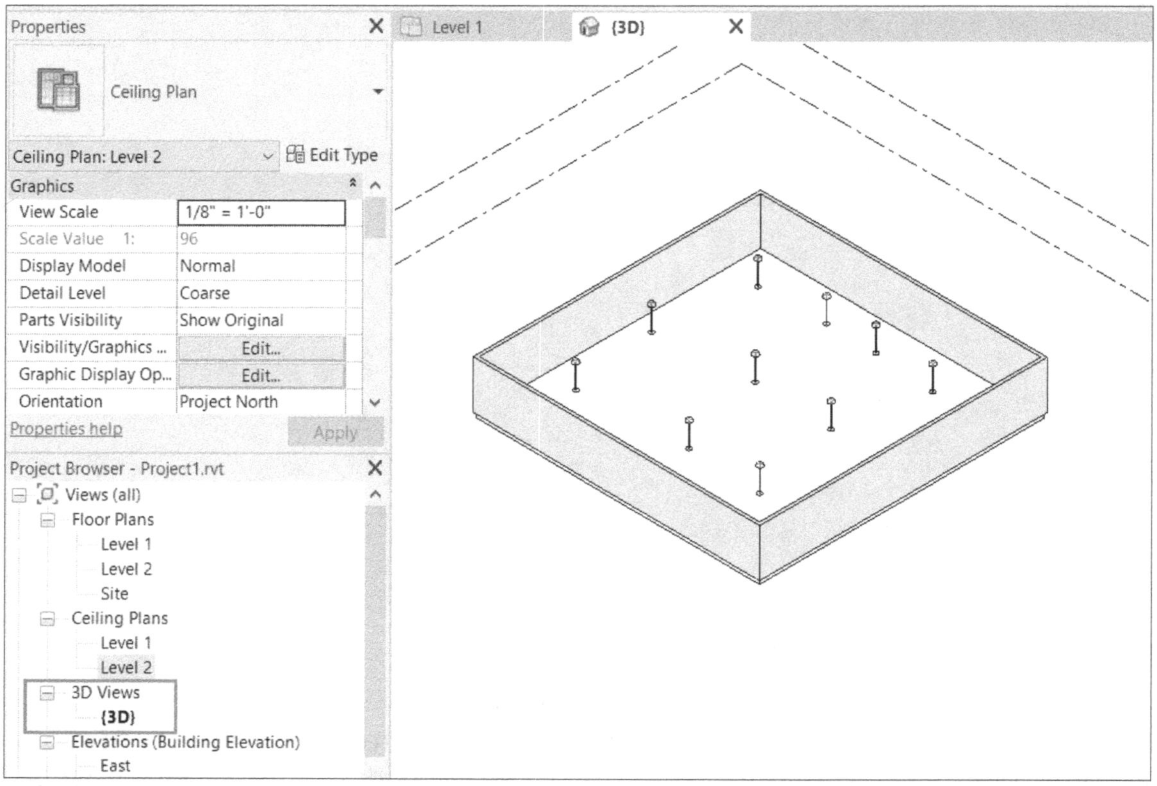

Figure-45. 3D view created

CREATING CAMERA VIEW

The **Camera** tool is used to create a camera view for displaying model at desired angle and offset height. The procedure to use this tool is given next.

- Click on the **Camera** tool from the **3D View** drop-down in the **Create** panel of **View** tab in the **Ribbon**. The options to place camera and define field of vision will be displayed; refer to Figure-46.

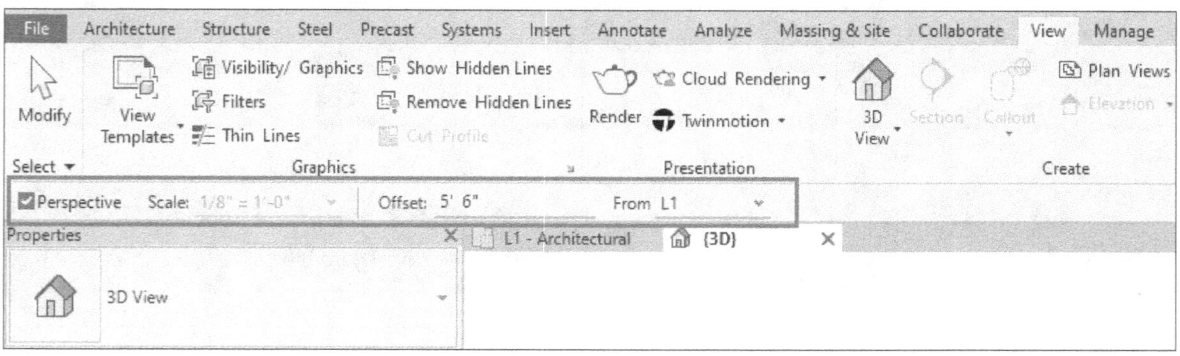

Figure-46. Options for placing camera

- Select the **Perspective** check box from **Options Bar** if you want to create perspective view.

- Set desired height of camera in **Offset** edit box of **Options Bar**. Note that height will be calculated from the level selected in **From** drop-down of **Options Bar**.
- Click at desired location to place camera. You will be asked to define the target point of camera; refer to Figure-47.

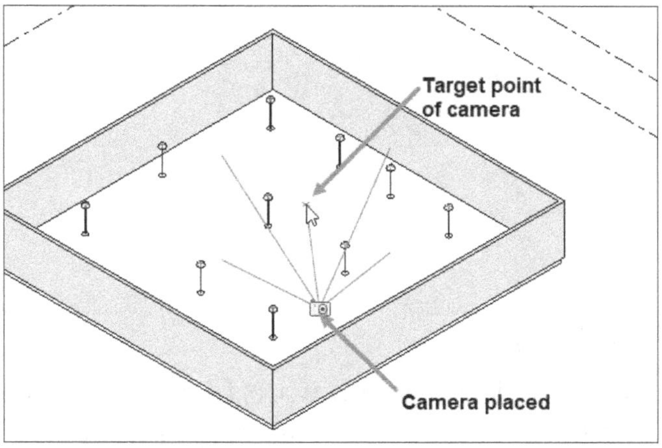

Figure-47. Defining target point of camera

- Click at desired location to define focus point. The camera view will be created; refer to Figure-48.

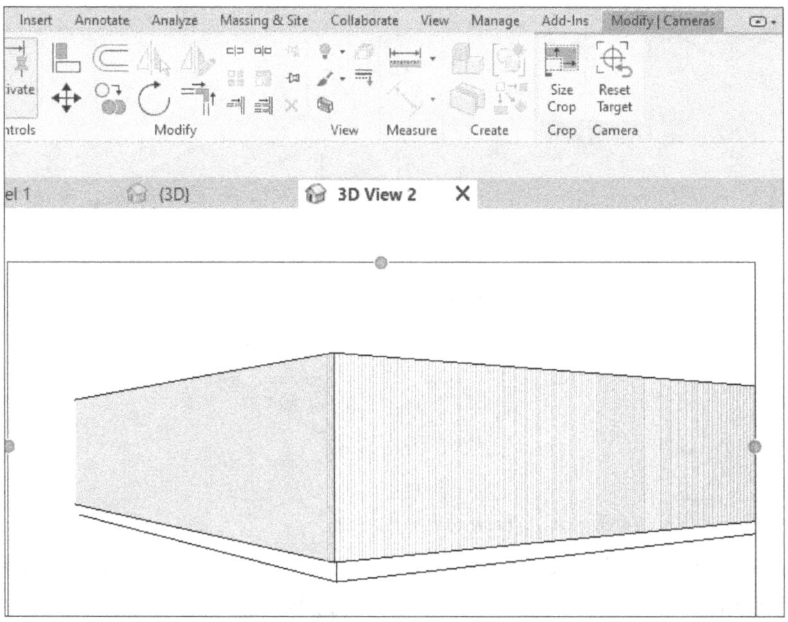

Figure-48. Camera view created

- You can change the size of camera view by moving boundaries using dots on the boundary.
- Click on the **Reset Target** button from the **Modify|Cameras** contextual tab after selecting the boundaries of camera view to restore camera target point to the middle of view.

CREATING WALKTHROUGH

The **Walkthrough** tool is used to create an animated 3D walkthrough of the model. The procedure to use this tool is given next.

- Click on the **Walkthrough** tool from the **3D View** drop-down in the **Create** panel of **View** tab in the **Ribbon**. The options to create walkthrough will be displayed; refer to Figure-49.

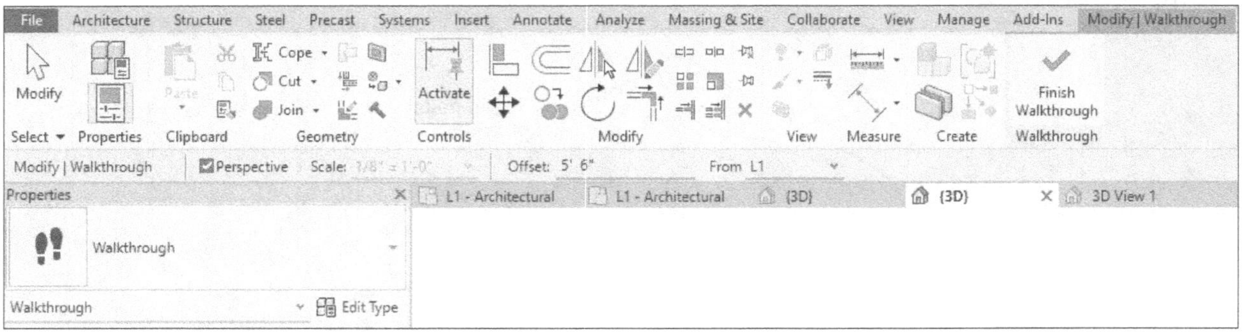

Figure-49. Options for creating walkthrough

- Select the **Perspective** check box if you want to create walkthrough in perspective view. Clear the check box if you want to specify fixed scale value.
- Specify the height from desired level at which you want to create the walkthrough in **Options Bar**.
- Click at desired locations to place the key frames of walkthrough; refer to Figure-50.

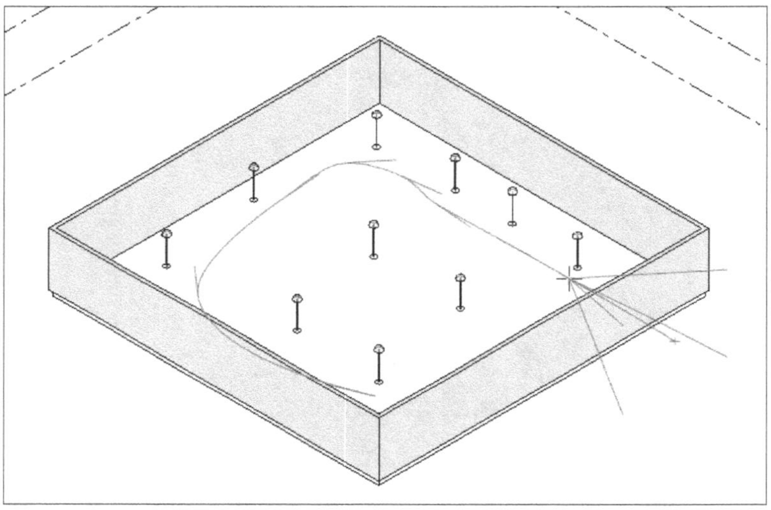

Figure-50. Placing walkthrough key frames

- Click on the **Finish Walkthrough** button from the **Walkthrough** panel of **Modify|Walkthrough** contextual tab in the **Ribbon**. The walkthrough will be created.
- Expand the **Walkthroughs** category in **Project Browser** and double-click on the **Walkthrough 1** recently created. The walkthrough will be displayed in the view area; refer to Figure-51. Select the boundary of walkthrough. The **Modify|Cameras** contextual tab will be displayed.

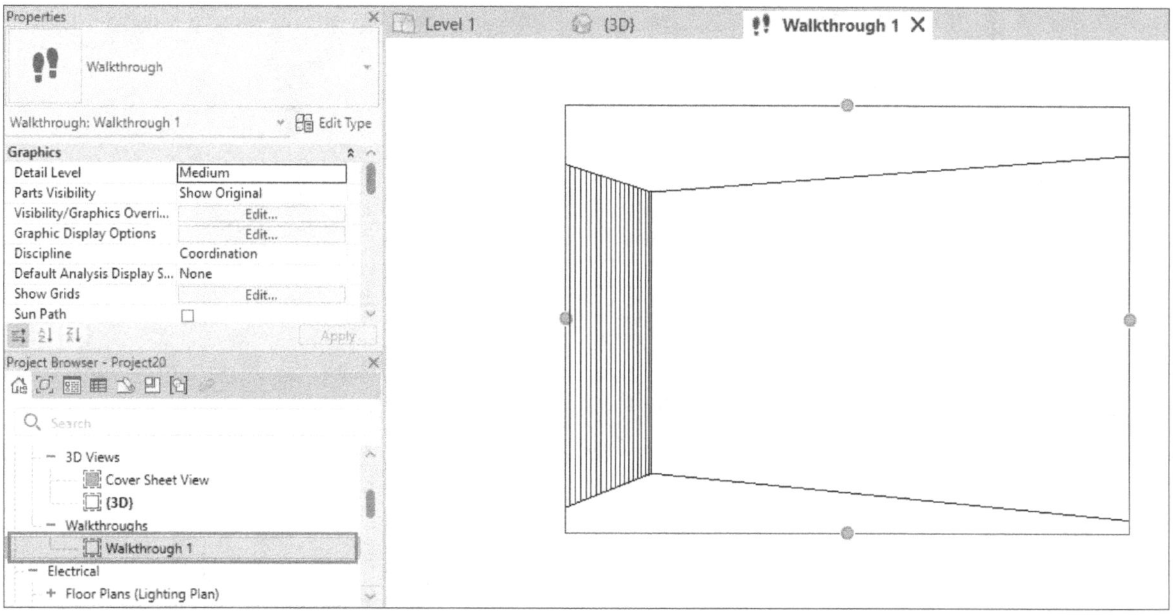

Figure-51. Walkthrough displayed

- Modify the camera boundaries as desired and then click on the **Edit Walkthrough** button from the **Walkthrough** panel of **Modify|Cameras** contextual tab in the **Ribbon**. The options will be displayed as shown in Figure-52.

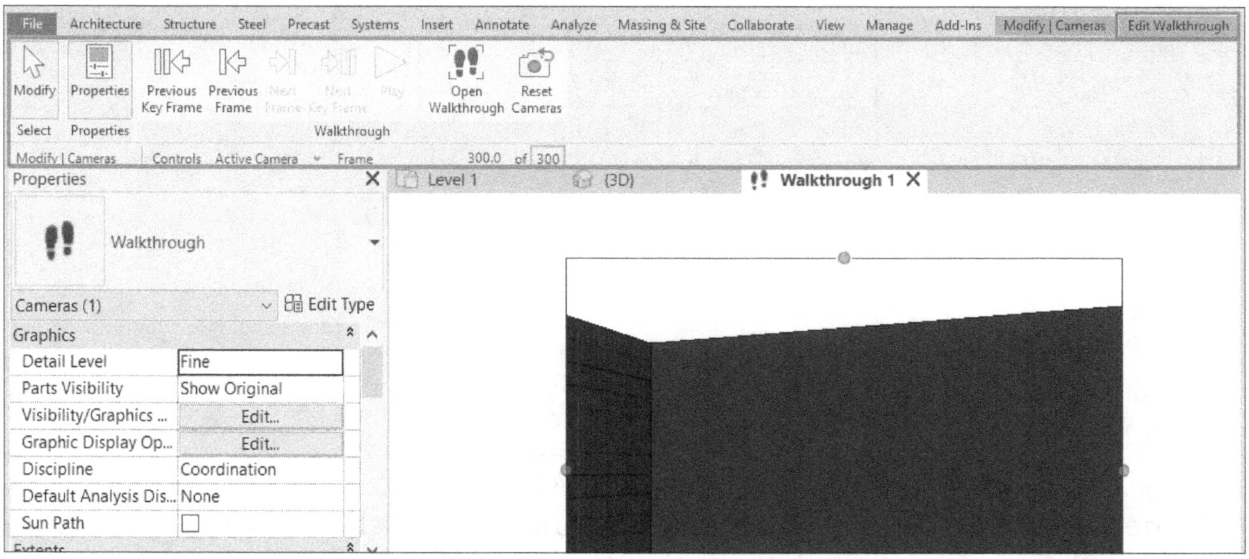

Figure-52. Edit Walkthrough contextual tab

- Set the frame to **1** in the **Frame** edit box of contextual tab and then click on the **Play** button from the **Edit Walkthrough** contextual tab. The walkthrough will be played inside boundaries.
- If you want to export the walkthrough, click on the **Walkthrough** tool from the **Images and Animations** cascading menu of **Export** menu in **File** menu; refer to Figure-53. The **Length/Format** dialog box will be displayed; refer to Figure-54.

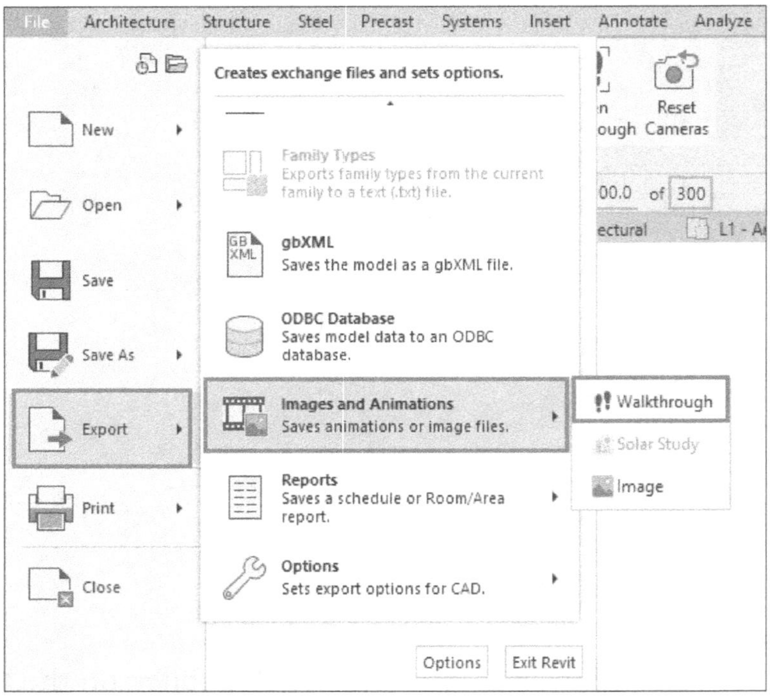

Figure-53. Walkthrough tool

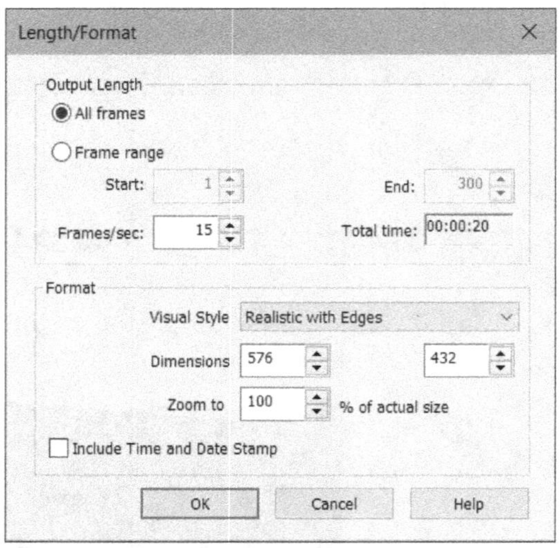

Figure-54. Length/Format dialog box

- Set desired parameters in the dialog box and click on the **OK** button. The **Export Walkthrough** dialog box will be displayed; refer to Figure-55.

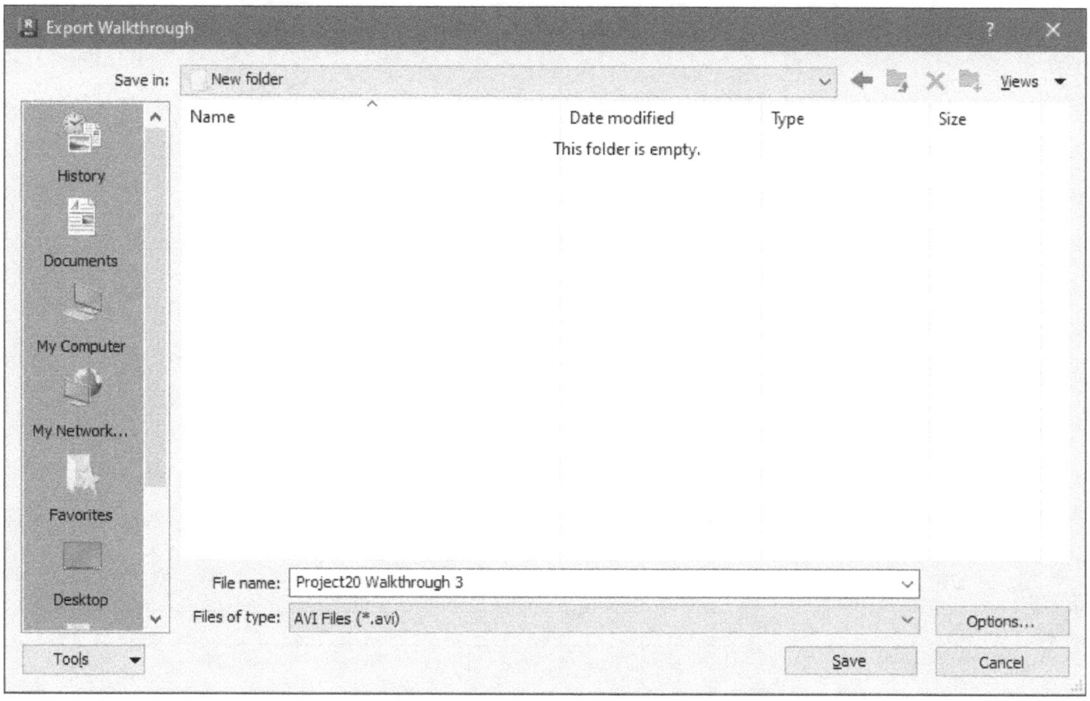

Figure-55. Export Walkthrough dialog box

- Click on the **Options** button from the dialog box to modify parameters for walkthrough.
- Specify desired name for walkthrough clip in the **File name** edit box and click on the **Save** button. The file will be created.

CREATING SECTION VIEW

The **Section** tool is used to create section of view at define line sketch. Note that this tool is not available for 3D views. The procedure to use this tool is given next.

- Click on the **Section** tool from the **Create** panel in the **View** tab of **Ribbon**. The options to create section will be displayed; refer to Figure-56.

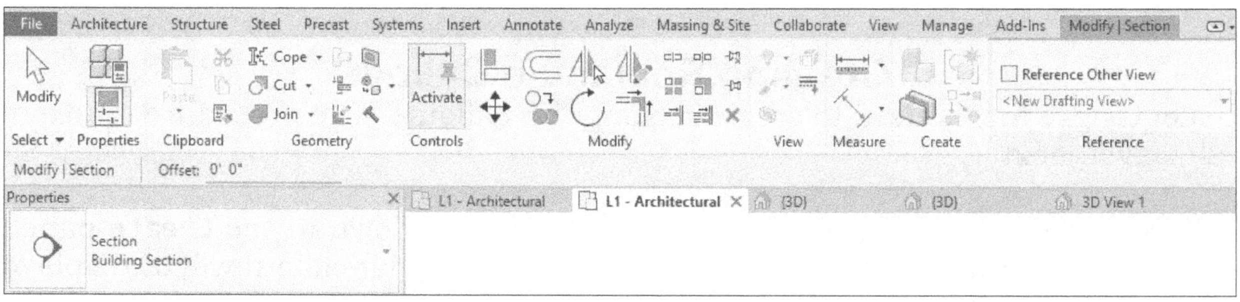

Figure-56. Modify Section contextual tab

- Set desired value of offset in **Offset** edit box. This will define the height of section from current level.
- Create a straight line passing through the region whose section view is to be created; refer to Figure-57. The section view will be created and added in the **Sections** category of **Project Browser**; refer to Figure-58.

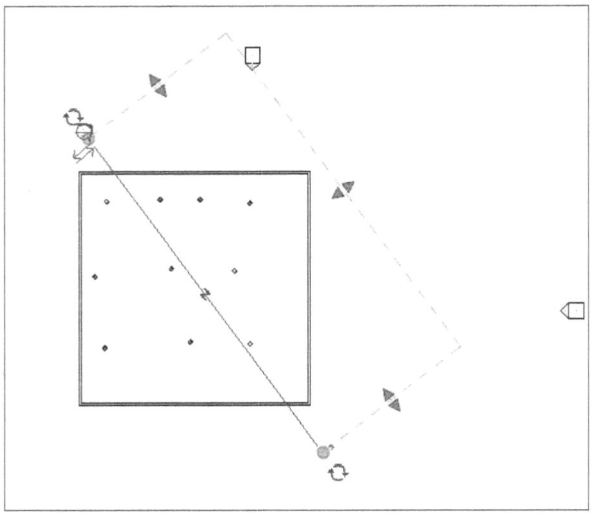

Figure-57. Line sketched for section

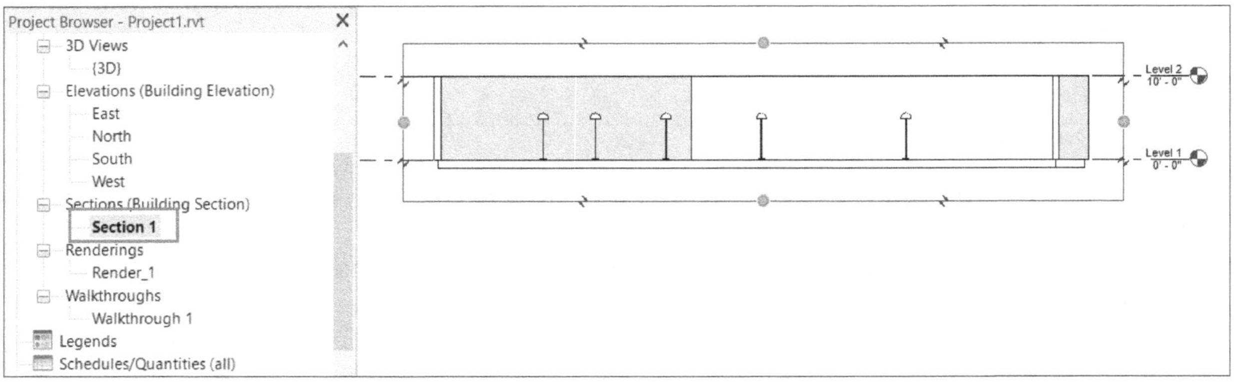

Figure-58. Section view created

CREATING CALLOUTS

The tools in the **Callout** drop-down are used to create different types of callouts. A callout is used to mark region on a building model and specify related information. These tools are not available for 3D views. Various tools in this drop-down are discussed next.

Creating Rectangle Callout

The **Rectangle** tool is used to create rectangular callouts. The procedure to use this tool is given next.

- Click on the **Rectangle** tool from the **Callout** drop-down in the **Create** panel of **View** tab in the **Ribbon**. The options to create rectangular callout will be displayed; refer to Figure-59.

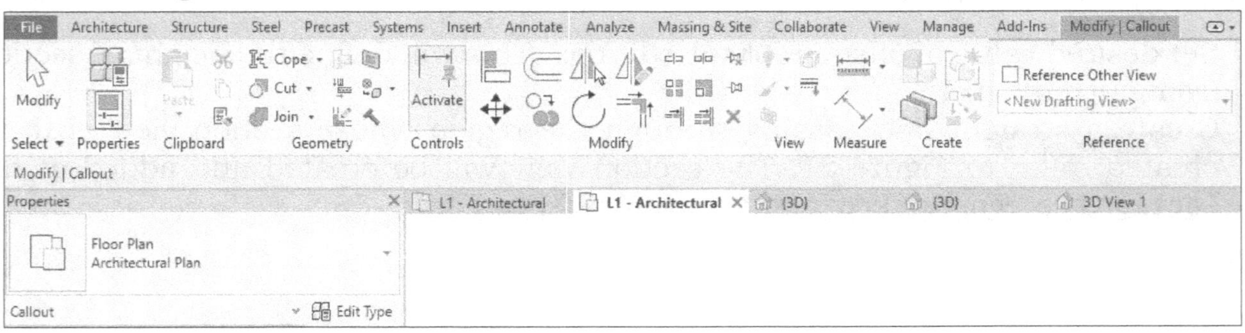

Figure-59. Options for creating rectangular callout

- Create the rectangular boundary at desired location. The callout will be created; refer to Figure-60.

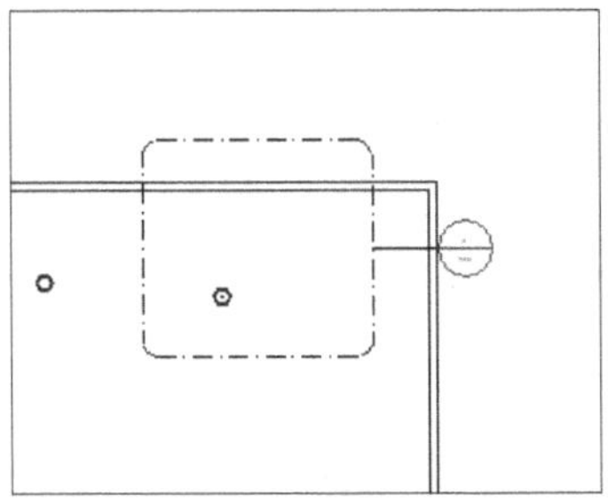

Figure-60. Rectangular boundary created for callout

- Double-click on the mark of callout to open the callout view.

Creating Sketched Callout

The **Sketch** tool in **Callout** drop-down is used to create callout with sketched boundary. The procedure to use this tool is given next.

- Click on the **Sketch** tool from the **Callout** drop-down in the **Create** panel of **View** tab in the **Ribbon**. The options to create sketched callout will be displayed; refer to Figure-61.

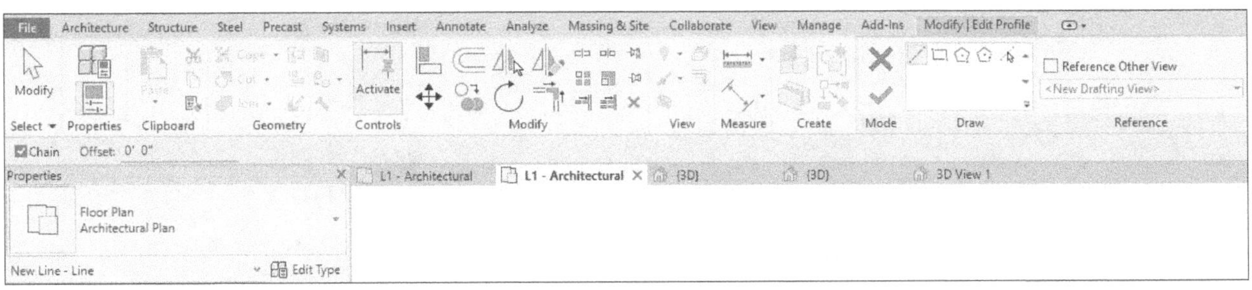

Figure-61. Modify Edit Profile contextual tab

- Select desired sketching tool from the **Draw** panel in contextual tab and create desired sketch boundary.
- Click on the **OK** button from the **Mode** panel in the contextual tab. The callout will be displayed; refer to Figure-62.

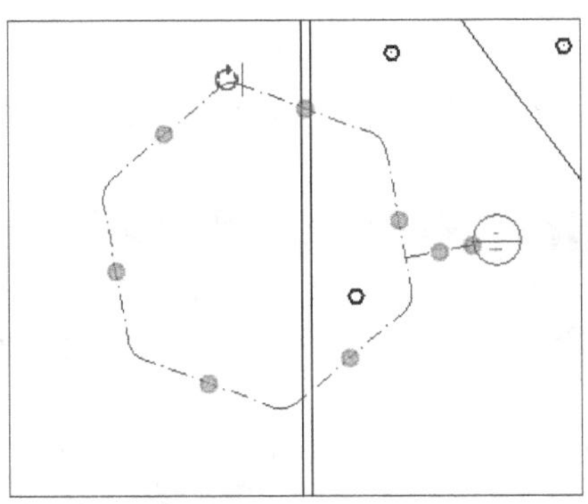

Figure-62. Callout created

CREATING PLAN VIEWS

The tools in the **Plan Views** drop-down are used to create different types of plan views; refer to Figure-63. Various tools in this drop-down are discussed next.

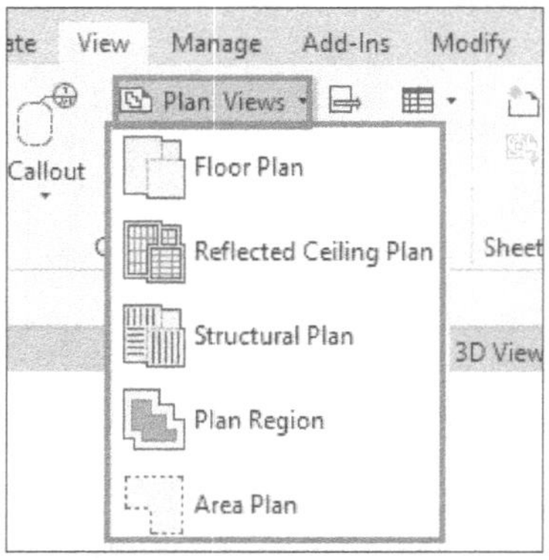

Figure-63. Plan Views drop-down

Creating Floor Plan

The **Floor Plan** tool is used to create different types of floor plans. The procedure to use this tool is given next.

- Click on the **Floor Plan** tool from the **Plan Views** drop-down in the **Create** panel of **View** tab in the **Ribbon**. The **New Floor Plan** dialog box will be displayed; refer to Figure-64. Clear the **Do not duplicate existing views** check box to create duplicate views.

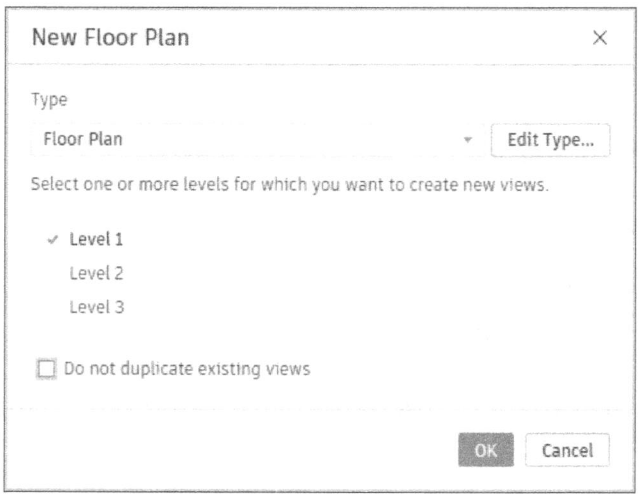

Figure-64. New Floor Plan dialog box

- The procedure to create floor plan has been discussed in previous chapters.

Creating Reflected Ceiling Plan

The **Reflected Ceiling Plan** tool is used to create ceiling plan displaying all the elements placed on ceiling. The procedure to use this tool is given next.

- Click on the **Reflected Ceiling Plan** tool from the **Plan Views** drop-down in the **Create** panel of **View** tab in the **Ribbon**. The **New RCP** dialog box will be displayed; refer to Figure-65.

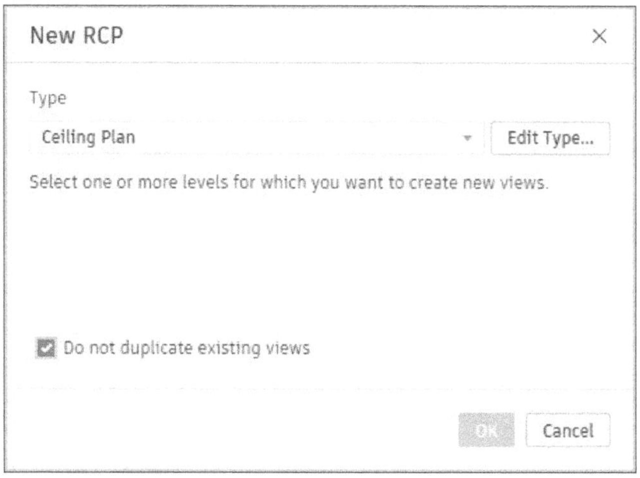

Figure-65. New RCP dialog box

- Clear the **Do not duplicate existing views** check box if you want to create a view using already used levels of model.
- Click on the **Edit Type** button from the dialog box. The **Type Properties** dialog box will be displayed as shown in Figure-66.

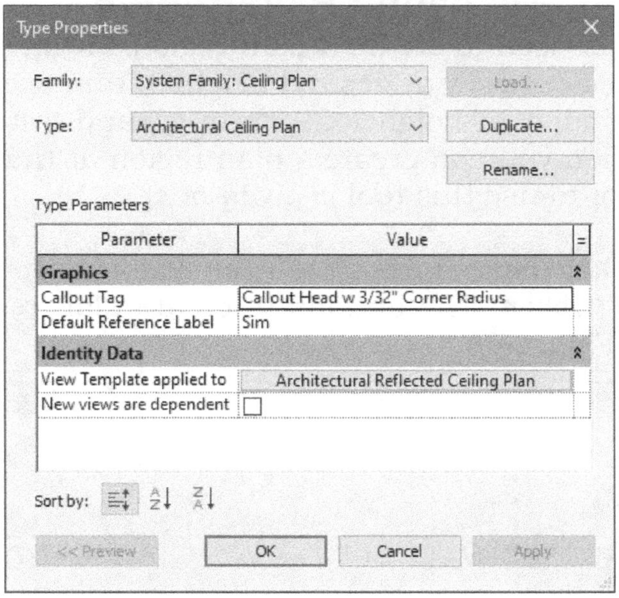

Figure-66. Type Properties dialog box

- Set desired parameters in the table. Click on the **<None>** button and select desired template. Click on the **OK** button from **Type Properties** dialog box to apply parameters. The **New RCP** dialog box will be displayed again.
- Select desired level and click on the **OK** button to create ceiling.

Creating Structural Plan

The **Structural Plan** tool is used to create structural plan view in **Project Browser**. The procedure to use this tool is given next.

- Click on the **Structural Plan** tool from the **Plan Views** drop-down in the **Create** panel of **View** tab in the **Ribbon**. The **New Structural Plan** dialog box will be displayed; refer to Figure-67.

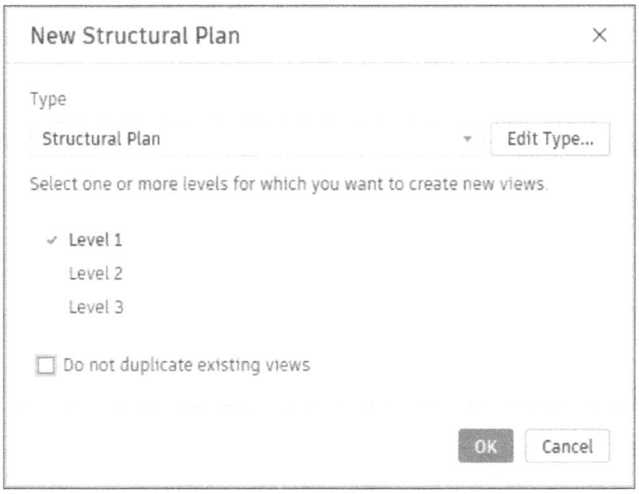

Figure-67. New Structural Plan dialog box

- Select desired level for which you want to create structural plan and click on the **OK** button. The structural plan for selected level will be created.

Creating Plan Region

The **Plan Region** tool is used to create a plan region within a view. Using the plan region, you can create a cut view at desired height within specified boundaries. For example, there is a window at height of 2' from ground but it is not displayed by default in plan view then you can create a plan region at that height to display the window. The procedure to use this tool is given next.

- Click on the **Plan Region** tool from the **Plan Views** drop-down of **Create** panel in the **View** tab of **Ribbon**. The options to create plan region boundary will be displayed; refer to Figure-68.

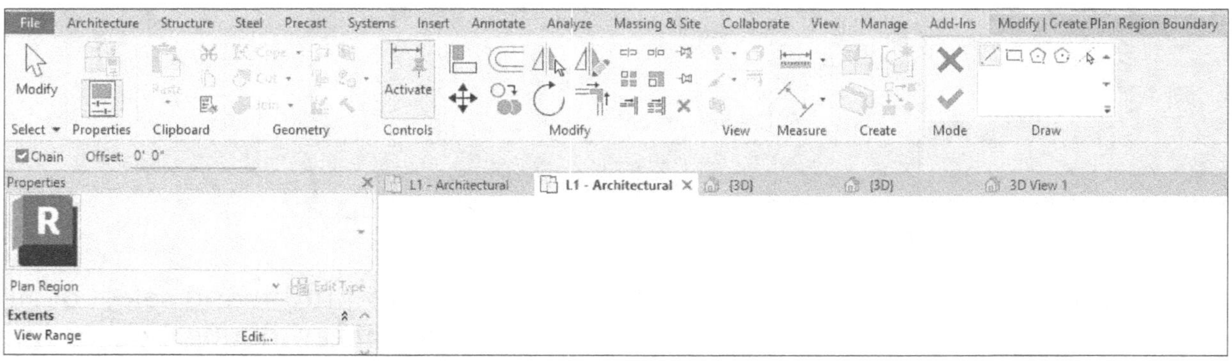

Figure-68. Options to create plan region boundary

- Create the closed boundary of plan region at desired location and specify desired offset value in **Options Bar**.
- Click on the **OK** button from the **Mode** panel in the contextual tab. The **Modify|Plan Region** contextual tab will be displayed with plan region created; refer to Figure-69.

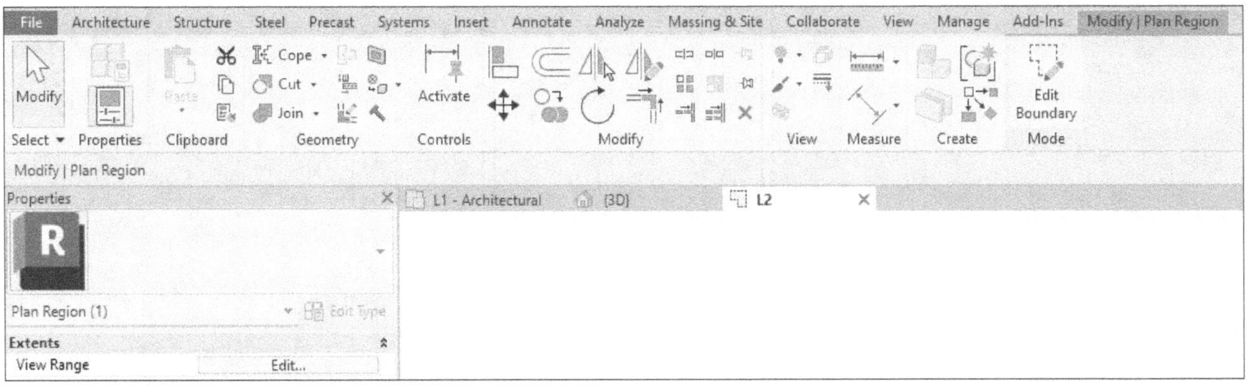

Figure-69. Modify Plan Region contextual tab

- Click on the **View Range** button from the **Extents** section in the **Properties Pallete** of **Modify|Plan Region** contextual tab in the **Ribbon**. The **View Range** dialog box will be displayed; refer to Figure-70.

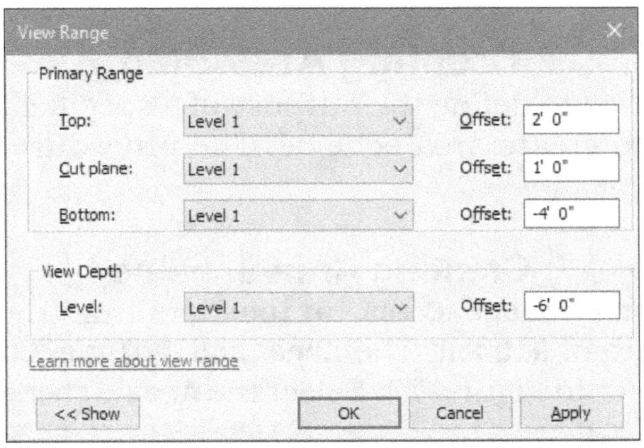

Figure-70. View Range dialog box

- Set desired values in various edit boxes of the dialog box. Make sure to set the height value for cut plane at the level where elements to be displayed in plan region are available. Like if window is available at 1' from bottom and has a height of 3' then you can create cut plane at 2'.
- Set desired value in **Top** and **Bottom** edit boxes to define top and bottom level of view region.
- Click on the **<<Show** button to check the sample view range.
- After setting desired parameters, click on the **OK** button from the dialog box. The plan region will be created; refer to Figure-71. Press **ESC** to exit the tool.

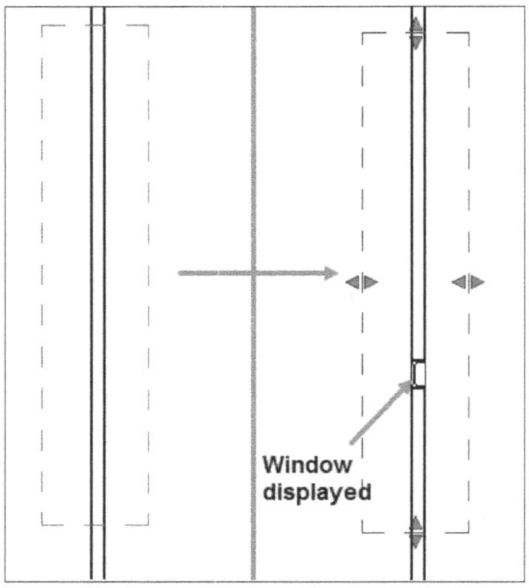

Figure-71. Plan region created

Creating Area Plan

The **Area Plan** tool is used to define the purpose of a specified region. Before creating area plans, you need to create area scheme. The procedure to create area scheme and area plan is given next.

Creating Area Scheme

- Click on the **Area and Volume Computations** tool from the **Room & Area** panel in the **Architecture** tab of **Ribbon**. The **Area and Volume Computations** dialog box will be displayed; refer to Figure-72. Select the **Area Schemes** tab in the dialog box.

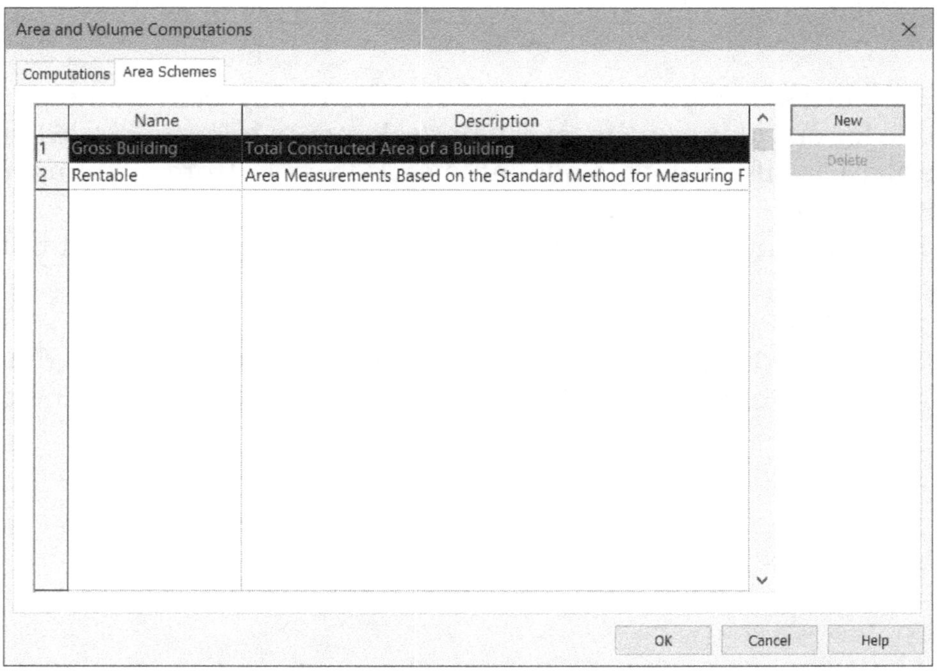

Figure-72. Area and Volume Computations dialog box

- Click on the **New** button from the dialog box. The **Area Scheme 1** will be added in the table; refer to Figure-73.

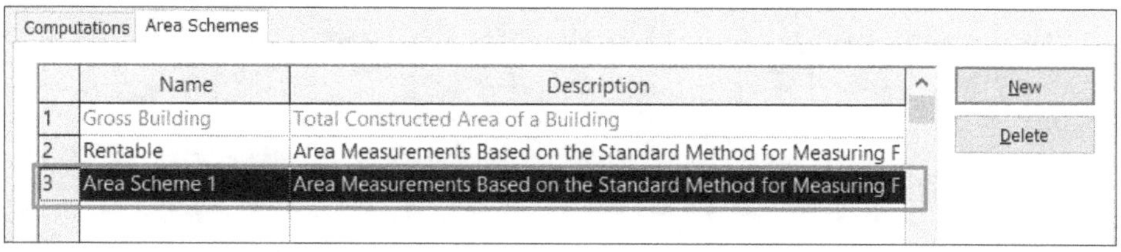

Figure-73. Area scheme added

- Click in the **Name** column and specify desired name for area scheme. Similarly, specify desired description.
- Similarly, you can create more area schemes by using the **New** button.
- Click on the **OK** button from the dialog box to create area schemes.

Creating Area Plan

- Click on the **Area Plan** tool from the **Plan Views** drop-down in the **View** tab of **Ribbon**. The **New Area Plan** dialog box will be displayed; refer to Figure-74.

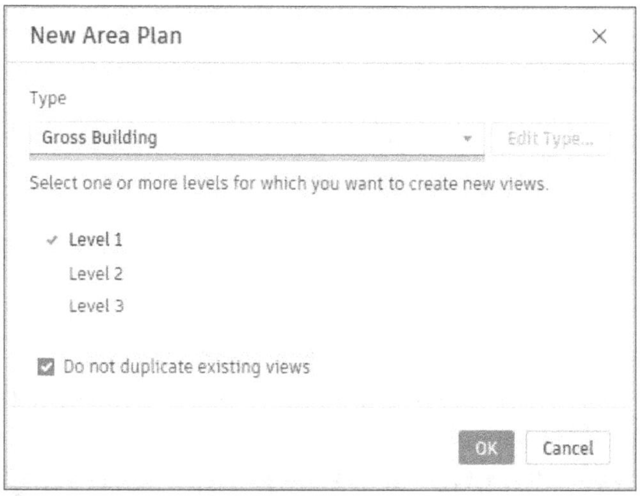

Figure-74. New Area Plan dialog box

- Select desired option from the drop-down. You will find all the area schemes earlier created.
- Select desired level from the list box and click on the **OK** button. A message box will be displayed; refer to Figure-75.

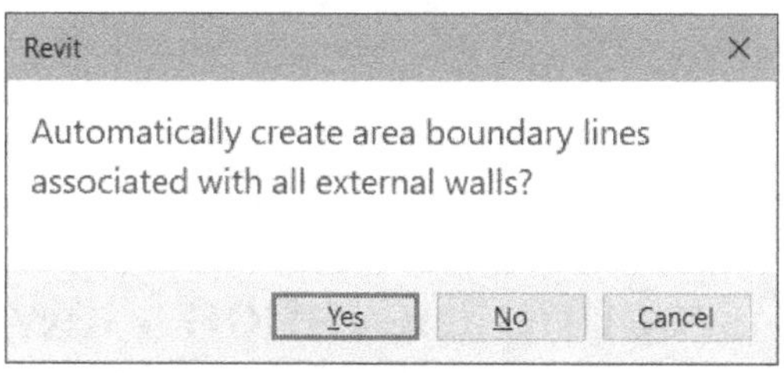

Figure-75. Message box

- If you want to create area boundary lines automatically along the external walls then click on the **Yes** button. If you want to create the area boundaries manually then click on the **No** button.

Creating Area Boundaries Manually

- Click on the **Area Boundary** tool from the **Room & Area** panel in the **Architecture** tab of **Ribbon**. The options to create area boundary will be displayed; refer to Figure-76.

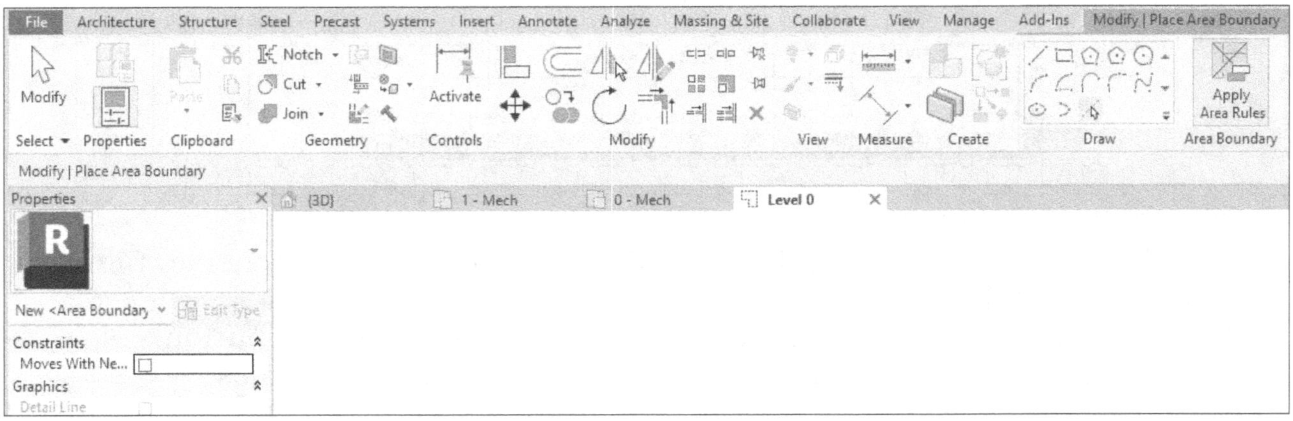

Figure-76. Options to place area boundary

- Select desired sketching tool and create the area boundaries; refer to Figure-77.

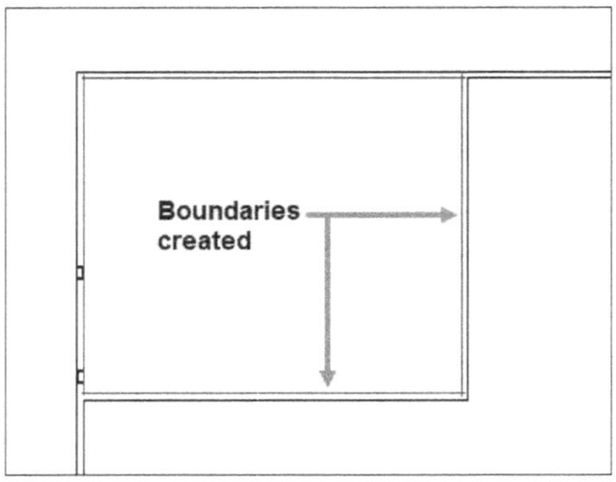

Figure-77. Area boundaries created

- You can apply the area tag as discussed in previous chapters.

CREATING ELEVATION VIEWS

The tools in the **Elevation** drop-down are used to create different types of elevation views; refer to Figure-78. These tools are discussed next.

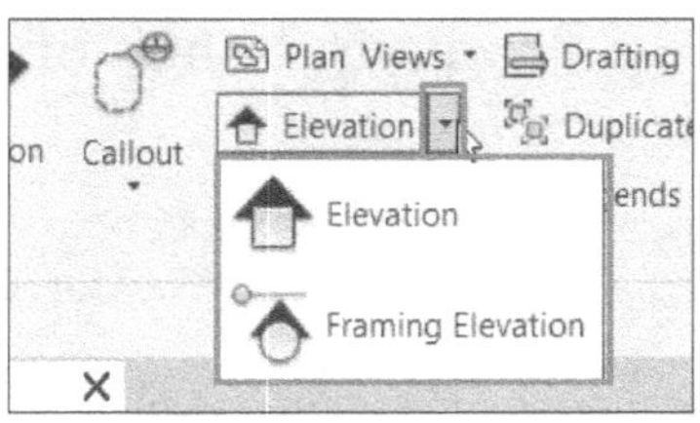

Figure-78. Elevation drop-down

Creating Elevation View

The **Elevation** tool is used to create inside or outside elevation view of the building. The procedure to use this tool is given next.

- Click on the **Elevation** tool from the **Elevation** drop-down in the **Create** panel of **View** tab in the **Ribbon**. The options to create elevation view will be displayed and elevation symbol will get attached to cursor; refer to Figure-79.

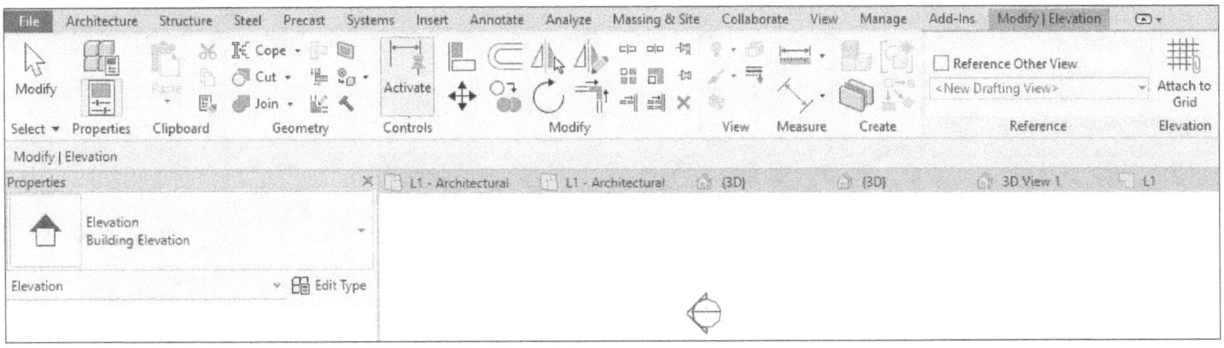

Figure-79. Options to create elevation

- Click at desired location to place the elevation mark. The elevation view will be created; refer to Figure-80.

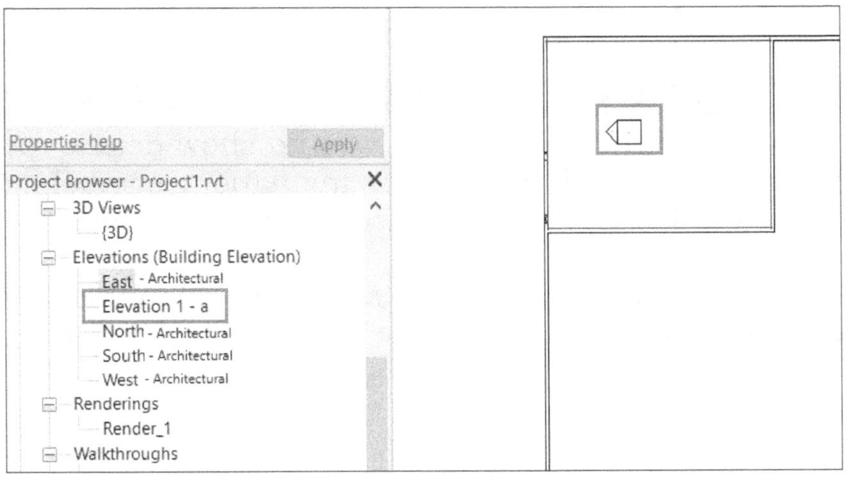

Figure-80. Elevation created

- Double-click on newly created elevation from the **Project Browser**.

Creating Framing Elevation

The **Framing Elevation** tool is used to create elevation view for frame members. The procedure to use this tool is given next.

- Select the **Framing Elevation** tool from the **Elevation** drop-down in the **Create** panel of **View** tab in the **Ribbon**. The options to create framing elevation will be displayed and you will be asked to select grid or reference plane.
- Click at desired location on grid or reference plane. The elevation will be created under Elevations category; refer to Figure-81.

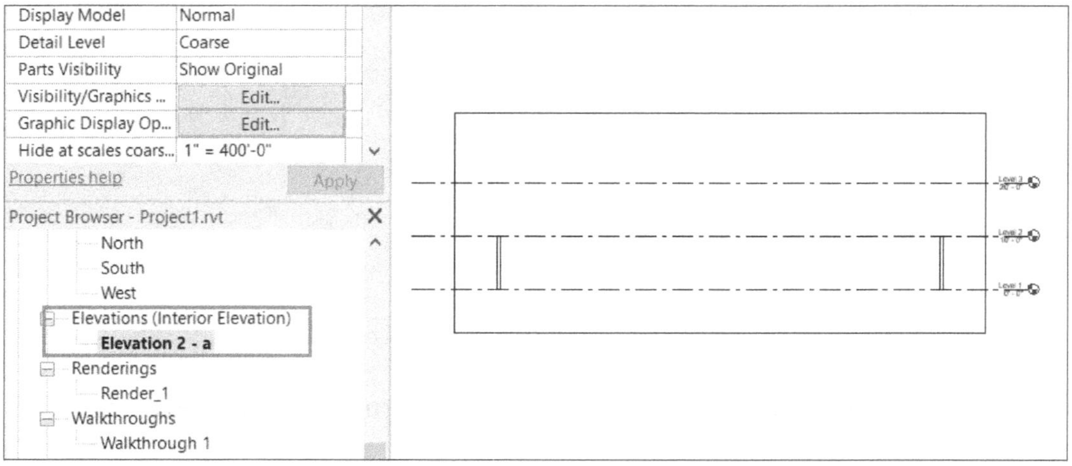

Figure-81. Interior elevation created

CREATING DRAFTING VIEW

The **Drafting View** tool is used to create a view to show details of building which are not directly associated with model like insulation, symbols, legends, detail components, and so on. The procedure to use this tool is given next.

- Click on the **Drafting View** tool from the **Create** panel in the **View** tab of **Ribbon**. The **New Drafting View** dialog box will be displayed; refer to Figure-82.

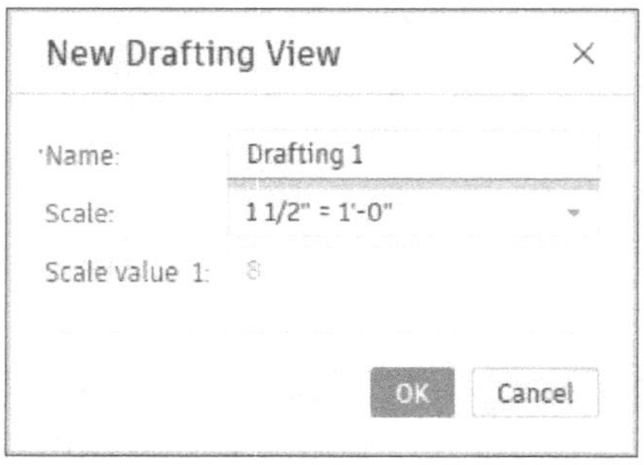

Figure-82. New Drafting View dialog box

- Set desired name and scale in the dialog box, and click on the **OK** button. The drafting view will be displayed; refer to Figure-83.

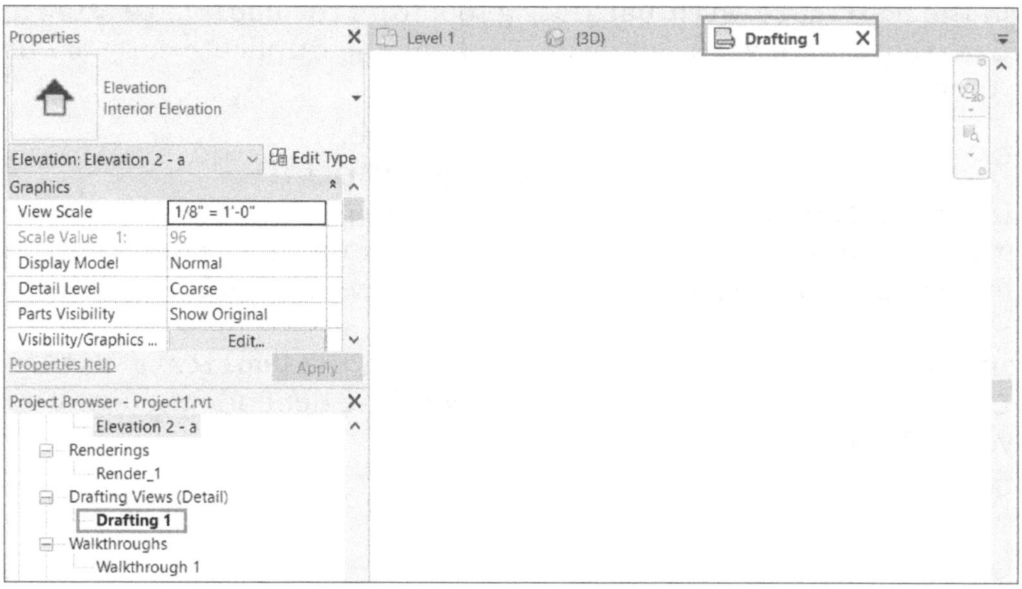

Figure-83. Drafting view created

- Copy the elements which are important for drafting view and use the tools in **Annotate** tab of the **Ribbon** to create drafting.

CREATING DUPLICATE VIEWS

The tools in **Duplicate View** drop-down are used to create duplicate view of selected view with/without annotations, dimensions, and detail elements; refer to Figure-84. These tools are discussed next.

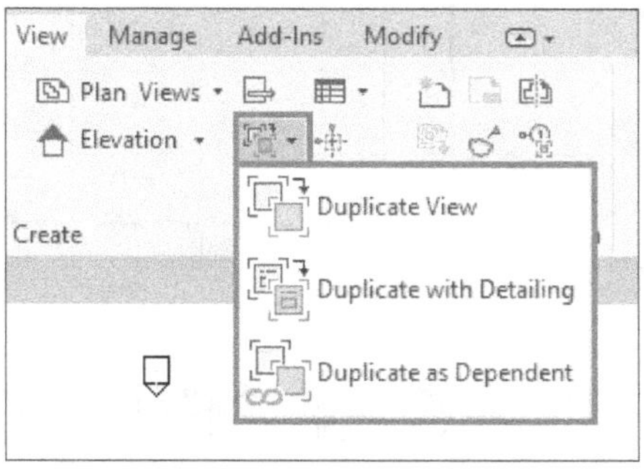

Figure-84. Duplicate View drop-down

Creating Duplicate View

The **Duplicate View** tool is used to create copy of selected view without annotations. The procedure to use this tool is given next.

- Click on the **Duplicate View** tool from the **Duplicate View** drop-down in the **Create** panel of **View** tab in the **Ribbon**. The copy of current view will be created.

Duplicate with Detailing

The **Duplicate with Detailing** tool is used to create duplicate view of current view with detailing elements like annotations, detail components, detail lines, and so on. The procedure to use this tool is given next.

- Click on the **Duplicate with Detailing** tool from the **Duplicate View** drop-down in the **Create** panel of **View** tab in the **Ribbon**. The duplicate copy of current view will be created with annotations applied.

Duplicate as Dependent

The **Duplicate as Dependent** tool is used to create a duplicate view of current view dependent on original view. Any changes made in original view are automatically reflected in the duplicate view. The procedure to use this tool is given next.

- Click on the **Duplicate as Dependent** tool from the **Duplicate View** drop-down in the **Create** panel of **View** tab in the **Ribbon**. The dependent copy of view will be displayed; refer to Figure-85.

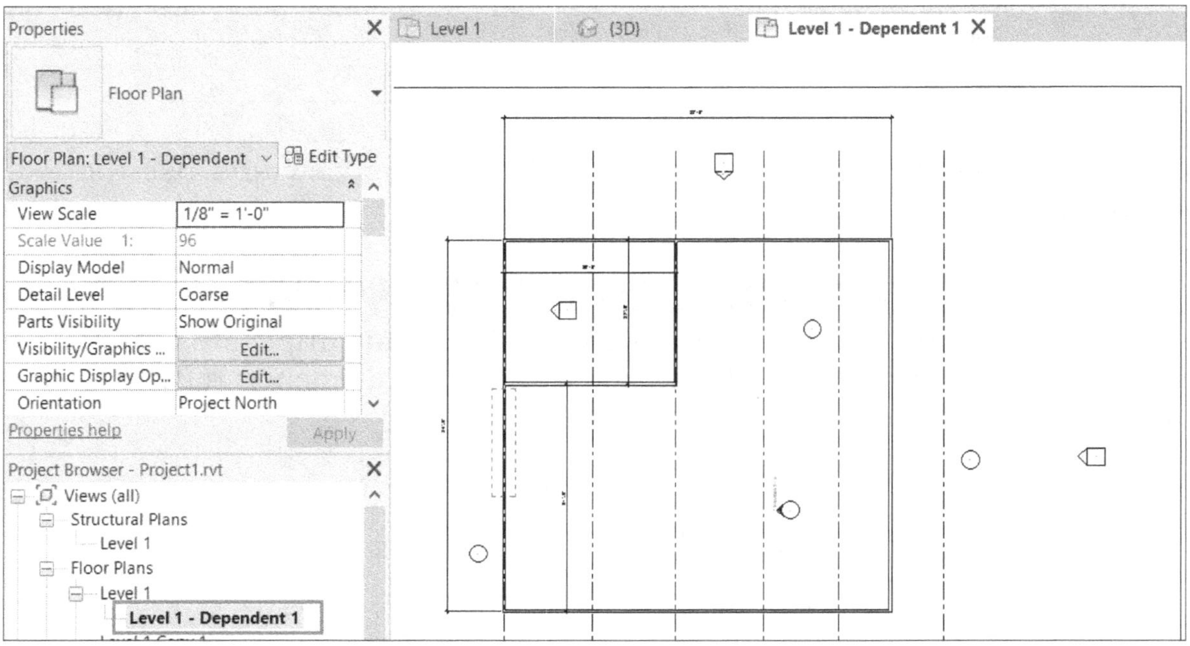

Figure-85. Dependent copy created

CREATING LEGEND VIEW

The **Legend** tool is used to create legend view where you can define legend for various detail components. The procedure to use this tool is given next.

- Click on the **Legend** tool from the **Legends** drop-down in the **Create** panel of **View** tab in the **Ribbon**. The **New Legend View** dialog box will be displayed.
- Set desired parameters and click on the **OK** button. The legend view will be created.
- Place desired detail components and apply annotations using the tools in the **Annotate** tab of **Ribbon**; refer to Figure-86.

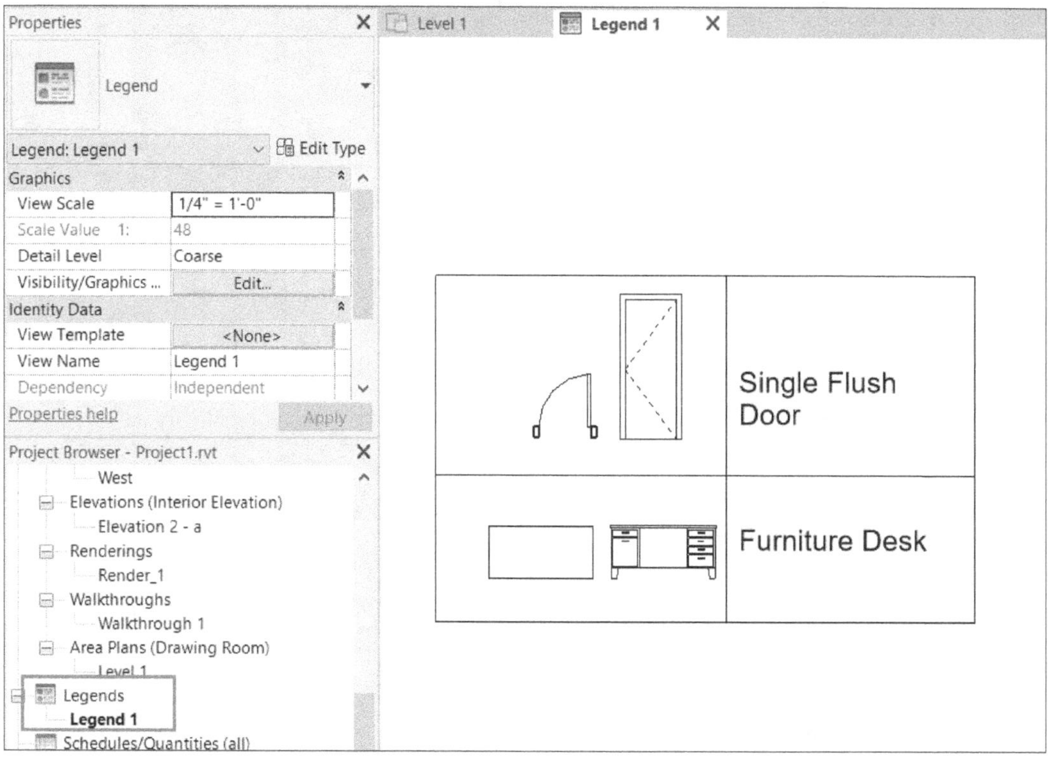

Figure-86. Legend view created

CREATING KEYNOTE LEGEND

The **Keynote Legend** tool is used to create legend view in which all the keynotes of project are described. The procedure to use this tool is given next.

- Click on the **Keynote Legend** tool from the **Legends** drop-down in the **Create** panel of **View** tab in the **Ribbon**. The **New Keynote Legend** dialog box will be displayed; refer to Figure-87.

Figure-87. New Keynote Legend dialog box

- Specify desired name for view in the edit box and click on the **OK** button. The **Keynote Legend Properties** dialog box will be displayed; refer to Figure-88.

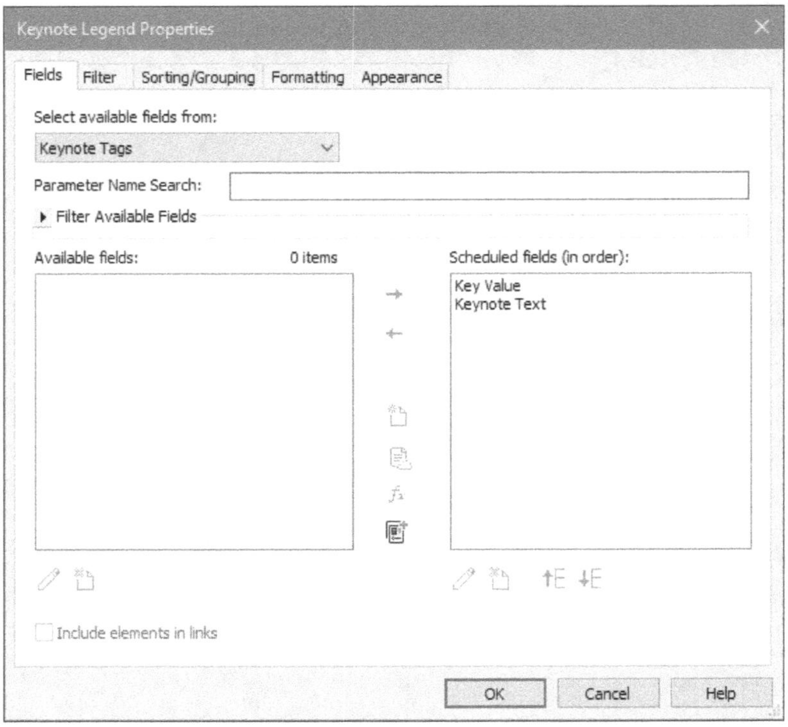

Figure-88. Keynote Legend Properties dialog box

- Set desired parameters in the dialog box and click on the **OK** button. The keynote legend table will be created; refer to Figure-89.

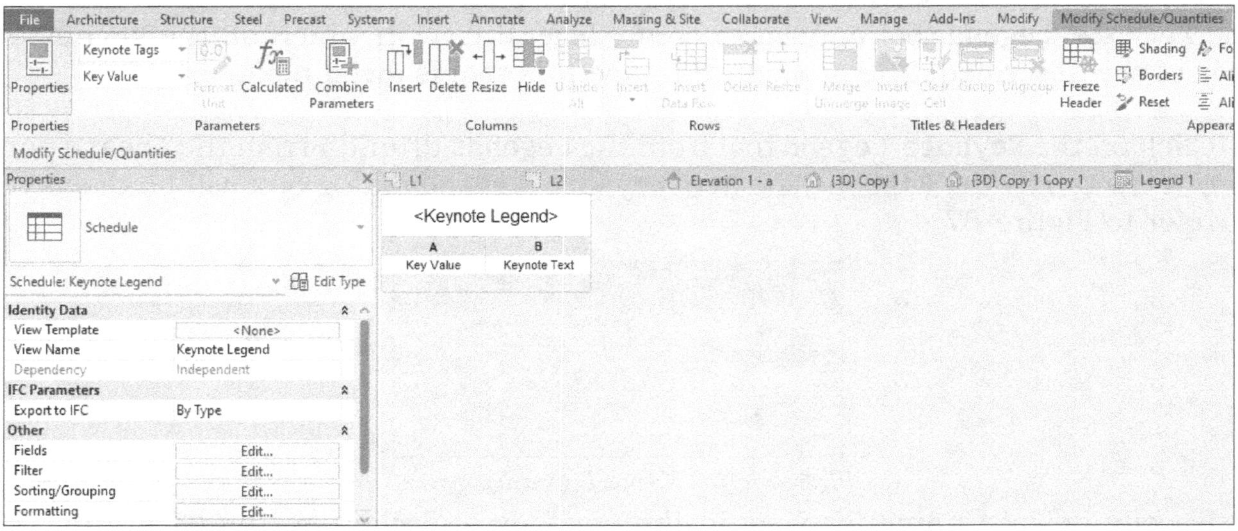

Figure-89. Keynote legend table created

CREATING SCHEDULES

The tools in the **Schedules** drop-down are used to create different types of schedules and tables in the view; refer to Figure-90. Various tools in this drop-down are discussed next.

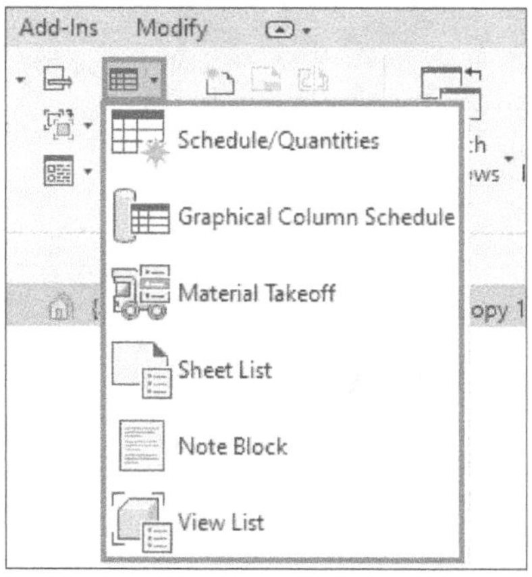

Figure-90. Schedules drop-down

Creating Schedules/Quantities

The **Schedule/Quantities** tool is used to create a table of objects used in the model. The procedure to use this tool is given next.

- Click on the **Schedule/Quantities** tool from the **Schedules** drop-down in the **Create** panel of **View** tab in the **Ribbon**. The **New Schedule** dialog box will be displayed; refer to Figure-91.

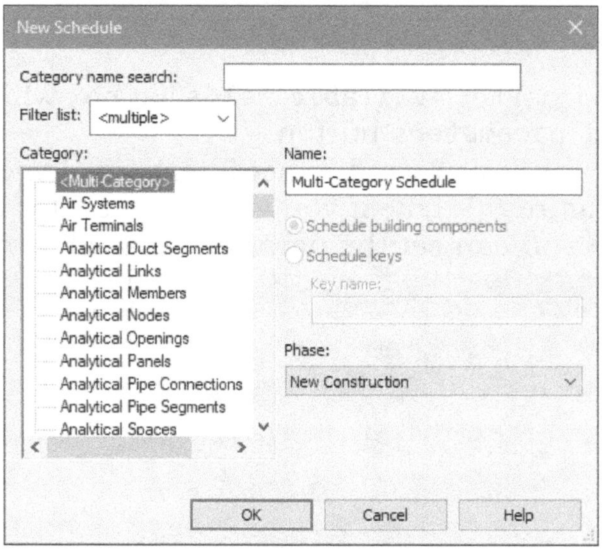

Figure-91. New Schedule dialog box

- Select desired category from the **Category** list box and click on the **OK** button. The **Schedule Properties** dialog box will be displayed; refer to Figure-92.

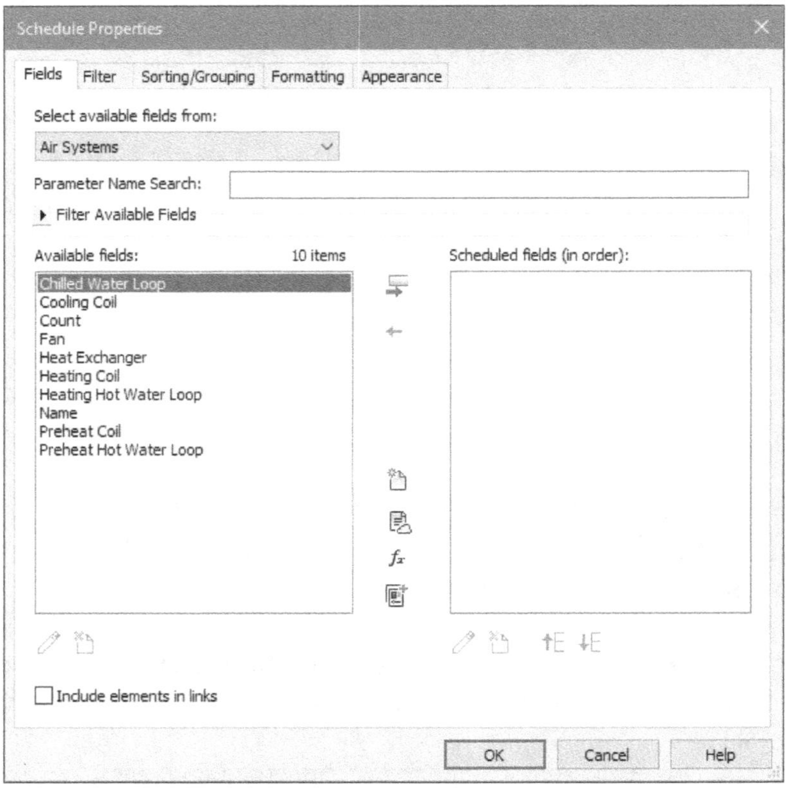

Figure-92. Schedule Properties dialog box

- Select desired fields from the **Available fields** list box while holding the **CTRL** key and click on the **Add parameters** button.
- Click on the **Filter** tab if you want to set filters for elements to be added in the schedule; refer to Figure-93. Like if you want to set filter for height of door to be greater than 2' then you can set the parameters as shown in Figure-94.

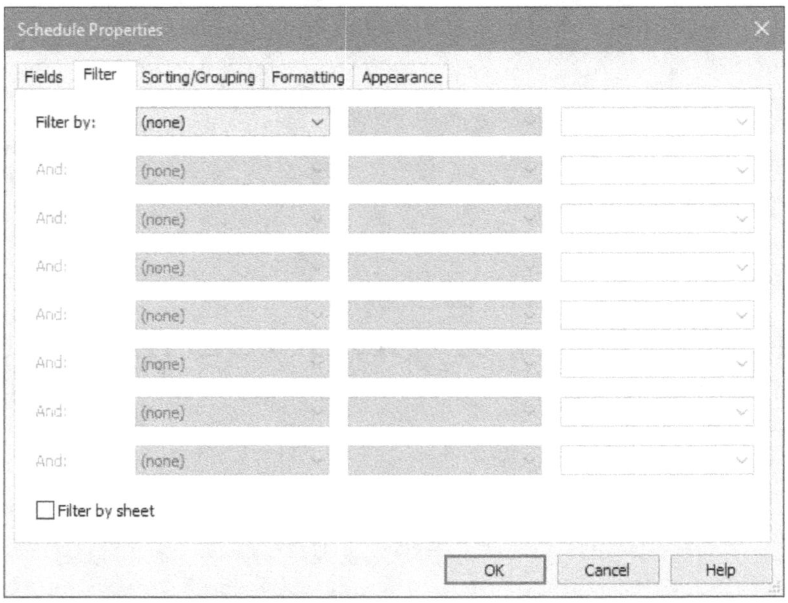

Figure-93. Filter tab in Schedule Properties dialog box

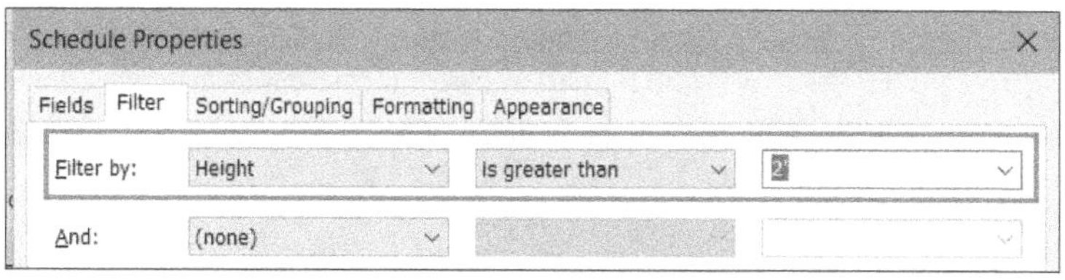

Figure-94. Setting filter

- Click on the **Sorting/Grouping** tab of dialog box to define sorting order of elements in schedule. Set desired option in the **Sort by** drop-down and set the other parameters as desired.
- Similarly, you can set other parameters in **Formatting** and **Appearance** tabs of the dialog box.
- After setting desired parameters, click on the **OK** button. The schedule will be created; refer to Figure-95.

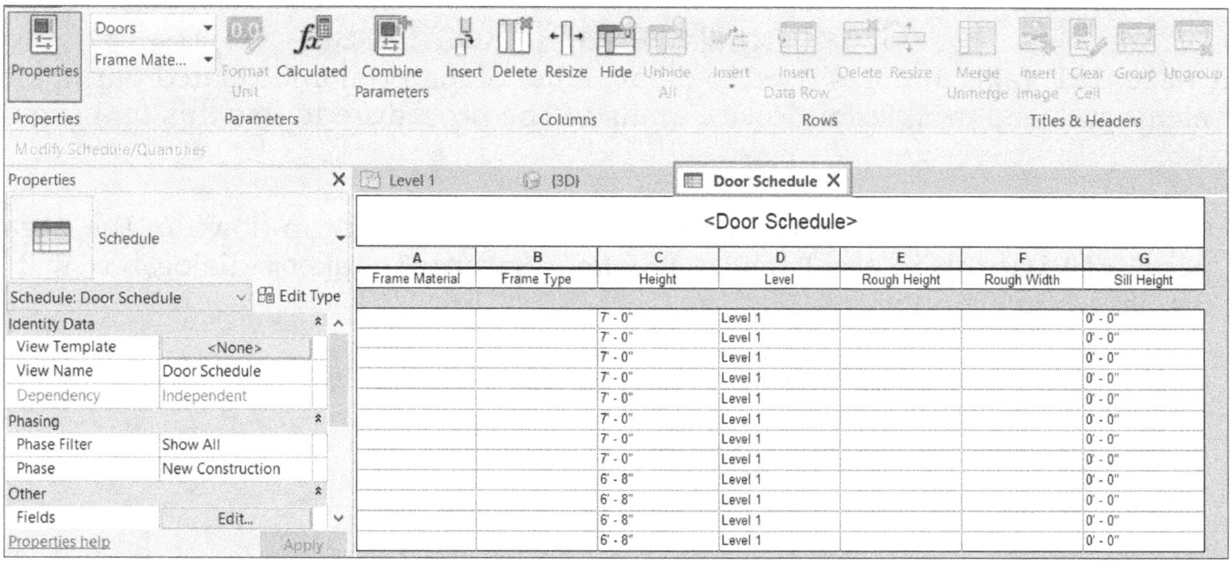

Figure-95. Door schedule

Creating Graphical Column Schedule

The **Graphical Column Schedule** tool is used to create a schedule of columns used in the Project using graphical format. The procedure to use this tool is given next.

- Open the structural drawing for which you want to create column schedule and click on the **Graphical Column Schedule** tool from the **Schedules** drop-down of **Create** panel in the **Ribbon**. The graphical column schedule will be created; refer to Figure-96. Make sure the columns are placed on grid intersections otherwise they will not be included in the schedule.

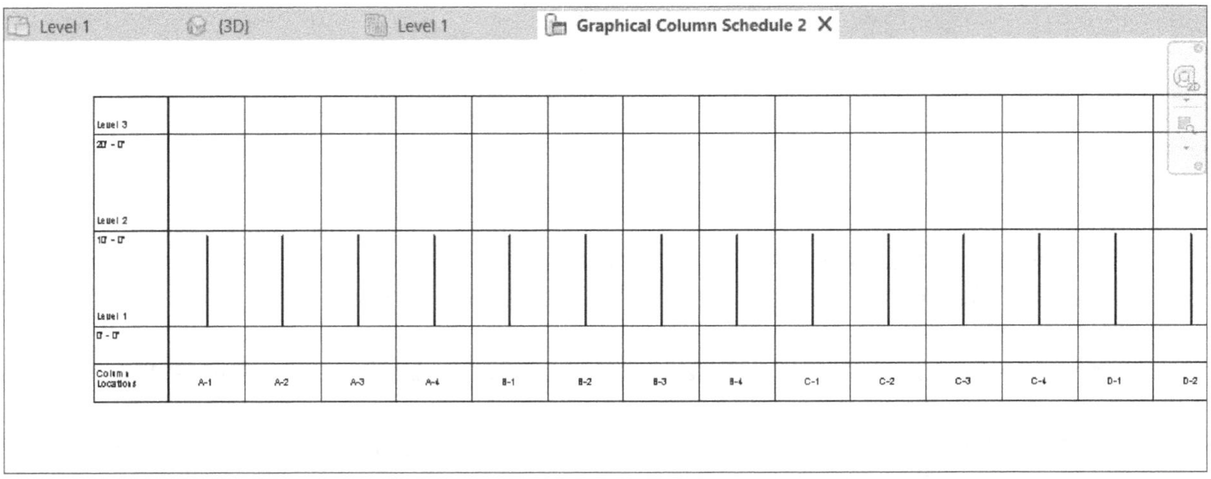

Figure-96. Graphical column schedule created

Creating Material Takeoff List

The **Material Takeoff** tool is used to create a list of material and related parameters for elements used in different Revit Families. The procedure to use this tool is given next.

- Click on the **Material Takeoff** tool from the **Schedules** drop-down in the **Create** panel of **View** tab in the **Ribbon**. The **New Material Takeoff** dialog box will be displayed; refer to Figure-97.

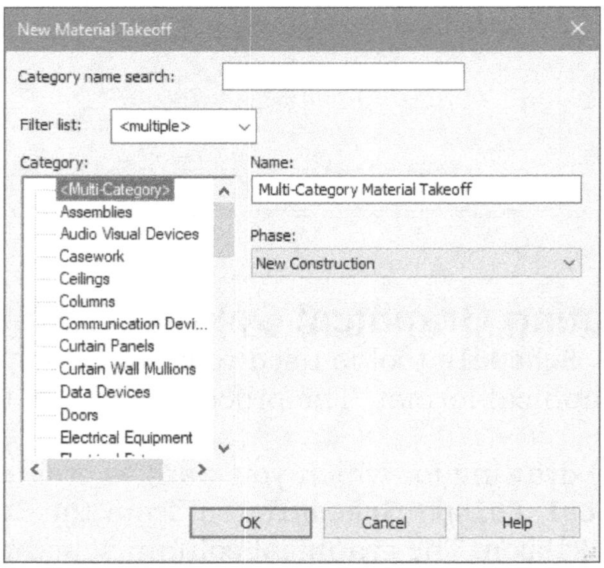

Figure-97. New Material Takeoff dialog box

- Select desired category from the dialog box and set the other parameters as desired. Click on the **OK** button from the dialog box. The **Material Takeoff Properties** dialog box will be displayed; refer to Figure-98.

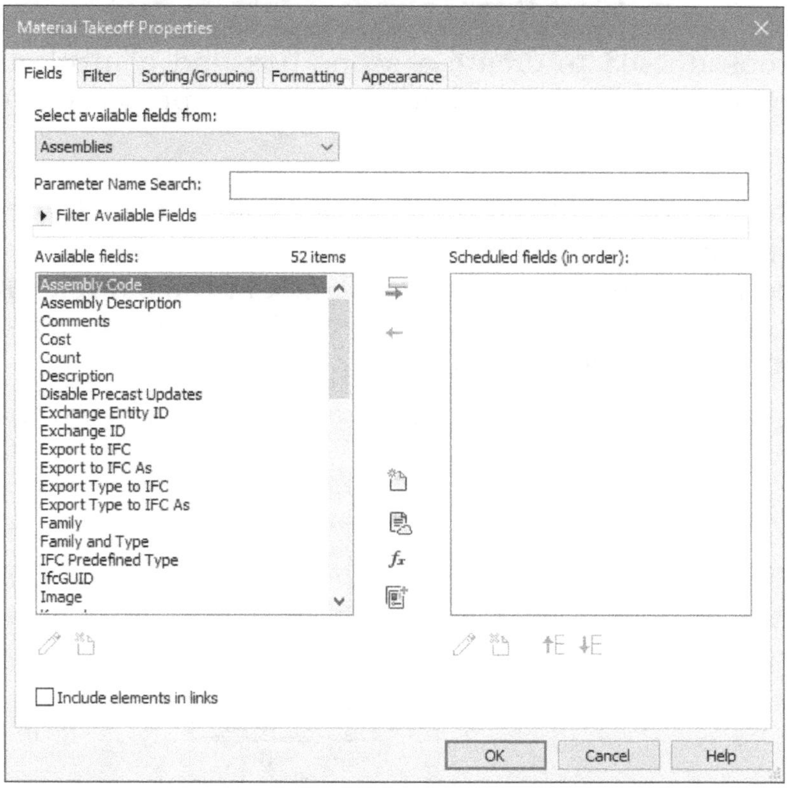

Figure-98. Material Takeoff Properties dialog box

- Select desired fields to be included in the schedule like assembly code, material name, and so on; and click on the **Add parameter(s)** button. The selected fields will be included in the schedule.
- Click on the **OK** button from the dialog box. The material takeoff list will be created; refer to Figure-99.

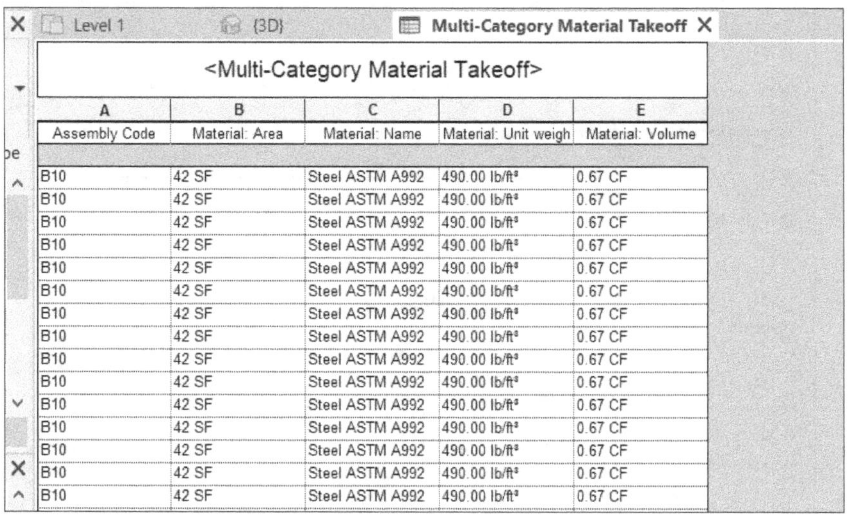

Figure-99. Material takeoff list created

You can use the **Sheet List**, **Note Block**, and **View List** tools in the same way as other tools of **Schedules** drop-down are discussed.

CREATING SCOPE BOX

The **Scope Box** tool is used to create a scope box and control visibility of datum elements within specified scope box boundaries. The procedure to use this tool is given next.

- Click on the **Scope Box** tool from the **Create** panel in the **View** tab of **Ribbon**. You will be asked to draw a scope box.
- Specify desired name and height for scope box in the **Options Bar**.
- Create the boundary of scope box as desired. The related options will be displayed in the **Properties Palette**; refer to Figure-100.

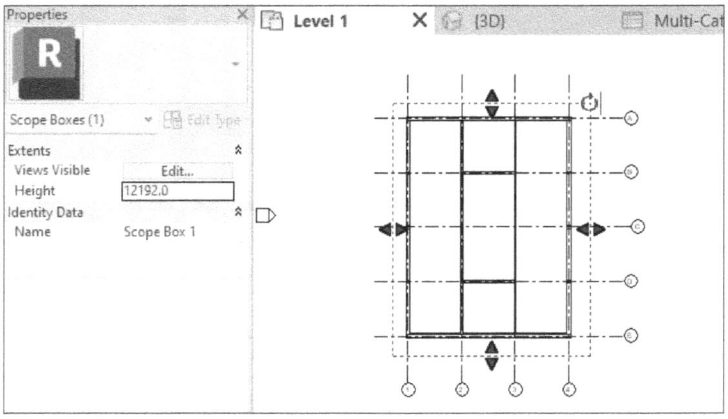

Figure-100. Options for scope box

- Click on the **Edit** button for **Views Visible** field in the **Properties Palette**. The **Scope Box Views Visible** dialog box will be displayed; refer to Figure-101.

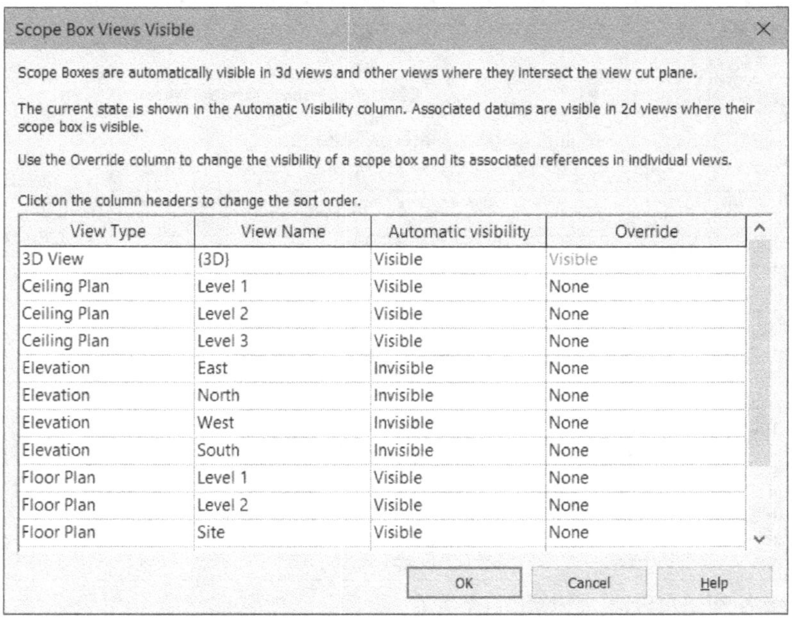

Figure-101. Scope Box Views Visible dialog box

- Set desired option in **Override** column for desired view and click on the **OK** button from the dialog box. The scope box will be displayed in different views based on specified settings.

CREATING SHEETS

The **Sheet** tool is used to add a sheet to document set. The procedure to use this tool is given next.

- Click on the **Sheet** tool from the **Sheet Composition** panel in the **View** tab of **Ribbon**. The **New Sheet** dialog box will be displayed; refer to Figure-102.

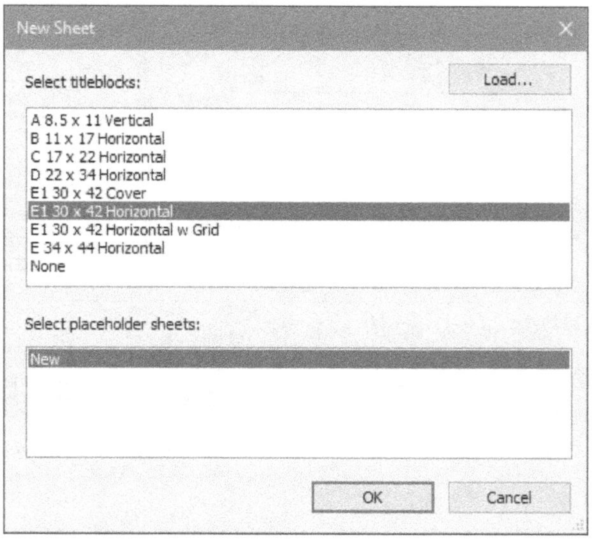

Figure-102. New Sheet dialog box

- Click on the **Load** button from the dialog box to load desired template. The **Load Family** dialog box will be displayed; refer to Figure-103.

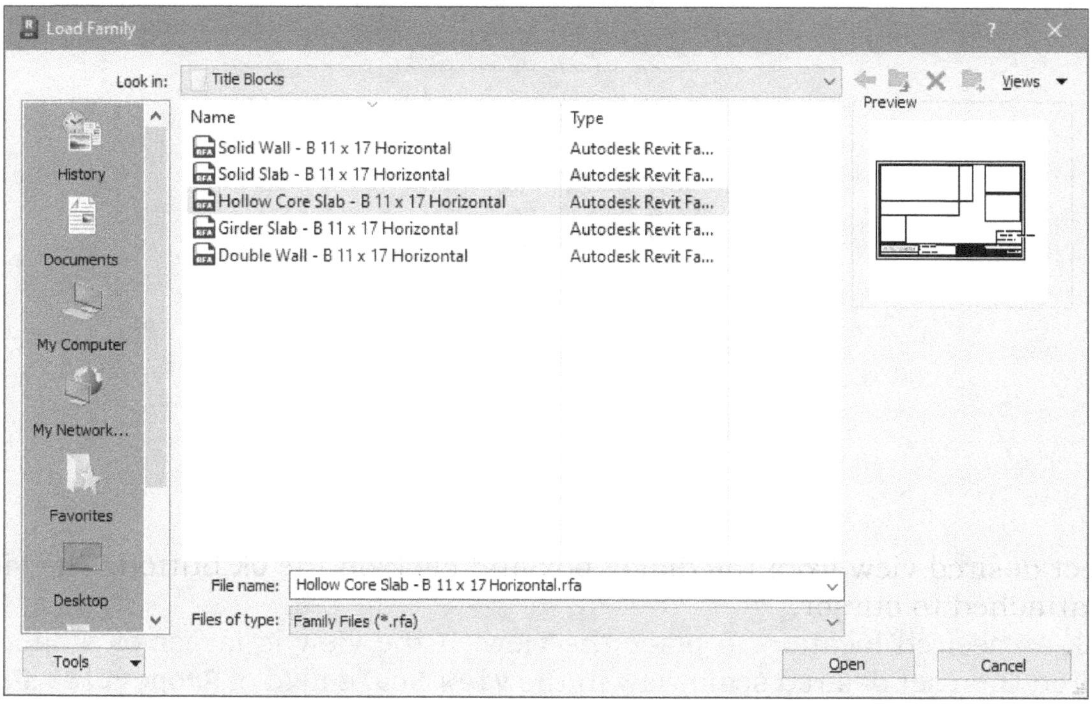

Figure-103. Load Family dialog box

- Select desired template from the dialog box and click on the **Open** button. The new title block will be added in the **Select titleblocks** list.
- Select desired title block placeholder sheet from the dialog box and click on the **OK** button. The sheet will be created; refer to Figure-104.

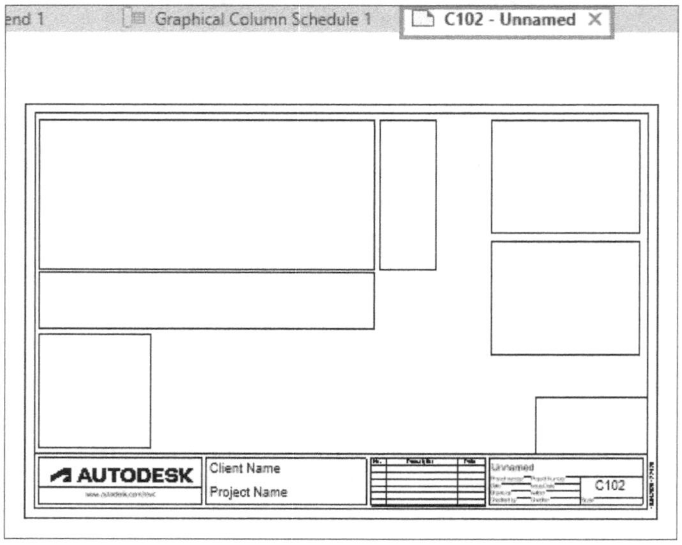

Figure-104. Sheet created

PLACING VIEW IN SHEET

The **Place View** tool is used to place selected view in the sheet. The procedure to use this tool is given next.

- Click on the **Place View** tool from the **Sheet Composition** panel in the **View** tab of **Ribbon**. The **Select View** dialog box will be displayed; refer to Figure-105.

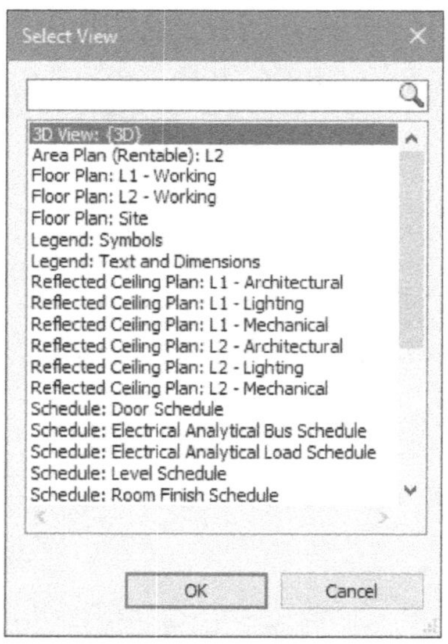

Figure-105. Select View dialog box

- Select desired view from the dialog box and click on the **OK** button. The view will get attached to cursor.
- Click at desired location to place the view. If the view is larger or smaller than desired then set desired scale view in the **View Scale** field of **Properties Palette**; refer to Figure-106.

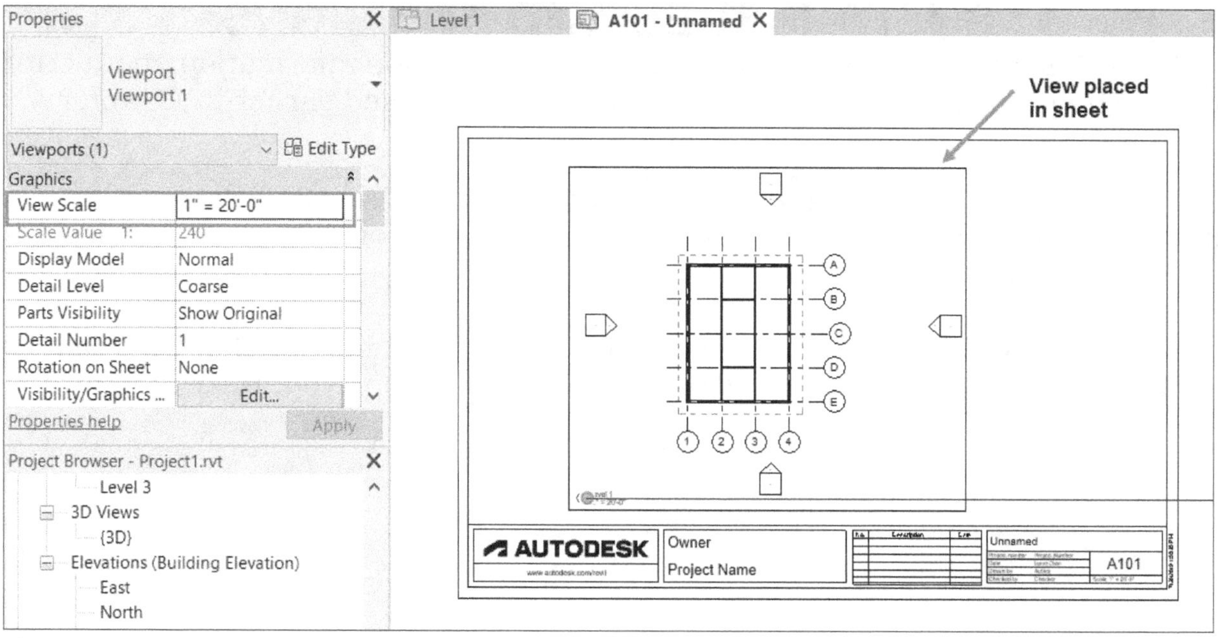

Figure-106. Placing view and defining view scale

- Similarly, set the other parameters as desired in the **Properties Palette** and click on the **Apply** button.

PLACING TITLE BLOCK

The **Title Block** tool is used to place desired title block in the sheet. The procedure to use this tool is given next.

- Click on the **Title Block** tool from the **Sheet Composition** panel in the **View** tab of **Ribbon**. The title block will get attached to cursor and related options will be displayed in the **Properties Palette**; refer to Figure-107.

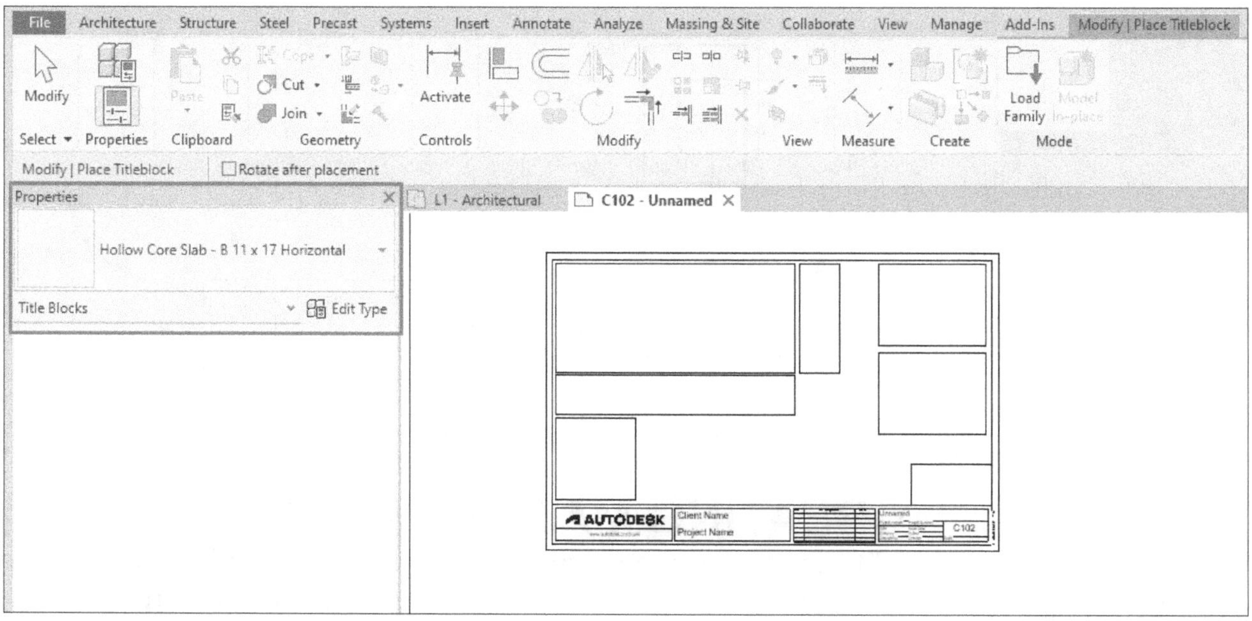

Figure-107. Options for placing title block

- Select desired title block from the drop-down at the top in the **Properties Palette** and click at desired location to place the title block.

SHEET ISSUES AND REVISIONS

The **Sheet Issues/Revisions** tool is used to specify revision information about current project. The procedure to use this tool has been discussed earlier in Chapter 4.

CREATING GUIDE GRID

The **Guide Grid** tool is used to create grids in the sheet for reference. The procedure to use this tool is given next.

- Click on the **Guide Grid** tool from the **Sheet Composition** panel in the **View** tab of **Ribbon**. The **Assign Guide Grid** dialog box will be displayed; refer to Figure-108.

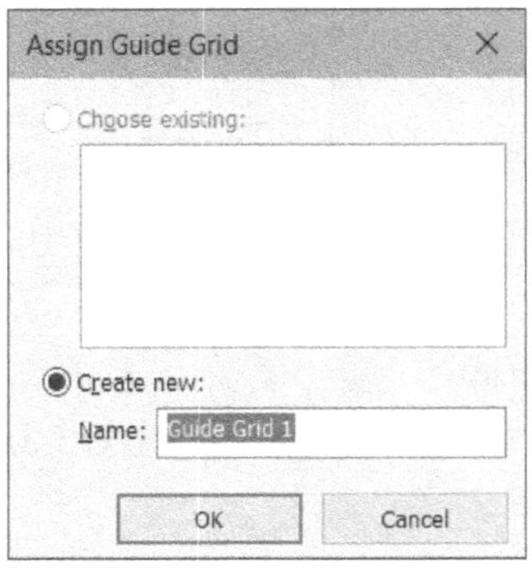

Figure-108. Assign Guide Grid dialog box

- Specify desired name for guide grid in the **Name** edit box and click on the **OK** button. The guide grid lines will be created; refer to Figure-109.

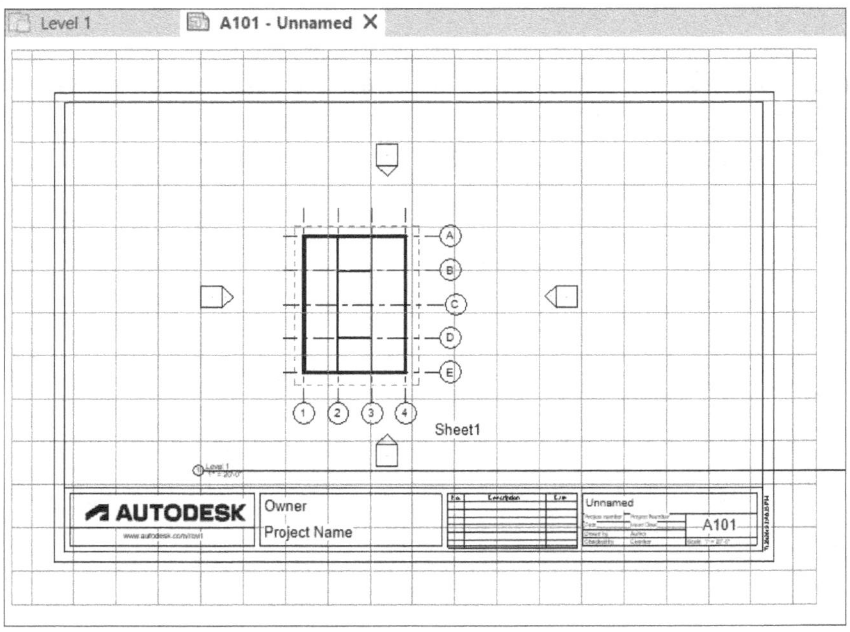

Figure-109. Guide grids created

CREATING MATCHLINE

The **Matchline** tool is used to create line in elevation or plan view to define the location where splitting of views occurred. The procedure to use this tool is given next.

- Create a duplicate view as dependent in the project and crop it to create split view from the primary view; refer to Figure-110.

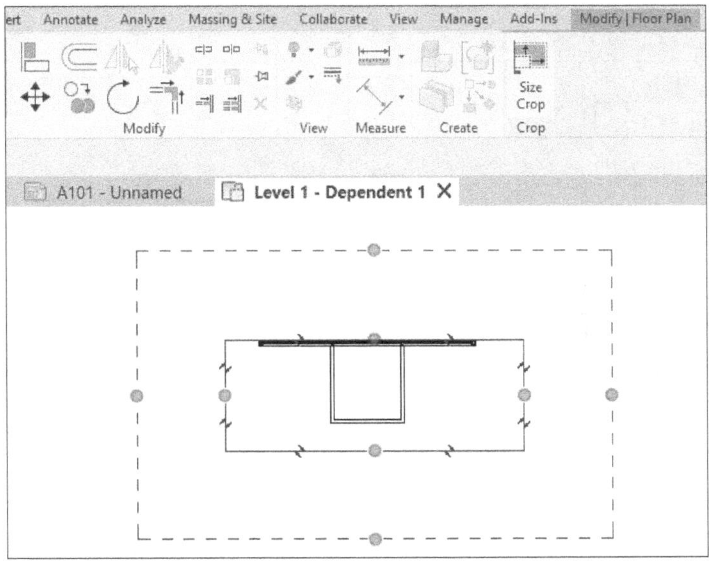

Figure-110. Dependent view created

- Click on the **Matchline** tool from the **Sheet Composition** panel in the **View** tab of **Ribbon**. You will be asked to specify start point of matchline and the options to create line will be displayed; refer to Figure-111.

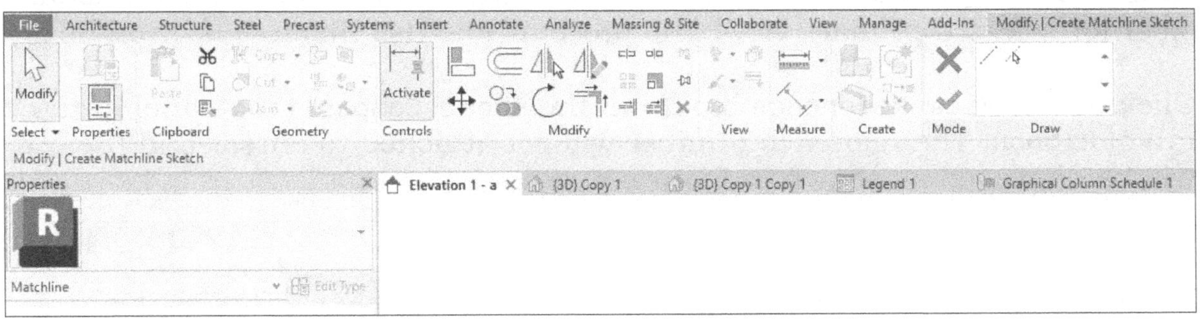

Figure-111. Options to create matchline sketch

- Create desired line sketch for matchline at the location where views split; refer to Figure-112.

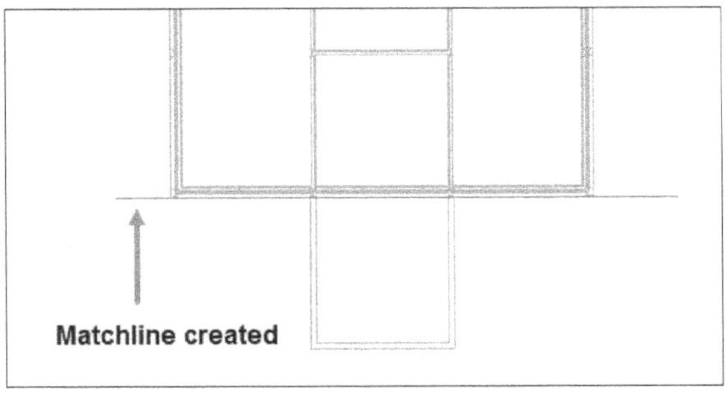

Figure-112. Matchline created

- Click on the **OK** button from the **Modify|Create Matchline Sketch** contextual tab in the **Ribbon**. The matchline will be created; refer to Figure-113.

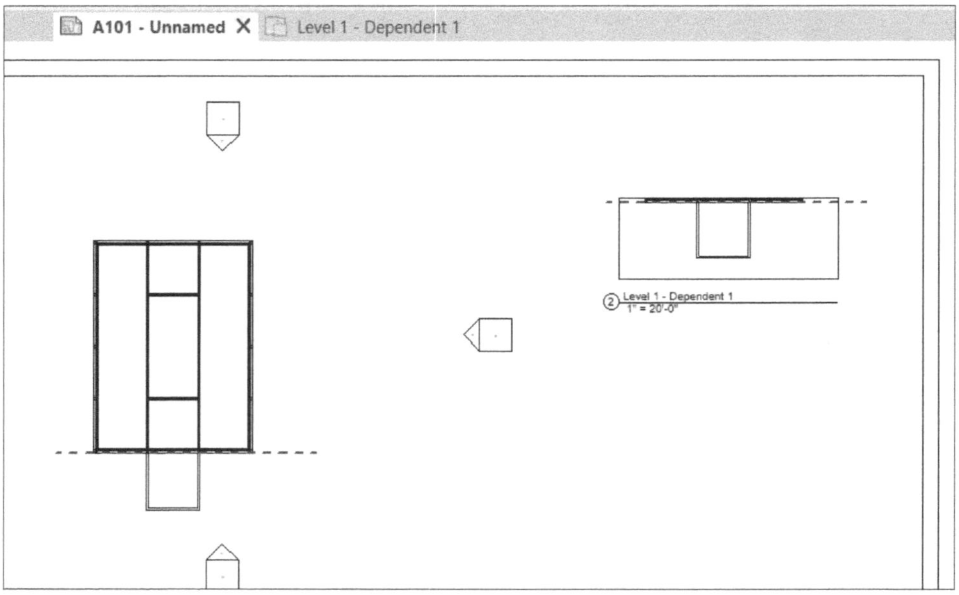

Figure-113. Matchline created in views

PLACING VIEW REFERENCE

The **View Reference** tool is used to place indicator of sheet number and detail view number for selected primary view. The procedure to use this tool is given next.

- Click on the **View Reference** tool from the **Sheet Composition** panel in the **View** tab of **Ribbon**. The reference number will get attached to cursor and the options will be displayed as shown in Figure-114.

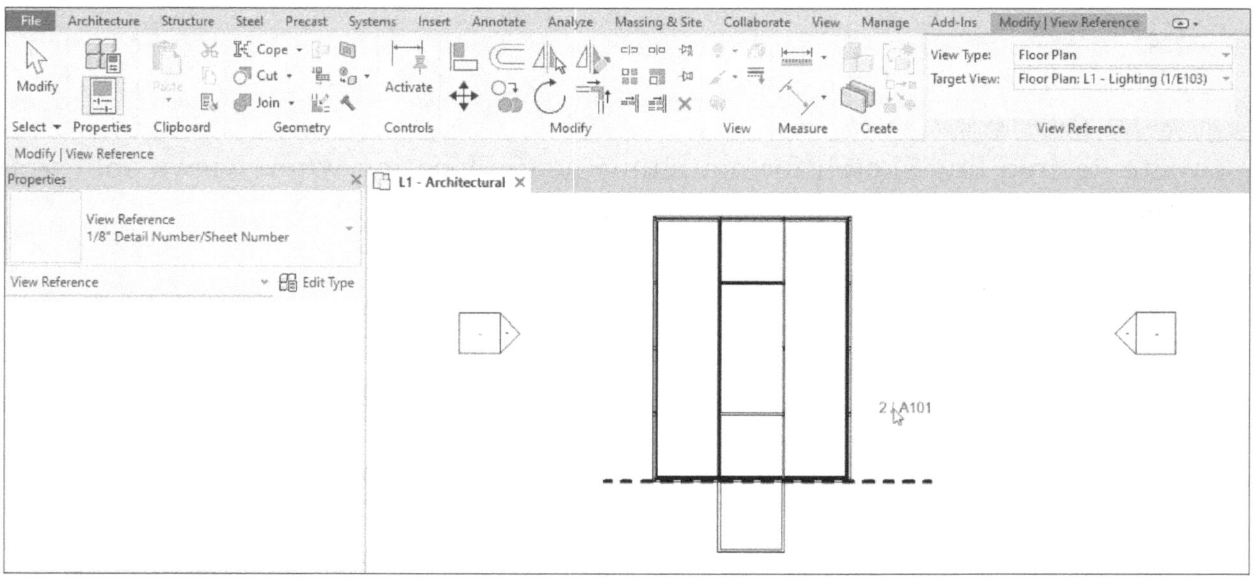

Figure-114. Options to place view reference

- Click at desired location to place the marker.

ACTIVATING AND DEACTIVATING VIEWS IN SHEETS

To activate a view for modification, double-click on the viewport in sheet.

To deactivate a view, click on the **Deactivate View** tool from the **Viewports** drop-down in the **Sheet Composition** panel of **View** tab in the **Ribbon**; refer to Figure-115.

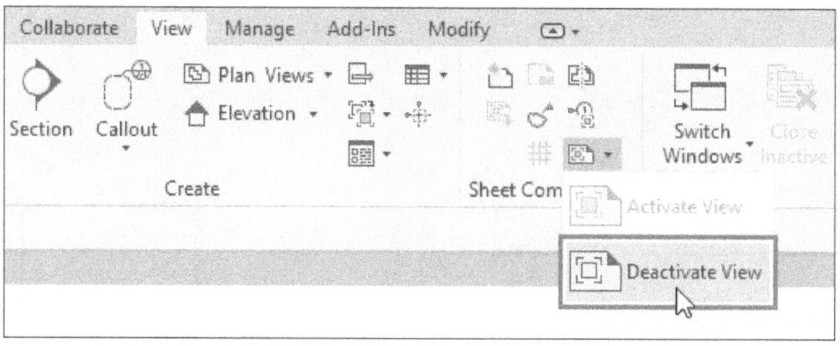

Figure-115. Deactivate View tool

MANAGING WINDOWS

The tools in the **Windows** panel are used to arrange views in the application window; refer to Figure-116.

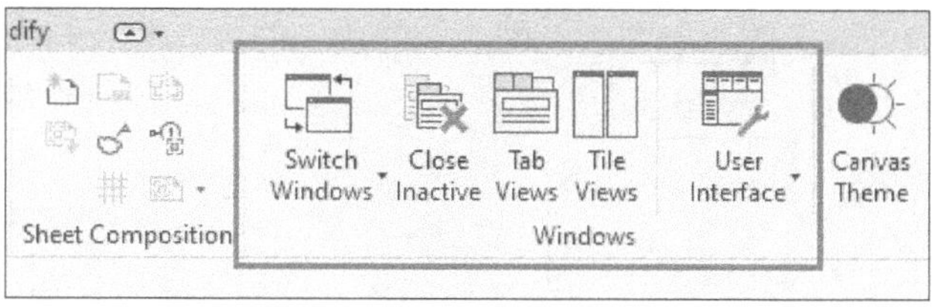

Figure-116. Windows panel

Various tools of this panel are discussed next.

Switching Windows

Select desired view from the **Switch Window** drop-down to activate it. Note that all currently open views will be displayed in the drop-down.

Closing Inactive Views

The **Close Inactive** tool is used to close all the views except currently active view.

Tab Views

The **Tab Views** tool is used to arrange all open windows into tabs. By default, all the views are arranged in tabs; refer to Figure-117.

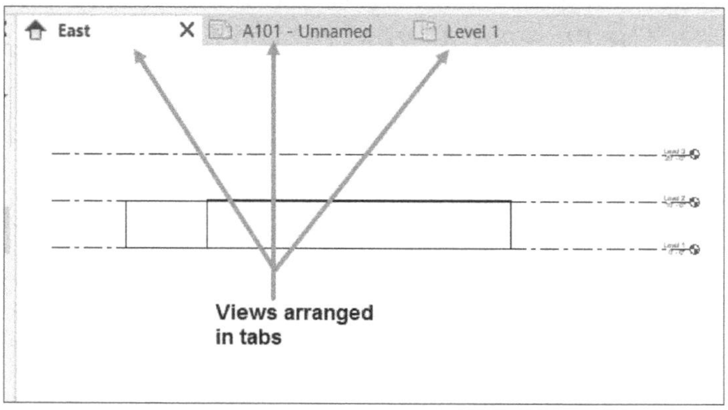

Figure-117. Views arranged in tabs

Tile Views

The **Tile Views** tool in **Windows** panel of **View** tab is used to arrange all the open windows in tiles; refer to Figure-118.

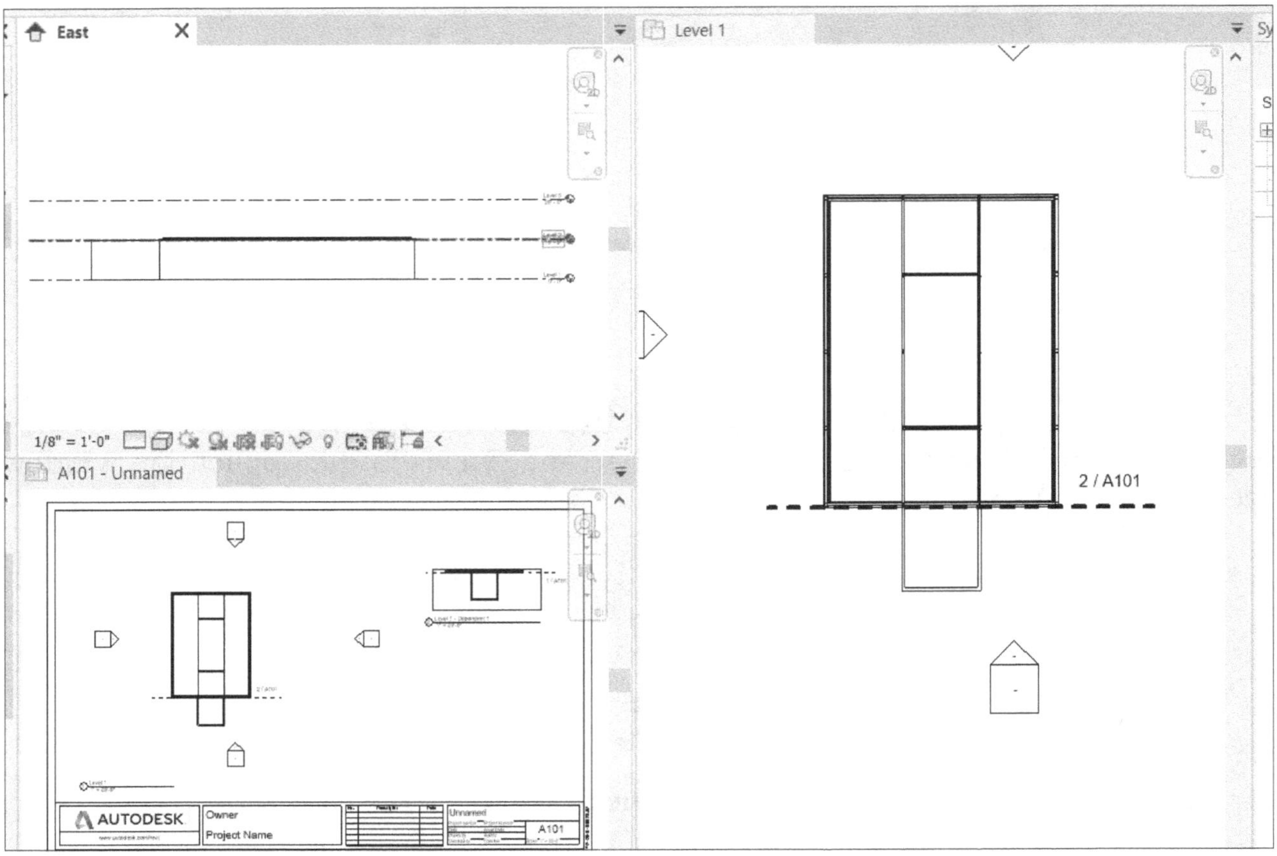

Figure-118. Views arranged in tiles

MANAGING USER INTERFACE

The options in **User Interface** drop-down are used to activate and deactivate various elements of user interface. Select the check box for user interface element to be displayed in application window.

Browser Organization

The **Browser Organization** tool is used to define how views and elements of project are arranged in **Project Browser**.

- Click on the **Browser Organization** tool from the **User Interface** drop-down; refer to Figure-119. The **Browser Organization** dialog box will be displayed; refer to Figure-120.

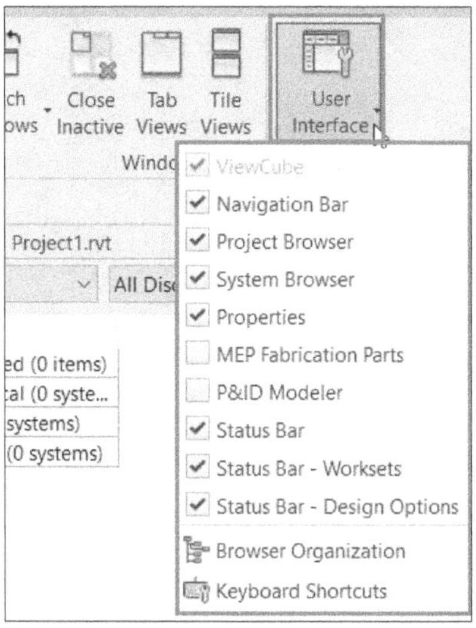

Figure-119. User Interface drop-down

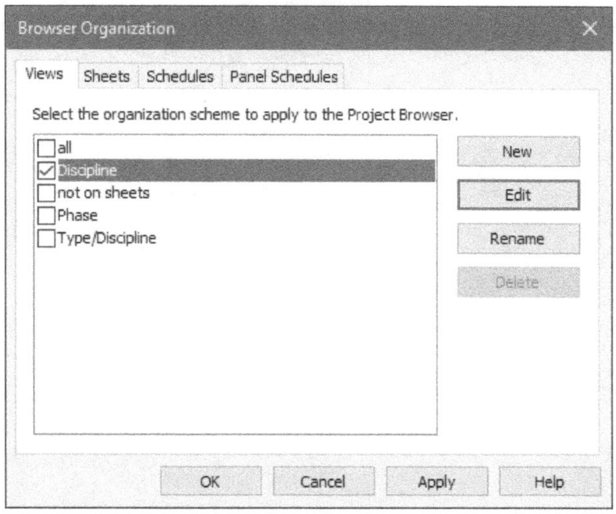

Figure-120. Browser Organization dialog box

- Select check box for property by which you want to arrange views in the project.
- Click on the **Sheets** tab to define arrangement of sheets in project.
- If you want to create a new parameter for organization of views/sheets/schedules then click on the **New** button in desired tab of dialog box. The **Create New Browser Organization** dialog box will be displayed; refer to Figure-121.
- Specify desired name in the **Name** edit box and click on the **OK** button. The **Browser Organization Properties** dialog box will be displayed; refer to Figure-122.

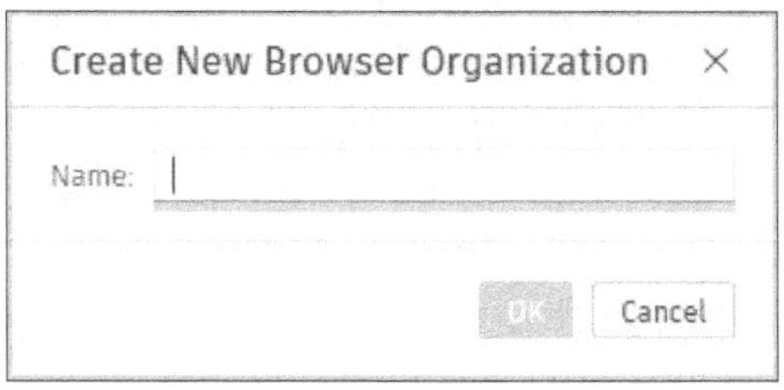

Figure-121. Create New Browser Organization dialog box

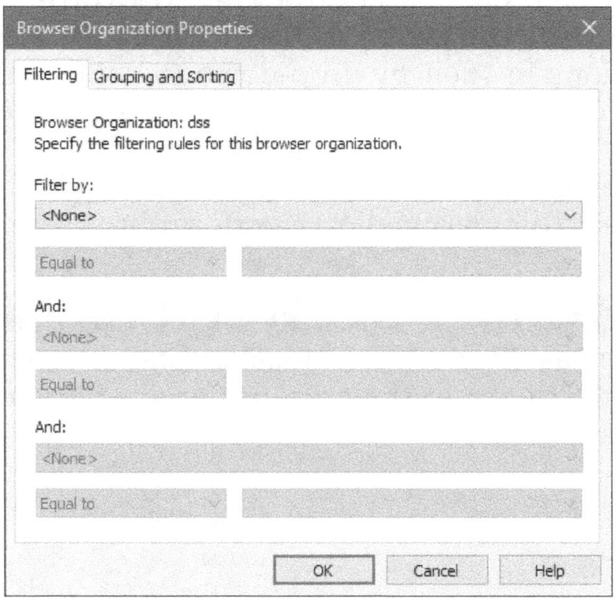

Figure-122. Browser Organization Properties dialog box

- Set desired parameters in the **Filtering** tab to apply filters on the views/sheets/elements which are to be displayed in **Project Browser**. If you do not want to apply filters then leave these parameters unchanged.
- Click on the **Grouping and Sorting** tab to define how elements will be organized in the **Project Browser**; refer to Figure-123.

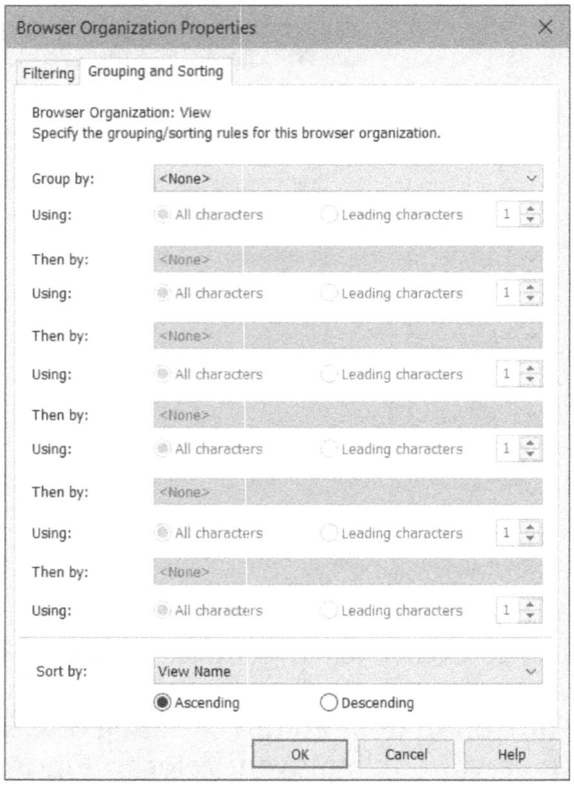

Figure-123. Grouping and Sorting tab

- Select desired option from the **Group by** drop-down to define how elements will be grouped. Like, select the **View Template** option from the drop-down to group all the elements based on view templates used by them. Similarly, you can use the options in **Then by** drop-down to define further grouping parameters.
- From the **Sort by** area of the dialog box, define the parameter by which elements will be sorted in ascending or descending order in the **Project Browser**.
- Click on the **OK** button from the dialog box to create the parameter. Now, you can select this parameter to perform browser organization.

SWITCHING BETWEEN DARK/LIGHT CANVAS THEME

The **Canvas Theme** tool in **Windows** panel of **View** tab is used to switch between dark and light theme in the graphics area where model is displayed.

SELF-ASSESSMENT

Q1. Which of the following properties are not part of View template?

a. Detail Level
b. View Scale
c. Shadows
d. Texture

Q2. Press **V** twice from keyboard to access Visibility/Graphic Overrides dialog box. (T/F)

Q3. On selecting the **Thin Lines** toggle button in **Graphics** panel, all the lines of model are displayed as per their line weight in drawing area. (T/F)

Q4. The **Show Hidden Lines** toggle button is used to permanently display the hidden lines in current view. (T/F)

Q5. Select the **Still** radio button to capture light of Sun at specified location, time instant, and day in the **Sun Settings** dialog box. (T/F)

Q6. You can create a section view of model in 3D view by using the **Section** tool. (T/F)

Q7. Discuss the difference between ceiling plan and reflected ceiling plan views.

Q8. Using the **Drafting View** tool, you can create drafting view to modify lines and symbols of the model. (T/F)

Q9. What is the primary function of the "Apply Template Properties to Current View" tool?

A. It creates a new view template from scratch
B. It deletes view templates from the project
C. It applies predefined view properties to the current view
D. It allows you to render a 3D view

Q10. How can you create a view template using current view properties?

A. By using the Manage View Template tool
B. By clicking on the Cut Profile tool
C. By using the Create Template from Current View tool
D. By modifying material properties

Q11. Which tool allows users to control the visibility of model elements in a view?

A. Graphic Display Options
B. Visibility/Graphics
C. Render
D. Object Styles

Q12. What does selecting the "Halftone" checkbox do to an element?

A. Highlights it in red
B. Hides the element completely
C. Sends it to the background in a light gray shade
D. Makes it bold and visible

Q13. Which tab in the Visibility/Graphics dialog box is used to control visibility based on filters?

A. View Templates
B. Object Styles
C. Detail View
D. Filters

Q14. What happens when the "Thin Lines" toggle button is turned ON?

A. All lines appear bold
B. Hidden lines are removed
C. All lines are displayed as thin, but print according to their settings
D. Lines disappear from the view

Q15. What is required to apply a material to a surface using the Paint tool?

A. Activate the Cut Profile tool
B. Create a new render style
C. Select a material from the Material Browser
D. Turn on the Thin Lines tool

Q16. In the Rendering dialog box, what does selecting the "Printer" radio button in the Output Settings do?

A. Disables artificial lighting
B. Creates a high-resolution render image
C. Shows background settings only
D. Crops the render to the view

Q17. What is the first step to adjust image exposure in the dialog box?

A. Click on the Render button
B. Click on the Save to Project button
C. Click on the Adjust Exposure tool
D. Click on the Export button

Q18. What should be done after setting the desired parameters in the Exposure Control dialog box?

A. Save the image
B. Export the file
C. Click the Render button
D. Click the Show Model button

Q19. What does the 'Save to Project' button do?

A. It exports the rendering image to a cloud storage
B. It saves the rendering image into the current project
C. It renders the current model in the cloud
D. It creates a default 3D view

Q20. How can an image be saved in a local drive?

A. Click on the Save to Project button
B. Click on the Export button and define the name and format
C. Click on the Adjust Exposure tool
D. Use the Post-processing button

Q21. What is the purpose of the 'Render in Cloud' tool?

A. To export walkthrough videos
B. To use Autodesk Cloud for rendering
C. To edit image post-processing
D. To adjust exposure locally

Q22. What option should be selected to get an email after cloud rendering completion?

A. Notify me box
B. Start Rendering checkbox
C. Email me when complete checkbox
D. Download Rendering checkbox

Q23. What is the function of the Panorama button in the cloud rendering tools?

A. To create walkthrough animations
B. To render model as a stereo image
C. To create a panoramic image
D. To edit exposure

Q24. What is the main use of the 'Render Gallery' tool?

A. To create camera views
B. To display renderings on Autodesk Cloud
C. To adjust exposure settings
D. To view walkthroughs

Q25. What does the Twinmotion tool do?

A. It edits exposure values
B. It creates section views
C. It integrates Revit with Twinmotion for visualization
D. It creates 3D walkthroughs

Q26. What happens when you click on the Default 3D View tool?

A. A panoramic view is created
B. A 3D view is created and added to the Project Browser
C. A walkthrough is started
D. A cloud render is initiated

Q27. What is the function of the 'Reset Target' button in Camera View?

A. To change the render mode
B. To adjust exposure
C. To set camera height
D. To restore target point to the middle of view

Q28. How is a Walkthrough animation finalized?

A. By exporting it from the Cloud
B. By pressing the Reset Target button
C. By clicking the Finish Walkthrough button
D. By using the Render button

Q29. How can a Walkthrough animation be exported?

A. Using the Render Gallery tool
B. From the Walkthrough tool in Export menu
C. By clicking on Post-processing
D. Using the Panorama option

Q30. What tool is used to create a section view of a model?

A. Camera tool
B. Section tool
C. Walkthrough tool
D. Post-processing tool

Q31. Which type of view cannot use the Section tool?

A. Elevation views
B. Detail views
C. Plan views
D. 3D views

Q32. What is a Callout used for?

A. To create camera animations
B. To adjust lighting
C. To mark region on model and add info
D. To export render

Q33. What does the Rectangle Callout tool create?

A. A circular region marker
B. A sketched boundary
C. A rectangular callout
D. A walkthrough frame

Q34. How is a Sketched Callout finalized?

A. Clicking on Apply
B. Clicking on OK in the Mode panel
C. Clicking on Save
D. Using the Render button

Q35. What is the Plan Views drop-down used for?

A. Exporting views
B. Creating section views
C. Creating different types of plan views
D. Setting panorama parameters

Q36. What is the purpose of the Floor Plan tool?

A. To create 3D models
B. To create floor plans for different levels
C. To design elevation views
D. To assign structural properties

Q37. Which checkbox should be cleared to create duplicate views in the New Floor Plan dialog box?

A. Duplicate levels
B. Show template
C. Do not duplicate existing views
D. Copy from existing

Q38. Which tool is used to create a plan showing ceiling elements?

A. Structural Plan
B. Reflected Ceiling Plan
C. Elevation
D. Plan Region

Q39. What should be done before creating an Area Plan?

A. Assign a template
B. Create a plan region
C. Create an area scheme
D. Duplicate a floor plan

Q40. What is the use of the View Range button in the Plan Region tool?

A. To rotate the view
B. To apply lighting effects
C. To set view levels and cut planes
D. To change rendering options

Q41. Which of the following tools creates a duplicate view without annotations?

A. Duplicate with Detailing
B. Duplicate as Dependent
C. Drafting View
D. Duplicate View

Q42. What is created by the Framing Elevation tool?

A. Floor elevation views
B. Structural plans
C. Elevation for framing members
D. Drafting view for details

Q43. What happens when you choose 'Yes' while creating an Area Plan?

A. The plan is not created
B. It opens a new drafting view
C. Area boundaries are created automatically along external walls
D. A schedule is generated

Q44. Which tool is used to show project elements in a tabular form?

A. Keynote Legend
B. Legend View
C. Schedules/Quantities
D. Elevation View

Q45. What kind of elements are typically added using the Drafting View tool?

A. Doors and windows
B. Grids and levels
C. Non-model elements like insulation and detail components
D. Load-bearing walls

Q46. What is the function of the Duplicate as Dependent tool?

A. It creates an independent copy of the view
B. It creates a view that updates with changes made in the original
C. It duplicates only annotations
D. It opens the view in a new window

Q47. How are graphical column schedules generated correctly?

A. By tagging every column manually
B. By ensuring columns are placed on grid intersections
C. By selecting all columns in the model
D. By using the drafting view

Q48. What dialog box appears when the Schedule/Quantities tool is selected?

A. Filter Properties
B. Schedule Properties
C. View Options
D. Element List

Q49. What is the purpose of the Keynote Legend tool in Revit?

A. To display schedule of materials
B. To show only graphical elevations
C. To list and describe all keynotes used in the project
D. To duplicate elevation views

Q50. Which tab contains the Area and Volume Computations tool used to create area schemes?

A. View tab
B. Insert tab
C. Annotate tab
D. Architecture tab

For Student Notes

Chapter 13

Annotating Model

Topics Covered

The major topics covered in this chapter are:

- ***Annotations***
- ***Detailing Tools***
- ***Applying Tags***
- ***Placing Symbols***

ANNOTATIONS

Once you have created the building model, the next step is to annotate it. Annotations are used to apply dimensions, tags, and other related parameters to the model. There are various types of annotations like dimensions, texts, tags, and so on. The tools to apply annotations are available in the **Annotate** tab; refer to Figure-1.

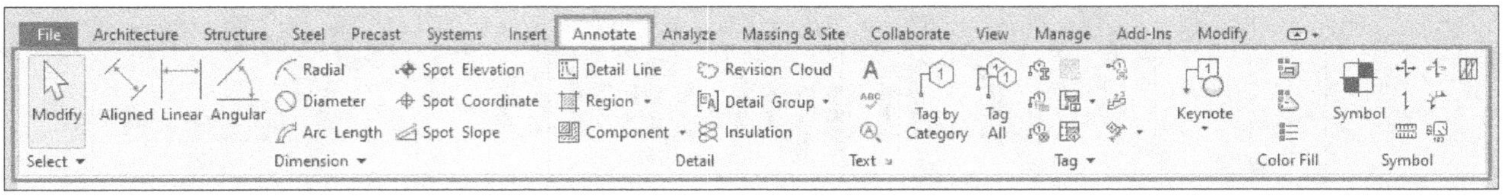

Figure-1. Annotate tab

Various tools in this tab are discussed next.

Creating Aligned Dimension

The **Aligned** tool is used to create dimension aligned along selected walls. The procedure to use this tool is given next.

- Click on the **Aligned** tool from the **Dimension** panel in the **Annotate** tab of **Ribbon**. You will be asked to select references for creating dimension.
- Select desired option from **Prefer** drop-down in the **Place Dimensions** panel of the **Ribbon** to define which elements of the wall will be used as reference for creating dimensions; refer to Figure-2. Select the **Wall centerlines** option to use centerlines of selected walls to create dimension. Select the **Wall faces** option from the drop-down to use front or back faces of walls as reference for creating dimension. Similarly, select the **Center of core** option to use center of core of wall to be used as reference and select the **Faces of core** option to use faces of core of wall as reference. Note that you can press **TAB** to switch between different references when selecting wall for creating dimension.

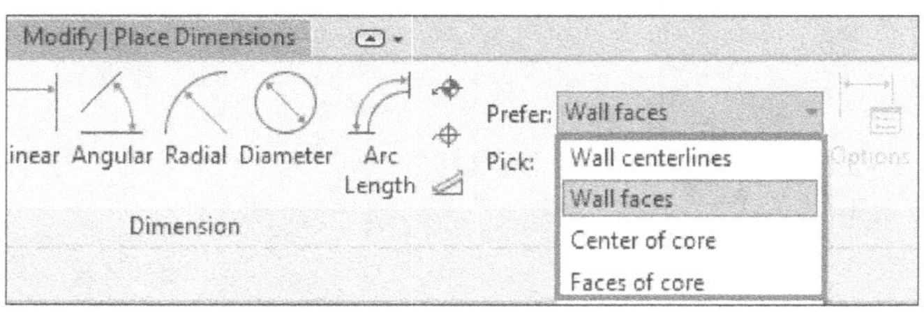

Figure-2. Reference drop-down

- Select **Individual References** option from the **Pick** drop-down in the **Place Dimensions** panel of the **Ribbon** to select two references on walls to create dimension. Select the **Entire Walls** option from the **Pick** drop-down if you want to select the wall to be dimensioned. If you have selected the **Entire Walls** option then **Options** button will become active in the **Place Dimensions** panel of the **Ribbon**. Click on this button to define advanced wall selection options. The **Auto Dimension Options** dialog box will be displayed; refer to Figure-3. Select the **Openings** check box from the dialog box to use openings of wall as reference. By default, **Center** radio button is selected on selecting the **Openings** check box. Select the **Widths** radio button to use sides of openings as reference for creating dimensions. Select the **Intersecting Walls** check box to use intersection points of walls as reference for creating dimensions. Select the **Intersecting Grids** check box to use intersection points of grids as reference for creating dimensions.

- If **Individual References** option is selected in the **Pick** drop-down then select two references for dimensioning. The dimension will get attached to cursor; refer to Figure-4.

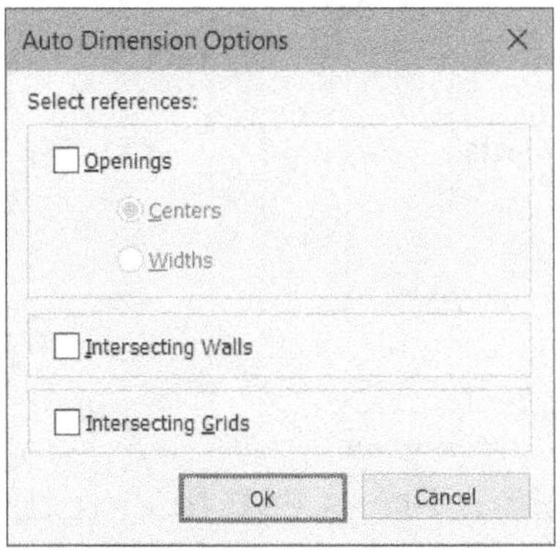

Figure-3. Auto Dimension Options dialog box

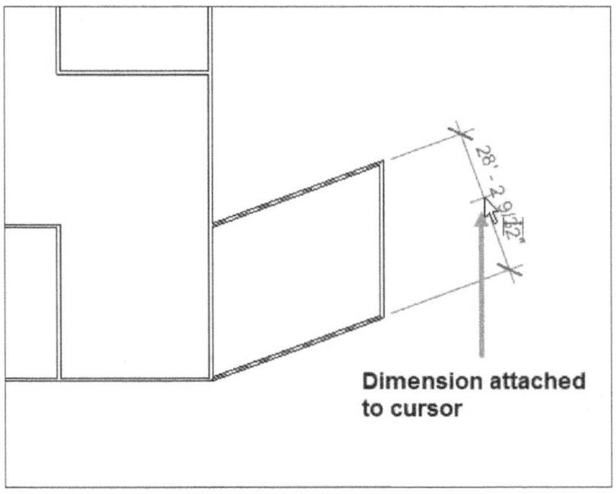

Figure-4. Dimension attached to cursor

- Click at desired location to place the dimension.
- Press **ESC** to exit the tool.

Creating Linear Dimension

The **Linear** tool is used to create linear dimension between two selected references. The procedure to use this tool is given next.

- Click on the **Linear** tool from the **Dimension** panel in the **Annotate** tab of **Ribbon**. You will be asked to select reference points.
- Click on two reference points between which you want to create linear dimension; refer to Figure-5.

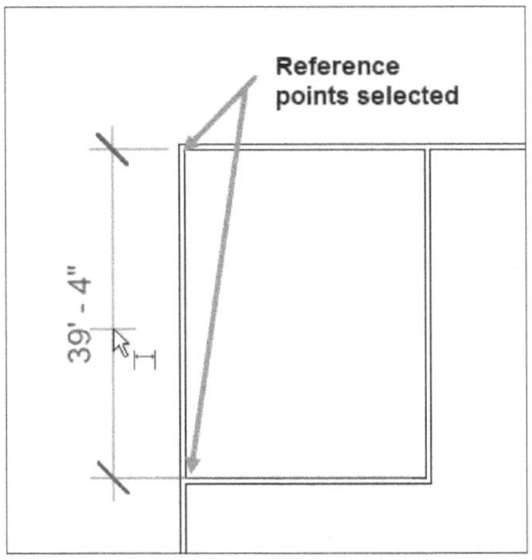

Figure-5. Reference points selected for linear dimension

- Click at desired location to place the dimension.
- Press **ESC** twice to exit the tool.

Creating Angular Dimension

The **Angular** tool is used to create angular dimension between selected references. The procedure to use this tool is given next.

- Click on the **Angular** tool from the **Dimension** panel in the **Annotate** tab of **Ribbon**. You will be asked to select references for angular dimensioning.
- Select two references between which you want to create angular dimension. The dimension will get attached to cursor; refer to Figure-6.

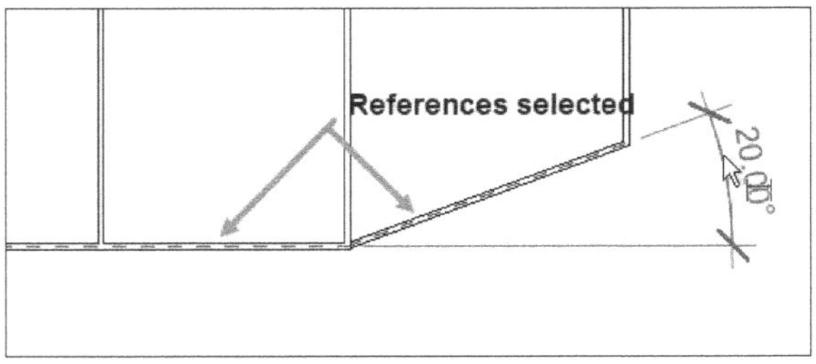

Figure-6. References selected for angular dimension

- Click at desired location to place the dimension. Press **ESC** to exit the tool.

Creating Radial Dimension

The **Radial** tool is used to create radial dimension for selected object. The procedure to use this tool is given next.

- Click on the **Radial** tool from the **Dimension** panel in the **Annotate** tab of **Ribbon**. You will be asked to select an arc to be dimensioned.
- Select desired arc element. The dimension will get attached to cursor; refer to Figure-7.

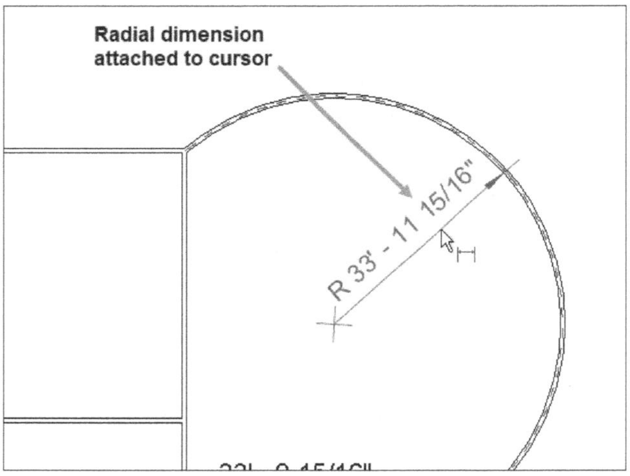

Figure-7. Radial dimension attached to cursor

- Click at desired location to place the dimension.

Creating Diameter Dimension

The **Diameter** tool in **Dimension** panel is used to create diametrical dimension for arcs and circles. The procedure to use this tool is given next.

- Click on the **Diameter** tool from the **Dimension** panel in the **Modify|Place Dimensions** contextual tab of **Ribbon**. You will be asked to select an arc or circle element to be dimensioned.
- Select desired element. The diameter dimension will get attached to cursor; refer to Figure-8.

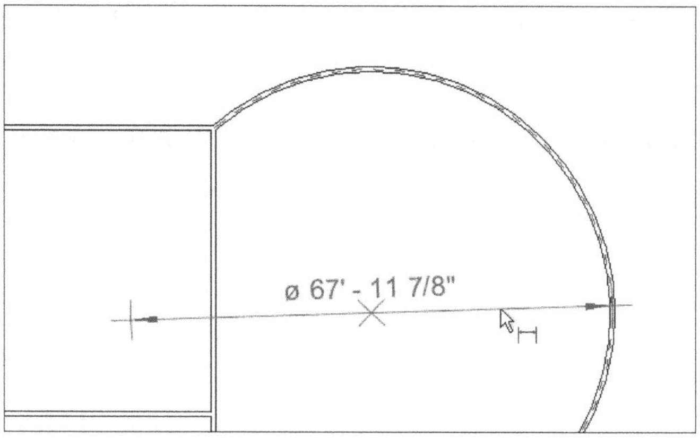

Figure-8. Diameter dimension attached to cursor

- Click at desired location to place the dimension.
- Press **ESC** twice to exit the tool.

Creating Arc Length Dimension

The **Arc Length** tool is used to create arc length dimension of selected arcs. The procedure to use this tool is given next.

- Click on the **Arc Length** tool from the **Dimension** panel in the **Annotate** tab of **Ribbon**. You will be asked to select the arc along which the dimension will be measured.
- Select desired arc. You will be asked to select intersecting walls.
- Select desired walls. The dimension will get attached to cursor; refer to Figure-9.

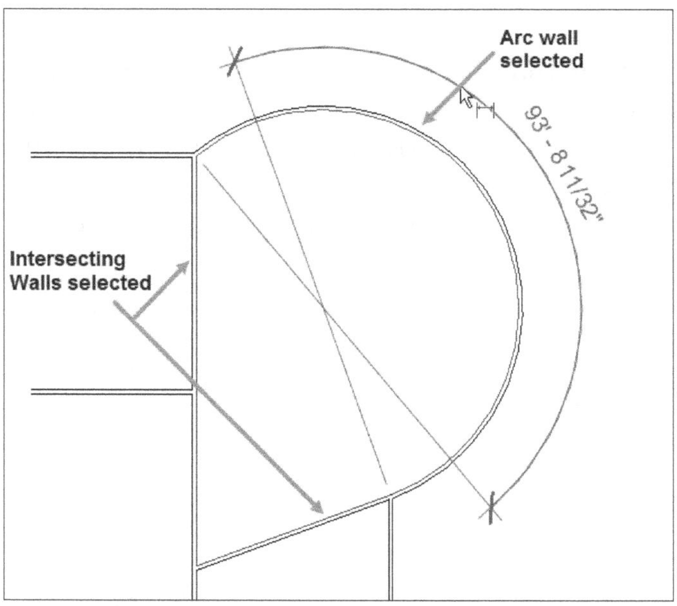

Figure-9. Arc length dimension created

- Click at desired location to place the dimension.

Spot Elevation Dimension

The **Spot Elevation** tool is used to display elevation values of selected points. The procedure to use this tool is given next.

- Click on the **Spot Elevation** tool from the **Dimension** panel in the **Annotate** tab of **Ribbon**. You will be asked to select a location where you want to place spot elevation value.
- Click at desired location. The spot elevation will get attached to cursor; refer to Figure-10.

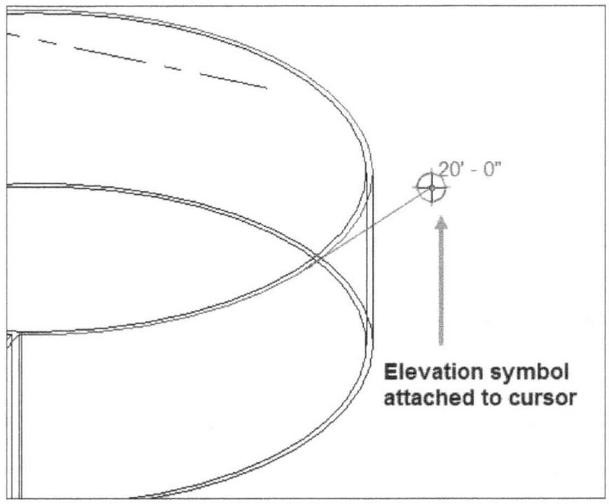

Figure-10. Elevation symbol attached to cursor

- Click at desired location to place the landing and then value of elevation.
- Press **ESC** twice to exit the tool.

Spot Coordinate Dimension

The **Spot Coordinate** tool is used to display coordinate value for selected point. The procedure to use this tool is given next.

- Click on the **Spot Coordinate** tool from the **Dimension** panel in the **Annotate** tab of **Ribbon**. You will be asked to select a point on the model.
- Click at desired location to place the coordinate dimension. You will be asked to specify location of leader landing.
- Click at desired location to place landing and then click to place the value; refer to Figure-11.

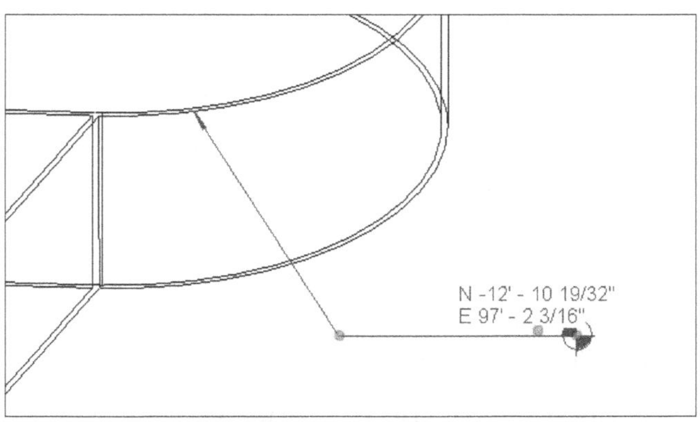

Figure-11. Placing spot coordinate

- Press **ESC** twice to exit the tool.

Spot Slope Dimension

The **Spot Slope** tool is used to display slope dimension at selected point. The procedure to use this tool is given next.

- Click on the **Spot Slope** tool from the **Dimension** panel in the **Annotate** tab of **Ribbon**. You will be asked to select a point on the inclined wall whose slope is to be measured.
- Click at desired location on wall. You will be asked to define the side on which dimension is to be placed.
- Click on desired side of wall. The dimension will be placed; refer to Figure-12.

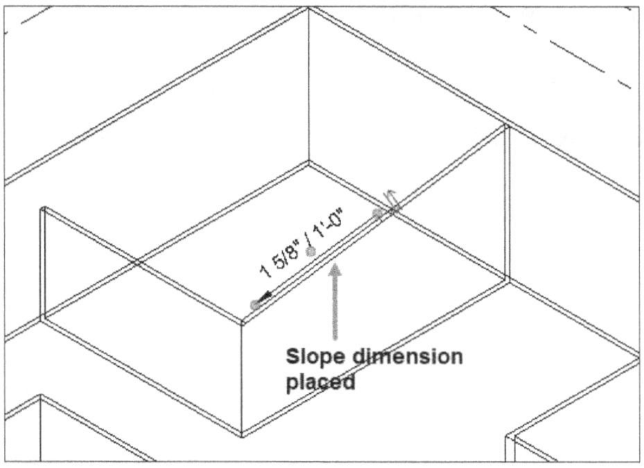

Figure-12. Placing slope dimension

DETAILING TOOLS

The tools in the **Detail** panel are used to apply detailing annotations like detail lines, regions, detail components, and so on; refer to Figure-13. Various tools in this panel are discussed next.

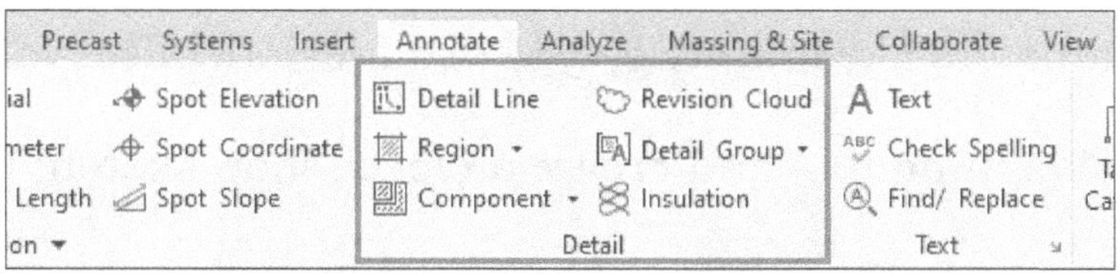

Figure-13. Detail panel

Placing Detail Lines

The **Detail Line** tool is used to create different type of detailing lines. The procedure to use this tool is given next.

- Click on the **Detail Line** tool from the **Detail** panel in the **Annotate** tab of **Ribbon**. The options to create detail lines will be displayed; refer to Figure-14.

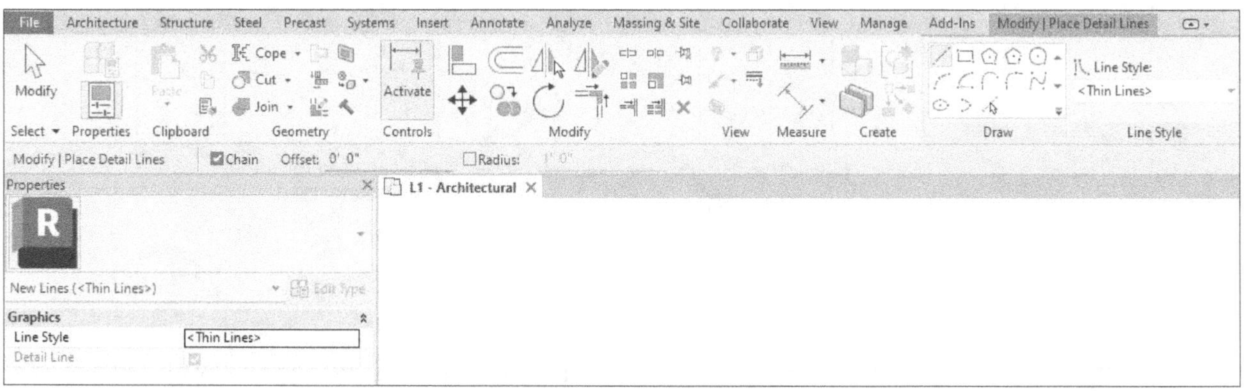

Figure-14. Options to create detail lines

- Select desired option from the **Line Style** drop-down.

- Set desired offset value in the **Offset** edit box.
- Create desired sketch for detail lines.
- Press **ESC** twice to exit the tool.

Creating Filled Region

The **Filled Region** tool is used to create 2D graphic region with fill pattern. The procedure to use this tool is given next.

- Click on the **Filled Region** tool from the **Region** drop-down in the **Detail** panel of **Annotate** tab in **Ribbon**. The options to create filled region will be displayed; refer to Figure-15.

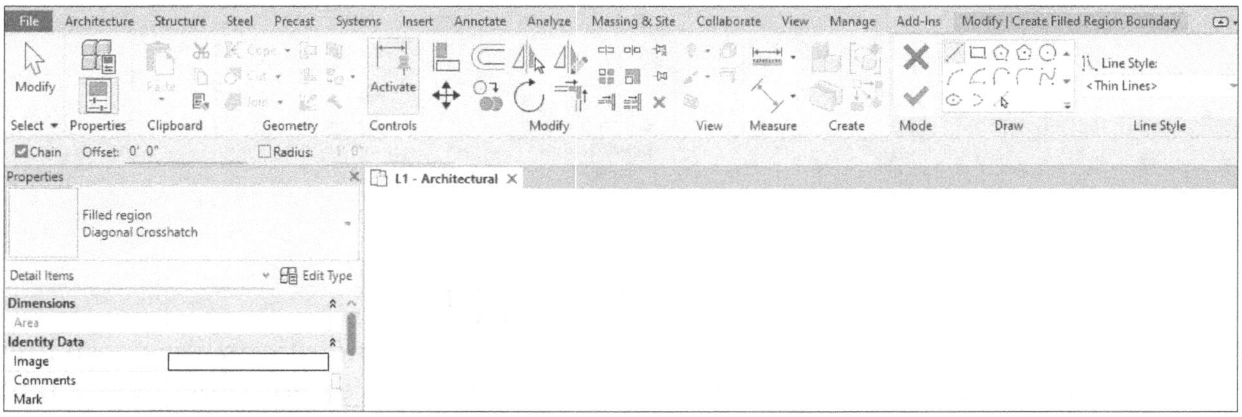

Figure-15. Modify Create Filled Region Boundary contextual tab

- Set desired parameters like line style, type of fill region, offset value, corner radius, and so on.
- Select desired sketching tool and create a closed loop sketch; refer to Figure-16.

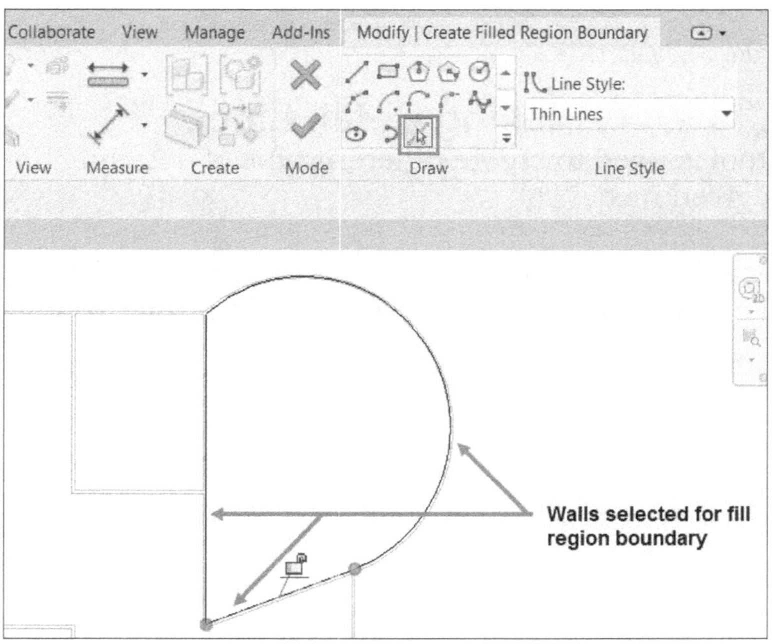

Figure-16. Creating fill region boundary

- Click on the **OK** button from the contextual tab. The filled region will be created; refer to Figure-17.

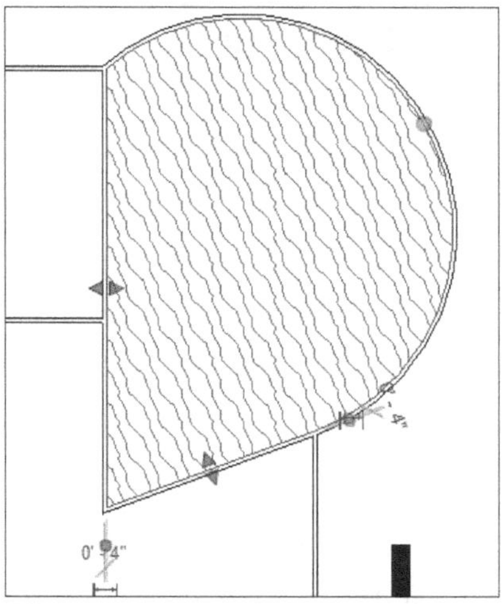

Figure-17. Filled region created

- Press **ESC** to exit the tool.

Creating Masking Region

The **Masking Region** tool is used to create a 2D or 3D masking region that obscure elements. The procedure to use this tool is given next.

- Click on the **Masking Region** tool from the **Region** drop-down in the **Detail** panel of **Annotate** tab in the **Ribbon**. The options to create masking region boundary will be displayed; refer to Figure-18.

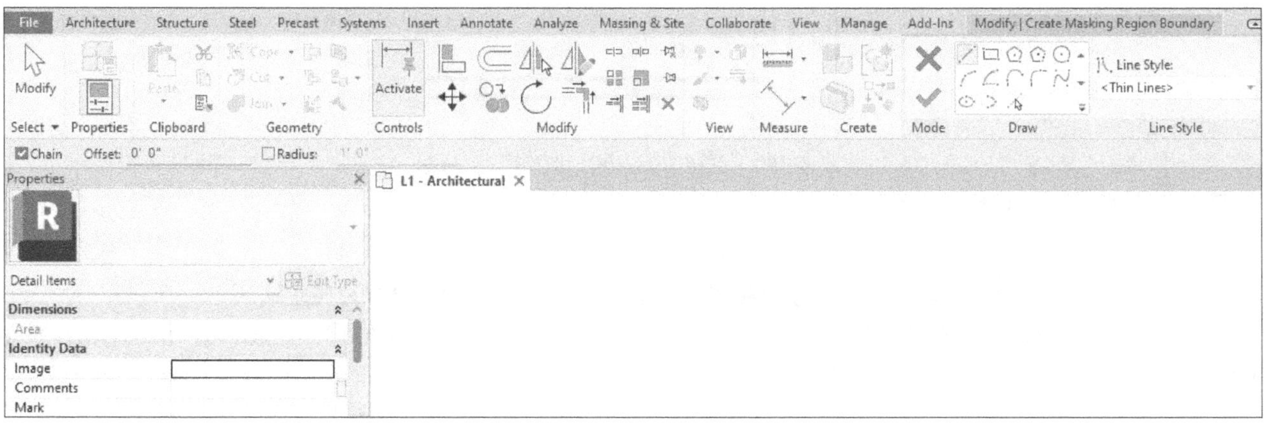

Figure-18. Options for masking region

- Set desired line type from the **Line Style** drop-down and set other parameters as desired.
- Create a closed loop sketch on the elements to be obscured.
- Click on the **Finish Edit Mode** button from the **Mode** panel in the contextual tab of **Ribbon**. The boundary will be created.

Placing Detail Component

The **Detail Component** tool is used to place different type of detailing components. The procedure to use this tool is given next.

- Click on the **Detail Component** tool from the **Component** drop-down in the **Detail** panel of **Annotate** tab in the **Ribbon**. The options to place detail components will be displayed; refer to Figure-19.

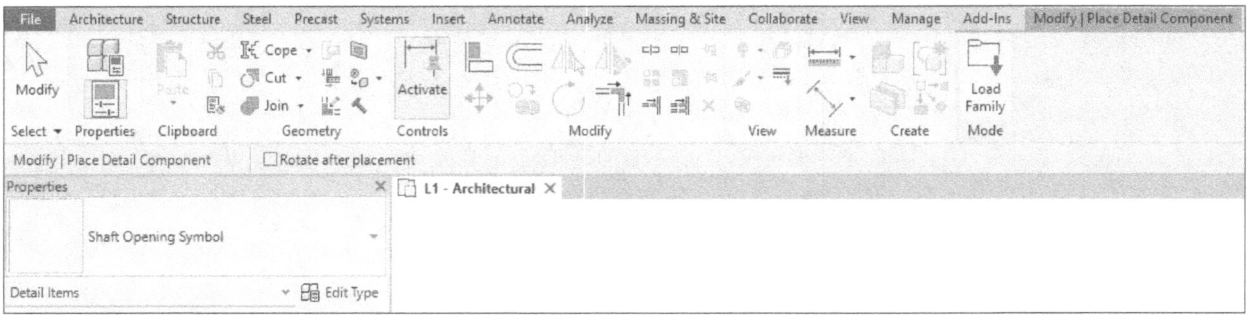

Figure-19. Modify Place Detail Component contextual tab

- Click on the **Load Family** tool from the contextual tab and load desired detail components.
- Click at desired location to place the component. Like, place detail component of brick in a brick wall; refer to Figure-20.

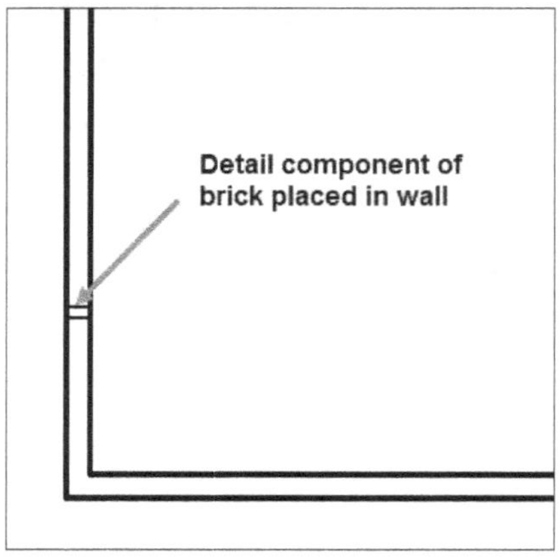

Figure-20. Placing detail symbol

- Press **ESC** to exit the tool.

Placing Repeating Detail Component

The **Repeating Detail Component** tool is used to place an array of detail components. The procedure to use this tool is given next.

- Click on the **Repeating Detail Component** tool from the **Component** drop-down in the **Detail** panel of **Annotate** tab in the **Ribbon**. The options to place repeating detail components will be displayed; refer to Figure-21.

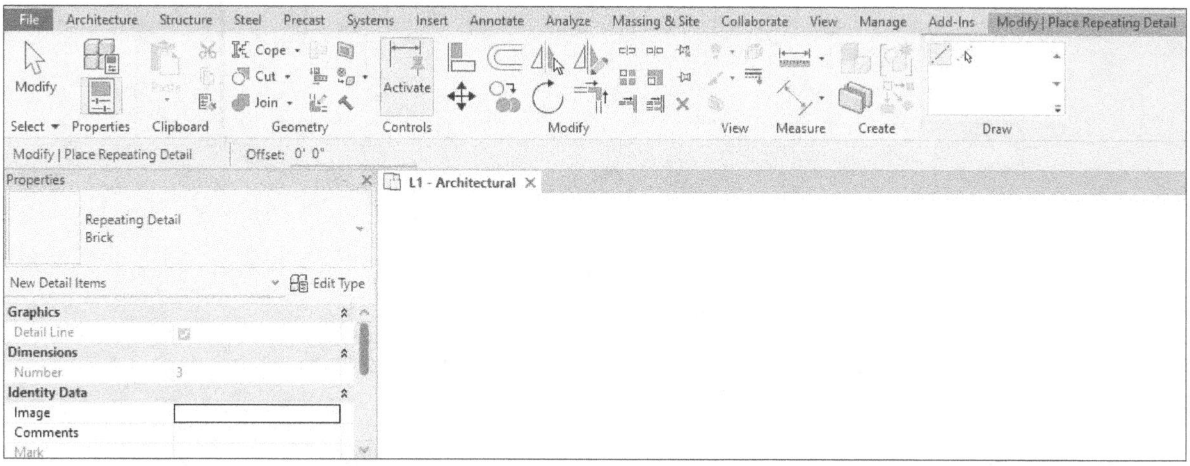

Figure-21. Options for placing repeating components

- Click on the **Edit Type** button from the **Properties Palette**. The **Type Properties** dialog box will be displayed; refer to Figure-22.

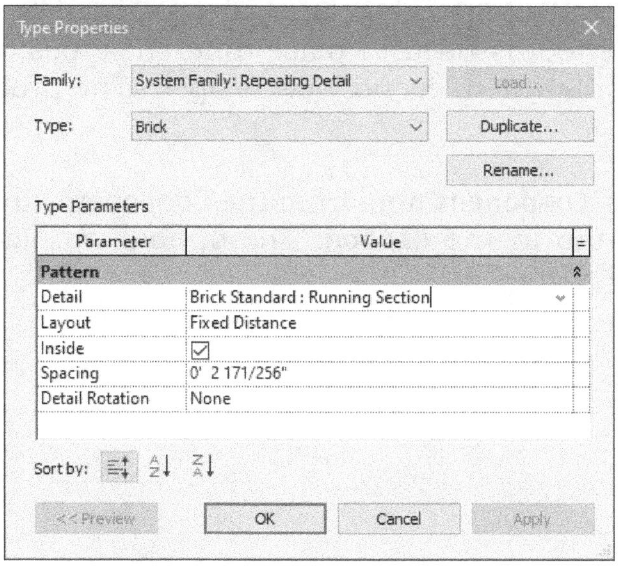

Figure-22. Type Properties dialog box

- Select desired component type from the **Detail** field in the tab and set the other parameters as desired.
- Click on the **OK** button from the dialog box.
- Create a line or pick the line to place repeating detail components; refer to Figure-23.

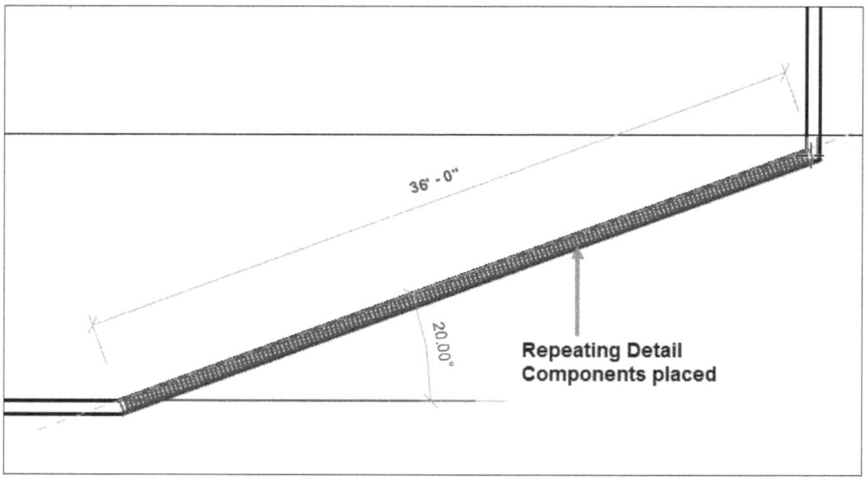

Figure-23. Placing repeating detail components

- Press **ESC** twice to exit the tool.

Placing Legend Components

The **Legend Component** tool is used to place different types of legend components. This tool is available only when legend view is open. The procedure to use this tool is given next.

- Click on the **Legend Component** tool from the **Component** drop-down in the **Detail** panel of **Annotate** tab in the **Ribbon**. The options to place component will be displayed; refer to Figure-24.

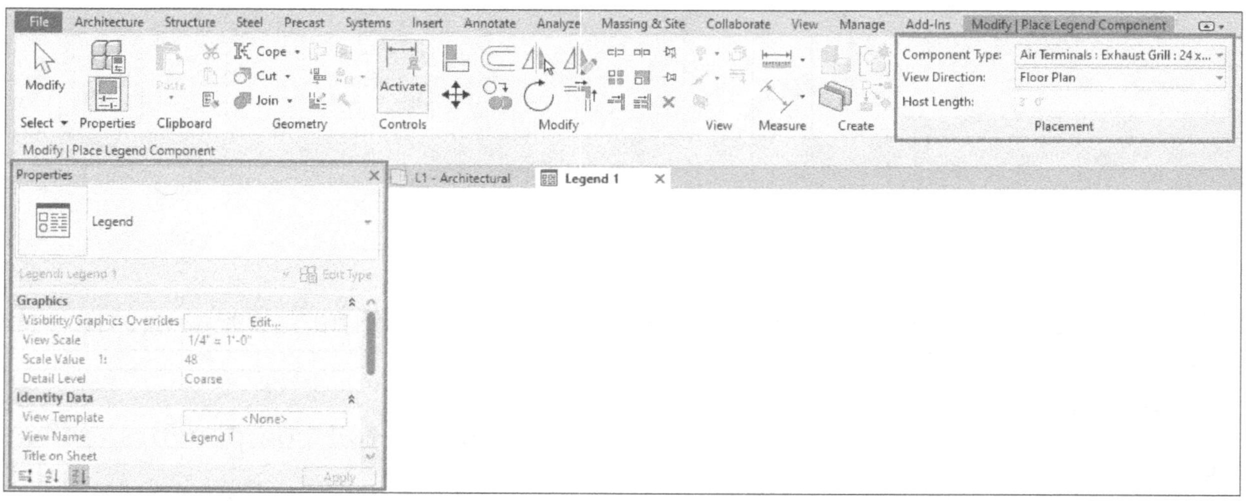

Figure-24. Options to place legend components

- Select desired option from the **Component Type** drop-down in the **Placement** panel of the **Ribbon** and set desired parameters.
- Click at desired location to place the legend component.

Placing Revision Cloud

The **Revision Cloud** tool is used to place cloud boundary around the elements which have changed by you or other users when collaborating on the model. The procedure to use this tool is given next.

- Click on the **Revision Cloud** tool from the **Detail** panel in the **Annotate** tab of **Ribbon**. The options to create revision cloud boundary will be displayed; refer to Figure-25.

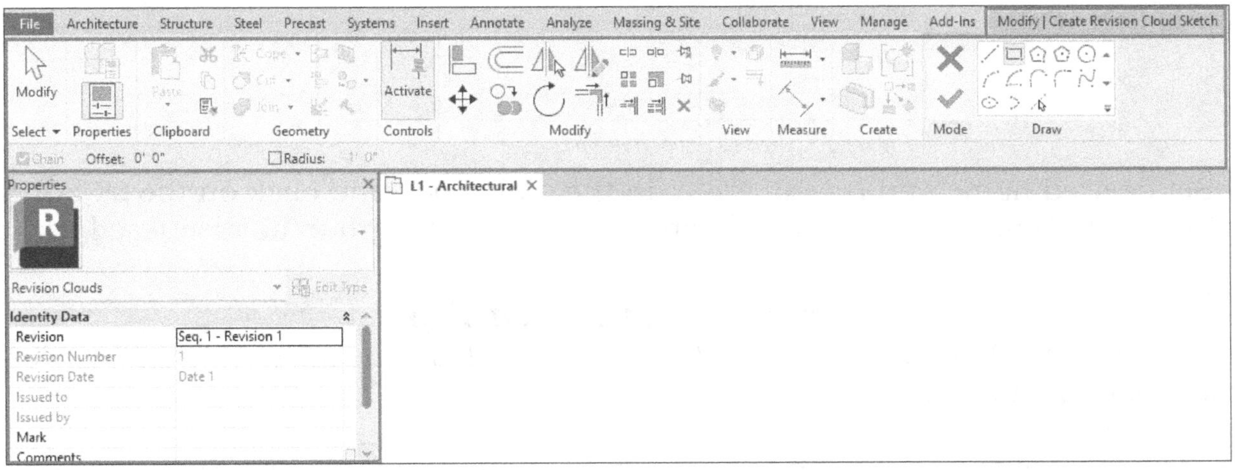

Figure-25. Modify Create Revision Cloud Sketch contextual tab

- Create desired closed loop sketch; refer to Figure-26.

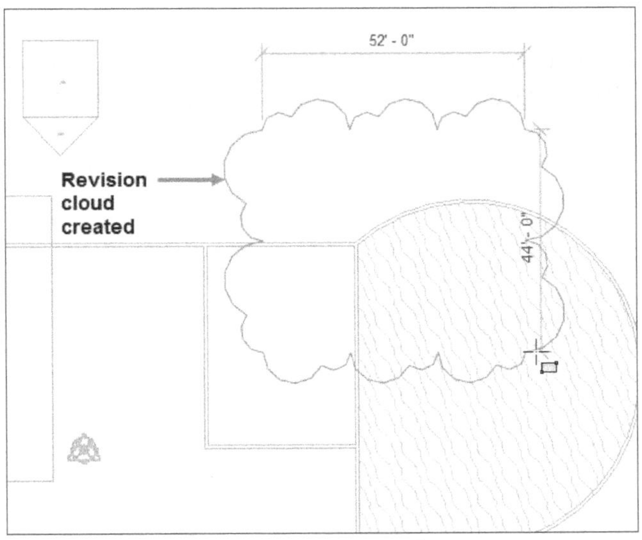

Figure-26. Revision cloud created

- Click on the **Finish Edit Mode** tool from the **Mode** panel in the contextual tab of **Ribbon** to create the revision cloud.

Creating Detail Group

The **Create Group** tool is used to create group of selected detail elements. The procedure to use this tool is given next.

- Click on the **Create Group** tool from the **Detail Group** drop-down in the **Detail** panel of **Annotate** tab in the **Ribbon**. The **Create Group** dialog box will be displayed; refer to Figure-27.

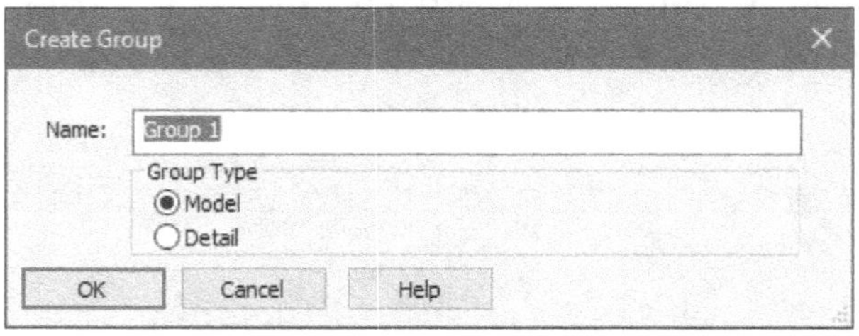

Figure-27. Create Group dialog box

- Set desired name and type of group in the dialog box and click on the **OK** button. The **Edit Group** toolbox will be displayed. Create the group as discussed earlier.

Placing Detail Group

The **Place Detail Group** tool is used to place detail group earlier created by **Create Group** tool. The procedure has been discussed earlier.

Creating Insulation

The **Insulation** tool is used to create insulation for different elements. The procedure to use this tool is given next.

- Click on the **Insulation** tool from the **Detail** panel in the **Annotate** tab of **Ribbon**. The **Modify|Place Insulation** contextual tab will be displayed; refer to Figure-28.

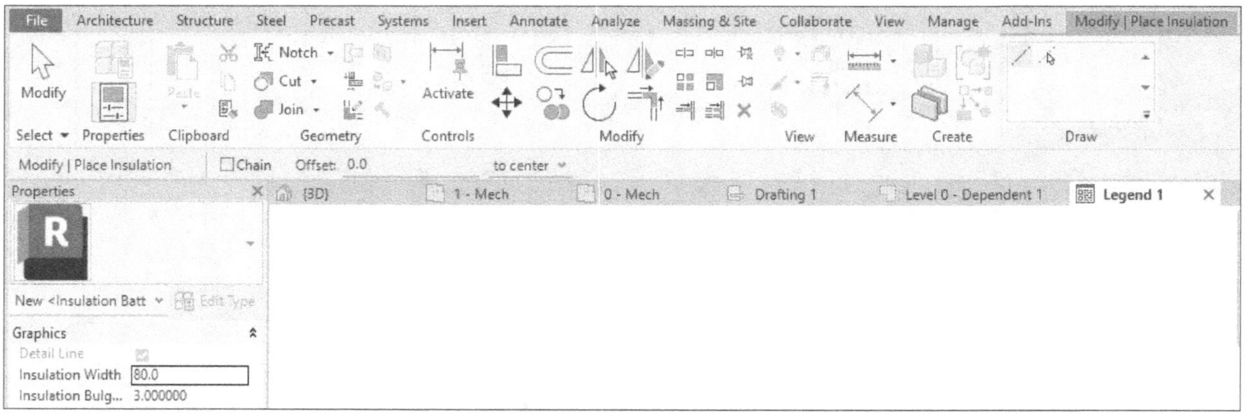

Figure-28. Modify Place Insulation contextual tab

- Set desired parameters in the **Options Bar** and **Properties Palette**.
- Create the insulation at desired location; refer to Figure-29.

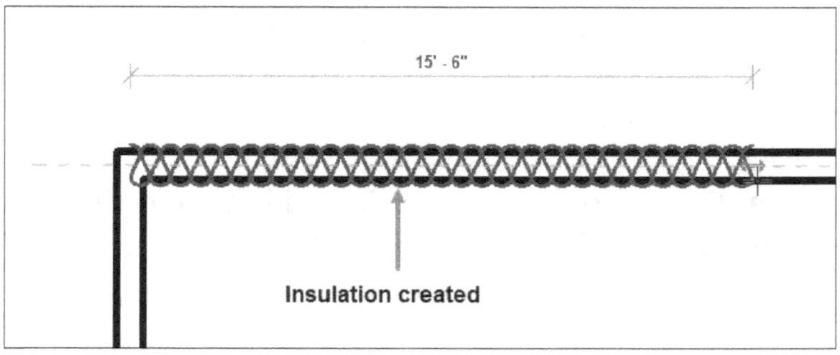

Figure-29. Insulation created

- Press **ESC** twice to exit the tool.

Creating Text

The **Text** tool is used to create text in the detailing view. The procedure to use this tool is given next.

- Click on the **Text** tool in the **Text** panel of **Annotate** tab in the **Ribbon**. The options to create text will be displayed; refer to Figure-30.

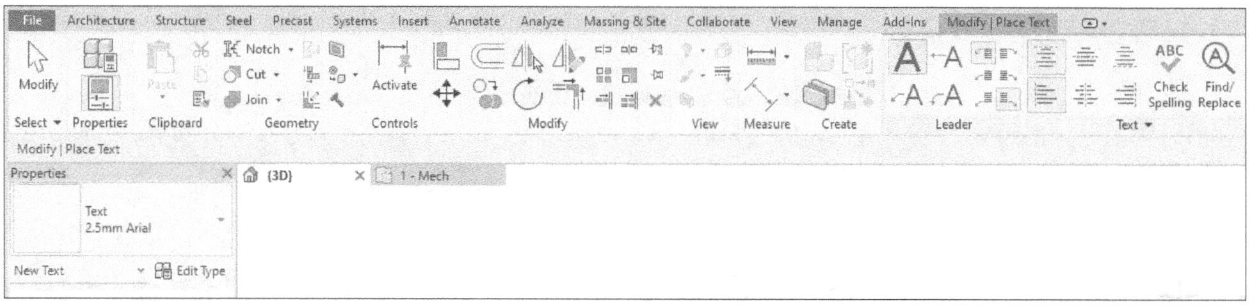

Figure-30. Modify Place Text contextual tab

- Select desired text size from the drop-down at the top in the **Properties Palette**. If you do not find desired size, click on the **Edit Type** button from the **Properties Palette** and set desired text size.
- Create a rectangular text box within which you will write the text. The **Edit Text** contextual tab will be displayed and you will be asked to type text; refer to Figure-31.

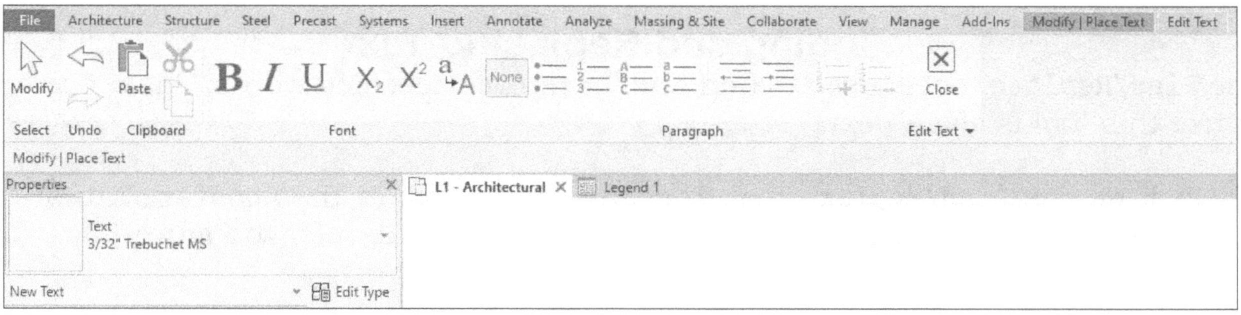

Figure-31. Edit Text contextual tab

- Set desired parameters in the contextual tab and type desired text.
- Click on the **Close** button from the contextual tab.
- Press **ESC** twice to exit the tool.

Checking Spelling

The **Check Spelling** tool is used to check spelling errors in selected notes or current view/sheet. The procedure to use this tool is given next.

- Click on the **Check Spelling** tool from the **Text** panel in the **Annotate** tab of **Ribbon**. The **Check Spelling** dialog box will be displayed; refer to Figure-32.

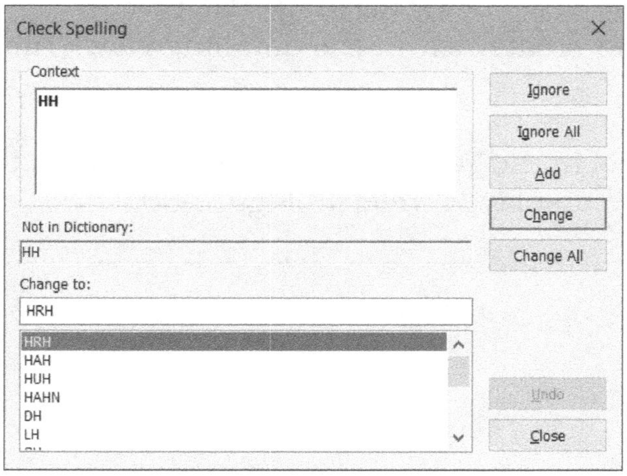

Figure-32. Check Spelling dialog box

- Select desired option from the **Change to** area if you want to replace the selected word in the **Context** area and click on the **Change** or **Change All** button.
- If you want to add error word in dictionary then select it from context area and click on the **Add** button.
- If you want to ignore the selected word then click on the **Ignore** button.
- Click on the **Ignore All** button from the dialog box if you want to ignore all wrong words.
- Click on the **Close** button to exit the dialog box.

Finding and Replacing Text

The **Find/Replace** tool is used to find and/or replace specified words. The procedure to use this tool is given next.

- Click on the **Find/Replace** tool from the **Text** panel in the **Annotate** tab of the **Ribbon**. The **Find/Replace** dialog box will be displayed; refer to Figure-33.

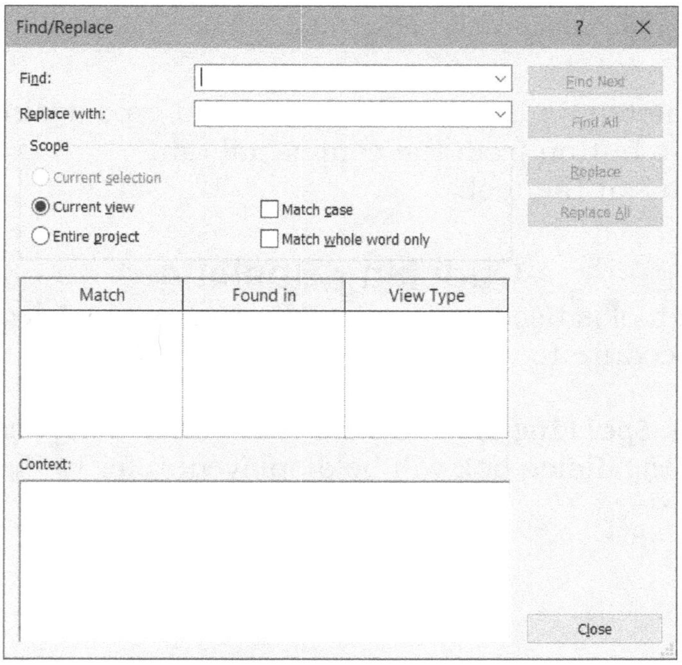

Figure-33. Find Replace dialog box

- Type desired word to be found in the project and click on the **Find Next** button. The text found will be displayed in the dialog box.

- Click on the **Find All** button to find all the matching text in the dialog box.
- Select desired radio button from the **Scope** area to define where to find the text.
- Specify desired text in the **Replace with** edit box to define the text by which searched text will be replaced and click on the **Replace** button. If you want to replace all the matching text then click on the **Replace All** button.
- Click on the **Close** button to exit the dialog box.

Defining Text Properties

The options in the **Type Properties** dialog box are used to define settings for creating text. Click on the inclined arrow of **Text** panel in the **Annotate** tab to display **Type Properties** dialog box for text. The options in this dialog box have already been discussed.

Applying Tags by Category

The **Tag by Category** tool is used to apply tags to various elements of model based their category. The procedure to use this tool is given next.

- Click on the **Tag by Category** tool from the **Tag** panel in the **Annotate** tab of **Ribbon**. The **Modify|Tag** contextual tab will be displayed to apply tags; refer to Figure-34.

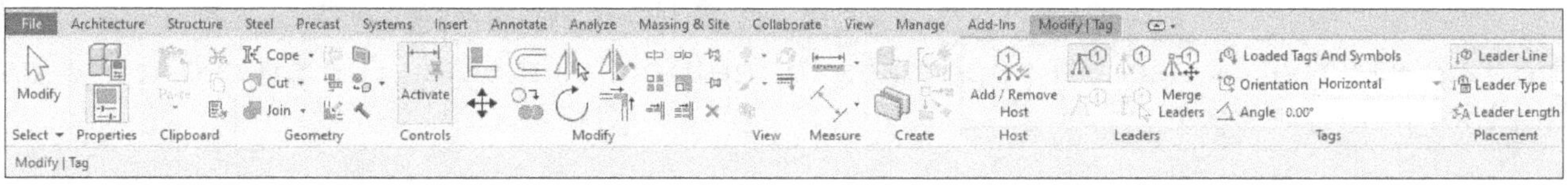

Figure-34. Modify Tag contextual tab

- Select the **Horizontal** option from **Orientation** drop-down in the **Tags** panel to align text of tag horizontally. Select the **Vertical** option from the drop-down if you want to align text of tag vertically.
- Click on the **Loaded Tags And Symbols** button from the expanded **Tags** panel of the **Ribbon** to set tags to be applied in model. The **Loaded Tags And Symbols** dialog box will be displayed; refer to Figure-35.

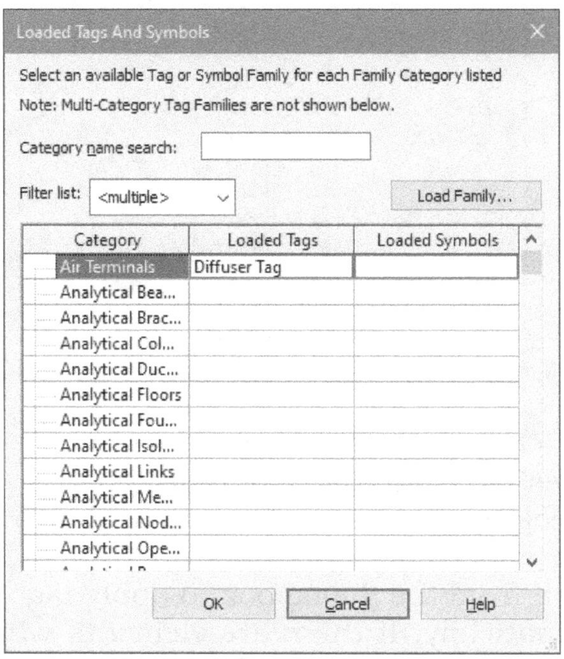

Figure-35. Loaded Tags And Symbols dialog box

- Click on the **Load Family** button from the dialog box and load desired tags. After loading tags, click on the **OK** button from the dialog box.
- Set desired text height and leader end condition in respective options in the **Ribbon**.
- Select desired button from the **Leaders** panel in contextual tab of **Ribbon**. Click on the element to which you want to apply tag; refer to Figure-36.

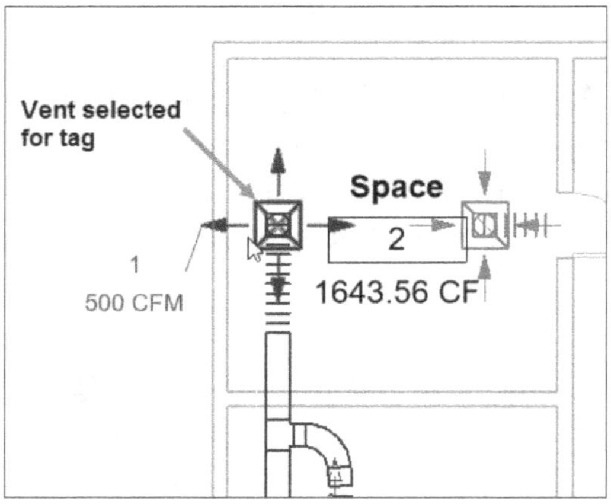

Figure-36. Placing tag on vent

- Press **ESC** twice to exit the tool.

Applying Tags to All Elements

The **Tag All** tool is used to apply tags to multiple elements. The procedure to use this tool is given next.

- Click on the **Tag All** tool from the **Tag** panel in the **Annotate** tab of **Ribbon**. The **Tag All Not Tagged** dialog box will be displayed; refer to Figure-37.

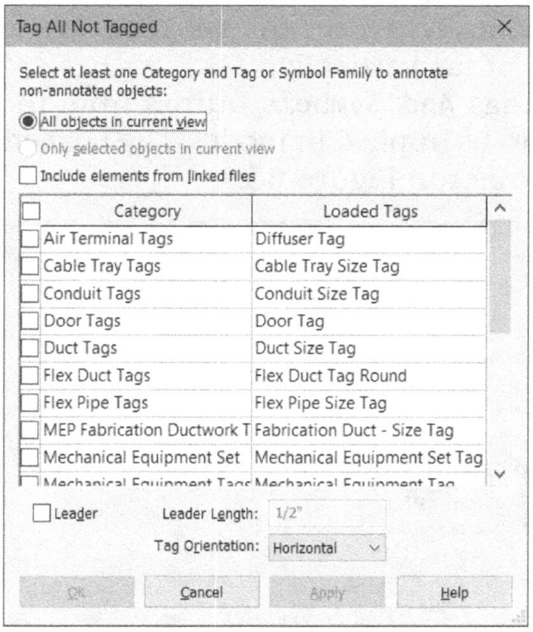

Figure-37. Tag All Not Tagged dialog box

- Select the check boxes for elements to be tagged.
- Select the **Leader** check box if you want to add leader to the tags and set desired parameters.
- Click on the **OK** button from the dialog box to apply tags automatically. The tags will be applied automatically. If there are elements which are not visible then **Category Visibility is Disabled** dialog box will be displayed; refer to Figure-38.

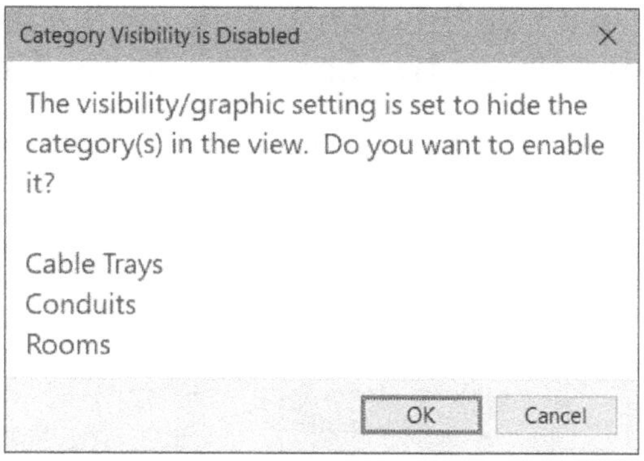

Figure-38. Category Visibility is Disabled dialog box

- Click on the **OK** button from the dialog box. Type **VV** and select the check boxes for elements which are not displaying. Click on the **OK** button from the dialog box.

Applying Beam Annotations

The **Beam Annotation** tool is used to apply tags to structural frames. The procedure to use this tool is given next.

- Click on the **Beam Annotations** tool from the **Tag** panel in the **Annotate** tab of **Ribbon**. You will be asked to load tags.
- Load desired beam annotation tag from the **Load Family** dialog box and click on the **Open** button. The **Beam Annotations** dialog box will be displayed; refer to Figure-39.

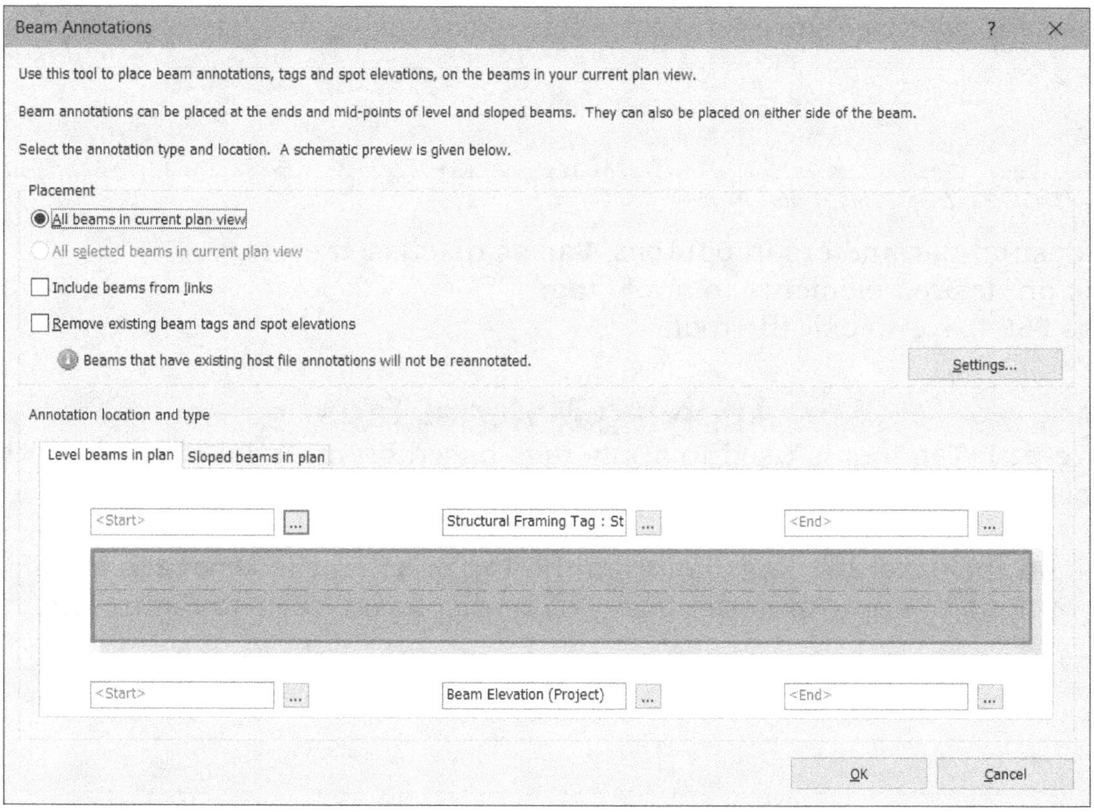

Figure-39. Beam Annotations dialog box

- Select desired check boxes from the **Placement** area to define whether to include beams from linked models and remove existing beam tags & spot elevations.
- Set desired annotation types and their locations from the **Annotation location and type** area.

- Set the other parameters as desired and click on the **OK** button. The annotations will be applied automatically on the beams; refer to Figure-40.

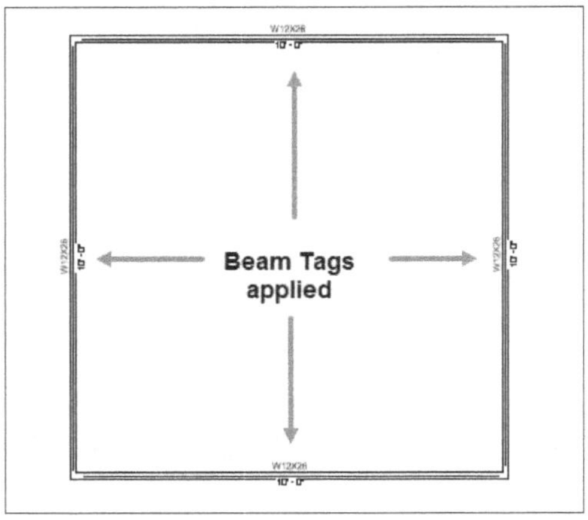

Figure-40. Beam tags applied

Applying Multi-Category Tag

The **Multi-Category Tag** tool is used to apply tags on elements of multiple categories. The procedure to use this tool is given next.

- Click on the **Multi-Category Tag** tool from the **Tag** panel in the **Annotate** tab of **Ribbon**. The **Revit** dialog box will be displayed asking you to load multi-category tags if no tags are loaded.
- Load desired categories as discussed earlier. The options to apply tags will be displayed; refer to Figure-41.

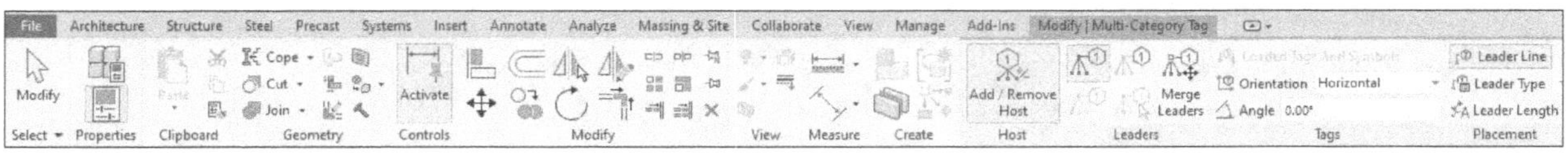

Figure-41. Options to apply multi-category tags

- Set desired parameters in **Options Bar** as discussed earlier.
- Click on desired elements to apply tag.
- Press **ESC** twice to exit the tool.

Applying Material Tags

The **Material Tag** tool is used to apply tags based on material of selected element. The procedure to use this tool is given next.

- Click on the **Material Tag** tool from the **Tag** panel in the **Annotate** tab of **Ribbon**. The options to apply material tags will be displayed; refer to Figure-42.

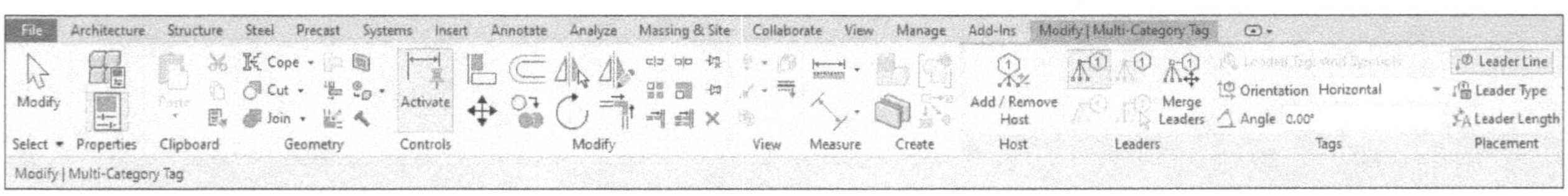

Figure-42. Options to apply material tags

- Set desired parameters for tags as discussed earlier.
- Select desired element to which you want to apply material tag.
- Press **ESC** twice to exit the tool.

Applying Area Tags

The **Area Tag** tool is used to apply tags to areas defined in the model. The procedure to use this tool is given next.

- Click on the **Area Tag** tool from the **Tag** panel in the **Annotate** tab of **Ribbon**. The **Revit** dialog box will be displayed asking you to load area tags. Load desired tags. The area tag will get attached to cursor.
- Click at desired locations in different areas to place the tags.
- Press **ESC** to exit the tool.

Applying Room Tags

The **Room Tag** tool is used to apply tags to rooms created in the building. The procedure to use this tool is given next.

- Click on the **Room Tag** tool from the **Tag** panel in the **Annotate** tab of **Ribbon**. The options to place room tag will be displayed; refer to Figure-43. If tags are not loaded already then load them.

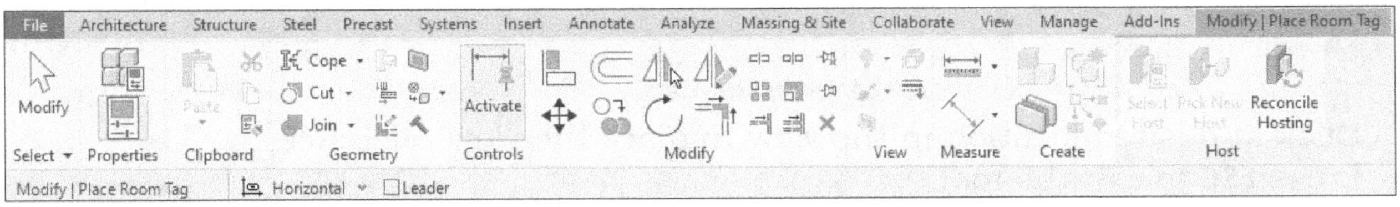

Figure-43. Modify Place Room Tag contextual tab

- Set desired parameters in the **Options Bar** and click at desired location to place the room tag.
- Press **ESC** to exit the tool.

Applying Space Tags

The **Space Tag** tool is used to apply tags to earlier defined spaces. The procedure to apply space tag is given next.

- Click on the **Space Tag** tool from the **Tag** panel in the **Annotate** tab of **Ribbon**. The options to place space tag will be displayed; refer to Figure-44. If space tags are not loaded then load them as discussed earlier.

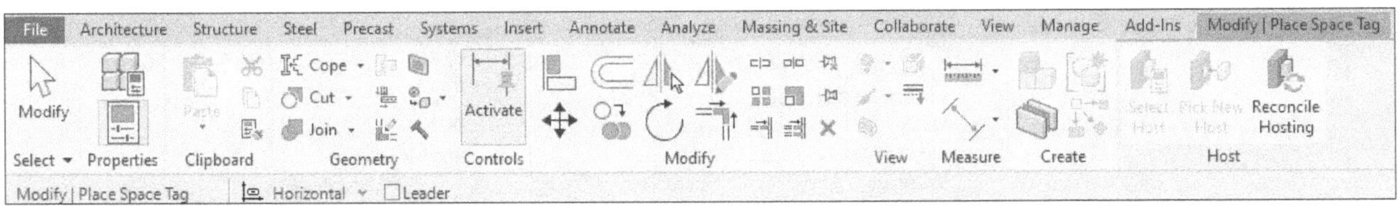

Figure-44. Options to place space tags

- Set desired orientation and leader settings in the **Options Bar**.
- Click in desired space areas to apply tags.
- Press **ESC** to exit the tool.

Applying View References

The **View Reference** tool is used to create an annotation of sheet number and detail number of selected view. The procedure to use this tool is given next.

- Click on the **View Reference** tool from the **Tag** panel in the **Annotate** tab of **Ribbon**. The options to apply view reference will be displayed; refer to Figure-45.
- Select desired options from the **View Type** and **Target View** drop-downs in the contextual tab.

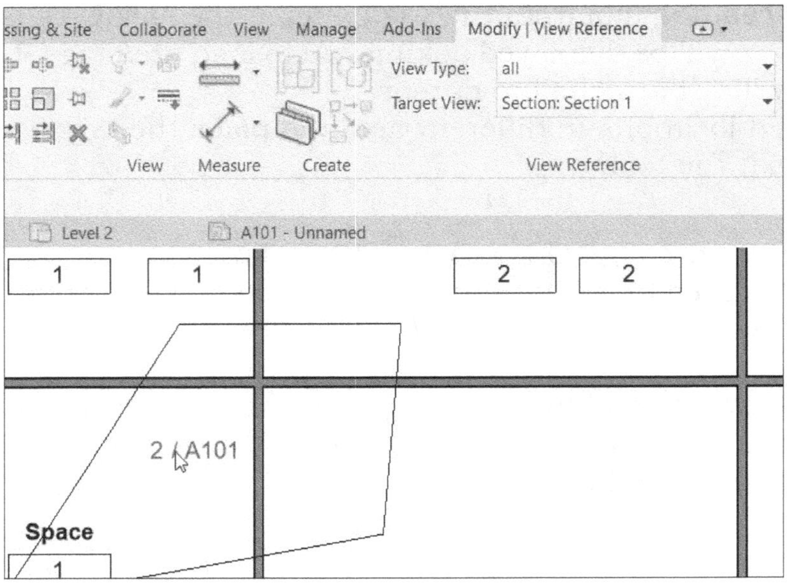

Figure-45. Options to apply view references

- Click at desired location in the view to place the view reference.
- Press **ESC** to exit the tool.

Applying Tread Number

The **Tread Number** tool is used to apply stair/riser numbers to selected stair runs in the plan, elevation, or section views. The procedure to use this tool is given next.

- Click on the **Tread Number** tool from the **Tag** panel in the **Annotate** tab of **Ribbon**. The options to apply tread number will be displayed in the **Properties Palette**; refer to Figure-46.

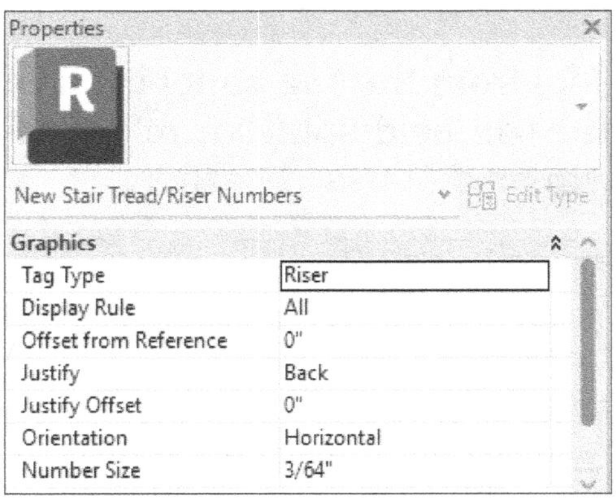

Figure-46. Options for applying tread numbers

- Set desired parameters in the **Properties Palette** and click on desired reference line of stair to apply tread numbers. The tread/riser numbers will be displayed; refer to Figure-47.

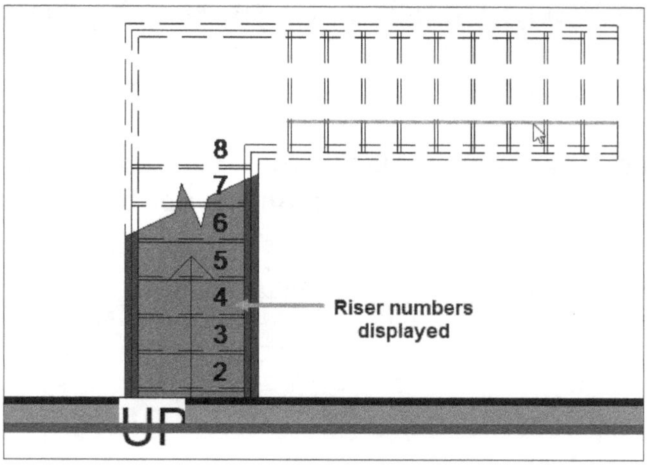

Figure-47. Riser numbers applied to stairs

- Press **ESC** to exit the tool.

Applying Aligned Multi-Rebar Annotations

The **Aligned Multi-Rebar Annotation** tool is used to create multiple annotations aligned to multi-rebar. The procedure to use this tool is given next.

- Click on the **Aligned Multi-Rebar Annotation** tool from the **Multi-Rebar** drop-down in the **Tag** panel of **Annotate** tab in the **Ribbon**. You will be asked to select the references to be dimensioned.
- One by one click on references to which you want to apply dimensions. The dimensions will get attached to cursor; refer to Figure-48.

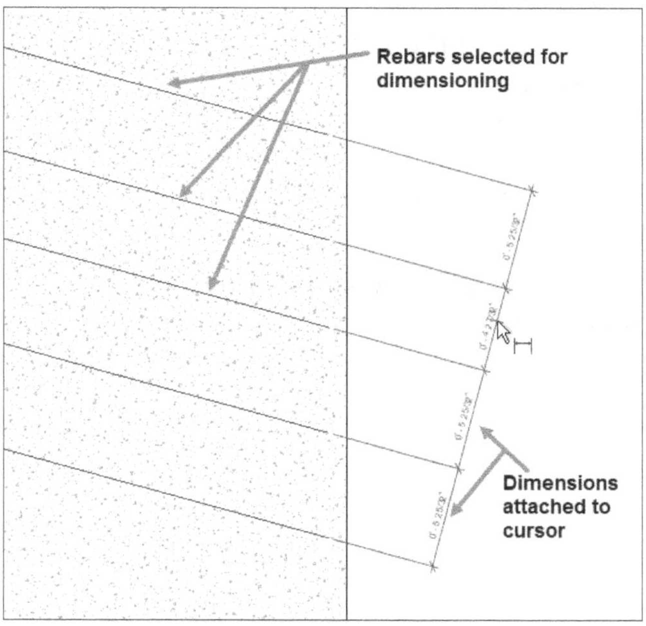

Figure-48. Aligned dimensions attached to cursor

- Click at desired location to place the dimensions.

You can use the **Linear Multi-Rebar Annotation** tool in the same way for linear rebars.

Checking Loaded Tags and Symbols

The **Loaded Tags And Symbols** tool is used to check the loaded tags and symbols in the project. The procedure to use this tool is given next.

- Click on the **Loaded Tags And Symbols** tool from the expanded **Tag** panel in the **Annotate** tab of **Ribbon**. The **Loaded Tags And Symbols** dialog box will be displayed; refer to Figure-49.

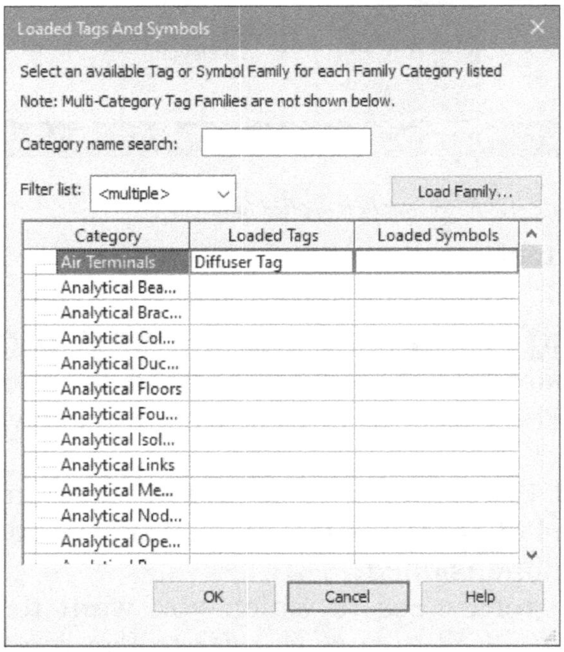

Figure-49. Loaded Tags And Symbols dialog box

- Load desired families of tags and click on the **Load Family** button. The **Load Family** dialog box will be displayed.
- Select desired tag family and click on the **Open** button from the **Load Family** dialog box to load the tag.
- Click on the **OK** button from the dialog box.

Applying Keynotes

The tools in the **Keynote** drop-down are used to apply notes related to elements, material, and other user defined keynote features; refer to Figure-50. Various tools of this drop-down are discussed next.

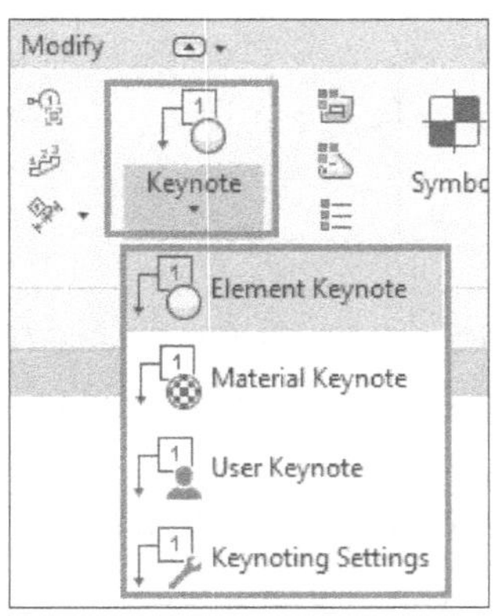

Figure-50. Keynote tools

Keynote Settings

The **Keynoting Settings** tool is used to define location and parameters of key note table. The procedure to use this tool is given next.

- Click on the **Keynoting Settings** tool from the **Keynote** drop-down in the **Tag** panel of **Annotate** tab in the **Ribbon**. The **Keynoting Settings** dialog box will be displayed; refer to Figure-51.

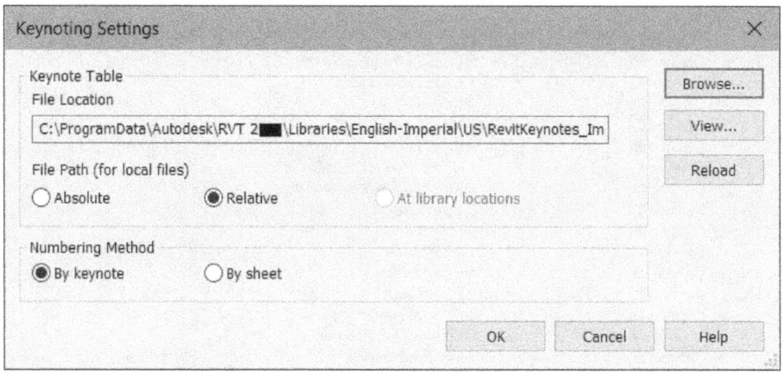

Figure-51. Keynoting Settings dialog box

- Set desired path for keynote table using the **Browse** button.
- Click on the **View** button from the dialog box to check the table. The **Keynotes** dialog box will be displayed; refer to Figure-52.

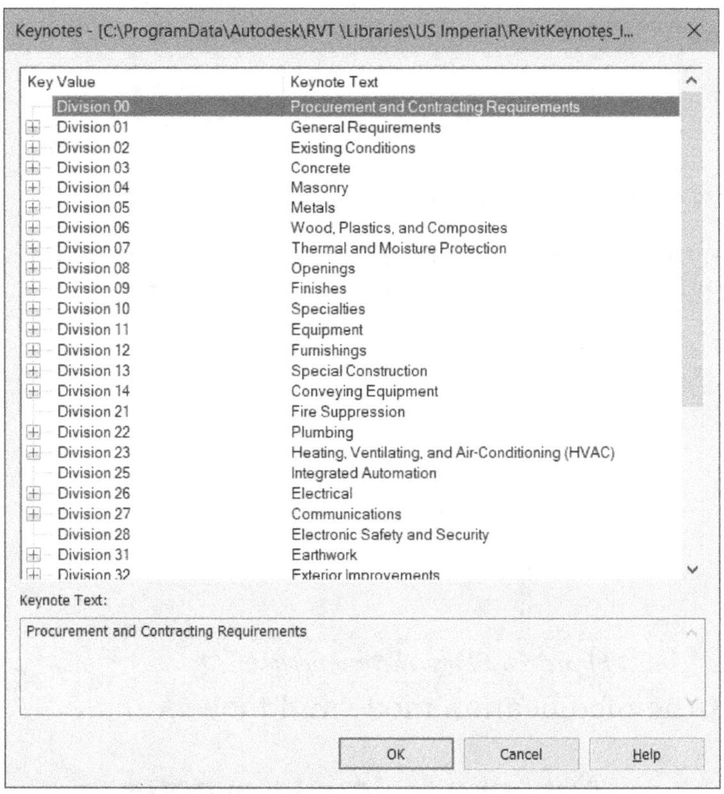

Figure-52. Keynotes dialog box

- Click on the **OK** button from the dialog box to exit.
- Set the other parameters as desired in the dialog box and click on the **OK** button.

Applying Element Keynote

The **Element Keynote** tool is used to place keynote tags for selected elements. The procedure to use this tool is given next.

- Click on the **Element Keynote** tool from the **Keynote** drop-down in the **Tag** panel of **Annotate** tab in the **Ribbon**. You will be asked to select the element to which you want to apply keynote tag.
- Select desired element and place the tag at desired location. The **Keynotes** dialog box will be displayed; refer to Figure-53.

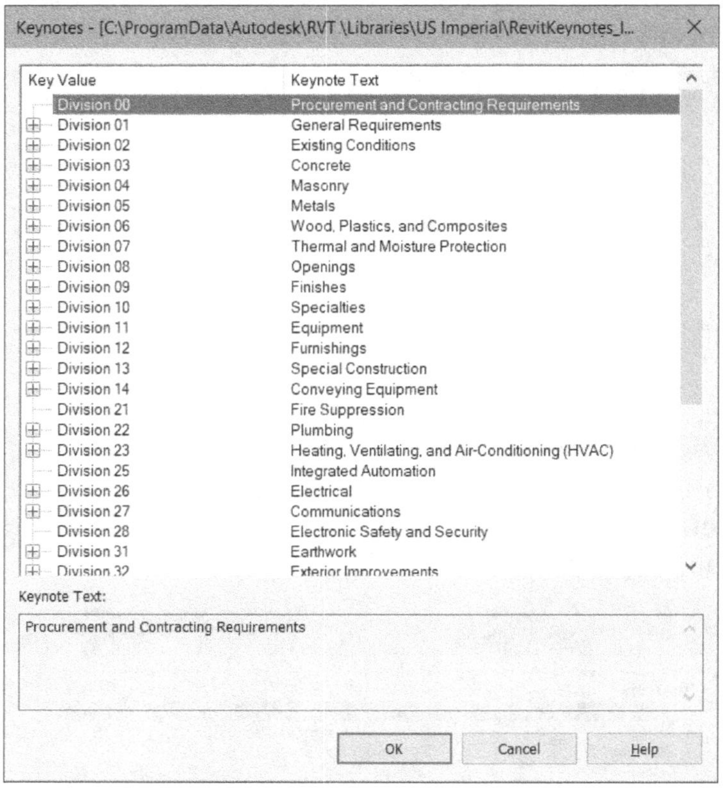

Figure-53. Keynotes dialog box

- Select desired keynote from the dialog box and click on the **OK** button. The keynote tag will be applied; refer to Figure-54.

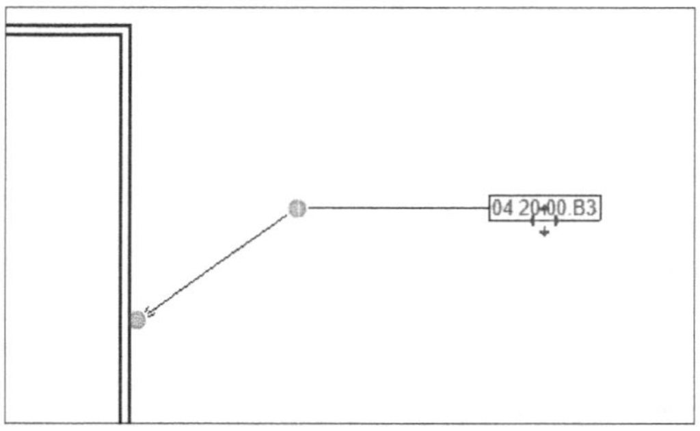

Figure-54. Element keynote applied

- Press **ESC** to exit the modification mode and tool.

Applying Material Keynotes

The **Material Keynote** tool is used to place material keynote for selected element if material is applied on it. The procedure to use this tool is given next.

- Click on the **Material Keynote** tool from the **Keynote** drop-down in the **Tag** panel of **Annotate** tab in the **Ribbon**. You will be asked to select the object to which you want to apply material keynote.

- Click on desired face of element whose material keynote is to be created and place the tag at desired location.
- Press **ESC** to exit the tool.

Placing User Keynote

The **User Keynote** tool is used to place user defined keynotes on selected elements. The procedure to use this tool is given next.

- Click on the **User Keynote** tool from the **Keynote** drop-down in the **Tag** panel of **Annotate** tab in the **Ribbon**. The options to place user keynotes will be displayed; refer to Figure-55.

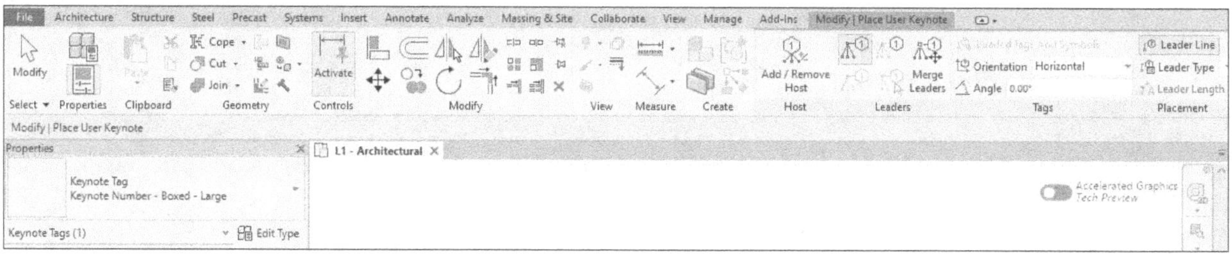

Figure-55. Options to place user keynotes

- Set desired parameters in the **Ribbon** and **Properties Palette**. Click at desired element and define location of tag. The **Keynotes** dialog box will be displayed.
- Select desired keynote tag from the dialog box and click on the **OK** button.
- Press **ESC** to exit the tool.

Placing Symbols

The tools in the **Symbol** panel are used to place symbols and define various parameters for symbols. Various tools in this panel are discussed next.

Placing Symbol

The **Symbol** tool is used to place different types of 2D symbols in the drawing. The procedure to use this tool is given next.

- Click on the **Symbol** tool from the **Symbol** panel in the **Annotate** tab of **Ribbon**. The options to place symbols are displayed; refer to Figure-56.

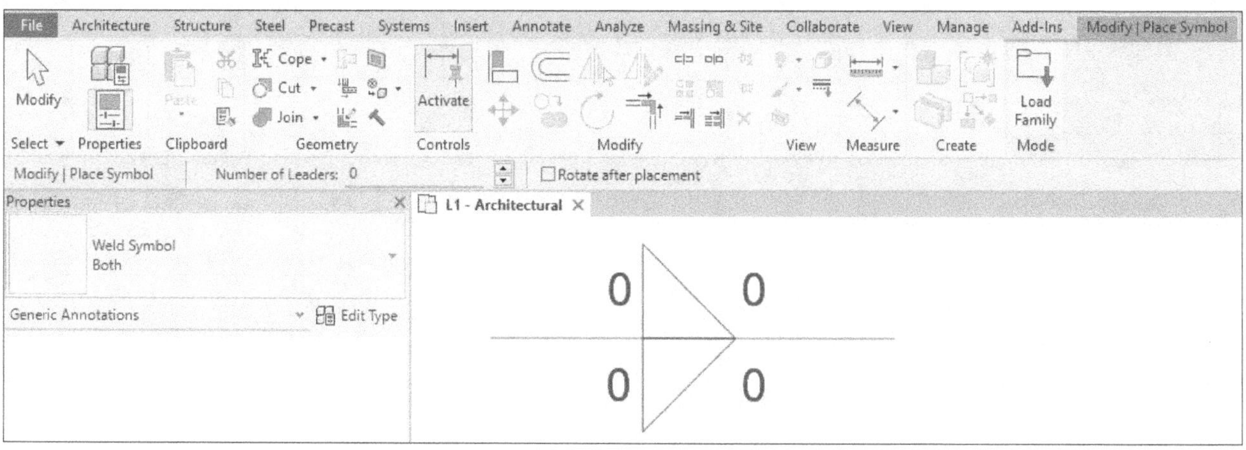

Figure-56. Options for placing symbol

- Load desired symbols if not available by default in the top drop-down of **Properties Palette**.

- Select desired symbol from the **Properties Palette** and set desired parameters in the **Options Bar**.
- Click on desired location where you want to place the symbol.

Placing Span Direction Symbol

The **Span Direction Symbol** tool is used to place symbol for span direction on structural floor. The procedure to place symbol is given next.

- Click on the **Span Direction Symbol** tool from the **Symbol** panel in the **Annotate** tab of **Ribbon**. The options to place the symbol will be displayed; refer to Figure-57.

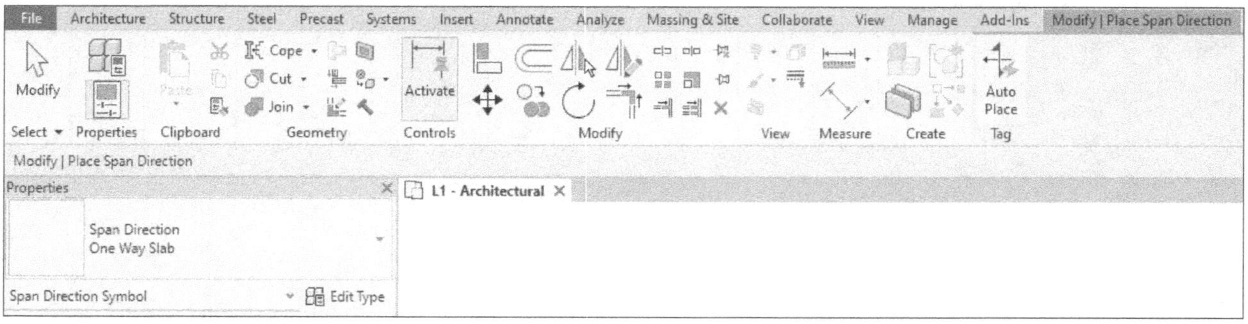

Figure-57. Options to place span direction symbol

- Select desired option from the drop-down at the top in the **Properties Palette** and click on the boundary of structural slab. The symbol will get attached to cursor.
- Click within the boundaries of floor to place the symbol.
- Press **ESC** to exit the tool.

Placing Area Reinforcement Symbol

The **Area Reinforcement Symbol** tool is used to place reinforcement symbol on the selected area reinforcement. Note that you can apply area reinforcement symbols only structural plan. The procedure to use this tool is given next.

- Click on the **Area Reinforcement Symbol** tool from the **Symbol** panel in the **Annotate** tab of **Ribbon**. The options to place area reinforcement symbol will be displayed; refer to Figure-58.

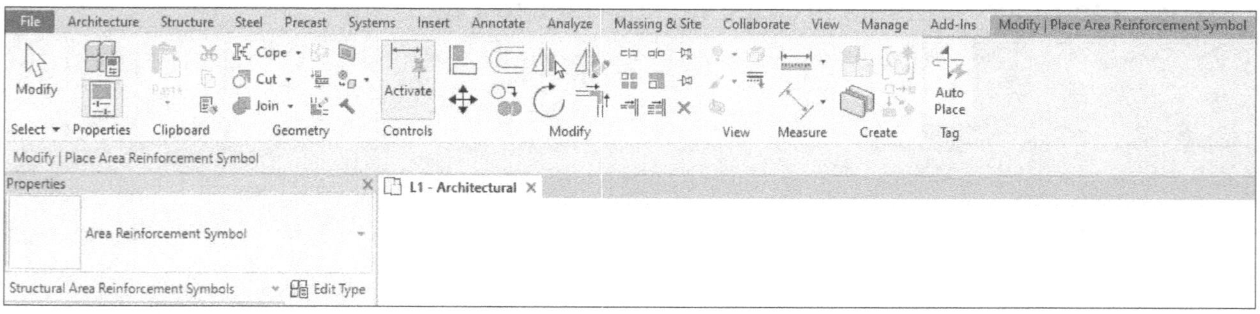

Figure-58. Options for placing area reinforcement symbol

- Select desired area reinforcement. The symbol will be placed on it automatically; refer to Figure-59.

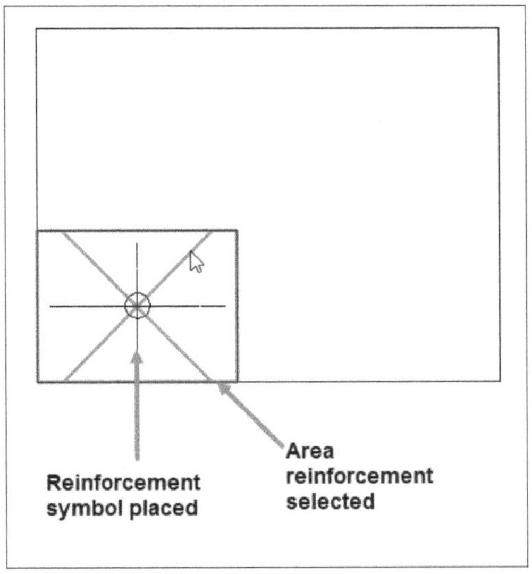

Figure-59. Area reinforcement symbol placed

- Press **ESC** to exit the tool.

Applying Path Reinforcement Symbol

The **Path Reinforcement Symbol** tool is used to place symbol on path reinforcements. The procedure to use this tool is given next.

- Click on the **Path Reinforcement Symbol** tool from the **Symbol** panel in the **Annotate** tab of **Ribbon**. The options to place path reinforcements will be displayed; refer to Figure-60.

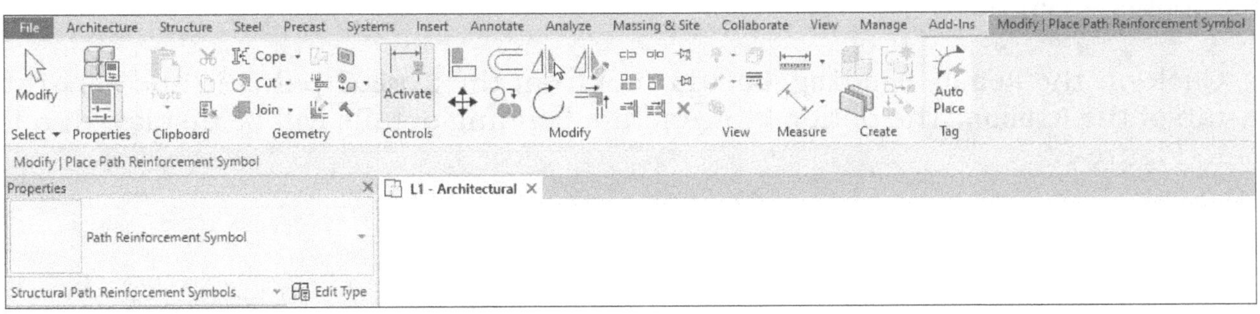

Figure-60. Options to place path reinforcement symbol

- Load the symbol for path reinforcement if not loaded by default.
- Click on the boundary of path reinforcement. The symbol will be placed on the path reinforcement; refer to Figure-61.

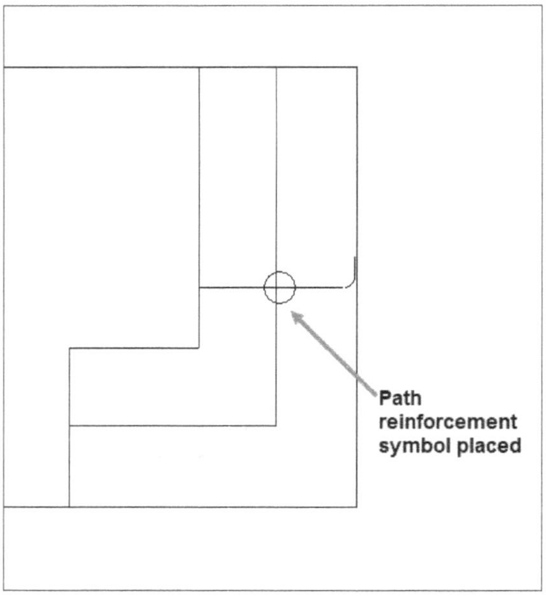

Figure-61. Symbol placed for path reinforcement

- Press **ESC** to exit the tool.

You can use the **Beam System Symbol**, **Fabric Reinforcement Symbol**, and **Stair Path** tools in the same way.

Rebar Bending Detail

The **Rebar Bending Detail** tool is used to generate either realistic or schematic bar bending details for selected individual rebars or rebar sets. The procedure to use this tool is given next.

- Click on the **Rebar Bending Detail** tool from the **Symbol** panel in the **Annotate** tab of the **Ribbon**. The options to generate bending details will be displayed; refer to Figure-62.

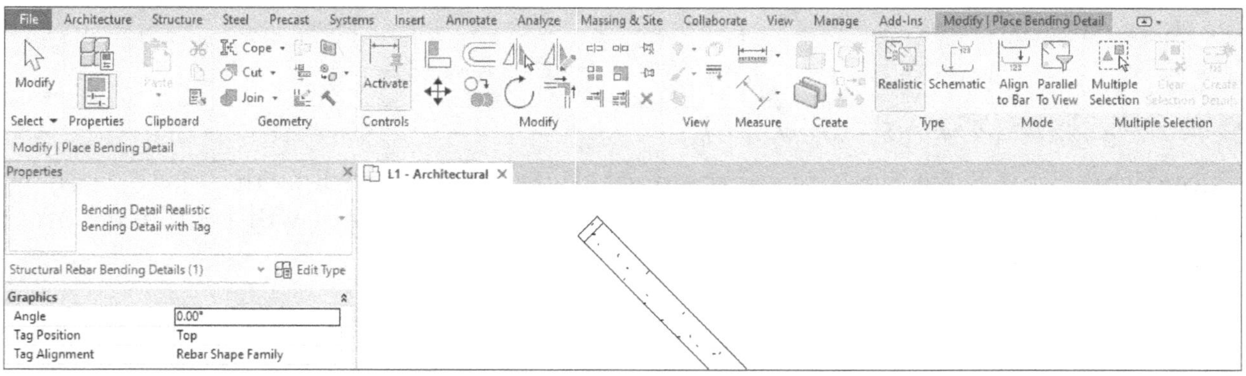

Figure-62. Options to place rebar bending details

- Select desired rebar or rebar sets from the graphics window. The rebar bending details will be displayed; refer to Figure-63.

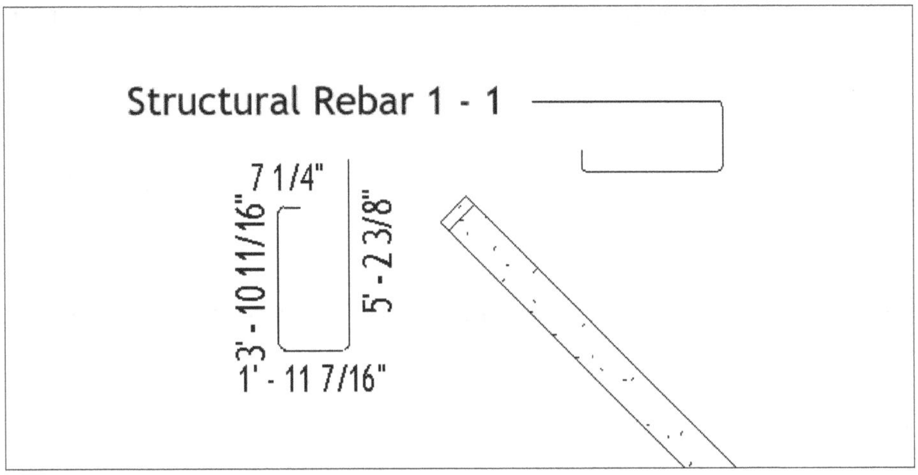

Figure-63. Rebar bending details displayed

- Press **Esc** to exit the tool.

SELF-ASSESSMENT

Q1. Discuss the use of **Aligned** tool and Linear tool for creating annotations.

Q2. Using the **Radial** tool, you can create diameter dimension for arc walls.

Q3. The .... tool is used to display coordinate value for selected point.

Q4. Discuss the use of **Material Keynote** tool.

Q5. What does the Aligned tool in the Dimension panel allow you to do?

A. Create circular dimensions on arcs
B. Create dimensions aligned along selected walls
C. Add slope measurements
D. Place components in model view

Q6. Which reference option should you select to use the centerlines of walls for aligned dimensions?

A. Faces of core
B. Wall faces
C. Wall centerlines
D. Center of core

Q7. What does the Auto Dimension Options dialog box appear after selecting?

A. Individual References
B. Entire Walls
C. Line Style
D. Openings

Q8. What tool is used to create a dimension between two selected reference points in a straight line?

A. Aligned
B. Angular
C. Radial
D. Linear

Q9. Which tool is used to create an angular dimension between selected references?

A. Radial
B. Arc Length
C. Angular
D. Linear

Q10. What is the first step when using the Radial tool?

A. Select intersecting walls
B. Choose dimension type
C. Select an arc to be dimensioned
D. Pick a closed loop

Q11. What type of elements does the Diameter tool work with?

A. Straight lines only
B. Arcs and circles
C. Grid intersections
D. Text labels

Q12. Which tool is used to show elevation value at a point in the model?

A. Spot Slope
B. Spot Coordinate
C. Spot Elevation
D. Spot Detail

Q13. What must be selected when using the Spot Coordinate tool?

A. A wall corner
B. A model point
C. A filled region
D. A detail group

Q14. Which tool allows you to show slope information on inclined walls?

A. Spot Slope
B. Spot Elevation
C. Spot Coordinate
D. Text

Q15. Which tool is used to create a 2D graphic region with a fill pattern?

A. Masking Region
B. Filled Region
C. Revision Cloud
D. Text

Q16. What is the purpose of the Masking Region tool?

A. Show topography
B. Create shadows
C. Obscure elements behind a region
D. Display insulation

Q17. Which tool is used to insert standard components like bricks or blocks for detailing?

A. Repeating Detail Component
B. Detail Line
C. Detail Component
D. Legend Component

Q18. What does the Repeating Detail Component tool allow you to do?

A. Create a 3D model
B. Place a group of legends
C. Place an array of detail components
D. Add multiple text boxes

Q19. Which tool is only available when a legend view is open?

A. Revision Cloud
B. Detail Group
C. Legend Component
D. Masking Region

Q20. What is the use of the Revision Cloud tool?

A. To mark important annotations
B. To obscure geometry
C. To indicate model changes
D. To measure dimensions

Q21. Which tool allows grouping of detail elements for reuse?

A. Place Group
B. Create Group
C. Repeating Detail
D. Fill Region

Q22. What does the Insulation tool help you create?

A. Detail groups
B. Closed loops
C. Insulation for elements
D. Core wall dimensions

Q23. How do you define the text size when using the Text tool?

A. Through the Annotate tab
B. Using the Ribbon
C. From the Properties Palette
D. By selecting the wall type

Q24. What is the purpose of the Check Spelling tool?

A. To check for grammar errors in the project
B. To replace images in a view
C. To check and correct spelling errors in selected notes or views
D. To change font styles in annotations

Q25. Which button is used to add a misspelled word to the dictionary in the Check Spelling dialog box?

A. Change
B. Ignore All
C. Add
D. Close

Q26. What does the Find/Replace tool help with in a project?

A. Replacing view templates
B. Editing view scales
C. Finding and replacing specified words
D. Creating tags for annotations

Q27. Which radio buttons are used in Find/Replace to define the search area?

A. Format options
B. Replace All buttons
C. Scope area options
D. Selection filters

Q28. What is the function of the Tag by Category tool?

A. Tag elements based on their materials
B. Tag elements based on their category
C. Tag rooms by area
D. Tag views based on visibility

Q29. Which key should you press to exit the Tag by Category tool?

A. Enter
B. ESC twice
C. Delete
D. Ctrl+Z

Q30. When using the Tag All tool, which box must be selected to add a leader to the tag?

A. Category
B. Scope
C. Leader
D. View

Q31. What dialog box appears if elements are not visible after applying tags with Tag All?

A. Tagging Failed
B. Elements Missing
C. Visibility Error
D. Category Visibility is Disabled

Q32. Which tool is used to tag structural frames?

A. Room Tag
B. Beam Annotations
C. View Reference
D. Keynote Settings

Q33. What is the use of the Multi-Category Tag tool?

A. Apply multiple tags to a single category
B. Apply tags to one selected element
C. Apply tags to elements of different categories
D. Apply symbols instead of tags

Q34. What do you click to tag areas in a model using the Area Tag tool?

A. Floor level
B. View boundary
C. Area boundaries
D. Room center

Q35. What happens when you click Re-center Reference in room tagging?

A. Room tag is deleted
B. Reference line moves to door
C. Reference line moves to the center of the room
D. Tags are removed

Q36. Which tool is used to create annotations showing sheet and detail number of a selected view?

A. Material Tag
B. View Reference
C. Room Tag
D. User Keynote

Q37. What do you select to apply tread numbers to stairs?

A. Stair boundary
B. Room center
C. Reference line of stair
D. Tag panel

Q38. Which tool creates aligned annotations for multi-rebar elements?

A. Beam Annotations
B. Path Reinforcement Symbol
C. Aligned Multi-Rebar Annotation
D. Fabric Reinforcement Symbol

Q39. Where can you check what tags and symbols are already loaded in a project?

A. View Settings
B. Loaded Tags And Symbols
C. Tag by Category
D. Annotate Options

Q40. What is the purpose of Keynoting Settings?

A. To delete unused keynote families
B. To define parameters of tag alignment
C. To set location and parameters of keynote table
D. To reload symbols

Q41. Which keynote tool is used to place tags for materials applied on elements?

A. Element Keynote
B. User Keynote
C. View Reference
D. Material Keynote

Q42. What do you use to apply a custom user-defined keynote?

A. Element Keynote
B. Room Tag
C. User Keynote
D. Area Tag

Q43. What is the Symbol tool used for?

A. Applying dimension lines
B. Placing 2D symbols in drawings
C. Placing structural loads
D. Assigning materials

Q44. Which tool places a symbol to indicate span direction on a floor slab?

A. Span Direction Symbol
B. Area Tag
C. Tread Number
D. Beam Symbol

Q45. On which type of view can Area Reinforcement Symbols be applied?

A. 3D views
B. Section views
C. Structural plans
D. Elevations

For Student Notes

Chapter 14

Macro Management and Visual Scripting (Introduction)

Topics Covered

The major topics covered in this chapter are:

- ***Creating and Managing Macros***
- ***Macro Security Settings***
- ***Visual Scripting with Dynamo***

MANAGING MACROS

Macros are small programs used to extend the capabilities of software or automate a task. In Revit, you need to write the whole codes manually to create a macro. There are four different languages in which you can create macros viz. C#, VB.NET, Ruby, and Python. To write code of macro, you need to have basic understanding of programming in any one of these languages. The **Macro Manager** tool is used to create, edit, and manage macros. You need to make sure Visual Studio Code and .NET SDK 8.0 is installed before using the Macros. The procedure to use this tool is given next.

Macro Security Settings

The **Macro Security** tool is used to enable/disable application based and document based macros. The procedure to use this tool is given next.

- Click on the **Macro Security** tool from the **Extensions** panel in the **Manage** tab of the **Ribbon**. The **Options** dialog box will be displayed; refer to Figure-1.

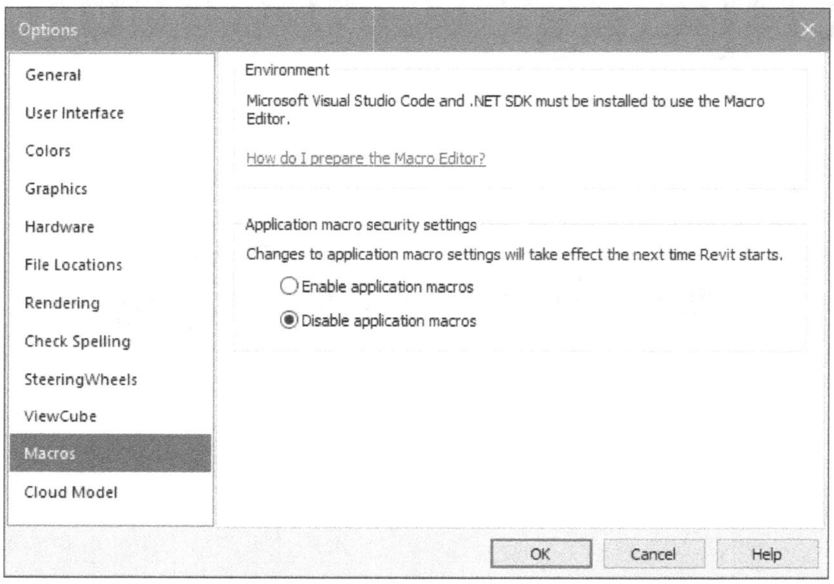

Figure-1. Macros options

- Select **Enable application macros** radio button form the **Application macro security settings** area to allow creation of application macros in the software.
- Set the other parameters as discussed earlier and click on the **OK** button.

Creating Macro Module

Macro Module is a group of macros. Macros in a macro module can share data with each other or they can be independent. There are two type of macro modules; Application based and Document based. The Application based modules are universal and can be applied to user interface as well as any project file. Application based modules do not need any project file to be open for functioning. The document based modules are specific to the document and do not function outside that document. The procedure to create macro module is given next.

- Click on the **Macro Manager** tool from the **Extensions** panel in the **Manage** tab of **Ribbon**. The **Macro Manager** dialog box will be displayed; refer to Figure-2.
- Click on the **Create new Marco module** button. The **Create a New Module** dialog box will be displayed; refer to Figure-3.

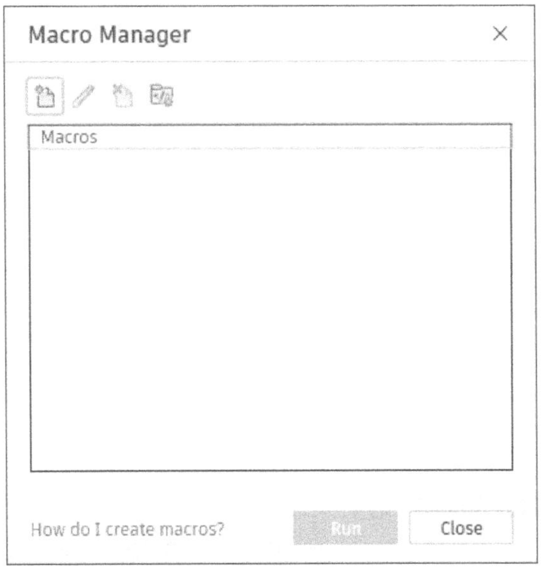

Figure-2. Macro Manager dialog box

Figure-3. Create a New Module dialog box

- Specify desired name of module in **Module name** edit box and select desired programming language from the **Language** drop-down.
- After specifying desired parameters, click on the **OK** button. The coding environment for the module will be displayed in the **Visual Studio Code** application; refer to Figure-4.

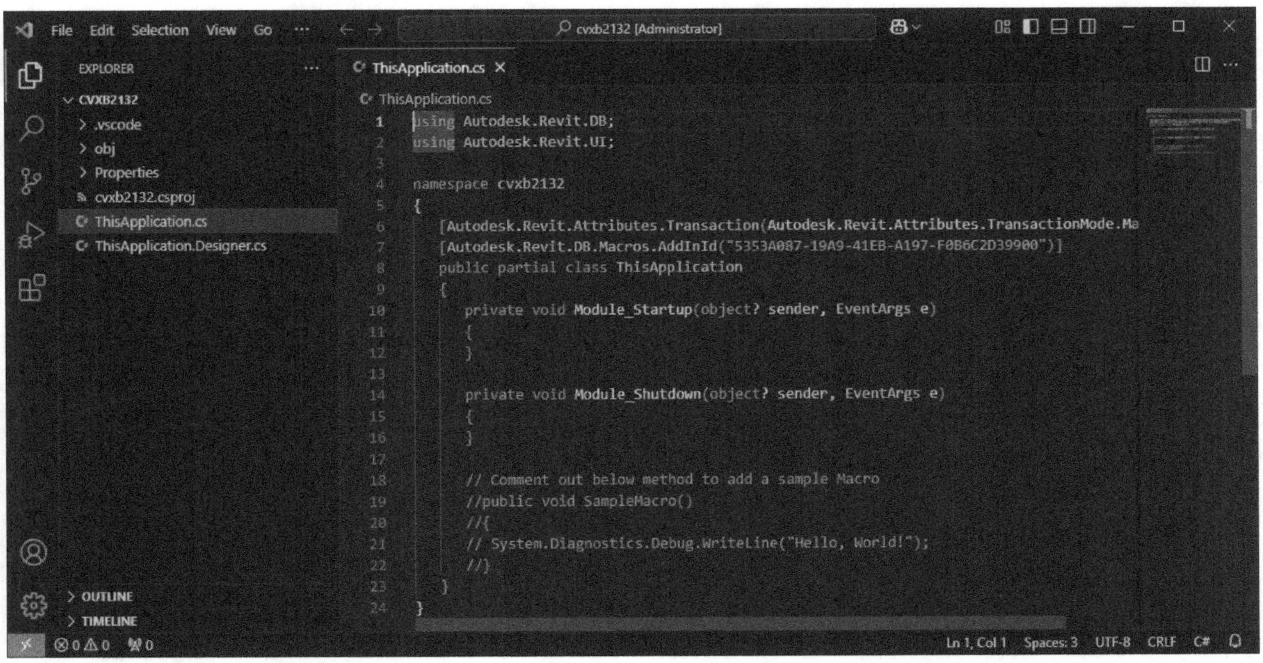

Figure-4. Visual Studio Code application

- If you have earlier worked on programming languages then you will find that Module is a program frame and various macros are functions created in this frame. Each macro can use variables defined in the module as well as variables defined inside the function.
- You either minimize the Visual Studio Code application or click on the **Close** button to return to Revit Application. The new module will be added in the **Macro Manager**; refer to Figure-5.

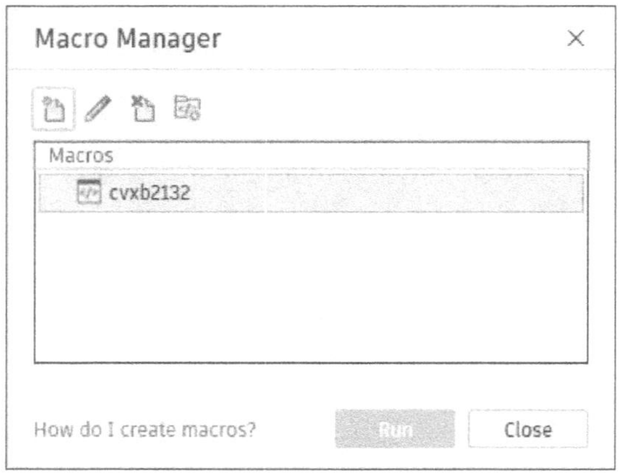

Figure-5. Module added in Macro Manager

Creating Macro

- Click on the **Create new Macro module** button. The **Create a New Module** dialog box will be displayed; refer to Figure-6.

Figure-6. Create a New Module dialog box

- Specify desired name of macro in the **Module name** edit box and click on the **OK** button. The container code for new macro will be added in the module coding and program will be displayed in Visual Studio Code. Note that the programming language of module will be automatically selected for the macro; refer to Figure-7.

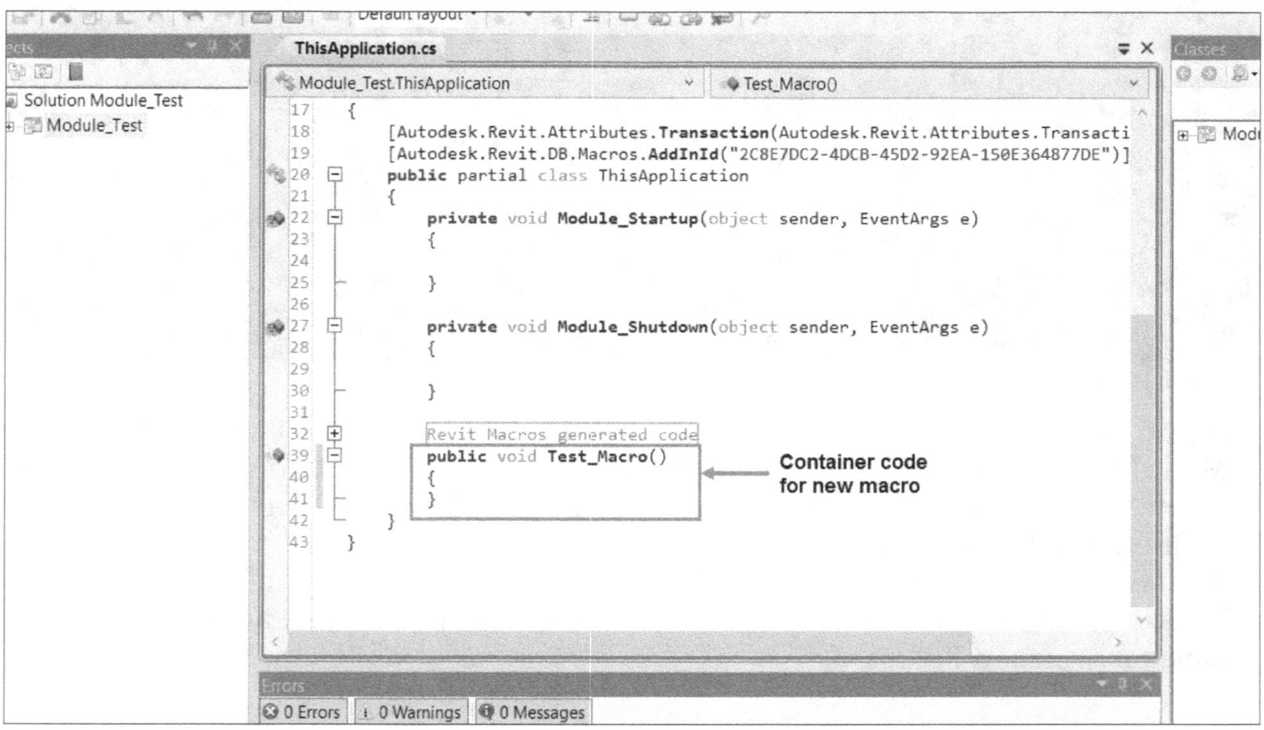

Figure-7. Macro coded added in module

- From this point, you can start to create, build, and debug codes for macros. There are various functions available in Revit API for direct use. To use these functions, you need to install Revit SDK (only once). Make sure you have closed the Revit application before installation. Visit the link **https://www.autodesk.com/developer-network/platform-technologies/revit** and click on the **Revit .NET SDK** link button on this webpage to download the SDK installer; refer to Figure-8. After downloading, run the installation package from your downloads folder and install at desired location.

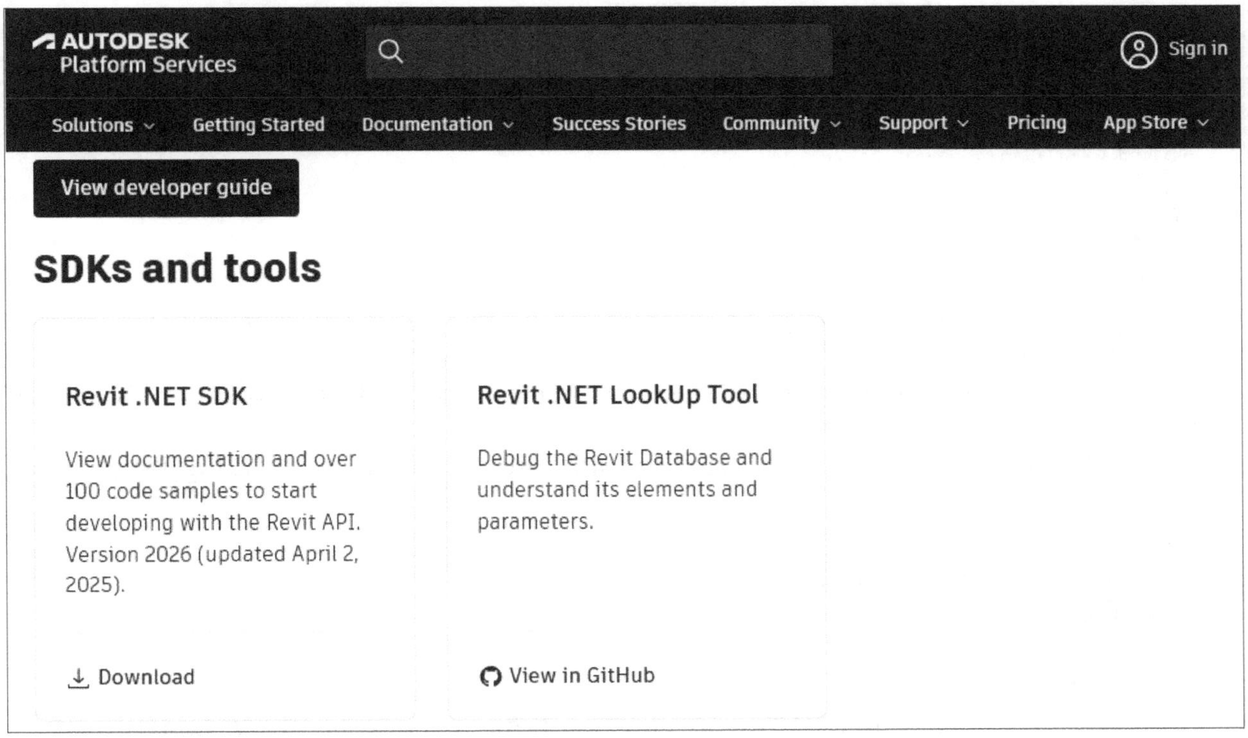

Figure-8. Revit SDK link

- After installation, open the SDK folder and open RevitAPI.chm file; refer to Figure-9. The Revit API help file will open; refer to Figure-10.

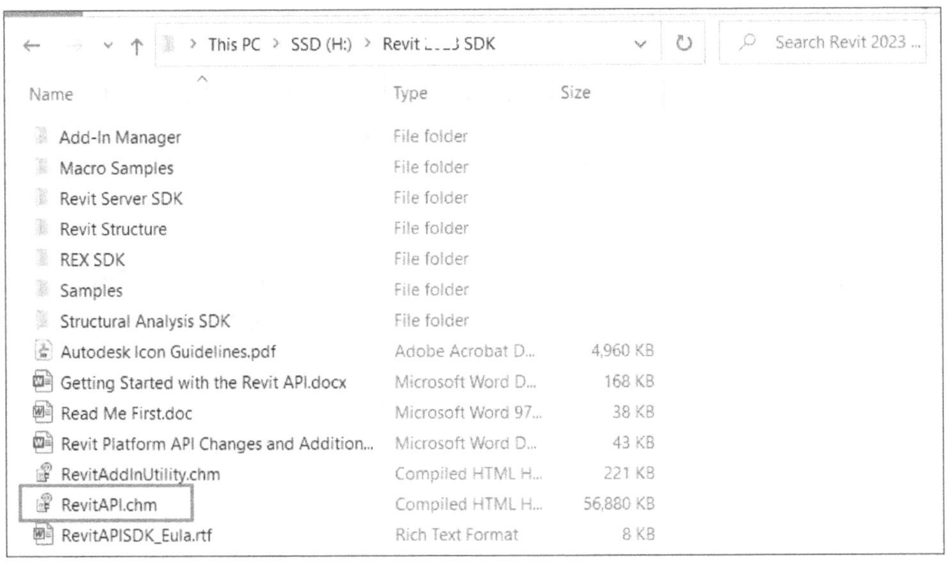

Figure-9. RevitAPI chm file

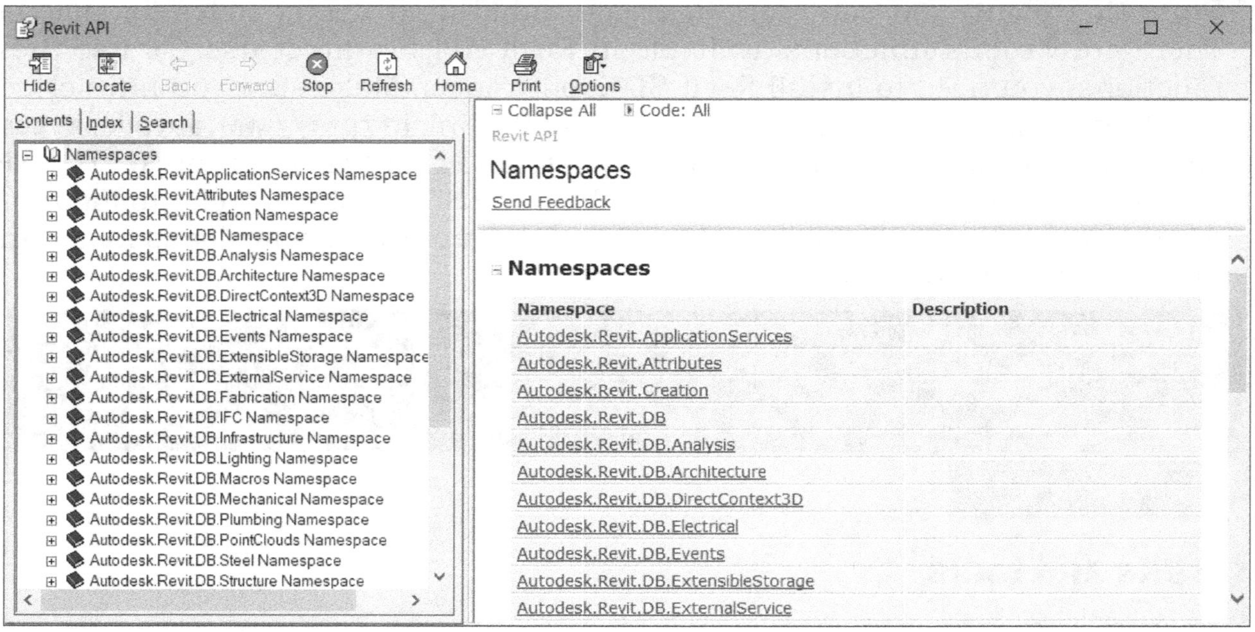

Figure-10. Revit API help

- Using this help file, you can learn about various functions available for use and then apply them in your macro codes.
- Here is sample code for macro that displays text output in a dialog box:

```
using System;
using Autodesk.Revit.UI;
public void Test Macro()

        {
                TaskDialog.Show("This is a test of macro", "Keep Learning");
        }
```

Here, TaskDialog is a class under Autodesk.RevitUI namespace and in this class, we are using Show function to display desired text note.

- After writing the codes, click on the **Build Solution** tool from the **Build** menu or press **F8**. System will convert the codes into machine readable codes for macro. If there are errors in the code then they will be displayed in the **Errors** area of the application window.
- Resolve the errors as guided by system and save the file.
- Now, open the Revit Application and run newly created macro by using **Run** button from the **Macro Manager** to check its functioning; refer to Figure-11.

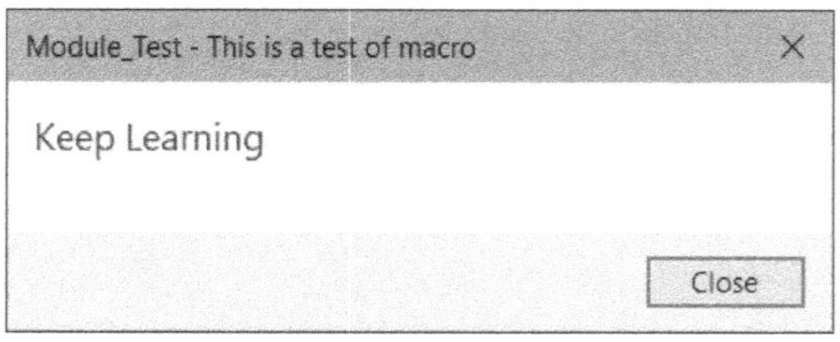

Figure-11. Output for specified macro code

Using Revit API Help file

The process to open Revit API help file has been discussed earlier, so we are not repeating the process. Click on the **Search** tab from the help interface and search TaskDialog members to see the functions available in TaskDialog class; refer to Figure-12. Double-click on the topic from search to check help.

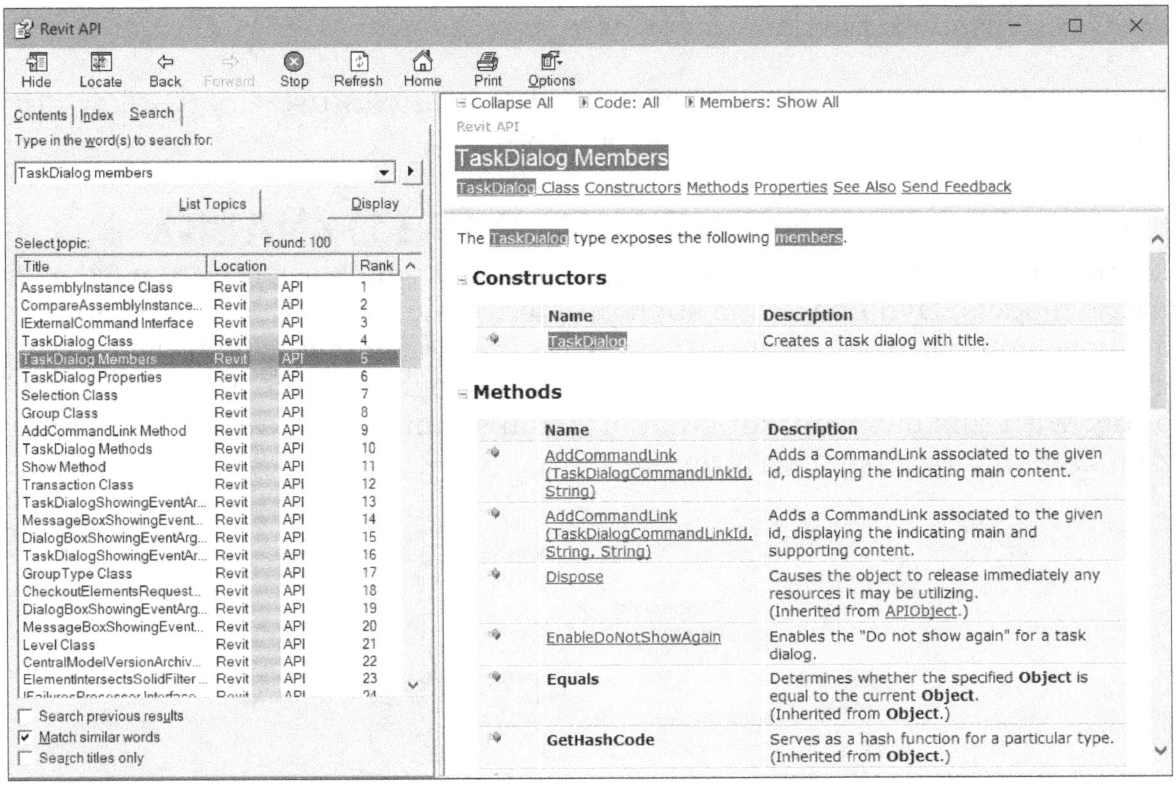

Figure-12. Task Dialog class members

Now, suppose you want to use Show(String, String, TaskDialogCommonButtons) function of TaskDialog class then click on the link button to learn more about it. After learning the codes from help file, you will get to know that you can also use following piece of code to display same information with **OK** and **Cancel** buttons. The same dialog box of macro will be displayed as shown in Figure-13.

```
public void Test Macro()
{
TaskDialog.Show("This is a test of macro", "Keep Learning",
TaskDialogCommonButtons.Ok | TaskDialogCommonButtons.Cancel);
}
```

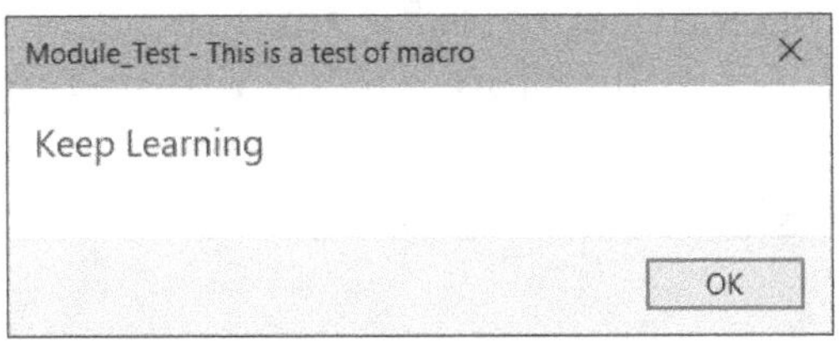

Figure-13. Updated macro

Common Operations in Macro Manager

- The **Run** button in **Macro Manager** dialog box is used to run selected macro. To use this button, select desired macro from the module and click on the **Run** button.

- The **Edit** button in **Macro Manager** dialog box is used to open source code of selected macro in Visual Studio Code application.
- The **Step Into** button is used to create break point in the source code for debugging. Use the **F10** key to check the source code line by line once the Sharp Develop application is displayed with source code.
- The **Delete** button is used to delete selected macro or module. Rest of the buttons have been discussed earlier.

Once you have basic understanding of Macros, you can use ChatGPT or other AI agents to generate codes using proper prompting.

VISUAL SCRIPTING WITH DYNAMO

The Visual Programming is a field of programming in which scripts are used to create geometric models. Dynamo is one such program which uses visual scripting. In this application, you can provide inputs using codes and nodes which act as base for other output code blocks/nodes. Figure-14 shows one example of node based visual scripting. With this basic introduction of visual scripting, you will now learn how to work on Dynamo for visual scripting.

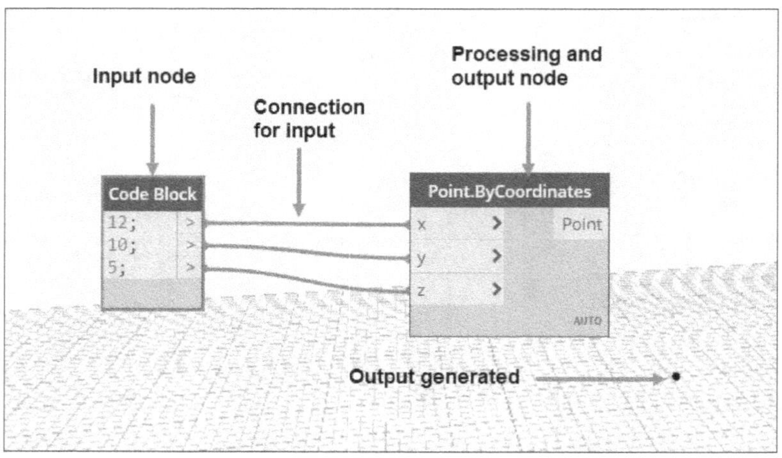

Figure-14. Example of node based visual scripting

Starting Dynamo

The **Dynamo** tool is used to start Dynamo application for scripting. The procedure to start Dynamo is given next.

- Open a document in Revit or start a new document.
- Click on the **Dynamo** tool from the **Visual Programming** panel in the **Manage** tab of **Ribbon**. The Dynamo application interface will be displayed; refer to Figure-15.
- The first page of Dynamo application is a common page having tools to get help resources, start a new file, open a file, and custom node creation tools. Click on the link button at the right side in application to get related help and resources.

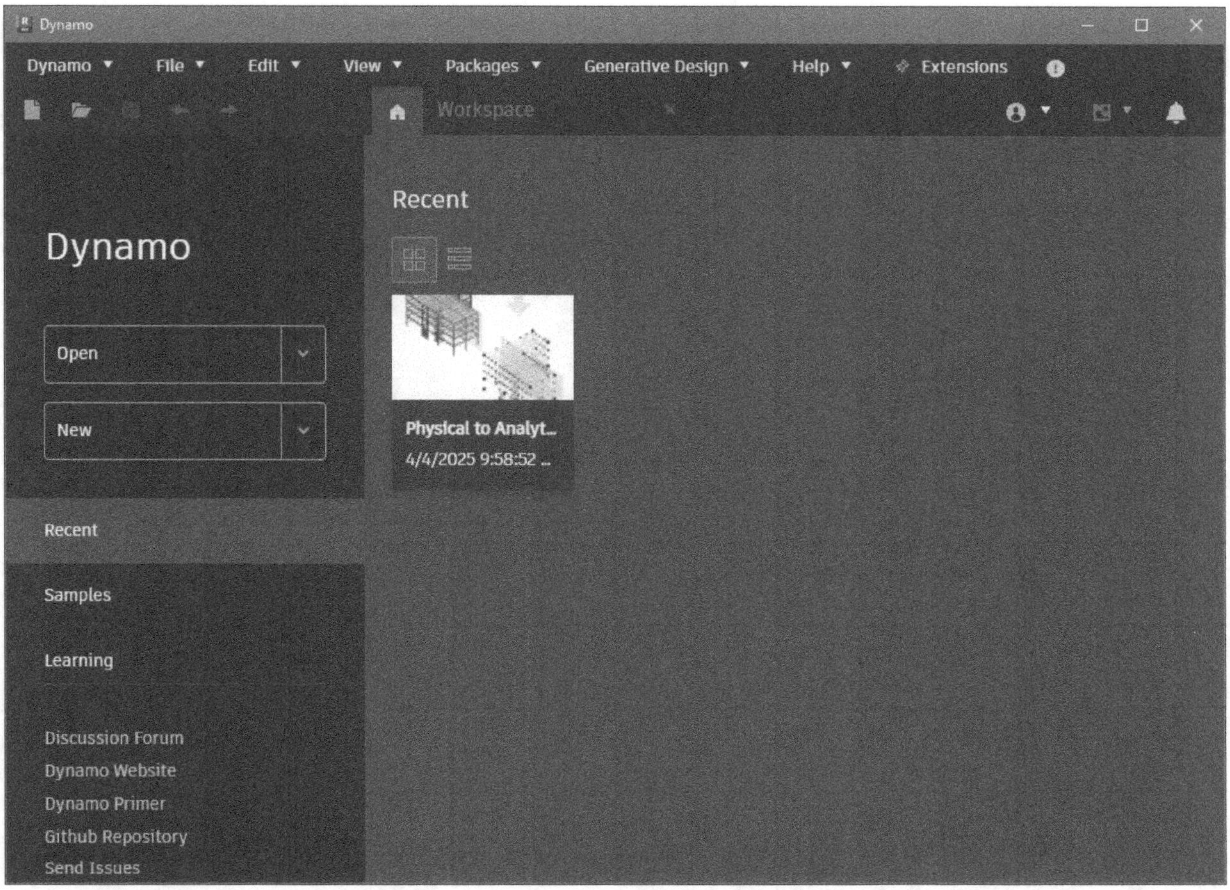

Figure-15. Dynamo application

Starting a New Dynamo Script

The **New** tool in **FILES** area of first page is used to create a new script of Dynamo. The procedure to start new script and basic user interface of Dynamo is discussed next.

- Click on the **Home Workspace** tool from **New** cascading menu in the **File** menu; refer to Figure-16. A new file will be created; refer to Figure-17.

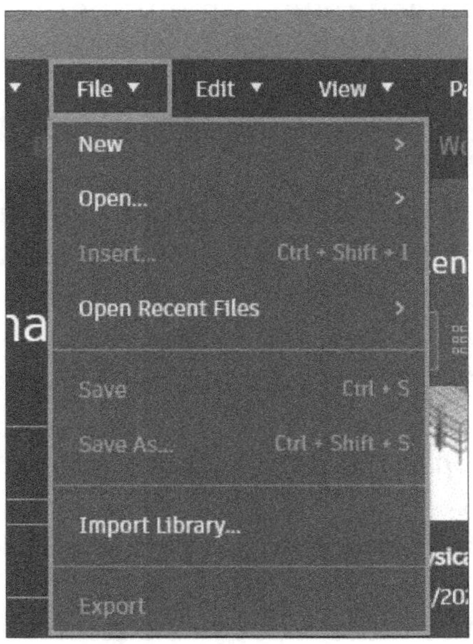

Figure-16. Home Workspace tool

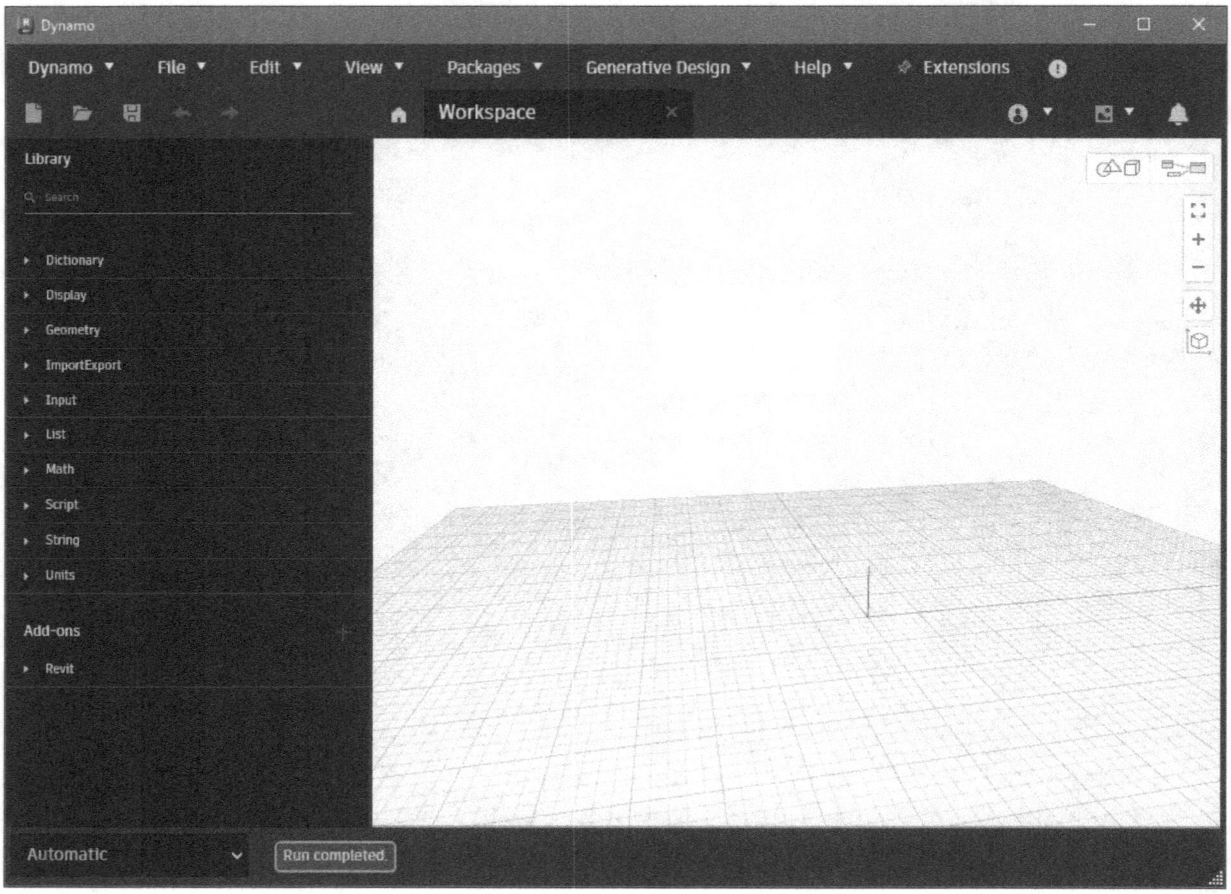

Figure-17. New file created in Dynamo

Various components of user interface are discussed next.

Menu Bar

The **Menu Bar** contains all the menus containing different tools to perform operations suggested by their names. For example, the **File** menu contains all the options related to file handling, the **View** menu contains tools related to view operations, and so on. Some of the most commonly used tools of menu bar are described next.

File Menu

- The **Home Workspace** tool in **New** cascading menu of **File** menu is used to create a new script.
- The **Custom Node** tool in **New** cascading menu of **File** menu is used to create custom nodes which can later be used to create model using visual scripting.
- The **Open** tool in **File** menu is used to open an earlier created dynamo script or dynamo custom node file.
- The **Insert** tool in **File** menu is used to insert earlier created dynamic script in the current design.
- Select desired file from **Open Recent Files** cascading menu to open recently worked files.
- The **Save** tool in **File** menu is used to save dynamo scripts and custom node files in storage drive.
- The **Save As** tool is used to create a copy of current file with new name at desired location.

- The **Import Library** tool is used to import a library of script files that can be used in Dynamo. The major formats available to import are DLL and DS.
- The **Export Workspace As Image** tool in **Export** cascading menu is used to take a capture of current workspace and save it in PNG format.
- The **Export Background 3D Preview as Image** tool in **Export** cascading menu is used to take a capture of background 3D preview of scripted model and save it as PNG format file.
- The **Export Model to STL** tool in **Export** cascading menu is used to save current 3D preview as model file in STL format. The STL file can be imported in many CAD/CAM/CAE software.

Edit Menu

- The **Undo** tool in **Edit** menu is used to reverse the latest operation performed in software. You can also press **CTRL+Z** to use this tool.
- The **Redo** tool in **Edit** menu is used repeat the operation dissolved by **Undo** tool. You can also press **CTRL+Y** to use this tool.
- The **Copy** tool in **Edit** menu is used to copy selected node. Note that this tool will be active only when a node is selected in the workspace. You can also use **CTRL+C** to copy selected node.
- The **Paste** tool in **Edit** menu is used to place duplicate of node earlier copied by the **Copy** tool. You can also use **CTRL+V** to paste selected node.
- The **Create Note** tool in **Edit** menu is used to create a text note in which you can type desired instructions as text. You can also use **CTRL+W** to create a text note; refer to Figure-18.

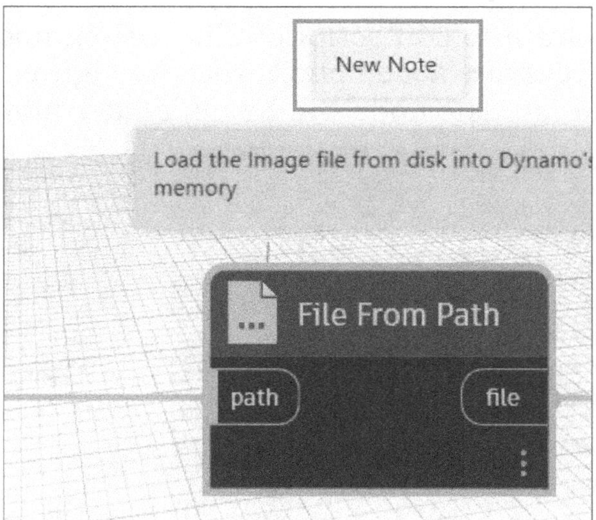

Figure-18. Writing text note

- The **Create Group** tool in **Edit** menu is used to create a group of multiple nodes. You can group nodes based on their output object. For example, there is a cone created by multiple nodes then you can group those nodes and mark them with description of cone. The **Create Group** tool is active only when a node is selected. Press and hold **SHIFT** key to select multiple nodes and click on the **Create Group** tool. The group will be created and you will be asked to define group title; refer to Figure-19. Double-click on **<Click here to edit the group title>** text and type desired name for group. You can also press **CTRL+G** key to activate the **Create Group** tool.

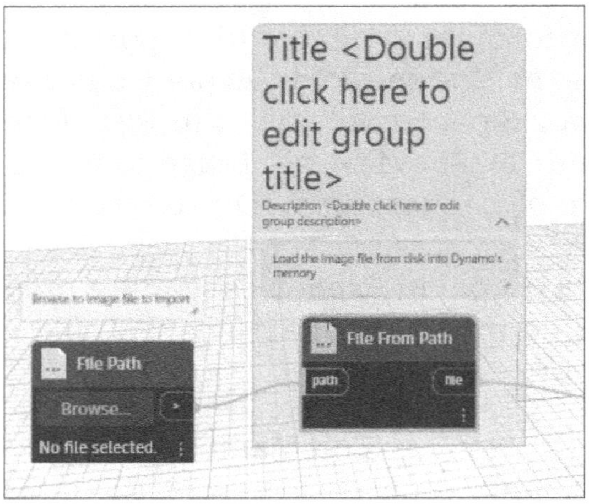

Figure-19. Group created

- The **Ungroup** tool in **Edit** menu is used to disband the group. This tool is active only when a group is selected. You can also use **CTRL+U** to active this tool.
- The **Create Custom Node** tool is used to create a custom node property. This custom property can later be used as node for the model. Note that the custom nodes created by this tool are placed in **Add-ons** section of library. On clicking this tool, the **Custom Node Properties** dialog box will be displayed; refer to Figure-20. Specify desired name, description, and category in the dialog box and click on the **Save** button. The node with specified parameters will be created; refer to Figure-21. Note that all the operations performed in the workspace prior to creating custom node will be combined in this node. For example, if you have created an inclined circle prior to creating this node then this circle will become the output of newly created node. If you want to edit script of this custom node then right-click on it and select the **Edit Custom Node** option; refer to Figure-22. Modify the node as desired and save the file. The node will be updated automatically in workspace.

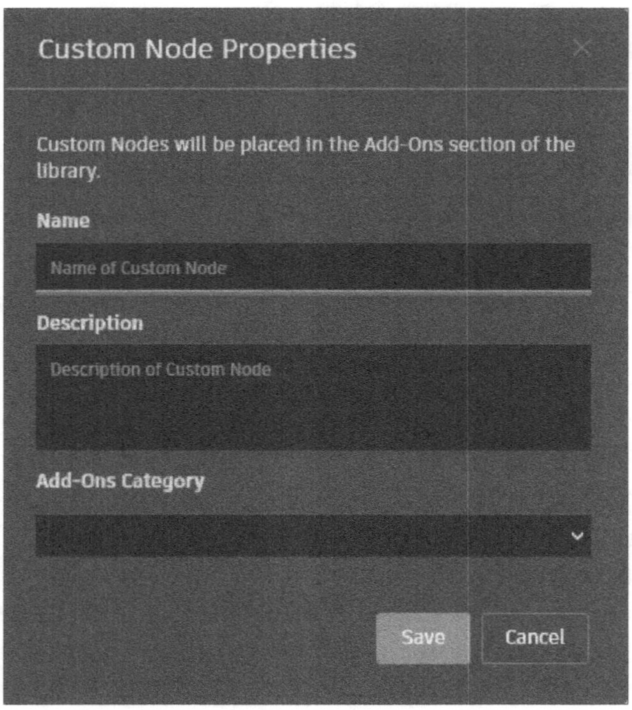

Figure-20. Custom Node Properties dialog box

Figure-21. Custom node created

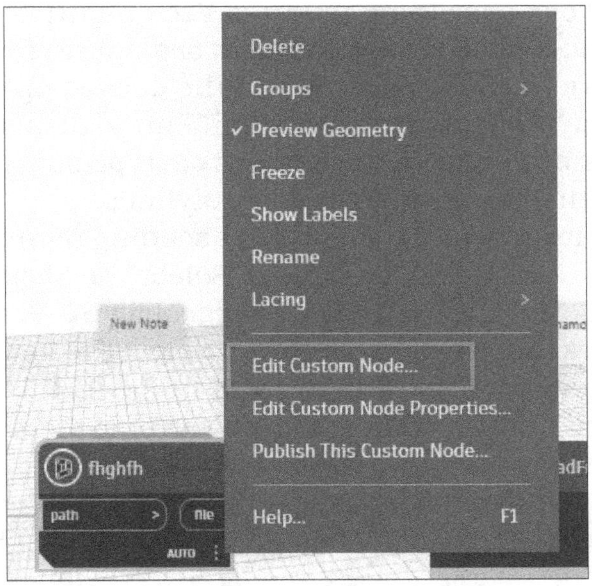

Figure-22. Option to edit custom node

- The **Select All** tool in **Edit** menu is used to select all the nodes and objects in the workspace.
- The **Unpin All Preview Bubbles** tool is used to unpin and collapse preview bubbles in the graph.
- The **Delete Selected** tool is used to delete selected nodes and objects.
- The tools in **Align Selection** cascading menu are used to align selected nodes at different alignment references. Select the nodes and click on desired tool to perform alignment.
- The **Set Phyton Engine** tool is used to specify python interpreter or engine will be used to run Python scripts within Revit environments.
- The **Cleanup Node Layout** tool is used to automatically arrange various nodes based on node links; refer to Figure-23.

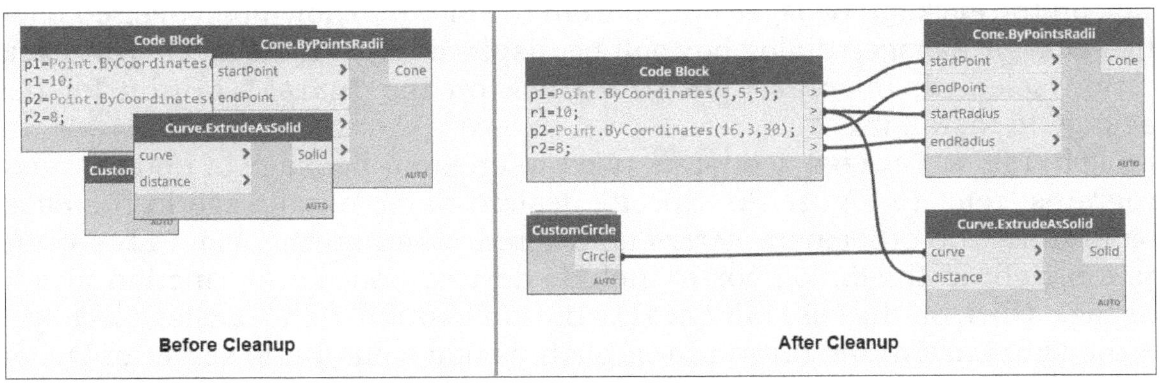

Figure-23. Applying cleanup

View Menu

The tools in the **View** menu are used to manage display of objects and interface elements. Various tools in this menu are discussed next.

- The tools in the **Zoom** cascading menu are used to zoom in and zoom out objects in workspace. There are two tools in this cascading menu viz. **Zoom In** and **Zoom Out**.
- The tools in the **Pan** cascading menu are used to pan objects in workspace. There are four tools in this cascading menu to pan left, right, up, and down.
- The **Show Console** tool in **View** menu is used to display console of file handling.

- The tools in **Connectors** cascading menu of **View** menu is used to change display style for connectors. Select the **Show Connectors** option from the cascading menu to display connectors in workspace. Select the **Curves** option from the **Connector Type** sub-menu in the **Connectors** cascading menu to display connectors as curves. Select the **Polylines** option from the **Connector Type** sub-menu in the **Connectors** cascading menu to display connectors as polylines.
- The options in the **Background 3D Preview** cascading menu of **View** menu are used to modify the model display in workspace. Select the **Show Grid** option to display grid in workspace. Select the **Navigate Background 3D Preview** option to activate model display in workspace and hide nodes. Select the **Revit Background Preview** option to display preview of resulting model in Revit. It is recommended to clear this option as it take a lot of computing power of system. Select the **Background Preview** option to display preview of model resulting from script; refer to Figure-24.

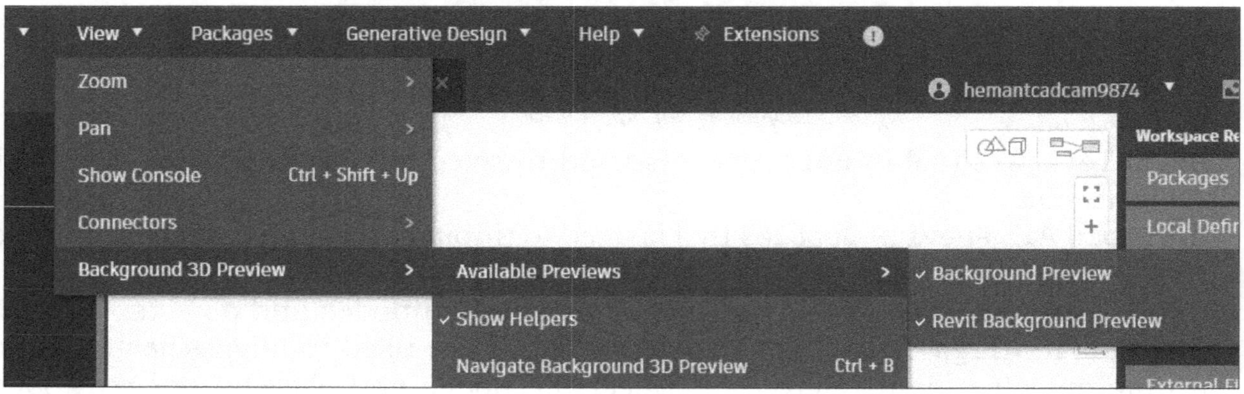

Figure-24. Background 3D Preview options

Packages Menu

The tools in the **Packages** menu are used to download, create, and manage packages containing node functions. The tools in this menu are discussed next.

- Click on the **Package Manager** option from the menu to download desired package. The **Package Manager** dialog box will be displayed with the **Search for Packages** section selected; refer to Figure-25. Click on the **Install** button for desired package to install it.
- The **Publish a Package** section is used to create a package of nodes and script programs; refer to Figure-26. Specify desired name of package in the **Name** edit box and set the other parameters as desired. Click on the **Add Files** button at the top-right in the dialog box to include desired nodes and function files in the package. Click on the **Publish Locally** button to publish the package locally. Click on the **Publish Online** button to publish package on online server of Dynamo.

Figure-25. Package Manager dialog box

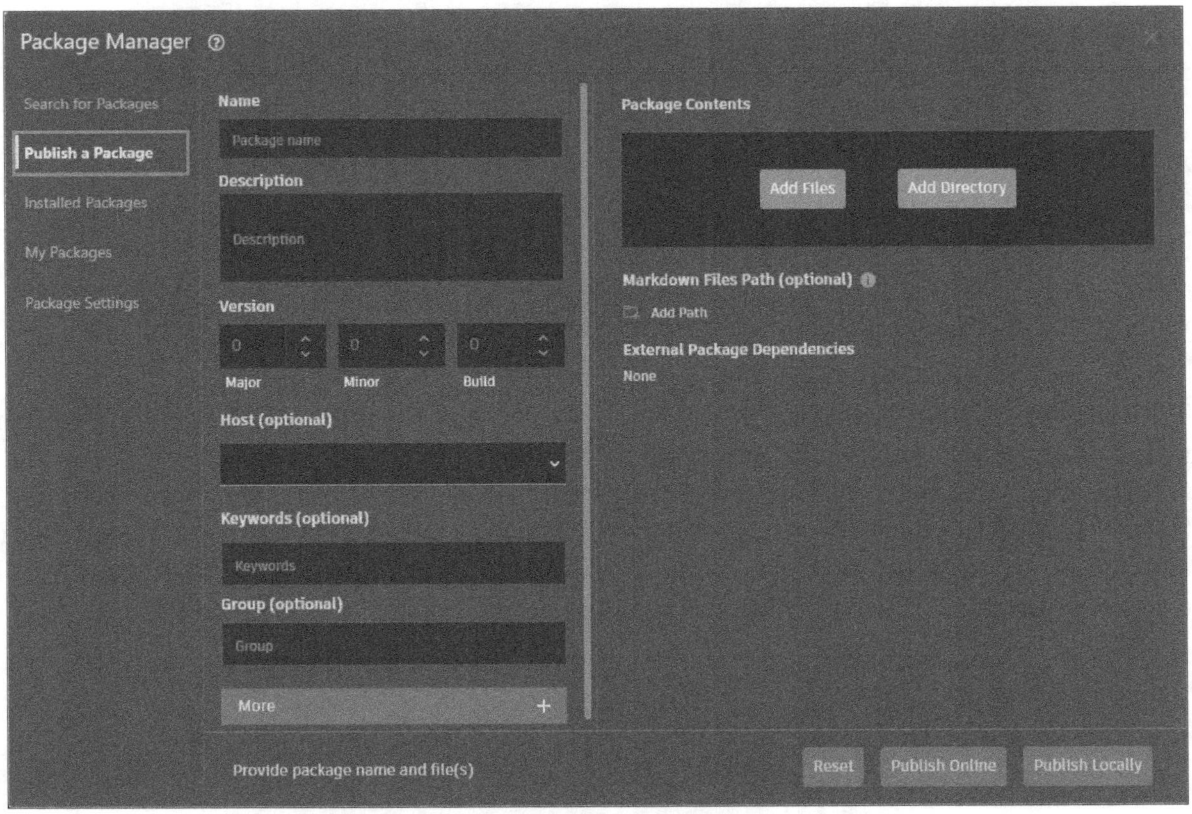

Figure-26. Publish a Package section in the Package Manager dialog box

- Select desired node and click on the **Publish Selected Nodes** option from the **Packages** menu. The **Publish a Dynamo Package** dialog box will be displayed with current selected node. Set the other parameters as desired and click on desired publish button.

Dynamo Settings Menu

The options in the **Dynamo** menu are used to manage various settings and parameters of software functioning. Some of the important options in this menu are discussed next.

- Select the **Agreements for Data Collection** button from the **Settings** menu to accept agreements of data usability. The agreement dialog box will be displayed. Select check boxes to enable anonymous summary reporting (Google Analytics) and detailed usability data reporting (Instrumentation) agreements.
- Select the **About** option to check information related to version of software.

Preferences

- Select the **Preferences** option from the **Dynamo** menu. The **Preferences** dialog box will be displayed; refer to Figure-27.

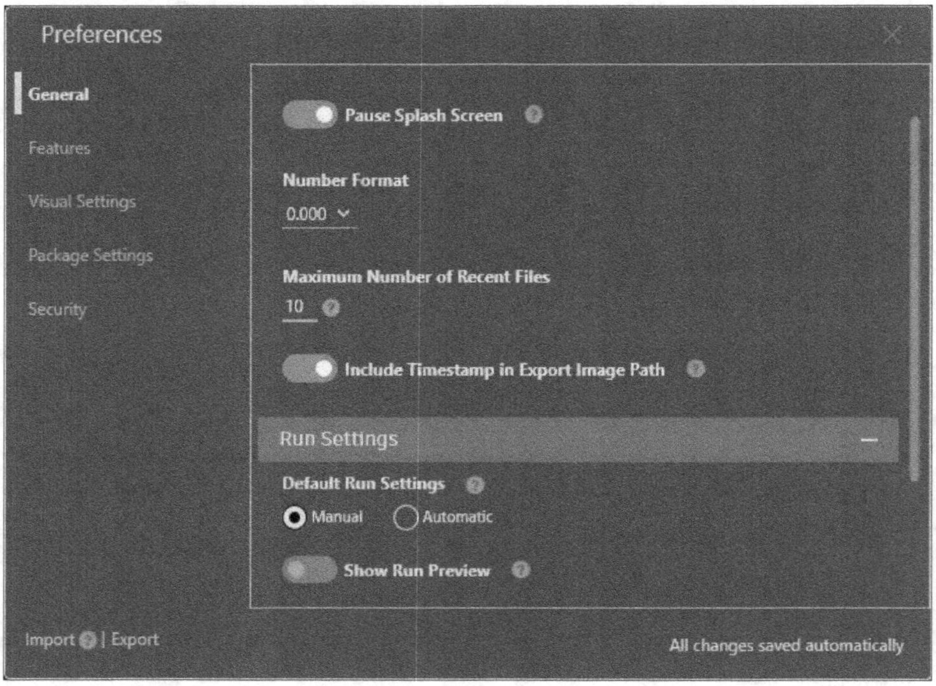

Figure-27. Preferences dialog box

- The **Show Run Preview** option is used to solve the nodes manually. This option is active only when **Manual** is selected in the **Run Settings** section.
- Set desired precision in **Number Format** drop-down.
- Select desired option from the **Default Geometry Scaling** section to set desired accuracy for geometric rendering and calculations; refer to Figure-28. Select desired radio button to define range for model values.

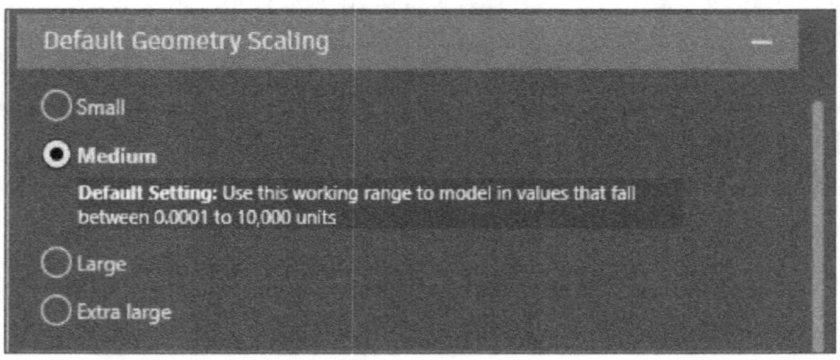

Figure-28. Default Geometry Scaling section

- Select **Features** option from the left area in dialog box to define settings related to Python and experimental Dynamo features. The options will be displayed as shown in Figure-29.

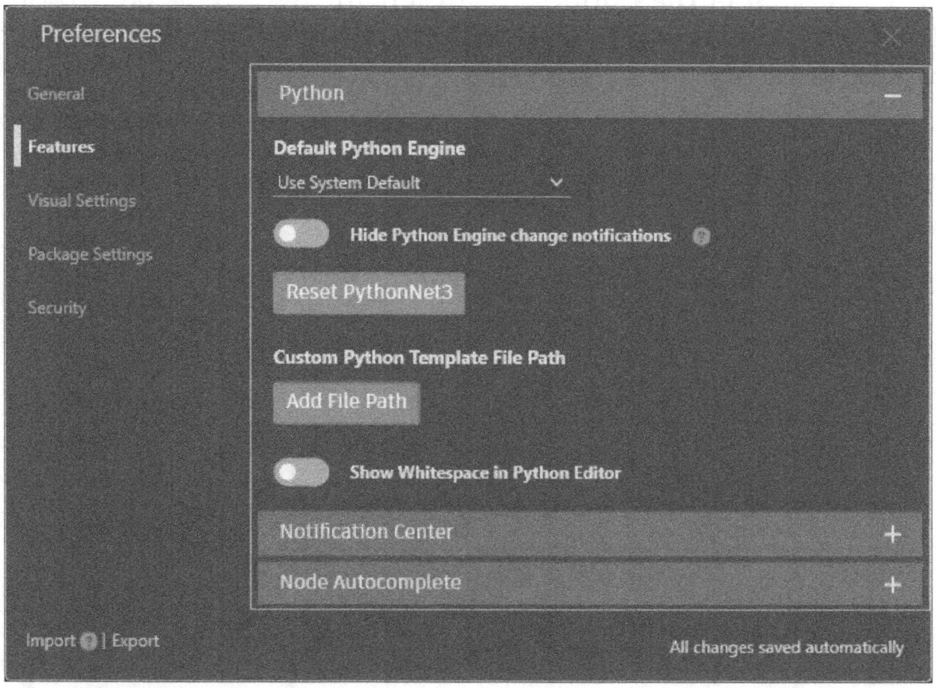

Figure-29. Features page

- Select desired option from the **Default Python Engine** drop-down to define which Python engine is to be used for calculates in visual scripting.
- Select the **Hide Python Engine change notifications** option from the menu to hide the notifications about the change of engine from CPython to PythonNet3.
- Click on the **Reset PythonNet3** button to reload default modules of PythonNet3.
- Click on the **Add File Path** button from the **Custom Python Template File Path** section to use already existing Python code file as template.
- Select the **Show Whitespace in Python Editor** option from the menu to display hidden characters in the Python Editor for created codes.
- Expand the **Notification Center** rollout and select **Receive notification** option to enable notifications.
- Expand the **Node Autocomplete** rollout to define settings related to auto complete suggestions displayed while creating nodes in program blocks. Select the **Enable Node Autocomplete** radio button to display list of possible functions for completing nodes while creating visual script. Select the **Node Type Match** radio button from **Default Ranking Method** section to display list of matching node options when you double-click on input/output node of a program block. Select the **Recommended Nodes** option from the **Default Ranking Method** section to display most used node options in suggestion list. If you have selected the **Recommended Nodes** option then you can specify the number of recommendations to be displayed in the **Number of results** edit box below the radio buttons.
- Select the **Preferred confidence level** option to set the recommendations which have confidence level below specified threshold value. The confidence level of an option in recommendation list defines its probability of being used based on machine learning algorithms.

- Expand the **Experimental** node to modify settings of experimental features of software. Select the **Enable Paneling nodes** option to allow creation of T-Spline nodes.
- Select the **Visual Settings** option from left in the dialog box to define settings like rendering quality and display of various entities. The options will be displayed as shown in Figure-30.

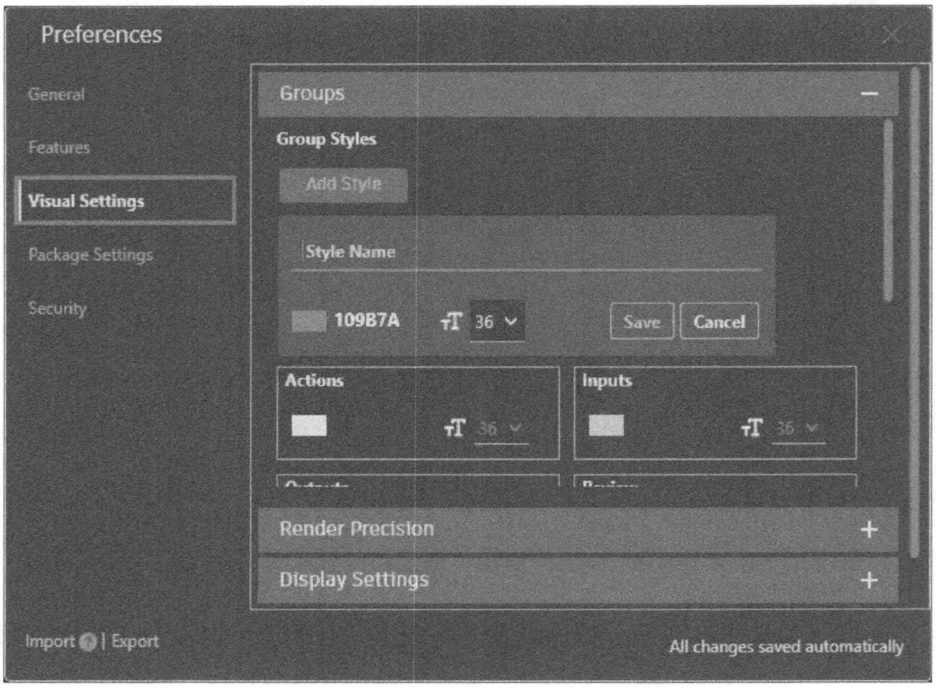

Figure-30. Visual Settings page

- Expand the **Groups** section to modify font and color styles of groups.
- Set desired precision value of rendering using the slider in **Render Precision** section of dialog box.
- Expand the **Display Settings** section to display/hide various entities of model. Select the **Use Hardware Acceleration** radio button to use GPU for enhancing graphics of model. Select the **Isolate Selected Geometry** button from the **Settings** menu to hide all other objects and display only selected geometry (selected by node). Select the **Show Edges** option to display edges in the model. On selecting the **Use Instancing (Beta)** option, some symmetric geometry types such as cubes, rectangles, or spheres will render faster due to multiple copies being drawn at once vs sequentially. Select the **Show CodeBlockNode Line Numbers** option from the menu to display line numbers in code blocks. Select the **Show Preview Bubbles** option from the **Settings** menu to display preview bubble. Select desired scale for the background graphic helpers (grids, axes) from the **Graphic Elements Scale** drop-down. On selecting the **Use Revit to scale background graphic helpers** option, the current host document units will be used to scale the background graphic helpers.
- Expand the **Zoom Scaling** section to adjust the library and python editor zoom parameters by dragging the respective zoom scale.
- Select the **Package Settings** option from left area in the dialog box to manage packages for Dynamo functions; refer to Figure-31.

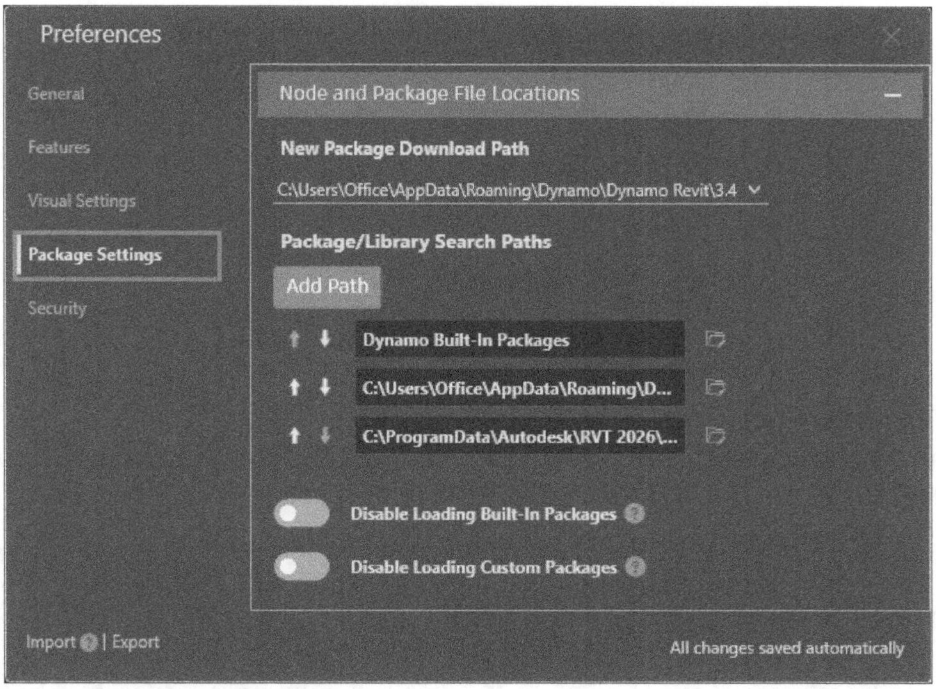

Figure-31. Package Settings option

- Expand the **Node and Package File Locations** section to define path for new packages to be downloaded.
- Click on the **Add Path** button to add more directories for searching packages.
- Select the **Disable Loading Built-In Packages** option if you do not want to load downloaded packages which are already built-in to the software.
- Select the **Disable Loading Custom Packages** option if you do not want to load custom packages.
- Expand the **Installed Packages** section from the dialog box and click on the **Package Manager** link to manage the installed packages in the **Package Manager** dialog box; refer to Figure-32.

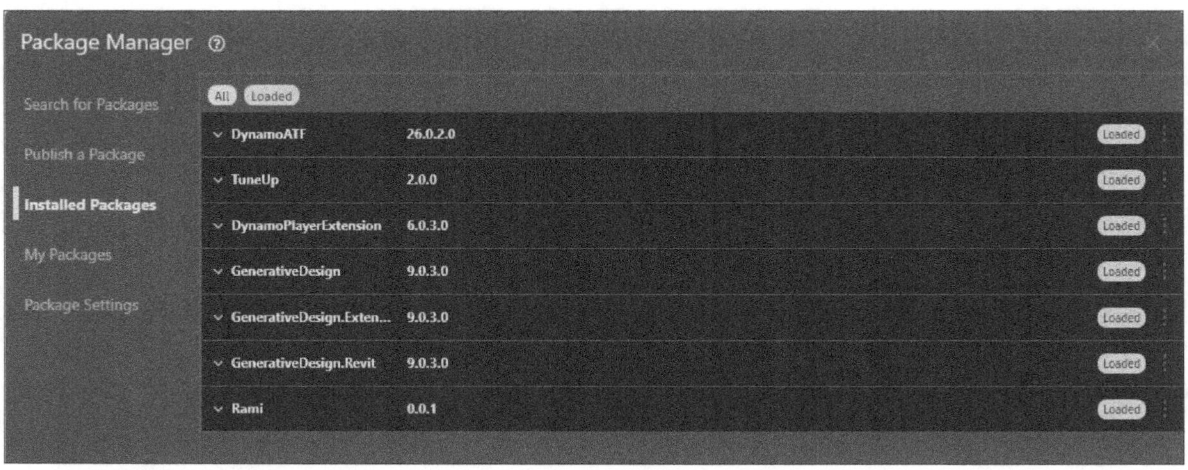

Figure-32. Installed Packages section in Package Manager dialog box

- Click on the ellipses button next to package for modifying it. A flyout will be displayed; refer to Figure-33. Select desired option to perform modification.

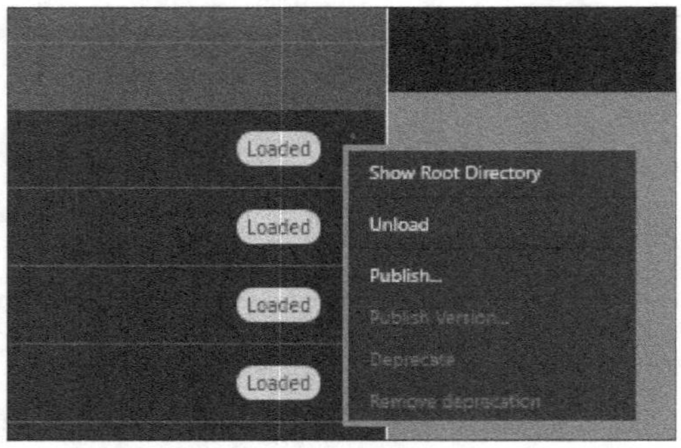

Figure-33. Flyout

- Close the **Preferences** dialog box to exit.
- Select the **Security** option from the left side in the **Preferences** dialog box to set trusted file location and enable/disable trust warning; refer to Figure-34.

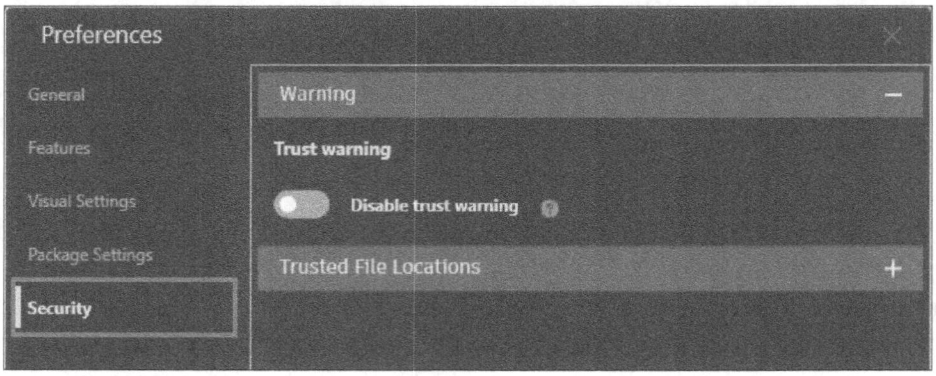

Figure-34. Security option

Generative Design

The options in **Generative Design** menu are used to create generative studies and perform analysis to get best possible generative model based on study parameters; refer to Figure-35.

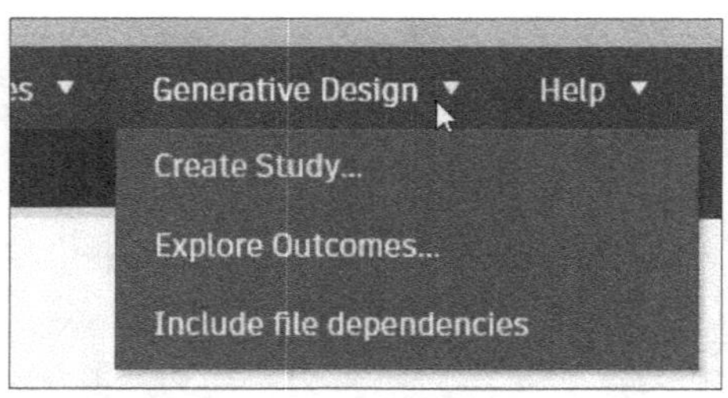

Figure-35. Generative Design menu

- Select the **Create Study** tool from the menu to start a new generative design study; refer to Figure-36. Select desired option from the list to start a new study. The options of Generative Design are out of scope of this book.

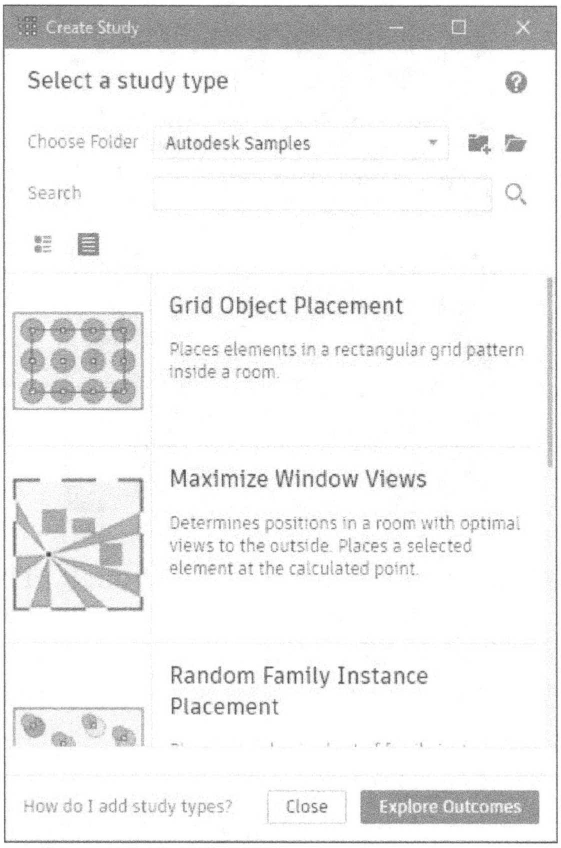

Figure-36. Create Study dialog box

- You can check the outcomes of generative design study by using the **Explore Outcomes** tool.
- Select the **Include file dependencies** option from the menu to include file dependencies in generative design study.

Creating Basic Script for Line

Before creating script, you need to understand the basic process required for creating line. For script, you need to create nodes for points and then create a line node which creates line joining two points. The procedure to create script for line is given next.

- Click in the Search box of **Library** and type **Point** (since we are creating points). The list of available nodes will be displayed; refer to Figure-37.

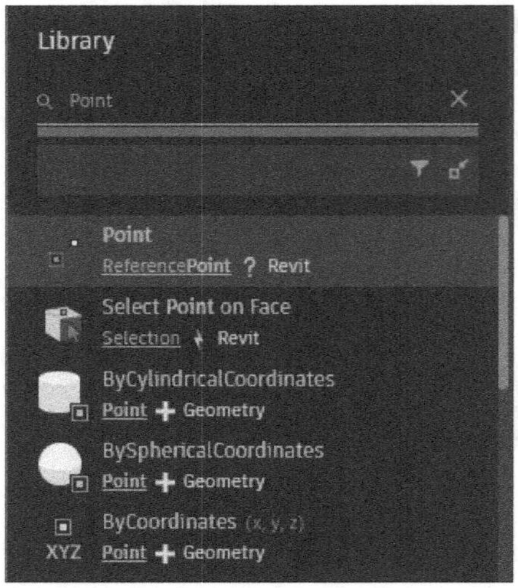

Figure-37. Nodes available for creating points

- Click on the **ByCoordinates** node from the **Library**. The **Point.ByCoordinates** node will be added in the workspace.
- Double-click in the blank area of workspace. The **Code Block** will be added. Set desired value for x, y, and z coordinates separated by semicolons (;). Refer to Figure-38.

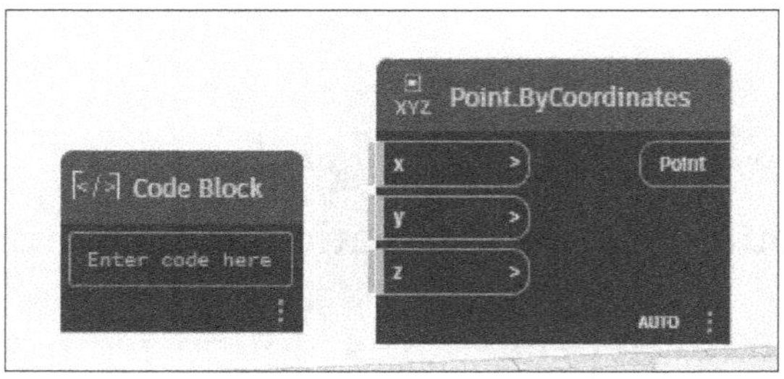

Figure-38. Code block created for coordinates

- Click on the blocks at locations as shown in Figure-39 to connect their respective nodes.

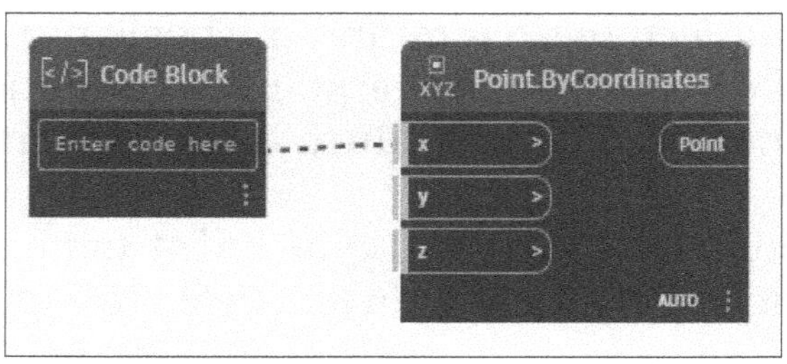

Figure-39. Connecting nodes

- Similarly, connect the other nodes as desired. The point will be created.
- Create another point by using the same procedure at **15, 15, 15** coordinate; refer to Figure-40.

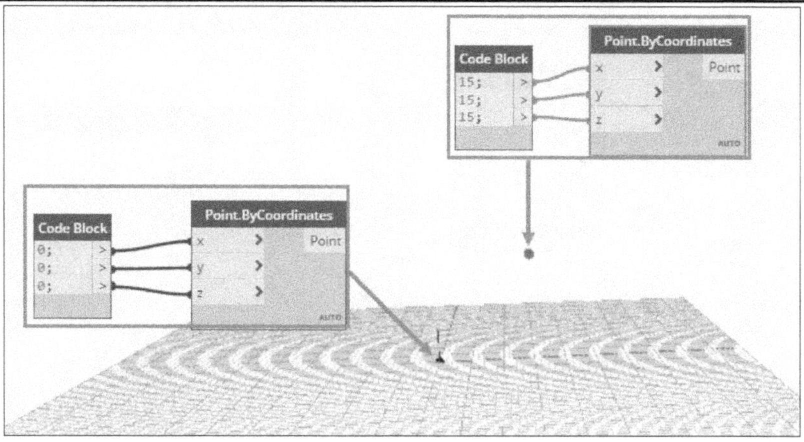

Figure-40. Points created by script

- Click in the Search box of **Library** and type line. The options to create lines will be displayed; refer to Figure-41.

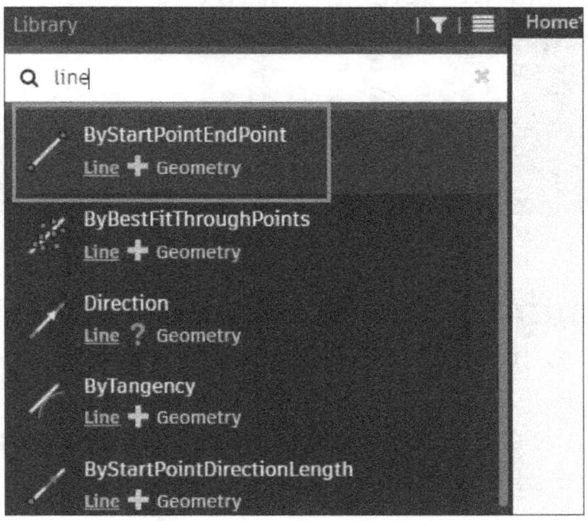

Figure-41. Line tools

- Click on the **ByStartPointEndPoint** option from the **Library**. The line node will be created be created; refer to Figure-42.

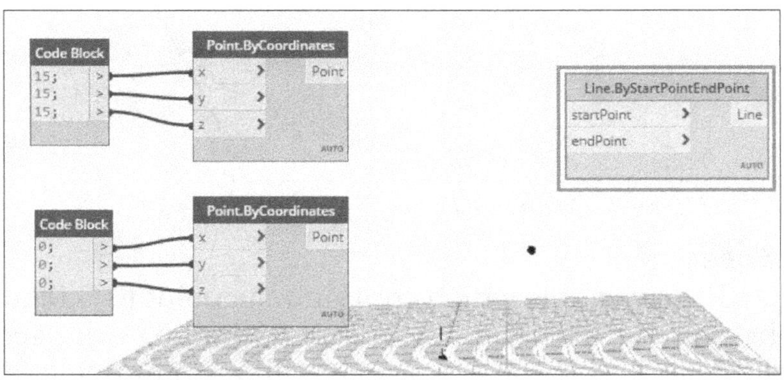

Figure-42. Line node created

- Connect nodes of **Point.ByCoordinates** code blocks to **Line.ByStartPointEndPoint** block; refer to Figure-43.

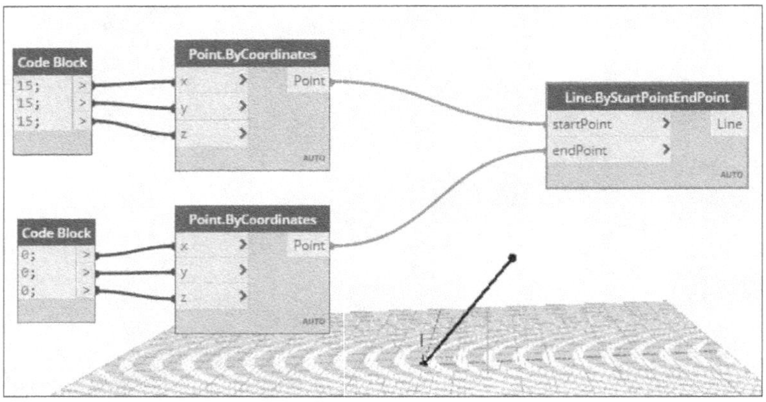

Figure-43. Creating lines by nodes

- If **Automatic** option is selected in the bottom bar of application then line will be created automatically. If the **Manual** option is selected then click on the **Run** button to check the output of script; refer to Figure-44.

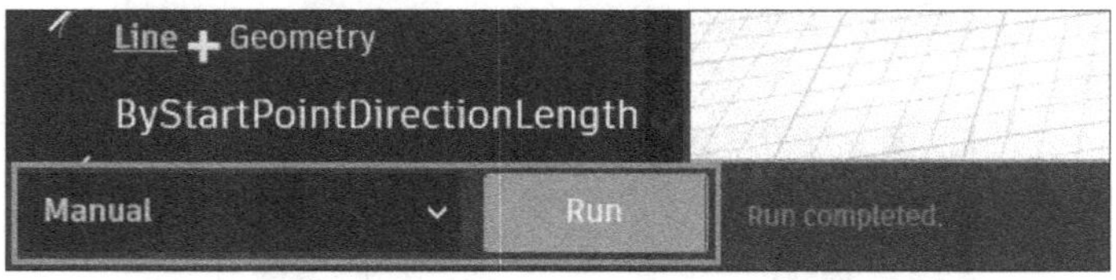

Figure-44. Run option for script

Creating Line with Single Code Block

- Click on the **New** button from the **Toolbar** or press **CTRL+N**. A new workspace will open.
- Double-click in the blank area of the workspace. A new code block will be generated.
- Type the codes in code block as shown in Figure-45.

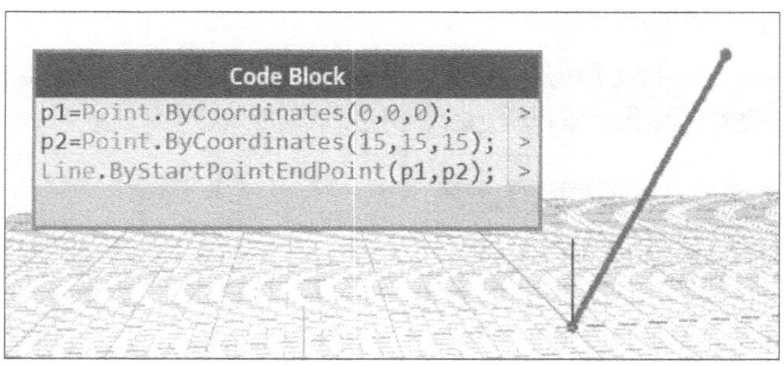

Figure-45. Code created for line

Explanation of Codes:

In this code block, p1 is a variable which contains the point (0,0,0) and p2 is a variable which contains the point (15,15,15). The points p1 and p2 are used as input for line code. Note that while writing the code, system will automatically suggest you codes based on typed characters.

Creating Solid Loft with Cross-sections and Guide Curves

- Click on the **New** button to start new workspace.
- Start a new code block by double-clicking in the blank area of workspace and type codes to create three points and two circles as shown in Figure-46.

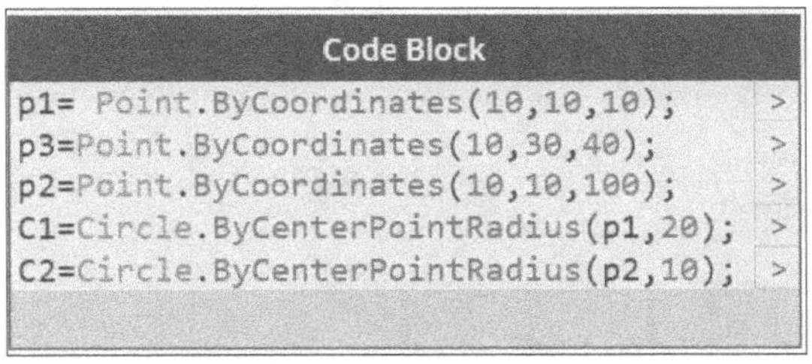

Figure-46. Codes for points and circles

- Now, search loft from the **Library** and select **ByLoft (crossSections, guideCurves) Solid** tool. The code block for loft will be created; refer to Figure-47. You can see that inputs of code block for loft needs cross-sections and guide curves. So, we need a list of cross-sections and guide curves to create loft.

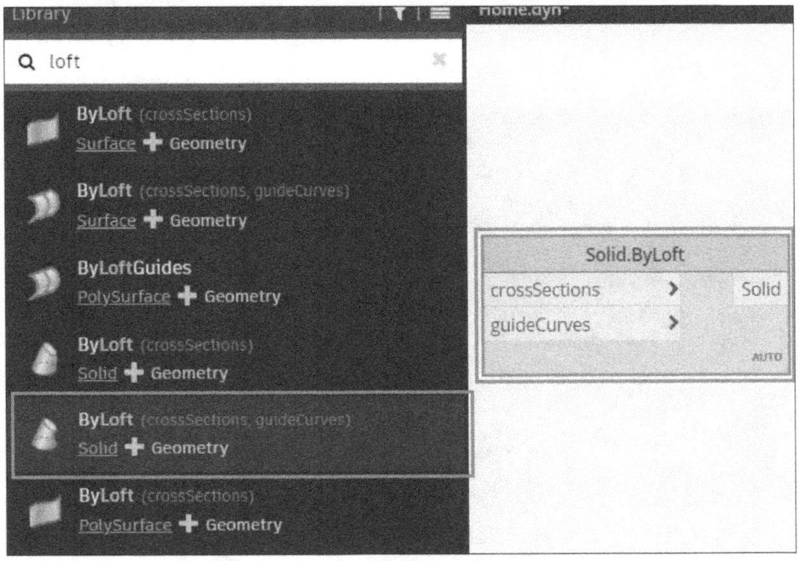

Figure-47. Code block for loft

- Type **List** in the **Library** search box and place a list for cross-sections; refer to Figure-48. We are not placing a list for guide curves as we will be using a single curve for guide.

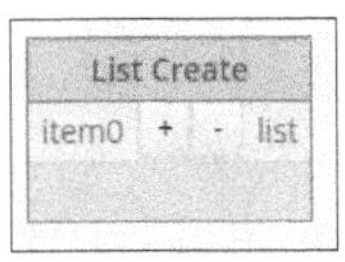

Figure-48. List create code block

- Click on the **+** button in code block to increase number of items and connect nodes of two circles; refer to Figure-49. Note that you can use **-** button to increase number of items in the list.
- Connect the output of this list code with crossSections input of **Solid.ByLoft** code block. Now, we need to create guide curve using p1, p2, and p3 points.
- Expand the **NurbsCurve** sub-category of **Curves** category in **Geometry** node of the **Library** and select **ByControlPoints** tool; refer to Figure-50.

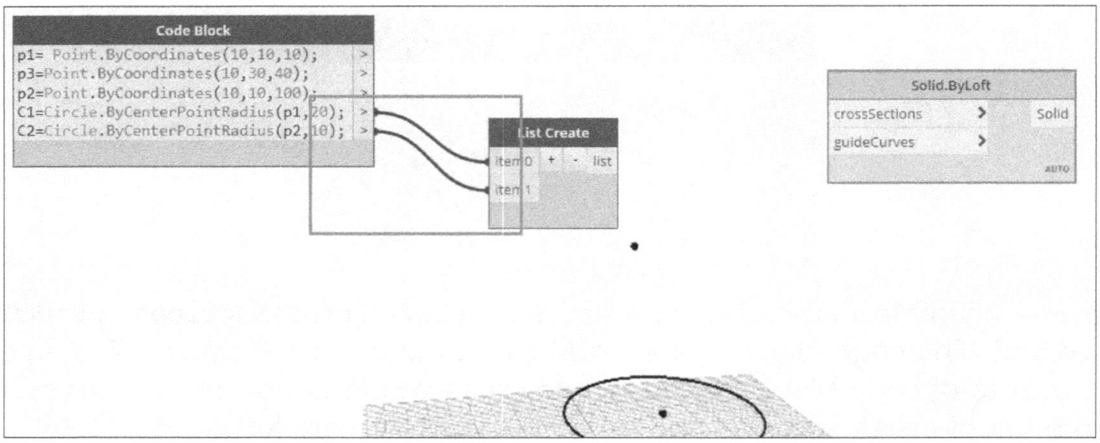

Figure-49. Connecting nodes of circles with list

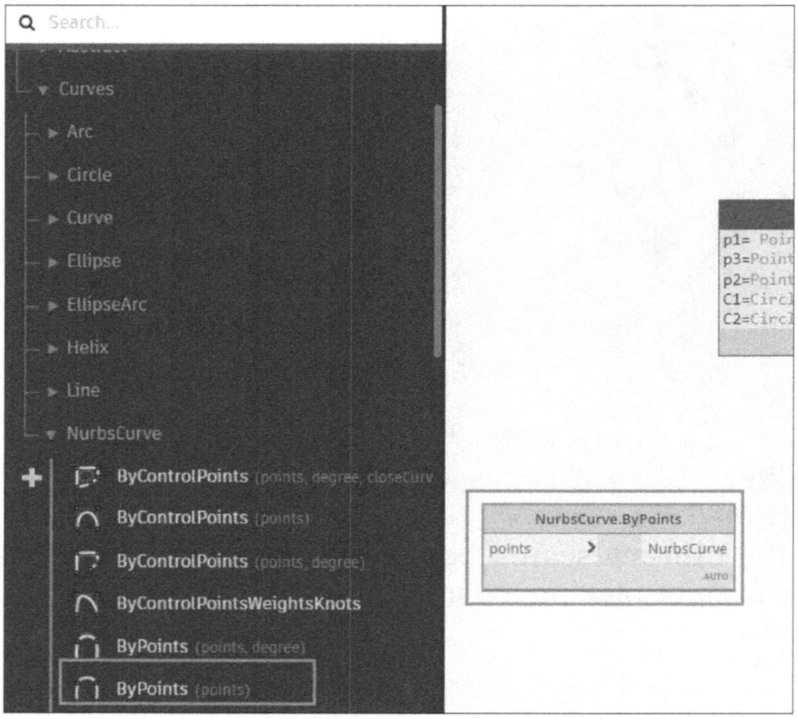

Figure-50. Code block for nurbs curve by points

- Note that the input for **NurbsCurve.ByPoints** code block is a list of points so, we need to create a list with 3 inputs as discussed earlier.
- Create the list and connect the points with list; refer to Figure-51.

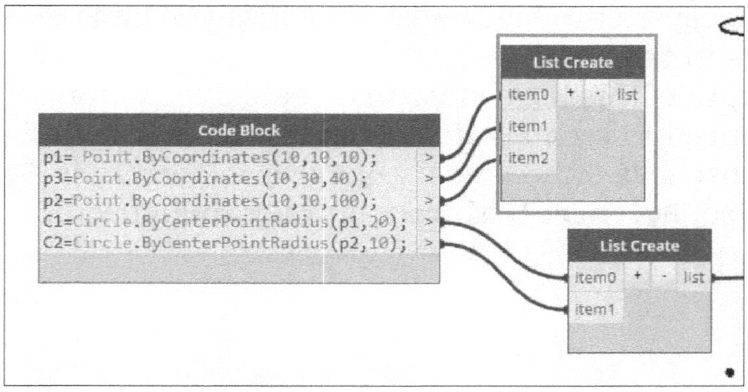

Figure-51. List created for points of nurbs curve

- Now, connect everything related to guide curve. Preview of model will be displayed; refer to Figure-52.

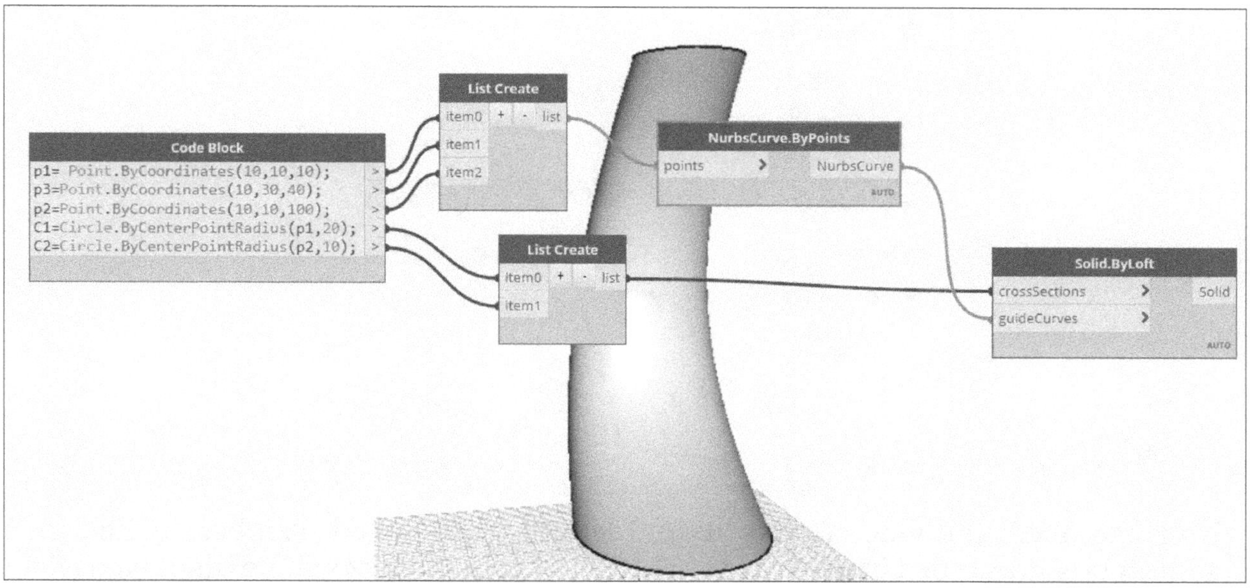

Figure-52. Solid loft created by script

Creating Path Array of Revit Objects

While working on Revit, you might have noticed that there is not direct method to create array of objects on specified path. We will now learn the procedure to create array of objects on path.

- Create the object that you want to pattern and model curve on which you want to pattern the object in Revit.
- Start Dynamo application by clicking on the **Dynamo** tool from the **Visual Programming** panel in the **Manage** tab of **Ribbon**.
- Start a new workspace.
- Place two **Select Model Element** code blocks to import path and object in Dynamo from Revit. Click on the **Select** button in first code block and select path from Revit. Similarly, click on the **Select** button in second code block and select object to be patterned; refer to Figure-53. Note that you may need to place both the application in tile form or overlapping form to perform selection.

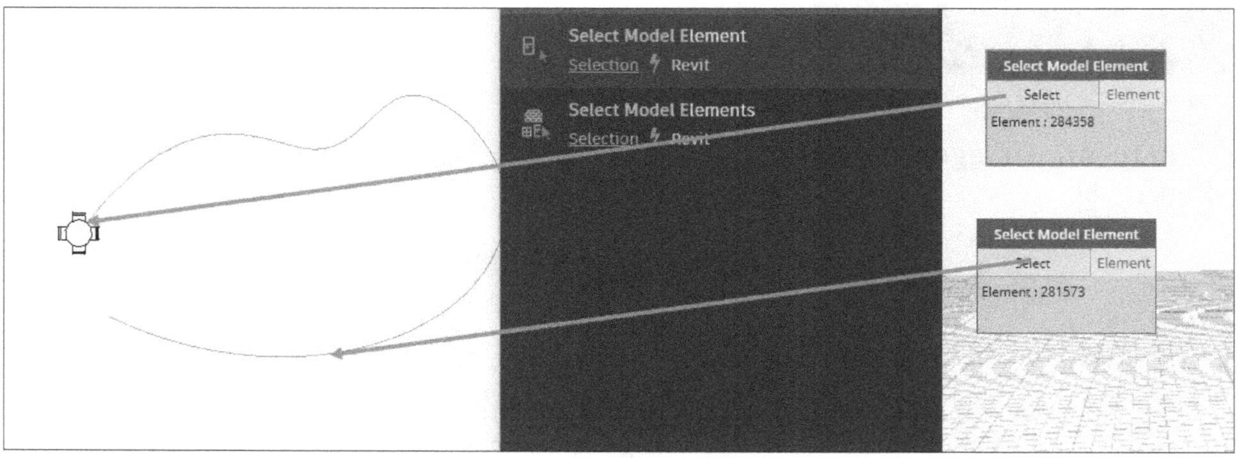

Figure-53. Selecting model elements

- Place the **Element.Curve** code block in workspace and connect the code block containing curve element. This will bring the selected path curve in workspace; refer to Figure-54.

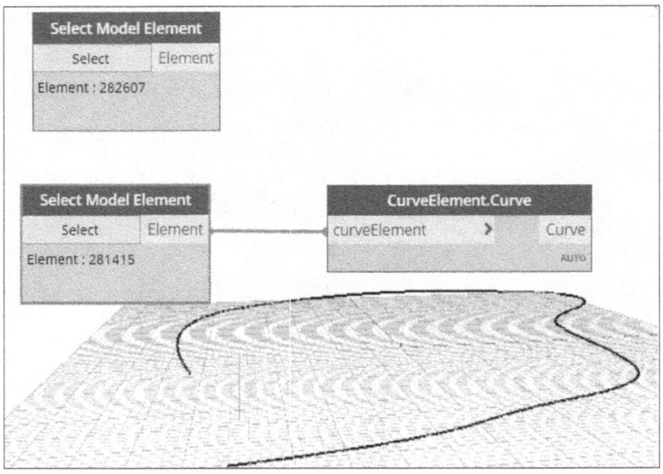

Figure-54. Path curve brought in Dynamo workspace

- Now, we need to divide curve at equal length in specified numbers. Click in the search box and type **`Curve.Points`**. The list of code blocks will be displayed. Select the **`PointsAtEqualSegmentLength`** code block. The code will be placed.
- Connect the curve as shown in Figure-55.

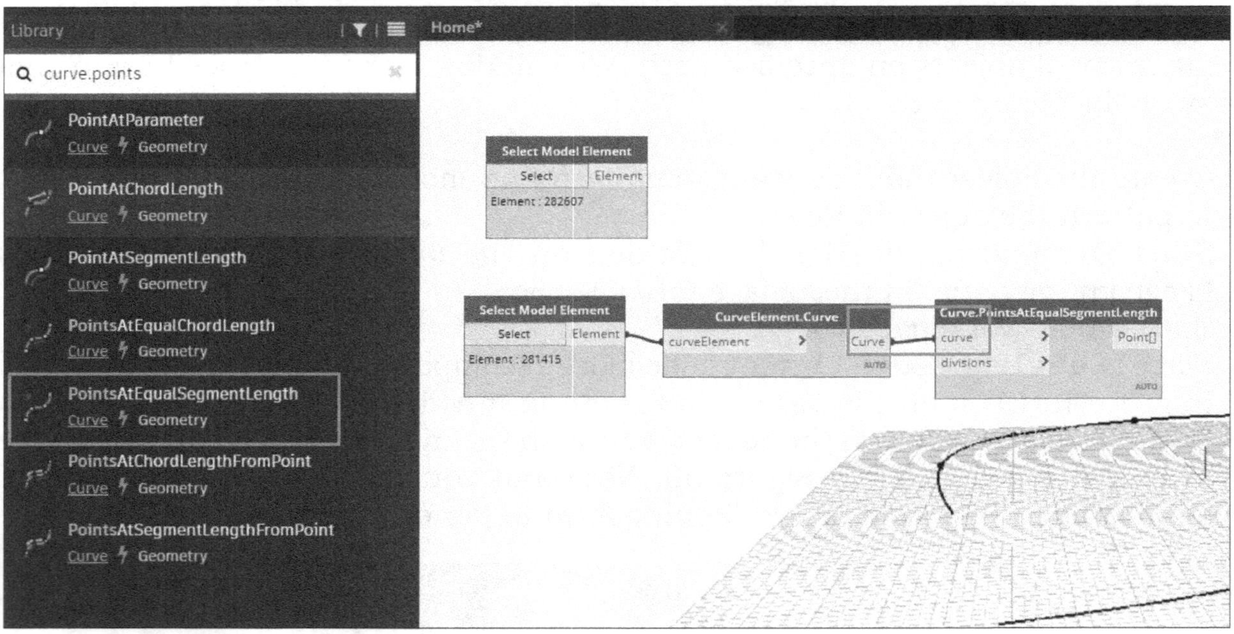

Figure-55. Dividing curve at equal length

- Create an **`Integer Slider`** code block and set the parameters as shown in Figure-56.

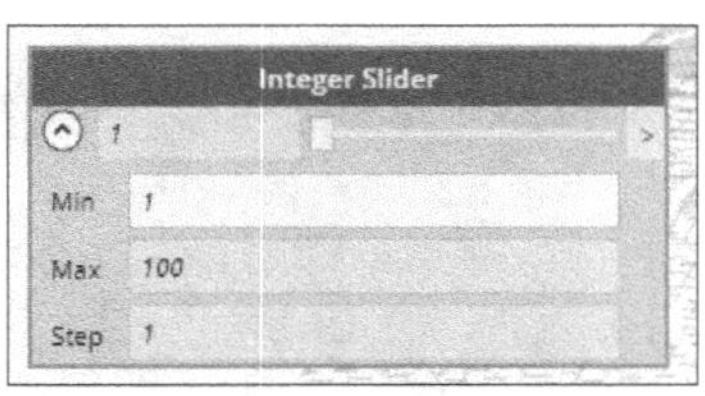

Figure-56. Integer Slider created

- Connect the output of **`Integer Slider`** to the **`divisions`** input node of **`Curve.PointsAtEqualSegmentLength`** code block and move the slide to create desired number of divisions. After division, the curve will be displayed as shown in Figure-57.

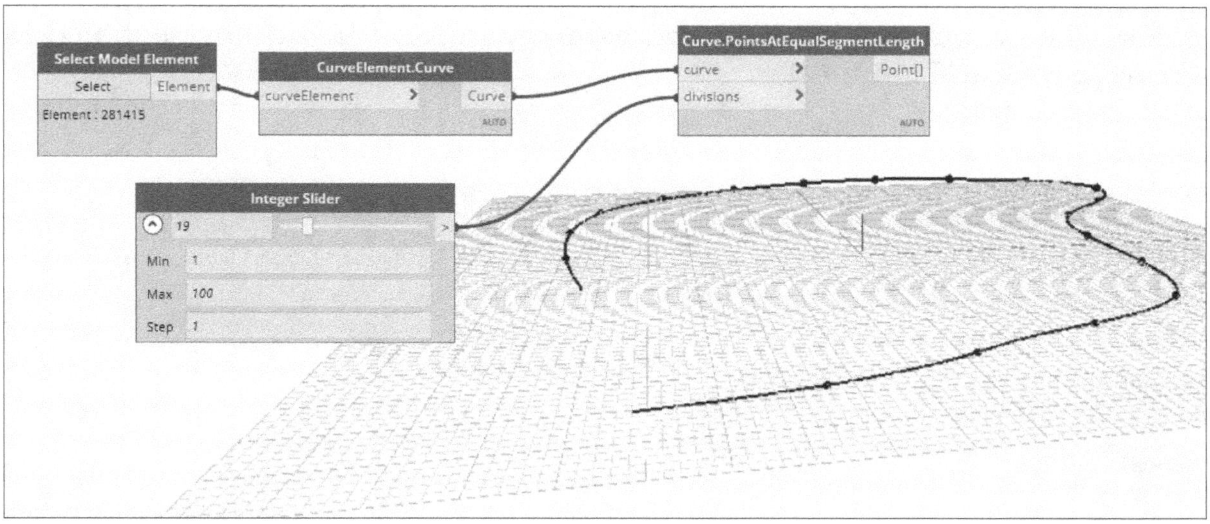

Figure-57. Curve after division

- Now, you will convert the selected object element (table) to family type because for creating array we need family type as input. To do so, type **element.element** in the search box and place **ElementType** code block; refer to Figure-58.

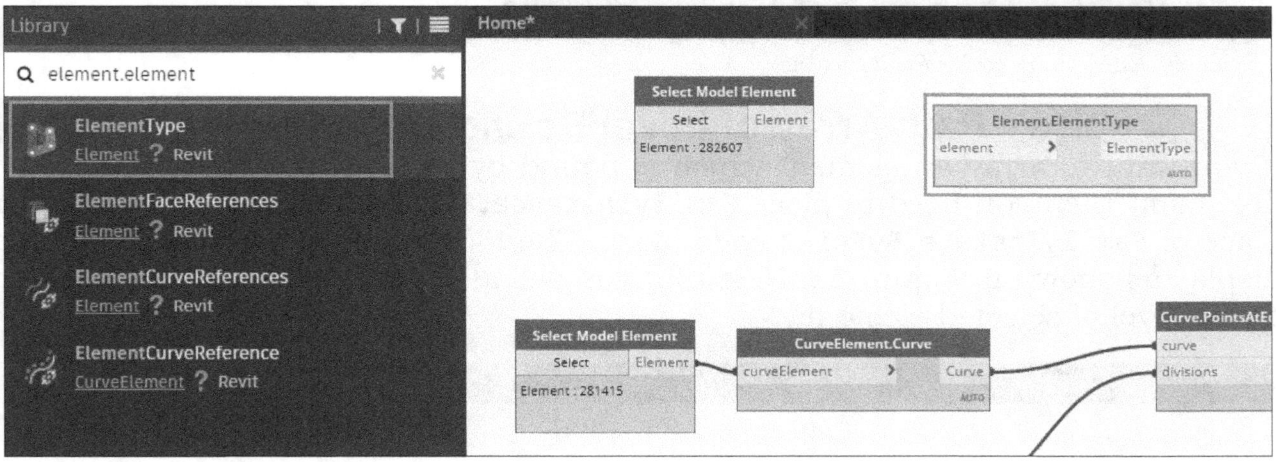

Figure-58. ElementType code block placed

- Connect the other model element to element input node of this block.
- Now, place the **FamilyInstance.ByPoint** code block; refer to Figure-59.

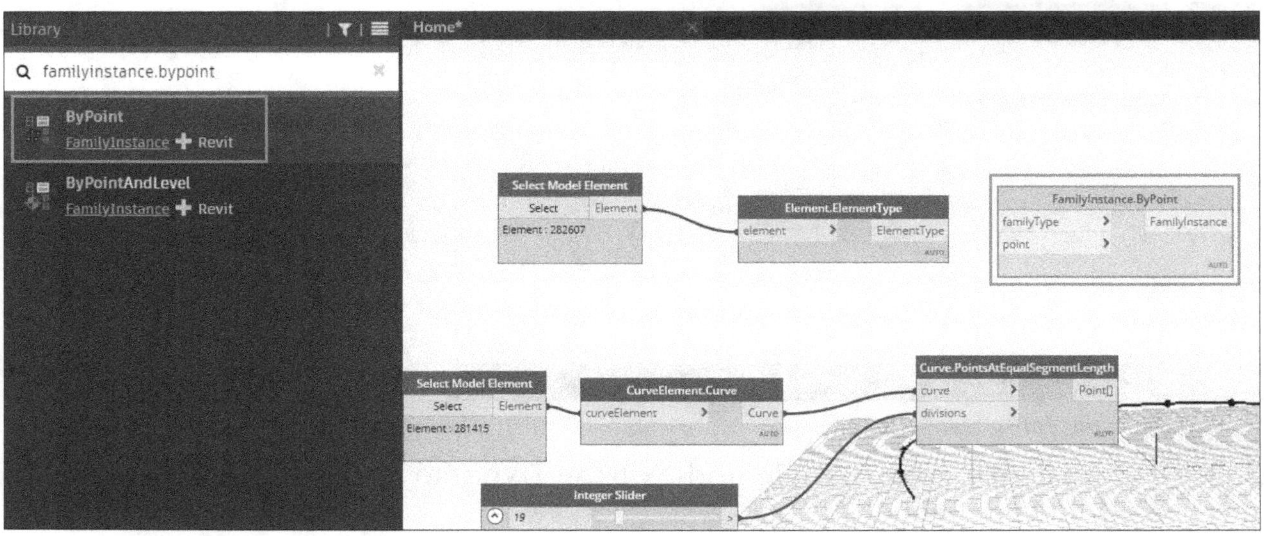

Figure-59. FamilyInstance ByPoint code block

- Connect the **ElementType** and **Point[]** nodes to **FamilyInstance.ByPoint** code block. The output will be displayed as array in Revit if you have enabled Revit Preview; refer to Figure-60.

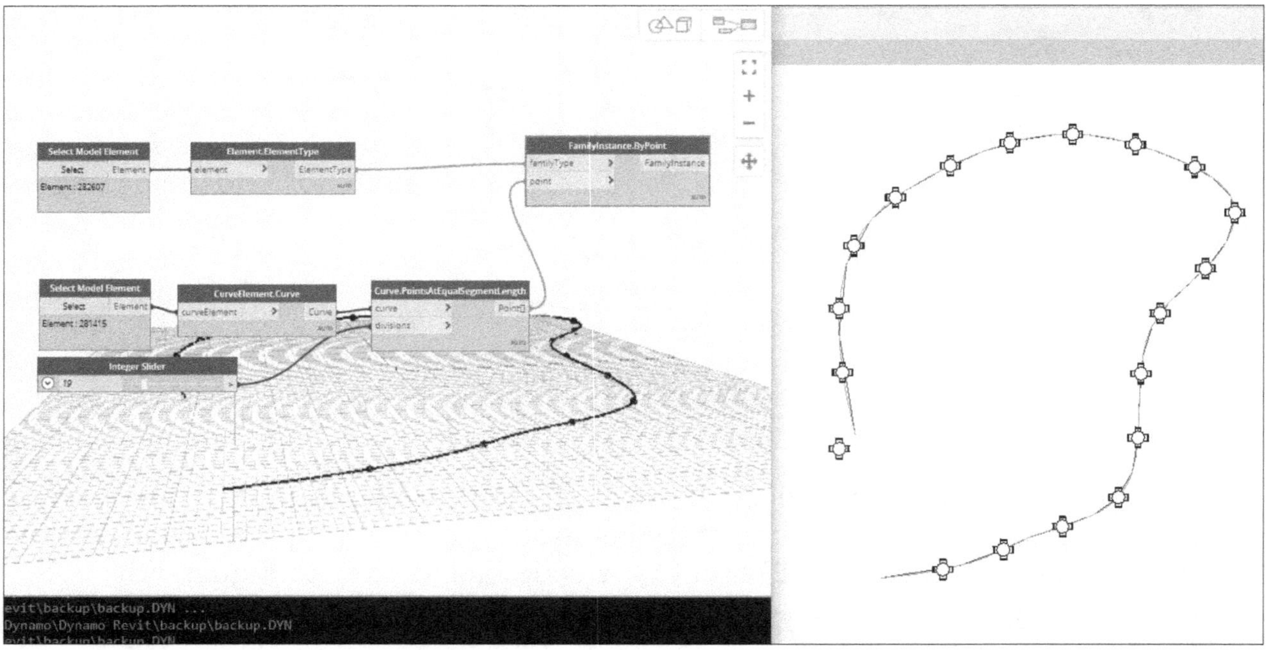

Figure-60. Path array created in Revit Preview

Path Array of Level Bound Objects

If you want to array an element which is bound by its level like columns in Revit document then you need to place **FamilyInstance.ByPointAndLevel** code block in place of **FamilyInstace.ByPoint** code block. The Flow chart of your nodes should display as shown in Figure-61. Note that you will also need a **Levels** code block to define level of selected element.

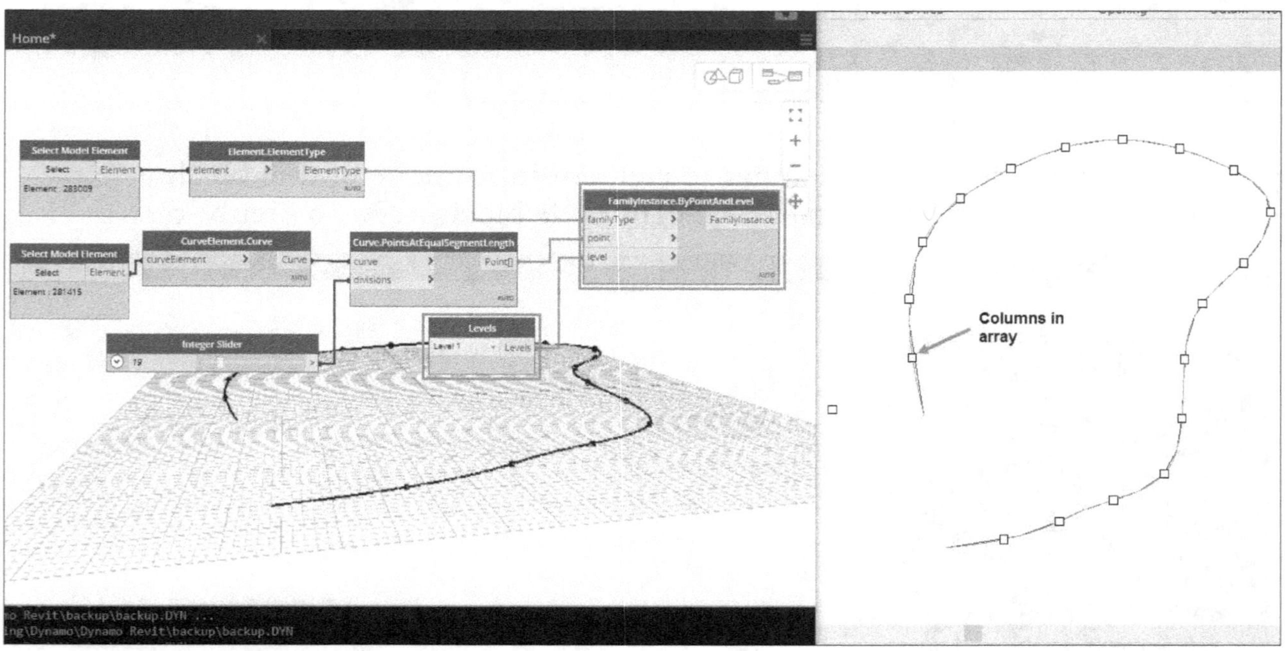

Figure-61. Creating path array of columns

After creating codes, save the file and exit the Dynamo application. The result will be reflected in Revit model.

Creating Scripts with User Inputs

You can modify or create a script that asks for user inputs during execution. To do so, you need to right-click on the code block which is input for your script and select the Is Input option; refer to Figure-62. You can convert the previously created Path array script to take user inputs of object selection, curve selection, and number of divisions. The procedure to use such scripts in Revit is discussed in next topic.

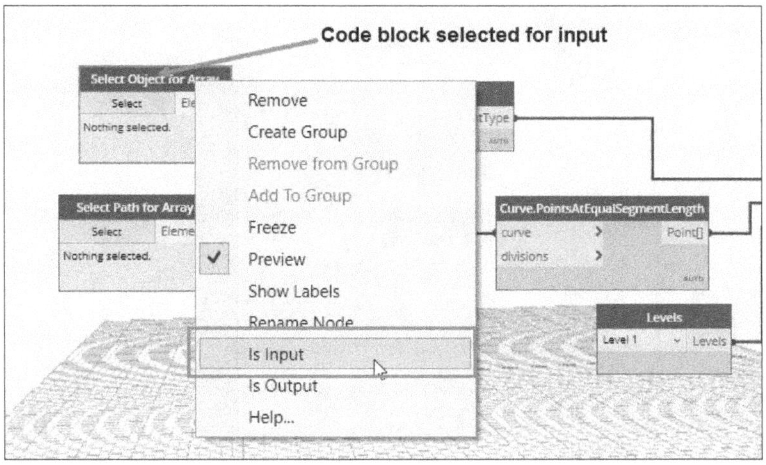

Figure-62. Setting Input for script

DYNAMO PLAYER

The **Dynamo Player** tool is used to run dynamo scripts saved in storage drive. Using this tool, you can run multiple scripts in a Revit project. The procedure to use this tool is given next.

- Click on the **Dynamo Player** tool from the **Visual Programming** panel in the **Manage** tab of **Ribbon**. The **Dynamo Player** will be displayed with sample scripts; refer to Figure-63.

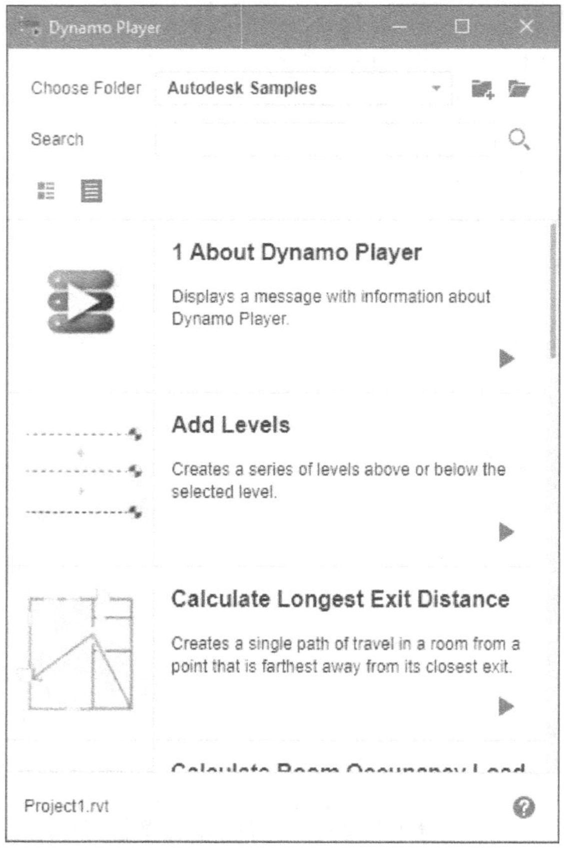

Figure-63. Dynamo Player

- Click on the **Add Folder** button and select the folder in which you have saved your scripts. The list of scripts will be updated automatically. Make sure to select the newly added folder in the **Choose Folder** drop-down.
- Click on the **Play** button for desired script to run it. If your script takes inputs then next page will be displayed in Dynamo Player to define inputs; refer to Figure-64.

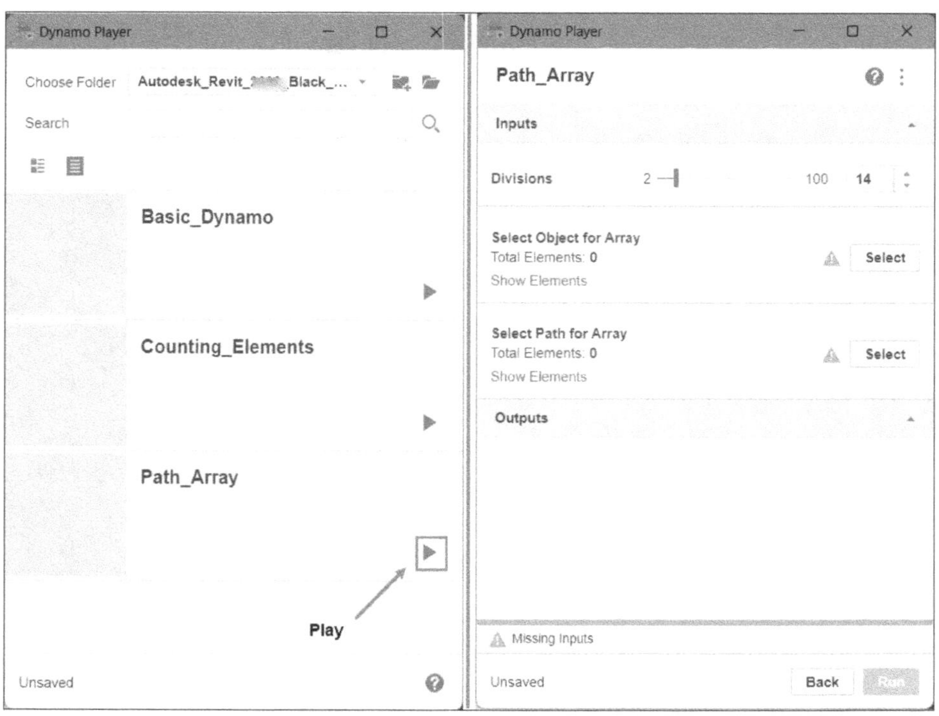

Figure-64. Specifying inputs in Dynamo Player

- Set desired parameters and select the elements as required by script; refer to Figure-65.

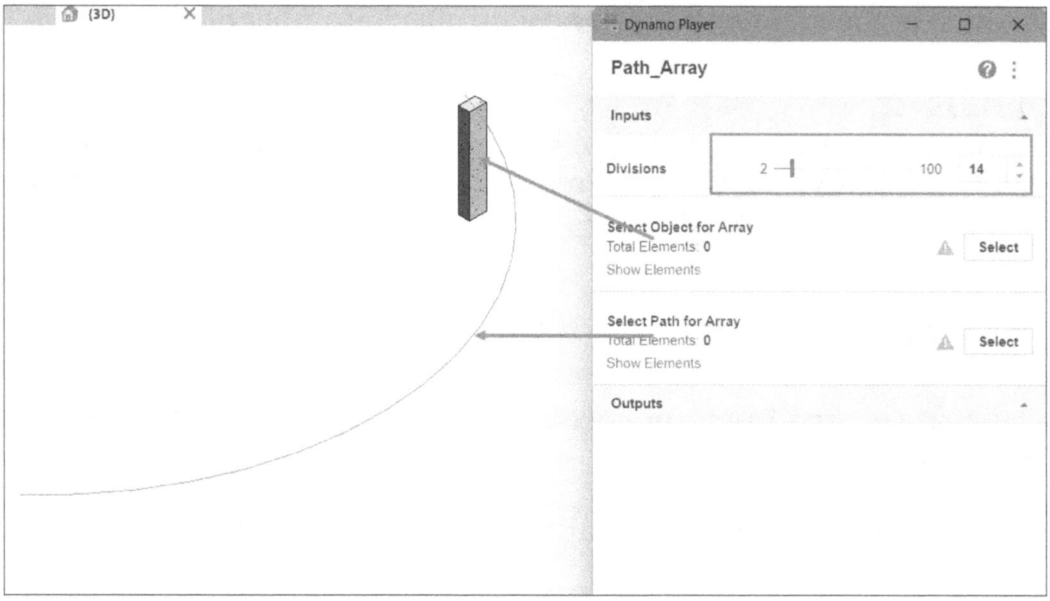

Figure-65. User inputs for script

- After defining inputs if required, click on the **Run** button displayed at the bottom in Dynamo Player. The result will be generated in Revit; refer to Figure-66. Note that **Run completed** message will be displayed below script name once it has run successfully.
- If there are errors in the script run then click on the **Edit in Dynamo** button below script name to edit the script.

Note that sometimes you may get some left overs of scripts like curves or 3D models created in Dynamo if you have enabled the Revit Preview option. In such cases, there is not need to trying hard deleting them. Save your file, close the file, and then reopen it. Those left overs will be gone.

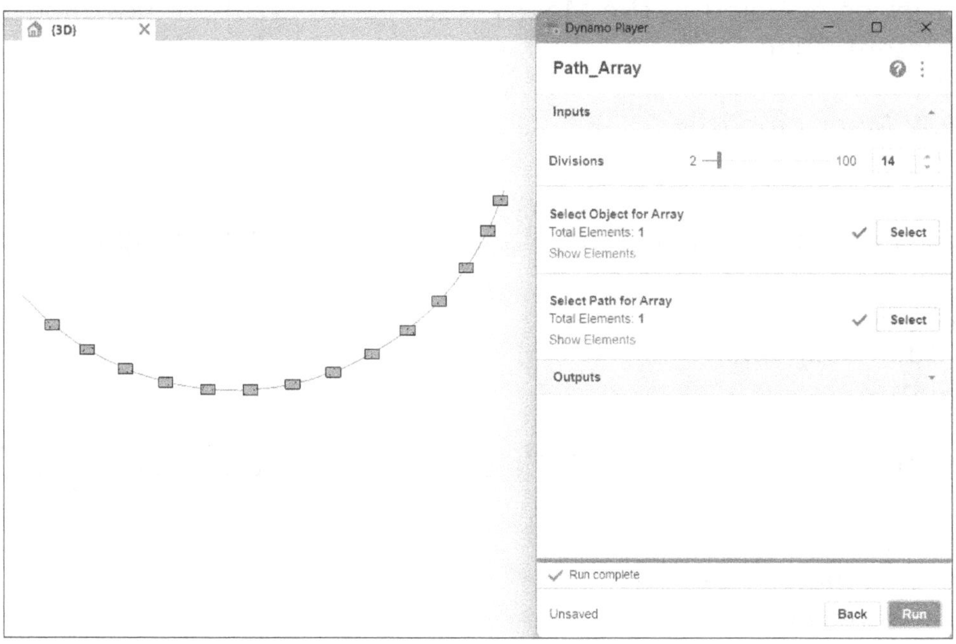

Figure-66. After running script

PRACTICE 1

Create a Dynamo script to display total number of elements of family same to selected element in current view. Note that you need to check number of elements in Dynamo.

PRACTICE 2

Create a Dynamo script for rotating objects about their Z axis in Plan view using a slider. There will be two inputs required in Revit; object selection and angle slider by which objects are to be rotated.

SELF ASSESSMENT

Q1. .... are small programs used to extend the capabilities of software or automate a task.

Q2. Discuss difference between Application based macro and Document based macro.

Q3. Discuss the concept of visual scripting.

Q4. Discuss the procedure to perform path array of Revit object using Dynamo.

Q5. Discuss the use of Dynamo Player.

Q6. What distinguishes an application-based macro module from a document-based one?
A. Application modules are only for specific files
B. Document modules run outside Revit
C. Application modules are universal and do not need a project file
D. Document modules can be reused across projects

Q7. What must be selected in the Macro Manager to create a new module?
A. Create Custom Node
B. Build Solution
C. Create new Macro module
D. Enable Macros

Q8. What file should be opened after installing the Revit SDK to explore API functions?
A. SDK.chm
B. RevitAPIFunctions.exe
C. VisualStudioSetup.exe
D. RevitAPI.chm

Q9. What is the purpose of the TaskDialog.Show function in a macro?
A. Create a 3D model
B. Export the file
C. Display a text dialog box
D. Import a macro module

Q10. Which button in Macro Manager is used to run a macro?
A. Edit
B. Run
C. Debug
D. Step Into

Q11. What is Dynamo used for in Revit?
A. Editing macros
B. Writing raw C# code
C. Visual programming using nodes and scripts
D. Running plugins from external sources

Q12. How can a user start the Dynamo application?
A. From the Home tab
B. Using the Visual Scripting panel under Manage tab
C. By right-clicking a macro
D. Through Macro Security settings

Q13. What tool is used to take a screenshot of the workspace in Dynamo?
A. Save As
B. Export Workspace As Image
C. Snapshot Tool
D. Print

Q14. Which menu in Dynamo contains the Copy, Paste, and Group functions?
A. File
B. Edit
C. View
D. Packages

Q15. What does the Cleanup Node Layout tool in Dynamo do?
A. Deletes unused nodes
B. Groups all selected nodes
C. Arranges nodes automatically based on links
D. Updates all node scripts

Q16. Which command is used to publish a node locally in Dynamo?
A. Save to Library
B. Publish Locally
C. Upload to Cloud
D. Share Workspace

Q17. What kind of files can be imported into Dynamo using the Import Library tool?
A. JPEG and PNG
B. STL and OBJ
C. DLL and DS
D. PDF and DOCX

Q18. What is the shortcut to undo the last action in Dynamo?
A. CTRL+W
B. CTRL+Y
C. CTRL+Z
D. CTRL+U

Q19. Which view option should be turned off in Dynamo to reduce system load?
A. Show Grid
B. Navigate Background 3D Preview
C. Revit Background Preview
D. Show Connectors

Q20. How can a custom node be edited once created in Dynamo?
A. Use the Edit menu
B. Right-click the node and select Edit Custom Node
C. Double-click the workspace
D. Open the File menu and choose Edit Node

Q21. When is the Show Run Preview option active in Dynamo?
A. When Automatic mode is selected
B. When the script is being saved
C. When Manual is selected in Run Settings
D. When Preview Bubbles are disabled

Q22. What does the Number Format drop-down allow you to do?
A. Change background color
B. Adjust node size
C. Set precision
D. Switch between Python and C#

Q23. Which section allows you to define accuracy for geometric rendering and calculations?
A. Render Precision
B. Default Geometry Scaling
C. Visual Settings
D. Display Settings

Q24. How do you define which Python engine to use in visual scripting?
A. By editing script manually
B. By using the Custom Template section
C. From the Default Python Engine drop-down
D. By enabling CPython

Q25. What is the function of the Reset CPython button?
A. Clears all nodes
B. Restarts Python engine and reloads default modules
C. Opens Python editor
D. Reverts to IronPython

Q26. What does Node Autocomplete help with?
A. Drawing curves
B. Showing color themes
C. Suggesting nodes during scripting
D. Resetting node settings

Q27. Which method in the Default Ranking Method section shows the most used node suggestions?
A. Node Type Match
B. Custom Match
C. Recommended Nodes
D. Auto Selection

Q28. What does the Preferred confidence level setting affect?
A. Script errors
B. Node color
C. Threshold for recommended nodes
D. Coordinate input

Q29. What happens when you enable the Use Hardware Acceleration option?
A. Enables scripting logs
B. Uses CPU for faster calculations
C. Enhances graphics using GPU
D. Runs script without preview

Q30. What does the Show CodeBlockNode Line Numbers option do?
A. Highlights syntax errors
B. Displays line numbers in code blocks
C. Enables logging
D. Adds comments

Q31. What happens when you select Use Instancing (Beta)?
A. Enables line numbering
B. Slows down rendering
C. Speeds up rendering of symmetric geometry
D. Runs preview scripts

Q32. How can you define the zoom parameters for the library and Python editor?
A. From Visual Settings
B. Using the Zoom Scaling section
C. By resizing window
D. With keyboard shortcut only

Q33. What does the Disable Loading Custom Packages option do?
A. Blocks all built-in packages
B. Prevents custom packages from loading
C. Deletes packages
D. Refreshes all packages

Q34. What is the purpose of the Create Study tool in Generative Design?
A. To generate default nodes
B. To start a new generative design study
C. To export a study
D. To reset node settings

Q35. What must be created before drawing a line using script?
A. Two curves
B. Points using Point.ByCoordinates
C. Grid system
D. Node group

Q36. Which node is used to create a line between two points?
A. Line.ByMidPoint
B. Curve.ByControlPoints
C. Line.ByStartPointEndPoint
D. Point.Connect

Q37. Which node creates a lofted solid using cross-sections and guide curves?
A. Solid.BySweep
B. Solid.ByLoft
C. Curve.ByLoft
D. Solid.BySection

Q38. What does the Element.Curve node do in path array scripting?
A. Creates a new path
B. Selects object to be copied
C. Brings selected Revit path into Dynamo
D. Divides the curve into segments

Q39. Which node is used to divide a curve at equal segment lengths?
A. Curve.DivideByLength
B. Curve.EqualSegments
C. Curve.PointsAtEqualSegmentLength
D. Curve.SegmentDivide

Q40. What is used in path array for level-bound elements like columns?
A. FamilyInstance.ByPoint
B. FamilyInstance.ByLevel
C. ElementType.ByLevel
D. FamilyInstance.ByPointAndLevel

Q41. How do you convert a code block input to take user input in a script?
A. Enable Auto Run
B. Use “Is Input” option
C. Add comment above input
D. Click on preview

Q42. What does the Dynamo Player allow users to do?
A. Edit Python scripts
B. Run saved scripts in Revit
C. Compile C# code
D. Edit Revit families

Q43. What should you do if leftover geometry is not disappearing after script execution?
A. Restart computer
B. Reinstall Dynamo
C. Save and reopen file
D. Use erase command in Dynamo

FOR STUDENT NOTES

Chapter 15

Residential Building Project

Topics Covered

The major topics covered in this chapter are:

- ***Creating Residential Building Model***

INTRODUCTION

A residential building is the one where people can live safe from environmental hazards. A residential building can be with or without cooking facilities. There are five major types of residential buildings; Individual Houses/Villas, Lodges, Dormitories, Apartments, and Hotels. Each type of building has its own design and construction needs. For example, a dormitory needs to accommodate sleeping facility for multiple individuals in same room. In this project, we will plan and design an individual house. Technically, each residential building passes through three phases: Planning, Design, and Construction. In this chapter, we are going to work on planning and design phases. The construction phase is not in the scope of this book. First, we will discuss the planning phase and then we will work on designing the building.

PLANNING

This is the first phase of building design. In this phase, we consider the size of land piece in which building will be created, direction of residential land, favorable conditions, unfavorable conditions, by-laws of locality, customer requirements, and so on. Various conditions of planning are discussed next.

Site Selection for Building

Following are some favorable conditions for site selection:

- Building site should be located in developed or under-development area. From developed area, we mean the area which has access to basic civic facilities like water, electricity, gas, sewer line, telecommunication lines, and so on.
- The site area should have good connectivity with city/town in terms of transport like bus and rail services.
- The soil in the site should be naturally good for building foundation. If you construct a building on bad soil then there are always chances of building cracks or even collapse. There are mainly six types of soils. Out of these soils, loam and rock soils are well suited for foundations of buildings. You can use the sand/gravel soil in foundation if you can control the water slipping in foundation and compact the sand/gravel in given region. The peat, clay, and silt soils are not suitable for foundation. These days you can add additives to different soils for making them suitable for foundation but that costs extra on building budget.
- The site should have enough space for abundant light and air ventilation.
- The ground water level should not be high at the site.
- If site is close to schools, hospitals, colleges and other public services then it is an added benefit.
- The site should be away from commercial institutions, manufacturing industries, and busy commercial roads.
- If you believe in ancient architectural system then according to ancient Indian architectural system Vastu Shastra, the main gate of house should be facing either North or East direction for prosperity. Apart from ancient architecture, you will get maximum Sun light in morning if your main gate faces East. If your main gate faces North and you are in Southern hemisphere then you will get maximum sunlight. If you are in Northern hemisphere then your main gate should face south to get maximum sun light. In simple terms, the building should get acceptable sun light in summers and maximum sun light in winters for energy saving.

Some of the unfavorable conditions for site are given next.

- Decaying or nuclear radiation affected locality.
- Sites with reclaimed soils.
- Polluted area due to heavy industries.
- Locations affected by heavy floods, frequent storms, tornados, or frequent earth quakes.
- Locations with high crime rates.
- Locations with unstable political environment.
- Locations with gun culture where any maniac can get guns and go on killing spree.

Residential Land Size

Once you have decided the site location, the next step is land size. The size of land depends on personal requirements of customer. It depends on how many rooms are needed by customer, what type of sanitary accommodations are needed, how many floors are to be constructed, and how much space is to be left vacant according to the Bylaws or building codes. You can also refer to International Code Council's International Residential Code 2018 manual for building codes generally acceptable in many countries. The manual is applicable for townhouses upto 3 storey. You need to always check the building codes in your state and your city.

Construction Type and Material

After considering the land size for residential building, you need to decide on the type of construction to be used in building. You need to also check the building codes for allowed construction types for your building. Like, you will be using steel structure, wooden structure, or concrete structure to construct your building.

As per the construction type, you need to decide on construction material like concrete, steel bars, wooden material, flooring material, bath fittings, and furnishing materials.

Once, you have planned your building in detail, the next step is to design the building. Here, **we are considering to design 2 storey building which has a parking garage. It uses concrete construction with beams and columns. The total area of building site is 2200 sqft (50 ft x 44 ft). The customer wants 4 Bedrooms with connected sanitary facilities, one hall, and one kitchen. The customer wants complete drawing set of architectural, structural, and MEP drawings.** The design step for building is discussed next.

DESIGNING

In this step, we consider various factors involved in designing the building. We consider size of beams and columns, size of staircase, sizes of different items, height of floors, thickness of floor slabs, heating and cooling requirements of building, and other building design related parameters. The columns and beams should be designed in such a way that they get mixed in the walls and do not spoil architectural aesthetic of the building. A thumb rule for columns is that for G+1 floor building, you can start with 9"x9" column with M20 grade concrete. Once modeling is complete, you can run the analysis and modify the sizes accordingly. The distance between two columns should not be more than 15 feet.

Now keeping notes of everything we have planned for the building, we will start creating the model in Autodesk Revit.

Creating Architectural Model in Autodesk Revit

As you have learned in previous chapters of this book, we can create architectural, structural, as well as MEP features of building model in Autodesk Revit. We will start with architectural aspect of model.

Starting A New Project

- Start Autodesk Revit from **Start** menu or using Desktop icon.
- Press **CTRL+D** and click on the **Project** tool from **New** cascading menu of the **File** menu. The **New Project** dialog box will be displayed.
- Select the **Architectural Template** option from the **Template file** drop-down and select the **Project** option from the **Create new** area of the dialog box.
- Click on the **OK** button from the dialog box. A new project file will open with architectural template.

Since we are working on a two storey residential building, it is not necessary to create grid lines at primary stage. We can start with creating walls and later when needed, we will create the grid lines as required.

Creating Walls

Since, we are going to use columns and beams in the building so we are free to use architectural thin walls in the building for room divisions. But we will need relatively thicker walls at boundaries of building because these walls have to bear the effect of outside weather. Note that architectural walls do not bear loads of the building.

- Make sure the **Level 1 Architectural** plan view is open and click on the **Wall: Architectural** tool from the **Wall** drop-down in the **Build** panel of **Architecture** tab in the **Ribbon**. The options to create architectural wall will be displayed in the **Ribbon** and **Properties Palette**.
- Set the height of wall to **Level 2 Architectural**, **Location Line** to **Finish Exterior**, **Offset** to **0**, and **Join Status** to **Allow** in the **Options Bar**.
- Select the **Generic - 8" Masonry** option from the top drop-down in the **Properties Palette**. The options should display as shown in Figure-1.

Note that if Level 0 and Level 1 are displayed in Floor Plans section of Project Browser in your case then assume Level 0 as Level 1 and Level 1 as Level 2 in this project.

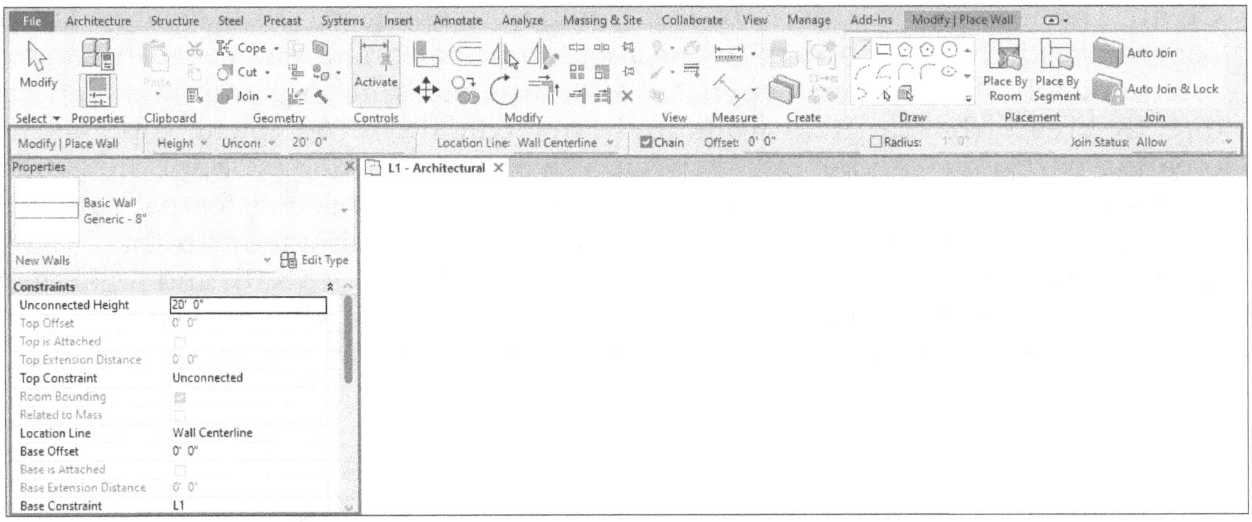

Figure-1. Options set for exterior wall

- Create the boundary wall as shown in Figure-2.

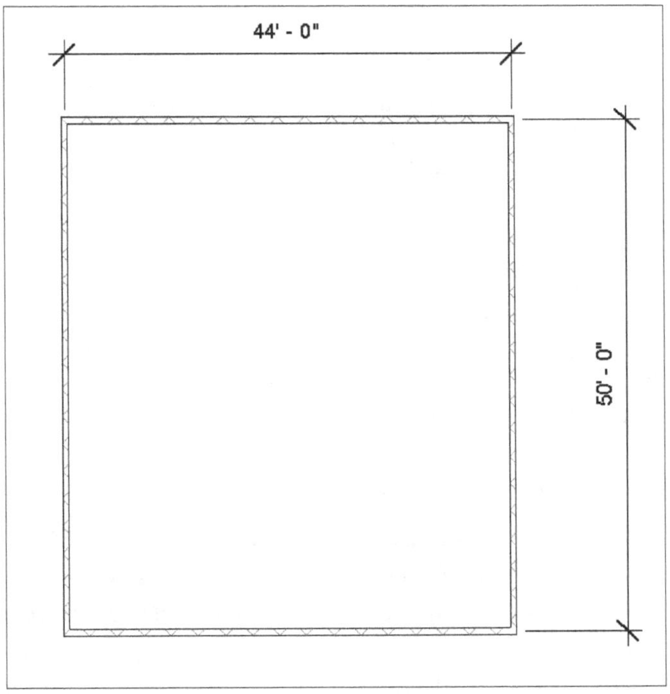

Figure-2. Boundary walls created

- Select the **Interior - 5" Partition wall** from the drop-down at the top in **Properties Palette** and set the **Location Line** to **Finish Face : Interior** in the **Options Bar**. Keep rest of the options same as set earlier; refer to Figure-3.

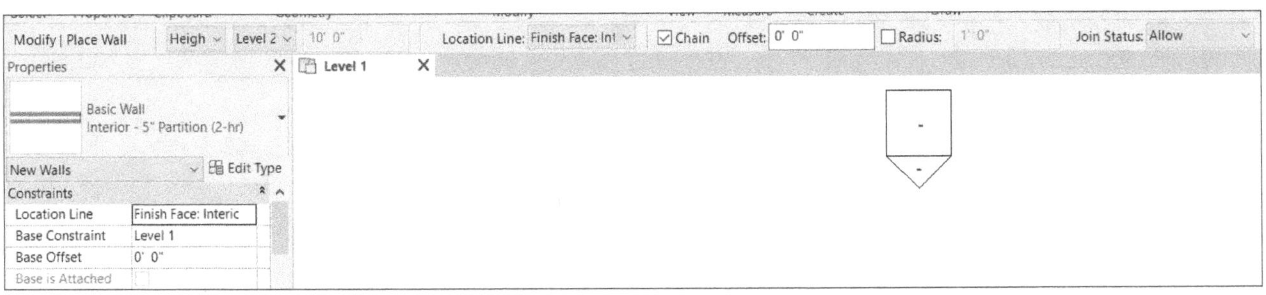

Figure-3. Options set for interior wall

- Create the interior partitions of the building keeping in mind desired size of bedrooms, kitchen, bathroom, living room, and parking area. You can create a rough sketch of rooms on paper, calculate the sizes in your mind, or you can directly create the partition walls and later edit them. A typical approach for creating partitions can be: Decide what size of bedroom do you want, how many rooms do you want on this floor, how much space is needed for parking, and then later you can adjust other rooms as per your requirement. In this project, we want to create two rooms on ground floor with size of 15'x15' and a garage of 20'x14' size on the ground floor. We also want to create a kitchen and bath room on the ground floor. The plan should display as shown in Figure-4.

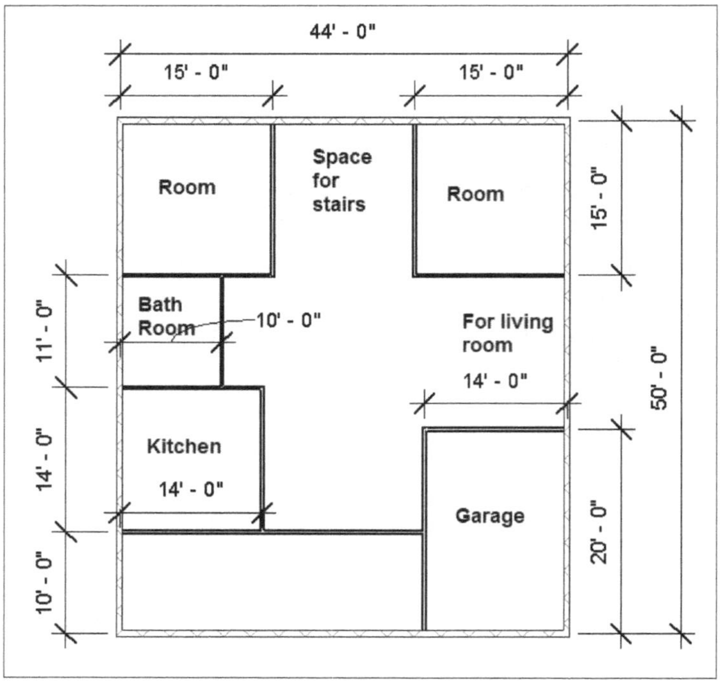

Figure-4. Plan for ground level

- Double-click on **Level 2 Architectural** from the **Floor Plans(Architectural Plan)** category in the **Project Browser**. The plan view will open.
- Click on the **Wall: Architectural** tool if not active. Select the **Generic - 8" Masonry** option from the top drop-down in the **Properties Palette** and set the parameters of **Options Bar** as shown in Figure-5.

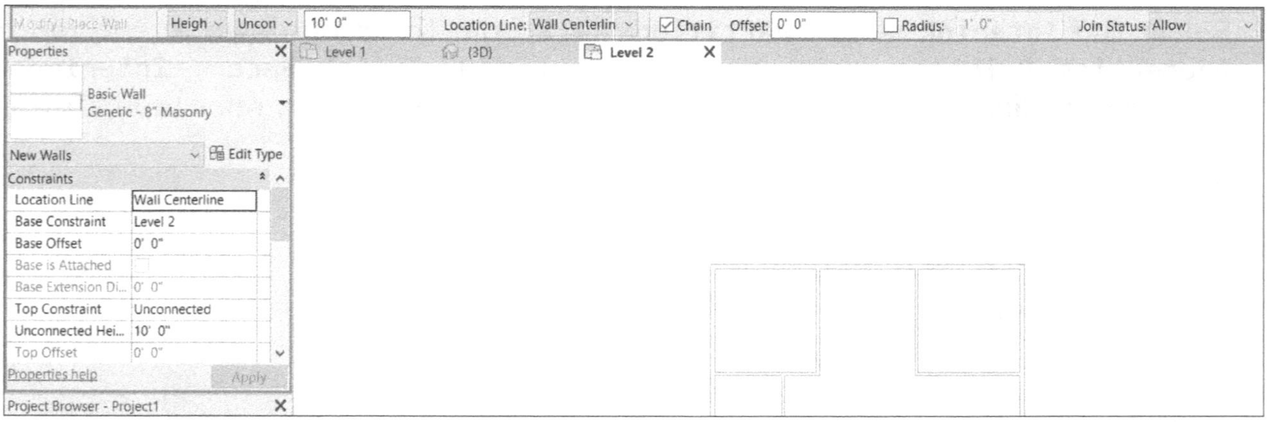

Figure-5. Options to set for exterior wall

- Create the exterior walls as shown in Figure-6.

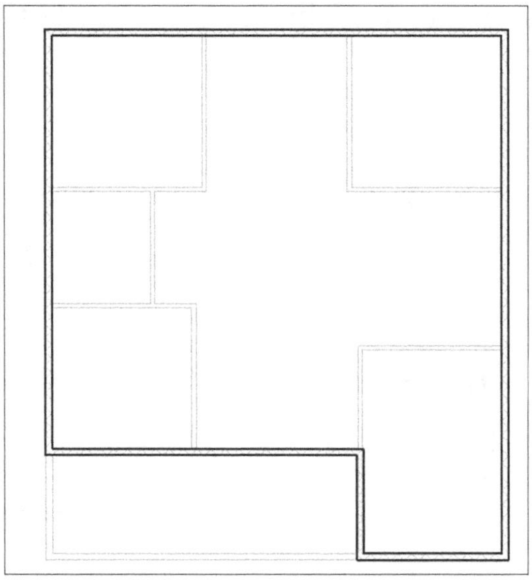

Figure-6. Creating exterior walls for Level 2

- Select the **Interior - 5" Partition** option from the drop-down at the top in the **Properties Palette** and set the other options in the **Options Bar** as shown in Figure-7.

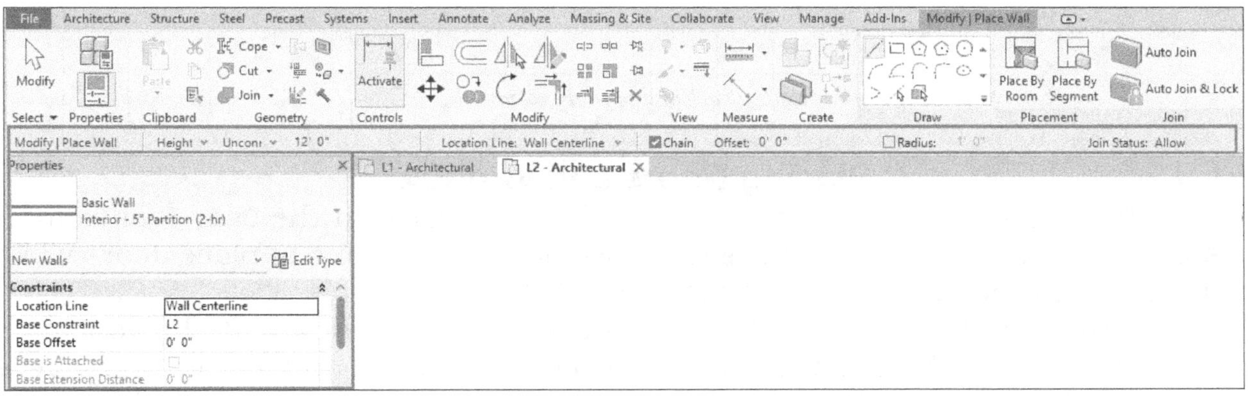

Figure-7. Options for wall on Level 2

- Create the two rooms as shown in Figure-8.

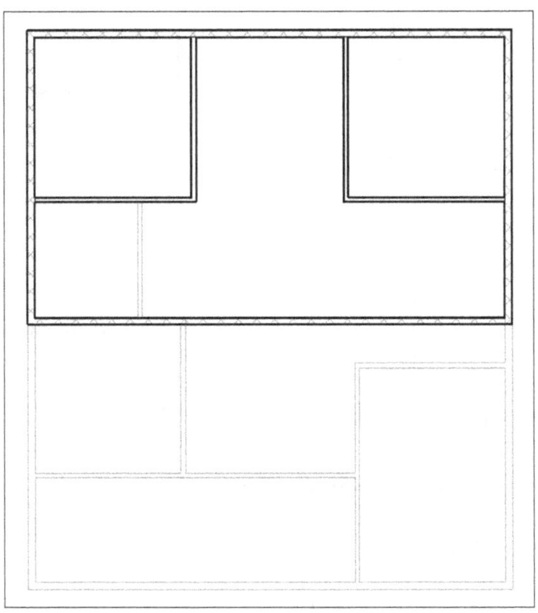

Figure-8. Creating rooms on Level 2

- Create the attached sanitary and bath rooms at both the levels using interior walls; refer to Figure-9.

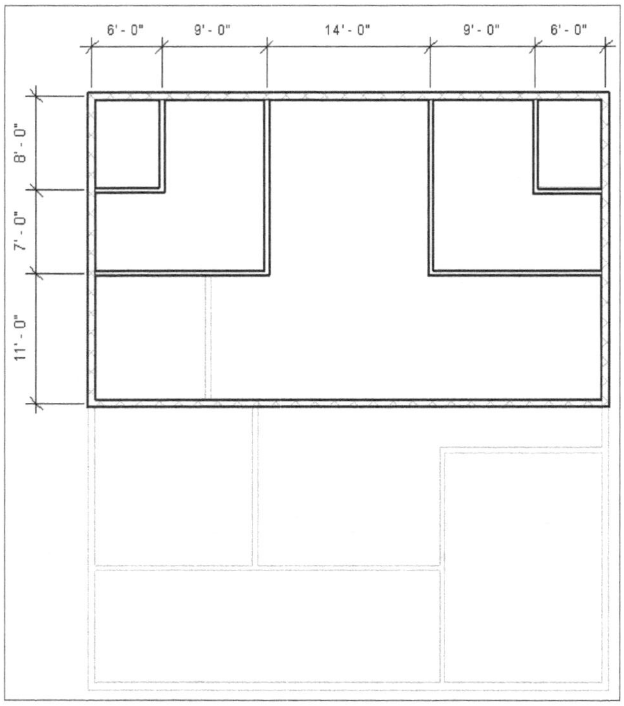

Figure-9. Attached bath and sanitary rooms

Placing Doors and Windows

- Switch to **Level 1 Architectural** plan view and click on the **Door** tool from the **Build** panel in the **Architecture** tab of **Ribbon**. The options to place doors will be displayed in the **Properties Palette** and **Ribbon**.
- Select the **Single-Flush 36" x 84"** door from drop-down at the top in the **Properties Palette** and place doors for rooms, kitchen, and garage in the **Level 1** plan; refer to Figure-10.

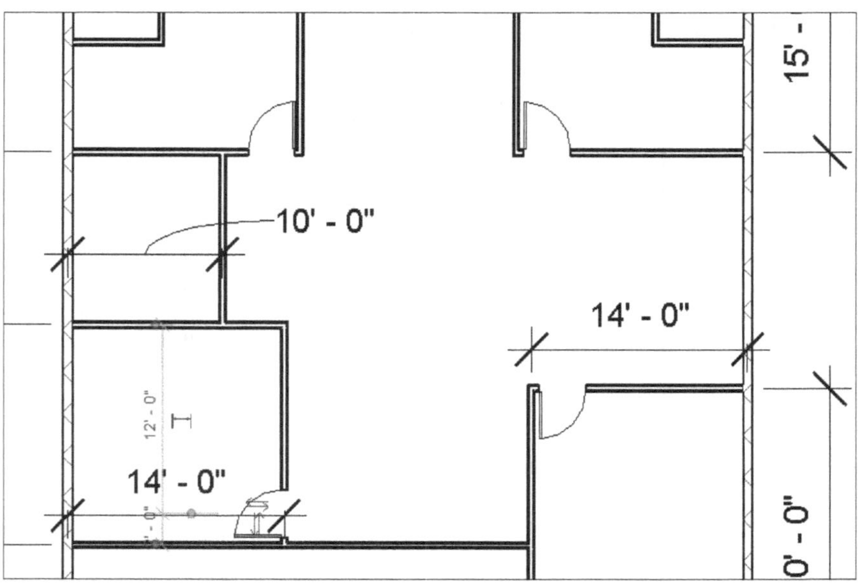

Figure-10. Interior room doors placed

- Similarly, create doors for rooms on Level 2.

- Now, select the **Single Flush 30" x 80"** door from the drop-down at the top in **Properties Palette** and place the doors in bath & sanitary rooms on both the levels; refer to Figure-11.

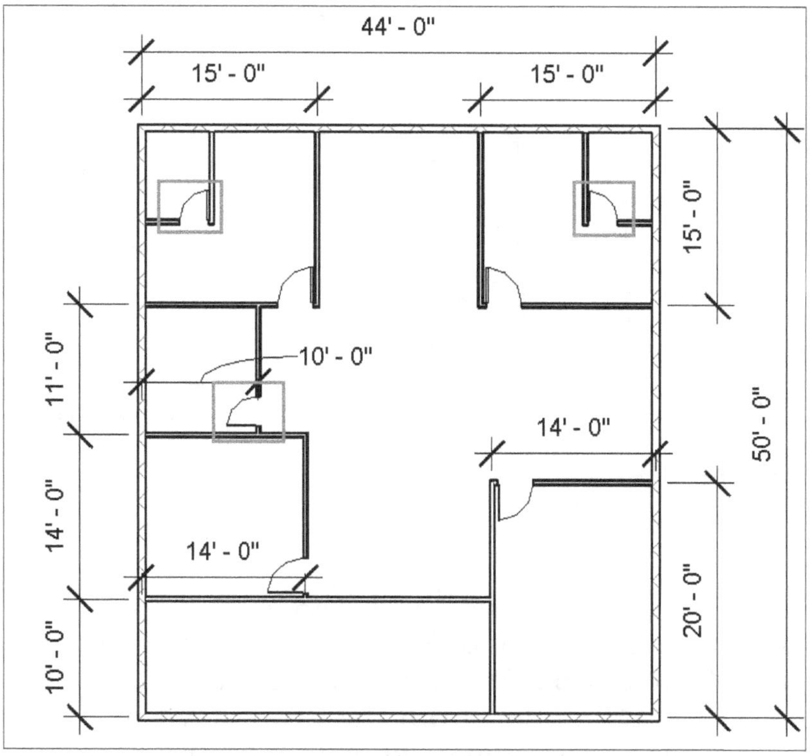

Figure-11. Doors created for bath and sanitary rooms

- Click on the **Load Family** tool from the **Mode** panel in the **Modify|Place Door** contextual tab of the **Ribbon**. The **Load Family** dialog box will be displayed.
- Select the **Door-Double-Flush Panel-Double-Acting.rfa** door type from the **Load Family** dialog box and click on the **Open** dialog box. The **Specify Types** dialog box will be displayed; refer to Figure-12.

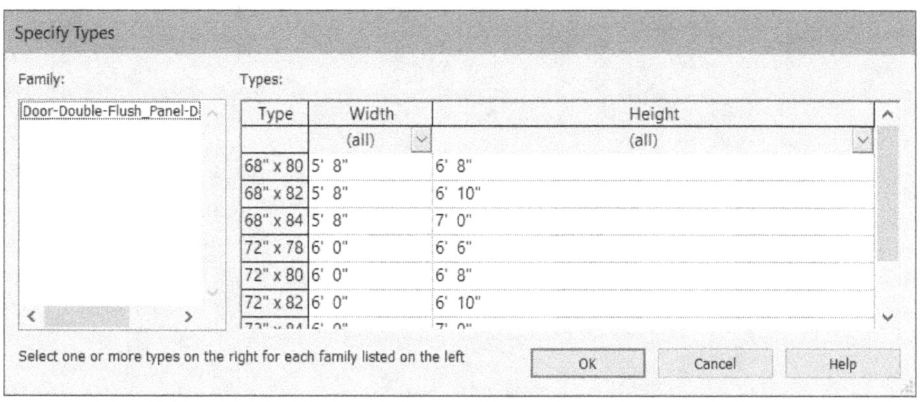

Figure-12. Specify Types dialog box

- Select desired **72" x 84"** door type from the list and click on the **OK** button. The door will be selected in **Properties Palette**.
- Click at exterior walls of building and place the doors; refer to Figure-13.

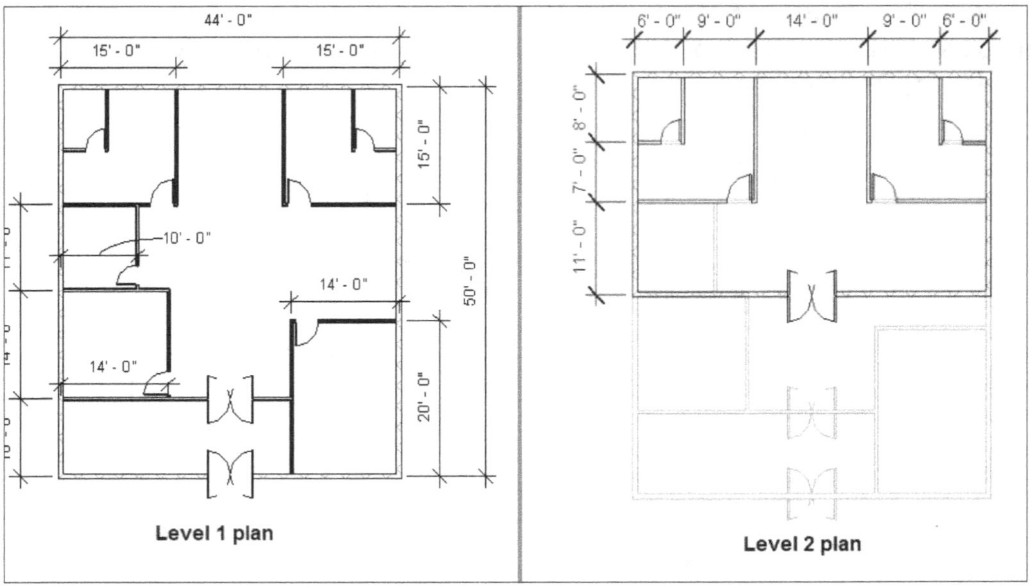

Figure-13. Main doors placed

- Press **ESC** to exit the tool.

Creating Floors

- Click on the **Floor: Structural** tool from the **Floor** drop-down in the **Build** panel of **Architecture** tab in **Ribbon**. The options to create floor will be displayed.
- Select the **Generic - 12"** option from the drop-down in the top of **Properties Palette** and create the line sketch as shown in Figure-14.

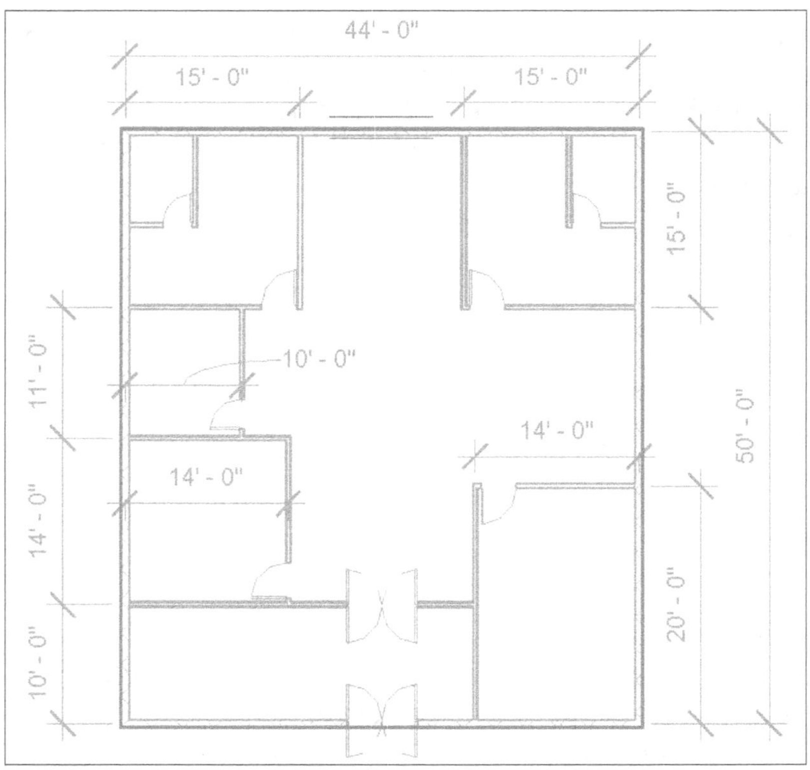

Figure-14. Line sketch for floor on level 1

- Click on the **Finish Edit Mode** tool from the **Mode** panel in the **Modify|Create Floor Boundary** contextual tab of **Ribbon**. The floor will be created.
- Double-click on **Level 2** option from the **Floor Plans** category in the **Project Browser** to open Level 2 Plan view.

- Click on the **Floor: Structural** tool as selected earlier. The options to create floor will be displayed same as discussed earlier.
- Create the line sketch for floor as shown in Figure-15.

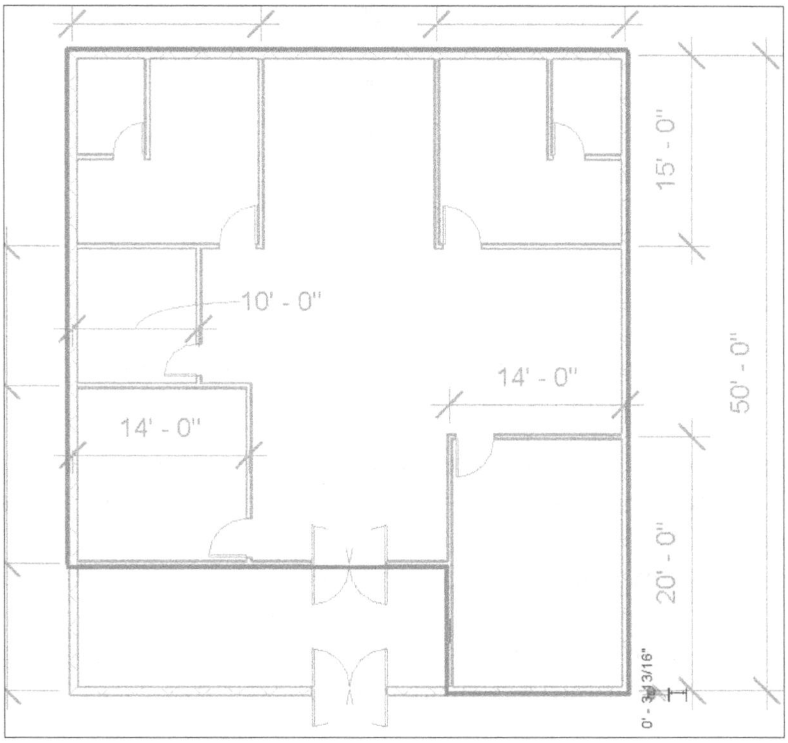

Figure-15. Line sketch created for floor

- Click on the **Finish** button from the contextual tab and select **Yes** if a message box is displaying asking you whether to connect floor with walls. The floor will be created.

Creating Level 3 and Roof

- Open the **East- Architectural** elevation view from the **Project Browser** and select the **Level** tool from the **Datum** panel in the **Architecture** tab of **Ribbon**. You will be asked to define the start point of level line.
- Create the level at **10'** elevation value as shown in Figure-16.

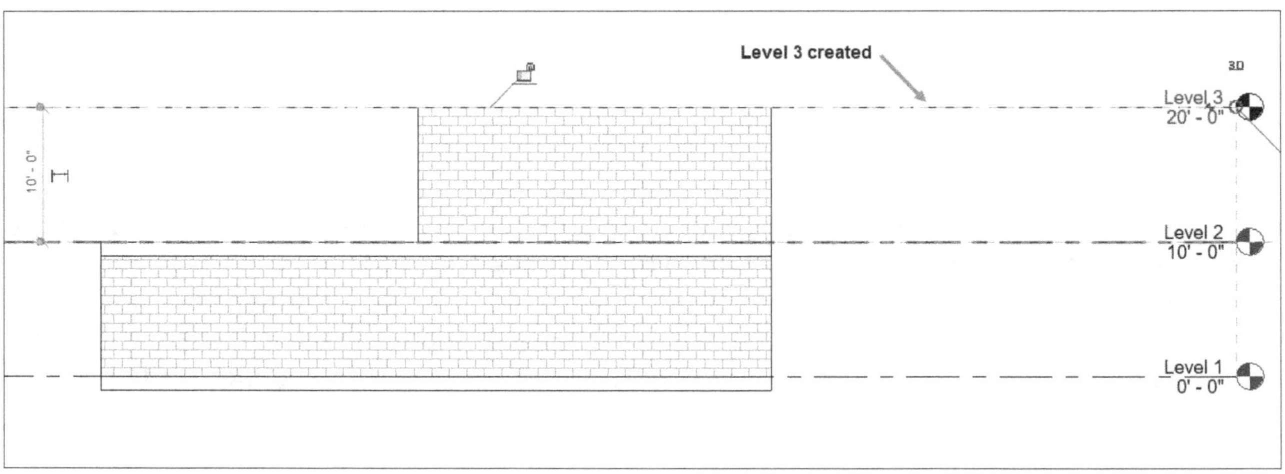

Figure-16. Creating level 3

- Select all the walls on level 2 and set the **Top Constraint** option to **Up to level: Level 3** in the **Properties Palette**; refer to Figure-17. Press **ESC** to exit the selection.

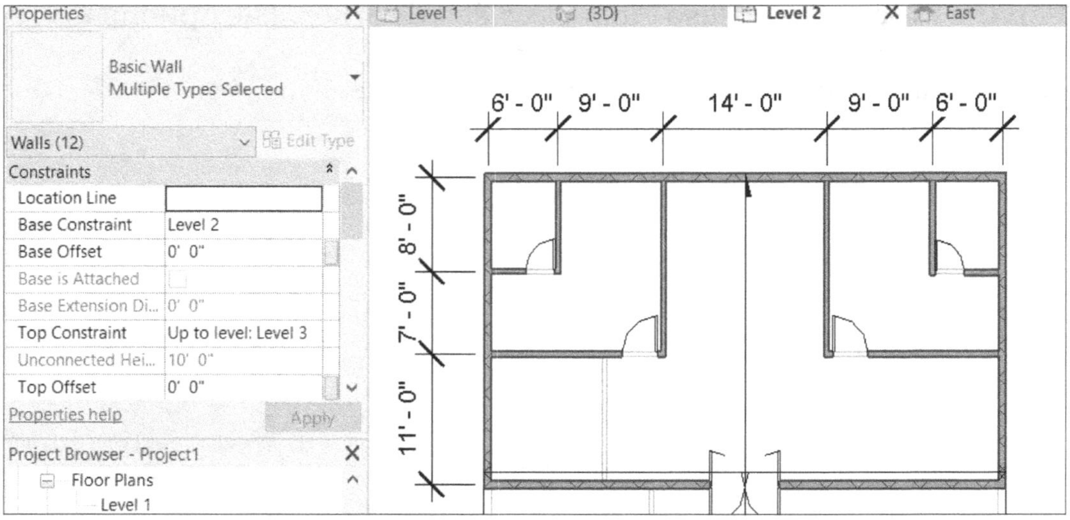

Figure-17. Top constraint setting for walls

- Open the Level 3 plan view by double-clicking on **Level 3** under **Floor Plans** category of **Project Browser**. The Level 3 plan view will be displayed without displaying walls of level 2.
- Scroll down in **Properties Palette** and set the ranges for Underlay as shown in Figure-18. (We need to do this step because without it the walls will not be displayed in Level 3 plan view). Click on the **Apply** button from **Properties Palette** if parameters are not applied automatically.

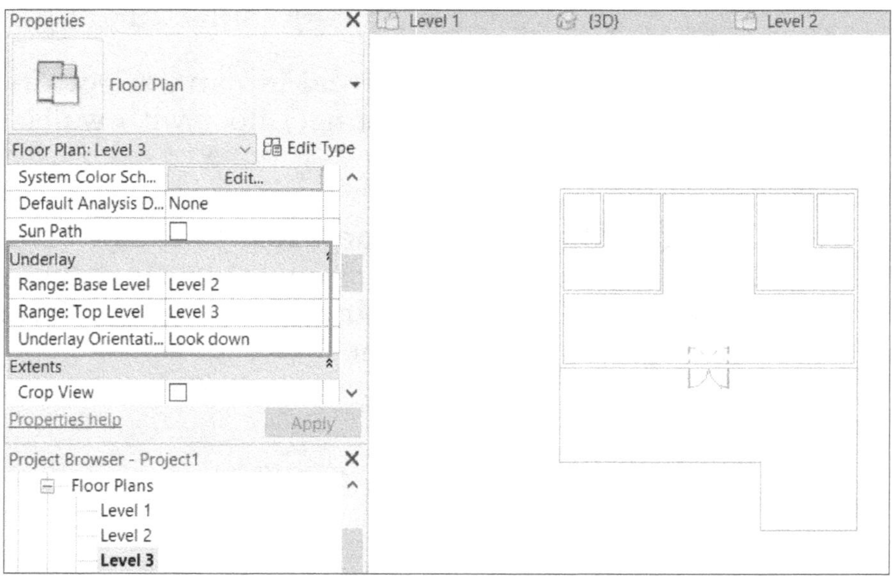

Figure-18. Options set for underlay range

- Click on the **Roof by Footprint** tool from the **Roof** drop-down in the **Build** panel of the **Architecture** tab in **Ribbon**. The options to create roof will be displayed in the **Modify|Create Roof Footprint** contextual tab and **Properties Palette**.
- Select the **Generic - 12" Filled** option from the **Properties Palette** and using the **Line** tool from **Draw** panel in contextual tab, create the line sketch for roof as shown in Figure-19.

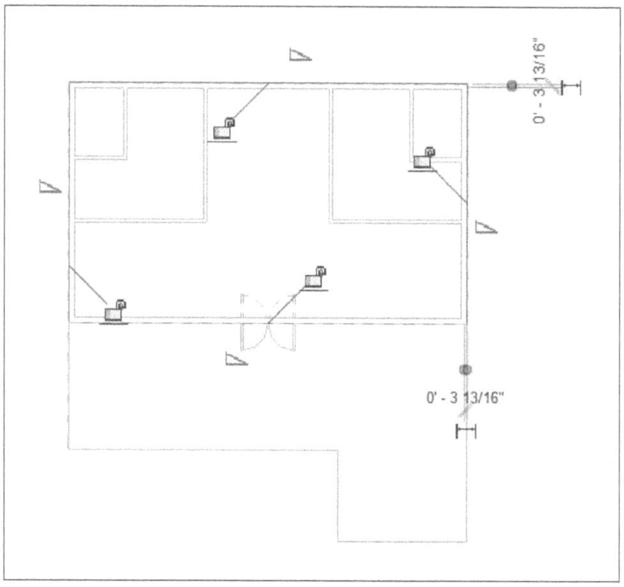

Figure-19. Line sketch roof

- Click on the **Finish Edit Mode** button from the **Mode** panel in the contextual tab and select **Yes** button if a message box is displayed asking you to attach walls with roof. The roof will be created; refer to Figure-20 (3D view).

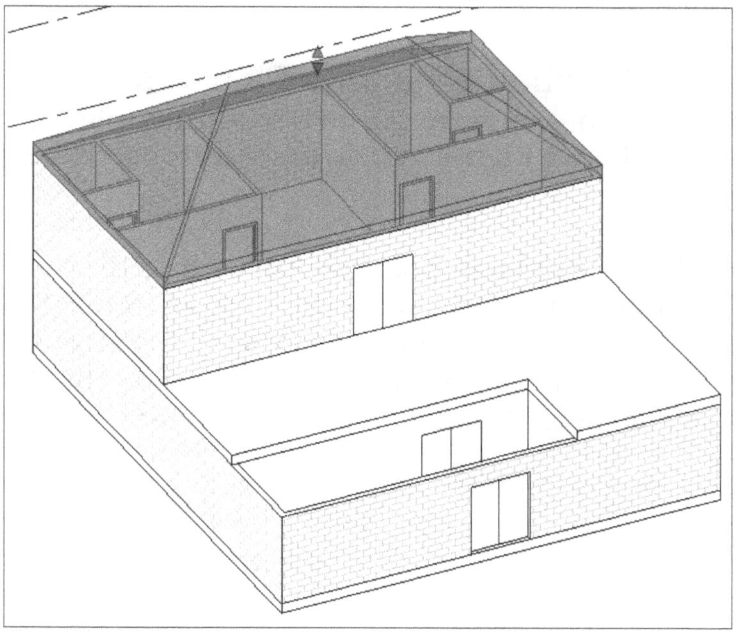

Figure-20. 3D view of roof

- Click on the **Roof: Gutter** tool from the **Roof** drop-down in the **Build** panel of **Architecture** tab in the **Ribbon** and select the three edges of roof as shown in Figure-21 to create gutter for water floor. Press **ESC** twice to exit the tool.

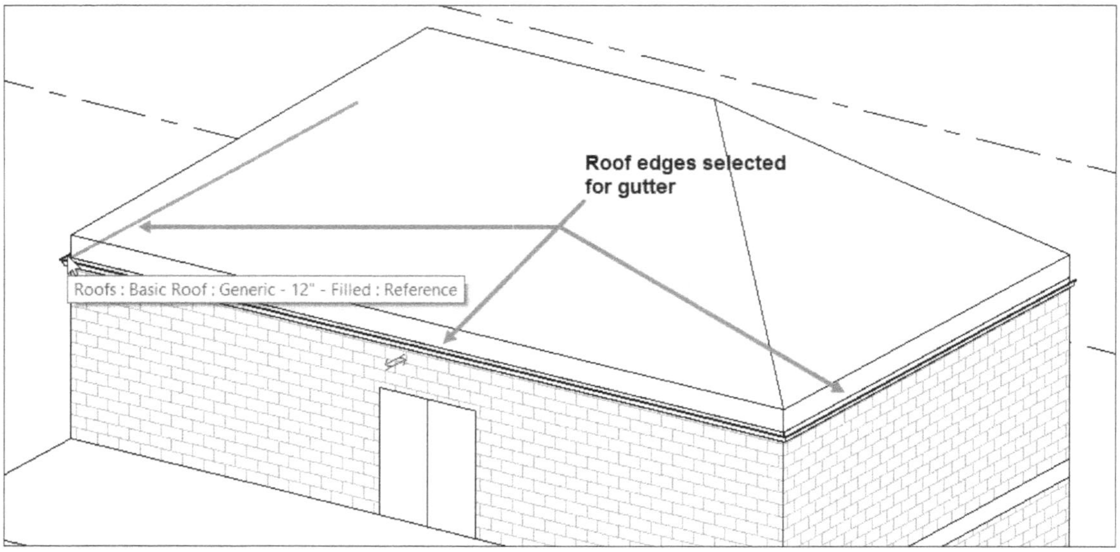

Figure-21. Edges selected for roof gutter

Creating Structural Model of Building

While creating architectural model, most of the walls were created as non-load bearing walls. To bear the load of building and objects in the building, we will create columns and beams in the model.

Creating Structural Plan Views

To keep architectural plans separate from structural plans, we need to create structural plans for Level 1 and Level 2. The procedure to create plan views is given next.

- Click on the **Structural Plan** tool from the **Plan Views** drop-down of **Create** panel in the **View** tab of **Ribbon**. The **New Structural Plan** dialog box will be displayed.
- Select the **Level 1** and **Level 2** options from the dialog box while holding the **CTRL** key; refer to Figure-22 and click on the **OK** button from the dialog box. The plans will be added in **Structural Plans** category of **Project Browser**.

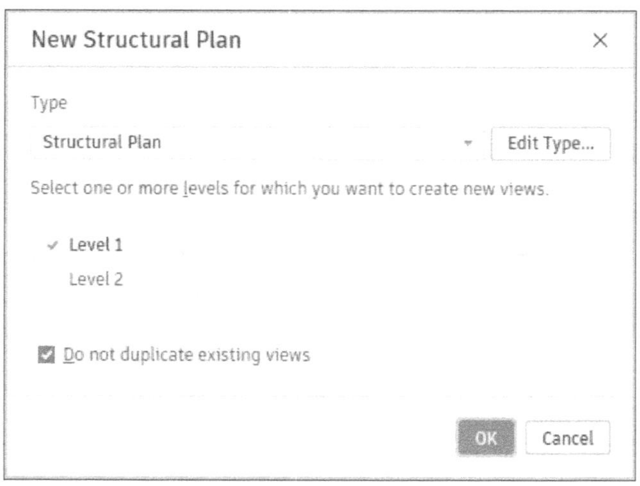

Figure-22. New structural plans to be created

- Open the Level 1 plan from **Structural Plans** category. The plan will be displayed.
- If architectural elements are displayed in dark lines then set everything halftone except structural elements in the **Visibility/Graphics Overrides** dialog box; refer to Figure-23.

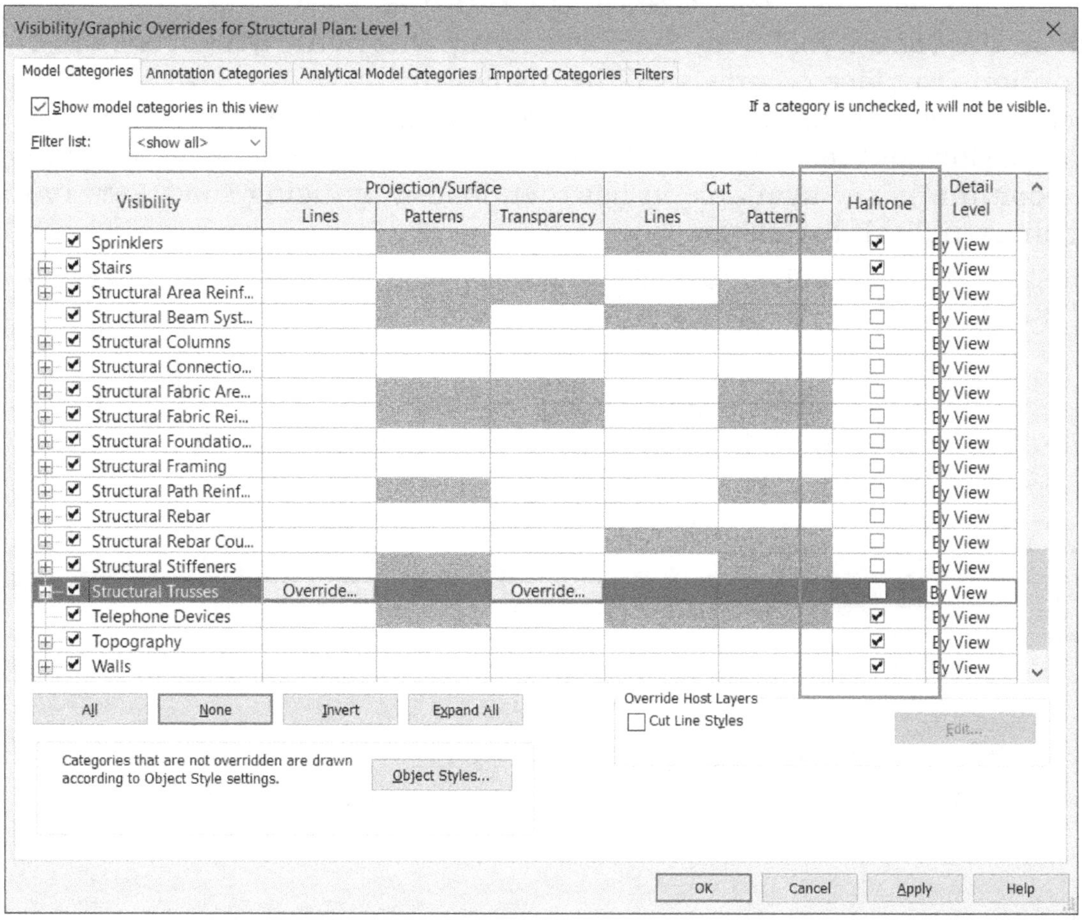

Figure-23. Setting all elements to halftone except structural

- Click on the **OK** button from the dialog box. The plan view will be displayed as shown in Figure-24.

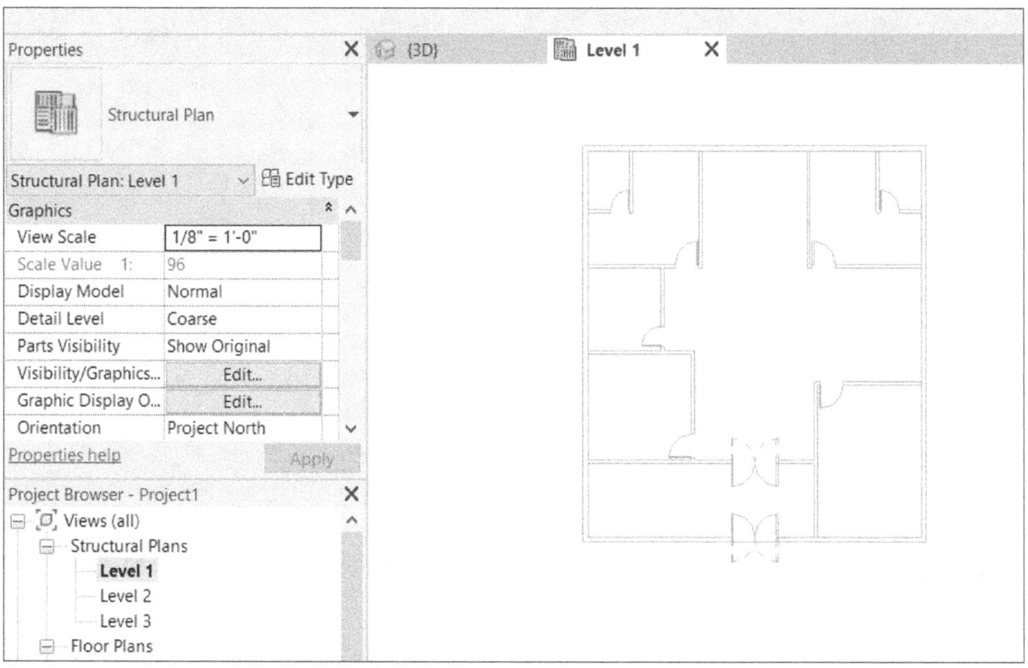

Figure-24. Level 1 structural plan view

Creating Columns

- Click on the **Column** tool from the **Structure** panel in the **Structure** tab of **Ribbon**. The options to place columns will be displayed.
- Select the **Concrete-Rectangular-Column 12 x 18** option from the drop-down at the top in the **Properties Palette** and set the other options as shown in Figure-25. If the column is not available in list then load it by using **Load Family** tool from the contextual tab in **Ribbon**.

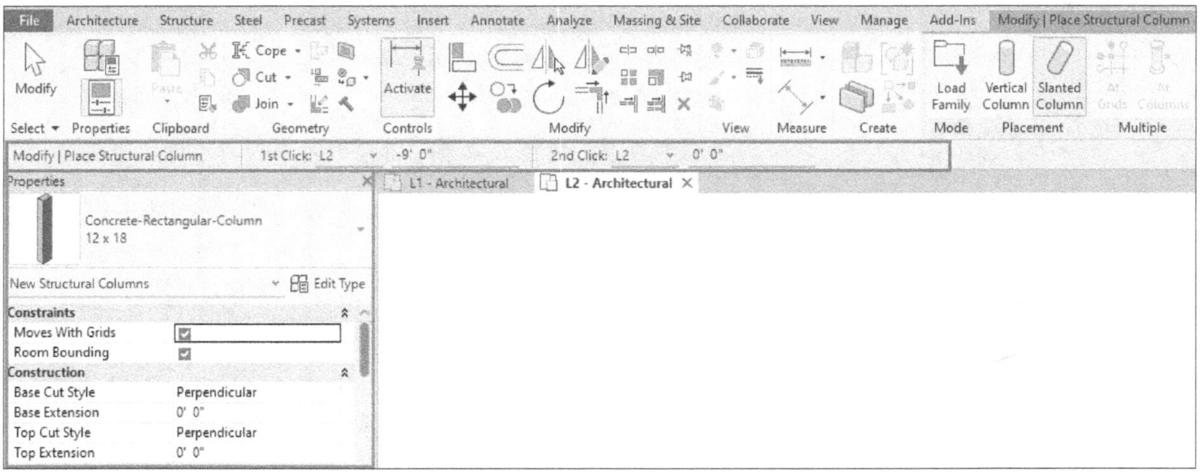

Figure-25. Options set for structural column

- Place the columns aligned with walls as shown in Figure-26.

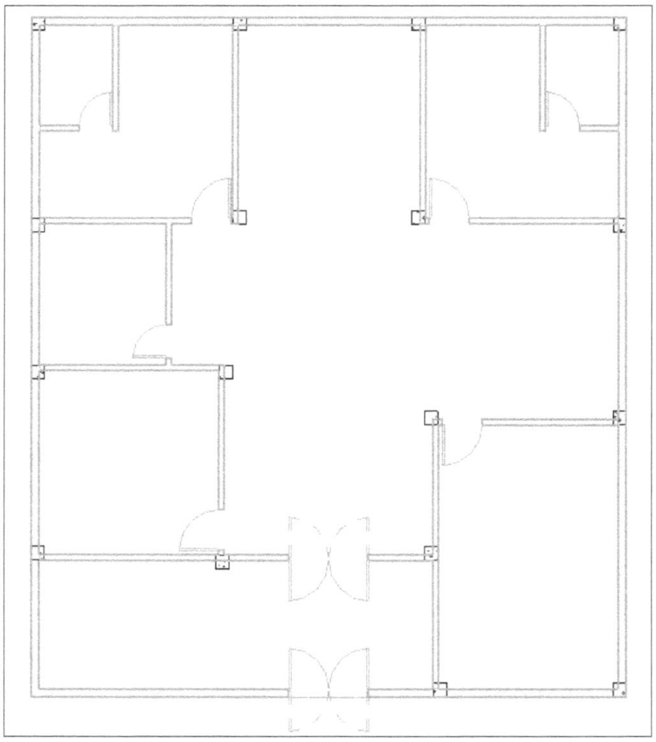

Figure-26. Columns created on Level 1

- Similarly, place the structural columns in Level 2 plan view; refer to Figure-27.

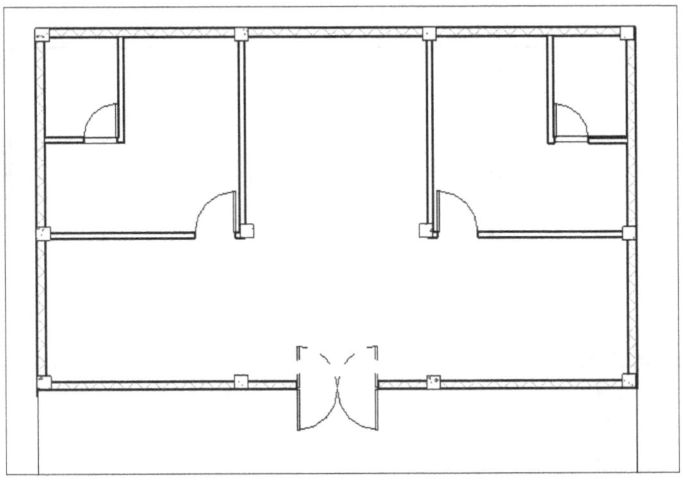

Figure-27. Columns created on Level 2

- Click on the **Default 3D View** button from the **Quick Access Toolbar**. The 3D view of building will be displayed; refer to Figure-28.

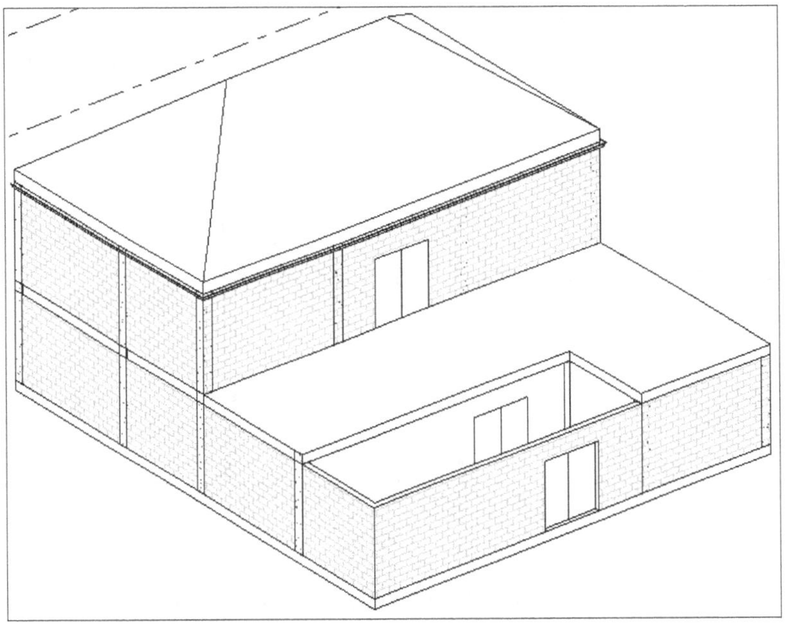

Figure-28. 3D model of building

Creating Plumbing System

- Open the Level 1 plan view of **Floor Plans** category in the **Project Browser**.
- Type **VV** to open **Visibility/Graphics Overrides** dialog box and make sure the mechanical, electrical, piping, and plumbing objects are checked for display. Click on the **OK** button from the dialog box.
- Click on the **Plumbing Fixture** tool from the **Plumbing & Piping** panel in the **Systems** tab of **Ribbon** and place different type of fixtures as required in the building on both floors; refer to Figure-29 and Figure-30. (Note that you need to change the -6" in the bottom range of **View Range** dialog box while placing the drain; refer to Figure-31.)

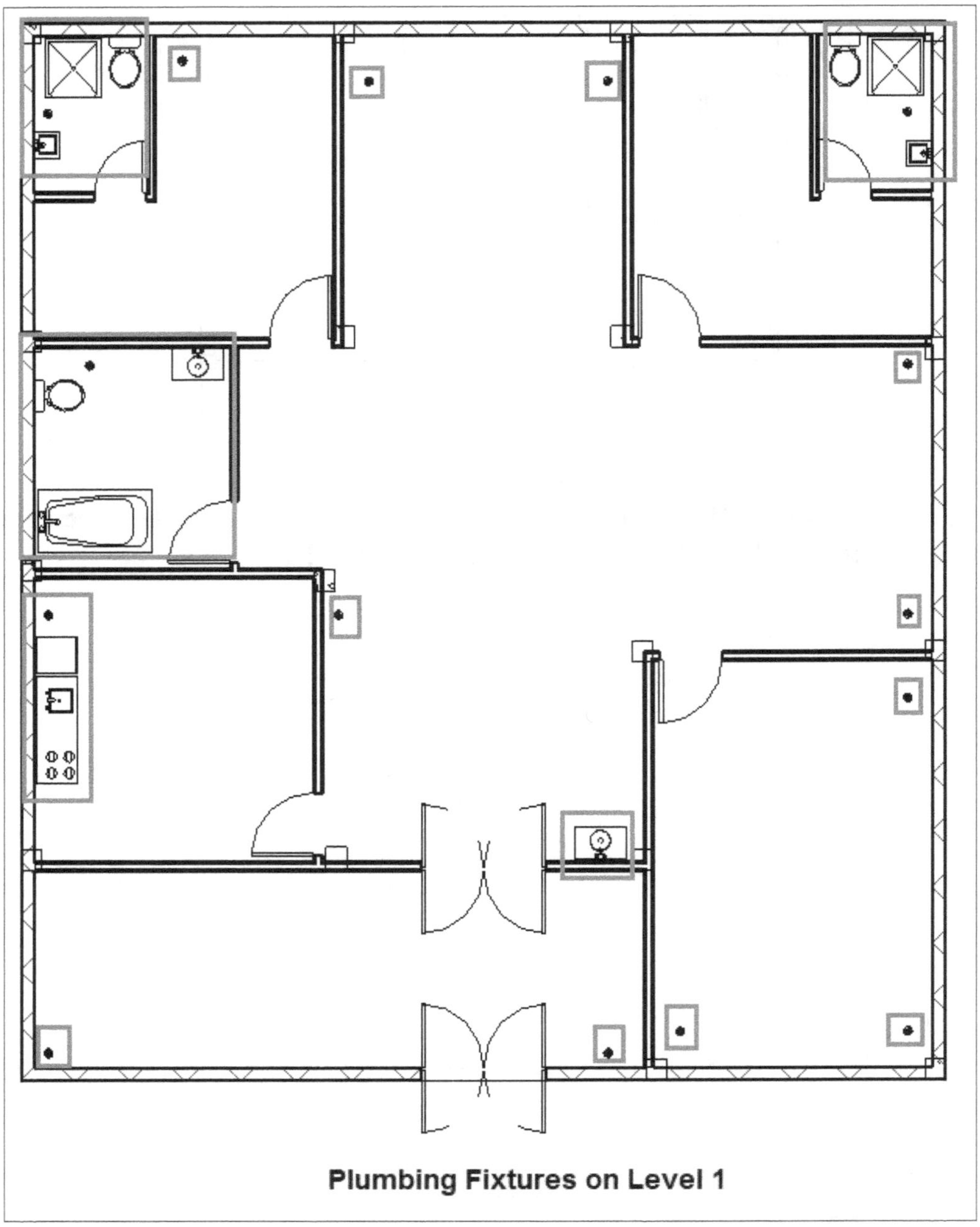

Figure-29. Plumbing fixtures on level 1

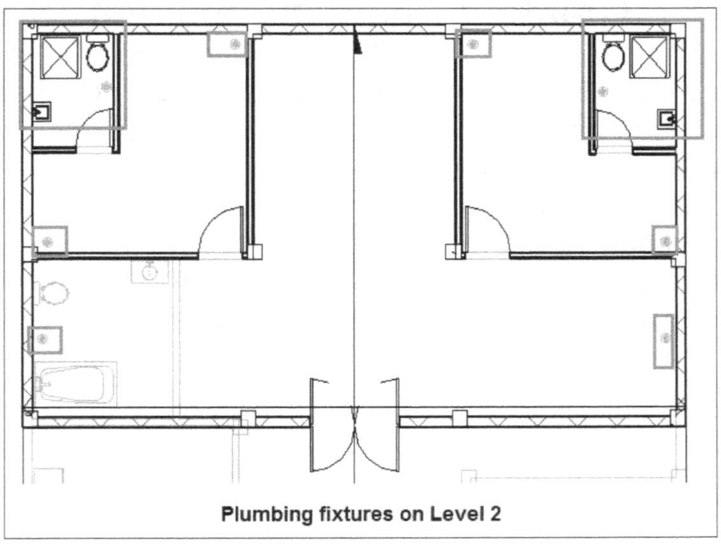

Figure-30. Plumbing fixtures on level 2

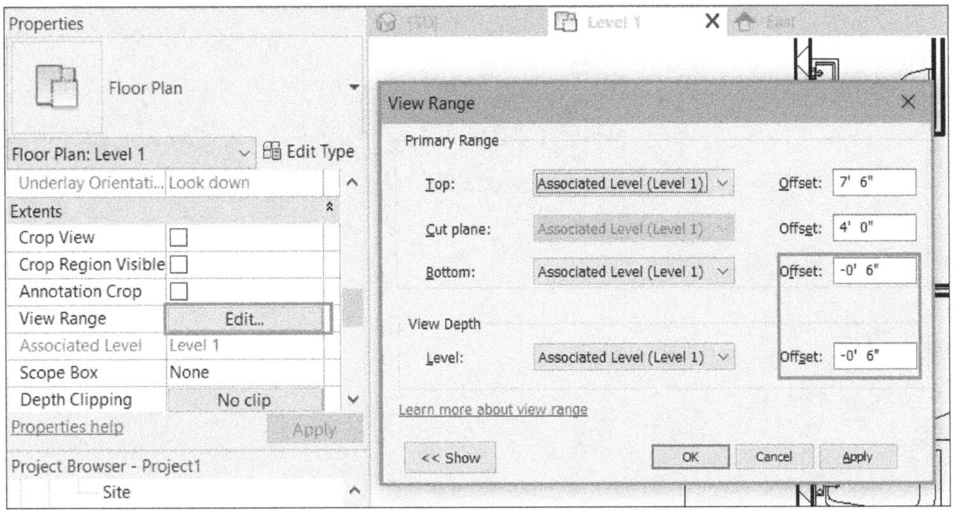

Figure-31. View range setting

- Open the **Level 1** plan view from **Floor Plans(Site Plan)** category and select all the plumbing fixtures. The **Modify|Plumbing Fixtures** contextual tab will be displayed.
- Click on the **Piping** tool from the **Create Systems** panel in the **Modify|Plumbing Fixtures** contextual tab of **Ribbon**. The **Create Piping System** dialog box will be displayed; refer to Figure-32. Make sure **Sanitary** option is selected in the **System type** drop-down and specify desired name for system in the dialog box.

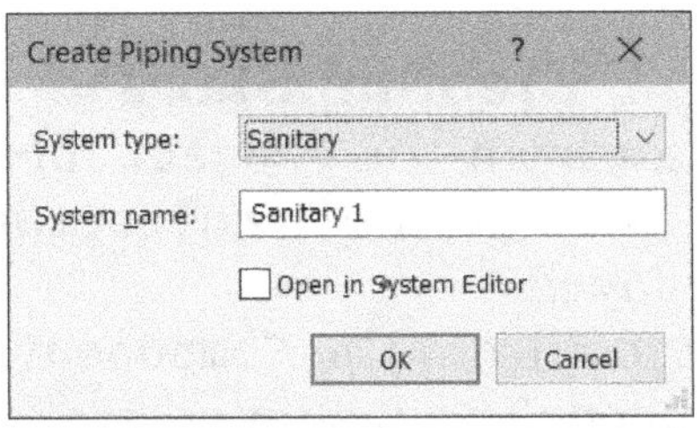

Figure-32. Create Piping System dialog box

- Click on the **OK** button from the dialog box. The **Modify|Piping Systems** contextual tab will be displayed in the **Ribbon**.
- Click on the **Generate Layout** tool from the contextual tab. The preview of layouts will be displayed.
- Click on the **Settings** button from the **Options Bar** and set desired offset level. If you want to create underground piping then set the offset value in negative for both main and branch pipes; refer to Figure-33.

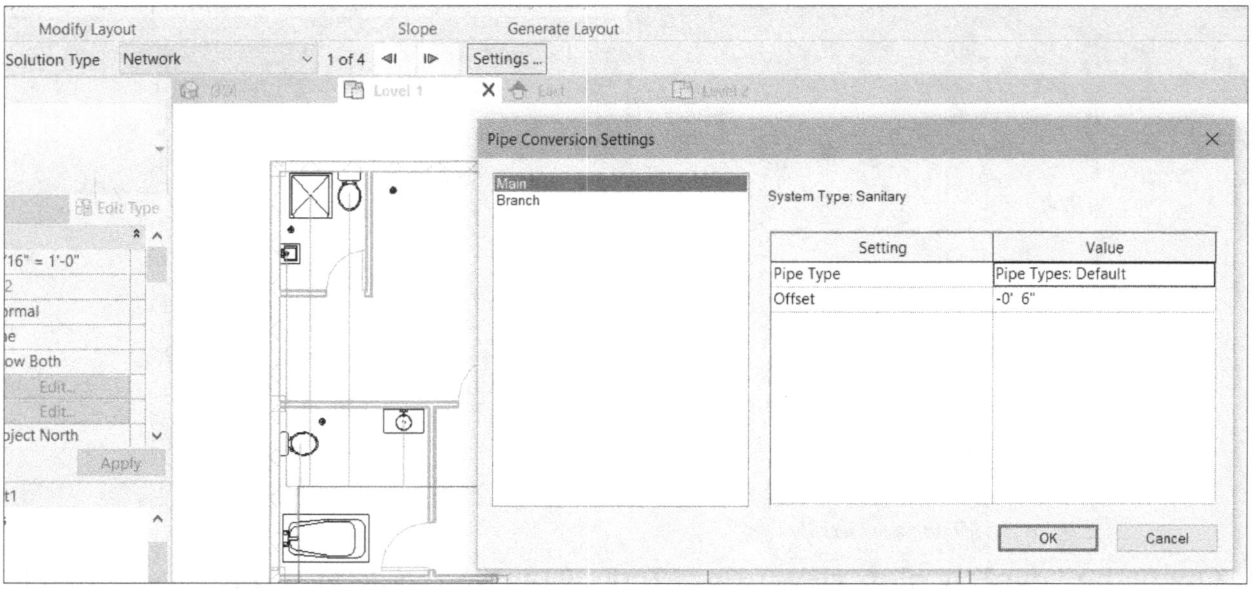

Figure-33. Settings for piping system

- Switch between different layouts and click on the **Finish Layout** button from the **Generate Layout** contextual tab in the **Ribbon**. Correct the warnings if displayed by following method discussed earlier in the book.

Similarly, you can create the electrical and piping system for the building.

Creating Stairs

- Open the **Level 1** floor plan from the **Project Browser** and click on the **Stair** tool from the **Circulation** panel in the **Architecture** tab of **Ribbon**. The options to create stairs will be displayed.
- Select the **L-Shape Winder** tool from the **Components** panel in the **Modify|Create Stair** contextual tab of **Ribbon**. The L shaped stair will get attached to cursor.
- Click on the **Railing** tool from the contextual tab. The **Railing** dialog box will be displayed; refer to Figure-34.

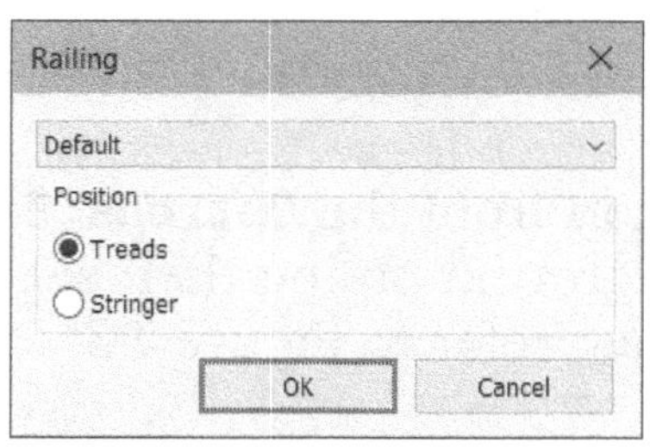

Figure-34. Railing dialog box

- Select the **None** option from the drop-down at the top in the dialog box and click on the **OK** button.
- Click at the location as shown in Figure-35 to place the stairs.

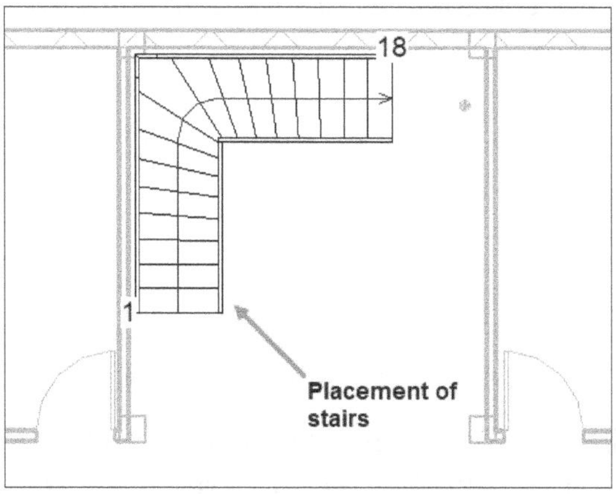

Figure-35. Placing stairs

- Click on the **Finish Edit Mode** tool from the **Mode** panel in the contextual tab of **Ribbon**.

We have created the stair but due to full slab of floor on 2nd level, there is not exit for stairs. So, we will create cut on the slab now.

- Open 3D view by click on the **Default 3D View** tool from the **Quick Access Toolbar** and select the roof of building. The **Modify|Roofs** contextual tab will be displayed in the **Ribbon**.
- Select the **Hide Elements** option from the **Hide** drop-down in the **View** panel of contextual tab in the **Ribbon**; refer to Figure-36. The roof will be hidden and you will be able to check slab as well as stairs; refer to Figure-37.

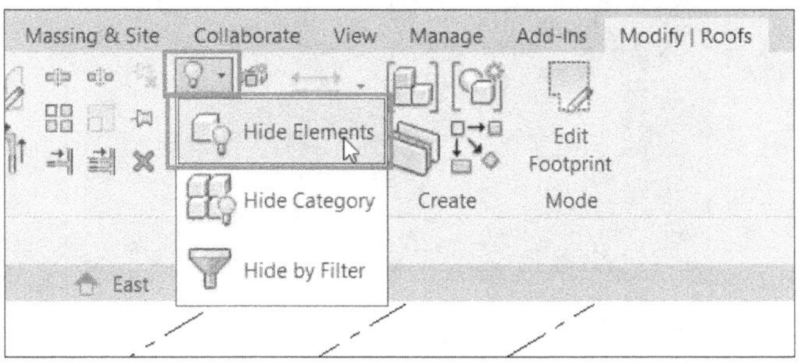

Figure-36. Hide Elements option

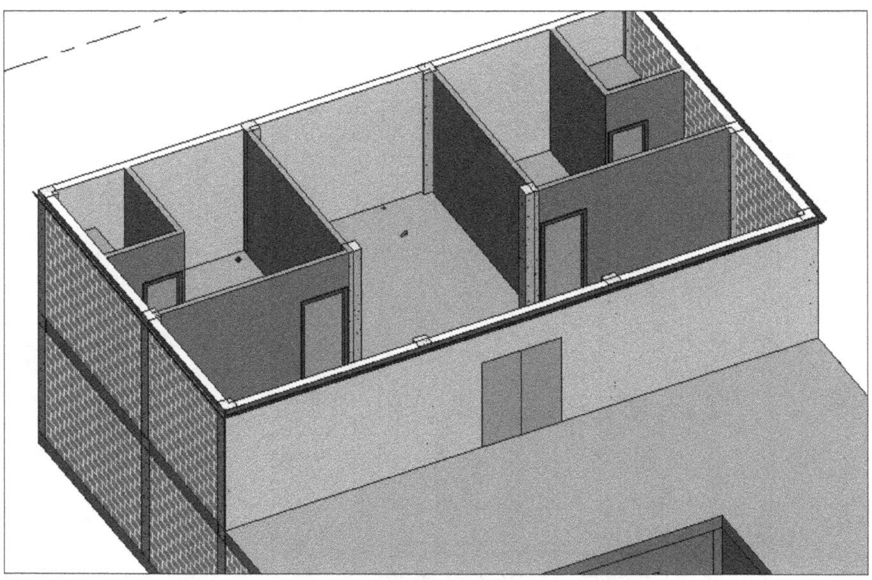

Figure-37. 3D view of building in Shaded style

- Click on the Top face of **ViewCube** to check Top view of model; refer to Figure-38.

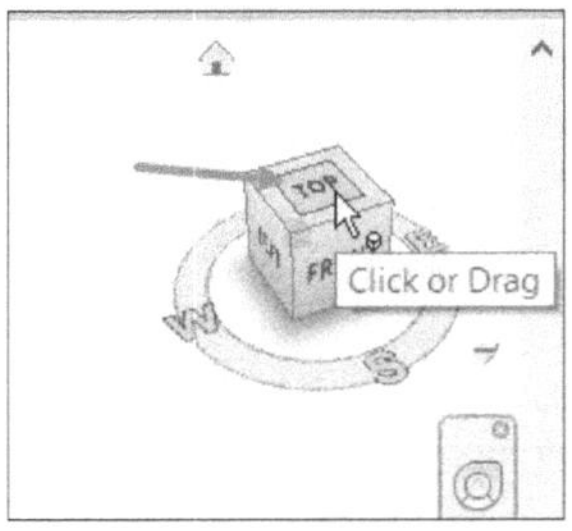

Figure-38. Top face of ViewCube

- Click on the **Vertical Opening** tool from the **Opening** panel of **Architecture** tab in the **Ribbon**. You will be asked to select the floor in which you want to create opening.
- Select the edge of floor created on Level 2; refer to Figure-39. The options to create opening boundary will be displayed.

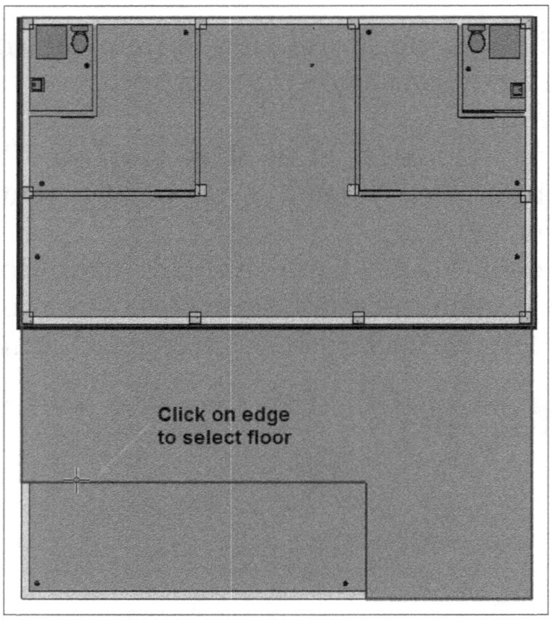

Figure-39. Selecting edge of floor

- Change the **Visual Style** to **Wireframe** from the **Bottom Bar** and create the boundary using **Line** tool as shown in Figure-40.

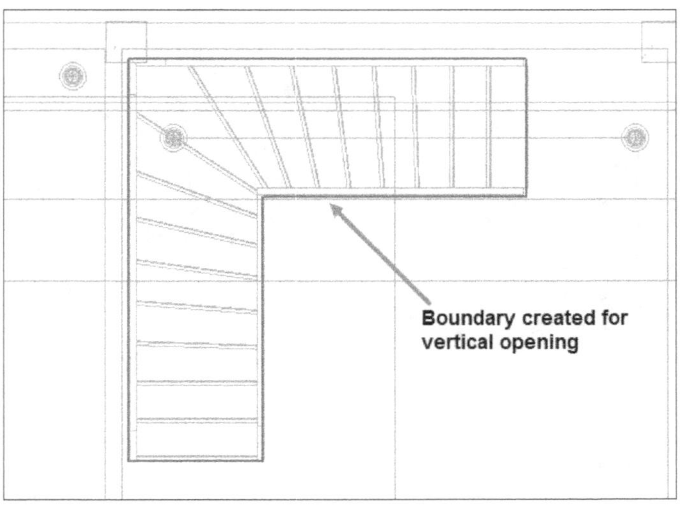

Figure-40. Boundary created for opening

- Click on the **Finish Edit Mode** tool from the **Mode** panel in the contextual tab. The vertical opening will be created. Press **ESC** to exit the selection.
- You can change the visual style to shaded and rotate the model to different orientation by holding **SHIFT** key & dragging mouse using Middle Mouse Button to check how this effects on stair ways.
- Click on the **Reveal Hidden Elements** button from the **Bottom Bar** to display roof temporarily. Now, select the roof and click on the **Unhide Element** tool from the **Reveal Hidden Elements** panel of **Modify|Roofs** contextual tab of **Ribbon**; refer to Figure-41.

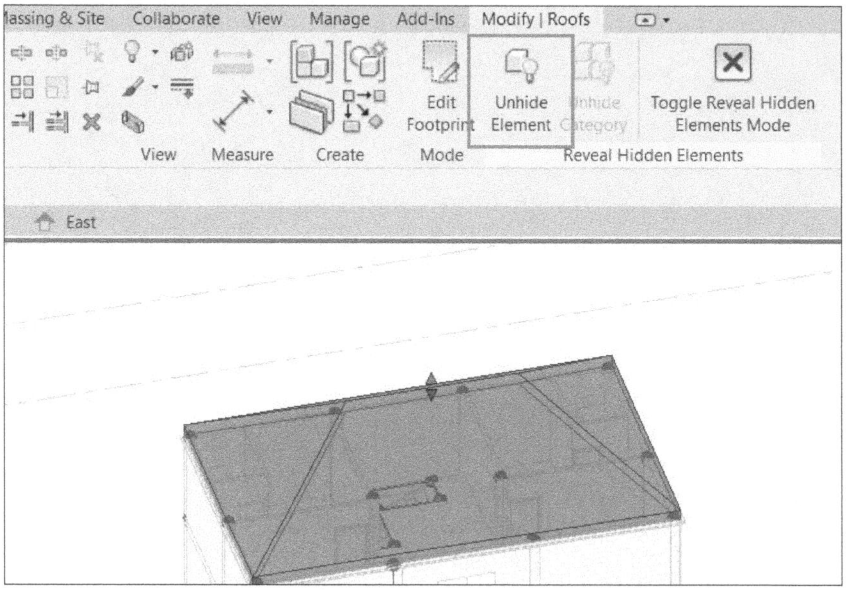

Figure-41. Unhide Element option

- Click on the **Toggle Reveal Hidden Elements Mode** button from the contextual tab. The final model will be displayed.

For Student Notes

Chapter 16

Precast

Topics Covered

The major topics covered in this chapter are:

- ***Performing Precast Splitting***
- ***Generating Mounting Parts***
- ***Generating Reinforcements***
- ***Generating Custom Fabric Sheet***
- ***Generating Shop Drawings***
- ***Exporting for CAM***
- ***Modifying Configurations***

INTRODUCTION

In this chapter, you will learn to convert the walls, floors, slabs, and other structural components into precast segments. Pre-casts are structural components in the form of segments which can be assembled to form walls, floors, and other structural elements of the building. The tools to create and manage precasts are available in the **Concrete** tab of the **Ribbon**; refer to Figure-1. Various tools in this tab are discussed next.

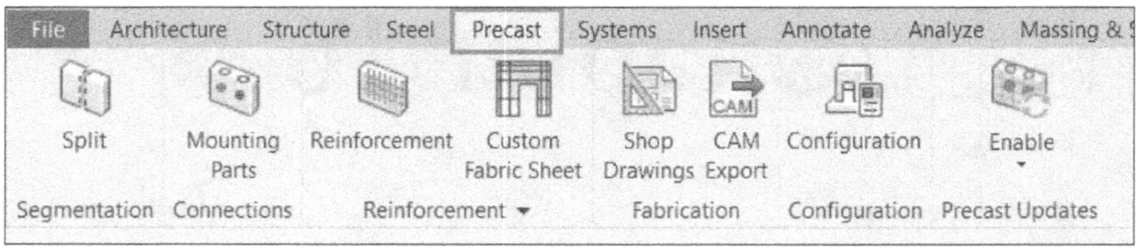

Figure-1. Precast tab

SPLITTING STRUCTURAL ELEMENTS INTO PRECASTS

The **Split** tool in the **Precast** tab of **Ribbon** is used to convert selected structure elements into precast segments. The procedure to use this tool is given next.

- Click on the **Split** tool from the **Precast Detailing** panel in the **Concrete** tab of the **Ribbon**. If you are running this tool for the first time, then an information box will be displayed telling you that system will first synchronize families. Click on the **OK** button from information box and then you will be asked to select the structural elements to be segmented into precasts.
- Select desired structural walls, floors, or slabs. Note that you can use windows selection for selecting objects.
- After selecting all desired objects, click on the **Finish** button from the **Options Bar**. Selected objects will be converted to precast objects; refer to Figure-2.

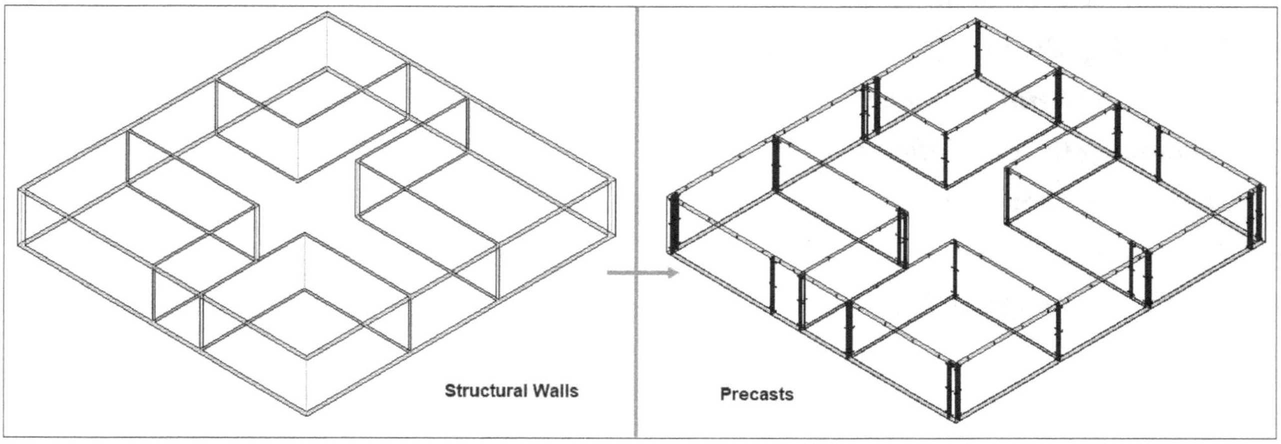

Figure-2. Converting structural walls to precasts

- Press **ESC** to exit the tool.

Placing Mounting Parts on Precasts

The **Mounting Parts** tool in **Concrete** tab of **Ribbon** is used to automatically generate required mounting parts for precast assembly. The procedure to use this tool is given next.

- Click on the **Mounting Parts** tool from the **Precast Detailing** panel in the **Concrete** tab of the **Ribbon**. If there is a need of additional mounting parts then they will be generated otherwise a message box will be displayed with "**No elements were added in the assemblies**" message.

CREATING REINFORCEMENTS FOR ASSEMBLY

The **Reinforcement** tool in **Concrete** tab of **Ribbon** is used to create reinforcement frame inside selected precast structures. The procedure to use this tool is given next.

- Click on the **Reinforcement** tool from the **Precast Detailing** panel of **Concrete** tab in the **Ribbon**. You will be asked to select elements for creating automatic reinforcement.
- Select desired elements (segments of precast) and click on the **Finish** button from the **Options Bar**. The **Wall Properties** dialog box will be displayed; refer to Figure-3.

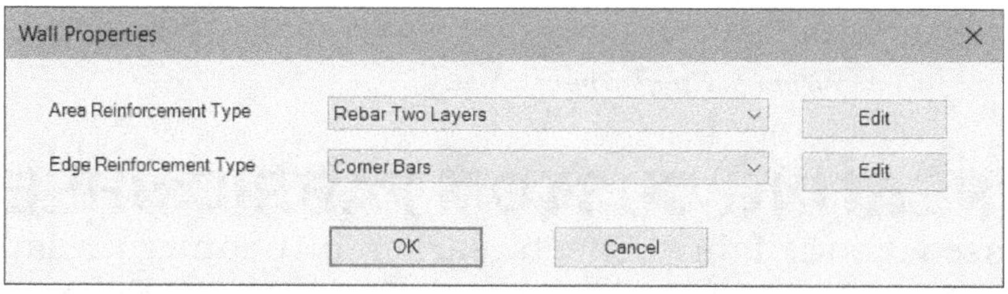

Figure-3. Wall Properties dialog box

- Set desired options in drop-downs to define type of reinforcements at the edges and in wall area.
- If you want to modify area reinforcement then click on the **Edit** button next to **Area Reinforcement Type** drop-down. The options to modify selected reinforcement type will be displayed in the dialog box; refer to Figure-4. Set desired parameters of rebar like rebar type, size, offset, bar direction, and so on. After setting parameters, click on the **OK** button from the dialog box.

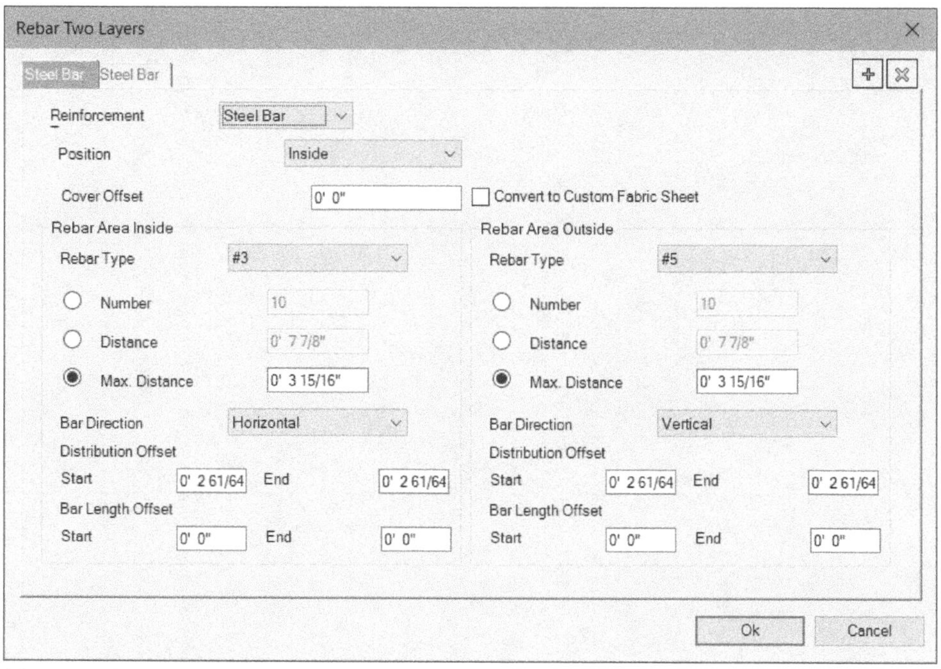

Figure-4. Rebar Two Layers dialog box

- Similarly, you can modify the edge reinforcement type using respective **Edit** button.
- After selecting desired reinforcement, click on the **OK** button from the **Wall Properties** dialog box. The reinforcement will be created; refer to Figure-5.

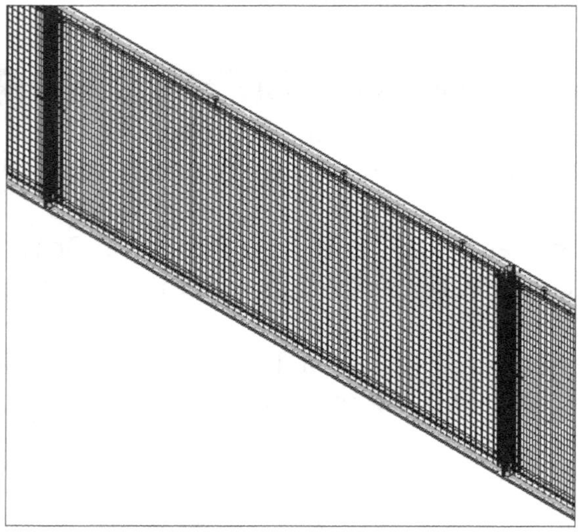

Figure-5. Reinforcement created

CREATING CUSTOM FABRIC SHEET

We have discussed about fabric sheets earlier in chapters related to structure designing. Here, you will learn to create custom fabric sheet. Before generating fabric sheet, it is important to specify parameters of the fabric sheet. The **CFS Config** tool in the expanded **Reinforcement** panel of **Ribbon** is used to define parameters of fabric sheet. The procedure to use this tool is given next.

Defining Custom Sheet Parameters

- Click on the **CFS Config** tool from **Precast Settings** panel of **Concrete** tab in the **Ribbon**. The **Custom Fabric Sheet Configuration** dialog box will be displayed; refer to Figure-6.

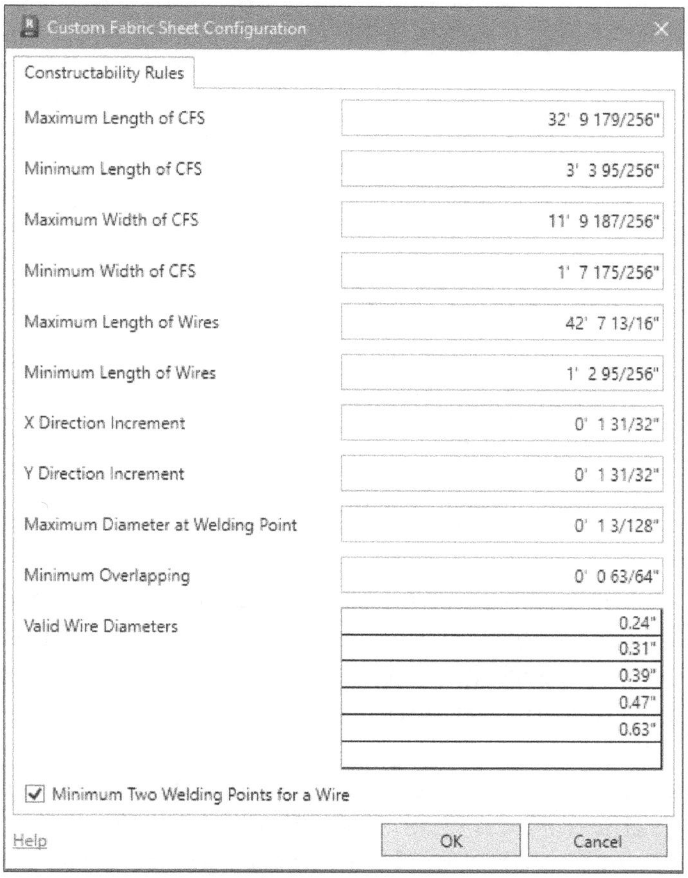

Figure-6. Custom Fabric Sheet Configuration dialog box

- Set desired parameters of fabric sheet like length, width, offset, and overlapping in custom fabric sheet. You can also set parameters of wires in the sheet using the options in the dialog box.
- After setting desired parameters, click on the **OK** button form the dialog box.

Creating Custom Fabric Sheet

The **Custom Fabric Sheet** tool in the **Reinforcement** panel is used create custom fabric sheet based on specified parameters. The procedure to use this tool is given next.

- Click on the **Custom Fabric Sheet** tool from the **Precast Detailing** panel in the **Concrete** tab of the **Ribbon**. You will be asked to select the assembly reinforcement for converting it into fabric sheet.
- Select the rebar assembly that you want to convert into fabric sheet. Note that you need to create rebars by using the **Rebar** tool from the **Concrete** tab in the **Ribbon**, then select all the created rebars and then create an assembly by using the **Create Assembly** tool from the **Modify** tab of **Ribbon**; refer to Figure-7.

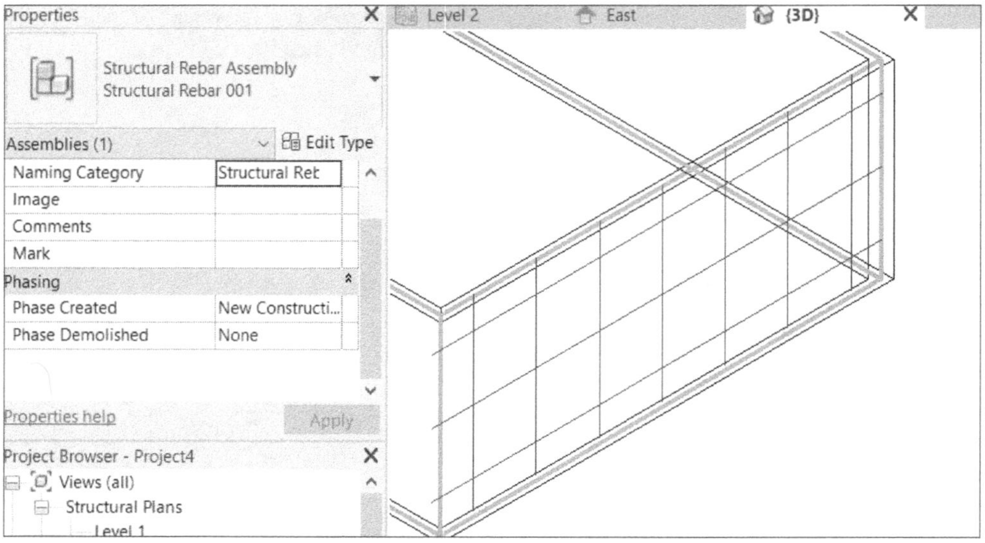

Figure-7. Structural rebar assembly created

- Make sure the parameters specified for rebars match with parameters specified in the **Custom Fabric Sheet Configuration** dialog box. After selecting the rebar assembly, click on the **Finish** button from the **Options Bar**. The selected bar assembly will be converted to custom fabric sheet.

Note that sometimes you might get an error telling you that wire diameter does not fit any of the input diameters. In this case, check the diameter of rebar and add it in the **Valid Wire Diameters** area of the **Custom Fabric Sheet Configuration** dialog box; refer to Figure-8.

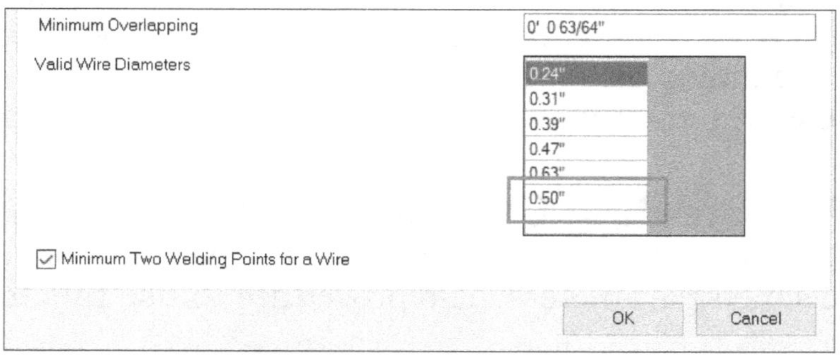

Figure-8. Size of rebar added in the list

Sometimes, you may also get the error telling you to have at least one weld point. In such case, make sure the end points of rebars are connected to edges of walls or floor.

MODIFYING PRECAST CONFIGURATION

The **Configuration** tool in **Concrete** tab of **Ribbon** is used to modify the parameters related to precast model. The procedure to use this tool is given next.

- Click on the **Configuration** tool from the **Precast Settings** panel in the **Concrete** tab of the **Ribbon**. The **Configuration** dialog box will be displayed; refer to Figure-9.

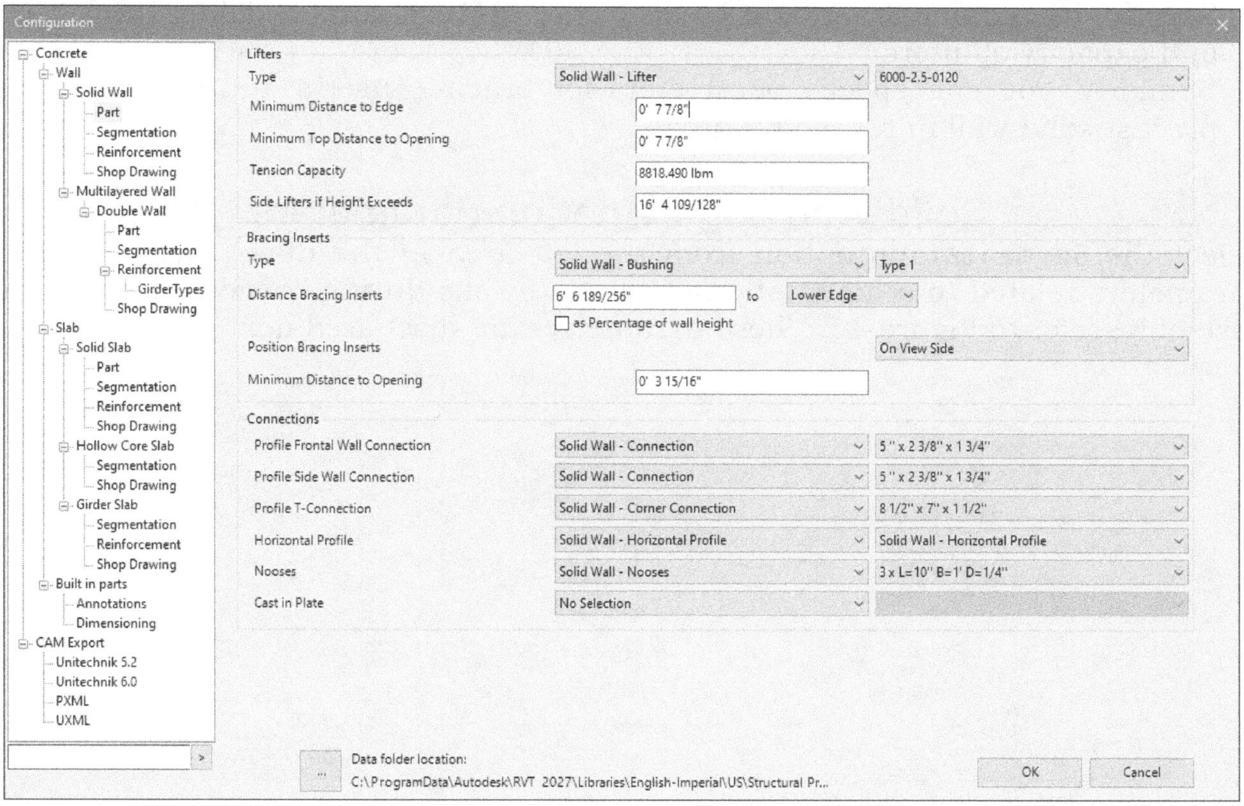

Figure-9. Configuration dialog box

Various options in this dialog box are discussed next.

Solid Wall Part Parameters

Select the **Part** option from the left area in the dialog box to display parameters related precast part.

- In the **Lifters** area of the dialog box, you can specify parameters related to lifting anchors of precast walls; refer to Figure-10.

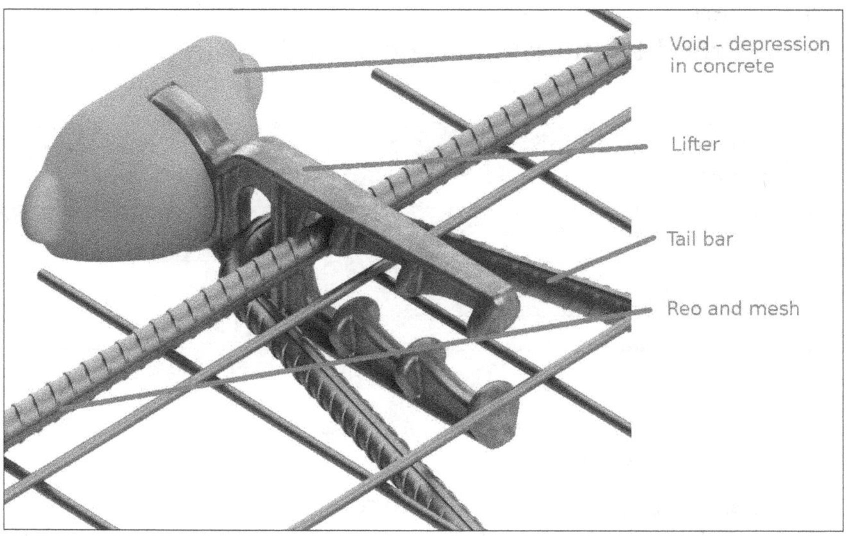

Figure-10. Lifter and other components of precast wall

- Select desired option from the **Type** drop-down to define type of lifter. In the drop-down adjacent to **Type** drop-down, select the sub-type of lifter.

- Specify the parameters in edit boxes of the **Lifters** area to define the location and capacity of lifters.
- Similarly, you can specify parameters for bracing inserts and connections of precast solid wall in respective areas.

Solid Wall Segmentation Parameters

Select the **Segmentation** option from the left area in the dialog box to display parameters related to segmentation of selected walls during conversion to precast assembly; refer to Figure-11. These parameters are discussed next.

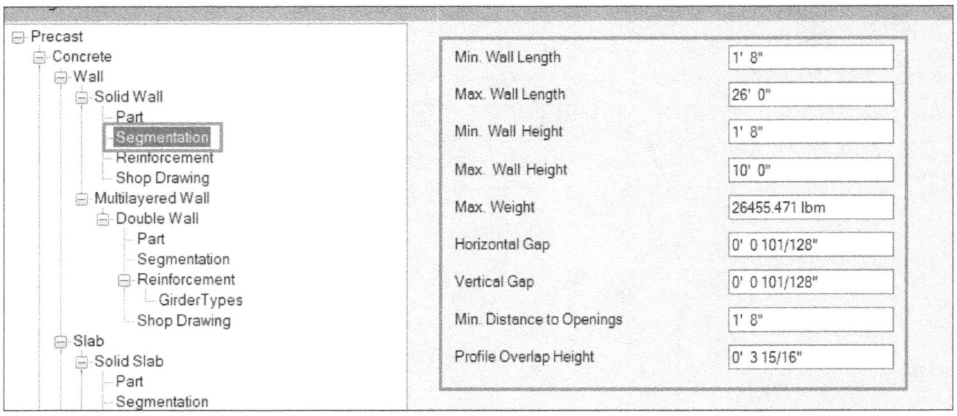

Figure-11. Precast Solid Wall Segmentation parameters

- Specify the minimum and maximum values of wall height and wall length in respective edit boxes of the dialog box.
- In the **Max. Weight** edit box, you can specify the maximum allowed weight of single precast wall. Once this weight is achieved, a new wall is created.
- In **Horizontal Gap** and **Vertical Gap** edit boxes, specify the gap between two consecutive instances of precast walls.

Solid Wall Reinforcement Parameters

Select the **Reinforcement** option from the left area in the dialog box to modify reinforcement type used in solid precast walls; refer to Figure-12. Using the options in this page, you can modify the rebar types used in area and edge reinforcement of precast.

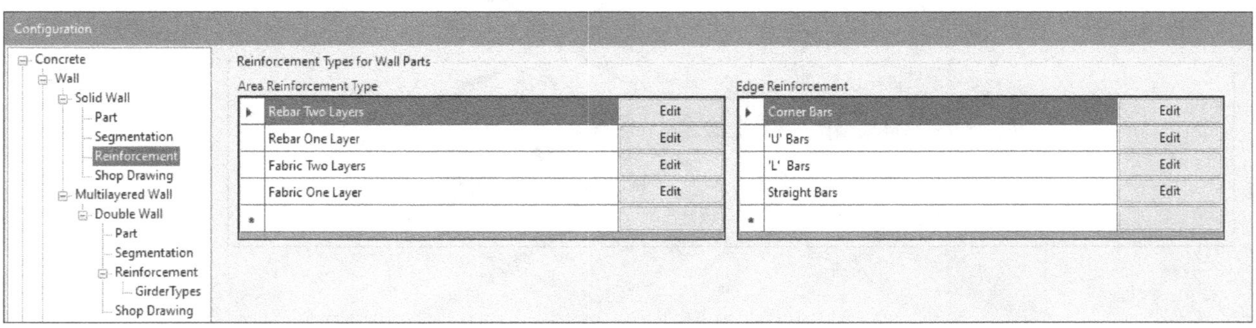

Figure-12. Reinforcement options for solid wall

- Click on the **Edit** button next to desired reinforcement type to modify its parameters. The dialog box to modify rebar parameters will be displayed.
- Set the parameters as discussed earlier and click on the **OK** button.

Solid Wall Shop Drawing Parameters

Select the **Shop Drawing** option from the left area in the **Configuration** dialog box to set drawing template and other related parameters; refer to Figure-13. Set desired parameters in the dialog box. Note that these parameters will be used when generating shop drawings of precast.

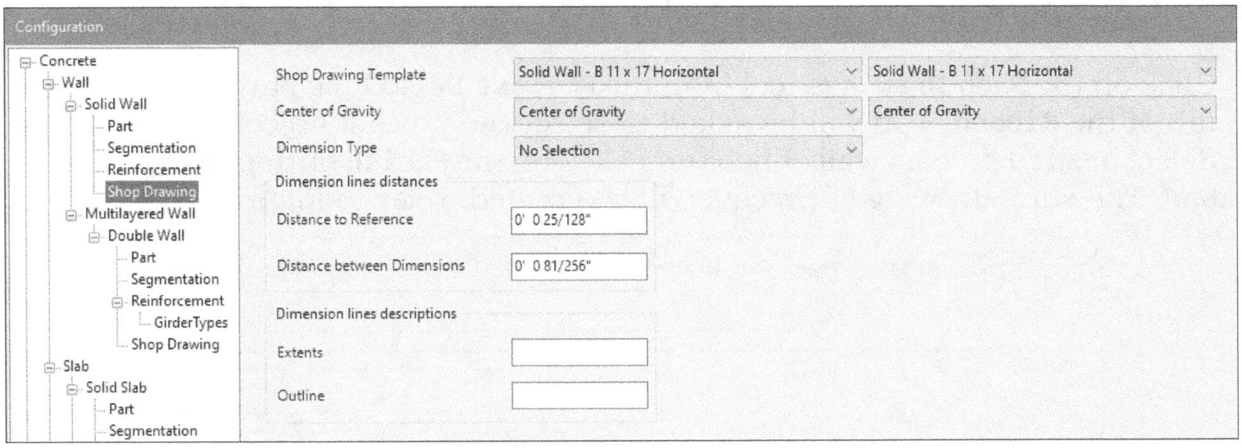

Figure-13. Shop Drawing parameters of Solid Wall

Similarly, you can set parameters for multilayered walls and slabs used in precast.

Annotation Parameters

Select the **Annotation** option from the left area in the dialog box. The options to set automatic annotations of precasts will be displayed; refer to Figure-14. These options are discussed next.

- Click on the drop-down in the **Category** column of the table. The categories of objects available in Autodesk Revit will be displayed.
- Select desired object category from the list.
- Click on the drop-down in the **Family** column and select desired family of category.
- Similarly, set desired options in other columns to define annotation match.

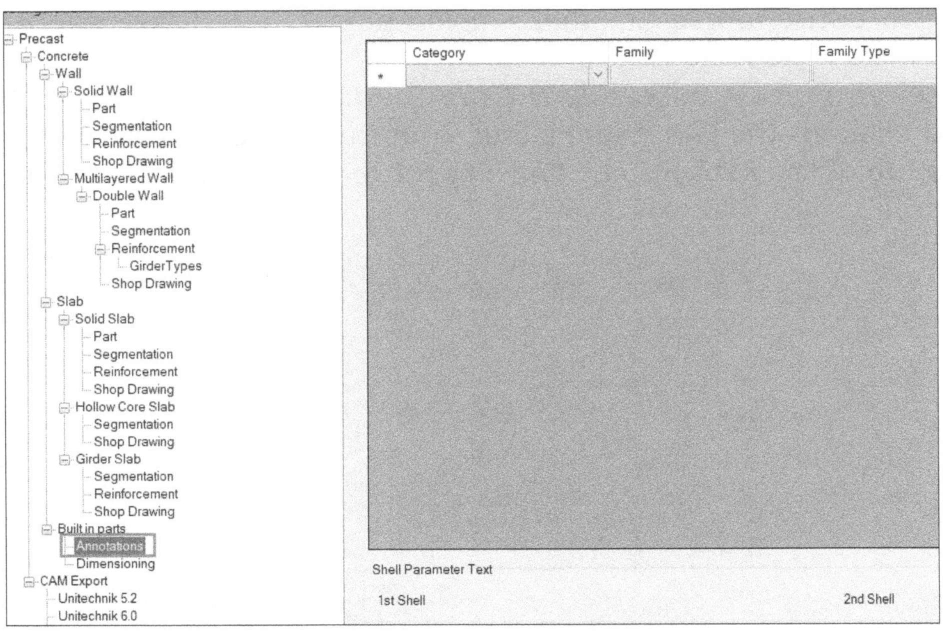

Figure-14. Annotations options for Precast

You can set the other options in the same way. After setting desired parameters, click on the **OK** button from the **Configuration** dialog box.

GENERATING SHOP DRAWINGS

The **Shop Drawings** tool in **Concrete** tab is used to generate shop drawing of selected precast. The procedure to use this tool is given next.

- Click on the **Shop Drawings** tool from the **Precast Detailing** panel in the **Concrete** tab of the **Ribbon**. You will be asked to select the precast object.
- Select desired precast wall or floor and click on the **Finish** button from the **Options Bar**. The shop drawing of precast will be created; refer to Figure-15.

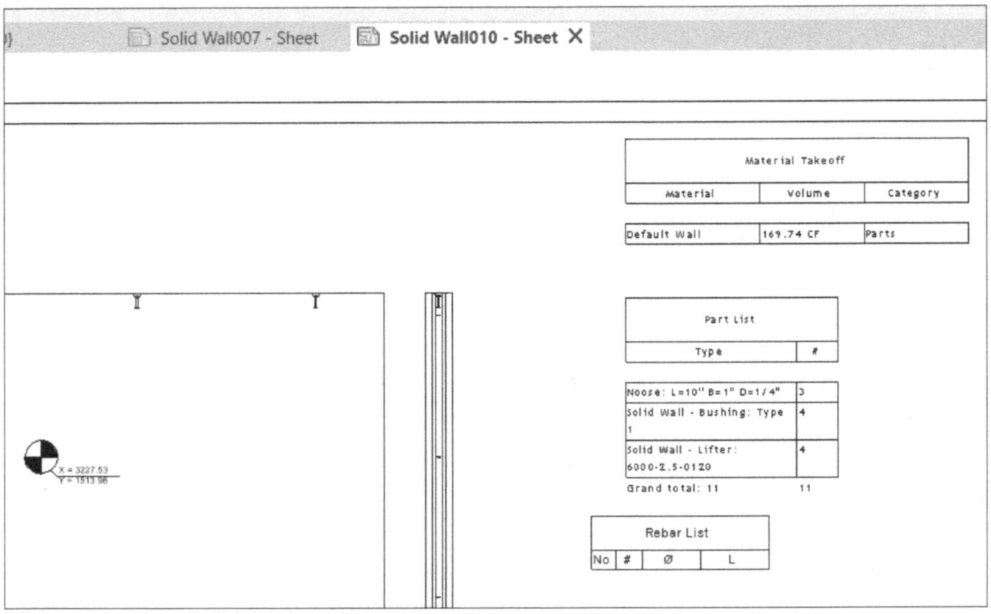

Figure-15. Shop drawing of a precast

EXPORTING FOR CAM

The **CAM Export** tool in **Concrete** tab is used to export CAM data of selected precast object. The procedure to use this tool is given next.

- Select desired precast assembly(s) from the model that you want to export for CAM and click on the **CAM Export** tool from the **Precast Detailing** panel in the **Concrete** tab of the **Ribbon**. The **CAM Export** dialog box will be displayed; refer to Figure-16.

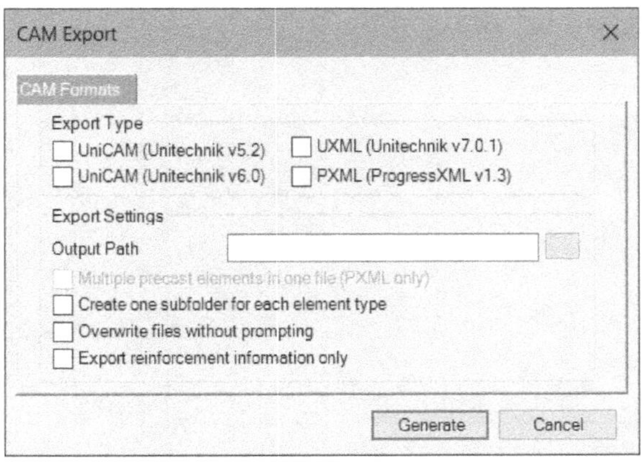

Figure-16. CAM Export dialog box

- Select desired check boxes from the **Export Type** area to define formats in which you want to export the model for CAM.
- If you have selected the **PXML** check box from the **Export Type** area then select the **Multiple precast elements in one file (PXML Only)** check box to export CAM data of multiple precast elements in a single file.
- Select the **Create one subfolder for each element type** check box to create subfolders for CAM data of each precast element.
- Select the **Overwrite files without prompting** check box to automatically overwrite previous CAM data files when exporting the same precasts.
- Select the **Export reinforcement information only** check box to export only reinforcement data of selected precast objects.
- Click on the **Browse** button next to **Output Path** edit box in the **Export Settings** area of the dialog box to specify location where CAM data files will be saved. The **Select Folder** dialog box will be displayed; refer to Figure-17.

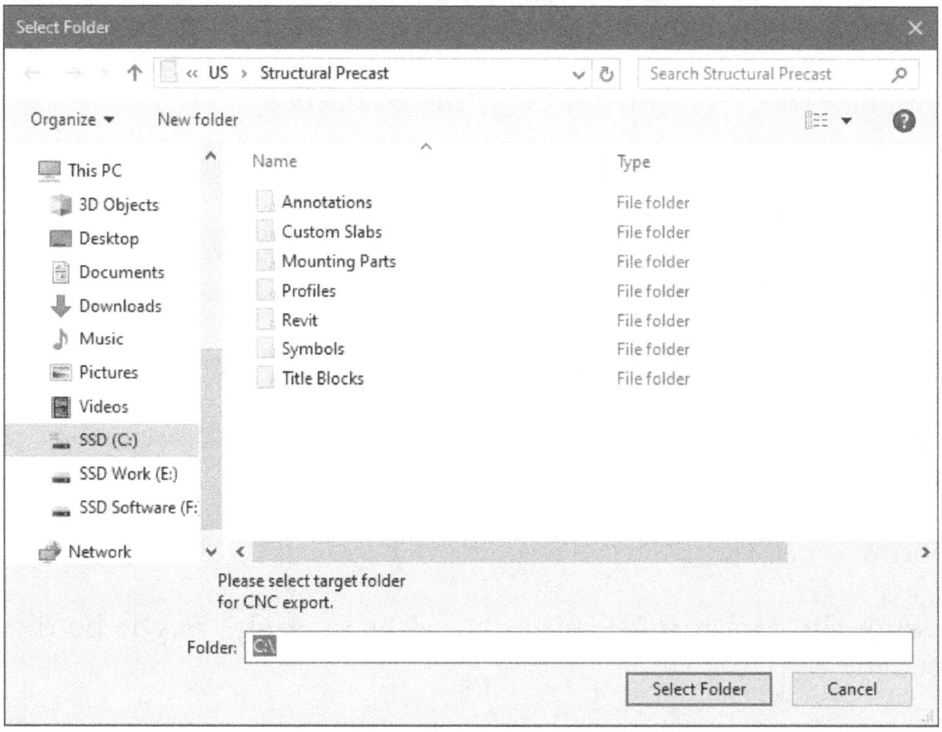

Figure-17. Browse For Folder dialog box

- Select desired location in the dialog box and click on the **OK** button.
- Click on the **Generate** button from the **CAM Export** dialog box. The files will be exported at specified location.

The **Disable** and **Enable** option in **Precast Updates** panel of **Precast** tab in the **Ribbon** are used to disable and enable the automatic update of precast on modifying parameters.

SELF-ASSESSMENT

Q1. What is a precast in construction industry?

Q2. The .... tool in the **Precast** tab of **Ribbon** is used to convert selected structure elements into precast segments.

Q3. Write a short note on various components of precast wall.

Q4. What is the purpose of the Split tool in the Precast tab?

A. To place mounting parts on precast objects
B. To convert structural elements into reinforcement
C. To convert selected structural elements into precast segments
D. To export precast objects to CAM

Q5. What happens the first time you run the Split tool?

A. System skips family synchronization
B. System automatically segments elements
C. System displays a message about family synchronization
D. System requests CAM export settings

Q6. Which panel contains the Mounting Parts tool?

A. Segmentation
B. Connections
C. Configuration
D. Fabrication

Q7. When using the Mounting Parts tool, what message might be displayed if no parts are needed?

A. “Tool not available for selected assembly”
B. “Elements failed to segment”
C. “No elements were added in the assemblies”
D. “No mounting parts can be created”

Q8. Which tool is used to create reinforcement inside selected precast structures?

A. Split
B. Mounting Parts
C. Reinforcement
D. CFS Config

Q9. What must you click after selecting elements for reinforcement?

A. Generate
B. OK
C. Edit
D. Finish

Q10. Where can you define parameters of a custom fabric sheet?

A. CAM Export dialog
B. CFS Config tool
C. Shop Drawing dialog
D. Segmentation panel

Q11. What must you do before converting rebar to a custom fabric sheet?

A. Use CAM Export
B. Place annotations
C. Create an assembly from rebars
D. Split the structure

Q12. If you get an error about wire diameter when creating a custom fabric sheet, what should you do?

A. Delete the selected rebar
B. Adjust wall parameters
C. Add diameter in Valid Wire Diameters
D. Create a new reinforcement type

Q13. What is the function of the Configuration tool in the Precast tab?

A. Export reinforcement information
B. Add annotations
C. Modify precast model parameters
D. Create fabric sheets

Q14. Which parameter sets the maximum allowed weight of a single precast wall?

A. Wall Height
B. Horizontal Gap
C. Max. Weight
D. Wall Length

Q15. What does the Annotation option in the Configuration dialog allow you to do?

A. Export annotation data
B. Set automatic annotations for precasts
C. Annotate fabric sheets only
D. Add reinforcement details

Q16. What must you select before generating shop drawings?

A. Reinforcement parameters
B. Custom Fabric Sheet
C. Precast object
D. CAM Export settings

Q17. What happens when you click the Generate button in the CAM Export dialog?

A. Opens annotation settings
B. Launches reinforcement tool
C. Files are exported to specified location
D. Custom sheet parameters are created

Q18. What does the Overwrite files without prompting option do in CAM Export?

A. Prevents overwriting
B. Prompts before overwriting
C. Automatically overwrites old files
D. Renames new files before saving

Q19. What is required before generating a custom fabric sheet from a rebar assembly?

A. Export CAM data
B. Place mounting parts
C. Match rebar parameters with configuration
D. Create shop drawings

Q20. What action should be taken if the error message "At least one weld point required" appears during fabric sheet creation?

A. Use a different rebar tool
B. Adjust wall weight
C. Ensure rebar ends connect to edges of walls or floor
D. Modify segmentation parameters

Q21. What tool is used to export precast assemblies for CAM processing?

A. Mounting Parts
B. CAM Export
C. Configuration
D. Shop Drawings

Q22. In the CAM Export dialog, which option allows exporting multiple precast elements into a single file?

A. Create subfolders
B. Export reinforcement only
C. Multiple precast elements in one file
D. Overwrite files

Q23. Which of the following is NOT a valid option in the Export Type area of the CAM Export dialog?

A. PXML
B. IFC
C. Export reinforcement information only
D. Create assembly

Q24. Which panel in the Precast tab contains the Shop Drawings tool?

A. Reinforcement
B. Connections
C. Fabrication
D. Configuration

Q25. What should be done to automatically update precast components after modifying parameters?

A. Click Enable in Precast Updates
B. Re-export the CAM file
C. Rerun the Split tool
D. Use the Edit tool in Reinforcement panel

Q26. What can be configured using the Solid Wall Reinforcement Parameters option in the Configuration dialog box?

A. CAM export format
B. Precast weights
C. Type of rebar used in area and edge reinforcement
D. Shop drawing file path

Q27. What kind of parameters can you define in the Solid Wall Part Parameters section?

A. Segment weights
B. Lifter type and location
C. CAM settings
D. Drawing templates

Q28. Which of the following is a function of the Annotation settings in Precast Configuration?

A. Define wall segmentation
B. Create CAM data
C. Set automatic annotation matches for objects
D. Adjust gap between precast elements

Q29. Which tool must be used to define custom sheet parameters before generating a fabric sheet?

A. Split
B. Reinforcement
C. CFS Config
D. CAM Export

Q30. What happens when you click the Finish button after selecting structural elements using the Split tool?

A. The software exits the tool immediately
B. Selected elements are converted to precast segments
C. Reinforcement is added to selected elements
D. A shop drawing is generated automatically

FOR STUDENT NOTES

Index

D

J

K

L

M

N

O

Ethics of an Engineer

- Engineers shall hold paramount the safety, health and welfare of the public and shall strive to comply with the principles of sustainable development in the performance of their professional duties.
- Engineers shall perform services only in areas of their competence.
- Engineers shall issue public statements only in an objective and truthful manner.
- Engineers shall act in professional manners for each employer or client as faithful agents or trustees, and shall avoid conflicts of interest.
- Engineers shall build their professional reputation on the merit of their services and shall not compete unfairly with others.
- Engineers shall act in such a manner as to uphold and enhance the honor, integrity, and dignity of the engineering profession and shall act with zero-tolerance for bribery, fraud, and corruption.
- Engineers shall continue their professional development throughout their careers, and shall provide opportunities for the professional development of those engineers under their supervision.

www.ingramcontent.com/pod-product-compliance
Lightning Source LLC
LaVergne TN
LVHW082005200926
848481LV00010B/2810

* 9 7 8 1 7 7 4 5 9 2 2 0 5 *